COMPILED BY THE
BROWN COUNTY HISTORICAL
SOCIETY

A reenactment in 1988 of train traffic to Brown County at Helmsburg. Engine 587 was on display for many years at Broadripple Park in Indianapolis, then the train was taken to Noblesville where it was restored. The line was formerly Illinois-Gulf Central Railroad; today's line is Indiana Railroad. Currently the train runs on special occasions between Indianapolis and Bloomington for football games at Indiana University. Recently diesel trains are coming to Brown County, especially during October, with bus tour groups from Michigan and other places, sight seeing the beauties of the changing leaf color. Occasionally the train goes further beyond Helmsburg and Bloomington to Elran (near Solsberry) to see the 5th largest viaduct in the U. S.. (Photo by Wayne Lowry)

Turner Publishing Company
Publishers of America's History

Author: Dorothy Birney Bailey

Copyright © 1991 by The Brown County Historical Society, Inc.

This book or any part thereof may not be reproduced without the written consent of the Author and Publisher

The materials were compiled and produced using available information; Turner Publishing Company, Mark A. Thompson and Brown County Historical Society regrets they cannot assume liability for errors or omissions.

Co-Produced by: Mark A. Thompson, Independent Publishing Consultant for Turner Publishing Company

Book Design: Elizabeth Dennis

Library of Congress Catalog Card No. : 90-71731

ISBN: 978-1-56311-025-2

Limited Edition of 1100 copies of which this book is number _____.

TABLE OF CONTENTS

Brown County Historical Society		4
Brown County Museum		7
Putting the Book Together		8
About the Author		9
History		
Chapter I	In The Beginning	12
Chapter II	Prehistoric and Historic Indians in Brown County	13
Chapter III	Pioneer Travel to Brown County	14
Chapter IV	Pioneers and Indians in Brown County	16
Chapter V	The Earliest Pioneers	17
Chapter VI	Brown County Land 1809 to 1836	23
Chapter VII	Organization of Brown County, 1836	25
Chapter VIII	A Visit to Brown County in 1836	29
Chapter IX	Brown County Courthouses, Jails, and Circuit Courts	30
Chapter X	Military History of Brown County	33
Chapter XI	Brown County Industries	45
Chapter XII	Brown County Villages and Inns	52
Chapter XIII	Artists in Brown County	60
Chapter XIV	United States Postal Service in Brown County	67
Chapter XV	Brown County 1836 to 1900	71
Chapter XVI	Brown County 1900 to 1990	79
Churches		95
Schools		109
Clubs, Organizations and Memorials		113
Businesses		125
Family History		131
Index		313

The Helmsburg-Nashville Taxi Hack stopping by the bungalow of Charity Dye en route to Nashville with a group of artists(from Alberta Shulz collection).

BROWN COUNTY HISTORICAL SOCIETY

The Society is now 33 years old. On September 16, 1957, a group of about thirty Brown Countians gathered at the Brown County Art Gallery to discuss the possibility of organizing the Historical Society. First elected President was Karl Ehrenschwender. Meetings were held in members' homes. A few of the homes in which they met were those of Leonard Welsh, Howard De Golyer, Marian Raisbeck, Onya LaTour, Gene Wilson and Jessee Crass. They also used the upper floor of the Community Building—now, part of the Museum Complex.

Property on Helmsburg Road was purchased. Plans were to have a Museum Complex there. However, distance from town and other complications led to the decision to sell the property and buy the present property known as the old Bowling Alley on Highway 135 north of Nashville.

It was at this time the Pioneer Women's Club was formed. The purpose of this club is to be a supportive group to the Historical Society. Gib Rogers was the first president. In the past thirty-three years they have earned and turned over to the Historical Society around $50,000.

The Historical Society has many fund raisers. Until 1982 the main event was the Antique Show. For many years it was held in the old Nashville Gym on Old School Way. The Society organized the first Log Cabin Tours. Quilt Shows (12th in 1990), Christmas Dinners (with entertainment) and Garage Sales are among present day fund raisers.

ARTICLES OF INCORPORATION

The Articles of Incorporation state the following purposes of our Society:
1. To collect and preserve manuscripts and other materials relating to Brown County history.
2. To collect and preserve relics relating to Brown County history.
3. To establish, maintain and perpetuate a Brown County Museum.
4. To mark and locate Historical Sites within Brown County.
5. To sponsor a History of Brown County.
6. To cooperate with the Brown County Board of Education in furnishing materials for the teaching of Brown County, Indiana, history.

Burning the Mortgage, December 3, 1973; Tom Woods, Pete Sturm and Bob Gregg.

ARCHIVES

In 1973 Dorothy Bailey was appointed the first archivist of the Brown County Historical Society. Archive holdings consisted of two small cartons of sundry papers, Brown County Democrats, and a few books. Recognizing that good intentions plus ignorance may result in irreparable mistakes Dorothy took a course in archival management at Notre Dame. The necessity to increase the archives was urgent. The search for historical data began. Donations of photographs, records and family histories was encouraging. Cartons of packed archival materials stacked in the Society's office and empty file cabinet drawers filled to overflowing posed problems.

George Kissling, president in 1977-1978 came to the rescue. He obtained a gift of building tile sufficient to enclose a space along the south wall on the upper level of the Historical Building for an archive room. The walls went up, but there was no electricity and not even a door. Tables were moved in, however, and the contents of the file drawers, and the cartons were transferred to the tables. All work was done in the Archive Room by flashlight!

Since the Society could not afford to pay for construction of an adequate archive room, Dorothy undertook to find grant money. It took over a year, but finally the Irwin-Sweeney-Miller Foundation donated $500, the Cummins Engine Foundation contributed $4,000, and the Historical Society gave $1,000.

With the guidance and specifications of State Archivist, John Newman, a double ceiling was installed with fire retardant material between the layers. Lights with ultra-violet shields were added. Walls were scrubbed and painted. A fireproof metal door was hung. Wide wooden shelves were built along the north and west walls. Supplies of acid-free folders and boxes were ordered. A wall to wall carpet was laid over the rough cement floor. The Dillman Heating and Air Conditioning Company in Columbus, set up a unit on April 7, 1981 that ensures a constant temperature of 65° and 50% humidity year round.

In the summer of 1987 shelf space had

CHARTER MEMBERS

Glen D. Anderson
Ida M. Anderson
Mable Bain Annis
Ellnita Bauer
Dr. Thomas B. Bauer
Mrs. Thomas B. Bauer
Grover G. Brown
Lura B. Brown
Mabel Calvin Burkholder
C. Earl Byrket
LaVerne Byrket
Marianna Cantrill
Elmer K. Congram
James Cordes
George (Bob) Cramer
Dr. Clyde Culbertson
Margaret Culbertson
Amelia DeWees
Joseph DeWees
Karl Ehrenschwender
Wayne Guthrie
Mark Hill
Jettie Isaacs
Edward D. James
Fred Bates Johnson

Helen Johnson
Dr. James Jones
Eudora Kelley
May Kimmick
Carrie Kensler
John Kensler
Kay Kensler
Maude Knight
Onya LaTour
Frederick G. Lorenz
Mary Jane Lorenz
Thelma Moffitt
Mrs. Carl McCoy
Joleen J. McGuire
Nova Mertens
Chattie Wade Miller
Lenore Mobley
Marietta Moser
M.S. Myers
Carolyn Ondreicka
Marian Pollack
Marian Raisbeck
Helen H. Reeve
Kenneth J. Reeve
Charles Roberts

Andy Rogers
Judith E. Rogers
Emma Catherine Roush
Joseph C. Schreiner
Mary Belle Schroeder
Adolph Robert Shultz
Rosemary Smith
Eleanor Snodgrass
Lillian Snodgrass
Walter R. Snodgrass
Hilda E. Sparks
Mahlon Sparks
Joseph F. Stockton
Mary Stockton
Edward D. Tanner
Mary Taylor
Mr. Timmerman
Charles G. Waltman
Virginia Weddle
Dr. Herman B Wells
Leonard F. Welsh
L.L. (Von) Williamson
Margaret Wyatt
Frank Yoke

Membership between September 16, 1957 and January 31, 1958 as reconstructed in 1989.

---

become so limited that new shelves were added along the south wall. Kenneth Reeve, John Wohler, John Lichtenberg and Paul Cutler contributed their time and skill to the work.

John Newman has told us that the Archive Room of the Brown County Historical Society built according to standard specifications is the only adequate archive space of a county historical society in Indiana.

At present the collection of Brown County school records, township trustee reports, 80 taped oral histories, courthouse records, county newspapers, photographs, census reports, books relating to Brown County, county history, maps, biographies, manuscripts and scrapbooks is more extensive than can be found elsewhere in Indiana—though the State Library has certain items the Brown County Historical Society archives do not have.

Numerous requests from people in Indiana and in other states are received for information from source material.

The assistant archivist, Ann Cole, has been trained in Chicago, by the Society of American Archivists.

CURATOR COMMITTEE

The items exhibited in the buildings in the Museum Complex—the Loom Room, Old Log Cabin, Blacksmith Shop, Dr. A.J. Ralphy's Office, the combination Gift Shop-Museum, and the Old Log Jail—reflect the individuality and uniqueness of Brown County. Some artifacts on display in the buildings have historical significance and relate directly to the community's history while others are commonplace, but necessary items used by early Brown Countians.

Through the years, persons devoted to preserving the culture of Brown County had accumulated items which they felt were of historic importance. Responsibility for collecting artifacts fell on the shoulders of volunteers, so before the Bowling Alley property of Rd. 135 was purchased by the Society, these items were stored in various places such as the upstairs of the Old Log Jail or in the homes and barns of the 1957 charter members.

The Secretary's minutes of the Society's meetings in the late 1950s were scanty and yield little information as to the names of the members who collected items but, in 1958, someone did label the artifacts and record the information on cards. Later secretary's minutes list Chairmen of the Archives as Mrs. Paul Seehausen and Olivia Toler.

The first Curator, Helen White, served from 1971-1978 and put into operation a methodical card catalog system in which was recorded every item in the Society's collection at the time. Succeeding Curators in the decade 1979-1989 were Margaret Mowery, Annabel Allen, Sally Schlick, Amelia DeWees, Sam Johnson and Tab Low.

Under the direction of the current Curator, Tab Low, and with the help of her assistants, Juanita Bainter and Amelia DeWees, and seventy-five other Society members, a detailed filing system was implemented—one which meets the standards of small museums nationwide.

Today's system includes 7,180 color-coded cards in seven separate files: Acquisition Ledger, signed Donor Releases, 2 Accession, Donor Unknown, Donor Known and Category. In addition to cataloging artifacts, the Curator is responsible for planning, updating, and

GENEALOGICAL COMMITTEE

In the fall of 1971, Ken and Helen Reeve began assisting with the task of surveying some of the county's cemeteries, work started by Linda Eastman and a group of Society members. On February 21, 1972, the Society's Board approved the project of reading all county cemeteries with the intention of publishing the results. The Reeves assumed the responsibility of completing the survey.

By 1977, ninety-five cemeteries had been surveyed, the data organized and published as BROWN COUNTY, INDIANA, CEMETERIES. This work was followed by BOND FUNERAL HOME RECORDS in 1978, SELECTED FUNERAL HOME RECORDS OF COLUMBUS, INDIANA in 1978, OBITUARIES (1914-1984) in 1986, MARRIAGE RECORDS (1836-1893) in 1987 and FEDERAL CENSUS INDEX (1840-1910) in 1988 – all Brown County records.

Ken and Helen Reeve were designated as the Genealogical Committee by the Society's Board in 1980. Many researchers have directed inquiries concerning their Brown County heritage to the Genealogical Committee which has provided information country-wide. Lineages of more than 300 Brown County families have been assembled from local sources. In return many researchers have placed their family histories in the growing library of the Genealogical Committee whose goal it is to provide other records, in book form, for the use of researchers. Works in progress are: more marriage records, abstractions of Probate, Wills and Guardianship Records, as well as an Index to Court Records, 1836-1945.

MEMBERS FOR THE YEAR 1990

The following persons are members of the Brown County Historical Society for the year 1990: Beulah Ackerman, Louise P. Allison, Dolores Altmann, Raymond G. Altmann, Vera M. Arnold, Dorothy Bailey, Eugene C. Bailey, Janet S. Bailey, Juanita Bainter, Robert T. Bainter, Shirley J. Banta, Helen Baptisti, Carl A. Barnett, Georgia Barnett, Martha Barnsfather, Robert V. Barr, Willa M. Barr, Kay Birk, Warren Birk, Robin Blanton, Samuel Bill Blanton, Juanita Boles, Robert Boles, Aileen Bolton, Walter Bolton, Roland A. Boughton, George A. Bredewater, Nancy Bredewater, Lawrence E. Brewer, Brown County Democrat, Carl Brummett, George Brunner, Floyd R. Bryan, Gladys Bryan, Patricia Burton, William Burton, Martha Carr, Ronald C. Carr, Wand Carr, Bob and Bea Clapp, Jerry Clark, Ronald Clark, Bea Clatworthy, Ellen Cobner, Ann Cole, Mary Collester, Sue Collester, Russ Condon, Gayle Cook, Anita Coyle, John Coyle, George (Bob)Cramer, John Crawford, Roberta Crawford, Jack Crouch, Clyde Culbertson, Melba Dailey, Robert Dailey, Hazel Davis, Carolyn DeTarnowsky, Pierre DeTarnowsky, Amelia C. DeWees, Joseph W. DeWees, Dave Elmore, Garnet Elmore, Betty Espenlaub, Ruth Espenlaub, David W. Foster, Douglas C. Fraker, Carl Heydon Franzén, Peggy Franzén, Robert A. Frederick, Elsie May Frenzel, Richard Frenzel, Judith Fulton-Stewart, Michael P. Fulton, Marie Fuson, Charles Gardner, Martha Gardner, David D. Girard, Mary Alice Girard, Ruth Goodrich, Marge Grimm, Joseph Gwinnup, Pat Gwinnup, Charles W. Hagen, Jr., Mary Hagen, John W. Hamblen, Virginia Hamblen, Nel Hamilton, Robert E. Hamilton, Madge A. Harlan, Bert Haviland, Emma Haviland, Hubert Hawkins, John Heidtke, Frances L. Himes, Robert W. Himes, Jeanne Holmes, Harriet Johnson, Sam Johnson, Ada M. Jones, Claire Jones, Jesse Jones, Robert Jones, William M. Jones, Lowell Joslin, Marcedes Joslin, Barbara Judd, Walter Judd, Claris Keaton, Laura Keaton, Verna Kilgore, Cecil F. King, George Kissling, Louise Kissling, Tudie Kuhn, Betty Jane Kyle, George Kyle, Heather Lawless, Judith Lawless, Rob Lawless, Amy Leskovec, John Lichtenberg, Virginia Lichtenberg, Alice Lorenz, Frederick G. Lorenz, Mary Jane Lorenz, Paul S. Lorenz, Beulah "Tab" Low, Edward Lucas, Mary E. Lusher, Robert W. Lusher, Dorothy McClain, George A. McClain, Mary Jane McCoy, Richard D. McCoy, Gladys McDonald, Jack McDonald, Nina Jo McDonald, Elmer L. McGuire, Mary Geneva McGuire, Louis E. Macon, Betty J. Markley, Roger B. Markley, Mary Maronde, Mary Agnes Monroe, May Monroe, Charles Wilbur Moore, Marie Oliver, Anne Olsen, Karen Olmsted, Arhtur W. Padish, Charlotte R. Padish, Garnet Parsley, Ralph Parsley, John Pelton, Mary Pelton, Gini Percifield, William Percifield, Rachel Perry, Mary E. Pogue, William H. Potter, Gene Powell, Joyce Powell, Virginia S. Pratt, Marian Raisbeck, Helen Reeve, Kenneth J. Reeve, Ruth Reichmann, Fern Reuter, Sandy Richards, Madeline K. Ritter, Charles T. Robertson, Rosita Robertson, Andy Rogers, George W. Rogers, Saramae L. Rogers, Onnalee Rose, Joan Rosen, Samuel R. Rosen, Phyllis Rotino, Gene Russell, Mary Lou Russell, Robert M. Seibel, Bea Seibel, Lois Shadle, Robert Shadle, Rosemary Smith, Cindy Snyder, W. Bob Snyder, Opal Spann, Norma Jean Stephens, Mary Sturm, Greg Temple, Lesta Thickstun, Millie Thompson, Fred Tilton, Ruth Tilton, Donald O. Tjomsland, Helen F. Tjomsland, Edmund W. Tratebas, Gladys M. Tratebas, Ann Varner, Frank Vincent, Patricia Vincent, Olive Voland, Doris M. Waldschmidt, Vera Walsdschmidt, Jeanie Walker, Myron Waltman, Opal Waltman, Theresa B. Waltonen, Elsie Wayman, Walter Wayman, Betty Weatherford, Louis Weatherford, Evon Weaver, Harrietta Weddle, Virginia Weddle, Barbara Weidner, Herman Weidner, Herman B Wells, Richard Wetzel, Charles H. White, Roy D. Wilkerson, John Williams, Mary (Mickie) Williams, I.L. Von Williamson, Roy Wininger, Frank A. Winninger, Mary M. Winninger, John F. Wohler, June M. Wohler, Marie Wolff, Art Wolpert, June Wolpert, Betty Woods, J. Ancil Woods, Helen D. Wythe, Jean N. Young, Roger Young, Albert Zimmerman, Hazel Zimmerman, Howard Zody.

PAST PRESIDENTS OF SOCIETY

Karl Ehrenschwender	Peter K. Sturm	Amelia DeWees
Frank Yoke	Harry Smith	Hank Weidner
Lowell Todd	George Kissling	David Welsh
Leonard Welsh	Helen White	Juanita Bainter
Helen Johnson	Ruth Woods	Gladys M. Tratebas
Howard De Golyer	Sheldon Pattison	Carl Heydon Franzén
Luther Coumbe	Hazel Davis	

---

arranging exhibits such as those found in the Museum Complex buildings.

BROWN COUNTY MUSEUM

This early barn was moved to Nashville and reconstructed by the Works Progress Administration (WPA) in 1935. After two end fireplaces were added, the building was used as a community building before title was transferred to the Historical Society.

The Blacksmith Shop - Early development of the new frontier areas often centered around blacksmith shops. They were the service stations of their time. This blacksmith shop is a replica of one about 1826 with authentic tools of the trade donated by interested local citizenry, including Carl Brummett.

Pioneer Cabin - First built in Jackson County, south of Brown County about 1844, this pioneer cabin's logs have been dismantled and rebuilt and still welcomes and shelters its visitors.

The Docter's Office - Built in 1898, the country doctor's office belonged to a Dr. Alfred J. Ralphy and was located in New Bellsville, in southeastern Brown County. The doctor never owned an auto, and all calls were made to the home with a horse and buggy or sleigh.

The Log Jail - At a cost of $1,500, the two-story log jail was built in 1879. Designed with two walls spaced one foot apart with one entrance consisting of three doors, one door requires a key that was ten inches long. The last prisoner to be kept here was in 1919.

Sketches by Kenneth J. Reeve and George Bredewater

Putting the Book Together

The group to the right got the history book project going in October 1989. Kenneth J. Reeve drew the logo and several maps contained in this book. Helen Reeve assisted 70 people with putting together their family history. Cleora Morgan made the sketch of the Parsley home on the cover of our first brochure to inform Brown County about this book project. Front and back inside cover done by George Bredewater.

Front: Helen Reeve, Gladys M. Tratebas, Garnet Parsley and Cleora Morgan. Back: Kenneth J. Reeve, Ralph Parsley and Roger Markley

Committee Members

Gladys M. Tratebas, Chairman, Roger B. Markley, Treasurer and members: Ian Engle, Heydon Franzén, David Girard, John Hamblen, Claris and Laura Keaton, George and Louise Kissling, Shelley Smith Law, Karen Norman, Ralph and Garnet Parsley, Mary Pelton and Sandy Richards. Additional people helping with the project: George Bredewater, Michael Fulton, Boots Gregory, Nel Hamilton, Frances and Robert Hime, Ada and William Jones, Fred King, Betty Jane Kyle, Judith Lawless, Mary Maronde, Cleora Morgan, John Pelton, Allen and Ruth Pickard, Helen and Kenneth J. Reeve, Gladys Rodgers, Phyllis Rotino, Barbara Sheehan, Harrietta Weddle, Thelma Wilkerson, John and June Wohler, The Brown County Library and The Brown County Democrat.

Committee Members - Front: Karen Norman, Garnet Parsley, Sandy Richards, Gladys M. Tratebas, Laura Keaton and Louise Kissling. Back: Ralph Parsley, George Kissling, Roger B. Markley, John Hamblen, Carl Heydon Franzén and Claris Keaton. Missing from photo: Ian Engle, David Girard, Shelley Smith Law and Mary Pelton.

About the Author

Dorothy Birney Bailey lived on Beacon Hill in Boston, when she was a child. Her father, Lauress John Birney, was a Dean at Boston University. When he was elected a bishop of the Methodist Episcopal Church, he chose to serve in China, and Dorothy accompanied her parents to Shanghai, China. After graduating from the Shanghai American High School, she returned to the United States and earned a B.A. at Ohio Wesleyan University. She continued to develop her musical talent in New York City, studying with two famous pianists before living in Leipzig, Germany, for work with the renowned Robert Teichmuller.

After returning to New York City and concertizing, she married Dr. Robert L. Bailey. In Richmond, Virginia, she continued to concertize, received graduate degrees from William and Mary and Yale Universities and taught at William and Mary.

Her two daughters, Barbara and Robin, were through school and married when Dorothy lost her husband. She decided to move to Indiana for a new life, and located in Nashville.

When she was asked to become the archivist for the Brown County Historical Society, she took a course in archival management at Notre Dame. Obtaining two grants she built the archive room with the help of then President George Kissling and the guidance of the State Archivist John Newman.

For over seventeen years she has collected Brown County history. In 1986 she published the book "Brown County Remembers" for which 41 manuscripts by Brown Countians were collected and edited.

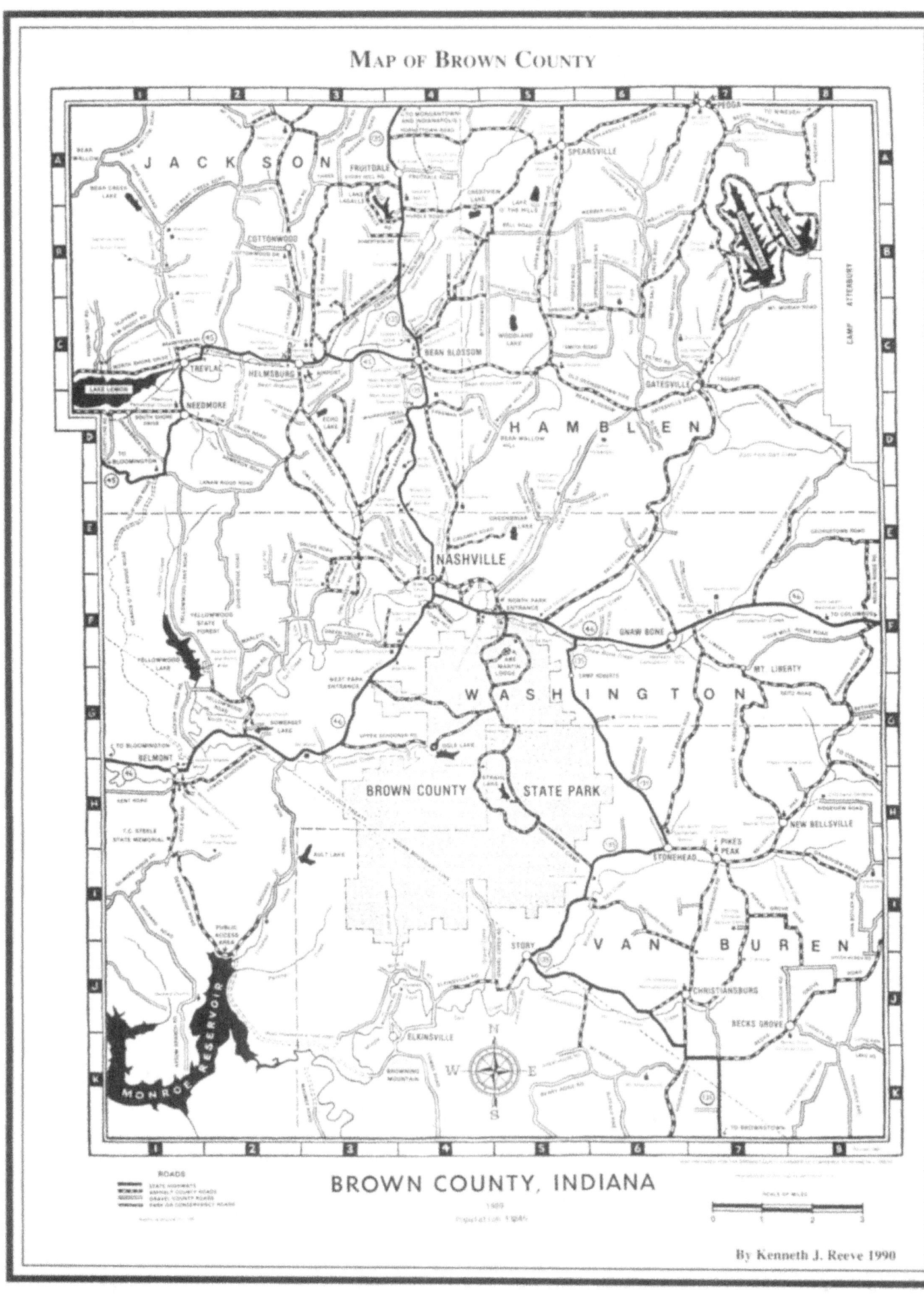

Brown County History

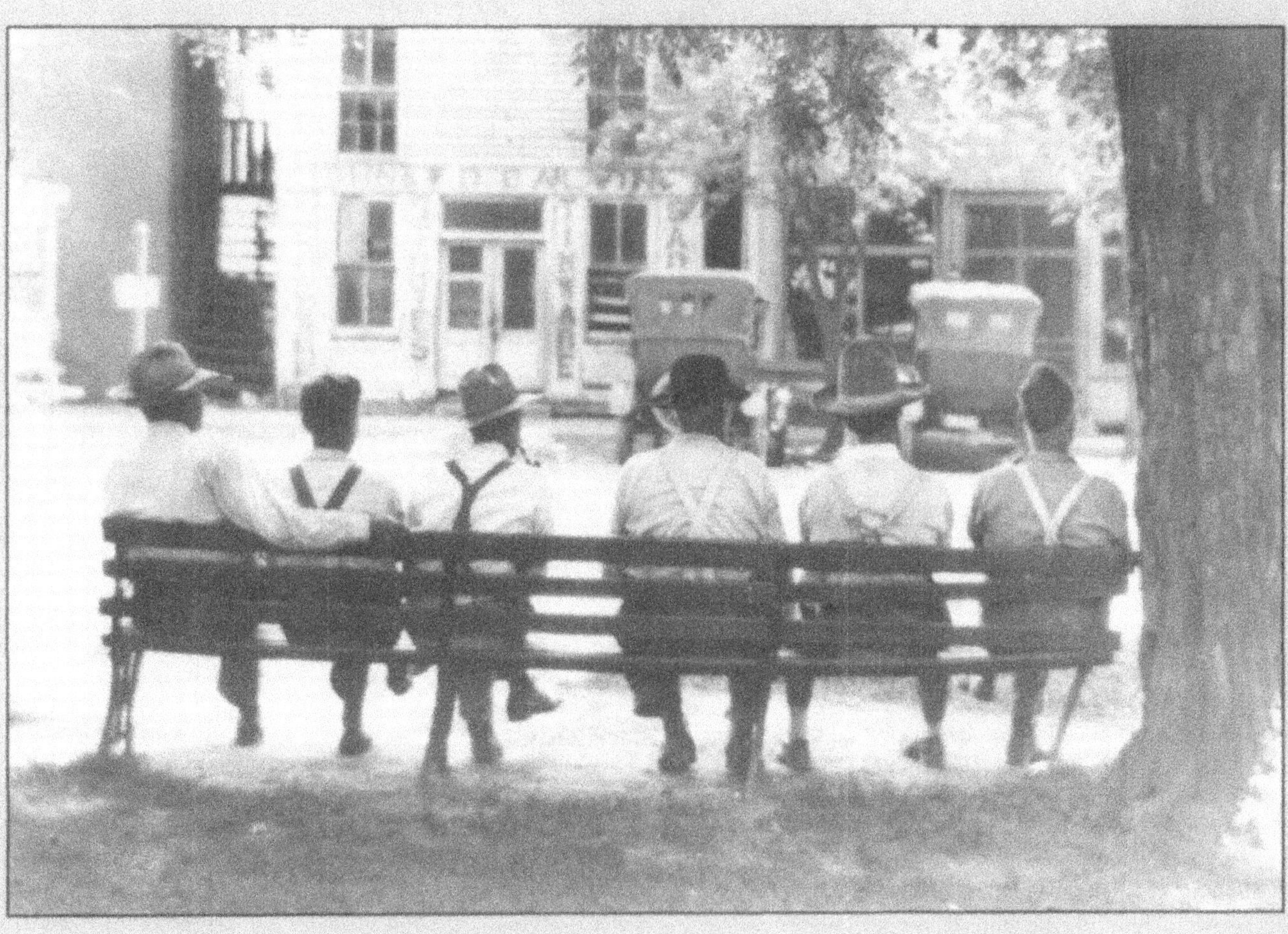

The "Liars Bench," 1923 Courthouse yard, facing Calvin Hardware. (Photo By Frank Hohenberger)

Chapter I
In The Beginning

Many millions of years ago there were no hills, valleys, forests, nor underlying bedrock of shale, sandstone and limestone in what is now Brown County.

In the geologic age named the Mississippian Period, 360 million years ago, the landmass to which present Indiana belongs was nearly on the equator. An extensive area of this land mass was covered by a shallow salt sea. The so-called Michigan River emptied into the sea over present south-central Indiana. When the river met the quieter salt water it deposited its sediments. As layers of river silt came under ever-increasing pressure, siltstone was formed. Clay deposits hardened into shale. A delta resulted after several million years.

Then the sea level rose. Calcium carbonate from the shells and sea creatures became carbonate sands and mud on top of the delta deposits, and through more millions of years hardened into solid limestone.

When the sea receded, a level rock surface was exposed over what is now Brown County, and adjacent territory. By this time the landmass had moved northward.

Erosion by rain, wind, sun, and frost began on the exposed rock. Through many centuries low hills and very shallow valleys, containing the clays, sand, and gravel of erosion were formed.[1]

About two million years ago a worldwide lowering of temperature ushered in the Ice Age, or Pleistocene Epoch. The enormous snowfalls turned into ice in what is now Canada. Under pressure of its own weight the Canadian icemass began to move south, southeast, and southwest.[2]

There were several advances and retreats of the ice. When the climate warmed the ice melted. When the cold returned the ice formed again. During the Illinoian glacial era the ice advanced east and west of what is now Brown County to the Ohio River and a portion of Kentucky, but it never covered the south-central section of present Indiana nor two-thirds of Brown County.[3]

The ice from the north was stopped at Bean Blossom Ridge which is the most northern point of the Knobstone Escarpment. This higher land extends south through Brown County to the Ohio River and is part of the higher land of the ancient delta deposited by the Michigan River so many million years ago.

The glacier ice crept through a gap in the ridge near the present village of Needmore, and it ploughed over a few areas in eastern Brown County leaving terraces of pebbles, gravel, and sand. But Bean Blossom Ridge was an effective barrier on the north and glacial till is not found on Brown County land directly south of the Ridge.[4]

When the Illinoian Ice Age ended with a warming of the climate, the melting ice caused floods that swept across the then low hills and shallow valleys of what is now Brown County. Erosion continued for thousands of years. Today's ridge-spines, steep slopes, V-shaped valleys and the wider valleys, are the result. In fact, erosion continues to this day, as the brown streams after rains testify.

The melting glacier left great piles of drift north of Bean Blossom Ridge over what is now northern Hamblen and Jackson Townships. And a terminal moraine was pushed against the north slopes of Bean Blossom Ridge.

Buried in the glacial drift near the surface and to a depth of 25 feet are small nuggets and flakes of gold, silver, diamonds, topazes, small garnets, tiny rubies, carnelian, greenstone, quartz and magnetite. After heavy rains these minerals wash out into Brown County streams. Such minerals are never found in sedimentary rock that underlies Brown County. They were brought in the masses of material scalped from Canadian land and pushed south under the glaciers as they advanced. They were, of course, deposited wherever the glaciers melted:[5]

The hills of northern Brown County over which the Illinoian glacier travelled to Bean Blossom Ridge are more rolling and less jagged than hills in the rest of Brown County.

Two of the streams that drain Brown County, the north fork of Salt Creek and Bean Blossom Creek, are believed to have originated when the Illinoian glacier melted.[6]

In The Beginning
Bibliography

[1] Hill, John, Department of Natural Resources, Geological Survey, State of Indiana. Letter to Dorothy Bailey March 22, 1984.
[2] Blatchley, W. S., Gold and Diamonds in Indiana, p. 13.
[3] Patton, John B., Map of Indiana: Unconsolidated Deposits, 1979.
Goodspeed, Weston A., Counties of Morgan, Monroe and Brown, Indiana, 1884, p. 73.
[4] Blatchley, W. S., Op.cit., p. 14.
[5] Ibid., p. 21.
[6] Lambert, Daryl. Survey of Brown County Soils, Brown County Democrat September 28, 1983.

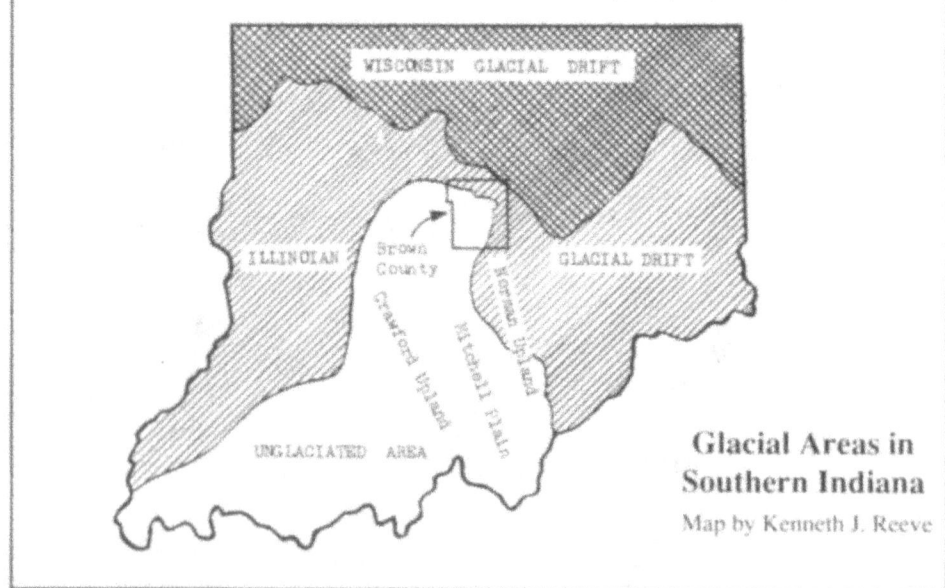

Glacial Areas in Southern Indiana

Map by Kenneth J. Reeve

Chapter II
Prehistoric and Historic Indians in Brown County

Prehistoric Indians

By the time the ice-age glaciers had retreated to central Canada for the final time, the earliest known Indian hunters, the Paleo, were wandering over what would be Brown County. They stayed for about 2000 years– 10,000 to 8,000 B.C.[1]

The Paleo hunted in small groups, their spears tipped with fluted points made of chert, a flint-like stone. These fluted spear points have been found in Brown County. The Paleo killed caribou and mastadon. It is supposed that they killed such animals in Brown County, although their spear points have not been found by archaeologists with the bones of their kills.[2]

By 1,000 B.C. enormous changes had come to future Brown County. The ice-age animals were extinct, the harsh climate had moderated, the tundra-like vegetation had been replaced first by coniferous forest, then deciduous forests of oak, hickory and maple. New species of fish had come to the streams. Deer, elk, bear, and turkey lived in the hills and valleys.[3]

The so-called Archaic Indians, instead of the Paleo, lived in the county from about 3,000 B.C. to 1,500 B.C. They lived in small camps on hilltops and stream valleys. The last Archaic Indians had larger base camps along Salt Creek, and Bean Blossom Creek. They made tools from bone and stone. They hunted with a variety of spear tips, and knives chipped from stone. The forests furnished food such as berries, nuts, fruits and roots, as well as game, and fish from the streams. It is not known what kind of shelters they built.[4]

The Woodland Indians came to what would become Brown County about 500 B.C. and stayed to 1,600 A.D. They hunted in the forests but it did not suit their life style to live in the narrow valleys and on the steep hills. They lived in settlements along rivers south and east of the county. They planted crops of maize, beans, sunflowers, and squash on flatter land that could be more easily tilled.

The Woodland were the first Indians to make pottery, shards of which are now found in the county. And from 500 A.D. to 1,500 A.D. they were the first Indians to make and use bows and arrows.[5] Countless arrowheads have been found in Brown County's ploughed fields, and in the streams.

By 1,600 A.D. all prehistoric Indians

had left Indiana. Why they suddenly left, and where they went is still an unsolved mystery.[6]

Historic Indians

By 1650 the Miami, Potawatomi, Kickapoo, Piankashaw and Wyandotte had filtered into Indiana.

About 1788 the Shawnee appeared from the east in southern, eastern, and northern Indiana. They were refugees driven west by white settlers.[7]

Though Shawnee and Miami may have hunted occasionally in the forests that covered future Brown County, it was the Delaware Indians who claimed the land for over forty years. The Delaware, once a powerful tribe whose original name was Lenni-Lennape, also arrived as refugees. They had lived in the Chesapeake Bay area. Powhatan and Pocohantas had belonged to the tribe, and it was the Delaware who captured John Smith.

In the early 1700s they were forced to flee Virginia. They settled in Ohio along the Muskingum and Mahoning rivers. Then again crowded out by settlers in 1770, they fled to eastern Indiana. The Miami and Piankashaw gave them permission to live on the land between the Ohio and the White River.[8]

Like the prehistoric Woodland, the Delaware hunted in the dense climax forest that covered Brown County. Their permanent settlements were built on the west fork of White River.

Early Brown County settlers found their wigwams, shaped like an inverted orange-half, made of saplings and covered with woven mats, hides, or grass. These they had used as shelters from rain and snow during their hunting expeditions.[9]

There have been innumerable accidental discoveries of Indian relics in Brown County, and there are certainly as yet undiscovered and undisturbed prehistoric sites. Casual removal of relics destroys accurate evidence of 12,000 years of prehistoric Indian life. The Glenn A. Black Laboratory of Archaeology at Indiana University, in Bloomington, would greatly appreciate people reporting their finds and allowing the Laboratory to record them.

Prehistoric and Historic Indians in Brown County
Bibliography

[1] Glenn A. Black Laboratory of Archaeology, Brown County Information Summary, August 8, 1982.
[2] Kellar, James H., An Introduction of Prehistory of Indiana, p. 25.
[3] Ibid., p. 27.
[4] Munson, Cheryl, (Glenn A. Black Laboratory), Letter to Dorothy Bailey, August 4, 1982.
[5] Peckham, Howard H., Indiana, p. 67.
[6] Voegelin, Erminie W., Indians of Indiana, Reprint from Proceedings of The Indiana Academy of Science, Vol. 50, pp. 27-32, 1941.
[7] Voegelin, Erminie W., Op. cit.
[8] Esarey, Logan, A History of Indiana, Vol. 1, Third Edition, p. 82, 1924.
[9] Bartholomew County Historical Society, History of Bartholomew County, Indiana 1888, 1976 Edition, p. 60.

Chapter III
Pioneer Travel to Brown County

The first generation of people in the colonies clustered near the coast. The second generation moved toward the Appalachians. Many of the third generation in Virginia, Delaware, Maryland, North and South Carolina pushed across the mountains into Kentucky and Tennessee. The fourth generation crossed the Ohio River and entered Indiana Territory a century or more after their ancestors crossed the Atlantic Ocean.[1]

The migration into Indiana, and to land farther west and north, became one of the greatest migrations in the history of the world.[2] In 1800 there were about 2,500 settlers in Indiana Territory. By 1825 there were an estimated 250,000.[3]

The pioneers who settled in what became Brown County were part and parcel of the thousands of people who came to Indiana during the pioneer era that lasted from 1800 to 1850.[4]

No bridges across river in early pioneer days. (A Frank Sohn painting)

The primary motive for this migration was the need to buy cheap, fertile land to own, to live on, to farm, and to pass on to their children. Pioneers were willing to undergo hardship, privation, loneliness and danger in order to acquire property. The opportunities to own land in the New World were very great by comparison with the system of land tenure and land ownership in the Old World. Consequently, the United States became a country of freeholders, rather than renters or tenants.[5]

Other contributing factors for moving to Indiana were the increasing scarcity of wild game, and the loss of land pioneers had believed to be their own in Kentucky, due to the insecurity of land titles. The desire for new land outweighed all other considerations.

The Ohio River was the great highway to Indiana in the early pioneer years before roads were built. It was far easier to float down the river than to trek through unbroken wilderness. Pioneers built their own flatboats, or bought them at the up-river ports of Cincinnati and Wheeling. They stopped at an Indiana river port, such as Vevay, Madison, New Albany or Jeffersonville, sold their flatboats for lumber, or abandoned them, loaded the family possessions into the wagons they brought with them, gathered up their livestock and commenced the arduous inland trip.[6] For pioneers moving into Indiana, a river town was the last outpost of civilization before they vanished into the wilderness.

When steamboats began to operate on the Ohio River in 1816 pioneers could journey to any Indiana riverport with their loaded wagon and livestock on the deck of a steamboat. After a canal was built to avoid the falls at Louisville in 1831, steamboats plied the entire length of the Ohio to the Mississippi and as far south as New Orleans.[7]

Pioneers could also cross the Ohio from Kentucky to Indiana on one of several ferries that were well established by 1816. To reach the ferries, migrating settlers from Virginia, the Carolinas, and Tennessee coming through the Cumberland Gap used the Wilderness Road through Kentucky to the Ohio River. In 1817 one observer wrote, "All America seems to be breaking up and moving westward. We are seldom out of sight, as we travel on the Grand Track towards the Ohio, of family groups behind and before us."[8]

Having arrived in Indiana by ferry, flatboat, or steamboat pioneers entered a thick, almost impenetrable climax forest. The sun hit the tops of giant trees seventy or eighty feet high, but near the earth it was always shady to the point of gloom.[9]

In 1817, the year after Indiana became a state, when travel and living conditions were still extremely primitive, an early traveler wrote, "There was not a foot of turnpike road in the State and plank roads had never been heard of. The girdled, standing trees covered the cultivated fields; the shovel plow (was) the only cultivator;...not a bridge in the State." This was only in the southern-most section of Indiana near the river, where people had lived since 1800.[10]

Since there were no roads, pioneers used Indian trails and traces the buffalo had left. Each important trail or trace leading east and west, or north and south, was as well known to pioneers in the 1820s and 1830s as the state highways are known to today's travellers. Other than these several trails and traces north from the Ohio River the wilderness was trackless.[11]

In the dim forest, trails and traces widened by constant and increasing wagon traffic, never really dried out. In wet weather they were deep in mud and almost impassable. A wagon often sank a foot and a half, and horses or oxen mired to their bellies in the mud. After such an experience drivers turned into the dense woods beside the trail maneuvering between trees, through tangled underbrush and around fallen logs.

There were fairly wide creeks to ford. The banks of small creeks were steep and difficult to negotiate. When water was high travelers had to wait, sometimes for several days, until the creeks could be crossed.[12]

Families who settled in Brown County frequently banded together to make the journey from the Ohio on the trace they chose, to help each other, and for protection in time of danger. William Murphy (1792-1891) the great-grandfather of William Romey Murphy (1877-1975) settled in Hamblen Township on a government land grant in 1835. The Murphys came from North Carolina. Together with the Brummetts, Stephens, and Mosers they made the trip from the Ohio River to Brown County.[13]

They followed a trail from Mauckport to Corydon and Salem, then veered northwest on a trail from Washington County to Jackson County crossing the East Fork of the White River at Sparks Ferry. Before bridges were built, the ferry played an important role for all settlers and travellers in western Jackson and Washington Counties.

From Sparks Ferry the pioneers followed the Sparks Ferry Trail to Freetown in northern Jackson County and to Christiansburg in southern Brown County, then north to present day Stone Head. The old road is now closed, though a few sections remain, and may be walked with difficulty. From Stone Head the trail continued, via Deadfall Creek, across Henderson (Gnawbone) Creek to the North Fork of Salt Creek, the town of Taggart in Hamblen Township, and north to Johnson County.[14]

Many Hamblen Township pioneers followed this same route from the Ohio River, especially those who settled near Gatesville and Taggart, or farther west in Jackson Township.

Jacob Walker (1788-1863) emigrated from Virginia with his wife, five sons, and a daughter. They crossed the Ohio on a ferry, and drove a covered wagon drawn by a pair of oxen to Nineveh in Johnson County in the early 1820s. Jacob Walker chose land along Salt Creek in Brown County. In 1825 since there was no road or trail, Jacob and his sons used their axes to cut down trees. For ten miles they made a path wide enough to bring the wagon and oxen to their destination. They cut down more trees to furnish the logs for their cabin, then cleared land for a corn crop.

Many other pioneers came south into northern Brown County from Johnson County. Settlers drifted into the county from Columbus, Bartholomew County, and from Bloomington, in Monroe County. All of the earliest pioneers had come from the Ohio River on a trail or trace through the dense forests.

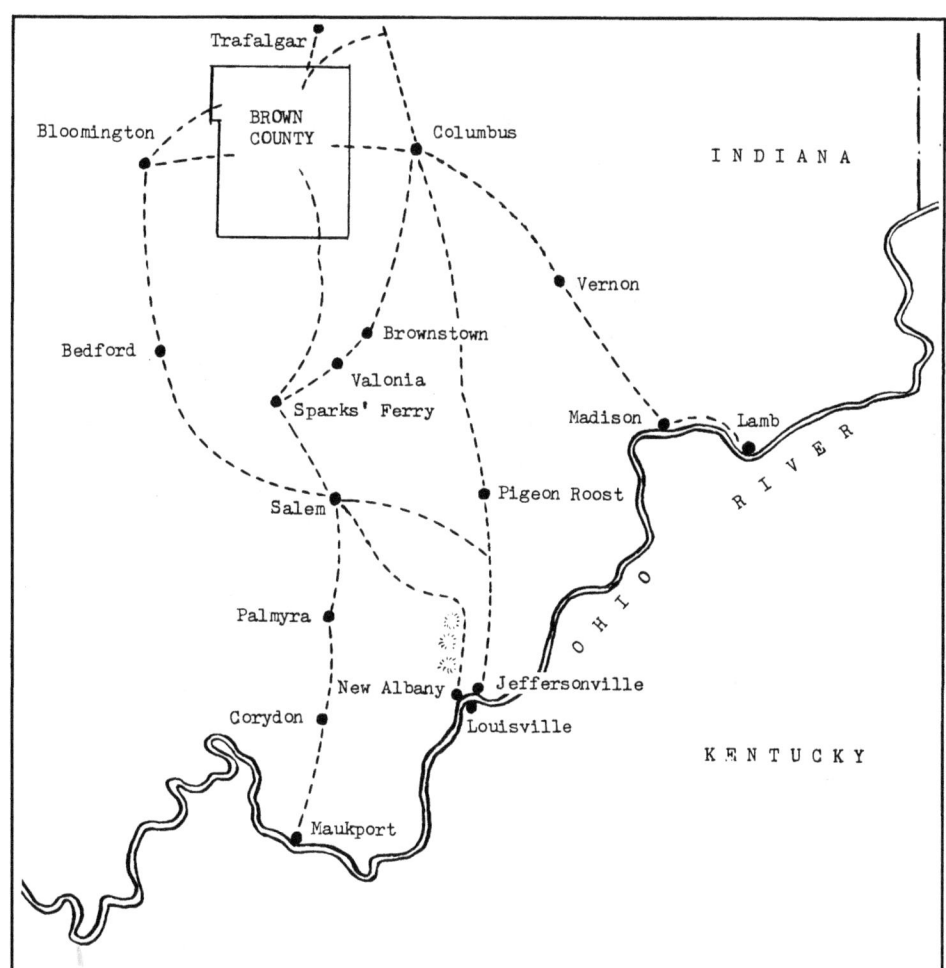

Pioneer Routes to Brown County. (Map by Kenneth J. Reeve)

Pioneer Travel to Brown County Bibliography

[1] Carmony, Donald F., Handbook on Indiana History, 1963, p. 16.
Esarey, Logan, A History of Indiana, Vol. 1, pp. 184-5, 1924.
[2] Rohrbaugh, Malcolm J., The Land Office Business in Indiana, 1800-1840, p.41.
[3] Esarey, Logan, Op. cit., p. 205.
[4] Carmony, Donald F., Op. cit., p. 29.
[5] Rohrbaugh, Malcolm J., Op. cit., p. 42.
[6] Zimmer, Donald T., The Ohio River: Pathway to Settlement, p. 64.
[7] Von Schweinitz, Lewis David, The Journey of Lewis David Von Schweinitz to Goshen, Bartholomew County in 1831, Indiana Historical Society Publications, Vol. 8, No. 5, pp. 222-224, 1927.
[8] Birbeck, Morris, Notes on a Journey in America Dublin, Ireland 1818.
[9] Zimmer, Donald T., Op. cit., p. 61.
[10] Cavinder, Fred D., Indianapolis Star Magazine, July 4, 1976, p.3.
[11] Wilson, George R., Early Indiana Trails and Surveys, Society of Indiana Pioneers, p. 24.
[12] Esarey, Logan, Op. cit., Vol. 1, p. 279.
[13] Murphy, Family History – Brown County.
[14] Goodspeed, Weston A., Counties of Morgan, Monroe and Brown, Indiana, 1884, p.719.

Chapter IV
Pioneers and Indians in Brown County

The United States acquired the Indians' land in Indiana by means of treaties, such as Harrison's Purchase in 1809, and the Treaty of St. Mary's in 1818. In 1821 the Delaware, and other tribes, were forced to march from Indiana over the infamous Trail of Tears to land west of the Mississippi. Therefore only a very few Indians remained in what became Brown County when the first settlers in 1820 began to trickle onto the land.

Information is scant, but there are tales concerning the Indians the pioneers told their children that have been handed down for several generations. Settlers did not call the Indians "Delaware," nor members of any other tribe. Apparently, Indians were just Indians to early pioneers.

In 1820 the Indians were peacable, but one story indicated that the few remaining Indians may not have been totally without malice. Emaline Helms Snider (1842-1907) came from Belmont, Ohio, when she was quite young. She married William Snider, known as "Tobacco Bill." Emaline told her daughter, Mary Jane Snider Wade (1861-1940), that a family named Marcum lived in a cabin on a hilltop near what is now Railroad Road. (William Marcum had entered land in Township 10 north, Range 2 east, Section 2, in 1837.) Early in county history the Marcums fled to the deep woods one night when a band of Indians seemed intent on marauding their cabin. No harm was done by the Indians but the cabin became a landmark and was known in Jackson Township as long as it existed as the log cabin that was almost attacked by Indians.[1]

However, peaceful association was the rule. More than a few pioneer families became accustomed to seeing smoke from Indian campfires "down the holler." Indians were inclined to move out of an area if pioneers came in. When the Petros came to Hamblen Township Indians camping near them promptly left. (Levi Petro entered land in Hamblen Township 9 north, Range 3 east, Section 14, in 1834.)[2]

Pioneers found, and used, Indian traces, and trails, that crisscrossed the county. Originally made by animals, deer and wood buffalo, the trails were five or six inches deep, and about five inches wide. One trace crossed western Brown County north to south, from Hendricks County, south to Lawrence County. Another trace crossed Brown County east to west, from Ohio to Illinois. Some of these traces were visible as late as 1955.[3]

Settlers found not a single Indian village but only scattered, temporary hunting wigwams. Occasionally they associated quite casually with a few Indians. Thomas Andrew Brown (1809-1879) came from Jackson County in 1830 to Brown County. He bought land and settled two miles southeast of Story. In time, he discovered a lone Indian living on his land. Thomas would find a gift of a rabbit or a couple of quail, cleaned and ready to cook, hanging on the rail fence near his cabin. He would return the kindness by leaving cornbread, butter, or vegetables on a stump. He and the Indian never talked together. Finally the Indian disappeared.[4]

Ransom Sturgeon lived in Schooner Valley half a mile from Duncan Cemetery. When he was a young man he was taught to plow by an Indian who planted a "truck patch" on his land every year.

Anna Jackson McGuire (1815-1892) wife of Alfred McGuire and mother of Seralvo McGuire, often saw Indian boys in a Salt Creek swimming hole near Hoover Mill about 1844. The boys would lie on logs, and when a white person showed up they dived into the water and swam with only their heads above water.[5]

Bands of Indians returned to Brown County for several decades to recover valuables they had buried and left behind them. They may have been Delaware since they were familiar with the land, but their tribal affiliations were not recorded. Richard M. Henderson (1857-1943) saw two Indians in the 1870s climb to the Mountain Tea Patch on a hill overlooking Salt Creek. They made no effort to hide their presence. It was a trip they made every year. Many people climbed the hill after the Indians left each year, but the earth was never disturbed and they never found as much as a footprint. The mystery of their yearly trip was never solved.[6]

In the 1880s or 1890s Hugh Tom Adams, (1868-1949) who farmed on Clay Lick Road and who was one of the first mail carriers in Brown County, came across several Indians digging at the foot of a large beech tree. A snake had been carved in the bark, head downward. After the Indians had gone, Hugh Tom found an empty iron kettle with the bottom missing at the base of the tree. Of course he never knew what had been buried there.[7]

A few Brown County people have Indian ancestors. Some early settlers had forefathers who mingled with Tennessee Cherokee, and had Indian blood in their veins when they arrived in Brown County. Some remember and are proud of their ancestry, others refuse to admit their heritage. More than one flyleaf listing births and deaths in a family Bible, bearing testimony of Indian ancestors, has been torn out and destroyed.

Pioneers and Indians in Brown County Bibliography.

[1] Oral History, Chattie Miller, Brown County Historical Society Archives, February 28, 1976.

[2] Ibid.
Hohenberger, Frank W., Down in the Hills O' Brown County, Indianapolis Star, September 26, 1925.
Goodspeed, Weston A., Counties of Morgan, Monroe and Brown, Indiana, 1884, p. 742.

[3] Guernsey, E. Y., Indiana, The Influence of The Indian Upon Its History, Indiana Department of Conservation, Map Publication, 122, 1932.

[4] Brown, Grover, G., Two Hundred Years with the Browns, 1964, p. 64.

[5] Mathis, Ray, Brown County History, 1936, p. 13.

[6] Hohenberger, Frank W., Down in the Hills O' Brown County, Indianapolis Star, December 17, 1949.

[7] Oral History, Eva Rogers Jarvis, Brown County Historical Society Archives, August 7, 1982.

Chapter V
The Earliest Pioneers

The first wave of settlers in future Brown County was almost entirely native born from Virginia, the Carolinas, Kentucky, and Tennessee. However "a sprinkling of Yankees were...enough to give the Northern spirit to all public undertakings."[1]

Many pioneers deliberately chose to live in the rugged county because they felt at home in the hills, having come from mountainous country southeast of Indiana. Others had fled from low, swampy land and came to the hills to escape malaria, the "ague" or "agger." In 1831 a man on horseback rode into Columbus, Indiana, and found a deserted village. Not a person was to be seen. Finally, the stranger discovered one solitary man working on the unfinished courthouse. Everyone else was at home in bed incapacitated by the "ague."[2]

In 1820 Congress passed a law that made it possible for Indiana settlers to buy a minimum of 80 acres (1/8 of a section) for $1.25 an acre at a government land office. Payment was strictly in cash. No credit was allowed as had previously been the case. In 1832 Congress passed a second law reducing a minimum tract to 40 acres.[3]

Settlers often lived in future Brown County for as long as ten years before visiting a government land office. Therefore the date of arrival and the date of land purchase rarely coincide. The stipulation of payment in cash was certainly one reason why pioneers delayed buying land, for settlers had very little money.

The Government Land Office at Jeffersonville was established in 1818. On August 14, 1820, when the survey of lands bought from the Indians in the 1818 Treaty of St. Mary's was completed, pioneers were allowed to settle on this new land and buy acreage from the government. After 1825 they could enter land at the Government Land Office in Indianapolis.[4]

Discovering accurate information concernng pioneers is often very difficult. The destruction of the early Brown County courthouse records in the 1873 fire compounds the difficulties. Names and dates of government land entries may be the sum total of information now known concerning the earliest pioneers.

Many settlers suddenly left the county and disappeared for a variety of reasons: sheer restlessness, the wish to join relatives who had traveled farther west, crop failures, or a disease like typhoid or diptheria that decimated a large family. The few who survived often hurriedly moved elsewhere to make a new beginning.

In this chapter a few of the earliest pioneers in each township are mentioned about whom information is available.

It is conceded that the first white man to enter future Brown County was the German, Johann Schoonover, though he was not a settler. He came north from the Ohio River to Jackson County on Indian trails or buffalo traces with a cart drawn by oxen. From Jackson County he made his way through the dense wilderness and settled on a creek in future Washington Township,

White oak on Albert Johnson Road, Hamblen Township, 1987. Planted by A. Porter Hamblen 1880. Standing (l. to r.) John Hamblen and Bob Hamblen indicating size of original trees in Brown County.

Aquilla "Quiller" Moore beside giant sycamore on his farm just south of Pikes Peak on Poplar Grove Road. Photo by Helen Ayres 1990.

sometime between 1818 and 1820.

He preferred to live alone, and traded trinkets, ammunition, and guns, for furs with the few remaining Indians. It is not known how long he stayed nor what became of him. However, he is firmly entrenched in Brown County history since Schooner Creek and Schooner Valley are named for him.[5]

JOHNSON TOWNSHIP

William Elkins was the first pioneer to settle with a family in what became Brown County. His history may be traced with authenticity since letters, personal records, the original deeds he received for land, tax receipts, and his will existed for many years.

William, born in 1796, came from Pulaski County, Kentucky to Lawrence County, Indiana, with his parents. During the War of 1812 the family fled to a blockhouse in Lawrence County, built at that time for the protection of pioneers from Indians. After the War, William lived with his parents in northern Jackson County until he married.

By 1820 he had built a log cabin for his family about a mile east of the former town of Elkinsville. The little village, founded in the 1850s, was named for William Elkins to honor the first settler in Brown County.

Elkins lived as a squatter until 1834. In that year new survey lines were run, and he discovered that the chimney of his cabin was not on the land he claimed as his own. Without waiting for supper he set out for Jeffersonville and promptly entered land in Township 8 north, Range 2 east, Section 36. He was determined not to lose his cabin, nor the farm he had spent years of time and effort hacking out of the forest.

William continued to live in his cabin until his death at ninety-two. The log cabin he built was later bought and moved to the hill just south of Nashville.[6]

David Johnson was the second pioneer to settle in Johnson Township, about 1821. In 1836, when the county was organized, Johnson Township was named for him.

David Johnson entered land in 1834 in Township 7 north, Range 2 east, Section 21. Little more is now known concernng this pioneer, except that in the 1840 census he was listed as between 80 and 90 years of age. His will, recorded in the Brown County Courthouse on October 3, 1845, was probated on April 1, 1846. This will still exists in a bound volume in the clerk's office.[7]

Only a few more pioneers drifted into Johnson Township during the 1820s.

VAN BUREN TOWNSHIP

Both Van Buren and Johnson Townships were settled more slowly than central and northern Brown County. However, in the 1830s there was an influx of pioneers in both townships and "log cabins were scattered in all directions."

Frederick Goss (1784-1868) was the first pioneer to enter land with the government in what became Van Buren Township, and furthermore, according to the Government Entry Record, he was the very first settler in all of Brown County to enter land. On May 30, 1821, Frederick took out 80 acres in Township 8 north, Range 3 east, and the west half of the southwest quarter of Section 22. In 1830 he entered more land in Section 22, and in 1834 land in Section 21.

Frederick Goss was the fourth generation of the Goss family to be born in the United States. The Gosses came from Germany and spoke their native language for three generations in the new country. They settled in Pennsylvania then moved to North Carolina where Frederick was born April 13, 1784, to Jacob and Phoebe Goss, in Rowan County.

Frederick left North Carolina for Indiana, and the 1820 census listed him, his wife Carrie, and four children, in Jackson County. By 1821 he was living in future Brown County.

He became a prosperous farmer, well known for his ability. In January 1834 Goss, J. Watson, and William Taggart were appointed as the committee to select public lots in Nashville on which to build county buildings. "Squire Goss" was a Justice of the Peace in 1836 and 1837. In 1844 he paid $5.50 in taxes and was listed as one of the highest taxpayers in Van Buren Township.

The Goss men were very large and strong. It was said that when Fredrick and his son, Nepthalian, walked through a snow storm "their big feet made tracks that looked as though two elephants had passed by ."

Frederick Goss decided to leave Brown County in 1846, when he was sixty-two. Accordingly, he sold his land on September 28, 1846, to James Williamson. Frederick, Carrie, and their eight children left in covered wagons for the long trip to Missouri to visit relatives. They took with them a letter, written by the clerk of their Brown County church, which has been carefully preserved by a descendant.

"To all whom these presents may come greetings. This letter gose (sic) to certify that our beloved brother Frederick Goss is a member in good standing in the Church of Christ at Friendship Meeting House Van Burren Township with his brethern and as such wherever his lot may be cast down by order of the Church this 22 Day of August 1846."

Thomas A. Brown, Clerk, Indiana.

The family settled in Wright County, Missouri. Carrie died in 1852, Frederick in 1868. They lie in Newton Cemetery, Wright County.[8]

Thomas A. Brown (1809-1879) was twelve years old in 1821 when he came from Burke County, North Carolina, to Jackson County, Indiana, with his father, Joshua (1774-1830), his mother, Phebe (sic), and his three brothers.

On June 13, 1830, Thomas married Mary O'Neal, daughter of Jacob and Elizabeth O'Neal, who had also emigrated from Burke County, North Carolina. As soon as they were married Thomas and Mary Brown came to Van Buren Township and settled two miles southeast of what is now Story. They carried their belongings, and walked through the wilderness to the site of their new home.

Thomas built a small log cabin and cleared enough land to plant his first corn crop. He traded a rifle for a blind mare in order to cultivate his corn.

In 1837 Thomas entered land in Township 8 north, Range 4 east, Section 7. Thomas and Mary Brown donated an acre of their land for the Shiloh, or Brown Cemetery, and for the Shiloh Methodist Episcopal Church. The church no longer exists.

Thomas, and a neighbor, cut down trees to make the first primitive road to the Nashville-Columbus, Indiana, highway. The road they made was only a trail through the forest. Horses, oxen and mules dodged innumerable stumps.

On this trail and the highway Thomas hauled six loads of chestnut oak bark to a tannery in Columbus (the tannery existed for over a hundred years) in one week with a four-mule team. No other pioneer achieved a similar record.

On one occasion, when driving home at night, Thomas failed to see a small tree that had fallen across the road. The oxen he was driving at that time climbed over the obstruction, but the wagon pinned his leg against the tree and Thomas arrived home with a broken leg.

Before the Civil War, Thomas built a more commodious tulip-poplar log cabin, consisting of two large rooms connected by a breezeway - later enclosed to make a bedroom. A picture of the large cabin, with the family standing in the dooryard, is an example of how the continual hard work of only one pioneer family could convert wilderness to a productive farm, and fairly comfortable, though primitive, living conditions. There was a large log barn back of the house, and several sheds. The barn was large enough for horses, cattle and sheep. Chickens, geese, turkeys, ducks, and guineas were also kept on the farm.[9]

Levi Noblet (1799-1872) born in Cumberland Gap, Virginia (now Tennessee), found his way to Brown County, built a log cabin, and cleared land in order to farm. In 1839 he entered land in Township 8 north, Range 3 east, Section 29. He is remembered as a trader who travelled between Van Buren Township and Louisville, for a number of years, carrying produce to sell. Like many other pioneers he was restless, and left Brown County for Osage, Missouri. In 1856 he returned and farmed as long as he lived.[10]

The Hattens, Hamptons, Bozwells, James Taber, James Williamson, were early pioneers in Van Buren Township in the 1820s, though they did not enter land until the 1830s and 1840s.[11]

WASHINGTON TOWNSHIP

Moses Williams was the second man to enter land on November 26, 1821, in what would be Brown County, at the Jeffersonville Land Office: 80 acres in Township 8 north, Range 1 east, and the west half of the northwest quarter of Section 12.

It may be that Williams was a land speculator – though this cannot be proved. The Monroe County Courthouse deed records show that he sold this land to Joshua O. Howe and Henry Wampler in 1825. Moses Williams apparently never lived on the land, and the Williams families of Brown County do not trace their ancestry to Moses Williams.

Land speculators had appeared in Indiana at an early date, and by 1830 were in very bad repute. They paid few taxes, did not help build roads, churches, nor schools, and did not "roll logs" to help pioneers build their cabins. If a settler failed, and sold his land, speculators were apt to buy it at the government price per acre, not paying for any improvements such as land clearing and buildings. Pioneers despised them, and they were considered as low as horse thieves. Fortunately, few speculators disturbed the settlers in Brown County.[12]

Edward David (1784-1880) entered 80 acres in 1828, at Jeffersonville Land Office, in Township 9 north, Range 3 east, Section 28, Washington Township.

Edward David came from Hardin County, Kentucky. It is recorded that he was a short man, and never weighed more than 130 pounds. Nevertheless, he was strong, active, courageous, industrious, and fully able to cope with the hardships and privations of pioneer living. He built a sturdy log cabin for his family, cleared land, and farmed.

Edward came to the county with an Indian wife. After her death he married three more wives: Polly who died in 1825, Patsey who lived until 1852, and Mary A. David who died in 1875. Edward David had 29 children, and his family was thought to be the largest in all of Indiana.

At the first Old Settlers Reunion held in Brown County at Georgetown (Bean Blossom), in September 1877, Edward David, then 95 years old, was awarded a cane as the man who had lived in the county the longest and was over 60 years of age. He danced a jig in appreciation for the tumultuous applause of the large crowd.

Edward David is buried in the David family cemetery on the farm he owned in Washington Township.[13]

Robert Henderson, Sr., (1795-1885) was fifteen years old when he emigrated in 1810 with his father, Joseph Henderson, from Virginia to Kentucky, and to Jackson County, Indiana.

One day, while hunting, Robert followed a deer into what became Brown County. The hills must have appealed to him for he promptly sold the 900 acres he had bought, loaded his wife, Permillie Newkirk, children and possessions on a wagon in 1829 and wended his way through the forest to future Brown County. Like many early pioneers Robert used his axe, cutting down trees, to make a path for his wagon and livestock. He settled on Henderson Creek, later named for him, now usually called Gnaw Bone Creek, built a round-log cabin, cleared land and developed a good farm with the usual immense amount of labor.

Robert Henderson knew Brown County when it was entirely covered by deep forest. He was one of the settlers whose land and cabin were described as "a mere niche" in the surrounding wilderness.

In 1835 he entered land with the government in Township 9 north, Range 3 east, Section 25. He built a second, more comfortable hewed-log cabin. The logs he readied with a whip-saw, a very slow and laborious process.

It is remembered that Robert Henderson was a Democrat of the "old Jacksonian school," and a member of the United Brethren Church.[14]

John Allcorn on February 22, 1832, entered 80 acres of land in Jeffersonville in Township 9 north, Range 3 east, Section 27. The year of his arrival in future Brown County is not known.

John Allcorn was a woodcutter by trade, and an enthusiastic coon hunter. One night, when he was hunting with a friend, the dogs found a coon in a hollow tulip poplar tree. John mentioned that he thought the poplar a most beautiful tree, and added "when I die I'd like to be buried in a tulip-tree coffin."

A few years later, about 1850, neighbors heard John's dogs barking continuously and his cows mooing. Knowing something was wrong they went to his cabin, found that the cows needed care, and the fire in his fireplace had burned out. They searched the woods until they discovered the place where John had been cutting wood. A large tree had fallen on him and killed him. His request was remembered, and a coffin was made from a tulip poplar.

The next spring both ends of the coffin sprouted, and the sprouts pushed through the earth. They grew to be large trees. One died, but the other still stands and is so enormous it takes three people to reach around it.[15]

Harden Holler in early days sheltered many pioneers. It is on the present Helmsburg Road near the western edge of the Nashville Corporation line. The Harden, Jones, and Williams families lived in the narrow valley as well as other settlers. By the early 1900s all traces of the homes of these early settlers had vanished with the exception of one stone well curb.

An intriguing story has come down through the years concerning a "Mr. Williams" of Harden Holler who drove a tall, gray horse hitched to a wagon with four solid wooden wheels, without rims, or tires. He was called "the wooden man."[16]

HAMBLEN TOWNSHIP

The name of the very first settler in what became Hamblen Township is unknown, but by 1824 there were ten or twelve families living in the area. Pioneers came from Jackson County by way of the old Sparks Ferry Road, or south from Johnson County, or west from Columbus and western Bartholomew County.[17]

James Taggart, Sr. (1774-1852) was the first settler to enter land with the government, 80 acres on March 22, 1828, in Township 10 north, Range 3 east, and the east half of the northwest quarter of Section 36. For this, and other land he later entered, James received government patents.

James and his wife, Rachel, came from east Tennessee. In 1836 he was appointed the first assessor in Hamblen Township, for which work he received $5.00. He was also the assessor in 1840 and 1841. The first election in the Township was held in his log cabin. In 1836 James Taggart, Sr., served as a Justice of the Peace. In the same year he and fourteen other settlers worked as road hands on the Sparks Ferry Road "near Owen Simpson's property."

James Taggart, Sr., buried in Taggart Cemetery, was the progenitor of the Brown County Taggarts.[18]

Job Hamblen (1762-1833) born in Worcester County, Maryland, one of the earliest settlers in Hamblen Township, was descended from George Hamblen (b. ca 1725) of English ancestry. The family later moved to Halifax, Charlotte and Pittsylvania Counties, Virginia, and by 1786 they were in Rockingham County, North Carolina.

Following his service in the Revolutionary War, Job finally settled in Lee County, Virginia where he raised his family. Job was living in 1821 near Clifford, Bartholomew County, Indiana. He was forced to move against his will. A. P. Hamblen, Job's great great grandson, wrote in 1938:

"grandfather Job settled on land near Clifford, Indiana, under the squatter's unwritten law of the frontier that when his means permitted he would purchase it from the government. But before he accomplished his aim, some other man of better means entered the land. Job had built a cabin and had cleared the land.

"This man came one day in 1825 to the Hamblen house and informed the family of his purchase and asked them to vacate. Job reached for his faithful rifle and made efforts to shoot the intruder, as he termed him, but was restrained by other members of the family. The matter was settled by the man's giving a horse to the Hamblens in exchange for the improvements on the land. This horse was used as the sole means of transportation to move the family over the roadless route to the place where he settled."

Job lived for eight years after his unexpected move. He built a one-room log cabin 145 yards east, and 15 yards north of the spot where he was buried in 1833, on his own land. In 1928 Job's descendents erected a monument over his grave to honor his memory. It was dedicated in a public ceremony. It is the only standing monument to a pioneer in all of Brown County.

Eliakim Hamblen (1796-1852), a son of Job, suggested to the three commissioners of Brown County in 1836 that the northeast township be named for his father, the Revolutionary War soldier, and the first settler in the area where he lived. The commissioners granted this request.[19]

JACKSON TOWNSHIP

By 1823 families began to settle in what would be Jackson Township, though they did not enter land until the 1830s. There were at least twelve round-log cabins by 1830, here and there in the forest that covered Jackson Township. James A. Baker, John Hubbard, John David, the Youngs, Fleeners, Weddels, and Robertsons were among the earliest pioneers.[20]

John Richards (1809-1894) became one of the best known and most successful pioneers in the county. Born in Hawkins County, Tennessee, John came with his parents, Michael Richards, a native of Germany, and Charity Hubbard Richards, to what became Brown County. The family settled in Washington Township.

Shortly thereafter in 1825, when John was sixteen, he returned to Tennessee to live with his grandfather. He made staves and worked as a hand on a flatboat on the Ohio River. In 1830 he made his way back to future Brown County and settled in the Bear Creek region, which he chose because of the excellent bear hunting. His first home was a log cabin. Later, when sawmills produced lumber, he built two frame houses. One of these was situated at an intersection of roads that led to Bloomington, Morgantown, and Nashville.

John Richards constructed chimneys and fireplaces, asking twenty-five cents for a day's labor. He sawed and sold firewood for twenty-five cents a cord, and built rail fences for twenty-five cents per hundred rails. He cleared land, farmed, hunted, and planted "good orchards."

In 1834 John entered land in Township 10 north, Range 3 east, Section 39. He continued to buy land until he owned 940 acres. At one time he was the largest land owner in the county. John found gold in Bear Creek, and was one of the first gold-panners. At one time he built a "gold placer" in the stream.

His ability and industry were recognized, and John Richards served as Constable, Justice of the Peace, and County Commissioner. In 1840 he assessed Jackson Township.[21]

William Snider (1802-1875) was one of the earliest pioneers in Jackson Township. He arrived in 1824 or 1825 from Kentucky, built a log cabin, a log barn, cleared land and farmed. In 1833 he entered land in Township 10 north, Range 3 east, Section 19 northeast of Georgetown (Bean Blossom). In 1836 he acquired more land in Township 10 north, Range 2 east, Section 36. He donated enough land in Section 36 for Snider Cemetery on the old Gosport Road.

When he first came to the county he brought his mother and a son, Harmon, born in 1822, with him. William, the seventh child of Herman and Elizabeth Bowman Snider, had married Jane Evans (1792-1882) but he and his wife had separated before he left Kentucky. A daughter, Eliza, born in 1823, remained with her mother.

After "Kentucky Bill" settled in his new location he decided to bring Eliza to his new Indiana home. In 1828 he made a trip back to Kentucky and kidnapped the child. William made the entire round trip by horseback. On the return journey five-year-old Eliza sat on a pillow in front of her father's saddle. William held her with one hand, and guided the horse with the other hand. He "experienced no little difficulty in making his way through the wild, unbroken country to his new home in the midst of a Brown County wilderness."

A second son, Washington, is said to have left Kentucky and joined his father in Brown County.

William set up housekeeping with Elizabeth Brummett (1812-1867) and they produced a second family of eleven children.

Kentucky Bill participated in numerous county activities and events. When Brown County was organized in 1836 William assessed Jackson Township, and with seven other men donated a tract of 50 acres for the site of the courthouse, the jail, and the village of Nashville in Township 9 north, Range 3 east, Section 19.

In April 1837 William Snider was selected for grand jury duty, and in the same year he was chosen as the contractor for the first log jail built on Lot Number 1 in Nashville. In September, 1837, William Snider succeeded William Taggart as surplus revenue and three percent fund commissoner. The surplus revenue fund paid for the cost of the log jail and log courthouse. The three percent fund accrued from fines of the "circuit, justices' and other courts." It was set aside to pay for a county seminary.

By 1835 Snider had established himself as a "leading man of business" in Georgetown. He opened a store and in 1847 apparently opened a second store. In 1848 he was listed as the heaviest taxpayer in Jackson Township. He paid all of $30.12. In that same year he was listed as paying a poll tax.

William did not neglect amusement and recreation. Georgetown was famous in the early days for horse racing on the long, level, open space near the village. William, and a group of men all over the county, owned "fast horses," and they met on certain days to test the merits of their steeds. Betting was carried to an "extravagant extreme very often," and whiskey was imbibed freely at these gatherings.

Kentucky Bill has been long remembered in Brown County.[22]

Pioneers who had the courage to brave the innumerable dangers of the wilderness should indeed be remembered. Their lives were rugged and difficult, but their never-ending hard work converted deep primeval forest to farms, roads, homes, and villages. Because of the labor of the first pioneers, life was easier for all who followed them to Brown County.

The early government land records have preserved the names of Brown County pioneers, the dates, and locations of their land entries. By 1836, when Brown County was organized, 105 land entries had been recorded for 98 settlers.

A primitive pioneer cabin. Bill Harden pictured on the right.

LAND ENTRIES RECORDED BY 1836 FOR THE PIONEERS OF BROWN COUNTY

Name of Settler	Date of Land Entry	Name of Settler	Date of Land Entry
Johnson Township		Thomas Brown	1834
William Elkins	1834	Luther Calvin	1831
David Johnson	1834	James Culley	1835
Adam Fleetwood	1833, 1834	Jonn Harris	1833
Thomas Fleetwood	1833	John Brown	1835
William Burroughs	1833	Benjamin Pitcher	1835
David Sively	1833	James Stewart	1833
Albert L. Gilstrap	1834	Levi Petro	1834
Solomon Fleetwood	1833	John Conner	1834
		George White	1833
Van Buren Township		James Bolt	1833
Frederick Goss	1821, 1830, 1834	William Murphy	1835
Benjamin Owens	1833	Josiah Goodwine	1833
Cornelius Hurley	1833	Franklin Walker	1834
James Sullivan	1833	Charles Walker, Jr.	1829
Hiram Rippe	1834	Samuel Walker	1833
John Hampton	1832	Michael Richards	1835
Isaac Shipley	1834	Caleb Kennet	1833
Alfred Young	1833	Wiley Guy	1834
William Rippe	1834	Conrad Kirts	1834
Asa Hatten	1834	Abe Chappel	1834
Daniel Hedrick	1834	Moses Tharp	1834
Hiram Mabe	1833	Preston Goforth	1835
John Rippe	1835	George Smith	1834
		Eliakim Hamblen	1834
Washington Township		Christopher Stump	1834
Joshua O. Howe	1826	Samuel Smith	1834
John W. Lee	1824	M.B. Weddle	1834
Henry Wampler	1824	Leah Martin	1834
Moses Williams	1821, 1824	Edward Duncan	1834
Samuel Dunn	1831	Patrick Sullivan	1829
William Johnson	1831	Daniel King	1834
Bezaleel McNully	1833		
Jonathan Fox	1831	**Jackson Township**	
Alexander Baker	1828	Jacob Fleener	1835
John Flinn	1830	Samuel Fleener	1835
Jerry King	1832	Thompson Weddel	1833
James Taggart	1828	Jonn Hubbard	1832
James Sullivan	1832	Jesse Ritter	1835
Henry Whittington	1834	Joseph Robertson	1835
John King	1833	Shad Robertson	1835
William Snyder	1832	James A. Baker	1833
John Alcorn	1832	Silas Young	1833
Edward David	1828, 1833	John Richards	1833, 1834
William King	1832	John David	1832
Joseph White	1833	James Mitchell	1834
Jacob Davis	1835	Joshua Brummet	1835
Cornelius Tucker	1835	Griffith Davidson	1835
Robert Henderson	1835	Aaron Fleener	1833
		Michael Fleener	1833
Hamblen Township		Merinda Kesterson	1833
Pleasant G. Weddle	1833	George Grove	1835
Robert Millsop	1833	William Snider	1833
James Taggart	1828, 1834		

The Earliest Pioneers
Bibliography

[1] Goodspeed, Weston A., Counties of Morgan, Monroe and Brown, Indiana, 1884, p. 746.
[2] William Terrell, John Beck, George Pence, History of Bartholomew County, Vol. I, 1976 Edition, p. 39.
[3] Carmony, Donald F., Handbook on Indiana History, p. 25.
Rohrbough, Malcolm J., The Land Office Business in Indiana 1800-1840, p. 47.
[4] Esarey, Logan, A History of Indiana, Vol. I, p. 389, 1924.
[5] Goodspeed, Weston A., Op. cit., p. 720.
[6] Mathis, Ray, Brown County History, 1936, pp. 10, 11, 23.
Goodspeed, Weston A., Op. cit., p. 751.
[7] Ibid. p. 752.
Nagley, Lester C., Sr., Brown County Vignette, Democrat February 14, 1963.
[8] Government Entry Record, Brown County Courthouse, p.80.
Goodspeed, Weston A., Op. cit., pp. 684, 748, 749.
Heuss, Lois Ione Hotchkiss, Frederick Goss of Rowan County, North Carolina, and His Descendents, pp. 71, 72.
[9] Brown, Grover G., Two Hundred Years With the Browns, pp. 7, 8.
[10] Bowen, F.B., Biographical Record of Bartholomew and Brown Counties, 1904, p. 394.
[11] Goodspeed, Weston A., Op. cit., p. 746.
[12] Mathis, Ray, Op. cit., p. 20.
Esarey, Op. cit., p. 397.
[13] Bowen, F.B., Op. cit., p. 467.
Mathis, Ray, Op. cit., p. 19.
[14] Bowen, F.B., Op. cit., p. 507.
[15] Weddle, William Jackson, Oral History, Brown County Historical Society Archives, June 25, 1979.
[16] Hohenberger, Frank, Down in the Hills O' Brown County, Indianapolis Star, March 18, 1930.
[17] Goodspeed, Weston A., Op. cit., p. 740.
[18] Government Entry Record, Op. cit., pp. 99, 100.
Goodspeed, Weston A., Op. cit., pp. 740, 741.
Joyce Ann Hall, Juanita May Burge, Historical Facts and Family Data in Hamblen Township, Brown County Democrat, March 1, 1962.
[19] Hamblen, A. Porter, The Hamblen Family.
Mathis, Ray, Op. cit., pp. 12, 23.
Bowen, F.B., Op. cit., p. 326.
Goodspeed, Weston A., Op. cit., p. 741.
Reed Dick, Brown County Folks, Brown County Democrat October 6, 1976.
[20] Goodspeed, Weston A., Op. cit., p. 735.
[21] Ibid. pp. 733, 735, 737, 781.
[22] Bowen, F.B., Op. cit., p. 476.
Goodspeed, Op. cit., pp. 735, 737.

Nashville's oldest house built by Banner Brummett

The Banner Brummett house when owned by Mollie Lucas in 1930.

Chapter VI
Brown County Land 1809 to 1836

Land which now comprises Brown County was obtained from the Indians by the Treaty of Fort Wayne, or Harrison's Purchase in 1809, and the Treaty of St. Mary's, or The New Purchase in 1818.

William Henry Harrison, Governor of the Indiana Territory carved from the Northwest Territory in 1800, enlarged the land area north of the Ohio River where pioneers could homestead, since they were not allowed to live on land owned by the Indians. At Fort Wayne on September 30, 1809, Harrison bought 3,000,000 acres for the United States from the Indian Tribes. The Indians received $10,000, a third of a cent per acre.[1]

The northern boundary of Harrison's Purchase, called the Ten O'Clock Line, crossed Indiana Territory from Vermilion County southeast to the East Fork of the White River. The boundary was chosen by Indian chiefs where shadow slanted in a southeast direction exactly at ten o'clock on the morning of September 30, 1809. The Indians who negotiated with Henry Harrison did not trust compasses and surveying instruments, but they trusted the sun.[2]

Brown County's share of the Fort Wayne Treaty was the southwest corner of the county; a straight line drawn on a Brown County map from Township 9 north, Range 1 east, Section 25 to Township 7 north, Range 4 east, Section 7 exactly coincides with the old Ten O'Clock Line.

According to the original government survey records, which still exist in the Land Department of the State Auditor's Office, Arthur Henrie and William Harris surveyed Harrison's Purchase. By October 23, 1815, the entire survey was completed.[3]

Henrie's field notes, written with goose-feather quill pens, show signs of snow, rain, and pocket wear. The surveyor's group included guards, hunters, tentmen, cooks, chainmen, flagmen, and axmen. They traveled on horseback through thick climax forest. Their work was demanding, rugged, and dangerous. Unfriendly Indians, catamounts that jumped from low tree branches onto the backs of horses, poisonous snakes constantly threatened.[4]

The rectangular system of mile-square sections, east and west congressional township lines, and north south range lines used by Arthur Henrie in his surveys, was invented by Colonel Jared Mansfield, United States Surveyor General from 1803 to 1814. It has been a blessing to Brown County, Indiana, and the United States. It is far more accurate and simpler than other survey systems.[5]

In 1816 a population of 60,000, the requirement for statehood, was reached in the Indiana Territory. Accordingly, Congress passed the necessary act and Indiana became the 19th state of the Union. The capitol was moved from Vincennes to Corydon. In 1825 the capitol was transferred to the more central location of Indianapolis.[6]

In 1818 land south of the Wabash River and north of the Ten O'Clock Line became the property of the United States. This included future Brown County's land. Jonathan Jennings, Governor of Indiana, Benjamin Parke the Federal Judge of the District of Indiana, and General Lewis Cass Governor of The Michigan Territory met with Indian tribes at St. Mary's in Ohio. The Treaty of St. Mary's, or The New Purchase, was negotiated with the Indians between October 2nd and 6th, 1818. The Indians ceded land comprising a third of Indiana to the United States. The price agreed upon was an annuity of $4,000, plus $13,312.25 in cash.[7]

The New Purchase was surveyed by James Hedges, Joseph Hedges, Edward Tiffin, and Thomas Brown. Future Brown

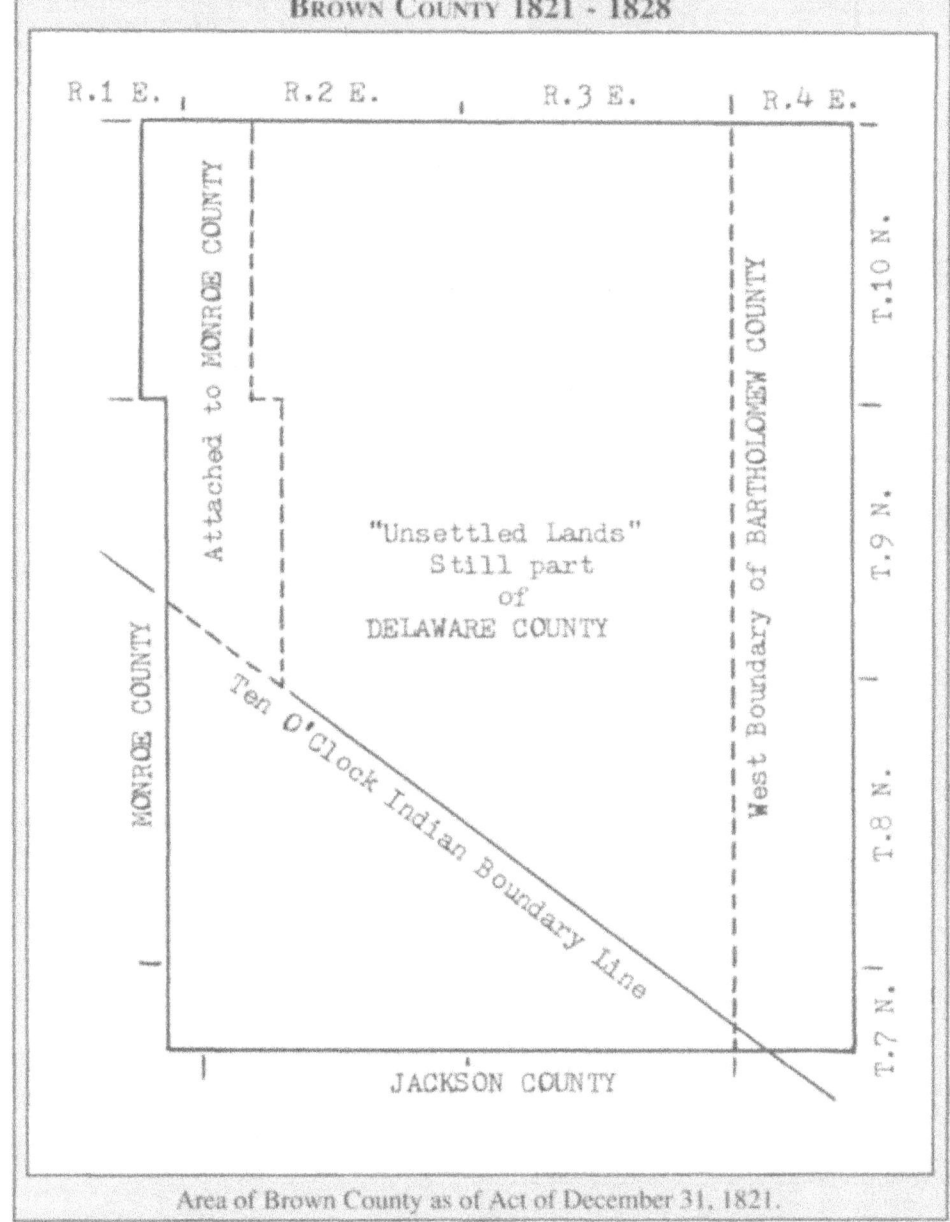

Area of Brown County as of Act of December 31, 1821.

County's land was surveyed in February and March of 1820.

The land of The New Purchase was almost entirely without settlers, and was covered by undisturbed primeval forest. The surveyors undoubtedly encountered the same difficulties and dangers Arthur Henrie had endured, except the Indians, subdued and disheartened by their defeat in the War of 1812 did not cause trouble.[8]

Following the New Purchase the General Assembly disposed of what became Brown County land in various ways:

1. On January 20, 1820, the General Assembly formed Delaware County from this land together with considerably more territory to the north.

2. Monroe County on December 31, 1821, received from the Legislature a portion of Delaware County in what would become northwest Brown County south of the present boundary between Morgan and Brown Counties.[9]

3. From 1821 to 1828 land between the eastern boundary of Monroe County and the western boundary of Bartholomew County was designated on maps of the period as "Unsettled Lands."[10]

4. On January 16, 1828, the Legislature gave a strip of land just north of the present boundary between Jackson and Brown Counties to Jackson County.

5. On that same day, January 16, 1828, the Legislature equally divided the remaining area of "Unsettled Lands," south of Morgan and Johnson Counties and north of Jackson County, between Monroe and Bartholomew Counties.[11]

Thus, by 1828 what became Brown County in 1836 was divided between the three counties of Monroe, Jackson, and Bartholomew.

Bartholomew County was not pleased by this addition of hilly country to its territory. People considered it poor, unfarmable, waste land.[12]

Before 1836 the earliest pioneers by necessity recorded their wills, land purchases, and marriages in the courthouses of Jackson, Monroe, and Bartholomew Counties. These records may still be found in those courthouses.[13]

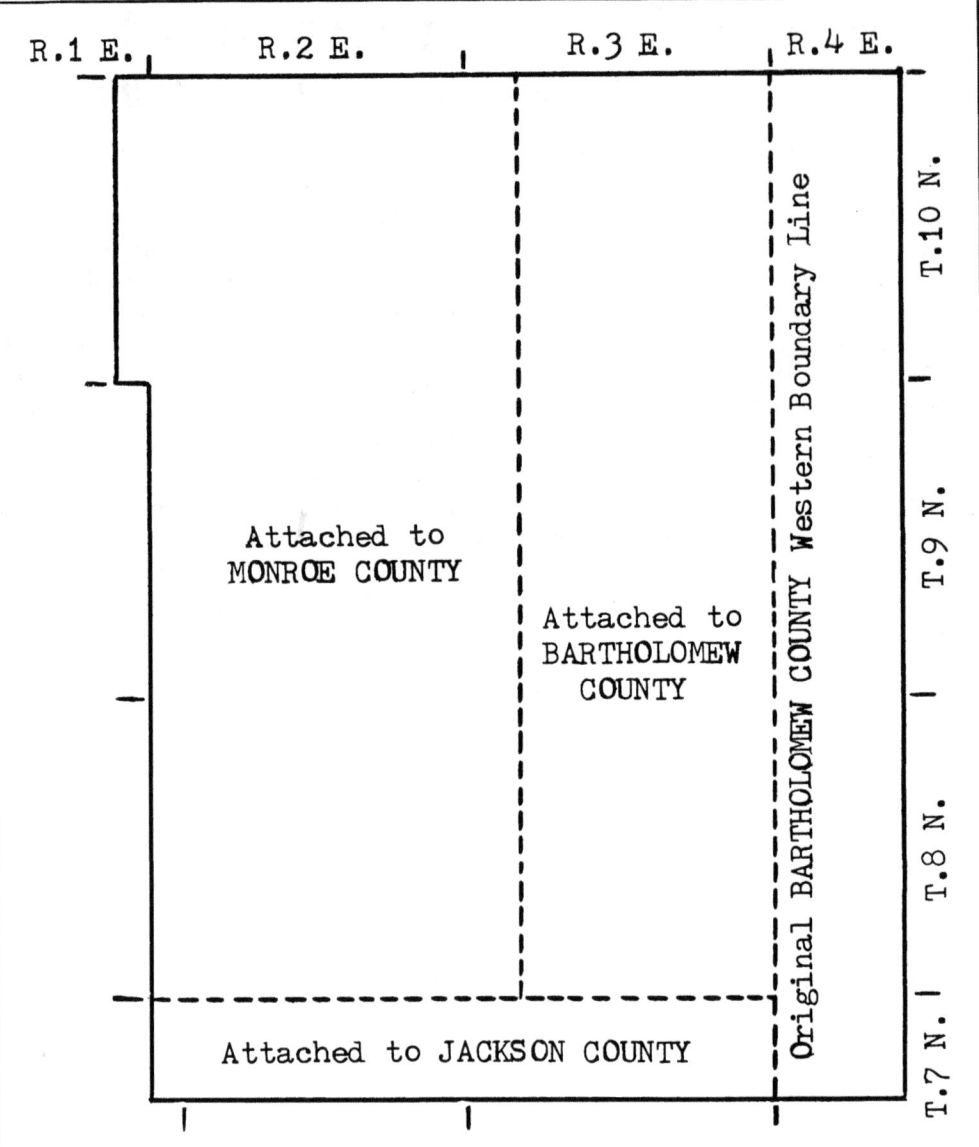

Area of future Brown County as of Act of January 16, 1828. (Map by Kenneth Reeve)

Brown County Land 1809 - 1836
Bibliography

[1] Esarey, Logan, A History of Indiana, Vol. 1, p. 207, 1924.
[2] Ibid. p. 259.
   Wilson, George, Early Indian Trails and Surveys pp. 76, 77.
[3] Brown County Abstract Office, Photocopies Original Government Surveys.
[4] Wilson, George, Op. cit. p. 71.
[5] Esarey, Logan, Op. cit. p. 386.
   Wilson, George, Op. cit. p. 65.
[6] Esarey, Logan, Op. cit. pp. 245, 270.
[7] Esarey, Logan, Op. cit. p. 260.
[8] Brown County Abstract Office, Op. cit.
[9] Goodspeed, Weston A., Counties of Morgan, Monroe, and Brown, Indiana, pp. 679, 680.
[10] Scott, John, Map of Indiana, 1826. Indiana Historical Society.
[11] Goodspeed, Weston A., Op. cit. p. 680.
[12] Terrell, Beck, and Pence, History of Bartholomew County. 1976 edition.
[13] Reeve, Helen H. and Kenneth J., Brown County, Indiana Cemeteries, p. V., 1977.

CHAPTER VII
ORGANIZATION OF BROWN COUNTY, 1836

It is not recorded, in any history of the county, why settlers in 1834 wished to form a new county. Pioneers may have found it too long a journey to the courthouses of Jackson, or Bartholomew, or Monroe counties. It was considered desirable, in early Indiana, for a man on horseback to reach his courthouse in one day from the most distant part of his county.

A few people, before 1834, had agitated for a new county in order to escape justice and protect themselves from the law in a new county. They counted on their friends to help them hide. Other counties in the 1830s had similar problems with settlers who had fled from arrest in eastern states.

Historical evidence corroborates that this element existed in Brown County for some years. A woman living in Brownstown, Jackson County, wrote a letter to relatives in Spencer in which she stated that she and her family would like to move to Spencer, but that it would be necessary "to cross the newly organized county of Brown which is a den of horse thieves and robbers." The family feared to make the trip. Little Blue Creek in southern Brown County did indeed, at that time, have an unenviable reputation as a place of rendezvous for horse thieves, ruffians, and fugitives from justice.[1]

However, the great majority of settlers, who apparently welcomed the possibility of a new county, were certainly law-abiding and hard-working pioneer citizens.

The United States census of 1830 estimated that there were 150 persons in what became Brown County. In 1834, when the first appeal was made to the State Legislature, there were at least 1800 settlers in the area.[2]

The petition presented in 1834 to the Legislature requested a county from parts of Bartholomew, Jackson, Monroe, and Morgan counties. The bill passed in the House, but died in a Senate committee.

In late 1835 a second petition was presented, and this was successful. House and Senate both passed the bill, and an act for the formation of Brown County from parts of Jackson, Monroe, and Bartholomew counties was approved on February 4, 1836.

The act was duly printed in the 1836 <u>Laws of a General Nature Passed and Published by the Twentieth Session of the General Assembly of the State of Indiana.</u> The ten sections of the act are reproduced here as they appear in a rare copy of this volume kept in a locked cabinet in the Indiana State Library.

CHAPTER XIX.
Boundary

Sec. 1. *Be it enacted by the General Assembly of the State of Indiana.* That from and after the first day of April next, all that tract of country included in the following boundary lines, shall form and constitute a new county, to be known and designated by the name of the county of Brown (in honor of the late Major General Jacob Brown.) Beginning at the north west corner of section one, in township ten north, of range one west of the second principal meridian; thence south, with the government land line twenty miles to the south west corner of section twelve, in township seven north, of the aforesaid range; thence east sixteen miles to the south east corner of section nine in the last named township, in range four east; thence north, with the government land line twenty one miles to the north east corner of section four, in township ten north; thence west, with the line dividing townships ten and eleven sixteen miles to the place of beginning.

Rights and jurisdiction

Sec. 2 That the new county of Brown shall, from and after the first day of April next, enjoy and possess all the rights, privileges, benefits and jurisdictions which to separate or independent counties do or may properly belong or appertain.

Commissioners to locate seat of justice. Sheriff of Monroe county shall notify commissioners.

Sec. 3. That James Alexander and Aquilla Rogers of Monroe county; and David Deitz and Hiram Wilson, of Bartholomew county; and Stephen Sparks of Jackson county be, and are hereby appointed commissioners agreebly to the act entitled "an act fixing the seats of justice in new counties hereafter to be laid off." The commissioners aforesaid shall meet, on the second Monday in August next, at the house of James Dawson, in the said county of Brown, and shall proceed, immediately, to perform the duties required of them by law; and it shall be the duty of the Sheriff of Monroe county to notify said commissioners, either in person or by writing, of their appointment on or before the second Monday in July next; and for such service he shall receive such compensation as the board doing county business, in said county of Brown, may, when organized, deem just and reasonable, to be allowed and paid as other county claims.

Courts where to be held.

Sec. 4. The Circuit Court, and the board of county commissioners, when elected under the writ of election from the Executive Department, shall hold their sessions as near the centre of the county as a convenient place can be had, until the public buildings can be erected.

Library fund

Sec. 5. The agent who shall be appointed to superintend the sale of lots at the county seat of said county of Brown, shall reserve ten per cent out of the proceeds thereof, and pay the same over to such person or persons as may be appointed by law to receive the same, for the use of a county library.

Attached for judicial and presentative purposes.

Sec. 6. The county of Brown shall be attached to the seventh judicial circuit of this state, for judicial purposes; and for representative purposes the citizens of said county shall vote with the counties of Bartholomew and Monroe in the following manner; those living within the territory of said new county, which was stricken from either of the counties aforesaid, shall vote with the respective counties from which they were stricken.

Times of holding circuit courts.

Sec. 7. That the circuit courts shall be held in the county of Brown, on the Mondays succeeding the week of the Monroe Circuit Court, and sit three days at each term, should the business require it.

Justices of the peace shall constitute county board.

Special sessions of the board

Sec. 8. That the justices of the peace in and for said county when elected and qualified, by a writ of election from the Executive Department, shall constitute the board of county commissioners; and the board of commissioners aforesaid shall hold special sessions not exceeding three, during the first year after the organization of said county, and shall make all necessary appointments, and do and perform all other business which may or might have been necessary to be performed at any other regular session, and to take all necessary steps to collect the state and county revenue, any law or usage to the contrary notwithstanding.

Certain acts to be in force in said county

Sec.9. That the act entitled "an act providing the mode of opening and repairing public roads and highways in the county of Monroe" (approved February 2d, 1833.) And the act entitled "an act to amend the several acts regulating the jurisdiction and duties of justices of the peace in the several counties herein named", approved February 7, 1835, be, and the same are hereby declared to be in force in the said new county of Brown.

Sec. 10. This act to be in force from and after its passage.

A mistake was made by the clerks of the Legislature in the wording of the Act in the eighth line of Section 1. On December 20, 1836, an amendment to the Act of February 4, 1836, was passed, correcting the mistake and substituting "east" for "west," thus making the boundary line east, instead of west, of the second principal meridian.

Chapter LVI

An Act to amend an act for the formation of the county of Brown, approved February 4th, 1836.

[Approved, December 20, 1836.]

Words declared misprint.

Sec.1. *Be it enacted by the General Assembly of the State of Indiana,* That the word *west* where it occurs in the 8th line of the first section of said act shall be, and the same is hereby declared a *misprint*, and that the word *east* shall be substituted in lieu thereof, and that the boundary lines of said new county of Brown shall be permanently established in accordance with said change. A second error was corrected by law on February 17, 1838, in which one Brown County boundary was redefined correctly. "Twenty-one miles to the north east corner of section four" in the first paragraph of the February 4, 1836, Act was changed to read "Twenty miles."

Jacob Jennings Brown (1775-1828), for whom Brown County was named, was a Major General in the United States Army

Major General Jacob Jennings Brown

during the War of 1812. His victories over the English in upper New York established his reputation as a war hero. After the war he became the General in charge of the United States Army in 1821, in Washington, D.C. It was the custom in 1836 to honor men who had served the nation, especially in a military capacity. Americans of that day were ardently patriotic.[3]

There may have been a second contributing reason for choosing the name of Brown County. Barton Stone Dunham, an early settler, before he moved to Missouri, met with a group of men in 1835 to discuss a suitable name for the new county they hoped would soon be granted by the Legislature. They decided the county should be named for Brown County, Ohio, because the land was as "mountainous" and "rough" as that of the Ohio county.[4]

The first necessity for a fledgling county was to elect officers for the management of county affairs, and the administration of justice. Accordingly, James Dawson was commissioned sheriff by Governor Noah Noble on April 20, 1836. Dawson was directed to order an election of a clerk and recorder, two associate judges of the Circuit Court, and three temporary commissioners. This first election in Brown County was held on the first Monday of June, 1836. John Floyd was elected clerk and recorder, James Taggart and Lewis F. Raper associate judges, Daniel Hedrick, William Jackson, and James Davidson county commissioners. Daniel Hedrick acted as president of the commissioners.

On July 25, 1836, the three commissioners, constituting the County Board, held their first meeting at the home of Sheriff James Dawson. Their first act was to divide the county into four townships of equal size: Hamblen, Van Buren, Johnson, and Jackson.

On July 25th the commissioners appointed Thomas Henson county treasurer, and selected township tax assessors.

On August 15, 1836, the three commissioners created a fifth township. The reason for this addition is not known. The new township of Washington received a two-mile north-south strip of land extending across the southern boundaries of Hamblen and Jackson Townships, a two-mile north-south strip from the northern boundaries of Johnson and Van Buren, plus a second two-mile strip from Johnson Township. This gave Washington an area of 80 square miles, and reduced Johnson to 48 square miles, the smallest of the five townships.[5]

The county seat, Jacksonburg, was no longer located in Jackson Township, but in Washington Township. The name was changed to Nashville. It is legend that the Banner Brummett family, having come from Nashville, Tennessee, was influential in choosing the new name.

An Act was passed at the 1836-37 session of the Legislature altering the name of the county seat to Nashville.

On August 11, 1836, four of the five locating commissioners from Monroe, Bartholomew, and Jackson counties had presented their report of the county seat selection and ordered it "spread upon the records."[6]

"We, the undersigned Commissioners appointed by the act of the Legislature of 1836, for the location of the county site of Brown County, Ind., do certify that according to said act we met at the house of James Dawson, in said county, on the 8th of August, 1836, and on the 11th of August located the site of said county of Brown on Section 19, Township 9 north, Range 3 east, on a tract of fifty acres of land donated by James Dawson, Banner Brummet, John Followell, Pierson Brummet, James Huff, William Snyder, John King and Henry Jackson. Also, we have received a donation of $150 to be paid in cash, for which we have received a note payable to the Commissioners of said county of Brown in the following persons, to wit: Banner Brummett, James Dawson, James Huff, Pierson Brummet and J. W. Dunning. We also certify that we have named the county site Jacksonburg. Given under our hands this 11th day of August, 1836.

Stephen Sparks
James Alexander   ⎤
David Dietz   ⎬ Locating Commissioners"
Hiram Wilson   ⎦

On August 15, 1836, the commissioners appointed Banner Brummet county agent with a bond of $4000. Brummet was directed to "lay out" the future town of Nashville into lots to be sold at public auction. James Dawson, named county surveyor, measured the lots and streets.

It was James Dawson who prepared the original plat of Nashville. This valuable plat unfortunately burned in the courthouse fire of 1873. The loss of the plat has caused endless trouble in the buying and selling of Nashville lots. Jonathan Watson and George Graves evaluated the lots as they were planned and measured.

The first auction of lots took place on September 12, 1836, the sale having been advertised in Brown, Monroe, Bartholomew, Johnson, and Jackson counties. Names of those who bought the original lots were not recorded, but by January 9, 1837, fifty lots had been sold for $694.87 $^{1}/_{2}$. Thereafter Nashville lots were sold quarterly.[7]

In the August election James Taggart became County Sheriff, William Followell Coroner, James McIntire Probate Judge, and John S. Williams County Treasurer. John Floyd continued as county clerk and recorder, although he employed a deputy, Avery McGee, to do his work. It was not until 1858 that both a county clerk and a recorder were elected. One person no longer could adequately serve in both offices.[8]

Since wolves were numerous and a menace to livestock, the commissioners agreed to pay one dollar to each person who presented a wolf scalp. A license for taverns selling liquor in the county was set at $5.00, stores selling merchandise or liquor were charged $10.00, and "wooden clock peddlars" paid $8.00 for a license.

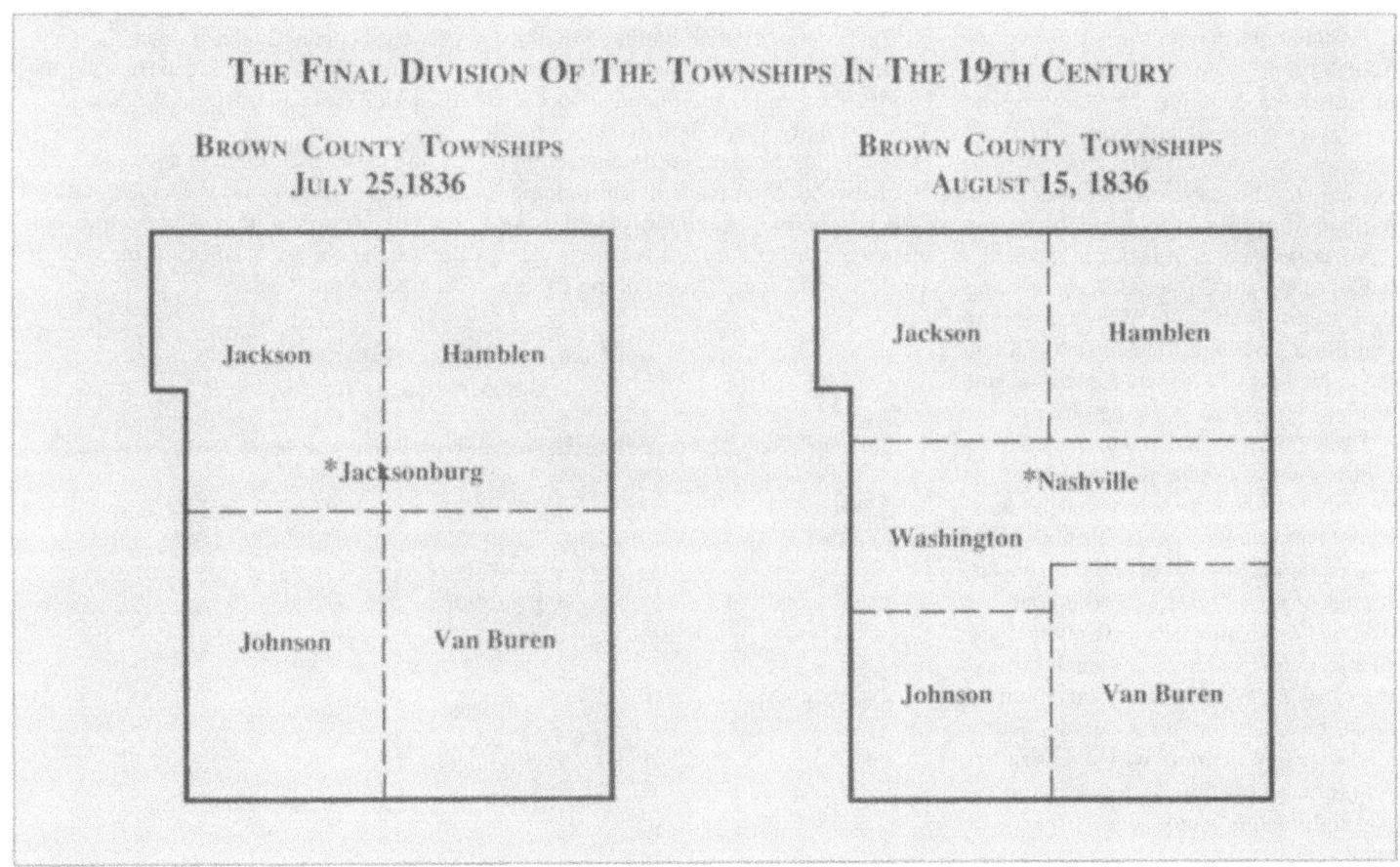

In all Indiana counties in 1836 "overseers of the poor" were appointed by the commissioners to care for the helpless who were placed in private homes. The townships, or the county board (commissioners), paid for this service. On July 25, 1836, William Murphy and John Hubbard were appointed overseers in Jackson Township, Daniel King and Cornelius Kirts in Hamblen, Hiram Mabe and William Rippe in Van Buren, William Johnson and William Davis in Johnson, Robert Henderson and William Jackson in Washington.[9]

Each county in Indiana took care of its own highways. There were few roads in Brown County but three received the attention of the commissioners. The famous old Sparks Ferry Road was traveled by any number of pioneers settling in the county or traveling north into Johnson County. It ran directly north from Jackson County through Van Buren, Washington, and Hamblen Townships. The commissioners divided the road into five districts with a superintendent for each district. Each superintendent selected enough "hands" to keep the road in repair.

The Bloomington-Columbus Road east of the "old county line" was divided into two districts, with a superintendent for each. The old county line, a short distance east of Nashville, had been the north-south boundary between Monroe and Bartholomew Counties before 1836. Early settlers remembered this county line for many years. The Brown County section of the Bloomington-Columbus road went straight east from Nashville, as it does now, to the boundary of Bartholomew County.

The third road from the salt licks, west of Nashville in Washington Township, running north to Bear Creek in Jackson Township, and on to Martinsville was one of the earliest roads in Brown County. One supervisor was chosen for this road.[10]

In November, 1836, the three temporary commissioners were replaced, in accordance with Section 8 of the act forming Brown County, by Justices of the Peace following their election and qualification by "writ of election" from the State Executive Department. This County Justices Court served for a number of years as the Board of Commissioners. They were empowered to make all necessary appointments, conduct county business, and collect state and county taxes. As many as ten and twelve justices met at each meeting in the home of James Dawson. In 1836 the justices were William Taggart, Jonathan Watson, George Graves, Nathan Davis, Banner C. Brummet, David D. Weddle, Jacob Hutsonpillar, Frederick Goss, and Hiram Weddle.

In June, 1845, the county was divided into three commissioners' districts, and after the fall elections commissioners took control of the county business in place of the Justices of the Peace.[11]

Organization of Brown County, 1836
Bibliography

[1] Mathis, Ray. Brown County History. 1936. Letter of Kate Milner Rabb, p. 25.
[2] Mathis, Ray. Op. cit., p. 16.
[3] Ibid. p. 26
[4] Miller, Ferd. Letter to Dorothy Bailey, February 7, 1983.
   David, Violet, Oral History, February 10, 1983.
[5] Goodspeed, Weston A., Counties of Morgan, Monroe and Brown, Indiana. 1884, pp. 682, 683.
[6] Ibid. p. 683.
[7] Ibid. p. 684.
[8] Ibid. p. 687.
[9] Ibid. pp. 719, 735, 740, 747, 753.
[10] Ibid. pp. 719, 735, 740, 747, 753.
[11] Ibid. pp. 684, 697.

Chapter VIII
A Visit to Brown County in 1836

There is an intriguing description of Brown County during the week when the locating commissioners chose the place for the county seat of Nashville. On February 6, 1869, in Brown County's newspaper, The Index, a man who called himself "An Old Settler" published an article concerning his trip to the county in early August, 1836. The Old Settler, who lived in Indiana, wished to discover where the locating commissioners placed the county seat.

Accordingly, he and a friend, Simon Taylor, traveled to Georgetown (now Bean Blossom). William Murphy, then living in the village, told them that three different locations had been under consideration for the county seat, and each had hoped for the honor. Georgetown, and Hedgesville three and a half miles east of Nashville, had already been visited and rejected. The commissioners were now at a site on Salt Creek about five miles south of Georgetown.

The travelers discovered that there was "nothing like a road" south of Georgetown. "A dim path led across Bean Blossom Creek then up a deep ravine and across the ridge dividing Bean Blossom and Salt Creek, then down on the south side and along Greasy Creek to near where it empties into Salt Creek. There was scarcely any settlement along the route. It was the forepart of August 1836; the ground was thickly matted with pea-vine and winter fern; around the heads of the ravines were to be seen numerous tracks of deer; wolves howled in the broad daylight, and the thick-set timber and foliage gave to the face of the country rather a gloomy appearance which made the distance seem to us much greater than it had been represented.

"At length, however, we came to Banner Brummet's residence; it was situate about one-fourth of a mile due east from where the court house now stands; there we halted to inquire our way. Mrs. Brummet came out. She had in the yard a scaffold erected, on which lay some flax drying for the brake. She informed us that we were near the place 'where the men were all gone to see about the laying out of the town'— pointed us the direction and said if Josh (who then came out) wouldn't brake out the flax he might go and show us the way. Joshua replied that he

Pioneer cabin on Helmsburg Road.

'didn't see any use of being in sich (sic) a hurry about the flax, when every body (sic) wanted to know whar the town was goin' to be, and ef the men'll wait till I get my jacket on I'll go with them.' We consented, Joshua got his jacket on and we proceeded. It was not more than half a mile to Dawson's who lived on the south bank of Salt Creek, about one-fourth mile south of what would be the public square of Nashville. There we found the commissioners and some fifty or sixty men, boys, and women congregated. Some of the men were shooting at a mark, some of the boys in the creek diving and swimming about; at the house was heard a fiddle — thither we bent our way.

"It was a log cabin, 15x20, the floor was hewn puncheons split from a large poplar, no particular pains had been taken to fit the joints or level them on the sleepers; in one corner stood a table made of a large hewed puncheon supported by wooden legs; and on it a jug, a tin cup and a bucket of water; in another corner of the house was a bed laid upon some poles fitted into the logs of the house, on which sat a barefoot man with a fiddle, who was making music to two other barefooted men, who were dancing upon the puncheon floor. We knew none of them, but I learned afterwards, that the fiddler was Rolla Sturgeon. The dancers we were never fortunate enough to know.

"The commissioners were financeering to obtain the largest donation for the location; we soon satisfied our self (sic) that the county seat would be located near where it is."

Hedgesville, mentioned as a contender for the county seat, was described by the "Old Settler" as he knew it in 1836. "Hedgesville was an embryo town, situate on the Bloomington and Columbus state road – near where David Crouch now lives. Its founder and proprietor was one L. M. Hedges. It contained one log cabin besides the proprietor's residence – and this additional structure was used for a family grocery which was carried on by David Randolph. Its stock consisted of a part of a sack of coffee, part barrel common whiskey and a few pounds tobacco. The stock, it is true was not extensive nor varied, but it embraced all its proprietor had the means to purchase, and the principal luxuries that his customers demanded. This place, as already stated, was a bidder for the location of the county seat, but failing in that, it flourished a short period and then disappeared; and at the time of this writing, there remains no monument to mark the spot where once stood Hedgesville."

The "Old Settler" stated that he intended to write a series of articles concerning early Brown County. He apparently moved to the county shortly after 1836. Unfortunately, there are no later copies of The Index in existence. What priceless information could be gleaned if the articles had survived!

Chapter IX
Brown County Courthouses, Jails, and Circuit Courts

In January, 1837, the commissioners appointed a committee consisting of F. Goss, J. Watson, and William Taggart to select two public lots in Nashville for a courthouse and a jail. Lot Number 1 was chosen for the jail, and Lot Number 2 for the courthouse. To this day these two lots contain a log jail and a courthouse, though not the original structures built in 1837.

On the first Monday in February, 1837, the County Board of Commissioners ordered Banner Brummet, the County Agent, to give contracts for building a courthouse and a jail to the lowest responsible bidders. The contracts were "sold" at "public outcry" on the 7th of March, 1837, between the hours of 10 a.m. and 4 p.m. William Snider won the jail contract and David D. Weddle the courthouse contract.

The courthouse was to be finished by the first Monday in September, 1837, and the jail by November 1, 1837. Both buildings were completed on time. The cost of the two buildings is not known, but has been estimated to have been not more than $700.

According to specifications the "court house was of hewed logs, 18 X 24 feet, two stories high, two rooms above, two stairways, one at each end, two windows above with twelve panes of glass each, one room below with one door, and one window with twelve panes of glass opposite to it; fireplaces in all the rooms, chinks (between logs) daubed with good mortar and weatherboarded on the inside; gable ends of building to have one window each, and to be weatherboarded."[1]

According to the Order Book of the County Commissioner the ceiling of the second story was raftered, the roof covered with (wood) shingles joined, 18 inches long, 6 inches to the weather, 3/4 of an inch thick, nailed to sheeting or lathing. The floors were laid down with seasoned plank an inch and a quarter thick, the lower floor jointed down rough upon twelve sleepers of good oak wood, laid an equal distance apart.

A partition ran through the upstairs room of seasoned plank, dressed, tongued and grooved together. Cracks between the logs on the inside were lined with boards or planks nailed on. "Sufficient" rock was placed under each corner of the building and in the middle of each sill. The sills were hewn to three faces of oak timbers and raised six inches from the ground, and were 10 X 12 inches thick.[2]

John S. Williams gave twelve chairs to the courthouse in September 1837, and D. D. Weddle furnished a table.

At this time the offices of Clerk and Recorder were held by one man. John Floyd had been elected in June 1836, but did not serve. He turned the work over to a deputy named Avery McGee. The County Clerk's

Nashville Courthouse 1909 (Built 1874)

Second Log Jail, 1880 (Built 1879)

office was established in one of the upstairs rooms of the courthouse on September 2, 1837.[3] Court was held in the lower room.

In 1853 the commissioners decided to build a brick courthouse. The old log building was sold, moved to a new location, and rebuilt as a stable. For a year or more the courts were held in the Methodist Church in Nashville.

In the fall of 1853 the courthouse contract was given to John Douglas. The cost was estimated at about $6,500. When completed and furnished the cost was a little more than $7,000.

In 1873 during a session of the Circuit Court the courthouse burned almost to the ground. Many valuable county records were destroyed but certain records, including the commissioners' records, were saved.

In June of 1874 a contract for rebuilding the brick courthouse on the ruins of the old foundation and a part of the old walls, was given to McCormack and Sweeney of Columbus, Indiana, for $9,000. When the building was under roof, $4,500 was paid and the remainder two years after the work was completed, with ten percent interest.[4]

The brick building is two stories high with the court and jury rooms above and the county offices on the first floor. Two iron stairways on the outside, over the front entrance, lead directly to the second floor.

This courthouse still serves the county, two additions having been added at the back of the original building.

Crowded conditions have made a new building absolutely necessary. Discussions and plans are underway at present. The old courthouse will continue to house court and jury rooms. A new building will provide space for other county business and offices.

Specifications for the first jail, recorded in the March 1837 Commissioners Order Book, state that the outside walls of the jail were to be of hewed oak logs 14 X 14 feet. A foot wide space between an inner and the outer wall was to be filled with square timbers hewed for the purpose and let down "end ways" between the two-story high walls. There were to be seven feet between lower and upper floors.

Square timbers a foot thick were to be laid on the floors. The jail was to be raftered, lathed, and shingled with a window in each side of the first floor criminals' room, nine inches square, "with good and sufficient grates each way." The door to the criminals' room was to be in the center of the floor of the upper debtors' room, the door two feet wide and four feet long. A ladder was to be let down through the opening in the floor to the criminals' room. When the sheriff's business was finished in the criminals' room he was to pull up the ladder and close and lock the door in the middle of the floor. There was no outside door to the criminals' room. A heavy iron door, with a heavy lock opened from the upper debtor's room to an outside stairway.

There is no mention of a fireplace or chimney in upper or lower rooms of the jail.

The 1837 log jail was used, with various repairs that were almost the equivalent of a new building, until 1879. The present log jail was then constructed at a cost of about

Sam Parks, Jailor. (Photo by Frank Hohenberger)

$1,500. The outside walls are 20 X 12 feet, two stories high with an outside staircase to the second floor. Both rooms have an entrance with an iron door and a large iron key.[5]

The second log jail still stands, and is a source of endless interest to tourists. It was used as a jail until 1912-1913, when for a short time prisoners were sent elsewhere for incarceration. Since then two different brick jails have been constructed and Brown County prisoners are safely and more comfortably housed in Nashville.

Two courts were established in the county in 1837 – a circuit and a probate court. Before the courthouse was finished in September 1837, court sessions were held in the home of James Dawson.

The first circuit court convened on April 20, 1837, before Judge Elisha W. Huntington, and Associate Judges James Taggart and Louis F. Raper. The first act was to administer the oaths of office to the judges. The next act was the consideration of a bastardy case. This was continued until the next term of court. The second case was one of slander: Pierson Brummet vs. Reuben Mathis. The plaintiff, by his counsel, moved to dismiss the suit, which was done by the court.

A seal for the court was then ordered. "Brown County Circuit Court" was to be inscribed in a circular form "near the margin of the seal, and in the center, the figure of a Western hunter leaning upon the muzzle of his rifle, with his dog lying at his feet, the whole to be engraved on the usual material of the proper diameter and thickness."

The second session began on October 19, 1837. The same judges presided. The bastardy case was continued at the cost of the defendant. Six cases were disposed of at this term of court. The grand jury returned ten bills of indictment – six gaming, three assault and battery, and one assault and battery with intent to murder.

The early gaming cases are interesting because they occupied a large amount of time in the circuit courts. Gambling in those days was considered a serious offense, though today it would be considered exceedingly trivial. In the second session of the circuit court, in the case of the State vs. Littleton Mathis, Mathis was indicted by the grand jury "for betting and wagering at and on a horse race the sum of $30 with John Whittington, and did then and there unlawfully win from John Whittington the same, contrary to the form and the statute and against the peace and dignity of the State of Indiana." Mathis was found guilty and fined five dollars to be used for the county seminary. This was an unusually large fine. Most fines were not over one dollar. Many of them were only one and two cents.

At the October term, 1837, "State vs. Banner Brummet, laborer, did by betting and playing at a certain game of cards commonly called poker the sum of twenty-five cents with Littleton Mathis and Stephen Gibson did then and there unlawfully win the same contrary to the form of the Statute in such made and provided and against the peace and dignity of the State." The defendant pleaded guilty and was fined one cent!

Another class of cases which appear often in the first records of the circuit court might be called nuisance cases. In the October term in the case of State vs. Luther Calvin, Calvin was indicted for "building a worm fence across the road, a common highway used for all citizens of said state with their horses, coaches, carts, and wagons to go, return, pass, repass, ride and labor at their free will and pleasure."

At the October court term in 1838 Edward David was indicted for "constructing a milldam across Salt Creek which placed on the state road between Nashville and Columbus a great quantity of water thus unlawfully and injuriously obstructing said highway for use of citizens with their horses, coaches, carts, and wagons." In both of these cases the defendant was acquitted.[6]

The first probate court convened on May 8, 1837, with Judge James McIntire on the bench. The Judge presented his commission from Governor Noah Noble and then opened court. There being no business, court adjourned. On the 4th of August the court appointed Alfred Young administrator of the estate of William Rippe deceased. The estate consisted of $608.15, besides considerable property. Alfred Young was directed to order a sale of the personal property.

At the February term 1838 Banner and Esther Brummet were called to answer for the administration of James Brummet's estate. They reported, under oath, that the estate consisted of two saddles and bridles, one horse collar and a pair of hames (part of a harness), a water pail, five crocks, a tin pan, seven tin cups, eight spoons, a coffee pot, three lavers (ladles), a set of knives and forks, a bread tray, a smoothing iron, a box, a razor, a horseshoe, three beds, bedding, and bedsteads, and $4.06, – a total of $26.06. Since James Brummet died insolvent it was ordered that the widow would have all the property, and pay no demands of the creditors.[7]

Many pioneers possessed exceedingly meager belongings. Some could carry all they owned to a new location.

The Common Pleas Court was established apart from the Circuit and Probate courts in 1853. The first session was held at Nashville on January 31, 1853, before Judge William G. Quick. Five attorneys were sworn into practice in this court: D. C. Dunning, Daniel McClure, Fred T. Butler, George A. Buskirk, and Shadrack Chandler. Rules governing the court were adopted. The first business "was the consideration of the petition for dower and partition of Jane Kelley and Zachariah Kelley vs. Nancy Hamblen et al." The next case was the examination of witnesses in the case of James Fleetwood for retailing liquor without a license. He was required to appear at the next term of court. Many similar cases followed in the early Brown County courts.[8]

Until 1972 Brown County's and Johnson County's courts were in the 8th Judicial Circuit. In that year the State Legislature split the 8th Judicial Circuit and created the 88th Circuit, called "Brown Circuit Court," for Brown County only.

The Brown Circuit Court has jurisdiction over all county legal matters – criminal, juvenile, probate, civil, and includes traffic violations. There is now a resident judge, elected for a six-year term.

The 88th Circuit Court became effective February 29th, 1972. The Governor appointed David T. Woods as judge for the balance of 1972. In November 1972, Judge Woods was elected and served until 1978. Judge Samuel R. Rosen, elected in 1978, served as judge until 1990.[9]

Brown County Courthouses, Jails, and Circuit Courts
Bibliography

[1] Goodspeed, Weston A., Counties of Morgan, Monroe and Brown, 1884, p. 686.
[2] Mathis, Ray, Brown County History, 1936, p. 34.
[3] Goodspeed, op. cit., p. 687.
[4] Ibid., p. 687.
[5] Ibid., p. 687.
   Mathis, Ray, op. cit., pp. 36, 37.
[6] Ibid., pp. 37-39.
   Goodspeed, op. cit., pp. 684, 685.
[7] Ibid., pp. 685, 686.
   Mathis, Ray, op. cit., pp. 39, 40.
[8] Ibid., p. 40.
   Goodspeed, op. cit., p. 686.
[9] Woods, David T., Phone conversation, April 18, 1990.

Chapter X
Military History of Brown County

Revolutionary War

Job Hamblen (1762-1833) was the earliest settler in what became southeastern Hamblen Township. Job had been a soldier in the Revolutionary War from 1779 to 1782. He served in Captain John Tabb's Company of Colonel Dabney's Virginia Militia. He took part in the siege and surrender of the British Army at Yorktown, Virginia, October 18, 1781.

After arriving in Indiana, Job tried to secure a land grant from the United States government because he had served in the Revolutionary War. His claim was rejected several times since it could not be proved that Job had served a minimum of three years in the war, a requirement for bounty land.

In 1928 a monument was erected over his grave in Hamblen Township by his descendants to honor the memory of this early settler and Revolutionary War soldier.[1]

In 1836 Hamblen Township was named for him.

Thomas Hatchett (d. 1863) was also a soldier in the Revolutionary War. He drove a baggage, or freight wagon, for the Army. He was frequently brought into contact with General George Washington, and a friendship developed between them. The General knew he could depend on Thomas' loyalty, and he respected the driver's hard work.

Thomas Hatchett arrived in Brown County in 1842, took out 15 acres of land, and farmed. He lived to be over 100 years old. It is believed he is buried in Duncan Cemetery, although there is no marker.[2]

War of 1812

John S. Williams (1787-1845), born in North Carolina, served as a Second Lieutenant in the Battle of New Orleans in the War of 1812.

After the war, Williams settled in Brown County, Washington Township.

In 1836 John Williams became the assessor of Washington Township, for which he was paid $3.00 "in full county orders." He received 50 cents for making a return of the September election in the Township. On November 7, 1836, he was appointed County Treasurer. In 1838 he served as the "Inspector of Elections."

By 1837 John Williams owned a business in the small village of Nashville. He sold liquor, as did most of the stores at that time.[3]

There were a few other survivors of the War of 1812 who settled in Brown County. They were cheered in Fourth of July parades, and various celebrations. Unfortunately, their names are not recorded.

The Mexican War

On May 18th, 1846, the President of the United States called for troops to carry on a war with Mexico. When the news arrived in Brown County, James Taggart, T. M. Adams, P. C. Parker, Williamson Wise, and Charles Bolt determined to organize a Company of volunteers.

A meeting was held at Georgetown and several men volunteered. At a second meeting, in Nashville, there were more volunteers, and by June 8th the Company was organized. James Taggart was elected Captain, Thomas M. Adams First Lieutenant, Patterson C. Parker Second Lieutenant, and Williamson Wise Third Lieutenant.

Formation of the Company was reported to the governor of Indiana. On the 14th of June orders were received from the Governor: The Company was to proceed to New Albany.

The next day the company left Brown County in wagons. A large crowd gathered to see them off. The men had bought bright blue uniforms and called themselves the "Brown County Blues." They were known by that name all through the war.

Reaching New Albany on June 17th the Company was mustered into the Third Indiana Regiment as Company E.

The Regiment arrived in New Orleans early in July, and was shipped across the Gulf of Mexico to Brazos Island. Here the Company performed guard duty, and later at Matamoras, Marine, Saltillo, and Nueva.

On Feburary 22, 1847, in the Battle of Buena Vista Pass 5,000 Americans fought General Santa Anna's 20,000 Mexicans. This was the only battle for Company E. Captain James Taggart was killed and Elias Weddle was severely wounded. "Squire" Stewart, and Matthew Mathews were also wounded.

Company E was commanded by Captain T. M. Adams after the battle, but saw no more fighting. Captain James Taggart was the only war casualty. However, a number of Brown County soldiers died of semitropical diseases, and could be considered war casualties.

On May 24th, 1847, the Third Indiana Regiment started north, and early in July the "Brown County Blues" reached Nashville. They were treated as heroes and given a warm welcome.[4]

> **Mexican War Veterans**
>
> The Mexican War veterans were gleaned from Weston Goodspeed's History of Brown County. Goodspeed mentioned that at least a company of men were sent to this war, but the following names were the only ones found in his record:
>
> Adams, Thomas M.
> Bidwell, Caleb*
> Bolt, Charles
> Brummett, Joshua*
> Brummett, Reese*
> Followell, John*
> Kennedy, Stephen
> Mathews, Matthew
> Parker, Patterson C.
> Stewart, "Squire"*
> Taggart, James*
> Weddle, Elias*
> Wise, Williamson
>
> An asterisk(*) after the name denotes killed in action.

Civil War

In 1860 the political campaign in Brown County was chaotic. The Wide-Awakes (Republicans), and the Democratic Clubs held noisy demonstrations and torchlight parades in all five townships.

When Abraham Lincoln was elected President, the Southern States, one after another, began to enact ordinances of secession. People began to understand that conflict between North and South was not far off. The slavery question had to be settled. The entire country was in turmoil.

1861

The news of the surrender of Fort Sumter in April, 1861, caused great excitement in Brown County. North and South were now at war, and there was an immediate call to arms from Washington, D.C.

A meeting was called at Nashville's courthouse. Several hundred Brown County citizens filled the courtroom to overflowing. Judge James S. Hester announced that it was the duty of the county to help "quell the Southern rebellion." W. W. Browning, T. D. Calvin, and Lewis Prosser spoke in favor of forming a Company of volunteers. The majority were in favor of this move in order to "preserve the Union and enforce the laws."

Within a few days following this meeting a Company of volunteers was formed. The men were called together to elect officers: James S. Hester was chosen Captain, W. W. Browning became First Lieutenant, and W. A. Adams Second Lieutenant. April 25th, 1861, Governor Morton received word that a Company of Brown County volunteers was ready. So prompt had been Indiana's response to the President's call to arms that Governor Morton sent word to the Brown County Company that they would be needed at a later date.

The call came early in July, 1861. The Compamy was to leave immediately for Madison to join the Twenty-Second Regiment. A spendid farewell dinner was given in the courthouse for the volunteers, and a beautiful banner was presented to them. They left for Columbus in wagons, then took the train for Madison. They became Company C of the Twenty-Second Regiment with three years enlistment service ahead of them.

At Madison, and at Indianapolis, the Regiment was subjected to the discipline of constant drilling. On the 17th of August, 1861, they were transferred to St. Louis, Missouri, where they were assigned to the army of General Freemont. The Regiment's first service was as a relief force to General Mulligan at Lexington, up the Missouri River. During the years of service the Regiment took part in twenty-four skirmishes and battles.

The officers of Company C during the war were: Captains— James S. Hester, W. H. Taggart, W. H. Fesler. First Lieutenants— W. W. Browning, W. A. Adams, V. P. Mason, W. H. Fesler, T. A. Pearce. Second Lieutenants—W. A. Adams, V. P. Mason, S. A. Kennedy and W. W. Gould.

Company C and the Twenty-Second Regiment were mustered out early in June, 1865, at Washington, D.C.

In 1925 a monument was erected by "Mabe, Hurley, and Freeze" at Pike's Peak to honor the first volunteers who left Brown county in 1861 for the Civil War. Their names inscribed on the monument are:

Jesse Ault
Henry Ault
G. W. Ayers
Paul Bucy
Joseph M. Breech
James Foreman
J. C. Freeze
John Hill
Cornelius Hurley
B. M. Hutchins
John Mobley
Hezekiah Mobley
Sylvanus Mabe
Augustus McDowell
Luther Powell
Mahlon Ward
David Ward
Theodore Ward
James T. Worley

Recruits:
James Ayers
G. W. Hurley
Silas Hurley

Due to the fact that the county was too small to complete many full companies, Brown County boys who were anxious to join the service left the county to enter companies organized in Bloomington, Columbus, Morgantown, and Indianapolis.

In August, and September 1861, sixteen, or eighteen boys near Elkinsville joined a Company of volunteers organized at Bloomington. They were mustered into the Thirty-First Regiment, as Company G, on September 20th at Terre Haute.

Company G and the entire Regiment took part in eight battles and ended up in Texas with the Army of Occupation. They were mustered out in 1866 and reached Brown County in 1866.

1862

On July 2nd, 1862, a call was made from Washington for 300,000 men, and on August 4th for 300,000 more men. An immediate effort was made to fill Brown County's quota. Meetings were held in all parts of the county to supply volunteers. Militia companies had been organized and it was from the militia that two full companies of volunteers were enlisted.

Brown County enjoyed the distinction of being one of only fifteen counties in Indiana to clear this draft. More than the required number of men enlisted. By the 19th of September, 1862, a total of 502 volunteers from Brown County were in the service.

The two full Companies were mustered into the Eighty-Second Regiment at Madison on August 30th, 1862. The officers of Company D were W. W. Browning Captain, D. D. Adams First Lieutenant, and John Calvin Second Lieutenant. The officers of Company H were John M. Methaney Captain, Jackson Woods First Lieutenant, and David S. Story Second Lieutenant.

The Eighty-Second Regiment saw three years of continual and active service in thirteen battles and skirmishes ending with Sherman in his march to the sea from Atlanta.

On June 9th, 1865, the Regiment was mustered out at Washington, D.C. and by June 15th had reached Indianapolis.[5]

1863

The "Brown County War" occurred in 1863. During this year many counties in Indiana experienced bitterly disloyal organizations opposed to the war. Brown County was no exception.

At a mass meeting in January 1863 it was resolved that "Our interests and inclinations will demand of us a withdrawal from the political association (to form) a common government with the New England States."

In August, at another meeting, it was resolved that "the present fratricidal and desolating war was unnecessarily forced upon the country by wicked, fanatical politicians, North and South....We are opposed to furnishing men or money to prosecute a war to free negroes....We demand an immediate armistice preparatory to a compromise of existing difficulties."

A war meeting was held in the northern part of the county. Lewis Prosser and a companion, who had been hunting squirrels in the woods, attended with their guns on their shoulders. A detachment of soldiers sent from Indianapolis, to arrest deserters hiding in the county, was present. Prosser made a remark that angered a soldier named Daniels. The soldier twisted Prosser's gun out of his hands. Prosser drew a revolver and shot the soldier dead. A bystander shot Prosser in the leg. Several more shots were fired without damage. Prosser later died from his wound.

During 1863 a band called "Knights of the Golden Circle" were causing considerable trouble in the county because of their opposition to the war. Together with a group of deserters and draft dodgers they were holed up in a log cabin on the top of the hill where Railroad Road joins Whitecap Road.

Women in the neighborhood, whose husbands were far from home fighting in the war, were becoming fearful. They were alone with the responsibility of children, farm and home. Their lives were difficult and money was scarce.

An older man in the neighborhood, a Mr. Whitman, was determined to rid the county of the Knights of the Golden Circle. He rode horseback to Fort Benjamin Harrison and pleaded for help. A company of Union soldiers started for Brown County with a horsedrawn canon. Their journey was half finished when the Knights and their cohorts learned of the approach of the soldiers and the canon. They hastily left the county, and disloyalty ended. The "Brown County War" was over.[6]

1864

No attempt was made to organize a company wholly in the county in 1864. Men recruited and drafted for war service were sent to older companies. However, voluntary enlistments in the county for 1864 were 183 men, and draft enlistments were 68.

1865

Under the last call of the war on December 19th, 1864, one full Company was raised in the county during January, and February 1865, for one year's service. The officers were Volney P. Mason Captain, John C. Hester First Lieutenant, Franklin P. Taggart Second Lieutenant. The Colonel of the Regiment they joned was W. A. Adams of Brown County.

The last Company became Company K mustered into the One Hundred and Forty-Fifth Regiment at Indianapolis on February 16th, 1865. The Regiment was mustered out in January 1866.

Brown County is officially credited with furnishng 996 men, or one Regiment (a regiment consists of 1000 men) for service in the Civil War. No county in Indiana is credited with a proportionately better record.[7]

Many Brown County women had an extremely difficult time performing all the necessary work on their farms during the war. When the need for financial relief became imperative in families of soldiers, the County Board (Commissioners) ordered a total of $2,976 distributed. A committee in each township dispensed this relief. The sum, which today seems so pitifully inadequate, stretched a great deal further in the 1860s.

In March 1865, in order to clear the county of the last enlistment quota, the County Board ordered the Auditor to issue $30,300 in bonds to be sold. Each man who enlisted was to receive a bounty of $300. By June of 1865 $26,100 had been paid out. The remainder was claimed after the war by returning soldiers.[8]

CIVIL WAR VETERANS

The following is a list of the Civil Veterans who lived in Brown County at the time 1861-1865. An asterisk (*) after the name denotes killed in action, and an # denotes a musician. The list is as complete as it can be at this date (July, 1990) and was prepared by Helen Ayers from the records from various courthouses, Goodspeed's History of Brown County, and military records accumulated by Helen and Ken Reeve.

According to Mr. Goodspeed there were about 996 men serving in the Civil War who claimed Brown County citizenship. From the records available at this date, 573 names with 94 killed in action. This discrepancy is caused by the fact that many of the men enlisted several times and were counted as a recruit each time they enlisted.

Acton, Drewry P.
Acton, Wilborn
Acton, William H.
Adams, Benjamin F.
Adams, David B.
Adams James W.
Adams, John W.
Adams, Thomas J.*
Adams, W. A.
Alexander, John B.*
Alexander, Robert H.*
Alexander, Samuel J.
Allender, John
Anthony, John
Antler, George W.*
Arwin, David L
Arwin, Thomas A.
Arwine, James N.
Arwine, Jesse
Arwine, Nicholas J.
Ault, Jacob
Ault, Martin*
Axam, Hezekiah
Aynes, Drewry
Aynes, Gabriel
Aynes, Peter
Ayers, Henry

Ayers, James
Ayers, Nathan*
Bailes, Alexander*
Baker, John
Bales, William
Bariff, John R.
Battin, John M.
Beavers, Samuel
Bebout, Citizen
Beck, William F.
Beightal, David
Belcher, Moses J.
Bell, Michael
Berry, Mathias
Bigtell, John
Boffing, Thomas
Bohall, John D.#
Bond, James
Bracken, Stephen
Bradley, Daniel D.*
Bradley, Francis M.*
Bradley, Garrison G.
Bradley, Gradison S.
Bradley, Jackson W.*
Bradley, Whitson P.
Brand, Austin
Brand, Peter

Breedlove, John A.
Breedlove, Thomas
Breedlove, William B.*
Bright, George B.
Bright John G.
Brock, Jacob
Brock John
Brown, Alfred
Brown, Elisha
Brown, Henry
Brown, John W.
Brown, Henry W.*
Browning, Amzi
Browning, Jesse
Browning, Nathan
Browning, William W.
Brumment, Harmon
Brumment, Joshua
Brummett, Christopher
Brummett, William
Bruner, Henry D.*
Bush, Isaac
Butler, Hugh R.
Callahan, Moses
Calvin, Green
Calvin, Jackson
Calvin, John

Calvin, Timothy D.
Campbell, Benjamin
Campbell, Humphrey
Campbell, John*
Campbell, William M.
Canary, Abram
Carmichael, Amos
Carmichael, Leander
Carnikle, Jacob B.
Chafin, John
Chambers, James H.
Chambers, John L.
Chambers, Nicholas P.
Chambers, William*
Chitwood, William G.*
Clark, Andrew
Clark, Morris M.
Clark, Timothy D.
Cochran, James S.
Coffin, George W.*
Coffland, Samuel
Coffman, John A.*
Coffman, William A.*
Collins, Isaac
Condon, Alexander
Conner, Peter
Conrad, Francis M.

Cook, Jeremiah B.
Cooper, Andrew J.
Cooper, Isaac P.
Cooper, Jasper*
Cooper, Richard J.
Copson, David
Cornett, Andrew J.
Cornett, Samuel
Comitt, Jesse
Coulson, Jefferson
Crider, Tilghman H.
Cross, Albert
Cross, James W.
Cross, Richmond M.
Cross, Solomon Z.
Crosslow, Joseph
Crouch, Hiram
Crouch, William P.
Curtis, Jonathan
Curry, James W.
Daggy, Charles W.
Daggy, Henry M.*
Daggy, Samuel
Dallsbury, Chesley
Dallsbury, William B.*
Daniels, Jonathan
Davis, John

Civil War Veterans (Continued)

Day, John C.
Day, William
Dean, Ephraim E.
Deckard, Jefferson
Denoon, Elias
Devine, Joshua
Dine, Peter, Jr.
Dine, Samuel
Dine, William N.
Donica, James M.
Drake, Peter
Drake, William M.
Dubois, George W.*
Dubois, Treat S.*
Duvall, Farling
Duvall, James R.
Duvall, William R.
Elkins, Andrew
Elkins, Drury
Elkins, George W.
Elkins, Granderson
Elkins, Joseph
Elkins, Richard*
Elkins, William
Elkins, Wirt
Elkins, Louis
Enos, Frederick
Falls, James M.*
Fergason, Caleb B.
Ferguson, Lorenzo D.
Fesler, W. H.
Fledwood, John
Fleener, Joseph N.
Fleener, Milton
Fleener, William*
Fleetwood, James
Fleetwood, Solomon
Fleetwood, Thomas
Florer, Robert
Floyd, Thomas N.
Followell, William
Followill, Fleming R.*
Foreman, John
Forrester, Amotis
Fox, Philip
Fraker, Joseph*
Franklin, Calvin
Franklin, William
Freeze, James B.
Frie, William
Gant, Henry B.
Garlock, David
Gee, William*
Gibson, George W.
Gosser, John*

Gould, Lemuel
Gould, William M.
Graham, Americus
Graham, Elijah
Graham, Moses
Gratton, William T.
Gray, Andrew B.
Gray, Cyrus N.
Gray, David L.
Greathouse, Peter
Greenlee, Amos
Greenlee, Sylvanus*
Griffin, William
Griffith, Reuben C.
Grose, John M.
Gwaltney, Aquilla D.
Hackney, William
Hall, Milton
Hamilton, James
Hamilton, William (MIA)
Hampton, James
Hampton, Nathan
Hampton, Willis K.
Hancher, Alexander
Hanna, Charles C.
Harding, Isaac*
Harper, Archibald
Harper, Thomas H.
Harper, William
Harvey, James A.
Hatchell, Bardell
Hatten, Marion
Hatten, Robert
Hatton, Samuel
Hatton, William H.
Hays, William W.
Heckman, Harvey
Hedrick, Francis M.
Hedrick, Joseph
Hedrick, Shelby
Helmick, Levi
Helms, Wilson
Helton, Andrew
Henderson, Henry*
Hendricks, Daniel J.*
Hendricks, J. W.
Hendricks, Thomas A.
Hendry, John
Henry, Joel A.
Herold, Ephriam P.*
Herold, Mathias
Hester, James S.
Hester, John C.
Hightower, William
Hill, William

Hilton, John S.
Hinsley, Henry*
Hines, Jonathan
Hobbs, William*
Hoff, Amos
Hoffman, John
Holly, Barton*
Honeycut, Daniel
Honeycut, Jacob*
Honeycut, Robert*
Hoover, Jacob
Hoover, James K. P.
Hoover, William N.*
Hudiburgh, Thomas
Huett, Jackson
Huett, Lawson A.*
Huffsteadler, John J.
Hurd, Charles W.
Hurley, Cornelius
Jackson, George H.
Jackson, John*
Jackson, Martin V.
James, Hugh*
Jones, Alexander
Kelley, Benjamin W.*
Kelly, John
Kelso, Robert C.*
Kennedy, Frank*
Kennedy, John D.
Kennedy, Stephen A.*
Kennedy, Thomas A.
Kent, Thomas
King, Conrad*
King, Henry W.
King, Hickman H.
King, John V.
King, Thomas J.
Kinsey, Allen T.
Kirk, Thomas P.
Kirts, George W.
Knight, Dempsey M.
Kreb, Joseph
Lamb, William
Lanam, Hugh
Lane, Ralph
Lang, Benton
Lankfort, William
Lathrop, William C.
Lauver, Joseph
Lawson, Druak
Lawyer, David*
Leal, William
Leifort, Jacob
Long, Andrew
Long, Elijah

Loudermilk, Daniel H.
Lucas, Albert
Lucas, Francis M.
Lucas, Henry*
Lucas, John R.
Lucas, John W.
Lutes, George
Lyons, Elijah*
McCarty, William H.
McCarty, William J.
McCleery, Will P.
McClung, David
McCord, Richard B.
McCoy, James*
McDaniel, William
McDonald, James D.
McDonald, William B.
McGankey, Abram
McGrail, Michael
McGuire, Alfred
McGuire(Maguire), John P.*
McGuire, Thompson
McIlhenny, Joseph K.
McIlvain, Leander J.
McIlvane, George
McIlvane, John W.
McIlvane, McClain*
McIlvain, Joseph A.*
McMahon, Elvin S.
McMahon, Oliver C.
McName, Michael
Mabe, James M.
Maloy, James A.
Markle, Gersham
Markwell, Abel
Marshall, Andrew J.
Marshall, George W.
Marshall, Randolph V.
Marshall, Robert
Martin, Edgar*#
Mason, Volney P.
Matheny, Andrew R.
Matheny, Francis D.
Matheny, James M.
Matheny, John M.
Matheny, Thomas J.
Mathis, George W.
Mathis, James K. P.
Mathis, Jeremiah B.
Mathis, John
Mathis, Mitchell
Mathis, Reuben
Mathis, Robert W.
Matlock, Wells
Matney, Clemment

Civil War Veterans (Continued)

Mead, Joseph*
Mead, Thomas E.
Meeks, David
Melvy, Ezra
Miller, Alexander H.
Mitchiner, John
Mobley, Thomas John*
Mohr, William
Moore, Emanuel H.
Moore, Eugene
Moore, Levi
Morrison, Jno
Mosier, Washington*
Mullis, Thomas
Murphy, William
Myers, James
Neal, David
Neff, Oliver A.
Neely, Jacob M.
Nelson, George
Newport, Ephraim
Nickerson, Henry P.
Noe, Jonathan A.
O'Haver, Joseph H.
Olmstead, John L.
Olmstead, Joseph S.
Onley, Alexander
Owens, Zachariah
Palmer, Elijah O.
Palmer, Robert
Panley, James W.
Parker, John
Parks, Edwin*
Parks, George W.
Parks, Jacob R.
Parmerlee, George*
Parmerlee, Marcus B.
Parr, Jacob
Parsley, Newton
Peake, Samuel*
Peck, Benjamin
Pender, John*
Percifield, Blevins
Percifield, Gilbert
Percifield, Samuel
Percifield, William J.
Petro, David
Petro, Francis
Petro, George
Phillips, Richard M.
Pierce, Thomas A.
Ping, John T.
Ping, Martin
Ping, Silas
Ping, William J.
Pitcher, Jacob F.
Plummer, Richard E.
Polen, Calvin W.
Polen, William P.
Polley, James W.
Porter, John H.*
Poulton, John G.
Powell, Alexander (MIA)
Powell, Richard
Price, Wilson*
Prosser, James J.
Prosser, Joseph K.
Pruett, Thomas
Prewitt, Aaron
Prewitt, William
Raper, Emery E.
Raredon, William M.
Rarridon, Henry
Rarridon, Thomas*
Redwine, George M.
Reel, William
Reeves, Eli M.
Reeves, James A.
Reynolds, Hiram
Reynolds, James
Reynolds, Jefferson*
Reynolds, Nelson A.
Rich, John W.*
Richardson, Frederick*
Richardson, Jacob
Richardson, James*
Roberts, William D.
Robertson, Charles
Robertson, George
Robertson, Henry
Robertson, Jacob*
Rogers, Henry
Rogers, James
Roundebaugh, Henry
Rusk, Thomas P.
Sanders, Hiram
Sandifur, John T.
Sattethwait, Oddy*
Schrougham, James
Scott, William M.
Scrogam, James
Scrougham, Thomas
Seals, William
Setser, Samuel H.
Settle, John
Sexton, James
Sexton, John H.
Shaffler, Arnold
Shaffler, John
Shepherd, Thomas
Sherrell, Levi
Shipley, Jesse
Shoup, Abraham
Shouse, James H.
Sipe, Alexander C.
Sipes, Albert F.
Sipes, James M.*
Skinner, Adonirum J.
Skinner, Joseph M.
Smith, Edward N.*
Smith, Francis M.*
Smith, George W.
Smith, John R.
Smith, John W.
Smith, Josephus
Smith, Leander
Smith, Philip S.*
Smith, Robert W.
Snider, John A.
Snyder, Frederick*
Snyder, George W.
Snyder, James*
Sowers, Alva A.
Spaulding, George W.*
Spurgeon, John W.
Spurgeon, Solomon D.
St. Clair, Alexander
Steadman, George W.
Steel, James William
Stephens, James J.
Stevens, Samuel
Stewart, James
Stogdill, William
Story, David S.
Strahl, Martin
Sullivan, Isaac
Sullivan, William
Sutherland, Fountain F.
Swain, Henry
Tabor, Joshua
Taggart, Franklin P.
Taggart, Patterson S.
Taggart, T.
Taggart, W. H.
Taylor, William H.
Teague, Elijah G.
Teford, John W.
Tever, John E.
Terrell, John
Thompson, Eli F.
Thompson, Samuel R.
Thompson, Thomas
Trick, Jacob
Truex, John*
Tryon, John
Tumbleson, Ezekiel M.
Tutrom, John
Varble, Henry
Vickers, Elijah J.
Vorheis, Simon L.
Waddle, Francis M.
Waddle, Michael*
Walker, Jacob C.*
Walker, Henry T.
Wall, James
Wallace, Thomas
Waltman, Hiram M.
Ward, Jesse P.
Ward, Leander
Watson, George W.
Watson, Tilghman H.*
Watts, Williamson D.
Weaver, Elza W.*
Weaver, James P.*
Weddle, John*
Weddel, Pleasant D.*
Weekly, John W.
Weekly, Joshua
Wells, Eli P. F.
Welton, James H.
Wendland, John
West, Michael
Wheaton, Fielding
Wheeler, Aaron H.*
Wheeler, Elihu
Whitaker, William
White, D. L.
White, Larkin
White, Minor
Whitehorn, David A.*
Williams, Alfred
Williams, Andrew J.
Wilson, James M.*
Wilson, John W.*
Winkler, John D.
Woods, Felix G.
Woods, Jackson*
Woods, Leander
Woods, William*
Worley, Robert*
Wright, Jacob A.
Wright, John C.
Yoder, James M.
Yost, James A.
Young, Andrew
Young, Joseph M.
Zimmerman, Jacob
Zimmerman, William J.

The Spanish-American War
1898-1899

President William McKinley declared war on Cuba April 22, 1898. Calls for volunteers to serve in the army were made on April 23 and May 25, 1898. Over seventy-five thousand men in the United States volunteered.

In the State of Indiana 7,421 men volunteered. The Spanish-American War affected Brown County very slightly. Only eight Brown Countians volunteered. The war was over within a year and no Brown County volunteer saw active army service.

The Record of Indiana Volunteers in the Spanish-American War lists the men who volunteered by name, town, township, or county where they lived, the enrollment date, and date they were mustered out. The list of the eight Brown County men were found in this record.[9]

1- Robert H. Burkhart, Georgetown
Enlisted April 26, 1898, as Sergeant Company C, First Regiment Indiana National Guard. Mustered out November 23, 1898.

2- James H. Cullen, Nashville
Enlisted July 29, 1898, as Corporal. Company H, First Regiment Indiana National Guard. Mustered out November 23, 1898.

3- Moses Stump, Brown County
Enlisted June 16, 1898, as Recruit Company H, First Regiment Indiana National Guard. Mustered out November 23, 1898.

4- Jesse M. Holmes, Van Buren Twp
Enlisted April 6, 1898, as a Private. Appointed Corporal March 4, 1899, Company D, Third Regiment National Guard. Transferred to Company A, Fourth Regiment. Mustered out April 25, 1899.

5- Harry F. Turner, Van Buren Twp
Enlisted April 26, 1898, as a Private Company A, Fourth Regiment. Mustered out April 25, 1899.

6- Lewine Gaiser, Van Buren Twp
Enlisted June 1898, as a Private. Appointed Corporal March 4, 1899, Company A, Fourth Regiment. Mustered out April 25, 1899.

7- Orval Gaiser, Van Buren Twp
Enlisted June 16, 1898, as Recruit Company A, Fourth Regiment. Mustered out April 25, 1899.

8- Henry Branaman, Becks
Enlisted June 27, 1898, as a Private Company K, Volunteer Company Organized at Columbus, Bartholomew County. (Regiment not named) Mustered out April 30, 1899.

World War I

List of Brown Countians who served in World War I as transcribed from the Memorial Honor Roll which is on display in the corridor of the Courthouse, Nashville, Indiana.

Adams, Paul
Allen, William M.
Allender, William A.
Altop, Edgar
Anthony, L. Herbert
Archambault, Leo H.
Ault, Albert
Ayers, William B.
Ayers, Bryan
Ayers, Carson
Aynes, Clarence A.
Bailey, Jesse A.
Barger, Nolan
Barger, Thomas
Bahan, Ralph
Barkes, Alvin E.
Barkes, Bert
Barkes, Walter
Barnes, Enos
Baughman, Harold
Baughman, Millard R.
Berry, Noble
Bitter, Harry J.
Bixler, William C.
Bond, Claude
Bond, Glenn
Bouska, Frank
Bradway, Daniel E.
Branson, Harry
Bright, William O.
Brown, James H.
Brown, Lawrence Glen*

Brown, Leonard R.
Brown, Martin
Brown, Ralph H.
Brown, Virgil E.
Bush, Charles
Butcher, Marshal E.
Butler, Homer
Calvin, Ernest
Calvin, Walter D.
Campbell, Virgil I.
Carmichael, Ernest E.
Carmichael, Ernest I.
Carmichael, Icel J.
Carmichael, Vernal H.
Carothers, Jesse
Clark, Al
Clark, Charles
Clark, Ephraim
Clark, Rex
Cloverdale, John C.
Connop, Thomas
Connop, Frank E.
Cooley, Walter O.
Cook, Ora
Coy, George
Crouch, Dorsey
Creamer, Warnia B
Crouch, John Melvin*
Crouch, Oddie*
Cummings, Adolphus
Dallas, Stanley
David, Andy

David, Daniel
David, Hershel A.
David, Roy V.
David, Shirley
Davis, Harry H.
Day, Colba R.
Day, Glen
Deaver, Ellice Borcie
Dosch, Russel M.
Dunham, Tracy
Duvall, Cecil
Duvall, James
Elkins, Arnold C.
Fleener, George R.
Fleener, Harley
Fleener, Homer D.
Fleener, John
Fleener, Leo L.
Floyd, Arnie
Ford, Donald Iros*
Ford, Elmer R.
Ford, Hiram
Ford, Reynold
Ford, Scott
Ford, Vernon
Fox, Isaac
Fritch, James E.
Gill, Hester O.
Gillaspie, Fascet
Gore, William J.
Greathouse, Lemuel James
Greathouse, Maley A.

Griner, Bryan J.
Griner, Charles E.
Griner, Elwood
Griner, Hugh T.
Griffin, Ralph E.
Griffin, Ray*
Groves, James M.
Harden, John W.
Hartsock, Herschel
Heidenreich, Charles E.
Henderson, Walter
Henthorne, Everett J.
Hill, Ervin R.
Hobbs, Guy
Hobbs, Washington M.
Howard, James E.
Hutchison, Perry M.
Jarrett, Ben
Jones, Jessie*
Kain, Oscar
Kaserman, Frank Sherman
Kennedy, James E.
Kent, Marion
King, Marcus
King, Reed
Kirts, Clifford Henry
Knose, Lewis A.
Lackey, Dwight
Lackey, Loren
Lawles, Ralph
Lawson, Hiram
Lawson, James

WORLD WAR I (CONTINUED)

Lawson, Ulyssis
Lemley, Clyde
Lemley, Herschel
Lemon, Walter
Loop, Emery W.
Lucas, Daniel J.
Lucas, Malcolm
Lutes, Thomas
Mann, Frank
Marlett, Joseph F.
Mason, Louie E.
Mason, Ora O.
Mason, Volney A.
Mathis, Phreno
Maxwell, Earl
Maxwell, Glenn M.
Maxwell, Jennings
Maxwell, Reno
McCoy, Clarence
McCoy, Harley
McCoy, Lawrence
McCoy, William T.
McDonald, Verl
McDonald, Virgil
Mead, Ira
Meade, Everett
Myers, Tyner
Miller, Dewey
Miller, Gordon
Miller, Vernon G.
Miller, Willie
Minton, Chester H.
Moberly, Herschell
Moberly, William I.
Mobley, Ivan
Moore, Arthur*
Moore, Clarence
Moore, Earl Chester
Moore, Harold
Moore, Watson T.
Monroe, Earl
Morlen, Roscoe
Morris, Benjamin Clarence
Mosier, Harry
Mullis, James
Mullis, Orvil
Murphy, Frank Ellsworth
Neal, Elmer
Neal, John
Neal, Omer Ray
Neidigh, Claude V.
Newmister, Melvin
Noe,
Parks, Homer
Parks, Otto
Parsley, Elmer A.

Patterson, Guy
Penrose, David V.
Penrose, Ellis E.
Penrose, Sylvanus
Percifield, Paul
Poling, Paul M.
Polley, Belvia
Polley, Neph
Prosser, Dan
Pruitt, Charles
Pruitt, Jesse
Purtlebaugh, William
Rains, James
Rariden, James W.
Read, Murnal
Reddick, John
Reddick, Mason W.
Reeves, Charles M.
Renard, Marquet
Richards, Leo P.
Richardson, Charley
Richardson, Ernest
Richardson, Henry
Richardson, Verlas
Robertson, Claude
Robertson, Floyd
Robertson, Leo F.
Robertson, Mason
Robertson, Sherman
Rogers, James
Rogers, William C.
Rude, Jacob B.
Rude, Joseph A.
Russ, Orvil
Sayer, William Elmer, Jr.
Schrock, Estel
Schrock, Joseph
Schrock, Lue Estel*
Scrougham, Harry
Selfrige, Raynolds Lever
Setser, Glen
Settles, Ira Elza
Shepherd, Arthur O.
Shepherd, Elda Grant
Shepherd, Thomas C.
Shepherd, William Bryan
Shepherd, William McKinley
Shipley, Thomas
Shultz, Ernest
Shulz, Walter*
Simons, Irven C.
Skinner, Icel R.
Slevin, James Messingham
Smith, James
Snow, Ora C.
Snyder, Frank J.

Spaulding, Martin
Spaulding, Otto
Stephenson, Cecil
Stark, William
Sturgeon, Charles G.*
Sturgeon, Clark H.
Sturgeon, Ralph W.
Swift, Ira
Sylvester, Van
Taggart, Thomas
Taylor, Alex
Taylor, Cecil
Taylor, Fred T.
Taylor, Walter
Thompson, George T.
Tipton, David L.
Tipton, William C.*
Tomlinson, James A.
Tracy, Clarence James
Tracy, Guy
Trisler, Carl

Truitt, Russel Clark
Turner, James Allen
Tutterow, Elmer Leo
Voland, Charles
Walker, Austin
Walker, Harold A.
Walker, James Bryan
Walker, Lawrence Leslie
Walker, Luna
Walker, Raymond
Waltman, Lowell C.
Waltz, Fred A.
Waltz, Walter
Watson, Thomas
Weddle, Ray F.
West, Arthur D.
Westbrook, Martin H.
White, John Raymond*
Williams, William
Young, Floyd
Zody, Vora

An asterisk(*) after the name denotes killed in action.

Omer Ray Neal (father of Louise Kissling)

WORLD WAR II
1941-1945

The following names of men and women serving from Brown County during World War II were taken from the plaques in the Brown County Courthouse. They were compiled and alphabetized by Helen Ayers in 1990 for use in the Brown County Veteran's Memorial to be constructed by 1991.

Abbott, Arthur
Abbott, Bernis
Abbott, Horace Glen
Abbott, Marvin
Allender, Omer Dale
Allender, Richard
Allender Thomas
Altop, Junior
Anderson, Robert E.
Arnold, Ellis Winfield
Arnold, Ralph Hughston
Artis, Arthur Floyd
Ashbaugh, Raymond
Ault, Albert
Ault, Kenneth
Ault, Robert C.
Axsom, Hershel Dewey
Ayers, Donald
Ayers, Herman Scott
Aynes, James Paul
Bailey, James Melvin
Bailey, Jesse Arda Jr.
Baker, Martin Clayton
Bales, William Robert
Barger, William S.
Barnes, Clarence Melvin
Barnes, Jack E.
Bartley, James Robert
Baughman, Millard Dale
Bay, Floyd Earl
Beach, Amos
Beach, Ernest
Beach, Ora
Beaver, Charles Edward
Beaver, Herbert Eugene
Beaver, Marion Leroy
Beaver, Robert Francis
Bennett, Daniel
Bingham, Merrel Robert
Bingham, Zack
Bock, Howard Martin
Bond, Allen Dale
Bond, Jack Jennison
Bond, James Wilson*
Bowden, Ralph
Bowden, Robert Allen
Bradley, Sammie P.
Bragg, Ralph Atwood
Brand, Bernard Forest
Bright, Billy Gene
Bright, Loren G.
Bright, Loren Mart

Bright, James Oakley
Bright, Robert Lee
Brock, HobertAgwert
Brown, Bernard Wayne
Brown, Berton Marshall
Brown, Delbert Ellis
Brown, Elmer C.
Brown, Ernest Carl
Brown, Glenn Ellsworth
Brown, James Robert
Brown, John Daniel
Brown, Leonard Ray
Brown, Robert Paul
Brown, Virgil Eugene
Brownfield, Herbert Emery
Brummett, Arza Nomman
Brummett, Basil Roscoe
Brummett, Carl H.
Brummett, Donald B.
Brummett, William Jr.
Bryan, Floyd Russell
Bryan, William Franklin
Burker, Wayne Louis
Bush, Leonard Burdett
Campbell, Byron Cornelius
Campbell, Curtis Wesley
Campbell, James Porter
Campbell, Jesse Thural*
Campbell, Kenneth
Campbell, Orval Dale
Campbell, Orville Edwin
Carmichael, Merrill
Carmichael, Neal
Carmichael, Robert Lee
Carothers, Harley
Carter, Lloyd
Cave, John D.
Childs, Walter Allen
Chitwood, Donald E.
Chitwood, Wendell Ora
Clampitt, Eli
Clark, Ralph
Clark, William Richard
Clephane, Harry
Clephane, Howard Julius
Cline, Marvin Louis
Cody, George Robert
Cody, William Frederick
Collett, James Lowell
Collins, Jesse Allen
Condon, Costa C.
Connell, John Latham

Cooley, Walter Howard
Cope, Raymond Ward
Crabtree, Joseph Harold
Crabtree, Kermit Quentin
Crabtree, Lee Dunn
Crawford, Paul
Creamer, Francis Ray
Creamer, Warnia Thomas
Cress, Chester Deryl
Cress, Robert
Crider, Carl Robert
Crider, Marlin
Crider, William Howard
Crump, John William*
Cullen, Robert Wilson
Cummings, Paul Edward
Curtis, Vernice James
David, Carl Edward
David, Charles, Jr.
David, Dale Clinton
David, Floyd Duane
David, Maurice
Davis, Marvin Orville
Davis, Theodore Henry
Deckard, Cecil
Deckard, Clarence Cecil
Deckard, Dewy
Deckard, Dillan Isaac
Deckard, Marion Allen
Deckard, Wayne Kenneth
Derringer, Arthur Leo
Derringer, Everett Dale
Derringer, Watter Asa
Dine, Arthur Dale
Dine, Herman
Dine, Morris Kenith
Dixon, Howard W.
Dobbs, Victor
Dobbs, Virgil T.
Dougherty, Robert Gene
Dupree, Louis Denzel
Dupree, William E.
Eaton, Edward
Eaton, Homer
Edwards, George Alfred
Edwardson, Harold Melvin Jr.
Elkins, Edgar Leon
Elkins, Robert Keith
Ellis, Howard Lee*
Emberton, James Edward
Exner, James William
Fesler, Dana Owen

Fishel, David Nelson
Fleener, Bessie
Fleener, Daniel Artie
Fleener, Guy Leon
Fleener, Martin Evans
Fleetwood, Dale Eugene
Fleetwood, Dorris
Fleetwood, Isom Chester
Fleetwood, Verlyn Leland
Fleetwood, Warren Lowell
Floyd, Edward Nolen
Floyd, Franklin Earl
Floyd, Joseph Jr.*
Floyd, Virgil R.
Followell, Aubrey Leon
Followell, Franklin Monroe
Ford, Arnold Jr.
Ford, Orval Ivan
Foster, Clyde Edward
Fowler, Thomas
Fox, Arnold Arthur
Fox, George
Fox, Charles Leroy
Fox, Charles Louis
Fox, Charles Wilson
Fox, Jessie Eugene
Fox, Russell Otto
Frazer, Allen
Frazer, Donald Dwight
Frazer, Lowell Keith
Frazer, William Lawrence
Frazer, William Warren
Freese, Glen
Freese, Neal
Freese, Paul
Fritch, Hughie Richard
Fritch, James R.
Fritch, Samuel Milton
Frownfelter, Ralph R.
Garloch, William E.
Gatewood, James Thompson
George, Roy
Glassburn, Loren Dale
Graham, Charles Edwin
Gray, Carl Nathan
Gray, Sameul Ernest
Greathouse, Alra
Greathouse, Elmer
Greathouse, Jacob
Greathouse, Ralph
Gredy, John Henry
Gredy, Lorenzo

WORLD WAR II (CONTINUED)

Gregory, Harold William
Griffin, Charles Edward
Griner, Alonzo
Griner, Charles
Guss, John Peter
Hacker, Hollis Carl
Hacker, Lowell Ray
Haggard, Harry Robert
Haggard, Howard Lester
Haggard, Morris
Hamblen, Vora Hustus
Hancher, Thomas
Harden, Earl*
Harden, Raymond Ellsworth
Harden, Roy
Harden, Walter James
Harsch, Fred Carl
Hatchett, Millard
Hatchett, Orval Loren
Hatton, Arnold Albert
Hawkins, Carl William
Hawkins, Joseph Marion
Hawkins, William R.
Hearth, Chester
Hearth, Francis O.
Hedrick, Burnell
Helms, Hershel Emerson
Hendershot, Ferrel Jr.
Hendershot, Robert Earl
Henderson, Charles Gordon
Hendricks, Paul
Hillenburg, Ansel
Hillenburg, Paul
Hobbs, Eugene
Hole, James H.
Holley, Oliver H.
Hooks, Harvey Lee
Horton, John Ryder
Houchins, Herman Gentry
Houchins, Robert Oscar
Houchins, Roy
Howard, Edgar E.
Howard, George Guffey
Hoy, Delmar Otis
Huber, Lee
Ingram, Jack R.
Jackson, Frell Eugene
Jacobs, Roy M.
Jarboe, Leo Jr.
Jarboe, Samuel Almon
Jones, George Richard
Jones, Robert Eugene
Jones, William Martin
Joslin, Leo Everett
Joslin, Lowell Ray
Kain, Oscar
Keaton, Earl Chester
Keaton, Lennis Carl

Kelp, Harold Wayne
Kemp, Alva
Kennedy, Charles G.
Kennedy, William Grant
Kent, Charles Edmond
Kent, Edward R.
Kent, Harry Clifford*
Kent, Leo Q.
King, Earl Charles
King, Fred Edmond
King, Harold Wesford
King, Rex Nolan
King, Robert Oliver
King, Virgil Gerald
Kinser, Ora Ansel
Kirts, Earl
Kirts, Mosier
Kirts, Russell
Kirts, Verl
Kleindorfer, Russell F.
Knose, Herman*
Krebbs, Virgil
Land, Eugene
Lawson, Charles Allen
Lawson, Charles Cecil
Lemen, Bernard Nelson
Lewis, Donald Eugene
Linke, Jean Millicent
Logsdon, Edward Lawrence
Logsdon, Paul Richard
Long, Albert Martin
Long, Jack Byron
Long, James Fremont*
Long, William Clarence
Loop, Max
Love, Norman Alexander
Lowman, Wesley Wandell
Lucas, Earl
Lucas, George Marion
Lucas, James Marion
McDonald, Carroll Clyde
McDonald, George Kenneth
McGrayel, William Harry
Malmgren, Paul Webster
Mann, Floyd James
Martin, Wesley Porter
Mathis, Harry Russell
Mathis, Mary Jane
Mathis, Maurice
Mathis, William Dale
Matlock, Noble Carlton
Merriman, Donald Lavere
Millard, Jesse Hollis
Miller, Ben Claudie
Miller, Charles D.
Miller, Clovis Woodrow
Miller, Herbert James Jr.
Miller, Ralph Daniel

Miller, Ralph William
Mitchner, Carl
Moberly, James Dale
Mobley, Bert Rex
Moore, Edwin Keith
Moore, Harold Eugene
Moore, John Henry
Moore, Julius C.
Moore, Loren Robert
Moore, Merrill Leon
Mullis, Charles
Mullis, Clinton Allen
Mullis, James Allen*
Mullis, William Gwin
Myers, Harry Edward
Myers, Thomas Warren
Neff, Jesse David Jr.
Newmister, Herschell
Noblitt, Glenn*
Ogle, Ernest Wayne
Oliver, Homer Amos
Osborne, Thomas H.
Owens, Eugene
Owens, James Henry
Palmer, Homer William
Parker, Loren K.
Parks, Homer Kenneth
Parmerlee, Harold
Parrish, Willard L.
Passenau, Charles Victor
Patterson, Verlys Cleo
Pearson, Challenor*
Peeples, William Jr.
Penrose, Thomas Jr.
Percifield, Grover Jr.
Percifield, Leonard
Percifield, Paul C.
Percifield, Wilber Allen
Petro, Cecil
Petro, Charles Ralph
Petro, Don Louis
Petro, Harold
Petro, Isaac Cortland
Petro, James Leslie
Phillips, Joseph Russell
Pierce, Paul Merril
Ping, Bennie F.
Ping, Bryce Dwight
Pitcher, Willie
Pittman, Alfred
Pittman, William Leon
Pogue, Leonard Mays
Poling, Allen
Powell, Herman Oliver
Powell, Homer Allen*
Powell, Luther
Powell, Wesley
Poyner, Everett Wyatt

Poyner, Roland Marion
Prinz, Charles Ernest
Pruitt, Dorman
Pruitt, Harlan Dale
Pruitt, Wayne Dewey
Rains, Everett
Rains, Marvin Louis
Rainwater, Glenn
Ratliff, Jesse J.
Rariden, James William Jr.
Rariden, John Earl
Rariden, Lee Alfred
Reed, Berl
Reeder, Sidney
Reeves, Dewey Dale
Richards, Harold Scott
Richards, Henry Byron
Richards, Melvin A.
Richards, Robert Paul
Richhart, Alvin Leroy
Richhart, Byron Cornelius
Roberts, Carson
Roberts, Chester
Roberts, Clarence
Roberts, Jack Junior
Roberts, Paul Wayne
Roberts, Raymond
Roberts, Warren
Robertson, Charles Edward
Robertson, Jasper
Robertson, Sherman
Robertson, Vernon P.
Rogers, Kermit Dale
Roller, Malcolm Herman
Rose, Earl
Rose, James Robert
Rose, Paul Leon
Rund, Delmer Earl
Rund, James Thurston
Rund, Melvin Forest
Russ, Harry
Russ, Richard Eugene
Russell, Thomas Edward
Russo, Frank William Jr.
Schild, Henry Bernard
Schilds, Henry S.
Schillingford, Herschel Eugene
Schrougham, Benton Jr.
Schrougham, Henry Ernest
Schrougham, Merrill Moris
Schrougham, Warren Marion
Scrougham, Lawrence
Scrougham, Robert Levonne
Seelmaer, Farris Dale
Seitz, Harold Allen
Seitz, Ivan Earl
Seitz, William
Sexton, Carl

WORLD WAR II (CONTINUED)

Sexton, Floyd
Shafer, James Jr.
Shepherd, Murnal Ellis
Shepherd, Thomas Marshall
Shepherd, Wilbur W.
Sherrill, Simmie Lavelle
Shipley, Andrew
Shipley, Edward Wayne
Shipley, James Isaac
Shipley, Mike
Simpson, Robert Louis
Sinkhorn, William Lloyd
Sipes, Clarence
Sisson, Alvin L.
Slevens, Lester
Slevin, Charles Sylvester
Slevin, William Curtis
Smith, Calvin Lewis
Smith, Charles Albert
Smith, Eligah
Smith, Horace
Smith, Isiah Harry
Smith, Phillip
Smith, Verlis Raymond
Smith, William Howard
Snider, Eustace Perry
Snider, Harold Roscoe
Snider, Harry Francis
Snider, Ivan
Snider, Marvin Lloyd
Snider, Paul Edward
Snider, Wendell Westford
Snyder, Elmer Louis
Snyder, Frank Jr.*
Snyder, Richard Allen
Snyder, William Allen
Snyder, William Victor
Sparks, Lloyd
Sperry, Ralph Anson
Spicer, Carl William
Spicer, Walter Thomas
Spiker, Harry Cline
Steel, Thomas Allen
Steele, Humphry Roosevelt
Stevens, Harold
Stillabower, Orville McNeal
Stillabower, Roscoe Emerson
Stillabower, Virgil O.
Stitt, John Leo
Stott, Jackie Lee
Sturgeon, Charles Wesley
Swift, James Earnest
Swift, Odie
Swift, Paul
Tabor, Fletcher Eugene
Tabor, Robert W.
Tabor, Russell Lowell
Taggart, Paul L.
Taggart, Raymond Strahl
Taylor, Harold Edwin
Taylor, Herschel Glen
Terrill, Layton John
Thickstun, Millard Dale
Thompson, John Thomas
Tilton, Fredric Lewis
Todd, James Harold
Torrence, Fred
Trisler, Earl
Tucker, George Clark
Tutterow, Leroy
Tutterow, Marvin Earl*
Tutterow, Raymond D.
Tutterow, Rex Eugene
Tuttle, Linton Harless
Voland, Elmo William
Voland, Howard Lewis
Voland, Richard Wilburt
VonKessler, Wilson
Waggoner, Cash
Walker, Alexander Laughlin
Walker, Charles Leslie
Walker, Claris Glen
Walker, Claude William
Walker, Paul Edwin
Walker, Ray William
Waltman, James Lowell
Waltz, Forrest William
Warford, Mildred
Watson, Arthur Dale
Watson, Jesse Levone
Wayman, Elmer Joseph
Wayman, Joseph Edward
Weddle, Billy David
Wells, Raymond
West, Ferrel Allen
West, Michael Howard
Wheeler, James Lemuel
White, James Keith
Whitley, Bert Phares
Whitley, Harold Joseph
Whitlock, Forrest O.
Wilkerson, Clifford
Wilkerson, Dale
Wilkerson, Hershel
Wilkerson, James Marshall
Wilkerson, Richard
Wilkerson, William Ralph
Williams, Walter Scott
Williamson, James Gerald
Williamson, Jean Elisha
Williamson, Lennis LaVaughn
Williamson, Paul Dwight
Williamson, Wendell
Willis, Nathan E.
Willoughby, Eugene
Wilson, Carl
Wilson, Olan Taylor
Woods, James Ancil
Wootton, Allen
Wrightsman, Charles E.
Wrightsman, Clifford A.
Wrightsman, James H.
Young, Everett Arthur
Young, Ira Russell
Young, Marion Louis
Young, Roger
Young, William S.
Zimmerman, Glen
Zody, Howard Sylvester
Zupancic, John Frank

An asterisk(*) after the name denotes killed in action.

Brown County boys returning from WWI. (Photo by Frank Hohenberger)

THE KOREAN WAR

The following veterans served in the Korean war. Their names were furnished to Helen Ayers in the summer of 1990 by the State Adjutant General's office.

Crabtree, Billie*
Crider, Acie Junior*
David, Kenneth Lee*
Dowell, Richard Lee*
Ford, Maurice E.*
Goe, Clyde*
McGee, Dale Alfred*
Ackerman, Paul Xavior
Adams, Herman Louis
Albright, Billy Eugene
Albright, Ray Everett
Allen, Robert
Ayers, Jr., Oscar
Ayers, Robert Eugene
Ayers, Roger Alan
Barrick, Marvin Lyndell
Bohall, Dale Eugene
Bohall, Lowell Edward
Bond, Ivan Lee
Bowden, James Ray
Bowden, William Lee
Bradley, Richard Ottis
Bradley, William Earl
Bright, Billy Gene
Bright, Charles William
Bright, James Oakley
Brown, Marshall Nolan
Brown, Noel Meredeth
Brummett, Jesse Omer
Buchholz, Jerald Stuart
Carmichael, Lowell Gene
Clark, Ralph
Clayn, Roy Henry
Clephane, Jr., Charles
Coffey, Donald Lewis
Coffman, John Edgar
Connor, Kenneth
Connor, Thomas
Crabtree, Lee Dunn
Crabtree, Richard L.
Craig, Shirley Eugene
Crawford, Jr., Cornelius
Cross, Albert William
David, Donald Robert
Dawson, Joe
Deckard, Harris Gale
Deckard, Melvon Dean
Dowell, Charles William
Emberton, Richard Eugene
Ferguson, Amanda Gertrude
Fleener, Kenneth Lee
Fleetwood, Robert Rose
Followell, Mallie Earl

Followell, Paul Leslie
Followell, Wilbur Donald
Ford, Denzil Leroy
Ford, Harold Edward
Frownfelter, Clarence Edward
Frye, Edward Ray
Garvey, Ralph Leon
George, Estil Verl
George, Harold Clayton
Graham, Jr., Clarence
Hancock, Kenneth
Harden, James Forrest
Harden, Thurman Eugene
Harding, Harold Eugene
Harvey, Jr., Harry Harold
Harvey, Laddie Leon
Hatchett, James Bennett
Hatchett, James Curtis
Hayworth, Donald Franklin
Hayworth, Max Kenneth
Hobbs, George Wayne
Hobbs, Mason Ellsworth
Houchins, Robert O.
Hunter, William Franklin
Inman, Jr., Edgar
Jacobsen, Richard Wayne
Jarboe, Leo Junior
Jarochovic, Jan
Johnson, Charles Robert
Jones, Rossie Elwin
Joslin, Herschel Paul
Joy, James Warren
Kelp, Donald Eugene
Kemp, Raymond Jacob
Kent, Robert Dale
Lauderdale, Alvin
Lawson, Francis Edward
Lawson, James William R.
Loop, Max William
Lucas, Edgar Dale
McCoy, John Lewis
McDonald, Bill Lee
Malan, Fredrick Louis
Mathews, Donald Jeann'e
Mathis, Harold Earnest
Merriman, Wayne
Moberly, Paul Eugene
Mobley, Max Ivan
Moore, Billie
Moore, Glenn Lee
Moore, Jimmie D.
Moore, John Rudolph
Moore, Loren Robert

Moore, Marion Paul
Mullis, Dale
Mullis, Russell Andrew
Myers, James Pat
Napier, Willlie
Northup, Gene Scott
Page, Paul Earl
Parker, Walter Lee
Penrose, Harold Eugene
Percifield, Charles Thurman
Percifield, George
Percifield, Robert Wayne
Petro, Floyd R.
Pointer, Robert Lee
Porter, William Allen
Quillen, Robert Lee
Rainwater, Charles Luther
Reed, Charles
Richards, Jerry Edwin
Richhart, James Alfred
Riser, Jack Dwain
Roberts, George Wesley
Robertson, Gilbert Hoover
Robertson, Morris Leon
Roller, Charles Eugene
Roller, Leland Earl
Sanders, Arthur Dale
Sanders, Kenneth Eithel
Sanders, Leslie Marlowe
Saylors, Leslie Lee
Schrock, James Allen
Schrougham, Leroy Edwin
Scott, Robert Homer
Scrougham, Harold
Seibel, Robert Marvin
Seitz, Emmett Robert
Seitz, George Max

Seitz, Gerald
Seitz, William
Shepherd, Lester Earl
Skinner, Ival Max
Slevins, Charles Sylvester
Slevin, Edwin Duaine
Smith, Donald Edward
Smith, Luther Mallary
Smith, Paul Loren
Smith, Richard Lee
Stevens, James Donald
Stines, Charles Arthur
Stines, Everett Russell
Stines, Paul Eugene
Stratton, Charles H.
Stratton, James Goodloe
Sullivan, Keith Alton
Tabor, James Lee
Taggart, Raymond Strahl
Taylor, Fred Eugene
Taylor, Maurice Franklin
Tuttie, Linton Harless
Voorheis, Elmer Dee
Walker, David Lee
Walker, Garnet Jonathan
Watson, Ernest Allen
Watson, James Robert
Watson, Raymond Eugene
Weaver, John William
Weddle, William Jackson
West, Orval David
Wilkerson, Kenneth Edgar
Williamson, Max Roderick
Williamson, Robert Dale
Williamson, Ronald Larry
Woods, Joseph Glen

An asterisk(*) after the name denotes killed in action.

Vietnam War

The following veteran's names were gleaned from Brown County Courthouse records by County Recorder Karen Olmstead by leafing through the discharge papers on file in her office; and many others were provided to Helen Ayers in the summer of 1990 by the veterans themselves or their families calling to record the names of those who fought in this war. There may be more names to this list, but as of September 1990, these were all that could be found. The National Archives provided the name of the one casualty from Brown County, Mr. Banks.

Adams, Ronald Cullen
Anderson, Charles Matthew Jr.
Arndt, Gerhard H.
Banks, Larry C.*
Beauchamp, Theodore Lee
Biddle, Kenny Joseph
Burker, Kenneth Wayne
Burrell, John Barton
Campbell, Danny Curt
Ennis, Carl O'Neal
Floyd, Jerry
Fox, Larry Dale
Greathouse, Daniel C.
Greathouse, Gary W.
Greathouse, Larry W.
Hanner, Terry Lee
Hardin, James Franklin
Harris, Dwight Douglas
Harris, Keith Ray
Hazelgrove, Ronald Eugene
Johnson, Jay
Jones, Jerry Lee
Lambert, David Gene
Lee, William Bernard Jr.
Lucas, Robert Wayne
Mattingly, John II
Meek, Michael Lee
Meriwether, Jeffrey
Meshberger, Harry
Murphy, Charles Milton
Nesbit, Philip Michael
O'Hara, Michael E.
Rains, Andy Michael
Roberts, John Wayne
Robinson, William
Rose, Roger
Rudd, John
Rudd, Marc James
Rund, James Anthony
Schroeder, Gustav Frederick Jr.
Seitz, James
Smith, Floyd Allen
Smith, Roy
Tolle, Anthony
Wachstetter, Raymond James III
Williams, James Wayne
Wrightsman, Edward A.

Panama Invasion

These names were provided Helen Ayers by the families of the men who took part in the invasion on December 20, 1989.

Burkhart, Brett
Lee, Chuck

Persian Gulf Conflict

The following names were called into the office of Helen Ayers during late summer, 1990, by the mothers of the men who were involved in this crisis.

Altop, Bryan D.
Baker, Everett Wayne
Betts, Scott E.
Blaney, Timothy
Bowling, Scott
Burkhart, Brett
Campbell, John M.
Chastain, W. E. (Billy)
Cooper, Robert
Dille, Geoffery A.
Fike, Jeffrey
Griggs, Andrew
Hopkins, Brian Ray
Howard, Dean
Kaserman, Scott
Keymon, Gary D.
Keymon, Jerry L.
Knapp, Joey
Kramer, Jason
Lawson, Jerry A.
Lee, Charles (Chuck)
Miller, Terry L.
Nevins, Garth Roman
Parker, Walter L.
Parsons, James A.
Perez, Maria J.
Popplewell, Williard L., Jr.
Reeve, Thomas
Reeves, Troy
Roberts, Jerry E.
Rodgers, Brian
Sipes, Travis D.
Sizemore, Randy
Sizemore, Sidney
Smith, Michael E.
Sparks, Tim
Thompson, Ryan
Thompson, Thomas A.
Vermillion, Frank
Voland, Michael L.
Williams, Christopher R.
Wood, Matt T.
Wright, Christopher
Wright, Eugene A.
Wright, Michael

Military History of Brown County Bibliography

[1] Hamblen, A. Porter, The Hamblen Family, 1940, Rev. 1985.
[2] Bowen, F. B., Biographical Record of Bartholomew and Brown Counties, 1904, p. 382.
  Reeve, Helen and Kenneth, Brown County Cemetery Book, p. 127.
[3] Goodspeed, Weston A., Counties of Morgan, Monroe, and Brown, 1884, p. 703.
[4] Ibid., pp. 703-705.
[5] Ibid., pp. 705-709.
[6] Ibid., pp. 709-710.
  Miller, Chattie Wade, Brown County Remembers, p. 143.
[7] Goodspeed, Op.cit., pp. 710-713.
[8] Ibid., p. 712.
[9] Record of Indiana Volunteers in the Spanish-American War 1898-1899 Issued by the Authority of the Sixty-first General Assembly of Indiana, Published by Wm. B. Burford, Indianapolis, 1900, pp. 68-364.

Chapter XI
Brown County Industries

Salt

The earliest industry in what became Brown County was the preparation and sale of salt. Salt licks were found near the junction of Salt Creek and Jackson Creek in Township 9, Range 2 East, Section 31, now western Washington Township. These salt licks were well known to the county's pioneers, and to Indians before they arrived.

As early as 1821, a settlement was established near the salt licks by people from Bloomington. The first road in the county was the road from Bloomington to the Salt Works. In 1823, William Jackson bored a well, 300 feet deep, pumped up the brine, and boiled it in eight to ten huge iron kettles. Cakes of salt formed in the bottoms of the kettles as the water boiled away. The salt was pulverized and sold in Bloomington and Monroe County.

The Jackson Salt Works flourished for some years. People traveled forty to fifty miles to buy salt. Two or three men were employed fulltime to cut wood for the fires under the kettles. The fires burned continuously night and day. At one time 2,500 bushels of salt were produced annually. Salt sold for $8.00 a bushel.

When the price per bushel decreased markedly, the Jackson Salt Works were abandoned in 1836.[1]

Later in the l9th Century, the salt licks again produced salt commercially. Seralvo McGuire's father, with Tom Richards, sank a second well, pumped up the brine and boiled it in large iron kettles. They cut the wood to feed the fires, pulverized the salt and sold it door-to-door in Bloomington. It is not recorded how long this business lasted. When it ceased, the iron kettles were distributed to Brown County farmers who used them to boil the water they needed for butchering.[2]

There was a third salt works in Brown County in Township 9 Range 9 East, Section 12. It was established by a company from Bloomington, headed by a Mr. Howe who sank a well in the 1820s. How long this venture lasted is not known, but the sixth United States Census of 1840 stated that 1,600 bushels of salt were produced annually in Brown County.[3]

Leather

The tanning of leather was profitable from 1840 to 1880. The 1840 United States Census listed $400 worth of sole leather, and $500 worth of other leathers tanned annually in the county. Six men were employed full-time, and the investment in tanning was $6,000.

According to the Indiana Gazetteer for 1849 there were eight tanneries in Brown County with an annual income of $50,000. Twenty-five people were employed in the industry.

Benjamin Huntington opened a tannery southeast of Nashville with four vats, later eight vats, in the early 1840s. The tannery was closed by the beginning of the Civil War.

T. S. Calvin started a tannery in Nashville in 1851 with six vats. It was later owned by Shotwell and Larkin, followed by Dow Head. As many as ten vats were used.

The most successful tanning business was that of James C. Parmerlee in Hamblen Township. Parmerlee came from Connecticut where he had operated a tannery. He settled in Nineveh, but moved to Brown County to be near the source of tanbark, and to leave the swampy, malarial country.

He chose land at the bottom of the hill on the road leading north from Fox's Corner. He built several vats as early as 1826. Walnut timbers were used to construct the vats. In 1935 they were destroyed and it was discovered that in 100 years the vats had deteriorated very little, and were in remarkably good condition. The building housing the vats was of brick. The tannery had been built near Bean Blossom Creek, east of Georgetown, for a convenient source of water.

A few hides were furnished by local people, but most of the hides were shipped to the tannery from Sydelia, Missouri. Parmerlee owned and operated a leather store in Sydelia. The hides were hauled by wagon from the railroad station in Morgantown, and after tanning, were taken back to the railroad station by a man named Goodin.

The tanning process required 5,000 "cords" of tanbark (chestnut oak) every year. Each spring, a large group of men was hired to camp in the forest for several weeks to peel the bark from the trees.

The 1876 Illustrated Historical Atlas of Indiana speaks of the , superior quality of leather tanned by Parmerlee. The leather won State, National, and International awards and prizes. The annual income of the tannery was $100,000.

Oliver Neff deserves mention as the finisher of the valuable hides. Before the leather was transported to the railroad, it was stamped by placing on each hide a thin piece of copper from which the name and address of the Parmerlee Tannery had been cut out. By painting over the copper the

Load of tanbark in front of courthouse, 1906.

name and address was transferred to the leather. Mark Parmerlee, the grandson of James Parmerlee, in 1936 owned one of these stamps:

"From
Parmerlee Bros.
Manufacturers of
Oak Tanned Leather
Tannersville
Bean Blossom P.O. Ind."

The location of the tannery for many years was called <u>Tannersville</u> by county people.

After James Parmerlee's death in 1872 his son, William, and his stepson, James, carried on the business as the "Parmerlee Brothers." The tannery was closed about 1879. William Parmerlee then moved to Sydelia to operate the Parmerlee store.

The <u>Jacksonian</u> of May 27, 1882, Brown County's newspaper, stated that "At the foot of the hill is a large brick tannery of Parmerlee and Sons, now in a dilapidated condition. A few years ago this was one of the most extensive establishments of its kind in the country, affording a splendid market for hides and tanbark and giving employment to a number of hands." In 1882 the walls were crumbling, and the roof was falling in.[4]

GOLD

The discoveries of gold flakes in the streams of Jackson and Hamblen Townships have caused numerous gold "excitements" in Brown County. Companies have been formed, land and stream areas leased, sluice-ways constructed, long-toms and rockers prepared, and elaborate mining machinery installed through the years. All attempts to mine gold in quantity have been doomed to failure.

If the source of the gold had been clearly understood, commercial efforts to mine gold, silver, precious and semi-precious stones would never have been undertaken. Gold is never found in the sedimentary rock that underlies Brown County. Gold found in the streams was brought by the glaciers, frozen into the masses of ice that scoured Canadian soil and rock for thousands of years. Bean Blossom Ridge, just south of the village of Bean Blossom, formed a high barrier against which the ice masses piled, unable to move directly farther south. Eventually the ice over northern Brown County melted, dropping the rocks and minerals.

Abandoned gold mining machinery at Upper Salt Creek in Hamblen Township in 1934.

Gradually, through thousands of years, the soil accumulated, burying the deposits to a depth of several feet. After heavy rains gold flakes, and small nuggets, and rarely, precious and semiprecious small stones wash out into the streams, Bear Creek, Bean Blossom, Plum, and Lick Creeks.

Gold in quantity, such as is found in South Africa, simply does not exist in Brown County.

John Richards, a pioneer who settled at Bear Creek in 1830, panned flakes of gold from the creek in small quantities. When stories of finding gold reached Indianapolis, a group of men leased a stretch of Bear Creek that ran through John Richards' farm. They constructed a long flume of oak timber for gold washing. Just as it was completed, a heavy rain swelled the stream and the flume was completely demolished. That ended the venture.

A few individuals who had had experience in the California gold rush came to Brown County and were more successful. By careful selection of location they panned out one to two dollars worth of gold per day. The most valuable nugget found was worth $1.10.

An estimate of gold found in Jackson Township by 1884 does not indicate that anyone became wealthy.

Richards Farm, Bear Creek	$400
Plum Creek	100
Lick Creek	150
Christopher Stump, Georgetown	500
Bean Blossom Creek	800
Total	$1,950

In 1875 the <u>Brown County Mining Company</u> was incorporated with capital of $10,000 divided into 2,000 shares of $5.00 each. This consisted of local county people only. The purpose was to prospect for, and mine minerals and precious metals in Brown County. In 1898 the <u>Indiana Mining and Investment Company</u> was incorporated with $100,000 capital divided into 20,000 shares of $5.00 each. This company consisted of leading business men over the State of Indiana. Their intent was to mine gold, silver, and precious stones. Both of these companies were to run fifty years. They did not average more than twenty-five cents of gold a day. Their efforts did not last long.

Considerable local gold activity occurred in 1901. The <u>Brown County Democrat</u> of September 6, 1901, printed an article concerning Colonel Calvert of Cleveland, Ohio, who had moved near Richards on Bear Creek. He had displayed in Nashville, a small piece of quartz laced with gold which he had found on his farm. He planned to mine gold extensively. He did not do so, however.

In 1901 farmers along Bean Blossom Creek from Spearsville to Needmore again searched for gold. A few, W. S. Richards, and a Mr. Young, found gold dust, gold flakes, and silver flakes, but never in quantity. Mr. Young discovered a diamond valued at $200 by an Indianapolis firm.

In 1930 a Nashville group organized the <u>Brown County Gold Mining Association</u> hoping to stimulate interest in placer and crevice mining. The members were active, and had a great deal of exercise and fun, but only occasional "color" showed when they panned for gold.

In July, 1934, a very large outfit came to Hamblen Township. Eugene Williams was the superintendent, as well as the inventor of the bulky machinery they installed. The investment cost $30,000. They leased 730 acres at the source of Upper Salt Creek, two miles southeast of Spearsville and thirteen miles northeast of Nashville. Kansas City men undertook the mining, but all efforts failed to produce gold in quantity.

Other attempts to mine gold commercially have been made, some fairly recently, but all without success.

Weekend panners are frequently present in Hamblen and Jackson Townships. They are not Brown County natives. As usual, they find little gold dust and few flakes.

John Dine (1882-1941), who lived in Hamblen Township, probably panned more gold than any other Brown County individual. A few gold rings and pins are owned by county natives made from gold found in the streams.[5]

STAPLES SPECTACLE FACTORY

George T. Staples came from Philadelphia to visit his sister, Mrs. Herbert P. Parmerlee, in Hamblen Township. He was greatly impressed by the beauty and quiet he discovered, and decided to move his spectacle factory from Philadelphia to Brown County. The date is uncertain, but Staples, a few miles east of Georgetown (now Bean Blossom), built a workshop, a home for his family, and houses for twelve or fifteen skilled workmen he brought from Philadelphia.

The spectacles were made completely by hand from glass and gold bars. The small, square pieces of glass were cut and ground into shape. The gold bars were melted and formed into wire for the frames. The gold was imported from Philadelphia, although Staples did buy scrap gold, gold money, rings, and other gold jewelry to melt down. He did not use gold found in Brown County streams.

One of the unusual features of the Staples spectacles were the sliding temples which made them adjustable.

The finished spectacles were sent to Philadelphia to Mr. Staples' distributing agent. The retail price for a pair of spectacles was $10.00.

George Staples worked in his spectacle factory until his death at fifty-six years of age in 1877. He had been in the county nearly fifteen years.

Zack T. Staples, son of George Staples, carried on the business for a number of years, but moved the factory to Bean Blossom. When the use of machinery caused handmade spectacles to become unprofitable, Zack closed the factory and moved to Indianapolis, where he worked in another spectacle factory.

In 1936, Mrs. Zack Staples and her daughter, Mrs. Anna S. Anderson, owned the original factory buildings, east of Bean Blossom. They used the old family house as a summer home and conducted tours through the factory.[6]

GRIST AND SAWMILLS

There were no grist mills when the first pioneers arrived in what became Brown County. Settlers were forced to take corn they grew to a neighboring county to be ground into meal. They traveled usually on horseback, with a bag or two of corn, to Tanahill Mill on Blue River in Bartholomew County, Arnold Mill three miles north of Columbus on the White River, Thompson Grist Mill at Edinburg in Johnson County, and later to Morgan County or Bloomington.[7]

Settlers found it an enormous help when corn could be ground to meal, and wheat to flour, in their own county.

The first grist mills were horse mills. A horse plodded around and around in a circle turning the millstones. A mill customer might be required to use his own horse to supply the power.

By 1828, Jonathan Fox, had installed a horse mill in what became east Washington Township, near Salt Creek. The Youngs ran a horse mill in western Jackson Township about that same time.

In 1835, George Grove's horse mill was doing business in Georgetown. The mill ran for almost ten years.[8]

In 1827, the first water mill was built on Salt Creek in Hamblen Township. The name of the owner is not known, but it is recorded that the mill was successful and ground meal until 1835. A second water grist mill was built by Eliakim Hamblen in 1838 in Hamblen Township. It is remembered that he used "a good set of buhrs"—the stones that ground the corn. That mill lasted for six years.[9]

It was soon discovered that native stone was too soft to withstand the constant grinding to which millstones were subjected. Buhr stones were imported from France. They were very hard stone and lasted for years.

Benjamin Cox's water grist mill was built in 1835 on Greasy Creek near its junction with Salt Creek, just east of Nashville. This mill proved to be exceedingly useful to county farmers.

In the 1830's, William Taylor's water mill, east of Georgetown on Bean Blossom Creek, ran for five years.[10]

During the Civil War, the Bartholomew water grist mill was active at Pike's Peak.[11]

The Adolph Schweitzer mill, on the bank of Salt Creek south and east of Nashville, was one of the best and busiest waterpowered buhr stone grist mills in Brown County for many years.

Schweitzer, a native German, came from Pennsylvania to the county in 1855. Although only eighteen, he understood the construction of a grist mill. He built his mill in 1857. The lumber he used came from the sawmill of Nicholas Petro. The dimensions of the mill were 34x42 feet. The building was two stories high with a front shed, and a "maple room" that housed a treadle wheel. Three sets of buhrs ground corn, wheat, and buckwheat. Bins stored meal and flour.

The mill dam was seven feet high across the creek from bank to bank. It was made of round, straight logs reinforced by poles reaching upstream. A "30 degree obtuse angle threw a stronger current of water on the treadle wheel."

Schweitzer ran the mill until his death in 1874.[12]

Beginning in the early 1830s, sawmills were also built in the county. A grist mill was often housed in the same building with a sawmill.

In 1830, Charles Sipes and Edward David owned a grist and sawmill on Salt Creek, three miles east of Nashville. This may have been the first sawmill in the county. A small, temporary dam and a race of perhaps 100 yards supplied additional head to the water, which furnished the power to propel the saw and the "niggerhead" stones for the grist mill. This early mill sawed logs into lumber. The grist mill was greatly improved when a set of French buhrs was installed and a stronger dam was built.[13]

In Van Buren Township the Goss sawmill was patronized in the 1830s by settlers. William Crouch in the late 1840s, operated a sawmill in the township.[14]

The Christopher Stump water grist and sawmill in 1848 was located on Bean Blossom Creek, two miles west of Georgetown, in Jackson Township. In the 1870s, Stephen A. Richards, son of pioneers John and Priscilla Richards, ran a successful saw and

47

grist mill at Richards, which became the town of Trevlac. In the 1870s and 1880s, there was a very active sawmill in the township owned by John Taylor and his son Ed. It was noted for its puncheon roof.[15]

In 1879 William P. Taggart, son of pioneers William and Sarah Taggart, ran a water sawmill in Hamblen Township. In 1880 he added a grist mill with the usual French buhrs.

Washington Township had a number of sawmills. In 1882, Wesley Kirts owned one on Salt Creek. In 1884 the Samuel Kent sawmill probably also on Salt Creek, was doing business as well as William Geary's grist and sawmill, and Benjamin Clark's sawmill in eastern Washington Township.[16]

The Hoover mill on Salt Creek, Washington Township, was built by John Hoover in 1866 and sold to Robert Howard in 1879. The structure housed an up-and-down sashsaw outfit before it became a grist mill. The timbers of the mill building were white oak and, as always, the water wheel was of wood. Late in the 1880s, a 60 horsepower turbine was added to Hoover mill. This ran for eight years when John Wrightsman had charge of the mill. The mill was well patronized, but it was abandoned in the 1890s.[17]

The only carding mill in Brown County was built in the 1840s by John Hight. The two-story building of yellow poplar was located on the west side of the Salt Creek grist mill, a quarter mile south of Nashville's public square at West Main and Jefferson Streets. It was operated by a treadwheel. The mill was run by W. H. Turner, and cleaned and separated wool to spin into yarn.

In 1874, the old carding mill was moved to East Main Street across from and slightly to the east of the courthouse. A third story was added. It was the skyscraper of Nashville, 45 feet tall. The building played an important part in Nashville's social and business life until it burned in 1939.[18]

The Nicholas Petro grist and sawmill south of Nashville on Salt Creek, built in 1855 was a three-story water mill. It was a very large, busy, popular mill. Nicholas Petro abandoned it in 1900 after steam mills had been introduced into the county and were causing problems for the water mills. In 1920 the dilapidated Petro mill was torn down. The mill stones were placed on the ground in front of the old log jail as a memento. The stones are still there.[19]

The buildings housing water-powered grist and sawmills, the gears, water wheels, and dams were constructed of wood in the 1800s. Hence, they had a short life span. When decay set in, mills were usually abandoned rather than rebuilt.

Many small mills were like sheds with a roof, a floor and three or even four sides open to the weather. They were all undershot mills: water flowed over the base of a mill wheel, turning it, and providing power for saw or buhrstones. Since there are no swiftly descending streams in Brown County, water never ran onto the tops of mill wheels.

Steam mills gradually replaced water mills in the latter 1880s, 1890s, and 1900s. Water mills could not compete with steam engines in quality nor quantity of cornmeal, flour, and lumber produced.

One of the earliest steam mills in the county was the Ed Taylor and T. D. Calvin grist and sawmill built in 1886 at the south edge of Nashville. An advertisement in the Brown County Democrat, June 30, 1892 stated:

"Ed Taylor, T. D. Calvin
Best flour – fresh at the mill. Pay cash for grain.
Sawing done just right."

The Calvert steam flour and sawmill, was considered one of the best in the county. Built and owned at Trevlac by Colonel Calvert, it was closed a few years after a depot was built at Trevlac for the Illinois Central Railway in 1906. Trevlac had been known as the community of Richards.[20]

Nicholas Petro, following the closing of his water grist and sawmill on Salt Creek, south of Nashville, built a steam grist mill in 1908 or 1909. It was on State Road 46 a mile southwest of Nashville, near Green Valley. The mill ground corn, wheat, and buckwheat.

On December 31, 1908, "Uncle Nick" built a roaring fire under the boiler which he thought contained water. When he discovered that the boiler was empty he began to fill it with cold water. There was a terrific explosion. The boiler was blown out of the mill as was Nicholas Petro (1839-1908) who did not survive the accident.[21]

After 1900, what had been Ed Taylor's and T.D. Calvin's mill at the south end of Jefferson Street, was owned by James Tilton and George Max McDonald. It was a flour mill. On a night in December 1917, church bells and the courthouse bell began to ring in the wee hours of the morning – a sign of fire. A large crowd gathered to watch the mill burn to the ground. It is said that the mill caught fire accidentally while a group of men were gambling in the mill.[22]

In 1919, Pete Thomas built and ran a steam sawmill where the Nashville Elementary School is now located. Pete kept his mules, wagons, and logging equipment in a barn on the southwest corner of Van Buren and Washington Streets.[23]

After Josh Bond's flour mill at Helmsburg burned in the early 1920s Stone Head mill was the only steam grist mill left in the county. It was built in 1870 by Cyrus Bartholomew as a waterpowered grist mill. When Charles Saffell of Van Buren Township bought the mill, he and Tom Hendricks installed a steel-roller to replace the buhrs, and added a steam engine. Four-foot oak wood was used as fuel to provide steam for the mill.

In 1910 the mill produced 2,000 pounds of cornmeal and 3,000 pounds of flour daily. Willard Fulks bought the very prof-

Nick Petro Mill on Salt Creek, south of Nashville in 1897.

Ewers Sawmill in 1906. Sam Ewers is on the left. (Photo by Otto Ping)

itable mill and managed it until it burned in 1914. The mill was rebuilt and sold to Alra Wheeler. It was known as the "Wheeler and Son Stone Head Roller Mill." The large, red, three-story building was situated where Pleasant Valley Creek emptied into Salt Creek at Stone Head. The mill burned for a second time in 1925, and was never rebuilt. The foundation stones are still visible.[24]

By 1925 flour and cornmeal could be bought readily and cheaply in local grocery stores. Small grist mills in Indiana ceased to be profitable.

The old water-wheel grist mills, besides meal and flour, had provided entertainment for county farm boys, who considered it a treat to be sent to a mill. During the wait for flour and wheat to be ground boys caught strings of fish in the stream or pond that provided water power for the mill. In slack times, or on rainy days, men drove wagons loaded with wheat or corn drawn by oxen, mules, or horses to a mill. It was a social occasion as well as a necessary chore. Everyone saw neighbors and friends while waiting their turn for wheat and flour, and learned the latest county and political news.

Steam mills, by contrast, made so much noise that conversation was nearly impossible. Steam millers kept ground flour and meal in bins, and farmers merely exchanged their grain for the finished product, without a long wait. Gone were the days of several hours of leisure at a mill.

Sawmills are not relegated to the past in Brown County. A few continue to function and are profitable though they differ from the old steam mills. Modern mills are electric and they possess infinitely more complicated machinery. At the present time, 1990, there are five working mills and at least three portable mills in the county.

Knight's sawmill on State Road 46, opposite the turnoff to Yellowwood State Park, is owned by Donald Knight. The mill saws logs to lumber and supplies whole logs for building cabins. The majority of the logs the mill uses come from Monroe and Green Counties.

The mill's chief occupation, however, is the making of wooden pallets. These shallow boxes hold supplies for shipment and are fork-lifted and stacked into trucks. After construction the empty pallets are taken to a factory in Edinburg, Indiana.

The "Brown County Forest Products" mill is located on Brown Hill Road near Gnaw Bone. This automated sawmill is owned and was built by John Booe in 1975. It has developed into a dimensional and finishing mill.

Red oak lumber, only, is bought for the mill from lumber sources all over the midwest. The mill kiln-dries the lumber and then processes it into stair treads, newel posts, banisters, handrails, cabinet panels and flooring. This mill is not a public mill and is a major Indiana processing mill. Its products are sold to a broker who in turn sells them to assembly plants in Canada and Germany. The mill employs fifteen people.

The "Bill Pool and Sons" sawmill in Helmsburg has had a checkered history. The first mill was built by Arthur West in 1940. Charles Richard bought it in 1951. In 1968 the mill burned. Richards constructed a new building and bought a new saw. He sold the mill in 1973 to Bill Pool. The mill burned again in October 1987 and was rebuilt by Pool in 1988.

The mill saws lumber for construction purposes. Lumber is also sold to a Logansport company. After kiln-drying, the lumber is used to make furniture and paneling. Hoosier Veneer in Trafalgar sends logs to Helmsburg from which "flitches" or strips are sawed. These are transported back to the factory in Trafalgar.

The Pool mill sells wood for the making of pallets, logs to build cabins, slab-wood to burn in fireplaces and wood bark, removed from logs with a debarker, for mulch.

The mill buys from loggers, but Bill Pool and his sons go to Brown County woods to cut down oak, beech, hickory, sycamore, ash, sugar maple, and poplar to saw into lumber.

Dale Wilkerson's sawmill is near Gatesville. Dale and his three sons are in partnership. They buy local logs which are brought to the mill, principally oak. The logs are sawed into lumber for building material. The pallets they make are trucked to Indianapolis and sold to the Ford Motor Company and R.C.A.

Robert McQueary's sawmill on Poplar Grove Road has, in the past, sawed crossties. At present the mill is involved in custom sawing – beams and red cedar for paneling which is sold to a Terre Haute firm. McQueary uses only hard woods. A five-man crew works in the sawmill, and he employs three men to cut timber in the woods and transport it to the mill.

Portable mills are still used in the county. Don Kelp, on Greasy Creek Road, has a portable mill with the trade name of "Woodmizer." It is a band saw and is pulled on a two-wheel trailer by a truck to the woods. After trees are felled, the woodmizer saws the logs into lumber: maple, oak, hickory, elm, poplar, and walnut.

Dale Rhoades, on Mt. Liberty Road, also has a portable band saw. He buys native lumber from timber cutters, oak and other hard woods, hauls the logs to his home, saws them into lumber to sell.

Jack Alltop on Salt Creek Road, works part-time sawing logs into lumber with his portable sawmill. He also hooks his mill to the back of a truck and heads for woods where trees have been cut.[25]

TIMBER

The early pioneers regarded forests as a hindrance to farming. Their chief concern

Portable sawmills just north of Hornettown Road in 1905-06 Logs were rolled down the hill into the log yard. The hills are devoid of forest due to the severe tree cutting all over Brown County.

was to dispose of unwanted trees as quickly as possible. A great deal of very valuable timber, while land was being cleared, was cut, rolled into large piles and burned in Brown County.

When settlers realized timber had a market value, trees from then on were cut recklessly: white oak, chestnut oak, hickory on the hills, and black walnut, yellow poplar, cherry and elm on bottom land.

In the mid-1800s logs were floated down Salt Creek to Shoals, Indiana. Trees were felled and axed into logs during the winter. Men with ox teams worked for days hauling logs to the bank of Salt Creek, east of Nashville. The logs were pushed into the stream and fastened together in rafts, forty logs to a raft.

When the spring freshets arrived three men were assigned to each raft. A large oar was used to steer a raft and keep it moving. It took three days and two nights to reach Shoals.[26]

When local mills sawed logs into lumber the woods still provided winter work for farmers. They brought the huge logs in wagons pulled by horses, mules, or oxen to the mills. Wooden brakes on wagon wheels enabled a farmer to control the descent of a wagon on the hills. The squeal of such brakes could be heard all over Brown County in winter.

Portable steam sawmills were taken to the forests to saw logs into lumber. Both lumber and logs were shipped as freight on the railways from Columbus, Bloomington, and Morgantown. From 1906 when a branch of the Illinois Central Railroad was opened in Jackson Township between Morgantown and Bloomington, logs and lumber were taken to Helmsburg, the main station in Brown County, to be freighted to Bloomington or Indianapolis. After 1935, when a paved road was built from Nashville to Morgantown, and on to Indianapolis, both lumber and logs were transported by truck and sold in the city.

A great deal of lumber was also used to build Brown County homes, barns, and other buildings. Fine old houses remain in Nashville built when walnut, poplar, and cherry were plentiful. Ornate scroll work, and gingerbread decorations were commonly used. The lumber could be an inch thick. County people spoke of their "native-sawed lumber" with pride. They boasted how well the lumber weathered.[27]

Examples of these houses are the Allison and Tilton homes on Jefferson Street, the Calvin house on Van Buren Street, the Mosier place on State Road 135 north of Nashville, and the Poling homestead, a mile west of Needmore built by Dr. Fleener.

By 1900 only a few small areas were still covered with the original large timber. From 1900 to 1936 smaller trees were cut to furnish wood for railroad crossties, spokes for wagon wheels, staves, and hoop poles for barrels; wood products that were readily sold.

Cutting and selling cordwood for Brown County stoves and fireplaces brought an income to many families in the early 1900s.

Orchards

From very early days apples, peaches, cherries, pears, plums, grapes, and berries were grown successfully in Brown County. Farmers planted orchards to supply their families with fruit. When the process of canning was introduced housewives industriously canned fruit and made jellies to use through the long winters.

In 1882 William Waltman planted the largest orchard in the county on the high hill south of Bean Blossom. He also built a family home on Bean Blossom Ridge. The orchard proved to be a profitable venture. Waltman apparently advertized his peaches, pears, and apples. People came from considerable distances to pick and buy the fruit.[28]

After 1906, when fruit could be shipped from Helmsburg on the railroad to Bloomington and markets in Indianapolis, orchards began to proliferate. By 1915 there were thirty-seven orchards in the county.

In 1914 Dale Bessire, one of the earliest artists, moved to Brown County from Indianapolis with his wife, Ruth, and baby son,

A. D. West and Sons Sawmill and Lumberyard, Helmsburg, 1940

Philip. He bought a thriving apple orchard from Sampson David, a thirty-acre tract on a hill at the northwest edge of Nashville. The orchard contained more than thirty varieties of apples.

At that time traveling salesmen sold fruit trees. Of course they praised the delicious new varieties. As a result orchards were planted with many kinds of apples.

Dale became a skilled orchardist. The apples furnished an assured income while he established himself as artist. Bill Quick, who built the home of T. C. Steele, built a house for the Bessires near the orchard.

Dale became noted for his apple cider. Every fall he sold innumerable gallons of cider to the ever-increasing number of tourists.[29]

By 1936 orchards appeared to be the most promising industry in the county. State Road 46 from Bloomington to Columbus had been improved. State Road 135 was constructed and paved from Nashville to Indianapolis. Trucking service was available and fruit could be transported very quickly to markets all over the state.

In 1936 there were several large orchards in eastern Brown County near a community known as Fruit Ridge. The most extensive orchards were in northwest Jackson Township. They belonged to Phillip Baker, Amos Gibson, James McGee, A.F. Steinheiser, B.W. Douglass, and Tyner Myers.[30]

The Douglass orchard, known as Hickory Hill, was the largest in the county, with thousands of trees. The display of blossoms in the spring was said to be the most spectacular in Indiana. Mr. Douglass also operated a canning factory.[31]

These orchards are no more. Mrs. Ruth Bessire gave two reasons for their demise. Hordes of parasites commenced to invade the orchards, resulting in constant tree spraying. Scores of local men had been employed to trim the trees, spray, and pick and pack the fruit for shipment. Increasingly, Brown County men rejected orchard work. They preferred the factories of Bloomington, Columbus, and Indianapolis. Better roads and the proliferation of cars made daily travel in and out of the county feasible. Also, factories had the advantage of year-round work, not seasonal activity.

Without the labor of local men orchardists were unable to raise fruit commercially.

Brown County Industries Bibliography

[1] Mathis, Ray, Brown County History 1936, pp. 55,56.
[2] Ibid., p. 47.
[3] Goodspeed, Weston A., Counties of Morgan, Monroe, and Brown, 1884, p. 726.
[4] Mathis, Ray, Op. cit., pp. 52-54, 55.
[5] Goodspeed, Weston A., Op. cit., pp. 726,732,733.
    Hohenberger, Frank M., Down in the Hills O' Brown County, 1956, pp.38,39.
    Mathis, Ray, Op. cit., pp. 45-47.
[6] Mathis, Ray, Op. cit., pp. 51-52.
[7] Baskin, Forster and Co., Illustrated Atlas State of Indiana, 1876.
[8,9,10] Goodspeed, Weston A., Op. cit., pp. 726, 737, 743.
[11] Hohenberger, Frank M., Journal, p. 511.
[12] Hohenberger, Frank M., Indianapolis Sunday Star, April 10, 1927, March 8, 1953.
[13] Goodspeed, Weston A., Op. cit., p. 726.
[14] Ibid., p. 749.
[15] Ibid., p. 737.
    Brown County Democrat, June 14, 1958.
[16] Goodspeed, Weston A., Op. cit., pp. 766,791.
[17] Hohenberger, Frank M., Indianapolis Sunday Star, April 10, 1927, Journal, p. 391.
[18] Goodspeed, Weston A., Op. cit., pp. 726,727.
    Hohenberger, Frank M., Journal, p. 284, Indianapolis Sunday Star, September 6, 1924, August 1, 1954.
[19] Indianapolis News, September 29, 1930.
[20] Nagley, Lester C., Sr., Brown County Democrat, Vignettes, May 31, 1962.
[21] Hohenberger, Frank M., Hohenberger Manuscripts, Lilly Library, December 3, 1908.
[22] Hohenberger, Frank M., Indianapolis Sunday Star, December 6, 1953.
    Bailey, Dorothy, Brown County Remembers, pp. 235,236.
[23] Reed, Dick, Brown County Democrat Column, Theron (Tubby) E. Clark.
[24] Nagley, Lester C., Sr., Brown County Democrat, Vignettes, January 17, 1963.
[25] Bailey, Dorothy, Oral Histories.
[26] Mathis, Ray, Op cit., pp. 44,45.
[27] Hohenberger, Frank M., Manuscript Collection, Lilly Library.
[28] Mathis, Ray, Op. cit., p. 56.
[29] Bailey, Dorothy, Brown County Remembers, pp. 149-154.
[30] Mathis, Ray, Op. cit., p. 57.
[31] Home Demonstration Club, A Guide to Brown County.

Chapter XII
Brown County Villages and Inns

Villages

Unfortunately it is not possible to write concerning all villages that do or do not now exist in the county because of a restriction on the length of this book. Villages such as Youno, Christiansburg, Elkinsville, Needmore, Spearsville, Fruitdale, Story served or are serving their communities and deserve to be included.

Buffalo

Buffalo on the Christiansburg Road in southern Van Buren Township became a village about 1857. There were two general stores, one owned by Dave Story, the other by Fletcher Wood, a Grange Hall, a blacksmith shop, several houses and a post office (1851-1861).

It was one of the few Brown County villages that had no church. By 1902 it was deserted and the sagging buildings were torn down and hauled away.

There is no recorded explanation for the name "Buffalo."[1]

Pikes Peak

Pikes Peak was founded about the time of the Civil War. When the gold fever was at its height in Colorado James Ward, who lived in the village, decided to take his family west. They prepared to journey in a covered wagon, or prairie schooner, as it was then called. A sign on the side of the wagon read "Pikes Peak or Bust."

They traveled the Madison Trail to Madison intending to go by boat down the Ohio River to Missouri. When they arrived in Madison the family was overcome with homesickness, and they returned to Brown County.

Ward opened a store next to Pikes Peak church. It became a joke in the community when someone was going to the store for supplies to say, "I'm going to Pikes Peak." Gradually Pikes Peak became the name of the village.

Thomas A. Hendricks ran the second general store and sold plows, corn planters, horse supplies, and groceries.

The location of the store shifted across the road and continued to serve the community under several different proprietors. Faun and Eleanor Clark were the last owners. The store closed in 1981, and the building was converted to a residence.[2]

Henry J. Ward, proprietor of grocery store at Pikes Peak, circa 1870, seventh from left.

Pikes Peak, 1900. Left foreground: George Foreman and Lon Clark.

Pike's Peak, 1980. Grocery Store.

Gnawbone

In 1874 John Ayers owned a sawmill on the road from Nashville to Columbus. He lived next to the mill. Early one morning, while he was eating breakfast, Jim Schrougham came by in his wagon on the way to Columbus. Ayres continuing to eat meat off of a bone, went to the door called to Schrougham and asked him if he would take a piece of mill machinery to be repaired in Columbus. Jim was quite willing to do so.

In the evening John was having supper when Jim returned. Again John went to the door, eating meat from a bone, to receive the machinery. Jim, much amused, said "This place ought to be called Gnawbone." The incident became common knowledge and people began to call the location Gnawbone until it became the official name of the village.[3]

This is apparently the authentic origin of the name, though there are half a dozen other explanations. Lately, in print, it has been stated that Gnawbone is a corruption of the French name Narbonne. This is pure fiction. Extensive research into the history of French explorers in Indiana from 1634 to almost 1800 confirms that the French were never in what is now Brown County. Certainly no written history has ever suggested that the French were in the county before or after it was formed in 1836.

Stone Head

At one time there was a small village and the last gristmill in the county near Stone Head, but the location is known for its unique road marker.

Henry Cross (1822-1864) was a Van Buren Township farmer, and a very talented carver of tombstones. He achieved considerable fame because of his carving. A few of his tombstones remain in Brown County cemeteries.

In 1851 it was required in Brown County that all able-bodied males spend six days a year working out their road tax by keeping the roads in at least passable condition. George Summa, the Van Buren road supervisor, decided Henry Cross should work out his tax by carving stone heads as direction markers, instead of hauling gravel.

Accordingly, Henry Cross carved three heads from sandstone. Two are lost, but one remains where State Road 135 turns sharply west to Story. The directions to Columbus, Fairfax, and Sparksferrie were indicated on the road marker. Originally the head was placed on a high cement milepost.

The head has been marred by whitewash on the face and black paint on the hair. It now rests on a very low pedestal.[4]

Stone Head, 1914.

Kelp

Kelp was once named Bird's Run, then Hobb's Creek. In 1896 during President Cleveland's second term, the postmaster at Nashville, Lon Allison, received a letter from the Postal Department in Washington D.C. asking him to recommend a short name for a post office to be established at Hobb's Creek in Van Buren Township. A boy named Harry Kelp walked into the post office as Allison was reading the letter. The postmaster liked the boy who had done odd jobs for him. He asked Harry if he objected to a new post office being named Kelp. Harry did not object and the new name was given to the post office and village.

Kelp served the surrounding neighborhood of farmers until the 1920s. There was a general store, a church, a one-room school, a blacksmith, a wagon maker, a cooper who made hoop poles, the post office, and a number of houses. At one time there had been a watermill.

In the 1920s land was being bought for the Brown County State Park. Kelp villagers and people on the surrounding land sold their property to the state. The post office closed in 1924. By the time the park opened in 1929 all families in and near Kelp had moved away.

Kelp School and Church, 1920. (Photo by Frank Hohenberger)

The empty buildings in the village deteriorated rapidly and by 1937 they had been removed. The location of Kelp was a short distance southeast of the present fire tower.[5]

TREVLAC

Colonel Calvert and his wife came to Brown County shortly after 1900 with the intention of building a resort. Calvert bought land near the village of Richards in Jackson Township, built a hotel, a number of small cottages, a bath house, and a club house. He rented the cottages to Indiana University students for weekends. Meals were served in the hotel dining room.

At that time, 1905, the Illinois Central Railway was building a line across Jackson township. Richards was to become a railroad station. Colonel Calvert realized the publicity value for his resort if the station was named Calvert. He made more than one trip to Indianapolis to persuade railroad officials to name the station and rename the town Calvert. Inquiry revealed that there was already a post office in Indiana named Calvert. Taking second best the Colonel suggested the station and village be called Trevlac, Calvert spelled backwards. This was done.

The Richards post office, established in 1881, became Trevlac in 1907. The village of Trevlac contained a general store, a sawmill, a feed store, a blacksmith shop. The village still exists though trains no longer stop at the railway station.

The resort failed to attract enough people to make it a paying proposition. After a fire partially burned the hotel Colonel Calvert closed the buildings, and with his wife left the county. Ostensibly he returned to Cleveland where he had made the fortune he had invested in his resort.[6]

SHERMAN

Sherman was a small town on Salt Creek one mile northeast of the Washington-Hamblen Township line. From 1900 to 1917 there was a general store, a post office (1905-1909), a Methodist Episcopal Church, a one-room school, and two houses. These buildings were located near the farms of Emmett W. and his wife Anna Bright Brown, and Richard (Bub) and Ida Kent Henderson.

Emmett Brown owned the store and was postmaster. He was also a carpenter, and operated a huckster wagon route. He sold timber, railroad ties, shingles, tanbark, and hoop poles in Columbus.

Without the slightest warning in 1917 a tornado descended on Sherman and virtually destroyed the village. Ida Henderson was killed as was Bob Henderson's father, Jim Henderson. A daughter, Olive Henderson Clark, was severely injured. The church and school were swept away. A corner of a stone building was all that survived.

The tornado after demolishing Sherman moved south into Van Buren Township where it caused extensive damage to farm buildings.[7]

BEAN BLOSSOM OR GEORGETOWN

Georgetown was founded by George Grove, the first settler in the area in 1833.

In 1842 when a post office opened in the growing town it was discovered that there was another Georgetown in Indiana. The town was renamed Bean Blossom.

The creek near the town had been named Bean Blossom before Georgetown was founded. It ran from Brown County into Monroe County before Lake Lemon was constructed. In 1811 Captain Jack Beanblossom, fighting under General William Henry Harrison against the Indians, drowned while attempting to cross the flooded creek. Subsequently the creek was named in the Captain's memory.

Although the official name became Bean Blossom, Brown County folk continued to call the village Georgetown for many years.

The town grew rapidly. George Grove built a horse-powered mill in 1835 which operated for ten years. Adams and Kennedy opened the first store in 1836 with $1,500 worth of variety merchandise.

By 1839 Jacob McNeely's large tannery with forty to fifty vats was in business. His buckskin leather was sent to eastern markets and was well known. The tannery flourished until 1849 when McNeely was killed by lightning.

There were numerous stores selling liquor, groceries, and merchandise by 1850. A newspaper edited by A.S. Helm was published about 1870. In 1880 there was an excellent grist mill built by the Waltman family. Thomas Waltman had settled in the town in 1838.

By 1884 nearly 100 people lived in Bean Blossom. It was a prosperous community for many years. In early times it was famous for horse racing. On a long, level tract of ground near the town William Snider, Matthew Mathis, Edward David, the Brummets and the Grahams tested the speed of their horses.

Bean Blossom in 1900 was still a busy town with a grist mill, a tannery, a saloon, a Masonic Lodge, an undertaker, a post office, three general stores and a school. All have now disappeared.

However, the oldest family-owned and continuously operated business in Brown County still prospers in Bean Blossom. In about 1901 Charles Kessler (Kess) McDonald built a small grocery on the northwest corner of the junction of State Road 45 and State Road 135. The store sold dry goods, oil for lamps, crackers, sugar, beans, flour, salt pork, rice and vinegar. Fresh eggs and chickens were traded by farmers for sugar, coffee, rice, and flour. Kess also drove a huckster wagon. The business descended to Herbert, Kess's son, and Herbert's wife, Gladys McDonald. It is now run by Jack McDonald, the son of Herbert and Gladys. In 1962 a new grocery was built. Two additions have more than doubled the size of the store.[8]

HELMSBURG

The area of present day Helmsburg was long ago called Connard's Ford. By 1900 the name was no longer used nor remembered. Before the Illinois Central extended a railroad in 1905 across the northwest corner of Brown County in Jackson Township, from Indianapolis to Effingham, Illinois, there was no village, only farmland.

The Illinois Central planned to build a station in that locality since it was as near Nashville as the railroad would come. The county seat had no railroad and did not want one.

A name was needed for the station. John Setzer suggested the name "Helms" since the Helms family had lived in the vicinity for fifty years. The name was accepted and Helmsburg came into existence. It was anticipated that as the Brown County railroad center, Helmsburg would grow rapidly.

A small railroad station was built. The first passenger train ran on the new roadbed in 1906. And, as expected, the village of Helmsburg did grow rapidly.

Josh Bond built a flour mill on the main street. The Baughman store was directly across from the mill. John Setzer's large grocery was on the site of the present post office. Farmers for miles around brought butter and eggs to trade for coffee, sugar, and shoes.

There was a hardware store and a lumber yard. Dr. Selfridge's office building was on the main street. Bill Hughes built a large house and a general store. He bought crossties and hoop poles from all over the county to ship as freight on the railroad.

In 1916 C.H. Marsh, from Connecticut, started a sawmill. The mill grew to be one of the largest band mills in southern Indiana. At one time fifty men were employed.

The post office opened in 1905 and has never closed. John Setzer was the first postmaster.

The first class of the Helmsburg High School graduated in 1915. A Methodist Church was dedicated in 1916. A large three-story log structure on a hill just south of Helmsburg, called Friendship Cabin, became a summer hotel.

The railroad continued to contribute easy access to and from Brown County, as well as increasing prosperity. The wood products shipped out included the huge logs from the county's forests. Cattle were exported in cattle cars.

Two trains a day came south from Indianapolis and two trains north from Bloomington. The Helms Livery Stable furnished horsedrawn carriages to take passengers to Nashville, and two-horse wagons to transport freight to Nashville. Competing wagons and carriages lined up at the station for every train.

By about 1920 a hundred people lived in Helmsburg. Then came unexpected tragedy for the town. In 1924 Joshua Bond's flour mill burned as well as other buildings on the main street. It is known to have been arson. A second fire followed which burned more businesses. Helmsburg was almost destroyed. The days of the town's greatest prosperity were over.

In the 1930s, when roads were greatly improved in Brown County, trucks inherited the railroad's freight business. The increasing number of cars greatly reduced

Bean Blossom, 1933. (Photo by Frank Hohenberger)

Main Street, Helmsburg, 1923 (right) North side of street: Bert and Ray Baughman Groceries, Red Crown Gasoline and Redman's Lodge Hall (left) South side of street: Cafe, Dr. Selfridge's Office, Goldie Yoder's Restaurant, Rains Hotel, Dr. and Mrs. Selfridge's Home, Ray and Bert Baughman's mother's home.

Rigs and Hacks awaiting passengers at Helmsburg Railroad Station 1920. (Photo by Frank Hohenberger)

Helms and Son Livery Stable, 1920.

Mason Hotel on West Main by Frank Hohenberger. Fox Hunt (l. to r.): Frank P. Taggart, Dan Turner, William Kennedy, George Turner, Dan Gordon, Anderson Percifield.

passenger service. Finally, trains began to run very irregularly and the Helmsburg railway station was closed, as well as the stations at Trevlac and Fruitdale. The few remaining trains carried only freight.

By the 1940s Helmsburg had started to rebuild when the Cullum Broom and Mop Company, the McCoy Precast Concrete Company (1951), and the Arthur West Sawmill came into existence.[9]

Early Taverns and Inns

P.C. Parker was the first Nashville tavern keeper in 1837-1838. He built a double log cabin, and in that space he lived with his family, sold liquor and groceries, and took in wayfarers.

Elijah Preston was an early tavern keeper as was Thomas Chinn. A "hotel" was run by Chapman and Lowe about 1840 when there were eighty people in Nashville. The log building was taken over by Slyvanus Manville who called the hotel the "American Tavern."

William M. Mason came to Nashville in 1840. In 1844 he built a large two-story building and opened the Mason Hotel. It was located on lot 117 on the original plat of Nashville, on West Main. The building, known as the "old Mason property" was still in existence in 1900. A photograph shows a frame building. It may have been built of logs and later covered with siding when mills turned out lumber.

William Mason had studied medicine with his father-in-law Dr. Alexander Clark, at Bedford. He practiced medicine in Nashville. In 1846 he was Brown County's Representative in the Indiana General Assembly. He also served as Clerk of the Brown County Circuit Court, and County Recorder.[10]

The Wayside Inn

In Schooner Valley stands an old building originally known as the Wayside Inn. It was a freighting station and stagecoach stop for travelers from Bloomington to Louisville and Indianapolis. From the Inn the road crossed Weed Patch Hill, ran along Four Mile Ridge and down to the present Columbus-Nashville Road. At Columbus a road turned south to Louisville, and North to Indianapolis.

The hewed-log Inn was built by George Henry. A date of 1830 is found. At one time there were two buildings, one of which

Pittman's Inn opposite Courthouse on the corner of East Main and Van Buren Streets in 1914.

burned. A loft ran the length of the Inn where travelers slept. The owner cared for and fed the horses, as well as the guests, for fifty cents a night.

Several families owned the Inn at various times and the building was expanded to five rooms. In 1871 James Wise, father-in-law of Rufus Reddick, bought the old Inn. It became known as the "Reddick Place." The Reddick family consisted of twelve girls and one boy. The girls slept in the loft, six beds on each side of the room.

The surrounding community used Reddick Place as a center for barn dances, spelling bees and quilting parties.

In 1922 the old building was modernized. It is now deserted and in very poor condition.[11]

Pittman Inn and Sanatorium

When mineral water was discovered in a well in Nashville people began to talk about a Sanatorium. Perry Hanna, Dunbar and Musselman, William Mason, James N.E. Bond, Collins Calvin, William Pittman, Alfred Grindle, John P. Wright collaborated in buying property just south of the old Christian Church on Van Buren Street. John Voland in 1885 constructed a Sanatorium.

By 1907 the idea of a Sanatorium had been dropped and William (Bill) Pittman had become manager of what he called the Pittman Inn. For seven years the Inn was the center of a summer art colony. As stated in the following chapter, Bill Pittman was most influential in the decisions of several artists to move to Nashville permanently.

Maple Inn Hotel, former Pittman Inn, 1925.

Nashville House

In 1914 Bill Pittman left the hotel on Van Buren Street and moved as manager to the hotel on the corner of Van Buren and East Main. Bill also called this building Pittman Inn.

After 1914 Perry Hanna bought the Van Buren Street hotel and tried to restore the original purpose of a sanatorium. He wished to put a tub for mineral-water bathing in each room. The Town Board would not allow him to pipe water from the artesian well on the Town Square. Hanna drilled a well but the well went dry. A new casing driven into the well did not solve the problem and mineral water in quantity was never again obtained.[12]

In 1925 R.S. Moser bought the property, completely remodeled the building and opened it to the public as the Maple Inn. The Mosers operated it until 1947 when Paul Adams bought the Maple Inn. In 1948 Adams sold it to Myron Rees, and his wife. Rees ran the Inn quite successfully for twelve years.

On March 12, 1960, the hotel was bought from Rees by the Christian Church. The church promptly demolished the building and turned the property into a parking lot.[13]

NASHVILLE HOUSE

In 1867 John Watkins, who owned a water-powered gristmill on Salt Creek, decided to build an inn for travelers. A frame structure on the southeast corner of Van Buren and Main was the result. Perry Hanna's father constructed the foundation for the inn.

Through the years the inn was called Hampton Hotel, Hobbs House, Browning Hotel, King's Hotel, Pittman Inn and Nashville House depending on who owned the building.[14]

In late 1926 Fred Bates Johnson was in the hotel lobby talking to Clint Moore, the manager. He made the remark that what Nashville needed was a modern hotel. He immediately found himself in a real estate transfer. He and his partner, Jack Rogers, bought the hotel for $6,000 from James Tilton, the owner.

In the spring of 1927 Fred Johnson and Jack Rogers employed an architect to plan a change. The hotel was completely remodeled. The old building along East Main was divided into two wings and one wing was moved until both wings faced Van Buren. A new lobby connected the two sections.

The lobby ceiling contained beams from old oak trees found on Bear Wallow Hill. There were murals by George LaChance. Twenty-one guest rooms were upstairs. The Pioneer Room served as a breakfast room. The main dining room was cheerful with red-apple wallpaper. A store selling Brown County handcrafts was entered from the lobby or from East Main. Called the Brown County Folks Shop and run by Portia Sperry it became renowned.

The fireplace in the lobby was memorable. It was built from stones in the basement wall of the wing that had been moved.

Electricity for Nashville House was brought over from Columbus. Large tanks buried in the front yard contained water pumped from Salt Creek. All drinking water was carried in buckets from the pump on the courthouse lawn.

Dale Bessire, the well known artist, was foreman of the construction crew. Priscilla Johnson has recorded how she and her husband, Fred Bates Johnson, searched in Indiana for the antiques they bought for guest rooms and lobby.

The grand opening of the new Nashville House occurred on the first Sunday of October 1927. It was a most successful afternoon but Priscilla Johnson found herself washing dishes long after the guests had left.

In 1936 Fred Bates Johnson, who lived in Indianapolis, and Jack Rogers, of Bloomington, divided their Brown County holdings. Fred settled for land they jointly owned. Jack Rogers became the proprietor of the Nashville House.

The hotel was a valued center for visitors and tourists. There are many famous names on the old hotel registers.

On September 24, 1943, Nashville House burned to the ground. It might have been saved had there been sufficient water. Nashville's only fire-engine with a hand-operated pumping unit was not in working order. Salt Creek was dry. A bucket brigade without water could not save the hotel. The whole town turned out to help remove furnishings from rooms and lobby, and items for sale in the Brown County Folks Shop.

On July 17, 1947 the rebuilding of Nashville House began. It is now a restaurant with a country store. It is owned by Andy Rogers, the son of Jack Rogers.[15]

Alra Wheeler store at Story. (Photo was made by Frank Hohenberger, between 1914-18, shortly before it was destroyed by fire.)

Villages and Inns
Bibliography

[1] Hohenberger, Frank M., Brown County History, Down in the Hills O' Brown County, 1952, p. 18
Mrs. Susan Hedrick, Letter, 1990.
Martha Wadsworth, Letter, 1990.
Goodspeed, Weston A., History of Brown County, p. 749.
Guthrie, Wayne, Indianapolis News, Unknown date.
[2] Crouch, Norma, Letter, June 16, 1990.
Hohenberger, Frank M., op. cit., p. 16.
Brown, Grover, Democrat Meandering, October 5, 1961.
[3] Hohenberger, Frank M., Journal, p. 346, 1924.
Herschell, William, Indianapolis News, October 20, 1934.
[4] Hartley, W. D., The Search for Henry Cross, Indianapolis: Indiana Historical Society, 1966.
Hohenberger, Frank M., Brown County History, 1952, p. 16.
[5] Ibid. pp. 13-16.
[6] Ibid. p. 16
Nagley, Lester C., Sr., Democrat Vignettes, November 23, 1924.
[7] Brown, Wayne, Letter, June, 1990.
[8] Goodspeed, Weston A., op. cit. pp. 737, 738.
Indiana Historical Society, A New Historical Guide, 1989.
Brown County Democrat, October 14, 1937.
Bond, Jack, Bloomington Tribune, Bean Blossom, August 6, 1967.
McDonald, Gladys, Oral History, 1982.
[9] Reed, Dick, Brown County Democrat, Brown County Folks, Lawrence McCoy, November 5, 1975.
Hohenberger, Frank M., Manuscript, Connard's Ford Lilly Library.
Brown County Democrat, Connard's Ford, February 27, 1941.
Chitwood, Mrs. Frank, Church Messenger, 1950.
Hohenberger, Frank M., Brown County History, 1952, p. 17
[10] Goodspeed, Weston A., op. cit. pp. 725, 767.
Hohenberger, Frank M., Brown County History, p. 50.
[11] Robertson, Charles, Brown County Democrat, February 7, 1990.
[12] Hohenberger, Frank M., Journal, p. 316, 1924, Perry Hanna.
King, Fred, Nashville Christian Church, p. 19.
[13] Nagley, Lester C., Sr., Democrat, October 12, 1961, Centennial Year Data.
Nagley, Lester C., Sr., Democrat, September 21, 1961, Vignettes.
[14] Johnson, Gaar W., Notes on Nashville House, 1990.
[15] Johnson, Priscilla, History of Nashville House, 1950.

Chapter XIII
Artists in Brown County

The first artist known to sketch in Brown County was William McKendree Snyder. In the latter 1800s he was one of the best trained, and best known artists in Indiana. For years he lived and worked near Madison.

From 1870 to 1872 William Snyder was associated with his photographer brother in Columbus, Indiana. During those two years he made several sketching trips to Brown County and found the beauty of hills, forests, and fields outstanding. On one occasion Peter Fishe Reed, a poet-painter and art critic, accompanied him.

In October 1891 Fred Hetherington and Charles Nicoli, art students in Indianapolis, spent several days sketching, photographing, and exploring Brown County. Since there was no railroad in the county they took a train from Indianapolis to Morgantown, then hiked in Brown County on the almost impassable roads.

Fred Hetherington did not become a professional artist, but in the early 1900s he returned in the summers to Nashville from Indianapolis where he worked at the Hetherington-Berner Steel Company. He lived in a log house on Jackson Branch Road at the bend in the road as it turns west. He was greatly interested in the artists coming into Nashville, befriending and encouraging them.

In August 1900, an article appeared in a Chicago newspaper extolling the scenic beauty of Brown County, the virtues of the stalwart hill people, and the quaint log cabins in the valleys and the hills. Adolph Robert Shulz, a native of Delavan, Wisconsin, and an artist in Chicago, was greatly intrigued by this article. Since he was searching for a place reasonably near Chicago to live and paint, he decided Brown County might be worth investigating. In Indianapolis, he boarded a train to Columbus, Indiana, then hired a horse and buggy to spend several days leisurely traveling in Brown County.

Adolph Shulz wrote "Never before had I been so thrilled by a region; it seemed like a fairyland with its narrow winding roads leading the traveler down into the creek beds through the water pools and up over the hills. Everywhere there were rail fences almost hidden in Queen Anne's lace and goldenrod ... All this country was enveloped in a soft, opalescent haze. A sense of peace and loveliness never before experienced came over me."

In 1900 the inaccessibility, the very poor roads, the lack of a *good* hotel, and the absence of a railroad discouraged travel in the county.

However, by 1907 the Illinois Central had built a railroad across Jackson Township from Morgantown in Morgan County to Bloomington in Monroe County.

Learning of the new railroad three Chicago artists Louis O. Griffith, Wilson Irvine and Harry Engle in March 1907 took a combination freight and passenger train from Indianapolis to Brown County. The train moved slowly through towns, fields, and woods until it jerked to a stop at Helmsburg. The artists hired a surrey, a horse, and a driver to take them on the three hour, seven-mile trip to Nashville. The horse and surrey splashed through shallow creeks for much of the way. Finally they arrived at the Pittman Inn on Van Buren Street.

The three artists enjoyed two weeks of sketching and were so intrigued with Brown County that they determined to return as soon as possible.

In June, 1907, Adolph Shulz and a friend started from Martinsville for two weeks of hiking through southern Indiana. In Nashvllle Mr. Shulz discovered that Bill Pittman and his wife, Mandy, had recently taken over the old Sanatorium. Shulz was delighted with the good cheer, excellent food, and clean beds he found in what had become the Pittman Inn.

Bill Pittman mentioned that "artist Steele" was building a home ten miles from Nashville near Belmont. Shulz hiked to the building site on top of a hill and found Theodore C. Steele sitting on a pile of lumber, directing the construction of his house.

Mr. Steele was the first artist to live in Brown County. He came from Indianapolis to the rugged hills to work in peace and quiet. He had already achieved fame, national recognition, and the respect of the art world as a member of the "Hoosier Group" of artists. Theodore Steele, Samuel Richards, J. Otis Adams and William Forsyth had studied together at the Royal Academy of Munich in 1880.

During the formative years of the art colony in Nashville the artists infrequently saw Mr. Steele because of the difficulty traversing the unpaved road to the "House of the Singing Winds."

However, Mr. Steele was always interested in the progress of the artists and he was considered the most distinguished artist of them all, —the "Dean of Indiana artists."

Following his death in 1926 Selma Steele, his wife, transferred 211 acres, 300 paintings, the house, the large studio, a guest house, and a log cabin to the Indiana Department of Conservation in 1945. The "T.C. Steele State Historic Site" is now open to the public.

In May, 1908, Adolph Shulz brought his wife, Ada Walter Shulz a noteworthy artist

Pittman Inn, Van Buren Street 1910.

and their son Walter, to the Pittman Inn for the summer. They returned every summer until they moved permanently to Nashville.

Word spread rapidly among the Chicago artists concerning the new railway in Brown County, and the Pittman Inn. As a result, during the summer of 1908 there were at least twenty-five artists painting in and near Nashville. The number increased steadily until fifty to sixty artists were spending summers in Nashville.

Bill and Mandy Pittman greatly influenced the growth of the art colony. Year after year Bill Pittman kept hotel prices within reach of the artists. He went to no end of trouble to make them welcome and comfortable. He fitted up a neighboring house as a hotel annex. When the hotel and annex were filled to capacity, Bill trudged around Nashville and rented every available room in every house for the overflow.

The Pittmans continually suggested interesting places to go, or things to do. On at least one occasion Bill arranged for the village band to be on the hotel balcony to greet a group of artists when they arrived from the Helmsburg railway station.

The artists responded by painting a portrait of Bill, front and back, on the upper panel of a door. The portrait signed by John Hafen, Adam Emory Albright, and Adolph Shulz was framed and hung in front of the Pittman Inn for several years. In 1914 when Bill moved to the hotel on the southeast

Bill Pittman posing for portrait

corner of Van Buren and East Main. streets he hung the sign outside that building. After his death, Pearl Pittman Fushelberger, daughter of Bill and Mandy, presented the unusual portrait to the Brown County Art Gallery in 1968. An artist restored the weathered picture and in so doing covered over the names of the original artists.

Among the first artists from Chicago who came to Nashvllle, after 1907, were Frank K. Phoenix, Louis 0. Griffith, Wilson Irvine, Harry L. Engle, Adam Emory Albright, Rudolph Ingerle, Karl Kraft, John Hafen, J.W. Vawter, Mary Murray Vawter, Ada and Adolph Shulz.

Gustave Baumann arrived in 1909 from Chicago. He was the first artist after T.C. Steele to actually live in Brown County. He established a studio on the first floor of the Odd Fellows building on the northwest corner of Jefferson and West Main. He stayed at the Pittman Inn, or Alice Ferguson's boarding house. In 1916 Baumann left Nashville. Two years later he settled in Santa Fe, New Mexico, where he lived until his death in 1971. He became nationally known for his multicolor woodblocks.

Dale P. Bessire moved to Nashville from Indianapolis in 1914 with his wife, Ruth, and young son. He bought an apple orchard at the north edge of town which furnished an income while he established himself as an artist. He built a home near the orchard.

Other artists gradually moved to Nashville. Adolph and Ada Walter Shulz built a home in 1917 on Cheerful Hill, North Jefferson Street. L.O. Griffith lived in the old creamery building with his family on South Johnson Street, formerly called Blood Alley.

William Vawter, famous for his illustrations for James Whitcomb Riley's books of poetry, rented a studio above the Star Grocery on the northwest corner of West Main and Van Buren. He built a home on the hill directly north of the old log jail.

Marie Goth bought a log cabin on what is now State Road 135, north of Nashville. V.J. Cariani also built a home on State Road 135.

C. Curry Bohm, who moved to Nashville with his wife, Lillian, in 1932 lived on West Main Street beyond Jackson Branch road, then moved to a picturesque farm house on Greasy Creek road for about ten years, before moving permanently to a gracious old Victorian House on East Main Street.

By 1935 Carl Graf, George La Chance, Alton Coffey, Robert E. Burke, Musette 0. Stoddard, Edward K. Williams, Frank Humpel, Alberta R. Shulz and Anthony Buchta also lived in Nashville.

Other artists closely associated with the Brown County art colony who never lived in Nashville were Lucy Hartrath, Homer Davisson, Oscar Erickson, Alexis J. Fournier, Charles Dahlgreen, Thomas Lockie, George Mock, Frederick W. Polley, Simon Baus, Robert M. Root, Paul Sargent, James Topping, Othmar Hoefler, Angus Peter MacDonall, Joseph Chenworth, Mr. and Mrs. William Riddell, Doel Reed., Jack Spelman, Ray Trobough, and Joseph Birren.[1]

T.C. Steele signing portrait of Bill Pittman to verify authenticity of portrait.

Artists who lived in Nashville found an isolated community of townspeople, hardy souls living independent lives. The townspeople accepted the artists, although many of them could never understand why anyone would want to spend all of their time applying paint to canvas.

The artists respected the villagers and were able to concentrate on painting-each in his or her individual style. They loved the peace and quiet of the small town.

These early artists were neither amateurs nor dilettantes. They had had excellent training. Many of them achieved enviable reputations before they arrived in Brown County.

There was no formal organization of the artists for a number of years. They sent canvases to exhibitions in Indianapolis or Chicago once or twice a year and became known as the "Brown County Group."

As the art colony grew in stability, importance, and recognition, the increasing interest of Indiana art lovers caused them to journey to Nashville. They visited the artists in their studio to see and buy their pictures. Artists would often be exhausted on weekends by the constant stream of visitors to their homes. It became increasingly apparent that the opening of a permanent art gallery in a central location was becoming a critical necessity.

Brown County Artists' Gallery, Nashville, 1926.

Finally, on September 3, 1926, according to the first entry in the <u>Book of Minutes</u> of the Brown County Art Gallery Association "A meeting of the Brown County group

Local and visiting artists, October 16, 1927 (l. to r.) Front row: Homer Davisson (Ft. Wayne), L. O. Griffith, V. J. Cariani, C.Curry Bohm, Charles Dahlgreen (Oak Park,Ill.) George Mock (Muncie) Second row: Edward K. Williams, Ada Walter Shulz, Musette Stoddard, Marie Goth, Lucy Hartrath (Chicago),Robert Root (Shelbyville, Ill.) Adolph Shulz:Third row: Will Vawter, Paul Sargent (Charleston,Ill.) Carl Graf (Indianapolis). (Photo by Frank Hohenberger)

The Grandma Barnes Cabin. The early artists painted the cabin and the flower garden. Many tourists visited the place. Grandma Barnes on far right.

of artists was called at the home of Mr. Will Vawter for the purpose of forming an association and establishing an art gallery. Those present were Will Vawter, L.O. Griffith, A.R. Shulz, V.J. Cariani, Marie Goth, Mrs. Ada Walter Shulz, Carl Graf, and Dale Bessire. Carl Graf was elected president, William Wilkes Vice President, and Dale Bessire Secretary-Treasurer." [2]

William Wilkes, an executive in the Indianapolis based food industry of Kothe-Wells-Bauer, had built a summer home a short distance west of Nashville on a hill above the Helmsburg road. He had become interested in the artists and the necessity of an art gallery. He offered to help the artists financially. The offer was gladly accepted and a committee was formed to work with Mr. Wilkes.

William Wilkes bought an old, dilapidated grocery store with a leaky roof, that had been owned by Cecil Rogers. It was the last In a row of buildings on the north side of West Main between Van Buren and Jefferson streets.

In a short time the old grocery was transformed into a very respectable art gallery. The outside was greatly improved and painted. A new roof stopped the leaks. The west room was totally remodeled to accommodate picture hanging. The artists enthusiastically pitched in to help. They painted the walls and covered them with burlap, sanded and painted window frames and arranged display cases in the front windows.[3]

Mr. Wilkes, as manager of the gallery, opened an art store in the adjoining room where art objects and small pictures could be sold.

In early October, 1926, the new art gallery was opened to the public. Fifty paintings and several etchings were exhibited, contributed by Marie Goth, Lucy Hartrath, Ada Walter Shulz, C Curry Bohm, Adolph Shulz, Dale Bessire, F. Nelson Vance, L.O. Griffith, Mary Vawter, Oscar Erickson, V.J. Cariani, T.C. Steele, Homer Davisson, Paul Sargent and Edward K. Williams. Frank Hohenberger displayed six large photographs.[4]

The show was an immediate success. The Democrat of October 14, 1926, reported that there were well over one thousand visitors in the first few days. Many motorists said they had never seen traffic as heavy in Brown County. Dust raised on the unimproved roads by the automobiles was so thick drivers kept their lights on to prevent collisions. The first picture sold was a landscape, "Hill Cottage", by F. Nelson Vance.

Attendance and public interest constantly increased. Each year the gallery opened from April 10th to November 20th. Exhibits were changed three times a season. In 1931, as many as 2,500 people entered the gallery in a single day in the fall, when the greatest number of people visited Nashville. An estimated 25,000 came to the gallery that year.

In 1939, during the month of July, the guest register proved that visitors came from Indiana, Illinois, Kentucky, Wisconsin, Minnesota, Michigan, New York, Texas, Ohio, Pennsylvania, and California, as well as London, England.[5]

When increased space for pictures became critically needed an east room was converted to a gallery, and the addition of two rooms next to the alley more than doubled available hanging space.

These Brown County artists became famous. Exhibitions were shown in Indianapolis and in various Indiana towns, as well as other states.

By 1935 the Brown County art colony had "taken its place as the most significant and widely known in America." The Milwaukee Journal reported on July 17, 1949, that Nashville, Indiana, had the most important art colony between new England and New Mexico.

Through succeeding years paintings by Brown County artists have been bought by private collectors, institutions such as DePauw and Indiana University, and eventually by art museums.

The Ada and Walter Shulz home "Cheerful Hill," North Jefferson Street. Built 1917

The Brown County Art Gallery observed its 25th anniversary when the doors opened on April 14 for the 1951 season. Appropriately the spring exhibit presented a memorial showing of pictures painted by twelve deceased former members of the gallery. The pictures were on loan from relatives and friends of the artists.

Artists whose paintings hung in the memorial exhibit and their donors were Carl Graf (Genevieve Goth Graf), Glen Henshaw (Mrs. Henshaw), Paul Randall (Mrs. Randall), Paul Sargent, Alexis Fournier (Dr. and Mrs. Ernest Murry), Ada Walter Shulz (Brown County Library), Fred Nelson Vance (Mrs. Vance), E.K. Williams (Rosemary Wildermuth and Frank Russo), Will Vawter, James Topping (Dr. and Mrs. Merrill Davis), Robert Root (Heinie Moesch), and Clarence Staley (Virginia Staley).[6]

Two events changed the course of the Brown County Art Gallery Association. In 1952 a large fire burned almost the entire block of buildings east of the gallery on West Main Street. Melodeon Hall, the only movie theater ever built in Brown County, the Abe Martin Barber Shop, a pool hall, and Charlie Pogue's shoe-repair shop were destroyed.

An alley between the burning buildings and the gallery helped save the gallery. Though the building was severely scorched it did not burn. The artists rescued every painting.[7]

On August 10th, 1953, the Brown County Art Gallery Association's Book of Minutes stated that a letter read by Dale Bessire informed the artists that the gallery, then owned by William Wilkes' granddaughter, was for sale. Since the artists did not wish to buy the building they were suddenly without a place to hang and sell their pictures. In 1939 Adolph Shulz had offered a lot on the northeast corner of Artist Drive and East Main for a modern art gallery, to be built in the future. Certain artists believed the time had come to build on this lot. Other artists did not agree. A split occurred, with the result that those who did not agree decided to form a separate organization, an Art Guild.

Roy Wininger designed and built a very modern building for the Art Gallery Association.[8] The new gallery opened on October 19, 1954. Unfortunately an arson fire destroyed the building on August 6, 1966. A second larger gallery was constructed of redwood and stone and opened for business in August of 1968. This building continues to be used for exhibitions, and many activities.

The Art Guild members accepted an offer from Jack Rogers, proprietor of the Nashville House, to occupy the historic old Minor house on Van Buren Street. In 1857 Robert M. Minor and his wife, Rachel, had arrived in Brown County. They prospered, and eventually built their beautiful home in Nashville. Mr. Rogers had bought the house to foil a scheme for turning it into a skating rink.[9]

Most of the founders of the Brown County Art Gallery Association joined the Brown County Art Guild. The artists adapted the Minor house to function as a gallery. The first exhibit opened in 1954.[10]

Marie Goth, famed for her portraits, died in 1975 and left a very substantial gift from her estate to the Art Guild for the rebuilding of the Minor house. The building had been used as a gallery for twenty-one years and space had become limited and cramped. A completely new structure was the result, though the outside resembles the former house. The first exhibit opened in 1978.

The fate of the first gallery on West Main is of interest. When the artisits left the building it again became a grocery store run by Leo Knight, followed by Clarence White. Then Bill Snyder opened a bakery. A series of photographs published by the Brown County Democrat on February 22, 1968, showed the building as it was being demolished. A new building approximately the same size replaced it.[11]

The two major art galleries in Nashville—the Brown County Art Gallery Association, Inc. and the Brown County Art Guild, Inc. still exist in 1990 and are very active. They have as many as 20,000 visitors each year.

A number of artists live in Brown County

Brown County Art Gallery opened in August 1968.

Brown County Art Guild in Historic old Minor House 1954.

THE BROWN COUNTY ART GALLERY ASSOCIATION 1990

Resident Artists in Brown County

Melba Dailey
W. Harold Hancock
Gladys Jones
Sue McAllister
Amanda Mathis
Kaye Pool
Kenneth Reeve
Francis Rogers
Dwight Steininger
Maphajean White
L.L. Von Williamson
Hildegarde Donaldson

Non-resident Active Artist Members

Columbus, Indiana
Betty Boyle
Martha Callaway
Norval Fischvogt

Indianapolis
Evelynne Mess Dailey
Louis Johnson
Shirley Little
Mildred Niesse
Willa Bowen Van Brunt
Frank Vietor
Evelyn McConnel

Indiana
Donald Austin, Anderson
Sue Turner Chapman, Milltown
E. Gaye Eilts, Wabash
William Ferguson, Worthington
Shelby Harding, Richmond
Tamiko Oberholtzer, Bowling Green
Marian O'Haver, Carmel
Helen Potter, Washington
D. Omer Seamon, Rosedale
Phyllis Whitworth, Middeltown
Kenneth E. Knight, Shelbyville
Letha Gaskins, —

Florida
Donald Lemon, Longboat Key

Illinois
Beatrice Zerwekh, Peoria

The Brown County Art Gallery Association has three exhibitions each year, an art education program, painting workshops, special exhibitions, and tours to major art centers. There is an extensive permanent collection of paintings of early Brown County artists such as Adolph Shulz and Glen Henshaw.[12]

THE BROWN COUNTY ART GUILD 1990

Resident Artists in Brown County

Amanda Kirby
Sally Kriner
Fred Rigley
Neal and Lillian Dunnigan
Gordon Fiscus
Peggy Brown
Francis Clark Brown

Non-resident Active Artist Members

Indianapolis
Jeff Burris
Harry and Lois Davis
Crawford Donnelly
Rich Ernsting, Jr.
Roger Frey
James Lentz
Wilbur Meese
Anthony Pernell
Leach Traugott
Jean Vietor

Indiana
Henry Bell, Noblesville
June Burkholder, Lafayette
Dean Davis, Evansville
Emel Doner, Carmel
George Elliott, Noblesville
Marilyn Gerst, Evansville
Louise Hansen, Terre Haute
Jeanne McLeish, Monrovia
Rob O'Dell, Ladoga
Jerry Smith, Crawfordsville
Martha Stevenson, Noblesville
Sylvia Worman, Evansville
Robert Hoffman, Merrillville

California
Margaret Eifler, Salinas

Florida
Em Flanagan, Bradenton

Massachusetts
Ken Gore, Gloucester

Illinois
Walter Parke, Naperville
Mary Miller, Salem, Chicago
Jan Wills, Galena

The Brown County Art Guild has the reputation of high selectivity in its choice of artist members. Each year there are two exhibitions and five solo shows. There is a permanent collection of paintings by earlier Brown County artists.

The Art Guild sponsors educational classes for art students in Brown County schools, and other schools. Recitals for music students are also sponsored.[13]

who are not affiliated with a gallery. They show paintings in their studios or in various places in Nashville. In 1967 the Brown County Art Barn was founded. It is north of the courthouse on North Van Buren and displays the paintings of thirty-five artist members.[14]

There is, of course, infinitely more information to record concerning Brown County artists. The purpose of this chapter, however, has been to concentrate on the formation of the original Nashville art colony which is certainly of historical significance and is not well remembered.

The early art colony brought a new prosperity to Brown County beginning in the 1920s.. When the artists arrived in the early 1900s the county was one of the poorest in Indiana. In 1880 the population was 10,308 according to the United States census, but by 1930 there were only 5,168 people in Brown County. The lack of sufficient farming land prevented scores of people from achieving an adequate living. Brown Countians left by the hundreds to settle in other states.

The wide recognition and influence of the art colony brought fame to Nashville as well as a new prosperity. Those professional artists and the excellent paintings they produced, not only of county landscapes but of many localities in the country, as well as still lifes and portraits, enticed thousands of visitors to the art gallery after its establishment in 1926.

Tourism began in Brown County

The construction of more adequate roads—State Roads 135 and 46 —as well as county roads, the rapid increase of travel by car, and the opening of Brown County State Park ended the county's isolation. Gradually people moved back to Brown County.

Tourists have never stopped coming to Nashville. The number, — in the millions — increases every year. At present, at least in October, the tourist influx is almost overwhelming.

Adolph Shulz (Photo by Frank Hohenberger)

Artists In Brown County
Bibliography

[1] *Indiana Magazine of History* December, 1935, The Story of the Brown County Art Colony, Shulz, Adolph Robert. Hohenberger, Frank M., Down in the Hills O' Brown County, *Indianapolis Star* February 2, 1924.

[2] *Brown County Art and Artists* 1971. Published by Psi Iota Xi Sorority, Compiled by Barbara Judd.

[3] Ibid.
   Nagley, Lester C., Sr. Vignettes *Brown County Democrat* September 6, 1962.

[4] *Brown County Democrat* October 14, 1926.

[5] Brown, Grover G. Know Brown County 1939.

[6] *Brown County Democrat* April 12, 1951.

[7] Nagley, Lester C., Sr. Op. Cit.

[8] Barbara Judd. March 1991.

[9] Ibid.

[10] *Brown County Art and Artists* - 1971

[11] *Brown County Democrat* February 22, 1968.

[12] Charles P. Keefe - Executive Director Brown County Art Gallery Association, Inc., July 1990.

[13] Margaret Colglazier - Executive Director Brown County Art Guild, Inc. July 1990.

[14] *Brown County Almanack* 1989 p. 27.

Chapter XIV
United States Postal Service in Brown County

Collins Calvin, R.F.D. Mailman, 1907.

In 1837 the first Post Office was established in Brown County. Amos Kendall, United States Postmaster General, appointed Banner C. Brummett postmaster of a fourth-class post office in Nashville on February 25, 1837.

According to the 1840 census Nashville consisted of eighty people, a cluster of log cabins, and three stores. One store was owned by Banner Brummett who undoubtedly, as was the custom, installed a post office in his home or store.[1]

Indianapolis was the mail-distributing center for Indiana in 1837. Mail was sent by stagecoach from Indianapolis to Columbus, Indiana. From Columbus, mail went by stagecoach to Nashville, Bloomington, Spencer, Bowling Green, Christy's Prairie and Terre Haute. On the return journey mail was taken back to Columbus. This round trip was made three times weekly.[2]

The Indianapolis-Madison Railroad was completed in 1847, the first railroad in Indiana. It received a contract from Washington D.C. to carry mail between Indianapolis and Madison. Columbus was one of the stations where the train stopped. The Columbus Post Office hired a carrier to take the mail to Nashville by horseback, mail hack, or wagon and bring out-going mail back to Columbus.[3]

The building of railroads in Indiana effectually ended the era of stagecoach travel because trains carried passengers, and freight as well as mail. Trains were certainly more convenient, more comfortable and far faster than horse-drawn vehicles.

Beginning in 1874 a spur of the "Big Four," the Cleveland, Cincinnati, Chicago, and St. Louis Railway, brought Nashville mail to Morgantown and Mahalasville. Carriers from both towns took mail to and from Nashville by wagon or buggy.

Mail for all Brown County came to Nashville and was distributed to township post offices by horseback or cart. For instance, in 1874 Reuben Hunt was paid $260 annually to deliver mail from Nashville to Oak Farm and Needmore in Jackson Township. In 1889 Bob Pruitt carried mail to Wakeup post office, north of Bear Wallow Hill, near the Turner School, in Hamblen Township.[4]

By 1879 post offices had proliferated in Brown County. In addition to Nashville there were two more post offices in Washington Township, Mt. Liberty and Schooner; Bean blossom, Oak Farm, and Needmore in Jackson Township; Mt. Moriah, Cleona, Spearsville, and Ramilton in Hamblen Township; Christiansburg, New Bellsville, Beck's Grove, and Pikes' Peak in Van Buren Township; Elkinsville, and Peter Cooper in Johnson Township.[5]

Post offices in Brown County's small towns were invariably kept either in the store or in the home of the postmaster. They were moved to a different location each time a new postmaster was appointed.

These post offices were established by the United States Postmaster General, since each village was the center of a community with usually a church, a schoolhouse, one or two stores, a blacksmith shop, a few homes, and perhaps a water or steam-powered lumber or gristmill nearby. Roads were hazardous, rutted, slippery and icy in winter, deep in mud in rainy weather, or dust in summer. There was not a paved road in the county and in early days no gravel roads. Travel was extremely time consuming. For

Rural Mail Carriers, Van Buren Street, west of Court House, 1914.

busy farmers having the mail brought to their communities without the need of a journey to the post office at the county seat was almost a necessity.

By 1900 there were 19 post offices in the county. Eight more came into existence after 1900.

Beginning in 1851 post offices sold stamps, and letters were prepaid. Before that time letters had been sent collect, and the recipients paid for their mail. The system of money orders came to Brown County post offices in 1864.[6]

In 1902 Rural Free Delivery arrived in Indiana for mail routes of 25 miles and 100 families. Indianpolis was headquarters for Indiana RFD under the jurisdiction of the Civil Service. Carriers were paid $400 annually and this included hiring a horse.

By 1903 Michael Poling, the Nashville postmaster, had set up two rural routes in Washington Township. Collins Calvin accepted Route 1, south towards Story, and Hugh Tom Adams was given Route 2, north from the Nashville post office. Hugh Tom Adams carried the mail for six years and Collins Calvin kept his mail route until at least 1931.[7]

In 1905 there were four rural routes in the county. Everyone in Brown County thought it was wonderful to have mail delivered to their very own boxes.

Delivering mail at time of high water or bitterly cold weather was always difficult and sometimes dangerous. Many are the stories concerning mailcarriers who tried to cross flooded creeks, misjudging the depth of the water, and were swept down-stream in their buggies. One way or another they seem always to have been rescued as well as their horses, mail bags, and buggies. There were very few bridges in Brown County in the early 1900s.

Mailcarriers used closed-in rigs in the winter. They were like little houses on wheels. Each rig had a small wood stove.

When the Illinois Central Railroad across Jackson Township opened in 1906 the trains delivered mail to the three railway stations of Fruitdale, Helmsburg, and Trevlac. The mail bags were taken to the local post office in the three villages.[8]

However, the need for many small post offices ceased with the coming of RFD. Gradually, postal inspectors closed all county post offices except two — the main office in Nashville and the one in Helmsburg. It is questionable how long the Helmsburg post office will remain since no RFD routes begin in Helmsburg.

Mail has never been delivered to homes and businesses in Nashville. Residents must rent a box and make a daily trip to the post office.

Delivery of mail by horse and buggy continued until the 1920s. By then the first Model-T Fords were being used to deliver mail on RFD routes. But for twelve years, until 1932, carriers kept horses for emergencies when their cars broke down, or could not negotiate the roads in winter.

County roads had been very much improved by 1949 and cars were able to reach even remote sections of Brown County, but wear and tear on mail-carriers' cars is never-ending. John Sherrill wore out ten cars, five Model-T's, three Model-A's, and two V8's from 1920 to 1949.[9]

In the 1930s railroads were in trouble due to their over-expansion. Trucks delivered mail and freight formerly carried on trains. In 1936 the Trevlac and Fruitdale railway stations were closed and abandoned. Trains in Brown County ran infrequently and not on a regular schedule. By 1941 all trains in Indiana had ceased to carry mail. Mail is now delivered by truck to county post offices.[10]

In 1990 there are five RFD routes from the Nashville post office. Mail reaches and leaves Nashville and Helmsburg twice daily from Bloomington.

Surprisingly, mail also is delivered to Brown County residents as part of rural routes from Morgantown, Unionville, Columbus, Freetown, Bloomington, Nineveh, Trafalgar, and Seymour.[11] Many people living in Brown County do not have a Brown County address!

The location of the Nashville post office from 1837 to 1885 is not now known. From 1885 to 1889, when Timothy D. Calvin, Sr.

was postmaster, the post office was in the Calvin Hardware Store on East Main directly across from the courthouse.

From 1897 to 1907 the post office occupied the building adjacent to the old bank on East Main. Mike Poling was postmaster. William H. Percifield, postmaster from 1907 to 1913, moved the post office to a building on North Van Buren Street just north of the Star Grocery, which was on the northwest corner of Main and Van Buren.

In 1917 the post office was on the first floor of the Masonic Lodge and Knights of Pythias building, now known as the Village Green Building, on the south side of West Main. John F. Bond was postmaster in that location. For a very short time the post office was housed in the Kritzer Building on north Van Buren. In 1919 it was moved to the old bank building on East Main. It stayed in that location until 1954.[12]

On January 31, 1954, the post office was moved to the Richard Weaver building on North Van Buren, opposite the courthouse. The change was made because more space was needed, and there were the conveniences of better lighting, automatic heat, tile floor, and storm entrances with door closers. The post office was changed to a second class office in 1954.[13]

On July 24, 1958, The Brown County Democrat announced that the decision had been made to build a new post office. By November, 1959, it had been built in its present location on East Main.

Dedication of the post office took place on November 7, 1959, in the building. Field Service Officer Herbert J. Lekman delivered the dedication address. The Brown County High School band played and the local Boy Scouts formed a Color Guard for the flag-raising ceremony.[14]

In 1959 the Nashville postmaster was Howard Zody, assisted by clerks Fred King and Joseph DeWees. Rural route carriers were Ivan Seitz, Clarence Aynes, William Robertson, and George Howard. Stamp sales and money orders for 1959 were $27,100.[15] What a contrast to the pioneer days of 1837 when total postal receipts accounted to $350!

Bruce Gould is the 1990 postmaster at the Nashville Post Office. His two clerks are Joyce Myers and Tom Routes. Mail is delivered on Route 1 by Jim Campbell, on Route 2 by Keith Matlock, on Route 3 by Mary Ford, on Route 4 by Sue Moore, and on Route 5 by Susie Hendershot.

Business is brisk at the Post Office. There are 1050 post boxes for rent. Yearly sales of postage amount to approximately $500,000.

Soon all rural roads will have names, and the houses will have numbers. Rural Free Delivery will continue, and mail will be placed in existing boxes.

The Nashville Post Office has outgrown its present space. A new and much larger building is planned. The Post Office now in use is not government property. The building and the land it is on are privately owned. The government has paid rent since 1959. The United States Postal Service has bought land on Commercial Street, part of the former Singing Pines Motel property, for the future post office. Plans have not yet been made for construction of the building.[17]

Brown County Post Offices[16]

Washington Township	Opened	Closed
Nashville	1837	
Mt. Liberty	1856	1932
Schooner	1876	1903
Belmont	1884	1916
Jackson Township		
Bean Blossom	1842	1911
Gold Creek	1852	1862
Oak Farm	1862	1880
Needmore	1872	1919
Richards	1881	1907
Campbell	1882	1883
Linzey	1887	1894
Cornelius	1893	1907
Helms	1904	1905
Helmsburg	1905	
Trevlac	1907	1966
Fruitdale	1909	1937
Hamblen Township		
Mt. Moriah	1850	1905
Cleona	1855	1903
Spearsville	1855	1907
Ramelton	1874	1903
Mead	1887	1903
Wakeup	1889	1901
Peoga	1901	1903
Beveridge	1902	1905
Sherman	1905	1909
Van Buren Township		
Christiansburg	1850	1902
Milo (Buffalo Village)	1851	1861
New Bellsville	1856	1909
Beck's Grove	1868	1895
Beck	1895	1907
Marble	1868	1879
Pike's Peak	1868	1907
Story	1882	1922
Lockman	1885	1907
Kelp	1896	1924
Johnson Township		
Elkinsville	1860	1941
Necessity	1862	1864
Peter Cooper	1879	1894
Cooper	1894	1921
Youno	1903	1921

United States Postal Service in Brown County
Bibliography

[1] Certificate of Appointment of Banner C. Brummett as Postmaster, Nashville Indiana February 25,1837. Brown County Historical Society Archives.

[2] Indianapolis Democrat, August 30, 1837.

[3] Carter, John, The Hoosier Post: Then and Now, Indianapolis Star Magazine April 16, 1978.

[4] Guthrie, Wayne, Ringside in Hoosierland, Indianapolis News, Clipping no date.

[5] Baker, David, J., The Postal History of Indiana 1976. Vol. II pp. 886-1094.

[6] Ibid. pp. 103, 161.

[7] Ibid. pp. 671-674 p. 681.
Barnes, Sylvester, Scrapbook Vol I. p. 159. Brown County Historical Society Archives.
Sherrill, Cleve, Oral History, August 1984.

[8] Keaton, Claris, Oral History, November 25, 1981.
Strode, Elmer, Oral History, November 18, 1981.

[9] Brown County Democrat September 25, 1941.

[10] Baker, David J., Op. cit. p. 545.

[11] Adair, Robert, Postmaster Nashville, Oral History, January 14, 1982.

[12] Hohenberger, Frank, M., Down in the Hills O' Brown County, Indianapolis Star, May 31, 1953.
Sherrill, Cleve, Oral History, August 1984.

[13] King, Fred, Brown County Democrat, February 27,1954.

[14] Brown County Democrat, November 5,1959, Post Office Dedication.

[15] Ibid.

[16] Baker, David, J. Op. cit. Vol. II.

[17] Gould, Bruce, Postmaster Nashville, Interview September 10, 1990.

Otto Strahl carrying outgoing mail to truck, 1930. (Photo by Frank Hohenberger)

Chapter XV
Brown County 1836 to 1900

By 1834 the National Road had been built from Cumberland, Maryland, to Indianapolis. It was the first good road to the west: eighty feet wide with a track thirty to forty feet wide in the middle, macadamized by ten inches of stone. Culverts and bridges were of cut stone blocks.

It was the busiest wagon road in the nation. A steady stream of pioneers, covered wagons, cattle, hogs and sheep poured into Indiana. No longer did Brown County pioneers need to find their way from the Ohio River on primitive trails through dense woods.[1]

The population of Brown County increased steadily, but the land was still densely covered with primeval forest and pioneer life was a necessity.

The first pioneer cabins were made of round logs, put together without nails. The only tool a pioneer usually possessed was an axe to cut down trees, trim and chop them into correct lengths. Clapboards "rived" from white oak and held in place by weight poles served as roofs. Chinking between logs was made of wood chips and mud. Floors were dirt. Fireplaces with outside chimneys supplied heat for cooking and cabin warmth. Cabins were likely not to have windows.

Mattresses containing straw were placed on horizontal poles driven into the chinking and supported by upright poles. Quilts covered the mattresses. Children slept in a loft reached by a ladder, if there was a loft.

One or two iron pots and a frying pan, or spider, on three legs served the cooking needs. Wooden or pewter spoons, plates and cups were used.[2]

After land was cleared to grow corn, a log barn was built for the animals the pioneers brought with them, or soon acquired: a cow, a horse, a yoke of oxen, pigs and chickens.

Neighbors gathered for cabin and barn raisings. These were social occasions as well as work sessions. Men built the cabins, women did the cooking. The day usually ended with singing and folk dancing.

The second homes of the pioneers were larger and more comfortable. The logs were hewed and there were puncheon floors. They usually contained two or three rooms, or they were double cabins with a walkway between them. Windows were covered with

Henry Hardin's log cabin 1919. (Photo by Frank Hohenberger)

Log cabin and well sweep 1919

Brown County, Sehmer Hill territory, showing a typical old-time farm 1890.

Swingin' Bridge over Salt Creek (Photo by Frank Hohenberger)

glass. Fireplaces were enormous often five to ten feet wide.

When sawmills furnished lumber, boards took the place of hewed logs, or were nailed over logs which gave the appearance of a frame house. No more log cabins were built in Nashville and the small towns in Brown County. However, log cabins continued to be constructed on farms for many years.

The men supplied meat for their families by hunting. Pioneers, like Seralvo McGuire's parents, told of woods filled with deer, bear, squirrels, and rabbits. As many as 100 wild turkeys comprised a flock, or drove. Enormous flights of passenger pigeons darkened the sky. For several years thousands of robins passed through Brown County in spring and fall. Robins and pigeons roosted low in the trees and at night were clubbed to the ground. They were salted and stored in barrels.

By 1880-1890 wolves, wildcats or panthers were eliminated but so were the passenger pigeons, turkeys, bears, and deer. Ben Wise is credited with shooting one of the very last of the deer in 1895.[3]

As more and more land was cleared farms contained pasture for horses, mules, oxen and cows. Wheat was grown as well as corn. Tobacco became a staple crop, sold to markets in Louisville. Vegetables and fruits were raised in abundance.

Brown County was not industrialized. Farmers prospered and supplied their own food. They were independent people. But through the 1800s they were also isolated people. Travel continued to be difficult and the roads were constantly in poor condition. As a consequence small towns cropped up in Brown County. Each became the center for a surrounding community, and contained a school, a post office, a church or two, a few stores, a blacksmith shop, and several houses.

As a result people became used to isolation in hilly Brown County, and lagged behind the development found in certain other counties. There are authentic stories of people who never visited Nashville in their lives. For instance, Frank Hohenberger wrote of a woman seventy years of age who lived less than twenty miles from Nashville. She had heard Frank was a photographer and had arranged for him to take her picture. He learned that she had never been to Nashville. This was in the 1920s.

Of course such isolation abruptly ended with the proliferation of cars, and the improvement of roads.

SCHOOLS

Before the county was organized in 1836 the earliest pioneers in Brown County were concerned about their children's education. The very first school opened in 1835 at Hedgesville, a short distance east of Nashville. The school was taught in a deserted log cabin. Eight to ten children attended. It did not last long.

A few terms of school were taught at the Jackson Salt Works, near Jackson Creek, southwest of Nashville before 1836.

In 1837 the families in Nashville built a log school 12 x 16 feet, in the northwest part of town. Poplar logs were split for benches, slabs of wood served as desks. The only light came from the huge fireplace that occupied one end of the room, or on warm days from the open door. David Reddick was the first teacher.

The log school was used for five years then the school was held at the Followell grocery, and later in the log courthouse. In 1857 a new schoolhouse was built in Nashville, in 1869 a second school was added, and by 1889 a third one-room school was active.

In Washington Township in 1840 there was a school in the western part of the township, and one in the eastern section.

Jackson Township built a log church that doubled as a school in Georgetown in 1838. John C. Marshall taught in the school. Marshall was considered an excellent teacher because the "big boys" found him a master who kept strict discipline. He taught in other county schools.

A second school was built in the "Anderson neighborhood" and a third near the Richards' farm on Bear Creek.

In Hamblen Township a vacated log cabin served as the first school in 1835 in the Taggart-Hamblen area. A man named Edgington was the teacher. In 1837 the newly constructed log United Brethren Church on the Taggart farm housed the school.

In Van Buren Township a log school was built in the southwest section of the township. The teacher was an Irishman named Sullivan. A second early school was taught near Christiansburg. The log Shiloh Methodist Episcopal church in the early 1840s served for some years as a church and school.

There is no record of the earliest schools in Johnson Township.[4]

These first schools were largely subscription schools. Parents helped to pay the teachers, build and repair the schools, contribute the fire wood, and supply a few books. The teachers boarded in various homes in the communities where they taught.

When wolves, bears and panthers were fairly numerous in the county, boys who walked through the woods to school carried a rifle for protection. In the log schoolhouses teachers called on the older boys to help carry in the heavy backlogs for fireplaces that were six feet wide.[5]

By the 1860s one-room frame schools, painted white, began to dot the county. Large cast iron box-stoves sat in the middle of the school room. Later, pot-bellied stoves supplied more heat. There were very few wood-houses to keep the stove wood dry. Sometimes a teacher kept a pile of firewood in a corner of the schoolroom. Sometimes the wood was stacked under the schoolhouse and was kept reasonably dry. On very

Deckard School House built in 1890. The last year was the 1937-1938 class. In 1940 the building was taken down and rebuilt in Deckard cemetery.

cold days the children clustered around the stove until mid-morning.

These schools had blackboards, more books, and usually a platform for the teacher's desk. A pail of water from the well, with a common cup, occupied a table along the back wall.[6]

The township trustees had charge of the one-room frame schools. They supervised the building of the schools in their township, kept them in repair, hired and paid the teachers, bought the necessary books and other school supplies, bought the firewood. Funds came from the Treasurer's office in the courthouse.

Since there were no school buses before 1900, and roads were often deep in mud, or snow, children could not walk far to school. By 1895 there were 78 one-room schools in Brown County:[7]

Jackson Township 19
Hamblen Township 16
Washington Township 19
(Includes 3 in Nashville)
Johnson Township 8
Van Buren Township 16

CHURCHES

Circuit riders found their way to what became Brown County before the county was organized in 1836.

The first sermon was preached by a United Brethren minister, named Eckles, in the log courthouse in 1837.

Pioneers established churches of six denominations. By 1881 there were 37 churches and 29 church buildings. The total membership was 3,167.[8]

PHYSICIANS

In the 1880s physicians lived a very rugged life. A few patients who were able to travel over the rough roads came to a doctor's office. But doctors were expected to call on the very ill in their homes. There were no ambulances nor hospitals. Doctors traveled on horseback with medicines in saddle bags, or in a buggy with a hot brick or a small stove under their feet in freezing weather. If a doctor misjudged the depth of water in a flooded stream he, and his horse and buggy could be carried downstream for quite a distance.

THE CHURCH ROSTER BY 1881

Denominations	Churches	Buildings	Members
Methodist	15	12	1,350
Presbyterian	2	2	108
Baptist	7	4	634
United Brethren	1	1	45
Christian	10	8	950
New Lights	2	2	80
Totals:	37	29	3,167

Medical knowledge was extremely limited and it is remarkable that doctors helped patients as much as they did. In typhoid or diphtheria epidemics they were helpless, since the prevention of these diseases was unknown. In 1896 or 1897 a Petro family in Brown County lost twelve of fifteen children in a diphtheria epidemic.

Most villages in Brown County from 1880 to 1890 had at least one doctor, sometimes as many as three. In 1881 there were twenty-one doctors in Brown County.

Nashville
H.C. Conner   Marion A. Duncan
Arnold S. Griffith   John F. Genolin
A.J. Ralphy   Capt. T. Taggart
T.E. Warring

Bean Blossom
Enoch S. Arwin   A.C. Spencer
James G. Ward   A.F. Wright

Needmore
William H. Beatty   Joseph N. Fleener

Elkinsville
Nathan Browning   John H. Leonard

New Bellsville
R.E. Holder

Spearsville
James P. Moser

Schooner Valley
Stephen Mossop

Pike's Peak
George F. Story   Sammuel C. Wilson

Mt. Moriah
W.H. Roddy

The three midwives in Brown County were:
Pikes Peak - Amy Whitehorn
Schooner Valley - Lavina Hotchet
Ramelton - Sarah M. Merryman

On October 23, 1879, the Brown County Medical Society was organized at Nashville by a group of county physicians. The society was under the control of the Indiana Medical Society. Its purpose was to understand advances in medicine, to improve standards of medical education, and to decrease suffering in the county.

Meetings were held regularly and much interest was manifested, but by 1884 the Medical Society no longer existed. In these days of rapid transportation the few county doctors are able to attend excellent Medical Societies in Indiana.[9]

Horse Thief and Felony Associations

In the latter 1800s horse thieves were numerous in Brown County. One sheriff could not apprehend all offenders. Finally, residents of Hamblen Township formed an Association in self defense.

There may have been several Associations before 1878 but the burning of the courthouse in 1873 destroyed the records. However, on June 4, 1878 the formation of the "Horse Thief and Felony Detectives of Hamblen Township" was recorded in the courthouse. William Walker, James W. McIlvain, John Wiry, John P. Prosser, Jacob R. Walker, Uriah Nisby, George Petro, Joseph McYoung, Asa F. Duncan, and Joshua Metheny entered into a "firm league of friendship.. for our common protection and general welfare... to assist each other against all thefts, felons, and other outrages ... of person or property." Officers were elected, and members were taxed "to defray expenses in capture of stolen property."

The Association was formed for a five-year period.

On June 2, 1883 the Articles of Confederation were renewed, and again on June 2, 1888, June 6, 1893 and in February 1918. On March 9, 1907 the "Gold Point Horse Thief Detective Association" was formed at Spearsville. On July 7, 1918 the "Needmore Horse Thief Detective Association No. 119", in Jackson Township, recorded its Articles of Incorporation in the courthouse.

What occurred, how many thieves were apprehended, wild chases undertaken, and what danger the members of the Associations encountered is totally unknown. Perhaps further information will be discovered.[10]

Whitecappers

Since one sheriff could not keep the entire county in order in the days of bad roads and slow travel a secret organization of regulators called "whitecappers" came into existence. They took the law into their own hands to administer justice in the latter 1800s.

They punished offenses such as stealing chickens, non-payment of debts, cruelty to family members, and immorality. The culprit was warned by hickory switches he found on his doorstep. If he continued to misbehave he was visited on a dark night by a group of men, masked with white hoods. He was tied to a tree, or wagon wheel, and thoroughly whipped. One whipping usually brought reform.

By 1907 whitecapping had degenerated into a means of revenge on an enemy, or just pure devilment. Governor Frank Hanly instructed Attorney General James W. Bingham to assist in the prosecution of seven citizens of Brown and Monroe counties who were alleged to have taken part in a whitecapping. The governor firmly stated he would not sanction state laws to be defied. It was widely recognized that whitecapping had become unsafe for perpetrators, and punishable. Whitecapping abruptly ceased in Brown County, and in Indiana.[11]

Poor Farm

From the time the county was organized it was necessary to arrange care for people who could not care for themselves. Overseers of the Poor were designated in each township to look after the helpless.

The first claim in the spring of 1837 was made by Ambrose Cobb who was allowed 40 cents a week by the township trustee to care for someone. At first, such claims were not presented to the County Board. By 1858 when $488.35 was allowed by the Board for the poor it was recognized that a "Poor House" was becoming a necessity.

In 1859 the County Board endeavored to buy a poor-farm, but because of the cost, the project was abandoned. However, in 1869 the Board bought 244 acres on the east edge of Nashville from Thomas A. Adams for $5,000. The first payment was made on April 25, 1870 for $2,500, and a second payment on April 25, 1871 for an equal amount. The payments were in county bonds bearing six percent interest.

William Waltman contracted to build a frame house 30 x 60 feet for $1,474. The house was finished in 1870 at a total cost of $1,600.

James Taggart was the first superintendent. He received the use of the farm and $3,085 for caring for the poor for three years. The number of residents varied from eight to fifteen.

In 1896 when Clark Campbell resigned as superintendent there were twenty-three acres of corn growing on the farm, a patch of potatoes, hay in the barn and a large garden of turnips, cabbage and beans.

Through the years the able-bodied men residents helped with the farm work; the women helped in the kitchen and with housekeeping chores.

The County Board, that is, the Commissioners, financed the cost of groceries and necessities from stores in Nashville, as well as repairs for house and farm machinery.

There are records of Brown County people taking gifts of fruit, vegetables, and meat after butchering quite regularly to the Poor House.

After ninety-three years the county commissioners decided to close the home on April 1, 1963. An auction held on May 11, 1963, realized $2,589.40 for the county.

Two men and three women were living in the home when it closed. Carl Hobbs, Superintendent of the home, took the men into his own house for $120 a month. Relatives of the two women accepted responsi-

Old Poor Farm building, which is currently the school administration building.

bility for their care, and the third woman was placed in a home by the welfare department.

On September 7, 1965 the Brown County School Corporation bought the Poor House and fifteen and a half acres for $2,750. The building was remodeled into offices for the School Corporation. It is still used for that purpose.[12]

RAILROADS

Through the 1800s after railways came into existence various plans were made to build a railroad across Brown County.

In 1863 the Commissioners agreed to invest several thousand dollars worth of bonds in a proposed Columbus, Nashville and Bloomington Railroad. The railroad was never built.

In 1869 a petition signed by over one hundred Brown Countians was presented to the County Board, asking for a two-percent donation to be given to the Cincinnati and St. Louis Short Line Railroad Company. The railroad was to be built through the central part of the county. An election was held in December in the five townships but twice as many people voted against as for the donation. The railroad was not built.

There was considerable discussion in the county in 1876 concerning a plan to build an Indianapolis and Evansville Mineral Railway across Brown County. The county voted to supply $7,500 toward the railroad. Again, the road was never built.[13]

NASHVILLE

By 1840 eighty people lived in a rapidly increasing cluster of log cabins. The log courthouse and log jail had been built as had the first bridge over Salt Creek on the Columbus-Bloomington road. John A. Brown was paid $233 for the bridge.

Banner C. Brummet started a grocery and liquor store. W.S. Roberts opened a second store with a "stock of goods worth $1,500." Lorenzo D. Head, who was a gunsmith and blacksmith arrived in Nashville about 1837. P.C. Parker built a double log cabin for a tavern, and Sylvanus Manville opened the "American Tavern" for travelers.

A long list of merchants and grocers is recorded between 1840 and 1880 when 348 people lived in Nashville and 2,836 lived in Washington Township.[14]

About 1860 there was a group of saloons on the west side of Van Buren Street opposite the courthouse. They continued on the north side of West Main to the alley. On Saturday mornings men on horseback with knives in their boots rode into town, tied their horses in the saloon alley and spent the day at the bars. Brawls and fighting were inevitable. The story persists of two men chasing each other around the courthouse with knives.

Nashville was known as a wild town full of gambling, drinking, fighting and horse racing. Farmers would not come alone to Nashville to pay their taxes at the courthouse, or to shop. Two or three drove a wagon and came together,- and never on Saturdays.[15]

In 1852 John Hight sent a second flatboat down Salt Creek, loaded with grain and pork, from the dock near Nashville. The first flatboat contained bacon. The boats floated down the creeks to the Ohio River, reached Cairo, Illinois, hence down the Mississippi to New Orleans. Elijah Scarborough and Al Meadows sent two or three flatboats to New Orleans from farther down the creek.[16]

In 1872 the town of Nashville was incorporated. The petition for incorporation was signed by forty residents accompanied by the necessary plats and descriptions. It was presented to the County Board on the fifth of August. An election was ordered for September 23 to determine whether a municipal government was advisable. The vote for incorporation was favorable, and the village was declared to be the incorporated town of Nashville.

The first trustees of Nashville following incorporation were Frank P. Taggart, John Genolin and Charles Gibson. E.H. Cox was the first clerk, and Leander Smith the first treasurer. The trustees adopted a series of by-laws and ordinances for the government of the town. They determined that the municipal government would not be rigid but act in accordance with a Democratic policy of open instead of centralized government.

In 1880 general merchandise was sold in Nashville by Frank P. Taggart, Charles Gibson, the Patterson Brothers, Hugh Mason, and Taggart and Grattan. Cornelius and Calvin took care of drugs and notions. William Day sold groceries, boots, and shoes. John and T.D. Calvin had a harness and hardware store on the south side of East Main. J.E. Kennedy kept a grocery store and sold confectionery. W.A. Mason sold groceries and notions. O.J. Taggart was the town barber. Blacksmiths were Guthrie Patterson and George Stone. Carpenters were J.P. Gray and James Meyers. Leander Smith built wagons, the cabinet maker was John L. Dew, the butcher Robert Brown, and the town milliner Mrs. Jennie Allison.

The three doctors were Dr. E.T. Taggart, Dr. John F. Genolin, Dr. Alfred P. Ralphy. There were six lawyers: R.L. Coffey, W.W.

This building was built by Frank P. Taggart in 1873. It is the oldest business building in Nashville. The building was used for merchandise, groceries and as a butcher shop in the 1900's. It was bought by Herbert Miller in 1925 and continued as a drug store for many years.

"Red" and "Dave", with a load of cross ties and Old Peg Leg. (Photo by Frank Hohenberger)

Browning, W.L. Cox, Anderson Percifield, W.C. Duncan, and J.C. Hester.[17]

Nashville in 1880 was a town of neat white houses. Each house was enclosed by a white-washed picket or board fence to keep cows and horses out that roamed the streets at night. Sidewalks were graveled. Ox teams plodded the streets hauling loads of tanbark or hoop poles.

Screens for houses came in about 1887. Each house had its own barn for a horse and cow. The animals were pastured west and north of Nashville. There was no running water. Everyone had a well which frequently went dry in summer. There was a pump in every kitchen. Wood stoves were used for cooking, and heat in winter. There were only outhouses, no bathrooms.

Nashville had nine stores and one saloon. It was a prosperous town because the timber industry still thrived. The last stands of big trees in the hills were being cut and sold to buyers outside the county.

There was an iron fence around the courthouse. Many locust trees grew on the lawn. Wood for the cast iron box-stoves in each office was kept in a large woodshed. Coal-oil lights lit the streets at night.

The original Nashville House, built just after the Civil War, stood on the corner of Van Buren and East Main Streets across from the courthouse. In the 1880s the proprietor came out on the steps and vigorously rang a loud bell to announce meal times. There were three or four other places that took in lodgers including the Mason Hotel on West Main, but the Nashville House was the most popular. Traveling salesmen called "Drummers" came by train to Morgantown then hired a team and driver for the trip to Nashville. They were always debonair and smartly dressed in the latest fashions. They stayed in a house they favored and paid twice the price of the Nashville House. Drummers visited the stores in Nashville and in the villages of the five townships.

It was the custom during the 1880s for people to drive to Columbus once or twice a year to shop for dress goods and other supplies not sold in Nashville.

In the early 1880s there were two schools in Nashville. A third one-room school was built in 1889 for primary grades. Large playgrounds surrounded the schools enclosed by a board fence and a stile. There were no high schools in the county.

Beginning in 1886 a normal school for teachers met in Nashville for six weeks in the summers. The town gained a reputation as a "little college town." At the end of six weeks a county institute was held. Instructors came from various colleges for the week. Many town people attended. This might be the only instruction a young teacher received.

Mail came daily from Morgantown and twice a week from Columbus. The mail hacks carried passengers and packages for merchants. Nothing stopped them but high water. The man from Morgantown had the worst drive. He came through the covered bridge at Bean Blossom (built in 1880 by Capt. Joseph Balsey at a cost of $1,200) then climbed up to the ridge road a half-mile west of the present highway. The road was about the worst in Brown County. In 1869 the Morgantown and Nashville Gravel Road Company had been organized. The length of the road was thirteen miles and the estimated cost was $17,130. The project was abandoned before it was finished. In 1879 the plan was revived. Much of the road was put in fair shape and a toll gate was built at the northwest corner of Jefferson and Mound Streets. At that time there was no other road directly north from Nashville. By November 1883 toll-collecting had

Henshaw Gallery in the Old Odd Fellows Building, where Hohenberger had lived. It was built in the 1880's.

The Bean Blossom Bridge built in 1880.

ceased and the road building was halted.

Alonzo Allison published the weekly Brown County Democrat. There had been a merger of the Jacksonian published by George Allison, father of Alonzo, and the Democrat published by William Browning.

There was a spoke factory, owned by a Mr. Clevenger and his sons, in southern Nashville in the 1880s. The old buhr mill run by water power, a half mile southeast of town on Salt Creek, was still a busy mill. In 1887 a roller mill was built where an old tannery had operated. The engineer was a Mr. Reep.

The Methodist Episcopal South and the Presbyterian were the two churches active in Nashville until the Christian Church was built in 1888.

The most exciting events were the political rallies held every four years. Brown County had been staunchly Democratic since pioneer days. Democrats have always outnumbered Republicans. On rally days in the 1880s people crowded into Nashville in buggies, carriages, wagons drawn by horses with colts running by their sides. Mule teams displayed brass-trimmed harnesses.

There were parades. The day's speakers sat in elegant carriages in high silk hats and linen dusters. Brass bands, drum and bugle corps, glee clubs from the townships furnished music. Houses were decorated with bunting and flags. Speeches took place on the courthouse lawn. At noon there were innumerable picnics and the hotel dining rooms were filled. Speaking continued in the afternoon and speakers moved to the courtroom in the evening.

On one occasion there was a torchlight parade that Nashville never forgot. Bill Pittman had brought 300 coal-oil torches from Columbus. The Nashville brass band wore gold-braided grey uniforms with red plumes in their hats. Houses were decorated with Chinese lanterns.[18]

DISASTER

In 1890 the United States Census reported 10,308 living in Brown County. In 1900 only 9,727 were in the county, a loss of 581 people. It took almost one hundred years for 10,000 to again live in Brown County - not until 1980.

Brown County reaped the result of disregarding warning signs, and misusing natural resources. Only a third of Brown County land is suitable for farming under the best of circumstances, yet farming was the basic county industry for the first hundred years. Since there was not sufficient bottom land for all settlers, hills were cleared of timber and this exposed the relatively shallow soil to erosion. Farmers plowed the earth and planted wheat on the sides of hills. Erosion became totally uncontrollable. Every rain took its toll and the soil washed away by the tons. After rains the creeks were brown for days because of the soil in the water.

The result was predictable. In a few years hill farms were infertile, and practically worthless for farming, because of the relentless erosion. Soil that was not carried away in the creeks piled up in the valleys in huge mounds and fields could not be plowed or planted.

When hill farms became infertile, farmers could not pay taxes and their land was put on the delinquent tax list. Some issues of the Democrat during the 1880s and 1890s were almost completely devoted to listing tax delinquent land.

This raised the cost of county government higher for fewer people. Taxes on bottom land farms were so high that farmers could not make a profit. Therefore, much of the better land was vacated also, and left to grow up in weeds. If families in these circumstances did not leave the county and find employment elsewhere they were eventually placed on relief. Brown County citizens left their homes and land literally by the hundreds in order to find work in cities or in other farming areas.

By 1930 the census reported 5,168 people in the county. Half of the Brown County population had fled. At one time there was a sign in front of the courthouse that read "Log cabins in any direction."

Brown County will never support large farms nor many full-time farmers. However, the worst of the ravages have been healed due to United States government aid in the 1900s.[19]

Brown County 1836 - 1900
Bibliography

[1] Esarey, Logan. History of Indiana pp. 290, 291.
[2] Marrs, Betty, Pioneer Living as told to Jeanette Richart.
  Vogel, William Fredrick, Home Life in Indiana, Indiana Magazine of History, Vol. X No.2, 1914.
[3] Mathis, Ray, History of Brown County, p. 13.
  Brown, Grover G., Indiana History Bulletin March 1963.
[4] Goodspeed, Weston A., Counties of Morgan, Monroe, and Brown 1884, pp. 730,731,738,744.
[5] Henderson, Robert E. Letter February 8, 1958.
[6] Brown, Grover G., Brown County Democrat December 6, 1962.
[7] Ogle, Warren, Oral History Tape, 1976.
[8] Goodspeed, Op. cit. p. 693.
[9] Ibid. p. 695.
  Mathis, Ray Brown County History p. 83.
[10] Miscellaneous Books, Brown County Courthouse, I pp. 118, 242, 305; III p. 111; IV p. 104.
[11] Mathis, Ray, Op. cit. pp.67-69.
  Brown County Democrat, July 18, 1907.
[12] Goodspeed, Op. cit. pp. 690-691.
  Brown County Democrat The Old Poor Farm, Delores Hamm, August 17, 1983.
[13] Goodspeed, Op. cit. pp. 688, 689.
[14] Ibid p. 688, 725.
[15] Hohenberger, Frank, Journal.
[16] Goodspeed, Op.cit., p. 727.
[17] Ibid. pp. 727-729, 725, 726.
[18] Stump, Mrs. Charles, Tales of Old Nashville June, 1944.
[19] Mathis, Ray, Op. Cit. pp. 48, 57, 58.

The Old Methodist Church.

One-room school near Nashville, 1918.

Chapter XVI
Brown County 1900 to 1990

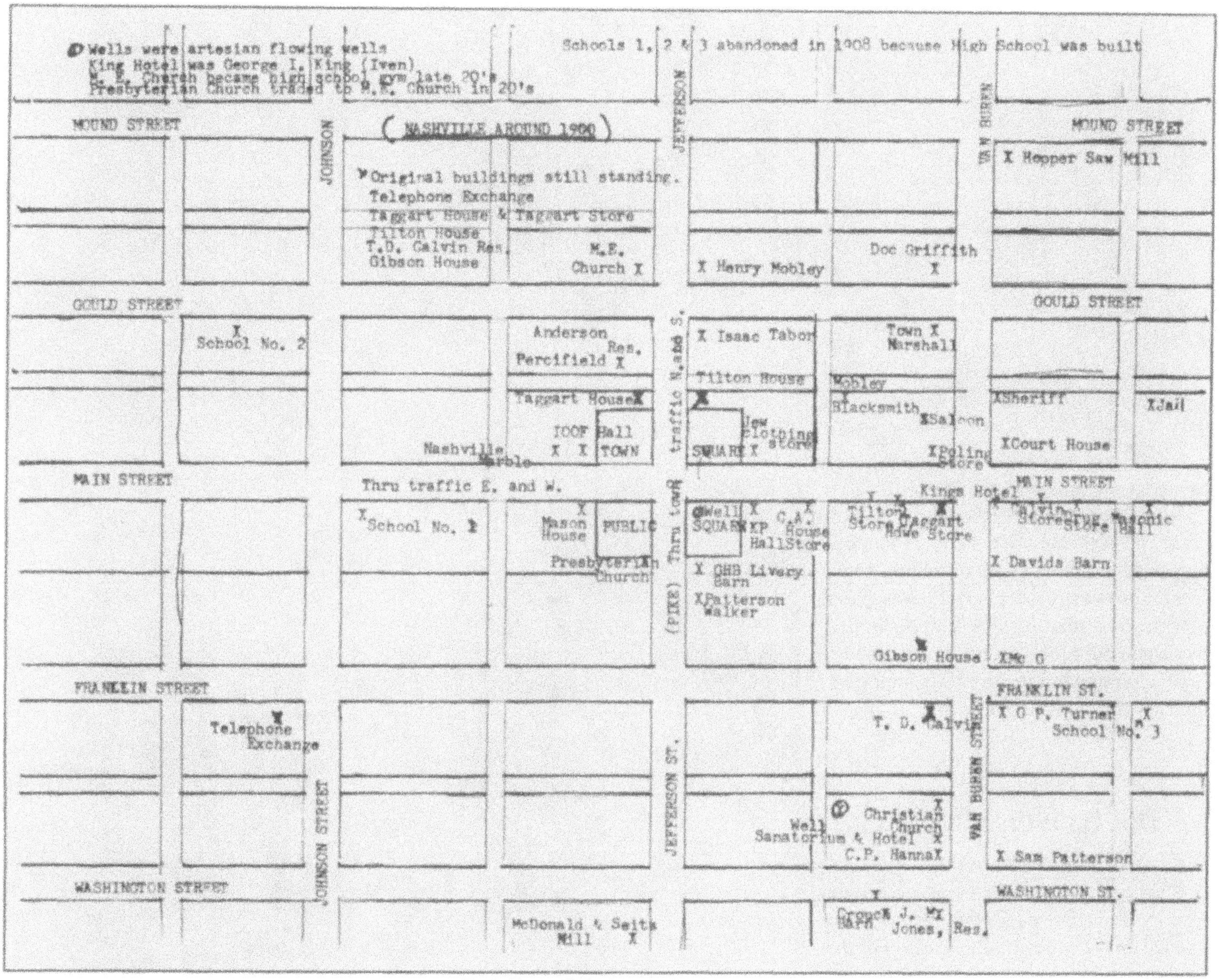

Nashville in 1900. (Map by Fred King)

In 1900 Brown County was known as the poorest, most backward, and isolated county in Indiana.

There were 581 fewer people in the county according to the 1900 census of 9,727 than in the 10,308 count of 1890. The exodus due to severe soil erosion and infertile farms had begun in earnest.

The deeply rutted roads in the townships did not encourage travel even to Nashville, the county seat. A trip to Bloomington or Columbus with a horse and buggy required a full day, longer with a team of oxen and a wagon. The return trip necessitated a second day of driving.

The streets of Nashville were "shoe-top deep in mud" in wet weather. On a breezy day in dry weather clouds of dust completely obscured the village from people

W. Main Street, 1911. Village Green Building on right.

A main road in Brown County in 1909.

Travel in Brown County in 1914.

living on the surrounding hills![1]

Since the valuable timber had been harvested by 1900 Brown County's economy depended to a large extent on cutting down second-growth trees for barrel staves, hoop poles, and railroad ties. These were shipped by wagon out of the county to a railroad.

Wagon-making was a rather important industry also in Brown County.

THE ILLINOIS CENTRAL RAILROAD

The coming of a railroad to Brown County proved to be a great blessing. It opened up the county to the world. For the first time in the county's history a quick and easy means of access was provided.

A line was built across Jackson Township in 1905 extending the Illinois Central's service from Morgantown to Bloomington, and on to the terminus at Effingham, Illinois. By 1906 two daily trains south, and two trains north to Indianapolis were in commission. The trains stopped at three Brown County stations, Fruitdale, Trevlac, and Helmsburg to deposit or load freight, mail, and passengers.

It was an event when trains stopped at Helmsburg. Carriages lined up to transport passengers to Nashville. Wagons waited to load freight for the county seat. It took wagons as long as six hours, and carriages four hours to make the trip to Nashville when the road was at its worst. Both wagons and carriages splashed through creeks en route.

Dave Harden and wife, Liza, travel with mules and wagon.

It never ceased to amaze visitors that Nashville did not have railway service. The railroad's original plan had been to lay tracks from Morgantown to Nashville and on to Bloomington. The county seat's townspeople rebelled and refused to accept the plan. They feared a railroad would cause quantities of dirt and smoke, bring undesirables to town, and endanger their children.

Nashville would not have opposed interurbans, however. The October 9, 1913 Brown County Democrat discussed a proposed interurban from Indianapolis to Nashville and Evansville. The Indianapolis, Nashville, and Southern Traction Company was incorporated with capital stock of $150,000. At a courthouse meeting Nashville citizens expressed considerable enthusiasm for the plan. The project failed as did other tentative plans for interurbans in Brown County.

Brown Countians greatly enjoyed spending a day in Indianapolis by taking the early morning train and returning on the late afternoon train.

The railroad encouraged outsiders to visit the county. Increasingly, vacationers came to Nashville for summer holidays.

A group of artists from Chicago and Indianapolis came to Nashville to paint. As has been stated in the chapter concerning artists, by 1920 artists were establishing homes in Nashville. Countless visitors came to the art gallery to buy the paintings of these excellent resident artists. By the 1940s and 1950s Nashville had become known as the home of the finest art colony in the midwest.

Had the Illinois Central never been built in Jackson Township there might never have been a recognized art colony in Nashville, nor an always increasing number of tourists in the county.

The railroad served Brown County reliably until the building of improved state roads in the 1930s. When trucks began to carry freight, and automobiles proliferated, the railroad's business dwindled rapidly. By 1934 the Trevlac and Fruitdale stations were closed and abandoned. By 1952 passenger trains were eliminated and the irregular service of the Illinois Central carried only freight.[2]

Waiting for train at Fruitdale, 1912.

THE 1913 FLOOD

The worst flood in Brown County's history occurred on March 24th and 25th 1913. In 24 hours 5.33 inches of rain fell. Every stream overflowed. Salt Creek rose six feet higher than ever recorded.

A high wind blew roofs off and rain poured into houses to a depth of five feet. Some houses were completely washed away as well as barns. Streams were filled with household furniture, fencing and hay. Stock drowned, and bridges were washed out. Telephones were out of service, mail could not be delivered, travel was impossible. Even trains of the Illinois Central stopped running.

Rowboats were used to rescue stranded people. The homeless in the county and Nashville were cared for by relatives or neighbors until houses were rebuilt.[3]

There was flooding elsewhere in the state, also. For other counties and for Brown County it was a very real disaster.

Helmsburg taxi to Nashville, 1918. Mr. Lutes, driver, with family in rear seat.

CHAUTAUQUAS IN NASHVILLE

In the early 1900s groups called Chautauquas traveled through the midwest during the summer from their headquarters on Chautauqua Lake, New York. They brought music, lectures on current issues, and drama to countless small communities in the hinterlands for almost thirty years.

An old livery barn and sales stable at the south end of Van Buren Street built in 1878, and owned by William Crouch, became known as the Chautauqua Pavilion. During Chautauqua week sawdust was spread on

W. Main Street Flood, Nashville, 1913.

Chautauquas Pavilion

the barn floor, and audiences sat on benches taken from churches. The overflow was relegated to the barn loft. One program each summer was turned over to local talent which presented a play or a concert.

During the rest of the year old autos were stored in the barn, the Nashville high school gave musical programs, the basketball team practiced there. When tomatoes were ripe the space was used as a canning factory.

In 1924 the Chautauqua Pavilion was torn down and the McDonald garage was built where the old barn had stood. In 1924 the Chautauqua was given on the first floor of the three-story carding mill on East Main Street

In 1927 and 1928 Chautauquas were held in a tent back of the Christian church. The first motion pictures in Nashville were shown in that tent.

With the arrival of cars, better roads, radio, and movies audiences faded away. Chautauquas were no longer needed for entertainment.[4]

COMMERCIAL CANNING

From 1915 to 1935 commercial canning in Brown County was successful. Fields of tomatoes, once called "love-apples" and thought to be poisonous, were grown specifically for canning as were corn and green beans, strawberries and blackberries.

Brown Countians canned in their homes, barns, backyards, and in buildings designed for canning. After fruit or vegetables were prepared, cans were filled, sealed, cooked, labelled, shipped to markets in Indianapolis, and sold.

In Van Buren Township by 1915 Otto and Clara Ping, Alex DuBois, Charles Hurley, Lou Clark, "Doc" and Nellie Crouch all had assembly lines in their family factories. Each family had its own label. The Crouch label read "Our Best" and the Ping label read "Tower Brand, Hand Packed, Green Beans." These families formed a marketing union to sell their products in Indianapolis.[5]

Jackson Township's factory near the railroad station at Fruitdale (east of Fruitdale's present location) canned tomatoes, strawberries, and blackberries. In 1917 the factory incorporated under the name "Fruitdale Canning and Preserving Society".[6]

In 1917 a large factory in Helmsburg - the Brown County Products Company - canned the "Abe Martin Brand" of berries and vegetables.

Howard Prince who owned the enterprise learned to can in a corncrib on his family's farm on Porter Road near Sprunica. By 1917 he had bought a building in Helmsburg and turned it into a canning factory. The factory was sizeable. Prince furnished lodging to employees who lived at a distance, and installed a restaurant. He even wrote, edited and published a chatty newsletter.

In 1918 Prince acquired several thousand dollars worth of orders. He transferred his canned goods by truck to Indianapolis and sold directly to the Emory Food Company, a branch of Swift and Company in Chicago.[7]

Prosperous years for Brown County canners were 1917 and 1918. The United States Army's and Navy's needs for canned foods had greatly increased since they were feeding the armed forces during World War I.

In 1929 Benjamin Wallace Douglass owned a large apple orchard, Hickory Hill, in Jackson Township. Douglass built a factory on his property to can apple butter.

The factory was most successful. During the fall apple season the factory kept open twenty-four hours each day to can apple butter.

In the middle of the Depression, 1935, when many people in Brown County desperately needed work, the canning business came to a crashing halt. The federal government's New Deal regulations became so strict and demanding that nobody in the county was able to run a canning factory profitably.[8]

BROWN COUNTY STATE PARK

The establishment of Brown County State Park in 1930 opened the county further to the outside world.

Richard Lieber, Director of the Indiana State Conservation Department, recognized the possibilities of Brown County as a recreation area early in the 1900s. While sitting on Fred Hetherington's front porch in the summer of 1913 he remarked that he hoped the beauty of Brown County, and other Indiana localities, could be preserved in state parks. Lieber lived to see his dream realized.[9]

Due to Richard Lieber's influence Indiana bought 16,000 acres of timber and farm land in 1923 for a game reserve and park. The land in central Brown County cost an average of $10.17 an acre.

Lee Bright of Nashville, a man concerned about conservation, persuaded farm owners to sell their land to the state. Many farmers barely eked out a living on their worn-out land yet they sold with great reluctance and moved out of the area. Later, Lee Bright learned that the land these farmers bought in neighboring counties was often far more productive. They were thankful for the change.

There was considerable opposition to the park. Brown Countians realized that land belonging to the state would never yield tax money for the county. Consequently it was feared that assessed county taxes would be considerably higher.

Nevertheless, on March 17, 1928 the county commissioners approved the state's proposal that the county acquire 1,000 acres for the park. The maximum amount allowed for land acquisition was $14,500. The auditor was ordered to purchase acreage.[10]

During the next two years after the park opened to the public in 1930, the Abe Martin Lodge and twenty guest cottages were built exclusively with Brown County labor. By May 1932 the buildings were ready for occupancy and a dedication ceremony took place.[11]

The Ramp Covered Bridge was rebuilt over Salt Creek at the park's north entrance in 1932. It was originally constructed near Fincastle in Putnam County by Henry Wolfe in 1838 for $300. It is a double-barreled, or two-lane bridge rare in Indiana. In 1932 the State Highway Department judged the bridge unsafe in its original location. The Indiana Department of Conservation's Division of Lands, Parks, and Waters ordered the reconstruction over Salt Creek.[12]

On June 1, 1934 two-hundred World War I veterans arrived in Brown County State Park. They comprised Company #1557 of the Civilian Conservation Corps—CCC. Their work was directed by the Forestry Service under the administration of the army.

It is due in great part to the work of the CCC that Brown County State Park is Indiana's outstanding park. The CCC lived in the park until 1942 when the entire Civilian Conservation Corps was eliminated during World War II.

The CCC built permanent barracks. Some of the buildings still exist. They created picnic areas, shelter houses, two lookout towers, a fire tower, two gate houses, and a saddle barn. The CCC constructed a stone amphitheater near Abe Martin Lodge and quarried the stone they used.

The CCC cleared 50 miles of trails, widened park roads, built a pump house and a 2,000 gallon reservoir for storing water, and wired all buildings for electricity. They planted well over 200,000 pine and black walnut seedlings to heal erosion, and cleared out a hollow for Ogle Lake.[13]

A game reserve was established. Two buildings near the fire tower housed an exhibit of wild animals and birds. Buffalo and elk were kept in large outdoor fenced areas. In the early 1970s the buildings were torn down and all captive animals removed.

A large swimming pool and a Nature Center now exist. The lodge has recently been considerably enlarged and more rental cottages added.

Brown County State Park of 15,641 acres, Indiana's largest state park, has considerable impact on the county's economy. In 1990 the payroll for the park staff, most of whom live in the county, was over a million dollars. Gate receipts of the million and a half annual park visitors, the lodge dining room, and overnight accommodations brought a two-million dollar profit to the park.[14]

STATE HIGHWAYS AND COUNTY ROADS

By 1930 the constantly increasing automobile traffic in Brown County made improved state roads an absolute necessity. Fortunately, they became adequate in the decade of the 1930s and the once extremely isolated county due to very poor roads became readily accessible.

The first road in Brown County via the Jackson Salt works to Columbus was hacked out of the wilderness by the Territorial Government as early as 1815. It was called a state road at that early date. By 1899 this road from Bloomington had been rerouted from Schooner Valley over Kelley Hill to Nashville. At Main Street the road turned east, now known as old State Road 46, to Columbus.[15]

In the 1920s automobile factories in Indiana tested the hill-climbing capacity of their cars by driving them up very steep Kelley Hill. Sometimes cars were driven backwards up the hill to accommodate the flow of gasoline to the engine.[16]

During 1929 State Road 46 from Bloomington to Nashville was greatly improved by the State Highway Department. Sharp, dangerous curves were eliminated. Dynamiting of Kelley Hill's bedrock reduced the necessity of a formidably steep highway. In 1935 the road was blacktopped.

By 1963 State Road 46 from Columbus to Nashville had been straightened and rerouted. Through traffic from Columbus to Bloomington by-passed the town of Nashville.[17]

State Road 135 from Nashville north to Bean Blossom was built in 1935. At Bean Blossom it joined State Road 135 which had already been constructed to Morgantown and Indianapolis. For the first time in Brown County's history there was an excellent road straight from Nashville to the state capital. For several years a bus made a daily round trip to Indianapolis from Nashville. Benton Schrougham was the first bus driver. Trucks carried freight to Indianapolis without the necessity of going

Richard Lieber Memorial, Fred Hetherington's Cabin.

to Columbus, and then turning north. Later, State Road 135 was extended south from Nashville to Jackson County.

The three state roads 46, 135 and 45 serve Brown County admirably.

Local Brown County roads have improved enormously but in the hinterland certain unpaved roads still are full of pot holes and driving is difficult.

In 1910 "Yankee" Bill Waltman of Bean Blossom drove a highwheeled, chain-driven car on the rutted county roads. Its coughing and sputtering caused horses to panic and bolt headlong down the road with carriages or wagons and their occupants. In 1913 there was a car in Nashville, and two motorcycles.[18]

Cars increased slowly in the county for their usefulness was strictly limited because of the poor roads. Care of township roads was the responsibility of the township trustees.

In 1932 the county commissioners ended care of roads by the township trustees and formed the County Highway Department. The commissioners appoint the Highway Superintendent. Financing for county roadwork comes from the gasoline tax of the State Motor Vehicle Highway Account.[19]

Depression Years in Brown County

The 1929 New York stock market crash did not cause a ripple in Brown County since nobody, apparently, owned any stocks bought on margin. Life continued as usual. However, during the 1930's the county was affected, for several reasons.

In 1930 the census reported 5,168 people in the county – half of the 1890 census count of 10,308. The exodus had reached its highest figure. As the Depression deepened during the next few years in the United States, people began to filter back to Brown County. Unable to find work in towns or cities to which they had moved they returned to their deserted homesteads.

Other people, who had never lived in Brown County, hearing rumors of empty houses and cabins came to the county to find shelter,- for which they did not need to pay rent. Knowing nothing about farming they were often reduced to great poverty and inevitably ended up on relief rolls.

People in established businesses in the county such as a drug store, a grocery, a dry goods store, the postal service, a garage, were not seriously affected by the Depres-

Mary E. Hamblen of Story pealing sassafras. The sassafras bark was tied into small bundles and shipped East. Some was peddled in cities as far as Richmond, Indiana. (Photo by Frank Hohenberger)

sion. Nor were farmers who had never left Brown County and lived on reasonably fertile land. They survived by raising the usual vegetables, fruits, pigs, chickens, and cows. The woods furnished firewood for cooking and heating.[20]

Those who could not farm performed odd jobs for very little money. Some ate meat because they owned a gun and a coon hound. They also trapped animals for fur. A raccoon pelt sold for $9.00, a skunk for $6.00, and a possum for $1.50. A night's hunting could bring in $28.00.

People scoured the woods and sold bittersweet for 15 cents a bunch, hickory nuts, black walnuts and persimmons.

The Works Progress Administration (WPA) arrived in Brown County in 1936. The Administration enrolled 500 unemployed men. A transient labor camp housed 225, but Brown County men lived in their homes. They were paid $50 a month, unbe-

lievably a living wage in 1936.

The WPA planted dogwoods at the north and west entrances of Brown County State Park, and helped the CCC work on 27 miles of park roads, and on the stone amphitheater. They built the first high school gymnasium back of the high school, then on Van Buren Street.

WPA labor constructed the first courthouse annex, after the commissioners voted on October 7, 1938, to employ them, and also the stone wall along the sidewalk on the west side of the courthouse.

WPA reassembled an old log barn found in Jackson County to serve as a community building. They added two fireplaces and two chimneys not found in the original barn. This building is now part of the Brown County Historical Society's Museum Complex.

In Helmsburg the WPA built a community center near State Road 45. They cleaned debris from Brown County cemeteries and constructed an airstrip on Weed Patch Hill. When jobs became plentiful during World War II the WPA ceased to exist.[21]

THE BEAN BLOSSOM LAND UTILIZATION PROJECT

The Bean Blossom Land Utilization Project of the United States Bureau of Agricultural Economics came to Brown County in 1935. The Project was a national effort during the Depression to promote constructive use of land, and to relocate people living in poverty on land unsuitable for farming.

In 1935 eighty-five families lived in western Washington, Jackson and Johnson Townships on eroded and worn-out land. Some owned the land and had lived in the region for years. Others came during the Depression to live in deserted cabins. They could not make a living and were in distressful poverty.

The Project proposed to buy 20,000 acres, prevent over-cutting of timber, eliminate farming on infertile land, relocate families and use the area for reforestation, conservation, and recreation.

At the end of three years considerable land had been bought and families relocated with the assistance of the Resettlement Administration. WPA labor planted two million trees on abandoned farm land and eroded hillsides. Fire lanes were cleared, miles of road repaired, and new roads built.

Land for a park had been selected. The WPA constructed a dam across Jackson Creek Valley impounding the water of Jackson Creek for a 133 acre Yellowwood Lake. Picnic tables, benches, and ovens were installed. A large, enclosed shelter house for tourists was built near the lake.

The Bean Blossom Land Utilization Project worked with the Indiana State Conservation Department. When the Brown County project ended in 1943 the State Conservation Department accepted management of what was then called Yellowwood State Forest and Yellowwood State Park. In 1990, according to Donald Duncan, manager of Yellowwood, the entire area is now designated Yellowwood State Forest and is under the Indiana Department Of Natural Resources.

Land is still being bought to add to the State Forest's 23,300 acres when owners of land within the boundaries of the State Forest wish to sell and the Department of Natural Resources has sufficient funds to buy the land.[22]

Thousands of tourists have enjoyed the forest and the lake for almost fifty years.

THE CENTENNIAL CELEBRATION 1936

The Centennial Celebration was held from August 29th to September 5th, 1936. Brown County remembered and reviewed its history of 100 years. The chairman of the Centennial Committee was Glenn Long. The committee spent many hours planning the events.

On August 29th an all-day church and Sunday School service was held in New Bellsville in Thanksgiving for having progressed from the hardships of pioneer days. Throughout the week various programs were given in the five townships by local clubs and organizations.

The Centennial had received considerable publicity in Chicago and Indianapolis newspapers. As a result, Nashville was crowded for the entire week. Exhibits of old pictures, newspapers and artifacts were displayed in Nashville's stores.

The culmination of the Centennial came on Saturday, September 5th with a pageant written by Glenn Long. It was a crowning achievement. The pageant depicted Brown County's history, and people from all over the county took part. The pageant was presented on the lots of the Community Club. Bleachers were installed to seat the crowd. Dignitaries from neighboring counties were invited.

The pageant was pronounced a great success, and Brown Countians believed the reputation of the county had been enhanced by the Centennial.[23]

COUNTY EXTENSION WORK

In 1862 the Land Grant College Bill was passed by Congress and signed into law by Abraham Lincoln. The bill provided for a college in each state to teach approved agricultural methods and home economics. Considerable land was to be given to each college for experimentation and research. Purdue became Indiana's Land Grant College.

In 1914 Congress passed the Smith Leaver Act signed by Woodrow Wilson. The act made it possible for an agent, employed with federal, state and county funds, to reside in each county to transfer information concerning farming from Land Grant Colleges directly to local farmers.

The first Purdue agent, R.E. Grubbs, arrived in Brown County in 1921. He taught farmers how to determine which hens would never lay eggs, and to cull them from a flock of chickens. This resulted in increased egg production in the 1920s. Extra eggs could be traded for necessities in local stores.

At first, Extension Work was discouraging. Many farmers were suspicious and hesitated to accept suggestions. As time went on and results of Extension Work became evident Brown Countians voluntarily sought advice.

For years, Mr. Grubbs discussed soil en-

Old barn reassembled by WPA in the 1930s, as a Community Building in Nashville.

richment by fertilization, and new methods of contour plowing to prevent soil erosion, in a weekly column in the Brown County Democrat. This resulted in improved wheat and corn crops.

In the 1930s Mr. Grubbs introduced soybeans and the exceptionally high-yielding variety of corn called hybrid corn. Slowly these became staple county crops.

Farm wives became acquainted with cold-pack canning, frozen foods, and new methods of home making and family care.

Emphasis was placed on livestock production. The first 4-H Clubs were organized and were most successful. In the 1950s and 1960s 4-H programs were expanded to include photography, forestry, electrical projects, care of household pets, and gardening.

Robert Himes, agent from 1963 to 1977, introduced annual 4-H Fairs, and various successful community programs.[24]

SOIL CONSERVATION SERVICE S.C.S.

The United States Agricultural Adjustment Act, or Triple A in 1933, was passed to place a government office in each county to teach water conservation and erosion prevention.

By 1935 Triple A had evolved into the United States Soil Conservation Service, or S.C.S. The field representative in the Nashville office travels to a farmer's field or woods only when advice is requested. He is trained to size up a problem situation and suggest a solution.

When the scarcity of water is discussed the agent frequently advises damming a small stream. The resulting pond furnishes water for livestock and can be piped into a farmer's house to supply water for the family.

Since 1935 over a thousand ponds and lakes have been constructed in the county—as many as 15 to 20 per square mile. The ponds not only furnish water but aid in preventing erosion by receiving runoff after rains, snow or storms.

In 1990 at least 80 percent of the fearful erosion of the early 1900s, when washed-out gullies 40 to 50 feet deep were all over the county, has been healed. Gullies have been bulldozed to make level land, planted in grass, alfalfa, or clover and heavily fertilized. This has resulted in excellent pasture on which to raise beef cattle. This program has been eminently successful. There are now 40 to 50 cattle farms, particularly in northeast Brown County where the land is better for pasture than for row crops.

In 1990 Brown Countians raise crops on a commercial basis on 250 farms: corn, soybeans, wheat, oats, hay, melons, tomatoes, and pumpkins.

Tobacco is the one crop controlled by allotment to farmers. Some plant and grow their own tobacco. Others lease land for a tobacco crop. The preferred market is Madison, in Jefferson County.

Christmas tree farming of scotch pine or white pine, has been commercially successful for thirty years. Trees must be carefully tended and trimmed. They sell in quantity readily in November.

Forest again covers much of Brown County, though not all trees are prime specimens. Many timber stands need improvement by cutting undesirable trees, eliminating vines and preventing cattle foraging which kills young trees. Logging is now a constant occupation. The forester's office at Atterbury is the source of information concerning care and growth of Brown County forests.[25]

UNITED STATES AGRICULTURAL STABILIZATION AND CONSERVATION SERVICE

The United States Agricultural Stabilization and Conservation Service - A.S.C.S.

Tobacco Barn

Remaining erosion northeast Brown County, 1981. James Eagleman, Naturalist, Brown County State Park

came to Brown County in the late 1940s, following World War II, on a full-time basis. A.S.C.S. manages cost-sharing programs. Farmers can borrow money to build a pond, plant a crop, fertilize fields, or whatever, but the money must be paid back. The goal of a balanced program for every farm is the purpose of both A.S.C.S. and S.C.S. The two agencies work together but have different responsibilities.

According to the present A.S.C.S. agent, Bill Miller, there are no full-time farmers in Brown County. Men farm after work and on weekends. To supply adequate income they may drive a school bus, become a carpenter, or plumber, or have a job outside the county. Apparently they farm because they enjoy contact with the soil and raising crops.

Land suitable for farming comprises only 12.5 percent of the county's 207,360 acres. Forest land totals 68 percent of the acreage. Since forests are now growing again in the county wildlife is returning- wild turkeys, grouse, foxes and deer.

The goal of complete elimination of erosion, and adequate care of forests has not yet been achieved. Streams are still muddy after rains, and the quality of forest trees is often poor, but by comparison with the Brown County of 1900 to 1930 tremendous improvement has been made. The County Extension Service, A.S.C.S., and S.C.S. have made this progress possible.[26]

MODERN CONVENIENCES IN BROWN COUNTY

The earliest telephones were fastened to a wall. A handle was turned to attract the attention of the operator at a switchboard. The operator connected the number requested with the caller's phone by long and short rings until the receiver was lifted. Switchboards were located in operators' homes.

Telephone wires were very likely to be strung on fences along roads. Phones didn't "talk" early in the morning until the sun dried the dew on the wires.

The Brown County Commissioners' Records state that on March 9, 1898, permission was granted to the S.W. Daugherly Company to construct a "telephone system" between Columbus and Nashville.

The Pike's Peak Telephone Company was incorporated on October 2, 1902. On May 2, 1912 a franchise was given to install

Home still standing at 227 W. Franklin Street, Nashville, was Jerry Wilson Telephone Exchange in 1917.

Union Telephone Company Office, Gift Shop, Nashville State Bank on West Main Street, Nashville, 1929.

a line to Nashville. The company served southeast Brown County for a number of years.

The Needmore Telephone Company constructed a line to Bloomington in 1902. The New Bellsville Telephone company recorded Articles of Incorporation on April 29, 1908. Its lines eventually reached Ogilville and Waymansville. In 1922 the company employed 22 linemen.

In Nashville the Jerry Wilson Telephone Company's switchboard was in the Wilson home at 227 West Franklin. In 1917 an advertisement in the Brown County Democrat stated that the company had "copper wire right to New York. All telephones fine talkers." An illustration proves phones were no longer attached to a wall. The receiver hung on the side of a small upright phone placed on a table.

In 1929 there were three telephone companies in the county: Bill Exner's line from Nashville to Belmont, the New Bellsville Company connected to Columbus, and the Union Telephone Company in Nashville installed in a small building between the bank on West Main and the Miller Drug Store on the corner of West Main and Van Buren Streets.

There was one long-distance line from

Burial of old town pump, July 2, 1949. (Photo by Lester C. Nagley, Sr.)

Nashville to Martinsville via Morgantown. It was often necessary to wait two or three hours for a call to go through to its destination.[27]

In 1953 Indiana Bell acquired a franchise to rebuild all telephone lines in Brown County. Indiana Bell bought the deserted old Methodist Church on the northwest corner of Gould and Jefferson, then used for high school basketball practice, tore it down, and built a thoroughly modern telephone exchange.

In 1990 all Brown County has Indiana Bell service except a small area near Monroe Reservoir where the Smithville Telephone Company at Elletsville operates, and a small section of northeast Brown County serviced by the United Telephone Company from Nineveh.[28]

In 1900 Nashville and all of Brown County used coal-oil lamps to light houses at night, cooking was accomplished on wood stoves and clothes were washed by hand on a scrub board in a portable wooden or metal tub.

On November 15, 1915, the Nashville Town Board passed a resolution to build a light plant. The plant supplied light from dusk to ten o'clock. Since there was no electric current during the day women ironed in the evening, if they possessed an electric iron. A sudden dimming of the lights warned townspeople the current would soon be turned off.

In 1927 the Town Board discontinued the light plant and contracted for electricity from H.F. Clevenger and Company of Columbus.

In 1948 the Town Board decided to buy electricity and all night street lighting from Public Service of Indiana. Public Service still supplies electricity to Nashville, Trevlac, Helmsburg, Bean Blossom and certain rural areas.

In 1941 Rural Electric Membership Corporation, established in Martinsville, brought electricity to northern Brown County. Jackson County REMC in Brownstown now serves southern Brown County.[29]

In June 1949 water was brought to Nashville in water mains from Lake Ogle in Brown County State Park and piped into the houses. No longer did townspeople need to depend on wells in their backyards that went dry in summer.

With the arrival of water Nashville citizens held a funeral service for the old town pump that stood for years by the Calvin Brothers hardware store in the Village Green Building.

It was a gala occasion on June 2, 1949. The event had been advertised in the Democrat and the story was repeated by the Associated Press and International News Service. A large crowd gathered in Nashville.

The old pump was placed in a black hearse drawn by two black horses. A "preacher" and two women "mourners" followed the hearse in a two-seat surrey. A procession of carriages passed a reviewing stand draped in red, white, and blue bunting. Men doffed their hats as the procession passed the stand west of the courthouse.

The purpose of the parade was to raise funds to buy fire hoses for the Nashville Volunteer Fire Brigade. An auction was held; individuals and businesses bought varying lengths of hose for a new fire truck. Fireplugs had been installed along the streets of Nashville. The days of water-bucket brigades to put out fires were ended.[30]

In 1990 the Brown County Water Utility brings water from deep wells in Morgan County to Nashville and parts of Jackson,

Hamblen, and Washington Townships. Monroe Reservoir water comes from Bloomington to houses along State Road 46, and surrounding Washington Township as far as the bridge across Salt Creek, south of Nashville.

Van Buren Township water is piped from Jackson County. The Bartholomew Water Corporation serves eastern Brown County along State Road 46 as far as Gnaw Bone.

Many residents in Brown County still depend on drilled wells, cisterns, ponds and lakes for water.[31]

THE HOOSIER NATIONAL FOREST AND DEAM WILDERNESS

By 1935 the Hoosier National Forest contained 195,000 acres in nine counties. Southern Van Buren and Washington Townships in Brown County have 35,000 of these acres.

In 1982 the Deam Wilderness of 3,000 acres was established in the southwest corner of Brown County and Jackson and Monroe Counties. The Wilderness is set aside as a completely undisturbed area for scientific study of the forests natural growth and diversity. No lumbering, planting, roads or recreation will be permitted.

From 1975 to 1990 constant and increased bitter adverse criticism in newspapers and publications protested the clearcutting, the construction of many roads, the off-road vehicles, gas and oil exploration permits in the Hoosier Forest. It took at least ten years of unrelenting effort on the part of many organizations interested in conservation to change the destructive policies, but apparently 95 percent of clearcutting, 80 percent of road building has been stopped, and off-road vehicles are totally prohibited.[32]

ATTERBURY RESERVE FORCES TRAINING AREA

In 1941, the Federal Government bought 3,000 acres in the extreme northeast of Hamblen Township, and 34,900 acres in Bartholomew County and Johnson County for the Camp Atterbury Military Reservation. The 83rd Infantry Division was the first army unit in World War II to train at Camp Atterbury. The 83rd Infantry saw action in Normandy in July 1944.

Renamed the Atterbury Reserve Forces Training Area in January 1969 Atterbury now serves the Army and the National Guard.[33]

CORDRY-SWEETWATER CONSERVANCY DISTRICT

The Conservancy in the northeast corner of Brown County is a private residential area. No businesses, restaurants, or retail stores are permitted. It is part of Hamblen Township and pays taxes to the county.

In the 1950s Howard Prince and Chester Cordry bought land and constructed Cordry and Sweetwater lakes. In 1959 2,700 acres and the two lakes became the Conservancy District with the approval of the State Legislature.

The Conservancy has an elected governing board, pays for its road upkeep, and snow removal, maintains a voluntary fire department, and two ambulances. The Conservancy manages its own water company. Mail is delivered from Nineveh.

A contract with the Brown County Sheriff assures a deputy sheriff at the expense of the Conservancy. A contract with the Brown County School Board sends buses to pick up children for Sprunica or Nashville schools and return them to their homes.

Residents who are not retired commute to work in Nashville, Franklin, Columbus and Indianapolis.[34]

A view of Nashville in 1910 with Pittman Inn and Christian Church on the left.

East Main Street in Nashville before the 1939 fire. On the far right is Bitters' home, Grover David's garage and restaurant and the old carding mill.

View of Nashville before the 1954 fire on West Main Street. (Drawing by D. Minturn)

Lawrence Frownfelter in the Nashville fire engine in 1930.

NASHVILLE

The business district of Nashville has been rebuilt several times following disastrous fires in the days of water-bucket brigades.

The first brick courthouse burned in 1873. Valuable early county records were destroyed.

In 1901 a long-established saloon on the northwest corner of West Main and Van Buren caught fire. The block of buildings west of the saloon also burned, including the store of a Jewish merchant.

The Presbyterian Church on Jefferson Street, where the Methodist Church now stands, burned in 1905. Across the street the livery stable built by Charlie Gibson and a half block of buildings known as Pauper's Row burned.

The Knights of Pythias Hall next to the village green on the south side of West Main, and James Tilton's furniture store burned in 1909. By 1910 the Masons and the Knights of Pythias had replaced the Hall with the brick Village Green Building, which is still being used.

In 1917 the George Max McDonald flour mill at the south end of Jefferson Street on Salt Creek burned to the ground.

In October 1931 fire consumed the old frame Christian Church on Van Buren Street.

In December 1939, on the south side of East Main opposite the courthouse, Grover David's garage, the Ford Agency, Laura David's small hotel and restaurant, Josh Bond's restaurant and the Bitter's house burned.[35]

The old Nashville House on the southeast corner of Main and Van Buren completely burned in 1943. The hotel had sheltered countless visitors for decades.

On January 13, 1954 a fire started in historic Melodeon Hall on the north side of West Main, where movies had been shown to crowds of Brown Countians. In 1954 it had become a pool hall, owned by Keith Skinner. The fire spread to Lauren Moore's grocery, the Abe Martin barber shop, and Charlie Pogue's shoe store. The Star grocery and butcher shop on the corner of West Main and Van Buren were spared because the building had been sheathed in metal.

The Art Gallery across the alley west of the fire and the row of burning buildings was scorched but not destroyed. Windows in the Bank and the Telephone Building across the street were cracked by the heat.[36]

In 1964 fire destroyed the Odd Fellows Lodge on the north side of Main Street between Jefferson and Johnson Streets, where the artist-photographer Frank Hohenberger had lived for many years.[37]

Fire hydrants now in Nashville and the Brown County Volunteer Fire Department will certainly aid in preventing future fires. Volunteer Fire Departments are also in Cordry, Fruitdale, Trevlac, Gatesville and Van Buren Township.

Incorporated towns in Indiana with less than 1,500 population are governed by a Town Council. Nashville incorporated in 1872 has a Town Council of three, elected by Nashville residents. The Town Council manages and is responsible for all town business. The Councilmen appoint a Town Attorney, a Town Marshal to enforce state laws and town ordinances, a Water Superintendent to oversee the town water, and a Sewer Superintendent to run the disposal plant.

At present the Water Superintendent also serves as the Street Commissioner. All street repair and construction is contracted to private firms. An elected Town Clerk is the Secretary and Treasurer of the Town Council.

Finances for the Town Council come from Nashville property taxes and state gasoline taxes.[38]

Nashville began to rely on tourism to bring money to the town in the 1930s following the opening of Brown County State Park. In 1990 tourism has become Nashville's accepted industry.

There are over 250 shops in the small town of Nashville. Every available old house is used for shops or businesses and the town is becoming crowded with new buildings. Fifty-six craft producers sell everything from musical instruments to soap with a "Made in Brown County" label.

Hotels, one Motel and one Bed and Breakfast are capable of lodging over 600 tourists in Nashville. There are also thirteen Bed and Breakfasts in the county. Cabins are rented to vacationers at various locations.

Of course there is a variety of restaurants. The Ordinary on Van Buren Street was once the Dinty Moore Restaurant owned by Sarah and Clint Moore. During the 1930s artists stayed there in the summer and were charged $30 a month for a room. This became the Old Hickory Restaurant. Andy Rodgers now owns The Ordinary.

The Hobnob Restaurant was formerly the Miller Drug Store. Frank Taggart built the store in 1873 to sell merchandise on the second floor, and groceries and meats on the first floor.[39]

Ski World, near Nashville, attracts skiers if and when there is sufficient snow. Nashville's Little Opry provides entertainment on weekends. In summer the Brown County Playhouse, under the auspices of the Indiana University's Theater Department, draws an audience from many localities in Indiana for its popular summer productions. In 1977 a thoroughly modern theater was built with the audience seated on three sides of a thrust stage. This developed from a stage in a barn opened to play to an audience sitting in wooden seats. In 1949 Lee Norvelle of Indiana University and Jack Rodgers teamed up to produce the first summer theater on the same location. A tent shielded the audience from rain. Andy Rodgers now owns the theater. The new theater is certainly far more comfortable than the first one!

Those who have lived in Nashville long enough to remember when the town was small, quaint, and charming realize that commercialism may destroy what is left of old Nashville. A few homes of charm and dignity remain and are privately owned. Many are now shops or businesses.

Warnings that tourists are becoming disenchanted by Nashville as it is today appear in letters published by the Brown County Democrat from time to time. Dismay and disappointment are expressed.

BROWN COUNTY 1990

Brown County's population remained through the 1800s almost entirely native-born Americans. For the first time the 1930 United States census listed 193 foreign-born in the county, from Ireland, England, Scotland, Germany, France and Poland. However, the great majority of the county's people were descendants of the pioneer stock.

In 1990 descendants of the county's pioneers still live in the county. Foreign-born are the exception. From 1980 to 1990 991 newcomers migrated to the county from other states and other Indiana counties, but they were not foreign-born. Retirees come to live in the county's peaceful surroundings. A new trend is evidenced by the number of young professionals and upper middle class individuals with growing families who deliberately are choosing to live in the county. They know before they arrive that they will commute to work outside of Brown County.

The migration rate to Brown County is the second highest in the state. County population increased from 12,377 in 1980 to 14,080 in 1990-the highest ever recorded. This is almost three times as high as the 5,168 in 1930 when half the population had fled.[40]

Schools in the county are no longer in the care of Township Trustees. In 1949 Brown County schools were consolidated. Seventeen township elementary schools and three high schools have been reduced to one high school in Nashville, a junior high, and four elementary schools in Nashville, Van Buren, Helmsburg, and Sprunica.

Shops along Van Buren Street - Shoppers' Lane in 1950. (Photo by Frank Hohenberger)

The schools are administered by a five-member School Board and an appointed superintendent. Funds for schools come from county property taxes, and a small amount of federal money. The state contributes the largest portion of school costs.

During the last few years Brown County schools have greatly improved.

In 1990 there are four townships in the county- Washington, Van Buren, Jackson, and Hamblen. In 1965 the people of Johnson township petitioned the county commissioners to "abandon" the township. Brown County State Park, the Hoosier National Forest, and Monroe Reservoir had absorbed a great part of Johnson Township, and relatively few people remained in the area. On January 1, 1966 the Board of Commissioners voted to divide what was left of the smallest township in the county between Washington and Van Buren Townships.

The four remaining townships each have an elected trustee. The trustees grant relief to those in need, or turn them over to the County Welfare program. They assess all real and personal property in their townships and administer the dog-tax fund. An Advisory Board of three members in each township reviews and adopts the trustee's annual budget, sets the tax rates, and levies the township taxes.

Brown County has always had difficulty financing its government. When the county was formed in 1836 pioneers had very little money. The new county government hoped that the sale of Nashville lots would furnish revenue. Financial difficulty occurred when the lots sold much more slowly than was expected.[41]

In the 1930s when half of the population had abandoned their land the county government was in a critical financial bind. Purdue University sent Harry Kohlmeyer to help raise the financial status at the courthouse. Mr. Kohlmeyer spent two years canvassing the County's tax delinquent land. When no owner could be found, the land was sold for taxes. The land was back on the tax rolls. More money began to arrive at the Courthouse. The financial situation was eased.[42]

In the 1980s Brown County continued to have trouble financing its government because less than half of the county's 205,160 acres are fully taxable. The Hoosier National Forest, Yellowwood State Forest, Monroe Reservoir, Brown County State Park, the T.C. Steele Memorial, and land owned by non-profit organizations or listed as classified forest have removed 110,142 acres from county taxation. Only 95,018 acres are taxable.

The records of the last two years provide a welcome change. Brown County has been able to pay all its bills without borrowing money. Township Trustees have discovered untaxed land in their bailiwicks. The land has been assessed and placed on the tax rolls. This has increased county income.

The elected officials of the county are the Clerk of the Circuit Court (County Clerk), the Auditor, Recorder, Treasurer, Sheriff, Coroner, Surveyor, Judge of the Circuit Court, Prosecuting Attorney, County Assessor, three County Commissioners and seven County Councilmen.

The Commissioners are responsible for directing all county concerns. The County Council manages the county funds.

County revenue comes from the state, a small amount of federal money, and Brown County property and income taxes. This finances county highway repair, the Sheriff and the county jail, the Circuit Court, schools, and the county administration.

There is a county Welfare Board and a Health Board. A Plan Commission issues new building permits and considers the advisability of subdivisions. Brown Countians apply to the Board of Zoning Appeals when dissatisfied with a Plan Commission Decision.

One of the unsolved Brown County problems is the fact that there are people in the valleys and hollows living in quiet desperation because of poverty. Landlords rent these people housing without the basic necessities of indoor running water and plumbing or electricity. Heat must come from a wood stove.

Brown County needs a housing code to force landlords to provide basic necessities.[43]

In 1990 twenty churches of sixteen denominations are listed in the Brown County Democrat.

Brown Countians are employed in the state park and state forest, in various jobs in the county and Nashville, but the majority of non-retired people commute daily to work in Columbus, Bloomington, Indianapolis, or other towns.

As stated at the beginning of this chapter, in 1900 Brown County was known as the poorest, the most backward, and isolated county in the state.

What a tremendous and remarkable change has occurred from 1900 to 1990!

Brown County has become one of the major recreation and retirement areas in the state, and it is a fact that Brown County is now Indiana's best known county, and most universally known county in other states.

Jefferson Street in 1930.

Brown County 1900 - 1990
Bibliography

[1] Hohenberger, Frank M., Journal p. 300.
[2] Mathis, Ray, Brown County History, pp. 73-76.
[3] Brown County Democrat, March 7, 1913.
[4] Hohenberger, Frank M., Op. cit., p.446. Indianapolis Star, February 19, 1927.
King, Fred, Oral History, November 1990.
[5] Miscellaneous Book IV, Recorder's Office, p. 337.
Sluss, Irene Ping. Otto and Clara Ping as Canners, 1990.
Crouch, Norma, Letter, 1990.
[6] Miscellaneous Book IV, p. 377.
[7] Hicks, Beatrice Prince Memories of Childhood, Sprunica.
Brown, Ruby Alice Prince, Helmsburg 1917, 1918.
Miscellaneous Book III , p. 546, January 22, 1917.
[8] Douglass, Benjamin Wallace, The New Deal Comes to Brown County, Doubleday Doran and Co. Inc., 1936.
[9] Mathis, Ray, Op. cit., p. 90.
[10] Brown County Democrat, January 8, 1986.
[11] Indianapolis News February 27, 1932.
[12] Herald Telephone Bloomington, September 13,1988.
Hohenberger, Frank M., Down in the Hills O' Brown County (History Booklet) p. 23, 1952.
[13] Indianapolis Star, April 5, 1981.
Mathis, Ray, Op. cit., pp. 96-98.
[14] Brown County Democrat, January 30, 1991.
[15] Brown County Democrat, November 23, 1967.
[16] Burkholder, Ralph, A History of Brown County Masonry, 1962, p. 21.
[17] Mathis, Ray, Op. cit., p. 76.
[18] Burkholder, Ralph, Op. cit., p. 21.
[19] League of Women Voters This is Brown County, p. 46.
[20] Miller, Maurice, Oral History, October, 1990.
[21] Mathis, Ray, Op. cit., pp. 95, 96.
[22] United States Bureau of Agricultural Economics, The Bean Blossom Land Utilization Project, 1935, pp. 1-5.
Mathis, Ray, Op. cit., pp. 92-95.
[23] Mathis, Ray, Op. cit., p. 102.
[24] Himes, Robert M., County Extension Work, 1990.
[25] Miller, William. Soil Conservation Service, 1990.
[26] Cline, Dorothea, The United States Agricultural Stabilization and Conservation Service, Brown County Democrat, January 11, 1981.
[27] Brown County Remembers 1986, Martha Synder Weddle, p. 283.
[28] Public Relations Department, Bloomington, Indiana, March, 1991.
[29] Indiana Rural Electric Cooperatives Fifty Years of Rural Electrification 1935-1985.
Hoosier Life, Brown County Farm Bureau, Winter, 1988/1989.
[30] Nagley, Lester C., Sr., Brown County Vignettes, Brown County Democrat, May 24,1962.
[31] League of Women Voters This is Brown County, p. 44.
[32] Hoosier National Forest - Oral History, William Miller.
[33] Brown County Democrat, September 20, 1989, March 7, 1990, February 7, 1990.
League of Women Voters, Op. cit., p.53.
[34] Cordry-Sweetwater Conservancy District Governing Board November, 1990.
[35] Brown County Remembers, Ruth Tilton pp. 235, 236.
[36] King, Fred, Oral History - March, 1991.
[37] Nagley, Lester C., Sr., Brown County Vignettes, July 23, 1964.
[38] Bainter, Juanita, Oral History, March, 1991.
[39] Brown County Almanack, 1990, p. 19.
[40] Brown County Democrat, September 5, 1990.
[41] Goodspeed, Weston A., History of Brown County 1884, pp. 699-700.
[42] Himes, Robert M., County Extension Work.
[43] Bainter, Juanita, Oral History, March 1991.

Rustic Inn of Joshua Bond on East Main in the fall of 1927.

Tourists beginning to arrive on West Main Street in the fall of 1927. (Photo by Frank Hohenberger)

Brown County Churches

Unity Baptist (1845-1990). Oldest active Brown County Church, Spearsville Road, Hamblen Township. The picture shows a gathering for a business meeting about 1895. 5th from left - Sarah Parsley (grandmother of Ralph Parsley), 6th from left - Columbus Parsley who was the church clerk for many years(grandfather of Ralph Parsley), 7th from left - Elsie Parsley (Ralph Parsley's aunt) Boy in middle front - Otto Parsley (Ralph's father), 7th from right - Mac Tracy, 8th from right - Cindy Long Flint, 10th from right with hat - Della Tracy (wife of Mac).

Bear Creek Church and Cemetery

Mrs. Likins moved from Indianapolis to Bear Creek in Jackson Township around 1911. She talked to the people in the community about starting church (1915). Tyner Myers said they could clear land and hold services on his property. Milt Richards donated lumber from his sawmill for seats. Later they held a meeting at the cemetery and talked about building a church. Milt Richards said "If you will build the church next to the cemetery, I will donate $50.00 worth of material, labor and money." Wilbur Mann said he would help, and everyone agreed.

Hannah Fritch Richards donated land for the church. Logs were donated by the community and cut into lumber at Milt's sawmill.

Milton Richards, Willis Richards, Frank Fritch, Wilbur Mann, Jim Russ, Sam Fleener and many others built the church. Benjamin Douglas, owner of Hickory Hill Orchard, donated the bell.

The congregation held a pound party, everyone attending brought a pound of nails. Naomi Bruce held a party for the young people. The girls brought dressed chickens and the boys dressed rabbits. Naomi sold the chickens and rabbits at Indianapolis, buying a heating stove for the church.

A funeral was held for Frank Fritch's sister, Savannah Thacker, before the church was completed. They carried in boards to sit on.

The church was dedicated September 25, 1917. The first minister was Henry Griffin, from Bloomington. He belonged to the Church of Christ and preached from 7 P.M. until midnight. Mabel Logston said you could hear him for miles and he scared Helen Richards so bad, Mabel had to take her outside.

The first trustees were Lelander Weddle, Frank Fritch, and Melt Richards.

The first organ was donated by Milt Richards. He had it shipped from Indianapolis by train to Trevlac.

Around 1949, Dudley R. Gallahue paid for a new roof and small chair for the Sunday School.

In 1978, David Weddle and Joe Rotino donated paint. Ray Fleener donated paint, brushes and ladders. Joe, Rick and Kevin Rotino, Marilyn Rotino, David, Walter, and Greg Weddle and Jay Logston painted the church.

From the early 1800 until early 1900 it was known as Tomey Cemetery. The first recorded grave was Thomas William Weddle (August 20, 1838).

The cemetery was taken care of by the community until late 1962.

On September 2, 1962, Ray Fleener, Roy McGuire, Leonard Zink, Arthur Fritch, and Orval Russ met to lay plans to set up a permanent fund for the care of the Bear Creek Cemetery.

October 21, 1962, at a called meeting, with 44 people present, it was decided that a corporation would be formed and filed at the Secretary of State Office. All moneys would be from contribution only, and that money from interest, only would be used for the upkeep and expenses of the cemetery. Mr. Grafton Kivett, an attorney at Martinsville, donated all his time in helping to set up and prepare for the filing.

The first Board of Directors was elected and filed. Chairman, Arthur Fritch, Vice Chairman, Leonard Zink, and Clarence Weddle. Jean McGuire Pieper, Secretary and Ruth Weddle Cody, Treasurer.

In 1970 a flag pole was set. Donations were from Fern and Rex Tutterrow, Mr. and Mrs. Ray Fleener, Mr. and Mrs. Orval Russ, Mr. and Mrs. Ernest Voorheis, and Mr. and Mrs. Clarence Chitwood.

Spring, 1980, a stone with the name, was erected at the entrance to the Bear Creek Church and Cemetery, donated by Mr. and Mrs. David Weddle and family and Mr. and Mrs. Joe Rotino and family.

Fall of 1988, Mr. and Mrs. Robert P. Richards built a picnic table to replace the old one. There has been a table present for those bringing a lunch basket for family reunions, to visit the cemetery, etc. for at least 75 years.

The present trustees of the cemetery are Lester McGuire, Robert P. Richards, and Joe Rotino; Jean Pieper, Secretary and Ruth Cody, Treasurer.

One Saturday in May is for clean-up for Memorial Day. The second Saturday in June is an annual meeting to elect officers.

Although the church building exterior still has a good appearance the interior has deteriorated and no services have been held there since the early 1970s. *Submitted by Phyllis Rotino and Harrietta Weddle*

Christiansburg United Methodist Church

The constitution of the Christiansburg Methodist Church now known as United Methodist was adopted on June 8, 1866 according to record books that still remain in the church. A Certificate of Membership shows William Franklin was taken in as a member October 30, 1866 by T.L. Brooks, Preacher in charge from the Houston Circuit, Indiana Conference.

John Parker came to Brown County, Van Buren Township from Ohio and since they were Christians it was called Christiansburg.

It is assumed this is the second church building. The land where the present church stands was deeded on June 7, 1887 to the church by Henry and Mahalia Wilson for $10.00.

John E. Bruce helped build the present church in 1880. At one time the Church had unfinished wood floors. A wood stove was in the center of the church. Kerosene lights hung from the ceiling. Electricity replaced the kerosene lights in 1949-50. A natural wood pine floor replaced the old floor in 1958. A gas furnace was installed. A vestibule was added in 1961-62 and concrete steps replaced the native rock step.

In 1976 a new addition to the Church including two rest rooms, two classrooms and a kitchen. In 1986 the Sanctuary and vestibule were carpeted and a new piano replaced the 50 year-old piano, which still remains in the Church.

In 1989 a new roof and belfry and steeple were redone. The bell still remains and can be heard every Sunday morning. It is a landmark church in the Valley on Christiansburg Road.

Ministers of the Christiansburg United Methodist Church

Year	Name	Year	Name
1876	Rev. A.T. Bright	1944	Rev. Galberth and Jewell
1892	Rev. Sterutt	1945	Rev. Galberth
1901	Rev. Barrett	1946	Rev. Galberth and Jewell
1903	Rev. Griffith	1947-1948	No record found
1904	Rev. Bolten	1949-1951	Rev. Austin
1908	Rev. Muchlon	1952-1953	Rev. James McCallie
1914	Rev. Jones, Rust, Schwartz	1954	Rev. Jarbo
1915	Rev. Embry	1955	Rev. Mark Beamer
1916	Rev. Bless	1956	Rev. John Roberts
1920	Rev. Proctor	1957	Rev. Robert Allred
1922	Rev. Grubbs	1958	Rev. Harry Allemang
1922-1925	Rev. Vennis Brown	1959	Rev. Samuel P. Worthington
1925	Rev. Chester Plummer	1960	Rev. William Ghering
1926-1928	No record found	1961-1962	Rev. John Rowe
1930	Rev. Adkinson (student)	1962 (Sept.)-1965	Rev. William Culbreth
1931-1932	Rev. Moreillon	1965-1970	Rev. Roy Huntsman
	Bro. Dale (Evangelist)	1970-1980	Rev. Kenneth Kritzer
1933	No record found	June 1980-1983	Rev. Hurshel Joslin
1934	Rev. Chester Plummer	1983-1987	Rev. Larry Stoops
1935-1937	No record found	1987-1989	Rev. Lester Ellis
1938	Rev. Galberth and Moreillon	1989-1990	Rev. Charles Todd
1939-1940	Rev. Galberth	Aug. 12, 1990	Rev. Mark Holmes
1941	Rev. Galberth and Jewell		
1942	Rev. Jewell		
1943	Rev. Galberth		

Rev. Morton Carmichael filled the pulpit in 1924-1925 when the regular minister was absent.

Cottonwood Christian Church

The Cottonwood Church is located about two miles north of Helmsburg on Lick Creek Road. At one time the Cottonwood neighborhood was known as the little town of Cornelius and was shown on the state map in 1920. Leo P. Richards spent several years gathering the history of the church from some of the "old timers" such as his grandfather, Elijah Long, Mr. Rittenhouse, John Hughes and others.

About the time of the Civil War or before, the Evangelist preachers of the Church of Christ began working in Brown County. As a result, school houses and even private homes were turned into places of worship.

The earliest services having a direct connection with the Cottonwood Church were held in the home of Christopher Stump. This place is located about 1/4 mile east of Helmsburg on SR 45. The meetings held at the Stump home were of a varied type ranging from a single meeting up to two or three days. At such meetings people came in wagons, on foot and horseback, bringing food and bedding along. The other necessities being furnished by Mr. Stump and his family.

Some time later two school houses were built, the "Long" and the "Ritter." The church class was divided and these school houses were used as places of worship. A preacher was hired by both places, the Rev. Wertz being one of these men.

In 1892 both churches joined together and agreed on the place for the erection of a church between the Long and Ritter school houses. The tract of land was received from the farm of William J. Long. The church house was built in 1892 and dedicated October 4, 1898 by Rev. Boles. It was named "Cottonwood" in honor of a large Cottonwood tree which stood near the road northeast of the building. This tree died and was cut down near 1910. The stump measured about five feet in diameter.

The church was originally heated by two wood stoves and oil lamps furnished the light. The original pews are still being used. Each Sunday a hand pulled bell is rung and the echos can be heard up and down the valley. A fellowship hall was added to the church in 1965. Then in 1983 restrooms, an office and Sunday School room were added. In the summer of 1969 the church members built a three-room parsonage. Two rooms and a bath were added in 1973. Today there is a new two-story parsonage to accommodate the Darrell Miller family, who have been ministering at Cottonwood since 1981.

The namesake of the church has been restored. In the spring of 1974, Rev. William Henry Hodge planted a Cottonwood tree in the back of the church. Although the tree gives meaning to the name of the church, the true identity of the church is found in the hearts of the members as Christ lives in them.

Harmony Baptist Church New Bellsville

Harmony Baptist Church of New Bellsville, IN was constituted on Saturday April 23, 1850 according to records copied from old books on March 22, 1890. At the same time new officers were elected and their duties restated. Trustees were: Robert Henderson, Frederick Froh and Hancher Campbell. Deacons were: Robert Henderson, Holden Cooper, David Ping and Cyrus Bartholomew. Benjamin Clark was Treasurer, J.T. Ping was Clerk and John Eddy was the Sexton. By Mar. 22, 1890 the church had served a total of 453 members. The membership at that time was 117; 45 had deceased, 120 were dismissed by letters (meaning that they had moved in good standing) and 171 had been excluded or dropped from membership. Most of those dropped had joined another church and the ones excluded had been guilty of immoral conduct, intoxication, dancing, profanity, selling intoxicating liquor, absence, etc.

The earliest record of the Sunday School at Harmony is dated Mar. 23, 1890 when it was reorganized with the following officers: Superintendent - Hancher Campbell, Assistant Superintendent - A. Hancher, Secretary - E.G. Ping, Assistant Secretary - Watson Carmichael, Treasurer - Ben Clark.

Today, March 22, 1990, there are 221 members. The trustees are: Darrel Kent, David Crabtree and James Butler. The Deacons are Max Henderson, Moderator, Plessie Hamblen, Richard Barkes, James Pruitt, Marvin Gorbett, Kevin Ault, Ben Harris and Kenneth Spath. Patricia Gorbett is the Treasurer and Karen Burgan is the Clerk. The Sexton is Ethel Stolle.

The current Sunday School Officers are as follows:

Superintendent - James Butler, Assistant Superintendent - Kenneth Spath, Secretary - Lou Ann Butler, Assistant Secretary - Mary Lou Barkes.

Since 1952 there have been two additions to the main building, the acquisition of additional acreage, the erection of a shelter house and the construction of softball and basketball courts. Harmony does not have a cemetery but is located adjacent to the New Bellsville Cemetery which is operated by the New Bellsville Cemetery Association with Lou Ann Butler of Columbus as Secretary/Treasurer.

Pastors for Harmony Baptist Church:

Richard W. Stolle	1968 - present
John David McGee	1966 - 1968
Robert Patrick	1962 - 1966
Richard Sutton	1960 - 1962
James W. Hendricks	1932 - 1960

Others who may have served as pastor and approximate dates were:

Francis H. Allbritten	1920s
Thomas L. Bush	1920s
Mayonord or Manard	1901 -
Pressley	July, 1900 -
Gates	1900 -
Alex Hancher	1899 -
W. Manard	1896 -

Mt. Zion Church and Cemetery

The earliest burial listed for Mt. Zion Cemetery in the book **Brown County, Indiana Cemeteries** by Helen and Kenneth Reeve is Sary (Sarah Allen) Matney, wife of Clement Matney. She d. 1834 and he d. 1838. A total of 566 burials were identified with 124 family names represented. Those with the most numerous burials are Brown (32), Ayers (29), Hurley (27), Hedrick (19), Moore and Skinner (16ea.), Reed (14), Freese, Noblit, Bradley, and Shepherd (13ea.), Williamson (12), Deaver (11), and Tipton and Whitehorn with (10) each.

The earliest land transaction occurred in 1868 when the Trustees of the Christian Church of the New Light Order, William Roush, James Williamson and William Tipton, purchased 130 sq. rds. of land from Jonathan and Catherine McKain for $10. A log church was first built and in 1876 a frame church was built. This building was still being used for funerals in the 1930s, but became unsafe and was removed in 1986. Trustees of the Mt. Zion Christian Church from 1898 to 1935 were James Reed, Sr. (d. 1914), David P. Noblitt and Winfield Noblitt. 1935 court records show also that William Reed, Samuel Anthony and James Brown were Trustees and others followed even though the Church was inactive. A shelter has been constructed where the church stood.

Other families involved in the sale or gift of land to make up the present cemetery were Newmister, Hurley, Ralphy and Deaver.

On March 19, 1936, L.J. Deaver and Elizabeth Deaver his wife Released and Quit Claimed the southern portion of the cemetery which lies in Sec. 22.

On October 10, 1975, Bob Allen, Brown Co. Surveyor, surveyed the portion of Mt. Zion Cemetery that lies in Sec. 15. This survey includes all land in Sec. 15 between S.R. 135 and the old road on the East side of the cemetery.

Until 1973 the Mt. Zion Cemetery was "looked after" by various interested parties. Cloyd Anthony, son of George Anthony, recalls "— that neighbors volunteered to help clean the cemetery at least once every year—always in late May, just prior to Memorial Day. Each family cared for the graves of their own family. Then most folk would help cut weeds etc. in areas where no one accepted responsibility. — I have seen as many as 20 people working the same day."

In 1973, Maxine Ayers Melton, as president of the Mt. Zion Cemetery Association, with the assistance of Warren Ogle, filed Articles of Incorporation with the Secretary of State. Other officers listed were G. Scott Ayers, Vice President and Esther Settle, Secretary/Treasurer. In addition to the officers, Rex Bond and Lawrence Strahl also served as Directors.

The current officers are Maxine Melton, President, Plessie Hamblen, Vice President, John W. Hamblen, Secretary, Esther Settle, Treasurer, and Bob Settle, Sexton. Other recent active members include Lawrence Strahl, Jim Wilkerson, Marge Craver, Lenore Ayers, Ollie Kritzer, Thelma Carmichael, Tressa Ayers, Burnell Hedrick, Virgil Hedrick and Dale Strahl.

Association policy is not to charge for burial lots but to encourage those who want lots to contribute to the Perpetual Care Fund. In 1989, 43 new lots were staked out in the front part of the cemetery.

Nashville Christian Church

The Christian Church universal had its beginning on the day of Pentecost when Peter preached the first gospel message. The Nashville Christian Church was formally organized April 9, 1888, although a group of Christian Church or Church of Christ members had been meeting in various places prior to this date. The organizational meeting was held at the Green Valley schoolhouse, a one-room school located about one mile southwest of Nashville. John F. Genolin was elected President and Charles C. Hopper, Clerk. The following men were elected Trustees: William Winchester, Samuel McClary and George W. Cornelius. All were Nashville residents except Mr. McClary who owned a farm nearby.

The congregation consisted of individuals who desired to worship God in a simple and sincere New Testament way. They believed, as we do now, that the true Bible is the divinely inspired word of God and is the final authority in doctrinal matters and daily living.

In believing that Jesus Christ is the son of the living God means that we believe in His virgin birth; His sinless life; His Miracles; His death, burial and resurrection; His Ascension to God the Father. Jesus Christ is the head of the Church and every congregation is directly responsible to Him and to no one else. While there may be differences of opinion or interpretation, the Bible is so plain that the essentials for Christian living, worship and salvation cannot be misunderstood when read with a true Christian spirit.

The congregation is led by the Elders and assisted by the Deacons, all elected by the congregation. The minister is called by the Elders with the approval of the Deacons and the congregation. The minister leads and teaches the congregation on spiritual matters and shows by precept and example the principles of Christianity.

The first church building was erected in 1888 and the frontispiece sign read, "Nashville Christian Church", and it has been known by that name only. It is the oldest continuing church organization in Brown County at the same location.

This building was used until 1926 when it was moved back from the street and a partial basement and a furnace were added. This re-modeled building was re-dedicated December 12, 1926, and on October 9, 1931 it was destroyed by fire thought to be caused by a defective flue.

Plans were immediately made to rebuild and on Sunday morning November 1, 1931, 89 members met at the Nashville High School across the street, all eager to sign pledges for a new building. With the insurance coverage and the pledges already made, a new church house was assured. The congregation continued to meet at the High School for a while but then moved into the Melodeon Hall, a vacated motion picture house.

Mr. A.A. Honeywell of Wabash, Indiana, was selected as the architect and he designed a building of the Christopher Wren type, which would be the only one west of the Appalachian Mountains at that time. Christopher Wren (1662-1723) was an English architect who had designed 52 churches in London alone. Mr. William T. Abraham of Seymour, Indiana, was the building contractor.

The new church building was dedicated November 13, 1932, and with matching funds from the Irwin-Miller-Sweeney Foundation of Columbus, Indiana, it was debt free. This Foundation, which had helped several area Christian Churches financially, continued to help us for several more years. This aid very definitely promoted this congregation to a good start and helped it establish a solid program which it now has.

In June 1956 a new parsonage was built just north of the church on land donated by the T.D. Calvin family. In 1960 the lot adjoining the church on the south was purchased to be used for parking. In 1982 a new parsonage was purchased in the Parkview Addition of Nashville and the old parsonage converted to offices and class rooms.

In 1962 an addition to the church had been made adding class rooms, kitchen and dining hall as well as rest rooms and a baptistry. In 1988, the 100th anniversary of the founding of the congregation, the entire interior of the church and the annex were completely renovated. New pews and full carpeting were added to the church as well as a new organ and piano. A wheel chair lift was also installed.

Since the very beginning of this congregation these phrases continue to express its position: "In matters of faith, unity; in matters of opinion, liberty; and in all things, love."

Nashville United Methodist Church

It was fifty-three years after the beginning of the Methodist Church in America that Methodism came to Brown County. In the year 1837, Eli P. Farmer was sent to the "Brown Mission," as it was then called, by the Indiana Conference to organize the first class of Methodists in the community of Nashville.

The first church building, a crude log structure, was built in the northwest section of the village on property donated by William Gould. It served as a house of worship for the early congregation until 1848 when a second church building was constructed on a lot across the street and just to the east of where the log structure stood. It was to worship in this building that Mr. Gould, who lived next door to the church and served as its janitor, would summon the Methodists to worship by the use of a long tin horn which could be heard to the far reaches of the village.

The second meeting house served more than one purpose. For two years during the 1850s, while a new Brown County Courthouse was being built, sessions of the County Court were held in the church building. At times, it was also used as a meeting place by Baptist, Christian and United Brethren congregations; but this arrangement did not please all Methodists. A trustee known as Squire Dow used to take possession of the door key when these "outsiders" were due to meet. The squire's wife, however, usually managed to slip the key from his pocket. Failing that, she saw that someone climbed through a window and unlatched the door from the inside.

A few years later, a more serious disagreement than this divided the little congregation. Here as elsewhere in the country, people who had been friends for years were bitterly divided by their convictions about slavery and secession. In 1860, the church split into "northern and southern Methodists." For eighteen years after that, groups met in private homes for worship services. During these years, the church building was sold to George Allison who moved it across the street and used it as a print shop.

In 1878, however, wounds were beginning to heal, and a Methodist Church South was organized in Nashville under the leadership of the Reverends Branstutter and Hunter. Late that year, a new church building was constructed on the site of the former building; and still later, the structure was moved to the corner of Jefferson and Gould Streets where it served the congregation for almost fifty years.

Meanwhile, in 1875, a Presbyterian congregation was organized in Nashville. This congregation built a church at Jefferson and Main Streets, but that building was lost in the great fire of 1909 which completely destroyed several buildings in the vicinity. The following year, a new church building was constructed on the same site.

In 1926, an exchange of properties was arranged between the Methodist Episcopal and Presbyterian churches. A Methodist Episcopal building in Boggstown, Indiana, was exchanged for the Nashville Presbyterian property. In November, 1927, the Nashville Methodist Episcopal congregation moved into the present building after some remodeling which included the digging of a new basement and installation of a furnace.

As Nashville and Brown County grew and the area became known as a mecca for artists, craftsmen and tourists, the church grew. In 1963, it was necessary to add the Education Building with its Fellowship Hall. It was dedicated in 1964. Ten years later, the sanctuary of the church was remodeled. In 1977, a further remodeling project provided a new church office and pastor's study in a space previously unused between the main church building and the educational unit, and included the renovation of the educational unit to allow for additional classroom space.

In 1968, the Methodist Churches and the Evangelical United Brethren Churches of the United States merged. The denomination is now known as the United Methodist Church; and from that date on, the official name of the congregation became the Nashville United Methodist Church.

The church endeavors to program and provide spiritual enrichment for the diversity of age groups, lifestyles and backgrounds which make up the church community. It functions as a good citizen in the community providing a meeting place for many community groups. It has an active Parents' Day Out program and helps to sponsor a Pre-School Kindergarten. Scouting programs for all ages of youth are a part of the total outreach.

A history of the church would be incomplete without a mention of FALLFARE which is held each year at the church and next door under gaily-decorated tents on the Village Green. Starting as a bazaar in October, 1972, it has grown in size each year until now many tourists plan their annual fall visit to Brown County to coincide with FALLFARE.

The church in this last decade of the twentieth century looks forward to the future. As it goes about carrying out the mission of the Lord, it seeks to prepare for the challenges of the twenty-first century.

Pleasant Valley Community Church

Sometime in the mid 1800s a group of people had a dream, to build a church with a steeple and bell. The congregation surely was only "hill folk" since Brown County then was not the tourist attraction it now is. One can only speculate upon the sacrifices that this beginning must have been for the people! Ground to buy, trees to fall, logs to haul to the saw mill, a bell to have cast, plus all the manual labor that it took after the raw materials were available. People with a dream to help other people, a church to call their own, a place where neighbors could meet and get the latest news, a place where "God's word" was to be taught and preached, a simple country church located in the hills of Brown County with a simple name, **Pleasant Valley**.

The earliest date that has been found in the old records is August 18th, 1867, when the membership entered into the Separate Baptist Church in Christ by an organizational letter, signed by Elder Joshua McQueen and Deacon Thomas Cline. Later a copy of minutes in Elmer Smith's Bible found in Mohawk, New York dated September, 1884 when they joined the Separate Baptists Indiana Central Association.

A dream continued to grow as did the membership listing 147 members as of May 18, 1913. Names that had their very roots and final resting places in the hills of Brown County. Were their dreams laid to rest with them? Do dreams ever die? As one walks among the named and nameless graves located upon the hill above the church and wonder what part they played in the history of the church and then look down and still see the steeple we know that their dream hasn't died, only passed from generation to generation! Many of their names and lives are still attached to the church in this present generation by relatives and friends.

Life continued for Pleasant Valley with many other ministers pastoring the church with a wide diversities of styles. Many of the "ol' timers" referred to the church as the "Old Clarks Church" because of the Clark school house that was next to it. Stories of humor also had their place in the church. One of the present members remembers when he was just a young lad the older boys decided to take one of the mules that was tied out back and stick his head through a window. What a sight that must have been, to have a mule braying at the preacher; the whole service was stopped by the laughter. Roots, dreams, and a place where God's word was to be preached haven't died — only passed to the present.

The future looks bright for Pleasant Valley; the dreams of a beginning haven't been forgotten or the labor that was toiled for the present. There has been some "rough ground to hoe" and all hasn't been easy sailing, but within the last few years a new interest of that dream has begun to grow in the hearts of the membership at Pleasant Valley Church.

In the late 1980s, after much prayer and concern, the membership decided to withdraw from the Separate Baptist Association and form as a community church of a nondenominational nature. Still holding to the word of God as the final authority for salvation and life. The old building was repaired as much as could be and new Sunday School rooms were built and at the present a dream of a new structure is in the working. New growth, a new generation, with their roots connected to the names and lives of the ones that started a beginning so long ago have only begun for the generations to come, still having the desire that the "word of God will be preached with such conviction that man will know that **he 'must be born again'**."

Our present pastor, Rev. John Cave and deacon, Clifton Bryant, along with all the members continue to share that dream started so long, long ago to keep alive a simple country church nestled in the hills of Brown County called **Pleasant Valley Community Church**. The original bell is still being rung as it has been for so many years, calling our neighbors and friends to come and share this dream with us each Sunday!

Pleasant Valley Community Church located on State Road #46, halfway between Nashville and Gnawbone, Indiana.

Shepherd of the Hills Lutheran Church 1966 - 1989

Shepherd of the Hills Lutheran Church 1990

SHEPHERD OF THE HILLS EVANGELICAL LUTHERAN CHURCH
- MISSOURI SYNOD -

Shepherd of the Hills Lutheran Church became the first formal attempt of Lutherans to begin a congregation in Brown County. Around the turn of the century, some outreach had been done in the far southeastern part of the county by the pastor of St. Peter, Waymansville. These efforts were not successful at the time. Further formal efforts by Lutherans were not started until 1964. Under the able leadership and counsel of Rev. Richard Tremain, Faith Lutheran Church, Columbus, and Rev. Kenneth Streufert, Faith Lutheran Church, Bloomington, it was decided that such a venture was definitely possible. The first service was held July 12, 1964, at the Episcopal Mission in Bean Blossom with the Rev. Wilbur Koenig, St. Paul's Lutheran Church, Indianapolis, as guest speaker. Rev. Streufert and Rev. Tremain served the Mission Church as interim pastors for the next year.

The first church home of Shepherd of the Hills was located one mile north of Nashville on Highway 135. Nestled among the trees of Brown County, Shepherd of the Hills portrayed very well the natural setting of the community! Sharing the Good News of Jesus Christ, to member and visitor alike, was and is the joy and purpose of this Lutheran ministry.

The property was purchased in June of 1965. With John Ackerman as general contractor, and volunteer help from members of the congregation, the building on the property was remodeled to make it suitable as a church home with the first worship service held on December 18, 1966.

On August 29, 1965, Rev. Daniel C. Bell was installed as the Mission's first called pastor.

The congregation was formally chartered on January 23, 1966. Charter members included: John and Beulah Ackerman and children, John David, Joseph, Timothy and James; Patricia Bell; Richard and Linda Downey and children, Lesa, Mark and Patrick; Boyd and Irma Helstrom and son, Joseph; Curt and Mary Holstein and sons, Bruce, Gary and James; Olive Dollinger Matthews; Vivian Miller and daughter, Maria; Martin and Beverly Saari and daughter, Jelene; Melusina Seehausen; Clarence and Marie Smith; Art and Dorothy Smith and sons, Ronald and Steven; Luther and Barbara Smith and children, Andrea, Kristy and Luther, Jr.; Elsie Snider; Richard and Sandy Stump and children, Gary and Roseann; and Ewald and Willow B. Wolff. Paul Seehausen was very active in the start of the congregation but was called home before Charter Sunday. Marjory Klusmeier was also very active in those early stages.

The dedication of the church was May 21, 1967 and had grown to a communicant membership of forty-one.

Several vacancy pastors have served over the years. The congregation has been served full time by Rev. Wayne Wilke, installed July 14, 1974, Rev. Hilmar Roschke, installed September 14, 1975 and lay minister Loren Cooper, installed August 17, 1977, ordained May 6, 1990, and currently serving as pastor in 1990.

Bruce Holstein, son of the congregation, was ordained in the former church home on June 30, 1974.

In the mid 1980s a building addition was discussed as a possibility to enhance the program and ministry of the church. In 1988 the opportunity arose to sell the first church home and build a new church home in a new location. The last worship service was held on Ash Wednesday, 1989, and for the next full year the congregation met in the Historical Society building on Highway 135 north of Nashville.

The new church home of Shepherd of the Hills, located one-half mile north of Bean Blossom, was built by the congregation and dedicated on June 17, 1990. Portions of the project were sublet, three retired men were hired to work on the project, and the balance of the work was done on a volunteer basis by members of the congregation. The stained glass windows, eight side windows and one 15' x 14' altar window, were designed and made by member Robert Cockrum, Martinsville. The spirit on the project was a joy for all and was gladly done to the glory of God! The first worship service in the new church home was held on Ash Wednesday, 1990.

1990 congregational officers include: Bill Krieg, chairman; Jeff Hawkins, vice-chairman; Judy Arndt, recording secretary; June Wohler, financial secretary; Barbara Bock and Kathy Roth, treasurer; Brad Baughman, Clayton Cooper, Peter Flokowitsch, Jim Roth, Don Schroeder and Jay Snider, elders; and Klaus Arndt, Paul Arndt, David Hendershot, Curt Holstein, Phyllis Keener, Bruce Koehl, Christian Miller and Amber Powell, trustees.

The congregation has grown to 251 baptized souls, and with the new worship and education center that God has given them, the members look forward to a meaningful and effective Lutheran ministry in Brown County in the future.

St. Agnes Chapel

In 1940 Mr. and Mrs. Joseph M. Nurre of Bloomington, Indiana, wishing to memorialize their gratitude to God for having blessed them with children, approached Bishop Ritter (later Joseph Cardinal Ritter) with their desire to build a church.

Although the Nurre's expected to build in Bloomington, the town in which their happiness and prosperity had been realized, the Bishop suggested Brown County and his reason was twofold: a chapel along the highway into Nashville would be easily accessible to the increasing thousands of tourists; and a church was needed where Catholics were so few. In fact, at that time, Brown County boasted only six Catholic households.

The Bishop's foresight has become a reality. In fifty years the number has increased to over 250 registered families in the parish and the tourist attendance can only be surmised.

On Friday morning, October 11, 1940, Bishop Ritter solemnly dedicated the chapel, putting it under the protection of St. Agnes, Mrs. Nurre's patroness. The following Sunday, Father Francis Kull, first pastor to this mission, welcomed hundreds of visitors who came to admire Brown County's only Catholic Church.

In adhering to the traditional Brown County rusticity and by using only native materials, the Nurres and the Bishop, in collaboration with architect William Strain and contractors McDaniels and McDaniels, achieved a structure which is one of the county's most attractive landmarks. Placed into a background of big old trees, the chapel is almost a replica of the first log churches which bravely dotted the frontier.

When parish expansion called for growth, the hillside was utilized to advantage. In 1972, under the guidance of Father Vogelsang, a two-story annex was built to provide facilities for children's religious instruction and parish meetings, as well as an apartment for the pastor.

Continued growth called for a second phase of expansion which began in 1980 under the direction of Father Mark Svarczkopf. There was a need for a larger worship space and more adequate facilities. Thus a large room was attached to the west wall of the chapel and atop the two-story annex. The windows, skylight and glass doors opening into a deck on the west side make this a pleasant room for many different functions. The pitch of the ceiling follows the same line of the chapel. Large exposed beams and a pinewood ceiling carry through the rustic warmth of the entire structure. On some weekends the number of worshippers necessitates the use of this room for Mass.

On the southside an extension was added for kitchen and bathroom facilities. One story below, a parish meeting room was added and on the ground level an office and storage space.

Logs were also used for this annex and the entire structure was painted in a warm brown with white mortar that unites both old and new structures.

Likewise, during this last expansion, a Marian Shrine was erected on the hillside in back of the parish building. This was made possible through the generosity of one of the parish's many patrons. Wooden benches built into the hillside and a sound system have made this a lovely spot for meditation and reflection. This hillside is also used in the summer and fall months for celebrating the Liturgy when crowds become large. This last addition and the Marian Shrine were dedicated by Archbishop Edward T. O'Meara on August 15, 1982.

Growth in the number of parishioners and tourists continues. Yet the warm and intimate spirit of the people of Brown County gives to all who come the feeling of hospitality that has been such a part of the history of St. Agnes parish.

Priests who have served St. Agnes Parish

Rev. Francis Kull (1940-45)
Rev. Charles Sexton (1945-55)
Msgr. Thomas Kilfoil (1955-58)
Rev. Paul English
Rev. Kenneth Smith
Rev. Victor Wright (1958-63)
Rev. Joseph McCrisaken (1963-67)
Rev. James Dorety (1967-68)
Rev. Laurence Lynch (1968-69)
Rev. Clifford Vogelsang (1969-72)
Rev. Stanley Herber (1972-74)
Rev. Robert Scheidler (1974-77)
Rev. Robert Morhaus (1977-79)
Rev. Mark Svarczkopf (1979-81)
Rev. William Munshower (1981-85)
Rev. Clem Davis
Rev. Richard Mueller
Rev. Herman Lutz
Rev. Theo Mathias
Rev. David Coons
Rev. Paul Koetter (current)
Resident ministers
Sister Marsha Speth, S.P. (1979-86)
Sister Mildred Wannemuehler, OSB (current)

CHRISTIAN SCIENCE SOCIETY

The Christian Science Movement in Nashville began in 1914 by a Christian Science Practitioner with three couples in attendance. No Christian Science meetings were held in Nashville from 1927-1935.

In 1935 a new couple came to Nashville and invited those interested in Christian Science to meet in their home. Meetings were held in the homes of students from 1935-1939. At that time a room in the Bartley House was rented and services were held under the name of "Informal Christian Science Society."

In 1944 one of the members of the informal society offered a piece of ground just north of Nashville on State Road 135 as a building site for their church.

In October 1945 ten students, as charter members, formed Christian Science Society, Nashville, In. The Society was formally accepted as a branch of The Mother Church in a letter of December 1946.

The ground donated for the building was deeded to the Society on July 11, 1947. Ground was broken for the new edifice in December 1949. The structure was completed in eleven months and the first service was held in the church in November 1950.

The Society was incorporated under the laws of the State of Indiana on August 29, 1952. Dedication of the new building was held following the Sunday Service on October 24, 1954.

In August of 1978 the Society purchased the adjoining property to the north of the Society in order to expand the parking lot.

North Salem United Methodist Church ca. 1900

North Salem United Methodist Church 1990

NORTH SALEM UNITED METHODIST CHURCH

North Salem United Methodist Church, located on State Road 46, began in 1860 when the Methodist Episcopal Church acquired 2 to 3 acres for $20 from John and Christina Joslin. The first church was a crude log structure. The deed, given to the church trustees, John Solomon Dobbs, Israel Joslin, Thornton F. Bright and Rasmus Nelson, was dated September 27, 1860.

For the next 40 years this log structure, with its hand-carved seats and rough floor, invited the community to gather for worship and fellowship. By the turn of the century it had become too small. The second church, a frame structure, was constructed in 1900.

In 1923, the church bought the Green Valley Baptist Church (located 1 mile up Green Valley Road, now Hoover Road) and used the lumber to add a room and vestibule onto the church.

One of the great events for the churches in the community was an all-day picnic with singing and preaching. In 1926, North Salem would have their picnic in the church yard one month, and the next month they would go to Becks Grove and fellowship with them. Each family, bringing their own dinner, would gather in the grandstand to hear the ministers preach and enjoy a hymn sing.

The second church served the community for 80 years. In 1980, using mostly volunteer labor, it was replaced by the present church building.

For 130 years "the church by the side of the road," North Salem, has been a constant witness to the passerby of the power of a Living God.

Christian Science Society

Nashville Parkview Church of the Nazarene

PARKVIEW CHURCH OF THE NAZARENE

The Church of the Nazarene began in Nashville under the ministry of Mrs. Naomi Downs in 1949. At that time services were held in the Brown County Court House. Ground was purchased ($1,000) on the corner of Locust and Gould Streets. On this location missionaries Elton and Margaret Wood held a tent meeting.

The church was officially organized February 26, 1950 by District Superintendent Leo C. Davis with 17 charter members. The first building was erected in 1951 at a total cost of $2,500. Labor was donated by the members. Dr. Ralph Earle dedicated the building.

By 1964 the first building was doubled in size with a new sanctuary built and the former sanctuary converted into classrooms and a pastor's study. In 1971 a parsonage was purchased in Parkview Addition of Nashville. With an increase in church attendance and parking as a problem it became necessary to expand church facilities.

Land across from the north entrance to Brown County State Park was bought in 1984. Contractor Lee Waltman purchased the downtown property. A relocation committee then began to develop plans for the new church building, to be called Parkview Church of the Nazarene. Steven V. Miller was hired as architect. Ground breaking took place in September, 1985. Construction of the new building was given to Steven A. Miller with work beginning the same month.

The final service in the old church was on June 2, 1985. During the interim, meetings continued at the Seasons Convention Center, 4-H Building and Historical Society Building.

On Easter Sunday, 1986 the congregation met for the first time in the new Parkview Church with 193 people present. On June 1, 1986 a dedication service and open house was held. District Superintendent Dr. B.G. Wiggs brought the dedicatory message.

The Church of the Nazarene at Nashville celebrated its fortieth anniversary September 1, 1990 with a banquet at Abe Martin Lodge in Brown County State Park. General Superintendent Jerald Johnson was keynote speaker of the evening.

ST. DAVID'S EPISCOPAL CHURCH

In October of 1959 meetings were held at various homes for the purpose of establishing an Episcopal Mission in Brown County. In that original group were James, Marion, James, Jr., and Syd Mara, Lennis and Judith Baughman, Andy and Judith Rogers, Frederick and Jeannette Rigley, Elizabeth Percival, Dr. Robert and Betty Percival, Thomas and Roxenna King, Nellie Meyrick and John and Mary Lynn Williams. Guidance for the procedure was given by Father William Casady of Columbus.

In November the Diocese of Indianapolis granted permission to establish the mission and the old schoolhouse in Bean Blossom was selected as the place of worship. Regular Sunday services were conducted by lay readers. The first Communion service was celebrated on Christmas Day, 1959, with the Rev. R. Stewart Wood officiating.

In March of 1960 the schoolhouse was purchased. The Right Rev. John P. Craine conducted the first Confirmation class. In April the first parish meeting and election of the Bishop's committee was held. Then in July the Rev. R. Stewart Wood was appointed priest-in-charge and served the mission until August of 1963 when he was called to Grace Church in Muncie, Indiana. The Rev. William R. Detweiler was appointed Vicar the following month and served for a two year period.

The Rev. Ralph E. Dille began his service to the parish in 1965. It was in June of 1968 plans for a new church were approved by the Diocese and permission to proceed was granted. Ground breaking for the new church was in September with a parish decision to change the name to St. David's Episcopal Church. The first worship services were held in the new church on Good Friday of 1969. The dedication service was held on July 6, 1969.

The Rev. Dr. Harold E. Taylor has served St. David's since 1975 with the exception of a short interim in which the Reverends Sacksteder and Hall guided the parish. St. David's has contributed to the community in various ways and been actively involved in the Ecumenical movement of Brown County. In 1987 outreach took the form of End-of-the-Month free Saturday evening dinners for all who wish to share an evening of good food and fellowship. In 1988 the church school was reorganized and an adult education program was initiated. In addition St. David's is sponsoring Boy Scout Troop 193 in June of 1990.

PASTORS WHO SERVED:
Naomi Downs 1949-1952
Emerson Chapman 1952-1953
Enoch Ralph 1953-1956
Howard Small 1956-1974
Richard Fisher 1974-1978
Don Ratliff 1978-1980
Jack Suits 1980-1984
Lyle Pettit 1984-1986
David Hayes 1986-

St. David's Episcopal

Unity Baptist Church

Unity Baptist Church is one of the oldest Baptist Churches in Brown County, having been founded in January of 1845. The devout group of Baptists who formed the members of the Church met in their various homes every fourth Saturday of the month. Ground for a building was obtained when William and Louiza Murphy deeded to the Church the present site in 1849, although the actual deed was not signed until 1850.

The first building was built under the supervision of B.W. Zook, Calvin Skinner and S.S. Parsley, the trustees at that time. It was 22 x 24 feet in size. That building remained until sometime in 1860 or 1861. The present building was remodeled in 1889. In 1891, through a sum of money willed to the Church by Solomon Wiatt a new roof, bell and belfry were added.

In 1949 a complete remodeling was done. The roof was changed to permit the removal of the support post within the Church. The doors and heating system were also changed. Members donated money for stained glass windows at that time.

In 1958 the Sunday School annex was added on the north side of the Church. Additional class rooms, kitchen and bathrooms were added to the west side of the Church in 1961. The foyer was added in 1972.

A History Time Capsule was buried in the cemetery in 1976 containing articles from each Church family to be opened in 2076.

Eight acres to the east of the Church was purchased in 1984 and is being developed for Church programs. A shelter house is nearly finished and a summer program for youth is planned to begin in June, 1990.

At the present time there are 107 resident members. Unity Baptist is affiliated with American Baptist Churches, USA. Rev. Fred Harrison is pastor.

Unity Baptist Church in the early 1900's.

Unity Baptist Church in 1990.

Mt. Nebo United Methodist Church

On March 21, 1891, Mt. Nebo Church was founded. A school house was used for services until a church house could be erected. The plot of land was donated by William Calvert and Susan Carmichael. Down through the years many additions have been made to the one-room church.

The members of the church that sets nestled in the woods of Nebo Ridge Road welcome all who would like to come and worship with us.

Mt. Nebo United Methodist Church

Brown County Schools

Old Log School House that stood for many years near Crooked Creek, Washington Township (then Johnson Township).

THE BEGINNING

The first settlers came to Brown County around 1820. There were no formal schools until 1835 when a house in Hedgeville, a community which no longer exists in the eastern part of the county, was used as a school. This was the first school in Brown County's history although it only lasted a very short time. The second school was constructed in Nashville two years later. This school was built of native logs and lasted five years.

In 1817, one year after Indiana became a state, the state legislature began a system to provide some type of supervision over the schools in each community. The intention was to insure that children would be taught correctly and in the proper environment. As a result the five townships in Brown County each had a township trustee who supervised the schools and teachers once this system was established locally. With this plan it was intended that a school house be established within walking distance of each child's home. In Brown County this could mean a walk of several miles. The trustees were paid a salary by the county and out of their salary they paid teachers, bought the textbooks, and took care of the buildings.

If Brown County children wanted to further their education by going to high school, they had to commute to Bloomington until 1907 when the first high school was built in Brown County. This caused a common problem for the children of the community because they had to furnish their own transportation. Since the roads were poor and people relied on horses and carts for transportation not many children could get back and forth to Bloomington, even though it was only fifteen to twenty miles to travel. Most children only went to school through eighth grade.

The population of Brown County had a definite effect on schooling. In 1840, four years after it was founded, the population was 2,364, a small figure compared to the 1980 census figure of 12,377. There were also problems because there were so few students. The families of the children helped to finance the schools so the schools with more children had more money and consequently were generally better equipped.

In August of 1949 Brown County became the first county in Indiana to create a school corporation. Elected members of a county school board and a corporation superintendent took the place of the trustees.

SCHOOL LEADERS

Grover G. Brown was the County Superintendent for Nashville Schools when all

Nashville's Old School Building - Relic of the past

The New $12,000 High School Building at Nashville in 1907.

Brown County Junior High School in 1990.

Brown County High School, Renovation and additions complete, December 1990.

county schools became one school corporation.

He served as Superintendent of Schools from 1933-1953. His successors were as follows: Claude M. Neidigh 1954-57, Ira Hunnington 1957-58, Warren Ogle 1958-70, Callison Simon 1970-75, Dennis Lacy 1975-78, John O'Dell 1979-81, Carol Walker 1982-90, I.E. Lewis 1990- .

Prior to incorporation trustees were responsible for schools in their township. The following is a partial listing of Nashville superintendents obtained from available state reports, Robert C. Kennedy 1930-31, W.C. Goble 1927-29, A.J. Reynolds 1921-23, Effie A. Patee 1919-21, Grover G. Brown 1917-19, Wm. L. Coffey 1910-?.

Many, probably most, of this group also taught classes.

ELEMENTARY SCHOOLS

In 1954 Sprunica Elementary was built north and east of Bean Blossom. Additions were made to Sprunica School in 1971 and again in 1982 to keep up with growth in the area and needed programs.

In 1958 and 1959 Helmsburg, Nashville and Van Buren Elementary Schools were built. Helmsburg west of Bean Blossom, Nashville located adjacent to the present high school and Van Buren south and east of Nashville were all built from the same plans. Van Buren and Helmsburg were slightly smaller than the Nashville building reflecting the population at that time.

An addition and renovation to Nashville Elementary was completed during 1988 and 1989.

Helmsburg, Sprunica and Van Buren will be expanded and upgraded in the next few years.

HIGH SCHOOLS

For over fifty years Brown County had three high schools. Nashville and Helmsburg High Schools were constructed in 1907. Van Buren High School's first graduating class was the class of 1913.

Van Buren, Helmsburg and Nashville High Schools maintained their identity and local rivalry until consolidation into the present Brown County High School. The first graduating class from the consolidated Brown County High School was the class of 1961.

From 1961 to 1982 the high school housed grades 7-12. Over the years the population ranged from 800 to 1250 students.

By the late 1970s the existing building was bulging with students. To relieve the overcrowding and separate the 13 year olds from the 18 year olds plans were put in place to build a Jr. High School.

Brown County Jr. High School for grades 7 and 8 was opened in 1982 located adjacent to the high school to the north on the Nashville campus.

This gave some flexibility to high school programs, a bit of growing room and grades 7 and 8 a new beautiful building.

By 1984 it was obvious that the high school needed attention and upgrading of the facility was a must.

The first of several yearly projects began in 1984. The Science area was the first area to be addressed and included a greenhouse addition. Library and Guidance areas were projects for 1985. In 1986 the Music and Art and Home Economics areas were expanded and renovated by enclosing the courtyard. New restrooms and a locker commons area were also part of the project for 1986.

At this point a complete renovation of the remainder of the high school was planned. A piece by piece method was no longer feasible.

The addition of an Industrial Technology area, Publication and Language Lab areas, a Physical Education facility, Vocational Day Care, transforming the old gym into an Auditorium with large group instruction areas, complete upgrading of heating and plumbing systems and computer network systems throughout the building were all key components for the addition and renovation of Brown County High School which began in 1988 and completed in December of 1990.

SUMMARY

While the structures have changed dramatically over the years the purpose and primary concern remain constant. The purpose to guide and prepare children for their future, whatever path in life they choose.

We "society" must leave the "value of education" as a legacy to our most precious asset, the children of our community and nation, for this is truly our only future.

Submitted by: Linda L. Hobbs, Brown County School Board 1986-1994.

Acknowledgement: "Toeing the Line" One-room schools in Brown County [1985-86 Brown County Jr. High School Honor Class.]

Map of One Room Schools

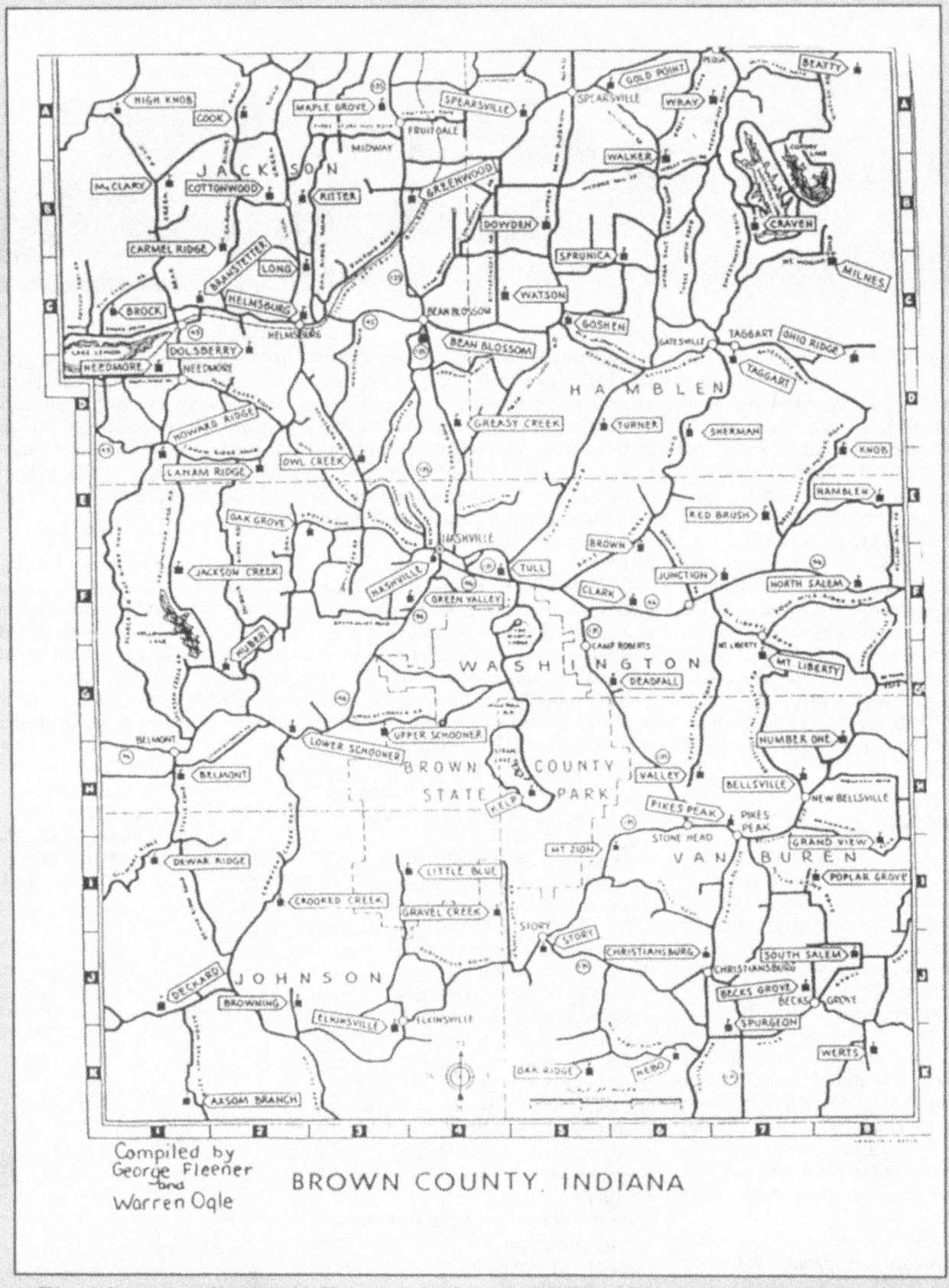

This map shows names and locations of the 76 one-room school houses that existed at one time or another in Brown County. During this era a total of 78 one-room schools existed, including three in the town of Nashville. A few of these structures are still standing including the Craven School near Sweetwater Lake, Lower Schooner School located approximately 3 miles west of Nashville on St. Road 46, the Branstetter School near the town of Trevlac, and the Cottonwood School at the junction of Carmel Ridge Road and Three Story Hill Road. (Drawing by Kenneth J. Reeve)

Brown County Clubs, Organizations and Memorials

Bean Blossom Home Makers in 1940 (L. to r.) Front Row: Wanda Rose Parsley and Helen Jane Smith. Middle Row: Roonie Wilkerson, Garnet Parsley, Opal Waltman, Blanche Waltman, Oma Zody, Ruth Parsley and Pauline Smith. Back Row: Jennie Clark, Bertha Zody, Naomi Curtis and Inez Wilerson.

Brown County Genealogical Society

Pays Tribute to Its Founder Gladys Tratebas and Its Forerunners Helen and Ken Reeve

Helen and Ken Reeve have devoted the past 17 years to Brown County genealogical research. They sorted through mountains of court house records, compiled, indexed and with the support of the Brown County Historical Society, published several reference books. Much of their daily work has been spent in assisting hundreds of present and former Brown Countians with their family research.

Gladys Tratebas is very active in and dedicated to Brown County History and genealogy and its preservation. Because of this interest Gladys organized the Brown County Genealogical Society. She led the first organizational meeting on Sept. 30, 1986 at the Brown County Public Library. There were fourteen people present. Officers elected on Feb. 3, 1987 were: Gladys Tratebas, President; Keith King, Vice President; Shelley Law, Secretary; Jeri Blackwell, Treasurer; Marcy and Lowell Joslin and Helen and Ken Reeve, Genealogists; and Hazel Zimmerman, Historian.

The purpose of BCGS "Shall be to encourage the science of genealogy, to help others gather genealogical information, to preserve and publish material of historical and genealogical nature - all for educational purposes."

The first project of BCGS was to index and record data from the Brown County Court House records.

Charter members are those who were members for 1987 and are as follows:

Jeri Blackwell, Linda Brown, Marguerita E. Grimm, Madge Harlan, Lowell and Marcy Joslin, Dale and Marguerite Kelley, Keith King, Russell King, Shelley Law, Maude Mings, Allen and Ruth Pickard, Mary Pelton, Kenneth and Helen Reeve, Linda, Arthur and Mae Robertson, Rosella Smith, Gladys M. Tratebas. Betty VanDerbilt, Hazel Zimmerman, Shirley J. Hannaford, Roberetta R. Amundsen, Gerald C. Storts, Delores M. Brenenstall, E. Lyle and Helen A. Tabor, Carolyne Stultz, Lorene Bond Prewitt, Linda Anne Zablatnik, Larry Ronald Fleenor, Kathleen M. Kinstler, Merlin P. Whiteman, Mary Gausman, and Juanita Burge.

The first BCGS Newsletter appeared on November 3, 1987 with a tree logo designed by Ken Reeve. The Newsletter is published four times a year and BCGS meets the first Tuesday evening of the month at 7:00 p.m. in the basement of the Brown County Library. In 1989 there were 51 members in 12 states.

The officers for 1990 are: President, Marge Grimm; Vice President, Betty VanDerbilt; Secretary, Mary Pelton; Treasurer, Marguerite Kelley; Editor, Gladys Tratebas.

The following 56 persons are members 1990:

Roberetta Amundsen, Agnes D. Bedient, Dorothy M. Benson, Delores McKinney Brenenstall, Loyd R. Brown, Juanita Burge, Robert O. Cameron, Sarah Clevenger, Don Condon, Marjorie Cooper, Ila Echstadt, Larry Ronald Fleenor, Douglas C. Fraker, Evelyn J. Gladding, Marguerita Grimm, Randall M. Grove, John W. Hamblen, Plessie T. Hamblen, Shirley Hannaford, Madge Harlan, Lowell and Marcy Joslin, Dale and Marguerite Kelley, Russell King, Kathleen M. Kinstler, Shelley Law, Marie McFadden, Susan G. Morris, George S. Jr. and Hazel Lemons Olive, William D. Peck, Mary Pelton, Bryce and Wilma Ping, Lorene Bond Prewitt, Kenneth and Helen Reeve, Chester G. and Jane W. Robertson, Mae and Arthur Robertson, Onnalee Rose, Rosella Smith, Carolyn Stultz, E. Lyle and Helen A. Tabor, Gladys Tratebas, Betty VanDerbilt, Larry Vehorn, Nancie Todd Webber, Merlin P. Whiteman, Doris R. Wilson, Linda Anne Zablatnik, and Hazel Zimmerman.

Brown County has been fortunate to have such dedicated people as Helen, Ken and Gladys.

Helen and Kenneth Reeve

Gladys M. Tratebas

Brown County Old Settlers

Brown County Old Settlers September 2, 1905.

The Brown County Old Settlers is the oldest continuous running event in Brown County. It has been a tradition here since 1877. It is a time when friends may gather and reminisce about the good old times, while enjoying the day's festivities.

Over the years, the location of the Old Settlers has changed and the occasion has become an event for folks of all ages, but the main purpose has stayed the same: to honor the old pioneers of the county.

The first Brown County Old Settlers was held in Georgetown, now Bean Blossom, in September, 1877. The Second and Third Annual Old Settlers were held on Greasy Creek Road near Nashville. The Fourth Old Settlers Reunion, in 1880, was moved to a grove of trees near Needmore. Goshen, three miles east of Georgetown (Bean Blossom), was the location of the Fifth Annual Old Settlers. The Sixth Brown County Old Settlers was moved back to Waltman's Grove, which is now Clupper's Grove, one-half mile northwest of Bean Blossom. This grove has been in the Clupper family since 1916.

Upon returning the location to Georgetown, the Old Settlers Association voted to have the reunion on the first Saturday in September. The Old Settlers then was held only on Saturday because there were no lights in the grove. The first Saturday in September still continues to determine the dates for the Brown County Old Settlers today.

In the beginning, folks would gather for the program and tell their stories and show family heirlooms and relics. Prizes were given for various things such as the man who had killed the most bears, person best in a foot race, couple with the most children, person who traveled the farthest; but prizes awarded almost always included the oldest man and woman present, person living in the county the longest and the couple married the most number of years. The prizes awarded varied from canes, fruit baskets, Bibles, rocking chairs, hats, Indian moccasins, and specs.

During the early years of the Brown County Old Settlers some of the awards were given to the following people: a Bible to John Prosser and wife for living together for 63 years, 1881; specs to Green Graham for being the oldest person present, 1881; hat to Brasillia Horner for best in a foot race, 1883; cane to John Richards, Sr. for killing the most bears, 1883; a cane to Milla Hamblem for having the greatest number of children, 1883; Bible to William Markum and wife for living together 62 years, 1885; cane to Jesse Hamblem for living in county the longest, 1885; hickory rocking chair to Mrs. Tucker for oldest female settler, 1885; pair of pants to A.A. Hudson for father with the greatest number of sons, 1885; a dress pattern to Rob Robison for mother of the greatest number of girls, 1885; cane to Louis Dupree for becoming a father at age 74, 1886; and a pair of pants to Andy Petro for being the lightest man present over 60 years of age (75 pounds), 1886.

Throughout history people have come from miles around to attend this annual event. In early days, families would come on horseback, in buggies, and by covered wagon and bring a picnic lunch. The coming of electricity to Brown County in the early 1950s had an everlasting effect on the Old Settlers. In 1953, the wooded grove area had to be changed from its original place in the south woods to its present location because of the addition of electrical power lines. The coming of electricity brought with it still another change. In 1954, the Old Settlers was held for the first time on Friday night and Saturday.

The festivities throughout the years have grown to include rides, games and food concessions. A grandstand program is now held on Friday night, Saturday afternoon and Saturday night. The grandstand activities include dance groups, auction, country music, baby contest, hymn sing, greased pole, and children's contests. The most important part of the Old Settlers is the Saturday afternoon program honoring the old pioneers. Recognition is given to the Oldest Lady and Oldest Man who are not previous winners, Couple Married the Most Continuous Number of Years, Person Attending the most Old Settlers, the Person Living in the County the Longest and the Oldest Person Attending.

The Brown County Old Settlers has continued for 115 years to be one of the leading events in Brown County. Each year the Old Settlers Committee works long and hard to make each Old Settlers a success. The Old Settlers Association is a non-profit organization whose members unselfishly donate their time and effort to this annual event. Each year the association is destined to make every Brown County Old Settlers an enjoyable time for everyone. The Old Settlers always features free admission, free parking, and free entertainment. You all come!

Community Club
1921 - 1959

A group of Nashville women organized to fill community needs. Martha Weddle writes in *Brown County Remembers* "when someone burned out, we usually managed to get them a few dishes, pots and pans, bedding, comforts and food. At Thanksgiving and Christmas, we fixed baskets of food. All the community helped."

The Club gave plays to raise money. The Brown County Democrat, March, 1921, says "The Old Maids' Convention," a one-act comedy, was given in the courthouse on April 2, 1921, admission 15¢ and 25¢. Repeated April 22, profit $97 was given to the Library. November, 1921, one-act farce, "Jayville Junction," November 1922, "The Suffragettes' Convention." January 1923, "The Old Maids' Convention" was given in Morgantown. Bake sales were held. Yearly dues was $1.00.

On December 28, 1922, praise was given the club for the beautiful electrically lighted Christmas tree at the south courthouse door.

The Club took a trip to McCormick's Creek State Park, August 16, 1923, with Helen and Olive Allison, Ella King, Olive Kelp, Olive Snyder, Ruth Bessire, Ruby McGrayel, Marietta Moser, and Leila David. Another trip was to Martinsville.

Marietta Moser guided the Club for many years. "Outsiders" were welcomed only after Victoria Coffey invited them to join. In February, 1923, Ruth Bessire entertained Carolyn Griffith, Olive Snyder, Mrs. A.J. Reynolds, Mrs. J.W. Sims, Clara Sayer, Florence Sayer, Marietta Moser, Mrs. Ira F. Poling and Sarah Moore.

July 11, 1935, reports 23 members had spent $3,000 on civic projects, and started reconstructing a log building on two city lots, donated by Olive Kelp. After an unsuccessful diligent search in Brown County for suitable logs, James Voland had located an old barn in Jackson County. Eddie Voland hauled the logs, some 60 feet in length, to Nashville and worked with other Volands to reconstruct the building near the old log jail. W.P.A. labor was also used. On March 9, 1936, the first meeting in the new building was held with four Charter members Marietta Moser, Tressa Taylor, Ella Rariden, Grace Turner present, and a total of 33 members were present. The Community Club operated the Old Log Jail for several years as a Curio and Antique Shop. Admission was 10¢ and half of the proceeds were returned to the county. After many inactive years, the Club met and deeded the land for a north exit street from the new Post Office, which was dedicated in 1959, and the remaining land and building to the county. Florence Bradley, attorney, assisted with this transaction. *Submitted by Marianne Miller*

Leppert Bus Line provided transportation for trip to Martinsville about 1930: (l. to r.) Front Row: Mrs. Harlan Clark, Alberta Shulz and Ruth Bessire. Middle Row: Jimmie Leppert, Sarah Moore, Marietta Moser, Margaret Bessire, Carolyn Griffith, Clara Sayer, Mildred Jones, Ruby McGrayel, Victoria Coffey, Olive Snyder, Olive Kelp, Leila David, unknown, Maude Calvin and James L. Tilton. Back Row: Leatha Walker and Laura David.

HILLTOP CAMP AND SUMMER SCHOOL FOR GIRLS
1925 - 1947

HILLTOP CAMP A CULTURAL AND PROGRESSIVE MOVEMENT

The fruit of the vision and foresight of a woman recognized as one of the leading educators of the State, this summer camp and school for girls is filling a need for Indiana parents in a fine way.

As director of a girl's camp Miss Kate Andrews is ably trained and experienced. Six years of steady growth attest her success. An alumni of Wellesley College with graduate study at Chicago and Columbia Universities and in Europe, she is ably equipped from an educational standpoint. She has taught in the high schools of Greensburg and New Albany in Indiana, Grand Rapids, Wisconsin, and was principal of Seymour high school for fifteen years. She has also taught at Western College and is now Dean of Women and Assistant Professor of English at Hanover College.

No safer or more desirable camp can be found for those desiring to send their daughters to a quiet, scenic place for a summer's outing. Their time is filled with useful pursuits, well directed by competent instructors. Horseback riding, hiking, swimming and all kinds of outdoor sports ably chaperoned are supplied for them.

A girl who has not had the privilege of a summer at Hilltop Camp has missed one of the happiest experiences of her young life.

ADVANTAGES

Hilltop Camp, amid surroundings of unusual charm, offers an ideal place in which your daughter may spend a healthful, happy summer. There is no better way for girls to rest their minds and strengthen their bodies than by a life in the open. Here they can learn to know better the great outdoors and to appreciate more the joys that nature has for those who study her. Here they will, in the "give and take" of camp life (under wise leadership), develop a power of adaptation that will always mean much; they will in the competition of sports, play, and work, learn to think more effectively and will grow initiative, resourcefulness and personality.

OVERSIGHT

The physical health, happiness, and welfare of the girls are always the first consideration. A physician and trained nurse, if needed, are within easy reach. Over each group of six girls is a counselor. As the number of campers is limited, Miss Andrews is always in close touch with them and has them in her personal care.

THE DRAMATIC DEPARTMENT

Under direction of Arthur J. Beriault

Tutoring.—"Hilltop" offers valuable individual work in high school and grade subjects under instructors who are college graduates and teachers in the leading schools of Indiana.

The State Board of Education has given Miss Andrews permission to grant high school credits for approved courses, subject to the supervision of the "State High School Inspector" and to acceptance by the superintendent and principal of the school from which the girl comes.

If a girl wishes to make advance credits toward graduation, to strengthen herself for the work of the following year in the grades, in high school, or in college, to secure credits lost from illness or other causes, "Hilltop" offers her an excellent opportunity to do this work under strong instructors and under delightful conditions. Too, in the midst of the varied activities of camp life, girls frequently discover interests that they might never have realized in the regular routine of school work but which may mean much to them in their school life and in their leisure time.

Hilltop Camp on State Road 46 South, top of Town Hill, 1928.

Terms.—Hilltop Camp opens Sunday, June 23, and closes August 18. The terms are $135 for the full season, $75 for each half season. $10 is payable with the application and the balance on entrance to the camp. In case of vacancies girls will be accepted for either term of four weeks. Special arrangements may be made for shorter periods.

The amounts above cover all expenses except laundry, personal expenses, and horses.

Equipment.—Attractive, roomy, and well ventilated rustic cabins afford ample room. Large screened porches furnish delightful sleeping quarters.

Large living rooms, pianos, easy chairs, couches, and other comforts increase the joys of social hours and rest.

Comfortable single beds are provided.

The camp sanitation is carefully looked after.

The drinking water is from a drilled well, 250 feet deep, and is tested by Purdue University before the opening of camp. Note: Kate Andrews Weaver 1869-1951 conducted Hilltop Summer Camps for Girls from 1925 to 1947. The Brown County Camp for Boys was opened about 1935 and continued until 1947. Kate Andrews married Thomas J. Weaver of Chicago in 1935. In the fall of 1948 they moved to Nashville after she had become ill. She died at the Robinson Nursing Home, Indianapolis. *(from Hoosier Magazine 1929 edited by Mabel Sturtevant)*

Brown County Lions Club

The Lions Club of Brown County was formed when the Club received its Charter from Lions International in February 1943. The Club held its first dinner meeting (Charter Night) in the Nashville United Methodist Church in March 1943, with the Methodist Women providing the meal. The Lions Club was sponsored by the Morgantown and the Martinsville Lions Clubs. In 1974 the name was changed from the Nashville Lions Club to the Brown County Lions Club.

The 31 Charter members were: Paul Adams, restauranteur; Ray Baughman, meat market; Walter Baughman, contractor; Joshua Bond, funeral director; Faun E. Clark, public welfare; James Davis, county assessor; the Rev. J.E. DeGafferelly, Christian minister; Melvin V. Flock, county agent; Russell M. Green, high school principal; Robert E. Gregg, service station; Walter Griffiths, pottery manufacturer; Fred King, public welfare; Kenneth Kunkel, State Fish & Game Director; Glenn R. Loop, federal employee; William McBeth, high school coach; Ival McDonald, Chevrolet dealer, Delmar R. Mills, federal employee, William Peeples, retired; Walter F. Snodgrass, real estate; Paul C. Snyder, farmer; Keith Taggart, service station; George C. Tucker, service station; Alonzo Weddle, State Park Superintendent; Edward K. Williams, artist; James Williamson, insurance agent; Howard S. Zody, banker; and Dr. Byron W. Marshall, physician (a transfer member from Pine Bluffs, Wyoming).

The Brown County Lions Club now has a membership of over 100 and is not only the largest Club in District 25 E-1, but is one of the largest in the State of Indiana.

The motto of Lions Clubs International is "WE SERVE." With the support of the community, Brown County Lions Club continues to abide by that principal to serve locally and around the world.

The Many Service Projects Performed by the Lions Club for Nashville and Brown County

Sponsors Annual 4th of July Fireworks Celebration
Sponsored the first free fair for 4-H Club Activity
Erected and dedicated the Veterans Honor Roll on Court House Square
Sponsored horse shows at Brown County State Park
Installed the town water system
Purchased eyeglasses for needy children and adults
Purchased a fire truck and built the Fire Station
Purchased the land for the city dump
Sponsored a free movies for the town of Nashville
School Projects -
  Two to four scholarships presented to graduating seniors
  Sent two boys to Boys State
  Sent students to France and Russia
Helped with Boy Scouts
Erected and installed wheel chair ramps in Nashville
Helped finance street signs in Nashville
Contributed to the Well Baby Clinic
Supported the purchase of a radio control system for the County's Fire Departments
Donated monies for the Senior Citizens Building
Contributed to construction at the 4-H Fair Grounds
Sponsored the calf scramble at the 4-H Fair
Donated monies for the construction and equipping of the Radiation Cancer Building at the IU Medical Center Indianapolis
Contributed to the revamping of the Library Bookmobile
Continued support of the Leader Dogs for the Blind School; Eye Care, Speech and Hearing; Lions Club International Foundation; as well as the many Lions District and State Projects
Supports Annual Arbor Day Project

Claris Keaton and Max Loop in a 1965 parade

Nashville Literary Club

During its more than fifty-six year existence, the Literary Club has made an important and continuing contribution to the social and cultural life of Brown County.

The first meeting of the Club was held January 18, 1934, at the home of Leatha Walker with nine ladies present. Charlotte Mathis was elected as the first president with Martha de Gafferelly vice president and Ferne Seitz secretary. The remaining charter members were Margaret Kelly, Dorothy Kennedy, Martha Weddle, Ruth Bright and Mrs. Crouch. The Club was to be an informal literary discussion group with meetings held every two weeks. The idea proved so popular that within a month the membership had grown to twenty. By September of its first year, it was thought necessary to limit participants to twenty, though the number was soon revised upward to twenty-five. During this period, officers served for only six months, dues were set at ten cents and meetings took place every two weeks.

From the time of the Club's inception, it has been the custom to begin each meeting with a roll call of the members. During the early days, members responded to their names with a verse, a brief literary allusion or a current event. At one meeting, one of the ladies no doubt astonished her fellows when she answered the roll call with a complete history of the life of Stephen Foster and concluded with a vocal rendition of "Somewhere My Love Lies Dreaming."

Although the Club has always adhered to the spirit of the purpose set forth by its founders, it has, as needs arose, expanded its activities to include patriotic, philanthropic and community service projects.

During World War II members entertained soldiers who were stationed in nearby Brown County State Park, knitted sweaters for men in the naval forces, sewed for the Red Cross and made efforts to conserve food by planting gardens and canning at home. One member recalled that the ladies were encouraged to bring mending and needlework with them to meetings in order to make the best use of their time. The practice was discontinued when it was decided that the sight of so much lingerie being mended was distracting to the speakers and not in keeping with the purposes of the club.

In addition to supporting patriotic and war-related activities, the Club has contributed to famine relief, helped the elderly needy of the County with gifts of dressing gowns and slippers and even anticipated present-day environmental concerns by placing a trash can in downtown Nashville.

Very early in the life of the organization, members began an active and continuing support for the Brown County Public Library through an annual contribution of books, augmented by additional volumes placed in the library as memorials to deceased members. This is still regarded as the Club's single most important project.

Because many of the early Club members were closely associated with the Arts, programs featuring musical entertainments and art topics were common. The delightful covers of the program books which have survived from the 1930s feature hand-painted Brown County scenes. Their modern counterparts are distinguished by the Club logo, designed by Melba Dailey and adopted in 1979.

The annual program schedule presently includes ten meetings, four of which are book discussions in which all members participate. The remaining programs are presented by individual members and cover a wide variety of topics suggested by the literary tastes and interests of the individual presenters. Membership in the club is limited to thirty-five and is by invitation.

Throughout its history, the organization has continued to grow and prosper. As we look forward to the 21st century, we are mindful of the club traditions of earlier times which we continue to observe and of members who are no longer with us, but who have, nevertheless, contributed so much to the present-day life of The Nashville Literary Club.

Members of the Nashville Literary Club

H.R. Almquist	Mary Alice Girard	Agatha Roberts Reed
Robin Blanton	Harriet Johnson	Barbara Rich
Mary Kathryn Burch	Mary Jane Lorenz	Mary Lou Russell
Betty Ann Buschmann	Dorothy McClain	Mary L. Seibert
LaVonne Coldren	Margaret McPherson	Joyce Shaw
Ann Cole	Florence Neill	Fran Snyder
Elaine Cooper	Anne Olsen	Marion Snyder
Melba Dailey	Charlotte Paddish	Mardi Swain
Hazel Davis	Mary Pelton	Betty Taylor
Betty Espenlaub	Florine Phipps	Helen Wythe
Ruth Espenlaub	Ruth Pickard	Barbara Zieg

This page is lovingly dedicated to the memory of
ELECTA CARTER CLARK
a member and devoted friend of the Nashville Literary Club.

Pioneer Women's Club

The 1990 Pioneer Women (l. to r.) Front Row: Gladys Tratebas, Marie Wolff, Madeline Ritter, Elsie Mae Frenzel, Juanita Bainter, Hazel Zimmerman, Anne Olsen, Tab Low, Elsie Wayman and Joyce Heiny. Back Row: Mary Alice Birkla, Mary Pelton, Kay Birk, Ruth Goodrich, Norma Jean Stevens, Nel Carley, visitor, Amy Leskovec, Mary Hagen, June Wolpert, June Wohler, Helen Wythe, Boots Gregory, Amelia DeWees, Linda Sage, Billie Barr, Marijane Litz, Juanita Boles & Ann Varner.

The Pioneer Club was organized in January 1965 to aid the Historical Society in the establishment of a Pioneer Village and Museum in Brown County. The By-Laws state, "The purpose of the club shall be to practice handcraft skills used by our forebears; to study and/or demonstrate old-time skills; to support and aid the Brown County Historical Society as resources will permit."

The first meetings were held at a small house owned by the Historical Society on Helmsburg Road. Items were made to sell at the Bazaars which were held every year. Breakfasts were served as some of the fund raisers in the small house. Meetings were usually held on the fourth Wednesday of each month in the members' homes until the Historical Society bought the bowling alley in December of 1970; then those facilities were used for meetings.

The following are excerpts from the first meeting held on January 30, 1965: "Despite sub-zero weather on Saturday, January 30, 1965, at 1:30 p.m. twenty brave ladies met in the cabin of the Brown County Historical Society to discuss formation of a club to enter into money-making projects for a bazaar in the fall. It was decided that the profits derived would be donated to the Society to reduce debt on the property.

"Officers were nominated from the floor and voted in by a show of hands: President Mrs. Lula Lee Rogers; Vice President Mrs. Ruth Fender; Secretary-Treasurer Mrs. Edith Forkner; General Chairman of the Bazaar Mrs. Ethel Mae Miller, assisted by Mrs. Bernice Burch. Enthusiasm and ideas poured in and if carried out it held much promise of success.

"Those attending the first meeting were: Kathryn Claussen, Fran Snyder, Melucina Seehausen, Lula Lee Rogers, Ruth Fender, Linda Eastman, Sara Buterff, Bernice Kleinefen, Ethel Miller, Bernice Burch, Helen Johnson, May Kimmick, Bertha Degelyer, Edith Forkner, Jessie Crass, Olive Dellinger, Birdie Miller, Marjorie De Golyer, Helen Kieser and Alberta Shulz."

Over a period of 25 years the Pioneer Women have given the Historical Society a total of $55,985.79, money earned from fall Bazaars and in later years from items sold at a gift shop located in the Museum Complex behind the Court House. Hand-woven rugs have been a special item that have been sold in the gift shop of late years. Also the women have made a quilt each year for the past five years to be raffled off at the annual Quilt Show put on by the Historical Society.

Many Brown County Women over a period of twenty-five years have put in long hours to make the Pioneer Women's Club the success it has been. Some of the faithful workers of the Club's early years are: Helen White, Anna Adsit, Vera Arnold, Lee Deming, Rozella Harris, Louise Kissling, Flord Burns, Genevive Lee, Gene Coumbe, Ida Anderson, Anita Burk, Marjorie Da Vee, Faith Wickard, Onya la Tour, Fran Snyder, Marjorie De Golyer, Irene Kinnane, Mary Ogle, Joan Rosen, Nola Todd, Annea Williams, Janet Bransworth, Edith McNany, Virginia Hamblen, Mary Simons, Jesse Cross, Helen R. Keiser, Clarissa Campbell, Babette Hufford, Olive Dollinger, and Esther Pimp.

Members 1990 are as follows: Kathy Adams, Juanita Bainter, Martha Barnsfather, Billie Barr, Kay Birk, Mary Alice Birkla, Juanita Boles, Wanda Bruner, Bimi Burch, Nell Carley, LaVonne Coldren, Margie Cooper, Joan Dalrymple, Hazel Davis, Amelia DeWees, Elsie May Frenzel, Karen Frenzel, Marie Fuson, Ruth Goodrich, Boots Gregory, Mary Hagen, Joan Harrod, Joyce Heiny, Jeanne Henderson, Louise Kissling, Marijane Litz, Amy Leskovec, Beulah "Tab" Low, Verl Lyon, Gladys McDonald, Mary Ann Mills, Mary Agnes and May Monroe, Karen Norman, Marie Oliver, Anne Olsen, Fonza Owens, Mary Pelton, Marie Ponader, Virginia Pratt, Fern Reuter, Sandra Richards, Madeline Ritter, Sharon Sadler, Linda Sage, Ada Sanders, Norma Jean Stephens, Ann Straughn, Lesta Thickstun, Mildred Thompson, Gladys Tratebas, Ann Varner, Theresa Waltonen, Elsie Wayman, Betty Weatherford, Evon Weaver, Ruth Wheeler, June Wohler, Marie Wolff, June Wolpert, Helen Wythe, and Hazel Zimmerman.

Brown County Community Closet

In the early 1970s a group of ladies of the Luthern Church under the direction of Marge Klusemeier established a small storage area in the log cabin building which is now known as the County Museum. Feeling the need of clothing items particularly for children they gathered used clothing, mended and laundered making it available where needed at no cost to the recipient.

By 1972 the accumulation of clothing had outgrown the small room at the west end of the building. It was at this time that the county commissioners started planning for the restoration of that building so that it could be ready for dedication by July 4th in 1976, our bicentennial year.

The commissioners asked Lenore Mobley to head up a committee to move the stock and relocate the shop. Lenore Mobley was widely known and respected county wide as the mother of five and a practical nurse. She travelled with the country doctor to assist with the birth of many Brown County babies.

Lenore was able to find a small house on South Jefferson Street across from Bond's Funeral Home which could be rented. The commissioners granted seed money of $150.00. There was no plumbing and previous tenants had left the house in a deplorable condition. Finally, with soap and water carried from the cistern and white paint the building was made respectable.

A board was formed including Mary Brock, Jean Mize, Rosella Smith, Sally Speelmon, Wilma Skinner, Elsie Wayman and Helen White. All of these ladies gave of their time and talents.

By selling clothing and household items at a very modest price enough income was generated to pay the rent and electricity. Welfare referrals and fire victims were served at no cost.

In 1978 the shop was moved to 61 North Johnson Street. Here there was plumbing. Additional shelving and clothes racks were purchased from shops in Bloomington and Columbus as those stores were terminating business.

During the years attrition took its toll on the original board members. The most faithful and loyal was Jean Mize who passed away on November 28th 1989.

The "Closet" is still in operation with volunteer help, a good gas heating stove, plumbing, parking space, a washing machine and a telephone. *Submitted by Lee Sparks*

During the 70s and early 80s Jean Mize was active in Girl Scout activities and was Cookie Sales Chairman, as well as doing work at the Community Closet.

Psi Iota Xi

Eta Alpha Chapter of Psi Iota Xi National Philanthropic Sorority initiated their twenty-two charter members at the Nashville Christian Church on May 1, 1966.

Prior to receiving the charter, several local ladies met at the home of Alice Ann McDonald to discuss with their co-sponsors from Bloomington and Columbus the forming of the sorority.

Nationally and locally, "Psi Otes" support philanthropic projects in the areas of art, speech and hearing, and music. Eta Alpha has been a supporter of the Hoosier Salon, Brown County Art Gallery and Guild, and Indiana Heritage Arts. Frank Hohenberger prints were purchased and are on permanent exhibition at the Brown County Library.

In 1971, an unveiling/autograph reception was held for the book *Brown County Art and Artists* which was published by Psi Otes under the direction of Barbara Judd.

Brown County Psi Otes have contributed greatly to different areas of the Brown County School System over the years. They were instrumental in establishing a speech and hearing program in the Brown County School System.

The first project for Psi Iota Xi was to give $500.00 to the Brown County High School Library. Psi Otes have continued to support all the school libraries and the Brown County Public Library, where a collection of Abe Martin Books which they purchased are on display.

Girls' State, Music and Drama Clinics, Band Uniforms, music records, symphony tickets, as well as substantial scholarships yearly are just a few of the school-related projects Psi Otes have sponsored. In the fall of 1990, Psi Otes announced the purchase of a grand piano for the Brown County High School Auditorium.

In order to fund these various projects, Psi Otes have worked hard. Fund-raisers include an auction, bake sales, ice cream socials, style shows, a Thrift Shop, flower sales, a Santa House, and the annual Log Cabin Tour which has been the most successful project.

Psi Otes are hard-working but have fun. Monthly meetings and social activities provide enjoyable, relaxing fellowship and the fund-raisers, though sometimes tiring, are filled with laughter. Psi Otes do all of this for one reason - for others.

Delta Kappa Gamma Society — International, Gamma Xi Chapter

Delta Kappa Gamma Society International, Gamma Xi Chapter, an organization honoring women in education, was installed August 30, 1980, at the Brown County Inn—the 86th chapter chartered in Indiana. Charter members included transfers from Tau Chapter, Bartholomew County, Fern Howe, Dorothy Jackson, Roberta Hill-Knapke, Leota Skirvin-Smith, Ruth Tilton, Carol Walker; and from Beta Lambda, Bloomington, Mary McGrayel. New initiates were Judith Allen, Martha Findley, Diana Igo, Sharon Rivenbark, Linda Roberts, Beverly Ulrey, and Norma Wood.

Kiwanis Club

Committed to working for and with the county's youth, the Kiwanis Club of Brown County, organized under the sponsorship of the Columbus Evening Kiwanis, received its charter June 26, 1987.

Through a number of membership and leadership changes the club has continued its work for young people through a number of programs including raising funds for the region's tertiary care center for children, Riley Hospital in Indianapolis. The men and women of the club work closely with and for Brown County's Big Brothers/Big Sisters organization, the Area XI Special Olympics and its own BUG (Bringing Up Grades) program at Brown County Junior High School.

In addition, the club encourages proper nutrition for county youngsters through its participation in the Brown County Food Pantry.

It also promotes educational opportunities by providing youth oriented reference materials for the Brown County Public Library.

Brown County Retired Teachers Association

The Association was organized July 5, 1972. Charter members included: Mary Alice Cairns, Aletha Chitwood, Olive Matthews, Warren Ogle, Josephine Tamney, Ruth Tilton, Virginia Updike, Gladys Whitaker, Virginia Weddle, Mr. and Mrs. Garret Weathers, Juanita Rains, and Earl Utterback. Most had taught in Brown County, and a number started their careers in one of the county's 78 one-room schools. Since that time, retired teachers from many other places have moved to Brown County and joined the Association, making this a truly special group.

Members still reminisce about spelling bees, ciphering matches, pie socials, wood stoves, the old outhouses, and salaries of $100 a month. Members who have shared experiences of those days include George Fleener, who in 1987, at the age of 94 drove his car to a meeting and recalled some highlights of a 44-year teaching career which began in 1915. Aletha Chitwood holds the distinction of having taught three generations of one Brown County family, and Mary Alice Cairns upon her retirement from IPS was presented with the key to the city by her former pupil, Senator Richard Lugar, who was at that time the mayor of Indianapolis.

BCRTA has among its goals and objectives volunteer service to the Brown County community, the continuing self-improvement of its members, and the support of legislation favorable to both teachers and pupils throughout the state.

Bean Blossom Homemaker Club

The Homemaker Clubs are a part of the Brown County Cooperative Extension Service - Purdue University, where they receive all their information and material. At the present time(1990) Barbara Bowman is the Home Economist and Jon Cain is the Extension Agent. There are seven active Brown County Homemaker Extension Clubs. The Bean Blossom Homemakers Club was organized in 1934 at Goshen Church in Hamblen Township with four women present: Blanche Waltman, May Oalden, Jennie Condon, and Edna Parmalee. Jennie Condon is still a member of the club which is now 56 years old (1934 - 1990) and is the oldest club in Brown County. The Bean Blossom Club was organized by R. E. Grubbs, the County Agent at the time.

The Club has been involved in civic and community projects such as heart fund and cancer crusade. They have prepared meals for bereaved families; given baskets and gifts to needy families; served meals to the election board; sponsored 4-H; worked at county fairs; and exhibited at fairs. In 1977 Garnet Parsley received the coveted "Jane" award from P.U. and received the "home maker of the year" honor. The Club always is striving to improve, endear and enlarge the greatest institution in the world - "The Home."

Present active members are: Dorothea Cline, Jennie Condon, Janice Fleener, Elsie Frenzel, Ruth Goodrich, Marge Huntsman, Dorothy Oliver, Garnet Parsley and Frances Wagler.

In Memory
George R. and Anna E. (Campbell) Fleener

George R. Fleener & Anna E. (Campbell) Fleener

No words can adequately express the love and appreciation the daughters of the late Geo. R. "Ray" Fleener and Anna Campbell Fleener feel towards them for giving us a nearly perfect setting in which to mature and grow.

That setting consisted of a small hilltop farm in Brown Co., Ind.: a woods to cool us in summertime, a winding creek in which to wade and swim, a small grocery store nearby, a large garden with giant tomatoes and yellow roasting ears, neighborhood children to play hide and seek, a school down the hill and across the railroad tracks, a church up on Bear Creek and the smell of newly cut Christmas trees. Add to all of these things two loving parents who gave of themselves for their children; not just daily work but from the richness of their mind and spirit.

How did they do this? Let us read this prayer written by Ray near the end of his life. "We are thankful for this beautiful Sabbath. Thank you for the resurrection of our Savior who died for us, that we may have everlasting life. What a gift from God! May we hear his message, Oh, God, instead of the evil all about us. Give me the power to teach the children that it is better to walk around the road in day light than to cross the field in darkness to commit an evil.

Bless the children of our community that they may live a life in Christ. Thanks, Oh, God, that most of our societies live in Christ. Bless our school. Thank God for my speedy recovery from a stroke."

In 1985 he was called on to say a few words in a Baptist church. He says, "As I walked down the aisle, every day of my life came in view. When I finished my walk I was standing in front of the pulpit. Each day of my life became brighter as God let it unfold.

I was very young when I told my mother my desires of life. As I grew older truth became evident. When I was six years old I found myself in the Brock School No. 8. There was a church in that old school which made God's Blessing unfold. (The school was like a church.) When I was twenty I came to fully realize Christ was calling me and I went with my sister (Minnie) to Christ in that old Howard Ridge Baptist Church. Industry came with truth and honesty followed, by self respect and respect for others."

Ronna Kay Walters, daughter of Carol Fleener McCracken, writes these verses in her poem, "A Tribute to Grandpa".

He shared his treasured knowledge,
To the kids, a living history, he had shown.
Now, his dedication was duly recognized;
As "Teacher of the Century," he is now known.

This man is George Ray Fleener,
My grandfather, who is so dear to me.
He had guided my lifetime values,
From the time that I sat at his knee.
RKW - 1988

An old Bear Creek Sunday School book of July 25, 1943, lists Anna Campbell Fleener as teaching the Adult Class. Her sister, Ruby Fleener, was teaching young people just as their mother and father did in 1908. Alice Fleener, daughter of Anna, was playing the piano. Ray was serving as superintendent a few years later.

In 1908 at the time Edith Campbell, sister of Anna Fleener, died the Indianapolis News writes in her obituary. "She had not a thought that was not a gentle one, not one that did not hold all the world in the arms of kindliness. She was sorely needed here. She was the light of the eyes of a great company of relatives and friends and that light has now gone out. To them she was what the sunshine is to the world and this eclipse to them brings forth both darkness and chill." All that was said of Edith can also be said of her sister, Anna.

Daughter Marjorie Fleener writes of her mother, Anna, in her poem, "Mama's Gift to Me"

Mama gave me my God
As she bounced me on her knee.
Always singing songs of Jesus,
How he loves you and me.

Mama taught of God's love
In each flower we would pick.
How he's with us in each rose,
Even with its thorns so thick.

Mama believed God's word
And lived his special way.
She's rejoicing as an angel now -
Singing praises all the day.

The children, grandchildren, and great-grandchildren of Geo. R. and Anna fondly remember the farmhouse at Trevlac and the precious memories it holds. By telling and retelling its story we can keep its lessons intact for yet another generation.

Geo. Ray once said, "The good Lord gave me five daughters instead of sons because he knew that daughters become mothers and they could best teach of the good life to the children." Ray and Anna taught best by example.

By looking backward and then looking forward we can give a sense of continuity, security and responsibility to the next generation. Let us pause to give thanks for all of the families represented on these pages and to the riches they have bequeathed to us. We reach back to the past with one hand and hold tightly to the future with the other.

George R. Fleener and great-granddaughter Julie Elizabeth Smith.

IN MEMORY

DUDLEY D. DAVIS (1912-1989)

Born: Indianapolis, Marion County, Indiana, January 22, 1912.
Died: Nashville, Brown County, Indiana, July 10, 1989.
Interred: Nashville Indiana, Greenlawn Cemetery.
Education: Graduate of Southport High School,
　　　　　Indianapolis 1931
　　　　　Indiana University Extension
　　　　　Butler University, B.S., 1936, major history
　　　　　Butler University, M.S, 1941, major economics

IN MEMORY

HAROLD E. BULLINGTON

Harold and Storm

NOVEMBER 7, 1934 - FEBRUARY 19, 1989

Old Log Church near Elkinsville erected by the Baptists of Johnson Township. Built around 1830. Some worshippers were the Sextons, Arwines, Maloys, Goodmans, Wilkersons and Davis. In the summer the puncheon seats were taken to the Beech Grove close by, where services were held. (Photo by Frank Hohenberger)

Brown County Businesses

Star Store on corner of Main and Van Buren Streets in Nashville. Ray Baughman, Paul Adams and Coach Doolittle. Lex Hollars behind meat case.

Brown County Art Barn

The Brown County Art Barn Gallery, opened by Judie Hurt in 1966, had its origins in a trailer built by her husband to house Judie's oil paintings. In 1973 the Hurts purchased the Gulf Service Station and began renovations. The building looks like a rustic Brown County barn in keeping with the look of Brown County atmosphere. The Art Gallery now houses the oil paintings, watercolors, and pastel art works of several well known local artists. These professional artists that exhibit along with Judie Hurt and her husband, Ray Scalf, are: Dwight Steininger, Joe Shell, Hielene Furlong, Anita Hoehne, Flora Yentes, Bruce Hume, Charles Handford, Joe Trover, Shirley Carr, Erin Pesavento, Maxine Lain, Henery Niles, Kathleen Niles, Jean Garro, Denise Farrar, Nancy Hayworth, Peter Brunning, Aileen Bolton, Bridget Moreno, Sandra Shroeder, Harold Davis, and Larry Schuller. Also the beautiful stained-glass artwork by local artist Kristy Richardson, and the fine lath-art by Mark Russell.

The Art Gallery is located on North Van Buren Street, just North of the Court House. Open from 11:00 to 5:00 P.M. daily. Closed January and February (but will open by appointment). Phone 812-988-2422.

The Brown County Art Barn Gallery prides itself on the originality of all the artist's work and the public can enjoy talking with at least one of the artists as they paint there on location. Throughout the summer and into the fall season the Brown County Art Barn supports other local craftsmen who set up their exhibit in front of the Gallery. Come and enjoy the friendly atmosphere.

Also visit our "Indian Trails Art Galley and Trading Post" located in front of the Brown County Art Barn Gallery. This is where you will find Southwest paintings by local artists. You will also find artist, William Piatt's handmade Indian Jewelry, along with handmade Indian rugs, blankets, wallhangings and placemats. Open daily from 11:00 - 5:00. Visitors welcome.

Rings and Things and Calvin Place

Peter A. Saurer, 1964, taken by Fred Sisson for the Bloomington Herald.

Rings and Things was founded in New York City in 1961 by Peter Saurer and Henri Leighton. They dissolved the partnership and Pete moved his store to Indiana in 1963. He rented the pink house behind the Old Ferguson House on Antique Alley and stayed there till 1965 when Alice Weaver asked him to vacate the shop so that two young men could have a place to live during the winter months. She got upset with them two weeks later and threw them out and asked Pete to stay.

He then decided to move and found a store being vacated by Carl Carpenter because the Old Nashville Liquor store went to a more spacious location. Alice Weaver found out about the new shop and gave him till eight o'clock the next morning to move out. At three the next morning the move was done to 35 S. Van Buren Street in 1966 where it can still be found next to the Nashville House on the corner of the Heritage Mall Building. In 1976 Pete and his wife bought the historic Calvin House built in 1895 by T.D. Calvin. They built the Calvin Place Complex in 1976. Pete opened the Brown County Rock Shop in 1976 in Calvin Place, and later sold it and opened the Brown Cow Cheese Shop in 1977 and it was sold in 1979. He then opened the Crystal Source in 1987 in Calvin Place where it is now. It is managed by Barb Davis. Rings and Things is still being run by Pete with Laurie Embry, Manager.

Gnaw Bone Camp, Inc.

In 1944 when Frederick G. Lorenz, Jr., saw the "Pittman Place," off of South State Road #135, he knew it was a perfect spot for a children's camp. Nestled in a valley were an old log cabin, a double log barn and a little stream known as Deadfall Creek. Fred bought 47 acres from the owner, Fred Bates Johnson, and named it Gnaw Bone Camp.

Over the years boy and girl campers helped construct sleeping cabins, a dining lodge, a recreational building, a covered foot bridge, a replica of the old one room Deadfall School, and recreated a Western town. There is a small lake for swimming, boating and fishing. More property was acquired for a total of about 1,000 acres, including a valley famous in the 1920s for Chief Eagle Feather's dance hall. 27 miles of trails were cut through the woods for hiking, riding, cross country skiing and mountain biking.

The Camp was certified by the American Camping Association in 1945 and was incorporated in 1973. Officers were: Fred Lorenz, board chairman; his wife, Mary Jane Lorenz, secretary-treasurer; daughters, Alice Sue Lorenz, president, Helen Marie Holdeman and Linda Jane Norton, vice-presidents. Fred's brother Paul S. Lorenz, joined the staff in 1977.

Together with a well qualified staff of former campers, the family business has provided thousands of children from all over the United States with wonderful camping memories.

Honeysuckle Place

Honeysuckle Place consists of five commercial shops. It originally was the James M. Jones' homestead, which he purchased for his family in 1914, and it is still owned by the family.

After the death of James M. Jones, few of the immediate family cared to commercialize the property, but they seemed to have little choice due to the location of it and the direction the surrounding properties were going. Even with commercialization of the property, a sincere effort has been made to maintain this century old house in its original style and architecture.

Three other buildings were placed on the property in 1968, 1973, and 1976 to add a primitive charm since the property originally had several out buildings on it which had to be torn down.

Numerous honeysuckle, wisteria, lilies, and shrubs on the property were cultivated by James M. Jones' wife, Mildred, and it is in her memory that her son William named the property Honeysuckle Place in 1970.

Brown County Art Gallery Association, Inc.

Presenting Fine Art Since 1926

* Exhibitors - 1990 - 1991 *
Betty C. Boyle - Martha Callaway - Sue T. Chapman - Melba Dailey - Evelynne Mess Daily - E. Gaye Eilts - William R. Ferguson - Elaine Fischvogt - Norval Fischvogt - W. Harold Hancock - Shelby Harding - Louise Johnson - Gladys Jones - Kenneth E. Knight - Shirley Little - Sue McAllister - Evelyn McConnell - Verne McKinzie - Amanda W. Mathis - Mildred Niesse - Tamiko Oberholtzer - Marian O'Haver - Kaye Pool - Kenneth Reeve - Frances Rogers - D. Omer Seamon - Dwight Steininger - Willa Van Brunt - Frank Vietor - Maphajean White - Phyllis Whitworth - Von Williamson - Beatrice Zerwekh.

* Guests Artists *
Thelma Frame - Shelley C. Frederick - Al Stine.

* Board of Directors *
Frank Vietor, President - Sue McAlister, 1st Vice Pres. - Martha Callaway, 2nd Vice Pres. - Heather Mollo, 1990 Exec. Sec. - Kathy Austin, 1991 Exec. Sec. - Board Members: Carol Bland - William Ferguson - Shirley Little - Amanda Mathis - Frances Rogers - Maphajean White.

Gallery Director
Charles P. Keefe, Associate, Edith B. Francis.

Crouch's Market

Located at Pikes Peak, Crouch's Market is owned and operated by Harry and Norma Crouch. They had sold produce at the same location of the blacksmith shop of Harry's father. In 1972 the produce shop was moved across the road. Enlarged, it now also sold feed and bait and was called Crouch's Feed and Bait Store. As the Pikes Peak community grew, customers' requests for more products developed the store into Crouch's Market. Now a country convenience store, it sells groceries, hardware, plumbing supplies as well as video rental, game room, sporting supplies and Notary service. *Submitted by Norma Crouch*

Morgan County REMC

Morgan County Rural Electric Membership Corporation, located in Martinsville, is a fast growing electric utility that serves the outlying areas of Morgan, Brown, Owen, Monroe, Putnam, Clay and Johnson counties. It has over 22,000 members and more than 2,500 miles of electrical lines.

But the REMC's beginnings were quite humble. In 1935, President Franklin D. Roosevelt created the Rural Electric Administration (REA) in order to provide funding to string electrical lines throughout the nation. On June 24, 1939, a group of farmers from Morgan, Brown, Monroe and Owen counties signed the Articles of Incorporation and Morgan County REMC was open for business. The purpose of the REMC was to provide electricity to the rural areas of those four counties. Late in 1939, the REMC received a loan from the REA of $150,000 — enough to string 24 miles of line to serve 54 farms.

Morgan County REMC

"Committed to Service Excellence in every customer contact."

The Totem Post

In 1952 Bill and Marielle Jockey, professional dancers, purchased Bud Austin's leather shop, one of five shops in town, and changed the name to The Totem Post. They continued to do custom leatherwork, adding handmade American Indian jewelry and eventually gifts and crafts from around the world. Liana, their daughter, returned to help run the business and Bill retired in 1982. Marielle's brother, Buz Dryfoose, retired Naval pilot, worked in the shop for 17 years.

Olde Bartley House & The Summer Kitchen

(circa 1886)

OLDE BARTLEY HOUSE & THE SUMMER KITCHEN
"GOODS IN ENDLESS VARIETY FOR YOUR HOME"
ON HISTORIC SHOPPERS LANE

John and Dotti Sheehan Proprietors since September 1983.

G. W. Rogers & Associates

**George and Saramae Rogers
Dunhill of Brown County
Consultant in Executive Search
in the Field of Engineering
Mechanical-Industrial-Electrical
Engineers
Nashville, Indiana**

Looking down Main Street showing Star Store. Paul Adams owned store for many years. On down street from the grocery is the Gables Restaurant, Shoe Shop, Barber Shop, Melodian Hall, Rogers' Grocery, Art Gallery and small part of Hohenberger Building. Paul Adam's truck is in front of store. He hauled groceries from the market in Indianapolis.

Brown County Family History

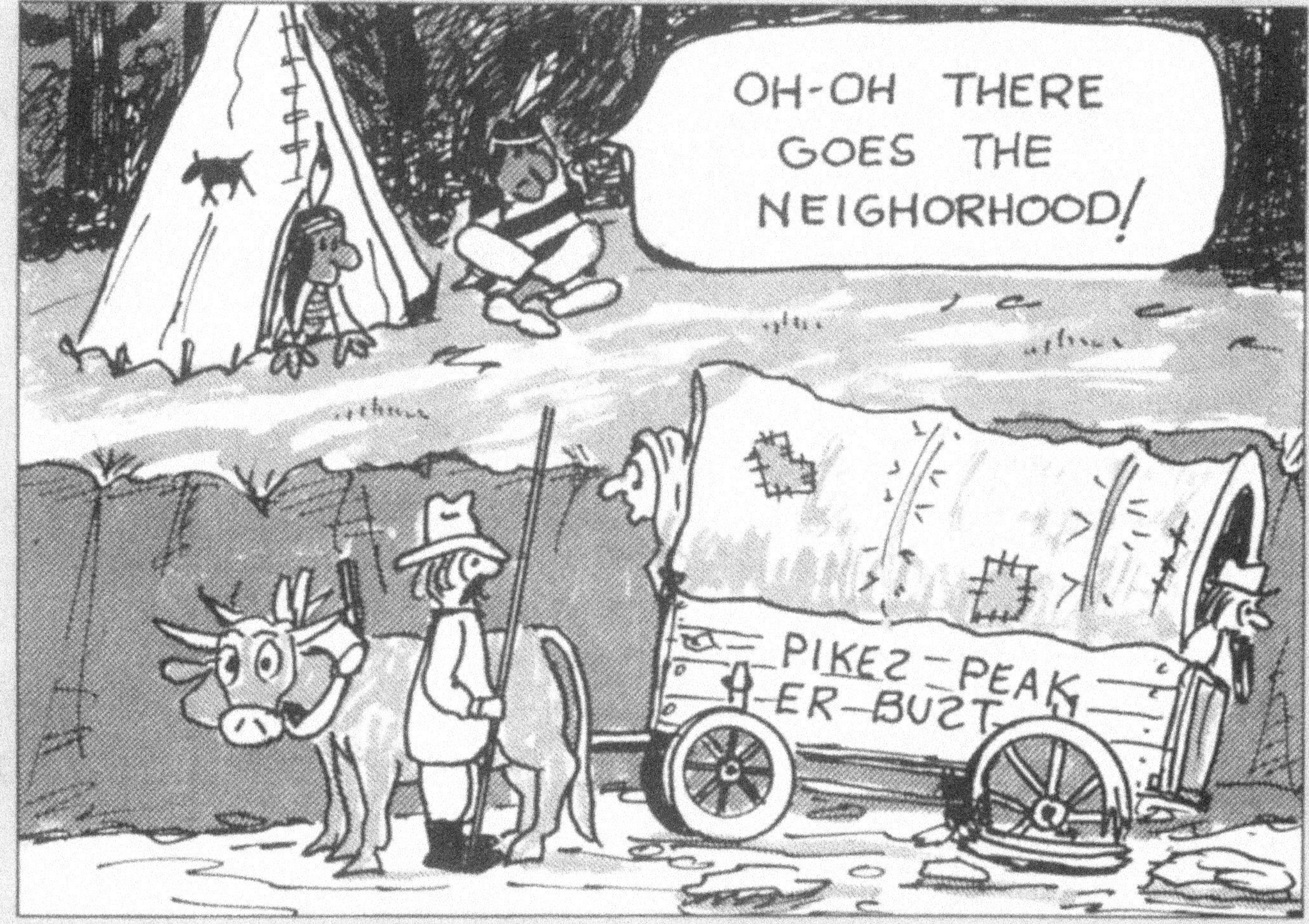

By Robert Bainter, Cartoonist for The Democrat

ABBEY - One family tradition was that James Pearl Abbey came from a foreign country. That is why his wife's father did not want her to marry him. But, records do show that James Abbey was born in Fairfield, CT in 1800. He was of German descent.

James went to Virginia. There he met and married Mary Hobbs. They migrated to Kentucky, then to Tipton Co., IN. They did not like the terrain of Tipton County. So they decided to move to Jackson Township, Brown County, because the terrain there was more like they had been used to in Kentucky. James and Mary came to Brown County about 1843.

James was primarily a farmer. A family story says he operated a huckster wagon business in western Brown County. He would make trips to Louisville to buy supplies to bring back to sell to the settlers. Also, a family tradition says James held a law degree from Yale University, and that he had been a school teacher. Another thing said was that James was a close associate of Martin Van Buren, eighth President of the United States.

Mary Hobbs Abbey was born in Virginia in 1804. Her father, Absalom Hobbs, fought in the War of 1812. Her mother was Susan Helvey (or Kelvey). Mary's paternal grandfather was Vincent Hobbs, an American Revolutionary War soldier. It has been reported that Vincent Hobbs was an indirect descendant of Thomas Hobbes (the "e" was later dropped), the 17th century English political philosopher who wrote the Levithan. Mary Abbey's paternal grandmother, Mary Shelby Hobbs is said to be related to Evan and Isaac Shelby, early American military and political leaders.

James and Mary had several children. Among them were Levi; Martin; Anna; twins Amanda and Armitta (married William Stump, who later became Justice of the Peace of Jackson Township). Elmina who married Robert Davis, and Adela who married Abraham Neideigh.

James died in 1852 while away on business in Illinois. He is buried there somewhere. Mary continued to reside in Brown County until her death in 1883. She was first buried in Brown County. Then, later she was moved to Morgan Co., IN.

There are no known descendants still living in Brown County, but there are several descendants living in nearby counties. *Submitted by Lorena L. Miller*

BEULAH AND JOHN R. ACKERMAN - Beulah and John met and fell in love, and were married on Sept. 14, 1945 by Captain U.S.A. Milford Barrick at a small chapel at Camp Atterbury. John was 1st Lieutenant in charge of the Clothing Warehouse. Beulah was manager of Service Club #3 Food Department.

As soon as John was out of service, they moved to Brown County and lived in a house over 100 years old - the old Edna Parmerlee house, two houses from where Beulah lives while they built the log house she lives in today. The logs for the house came out of her father's woods up near the Bean Blossom Overlook. They were cut and hand hewed by her husband, John. The lot they built on was bought from J.A. Waltman in Bean Blossom for $500.00. The money came from the State of New York. John, being a soldier, received $485.00 from the State for a new start.

Beulah and John had five children —four sons and one daughter, and, in addition, seven grandchildren, two daughters-in-law, and one son-in-law. John died May 29, 1980.

Beulah's parents were Clarence and Marie Ellerman Smith from Knox County. They all came here during the Great Depression. Her father, along with several other melon farmers, lost his farm in 1934. Dad and Mother Smith rented three places before buying the Tracy farm in Bean Blossom.

Beulah Ackerman

There were eight Smith children—three boys and five girls—and Arthur and Luther Smith of Brown County, and Clarence Smith of Florida; Donna Rhoades of Indianapolis, Mary Sluss of Greenwood, Dlema Baughman of Terre Haute, Louellen Pate of Fort Wayne, and Beulah Ackerman of Bean Blossom.

The Hoover Days made a straight and strong Democrat of Beulah. The Smith family helped to get the first Missouri Synod Lutheran Church, known as Shepherd of the Hills, in Brown County. Beulah was a charter member of that church, and also a member of the Brown County Business and Professional Women's Group, Brown County Historical Society, and Bean Blossom Boosters. Currently, Beulah is on the Bishop's Committee of St. David's Episcopal Church, where she has been a member for nearly two years.

Going back a few years, Beulah owned and managed The Family Restaurant in Bean Blossom from 1954 until 1973. She retired, after several odd jobs in Nashville, to being Bean Blossom's most loving babysitter. In Brown County, she is known as "Ma Maw Boodie" to several little ones. In June, a granddaughter, Stephanie Ackerman will graduate from Indiana University. In the fall of 1990 a grandson and his wife, Mr. and Mrs. Patrick Downey, are making her a great grandmother.

Living in Brown County has made Beulah very happy. She thanks God daily for yesterday, and today will take care of itself!

ADAMS - Thomas Martin Adams was a leading citizen of early Brown County. He was the son of John and Sarah Davis Adams and was born in Green Co., TN where he learned the potter's trade. He was married to Elizabeth Rose High in Johnson Co., IN on Oct. 25, 1832, and in 1837 moved to Brown County. He was very active in the early politics of the county. He served as auditor from 1841 to 1848, as clerk a total of 14 years and recorder in the 1840s. He served in the Mexican War as First Lieutenant and was promoted to Captain during the Battle of Buena Vista after the death of his friend Captain James Taggart. He was one of the heaviest taxpayers in 1848 when he paid $9.29. He was a state senator serving from Brown and Monroe Co.'s for four years, 1848-1853.

Thomas Adams was instrumental in organizing the Masonic lodge and served as its first Worthy Master. Thomas and Elizabeth had 12 children of which two died in infancy. Their children were:

Elizabeth Rose (High) Adams

Samuel (1833-1909) married Mary Calphurnia Medley; Susan Jane (1838-1912) married Valentine Griffith; Elizabeth Jane (1841-1902) who married Albert F. Sipes; Thomas Jefferson (1843-1862) who died in the Battle of Pea Ridge; James Watts (1846-1864) who died of tuberculosis contracted in the Army; John Walter (1848-1923) who married Amanda Butler; Joseph Warren (1850-) who married Jennie; Sarah Ann (1853-1924) who married Henry Banks; and David McIlvan (1855-1904) and Nancy Maria (1875-1903) who married D. J. Bryan. Elizabeth and Thomas moved to Montezuma, IA in 1869 and from there some of the younger children went to Oregon on the Oregon Trail. For descendants of Elizabeth Jane and Thomas Adams see the Sipes Family of Brown County. *Submitted by Sarah Clevenger*

WILLIAM ALLEN - This Allen family begins with two brothers, John and William, who became citizens in Philadelphia, PA in 1798 after emigrating from County Cork, Ireland. John owned property in the Southwark District of Philadelphia and was a drayman. During a Yellow Fever epidemic John left the area and settled in what is now Marshall Co., WV. John, his wife Rebecca and a daughter Rebecca are all buried in the Buchanan-Kelly Cemetery near Moundsville, WV.

The three known children who lived to maturity were William, John and Jane. William was a farmer and a lay minister and married many people in the Proctor, WV area. He was married to Sarah Brown and was the father of 14 children. Jane was married to Ephraim Hall and six children were born to this union.

Allen Family: Back: Matilda R. Coen, William H. Allen, Mary J., George Ira; Front: Joshua, William, Melissa with Frank, Sylvania with Elmer (Pittman)

John married Rebecca Goddard, daughter of Francis and Hannah Goddard of Green Co., PA. John and Rebecca were the parents of 12 children: Francis (married Hannah Martin), Dorcas (married James Wade and Eugenus Walker), Rebecca, Hannah (married Nelson Minor), William (married Mary J. Goddard and Melissa Truex), Elizabeth, John, Sarah J. (married Benjamin F. Postlethwait),

Soloman B. (married Jemima Wise), George W. (married Hulda Rambo), James Alexander (married Nancy Richmond), Daniel W. (married Martha Rosenberger).

William came to Brown Co., IN in 1863 after the death of his first wife. William's mother, Rebecca Goddard Allen, also came to Brown County with her second husband, William Coen. A few months after William's arrival he married Melissa J. Truex, daughter of Henry Truex and Saloma More. The Truex lineage has been traced back to Philippe du Trieux who was a Walloon and living in Roubaix, France, where he was a dyer and cloth maker. He came to New Amsterdam in 1624 and was one of the first settlers. He was the founder of the first Protestant Church in America.

William and Mary Jane had four children: Eunice and Emily who died young, Joshua and Sylvania (married William Pittman). William and Melissa had six children: Mary Jane (married Charles Gates), Matilda Rubertie (married James Judson Wilson), William Henry (married Pearl Williams), George Ira (married Mary Penrose), Coen Clark (married Minnie Ann Crouch) and Frank Reuben (married Viola Pike). Many of this family are buried in the New Bellsville Cemetery.

Coen and Minnie (Crouch) Allen were both born in Brown County. Minnie was the daughter of Daniel Crouch and Amanda Henderson. Daniel was the son of William Crouch and Amy Reynolds. William was the son of Aaron Crouch and Mary "Polly" Cassady. Aaron was an early settler of Bartholomew Co., IN arriving by 1820. He was the son of David Crouch of Montgomery Co., VA. Amanda Henderson was the daughter of John Henderson and Jane Steele who came to Brown County during the Civil War from Washington Co., OH.

Coen and Minnie had five children: Charles who died as an infant and is buried at New Bellsville, Jesse, W. (married Evelyn Printz), Ray (married Dorothy Manuel), Marie (married Lewis P. Smith) and Earl (married Clara Sweet).

It has been many years since our Allens left Brown County but it still remains close to our hearts. S*ubmitted by Shirley J. Hannaford*

CECIL AND RUTH ALLENDER
Cecil and Ruth were life long Brown County residents until their retirement years. He spent the majority of his life as a dairy and land farmer, but his true love was logging with mules. His son Bob and grandson Leon (Colt) are still logging with mules today. Part of their farming was done on the Monroe-Brown Co. line on Kent Road. Currently, his son, Bobby, and daughter Irene Schroeder, two grandchildren, two great-grandchildren and two great-great-grandchildren reside in this same area; and Bobby is still logging with horses. In the late 1920s, Ruth and Cecil lived in the Brown County State Park and cared for the Animal Shelter. Ruth also worked for the Abe Martin Lodge, Nashville House Restaurant and drove a school bus. Upon retiring, they sold their farm and moved to Monroe County and spent their winter months in Florida. Ironically, their daughters Mable Tucker, Mary Kirts Brown, Beryl Deckard, and son George Allender have retired in the same area as their parents did years earlier. Eldest son Glen Allender and youngest daughter Dolly Wodtke both reside in Indianapolis, IN. Ruth and Cecil were married June 7, 1911 and to this union of 60 years 12 children were born and eight still survive. Ruth died May 5, 1971, in Bloomington, IN. Cecil died Jan. 3, 1976, in Inverness, FL. Both are buried in the Bean Blossom Weeping Willow Cemetery and were life long members of the Pentecostal faith.

Cecil and Ruth (Snyder) Allender

Of this couple these facts are known of their ancestors: Cecil was the 7th of 12 children born, (March 15, 1888 in Brown County) to Thomas Henry (Koon) Allender and Elizabeth E. Turner. Cecil's father, Thomas H. Allender was born Aug. 15, 1850, in Ohio and died Dec. 11, 1938, buried in Bean Blossom Cemetery. His parents, Thomas Allender and Armilia Henry, were likewise born in Ohio, but after Thomas Henry's birth moved to Brown County. Cecil's grandfather, Thomas Allender died Sept. 1, 1901. His grandmother, Armilia Henry Allender died Sept. 11, 1906. Both are buried in the Unity Baptist Cemetery. Cecil's mother, Elizabeth Turner, was born in Helmsburg, IN, July 18, 1857, to Rebecca McCoy (died 1898) and Elisha Daniel Turner (died 1920). Elisha Daniel Turner was born in Maryland in 1828 and was a member of General Sherman's Union Army. Rebecca and Daniel are both buried in the Georgetown Cemetery.

Cecil's son Bob C. Allender with Cecil far left. Right: Debbie Allender Mathis and Larry Allender

Ruth Armintie Snyder Allender was the first of five children born, March 21, 1892, to Herman Vanstander Snyder and Mary Isabelle (Mollie) Parker. Ruth's mother, Mollie, was born Nov. 17, 1871, in Brown County to Martin V. Parker and Hannah M. Settle. Martin preceded Hannah's death of June 11, 1930 and both are buried in the Goshen Cemetery. Mollie divorced Herman between 1902 and 1905 and married Herman's brother, Joseph E. Snyder to which six children were born. Mollie is buried at the Rest Haven Cemetery in Edinburg, IN. Ruth's father, Herman Vanstander Snyder, was the second of eight children, born July 15, 1868, in Brown County to Uriah Snyder and Elizabeth Kinsey Snyder. Uriah was born Feb. 24, 1842, in Belmont Co., OH, to Frederick Snyder. According to the 1900 Census, Frederick was born in Germany and his wife in Ireland. Uriah died in Jan. 27, 1922 at 79 and was a Civil War Veteran. His wife Elizabeth was born Dec. 5, 1925, at her home three miles northeast of Nashville. Both Elizabeth and Uriah are buried in the Clark Cemetery along with their son Herman. S*ubmitted by Vicki Payne*

PAUL RICHARD AND LOUISE (PEARSON) ALLISON
James Allison and Eleanor Poulter were the parents of George W. Allison, born Mercer Co., KY in 1825. George married Rachel Rogers in 1850. They had nine children: George, William, Ed, Orion, Rachel, Nettie, Alice, Madie and Alonzo. George W. Allison was a brilliant man, was admitted to the bar on Dec. 3, 1859 and served as a Captain in the Civil War. He took his young son Alonzo along as drummer boy. George also served as Indiana State Rep. in 1882 and was a dedicated Christian layman and preacher. He helped organize a Methodist Church in Franklin, IN where he sometimes served as preacher. He was editor and publisher of the Franklin newspaper, The Jeffersonian. He later owned the Brown County newspaper, The Jacksonian.

George W. Allison's son, Alonzo, married in 1873 to Jane Elizabeth Minor, one of the seven children of Robert N. and Rachel Elizabeth Hoy Minor. In 1857 they had travelled by covered wagon from Belmont Co., OH to Schooner Valley in Brown County where they purchased land. Later, the family moved to Nashville where they ran a hotel. Located on the west side of Van Buren St., the building known as the Old Minor House is now owned by the Brown County Art Guild.

Thurle H. Allison Brown County Mail Carrier in front of Methodist Parsonage, Nashville, IN.

Alonzo Allison came to Nashville in 1870 from Franklin, IN where he was born. He purchased the Brown County Democrat Newspaper in 1885 which he ran until his death in 1926 when his wife, known as Jennie, took over as publisher. Alonzo and Jennie had six children: Cecil Alonzo, James Elmer, John Grover, George Arthur, Thurle and a daughter who died young. Alonzo built the family home in Nashville, now "The Allison Inn."

Thurle, born Nov. 6, 1887, son of Alonzo and Jennie E. Minor Allison, married in 1909 to Olive Campbell, daughter of Clark Augustus and Hattie Poling Campbell. Thurle and Olive Allison had six children: Pauline, Harriett, Carl, Jane E., Paul Richard and Dorothy. Thurle was a mail carrier for many years and was a valued correspondent for the Indianapolis NEWS and STAR. He was killed in a truck accident July 1921 on Taggart Hill when he and Orville Pittman were taking a mule to Columbus.

Paul Richard, son of Thurle and Olive Allison, lived with his grandfather, Clark Campbell and attended Nashville schools until 8th grade when he moved to Columbus to live with his mother. He graduated from Columbus High School in 1935, attended Indiana Extension School and worked at Noblitt-Sparks Industries, Columbus.

Paul Richard Allison and Louise met while her father, Dr. R.O. Pearson, was serving the First United Methodist Church in Columbus. They were married in that church where they had enjoyed singing in the choir. Paul served in WWII as Captain in the Airforce Signal Corps and spent five years in New Guinea. He returned to work as Safety Director at Arvin Industries in Columbus. Paul and Louise had four children: Paula Allison Brostrom, a registerd nurse and music major from DePauw University, James Richard, Ohio University and Boulder Law School, now Fed. Pros. Attorney, Denver, Nancy Louise Pegg, graduate of University of Evansville and Library Media teacher at Crescent City, FL and Deborah A. Stamper, graduate of Purdue with a M.A. in phys. ed from Indiana University. There are eight grandchildren.

Paul was known for his recitation of James Whicomb Riley poems and gave over 60 programs before his death on May 8, 1989. He is buried in Greenlawn Cemetery in Nashville in the Allison plot.

Louise's parents were Dr. R.O. Pearson and Naomi Fetzer Pearson who had served the United Methodist Church for over 50 years in the Indiana Conference. Dr. Pearson was the Chaplain at Methodist Hospital in Indianapolis for ten years. Louise graduated with a R.N. degree from Methodist Hospital in 1939. She is active in the Joseph Hart D.A.R. Chapter of Columbus, and the P.E.O. Sisterhood, as well as in the Women's Organization of the local Methodist Church.

Faith, Family, Loyalty and Love were the fundamental factors in their lives. S*ubmitted by Louise Pearson Allison*

JOHN ANDERSON - John thought to have been born in Wales about 1725, migrated to America before 1780 when he appeared in Rockbridge Co., VA, where he died. Joseph, son of John Anderson, was born 1757 and married Sarah Bess, born in England. Sarah had three brothers, George, John and Samuel Bess, of Kentucky. Joseph and Sarah Anderson had six children: James, Nancy, Isabell, Fanny, Polly and Joseph Anderson, Jr.

Joseph Anderson, Jr. was born near Fincastle, VA on Feb. 27, 1789. He married Christiana Britz of Augusta County Sept. 2, 1813. After living in Montgomery Co., VA for 25 years, Joseph Anderson, Jr. moved his family to Morgantown (1837), Morgan Co., IN where he died Jan. 27, 1870 and was buried in East Hill Cemetery. Joseph and Christiana Anderson had seven children:

1. Caleb Henry Renshaw Anderson married Barbara Lake, daughter of Timothy and Mary Lake. Caleb and Barbara had children: John, Amanda and Emily Anderson, live Ladoga, IN.

Allen Stover Anderson Home

2. Allen Stover Anderson, born July 24, 1815, married Sarah Canatsey in 1839. Their children were: Sampson Joseph; George Madison, born Oct. 31, 1849, married Margaret Terhune; Florentine Emaline who married Arnold Griffitt and had children: Paris Whitcomb Griffitt, Francis Marion Griffit and Queen Victoria Griffitt; Alias Anderson; Mary Anderson; Madison Britt Anderson who married Saloma Harshbarger, lived in Montgomery County and had five children; Charles Lewis Anderson who married Maria Howe, lived in California and had four children; Harriett Anderson who married John Jamison Kelso and had nine children.

Allen Stover Anderson, second child of Joseph Anderson, Jr. and Christiana Britz, was Surveyor of Brown County from 1839 to 1852, blazing the trail from Morgantown to Nashville. He entered land in 1837 in Jackson Twp., Sec. 13, T10N, R2E. Allen's wife Sarah was born in Kentucky, a daughter of Sampson and Nancy Richards Canatsey. Sarah entered land in Brown County in 1889 which passed to her son George Anderson. Allen Stover gave each of his children a farm. Each began with a one room log cabin, chinked and daubed with sticks and clay mud, with fireplace and dirt floor. Their meals were cooked outside, eaten on stumps and keeping close watch for Indians. Shingles were hewed with homemade tools, tiresome job. They had corner beds with ropes as springs and straw ticks. The surrounding woods supplied wild animals. They raised sheep for wool, flax for making clothing, found honey in bee trees, made corn cob molasses, burnt cobs on stones for potash to make biscuits rise, grew gardens, smoked meat and had a milkhouse to cool milk and butter. Allen later made a brick kiln, burnt red brick, built his own house and houses for others. If each brick didn't sound just right when he thumped it with his cane, it was taken out and replaced before going farther. The home he built for his family now overlooks State Rd. 135 north. It has an open porch on the second floor and was built between 1861 and 1864. His son, Sampson Anderson, later lived there. S*ubmitted by Mary Murphy Taylor*

WILLIAM P. AND SHARON L. ANDREWS - The Andrews (Bill and Sharon) were both born and raised in Indianapolis, IN. Bill Andrews was born Aug. 14, 1941. He was one of five sons of Louis and Agnes (Boyer) Andrews. Sharon (Jones) Andrews was born Oct. 23, 1943. She was one of four daughters and one son of Paul and Mary (McNeal) Jones.

Although Bill and Sharon attended the same high school (Emerich Manual Training High School), they were unacquainted at the time. Many years passed before they became close and fate would prove them to be inseparable. With God's blessings and an everlasting love they were married on Feb. 14, 1976.

William P. and Sharon L. Andrews

The Andrews' raised six children: Scott, Kim, Brent, Karen, Kyle and Julie before they decided to make a major change in their lives. Because of their shared desire of a more simplistic and wholesome lifestyle, they moved to Brown County in June of 1985. At that time they started clearing their property, and prepared to reconstruct a 150 year-old log cabin which is presently their home.

Sharon is an employee of Eli Lilly and Company. She is a Process Technician in insulin purification. Bill is a full-time organic gardener and orchardist while maintaining a woodlot and wildlife management program at their farm on Oak Ridge Road.

Their primary goal is to be responsible stewards of their land and to leave it better than it was found for prosterity's sake, so hopefully they can rest in peace in these rolling hills of Southern Indiana in the County of Brown.

LARRY AND GARY ANTHONY - Larry Gene and Gary Wayne Anthony are the last two native - born Brown and Jackson County descendants of Peter Anthony who immigrated to the United States in 1840 from Bern, Switzerland with his brother Christopher and two sisters, one of which died in route and was buried at sea. Reportedly, the surviving sister went to Missouri, Christopher to California as a 49er, and Peter settled in Powhattan Point, Belmont Co., OH.

In 1842, Peter married Mary Jane Meeks, of Virginia, at St. Clairsville, OH. After buying land in York Township, they parented 11 children while Peter worked as a farmer and millwright until he and his two oldest sons, John and William Christopher, served in the Civil War.

Following the war, in October of 1866, Peter bought 160 acres in Van Buren Township, Brown Co., IN and sold their land in Ohio. Samuel, the fourth son, said that Peter and the six women folk embarked from Powhatten Point, OH on a flatboat built by William Christopher Anthony who was an experienced boatsman. They landed at Madison, IN and moved on by wagon teams to their land near Christiansburg in Brown County. The six sons that came made the trip from Powhattan Point, OH to 160 acres of section 26 in Brown County by wagon train. There, where Peter and Mary Jane lived until their deaths, the Anthony family began their Brown County beginnings.

Larry and Gary Anthony, 1990

Feb. 21, 1869, William Christopher Anthony, second son of Peter and Mary Jane Anthony, married Nancy Helms in Brown Co., IN. On Dec. 6, 1871 he purchased 40 acres located about half way between Houston and Mt. Nebo, IN from his parents.

Located on land just north of the Brown - Jackson County line was a log cabin where John, Jim,

Harley, and Ray were born. After the cabin burned in 1885, Nancy and William had a new white two-story four bedroom weatherboard house built during April-September of 1886 just about 200 feet southeast in Jackson County.

Following their respective deaths in 1893 and 1896, oldest son, John Wadsworth Anthony and Nora Ellen Hashman began their married life in this same house in 1899. Subsequent to the birth of a daughter, Virta Mae in 1901, a second daughter, Mildred in 1906 and a son, John Daulton Anthony in 1914 this farm couple lived in the William C. Anthony house until 1944, five years after John Daulton Anthony and Mary Ellen Cobb began their married life there. To that marriage, two sons, Larry and Gary were born. Larry, wife Janet, and daughters Janalyn Renee and Elysa Ellen live near Ogilville, IN. Gary lives part time with his mother, Mary in the house built by his great-grandfather, William C. Anthony, son of Peter Anthony who was the original progenitor of the "Brown County" Anthonys. *Submitted by Larry Anthony*

PETER ANTHONY - Was born in Switzerland in 1819. In 1839 he, with a brother Chris and two sister, migrated to America. Enroute one sister died. The survivors settled first in Belmont Co., OH.

In 1842 Peter married Mary Jane Meeks. Their home was farm in Belmont County near Steinersville and Powhatten Point on the Ohio River. They had 11 children: John (1843), William C. (1843), Henry (1846), Peter (1848), Samuel (1849), David (1852), a son stillborn, Charlotte (1855) Jeanette (1857), Arena (1859), and Alice (1863).

Peter was a farmer and millwright. During the Civil War, Peter and two sons, John and William, served in the Union Army. After the War John married Lucretia Knightler. Henry married Sarah Wright.

Peter and Mary Jane (Meeks) Anthony

In 1866 Peter purchased land near Christiansburg, Van Buren Township, Brown County, an area which attracted the Tipton, Roush, Read, Carmichael and other families from Belmont County. In the fall of 1866 Peter embarked a flatboat constructed by his sons on the Ohio River at Powhatten Point. With him were Mary Jane, their four daughters, age 3 to 11 and the two daughters-in-law. Also on the boat were possessions including a team and wagon. At Madison, IN ,400 miles down river, they disembarked and travelled 70 miles by wagon to the new home. Meanwhile, the six sons, ages 14 to 23, made the move overland by wagon train.

In Brown County, Peter was farmer, orchardist and woodsman as were the sons. Descendants of Peter and Jane; children of John and Lucretia: Margaret, Florence, John W., and Harvey. William C. married Nancy Helms. Children: John, James, Harley and Vandaver Ray.

Children of Henry and Sarah: Mary, Emma D., Amanda, Jeanette, Martha, George A., Cora, Amos, Olive, and Myrtle.

Peter Jr. married Mary Carmichael. Children: Wesley, Scott, Rose and Orville. Samuel married Mary Elizabeth Roush. Children: Almeda, George W., William T., James, Sina and Bert.

Charlotte married Amos Carmichael. Children: Mary, Ada, Harley, Adolph and Bessie.

Jeanette married Vandiver Mabe. Children: Willie, Bessie and Lawrence.

Arena married Wilson Ross Read. Children: Alonzo and Mary.

David and Alice died young. Never married.

Peter died 1891; Mary Jane, 1893. They and nine of their children and several grandchildren are buried in Christiansburg Cemetery.

All of Peter's 40 grandchildren are deceased. Two of them were centenarians: Margaret Garlock age 107 died 1974. George W.. Anthony died in 1984 age 109.

George W. Anthony by log home of grandfather, Peter Anthony, 1979 (George is 105 years old)

Ten of Peter's 60 great-grandchildren are living: Elva McKain, daughter of Margaret Garlock, lives near Seymour. Wanda Dobbs, Henry's granddaughter lives in Florida. Delphine Read McCalmon, Arena's granddaughter, Michigan.

Seven of Samuel's grandchildren:

Grace Hall and Rada Brown live in Columbus.

Lillie Ayers Smith and Olive Ayers Hastings live near Evansville.

Herbert Anthony, WWI veteran and retired teacher, Edmonton, Alberta. Cloyd Anthony, Terre Haute.

Wilma Spiker, road 135 South. Wilma, her children, and the children of Hesper Beauchamp (deceased) are the descendants of Peter still living in Brown County. Many others left their place of birth and resumed Peter's migratory pattern. When they re-visit scenes of childhood they are "strangers in a foreign land." *Submitted by Cloyd Anthony*

BELLE (CHITWOOD) HAWLEY ARNOLD - Nora Belle Chitwood, daughter of Richard and Ida May Chitwood, was born Dec. 7, 1891

Belle Chitwood Hawley Arnold about 1922 with Ivan Hawley and Robert Arnold in chair

near Needmore, IN. She grew up on the family farm west of Needmore, married Harry Hawley in 1910 and had one son, Ivan, born 1911. After her husband's death from tuberculosis in 1916, Belle found that she also had contracted the disease and moved back to her parents' home with Ivan until the tuberculosis appeared to be cured.

In 1917 Belle married William Arnold, son of John and Ellen Hawley Arnold. One son, Robert Warren Arnold, was born in 1920 to this union. The Arnolds moved to Sioux City, IA.

Nora Belle died of tuberculosis in 1930 and her son, Ivan Hawley, also died of the same disease about 1940. Bill Arnold raised Robert in Sioux city but Robert spent many summers in Indiana with his grandmother Ida May, his Aunt Blanche Neal, and his Aunt Maude Martin. Robert married Margene Le Moine, daughter of Wilford and Ilo Grapp Le Moine. Margene died in 1979 and Robert married Alice Davis.

CHARLES EUGENE AND VERA (CAMPBELL) ARNOLD - Dr. Charles Eugene Arnold (known by his friends and family as "Doc"), a dentist by profession, was the eldest son of Charles Albert and Sara Collins Arnold. He was born Feb. 11, 1891, in Madison Co., IN. Upon graduation from Greenfield High School, Doc attended Butler University and received the degree of Doctor of Dental Science from Indiana University School of Dentistry in 1918. Dr. Arnold was also a graduate of the Indianapolis Conservatory of Music. He gained recognition for his rich and well-trained baritone voice, singing on the concert stage, and for 15 years did choir work at the First Baptist Church. He did choral work in the United States Army, singing in a production of "H.M.S. Pinafore" staged by the armed forces while serving in the Army during War I.

The Arnold Brown County Cabin.

In 1931, Dr. Arnold married Vera M. Campbell, daughter of Joseph Martin and Mary Cheek Campbell of Chatham County, NC. The Arnolds reconstructed a log cabin (from 1843 hand hewned yellow poplar logs purchased from the Brummetts of Bean Blossom for $50) atop a hill near Nashville, Brown Co., IN, and there he installed an open-air dentist's chair. His dental kit was always with him, and at all hours of the day or night, in about every conceivable situation, he was called upon to practice dentistry. He had offices at 5412 East Washington, Indianapolis, and a parttime office in Morgantown, but there was not a crossroads from Indianapolis to Stone Head where he hadn't pulled teeth. Once he improvised a dental chair out of fence rails. He sat the patients on stumps, milk stools and rocks while he went about the work of extraction. He wasn't always paid money for his services, but he felt he never failed to receive ample pay. He pulled teeth for country butter and eggs, filled teeth for fried chicken, rabbit stew, froglegs, roasting ears and bird dog pups.

It was in this rustic, picturesque cabin (their week-end home) that friends came from far and near to be entertained by the Arnolds. The cabin, furnished with antiques, quilts, three-corner cupboard, lamps, a very fine collection of paintings of William Forsyth, a long-time friend of the Arnolds, and added works of art by other artists (including Charles Townsend, Alton Coffey, Mary Vawter and Frank Hohenberger) was merely a part of the whole. Rich and poor visited the Arnold cabin, educated and uneducated, artistic and unartistic, well fed and hungry, and the atmosphere and the personalities of the owners were such that always the hosts and guests parted the richer for having met. Doc's sense of humor, his friendliness and joviality will be remembered by many who visited.

Dr. Arnold died in September 1950, son, Charles, died in 1982 and daughter, Sara Walters, died in 1986. Vera retired in 1969 and lived in Brown County until 1980, and after 49 years of pleasurable log cabin living, moved to Oxford, MS, where she now resides.

DONALD AND MARTHA LEE (NEFF) AULT

Donald George Ault's ancestors arrived from Emmushauer, Germany on the ship "Davy" Oct. 25, 1738. Valentin Alt (born 1710) and Marie Catherine Schmidt took their oath at the courthouse in Philadelphia, and moved to Falkner Swamp (Mongomery Co., PA).

Their son, Valentin II, was born in 1750, and became an indentured servant after his mother's death in 1759. Valentin served in the Revolutionary War as an Ensign in the Militia 7th Company (York County).

Valentin's son George (born 1793) anglicized his name to "Ault" and married Margaret "Polly" Ault, his cousin. They moved to Belmont Co., OH and had 11 children. Polly died after 1833. George married Emma "Amy" Battin on June 14, 1836 and had seven children. The family moved to Pikes Peak, Brown Co., IN in 1854.

Six of George's sons served in the Civil War: Andrew, Valentine, Martin (KIA), Henry, Jacob, and Jesse. The story in the Ault family is that "they all got together in camp one night...all six were six feet tall, and each weighed over 200 pounds, with less than ten pounds difference in their weights!"

Andrew Ault married Mary Ann Snively July 15, 1838. He died in Brown County in 1894. Valentine lived in Belmont Co., OH. Henry moved to Los Angeles, CA. Jacob, severely wounded in the war, lived in Brown County.

Donald George Ault Family: D. Gregory, Douglas L., Martha Lee (Neff) Donald and Jaquelyn L.

Jesse Ault married Tina Hill Oct. 22, 1864 in Brown County, the day he received his discharge from the Union Army, Co. C, 6th Indiana Reg., Infantry. Jesse was the first volunteer in Pikes Peak; his name heads the list on a monument erected to the soldiers in the Pikes Peak area. Tina and two children died within three years.

Jesse then married Jane Pruitt on Jan. 30, 1868 in Pikes Peak. Jane (born April 11, 1850) was the daughter of Samuel and Deborah Bridgewater Pruitt, who lived in Brown County and are buried at Beck's Grove. Jesse and Jane lived in Brown County when their son George Samuel was born (Dec. 4, 1870); they later moved to Morgan County, then to Tipton County.

George Samuel Ault married Nellie Frances Shaw in Muncie, IN. They had eight children, including Thomas Gola (born Aug. 29, 1896).

Thomas (Jake) married Hazel Verona Heflin on Feb. 2, 1918 in Tipton Co., IN. They moved to Kosciusko Co., IN in 1942, where Jake was a Livestock Dealer and Auctioneer, founding the Claypool Sales Barn. Jake and Hazel had five children: Phyllis Christina, Lloyd Joseph, Thomas Hobart, Wilma Jean, and Donald George.

Donald George Ault (born Aug. 15, 1928 in Summitsville) married Martha Lee (Marty) Neff (born Aug. 16, 1927) on Nov. 7, 1948 in Claypool, IN where they reside today. Don and his brothers are well-known Livestock Dealers in the northern Indiana area; Marty is a registered nurse.

Don and Mary Ault have three childen: Douglas Lee, Jacquelyn Lynn, and Donald Gregory.

Douglas (born Aug. 22, 1949) married Janet Heberling (born Feb. 16, 1953) and reside in Claypool, IN. They have two sons, Ryan Douglas (born Sept. 3, 1975) and Kevin Gregory (born Dec. 1, 1977).

Jacquelyn (born Aug. 27, 1951) married Jon Keith Negus (born Nov. 8, 1960) on Aug. 14, 1982 and reside in Chicago, IL. They have three children: Jeffrey Keith (born Jan. 18, 1984), Jessica Lynn (born Feb. 17, 1986) and Joel Kristopher (born May 26, 1989).

Donald Gregory (born Nov. 14, 1955) married Cindy Louise Reppert (born Jan. 23, 1953) on Aug. 21, 1982, and reside in Baltimore, MD. They have one child, Stephanie Kane, (born Aug. 12, 1986). *Submitted by D. Gregory Ault*

GARLAND AND TRESSA AYERS

Garland, son of Edmond and Georgia Baker Ayers of Gravel Creek, married Tressa Hamblen, daughter of James and Mary Morrison Hamblen of Story, Aug. 30, 1930. Garland died 1968 and Tressa died 1989. They lived first on the Bruce place near Kelp while Garland worked at the Brown County State Park. From 1932 until 1972 they lived on Gravel Creek near Garland's parents where they raised 12 children. In 1972 Tressa moved to near Christiansburg and in 1987 she moved to Columbus. Garland was a farmer, logger and seasonal canning factory worker. Tressa was custodian at VanBuren Township Elementary School, cook at the Nashville House and eight years as custodian at Jim Good Custom Cabinets. Garland and Tressa are buried at Mt. Zion Cemetery with son, Garland Junior, and daughter, Mary Louise.

Their eldest is Robert Ayers of Columbus, born 1931. Bob works for Arvin Industries in Columbus. He married Violet Wyant in 1954 and has five children, Robert Leon, Rhonda Lynn, Laura S., Jeffry Scott and Roger Dale.

Garland Junior, born 1932, died, 1979, retired U.S. Army, Ft. Carson, CO and was living in Colorado Springs when he died. He married first Gladys and had one daughter, Tressa Elizabeth. He married second Neftal Catt and had sons, Jack and Lyndal, and daughter Stacy.

Left to right, Tressa, Michael, Maxine, Edna, Ruth, Linda and Janet

Betty Jane, born 1934, married Warren K. Shaw, 1952. He is a GE retiree and farms near Flat Rock and she worked for Western Electric in Indianapolis for many years. They have sons, Michael.

Edna Mae, born 1949, married Darrell Thomas, 1971, and have daughter, Melanie Ann, and son, Scott Darrell. They reside in Mohawk, IN. Edna received a BWP of Nashville Scholarship, is a Beautician and Darrell is part owner of Classic Kitchens in Indianapolis.

Helen Anita, born 1951, married Michael Gregg, 1974, and has daughter Michelle Leigh. Michael is Damage Control Chief Petty Officer in the U.S. Navy and Helen is Benefits Systems Analyst with the Sovran Bank in Norfolk, VA.

Michael Keith, born 1956, married Marilyn Moore of Nashville, 1981. Michael is a graduate of Taylor University and is currently an FAA Air Traffic Controller at the Indianapolis Air Route Traffic Control Center. Marilyn graduated from Cincinnati Bible College and Ft. Hays State University (KS) and taught at the Lawrence Christian School. They now live in Annendale Estates in Nashville. *Submitted by Maxine Ayers Melton*

JOHN AND SARAH (CROUCHER) AYRES

John Ayres was born March 4, 1840 in Van Buren Twp., Brown Co., IN, a son of Samuel C. and America McKinney Ayres. He was a farmer by occupation and spent his early adult years in Jackson Co., IN.

John married Susannah Croucher on Feb. 12, 1857 in Jackson County. She was born on Oct. 17, 1839 in Owen Twp., Jackson County, the daughter of James W. and Margaret C. Scott Croucher. Her ancestry includes the Zike, Maxwell, Dele and Avery family names. Susannah died in childbirth between 1861 and 1864, according to family tradition.

Sarah (Croucher) Ayres and John Ayres

In 1863, John Ayres migrated west by wagon train with his uncle, Rev. Daniel McKinney, and his brothers-in-law, Joshua McQueen and William Croucher. After his wife's death, John returned to Jackson Co., IN and married his sister-in-law and married his sister-in-law, Sarah Croucher in 1865. She was born in 1841. John and Sarah made their home in Shelby Co., IL.

His children by Susannah were: Margaret C. who married Francis McQueen (through whom the submitter is descended); Samuel C. who died young and Mary Ann who married Elza Propeck.

His children by Sarah were: Elizabeth who married Ben Camp; America who married Tom Tolliver; Delila E. and John W., both of whom died as infants; and Susannah who married Douglas Miller.

John Ayres died Oct. 22, 1909 in Shelby Co., IL and Sarah died in 1919. They are buried in Antioch Cemetery near Henton, IL. Descendants of these pioneers are scattered throughout the United States. Some members of the Ayres family spell their surname Ayers. (See Samuel C. and America McKinney Ayres). *Submitted by Russell L. Layhew*

SAMUEL C. AND AMERICA AYRES -

The Ayres family appears in the 1840 Van Buren Twp., Brown County Census. Samuel C. Ayres was born in 1804 in Virginia. His parentage is unknown, but it is known that his brothers were George Washington Ayres who married a Bales; Edward E. Ayres who married Dorcas Dotson, and William Ayres. According to Brown County records these Ayres men helped build roads near the Jackson County line in 1836.

Samuel C. Ayres married America McKinney on Feb. 25, 1836 in Bartholomew Co., IN. America was born in 1818, the daughter of John D.W. and Elizabeth Mullis McKinney. Both of America's parents died in Vermillion Co., IL in December of 1863.

Samuel C. and America (McKinney) Ayres

Samuel C. and America Ayres settled in Jackson Township, Bartholomew County and raised their family on a small farm outside of Freetown, IN. Their children were Margaret Amanda who married James Harvey; Elizabeth who married Joshua X. McQueen and settled in Shelby Co., IL; John who married Susannah Croucher, then her sister, Sarah Croucher; Samuel who died in 1870; America who married William F. Croucher (a brother of John's wives) and settled in Shelby Co., IL; James who married Amanda J. Logsdon and settled in Kansas; William who married and died young in Kansas; Malinda G.; Delila who married James T. Gray; and Daniel R. Ayres who married Susanna Barker.

It is not known when Samuel Ayres died. He is listed on the 1870 Bartholomew County Census but is absent from the 1880 census. Family tradition states that Samuel is buried in Jackson County in Sutherland Cemetery. His wife, America Ayres, went west with some of her children and died there. (See John and Sarah Croucher Ayres. *Submitted by Mrs. Dorothy Helton Layhew*

ROBERT AND JUANITA (MILLER) BAINTER -

The Bainter family came to Brown County in 1961 from central Illinois. They reside on Coffey Hill outside of Nashville.

Robert Bainter was born June 23, 1918 in Galesburg, IL and grew up in Illinois. Although a city boy, he decided to be a farmer and did so after high school. When WWII began, he sold everything and joined the Army Air Corps. He served in the South Pacific for four years. He was discharged in 1946 and married Juanita Miller. He returned to school and later rejoined the Air Force until 1965. After his military stint, he was employed for 18 years by the Department of Defense as a Quality Engineer on Aircraft Engine programs and the Apollo Space program. He retired in 1978 and has since devoted himself to various Brown County activities such as Brown County State Park Gate Attendant and Cartoonist for "The Brown County Democrat" newspaper.

Robert and Juanita Bainter

Juanita (born Aug. 16, 1919, Shelby Co., MO) was owner and operator of a homemade candy and popcorn shop until their marriage at the conclusion of WWII. She then devoted herself to rearing three children and doing volunteer work in the community and working in politics. She served four years as Brown County Republican Vice-chairman, and Governor Orr designated her as "A Sagamore of the Wabash" in 1984. She was elected to two terms as Brown County Treasurer and to three terms to the Brown County Council, being the first woman ever elected to the County Council.

In volunteer work, she served the Brown County Historical Society as two terms as treasurer and two terms as president. She is now in her second term as president of the Pioneer Women's Club. She frequently serves as a docent at the Brown County Historical Society Museum. She has served as Sunday School teacher, Bible School teacher and as Den Mother at the United Methodist Church in Nashville. During the childrens school years, she served in PTO and in Band Boosters. She has walked her neighborhood many times, collecting for Heart Fund, Cancer Fund, Leukemia Fund, etc.

The Bainter children are: Jeffrey W. (born Canton, IL, Dec. 28, 1946) who operates a restaurant in Castle Rock, CO; Lynnette G. (born Canton, IL, Oct. 13, 1949) married to Michael L. Miller son of Rupert and Birdie Miller. Lynnette is raising a family of two boys: Adrian J. (Jan. 20, 1978) and Galen G. (Aug. 13, 1983). They live in York, SC. Eric L. Bainter (born Nov. 4, 1959 at Franklin, IN) is a Captain in the United States Air Force, serving in West Germany.

Bob's parents were: Harold G. Bainter, 1894-1967 and Stella Jane Werdebaugh, 1893-1963.

Juanita's parents were Thomas W. Miller, 1882-1975, and Cora Mildred Herrick, 1888-1953.

OWEN BARGER -

Among the early settlers of Brown County were the ancestors of Owen Barger. In Washington Township lived his great-grandparents, Joseph and Hannah Barger. Joseph was born circa 1831 in Bartholomew Co., IN to John S. and Tabitha (Kinnear) Barger. Hannah was born circa 1834 in Indiana to John and Letitia Jackson of Brown Co., IN. Hannah's father, John Jackson was born circa 1791 in Virginia, and his wife, Letitia was born circa 1790 in Kentucky.

Joseph and Hannah Barger had children; James, Joseph, Oliver, Anna, and Ira who was the grandfather of Owen.

Ira Elsworth Barger and his wife, the former Eva Ella Bradburn, were parents of Martin, John, Clarence, William, Mary, Bertha, Verna, Dolly, Allen, Anna and Beatrice.

Owen "Mickey" and Donna (Stigdon) Barger

Allen Lorain Barger was the father of our subject. Allen was born Sept. 22, 1905 and died May 7, 1987. He was married April 27, 1925 in Morgan County to Lena Jane Owens, the daughter of James Lawrence and Pearl (Hacker) Owens. Lena was born March 6, 1909 and died April 24, 1983. Allen and Lena are buried at the New South Park Cemetery in Martinsville, IN. Their children are Alice, Carol, Merrill, Janice, Owen, Gary, Judith, Mary, Karen and Doris.

The fifth child of Allen and Lena Barger was our subject, Owen Mitchell Barger who was born Feb. 9, 1941 near Taggarts Crossing in Morgan Co., IN. He is called "Mickey" by family members, but many friends know him as "Chainsaw", the codename he adopted when he operated a citizens band radio. He attended schools in Morgan and Shelby Counties through the 11th grade, then his family moved to Seymour, IN and he engaged in farming with his father. Owen had his National Guard training in Oklahoma then returned home to continue farming with his father on the dairy farm where they also raised hogs, chickens and grain.

Owen was age 26 when he married Donna Hunt at Franklin, IN on Feb. 18, 1967. She was born May 30, 1934, at Seymour, IN, the daughter of Ross Stigdon and Doris (Mellencamp) Stigdon. Donna had a 14 year old daughter, Vanessa Dale Hunt, from a previous marriage, and Owen took full financial responsibility for her upbringing until she graduated from Seymour High School in 1972 and moved to Indianapolis to take a job at the State

Office Building. Vanessa still resides in Indianapolis where for the past ten years she has been employed with the law firm, Hall, Render, Killian, Heath and Lyman.

Besides farming, Owen has worked as a heavy equipment operator, then on Dec. 3, 1968 he started a job with Cummins Engine Co. where he is still employed. His wife, Donna, worked as a secretary for 25 years, retiring in 1978 to become a full-time homemaker.

In September 1975 Owen and Donna purchased Brown County land from her father and they still reside in Van Buren Township. They each play several musical instruments and have pets, dogs, chickens and cats. *Submitted by Mrs. Owen M. Barger*

DEMAREE BARNES - William Barnes (1795-1882) arrived in Brown County from Belmont Co., OH around 1858. The 1860 census in Jackson Township of Brown County, Georgetown Post Office (now Bean Blossom) listed William as 63 years old, a farmer, born in Pennsylvania, wife Elizabeth with 11 living children.

It is said that the Barnes family came from the Old Country on horseback. They came over on a cattle boat and he rode on the back of a horse corraling the cattle most of the way.

They settled on West Owl Creek, along with some of their friends, the James M. Yoder and Efram Carter families.

Morton Barnes, the 11th child of William and Elizabeth married Emma Crider, having three sons, Charles, Bert and Demaree.

Morton Barnes was trustee of Jackson Township in the 1920s. He also operated a steam engine for threshing and sawmill. One location of the sawmill was east of Bean Blossom on a farm now owned by Carl Brummett. Demaree was running the engine for his dad the day J.I. Yoder got both hands cut off. Bert lost two fingers while helping his dad with the sawmill.

Demaree (Dump) Barnes, Blacksmith

Demaree Barnes, a blacksmith, known to many as Dump Barnes, first operated a shop in Morgantown, then traded his shop for one owned by Ernest Beaver in Helmsburg in the 20s and had his business there until his death in 1957. Helmsburg was a big logging town due to the railroad there. Dump would shoe as many as 18 head of horses in a day, finishing one day with Harry Bell's team of mules at 10:00 at night.

The blacksmith shop was a gathering place for hunters and ball fans on Saturday morning. Dump made much of the ornamental iron work in Brown County, including the Leota Loop Artist Studio and the Witch House.

Demaree was a Deacon and Licensed Minister at Unity Baptist Church. He and his wife, Hazel Jones, had six children, of which two still live in Brown County.

Leona married Russell Kelso and had two sons, William and Daniel. They lived in Indianapolis. Leona retired after 21 years working at American Fletcher Bank.

Mary Avis married Edward Mayhew and had one son, Eddie, who died at age 13. Mary retired after 26 years working for American Fletcher Bank. She and her husband made their home in Indianapolis.

Dalton married Margery McCreery, had five children, three now living in Brown County, Douglas Barnes, Margaret Crabtree and Beth Richhart. Donald lives in Indianapolis and Madonna Taylor lives in Decatur, IL. Like his dad, Dalton loved sports, especially baseball. He retired from Eli Lilly after 35 years.

Joan married a Baptist minister, Rev. John Honeay and raised four daughters, Barbara Ranard, Rebecca Turley, Teresa Hall and Julie Miller. After her husband had a stroke they retired and moved back to Brown County.

Bertha Rose died at the age of six months.

Maurice has lived in Brown County all of his life, commuting to Indianapolis as a printer for 43 years. He followed his dad's footsteps as a Deacon at Unity Baptist Church. Also his love for hunting and sports. Would much rather be home in Brown County than any place else. He married Catherine Walker and raised a son, Mark and a daughter Carol. *Researched and written by Maurice Barnes*

BARNES FAMILY - Left England to settle in Barnesville, OH and in 1860 came to Brown Co., IN as had other families from that area who arrived in 1827. Among those coming were Washington and his parents William (1795-1882) and Elizabeth (1815-1901). They settled along Owl Creek in the hills reminding them of those they left in Ohio.

George and Nelda Barnes

Washington (Wash) (1854-1929) one of 14 children married Mary Ann Wright (1853-1940) who was later known as Grandma Barnes. Both are buried at Lanam Ridge Cemetery. There were seven children born in the log cabin where they lived on Grandma Barnes Road. They farmed and Wash made brooms to sell or trade. The beautiful flower garden of Grandma Barnes was a showplace for artists to paint. Many stopped enroute to Nashville from the Helmsburg Railroad Station.

She became so well known that she was chosen the first Blossom Festival Parade Queen.

One of their children, Sylvester (1879-1966) became a well-known school teacher throughout the area. He taught in one-room schools including Georgetown and 8th grade at Helmsburg for 45 years. He is buried in Bean Blossom Cemetery. Included in his career was County Superintendent of Schools. Another son Oda (1885-1964) married Della Pryor. Three of their four children were teachers.

Grandma Barnes as Festival Queen

George (1911-1984) a graduate of Central Normal College, also did graduate work at Indiana University. He taught 43 years in one-room schools at Georgetown and Needmore and was a well-known coach at Helmsburg High School and Elementary School. Many former students became teachers. He served as a Medic in the Army in WWII in Europe and Japan. He married Nelda Eisenmenger also a graduate of Central Normal College and teacher at Nashville and Helmsburg Elementary Schools. Nelda is a WWII veteran having been in the Navy (Waves). They lived on the former John Waltman farm on Spearsville Road with their children Judith K. and John R. Judith is a graduate of Indiana Central College and now teaches in Texas. She married Claude Pass. John is a graduate of the University of Arizona and serves as Director of a Social Services Agency. He is married to Jodelle Earll and their son is Jason.

The John and Pearl Waltman place as it looked when purchased by George and Nelda Barnes in 1950.

Education is a Barnes tradition and hopefully will continue with Jason a sixth generation of Barnes since they first came to Brown County. *Submitted by Nelda Barnes*

BAUGHMAN - Although Swiss/German in origin, the Baughman family name came to be identified with that group of early Americans known as "Pennsylvania Dutch." This name was given to those Swiss, German and French Huguenot immigrants who arrived in America in the 1700s, settling in south-central and eastern Pennsylvania. In the latter part of the 18th century the Baughman families began migrating to Maryland, Virginia, North Carolina and Ohio.

The Baughman family settled in Byrd Township, Brown Co., OH in the early 1800s from Pennsylvania.

Jacob Baughman, farmer, was born on Feb. 22, 1818. He came to Brown Co., IN where he married Eliza Jane Snider, daughter of William and Jane

(Evans) Snider, on March 23, 1846. Jacob and Eliza Jane Baughman bought a farm in Jackson Township where they raised their children: William, John, Mary, Eliza Jane, Amanda Ellen, Lidda, Lurena and Sarah Catherine.

Jacob's eldest son, William (1848-1910) married Margaret Branum on April 6, 1873. William continued the family tradition of farming in Jackson Township where his ten children were born: Rosa (1874-1953), Laura (1875-1964), Nettie (1877-1877), Jacob (1879-1954), Bert (1881-1942), Cecil (1884-1967), Frances (1886-1982), Nellis (1889), Joseph (1891-1982) and Millard (1895-1953).

William's sister, Eliza Jane (1853-1934), married James Yoder (a politician and a Civil War Veteran) on Sept. 11, 1872. Their children were Jacob (1873-1963), Ida, Cyrus (1877-1877), Myrtle (1879), Edith (1883-1903), Maude, Daniel, Leroy (1889-1976), Ralph (1891-1980), Dorval (1894), John (1897-1907) and Pearl (1899).

Amanda Ellen Baughman (1858-1943) married James Chitwood on May 31, 1883. Both are buried in Unionville, IN, Baptist Church Cemetery.

Lidda Baughman married Patterson Snider on Jan. 28, 1890. No further information can be found on Lidda or Patterson Snider.

Lurena Baughman (1864-1930) married Marion Lee Brown on April 21, 1889. Lurena and Marion's children were Lawrence Glenn (1890-1919), Leonard Roland (1892-1975), Olive (1894), Mary Jane (1896-1976), Maude (1898), Burrell (1900), Paul (1901-1930) and Mark (1908-1908).

Sarah Catherine Baughman (1856-1929) married Martin Luther Morrison, a Jackson Township farmer, on Feb. 19, 1880. They were the parents of John (1886-1966) and Myrtle (1887-1960).

Of the eight children born to Jacob and Eliza Jane (Snider) Baughman, no information can be traced for John Baughman (1850).

Jacob (1818-1889) and Eliza Jane (1823-1906) Baughman are buried in the Lanam Ridge Cemetery.

Jacob's younger brother, William M. Baughman, settled in Acton, IN in 1869. William was born on Sept. 30, 1822 in Brown Co., OH where he married Mary Bassett on Feb. 26, 1846. William and Mary also raised a large family on their farm in Franklin Township, Marion Co., IN. They were the parents of Jacob (1846), John (1848), Hester (1851), Nancy (1854), Robert (1855), William (1857), Samuel Walker (1859), George (1862), Willis (1864), Mary Irene (1867), Minnie (1869), and Lillie May (1873).

William (1822-1894) and Mary (1830-1874) Baughman are buried in the cemetery at Acton, IN. *Submitted by John E. Smith, great-grandson of Samuel Walker Baughman*

DALE BAUGHMAN FAMILY

Bachman-Baughman, a family name of Swiss-German origin, known as early as 1672 apparently originated at Bottenstein in the Canton of Aargau, Switzerland. Some members of one such family moved to Palatinate, Germany and shortly thereafter, Andreas Bachman was the first to immigrate to Pennsylvania. The date was 1742. Although it is historically unverified, it is most probable that Jacob Baughman, born Feb. 22, 1818 somewhere in Ohio was a direct descendant. Jacob died Dec. 13, 1889 and is buried in Lanam Ridge Cemetery. Jacob was Dale's great-grandfather. As a young adult he moved westward to the settlement which is now Indianapolis. There he witnessed illness and death from ague, a fever similar to malaria. He was advised to head for high country, and he did, to Brown County.

There he married Eliza Jane Snyder born Nov. 15, 1823 and died Aug. 10, 1906 and is buried in Lanam Ridge Cemetery. Eliza gave birth to a son William; 1848; William was Dale's grandfather. The census of Brown County in 1850 reveals that Jacob was a landowner, farmer and head of a household. The census also included a son, John, five months of age. Subsequently, five daughters were born to "Billy" and "Liza." Their names were Katherine, Amanda, Lydia, Lorene, and Jane.

"Billy" Baughman, a cattle and grain farmer, married Margaret Branyan of Brown County. To that union ten children were born; Anna, Clementine, Rosa, Nellie, Netty (died in infancy), Jacob, Bert Orin (Dale's father), Cecil, Joseph, and Millard Ray. Of the ten children only Bert and Ray remained for any appreciable length of time in Brown County after their marriages. Ray served his country in France during WWI and upon his return joined Bert to operate Baughman Brothers General Store until 1926 when the store burned to the ground with few contents saved. Ray's son, Lennis, lives with his wife, Judith, in Brown County.

Bert Baughman married Josephine Browning, daughter of Nathan Browning who practiced medicine in Story and Needmore. Bert and "Jose" reared three children; Verna, 1902-1975; Walter, 1905-1951; and Dale, 1919 and living. Walter, except for occasional wandering to all points of the compass, spent his entire life in Brown County. Bert Baughman died in 1962 in the Morgantown Nursing Home; Jose Baughman passed away in 1948 at Bloomington Hospital.

Dale Baughman and D'Lema Smith were wed in 1950 and three children were born in the next seven years, the birth order being Dala, Dlynn and Brad. Dala teaches school in Baton Rouge where her husband, Dr. John Beard, is a Professor of Mechanical Engineering at Louisiana State University. Dlynn is a teacher of Critical Care Nursing at Ball Memorial Hospital in Muncie. Brad currently teaches English and serves as Athletic Director at Brown County High School.

D'Lema and Dale Baughman

As a WWII Navy Petty Officer First/Class, Dale was both a Medic and Chemical Warfare Instructor in the Asiatic-Pacific Theatre for two years, mostly in the Aleutian Islands. Later he was assigned to the 5th Amphibian Training Unit at Oceanside, CA where in August, 1944 while engaged in simulation exercises he severely injured both legs and was hospitalized for four months at Santa Margarita Ranch Naval Hospital at Camp Pendleton Marine Base. Three days later his outfit sailed for Saipan and further training and Dale was left behind to wonder, to hope and to pray for his comrades. The Iwo Jima Project was successful but several of Dale's former buddies were among the casualties. On Aug. 9, 1945 he received a medical discharge for injuries suffered in line of duty at Attu and again at Oceanside.

During his experience in three Indiana school systems, Dale functioned at grade levels 1 through 12, teaching, coaching all major sports, being a Guidance Director, Principal and Athletic Director. In 1956, after completing his Bachelor's, Master's and Doctor's Degrees in Education at Indiana University, he spent the next 28 years as Professor of Graduate and Undergraduate Education at the University of Illinois and Indiana State University. He found time to accept "Visiting Professor" assignments (summers only) at six major universities in the South and West. He authored seven books and 100+ articles for educational journals, provided many consulting services to public schools and universities and to state and federal, as well as private agencies. He filled more than 2,000 major speaking engagements in 44 states and seven foreign countries and worked abroad while on Sabbatical Leaves as Consultant in most of Western Europe. His educational travels took him to ten more countries including Greece, Finland, Sweden, Soviet Union, Czechoslovakia, Spain and England. He is listed in **Who's Who in America, Who's Who in the World,** and the **International Speakers Platform Association**.

Since Dale's retirement in 1982, he and D'Lema have resided on Terre Haute's East Side nine months of the year, the remaining three being divided between Florida, Louisiana, and Brown County. Their church membership is with Shepherd-of-the-Hills Lutheran Church in Bean Blossom. *Submitted by Dr. Dale Baughman*

ROSEY AND LEON BEAUCHAMP

Rosey Elizabeth Merriman was born in Brown County on July 21, 1939, the seventh child of Hallie Josephine Fleener and Clarence Merriman, who lived on Bear Creek in Brown County. Rosey attended the Brown County schools and married Richard Leon Beauchamp in 1957. They lived in Chicago, IL and west of Nashville, IN; in Johnson County; and later in Henderson Co., KY.

Leon was born Aug. 1, 1936, in Owen County. He was the son of Charles and Vina Marie Ewers Beauchamp. Vina was the daughter of George W. and Estella Wilson Ewers. He had brothers George, Francis, Marshall, Wendell and Donald; sisters Estella, Joyce, Barbara and Wilma. Leon died in a truck accident on Aug. 25, 1971. He was employed as a driver for the P.B.S. Chemical Company in Henderson, KY when he was thrown from the truck he was driving three and a half miles north of Sebree on the Pennyrile Parkway.

Rosey and Leon Beauchamp

Rose and Leon were the proud parents of five children: Elizabeth Ann, Robert Leon, Jeannette Kay, Donna Jean and Brenda Gail. Shortly after their father's death, they returned to Indiana and lived at Quincy and later at Cloverdale where they attended the Cloverdale High School.

Elizabeth Ann was born Sept. 30, 1957 in Monroe County and married Max Wilbur Cassida in Quincy, IN on Oct. 17, 1975. Their son Bartholomew was born Aug. 21, 1977. Elizabeth and Max were divorced and she later married Robert Michael Cross and they have a daughter, Bobi Ann. They lived in Indianapolis.

Robert Leon Beauchamp was born March 19, 1959 in Johnson County and married Juanita Walker in Owen County. They had two children: Nicole born Feb. 15, 1978 and Ryan born Feb. 3, 1980. Robert later married Cindee Sherman in Owen County in 1985 and they have two children: Robert, Jr. born Feb. 23, 1987 and Rachel Lynn born April 24, 1989. They live in Quincy, IN.

Jeanette Kay Beauchamp was born Dec. 18, 1960 in Johnson Co., IN. She is a single parent to Zachary Lyle Smith born Nov. 20, 1988 in Georgia where Jeanette now resides.

Donna Jean Beauchamp was born July 28, 1963 in Johnson County and married Tim Zook in Owen County July 2, 1989. They have one child, Emerson Cory, born Feb. 12, 1990 in Bloomington. They live RR#3 Cloverdale.

Brenda Gail Beauchamp was born April 9, 1965 in Henderson, KY and married Steven Edward Eckerman on Dec. 17, 1983. They divorced and she presently lives and works in Bremerton, WA. *Submitted by Rose Beauchamp*

BECK FAMILY - Originated in Germany and immigrated to the United States, settling in Rowan Co., NC. Dewalt Beck and Catherine had three sons in the American Revolution. One son, Michael Beck Sr., married Margaret Daniels and they had eight children. One son, David Beck, Sr., (born June 19, 1796 in Rowan Co., NC) came to Pinhook, IN, married Elizabeth Phillips and had nine children.

Elder David M. Beck was born Feb. 4, 1836, in Lawrence Co., IN, and is the sixth of ten children descended from David Beck and Elizabeth Phillips who relocated in Brown County to a place later known as Beck's Grove in 1850 where he remained until his death, May 3, 1856, having given up his ministry of 30 years.

Marie (Wheeler) McFadden, granddaughter of Emma J. (Beck) Wheeler

David M. Beck, Jr., (born Feb. 4, 1836) married (1) Mary J. Litten who died, and then he married (2) Mary Jane Allen, March 22, 1862 and had eight children. Elder David M. Beck lived on a farm, received a practical education, after which he began teaching in Lawrence and Brown Counties. August 1872 he commenced his ministering in the Christian Church. In 1877 he was appointed Superintendent of Brown County and in 1879 re-appointed.

One daughter, Emma Josephine Beck, was born Nov. 5, 1861, Brown County, married Aug. 1, 1886 to Abel Alvin Wheeler and had two children, Mary and Oscar. Oscar married Drusilla Jackson April 24, 1920, and had one daughter, Marie (born Feb. 23, 1922), who lived in Bartholomew County until 1985 when she moved on Beck's Grove Road in Brown County. Oscar lived and farmed in Bartholomew County until death Sept. 17, 1973. Marie's daughter, Mona (born Jan. 6, 1955), married Martin Peterson on June 24, 1973, and bought a place on Beck's Grove Road in Brown County in 1978. They have two children, Patrick (born Sept. 16, 1981) and Kathleen (born Feb. 27, 1983), who attend Van Buren Elementary School. *Submitted by Marie McFadden*

DAVID LOUIS AND MARGARET LOUISA (WAGGONER) BECK - David Louis Beck, born ca. 1830, was the son of John Beck and Mary Catherine Fipps. David's siblings were: Solomon N., William P., Daniel Boone, Elizabeth Ann, James P., John Benton, Martha, Serelda or Carolinda and Charlotte A. Beck. The family lived in the Beck's Grove-Buffalo area.

On May 14, 1853 David married Margaret Louisa Waggoner (born May 30, 1836 died May 7, 1910). Margaret was the daughter of David Waggoner and Margaret Beard, also of Brown County.

David Louis and Margaret Louisa (Waggoner) Beck

From this union six children were born in Brown County.

William Benton "Billy" Beck, born May 21, 1853, died Feb. 25, 1926; Serane E. Beck, born Jan. 11, 1856, died Feb. 5, 1874, buried in Buffalo Cemetery; Mary Katherine "Kate" Beck, born Aug. 25, 1857, died Feb. 27, 1933; Ashbel P.W. "Willard" Beck, born Dec. 11, 1858, died ?; Surilda H. Beck, born Sept. 27, 1860, died ?; David Louis Beck, Jr., born June 29, 1863, died 1937.

David was a religious, hard working farmer who had strong beliefs. He enlisted in the Union Army, Co. H, 50th Reg. Indiana Volunteers on Dec. 1, 1861.

During the siege of Munfordville, KY, Sept. 17, 1862, the Federals surrendered in formal ceremonies. There were 4200 Union soldiers, David among them, taken prisoner. They were disarmed, paroled and sent toward Nashville, TN.

Shortly after re-enlisting he was killed at the Battle of Spoonville, AR on April 2, 1864.

David and Wiley Spurgeon of Brown County were close friends. In a letter to Wiley, from a Camp near Lewisburg, AR and dated Jan. 26, 1864 David writes:

"The Rebs will knot stand and fight so we haft to keep in Pursuit of them. We had a pretty hard winter. A Majority of the Citizens here are for the Union. Well Wiley I would like to se you but my business detains me for a little season. Yet I would rejoice to hear of Peace on fair terms but any other way would be worse than no Peace."

After David's death Margaret and her children left Buffalo and settled in Jackson Co., IN. *Submitted by great-great-granddaughter Betty Lou Thornton Miller*

DALE AND RUTH BESSIRE - Dale Philip Bessire (1892 Columbus, OH-1974) and Ruth Sabina Sayer Bessire (1892 Chicago, IL) brought their six week old son, Philip Dale Bessire (1914-1979) to Brown County from Indianapolis in June, 1914. They had rented a log cabin north of Nashville from the Nashville State Bank, and an apple orchard from Sampson David. A good crop of apples was shipped by rail from Helmsburg to Indianapolis. They bought the orchard that fall and started building a house. Ruth and the baby returned to Indianapolis for the winter but came in the spring to the new house, presently located at the north end of Johnson Street.

The log cabin was later purchased. There was a hand pump on the porch from a cistern, but no plumbing in the cabin. An ice box was on the porch and ice was brought from Columbus by Nick Roberts. A log ice house near the cabin was later torn down and the logs used for the orchard sales cabin on state Road 135.

A second son, William Sayer Bessire (1915-1962) and a daughter, Marianne Ruth Bessire Miller (1917-) were born. All three children started their married life in the log cabin.

Ruth's parents, William Elmer Sayer (1861 Oswego, NY-1945) and Clara Hannah Sayer (1863 Cambridge City, IN-1962) moved to Brown County from Indianapolis in 1916. They bought a house from William Goble and an orchard which is now the Sayer addition to Nashville.

Dale and Ruth Bessire with son Philip by Moore Log Cabin, Bessire's first home in Brown County.

Dale's parents, Jules Philip Bessire (1863 Perry, Switzerland-1955) and Margaret Salome Ritzler Bessire (1867 Kenton, OH-1954) bought a summer home in Nashville in 1925. J.P. Bessire, after retiring from Bessire and Company, a baker's supply house in Indianapolis, opened the first Nashville Curio Shop.

A second orchard on Plum Creek Road in Jackson Township was purchased. The Nashville Orchards, Inc. was organized by Jack Rogers, Fred Johnson and Dale Bessire, and additional peach and apple orchards were planted. After Jack and Fred sold their interests to Dale, he managed the orchards until his sons were graduated from Indiana University. Dale was able to devote full time to his painting of landscapes. He was a charter member and first secretary of the Brown County Art Gallery and later an exhibiting member of the Brown County Art Guild. The Bessire sons also bought and operated peach and apple orchards on Lanham Ridge.

Philip married Kitty Ditts (1915 Winamac, IN-1939) in 1937. Kitty died in childbirth when their son James Philip Bessire was born in 1939. Philip married Fern Connell, daughter of Latham and Sybil Connell, in 1940. They had three daughters - Janet Higgins, Judy George and Jennifer Fernandes, and three sons - David, Richard and Jack.

William married Grace Tracy, daughter of Everett and Blanche Tracy, in 1940, and they had a daughter, Barbara, and a son, Jed.

Marianne married Maurice "Pods" Miller, son of Herbert and Clara Miller, in 1939, and they have two daughters, Susie Roush and Marilyn Rudd, and two sons, John and Stephen. (See Miller, Maurice) *Submitted by Marianne Miller*

LAURA (BROCK) BINGHAM

Laura born July 9, 1889 in Pineville, KY, was the oldest of six children born to Zack and Martha Brock.

Laura and her husband Robert Bingham were living in Columbus, Bartholomew Co., IN when they began their family with the birth of Frances Bingham Jan. 27, 1913. Sylvester born May 23, 1914; Lessie born Dec. 6, 1916; and one infant born and died 1915 before the family moved back to Kentucky. On April 29, 1919, Zack Bingham was born in Pineville. Shortly after her husband's death, son Robert Mearl would be born on March 30, 1921. In less than a dozen years Laura had gone from blushing bride to a widow with five small children.

Laura was desperate to move her sons away from Pineville and the frequent underground coal mine accidents. In 1938, Laura Bingham and her family, upon the advice of Aunt Myrtle Brock Miller, moved to the hill country of Brown Co., IN. The Bingham boys farmed just a few years before answering Uncle Sam's call for volunteers in WWII.

With Zack in the Army and Robert Mearl in the Coast Guard the family received eight different telegrams since each was injured four times. Although scarred for life, their deaths, Zack Feb. 2, 1958 and Robert Mearl on Oct. 26, 1980 in Bartholomew County Hospital, were not service related.

In Pineville, KY, Frances Bingham married Willie Messer and gave birth to two girls, Alberta and Maxine Messer. In 1939 after her divorce became final, she and her daughters joined the Bingham family in Brown County.

While working in a Columbus restaurant, Frances met and married a young man from Des Moines, IA, Fred Strong. Many of the motels, restaurants and apartments in Brown County, as well as nearby Bloomington, Columbus and Indianapolis were roofed by Fred Strong and his crew. Fred suffered a fatal heart attack Oct. 18, 1980, while on the roof of a neighbor's small building near his home at Gnaw Bone, IN. Following a long illness Laura Brock Bingham died June 28, 1979 in the Convalescent Center, Columbus, IN. *Submitted by Frances Strong*

BISEL FAMILY

came to Hamblen Township, Brown Co., IN in 1876 from a small community in Western Bartholomew County called "Ohio Ridge." Joseph Bisel was born in Bedford, PA, married ? Moon. Their son Noah Bisel was born there also in 1826. They went from Pennsylvania to Tuscarawas Co., OH where Noah married in 1854, Mary Jane Wright, daughter of J.E. and Nancy Smith Wright, also natives of Bedford, PA. In 1855 Noah, his wife and infant son, Benjamin Franklin, came from Tuscarawas Co., OH to the "Ohio Ridge" community where before them in 1845, some 15 families had traveled the same route, by boat from Stubenville, OH down the Ohio River to Madison, IN. From there they traveled by train to Taylorville, IN.

Several of the names who helped to build a church and formed a cemetery association at Ohio Ridge were: Long, McKee, Milnes, Stillabower, Geotz, Waltz, and Noah Bisel. The Lutheran and United Brethern both held services in the church for several years. The Bisels were of German origin, as were many other families that settled there.

John R. Bisel, 1950

Noah enlisted in the Civil War Oct. 8, 1864 and was mustered out in Greensboro, NC in July 11, 1865. He died May 24, 1895, buried at Ohio Ridge, later moved to North of Edinburg near St. Road 31, when Camp Atterbury took over the land.

Noah and Mary Jane had five more children: John C., Nancy, Theodore, Mary and George. John C. Bisel was born in 1857, married Nancy E. Roberts, daughter of Joseph and Jane Hiat Roberts of Brown County. John C. and Nancy lived in the Mt. Moriah neighborhood in Hamblen Township where their seven children were born: Ritta, Lestie, Vincent, Florence, Lillie, Anna and John R. Bisel. Vincent married Mary Anderson and they were known around Brown County as "Doc and Dinah," and played music for any occasion that called for it. John R. Bisel was born July 14, 1896, married Iva Mullis and four children were born to them: Ruth, Alice, Rosemary and a son who died in infancy, buried in Taggart Cemetery. Ruth married Leonard Boaz, he died 1970. Ruth still lives on upper Salt Creek Road near where she was born. Iva Mullis was daughter of Silas and Elizabeth Saffel Mullis and died 1949. John R. died Feb. 18, 1979 and is buried at Rest Haven, Edinburg, Johnson County. The Bisel men were all farmers and sawmill workers. The name has had several different spellings: Bisel and Bissell. *Submitted by Ruth (Bisel) Boaz*

LEWIS BISHOP

Charlie Bishop came to Indiana from New York where he owned and built ships. He came from a seafaring family. When his wife died an Indian lady was his housekeeper. Charlie settled in Union Township, Bartholomew Co., IN. His son, Alance Bishop was a blacksmith and served in the Civil War. Alance married Hannah Crail, daughter of Thomas Crail who was an early settler of Harrison Township, Bartholomew County. George Washington Bishop, a son of Alance and Hannah Bishop, ran steam engines for various factories and mills around the area. It was George W. Bishop who moved to Brown County in 1930.

George W. Bishop (July 4, 1873-Feb. 7, 1963), Bartholomew County; he married on Oct. 20, 1913 to Mary Ida Thompson (Feb. 12, 1888-Feb. 25, 1963), daughter of Martin Sandy Thompson (Oct. 4, 1859-Dec. 29, 1930) and Elsie Miranda Taylor (Feb. 14, 1862-May 29, 1942). Martin Thompson's parents, Thomas and Lucinda (Matney) Thompson came to Stone Head, Brown County from Marietta, OH. Elsie Taylor's parents, Benj. and Mary E. (Mobley) Taylor came from Washington Co., OH. Martin Thompson was a farmer, made hoop poles, barrel staves and tan bark. He and two others also owned and operated the first motion picture machine in this area.

Lewis Bishop; son Tom Bishop; grandson Tom Lewis Bishop, Bethany Jones (great-granddaughter); Rebecca Bishop Jones (granddaughter) holding great-grandson David Jones.

Lewis Bishop, born June 16, 1916, was the son of George W. and Mary Ida Thompson. He attended Junction School and Nashville High School. In January 1936 Lewis married Louise Hellenburg. They had three children, two of whom died as infants; the third child, Thomas O. Bishop, was born February 1943. In 1941, Lewis Bishop graduated from the National Radio Institute, served in WWII as a Sergeant in the Army Corps of Engineers and was stationed in the South Pacific. In September of 1946, he married Dorathy M. Hull. They had three children: Norma J. Bishop, born 1947; Vicki L. Bishop, born 1954 and Larry A. Bishop, born 1955. Lewis worked as an electrician for Cummins Engine Co. as a trouble shooter. While working there he started his own Radio and TV sales and service which he eventually went into full time. He also worked at Arvin's as an electrical parts inspector on Government jobs. He worked for Montgomery Ward as an electronics tehcnician for the southern half of Indiana. In 1965 Lewis Bishop bought land in Brown County; in 1970 he and his family moved here. He has always lived in and around Brown County. He is now retired and is enjoying gardening and woodworking. Being the last of a rare breed who has the true pioneering spirit, living and communing with the beautiful land he lives on, who would love to pass on his knowledge of the land to his nine grandchildren and eight great-grandchildren, knowledge which is sadly becoming a lost art in our country today. *Submitted by Vicky Bishop Wallace, daughter of Lewis Bishop*

DENNIS AND MARY JANE BLAKE

Dennis Lee Blake was born July 3, 1940 at home in Marion Co., IN. He was the middle child of five. While growing up he found interest in the outdoors and especially farming.

In the summer of 1959 he met Mary Jane Pearson. She was born Oct. 5, 1942 also in Marion County, at St. Francis Hospital, Marion County, Beech Grove, IN. Mary Jane was the oldest of six children born to Alex V. and Estelle Pearson. Alex and Estelle were born in the state of Kentucky.

Some of Mary's preteen years was farm living and after meeting Dennis, the interest of the outdoors and farm living proved to be a goal they both wanted. They were married Oct. 27, 1961 at Lynhurst Baptist Church, Marion Co., IN by Rev. Wright.

Christmas 1989 First row: Dennis Lee Blake holding David Joshua Whitaker, Nicole Estelle Whitaker, Mary Jane (Pearson) Blake. Second row: Timothy W. Blake, Teresa Estella Blake Whitaker and David Mark Whitaker.

After ten years of marriage and two children and many Sunday drives looking at farms they settled in Brown Co., IN, April 1972. They enjoyed several years of farming and remodeling the old farm house. Dennis spent several years in full service of the Gatesville Vol. Fire Dept. Assistant Leader in 4-H, four years on the Board of Trustee of Hamblen Township of Brown County. Mary was active in the volunteer fire department and 4-H leader for nine years.

After Mary chose full time employment, they both cut back on the farming. Their main project pushed ahead, that of raising two children, Teresa and Timothy. Both born before they moved to Brown County. After very active school years, both graduated from Brown County High School, Teresa in 1981 and one year later married David Mark Whitaker also of Brown County. They have two children and have a trailer on the farm. Timothy Wayne graduated 1983 and still lives at home. After trying other fields of work, he settled into electric work. He has been five years with Frye Electric now. He plans to build on the home place and has picked out the location already. Dennis and Mary hope to go back to light farming for fun when they retire. Blakes' Briar Patch is the family name for their farm.

Teresa Estelle Blake moved to Brown County with her parents and brother in the Spring of 1972. Her parents bought the Wilkerson home place on upper Salt Creek, Hamblen Township. A former County Commissioner, Orville Wilkerson was raised on this farm with his brothers and sister. The U.S. Government sold the property to Petro's in 1840. Teresa was very active in all levels of school and 4-H. After graduation she went into retail sales.

The year after graduation she married David Mark Whitaker, from Brown Co., IN.

May 24, 1985 the daughter Nicole Estelle was born.

November 1988 they moved a trailer to her parents' farm in Hamblen Township. David is a carpenter by trade. In March 1989 their son David Joshua was born.

WILLIAM AND ROBIN BLANTON -
Samuel William (Bill) Blanton was born on a farm near Darlington, IN. His mother and father were native Hoosiers. Bill's mother and father were married in Darlington and spent all of their lives on a farm near Darlington. Bill was the youngest of their four children. He knew from the time he was a little boy that he wanted to go to Purdue University, which he did. He had a commission in the Army Reserve and the National Guard. He received his engineering degree in 1934 and got a job at Delco Products (a division of General Motors) in Dayton, OH.

Robin and Bill were married in Dayton, OH, in 1939. They moved to Bay Village, OH, and then Birmingham, MI, where Bill worked in the General Motors headquarters in Detroit. While living in both Ohio and Michigan, he was active in professional and community organizations: he was a member of the Society of Automotive Engineers (SAE), chairman of the Boy Scouts of Bay Village, OH, and on the vestry of St. Philips Episcopal Church in Rochester, MI.

During World War II, he was assistant chairman of the Ordinance Industrial Committee which overlooked the making of ammunition shells. He was discharged from the National Guard in 1940 while in a hospital bed due to complications from a ruptured appendix.

After an angina attack and 38 years with Delco, he retired in 1968.

Olive (Robin) Blanton was born in Monroe, OH. Her father, Will James Rodgers, was a farm boy from Madison Co., IN. He did not like the farm. He wanted a college education. He walked from Indiana to Cincinnati to enroll in the University of Cincinnati. He worked for a professor and his family to earn money for his books and schooling. He received a two-year degree in horticulture and got a job with the Highway Department of Ohio. He laid out and made the first highway park areas on the main highways of Ohio. These were the forerunners to the "Rest Areas" on the interstate highways of the United States. He later opened his own florist shop in 1915.

Robin Manetta, Bill Blanton, Maureen Blanton, Robin Blanton, Peter Blanton, Geneva Stewart, Maureen Blanton, Ed Manetta and Bill Blanton.

Her mother, Martha Meyer, was the daughter of a wealthy furniture manufacturer in Cincinnati, OH. Will and Martha were married and lived there until 1909 when they moved to Dayton, OH. Robin was one of four children born to them.

Robin spent all of her school years in Dayton, graduating from the Dayton Junior Teachers College in 1932 when the college closed because the city ran out of money to run it. She worked at the McCall Magazine Publishing Company, which was located in Dayton, OH, at that time. She worked there until there was an elementary teaching job open.

After their years in Bay Village, OH and Rochester, MI, and raising three children (Bill, Peter and Robin), Bill and Robin moved to Nashville, IN when Bill retired from G.M. in 1968. They had a home built for them on Red Bud Lane. They joined the Brown County Historical Society and the Nashville United Methodist Church. Robin enjoyed joining every class that was offered in weaving, basket-making, quilting and rug hooking. Bill enjoyed getting back to his farm background. He has a garden each year, growing most every vegetable, including a special lettuce and garlic. He also has two colonies of bees. Robin spends most of her time growing flowers and herbs. Nashville has been the perfect spot to fully enjoy their interests and their retirement!

Their three children and four grandchildren live not too distant from them: Bill in Centerville, OH; Peter in Newton, NJ; and Robin (Manetta) in Carmel, IN.

CHARLES EDGAR BOCK -
Was born in 1882 to John Franklin Bock and Rebecca Hanna Poling Bock. He was a railroad worker but retired early because of his health and died in 1952. He was known for being organized and caring well for his home and personal possessions. As examples, he had the first radio set in Trevlac-Needmore area and he left behind a shiny 1939 Plymouth that looked like new. He and his wife Maude Catherine (Martin) Bock, reared three children: Zella Bock Warford, born in 1911; Harold Bock born 1913; and Howard Martin Bock born in 1916. Howard Bock died in 1962. Zella married Cecil Warford (the son of Jessie and Edgar D. Warford) and had two children: Donald Maurice born in 1928 and Deloris Lavon born in 1930. Harold married Lillian Steele in 1935, and they had one daughter, Rita Lynette.

Howard Martin Bock had three children: Martin Lee born in 1938, Tracy born in 1939 and by a second marriage in Elwood, IN a third son, Charles Robert born in 1945. Charles Bock managed things so well and was very conservative. When he bought gasoline for his car from World War II until the last he bought, it was always five gallons. A habit carried over from ration days when you didn't buy without stamps. Tracy remembers one time going with him to the license branch (then a part of Zody's IGA Store) to get his plates. When he got home to put them on he found he had outdone himself. Wanting a low number I suppose, or just being on top of things as he was, he bought 1948 plates on Dec. 28, 1947 only to find they had given him 1947 plates. Charles Edgar Bock was a diabetic and for as long as family can remember he gave himself an injection of insulin prior to each meal. When it finally got him he was ready. He was a practicing Methodist and Tracy remembers him saying from his hospital bed " I wish it (death) would just come on." At the turn of the century there were lots of ancestors named Bock. Today, Martin and Tracy and Tracy's son, John Paul Bock, carry the name and remain in Brown County and John Paul is the most likely one to carry on this branch of the Bock name.

MAUDE (MARTIN) BOCK -
Maude was born July 1, 1887 to Hiram La Rue Martin and Millie Frances Richardson Martin. On Nov. 25, 1909 she married Charles Edgar Bock. Their children, grandchildren, etc., are listed in this publication under Charles Bock. Knowledge of the Martins goes back to Barbour Co., WV, where Joseph and Catherine (Squires) Martin had five children. Hiram, Maude's father; William, who was killed by Confederate soldiers; Mary Ann, who married Alexan-

der Lindsey, also lived in Brown County; and Clarissa and Sarah of whom nothing more is known. Hiram was born July 8, 1853. He married in Brown County Nov. 20, 1878 to Millie Frances Richardson the daughter of Jeremiah and Mary (Fleener) Richardson. Millie was born Nov. 26, 1860. They had six children, William Nelson, born Aug. 19, 1880, Permelia born in 1881, John Allen born June 12, 1882, Sara Myrtle, born Sept. 12, 1884, Maud born July 1, 1887 and Nora Larue born April 13, 1890. Permelia's name may have come in some way from the fact that Millie according to their calculations, was pregnant 27 months out of a 31 month period.

Hiram was killed on Sept. 2, 1889 while hauling logs. His death occurred about seven months before his last daughter Nora was born. Several years later Millie remarried to Morgan Hawley. They had three children; Ola, Alvey and Ada. While these three were quite young, Morgan died. A few years before her death Millie married once more to Taylor Richey and spent her last years in Greenwood, IN. Maude was a person who cared for people and things. She cared for house plants and had lots of them. She raised a big garden and canned not only every kind of vegetable she raised but also canned pork, whole chickens and anything else that could keep her out of the grocery store. She liked a pretty lawn and had one. She cared for a severe diabetic husband and kept him until he died at age 70. She once said to a young daughter-in-law who was being divorced by her son, "You may not be my son's wife, but you'll always be my daughter-in-law." She cared for a home and kept her's spotless. She cared for a bank account and kept one of those also. One particular year she hinted to her three children that she would like to have one of those big kitchen mixers. In those days $39.95 was a lot of money and more than any of her kids was used to spending on her. They got together, gave her collectively $40.00 and a picture of the mixer she wanted and unless my memory fails me, she put the money in the bank and for the rest of her life went without a mixer. Maude cared also about her spiritual life, she was a member of the Eastern Star and a practicing Methodist. She died Nov. 27, 1968 and is buried beside her husband at Needmore. She was preceeded in death by one son, Howard, and a grandson, Donald Warford.

TRACY EARL BOCK - Born Sept. 8, 1939 in a small burg in Northwestern Brown County called Helmsburg. He was born to Howard Martin Bock and Mary Tracy. Howard was born Aug. 3, 1916 in Trevlac a near-by burg and Mary was born in another little one called Bean Blossom on Feb. 27, 1920.

Tracy has an "older" brother, Martin Lee Bock born Jan. 19, 1938 also in Bean Blossom. Tracy attended school here in Brown County and graduated from Brown County High School in 1958. He married Sharon Anderson and had one daughter, Ronni Lynn on Oct. 9, 1959. A divorce followed soon and Tracy left Brown County for Indianapolis and hopefully some kind of work. The work he found took him to Minnesota for a while and then to Kokomo and Ft. Wayne where he met and married Beth Moltham and she and Tracy had two children, John Paul Bock born Sept. 10, 1968 and Mary Elizabeth Bock born Sept. 1, 1979. Tracy and Beth parted company and a few years later he married again to Barbara Melton Bock and now has three step children Jason, Tressa and Mary Elizabeth.

Overall, Tracy spent about ten years of his adult life away from Brown County but he, like most of us who were reared here, wasn't happy with his life style and it didn't seem to matter where he was located it wasn't Brown County so it wasn't home. After opening and managing a farm store in Fort Wayne and setting up and managing the Auto Centers of several Sears stores he finally found his way back to Brown County. Late in 1980 he hung out his own shingle "Tracy Bock Realty" and has been here ever since and yes still with the same shingle.

Tracy is the grandson of the late Blanche Tracy, has much of her sense of humor and enjoys writing "Barnyard Butch" weekly for the Brown County Democrat. He has two grandchildren of his own; Jeremy Brattain born Jan. 25, 1977 and Emily Renae Bock born Jan. 1, 1990 to Melissa and John Paul.

DR. HAROLD W. AND EVANGELINE C. (ROATH) BOCKSTAHLER - The Bockstahlers purchased a building spot in Brown County in 1971. At retirement time in 1973, they built and moved into their new home on a hilltop across from the Little Opry.

Dr. Harold was a son of Reverend Wm. J.G. Bockstahler, a Methodist Minister, and was born in Booneville, Sept. 27, 1906. His grandfather fought in the Civil War and died from his wounds soon after returning home. His great-grandfather purchased land in what is now Santa Claus, IN in 1830, after coming to Indiana from Eichstetten, Germany. After graduating from Purdue with degrees of BS and MS in Plant Pathology, Harold later earned his doctorate at the University of Minnesota. He entered USDA service and became Regional Director of Sugar Beet Research. This work was done in cooperation with Colorado State University, Ohio State University, USDA at Beltsville, MD, the University of Minnesota and Michigan State University.

Dr. Harold, Mrs. Bockstahler, granddaughter Katrin

Evangeline, also a graduate of Purdue in Science and Home Economics, was born in Pittsburgh, PA Oct. 27, 1905 to Albert J. and Lydia (von Monninger) Roath who returned to Indiana when Evangeline was one year old. Her father was a Canadian of English and Irish descent born and reared in St. Catharines, Ontario. Evangeline is the great-granddaughter of George Stumpf, who purchased a Quarter Section of land on the Three Notch Road (now S. Meridian St.) in Indianapolis. This homeplace is now one of the historic homes of Indiana. Her grandfather, Gottfried Peter von Monninger, was a turn of the century business man of Indianapolis. He had a German Cafe in the Brevort Hotel. He married Katerina Stumpf in 1878 and for a time returned with her to his native Rhineland in Germany so she could learn to prepare the cuisine of that area and understand the wine making business of his extended family.

At Purdue, Evangeline took extra courses in home planning and building. While living in Michigan she developed two subdivisions, planned and built homes in them. The Bockstahler's present home is a copy of their home in Michigan.

Their son, Dr. Larry E. Bockstahler, a Bio-Physicist, working for the U.S. Government, resides in Rockville, MD with his wife, Rotraut, and daughter, Katrin, who is completing her Masters Degree in Marine Biology.

Harold was deceased July 10, 1987. Evangeline still lives in their home in her beloved Brown County.

AILEEN AND WALTER BOLTON - Walter Bonar Bolton was born in Hendricks Co., IN in 1925, the eighth child born to Elva Smith and Lee Bolton. The Bolton family have been residents of Hendricks County since 1884. Lee Bolton was owner and operator of a painting and wallpapering business and developer of real estate. Walter Bolton graduated from Danville High School and then worked for Bridgeport Brass, Chambers Range and Danville Plumbing and Heating.

In 1950 Aileen and Walter were married and began their home on the west side of Indianapolis. Shortly after marriage Walter began working for Western Electric Company as a pipefitter and was promoted to Order Analyst and Maintenance Supervisor. He received numerous awards for his suggestions on improvements to the manufacture of telephones.

Aileen and Walter Bolton

Aileen Marie Bolton was born to Eleanor Haag and Ray Unversaw in Indianapolis in 1928. She has one sister Marilyn Tharp. The Unversaw family came to the United States from Germany in 1837. They settled on the southside of Indianapolis in 1854. The family owned and operated meatmarkets in Indianapolis. The Ray Unversaw family raised tropical birds and had the largest aviary in the midwest. Aileen and her sister performed for various groups throughout Indiana by singing and playing the Hawaiian guitar. Aileen graduated from Broad Ripple High School and studied at Butler and Indiana University. After marriage to Walter, Aileen worked as a bookkeeper and reception secretary.

Aileen and Walter had two daughters. Arleen was born in 1951. She received her degree from Indiana University in Public Broadcasting. She married Andrew Finlayson in 1989 and is Executive Producer of KCBS Radio of San Francisco, CA. She has one daughter Lauren.

Donna was born in 1953. She received her degree from Indiana University in Public and Environmental Affairs and did post-graduate work at

Georgia Tech and ICMA. Donna married John Chester Kupferer of New Albany, IN in 1974. She worked for the Columbus/Bartholomew Planning Department as an Associate Planner and currently is owner operator of Kupferer Glass Design. Donna and John have three children: Elgin Andrew, Tyler Johnathan and Alysha Marie. The Kupferer's reside on Grandview Lake in Bartholomew Co., IN.

Aileen and Walter were members of 7th and 8th United Christian Church of Indianapolis. She was a member of the choir and he was an usher for 25 years. Aileen is a professional artist in oil and water colors. She maintained a shop/studio in Nashville for five years and taught oil classes in Indianapolis. Her artwork is currently shown in various gallery displays throughout the state and at her studio/home on Coffey Hill Road in Nashville.

Aileen and Walter moved to Nashville in 1983. Walter retired in 1985 from Western Electric with a near perfect 35 year attendance record. They are now members and workers in Nashville Christian Church, Brown County Historical Society and Indiana Heritage of the Arts. Aileen belongs to Hoosier Salon, Brown County Art Guild, Brown County Art Gallery, Women in the Arts of Washington, D.C. and Zeta Tau Alpha Sorority. Walter is a member of Telephone Pioneers of America. *Submitted by Aileen Bolton*

BOND-DECKARD - Joseph Walter Bond was born March 13, 1916 on Schooner Valley in Brown Co., IN. He was the son of William Thomas and Bertha Ann (Robertson) Bond. Named for his Uncle Walter Robertson, he went by Walter all his life.

On Aug. 7, 1937 he married Mary Ellen Deckard, daughter of Cecil and Mary Rosetta (Sinn) Deckard of Brown Co., IN. They were married in Monroe County by Paul Harvey in his home. Walter's niece, Helen Louise (Sturgeon) Welch and Mrs. Harvey were witnesses to this union.

They began their married life on a farm in Orange Co., IN. While living there their oldest son William Cecil was born July 28, 1938. In 1939 they moved back to Brown County in the Elkinsville area. While living in Elkinsville two more sons were born. Joseph Paul born March 7, 1940 and David Dale born Oct. 4, 1942. While David was still a baby they moved to Schooner Valley to the family farm. The farm has been in the Bond family since Walter's father bought the farm in 1899. Three daughters and one more son were born on Schooner Valley. Phyllis Ann born July 26, 1944, Mary Faith born March 13, 1946, Florence Marie born Dec. 14, 1947 and James Frederick born July 10, 1949.

Walter Bond

An excellent cook, Mary has been a homemaker all her life. She always provided three abundant meals daily for her family. There was always plenty for the many people that Walter invited to stay and eat. Walter always told people of the great pies Mary made and one time during a truck trade two of Mary's pies were part of the deal.

Walter was always a farmer but worked at many other jobs to provide for his family. He operated bulldozers and graders for Crider's and for Meshberger Stone. While with Meshberger's he worked in Kentucky and Michigan as well as Indiana. He hauled coal, livestock, grain and Christmas trees. He sold fertilizer and seed corn for many years. At various times he worked in the log woods, sometimes for himself and other times as a hired man. He was a school bus driver from 1970 through 1982.

Always a staunch Democrat, he was a Township road man in the 40s, served as Precinct Committeeman, elected County Commissioner from 1956 to 1960 and again from 1976 to 1980, and hired as County Road Superintendent in 1973.

Walter and Mary were extremely proud of their children and having them all graduate from high school. Walter told many people that he was worth seven million dollars in that each child was like a million dollars to him. This is a list of their children, their children's spouses, their grandchildren and great-grandchildren. William Cecil, married Feb. 5, 1977 to Judith Ann Davis of Monroe Co., IN. No children; Joseph Paul, married Sept. 23, 1961 to Marilyn Joan Goforth of Jackson Co., IN. Joseph has two sons, Jeffry Paul born Sept. 28, 1962 and Roger Dale born March 1, 1965. Jeffry married April 16, 1982 to Doris Diane Martindale of Jackson Co., IN. Jeffry has two girls, Diana Marie born Oct. 22, 1985 and Pamela Sue born Dec. 12, 1987. Roger Dale married June 21, 1986 to Sharon Kay Tatlock of Jackson Co., IN. Roger has a daughter, Amanda Jo born Aug. 6, 1988. David Dale married Aug. 24, 1963 to Lucille Phillips of Wayne Co., KY, living in Monroe Co., IN. David Dale has two children, Paula Lynn born Jan. 9, 1963 and David Bruce born Aug. 20, 1965. David Bruce married Aug. 20, 1988 to Amy Lynn Deckard of Monroe Co., IN. Phyllis Ann works for Eastern International and is presently unmarried. Mary Faith married April 12, 1969 to Jerry Ralph Floyd, born in Muskogee, OK, however he spent most of his life in Brown Co., IN. No children. Florence Marie married Sept. 11, 1971 to Miles Ray Barnes of Greene Co., IN. One son Daniel Ray born May 20, 1982. James Frederick married Nov. 26, 1971 to Linda Lee Applegate of Brown Co., IN. James had five children: James Douglas born Oct. 29, 1972 died Oct. 29, 1972, Leanna Renay born Sept. 20, 1973, Joseph Wayne born Oct. 19, 1976, Lorelle Marie born June 15, 1983, and Joshua William born Nov. 6, 1984.

Walter and Mary were members of the Belmont Church of Christ. Walter died June 19, 1984 at Bloomington Hospital after suffering a massive stroke five days earlier. He is buried in the Hickory Grove Cemetery in Brown County. Mary still lives at the family farm on Schooner Valley. *Submitted by James Fredrick Bond*

EARL AND GRACE BOND - Had it not been for a flu epidemic, school teacher Joshua Jennison Bond, might never have purchased a Funeral Home business in Nashville, IN. The funeral home director was afraid and sold the business to Joshua Bond. The death toll worldwide was 20 million people. Over 100 of those lived in Brown County. Joshua Bond lived in Schooner Valley along with his wife, Myrtle Irene Yoder Bond, and three children, Ivan, Ruth, and Earl.

Earl and Grace Bond

Estle Earl Bond was born Feb. 8, 1900 on Schooner Valley Road in Washington Township. In 1905, when Earl was five the family moved to a farm near Helmsburg. Eight years later, 1913, Joshua opened a funeral business there. Funeral directors went to homes then. At age 14, Earl began to assist his father in business. Helmsburg was the railhead for the surrounding area. Joshua Bond opened a livery business service in conjunction with the funeral business and railroad transportation and a grocery. Earl drove horses all over Brown County. In 1917 a Model-T chassis was purchased and mounted on a two-horse hearse body. It worked well. In 1946, Earl and son, Jack purchased the funeral business and home from Joshua Bond. Earl journeyed from Schooner Valley farm to Nashville by way of Helmsburg.

On May 23, 1918, Earl married Grace Lodema Barkes. Grace Lodema was born Aug. 25, 1895 to John H. Barkes and Hester Ann Brown. Eight children were born to Earl and Grace. Jack, James (2nd Lt. Air Force, Navigator; shot down over Germany in WWII; July 21, 1944; Awarded the Purple Heart), Dale, Betty, Ruth, Susie, Dick, and Bill. All children reside in Brown County. Grace attended Central Normal College at Danville to become a teacher. She taught at Carmel Ridge and Dollsberry in Brown County before marrying Earl.

Earl Bond, 88, died at 3 a.m. on March 31, 1988 at his home on Jefferson Street in Nashville. He operated the Bond Funeral Home with son, Jack from 1946 until 1982. He was treasurer of Brown County from 1933 to 1936. During World War II, he was a defense worker. He worked for Indiana State Conservation Department and served as coroner of Brown County for several years. He was a 50 year member of Nashville Masonic Lodge, a member of Nashville Christian Church and a Life Member of the Brown County Lions Club. Earl was recipient of a 50 year pin award from Indiana Funeral Directors.

Grace Bond, matriarch of the Bond family, died at the age of 90 on Dec. 15, 1985 at home on Jefferson Street in Nashville, IN. Grace was a former school teacher, served for two terms as treasurer of Brown County. She was a member of the Nashville Christian Church, the Order of Eastern Star, the Brown County Historical Society, The Brown County Homemakers Club, of which she was a past President. *Submitted by Marilyn Bond*

BILL AND MARILYN BOND FAMILY - Billy (Bill) Hugh Bond, the youngest son of Estle Earl Bond and Grace Lodema Barkes, was born on the Bond farm near Helmsburg, IN in Brown County. He was born Feb. 13, 1937. Bill had seven brothers and sisters: Jack, James (killed in WWII), Dale, Betty, Ruth, Susie, and Dick.

November 21, 1955, Bill started to work for the telephone company. He traveled for two years exchanging crank telephones for dial telephones. In 1958, he went to Bloomington as a Frameman, later as a Switchman. Bill holds a life long radio license. He helped to install one of the first Digital Switching offices in Indiana in Nashville, IN on Nov. 14, 1987.

Bill coached Little League baseball, Biddy Basketball, and Elementary Basketball. He served on the Brown County Council for several years. He was a member of the Nashville Masonic Lodge, a charter member of the Brown County J.C.'s and a member of the Nashville Christian Church.

Top row/standing: Brenda, Brad, Barbara; Second row/sitting: Bill, Marilyn, Gregory.

Bill, along with all of his brothers and sisters at one time or another helped his father, Earl Bond, with the Bond Funeral Home Business.

Bill married Marilyn Sue Hine on Oct. 17, 1964 at Eminence, IN in Morgan County. Marilyn, the fourth child of Scott C. Hine and Wilma L. Clarkston, was born Sept. 13, 1943 at Eminence, IN on the Hine farm. Marilyn had two brothers and twin sisters: William G. Hine, Shirley Ann Hine Hubbard, Charlene Jo Hine Brown, and Charles (Bob) Robert Hine.

In 1961, Marilyn started to work for Indiana Bell Telephone Company in Bloomington, IN. August 1974, she became the Secretary/Treasurer of Helmsburg Elementary School. She was a member of the Eminence Christian Church and later transferred to Nashville Christian Church.

Children blessed Bill and Marilyn's marriage. Barbara Sue, was born March 1, 1960. Barbara married Gregory D. Rea Dec. 27, 1983. To this marriage was born Gregory Dale Jr., Oct. 31, 1984. She received her Realtors License March 1989. Barbara was a member of the Nashville Christian Church.

Sitting: Tony, Sundi, Ty

Bradley Scott was born Oct. 8, 1966. Brad later attended Vincennes University, and Indiana State University. He played center field on his college baseball teams. Brad was a member of the Nashville Christian Church.

Brenda Susanne was born March 22, 1969. She attended Purdue, IUPUI, and Indiana University. Brenda was a member of the Nashville Christian Church.

In June 1987, Charles (Tony) Anthony Payton came to live with the Bond family. Tony married Sundi Marie Hilbert on June 25, 1988. To this marriage was born Ty Michael, Jan. 21, 1989. Tony was a member of St. Agnes Catholic Church and Sundi was a member of New Life Christian Church. *Submitted by Marilyn Bond*

EARL AND GRACE BOND'S CHILDREN

- Estle Earl Bond, the son of Joshua Jennison Bond and Myrtle Irene Yoder was born Feb. 8, 1900 and died March 31, 1988. Grace Lodema Barkes Bond, the daughter of John H. Barkes and Hester Ann Brown Barkes, was born Aug. 25, 1895 and died Dec. 15, 1985. They were married May 23, 1918. To this marriage was born eight children: Jack, James, Dale, Betty, Ruth, Susie, Dick, and Bill Bond.

Jack Jennison was born Nov. 19, 1918 at Helmsburg, IN in Brown County. He married Patricia Irene Austin, the daughter of Rev. James Monroe Austin and Grace Hickerson, on Oct. 14, 1950. To this marriage was born Peggy, Susie, Rebecca, Cindy, and Jeff Bond. Peggy Jane born Nov. 1, 1951. Peggy married Michael Eugene Thompson on Aug. 30, 1970. To this marriage was born Michael Eugene Jr., Oct. 29, 1973; Gregory Lewis, July 2, 1976; Rebecca Ann, Oct. 12, 1978; Bryce Andrew, Jan. 13, 1986/died March 5, 1986; and Brayton Patrick, July 17, 1987. Carol Sue (Susie) was born Feb. 21, 1954. Susie married Gary Richard Owens June 17, 1972. To this marriage was born James Scott, Oct. 19, 1973; Elizabeth Ann, Sept. 11, 1978, and Joshua Ross, Sept. 9, 1988. Rebecca (Becky) Ann was born April 25, 1955. Cindy Lou was born July 19, 1958. Cindy was married to Kevin Wilson Speas on July 7, 1979. To this marriage was born Todd Wilson, Jan. 15, 1981; Kayla Brooke, Oct. 24, 1982; and Austin Tyler, Oct. 18, 1984. Jeffery Scott was born Feb. 15, 1972.

James Wilson was born Sept. 5, 1920 on Miller Road in Brown Co., IN. James died in World War II on July 21, 1944. He was a 2nd Lieutenant and a Navigator in the United States Air Force. He was awarded the Purple Heart Sept. 4, 1945.

Top row/standing/ Dale, Jean, Dale (Footsie), Betty, Loren, Ruth; Middle Row: Dick, Lois, Jr., Susie; Bottom row/sitting: Jack, Pat, Bill, Marilyn.

Allen Dale was born Sept. 4, 1922 on Miller Road in Brown Co., IN. He married Lois Jean Chitwood Oct. 15, 1947. Lois Jean was the daughter of Ralph Ivan Chitwood and Lillian Lee Peavler. To this marriage was born James, and Robert. James (Jim) Dale was born Dec. 16, 1948. Jim married Donna Elaine Rund on Aug. 6, 1972. To this marriage was born Dorinda Kay, March 28, 1975, and Jebadiah Allen, Nov. 25, 1978. Robert (Bob) Lance was born Feb. 4, 1954. Bob married Kathy Lyn Moberly on Sept. 8, 1973. To this marriage was born Ryan Lance, April 3, 1975.

Hilda Ann (Betty) was born Oct. 21, 1926 on Miller Road in Brown Co., IN. Betty married William Dale (Footsie) Mathis Sept. 13, 1947. Dale is the son of William Mathis and Mary Ann McLary. To this marriage was born Joyce Ann and John. Joyce Ann, born Aug. 28, 1948. Joyce married Michael Roy Boulton March 16, 1968. To this marriage was born Melissa Anne, Sept. 8, 1968 and Matthew Chasteen, April 8, 1971. John William was born Oct. 28, 1952. John married Amanda Wallace on Jan. 22, 1974. To this marriage was born Nathan Andrew, June 24, 1974, and Eliza Ann, June 18, 1976.

Ruth Irene was born May 1, 1928 at Goshen (Foxes Corner) in Brown Co., IN. Ruth married Loren Robert Moore Sept. 1, 1951. Loren is the son of Harold Moore and Elma Bright. To this marriage was born Marcia Kay June 25, 1953; Marilyn Sue, July 8, 1954; and Mary Beth, June 28, 1956. Marcia married James Beery Aug. 19, 1972. To this marriage was born Jennifer Kay, Feb. 11, 1974, and Christie Jolene, Feb. 7, 1975. Marcia married John Boyd May 3, 1985. Contess (Tessa), born Feb. 1, 1974, is the daughter of John Boyd. To Marcia and John was born Lauren Grace, Aug. 16, 1986. Marilyn married Michael Keith Ayers July 18, 1981. To this marriage was born, triplets, Conner Keith, Brooks Michael, and Allyson Sue, May 23, 1990. Mary Beth married Steven Craig Fisher July 28, 1979. To this marriage was born Daniel Lee, March 14, 1983, and Holly Nicole, Jan. 22, 1987.

Susabel (Susie) was born July 5, 1930 at Goshen (Foxes Corner) in Brown Co., IN. Susie married Harry Emil Poling, Jr. on Dec. 17, 1949. Harry is the son of Harry Emil Poling Sr., and Mittie Stephens. To this marriage was born Nancy Sue, July 7, 1950; Judith Irene, Jan. 27, 1952; Harry David, March 31, 1953; and Joseph Lee, Jan. 29, 1961. To Judith (Judy) was born Anna Irene on Aug. 12, 1986. Harry David married Judy Ann Holton on May 15, 1971. To this marriage was born Brian David, Oct. 29, 1971, and Amanda Sue, April 15, 1976. Dustin Joseph, Aug. 29, 1987, and Jessica Lynn, July 14, 1989 are the children of Joseph.

Richard (Dick) Earl was born March 15, 1932 at Goshen (Foxes Corner) in Brown Co., IN. Dick was married to Lois Ann Wilkerson on June 13, 1953. Lois is the daughter of Winfer Wilkerson and Goldie Mae Finn. To this marriage was born Shirley Ann, March 20, 1954; Melinda Lea, July 6, 1958; Richard (Rick) Allen, Nov. 22, 1967, and Amy Lynn, Aug. 8, 1969. Shirley married Mark Manley on Oct. 5, 1986. Neill, May 28, 1984, was the son of Mark.

Billy (Bill) Hugh was born Feb. 13, 1937 at Helmsburg, IN in Brown County. Bill married Shirley Ann Baldrige Sept. 13, 1958. To this marriage was born Barbara Sue, March 1, 1960. Bill married Marilyn Sue Hine Oct. 17, 1964. Marilyn is the daughter of Scott C. Hine and Wilma Lee Clarkston. To this marriage was born Bradley Scott, Oct. 8, 1966, and Brenda Susanne, March 22, 1969. Barbara married Gregory Dale Rea Dec. 27, 1983. To this marriage was born Gregory Dale, Jr., Oct. 31, 1984. *Submitted by Marilyn Bond*

JACK BOND FAMILY

- November 19, 1918, the town of Helmsburg, IN had a population increase when Jack J. Bond made his appearance to Earl and Grace Barkes Bond in an upstairs room over the Helmsburg flour mill, operated by his grandfather, Joshua Bond.

Joshua was the local undertaker and also ran the livery stable in town and met the trains and drove people all over the county. Earl while in the eighth grade, joined him in the operation of this business.

The family soon moved to a farm north of Bean Blossom where Rupert Miller family now lives. They lived there until Jack was in the third grade and then moved to what is now known as Fox's Corner. He attended the Goshen one-room school until it burned during his eighth grade year.

Jack came to Nashville to live with his grandparents, Joshua and Myrtle Bond. They operated a funeral business and had opened the Rustic Inn Restaurant. Jack attended Nashville High School 1933-1937 when he graduated.

Jack attended the Indiana College of Mortuary Science in 1939-1940, receiving his embalmer's license in May and his draft notice in October 1940.

The 1st Armored Div. and the 47th Armored Medical Battalion were his home for the next five years, serving in Africa and Italy. In May 1945 Jack returned to Nashville and the following month purchased the Bond Funeral Home from Joshua in a partnership with his father Earl. They operated it until March 1982 when they sold to Dave Mitchell and retired.

October 14, 1950 Jack and Patricia Irene Austin were married in the Nashville Methodist Church by her father, Rev. James M. Austin, then pastor of the church.

The family soon included four daughters. Peggy born in 1951 arrived while the family was living in two rooms above the funeral home. They quickly concluded that if other children were going to arrive they would need to build a house. On Aug. 12, 1953 the family moved into a new home on South Jefferson Street.

Carol Sue (Susie) arrived in February 1954 and about a year later Rebecca Ann (Becky) made a grand entrance in the front seat of a 1953 Chevrolet in front of the Witch House five miles north of Nashville. A crinkley crepe gown was her receiving blanket. Following birth they continued towards Franklin Hospital finding State Policeman Charles McCarter who had a speeder stopped along the highway. He jumped into his car and escorted them to the hospital passing the doctor, Dr. Kenneth Schneider enroute. They stopped at the roadside and found that the mother and new baby were fine and continued to the hospital.

Cindy Lou, the baby of the family for 13 years came along in July 1958. She was in eighth grade and Peggy was a junior at Franklin College when the biggest surprise occurred. Dr. Schneider informed Pat she was pregnant again.

Pat was now operating the Village Florist and Valentine's Day was approaching—the same day the baby was scheduled. Postponing birth until Feb. 15, 1972, Jeffrey Scott arrived via Batholomew County Hospital. That was the real news around Nashville that day—the Bond's got a boy this time.

June 1990, Jeff is graduating from Brown County High School currently planning to attend Franklin College Fall 1990. Jack is now retired after completing 55 years as a licensed funeral director in the Hills of Brown County—a record for some time to come.

Jeff kept his old parents entertained for many years in little league baseball, basketball and especially football. Becoming a father again at age 53 really paid off. Jack and Pat have four more years of college athletics to enjoy with Jeff.

Meanwhile action has continued on the girls' side of the fence. Ten grandchildren - three girls and seven boys. Some are almost as old as Jeff. Jeff certainly enjoyed having them around to play with and they have enjoyed having Uncle Jeff keep an eye out for them.

BOND-PATTON - James Bond was born May 25, 1844 near Belle Valley, OH. One of eight children born to Joshua and Catherine (Harkins) Bond, he came to Brown County about 1860. He was married to Sarah Loyd Patton of Woodsville, OH on Nov. 23, 1865 in Schooner Valley, Brown Co., IN by Charles Hanna. Sarah was born April 30, 1839 in Pittsburg, PA, the daughter of Thomas W. and Mary E. Patton. The family moved to Ohio in 1850. As a young woman she was a school teacher. Her sister Nancy Erickson lived in Brown Co., IN on Schooner Valley. Her father said he would pay her way if she would go to Indiana to visit her sister. She came by train to Columbus, IN and was met there by her folks. They brought the buckboard wagon to pick her up in. She met and married James Bond on this trip. She did not get back home for ten years and then took five sons back with her.

James Bond was a Civil War Vet No. 110976 Co. H 82 Indiana Infantry. He enlisted as a Private at 18 years on July 30, 1862 and served until war's end. He was captured and held in the Libby prison for six months, later released by an exchange of prisoners. Rejoining, he was wounded in the battle of Chicamauga, hospitalized and later returned to the Army, joining Sherman in his "March to the Sea". He was honorably discharged.

James and Sarah (Patton) Bond

James and Sarah Bond were the parents of seven children, they are: George Weir, born Oct. 21, 1866, married Elizabeth Lane. They were the parents of Tressa and Ralph Bond. James Noah Elsworth Bond, born April 14, 1868, married Louella Wheeler. They were the parents of Claude, Elihu, Gladys, Muriel, Carl, Sally and Ruth Hold. William Thomas Bond, born Oct. 5, 1870, married Bertha Ann Robertson. They were the parents of Florence Edith, born Oct. 5, 1898; Wilma Faith, born May 20, 1900; Sigeal Monroe, born Jan. 24, 1902; Golden Rex, born July 27, 1904; Nellie Pearl, born April 3, 1906; William Everett, born June 23, 1908; Ira Patton, born June 17, 1910 (Everett and Ira died in 1915 of diptheria, 11 days apart); Mary Marguerite, born Jan. 24, 1914; Joseph Walter, born March 13, 1916; Ruby Gail, born July 25, 1919; and Bertha Pauline, born April 29, 1926. John Franklin, born Jan. 29, 1873, married Otta Lane. They were the parents of Pearl, Glenn, Sarah Jane, Velma and Lane Bond. Joshua Jennison, born Nov. 12, 1874, married Myrtle Yoder. They were the parents of; Earl, Ivan and Ruth Bond. Ella Florence, born Feb. 9, 1877, married David Morgan Hamilton. They were the parents of: Faith, Blanche, Bonde, Florence, Madge, Martha Neal, Iris, George and Helen. They raised their family at South Tunnel, TN. Clyde Arthella, born Sept. 5, 1878, married Setta Hatchett. They were the parents of Lloyd, Harry, Ray, James, Alvin, Wayne, Nona, Sarah and Marjorie. They raised their family in St. Paul, KS.

James and Sarah planned to move to South Tunnel, TN to live with their daughter Ella Florence. While James was moving their belongings to Tennessee, Sarah was staying with their son William Thomas. She was there when she became ill and died on April 27, 1923. Sarah Bond was buried in the Hickory Grove Cemetery (Bond Cemetery). James finished the move to Tennessee and lived there until his death on Feb. 10, 1932. Funeral services were held in South Tunnel, TN and at the home of his son, Joshua in Nashville, IN. Joshua had traveled to Tennessee in his own hearse to return his father's body to Brown Co., IN. A military service was given for James Bond and burial was in Hickory Grove Cemetery. *Submitted by Byron Wilson, great-grandson of Ella Florence Bond Hamilton Pearson*

BOND-ROBERTSON - William Thomas Bond was born in Brown County on Oct. 5, 1870. He was the son of James and Sarah Lloyd (Patton) Bond. Bill Bond was a farmer and ran a threshing machine. He traveled in the area with a threshing crew. He loved his babies and always requested they be seated by him at the table. He would feed them while he ate his own meal. He was a good Chrisitian man and was (as was his family) a member of the Church of Christ.

On March 6, 1898 he married Bertha Ann Robertson in Brown County. Bertha was born Aug. 7, 1881, the daughter of James Monroe and Sally (Young) Robertson. Her father had a blacksmith shop in the Belmont area.

Their children were: Florence Edith, born Oct. 5, 1898; Wilma Faith, born May 20, 1900; Sigeal Monroe, born Jan. 24, 1902; Golden Rex, born Aug. 27, 1904; Nellie Pearl, born April 3, 1906; William Everett, born June 23, 1908; Ira Patton, born June 17, 1910; (Everett and Ira died of diptheria in 1915, 11 days apart.) Mary Marguerite, born Jan. 24, 1914; Joseph Walter, born March 13, 1916; Ruby Gail, born July 25, 1919; and Bertha Pauline, born April 29, 1926.

William Bond Family, Back: Sigeal Monroe, Nellie Pearl, Wilma Faith and Florence Edith; Front: Joseph Walter, Ruby Gail, William T., Bertha Ann Bond and Mary Marguerite

Florence Edith married Dec. 26, 1916 to William Cecil Sturgeon. They had three children: Helen Louise, born June 7, 1918; William Paul, born July 11, 1924 died Dec. 31, 1989, and Venetia Rose, born Jan. 8, 1927. William Cecil Sturgeon died

March 30, 1927. Florence then married Everett Isaac Henthorne and after his death married Lloyd Bush. All three husbands preceded her in death. Florence died May 11, 1979.

Wilma Faith married Quentin H. Gwin on April 15, 1922. They had two children: Quentin H. Gwin, Jr., born July 2, 1924 and Helen Deloris, born April 7, 1934. Quentin, Sr. died April 7, 1980 and Faith is still living in Indianapolis, IN.

Sigeal Monroe married Mary Olive Rogers on April 19, 1924. They had three children: Harold Edward, born March 16, 1925 died Dec. 12, 1946; Etta Marie, born Aug. 4, 1927 died May 6, 1971; Martha Joan, born Aug. 30, 1929 died May 22, 1944. Sigeal died Nov. 8, 1981. Mary died March 9, 1990.

Golden Rex married Blanche L. Shepherd in 1926. Blanche died Aug. 20, 1937. His second marriage was to Cynthia Virginia Blackaby in 1938. They had three children: Blanche Lavina, born Oct. 12, 1939; Elizabeth Ann, born April 19, 1941; and Dorothy Marie, born May 7, 1943 (died immediately after birth). Rex died Feb. 25, 1979; Virginia still lives in Indianapolis, IN.

Nellie Pearl married James Woods on June 2, 1923. They had three children: Wilma Jean, born April 25, 1924; James Lester, born April 25, 1928 and Robert Earl, born March 20, 1934. Jimmy died Aug. 13, 1986 and Nellie still lives in Bloomington, IN.

Mary Marguerite married Charles Nathan Bradley on July 5, 1933. They had one son: Billie Lee, born June 3, 1935. She died Jan. 18, 1943. Charles was remarried to Geneva Harden and died June 9, 1971.

Joseph Walter married Mary Ellen Deckard on Aug. 7, 1937. They had seven children: William Cecil, born July 28, 1938; Joseph Paul, born March 7, 1940; David Dale, born Oct. 4, 1942; Phyllis Ann, born July 26, 1944; Mary Faith, born March 13, 1946; Florence Marie, born Dec. 14, 1947, and James Fredrick, born July 10, 1949. Walter died June 19, 1984. Mary still lives on Schooner Valley in Brown County.

Ruby Gail married Clifford Petro. They had four children: Anna Mae, born June 27, 1935; Charles Thomas, born Dec. 28, 1937 died May 23, 1968; David Lee, born Jan. 28, 1943, and Bonnie Kay, born Feb. 7, 1951. Ruby Gail lives in Indianapolis, IN.

Bertha Pauline married Elza Morton Lucas Dec. 12, 1942. They had three children: Gwendolyn Fay, born Nov. 12, 1943; Larry Ray, born Jan. 4, 1945 and Linda Kay, born June 5, 1947. They live in Columbus, IN.

William Thomas and Bertha Ann (Robertson) Bond both died at their daughter Florence's home in Bloomington, IN. William Thomas died May 1, 1931 and Bertha Ann died Sept. 17, 1951. Both are buried in the Hickory Grove Cemetery in Brown Co., IN. *Submitted by Florence Bond Barnes, granddaughter of William Thomas Bond*

DEBRA ANN BOYER - Debra is a sixth-generation Hoosier on both sides of her family. She was born in Indianapolis on Aug. 4, 1951, the oldest of six daughters of William Richard and Mary Helen Beyke Boyer.

Her line can be traced to the York Co., PA, Boyers (Bayers) who emigrated from Germany in the early 1700s. Jacob (born 1789) and his English wife, Lucy, moved from Maryland to Kentucky. Their son, Henry Milton (born 1826), came to southern Indiana to study ministry at Mars Hill College. He was a Methodist circuit rider in southern Indiana and married Amanda Griffin of Decatur County, whose father, Charles, surveyed the town of St. Omer.

Charles Theodore Boyer, born 1856 at Greenwood, met his future wife, Martha Jane Shipp, at Amity's Jollity Methodist Church where his father preached. A realtor and inventor, Charles sold his patent to the Boyer Clover Buncher around 1900 when he moved the family to Indianapolis.

His son, Walter Thomas, born in 1885 in Franklin, married Hazel Vivian Campbell (1888) of Fairmount in 1906. Her father, William, came with his father from Greenwood, LA, to fight for the North in the Civil War. When his father returned to the family farm, William stayed behind to become the first postmaster of Fairmount and marry Emma Makepeace of Daleville. Emma's family originated in New England; her mother was a Pierce, first cousin to President Franklin Pierce. The Makepeaces were a literary family, and Emma became a published songwriter.

Walter was an entrepreneur who opened Boyer's Rent-a-Car, the first car rental business in Indianapolis. He ran for the Indianapolis City Council and was an organizer of the city's Lindbergh welcoming parade. His son, William, Debra's father, born 1926 in Indianapolis, served in World War II, graduated from Butler University, and started the Boyer and Gatewood Steel Company. Debra's mother, Mary Helen Beyke, was born in 1926 in Jasper, Dubois County, an area settled in the 1840s primarily by German Catholics from the Black Forest. Mary Helen's father, Joseph (born 1894), was the son of Christotom (Christ) Beyke and Catherine Spellmeyer. Joseph served in World War I, returned to marry Dorothy Fehribach in 1921, and operated a laundry in Jasper. The Beykes and Fehribachs were farmers.

Dorothy (born 1901), an accomplished quilter, was the daughter of George Fehribach (born 1869) and midwife Rosa Meschede (born 1878). George's father, Raymond (born 1841) was a Civil War veteran who married Elizabeth Strotman (born 1851). Rosa was the daughter of Henry Meschede and Elizabeth Seiler (both born 1855). All the parents of these four great-great-grandparents were immigrants. The German name of Fehrenbach was changed to Fehribach; Debra is related to all bearing this name.

Debra Ann Boyer

Debra attended Catholic schools in Indianapolis, representing St. Lawrence in the 1964 Central Indiana Spelling Bee finals. She received a full scholarship to St. Agnes Academy; as a member of a vocal group there, she competed at the state level. Upon entering Indiana University in 1969, she qualified for the honors program in math, English, Latin and chemistry. Her 1973 degree in biological sciences is completed with minors in math, German, chemistry and classics.

After graduation, Debra worked in Pediatric Genetics, Riley Hospital, at the Indiana University Medical Center. There she performed the labwork for a statewide genetic screening program. Following that, Debra was a research assistant in genetics at Indiana University.

In 1979, Debra decided to test her creative talents by freelancing in calligraphy, a hobby for ten years, and in graphic design. At the same time she moved to Brown County.

She joined the staff of the Brown County Democrat in 1980 and for the next five years was able to work in every capacity of newspaper production. In 1981, she took a seven-week, solo backpack trip to Europe and interviewed Brown County servicemen there. When Woman's World magazine featured Brown County in 1985, Debra's photo of the Dillinger Museum was used in the piece. Ironically, her great-great-grandparents Makepeace are buried 30 feet east of Dillinger in Crown Hill Cemetery.

The year 1986 marked the Brown County Sesquicentennial when Debra served as secretary-treasurer officer of its commission. Later that year, she began her business, Brochures Unlimited, a division of Ridgetop Communications. Since Debra began freelancing in 1979, the word "Ridgetop" has always been used in conjunction with her work to represent a Brown County point of view and state of mind.

Debra's permanent home is Brown County, a place she finds conducive to creativity yet centrally located for operating a business. Her long-range goals include painting watercolors and writing fiction.

DANIEL BRANSTETTER FAMILY - Magdalena Branstetter was born ca. 1758 and is buried in Harbaugh's German Reformed Church Cemetery in Franklin, PA. Her son, Daniel Branstetter, was born ca. 1781 in Washington Co., MD. He married Catherine Geiser, born 1783 in the same county. They were parents of several children including Daniel W., born 1815. The Branstetters probably came from Germany. Daniel W. moved to Wooster, OH and married Rebecca Mortice, born 1824 in Pennsylvania, there in 1843. Daniel and Catherine are buried in the Plains Church Yard at Wooster, OH and Daniel's stone reads "War of 1812".

Daniel Branstetter

By 1850 Daniel W. and Rebecca had moved to Brown Co., IN and had a land grant signed by President Taylor. He built a house in a valley north of Pine Bluff, facing what is now SR 45. Brick for the house were made on the property. The double fireplace had built-in equipment for cooking. A large barn was built across the road. By various means Daniel acquired more land and when he was home he could look in any direction and scarcely see land which did not belong to him.

Daniel is mentioned frequently in the Brown County Commissioners' records as road viewer. Even though he could not read or write he loaned money to people, keeping his reserve money hidden in the barn. He kept a chest of gold and other coins in the house. Sometimes children were allowed to play with them.

Daniel's feet matched his large frame. Once Fritch was making shoes for Daniel and told bystanders he thought he would take a trip around Daniel's shoes. Daniel had just come in and heard the remark. It was quite some time before Daniel paid for the shoes.

Rebecca was a quiet but busy person. She made quilts and some bits of her weaving still survive. She knew about both wool and flax. Her daughters grew up knowing such outdoor work as lye soap and apple butter making. Rebecca is listed in the Georgetown Church Book, Brown County (1859-1897), as a deceased member.

One son died when a child. The other, who resembled Daniel in looks, tall and ungainly, was sometimes depressed because he felt he was not as neat looking as he wished to be, died from a gunshot wound (supposedly self-inflicted) at age 20.

Daughter Julia married Alfred Brock, Sarah married Oscar Warford, Mary married Sam McClary and Catherine married T.H. Lester. Catherine and her only child died in 1871. Rebecca died in 1875. Daniel married Mary Brock, the mother of his son-in-law, Alfred. A granddaughter once stated that "Mother said that German was spoken in her household." Rumors travelled in the family about treasure, royalty, and an illegitimate child while in Germany.

Daniel died 1884, the death report gives the cause as rheumatism of the heart. He was not ill ahead of time.

BREECE FAMILY - Charles A. Breece Jr. has many early childhood memories of Brown County: the long drive from Indianapolis over the old roads, hikes in the woods with his father, and those family style chicken dinners served at Abe Martin Lodge or the Whip-Poor-Will's Nest.

Charles Breece, Sr., Unidentified man and Charles Breece, Jr.

Charles Jr.'s mother, Georgia Breece, was a budding artist studying with Leota Loop and he can recall the visits to her studio and also the visits with Adolph Shulz and Dale Bessire. Many times the family stayed with Dr. Walter and Lottie Grow at their Brown County log cabin. This may be how we became "cabinized." In 1936, Ben Hitz and Fred Bates Johnson completed six log cabins on Freeman Ridge and all had a commanding view of the hills and valley. The old hewn poplar logs were numbered on the ends when they were disassembled at the original location. A porch and kitchen room were added along with a brick cistern and an outhouse. Charles A. Breece, Sr. leased one of the cabins and the family finally had their very own Brown County log cabin. Because the concrete vault privies were partially built with WPA labor, Dad called ours the "Roosevelt House." In the Greasy Creek valley below the cabins Charles Jr. hunted fox and raccoon. An elderly gentleman whose name he cannot recall, came to their place occasionally to help tan some of his pelts. The photograph, taken in 1937, shows Charles Breece, Sr., this man and Charles Breece, Jr. with part of a season's catch. The cabin had no telephone, city water or electricity. With old telephone wire and magneto crank telephones Charles Sr. connected four of the cabins by phone. Someone would arrive on the ridge then crank the phone to see who else had made it.

After World War II, Charles Sr. purchased another of the cabins, sold their city home and made Brown County their permanent residence.

Charles A. Breece, Sr., retired in 1949 after 46 years with AT&T and Indiana Bell. He became active in local affairs, was a lifetime member and director of the Brown County Art Gallery Association and had been chairman of the Community Fund Drive. He died in 1976 at age 93. He was one of the incorporators and member of Indiana Bell's first board of directors. Georgia Breece died in 1956.

Although Charles Jr. and wife, Anne, were living in Dayton, OH they were regular week-enders throughout the 70s. They moved to Brown County permanently in 1979.

One of the six original cabins burned in 1939. The five that remain have all been remodeled and enlarged. The Breece cabin may be the only one with the old crank telephone still hanging on the wall. Most will agree that Brown County has changed, but once after a storm when they had no power, no water and no telephone, it was again the same. The wind in the tall oaks, the rain, the Whip-Poor-Will's song unchanged from the Brown County known more than half a century ago. *Submitted by Charles A. Breece Jr. Col., U.S. Army, retired*

BREEDLOVE FAMILY - The Breedlove family living in Brown County before 1840 probably came here from Kentucky. It appears that John Breedlove married three times. It is believed that his first marriage was to Cynthia Mitchner, March 26, 1832 since this shows (1) Thomas (born ca. 1834) and (2) Nancy born in Jackson Co., IN. John then married Orinda Followell in 1837 and they had (3) William (born ca. 1837), (4) John (born ca. 1840), (5) Francis M. (born ca. 1842), (6) Lewis B. (born ca. 1846) and (7) Albert M. (born ca. 1849). John then married Mrs. Jerusha Miller and they had (8) Orinda (born ca. 1864) and (9) Mary J. (born ca. 1866). In the 1840 era census records show the family living in Washington Township, Brown County.

Thomas Breedlove, first-born son of John, born January 1832 and who died Oct. 6, 1901 in Brown County is buried at Greenlawn Cemetery. Thomas has a Civil War shield stone Co. I, 120 Ind. Inf. He married Elizabeth Graham Oct. 8, 1856 and she was the daughter of Green and Margaret (Petro) Graham. Elizabeth was born May 8, 1847 on the Whittington Farm in Bartholomew County. She died Feb. 18, 1922 at her home five miles southwest of Nashville and is also buried in Greenlawn Cemetery. They had 13 children: John William Breedlove (1858); Felix Preston (1860-1951), Thomas Monroe (1862-1936) Charles F. (1864-1924), Jacob Sherman (1867-1931), Ulysses Grant (1869-1919), Susan Alice (1871-?), Albert E. (1873-1936), Louis Edward (1875-1892), Ida Mae (1876-?), Mary Etta (1877-?), Oliver E. (1878-1931), Columbia B. "Lumie" (1879-?)

Back: Roscoe and Mildred Breedlove; Front: Roscoe Breedlove, Jr. and Charles Breedlove and Tootie Bug (dog)

Charles F. Breedlove, fourth child of Thomas and Elizabeth was born Sept. 10, 1864 in Washington Township and died May 23, 1924 and is buried in Duncan Cemetery. Charles married Dec. 21, 1890 Sarah Ellen Hatchet (daughter of William Green Hatchett and Alvira Earl). Sarah was born Sept. 10, 1865 Brown County and died Oct. 21, 1951 at home of her son, Roscoe in Bloomington and is buried in Duncan Cemetery. Charles and Sarah had four children: Louis E. (1895-), Esta Viola (1896-), Harry Roscoe (1899-1982) and Flora Elizabeth (1905-1968).

Roscoe, third child of Charles and Sarah, was born July 2, 1899 in Brown County and died Sept. 1, 1982 at Bloomington and is buried in the Duncan Cemetery. Roscoe married Mildred Hornung of Deer Park, IL at Ottawa, IL and at this time Roscoe was a resident of Haviland, OH. Mildred was born Aug. 29, 1901 and died Dec. 15, 1989 and is buried in Duncan Cemetery. Roscoe and Mildred had two sons: Roscoe, Jr. (born Sept. 20, 1931 at Decatur, IN) and Charles G. (born Dec. 20, 1933 at Decatur, IN) and Roscoe adopted Mildred's daughter, Violet V. (born April 16, 1921).

The State of Indiana bought Roscoe's acreage around 1936, as well as other Breedlove property in the Weed Patch area of what is now Brown County State Park and Roscoe and his mother settled in Monroe County. Roscoe and his mother would pick peaches and other farm produce when living at Weed Patch and leave their home at 2:00 a.m. and go to Bloomington, Court House Square Market, to sell this produce and return home about midnight.

Charles G. Breedlove was the second child of Roscoe and Mildred, and married Shirley Hoffa, April 24, 1953 in Bloomington. Shirley was born March 10, 1935 in Owen County (daughter of Walter Hoffa and Mildred Rubeck). Charles and Shirley have three sons: Harry (born June 10, 1954) married Debra Kelley June 16, 1972 and have Christopher (born Jan. 10, 1975) and Emily (born June 9, 1984); Charles K. born April 30, 1956 and is unmarried. Mark born July 8, 1960 and who married Monagale Whitehead July 30, 1982 and have daughters Sarah (born Sept. 27, 1984) and Ashley (born Aug. 1, 1987), both born in Bloomington. *Submitted by Charles G. Breedlove*

BREEDLOVE AND STIDD FAMILY - The Breedlove family was proud that they were from Brown County, although they ended up in Monroe County. They always talked of old neighbors and happenings in Brown County. David Stidd (born May 8, 1844-died April 11, 1919) and Rebecca Rody (born Jan. 18, 1847-died May 5, 1925) were married Aug. 14, 1864 in Belmont Co., OH and settled in Brown Co., IN. They were the parents of eight children, and in 1893 they moved to Monroe County.

Thomas Monroe Breedlove, Sr. (born January 1832 - died Oct. 6, 1901) and Elizabeth Graham (born May 8, 1842 - died Feb. 18, 1922), both from Brown County, were married Oct. 8, 1856. They were the parents of 13 children.

These two families were joined when Thomas Monroe Breedlove, Jr. (born Aug. 4, 1862-died Jan. 28, 1936) and America Stidd (born Oct. 15, 1875-died May 3, 1965) were married Sept. 19, 1895. Two of their children died as infants: Elizabeth Ann and Alra Lawton. Helen Chitwood's mother, Ida Mae Breedlove, was born to this marriage March 13, 1898. She had one sister and two brothers: Elsie Lenore Breedlove Gillespie (born Nov. 22, 1902-died Dec. 18, 1984); William Roosevelt Breedlove (born Feb. 7, 1904-died April 17, 1977); and Noah Anderson Breedlove (born July 28, 1907-died June 16, 1976).

Front: Thomas Monroe Breedlove, Jr., America Stidd Breedlove Back: Elsie Lenore Breedlove Gillespie, William Roosevelt Breedlove, Noah Anderson Breedlove, Ida Mae Breedlove Wampler, 1925.

About 1911, Thomas and America Breedlove, Jr. moved from the Oak Grove neighborhood to Monroe County with their four living children. Thomas worked at the Monon Railroad yards until he was injured.

Ida Mae met and married Basil Glen Wampler (born Nov. 25, 1892-died June 12, 1954) on Dec. 20, 1915. They spent the rest of their lives in Monroe County, except for two years at the George Setser Farm on State Road 45 just East of Helmsburg in 1933.

Ida Mae and Basil made sorghum the two Falls they lived at the Setser Farm, just as they had done in Monroe County (except the sorghum wasn't black). They learned that the type of seed and ground had much to do with the finished product. They also had a cider mill and made cider each fall which was sold to Brown County sight-seers. Earl and Grace Bond, Al and Mable Neal and Grandpa and Grandma Turner were close neighbors.

Donald Edwin Wampler (born Dec. 25, 1928), now living in California, started to school at Helmsburg with Katherine Morrison, teacher. This was in the days of John Dillinger. One day Donald's older brother, John Dale Wampler (born March 1, 1918-died Dec. 16, 1984) walked home from school for lunch; a car stopped to ask if he wanted a ride. Dale told him, "No." The man told him he was John Dillinger! He did look like the newspaper picture.

In 1940 the family lived just over the line in Brown County on the Vannie Fleener farm, when Mae Wampler died, June 27, 1940.

On Dec. 20, 1940, Helen Iris (born Aug. 9, 1920) married Charles Corbitt Chitwood (born May 23, 1917). Charlie was first cousin to Clarence Chitwood.

Helen and Charles' only child, Patricia Mae Chitwood (born Sept. 7, 1942) married Jack Stultz (born Oct. 3, 1941) on Jan. 11, 1963. They had two children: Daniel Paul Stultz (born April 6, 1964) and Paula Elaine Stultz (born Nov. 11, 1965). Daniel married Amy Summit (born Nov. 18, 1968) on May 30, 1987; and Paula married Tom Todds (born May 13, 1961) on May 3, 1986. Paula and Tom Dodds have two children: Joshua Wayne Dodds (born Oct. 19, 1986) and Jacob Allen Dodds (born March 16, 1988). *Submitted by Helen Iris Wampler Chitwood*

LOUIE EDWARD BREEDLOVE - Louie was a son of Charles F. Breedlove (1864-1924) and Sarah Ellen Hatchett (1865-1951). Charles, in turn, was a son of Thomas Monroe Breedlove (1832-1901) and Elizabeth Graham (1842-1922) who were the progenitors of the Breedlove family of Brown County. Louie Edward, born Feb. 3, 1895 at Belmont in Brown County, married Oct. 17, 1917 at Lowell, IL to Ada Josephine Brittingham who was born Sept. 22, 1895. Louie Edward died Aug. 23, 1975, his wife, Ada, died June 30, 1961. Both are buried in Blue Creek Cemetery, Haviland, OH. They had four children: Carma Ellen Breedlove; Gaylord Louie Breedlove; Norma Irene Breedlove and Doyle Duane Breedlove.

Carma Ellen Breedlove, born March 5, 1921, Scott, OH married Kenneth Ira DeVore on Nov. 23, 1939 at Haviland, OH. He was born Sept. 9, 1912 at Ohio City, OH. Ken and Carma DeVore had five children: Brenda Joyce, Lowell Kenneth, Dale Gene, Cedele Sue and Richard Glen DeVore. Brenda Joyce DeVore, born Aug. 26, 1940, married Carl Raymond Howard at Latty, OH on June 25, 1960. Carl and Brenda Howard had three children: Caren Kay, born Jan. 22, 1966, Fort Wayne; Edward Paul, born Aug. 24, 1967, Fort Wayne; and Amy Sue Howard, born June 1, 1973.

Lowell Kenneth DeVore, born May 5, 1942, Haviland, OH, married Mary Kathryn Kruger of Celina, OH, on Nov. 30, 1963. They divorced in 1974. Their child, Janis Marie DeVore was born Nov. 3, 1968 at VanWert, OH. Dale Gene DeVore, born Dec. 17, 1947, Mt. Clemens, MI, married Carol June Buelher in Toledo, OH on May 20, 1967. Their son, Brian Keith DeVore was born Dec. 9, 1967 at Oregon, OH.

Cedele Sue DeVore, born May 27, 1951, Parsons, KS, married William Harold Emch in Woodville, OH on Sept. 23, 1978. They had two children: Jennifer Marie, born Dec. 13, 1980, Oregon, OH and Jacqueline Nicole, born March 10, 1984, Toledo. Richard Glen DeVore, born Nov. 13, 1956 at Parsons, KS, is unmarried.

Gaylord Louie Breedlove, born March 20, 1924, Scott, OH, died June 15, 1980, buried at Blue Creek Cemetery, Haviland, OH. He married Ruth Mabel Simpson (born April 5, 1928), on April 5, 1947 at Cecil, OH. They had three children: Bonnie, Ronnie and Tommie. Bonnie Sue Breedlove, born April 27, 1948, married on Oct. 8, 1966 at Paulding, OH to Douglas Weller. They had two children, Ryan and Troy. Ryan Jay Weller, born Oct. 11, 1967, married Christina Sprouse on Nov. 7, 1986 at Melrose, OH. Their child, Rhamsey Thor Weller, was born Aug. 26, 1986. Troy Linn Weller was born March 17, 1970.

Ronnie Gene Breedlove, born Jan. 22, 1952, Paulding, OH, married Angela Jill Robinson. They had two children: Myka Michelle Breedlove, born July 2, 1975 and Chad Christopher Breedlove, born Dec. 24, 1980, both born Paulding, OH. Tommie Gayle Breedlove, born July 25, 1967 at Paulding, OH, is unmarried.

Norma Irene Breedlove, born Dec. 6, 1926, Scott, OH, died July 19, 1988, buried Blue Creek Cemetery, Haviland, OH. She married James Arnold Barkley at Winchester, IN on Nov. 17, 1956. James was born Sept. 3, 1926 at Conway, OH. They had three children: Jerry, John and Ann. Jerry Duane Barkley was born Jan. 28, 1959, Ft. Wayne, IN. John Kent Barkley, born July 19, 1961, married Lori Kay Drayer on June 28, 1986 at New Haven, IN. Their child, Jessica Lynn Barkley was born Sept. 20, 1988, Ft. Wayne. Ann Louise Barkley, born July 27, 1962, married Steven Scott Harry on Oct. 4, 1986 at Ft. Wayne.

Doyle Duane Breedlove, born Oct. 8, 1932, Haviland, OH, married Rosemary Elna Noneman at Paulding, OH on July 19, 1959. They had two children: Melissa and Lori. Melissa Ann Breedlove was born Aug. 11, 1960. Lori Kay Breedlove was born March 25, 1963, both born at VanWert, OH. *Submitted by Carma (Breedlove) DeVore*

ROBERT LEE AND BETTY RUTH BRIGHT - Robert and Betty live at 404 N. Jefferson Street, Nashville, IN, in the house Lee and Ruth Bright bought from Laura Duhm, the builder (a retired Army nurse). The house was built in the late 1930s.

Robert Lee and Betty Ruth Bright

Robert Lee Bright married Betty Ruth Detering, Sunday, Sept. 7, 1947, in Central Methodist Church, Evansville, IN. He was graduated from Nashville High School in 1938, and from Indiana University in 1942 with a degree in Business Administration, major in insurance and minors in speech and economics. Enlisted in the Army Air Corps, June 30, 1942, and entered active service Dec. 7, 1942, as an aviation cadet. Honorably discharged with the rank of staff sergeant, Dec. 20, 1945. Son of Lee Bright and Ruth Williams Bright. Born Jan. 10, 1921, in house across the road from the old Brown School, located on Salt Creek Road. Father, Lee, taught in the school there and was later responsible for the establishment of the Brown County State Park. Father of Ruth Ellen and Beth Ann Bright. Spent working years in radio and television broadcasting as an announcer and later in management and sales positions, before retiring in 1986.

Betty Ruth Detering Bright, married Robert Lee Bright, Sunday Sept. 7, 1947, in Central Methodist Church, Evansville, IN. Graduated from Freelandville High School in 1942, and from Deaconess Hospital Nursing School in 1945, becoming a registered nurse. Daughter of Ellen Harper Detering and August Albert Henry Detering. Sister of Elnora, Mary and Donald Albert Detering. Mother of Ruth Ellen and Beth Ann Bright. Born March 4, 1924, two miles south of Freelandville, IN, in Widner Township, Knox Co., IN.

MARTHA (RODGERS) BRITT FAMILY

- Winfield Scott Richards (born 1847) son of John Richards and Joanna Stipp and Hannah Ellen Fritch (born 1849) daughter of Lewis Fritch and Ellen Aldrich Folsum, were married March 10, 1866 in Brown County. They had ten children: John Lewis (born 1867), Naomi (born 1869), Julius (born 1872), Mary Helen (born 1873), Scott (born 1875), Milton (born 1878), Conrad (born 1882), Calvin (born 1884), Anna Ellen (born 1887) and Leonard (born 1890).

Winfield was a colorful character and panned for gold in Brown County. Hannah was a strong woman in spirit, raising her children in a Christian home. She gave 1/2 acre of land on which Bear Creek Church was built.

Allen Albert Collins (born 1864, son of Ephraim Collins) and Tillie Mae Wilson (born 1879, daughter of Joseph Woodrow Wilson and Screlda Dillon) were married April 23, 1903. They moved to Brown County, raised a large family; including Flossie Edith Collins (born 1912).

Seth, Justin, Mattt Britt, 1984

Milton Richards, married Viola Robertson (born 1878) on Dec. 21, 1899. They raised seven children: Mabel (born 1901), Melvin (born 1903), Jesse (born 1906), Helen (born 1908), Naomi (born 1910), Robert (born 1912), and Harold (born 1921). After Viola's death in 1932, Milton married Flossie Collins, March 17, 1933 in Brown County. They raised four children: Elmer Ray (born 1935), Faye Louise (born 1937), Kathern Darlene (born 1942) and Viola (born 1946).

Milton owned a sawmill on Bear Creek Road; in early 1950 he operated a grocery and cafe in Trevlac, later starting an auction. Milton was a Trustee and Deacon at Bear Creek Church for many years.

John Wesley Rodgers (born 1875), son of Johnathan Rodgers and Mary Jane Crum) was married Dec. 27, 1907 to Millie Jane Harris (born 1881, daughter of Samuel Harris and Martha Ellen Shela). Their son, Ray Edward Rodgers (born 1913), moved to Brown County with his former wife and four children: Ray Jr., Mary Jane, Ruth and Nancy. Faye Richards married Ray Rodgers, Sept. 1, 1955. They have two sons: David (born 1968) and Scott (born 1972).

Martha lived her early life in Brown County and attended Helmsburg School. Martha and her sister, Linda, contracted polio in 1960 leaving Martha on braces. Many of Martha's relatives still reside in Brown County.

After moving to Morgan County, Martha Rodgers married Daniel Alan Britt (born 1958) on June 21, 1979. They have three sons: Seth Alan (born 1980), Daniel Justin (born 1981) and Matthew Tanner (born 1982). *Submitted by Mary Jane Richards*

LOYD CLIFFORD AND MARY MARTHA RHUDE BROCK

- Loyd Clifford Brock was born Jan. 20, 1921 in Crab Orchard, KY, the son of Sim France and Virgie (Simpson) Brock. Mary Martha (Rhude) Brock, born April 1, 1922, on one of the Rhude Farms near Peoga, now known as Green's Lake, in Hamblen Township, Brown County, IN, was the daughter of Jacob Douglass Rhude, Jr. and Cassie Mable (Trisler) Zimmerman Rhude. Loyd and Mary were united in marriage in Franklin, Johnson Co., IN July 3, 1941 by the Rev. Cecil Parkhurst.

Loyd and Mary resided in Franklin, IN prior to moving to Spearsville, Trevlac, and south of Peoga in Hamblen Township, Brown Co., IN, in 1944, where she still lives. Loyd worked for General Motors, Indianapolis. He died May 25, 1956, result of an automobile accident, coming home from work. He is buried at Greenlawn Cemetery, Franklin, IN.

Mary attended the one-room elementary schools (Wray and Walker) in Hamblen Township, near Peoga, first walking then later riding in the first horse-drawn school hack in the area, owned and driven by her father. She attended Trafalgar High School, Trafalgar, IN and Redland High School, Dade Co., FL.

The watershed from Peoga to Upper Salt Creek, an area now known as Rhude Hollow, through which Rhude Creek flows, was mostly owned by the Rhudes and members of their families in the 1800s and 1900s—thus it got its name.

Mary Martha (Rhude) Brock, 1990

Mary is a fourth-generation Brown Countian, descending from William Henry Harrison, Martha Ellen (Harrison) Rhude, and Jacob Douglass Rhude, Jr. Three generations of her descendants also live in Hamblen Township, Brown County, i.e., son Garland Brock; grandson, Alan Brock; great-granddaughter, Justina, and great-grandson, Brandon Brock.

Mary and Loyd had seven children:
Martha Louise, born June 8, 1942, married Eugene Napier Aug. 19, 1962. Presently lives near Edinburg, IN; Garland Lee, born Aug. 25, 1943, married Zuba Napier, June 6, 1961; Wanda Jean, born Nov. 27, 1945, married Marshall Batton, Jan. 28, 1964; Marvin Dale, born June 20, 1949, married Barbara Bowling July 28, 1967; Deborah Joan, born March 8, 1953, married Boyd Emerson, April 2, 1971. Presently lives in Edinburg, IN; Bruce Wayne, born April 9, 1954, married Robin Fitzer, Aug. 31, 1974; James Allen, born Jan. 18, 1956, married Mary Lou White Oneal, Feb. 11, 1984. They divorced.

Garland, Wanda, Marvin, Bruce and James all live in Hamblen Township, Brown County. Garland works at Allison's Indianapolis; Wanda works at Methodist Home Franklin; Marvin is self-employed logging; Deborah works for H&R Block Income Tax Office; Martha works at Arvins, Franklin, and H&R Block Income Tax Office; Bruce is self-employed building construction; James (Jimmy) is an apprentice marble layer. Garland served four years, nine months in U.S. Air Force. Bruce served six years in Indiana National Guard.

Mary owns and operates Brock's Grocery at the west end of Peoga, IN. Her grandfather, Jacob D. Rhude, formerly owned and operated a general store at the east end on Brown County side of Peoga. Her son, Marvin, previously owned and operated Brock's Grocery. Later, Garland and Mary bought the land and erected the present building. Garland was also working at Allison's where he has been an Area Manager for some time. Mary bought his interest in the store. Jacob D. Rhude Sr. (grandfather) also worked in timber, operated a steam engine powered sawmill, and farmed, as did her father, Jacob D. (Bob) Rhude, Jr. Garland Brock served as trustee for Hamblen Township.

Mary lives on the property where her father grew up and was previously owned by her father, grandfather, and great-grandparents. One of her grandsons, Lloyd, son of Marvin and Barbara Brock, and his wife, Janette, and their daughter, Heather, also live on this property, making seven generations which have occupied homes on the same property in Hamblen Township, Brown County. *Submitted by Mary Martha (Rhude) Brock*

BROWN FAMILY - Thomas Brown and his wife, Susanna McKinney, both born in 1803 in Davis Co. NC, came to Pekin, IN at an unknown date. In 1834 they moved to the Stone Head area in Brown County. Their children were Sarah, born January of 1827, Catherine, also born 1827, Sandy 1829, Henry 1831, Mary 1835, Elizabeth 1838, Lewis 1841, and George 1844. Thomas died in 1847, Susanna in 1869. Both are buried in Mt. Zion Cemetery, Brown County.

Drusilla Gordon Williams, daughter of Evelyn and Ray Brown Gordon. She was crowned Brown County Queen for the Indiana Sesquicentennial celebration in 1966 and led the Brown County Spring Festival Parade that year. She is wearing a suit and hat belonging to the wife of the well known Dr. Ralphy. Note the feather plume on the hat.

Sandy Brown, son of Thomas and Susanna, married on Oct. 25, 1850 to Mary Ann Lawles, born

1833 in Maryland. Mary Ann died in 1855 and is buried in Lawles Cemetery with their two infants. In 1857 Sandy married Nancy Matney. Their children were Thomas born 1857, John 1860, Mary 1862, Henry 1864, Martha 1867, Lydia 1873 and Charles 1876. Mary was killed by lightning in 1873. Her father died in 1907, her mother died in 1917. All three are buried in Mt. Zion Cemetery.

Henry Brown, son of Sandy and Nancy Brown, married first to Lucy Hines in 1886. They had two children: Clyde Brown who married Fannie Percifield and had Harold and Wanita; Nellie Brown who married Forest Gordon and had a daughter, Faye, who married Sandford Strough; and a son, Ray Brown Gordon who married Evelyn Nash and had four children: twins, Jayenna Faye, died at four months and Forrest Ray who married Nancy Beaver and had a daughter, Jane. He served in the U.S. Army. Drusilla who married Larry Fender and had a son, Brian. Drusilla won the Indiana State Sesquicentenial Queen Contest from Brown County in 1966. Angela Rose who married Conan Gill and had a child, Chelsea Gill.

Clyde Brown and his sister, Nellie Gordon, are buried in Indianapolis. Their father, Henry Brown, married second to Nancy Palmer. They had five children: Lydie, Martha, Dorothy, Walter and Lewis.

Charles Brown, son of Sandy Brown and Nancy Matney, married on Jan. 1, 1906 to Gertrude Alta Moore. Charles and Gertie Brown had five children:

Clifford Brown who married Goldie Aynes and they had Maxine, Michael, Benny and Barbara. Barbara married Jim Brinegar and had Jeff, Robin, Lydia.

Hazel Brown who married first to Irvin Kelley, second to Ed Covey, third to Ernest Rambo.

Berton Brown who married Goldie Smith and had Walena, Barbara and Gerald.

Clarence Brown who married Betty Voorhees and had Robert, Patricia, Karen, Bonnie, Nora and an adopted daughter, Toni.

Earl Brown married Betty Joy and had three children: Darwin, Gary and Cathy.

Members of the Brown family attended school at Valley Branch, Chrisitansburg, Pikes Peak and Nashville High. Churches attended were Mt. Zion, Church of Christ or Harmony. Deceased members are buried at Mt. Zion, Nashville, Columbus or Indianapolis. *Submitted by Evelyn Nash Gordon.*

GROVER G. BROWN - Grover's oldest known ancestor was Joshua Brown, born in North Carolina in 1776. He and wife Phoebe had four sons and moved to Houston, IN in 1823. Of these four sons, Thomas married Mary O'Neal in 1830, six years before Brown County was organized. They built a crude log cabin two miles southeast of Story, which location was later known as the Isaac Tabor Farm. Two abandoned Indian wigwams near the Brown cabin were used by roving hunters. Thomas and a neighbor cut the first road from the Story area that joined up to the Columbus Road. It was just a trail through the woods. To this marriage was born 16 children which incluced Thomas Hill Brown, the youngest, born in 1849. James Brown, son of Thomas Hill Brown was born in 1866. Grover G. Brown, oldest son of James and Nancy Brown was born near Story in 1886.

Grover's childhood years were spent on Gravel Creek. Since the school terms were only five months he attended a one room school 11 years before graduating from the eighth grade. He never attended any high school as there were none in the county then. He attended a ten week County Normal at Pikes Peak for a teachers license and began teaching at age 17. Little did he know that one of his pupils ten years later would become his wife. Later he spent two years in Central Normal College at Danville, IN, and graduated from State Teachers College, Terre Haute. He also graduated from Zanerian College of Penmanship in Ohio and took extension and correspondence at Indiana University.

Grover G. Brown

He served 51 years in the Brown County Schools as teacher, principal, and superintendent. Grover was a man of many interests and talents. He memorized over 6000 lines of poetry, split over 400 fence rails after age 74 — walked 48 miles in one day after age 57. Served as State Grange Lecturer of Indiana four years. Served as church elder for over 20 years. Wrote a Brown family history over a period of 32 years. Was Secretary of the Tuberculosis Association for more than 30 years. Wrote newspaper columns for the Brown County Democrat and the Republic for several years.

He required about 2500 eighth grade pupils to write him a letter to high standards before they could graduate. These letters from 1936 to 1952 have been bound and preserved. He answered every letter personally. His goal was to write one surprise letter each week, to a five year old or 100 year old, to an old friend or a perfect stranger. He will be remembered longest by most people for his story telling, especially "The Taleypo." This story was told in 12 states to white, black, Indian, kindergarten, elementary, high school and even college students. In 1913 he married Lura Browning and they had four children, Lenore, Glenn (deceased), Wilma and Norma, eight grandchildren, 11 great-grandchildren and one great-great-grandchild.

The Brown Family Bible. — Thomas A. Brown had an old family Bible with records of births and deaths. It was discovered one day in 1962 to be in the possession of Jessie Potter, granddaughter of Thomas A. Brown, now living in Bloomington. The Bible contained the following information: Thomas Brown and Mary O'Neal married June 13, 1830. Thomas Brown, son of Joshua and Phebe born Dec. 10, 1809. Mary, daughter of Jacob and Elizabeth born Sept. 19, 1812. Children: Sarah Ann Brown born May 16, 1831; Elizabeth Jane Brown born Oct. 1, 1832; John H. Brown born Sept. 24, 1833; Julia Ann Brown born Jan. 1, 1835; Wilburn E. Brown born March 31, 1837; Mary Ann Brown born May 22, 1838; William Manson Brown born Sept. 14, 1839; Elisha Brown born Jan. 21, 1840; Phebe Brown born April 21, 1841; Alfred Brown born June 22, 1843; Amanda Brown born Dec. 25, 1845; George Washington Brown born June 22, 1847; Andrew T. Brown born March 20, 1849; Thomas Hill Brown born March 20, 1849. Andrew T. Brown departed this life Sept. 27, 1849.

Note. It seems that all of the above records were made at one time about 1850 by John B. Hayward, an Evangelist. The next record is about 30 years later and is in a different handwriting. It reads "Thomas Brown departed this life Feb. 27, 1879." "Mary Brown departed this life March 22, 1894, in the morning 8:25." It was told that Thomas A. Brown and Mary (O'Neal) Brown had 17 children. Only 14 are listed in the Bible record. Another source mentions two more born after 1849 who died in infancy. Nothing known about the 17th child. This Bible information is taken from Grover Brown's book "Two Hundred Years with the Browns."

Helen Enslow of Bloomington is the daughter of Jessie Brown Potter who was a daughter of Alfred Brown listed in the above Bible record. *Submitted by Wilma Pittman and Lenore Engle*

LURA D. (BROWNING) BROWN - The Brownings came from England to Virginia. To the marriage of Nathan Browning and Obedience McPike was born a son, John Rufus, in 1818. In 1825 they moved to Indiana and in 1839 John married Phoebe Hunter and 18 children were born including three sets of twins and one set of triplets. Nathan Browning, the fourth child, became a doctor, locating in Needmore. He married Amanda Elizabeth Carothers. Lura Dell and Tura Bell were the youngest of ten children.

When they were nine days old their mother died. A month later, a sister, Nora, married Oren Jones and they assumed the responsibility of rearing the twins. It was a little unusual for newly weds to have twins with them on their honeymoon. The trip from Needmore to Bloomington was made by horse and buggy. The twins ran out of milk and made quite a fuss. Oren spied a cow and borrowed enough milk for the twins' bottles. After Dr. Nathan Browning remarried the twins returned to Needmore. When they were nine years old their father died. Tura Bell died at the age of ten.

Lura Brown

Lura then lived with her sister, Dora Ault, and went to school at Gravel Creek. Her teacher was Grover G. Brown who would later become her husband. After the death of Dora, Lura lived with various brothers and sisters until she began working as a housekeeper in private homes. In the meantime a romance developed between her and Grover G. Brown. He graduated from Indiana State Normal on June 25, 1913 and 31 days later they were married.

Lura's practical experience in housekeeping made her an excellent manager of the household. Her cooking was envious. She could make crispy, white kraut in a 12 gallon jar. Keeping the children from raiding it for cabbage stalks was her only problem.

Although Lura's formal schooling ended at the 6th grade her talents and hobbies were many. She did woodworking that ranged from tablemaking to a back porch for their home. She was an excellent seamstress and quilter. She was active in the Nashville Christian Church's Ladies Aid, quilting to help the needy. She demonstrated quilting at the Indiana State Fair to thousands of people. Even into her late 90's she worked at quilting and embroidering.

Lura loved music and was an enthusiastic guitar player, specializing in instrumental music. She sang with the Home Demonstration Choir at Purdue University. After she was past 90 she had a season ticket at the Little Nashville Opry for five years, almost never missing a show in spite of bad weather, her wheel chair and oxygen bottle.

Lura was the mother of four children, Lenore Engle, Glenn (deceased), Wilma Pittman, and Norma Nentrup. She had eight grandchildren, 11 great-grandchildren, and one great-great-grandchild when she died at age 99 on Jan. 1, 1990.

NOEL M. BROWN - Noel, a fifth generation Brown Countian, was born on Salt Creek Road, June 24, 1934, the son of Virgil Emmett and Ruth E. Neff Brown. Jennifer Lynn Brown Rollins, a daughter by his first marriage, resides in Colrain, MA, with husband Douglas and their three children, Justin, Alexander and Emily. He and his present wife of 30 years, Sarah Haase Brown, are the parents of four children, Vincent, Michael, John, and Suzan, all of Indianapolis. Noel attended the one-roomed Brown and Clark Schools and Nashville High School in Brown County prior to furthering his education at the Universities of Maryland and Missouri. He is a veteran of the Marines and served in Korea and Japan during the Korean War.

He is Director of Operations of the Indiana State Commission on Vocational and Technical Education and served on the Governor's Youth Committee for eight years. He is also active in the Indiana Adult Literacy Coalition. Noel has served in the administrations of Governors Branigan, Whitcomb, Bowen, Orr, and Bayh, and has received several awards for outstanding service to the State of Indiana.

Noel is the great-great-grandson of Reverend Thornton Flemmon Bright, born circa 1805, in Virginia and a preacher of the Methodist faith. Thornton came to Brown County circa 1850. He, his wife, Mary Frail Bright, born circa 1806 in Virginia, and four of their nine children, William, Luzannah, Jane, and Lewis came to Brown County from Virginia (now Wheeling, WV) via flatboat to Cincinnati, then northwest to Brown County by team and wagon. The eldest son John preceded the family to Brown County.

Thornton was on the first Board of Directors of the North Salem Methodist Episcopal Church in Brown County, and his last preacher's license for that church dated July 24, 1886, remains in the possession of Noel. Being a circuit riding preacher, Thornton served many other churches in the county, and as a Justice of the Peace he performed many marriage ceremonies.

Noel's great grandfather, Lewis Bright, operated the post office and general store at Mt. Moriah in Hamblen Township. His grandparents Emmett and Anna Bright Brown also operated a post office and general store at Sherman, where the building stands today.

Noel's mother resides in Columbus, and his father Virgil, a veteran of WWI who taught school and farmed in Brown County, was killed in 1944 as a result of a farm accident.

Noel is an amateur genealogist and enjoys writing family histories and communicating with family genealogists world-wide. Noel and other Bright researchers plan to compile a history of Thornton Bright, his ancestors and descendants.

ORVAL AND WANDA (MEDCALF) BROWN - A few years ago a scholar said that English in its purest form, as descended from Elizabethan English was probably spoken with most authenticity in the hills of southern Indiana. He surely meant Brown County where the colorful phraseology and rhymical speed patterns, sparkling with humor, have been noted by Kim Hubbard, Ernie Pyle and others. One of the genuine originals was Orval Brown whose ancestors have lived in Brown County since 1828. They came from North Carolina, Tennessee and Kentucky. Orval's early memories were of hunting, farming, log cabin building, shinglemaking, railroad tie cutting, and bronco busting. (They would buy several wild horses at a time at the Railroad station auction in Franklin.)

Orval was one of the founders of the football program for Nashville High School and helped build the stadium where football is still being played.

Orval and Wanda Brown

Wanda graduated from Indiana University in 1947 as an Art major. She taught for 30 years, 15 in Brown County and the rest in Indianapolis, Whiteland, Trafalgar, and others. As an artist she has exhibited in many places. She is the Calabash Lady of Brown County who raises and designs ornamental gourds.

Orval Brown, builder, bronco buster, amateur boxer, pilot, stock car racer and school bus driver, was born Oct. 21, 1922 in Brown County, the son of Eber and Jessie Corley Brown. Eber (1890-1965) was the son of John A. (1855-1953) and Mary Ann Crouch Brown. John was the son of Henry W. (1831-1865) and Elizabeth David Brown and Henry, died in the Civil War, was the son of Thomas A. (1803-1847) and Susanna McKinney Brown. Thomas and Susanna are buried in Mt. Zion Cemetery. Mary Ann Crouch was the granddaughter of Aaron and Mary Casady Crouch, Sr. Aaron Crouch (1786-1848) served in the War of 1812.

On May 20, 1957, Orval married Wanda Medcalf in Brown County. Their children are Patricia, Karen (Kitty), Ishmael, and Samuel Brown. Patricia married Frank Casale and they have children Giancarlo, Gabriele, and Mia. Ishmael married Darla Roberts and they have children Kile and Kyra. Wanda is the daughter of school teachers, Admer and Jessie Brooner Medcalf of Dale, in Spencer Co., IN.

Orval's paternal grandparents lived in the Pike's Peak area. Orval was raised in the Bean Blossom area. He and Wanda wrote "Growing Up in Bean Blossom" containing stories of his early memories and family folklore.

Edward (Ned) David, Orval's great-great-grandfather, came from Kentucky in 1830 and was offered "all the land he wanted" near Columbus in exchange for a pony. He refused the offer, preferring to come on to Brown County since the hills offered protection from chills and fevers common in the lower, swampier areas. He made the first bricks in Brown County, many were used in Nashville, and built a large brick home near the junction what is now SR 135 and SR 46. He lived to age 96 and was the father of 29 children.

Henry W. Brown's widow, Elizabeth, married Phillip Pike in 1868. They lived in Illinois, but some of the family returned to Brown County as it was considered a healthier place to live.

RAY AND LINDA BROWN FAMILY - Ray Brown, son of Carl and Marie Boaz Brown, was from Hartsville in Bartholomew Co., IN where the Brown ancestors settled in 1846 after leaving Warren Co., OH.

The Boaz ancestors left Ireland and came to Virginia and eventually Indiana. Thomas Boaz, born in Scotland in 1721, moved to Ireland and married Agnes. In 1747 or 1748 they came to America. Ray's great-great-great-grandfather, Abednego, their tenth child, was born in America. The DAR listed Thomas Boaz as a Pittslyvania County Patriot for his contribution to American Revolution.

Linda Baxter Brown, was born in Bartholomew County, the daughter of Floyd and Gladys Moore Baxter. Floyd's grandfather, Williamson Baxter, from Jefferson Co., IN, fought in major Civil War battles including Chickamauga and Missionary Ridge near Chattanooga, TN. Floyd's mother, Anna Painter Baxter, was born in Brown County. Gladys was also born in Brown County, the daughter of George Wesley and Mary Alice (Molly) Dobbs Moore.

Linda and Ray Brown

Molly's parents, Rebecca Magaw and Solomon Dobbs married in Brown County in 1860. Solomon was the son of John and Mary Dobbs. Family tradition alleges that Solomon and Rebecca had lived in Pennsylvania about 20 miles apart, but didn't know each other until they came to Brown County.

Rebecca's parents, Enoch and Matilda Haines Magaw moved to Brown County, sometime between 1857 and 1860 from Beaver Co., PA, owning 80 acres near Bartholomew County line. Enoch was the son of James and Eunice Dye Magaw, who were both born in Beaver County. James' father came to Pennsylvania from Ireland. James was a cobbler but spent most of his life as a farmer.

Molly married George Wesley Moore also from Brown County. Wesley was the son of William

Henry and Sarah Ann Hall Moore. Sarah was the daughter of Jesse and Rebecca Aynes Hall, another Brown County family. Sarah died when Wesley was only 12 years old, just three days after the death of her three month old son. Wesley's grandmother and grandfather was Sanford and Mary Morgan Moore.

Sarah's grandparents were Jesse and Rebecca Aynes Hall, Sr. Rebecca was the daughter of Gabriel and Sarah Aynes, Sr.

Gabriel Aynes, of North Carolina, and Sarah of Tennessee, settled in Brown County where they lived their remaining years.

Linda and Ray's children, Donna Eaton and Carl "Bucky" Brown both live with their families in Brown County.

RUTH ELIZABETH (NEFF) BROWN - Was born on a Clay Lick Road farm in Brown County in 1900. She is the daughter of James Daniel (Dan) Neff and Amanda Louisa Fowell Neff.

Ruth was married to Virgil E. Brown in 1920. A WWI veteran, he attended Indiana Normal School (now Indiana State University), taught at the Brown and Cravens elementary schools in Brown County, but could not lose his love for the farm. It would later cost him his life. He was killed on Memorial Day, 1944, in a farm accident. Ruth was left with five minor children and a farm to tend. After maintaining the farm for a few years, she spent the period from age 50 to age 71 as a cook at the Brown County CYO camp.

Ruth and Virgil were the parents of nine children: R. Ernestine, born 1921; V. Eugene, born 1922; B. Wayne, born 1924; J. Dale, born 1927; Marshall, born 1929; Mary, born 1930; Noel, born 1934; Kay, born 1936, and; Lou Ann, born 1938.

Ruth Elizabeth Brown

Ruth's maternal grandfather, Isaac Fowell came to the United States in the mid 1800s from the United Kingdom. He was married to Eliza Jane Burkhead. His lineage can be traced to William Fowell, a lawyer and "feoffee" - land owner from Totnes and a Member of Parliament (Commons House) in 1455-1456.

Ruth's paternal grandfather, Oliver Alexander Neff, born 1829 in New York City, served in the Civil War with the 17th and 82nd Indiana Infantry Regiments. As a result of injury, he received a military disability pension until his death in 1916. Oliver came to Indiana without relatives at age 13. He married Sarah Elizabeth Campbell in 1853.

Ruth's maternal great-great-grandfather John Birkhead who served in the Revolutionary War from Maryland. His family were among the early settlers of Maryland in the 1600s.

Ruth's brother Jesse Neff, an educator and farmer, taught school at Gold Point, Turner, Dowden and Sprunica in Brown County from 1912 to 1957 except for a period of 12 years while serving as a school superintendent in North Dakota. As a student at Indiana University he served on the President's Student Interest Committee.

Ruth attended Turner Elementary School in Brown County. Having no opportunity to continue her education, but with an intense desire for learning, she received permission to complete the eighth grade twice, both years being an A student.

As a child, Ruth walked over the hills to church at Goshen. About 1930, she became a member of the Gnawbone Holiness Mission. Later she became a charter member of the Nashville Nazarene Church until her transfer of membership to the First Church of the Nazarene in Columbus, where she was voted as Mother of the Year.

Ruth, now in her 90s, lived in Brown County for 56 years. She now resides in Columbus and spends her life in adoration of, and devotion to, her seven living children; 24 grandchildren and 29 great-grandchildren. She continues to be very active in the church. In May of 1990, the Mayor of Columbus, IN issued a proclamation naming her 90th birthday as "Ruth Elizabeth Neff Brown Day."

WAYNE AND ROSE BROWN - Wayne and Rose married in 1946, and are the parents of three daughters, Constance (Connie) Brown, Camille Willmore and Teresa Artman. There are seven grandchildren. They lived in Phoenix, AZ, Indianapolis, Greenwood and Morgantown, IN, before settling in the old Stoney Lonesome area west of Columbus.

Upon returning to Indiana from Arizona, they mixed public service careers with family raising and are both retired from the staff of the Indiana State Board of Accounts.

Rose was born in Greenwood in 1927 and spent most of her youth in Helmsburg. She is the daughter of Harold and Jessie Watson Harding. Harold was the son of Franklin and Mary Ann Pittman Harding, early Brown County natives. Jessie was the daughter of Seward and Sarah Martha Tracy Watson. Seward was the son of William Greene Watson and grandson of Jonathan and Elizabeth Seward Watson, natives of Kentucky, moving to Hamblen Township circa 1834 and settling on entered land (21-10-3).

Wayne and Rose Brown

William G. Watson settled on entered land in Hamblen Township (33-10-3). He was township assessor two terms, Brown County Sheriff, 1864-68, and elected Brown County Auditor in 1870. In 1859 he was married to Rachel Parsley, daughter of Solomon S. and Susannah Staples Parsley. Solomon, born 1803, was the son of Robert Martyr Parsley who migrated from England. The Parsley family also settled on entered land in Hamblen Township (33-10-3).

Wayne, born in 1924 in Brown County, is the son of Virgil and Ruth Neff Brown. Ruth, now age 90 and living in Columbus is the daughter of Daniel and Amanda Fowell Neff. Daniel's father, Oliver, was a disabled Civil War veteran from New York City. Oliver's wife was Sarah Elizabeth Campbell.

In his later years, Oliver was a frequent occupant of the Nashville liar's bench and guest at the Pittman Hotel. On authority of Squire Harry Kelp, Oliver was the subject of illustrations by Will Vawter for Riley's "Songs of Home." Amanda's father, Isaac, was the son of Isaac and Martha Jenkinson Fowell of England. Amanda's mother was Eliza Jane Birkhead Fowell from Ohio, and descendant of the Birkhead family of Anne Arundel County of Maryland.

Virgil Brown was the son of Emmett and Anna Belle Bright Brown. Emmett was the grandson of Jesse and Mary (Polly) Porter who settled on entered land in Washington township (22-9-3). Jesse was born ca 1805 and Mary ca 1806, both in Virginia. Emmett was Postmaster of Sherman, IN (Hamblen Township) and a farmer and merchant. Anna Belle was the daughter of Lewis and Mary Starr Bright and was the granddaughter of an early Brown County Methodist circuit preacher, the Rev. Thornton Flemmon Bright. Thornton and Mary Frail Bright settled on entered land in Hamblen Township (19-9-4) (Mt. Moriah) where they operated a store and post office. Thornton and Mary were the progenitors of the Bright families of Brown County.

BRUMMETTS - The roots of the Brummett family are found in Franklin Co., VA where James I was born in 1746. He married Agnes, whose maiden name is unknown in 1765-66. There are records of the births and marriages of James II born in 1765 in Franklin Co., VA (not state but Colony then) and married Feb. 17, 1786 to Sarah Riece in Pittsylvania Co., VA. He later moved to Adair County, which was in Kentucky Territory.

Children: Anne, born 1770, married Shadrack Chandler in Kentucky April 10, 1790. John married Prudence McKinney Nov. 19, 1787. Sally married James Bryant July 17, 1788. Renna born 1770 married Mary Estes April 10, 1790 in Franklin City, VA. Renna (also known as Reason) was in 1840 Brown County census. He was in the 1805 Land Records, Cape Girardeau, MO. He and Mary Estes had eight children. Renna was 70 years old in the 1840 Census. Information found in "Publication Brummetts All" published twice yearly and Edited by Mary Nipper of Amarilla, TX.

George (Grancher) born December 1780 in Franklin Co., VA married Mary French July 22, 1802.

The families of James II, Anne and George came to Monroe Co., IN before 1820 since they are in the Monroe County 1820 Census and James III, son of James II marriage record is recorded in Monroe County, 1819.

The families are later found among the earliest settlers in Brown County. They had settled on Brummetts Creek in Monroe County. Brummetts Creek Road runs north from Indiana State Road 46 to State Road 45 where it ends at Unionville. It is here that many of the Brummetts were buried in the cemetery that is by the Unionville Baptist Church. This church was founded in the home of James Brummett II and as the membership grew a log church was built on Brummett Creek. It was replaced by the present limestone structure. The name "Little Union" was given to the first church on Brummetts Creek.

George Brummett's oldest children: Joab, Elizabeth, William, and Langston were born in the Kentucky Territory. Robert and Solomon were born in Tennessee after the Kentucky Territory was divided into two states. All of George's children were among the first families in Brown County.

The Brummetts seemed to migrate whenever the area in which they lived became so densely populated that smoke could be seen rising from another residents' chimney on a clear morning.

The county of Brown was created by an Act of the State Legislature in 1836. All of its territory came from Monroe, Bartholomew, and Jackson County, the State Legislature appointed James Alexander and Aquilla Rogers of Monroe County, David Deitz and Hiram Wilson of Bartholomew County, and Stephen Sparks of Jackson County as Commissioners, who were to set up the government of the new county. The eastern township which was Jackson Township was now the northern part of Brown County. Banner Brummett, son of James II, and Pierson, were already living in this area. Banner had built a log cabin around 1835 or 1836 northeast of what became the County Farm where the paupers were housed. This house is now the office of the Brown County School Corporation. Banner C. Sr.'s home would have been in the area of the present Greenlawn Cemetery. The cabin on the corner of Mound and Johnson Street was the home of Banner C., Jr.

On Aug. 8, 1836, the commissioners met and appointed James Huff, William Dowson, Banner C. Brummett, Sr., John Followell, Henry Jackson and Pierson Brummett (Banner Sr.'s brother) as Commissioners of Brown County.

At this first meeting in July 1836, the Commissioners had set up the boundaries for the townships. Eight men donated the land for the County Seat: two of these were Banner and Pierson Brummett.

The Legislature ruled that the five Commissioners in charge of the organization of the county be paid for their services. They received a vote for $150.00 which was to be paid in cash to five men. Banner C., Sr. and Pierson Brummett were two of these men. At this meeting Banner Brummett, Sr. was appointed County Agent. He was directed to lay out the lots in this 50 acre tract to be sold at public auction. After the lots were surveyed, Banner chose lots #1 and 2 for the jail and courthouse. The name of Jacksonburg was chosen for the county seat. This name was suggested by Banner Brummett, Sr. in honor of General Jackson, the hero of New Orleans.

George A. Brummett

The first court was held at the home of James Dawson in February 1837; being ordered by the County Board, Banner Brummett, Sr., County Agent, let the contract for the building of the courthouse and jail. The courthouse needed to be furnished before it could be used. The county had little money so John S. Williams donated 12 chairs and Banner Brummett's Sr. donation to the county was 20 acres of land.

At a meeting of the First Circuit Court April 20, 1837, the second case on the docket was one of slander. Pierson Brummett vs. Reuben Mathis. The case was not heard, the plaintiff, by his counsel, moved to dismiss the suit.

Banner C. Brummett, Sr., David D. Weddle, and John Floyd were appointed commissioners to view and relocate so much of the Bloomington and Columbus State Road as it crossed the farms of Henry Newkirk and Robert Henderson.

William S. Roberts, one of the first Justices of Peace in Washington Township, had on his dockets many interesting items. Fighting to see who was the better man was as fashionable as drinking to see who could hold the most liquor. Many of the best citizens were involved. Fines resulting from these incidents went to swell the Seminary Funds. Fines were assessed for assault and battery, profane swearing, thrashing, etc. Banner got his name in this list for contempt of court.

Businesses were being established soon after the boundaries of the town were established. Stores were being opened and fees were set for licenses to sell merchandise. Banner C. Brummett, Sr. by 1837, was operating a store for the selling of groceries and liquor. The selling of liquor seemed to be a thriving business in 1837-1838. As there were five others selling liquor, among those were Pierson Brummett. He is listed as a charter member of the Little Union Baptist Church at Unionville, IN. Banner C. Brummett, Sr. sold groceries and liquor but when a minister, after having delivered a blistering sermon about the drinking of liquor, was told by the keeper of the inn, who also sold liquor, that he could no longer stay there, was taken by Banner to his home to spend the night.

Around this time Pierson, who had the blood of a Frontiersman in his veins, decided to move on. He died in Missouri, April 4, 1846. This and the death of his wife, Rachel, were recorded in the family Bible of his son, Lloyd, who is in the 1850 Brown County Census. The Early Land Entries in Jackson Township listed Lewis, 1835, Banner, 1837, Lewis, 1837 and Joshua, 1835. In Washington Township, George Brummett 1836 and Banner Brummett 1836 entered land.

Joseph, son of Banner, Sr., Robert and Solomon, sons of George had acquired land and were listed with the Toll Tax Payers in 1848. Robert (grandfather of Mildred Marshall) owned 320 acres in Washington Township, Sec. 9. This land was divided by Dubois Ridge Road which ran north from the road now known as Yellow Wood Lake Road. The Brummett Cemetery is on the left side of the road at the top of the hill just north of Yellow Wood Road. In the 1870 Census, Robert's land was valued at $2,500. The Real Estate had a value of $600.

Joab, the oldest of George's sons (George born 1780 Franklin Co., VA, died 1891 - a brother to Banner's father) was among this list of taxpayers of 1848. George was 80 in 1860 census and 90 in the 1870 census and was 111 when he died. There were 134 Poll Taxpayers in 1848, Banner C. Brummett, Sr. ranked ninth in the list of the highest.

On May 13, 1846, the President of the U.S. called for troops to carry on the War with Mexico. A few days after the news reached Brown County, Thomas Taggart (later lost his life in battle at Buena Vista, T.M. Adams, P.C. Parker, Wm. Wise and Charles Bolt decided to raise a company, if possible, in Brown County. These men headed the Enlistment Roll. The first meeting was in Georgetown where about 20 men responded. Among these were Joshua and Reice Brummett, sons of Banner C., Sr. The rest of the men, who formed the company volunteered at Nashville, on June 15, left for New Albany, IN. Here they became part of the Third Regiment and proceeded to New Orleans to embark for Mexico. An epidemic of measles caused the death of many of these soldiers. Joshua Brummett died and was buried on Brazos Island. Reice died, while crossing the Gulf, and was buried at sea.

From the beginning of the government of Brown County, Brummetts were performing official duties. Banner was one of the nine Justices of Peace appointed in 1836 to assume the duties of the county. From 1836-1882 there were 19 sheriffs that served the county. Some served more than one term. One of those was R.S. Brummett, who served 1839-41, again from 1848-52, and his last tenure was 1868-70.

Christopher Brummett (Robert's son) was serving as County Clerk during 1915-16. Wm. Enoch Brummett, known as Nick, was active in politics throughout his life. He was born at Bean Blossom in March 1872. He lived his entire life in that neighborhood. He was a farmer by occupation and a very successful one. He always kept up his yard and home.

Carl Brummett, 1989

Nick took an active interest in the affairs of the community. He served one term as county commissioner and also a term as county assessor. He had been for many years president of "The Old Settlers Association" and was president at the time of his death. His granddaughter, Janice Fleener, is now very active in "The Old Settlers Association" and is at the time of this writing, serving on many of the committees for this year's celebration which was always the first Saturday in September, but now begins Friday evening and continues throughout the weekend.

Nick's father, Hiram Brummett (son of "Whispering" Billy) served in the Union Army during the Civil War. Nick's mother died when he was quite small. Nick's two brothers Ed, father of Carl Brummett of Bean Blossom and well known at the present time, and John preceded him in death. Nick passed away, a few hours after suffering a stroke, at his home Feb. 10, 1947. Nick's grandfather was Wm. Brummett, the son of George and Mary French Brummett who came from Tennessee to Monroe County around 1818-19. Carl Brummett was county commissioner 1949-53.

Joab Brummett, born 1805 in Kentucky, the oldest of George and Mary's six children was the father of Henry, Nancy, William ("Whispering Bill") —great-grandfather of Carl Brummett. George Ab, Sabra, Sally, Langston, Elizabeth, Christopher, and James Payton (Pate).

George Ab Brummett remained living with his parents until he married on March 6, 1861 Martha Snider, the daughter of William and Elizabeth (Brummett) Snider. Elizabeth was the granddaughter of George and Mary (French) Brummett.

George Ab and Martha had five children: Eli born 1862, William McClelland born 1864, Arwine born 1868, Thena Catherine born 1871, and Effie born 1874. Thena Catherine died at a very young age.

Mrs. Martha Brummett died in September of 1875. In January 1877 George married Elizabeth, daughter of John and Elizabeth Brown. They had three children: Orval, Daisy and Mary Jane.

George had moved to a new residence between Georgetown and Helmsburg in 1861, it comprised 125 acres considerably improved, with good buildings, orchards and better land for farming. He continued to labor in the industry of farming until his death at the age of 81 years ten months.

Dates of births of all the children are not given but the Family Bible, furnished by Orval Brummett, listed the following: Effie Jan. 27, 1874, Mary Jane Dec. 18, 1885, Daisy Dec. 22, 1883, Orval Nov. 2, 1881. Effie married Richard Clark who operated the Clark Funeral Home in Morgantown, IN. They had one child, Emerson. He operated the funeral home several years but sold it and ran a nursing home until his death May 27, 1965.

Orval, who died March 3, 1968 married Agnes Parmerle Nov. 3, 1902. They had three children: Lloyd, Osa Brummett Warford and Catherine (better known as Katie) Robertson. Lloyd and Osa are deceased, Katie resides at the Community Care Nursing home at Nashville, IN. Daisy married Edgar Steele. They had three daughters: Beryl Rumsey, Bonnie Weddle, and Lillian Bock. Mary Jane married Carey Warford. They had a son Thurl, who is now deceased. *Submitted by Mildred Marshall*

BULLARD - Brown County residents Gilbert and Betty Bullard were married Oct. 6, 1953 at North Vernon, IN. He was born Gilbert Franklin Bullard, Nov. 29, 1915 at Milford, IN, the son of Orlie Bullard and Catherine (Creek) Bullard. She was born Betty Allene Stigdon, Feb. 22, 1927 at Seymour, IN, the first of six children born to Ross Stigdon and Doris (Mellencamp) Stigdon.

Gilbert was a gentle man. He worked as a long-distance trucker and made a comfortable living for Betty and the grandson they had adopted, plus her five children from a previous marriage. Gilbert died Nov. 26, 1977 at Seymour, IN and he is buried at the Hayden Cemetery in Jennings Co., IN.

Betty now makes her home in the Hayden Community. She had several hobbies and enjoys visits from her children and grandchildren. She is a member of the Seymour Christ Temple Church. Living with her is the adopted son, Baron Scott Bullard who was born Jan. 2, 1972 at Seymour, IN.

Gilbert and Betty Bullard

The father of Betty's other children is Melvin Leo Emily, who was born April 22, 1925 to Charles David and Mary Etta (Reynolds) Emily. That ten year marriage ended in divorce but produced the following children:

Doris Melba Emily, born June 17, 1944 was married to Merle Leslie Lacey and has four children. Melanie Sue Lacey married Jason Scott Alcorn and has children Gregory Scott Alcorn and Julie Ann Alcorn. Cheryl Ann Lacey married Kevin Matthew Birge and has children Matthew Scott Birge and Tristan Lynn Birge. Merlina Kay Lacey, Leslie Allen Lacey.

Darlene Jo Emily was born Feb. 11, 1946. She married Bobby Gene Mays who died Oct. 27, 1970. Next she married Hugh Francis Randall and her children are: Lauralee Mays married John Charles Crane. Starlene Mays married Robert William Walls, Jr., son of Robert William Walls, Sr. and Nettie Pauline (Roberts) Walls of Brown County. Two children were born to them before they divorced and Starlene later married Marty Dwain Jaynes. Her children are Robert William Walls III and Dillon Eric Walls. Baron Scott, Mark Anthony Randall.

Ross David Emily, born May 27, 1947 married Betty Pauline Heilman who already had sons Rick, Steve and Gary. Ross and Betty then became parents of Tamra Lynn Emily who married Brent David Ashpaugh.

Stephen Michael Emily was born Aug. 25, 1949 and died Jan. 8, 1985. He was married to Mary Katherine Campfield and had children: James Melvin Emily married Heather Massey. He has a son Cody James Emily and a stepdaughter Lacy Dawn. Felicia Susann Emily married Michael Bafumo and has children Richard Michael Bafumo and Stephen Allen Bafumo. Timothy Allen Emily.

Gregory Allen Emily, born April 27, 1950, married Constance Hudson and had a son Steven Michael Emily, then he married Veda Misner and had children Rebecca Ann Emily and Gilbert Paul Emily. *Submitted by Donna Stigdon Barger*

CHESTER H. BUNGE - Chester was born Oct. 13, 1904, of German parents, William and Rachale Bunge of Indianapolis, IN. He remembers little about the childhood years with his three brothers, and three sisters because of the tragic deaths of his parents. On Jan. 11, 1916, his mother died of tuberculosis and in the spring his father was killed while working on the levee at White River. With both parents dead, the children were split up. Chester moved to Brown County on May 27, 1916, to live with Miss Fae Patie and her elderly mother.

He was placed in the sixth grade at Dolsburg, in Jackson Township, where he finished the eighth grades. He attended Nashville High School and graduated in 1924. While in school he had his first job with the Nashville Orchard Corporation for 25 cents an hour. This included spraying, picking, and trucking apples, grapes, peaches and plums to the Southside Market in Indianapolis in a Model-T Ford. His next job was working at the sawmill in Helmsburg, Monday through Saturday at noon for $15.00. He ran the cut-off saw, edger and stacked lumber on racks.

In 1928 he married Hannah E. Richards in Brown County and worked for six months in 1929 at a steel mill in Indianapolis. He then returned home and started the job he would continue throughout most of his life, trucking. He worked for Americans Agragates until after WWII. He missed being drafted because he was born three days too early. After he left Agragates, he bought a truck and went to work independently. He helped in the construction of Highway 135 unloading a train car of stone and hauling it to the construction site. In 1930 he worked a dragline on the Wabash River in Posey County. In 1943 Mary Richards, Hannah's mother, died and the Julius Richards farm on Bear Creek was not to be sold out of the family. Chester and Hannah bought the farm and this was the beginning of 15 years of hard agricultural work for the family. They raised chickens, cattle, and most importantly, hogs. Chester said, "if you ever need any quick money, he could raise the cash by raising a bunch of hogs." They had a truck garden with tomatoes, beans, corn and other vegetables. Many times they would combine, along with a neighbor, enough green beans to make 100 bushels to haul in a dump truck to market. Times were hard. A small farmer just simply could not make enough to raise a family of seven and send them through school. During three years on the farm, between 1947-1950, Chester, in partnership, owned a feedstore in Trevlac. The store was the old depot with a platform which sided the tracks. They sold feed, fertilizer, eastern coal and grains along with a few groceries and sundry items.

In 1957, the farm was sold, and the family with three children moved into a house on Hwy. 45 West of Helmsburg which Chester and his sons had built. He was proud to say that when the house was finished, it was paid for and this became the base for his small trucking business. A big garden and many plants and flowers were typical of their home.

Front: Mary Johannah Renihan, Hannah and Chester H. Bunge, Dorothy Jean Young; Back: Sue Lynn Isley, Johnny Arthur Bunge, Kenneth Leon Bunge, Philip Richard Bunge, and Franklin Maurice Bunge.

Hannah passed on July 25, 1977 and Chester continued to live there alone. He retired from trucking in 1981 and kept quite busy with gardening, canning, working around the yard, cooking and housework. He enjoyed reading poetry and literature and could recite with great accuracy "The Rime of the Ancient Mariner" along with many other poems. He enjoyed the company of his family and friends and kept a daily diary and journal of accounts that go back as far as 1920. He was in good health up until the day he suffered a stroke in the kitchen of his home and passed on June 28, 1985. Chester and Hannah are buried in Bear Creek Cemetery, not far from where they spent most of their lives working, enjoying their children and as Chester stated, "We have a lot of ups and downs and a lot of good times."

This union bore seven children, four sons and three daughters: Dorothy Jean Bunge Young. Franklin Maurice Bunge, Philip Richards Bunge, Kenneth Leon Bunge, Mary Johannah Bunge Renihan, Sue Lynn Bunge Isley and Johnny Arthur Bunge. All their children married and had children. At this writing there are 23 grandchildren and 21 great-grandchildren with their third oldest grandson living in their home with his wife and two daughters in Brown County. *Submitted by Trudy M. Bunge*

ANCESTORS OF JENNIFER ANN BUSH

- Jennifer Ann born Aug. 22, 1979, is the daughter of James Ivan and Barbara Ann 'Alba' Bush. Barbara was born in Omaha, NB, 1945, to Abdias Lawrence, born Brown Co., KS (1923-1988) and Alberta, born Nebraska 1925. Alba, who moved to Brown County in 1978. Jennifer has many direct relatives with deep Brown County history on her father's side:

James I. Bush (born 1946) attended Nashville Schools 12 years, graduating from Brown County High School in 1964. He's a U.S. Air Force Veteran and employed at Cummins Engine Co. since 1968. Parents Ralph Edward "Scotty" and Mary Kathryn 'Bond' Bush had one other son, Allen Lee (1950-1953).

Ralph Bush, born Monroe County 1923, currently resides in Corydon. He's a decorated WWII 5th Army Veteran (Europe). His parents, James Willard, born Brown County 1893, died 1980, and Mary Margaret 'Owens', born Brown County 1893, died 1970, lived near Belmont James' parents were Thomas Jonathon, born Jennings County 1853, died Brown County 1929, and Margaret 'Clark' born 1860, died Brown County, 1929, Bush, daughter of Pleasant, born 1830, died Brown County 1904, and Elizabeth, born 1826, died Brown County, 1908, Clark. Thomas Jonathon's parents were William L. born Kentucky 1819, died Brown County 1882, and Elizabeth 'Hellman' Bush. William's father was Robert Bush, Minister of the Gospel, born Kentucky 1797, died Brown County 1868. Mary Margaret's parents were James Samuel, born 1870, died Brown County 1934, (son of Samuel and Elizabeth Owens), and Dora Alice 'Henthorne', born Brown County 1874, died Brown County 1939, Owens, Dora's parents, Isaac Eric, born 1826, died Brown County 1919, and Margaret, born 1828, died Brown County 1919, Henthorne, came to Belmont from Belmont Co., OH.

Jennifer Ann Bush

Mary Kathryn attended Helmsburg Schools and graduated from Nashville High School in 1944. Residing in Nashville, she's retired from 32 years Selective Service work (Nashville 1952-1967). She has two brothers, Harry Alvis Bond in Brown County and Ivan Lee Bond in Bartholomew County, and a sister, Oma Jean Kritzer in Brown County. Her parents were Ivan Yoder, born 1903, died 1950, and Katheryn Margaret McLary, born 1903, died 1961, Bond. Ivan worked for the county, State Park and State Road crews with reputable teams of horses and mules. His parents were Joshua, born Brown County 1874, died 1962, Myrtle 'Yoder', born Brown County 1878, died 1945, Bond. Joshua's parents were James, born Ohio 1844, died Brown County 1932, a Civil War Veteran, and Sara Loyd Patton, born Pennsylvania 1839, died Brown County 1923, Bond. James' parents were Joshua and Kathryn Harkins, born Ireland 1812, died Brown County 1899, Bond. Years of family business included mortuary, livery, restaurant, and transporting travelers to/from the Helmsburg Train Depot and Nashville Pittman House. Myrtle's parents were James M. born 1843, died Brown County 1931, a Civil War Veteran and Eliza Jane Baughman, born 1853, died Brown County, 1934, Yoder, daughter of Jacob, born 1818, died Brown County 1889, and Eliza Jane Snider, born Kentucky 1823, died Brown County 1906, Baughman. James was son of Jacob, born North Carolina 1816, died Brown County 1885, Yoder. Eliza's parents, William born Kentucky 1802, died Brown County 1875, and Jane Evans Snider, settled Jackson Township in 1836. Kathryn Margaret McLary Bond was daughter of John Daniel, born Brown County 1872, died Brown County 1918, and Allie Erseneth Mobley McLary, who was born in what is now Brown County State Park to James K. born Ohio 1843, and Emline Smittle Mobley. John's parents were Samuel L., born Brown County 1843, died Brown County 1930, and Mary Ann Branstetter, born Brown County 1847, died Brown County 1880, McLary. Samuel's parents, Hugh A., born Kentucky 1805, died Brown County 1887, and Savannah Lockridge, born 1808, died Brown County 1887, settled Jackson Township in 1839. Hugh's parents were Samuel and Jane Dollhouse McLary. Mary Ann's parents, Daniel, born Maryland 1815, died Brown County 1886, and Rebecca, born 1824, died Brown County 1875, Branstetter, settled Jackson Township in 1840.

LOWRY ELIJAH CALVERT

- Lowry Calvert was born Oct. 5, 1838 in either Dearborn Co., IN or Macon Co., MO the son of John N. and Sarah Sanders Calvert of Lanarkshire, Scotland, the father moving first to Toronto, Canada, Dearborn Co., IN and then to Missouri.

Late 1920s Alice, David, Mary, Annie, Daisy and Owen Calvert

The family returned to Aurora, IN where Lowry received his education. Lowry married in Johnson County Jan. 13, 1861 Amanda Melissa James, the daughter of Samuel Frank and Elizabeth Savage James. By 1870 Lowery and Amanda were living in Hamblen Township, Brown County. Their children were, Anne Elizabeth who married first John Neville and second Robert White; Samuel Edward who married Sadie Ohaakson; twins, Alice Charlotte and David Brewer, Alice marrying Samuel Frank James, Jr., and David marrying first Catherine Morris, second Annie White, and third Myrtle Wilhite; Mary Eliza married Isaac Jones; George Thomas, married Captola Taylor; Daisy Melissa married Edward Lonzo Walker; and Owen Marion married Stella Bennett. Amanda died Dec. 12, 1914, and Lowry died April 23, 1926. Both are buried in the Nineveh Christian Church Cemetery.

CAMERON-HURDLE

- Robert O. Cameron says, "Today my heart holds a place. My inner place is as real as the region folks call, Brown County. What can be shared about the evolution of my inner place?" Come, if you will, to the Bean Blossom overlook on Highway 135. A young boy of six is standing in the spring of 1940 with his mother and friends. The clean, fresh smells of the woods tell that birth is happening once again. The boy's mother, Goldie E. Cameron, breaks her silent gaze of the sweeping valley below, turns to the group and says in her usual jolly manner, "Aren't the redbuds more beautiful than usual?" Not a question but a triumphant exclamation is what the group heard! The boy is moved and embraced by Goldie's passionate utterance although he doesn't realize it at the time. The magic was given and received and the evolution of the boy's inner place began.

Brown County was home for Goldie. Her birth occurred in her parent's home, Oct. 21, 1898. The woman enjoying Bean Blossom Valley had been bathed early on in the magic and charm of Brown County similar to a baptism. All her adult life she was nudged irresistibly to share that spiritual bond with others.

What can be shared about Goldie's inner place? Pretend to leave the overlook and come to the place of James and Presha Hurdle in their modest house north of Bean Blossom in 1903 in wintertime. Thirty-eight years have passed since the young Hurdles arrived from Zanesville, OH, settling first in Schooner Valley. Presha had given birth to 13 children and ten survived infancy. In front of the hearth, held by the warm fire, sits grandmother and six year old Goldie who rests snuggly in the Presha's experienced lap. The innocent girl feels the gentle motion and occasional squeak of the sturdy rocker that held others before Goldie in the embracing and loving arms of Presha. The two sit silent and serene, sure and confident, moving ever so slightly to the currents of mutual devotion for each other. Like her son, 36 years later at the overlook, Goldie was moved by the sharing and receiving of her grandmother's loving enchantment and her inner place was begun.

Goldie, the redbuds are beautiful, as are the autumn fields of pumpkins, the dogwoods, the striking fall colors of the leaves, Yellowwood Lake, a covered bridge, hunting for soap stones and "thunder eggs" in a dry creek bed, "Old Settlers' Days," spirited weekend visiting, playing and eating with relatives and friends. *Submitted by Robert O. Cameron*

CAMPBELL FAMILY

- Thomas Campbell, grandfather of Iris Arnold Lee was born in Ohio in 1854, but came to Brown County as a young man. The Campbells built rude homesteads back in the hills and hollows. On May 18, 1878 Thomas married Elizabeth Brummett, daughter of Robert and Amanda Harris Brummett. Their log cabin was on Jackson Street, just north of where Yellowwood Lake is now located. They were parents of ten children, one dying in infancy. The others were Effie, Art, Lon, Archie, William, Grace, who was Thomas' mother, Mildred, Eva and Alice. Their home was in an isolated and lonely place, but they were hardy and independent. They kept to the old time ways for many years. Life was hard, but they grubbed and endured.

Thomas had a sorghum mill. When the sorghum was being made the aroma wafted into the Brown County hills. He also planted an orchard. Apples from this orchard were served with every meal, prepared as apple sauce, stewed dried apples or fried apples. Each winter night apples were brought up from the cellar and enjoyed by family around a wood burning stove, keeping warm on bitter cold nights with the snow blowing in around the windows. Floors were covered with woven rag rugs to help keep out the cold.

Lon, Archie and William Campbell

Nearly everything the family ate was raised on their own farm. Wheat and corn was taken to a grist mill and ground into flour and meal. Building a fire in the wood burning stove and getting the temperature just right to cook or bake a pie, cake or bread could be a tricky experience. Elizabeth baked great loaves of yeast bread. She made her own yeast from hops and cornmeal. A slice of home baked bread covered with a helping of home-churned butter was a real delight. A trip was made to Needmore in a buggy usually twice a month to get whatever other supplies were needed. Eggs and hens were sold to a huckster who came by each week in his wagon.

The well was dug and water brought up with a windlass. Every wash day, water from the well, or rain water, when available, was heated in a large black kettle. The only equipment needed was wash tubs, a wash board and lye soap, which Elizabeth made herself. If she used the kitchen for wash day, the wide ash boards were then scrubbed with lye soap water which ran out through a hole bored in the middle of the floor.

Thomas and Elizabeth found contentment and peace of mind in the hills of Brown County. They spent their lives helping others, and never a day passed but that extra people shared meals with them. Small crops in the cleared patches, small log houses and game from the forest were all that the early people of Jackson Creek had, but it was their life and they thanked God for it. *Submitted by Iris Arnold Lee*

CORNELIUS S. CAMPBELL - The oldest son of James B. and Catherine E. Campbell married Hannah J. Lindsey April 30, 1884 at Bloomington, IN. Hannah was the daughter of Peter I. and Rachel A. (Stark) Lindsey. She was born Dec. 8, 1860 at Georgetown, WV. Her father was of Irish descent and her mother was English. She had four sisters and three brothers.

Cornelius and Hannah moved to near Sprunica in Hamblen Township. They had 11 children; James P., (1885-1955), Charles C., (1886-1958), Herbert N., (1887-1943), John F., (1889-1959), Mary Edith, (1890-1908), Henry Harold, (1892-1966), Martha Edna Delph, (1894-1973), Anna E. Fleener, (1896-1982), Ruby C. Fleener, (1897-1980), Nathaniel C., (1900-1979), Nellie C., (1903). Nellie Watters is the only one still living.

Front: Ruby, Nathaniel and Nellie, 2nd row: Cornelius, Hannah (Lindsey) Campbell, 3rd Row: Anna, Edith, Edna, Harold, 4th Row: Herbert, John, James and Charles

The Campbell family was active in their church. A Salt Creek Sunday School book on June 7, 1908 records teachers: Mrs. Campbell Class No. 2, C.S. Campbell Class No. 5, Edith Campbell was the Sunday school secretary. By Aug. 23, 1908 her brother, Charles, was acting secretary, and the book reports she was absent on account of sickness. She died a few months later. At different times John also assisted with the records.

In 1909 Cornelius became assistant superintendent. Herbert began teaching Class No. 4 with his future wife Iva Abbett as secretary. He taught Class No. 1 in the years 1910 and 1911. By 1911 the attendance was up to 41 on several Sundays. Salt Creek was later called Sprunica.

Cornelius was a teacher in Hamblen Township as were his children James, Charles, Herbert, Anna and Ruby. He served as county superintendent in 1897 to 1899. He also conducted a normal school for the training of teachers and was a county deputy clerk for one year.

Cornelius, Hannah, John, Herbert and Edith are buried at Sprunica. *Submitted by Nellie Watters-James P. Campbell*

JAMES B. CAMPBELL - The earliest known records of James B. Campbell of Brown County were found in Zanesville, OH where the marriage of James B. Campbell and Catherine E. Stedman was recorded on Feb. 5, 1857. Cornelius Campbell in his journals of 1886 spells her name "Stidham."

James B., of Irish descent, and Catherine, of Welsh descent, began their family in Ohio. His oldest son, Cornelius S. was born at Zanesville on Oct. 2, 1859. There were a total of four sons and two daughters. At the time of this writing only the names of Cornelius, Alexander, (1872-1952), and Anna (Culver) are known. Anna Barrow was listed as a surviving sister in Cornelius's obituary in 1917, along with Alexander.

James Buchanan Campbell

James and Catherine moved to Indiana in 1860. They first moved to Bartholomew County and then to Lawrence County in the fall of 1869. From there they moved to Brown County in 1870. Cornelius in his journal tells of being at a Sunday school convention at Unionville in the fall of 1880 and an Inspector of spring elections in 1886 some time later.

The family moved to Monroe County in the fall of 1871 when Cornelius was 12, but it is thought that the family was living around Needmore in 1900.

In October, 1879 the Brown County Medical Society was formed and James B., a doctor, was listed in Goodspeed's history of 1884 as being one of the founders. He later moved to Bean Blossom and he and his wife are buried in Bean Blossom Cemetery. He evidently was interested in educating young people because Goodspeed reports that an Alexander C. Spencer entered on the study of medicine with Dr. Campbell. *Submitted by Alice Fleener-Smith Parmerlee*

CARMICHAEL FAMILY - After spending most of her married life in Columbus, IN, Lyle and Velma Carmichael built a home in SW Brown County in 1979 on land where Lyle was born on Dec. 10, 1927 and spent all of his childhood. Lyle graduated from Van Buren High School in 1946 in a class of eight. He married the former Velma Sterling of Brownstown in 1948, and spent 40 years in the insurance and real estate business in Columbus.

Velma and Lyle Carmichael, 1990

They are the parents of three children: Caren, born in 1950, is a teacher at Van Buren Elementary School and married to Don Senesac, Industrial Technology teacher at Nashville High School. They have two children—Amy, 14 and Matthew, 8. James L. Jr., born in 1953, is a minister and teacher in Cincinnati and married to Kathy McPheron. They have two children—Christy, eight and Melissa, five. Cindy; born in 1959, is married to Phil Krueger, Indy race car driver and mechanic. They have one son, Ilya, 14.

Lyle's parents, Harley (Bill) and Elva Jane Greathouse Carmichael were lifelong residents of Brown County, living all their lives in Van Buren Township. Lyle's brothers are: Robert Lee, Columbus; Lowell Gene, Indianapolis; Loren Harley, Jeffersonville; sisters, Vurlean Carr, Scipio; Virginia Spray, Brownstown and Shirley Wilkerson, Columbus.

Harley (Bill) was born Sept. 4, 1902 the ninth of ten children of William Calvert and Susan Caroline Goble Carmichael, who also lived their entire lives in SW Brown County. Two brothers were Grover (1885) and Orla (1893); seven sisters, Lola Tabor (1883), Delythia Eddy (1885), Vannie Davis (1886), Calsie Brand (1891), Fena Haws (1896), Veva Greathouse (1899) and Alta Newkirk (1905).

Elva Jane's parents were Jacob and Emily Ayres Greathouse. Brothers, Melvin, James, Lester, Jacob. Sisters—Vira Freese, Della Wray, Ollie Schwab, Rady Mae Waggoner, Dora Kritzer, Laura Wilkerson and Mary Wanicki.

Harley (Bill) farmed most of his life, drove a school bus, worked for the highway department, and served two terms as Brown County Treasurer.

The early Carmichaels came from Scotland around 1758 and settled in Pennsylvania. John Carmichael married Nancy Graham in Mercer Co., PA. Great-great grandfather William Carmichael, born in 1793 in Baltimore, served in the War of 1812 and married Louisa Powell in 1817. Her grandfather, Capt. William Powell, came from Wales to Pennsylvania in late 1700s and married Elizabeth Wells. Her parents were Andrew and Mary Moore.

William and Louisa moved to Belmont Co., OH and had 11 children. In 1850 they moved to SW Brown County. Son Andrew served four years in the Civil War, being only 21 at close of war. In 1868 Andrew was elected surveyor and was candidate for Secretary of State in 1900.

Great-grandfather William was born in 1824 in Ohio, married Nancy Snively Calvert born in 1828 in Ohio. They were married in 1852 in a double ring ceremony with her sister Hester. Nancy's parents, William and Rachel Snively Calvert, both died of cholera in the epidemic of 1854. The house was burned and the well sealed. William and Nancy Carmichael both died in 1910 and are buried in Houston Cemetery. They had seven children, including William Calvert, who was born in 1859. *Submitted by Velma Carmichael*

JOHN AND SARAH CARMICHAEL - John Carmichael and Sarah Ann Kenny were married in Ohio in the late 1840s. They came to Brown County about five years later. He was the son of Thomas Carmichael and Elizabeth Hope.

John and Sarah had three children: Leander, Joseph Thomas, and James M.

Joseph Thomas married Nancy Jane Berry, the daughter of John H. Berry and Rachel Adams and they had nine children: John, Alice, Sarah Oshie Anna, Will, Pearl, Dan, George, Lee and Rachel.

Sarah Oshie Anna Carmichael married Curtis Solomon Zike on Sept. 23, 1894. They had five children: William, Julia, Mary, Gertrude, and Susan Navilla.

Susan Navilla Zike married Clifford Hezikiah Wayt on March 17, 1928 in Freetown, IN and they had three children: Gerald Clifford, Glen Curtis and Gloria Sue. *Submitted by Larry Dean Wayt*

KENNETH C. CARMICHAEL FAMILY - Kenneth devoted most of his adult life to bringing out the potential he believed existed in every school child he taught and supervised. After receiving his undergraduate education at Danville College and his masters at Indiana University, he taught for three years in the Bartholomew County Schools. He then worked for 40 years in the Brown County School System, 25 as a teacher and 15 as an elementary school principal. Kenneth was a member of the Oddfellows Lodge and the Redmen Lodge. He served on the Brown County Zoning Board, the Brown County Planning Commission, the ASCS Community Committee and served on the board of the Tri-County Church Camp. He was a member of the United Methodist Church at Christiansburg.

The Carmichael family originally came from Scotland. Kenneth's great-grandfather, Thomas Carmichael was born in Maryland on May 18, 1801. They later moved to Ohio. In a later move to Indiana, Thomas and his two brothers were crossing the Ohio River when one brother, his family and oxen were drowned. In approximately 1850, Thomas founded Christiansburg, IN where he lived until his death on April 15, 1875.

Kenneth Carmichael

Kenneth & Jewell Carmichael; Phyllis & Sheila Carmichael

The Reverend Amos Worley Carmichael was born to Thomas and his wife Elizabeth on June 20, 1834, before they moved to Indiana. Amos served in the Civil War from 1862 to 1865 in the Indiana Volunteer Infantry. He was made a corporal on July 4, 1864.

Noble was born to Amos and his wife Susie on July 18, 1870 in Christiansburg. Noble began purchasing parcels of the current family farm in Van Buren Township in the late 1800s. He was married to Nancy Ellen Brown on June 29, 1895. To this family were born six boys, all of whom became school teachers. Noble was also a school teacher and in addition to his teaching, the family raised chickens, cows and pigs and farmed with a team of horses.

On April 7, 1934, Kenneth married Jewell Waggoner in Milford, OH because that was the first place they could find a Methodist minister to perform the ceremony. Jewell was born on Oct. 29, 1914, the daughter of Howard and Alice Waggoner of Jackson County. Kenneth and Jewell farmed with horses until purchasing their first tractor, an Allis-Chalmers, in the 1930s. Kenneth was born on the home farm, teaching and farming until he died May 14, 1982. Jewell continues to live and work there today. She is a member of the Parkview Nazarene Church and has served on the Brown County 4-H Council for several years.

Kenneth and Jewell had two children, Phyllis born June 28, 1935, and Sheila, born Oct. 13, 1937. Phyllis and her husband, Ed Lucas, son of Albert and Arlene Lucas, operate the Green Valley Motor Lodge in Brown County. They have four children, Teresa, Stan, Madeline and Michelle and three grandchildren, Ryan and Aaron Harden and Taylor Peters.

Sheila and her husband, Jack Lucas, also the son of Albert and Arlene Lucas, continue to operate the family farm along with Jewell in Van Buren Township, where they raise primarily corn and cattle. They have three children: J.D., Suzette and Aimee and three grandchildren: Jared Lucas and Danielle and Chad Sizemore. *Submitted by Jewell Carmichael*

L. NEAL AND VIRGINIA A. CARMICHAEL - The Carmichael family came from Scotland to Maryland. Two sons, Thomas (1801-1875) and William moved to West Virginia, then on to Ohio, and finally to Van Buren Township, Brown County arriving in 1849. The majority of land that was purchased around Story (within a five mile radius) was cleared and their living was made by the harvesting of timber and farming.

In 1850, Thomas (great-great-grandfather) founded Christiansburg and began purchasing land in the vicinity. Married to Elizabeth C. Holts of Pennsylvania in 1822 and from this union seven children were born. (John, Robert, Mary, Joseph, James, Amos, and George.)

Robert (1824-1893) (great-grandfather) married Hannah Powell in 1851 and to this union were seven children. (William Thomas, Nancy Catherine, Loretta Cassandra, Mary Louise, Otto Kenny, Meta Lena, and Otho Lessie.) The family lived on the 240 acre farm, the west one-half now known as "Cherry Hill", five miles east of Story.

L.N. Carmichael

William Thomas (1852-1926) (grandfather) married Susanna Helms in 1872 who died during the birth of a child and in 1875 he married second Amelia Knightler. To this union were born five children: Ival (1879-1931), Mary L. (1881-1900), Phillip (1887-1953), Ellra (1889-1909), and Bert (1893-1963). Amelia died in 1895, and he married Mary Pearl Roush, the daughter of George W. and Margaret Knightler Roush in 1897. To this union were born seven children and one unnamed infant. (Ira 1897, Estel 1899-1986, Virgil 1900-1976, Ruby 1901-1921, Howard 1906-, Olive 1910-1911, Blanche 1913-). He owned the land about .5 mile south and east of Story.

Estel Carmichael married Eva Fleetwood (daughter of William R. and Kate Saunders Fleetwood) in 1921. Leston Neal was born in 1922 and Esther Kathleen in 1926 on the Carmichael farm near Spurgeon's Corner, ("Cherry Hill," Van Buren Township.) The east one half (120-acre tract) of the land purchased by Robert Carmichael in 1850 is still owned by Neal and Kathleen. They were issued the Indiana Homestead Award in 1988.

The 20s and 30s were rough times for the Carmichael family. In 1927, the first buildings were constructed on the present farm using materials from three old school buildings, including Spurgeon school. Present barn was built in 1935 and the house in 1941. Income was generated from farming, using horses to bus children, working in timber and hauling gravel for country roads. Horse and buggy was a means of transportation for the family to Mt. Nebo and Christianburg churches. A 1926 car was purchased for use when roads were passable.

Neal attended the one room school at Becks Grove, Christianburg High School and graduated from Freetown High School in 1941. He enrolled in Purdue University School of Agriculture and completed two years prior to enlisting in the U.S. Army in 1942. Commissioned a Second Lieutenant, he served in the Pacific area until 1946. He completed his education at Purdue and taught vocational agriculture at Trafalgar High School in Johnson County for nine years.

Neal married Virginia Anne Fuller of Pine Village, IN in 1944 and they have two daughters, Sheryl Anne born in 1948 and Sue Ellyn in 1949. He moved to Columbus in 1956 and taught science in the high schools, retiring in 1982. He maintained his reserve commission in the U.S. Army after World War II, completing various levels of military training and retired in 1982 with 40 years of service and the rank of Major General. His last assignment was the command of the 123rd U.S. Army Reserve Command which included Indiana and Michigan Reserve units. He received many awards and decorations to including the Distinguished Service Medal.

The family still lives in Columbus. Sheryl is employed by Indiana State Board of Health. Sue Ellyn, an elementary school teacher, married David Walters in 1971 and has two daughters, Erin Elizabeth 1978 and Megan Elyse 1984.

Neal and Virginia, although retired, still participate in many local and state groups and boards.

CARTER - Family tradition says Joel Russell Carter as a young man went off to the Civil War. There, he stood guard in wet clothing. He developed arthritis from this. Later he became so crippled from the arthritis (he walked on crutches) he could no longer farm—an occupation in which he had engaged since early manhood. So he entered politics and ran for Recorder of Brown County. He was first elected in 1884. Later, he was elected to another term.

Joel was born in January, 1842 in Belmont Co., OH, the oldest child of Ephraim and Nancy (Millison) Carter. The father was a native of New Jersey and was of Scottish extraction. The mother was from Pennsylvania and was of German extraction. In 1852, Joel came with his parents to Jackson Township where he grew into manhood. He originally stood about six feet tall. But later, he became so crippled that he did not stand near six feet. He was a brother to John W. Carter, a well-known schoolteacher and a colorful character of the Brown County area during the latter part of the 19th century and early part of the 20th century.

In 1874 Joel married Elizabeth Hines, a young widow with two small children whom he helped raise. Elizabeth was born Ann Elizabeth (Joel changed her name to Elizabeth Ann) Taylor on Jan. 8, 1841 in southern Monroe Co., IN. Her father, William Taylor, owned a farm in Perry Township around where Lake Monroe now is. That farm was probably where she was born. William and Elizabeth's mother, Nancy (Smith) Taylor died while Elizabeth was still a child. Elizabeth and her sister and brothers, some grown by that time, continued to live on the family farm for several years. Elizabeth was a small woman, about five feet tall and had dark hair and grey eyes. How she met Joel is not known.

Four children were born to Joel and Elizabeth. They were Ida Jane, born 1875, married George Setser, a schoolteacher; Mary Lorena, born 1877, married Charles Stump, also a schoolteacher, as well as a minister; Daisy Myrtle, born 1879, never married. She was also a schoolteacher; and Courtland M., born 1882. He was on his way to becoming an established cartoonist when he was killed by a train at the age of 25 in 1907.

After Joel retired from politics, he and Elizabeth lived at what is now Helmsburg in the Stump-Carter House which is still standing. Joel died in 1898 and Elizabeth in 1904. Both are buried in the Lanam Ridge Cemetery.

There are no descendants living in Brown County now; however, there is a great-granddaughter who lives in neighboring Monroe County. *Submitted by Lorena L. Miller*

JAY AND ELLEN CARTER, Jay D. Carter, the son of James V. and Virginia Carter was born Oct. 12, 1942 in Anderson, IN. He graduated from Anderson Highland in 1960 and from Indiana University in 1964, where he was a member of the Sigma Chi Fraternity and rode in the "Little 500." While at I.U. his grandparents, Earl and Cliffie Carter often brought him to Brown County. After graduation he worked as a bank examiner.

In 1971, while visiting Brown County, he discovered that the Hugo Fechmans were going to sell their summer log cabin. That day he called the Fechmans and reached an agreement with them to purchase the home. Shortly, thereafter, he moved to his new home which had no heat or plumbing. Since that time, the cabin has been expanded and modernized. Extensive flower- and wild-life gardens have been added. The house has been on the Log Cabin Tour numerous times. Later he purchased the Orchard Hill Motel, built by William Gore, from Richard Acton.

Ellen K. Carter, the daughter of Frederick and Jeannette Rigley was born in Gloucester, MA on Nov. 2, 1946. She moved to Brown County when she was four and graduated from Brown County High School in 1964, attended Stephen's College for two years and graduated from Indiana State University. After graduation, she was a probations officer for Johnson County.

Jay and Ellen were married at the chapel at Waycross Camp on Jan. 6, 1973. Ellen was appointed the probation officer and bailiff of Brown County Circuit Court by Judge David T. Woods, when it was first established.

Jay started an antique business and did shows in the eastern part of the United States. On Nov. 11, 1975 they started their family when Shirley and Lynda Swift became their children. On June 30, 1978, their daughter Jessica Anne was born and on March 28, 1990 Hannah Elizabeth was an unexpected gift.

In 1977, Jay became an insurance agent and in 1981, with Robert Gredy and Edgar Freese they purchased the Bright and Williamson Insurance Agency. Jay and Ellen have owned Sunshine Inn and Kentucky Fried Chicken. They also built the Colony Shop complex. Jay became a director of the Nashville State Bank and is currently director of its successor, Trust Corp. He is also a member and past director of Independent Insurance Agents of Indiana and the Brown County Chamber of Commerce.

Ellen was actively involved in forming Big Brothers-Big Sisters and Parent's Day Out. She is a member of Psi Iota Xi Sorority and actively works on the Log Cabin Tour each year.

TOM AND TINA CAVE - James and Audrey Kay Stogdill decided to name their three daughters names beginning with the letter "T". They are Tammy (Murphy), Teresa Stogdill and Tina Cave. Tina was born June 13, 1961 in Bedford and spent her growing up years in Johnson County. While at a church skating party in October 1982 Tina met Tom Cave and they were married April 15, 1983. Tom was born in Johnson County July 16, 1958. They both work in Franklin. Tom is with Johnson Controls and Tina works at the Franklin United Methodist Home. Tom's parents are Daniel and Florence Cave. His living grandparents are John Cave and John and Zelma Shoenfield. Tina's living grandparents are Beulah Stogdill and Grace Hearth. Tina and Tom have lived in Northern Brown County on Sweetwater Trail for seven years and enjoy the peaceful surroundings. They are active members of the Midway Separate Baptist Church in Brown County.

Tina and Tom Cave

CLARENCE AND GOLDIE CHITWOOD - Katie Leona Miller, born in 1873, married Charles Mason Gill in 1895. To them seven children were born in a little log cabin, and raised on a rough rugged, 190-acre farm at Trevlac. Their oldest son, Everett, died during World War I in 1918 at the age of 22. Their only daughter, Goldie, born March 18, 1905, married Clarence Chitwood of Monroe County in 1923.

Clarence was a very busy man because in 1922 at the age of 20 years he had purchased a small garage and repair shop in Helmsburg. Clarence worked long, hard hours to make ends meet. Cars were mostly Model T Fords. Clarence enjoyed his work. He seemed to be a natural-born mechanic.

Clarence and Goldie went to housekeeping in a neat three-room house in Trevlac. There, on Jan. 11, 1925 a healthy beautiful daughter was born. She was named Lois Marie. According to all the neighbors, she was the most perfect, beautiful baby they had ever seen. Her parents thought so too! During October of that year they packed up the baby and moved to a larger, better home in Helmsburg nearer Clarence's work.

Goldie and Clarence Chitwood

Clarence's business grew and grew until 1927. He then realized that his business had outgrown his building. He purchased two lots in Helmsburg and built a 46 x 60 square foot concrete block building. Electricity was not available in Brown County at that time. Clarence bought a power plant and made his own electricity. He ran wires to his home two blocks down the street. They enjoyed the convenience of electricity in their home.

Clarence bought a lathe and welding torch, on which he manufactured many of the parts and pieces he used in his repair work. Clarence always had the desire to build and manufacture things. During the years 1931 and 1932, he built from parts of other machinery, three tractors. One of them he gave to his dad, Michael E. Chitwood. The tractor could pull a 16-inch breaking plow or cultivator and do odd jobs around Mike's farm near Unionville. The farm is now covered by Lake Lemon.

Goldie kept busy with the care of daughter and helping Clarence with his business. When Lois went away to college in 1942, Goldie started adding bits and pieces of hardware items to Clarence's line of parts and supplies. Almost every weekend they would go see Lois, or she would come home, because she was mistress of ceremonies at the Brown County Jamboree in Bean Blossom. She was cheerleader during her four years in Helmsburg High School and also her four years at Indiana University. She was chosen Miss Indiana in her senior year at the University, and competed in finals at Atlantic City. After graduation she taught in the public schools for six years until she married Milton B. Learner of La Crosse, WI, in May 1954.

Their business grew. They sold appliances, cars, radios, machinery, International Harvester farm tractors, etc. Repair service was in great demand. They hired Chelsea Sisson in 1952 to handle the demand for repair service. He stayed with them until they sold the business in August, 1982. Clarence died June 29, 1986.

This material excerpted from "Brown County Remembers." *Compiled and edited by Dorothy (Birney) Bailey, 1986. Revere Press, Indiana*

IRA AND ELLA McCOY CHITWOOD -

Ira Chitwood, son of Richard and Ida May Chitwood, was born Sept. 23, 1888, near Needmore, Brown County. He moved in 1899 with his parents to the family farm west of Needmore. In 1906 he went with his brother, Walter, to Montana to work on the Big Ditch near Glendive. Discouraged by a deep snow in May, he returned the following year to Indiana. After working on drainage projects in Illinois, he made his home in Brown County.

Ira Chitwood, Ella Chitwood about 1965

Ira married Ella McCoy, one of eight children of Dave and Margaret McCoy of Monroe County in 1912. They had seven children, Mable (born 1916) married Woodrow Fritch; Donald (born 1919) married Ima Jean Henderson; Rosabelle (born 1921) married Leonard Ruggles; Glodine Helen (born 1924) married Irvin Lawson; Allen Eugene (born 1926) married Jean Logsdon; Walter Joseph (born 1929) married Bethel Duck; and one child who died in infancy. Ira owned land in Needmore and raised his family in the log house now the home of Red and Glodine Lawson. He did road maintenance work and was a coon hunter who bought and sold furs. He loved to roam the woods hunting ginseng, yellow root, and sasparilla bark for which there was a ready market. He was very family-oriented with a great sense of humor. Both he and Ella were witty people, and their children will always remember Ira and Ella as fun people as well as responsible parents. During the depression years of the 30s when Ella was coping with six children, Ira once introduced a relative to Ella saying, "This is my wife. When I married Ella, she didn't have a rag to her name. And now she's all rags!"

Ira passed away in May of 1968, closely followed by Ella in 1969.

ORA J. CHITWOOD -

Ora J. Chitwood was born Dec. 16, 1895 in Jackson Township, Brown Co., IN. He was a descendant of Mathias Chitwood who came from England in the 1600s. His ancestor, David Chitwood, was the first one to settle in Indiana.

Ora was one of eight children born to Richard and Ida Day Chitwood. They were brought up, first in a log cabin; then Richard built a frame house for his family near the same spot. Part of their farm is now Lake Lemon—originally named Bean Blossom Lake.

Ora attended school in Needmore. At that time, the town was large enough to have its own school, two churches, and two general stores.

On Aug. 23, 1913, Ora married Violet Lincicome from Monroe County. She died in May, 1961. He later married Irene Walker.

Ora was a man of many talents. He was a farmer, owner and operator of the general store, builder of log cabins, and a developer of Lake Lemon. He also bought and sold cattle, and operated a Christmas tree farm. He dredged channels at Lake Lemon and developed Chitwood's Fishing Camp which included a dining room, boat launching facilities and dock rentals, fishing tackle sales and cabin rentals.

For many years, Ora and his wife Violet operated the Needmore general store. While Violet ran the store, Ora would run the huckster truck over the hills and back roads to serve families who were unable to get to the store. He later sold the store to his son and daughter-in-law, Wendell and Marty.

Ora was politically active in the Democratic party, as well as in many civic affairs. He was a Brown County Commissioner and later served as sheriff. He was instrumental in bringing R.E.M.C. and served as a Director of the R.E.M.C. at Martinsville, IN. He was also instrumental in the establishment of the Brown County water systems.

Chitwood Grocery (Needmore)

During the depression, he was a W.P.A. Supervisor of Maintenance on the State Road 46 project. Friends and relatives called him the "Mayor of Needmore", and his friendship was cherished by all who knew him. Ora loved to "coon hunt" and spent many hours hunting with his brother, Ralph and their dogs.

He had two children: Veva B. Waltz, now of Greenwood, IN and Wendell O. Chitwood, Punta Gorda, FL.

His daughter, Veva, had four children: Darryl, Donna, Dianna, and Douglas. Donna had two children: Charles (Chip) and DeMaris Henderson. Darryl has one son, Brent. Dianna's children are: Lisa, Jason, and Michael, and Douglas' children are Philip, Laura, Kevin, and Jeffrey.

His son Wendell is the father of two sons: Ronald and Robert. Ronald's sons are Richard and Wendell. Robert was born later in life and has not married yet.

Ora left his friends with many happy memories of all the times he played his fiddle for dances and at other times when friends and neighbors would gather to hear him play outside his general store. He would often be heard singing and he had a great voice. He was known for his beautiful penmanship-Spencerian style. He died Aug. 1, 1983 at the age of 87. *Submitted by Veva B. Waltz*

RALPH IVAN CHITWOOD -

Ralph, son of Richard and Ida May Chitwood, was born May 29, 1904, at the new house built by his parents west of Needmore, Brown County. He spent most of his life in Brown County farming, owned a grocery store in Needmore at one time, and was a bricklayer by trade who was foreman of many brick-laying projects at Indiana University in Bloomington, Indianapolis and surrounding communities.

Ralph married Lillian Peevler in 1926 and one child, Jean, was born in 1926. Jean is married to Dale Bond. Ralph started his life-long interest in hunting dogs with two dogs bought from a Kentucky uncle of Lillian's. He has dozens of trophies collected over the years when his dogs were rated the best at field meets all over Indiana and surrounding states.

Ralph Chitwood and trophies from Dog Meets, 1982

Although Lillian had had no experience with hunting dogs, she soon became a partner in the dog business. Ralph's most memorable dog, a pointer named Sport, was one given to him. Ralph says Sport was the poorest-looking dog he and Lillian had ever seen walking, but he accepted the gift because the dog seemed so hungry and pitiful. But Sport turned out to be the smartest dog they ever had and was easily trained. Ralph hunted everywhere with him, including Arkansas, and he was never beaten. One quail season, a fellow from Indianapolis who had bought dogs from the Chitwoods before, saw Sport's pointing action and wanted to buy Sport. When Lillian heard the big offer, she told Ralph she liked Sport better than any dog Ralph had ever owned. There upon Ralph gave Lillian the dog, and that was the only dog they ever kept until it died.

Lillian passed away in 1973. Ralph later married Mabel Rogers. Because of recent poor health Ralph has had to give up caring for the last of his dogs and is living in Nashville.

RICHARD AND IDA MAY (DAY) CHITWOOD

The first proven ancestor of the Brown County Chitwoods was Mathias Chitwood (Cheatwood) who, at the age of 14, came from England to Goochland Co., VA, in 1695. Subsequent generations migrated to Rutherford Co., NC; Scott Co., TN, and in 1828 David Chitwood, son of Pleasant, came with his wife, Sarah, and his family to Monroe Co., IN. They were accompanied by his wife's parents, Thomas and Nancy Quesenberry Richardson, and the Richardson offspring. David and Sarah's children were: Elizabeth, Emanuel, Nancy Ann, John O., Henry J., Andrew J., George W., Jonathan, William, Isaac, Noah, and Greenberry.

John O. and Martha (Neal) Chitwood

John O. Chitwood, fourth child of David Chitwood, married Martha Neal, daughter of Samuel and Abigail Neal. In 1850 they moved to a farm near Needmore, Brown County and raised children Sarah, Isaac, Nancy C. (Kit), Richard, David, Linzey, and Rebecca.

Richard Chitwood was born July 12, 1862, son of John O. and Martha, in Brown County and married in 1885 Ida May Day, daughter of Thomas R. and Margaret Rogers Day of Brown County. Richard and Ida May lived on a farm near Needmore until about 1899 when he bought a farm west of Needmore which later became part of the Lake Lemon Reservoir Project. The land had a large log inn on it, and Richard took the inn apart, sold the hardwood logs, and paid for the land and a new frame house which is still in use near the Marina at the lake.

Richard and Ida May (Day) Chitwood

Richard and Ida May had eight children: Maude May, born 1886; Ira Charles, born 1888; Walter James, born 1890; Nora Belle, born 1891; Ora John, born 1895; Nellie Ann, 1898; Viola Blanche, born 1900; and Ralph Ivan, born 1904. Blanche was born in the log inn, but Ralph always claimed that his folks built the new house specially for him, the eighth child, to be born in.

Richard was known as a hard worker and a good provider, and everyone, even the professional railroad hoboes, knew that Ida May never turned away a hungry visitor. The family was very musical and Richard was asked to sing for one of the first Edison phonograph records cut in Indianapolis. He was a school trustee and campaigned in the district on foot, walking to all the homes. At one time Ida May had both her widowed mother and her widowed mother-in-law living in her home and her children always commented on her graceful acceptance of the situation. She liked lots of people around.

Richard Chitwood died in 1918. Ida May married Taylor Richey in 1923 and was widowed again in 1930. Ida May led a long useful life with various families moving in with her on the farm during the Depression of the '30s. Her later years were spent in a home in Needmore and at the home of her daughter, Blanche Neal Riggins in Indianapolis. She died in 1958.

John Allen and Maude (Day) Martin

Three sons, Ira, Ora and Ralph, lived almost all their lives in Brown County. Maude lived near Greenwood, IN; Walter homesteaded in Montana; Belle moved to Iowa; Nell to California and Chicago; and Blanche lived in Bloomington and Indianapolis.

WALTER AND JOSEPHINE CHITWOOD

Walter James Chitwood, son of Richard and Ida May Chitwood, was born Jan. 28, 1890, near Needmore, Brown County. He moved to the Chitwood farm west of Needmore about 1899. He worked as a water boy at the age of 12 when the railroad line was constructed through Brown County. At age 15, while employed by the railroad, he was badly burned on one side of his face when a hot tar vat tipped over on him. While recuperating at his parents home, Walter dreamed of going West which seemed impossible. However, his brother, Ira, age 18, had jobs lined up working on the Big Ditch Irrigation Project near Glendive, MT. Ira sneaked Walter's few clothes out in his one and only suitcase, and the two brothers left.

Josephine and Walter Chitwood, 1912

After the summer's employment, Ira and Walter were a welcome addition in homesteading-bachelor Billy Hibbard's log cabin at Limestone in Stillwater Co., MT. They stayed the winter, hunting deer and helping Billy cook. Ira left with a deep May snow but Walter, always known locally as Chick, stayed, homesteaded near Absarokee, prospected and developed various mines, and returned several times home to Indiana with the cattle shipments to Chicago.

Walter married school teacher Josephine Bryant, daughter of Frank and Sarah Bryant, who also had homesteaded, and they had five children: Beth (born 1915) who died in the flu epidemic of 1918; Jean Bryant (born 1917) married Ed Bolin; Guy Clifford; Julia June (born 1920) married Verle Trees; Walter Joe (born 1921) married Blythe Kennedy; and Richard Day (born 1925) married Willa Skok. Except for a short stay in B.C., Canada, a few years in Washington and one year (1928-1929), they lived in Absarokee where Walter died in 1961. Josie, editor and owner of a weekly newspaper for 21 years and school clerk for 17 years, passed away in 1969.

CLARKE FAMILY

Louis A. and Betty L. Weatherford moved to Bittersweet Road (R.R. 4, Box 109), which is about two miles northeast of Bean Blossom, in May 1979. They had begun construction of a weekend home in 1961 on five acres with a one acre pond. This acreage, and later 55 more, was purchased from Arthur and Florence Bradshaw, Betty's uncle and aunt. Art's father, Millard Bradshaw, had owned the property since the 1940s.

Lou and Betty have two daughters, Kathleen Sharp and Jane Lawson to whom they deeded 20 acres each in 1982. Kathy lives near Zionsville, IN and Jane is living in Brown County.

Samuel Clark

The Weatherford's have enjoyed having their annual family reunions and having friends visit them at their home. They also enjoy the birds, wildlife and scenery of Brown County. Lou and Betty have been active in the Humane Society, Historical Society, and the Pioneer women while living in Brown County.

Betty (Clark) Weatherford was the granddaughter of Samuel Clarke. He came from Bristol, England, and settled in Pennsylvania. He lived from 1870-1952. He was a millworker and married Ellen Gibson Ashman. They lived in Elwood, IN with Ellen's children, Laura, Robert and Ethel Ashman. Samuel and Ellen had four children, Charles, Lucy, Florence and William Clarke.

Samuel and Ellen and their family moved to Woodland Lake Road, just east of Spearsville Road in 1910. Samuel worked for the highway department, the railroad during World War I and farmed.

He enjoyed all his animals and his daily walk to the mailbox at Bittersweet Road.

Laura Ashman married David Webb and they had four children, Mary, Ruth, Dorthea and Walter. Ruth married Ralph Goodrich, and they owned the variety store in Morgantown for several years. Dorthea married Davie Cline. She worked for the ASCS office in Nashville for 25 years. Both Ruth and Dorthea are living on Spearsville Road in Brown County.

Robert Ashman married Maude West and had nine children.

Ethel Ashman married Newton Hutchison and had one daughter, Cornelia. Ethel enjoyed sewing for the Pioneer Women's annual bazaars. She is currently living in Nashville. Cornelia married Melvin Korte and lives on Woodland Lake Road next to the old home place of Samuel and Ellen Clarke.

Charles Clark married Grace Roberts and had two daughters, Maxine L. (Clark) Paton and Betty L. (Clark) Weatherford.

Lucy Clarke married Albert Birr and lived on Spearsville Road for 35 years.

Florence Clarke married Arthur Bradshaw. They lived on Bittersweet Road about 50 years. Florence is now living in Nashville. Art was very active in many community organizations including the Farm Bureau, Humane Society, and AARP.

William Clark married Jenny Slavens and lived on Woodland Lake Road. He worked at the Brown County State Park.

The Clarke family has enjoyed many, many, years in this county and several of the family members continue to cherish the beauty and peacefulness of Brown County. *Submitted by Betty Weatherford*

CLEVENGER FAMILY - This family descends from George Clevenger who married Sarah Hadden in New York about 1654. Their son John moved to New Jersey and from there the Clevengers moved to other parts of the colonies. Sylvester and Sarah McCoy Clevenger were married in New Jersey and moved to Southwestern Ohio about 1806 and to Wayne Co., OH by 1820. Their children were: William Louis (1804-1880) who married Susannah Lynn; Charles (1805-) who left home when a young man; twins, Amy (1807-1870) who married Alexander Lewis and Anna who married Samuel Reynolds; Job who died in infancy; Jonathan (1811-) who married Celia Peel; Mary (1814-1895) who married Robert Canada Lynn; George Washington (1818-1899) who married first Catherine Ebersole, then Elizabeth Briney; Margaret (1820-1854) who married George Horner; and Hope Jane (1822-??) who married Jarus Ward.

William Henry Harrison Clevenger

William Louis Clevenger married Susannah Lynn in Warren Co., OH on Feb. 16, 1826, and they lived in Warren and Preble Counties. They had eight children: Sarah Jane (1828-1901) who married James C. Hayes; Francis Marion and Mary C. about whom nothing is known; Sylvester Alexander (1832-1905) who married Anna Utz; Margaret (1834-1869) who married Elias Bringman; William Henry Harrison (1836-1893) who married Elizabeth Wertz; George Washington Runnels (1840-1901) who married Catherine Musser; and Susannah C. (1845-1902) who married Adam Stillabower.

About 1860 William Henry Harrison Clevenger moved to eastern Brown County. The log house that he built still stands near the Brown County entrance to Camp Atterbury. Henry was a master carpenter and made hickory spokes for Studebaker wagonwheels. Henry and Elizabeth had seven children: Sarah Margaret (1860-1939) who married Nelson Ford; Oliver Perry Morton (1863-1920) who married Ida Wilkerson; Mary (1867-) who married Willam Hamblin; Franklin Henry (1870-1940) who married Emma Susan Sipes; James Louis (1873-1955) who married Alma Percifield; William Adam (1878-1941) who married Lydia Van Arsdale; and America May (1882-1946) who married Matson Percifield.

Henry's sister Sarah Hayes was the mother of Franklin William Hayes who was the life-long physician friend of the Hossier poet James Whitcomb Riley. The Riley poem entitled "Old John Clevenger on Buckeyes" quite possibly is a portrait of Henry Clevenger.

Franklin and Emma Susan Sipes Clevenger had four children: Edgar, Cyrus, Blanche and Henry. Cyrus was born in Brown County before the family moved to Columbus. Cyrus Clevenger married Mary Beth Stevens and their two daughters, Janice and Sarah Clevenger, live in Bloomington. *Submitted by Sarah Clevenger*

SAMUEL AND FLO (PRYOR) CLINE - Charles and Nancy Cline were immigrants, from Ireland. They settled in the Bartholomew County Community of Kansas, now known as a part of Camp Atterbury, where they were farmers.

Samuel Taylor Cline, one of four children, was born on April 13, 1894. The family moved to Nashville two years later. Due to a severe injury to Charles' legs, he was unable to support his family, so they were forced to live at the Brown County Home for the Poor. Charles died there and is buried in the Nashville area.

Sam and Flo Cline

Sam and his family had a very hard life. He learned the trade of farming and logging as a young boy and thus did not have the time for a formal education.

On Sept. 20, 1913, Sam married Flo Pryor of Martinsville, IN. Flo was of Scottish descent. They moved to northern Brown County where they were tenant farmers. Later they purchased a farm in Hamblin Township.

The Clines had a large family, 17 children, all born at home. The children were educated in a oneroom school house by one teacher who taught first through eighth grade levels.

In the early 1900s, electricity and telephones were unavailable in this region. It was not until the 1950s that electricity lines came through. Travel was primarily by horse-drawn wagon.

During World War II, Sam was a guard of prisoners of war at Camp Atterbury. After the war, he worked for B&O Railroad at Beech Grove, where he retired in 1959.

Flo was the family seamstress. She enjoyed cooking, canning and crocheting. She was a member of the Neighborhood Church of God, located on Peoga Road.

The Clines have 50 grandchildren, 104 great grandchildren and 34 great-great grandchildren.

Sam died at home on Aug. 29, 1971. Flo passed away on July 16, 1973. The couple were married 58 years. *Submitted by Deborah Lou Goodwin Sanders, granddaughter of Samuel and Flo (Pryor) Cline*

C. CAREY CLOUD FAMILY - Carey, himself a Legend—Artist, Author, Cartoonist, Inventor was born in 1899 on a small farm in north-eastern Grant Co., IN. As a small child hoeing endless rows of corn, he was given the best fatherly advice of his colorful life: "Son, you are going to learn that throughout life you are going to have to hoe out your own row."

C. Carey Cloud

This he did many times. As a young man, Carey worked on a farm, labored on a railroad, worked in midwest oil fields, in a shoe factory and a glass factory, in a player piano factory, and in a steel mill during the First World War.

He started his career on the art staff of the CLEVELAND PRESS when he was 19 years old, after studying a 25 dollars correspondence course in art. Later he worked in an advertising agency, then as an art director of a calendar company and a greeting card publisher.

C. Carey Cloud

Carey Cloud designed premiums for "Little Orphan Annie," "Superman," and other radio shows. His big success came when he started designing toys for the Cracker Jack Company in 1937, prizes that were found in the Cracker Jack boxes. He was called "The Cracker Jack King" by many. Ideas were always rattling around in the back of his head and, according to his own estimate, he probably created, produced and delivered to the Cracker Jack Company 700 Million toys — spinning tops, puzzles, rings, Mother Goose characters, others we all remember.

Carey and his wife Vera had been high school sweethearts. He was witty, creative and sensitive; she was full of laughter, artistic and knowledgeable about many subjects. In October, 1947, they traveled from their home in Chicago to Nashville, IN, where they met Herb Miller, Sr., just locking his drugstore. Since there were no places open for eating, the Clouds were invited to eat with the Millers. As Herb Miller put it, "I've eaten Clara's food for 50 years. You can stand it for one meal." According to Carey, Clara was one of the **best** cooks in Brown County. That's the way it was in those days.

The Clouds bought the high hill one mile south of the village of Nashville, consisting of 195 acres separating 15,768 acres of State Park and forest preserve from the village. The view was grand! The place had a lovely chalet-type home and a 100-year-old caretaker's cabin, which Carey later used for his studio for over 30 years, and where millions of toys were designed. Wonderful years were spent there at Cloudcrest Hill with two sons and a daughter Mary. Harold later moved to Chicago, Donald to Bloomington, and Mary (Smith) to Texas. Also, during this period Carey served as President of the Brown County Art Gallery for three years, doing much to procure a building to display the works of great artists; and as member of the Brown County Lions Club, he created designs for club medals.

Nineteen-hundred-sixty-four, in that unique cabin, was the beginning of his serious commitment to painting: first pallette knife painting, then surrealism, and finally realistic detail in acrylics, or "Realism in Depth." One critic wrote in the Bloomington HERALD-TELEPHONE, "He creates such an illusion in his paintings of old buildings that it seems a mere touch will result in a splinter." Dr. Karl Bookwalter of Indiana University remarked, "Cloud's work is meticulous. His paintings might be classed as collectors' art and museum pieces." Wayne Guthrie, columnist, once wrote: "Because of the near microscopic detail and sharpness, Cloud's work fairly jumps out at the viewer with what he calls 'realism in depth' that produces almost a third dimension. Cloud sees the Brown County scene through different eyes than most painters; he is interested in more intimate subjects, such as minute detail of weather-sculptured old wood, contrast of light and shadow playing on old buildings." Carey Cloud, himself, said, "I have found strength and beauty in these subjects and joy in making others aware of the passing scene, bringing back quiet memories of a more vibrant past."

Vera's death in 1971 heightened and deepened Carey's art; perhaps his best paintings were in sadness of heart. At age 80-82, he put his nostalgic memoirs into his book CLOUD NINE—The Dreamer and The Realist. His words (like his paintings) deeply expressed his love for the hills, quiet valleys, old buildings, people, winding roads, the Stoney Lonesomes and Gnawbones, wildlife and lush foilage. C. Carey Cloud—Artist, Author, Cartoonist, Inventor—died in November of 1984 leaving Brown County richer in heart, mind and soul. *Submitted by Bobbie Hill-Cloud Knapke*

CLUPPER FAMILY - The Clupper family migrated from Germany to America in 1750. They settled in York Co., PA. The spelling of the Clupper name at that time was Klopfer, which later changed to Klopper, Cupper and then to the current spelling of Clupper.

Christian Clupper came to Wabash Co., IN in 1849. He traveled for three months in horsedrawn wagons and settled on land near a trading post at Treaty, IN.

Lewis Clupper, Doc's grandfather, was the son of Christian and Margaret Clupper. He was one of ten children. Lewis was born in 1846 in Pennsylvania and traveled with his family to Wabash County. Lewis served in the Indiana 138th and 153rd Volunteer Infantry. He later became a farmer and in 1873 married Mary Shranze who was born in Switzerland and came to the United States in 1849. They had two children William Frank Clupper and Charles Clupper. After his first wife's death in 1877 he remarried Maria Putnam in 1881. They had four children: George Leonard Clupper, Harley G. Clupper (Doc's father), Hugh E. Clupper and Ralph C. Clupper.

Doc and Judy Clupper

Harley Clupper farmed his father's homestead in Wabash County. In 1906 he married Grace Edith Unger, and they had one daughter. After only two years of marriage his wife died of complications from a tooth extraction. The daughter, Leona Murl Clupper, died at age three from diptheria.

In 1915 Harley married his second wife Rose Evelyn (Crouch) Norvell. At the time of their marriage she had two young daughters from a previous marriage, Gladys M. Norvell (McLarry), and Golda Virginia Norvell (Brummett) who died in childbirth at age 18. Harley and Rose had two daughters and one son: Harold "Doc" Clupper, Mae Clupper (Smith), and Sarah Frances Clupper (White).

The Clupper family came to Brown County in the early 1900s. Lewis Clupper, Doc's grandfather, purchased two large parcels of land near Bean Blossom (Georgetown). Hugh Clupper, Doc's uncle, settled on the east tract of land and later in 1917 Harley Clupper, Doc's dad, settled on the 200 acre tract west of Bean Blossom (Georgetown). The land east of Bean Blossom extended from what is now Gatesville Road up to Bear Wallow. This homestead was later sold to Tom Waltman. The land west of Bean Blossom in Jackson Township which was purchased by Harley's dad came from the Haram Waltman and Moore properties. The majority of this tract of land still remains in the Clupper family today.

Harley Clupper and his wife, Rose Evelyn Crouch Norvell Clupper, came to Brown County with their one year old son Harold "Doc" Clupper who had been born in Kokomo, and Rose's two daughters Gladys Norvell (McLarry) and Golda Norvell (Brummett). It was here in Brown County that Doc's two sisters, Mae Clupper (Smith) and Sarah Frances Clupper (White), were born.

Harley and his family were grain and stock farmers. They raised hogs, cattle, corn, soybeans and hay. This land is still farmed today by Harold "Doc" Clupper and his wife Judith (Scrougham) Clupper, daughter of Ernest and Velma Scrougham.

Doc retired from the federal government after 28 years of service at Camp Atterbury and Bakalar Air Force Base. He is now semi-retired and works in real estate and farms. Judy is a teacher at the Helmsburg Elementary School in Brown County.

The northeast corner of the Clupper farm has been used for approximately 115 years as the site of the Brown County Old Settlers. This event has been a tradition in Brown County since 1877. People come from miles around to attend this annual event. In early days they came on horseback and in wagons bringing baskets and boxes of food for a picnic lunch. It was a time to visit with family and friends. The Brown County Old Settlers has seen many changes since the coming of electricity in the early 1950s but it still continues to be one of the leading events in Brown County today. *Submitted by Judy Clupper*

GEORGE AND LAVONNE COLDREN - George D. Coldren was born Feb. 4, 1907, in Kokomo, IN to J. Riley and Mae Littler Coldren. George was a graduate of Kokomo High School and Indiana Central College (now University of Indianapolis) where he majored in finance and economics. Following graduation in 1931, he worked at Coburn Warehouse and Bankers Trust before joining Railroadmen's Savings and Loan Company in Indianapolis. After many years of service, he retired from Railroadmen's in 1972 where he was assistant treasurer.

Clara LaVonne Coldren was the daughter of Alonzo E. and Lona May Sherrill Thompson of Parke Co., IN. She was born on June 7, 1908, in Princess Anne, MD. LaVonne and her parents returned to Indiana in 1913 and settled on the east side of Indianapolis where, five years later, a son, Almon (Bill), was born. In 1922 the family moved to University Heights. LaVonne graduated from Emmerick Manual High School in 1926 and Indiana Central College in 1929.

LaVonne and George Coldren

George and LaVonne met during psychology class in 1929 and were married on May 1, 1932, in

163

Indianapolis. They were the first couple to be married in the University Heights Evangelical United Bretheren Church. LaVonne taught art and music at several elementary schools and retired from Perry Township, Indianapolis, in 1971.

George and LaVonne first became interested in Brown County in 1962 while looking for a retirement location. They found and purchased a lot on Lake LaSalle in 1962. They began building in January 1967 and moved into their new home in June 1967. While residents of Brown County, George and LaVonne were active in the Brown County Historical Society, Friends of the Library, the Brown County Art Gallery, and Nashville United Methodist Church.

George was also active in the Brown County Lions Club, Nashville Masonic Lodge, Indianapolis Scottish Rite, and Murat Shrine. LaVonne was active in the Nashville Literary Club, Brown County Garden Club, Brown County Pioneer Women and sang in the church choir.

George and LaVonne had two children: David Lawrence, born in Jan. 19, 1936, and Georgann Ruth, born on Oct. 14, 1941. David currently resides in San Bernardino, CA, with his wife and two sons, David Lynn and Chris Allan. Georgann lives in Brandon, FL, with her husband, LaWayne Wyatt. Their daughters, Cynthia June and Denise Ann, live in Bloomington, IN.

Prior to moving to Brown County, George was a volunteer with the Indianapolis Council of Boy Scouts and Girl Scouts and received the Silver Beaver award from the Boy Scouts. He had a 43-year perfect attendance record with the Lions Club, attending meetings in other locations when he was traveling or visiting. He was president of the Southport and Nashville Lions Clubs, had received awards from the organizations for inducting numerous new members and was devoted to the club's Seeing Eye and Eye Bank programs.

George died on Sept. 19, 1988, and is buried in Greenlawn Cemetery in Nashville. On Feb. 1, 1990, LaVonne moved to the Franklin United Methodist Retirement Home, Franklin, IN. *Submitted by LaVonne Coldren*

JOHN H. AND MARY JANE COMBS -

John H. Combs, one of seven children was born in Brown County in 1854. His parents were William Riley and Lucinda Sipes Combs. William was born Aug. 10, 1810 in Kentucky, married July 17, 1841 in Jackson County and died Jan. 9, 1899 in Jackson County. His wife Lucinda Sipes was born July 18, 1819 in Indiana and died Aug. 23, 1885 in Jackson County. Mary Jane was the daughter of Drury and Nancy Uley Elkins.

Every spring, Mary Jane carried buckets of water from the stream to scrub down the outside of her log cabin. Her floors were covered with woven rags that she had sewn together. When she wanted to clean them, she cut them apart and took them to a nearby stream. This stream was shallow and had a flatrock bottom. After they were cleaned with lye soap, she hung them over her yard fence to dry. Finally, she took them back to the cabin and sewed them together again.

There were nine children who lived to adulthood: Alfred married Anna McMahan, six children; Laura married Oscar Lutes, five children; Lilly married Fredrick Jones, three children; George I. married Tena Hegwood, two children; Luda married Ora Winkler, one child; Benjamin, three children; David; and twins Eller and Ellis. There were also five children who died while quite young: Rolley, Dillen, Lina, Lucy and one other child.

Laura Combs, born Sept. 26, 1877, married Oct. 3, 1904 to Oscar Lutes, born Sept. 6, 1879 in Brown County. They had William, born July 8, 1905; John E., born Nov. 29, 1906, married Elizabeth Kerkhof on Jan. 10, 1933, died March 2, 1985, three children still living: June, Ray, and Laura; Winfrey, born Jan. 15, 1909, married Grace Schroer, died March 26, 1987; Waldon, born Nov. 10, 1910, married Emma Douglas; Fred, born Feb. 19, 1913, married Edna Behrman, three children. Laura died Sept. 14, 1964 and Oscar died Jan. 28, 1957.

John H. died in 1934 and Mary Jane died in 1925. They are both buried in the Robinson Cemetery in Maumee, IN. *Submitted by Elizabeth Lutes*

CONDON FAMILY -

Perry Green Condon was born in Maryland in the year 1800. He moved to Belmont Co., OH, at an early age. There he met and married Elizabeth Campbell (born Belmont Co., OH, 1804). Perry died in 1857, and was buried there, in Belmont County. After his death, his widow came to Indiana along with several of their children. They arrived and settled in Columbus (Bartholomew Co.,) IN, in 1860. Elizabeth died there in 1862. Perry and Elizabeth's children were: (1) John Henry (born 1830), (2) Alexander (born 1832), (3) David Chandler (born 1834), (4) Perry Green, Jr. (born 1836), (5) William Henry (born 1839), (6) Joseph Campbell (born 1840), (7) Samuel D. (born 1842), (8) George Riley (born 1846), (9) Anna Belle (born 1848) (10) Elizabeth, (11) Matilda, (12) infant and (13) infant. Several of the children moved on West to find a new, and perhaps better way of life. Samuel D. became a very successful drygoods merchant in Paoli, KS. His brothers and sisters scattered to various locations, including California and Oregon.

At least three of Perry and Elizabeth's sons settled in Brown County. Each of them married women of the Bailey family, from Belmont Co., OH.

The family of Emma Condon Belcas (fourth from right) gathered near Gatesville in 1913 when she was 12 years old. Pictured are (left to right, with their relationships with Mrs. Belcas), Uncle John Condon, Uncle Bill Condon, Uncle Wesley Settles, first cousin Virgil Condon, brother Ralph Condon, grandfather Alexander Condon, brother Jessie Condon, Aunt Jennie (Mrs. John) Condon, first cousin Pearl (daughter of Bill) Condon, father Oliver Condon, first cousin Ruth (daughter of John) sister Mable Condon, Mrs. Belcas, Rachel (Mrs. Bill), mother May Condon and grandmother Selena Condon, at whose home the photograph was taken. In the foreground with the dog are (left to right) Elnora and Harold Settles, children of Uncle Wesley.

John married Rebecca Emily Bailey, Belmont County on April 29, 1854. Alexander married Selena in Belmont County on July 5, 1855 and Joseph married Mary Elizabeth Bailey at Columbus, IN on Jan. 23, 1862.

One of the brothers who remained in Brown County the rest of his life was Alexander. He and Selena lived on Salt Creek, near Gatesville, where they had six children: (1) Minora Lodena (born May 3, 1856, died April 22, 1945, married David Hamblen Curry), (2) John Henry (born July 28, 1858, died Feb. 5, 1947, married Louisa E. Mead and Jennie Black), (3) Willie Anderson (born Oct. 5, 1861, died April 30, 1938, married Rachel Walker) (4) Oliver Perry Morton (born Jan. 25, 1863, died April 8, 1932, married Anna Taylor and Mahala Weaver), (5) Mary Lorena (born June 17, 1867, died Feb. 8, 1952, married Edward E. Clark and Manford Walker), and (6) Hattie Belle (born Nov. 8, 1871, died Nov. 11, 1876 - only five years old).

Alexander also took in four grandchildren and helped to raise them after the death of his son-in-law, David Curry, who died of tuberculosis at an early age. The grandchildren were: Myrtie Leona, Lee Omer, Mary Belle and Henry Edgar Curry.

Alexander joined the Union Army on Jan. 26, 1865, at Bloomington (Monroe Co.,) IN. He was a private in Co. E, 145th Regiment of the Indiana Volunteers. He served for one year, during which time he marched with his regiment into the deep South, enduring many hardships. He was discharged at Indianapolis on Dec. 2, 1865. Alexander came home with many health problems brought on by his military service. Since he was partially disabled, he received a government pension for the rest of his life. He died April 15, 1915.

Alexander's wife, Selena, was born in Belmont Co., OH on Feb. 3, 1832. She was the daughter of Malon and Charity (Davis) Bailey. She died in September 1914. They are buried side-by-side at Goshen Church Cemetery, Brown County.

Some of Alexander and Selena's children moved away and others remained in Brown County. One of the sons who stayed was Oliver Perry Morton Condon. He married Anna Taylor and they had two sons: Elmer Otto (born May 11, 1885, died Nov. 29, 1959) and Alvey Edward (born Nov. 7, 1886, died 1919).

Oliver's wife, Anna, was born Oct. 9, 1867, and died a few years after their marriage. Oliver then married Mahala Ellen Weaver on Jan. 8, 1892. She was the daughter of Jacob and Sarah Weaver and was born April 23, 1858, in Bartholomew Co., IN. She died on Jan. 29, 1937. They are buried together at Goshen Church Cemetery, Brown Co., IN.

Oliver and Mahala Condon's children were: (1) Harry Alexander (born March 12, 1894, died May 1979, married Jennie Moser); (2) Earl Dolan (born March 24, 1894, died August, 1957, married Ada Parsley (divorced) and Ethel Stokesberry); (3) Leonard B. (born 1896, died 1897); (4) Ralph Weaver (born June 4, 1897, died Oct. 8, 1967, married Reba Schrougham (divorced) and Lois Clinton; (5) Mabel Clare (born 1899, died 1980, maried Harry Schrougham (brother of Reba); (6) Emma Florence (born March 9, 1901, died April 8, 1988, married George Belcas, Florina, Greece); (7) Jesse Wayne (born Aug 20, 1905, died March, 1988, married Lula Pitts).

Oliver was a man of many dreams and ambitions. He moved around several times in search of the proverbial "pot of gold at the end of the rainbow." His business ventures once included running a grocery store south of Spearsville. When he was older he and Mahala moved to Indianapolis, near their son, Ralph and his family. Ralph also married a "Brown County girl," Reba. A few years later

Oliver and Mahala moved again, back to their beloved Brown County, where they lived the remainder of their lives with their oldest son, Harry, his wife Jennie and their children. They are buried together at Goshen Church Cemetery.

Descendants of Oliver and Mahala Condon include: Harry and Jennie Condon—children, Russell Vernon, Arnola and Hila Star; Earl and Ethel Condon—Barbara and Linda; Ralph and Reba Condon—Victor Eugene, Violet (Vi) Bartram/Walton, Donald Duane; Mable and Harry Schroughan—children include: Robert, Vernon, Harry Jr. and Myrna (three other children died in infancy); Emma and George Belcas—Mary, Paul, James Oliver and Theodore Glen; Jesse and Lula Condon—one daughter.

Note: Linda, Earl and Ethel Condon's daughter, was raised by Harry and Jennie Condon, as her mother, Ethel, died shortly after she was born; Barbara was raised by her mother's family, Mr. and Mrs. Fritz. They also had a half-sister, Shirley Stokesberry, who was raised by her father's family. Shirley was Ethel's daughter by a previous marriage. *Submitted by Donald Condon*

BENJAMIN COOK FAMILY - Benjamin W. Cook was born Jan. 5, 1792, in New York State. He was first married to Lydia Howell and had a large family. Their oldest son, Steven B. Cook, was born in 1818 in West Virginia; their youngest, Ebenezer, was born in Ohio in 1838. After the deaths of both his first and second wives, Benjamin married a third time, to Catherine E. Sipe Truex, in 1847. In March of 1852, they moved to Indiana from Belmont Co., OH, with these six children: his son, Ebenezer Cook; her children, Joseph and Julia Anne Truex; and their younger children, Lydia, Sarah E., and Christopher Sipe Cook, who was just six weeks old.

The family floated down the Ohio River on a flatboat from Bellaire, OH to Madison, IN. They came to Columbus on the then-new railroad, bringing two cows, a team of horses, a wagon and household goods. They made their way by wagon to VanBuren Township, Brown County, to a 40-acre homestead on Salt Creek, east of New Bellsville. Benjamin's oldest son, Steven had already settled in the area sometime earlier.

Life was very hard. The old man, now past 60, had to clear woods in order to farm. Only about half of the homestead was good bottom land, the rest steep hillside. However, the woods was full of game (as well as timber wolves and "painter" cats), and the streams teamed with fish, so there was always food on the table.

Benjamin Cook died Aug. 9, 1873, and is buried at South Bethany Christian Church in Bartholomew County. Catherine died in October, 1899. In three months, she would have been 86.

Steven B. Cook had married Olive Mercer in Ohio in 1841. Their children were Sarah A., Joseph M., James M. and William J. Joseph was a doctor in Brown County. William was president of the Nashville State Bank. Their descendants continue to reside in the area, and hold a Cook reunion each summer.

Ebenezer Cook married Sarah Cooper in 1857.

Joseph Truex married Malissa E. Cooper in Bartholomew County in 1860. His sister, Julia Anne Truex, married a Brown County preacher, William H. Harrison in 1861.

Lydia A. Cook married Simeon B. Crider in 1871.

Sarah E. Cook married Solomon Seal in 1869.

Christopher Sipe Cook married Evaline Ward of nearby Pike's Peak, in 1878. Evaline had a three year old daughter, Rosa Smith. Shortly after their marriage, the family moved to Ellinwood, KS with some of Evaline's kinfolk. They made the trip in a covered wagon. Their son, Joseph L. Cook, was born in Kansas in 1879. They returned to Brown County in the fall of 1879 on the train. Two more children were born in Brown County, Walter E., and Iva Cordelia. Iva died of diptheria at age three. Descendants of Joseph L. Cook live in Bartholomew County. *Submitted by Evelyn Cook Cleland Sanborn and Donna Cleland Kuhlman*

THE COOLEY FAMILY - William N. Cooley was born March 23, 1868 at Blue Creek, near Elkinsville, in Brown County. He was a son of Abraham Cooley and Elvira Richards. Family tradition says Abraham came from Ireland and returned to that country.

William Cooley married Elnora Adaline Petro, daughter of Nicholas Petro and Luvisa Mullis, on June 25, 1887 in Brown County. William died Dec. 26, 1951; his wife, Elnora, died March 1, 1936 age about 70 years. Both are buried in Mt. Zion Cemetery, Van Buren Township.

William and Elnora Cooley lived and reared their family near Gatesville in Hamblen Township. They had nine children.

(1) Mary Elizabeth Cooley (May 10, 1888-Aug. 9, 1905), married Samuel Ayers; they had a son, Verlyn Ayers, born 1905.

(2) Died in infancy.

(3) Alfred Otto Cooley (April 5, 1892-Jan. 12, 1919), unmarried.

(4) Walter Otha Cooley (Feb. 1, 1895-Aug. 7, 1980), married first to Mary E. Saffell. They had four children: Ruey, born 1919; Howard Walter, born 1923; Geneva Nolena, born 1926 and Alfred Eugene Cooley, born 1928, died 1929. Walter married second to Dorothy M. Ault and third to Bessie May Ferrenburg.

(5) Died in infancy.

(6) Arthur McClellan Cooley born Feb. 20, 1900, married Lottie M. Harden (Dec. 15, 1906-Aug. 18, 1966), daughter of Jesse Harden and Bessie Hurley. Arthur and Lottie Cooley had three children: Dessie Paulina (Cooley) Del Vecchio; Clinton McClellan Cooley who married Charlotte Martin; Esta Minnie Marie (Cooley) Heck.

(7) Abraham N. Cooley (March 24, 1902-Dec. 20, 1968), married Grace A. Lucas, daughter of William Lucas and Martha E. Petro. Among the children of Abraham and Grace Cooley were Orville, Martha, Kenneth and a daughter, Ruhama who died as an infant in 1928.

(8) Ernest Cooley (Sept. 19, 1905-July 21, 1968), married Maggie Etta Collins, a daughter of Allan Collins and Tillie Mae Wilson. Ernest and Maggie had a daughter Loretta Mae who married Billy Jo Stringer.

(9) Sarah Elsie Cooley (Dec. 22, 1909-May 9, 1988) married Fred Lucas (May 10, 1899-June 4, 1947) and had a son, Carol A. Lucas. Sarah Elsie married second to Jesse M. Asher.

Clinton Cooley, son of Arthur and Lottie Cooley, served in the Navy for two years. He then worked as foreman at the C.P. Electronics Company in Columbus before returning to Brown County, starting the Cooley Salvage Company about 1960, a business which he sold in 1986. At Gnaw Bone he also had a gift shop, a tourist's camp which he began in 1983 and a flea market begun in 1987. *Submitted by Clinton McClellan Cooley*

JOHN AND ANITA COYLE - John Allen and Anita Coyle live near Fox's Corner in Hamblen Township. They moved to Brown County from Indianapolis in October, 1986.

John Allen Coyle is the son of John Franklin and Beatrice Goodnight Coyle. He was born Dec. 9, 1933, in Indianapolis. John Franklin was the son of Isaac Wesley and Sophia James Coyle of Berea, KY. Beatrice is the daughter of Frederick Harvey and Mary Jane Rector Goodnight of Circlesville, IN.

John Franklin was a pipefitter for 48 years. Beatrice is now living in Unionville, Monroe County. John Allen followed in his father's footsteps and has been a plumber/pipefitter for 38 years.

John grew up in Indianapolis, near the Twin-Air area. He attended Tech High School and later became an apprentice steamfitter. He joined the United States Navy in 1952. He served during the Korean Conflict and saw action aboard the USS *Herbert J. Thomas* DDR-833. Returning to his family in 1954, he married and had two children, Jill Ann and John Alexander.

Anita Claire Coyle is the daughter of Chester Leonard and Virginia Katherine Bunch Sturgeon. She was born Feb. 16, 1935 in Indianapolis. Chester Sturgeon was the son of Frank and Rosa Phelps Sturgeon, and was also born in Indianapolis. Chester Sturgeon was an Indianapolis Policeman for over 25 years. Virginia was the daughter of John Wesley and Catherine Kiser Bunch, and she was born in Camby, IN.

Anita grew up in the Brookside Park area, and graduated from Tech High School. She worked a short while at the Charles Mayer & Company department store until it was sold to L.S. Ayres and two more years at the Ayres downtown store.

Anita married and had four children, David, Mark, Christine and Julie Fly. During this time, she attended the Indiana University Extension and, after the new campus of IUPUI was built, was in the first class to receive a B.S. in Education at Indianapolis. She began teaching in 1970, received a M.S. in Education in 1973. She has taught in the same school where she began teaching for 20 years.

John and Anita met at a square dance and were married in January, 1983. They began building on 20 acres of land. First a barn was built, and then a house. This construction took three years. During this time, they held their full-time jobs and spent every week-end staying in the barn, in Brown County to complete this project. They did much of the work themselves, wiring, plumbing, insulating, woodwork trim, and the concrete work around the house.

The first week after they moved in they noticed a red fox trotting around the house, and she became almost a pet. She came for food on the porch, brought her offspring to meet them, and even climbed on the roof to survey the surrounding territory. Because of these activities, "Mother," as she was called, was immortalized in the Brown County Democrat.

CRABTREE FAMILY - The children of Garvin Preston Crabtree and Sarah Louise (Adams) Crabtree Kritzer have deep roots in Brown County. Larry, the oldest of five children was born in Nashville and delivered by his grandfather, Doctor L.R. Crabtree. Larry Crabtree is an Indiana Conservation Officer and resides on Plum Creek. Danny Crabtree, the second eldest, lived in Nashville until 1968 when his high school coaching job took his family, wife Jennifer and two sons, Brian and Matt, to Greentown and eventually to Whiteland. Sheila Jane (Crabtree) Oliver the third eldest lives with her family, husband Gary Oliver, son Ryan, and daughter Jannaka, in Van Buren Township from where she travels daily to her job as principal of Sprunica Elementary. Deborah (Crabtree) Asbury the fourth child, lived in Brown County until 1979 when a move closer to her husband John Asbury's work took them to Greenwood along with their sons Seth, Rett, and Joel. Steve Crabtree, the youngest, lives with his family, wife Sally, daughter Erin, and son Clint, in Las Vegas, NV, and works at Circus Circus R.V. Park. Four of the five Crabtree children married Brown Countians so not only do they have roots but also many branches.

Kay and Larry Crabtree

Preston's family came to Brown County from Monroe Co., KY, in 1929. His father, Louie Richard Crabtree was a doctor and had heard of the need for one in Nashville. He brought his eight children and wife, Sara Belle (Grinestaff) to Brown County. Sara Belle died in 1935. He later married Beulah (Taggart). She bore him two more children, Mary Elizabeth Crabtree and Rudy Crabtree.

After serving in the Navy during WWII, Preston supported his family as part-owner of the Gable's Restaurant. He was elected sheriff in 1949 served 2-1/2 years, then became an Indiana State Trooper in 1952. In December, 1958, Preston had a fatal heart attack at the age of 38.

The Crabtree children have all added another generation with Brown County ties. Larry's first marriage ended in divorce in 1974. He and his two children remained on Plum Creek Road. In 1976, Larry married his high school sweetheart, Kay (Percifield) daughter of Bill and Beulah. Kay had two children by a previous marriage. Larry's children, Preston and Robin, ages 13 and ten were united with Kay's children, Greg and Stacy Miller, age 13 and ten, and in 1978, Benjamin Adams Crabtree was born into the family. The three older children are married, Greg has two sons and his wife is expecting. Both Preston and Robin are expecting their first child this year (1990) and Stacy will be married this summer.

Dan Crabtree's two sons are in college and not yet married. Shiela's oldest, Ryan Oliver is a junior in high school. Deborah Asbury's oldest is 13 and Steve Crabtree's oldest is nine years old. *Submitted by Larry Crabtree*

DR. LOUIE RICHARD CRABTREE FAMILY - In the fall of 1929, Brown County needed a physician. Louie Richard Crabtree answered the call from Akersville, KY, where he had practiced medicine since graduating from the University of Tennessee Medical School in 1910. One of the attractions of Nashville was a high school his children could attend without boarding away from home, as his oldest son had done. He brought with him his wife, Sarah Belle (Grinestaff), and their children: Joseph Harold, 19; Lee Dunn, 17; Emma Mae, 14-1/2; Lillian Pearl, 12; Garvin Preston, 9-1/2; Kermit Quentin, 7; Elois "Nip", almost 5; and Billy Richard, 2-1/2.

Dr. L.R. Crabtree, Belle Crabtree, son Billy

The new house on Jackson Branch had electricity, which some of the children had never seen, but no running water—not unusual even for homes in town at that time. Like most country doctors of that era, Dr. Crabtree was very busy, but his pay was always small, often late and somtimes nothing at all. His wife Belle was a shy person who stayed close to home. She died in 1935, after seeing only the first three or four of her 24 grandchildren. Dr. Crabtree remarried in 1937, to Beulah Taggart of Nashville. They had a daughter, Mary Elizabeth and a son, Louie Rudolph.

In the early 1940s Dr. Crabtree moved his medical practice to Columbus and was on the hospital staff there, but he returned to Nashville one day a week to see patients. He died of a heart attack in the summer of 1946 while fishing in Brown County. His oldest son, Harold, had a brief try at a singing career on radio station WOWO, Fort Wayne, but came home to marry a Brown County girl, Ruth Seitz. Harold was the first of four Crabtree boys to serve with the Navy in World War II and the first of three to join the Indiana State Police. He served a term as Brown County Assessor before his death in 1974. Ruth died in 1989. They had two sons, Richard Lee and Jack Alvin, and a daughter, Sue Caroline.

Lee served a brief stint in the Marines. While in the Marines he married Marie Purtlebaugh of Columbus. An Army Air Corps bomber pilot in World War II, he was shot down on Sept. 1, 1943, over France, and was a prisoner until April 1945. He stayed in the Air Force until his medical retirement in 1964, and he died in 1967. Lee and Marie had two daughters, Kay Frances and Janet Clair.

Mae graduated from Nashville High School in 1933 and married Charles Miller, a civil engineer and son of pharmacist Herbert Miller, who had come to Nashville just five years before the Crabtrees. They had eight children: James Richard, Judith Ann, Charles Norman, Carol Jeanne, Joseph Lee, Mary Esther, Tom David and Margaret Elizabeth. Charlie, who also served in the Navy during the war, retired from the Indiana Highway Department in 1977 and died in 1978. Mae lives near Monrovia.

Lillian married James Richards of Greenup, KY, and they had a son James Michael, and a daughter, Anne. Lil died in 1980.

Preston served in the Navy in World War II and later became the youngest elected county sheriff in Indiana history. He then joined the State Police and died on duty while serving as a pallbearer for a fellow policeman's father. He was married to Sara Louise Adams of Nashville and they had three sons and two daughters: Larry Denton, Loren Danny, Sheila Jane, Debbie and Steve.

Quentin, known to his friends as "Joe," returned from the Navy service after the war and married Lola Keene of Nashville. They have two daughters, Barbara Kay and Joyce Ann. He became a state policeman and is now retired and works as a security guard for Pillsbury in Clarksville, IN.

Dr. L.R. Crabtree

Nip graduated from the Methodist Hospital School of Nursing in Indianapolis and married Roy Jones of Brownsburg, where they owned a mortuary. They had two daughters, Jennifer Ann and Cindy Jane. Roy died while the girls were young and Nip was later reunited with her high school sweetheart, Keith Skinner, who was by then an Indianapolis businessman. They were married in 1971 and Keith died in 1983. Nip still lives in Brownsburg.

Billy graduated from Columbus High School and entered the Navy just before World War II ended. After finishing his enlistment, he was accepted for pilot training in the Air Force and became one of the first jet fighter pilots. He was shot down over Korea in September 1950.

Mary Elizabeth married David Banister and they live in Columbus and have two children; Robert and Michelle. Louie Rudolph (Rudy) married Cheryl Leslie and graduated from Indiana State and taught and coached at Brown County High where he is still teaching. He has two daughters; Lisa and Amy.

The Crabtree grandchildren have become nurses, teachers, lawmen, engineers, business executives and career servicemen, but not doctors. However, a great-granddaughter (daughter of Janet) and a great-grandson (son of Jim Miller) are on the way to medical school, so "Doc" Crabtree's descendants may yet include at least two physicians. *Submitted by Mae Miller*

BOB AND JEANADELLE CRAMER FAMILY - Bob and Jeanadelle (Russell) Cramer are natives of Martinsville, IN and came to Brown County a few years after Bob joined the staff of the Brown County Democrat in 1955.

Born George Frederick Cramer, May 1, 1914, to Ira E. and Alpha June (Kelso) Cramer, a sister called the new baby Bob which has been his name ever since. His Cramer ancestors came from Germany via Philadelphia in the early 1700s and his Kelso ancestors came from Kelsoland, Scotland, via Baltimore also in the early 1700s. A sixth generation ancestor Abraham Cramer is listed as a 1748 freeholder in Monmouth Co., NJ. An eighth generation ancestor, Reverend John Kelso, wife, and children landed in Maryland. John's son Rev. Alexander Kelso, a direct ancestor, married Mary Blair of the Blair who founded William and Mary College and Princeton University.

Back: James Cramer, Julia (Cramer) Voland, Susan (Cramer) Brewer, Philip Cramer. Front: Jeanadelle and Bob Cramer.

Jeanadelle was born Oct. 17, 1916 to Lewis Samuel and Anna Merle (Baughn) Russell. The Russell ancestors came from Britain and the Baughn ancestors are traced from Germany emigrating via Virginia and Kentucky. The Russell and Baughn families were God-fearing farmers, artisans, merchants, and professionals.

Kelsos fought in the Revolutionary War and migrated west via the Carolinas establishing a mill east of Knoxville, TN. Being abolitionists they were uncomfortable in a slave state so moved on to a homestead just east of Morgantown. Besides millers, through the centuries the Kelsos have been farmers, merchants, artisans, ministers and professionals.

Jeanadelle and Bob were wed in 1936 and are parents of two sons and two daughters: Philip, born 1944, owner of ImageAccess, Inc., Indianapolis; James, born 1952, Project Manager for SAE Corporation, Houston, TX; Susan, born 1946, Manager, Research and Development, Health Maintenance of Indiana, Inc., Indianapolis, wife Dr. Gene Brewer, Bloomington; Julia, born 1949, Computer Programmer in the Comptroller's Office of the State of Texas in Austin. Philip is a graduate of Martinsville High School and Ball State University. The other three are graduates of Brown County High School, Jim a graduate of Purdue University, Susan and Julia graduates of Indiana University. There are four grandchildren.

Since coming to Brown County Jeanadelle and Bob have resided on Artist Dr., Carmel Ridge Rd., and now live in a century-old cabin on the Old Helmsburg Rd. one mile west of Nashville. Jeanadelle is an artist and a former Nashville shop owner. Bob is a member of the Lions Club of Brown County and is claimed by the Brown County Historical Society as a charter member. He is also claimed by the Brown County Democrat as staff member. They and their family are ecumenical Christian.

JOHN BURNETT CRAVEN - Born in 1848 in Yorkshire, England, John Burnett Craven was a son of William and Mary Burnett Craven. The Craven family emigrated to America in October of 1853. Before coming to Hamblen Township, Brown County, the family had lived in Ohio for a few years.

John Craven married Martha Adaline Hamblen, born 1854, daughter of Rev. William Hamblen and Nancy Ann Goforth, in Brown County on Sept. 7, 1872. John and Martha had five children: (1) Mary Alma (1873-1945) who married William S. Walker; they are the grandparents of the submitter, Marcedes Walker Joslin (2) Nancy Olive, born 1875, married Elza Hague in 1894 in Brown County; (3) Essie Myrtle, born 1881, married Ernest Walker in 1901 in Brown County. (4) William Cleveland (1884-1908); (5) John Christopher, born 1890, married Ruth E. Scovell in 1914.

John B. Craven

John Burnett Craven was active in the Democrat Party and was elected chairman of the Democrat Central Committee. He was elected Trustee of Hamblen Township, in 1894 and was President of the Hamblen Township Fair Association which held agricultural and racing fairs at Sprunica for several years. He was also a member of Odd Fellows and Knights of Pythias Lodges. His wife, Martha, was a member of the Daughters of Rebecca Lodge. John died in 1937, Martha died in 1902. Both are buried in Nineveh Cemetery, Johnson Co., IN. *Submitted by Marcedes L. (Walker) Joslin, great-granddaughter of John B. and Martha (Hamblen) Craven*

DANIEL CROUCH FAMILY - Daniel, great-great-grandfather of Bernadine S. Acker, was born in 1832 in Brown Co., IN. He was the second child out of ten born to William Crouch and Amy Reynolds Crouch. He died March 28, 1894 in Brown Co., IN. William and Amy are probably buried in Brown County also. William died between 1850-58, and Amy in 1868. They had the following children: Polly, Daniel, Aaron, Anna, David, Elizabeth, Hila Ann, William R., James A. and Even. (A George W. Crouch lived next door to Wm. and Amy in the 1850 Census, and could be a son of theirs also).

On a genealogical trip to Nashville, IN in 1978, Bernadine Acker and her mother, Marie Allen Smith were wandering about the Crouch-Roberts Cemetery. Bernadine tripped over a headstone way beyond the regular graves. Not realizing there were any more headstones in that area, she pulled the weeds and brambles away and discovered Daniel's gravestone. It was unknown to us until then where he was buried.

Children of Minnie Ann (Crouch) and Coen Clark Allen. Back: Jesse Willard Allen; Middle: Twin sons: Ray and Earl Allen; Front: Marie Estella Allen.

Daniel was quite a character in the Brown County Courthouse records. He was administrator for the Estate Record of Amy Bird: Book #1 Page 303, 11-4-1868. The Courthouse records are sprinkled with legal episodes of Daniel. He loved to go to court.

Daniel was a farmer and a "quack" doctor. During the Civil War, he was a substitute for Hamilton Clipp. He served in Co. "G",. 32nd Regiment for one year. He enlisted Oct. 19, 1864 at Columbus, IN and was mustered out on May 8, 1865. When inducted, his age was 33. He had blue eyes, dark hair and was 6'3" tall, with a fair complexion.

In 1861 Daniel was on the Washington Township Committee to expend relief for families of men who were in service.

He was married five times. Marriage #1 was to Nancy Ping and they had five children.

Daniel and Amanda Melvina Henderson (#2) had two children. George W. born in 1872 and Bernadine's grandmother (always called "Granny" by her grandchildren), Minnie Ann Crouch, born Nov. 21, 1870 in Gnawbone (Stonehead) and she died March 12, 1938 in Frankton, IN. She is buried in Parkview Cemetery, Alexandria, IN. She married Coen Clark Allen on July 4, 1896 in Columbus, IN. Charles was their first born on Aug. 6, 1897. He died July 30, 1898. He is buried in the New Bellsville Cemetery. The largest pine tree is his headstone, planted by Coen. Jesse Willard was born June 1, 1899 in Hadley, IN. He married Evelyn Printz on May 29, 1930 and they had one daughter, Fonda Lou. Jesse died in 1980. Minnie and Coen then had twins, Earl Edgar and Ray Edwin on Sept. 25, 1903 in Columbus, IN. Earl married Clara Sweet and they had one son, Francis Coen (died) and Shirley Jean. Earl died April 4, 1964. Ray married Dorothy Manuel and they had one daughter, Fern. Ray died Sept. 28, 1989. Coen and Minnie's last child was their only daughter, Marie Estella, born May 21, 1905 in Columbus, IN. She married Lewis Smith and they had five children: Vernon Willard, Dwight Richard, Wallace Galen, Wanda Lee and Bernadine Lou. Marie died Aug. 28, 1989, one month earlier than Ray. Marie is buried in Parkview Cemetery in Alexandria, IN. That was the end of that Allen generation. *Submitted by Bernadine S. Acker*

ELSWORTH AND BEULAH CROUCH - James Elsworth Crouch was born Aug. 24, 1901 at Kelp, which is now part of Brown County State Park. He was the son of Joseph Wm. and Sarah E. Roberts Crouch. Joseph was born Feb. 13, 1876, died March 3, 1930, and is buried with his wife, Sarah, in the Reeves Cemetery, Van Buren Twp., Brown County. Joseph and Sarah were married July 29, 1899. Sarah born Jan. 26, 1881 and died March 21, 1908.

Elsworth married Beulah Hobbs, born July 12, 1905 near Kelp, the daughter of George and Lula Hamblen Hobbs, on May 14, 1921. (Lula was a sister of James W. Hamblen.) Elsworth built a house on a hill East of Kelp which was later owned by George and Lula until it became a part of the park. Elsworth and Beulah moved to Columbus ca. 1927. Elsworth was a mechanical whiz with steam engines, tractors, automobiles and later diesel engines. In the '40s he traveled widely for Cummins to repair large diesel engines on seagoing vessels. He was a much sought after auto mechanic for 35 years, mostly for the Reeves (Ford) Garage in Columbus. After retiring, he worked for seven years as maintenance engineer at the Irwin Union Bank and Trust Company.

Elsworth and Beulah Crouch

Elsworth and Beulah were very kind and generous people. In particular, when Beulah's uncle, James Hamblen, died in 1933 they did much to assist the widow, Mary, and her nine children. Their home was always open to Mary and the children. They arranged for them to rent a home with Beulah's mother, Lula Hobbs, at Waymansville, IN, Bartholomew County for a few years. Elsworth died April 24, 1984 and Beulah died July 6, 1960. They are buried in Garland Brook Cemetery, Columbus, IN. Their children are:

(1) Grace Louise, born April 9, 1922 married Rev. Grover J. Myers, born March 13, 1916, on May 22, 1941. They live in Edinburgh and have seven children: James Leon, Marcella Dorette, Stephen Wesley, Timothy Jack, Paul Eugene, Mark Jeffery and Nathan Robert.

(2) Lela Alice, born Aug. 26, 1928, married James Robert Fleetwood born July 3, 1929, died November 1989. Alice lives in Bethel Village. They had children Terry Mark, Sheryl Jolene, Cynthia Dalene and Ronald James.

(3) Imogene, born May 22, 1931, died Oct. 6, 1975, married Roy Combs and had one child Yvonne Gail. Imogene is buried in Garland Brook Cemetery.

(4) Cloyce Dale, born Jan. 5, 1943, died March 23, 1943, also buried in Garland Brook Cemetery.

(5) Jacob Elsworth, born June 3, 1944, married Barbara Jean Kelley, born June 3, 1946. They live in Georgetown, KY and have two children, James Robert and Gina Lynn.

Elsworth's grandparents were John R. Crouch, born Sept. 22, 1853, in Brown County and Rebecca Reeves (daughter Wm. Reeves and Eunice Steel) born ca. 1857 in Ohio and died 1906, both buried in Reeves Cemetery. His great-grandfather was Daniel Crouch, born ca. 1832, died March 28, 1884 in Brown County. Daniel is buried in the Crouch-Roberts Cemetery, Brown County. Daniel married ca. 1850 to Nancy Ping, born Nov. 9, 1832, Pulaski Co., KY, died Feb. 13, 1865, buried in New Bellsville Cemetery, Brown County. His great-great-grandfather was William and his great-great-great-grandfather was Aaron. The Crouch family was one of the first families to settle in Washington Township in the 1830s. *Submitted by John W. Hamblen*

HIRAM CROUCH FAMILY - Hiram E. Crouch (Feb. 4, 1839-March 3, 1912) was born in Bell Co., KY, a son of James Crouch and Elizabeth Simons. He married in Claiborne Co., TN on Sept. 7, 1857 to Elizabeth Jane Taylor. Hiram was a Civil War veteran, having served as a corporal in the 49th Kentucky Infantry, Co. C.

Hiram and Elizabeth Jane Crouch journeyed to Brown Co., IN in 1868. They had 12 children. The seventh child, born 1869, was Joseph W. Crouch who married Lillie May Shepherd in Brown County on Sept. 10, 1892. She was a daughter of Thomas Shepherd and Christena Lucas. Joseph and Lillie May set up housekeeping in a log home on Valley Branch in Van Buren Township. They took crossties to Freetown to sell. They also were farmers and took cream and eggs to Columbus by horse and wagon. Because the trip was too long to do in one day, they would spend the night at Two Mile House, just west of Columbus.

Nellie Moore and Doc Crouch wedding picture, Feb. 24, 1916.

Joseph and Lillie May Crouch had nine children. The second oldest was Alfred Ralphy Crouch, called "Doc" because the local physician was Dr. Alfred J. Ralphy, and a good friend of the family. Doc married Nellie Esther Moore on Feb. 24, 1916, daughter of James Leroy Moore and Caroline Mackey. Caroline was a midwife and was with Dr. Ralphy when most of the children of the community were born. Doc and Nellie were truck farmers on land at Pikes Peak where they made their home. They had a canning factory and Doc operated a Blacksmith Shop on the southeast corner of New Bellsville Road and Poplar Grove Road. Doc made everything from tobacco knives, garden hoes, butcher and paring knives to hay hooks. He also shod horses and made wagon wheels, including those belonging to Dr. Ralphy.

Doc and Nellie Crouch had three children: Gwendola, born May 24, 1919, who married Densel Anthony Truex; Lois Delphine, born March 24, 1926, who married Harold Hatton; and Harry Wendell Crouch, born June 29, 1928, who married Norma Rosanna Eggeman. Harry and Norma Crouch have three children: Caroline Ann, born May 22, 1962; Steven Wendell, born Oct. 15, 1964; and Connie Anita Crouch, born Aug. 27, 1968. *Submitted by Connie Crouch*

JOSEPH WILLIAM CROUCH - Aaron Crouch (1786-1848), William Crouch (ca. 1810-ca. 1855), Daniel Crouch (ca. 1832-1894), John R. Crouch (1853-1923), Joseph William Crouch (1876-1930), make up five generations of the Crouch family who lived in this area and who are buried in various cemeteries here.

Joseph Wm. Crouch, born Feb. 13, 1876 in Brown County, married Sarah E. Roberts. They had three children, James Elsworth, Ina May and Effie Leanna. All three spent most of their lives in Brown County. Effie lives in Columbus. After Sarah's death, Joseph married Amanda Skinner Fitzgerald. They had two daughters, Amanda M. and Ruth. Ruth spent her young years in Brown County. Their mother died in 1913 and is buried in Brown County.

Joseph then married Ora F. Petro, daughter of Preston and Ellen Sullivan Petro, on Sept. 19, 1914 in Brown County where they lived and raised a family: Melvin, born and died June 14, 1918; Grover W., born June 12, 1919, lived in Brown County and Columbus until he joined the Navy, was at Pearl Harbor, serving on the USS *Pennsylvania* when attacked by Japan, died February 1987; Goldie F., born and died Nov. 22, 1921; John R., born June 16, 1923, his early years spent in Brown County, now lives in Columbus area; Kenneth Woodrow, born May 5, 1926 in a log cabin built by his parents, Joseph and Ora, in what is now the Horseman's Camp in Brown County State Park. Woodrow lived just four years here, then lived in Indianapolis.

He and his wife Mary C. live in Greenwood. The youngest child, Freeman Donald was born June 10, 1929 in the Old Kelp Post Office. When the State bought the land for the Brown County State Park, his and Woodrow's birthplaces were torn down to make way for wildlife and bird sanctuaries. Don and his wife Carol live near Columbus.

Joseph William Crouch in his first Auto

Joseph Crouch and his first son, James Elsworth, were known for their mechanical skills. Together they kept machinery in running condition for many farms in Brown County. Joseph also had a blacksmith shop on his farm and an ice-house where he stored ice he cut from the creek. Joseph lost an arm in a corn shredder in November of 1919 but still carried on and supported his family. He died in Robert Long Hospital on March 3, 1930. After his death the family was separated and the two youngest children adopted, becoming Kenneth Woodrow Robbins and Donald Fremont Chandler. Fifty years later the family was joyously reunited. Joseph's widow, Ora, continued to live in Brown County, remarried and had five more children. She lives at the Brown County Community Care Center in Nashville as Ora Mathis.

Many of the family members have wonderful memories and love for the old home places and still visit them. The Crouch and Petro families hold family reunions at the Hoosier's Nest, the log cabin in the State Park where Joseph Crouch first set up housekeeping and where his first son Elsworth was born. (see Preston and Ellen Petro) *Submitted by Kenneth Woodrow Robbins*

CULLEN FAMILY - James Emmett Cullen's direct ancestor was born Nov. 12, 1811 in Queens Co., Ireland. He came to America around 1827-34, met and married Rozannah Haeffer July 1840 in Guernsey Co., OH. While living in Sarahsville, OH, James and Rozannah had ten children, Peter, Mary A., Harriett, Samuel, John, Elizabeth, Hester Al, Catherine, Rhoda E. and Susan M. In 1864 they moved to Brown County on Howard Ridge (above Needmore). James was a stone mason. Many of the fine bridges and arches along the B&C Railroad and over Salt Creek and Bean Blossom Creek will remain as evidence of his handiwork and skill. He was several times elected to the office of Assessor of his township. He was known as a kind husband, a loving father and a true friend. He is buried at Old Unionville Cemetery in Monroe County July 8, 1887.

Peter Wilson Cullen

Peter W. Cullen born Dec. 12, 1841, died Dec. 18, 1932, was the great-grandfather of Mary Ann Walker all she knows of him was told to her by her grandmother, Mary Catherine Cullen Robertson. Peter married Mary Ellen Neal Singleton born Aug. 13, 1852, died Dec. 31, 1914. They lived near Needmore in Brown County. Their children were: Samuel born Feb. 24, 1877, died Oct. 14, 1958; Mary Catherine born April 17, 1879, died July 29, 1975; John Walter born Aug. 16, 1881, died Aug. 25, 1955; Jessie Elizabeth born April 12, 1884, died Jan. 11, 1957; Rosanna born Feb. 2, 1889. She and a baby died in childbirth Jan. 11, 1920.

Peter Cullen served as county commissioner of Brown County several years ago and made an enviable record as such officer. The Cullens were truly a religious Catholic family. James Henry Cullen, born Aug. 1, 1865, died Sept. 15, 1951 and wife, Emma Legge Cullen, born Dec. 14, 1876, died Dec. 1, 1952, lived on Highway 135 north of Bean Blossom, IN in a lovely brick home that is still standing. Their son, Henry Terrance (Tat) Cullen born Oct. 6, 1904 still lives in Morgantown. *Submitted by Mary Ann Walker*

J. ROBERT AND MELBA DAILEY -
The Daileys are former residents of Kokomo, IN and have been associated with Brown County since the early 1960s, when Melba joined the Brown County Art Gallery as an Associate Artist Member. Enchanted with the area, its people and pace, they purchased a precious little cabin on North Jefferson Street where, for several years they spent as many holidays and long weekends as possible.

Melba Dailey was born Melba Pauline Hall on April 28, 1909 in Akron, OH to Virginia Susan Cline Hall and Adonias Wateland Hall. Melba is a descendant maternally of Peter Cline, Sr. He was of German descent and in 1774 lived in Tazwell Co., VA and paternally of Peter Hall (1831) and Ida Fore and Ida's connection to George W. Fore (1828) of Prince Edward Co., VA of English descent.

Melba has been active in the field of fine art since the early 1950s. She trained at Indiana University, Kokomo, Purdue, Indianapolis Art League and the Venice Area Art League. Through the years she continued her art education, attending special classes and workshops taught by recognized artists and sculptors. Mrs. Dailey is an exhibiting artist member of the Indianapolis Hoosier Salon and Indiana Artist Club. She is a past president of the Kokomo Art Association, and a charter member and past president of the Sculptor's Guild. Inventive and versatile the artist works in several mediums. Melba originated "Wall Jewels," small expressionistic bas'-reliefs in precious and semi-precious metals embellished with gemstones. She also pioneered and was self-taught in the art of fused cathedral glass.

Throughout the years Melba has won awards, had one and two-artist exhibitions and served on the executive boards of several Indian organizations associated with the arts. She has been an active exhibiting artist member of the Brown County Art Gallery for a number of years where at age 75 she accepted an Emeritus Artist status; continuing to exhibit, but fewer pieces. Her work is in collections in the United States and Europe. Melba is one of the founding members of Indiana Heritage Arts, an associate member of the Brown County Art Guild, member and past president of the Nashville Literary Club, and a member of the Nashville United Methodist Church. In 1981 Melba received a citation "for outstanding cooperation with the Red Cross Blood Bank" for her 40 years of service.

Melba Dailey and J. Robert Dailey about 1975.

In Kokomo, Melba is a member and past president of St. Joseph's Hospital Cheer Guild Board, serving 12 consecutive years. She is co-founder and past president of the Howard County Mental Health Association. Melba is one of the founding members of the Kokomo Sunrise Easter Pageant—past president and honorary member of the Symposium, past president and honorary member of the Devon Woods Home and Garden Club which she founded in 1965.

Patrick Dailey, a native of County Cork, Ireland, migrated to Lindsy, Ontario, Canada. His two sons were Frank and Joseph W. Dailey. The family then migrated to Bay City, MI. Joseph W. Dailey married Ella M. Campbell of Scotch-Irish descent. Joseph and Ella had three children: Edward, James Robert, and Helen. J. Robert (Bob) Dailey was born Aug. 3, 1902 in Bay City, MI.

In the early 1900s the family moved to Lansing, MI where Bob grew up. He attended St. Mary's grade and high school. His higher education was gained at the University of Detroit and General Motors Institute of Technology. His life-long interests and employment were associated with the automotive industry. In 1971, after 30 years as General Manager of the Ford Motor Company Automotive Parts plant in Kokomo, IN, Bob retired.

Both Melba and Bob having led very active lives found themselves spending much more time at their Nashville cabin, than in their Kokomo home. 'Twas then they decided to make Brown County their permanent home. They bought a pleasant place on 135N, high on the ridge, half way between Nashville and Bean Blossom, at the corner of Red Bud Lane. They named it "Whippoorwill Hill." Since retirement Bob has maintained a very active interest in business. The first two years he spent as a business consultant. He became very active in the Service Corps of Retired Executives (SCORE) and was chairman of the Kokomo Chapter before moving to Nashville. He also founded the SCORE chapter in Columbus, IN and served as its chairman for two years. Still active in the organization, he has received numerous citations for his contributions to the Small Business Community. Bob also serves on the advisory board of the Columbus Enterprise Development Corporation.

Mr. Dailey is a member of St. Agnes Catholic Church; a life member of the Elks Club, Brown County Historical Society; the National Taxpayers Union and the Heritage Foundation. He is a past director and associate member of the Brown County Art Gallery, also a past director and member of the Country Club of Brown County.

The Daileys were married in 1941, each having a son from a previous marriage. Both boys lived in Kokomo with their parents and graduated from grammar and high school there. They attended Indiana University (Bloomington) where Melba's son, Markolf Donald Schickendantz II (Mark) earned a B.S. degree in Business and Bob's son, James Barton (Jim) Dailey, received a B.S. in Business and a Masters in Geology. Both sons are married and live in California's San Francisco Area. Mark is owner of Asset Management Associates and Jim, a now retired Senior Geologist, is owner and operator of Shilo West, an Equestrian Estate accommodating over 90 riding horses.

Jim has one son, two daughters and four grandchildren. Mark and his wife (Nashville born, Judith McQuire) have two sons, two daughters and four grandchildren. *Submitted by Melba P. Dailey*

DUDLEY D. AND HAZEL S. DAVIS -
The Davises adopted Brown County as their retirement home and in 1974 built "Seasons' Watch" on Greasy Creek Road. Both Hazel and Dudley were born in Indiana—Dudley in 1912, the oldest child of Orange and Florence (Diggs) Davis in Indianapolis and Hazel in 1917, the oldest child of Clarence and Muriel (Krout) Smith in Montgomery County.

Dudley was of English ancestry and they came westward from Virginia (Williamsburg area). Hazel is German/English and early family members came to Indiana from Ohio.

Dudley and Hazel Davis

At the time of Dudley and Hazel's marriage in 1943, they moved to Washington, D.C. and Dudley served 30 years with the Federal Government, first in World War II connected agencies and then in overseas posts in the Far East, Middle East, and Vietnam. Their daughter, Linda was born Nov. 3, 1948 in Tokyo, Japan and now resides in northern Virginia (Woodbridge). Linda married Ernest E. Green. Their daughter Valerie Nicole Green was born June 29, 1977.

Growing up during the great depression of the 30s, money for a college education was hard to acquire, but Dudley was a dedicated student and worked all summer for 10¢ an hour on an Indiana Game Farm so he could attend Indiana University extension classes in Indianapolis. He then transferred to Butler University and received a B.S. in history in 1936 and in 1941 was awarded a M.S. degree in economics. He was elected to Phi Kappa

Phi, an honorary scholastic fraternity. He wrote "The History of the Indiana Farm Bureau Cooperative" and "The History of the Southport Presbyterian Church" on the occasion of its 100th anniversary.

Hazel graduated from Indiana Business College in 1936 and thereafter followed a career in business.

Having seen a lot of the world devastated by war, pollution and abuse, Dudley and Hazel were environmentalists, interested in the preservation of land and trees and saving the habitat of birds and animals. Both were members of the Nashville United Methodist Church. Dudley was a Life Member of the Brown County Historical Society and Hazel is an Honorary Life Member. Hazel served as President of the Historical Society.

Dudley died in July 1989 and is interred in Greenlawn Cemetery in Nashville, IN. Hazel still resides at Season's Watch, the family Home, midst the trees and hills of Brown County.

FRANK AND DELPHA DAVIS

After living near Nashville for 13 years, the Davises moved to a house at the Methodist Home at Franklin October of 1979. Soon after moving to Nashville, Frank and Delpha operated a crafts and antique shop in their home—Americana Crafts—located one mile north of Nashville on Route 135. After a year or so the shop was moved to downtown Nashville. It was located back of Bartram's Original Gift Shop and owned by them.

Delpha's brother and wife, Bob and Pearl Simpson had a rock shop in the same building. After a few years they became tired of being there seven days a week with no opportunity to travel very far or be away for very long, so the shop was sold.

Frank and Delpha Davis 53rd Wedding Anniversary, March 1987

Frank and Delpha were members of the Methodist Church and the Historical Society. When they moved to Franklin, they moved their church membership and no longer belonged to the Historical Society.

They miss "Brown County" and all of its beauty. Most of all they miss good friends that were made at the Church and at Historical Society and at other activities. They have very pleasant memories of square dancing and still keep in touch with friends there. They felt sad to leave Brown County but felt it was the right thing to move to the Methodist Home since it is an enjoyable and lovely place to live. There are many programs and activities at the Home. There is a large yard and they can work in it in the summer and have many flowers.

ROBERT AND VIRGINIA DAVIS

In 1850, Jerimiah and Anna Gredig and their two children emigrated to the United States from Graubunden Canton, Switzerland. After a two-month voyage they settled in Maryville, TN. Their daughter Rose Ellen Gredig married Edgar Adam Davis in 1926. Edgar's family, in Blount Co., TN dates back to the 1800s. Edgar and Rose had five boys one of which was Robert Glen.

Virginia's parents, Ethel Lee Wilburn and Lonzo Robert Abrams lived in Carter Co., KY. Both families were clay miners and farmers. Ethel Lee and Lonzo Robert were married May 4, 1923 and had nine children. Virginia, the oldest girl, quickly learned to cook, farm and take care of her younger siblings. She enjoyed going to quilting bees with her mother and friends. She attended a one room school house in Jacobs, KY.

Robert and Virginia Davis, 1953

At the age of 17 she moved to Richmond, IN and put her skills to work in a glove factory. Every evening after work she would sit on her porch swing and glance at the boy next door on his swing. Eight months later on March 27, 1953, they became husband and wife.

In 1956, Robert and Virginia moved to Indianapolis, IN returning from South Carolina where Robert was stationed with the U.S. Army for two years. At this time, Brown County became a weekend ritual; for Robert it was the hilly countryside and for Virginia it was the privacy and friendly people. They decided to raise their two daughters Sue and Marti in the country. In 1965 the Davis family moved to Brown County and purchased the Lowell Long homestead north of Helmsburg on Oak Ridge Road where Robert built their home.

Robert is a skilled craftsman. He has worked in construction all his life. Today he works as a General Contractor. He retired from the A.E. Pitcher Construction Company in 1985 where he worked for 30 years. He was Vice President and a partner in ownership.

Front: Marlene (Marti) Reynolds and Katharine (Sue) Rejko. Back: Della Virginia (Abrams) and Robert Glen Davis, 1989.

Virginia still enjoys the country and relaxes with her many hobbies which include cooking, sewing and gardening.

Sue and Marti both graduated from Brown County High School. Sue lives in Brown County with her husband Jesse Rejko and Marti resides in Bloomington with her husband Bob Reynolds.

THOMAS R. AND MARGARET (ROGERS) DAY

Thomas Reynolds Day was born Jan. 10, 1843 in Delaware Co., OH. His mother, Celinda Reynolds, born 1817, in Pennsylvania was the daughter of Ingham and Mary Reynolds of Delaware County. His father, Presley, born 1814, was the son of Charles and Mary Rawlings Day who married in 1806 in Fleming Co., KY and moved to Licking Co., OH adjacent to Delaware County, when the Ohio country was first being settled. Charles' father, William Day, had moved to Kentucky from Virginia as had Mary's father, William Rawlings, with their families. Nine children were born to Presley and Celinda in Ohio: Jane, William, Ingham, Charles, Thomas R., John, Sarah, Julia, Hester, and Alwelda. All five sons served in the Civil War. Ingham died of disease in 1862. After the war William, Charles, and Thomas moved to Brown County where they farmed, married, and raised their families.

Thomas Day Family: Back: Charles, John, Morten, Frank, Arlie. Front: Ida May Day Chitwood, Thomas, Margaret Rogers Day, and Olive Day Rose.

The military record of Thomas Day states that he was 6' 1-1/2" tall with black hair, dark eyes, and light complexion. He entered Co. H of the Ohio Volunteer 121st Infantry Unit at the start of the Civil War and served the four years of the war in that organization. The first battle that the 121st engaged in was Perryville, which was fought after the unit marched with Buell's army in pursuit of Bragg, having never had an hour's drilling after organizing. They took part in many engagements and major battles, Chickamauga, Lookout Mountain, Mission Ridge, Kennesaw Mountain, and were on Sherman's March through Georgia. At the battle of Kennesaw Mountain, GA in June of 1864, while engaged in a charge, Thomas suffered a type of stroke and was carried off the field. He managed to finish his war service but the experience contributed to his death of heart and stomach trouble in 1908.

In 1866 Thomas married Margaret Rogers, born 1845 daughter of Lewis and Parilda Siscoe Rogers, and they raised seven children on a farm three miles west of Nashville: Ida May, Charles, John, James Morten, Joseph Frank, Olive, and Arlington. Three babies died in infancy. Margaret lived until 1923, sometimes with daughter, Ida May Chitwood, and later with daughter, Olive Rose, on the home place.

The Rogers family were early settlers in Indiana. Lewis' father, James, was the son of Aquilla Rogers who built the first log cabin in Jackson County. Aquilla and his brother, Henry, were born in Chester Co., PA, sons of David and Hannah Rogers, and came to Indiana after serving in the Revolutionary War.

Parilda Rogers was the daughter of William and Elizabeth Sullens Scisco who had come to Monroe County from Kentucky about 1830.

Lewis and Parilda had a great deal of land in Brown County and are buried in the Rogers-Day Cemetery.

DECKARD FAMILY

The Deckard family came to America from Metz, Germany, via New York City about 1775. They then went into Virginia and by 1830 they had moved into Monroe and Brown Co., IN.

Jacob Deckard, the great-great-grandfather of Raleigh, was born in 1757 in Germany and served with the Army in Virginia in the Revolutionary War. He married in Virginia and had 11 children.

One of his sons, Jacob Deckard, Jr. came to Monroe County. He was born 1791 in Wytheville, VA and married Sallie Hillenborg in Virginia. They had five children in Virginia before moving to Monroe County. They had seven more children in Monroe County.

Raleigh and Bessie in the 1940s in front of their house.

Hezekiah Deckard was their oldest child and Raleigh's grandfather. In the 1850 census of Brown County, it says that the value of his real estate was $75,000. He married Barsheba Ann Pennington and they had 14 children.

Jacob, born May 9, 1848 in Johnson Township, Brown County, married Sara Elizabeth Hanson. They had nine children with only five living to marry and have a family. They were: Thomas, Anna, May, Iva and Raleigh.

Raleigh went to school at Central Normal College in Danville for six weeks to become a teacher. At the age of 16 years, he began his teaching career at Dewar Ridge. He taught for 43 years in Brown County. He married Bessie Woods who was in the eighth grade when he taught his first school. They raised six children. The oldest became a school teacher. She also taught in the county.

When the Deckards moved to Brown County they built their houses somewhat the same way and the one known as the Raleigh Deckard house on Deckard Ridge, as it is known now; but years ago it was known as the Deckard settlement. This house is the only one still standing and it is over 100 years old. *Submitted by Dean and Lois Carter*

HEZEKIAH DECKARD

Hezekiah Deckard married Bashie Pennington and settled in Brown Co., IN in a one-room log cabin. The floor was of dirt, and there was no cook stove. The bed consisted of four forked sticks. They had no knives and forks.

Hezekiah's first team was a yoke of calves. One died leaving him only one with which to bring to work. He would tie a turn of corn on a shock of wheat on the back of the ox, walk and lead it to the old Ketcham Mill about 20 miles west of the house. There were mud roads only. Later he could afford a team. He used hickory bark lines for harness. They were soaked in water at the noon hour to keep them soft. He owned the first new wagon in Johnson Township.

Hezekiah Deckard could neither read or write, but he could work problems in arithmetic faster in his head than many people can with pencil and paper.

He raised a large family. After his death, the sale of personal property took two days. He left 2,300 acres of land. His heirs sold 70 head of three-year olds at $30.00 a head. He kept between 20 and 30 milk cows, three pair of mules, two yoke of oxen, and three or four teams of horses. He kept two hired hands and two hired hand girls. They got up at 3:00 a.m. to start work. All the boys helped until they were married.

There were salt springs in the bed of Salt Creek by the Cutright Bridge. People boiled the water there and took out the salt. There were also the Deer Lick Springs in Polk Township (Monroe County) where people hid and caught deer. Wild turkeys, catamounts, and bobcats, were plentiful in Brown County at that time. Wild pigeons were so plentiful, they broke off limbs of trees where they roosted. People killed squirrels and salted them down as they did pork meat. As late as 1889 a wild turkey gobbler came in and fought the tame gobblers. He could take off in flight from a running position and fly for one-half mile like a bird.

The little log school house was across the road from the family house. John's (Hezekiah's son) mother had a spelling and an arithmetic book. Many times there was no other person at the school except the teacher and one pupil.

No records of any deeds made by Jacob Deckard Sr. (Hezekiah's father) have been found in the Monroe County courthouse. He may have lived with his children until his death in 1840. His place of abode and burial place are not known. Who can say that his restless pioneering spirit does not hover over the ancestral home of one of his children. *Submitted by Josephine Aubin and John Hays, grandson*

JOHANNES JACOB DECKARD

Johannes Jacob Deckard was born in 1757, Metz, Germany and died in 1842 in Monroe Co., IN. His wife, Mary Vance, was born in Botetourt Co., VA. Jacob served in the Revolutionary War as a soldier of Virginia.

Jacob, Sr. moved to Monroe Co., IN with his children. They were: Jacob, Jr. (born 1791, died 1878); John (born 1794, died 1869); Michael (born 1781, died 1839); Adam (born 1808, died 1881); Jesse W. (born 1809, died 1886); William (born 1799, died ??); Daniel (born 1801, died ??); Henry (born 1795, died 1879); Catherine Deckard (born 1815, died ??).

John and Nancy (Ping) Deckard

Henry Deckard, son of Jacob, Sr., married Elizabeth Etter, born 1811, died 1870. Their children were John, David, Milton, Albert, Thomas, Stephen, Wade, and Henry.

John Deckard, son of Henry, married (1) Caroline Clark, (2) Nancy Ping. Nancy Ping was a daughter of Richard Ping and Sarah Rogers. John and Nancy's children were Lydia Elva and Aaron Deckard. Lydia Elva married Isaac C. Lemasters. Lydia and Isaac Lemasters' daughter Pearl married (1) ?? Cooper and (2) James V. Cummins, Sr. Pearl's children were Richard Cooper Cummins and James V. Cummins, Jr.

Adam, son of Jacob Deckard, Sr., married Sarah Stuart. Their daughter Mary married William Deckard, a son of Mary Deckard who was a daughter of Jacob Deckard, Sr. Polly A., daughter of William and Mary Deckard, married John F. Nilson. Lula Mae, daughter of Polly and John F. Nilson, married William Sherman Stogdill. The children of William Sherman and Lula Mae Stogdill were Fairney (Mrs. Earl Bowman), Cecil, Otto, Brady E., Dorothy (Mrs. Hurshel Stines), Kathryn M. (Mrs. Albert H. Cross), Lucy (Mrs. Glenn Hanners), Frona (Mrs. Lloyd Bruce), Lester and Mary E. Stogdill. Fairney's husband, Earl Bowman, was a son of Jefferson and Nora Chasteen Bowman. Nora Chasteen was a half sister of James V. Cummins, Sr.

John, son of Jacob Deckard, Sr., married Catherine Hildonborg. Martin, son of John Deckard, married Malinda Eads. Daniel, son of Martin Deckard, married Melinda Stepp/Stipp, then married (2) Malissa Jane Baxter, daughter of William and Julia Wilson Baxter. The children of Daniel and Malissa Jane Baxter Deckard were Vina Viola (Mrs. Earnest A. Cox), Charles, John Eliot and Minnie Irene Deckard. Minnie Irene married Bart Short. They had three boys who died in infancy. Minnie Irene then married Ray Bowman, brother of Earl Bowman. Minnie Irene and Ray Bowman adopted Thomas R., who died as a boy. *Submitted by James V. Cummins, Jr.*

LESTON AND EDITH DECKARD

Jacob Deckard, Sr., born near Metz Lorraine, France, in 1757, was one of ten children. The family moved from France to the Netherlands, then to the United States about 1775-76, and later settled in Wythe Co., VA. In 1830-32, they moved to Indiana, making their home in Lawrence, Brown, Green, and Sullivan Counties. Jacob Deckard, Sr. was Leston's great-great-great-grandfather.

One of the sons of Jacob, Sr., Jacob, Jr. was born in 1791 in Virginia. He and his first wife had five children born in Wythe Co., VA, before moving to near Smithville, IN. Their oldest son, Hezekiah, was born in 1819.

Home of Hezekiah and Barsheba Deckard built in 1870, remodeled in 1975.

Hezekiah married Barsheba Ann Pennington in 1840. She was Irish. They moved to Johnson

Township, Brown County, to live. Hezekiah and "Bashies's" first home was a one room log cabin, with a dirt floor, no cook stove or furnishings. Hezekiah used hickory bark for a harness and his first team was a yoke of calves; one died. Hezekiah could not read or write, but he knew and appreciated good soil, and later owned 2,300 acres where they raised beef cattle, milk cows and horses. Their last home is still standing.

The huge barn was destroyed by the tornado in May 1917, but was replaced by his family. They were parents of 14 children. Their fourth son, William Deckard, born in 1845, was Leston's grandfather.

William Deckard married Retta Izilla Fleetwood Jan. 1, 1870. They owned, 1,050 acres of land. William was the veterinarian for the community and also raised cattle, horses, and sheep. Their new home was on a high hill because of Izilla's health. They were the parents of seven children. One son, Vernon Deckard, was Leston's father.

Vernon Deckard was born in Johnson Township on July 25, 1881. He married Daisy Pearl Strain. They owned 530 acres where he farmed and grew timber. He and Daisy were parents of seven children. Vernon taught school for 42 years. Three sons were also teachers. One son, Leston, was born on Feb. 21, 1913, the year of the "great flood" in Indiana. Leston Deckard attended the Deckard School for seven years. He had teachers named Deckard every year. Vernon and Daisy were blessed with longevity. Today, Monroe Reservoir owns their acreage.

Leston Deckard graduated from college and began teaching school in Hamblen Township, in 1932. On March 20, 1937, Leston and Edith Sipes were married. Leston spent 40 years in the educational system, and Edith spent 34. Summers were spent making hay, trucking, and raising cattle. In November 1949, they became members of Unity Baptist Church, working in Sunday School, helping with the cemetery and Leston served as a deacon. They had one daughter, Janet Kay Deckard Yoder, four grandchildren, and two great-grandchildren. Janet Kay and John David Yoder are parents of Kathy Ann Yoder Porter, John Andrew, Steven Louis, and Nancy Jane. John Andrew and his wife Mary Helen Webster have two children, Rachel Lynn and Ryan Andrew Yoder.

DECKARD-SEXTON - Hezekiah Deckard was born Jan. 1, 1819 in Wythe Co., VA, the son of Jacob Deckard, Jr. and Sallie Hildonborg. Jacob Jr. and Sallie were married May 8, 1817 in Virginia. Hezekiah married Barsheba (Basha) (Bassie) Jane Ann Pennington of North Carolina. They were early settlers of Brown County, living in the Crooked Creek area.

Middle Front: John Henry and Rachel (Sexton) Deckard. Far Right: Youngest child: Cecil Deckard.

They were the parents of 11 children. John Henry Deckard, born Nov. 25, 1840, died Aug. 15, 1904; William, born 1845, died April 22, 1929; Jacob, born May 9, 1864, died June 30, 1923; George (tombstone has last name as Dickard), born May 3, 1864, died Aug. 25, 1870; Isaac Dunn, born Feb. 14, 1841; Phillip; Andrew, born May 3, 1852, died 1934; Matilda (Tilda), born 1858; Amanda Ellen (Manda), born 1855, died June 23, 1932; Sarah Clementine, born 1867; James Madison, born July 9, 1842, died Aug. 6, 1912.

Hezekiah died on March 28, 1889 and Basha Ann (Pennington) Deckard died on June 27, 1909. Both died in Brown County and are buried in Deckard Cemetery in the Crooked Creek area of Brown Co., IN.

John Henry Deckard was born in Brown County, the eldest of the 11 children of Hezekiah and Basha Ann Deckard. On May 3, 1860, in Brown County, John married Rachel Sexton, daughter of David and Anna Rogers Sexton. Their children were: Sarah Elizabeth (1862-Sept. 3, 1907), married George Robertson; Martha Jane (April 12, 1863-??), married Oliver Fleetwood; Mary Alice (Dec. 21, 1865-Feb. 22, 1943), married April 9, 1882, Brown County, to Daniel Miller; Amanda Ellen (Feb. 25, 1868-October 1945), married Perry Robertson; Ollie (Sept. 26, 1870-??), married Charles Winkler; Hezekiah, (Sept. 9, 1872-Dec. 3, 1932), married Rosetta Lutes; Enoch (Nov. 15, 1874-June 24, 1944), married (1) Leotta Wilson, married (2) Pearl Mitchner; Cecil (July 14, 1877-Aug. 6, 1947), married Mary Rosetta Sinn on Sept. 15, 1895; George Washington (Aug. 7, 1880-Sept. 29, 1958), married Mary Ellen Ross on Sept. 28, 1902; Charlotte (1884-1950), married Ival Carmichael; Lonie (April 22, 1886-March 5, 1934), married Flora Terrill on April 3, 1906.

John Henry Deckard died on Aug. 15, 1904 and his wife, Rachel Sexton Deckard, died on May 31, 1914. Both are buried in Deckard Cemetery in southwest Brown County, near the Monroe Reservoir. *Submitted by Mary Deckard Bond, granddaughter of John Henry Deckard*

DECKARD-SINN - Cecil Deckard was born in Brown County on July 14, 1877, the son of John Henry and Rachel (Sexton) Deckard.

On Sept. 15, 1895 he married Mary Rosetta Sinn. She was born March 30, 1876 in Brown County to Frederick and Nancy Jane (Hall) Sinn. They were farmers and lifelong residents of Brown County. The home was on Kent Road near Monroe County.

They were the parents of eight children: Iva, born April 10, 1896, died Sept. 10, 1973; Lonnie, born Oct. 13, 1899, died Oct. 9, 1967; John Wesley, born Dec. 12, 1901, died Feb. 28, 1980; Janie, born July 3, 1903, died May 20, 1987; Rachel, born Aug. 28, 1906; Estella, born July 7, 1909; Ella Inez, born Oct. 24, 1911; and Mary Ellen, born Nov. 22, 1914.

Iva married Lobie D. Kent, son of Sam and Ellen Kent on March 15, 1915. They had four children: Edna, born Oct. 2, 1915; Cecil, born April 7, 1917; Edward, born Nov. 8, 1919; and Clifford, born April 26, 1924.

Lonnie married Elsie Mae Floyd, daughter of Joseph and Cora Floyd on May 31, 1920. They had nine children: Leslie, born June 8, 1921; Herman, born Dec. 19, 1923; Cecil, born March 23, 1926; Maxine, born May 10, 1931; Louie, born Oct. 23, 1933; Joe, born Nov. 23, 1935; Lucille, born Dec. 27, 1937; Peggy, born Sept. 5, 1943; and Lonnie, Jr., born Jan. 22, 1946.

Cecil and Mary Rosetta (Sinn) Deckard

John Wesley married Leona Mae Leffler, daughter of Fay and Efie Leffler on Oct. 6, 1923. They had two children: Clarence Cecil born June 4, 1924 and Dorothy Irene born June 1, 1926.

Janie married Floyd Mullis, son of George and Sarah (Fleetwood) Mullis, on Feb. 28, 1925. They had nine children: Clyde, born June 30, 1925; Dale, born Feb. 1, 1927; Mary Lucille, born Sept. 9, 1928; Pauline, born Feb. 18, 1931; Delmar, born Jan. 26, 1934; Donald Wayne, born March 14, 1936; Cecil, born Feb. 21, 1939; Ruth, born July 18, 1941; and Floyd, Jr., born March 4, 1944.

Rachel married Harley Sturgeon, son of Gil and Elizabeth Sturgeon on March 19, 1923. They had six children: Charles, born Sept. 23, 1923; James, born May 24, 1925; Cecil, born June 4, 1927; Dorothy Mae, born Sept. 20, 1929; Mary Doris, born July 24, 1935; and Lois Marie, born June 16, 1938.

Estella married Stacy Mason Dewar, son of John William and Sara Annos (Aynes) Dewar on Nov. 12, 1932. They had three children: James Fredrick, born Nov. 18, 1933; Wesley Dale, born April 4, 1939; and Wilma Jean, born July 4, 1944.

Ella Inez married Harold F. Shields on Feb. 27, 1932. They had three daughters: Rosetta, born Oct. 8, 1932; Mary Jane, born Oct. 24, 1933; and Madeline, born May 23, 1941.

Mary Ellen married Joseph Walter Bond, son of William Thomas and Bertha Ann (Robertson) Bond on Aug. 7, 1937. They had seven children: William Cecil, born July 28, 1938; Joseph Paul, born March 7, 1940; David Dale, born Oct. 4, 1942; Phyllis Ann, born July 26, 1944; Mary Faith, born March 13, 1946; Florence Marie, born Dec. 14, 1947; and James Fredrick, born July 10, 1949.

Cecil Deckard died Aug. 6, 1947 and Mary Rosetta died April 9, 1958. Each died as a result of a stroke. They are buried in the Duncan Cemetery in Brown County. *Submitted by Mary (Deckard) Bond, daughter of Cecil Deckard*

JAMES W. DERRINGER - James W. Derringer was born in Wales on Jan. 5, 1836. He married Jane Markum and had three children: James Napoleon, born September 1865, died October 1936; Etta Joy and Clara Henning. He later married Mary E. Phillips Waltman, who had three daughters. James W. and Mary had two children: Verna (Mrs. Bramble Mosier) and Roy who lived in Indianapolis.

James W. was a carpenter, cabinet maker, undertaker and teacher. He brought his carpenter tools with him from Wales. He lived his early life near Oak Ridge, and built the Long School House on Oak Ridge. He built and lived in the house where Short's Market is located now and had his undertaking office in the very small second building to the north of the market. In 1932 when State Road 135 came through town, the house was moved back and remade into a filling station.

He made his own caskets—Mary (Derringer) Porter heard her mother say that she, her sisters and friends would walk by the building after school and he would be working on a casket. They would yell and run and he just laughed at them. He also built Carl Brummett's house located 1/2 mile east of Bean Blossom. Some of the furniture he made is still in use by relatives.

James N. Derringer family, left to right, Maggie May, Walter Ray, Cordelia, James N., Willie Earl, Rex Edgar. In front: Archie Leroy.

He lived at Bean Blossom 41 years, was a good Brown County Democrat and Justice of the Peace for 20 years. He and all of his children were avid readers of everything. One upstairs bedroom in James Napoleon's house was filled with book cases, all four walls except for one door and one window.

He died of Bright's Disease at his son's house (James Napoleon) on July 22, 1912 on Landfill Road, near Oak Ridge. The farm had been in the Derringer family a long while. His wife, Mary, died June 18, 1924, and both are buried in the Bean Blossom cemetery.

James Napoleon Derringer was married on March 16, 1890 to Cordelia Snider, (born March 27, 1870) the eighth child of George and Nancy Snider. He was a farmer and raised mules.

James N. and Cordelia had five children: Maggie May Everling, William (Willie) Earl, Rex Edgar, Walter Ray and Archie Leroy.

Cordelia died May 9, 1920, and James N. died Oct. 24, 1936 and both are buried at Oak Ridge Cemetery in Brown County.

Willie Earl Derringer, the second child of Cordelia and James N., was born July 14, 1892 in Brown County. On Jan. 27, 1915 he married Ruby Letha Turner, also of Brown County. Their children were born between 1915 and 1927: Mary Cordelia Porter, James William, Arthur Leo, Lillie Mae Reidinger, Edgar Lewis (died at two and one-half months old), Everett Dale and Elmer Lennis.

Ruby Letha Turner was born on April 7, 1898 and died Aug. 29, 1949. Willie died on Feb. 28, 1965 and was buried beside his wife at the Bean Blossom Cemetery, formerly known as Weeping Willow and Georgetown Cemetery in Brown County. *Submitted by Mary Cordella (Derringer) Porter and Genevra Owens*

REX AND VINNIE DERRINGER

Rex was born on his father's farm (James N. Derringer and Cordelia (Snider) Derringer) June 10, 1894 and was married to Vinnie Rariden on Jan. 3, 1916 at Nashville. Vinnie was born July 12, 1894. He helped his father on the farm and his grandfather (James W. Derringer) until grown, and when the railroad came to Brown County he and others worked there. During World War II he worked at Cummins Engine Company in Columbus and retired from there.

He also was a carpenter and realtor and he and his wife built and sold several log cabins on land they owned on Helmsburg Road and nearby. He shared the love of working with wood and reading with his father and grandfather.

They rented a house in Helmsburg when first married and where Genevra was born Aug. 24, 1917. They bought land on Helmsburg Road and he and his father built a house there, hauling the lumber from Morgantown by mule team.

Rex and Vinnie were both licensed realtors (Vinnie was the first licensed woman realtor in Brown County).

They always raised a big garden and canned lots of food. They also kept a cellar for potatoes and apples.

Rex died Feb. 24, 1963 and is buried at Oak Ridge Cemetery.

Vinnie died April 9, 1986 (born July 12, 1894) and is also buried at Oak Ridge Cemetery. *Submitted by Genevra Owens*

WALTER ASA, WILBUR AND VERLIS DERRINGER

Walter Asa was born Jan. 31, 1922 while family lived on Railroad Road and died Aug. 17, 1988. He married Rebecca McCay on May 9, 1942 in the Methodist Church Parsonage, now an Ice Cream parlor on Main Street, Nashville. Rebecca was born Sept. 12, 1923 in Indianapolis and they have three children: (1) Asa Ray (born March 2, 1943 in Indianapolis), (2) Mary Gladys (born March 6, 1946 in Indianapolis,) and (3) Denise Ann (born Jan. 18, 1955). All of whom live today in California.

Front: Verlis Derringer. Back: Walter and Wilbur Derringer.

Walter Asa learned his carpenter trade from Elmer Strode and pursued it until his retirement. They lived most of their lives in California. Walter served with the Navy in W.W. II as a carpenter's mate 2/c, 1942. He died in his "vacation home" on what is now known as Three Brothers Road, one and one-half miles north of Bean Blossom. Walter is buried in San Diego, CA. They have four grandchildren. Asa Ray has three children: (1) Terra Annette, (2) Shawna Marie, and (3) Daniel Asa. Mary Gladys married David Lawson and has one daughter, Sarah Delcina.

Wilbur A. was born on the home farm two miles east of Helmsburg on Railroad Road Jan. 13, 1924 and was taken to Boone, IA after the untimely death of his parents. After living there for 13 years and serving with the Army during W.W. II, he came back to live in the house he was born in in Brown Co., IN. He was married Oct. 30, 1949 and divorced after 28 years of marriage. He has a son Jerry Wayne, and a daughter, Doris Ann. He was a machine operator for Cummins Engine in Columbus for 31 years and is now retired. He has four grandchildren. Jerry Wayne Derringer (born Dec. 23, 1949 in Franklin, IN) and Jerry Douglas born Aug. 12, 1974 in Columbus, IN. Currently the family lives in Gnawbone.

Ray and Ruth Derringer

Wilbur's daughter, Doris Ann (born March 29, 1953 in Franklin, IN) married Gregory Brinegar, Dec. 29, 1972 and they have two children: Zachariah Daniel (born July 23, 1980 in Bloomington, IN) and Rachel Nicole (born June 21, 1987).

Verlis C. was born Sept. 12, 1926 and died Aug. 18, 1989. He was married to Marjorie Lawson on July 3, 1950. They spent their married life in the home where Marjorie still lives north of Bean Blossom on the Three Brothers Road. He was a machinist in Columbus, IN and served with the Air Force during W.W. II. They have four children: William, Mary Ruth, Margie, and Rebecca, all of whom live in Brown County. They were blessed with nine grandchildren. *Submitted by Wilbur A. Derringer*

DEWEES FAMILY

The DeWees forebears must have felt some urgency to "Go West, Young Man," for so it was that following the Revolutionary War early DeWees family members left the Philadelphia area and fanned out westward. Young Joseph DeWees (father of Joseph W. of this history) forsook Belmont County in Eastern Ohio for Zanesville, and his son Joseph W. left Zanesville to attend Purdue University and stayed on in the Hoosier State to marry Amelia Cherry of Greenfield.

DeWees graduated from Purdue in 1935 and worked as a forester in many of the State Forests during the depression years, when the Civilian Conservation Corps was in full swing. During this time he became acquainted with Brown County through friendship with a local Forestry School graduate, Glenn Allison.

The clouds of WWII were rapidly gathering. A year before Pearl Harbor, DeWees volunteered for duty with the fledgling Army Air Corps. His WWII experience included supply depot management. Eighteen months were spent with the 15th Air Force in Italy. After VJ Day Joe returned to the States, to Kelly Field, and was returned to reserve status and retired in 1971 as a Lt. Col. USAF.

Joe and Amelia DeWees

Joe and Amelia moved from Greenfield in 1947. He served from 1950 to 1975 in the Nashville Post

Office, retiring as postmaster. Upon settling in Brown County the DeWees family consisted of Joseph Eugene and Donald James, but in 1954 increased with the arrival of Dallas Daniel.

Amelia assisted Marianne Miller, Dick Jones, Gene Keller, among others from the PTA group in helping to build the Nashville School Cafeteria. Under the leadership of Bill Bessire and Evelyn Coffee and the expertise of teacher Virginia Weddle, Amelia and PTA members operated the first school cafeteria in Nashville.

Amelia helped Fort Joseph Koons in his drapery work, a home industry a few doors away on Road 46 East, and later assisted Mrs. Gene Wilson in her interior design business.

Keith and Nina Taggart introduced Amelia and Joe to square dancing and this has become an important part of their spare time activity. It has opened the way to very interesting travels - to Poland and Russia, arranged by Friendship Ambassadors, a people-to-people project of President Eisenhower, and to Europe one summer, the high point being a dance at an army base in beautiful Heidelberg, Germany. They have also attended dance conventions in many states.

Amelia and Joe's eldest son Eugene met with a tragic accident in 1984; his widow Marilyn (Snyder) DeWees lives at Route 2, Nashville, and has three children; Joe and family in Bedford, and Jim and Beth at home. Donald and Bette (Joyner) DeWees went West and live near Tacoma, WA and have three children, Angela, Bradley, and Casey. Dallas and Laurie (Joy) DeWees, daughter Haley, and stepson Corey Joy and family live near Nashville.

Joe is a member of the Lions Club. He and Amelia are charter members of the Brown County Historical Society. She served as president two years, and they both serve as docents in the museum complex during the summer. Joe is a member of the Central Trinity Methodist Church in Zanesville and Amelia is a member of the Nashville Christian Church. They celebrated their 54th wedding anniversary April 12, 1990.

SAMUEL DINE - Samuel's grandparents, John and Rachel (Cole) Dine had 14 children. John was born and raised in Hunterdon Co., NJ. Before his 17th birthday he served as a Minute Man in 1779. He fought in the Battle of Springfield, NJ in 1780. A detailed account of the fight is on record at the Court of Common Pleas October Term 1836 in Butler Co., OH. Rachel was born in South Carolina. They lived in Mercer Co., KY for five years, then moved near Middletown, OH, Butler County in 1805. Three of their sons, John Jr., Peter and Cornelius married in Ohio then moved to Decatur Co., IN in 1820. Peter and Cornelius moved on to Hensley Township, Johnson Co., IN a year later. Cornelius and family then moved to Hamblen Toenship, Brown County in 1822 where on 33 acres he farmed.

Cornelius and Rebecca (Tietsort) Dine had six children. Samuel was their third. Peter and Hannah (Tietsort) Dine had seven children. Rebecca and Hannah were sisters. Samuel married Mary Ann Pitcher, neighbor to the Peter Dine family. They had 11 children, and lived on the same 33 acres where he farmed and did blacksmithing. He served a gallant three years in the Union Army during 1862-65. Co. "D" 82nd Infantry Regiment, Indiana Volunteers was mostly Brown County men. Those from the Spearsville area were Corporal Jonathan Daniels, Wagoner Charles W. Hurd, and Privates Abram Canary, Samuel Dine, Peter Dine Jr., William N. Dine, John Hendry, William McDaniel, George Petro, Jacob F. Pitcher, William M. Raredon, Henry T. Walker, Jacob C. Walker and Jacob A. Wright. All were mustered in on Aug. 30, 1862. Samuel Dine was in battles in Kentucky and Tennessee in 1862 in the pursuit of Gen. Bragg; in Gen. Rosecran's campaign in Tennessee in 1863; against Chattanooga and in the "Battle in the Clouds" in 1863; against Atlanta and the pursuit of Gen. Hood in 1864; with Gen. Sherman's march to the sea in 1864, and through the Carolinas in 1865. Sgt. Sam Dine was in the Grand Review in Washington, D.C., and was mustered out at a Philadelphia Army Hospital on June 12, 1865. He resumed his farming and blacksmith work in Brown County.

In 1887, Sam Dine and several other local area men built the Spearsville Church of Christ. Sam died in 1901, and Mary Ann in 1919. Both are buried in the cemetery adjacent to the church he helped build. A grandson, John Herman Dine lives on a farm which includes the original 33 acres of Cornelius Dine. Retired, he spends a lot of time teaching the art of goldpanning to visitors. *Submitted by Arvilla (Dine) Kibler, granddaughter of Sam Dine*

KEITH DONALDSON FAMILY - Keith moved to Van Buren Township in Brown County in 1935 from Maywood, IL. His father, D.C. Donaldson and his mother, Vera (Edminston) Donaldson, were acquainted with Olive Cope of New Bellville and had visited with her several times. The scenic beauty and the general type farming influenced Keith to purchase the Donaldson Farm. Soon cooking on the wood cook stove and carrying water formed his daily routine.

Mail delivery from the Waymansville Post Office was delivered three days per week. Reading the daily newspaper offered quite a challenge to Keith with holidays and the muddy road conditions affecting the delivery.

Keith's friends always liked to get together on Thanksgiving Day and go rabbit hunting because the Donaldson Farm was so far out in the country that they always had to hunt towards town.

The Donaldson ancestors immigrated to the United States in 1847 from Ireland. William Donaldson, born in Scotland in 1795 moved to Ireland and married Susan Hendren in 1819 at Markethill in County Armagh, Ireland. They and their children settled in Buffalo, NY. Three of their sons, Oliver, John and William Hendren, later moved to the Chicago, IL area and founded the Donaldson Brothers Company. They specialized in shipsmithing and blacksmithing at the corner of N. Water and N. LaSalle Streets in Chicago. William Hendren's son, Daniel Batten of Maywood, IL was D.C.'s father.

1944 D.C. and Alan on 1936 Fordson Tractor cultipacking crop field on Keith Donaldson's Farm.

Following his retirement from Eastman Kodak and the death of Vera Donaldson, D.C. married Hildegarde Beck and they moved to Brown County. D.C. was a very talented landscape artist and photographer. Salt Creek and Lake Lemon were two of his favorite spots. Hildegarde enjoyed painting and made many of the trips with D.C. The Brown County Art Gallery Association became a reality with leadership from D.C. and other local artists.

Keith married Dorothy Schrougham of Brown County on May 8, 1937. The Schrougham family lived in Hamblen Township and later moved to Nashville. Keith and Dorothy had two children, Alan and Janet.

Alan graduated from Van Buren high school and received his Bachelor of Science Degree from Purdue University. Following his military service as an Officer in the U.S. Air Force, Alan has made a career with the Soil Conservation Service, USDA. Alan is married to Catherine Smith of Brown County and they have three children. Mark lives in Hendricks County and is married to Jane Roe. They have two children, Amanda and Daniel. Lynn lives in Tennessee and is married to Philip Adams. They have one son, Nicholas. Susan attends Van Buren elementary school.

Janet graduated from Nashville high school and received her Bachelors and Masters degrees from Indiana University. She is married to R. Philip Loy of Grant County. Janet has made teaching her career and she is now the Head of the Foreign Language Department at Taylor University. Their daughter Lisa attends Taylor University.

Following Dorothy's death in October 1961, Keith later married Kathryn Harvey in July 1963 and they reside on the Donaldson Farm. In addition to producing quality crops and forages, Keith has managed and produced high quality timber products and Christmas trees. He received a 25 year Tree Farm Award recently for his well managed woodland. Keith's keen interest in wood is demonstrated in his shop as he refinishes and restores antique furniture.

Keith has been very active in local politics. He served two terms as Trustee in Van Buren Township and County Commissioner. He was also County Chairman of the Democrat Party for eight years.

DOWELL, BERNIGER, VENABLE - Myrtle Iva Griffin, daughter of Irvin Griffin and Elizabeth Steinbarger, was born Jan. 3, 1905 in Brown County. She married Roy Dowell who was born Nov. 8, 1899 in Brown County and died Aug. 21, 1982 at Lafayette, IN and they had 13 children. (1) Helen Geneva, born Nov. 26, 1923, Brown County; (2) Thelma Ruth, born Aug. 16, 1925, Brown County; (3) Edna Mae, born Aug. 18, 1927, Benton County; (4) Mary Elizabeth, born Sept. 21, 1929, Tippecanoe County as were the following children; (5) Albert Lee, born Oct. 20, 1931; (6) Betty Lou, born Dec. 30, 1933, died March 7, 1935; (7) Delbert Roy, born Nov. 29, 1935; (8) Kathryn Louise, born July 15, 1939; (9) William Dale, born May 13, 1941, unmarried; (10) Carol Sue, born March 12, 1943; (11) Donald Wayne, born Jan. 24, 1945; (12) Linda Marie, born July 31, 1946; and (13) Judy Ann, born Sept. 28, 1947.

Helen Geneva Dowell, first child of Roy Dowell and Myrtle Iva Griffin, married Charles Paul Berniger who was born July 27, 1920. Their children were Charles Paul Berniger, Jr. who was born Feb. 25, 1944. Charles, Jr. and his wife, Rose, had children: Paul Brian Berniger, born Nov. 25, 1970 and Gina Marie, born July 18, 1975. Robert Owen Berniger, second child of Helen and Charles Berniger, was born March 3, 1948, married Jeann Ann Hawk, born July 17, 1948. Their children were: twin sons, Matthew Scott, born and died June 11, 1970 and Steven Wesley, died June 12, 1970; Amy Susan Berniger, born April 22, 1972; Zackaire R., born May 16, 1980; Grace Elizabeth Berniger, born Nov. 29, 1984. Michael Lee, third child of Helen and Charles Berniger, was born Feb. 5, 1954. He and his wife Ann had two children: Annabelle Lea Berniger, born October 2 and Ariel Noelle Berniger, born Dec. 29, 1985. Jeannie Elaine, youngest child of Helen and Charles Berniger, was born May 5, 1957. She married Larry Logsdon, born Dec. 26, 1948. Their child is Jessica Leigh Logsdon, born April 17, 1987.

Roy Dowell and Myrtle Griffin Dowell

Thelma Ruth Dowell, second child of Roy Dowell and Myrtle Iva Griffin, was born in Brown County on Aug. 16, 1925. She married Evertle Martin Venable, born June 10, 1925. They have daughters Joyce Eileen and Janet Marie. Joyce Eileen Venable, born Aug. 26, 1947, married Oral Eugene Flynn who was born May 28, 1947. They have two children: Regina Ann Flynn, born Aug. 14, 1967 and Wesley Arrin, born June 10, 1971. Regina Ann Flynn married Mark Vaughn, born April 1, 1969. They have twin daughters, Rebecca Ann and Rena Marie, born Dec. 31, 1988. Janet Marie Venable, born Oct. 8, 1952, married Jack Halsema, born Oct. 18, 1950. They have three daughters: Rissa Marie, born July 29, 1973 and twins, Angelo Rena and Andrea Lynn, born May 10, 1977. *Submitted by Helen Dowell Berniger*

DOWELL, CLOUSE, RITCHIE - Edna Mae Dowell, third child of Roy Dowell and Myrtle Iva Griffin, was born on Aug. 16, 1927 in Benton Co., IN. Her parents had left Brown County and with their two daughters, Helen and Thelma, had traveled by wagon to Lafayette where they farmed and made their home. Edna Mae married Donald Gordon Clouse, who was born April 8, 1927. They had three children: (1) Ronald Lee Clouse, born June 15, 1950, married Mary Richle. They had twins, Jamie and Jeremy, born Feb. 3, 1976 and two more sons, Christopher and Eric. (2) Steven Michael Clouse, born Feb. 15, 1954, married and has four children: Elisa, Rechelle, Jason and Amanda. (3) Debra Kay Clouse, born Jan. 3, 1957, married, has children, Megam Nicole, born Dec. 22, 1986 and Andrea Mae, born in August of 1988.

Mary Elizabeth Dowell, fourth child of Roy Dowell and Myrtle Iva Griffin, was born Sept. 21, 1929, Tippecanoe Co., IN. She married James Lemont Ritchie who was born Nov. 11, 1923. They had two children: (1) James Mark Ritchie, born Sept. 18, 1954. He married Terry Miller who was born April 7, 1957. They had two children: Heather Noelle Ritchie, born Dec. 5, 1974 and Stephanie Lynn Ritchie, born June 17, 1977. (2) Cathy Lynn Ritchie, born Jan. 16, 1956, married Ed Baumgard. They had three sons: Otis Allen Baumgard, born Dec. 28, 1973, Craig Baumgard, born Aug. 7, 1976 and Benton James Baumgard, born Nov. 5, 1982. Their father was killed in an accident.

Albert Lee Dowell, fifth child of Roy Dowell and Myrtle Iva Griffin, was born Oct. 30, 1931. He married Joan Alberta McKinney who was born Sept. 25, 1931. They had five children: (1) Danial Lee Dowell, born April 25, 1957, married Kristie White, born May 31, 1957; (2) Phyllis Joan Dowell, born Dec. 22, 1958; (3) John Edward Dowell, born Feb. 16, 1961, had child Meghan Lindsey Dowell, born Nov. 30, 1982 by his first wife. He married second to Amy Brooks. (4) Margaret Louise Dowell, born Sept. 21, 1962, married Todd Gish; (5) Nancy Eileen Dowell, born Feb. 5, 1964.

Delbert Roy Dowell, seventh child of Roy Dowell and Myrtle Iva Griffin, was born Nov. 29, 1935, Tippecanoe Co., IN. He married Mary Agnes Whilarant who was born Feb. 16, 1941. They had three children: (1) Michael Roy Dowell, born Sept. 5, 1960, married Julia Moore. They had a daughter, Nicole Marie, born July 15, 1985 and a son, Adam Roy, born Feb. 26, 1989. (2) Christina Ann Dowell, born Nov. 7, 1965. (3) David Wayne Dowell, born Oct. 31, 1967. *Submitted by Ronald Lee Clouse*

DOWELL, WRIGHT, NANGLE, BILYEU, RIDDLE - Kathryn Louise Dowell, eighth child of Roy Dowell and Myrtle Iva Griffin, was born July 15, 1939, married James Allen Wright, born Sept. 8, 1929. They have three children: 1. Jeffry Allen Wright, born March 31, 1957, married Jean Barker, born January 1959. They have three sons, Jarrad Max, born Feb. 5, 1981, Jedidiah Paul, born Sept. 11, 1983 and Jonas Dale, born May 18, 1986. 2. Kimberly Lynn Wright, born Jan. 23, 1961. 3. Kirk Lee Wright, born Sept. 17, 1963.

Carol Sue, tenth child of Roy Dowell and Myrtle Iva Griffin, was born on March 12, 1943. She married Arne Eugene Nangle who was born Sept. 9, 1942. They had three children: (1) Bradley Steven Nangle, born April 12, 1962; (2) Arlene Marie Nangle, born Sept. 9, 1964, married Kristen Jay Baldwin; (3) Tracy Jo Nangle was born Feb. 4, 1968.

Donald Wayne Dowell, 11th child of Roy Dowell and Myrtle Iva Griffin, married (1) to Nancy Reed Currian, born Oct. 14, 1947. Their children are Anthony Edward Dowell, born March 26, 1966, married on June 24, 1989 to Patricia Elizabeth Carter. Delissa Diann, second child of Donald and Nancy Dowell, was born March 28, 1968, died March 29, 1968. Denesia Deann, third child of Donald and Nancy Dowell, was born Aug. 15, 1969. Donald and Nancy Dowell divorced.

Linda Marie Dowell, 12th child of Roy Dowell and Myrtle Iva Griffin, was born July 31, 1946 in Brown County. She married Arthur George Stover Bilyeu, born March 13, 1944. They have three children: 1. Cynthia Lynn Bilyeu, born April 3, 1966, married David Joseph Badaszewki, born March 10, 1965. 2. Bryan Arthur Bilyeu, born Oct. 12, 1968, married Shari Lynn Hahn, born Jan. 2, 1970. 3. Roy Eugene Bilyeu, born Nov. 8, 1973.

Judy Ann Dowell, the 13th and youngest child of Roy Dowell and Myrtle Iva Griffin, married James Harold Riddle, born Dec. 20, 1946. They have three children: Jennifer Ann Riddle, born Sept. 27, 1970; Jill Susan Riddle, born May 24, 1972; Janae Leeann Riddle, born June 12, 1976. *Submitted by Brian Arthur Bilyeu*

DOWNEY FAMILY - The Downey family came from Ireland, Tyrone County. Joseph Downey (March 12, 1806-July 2, 1878, Brown County), lived at Zanesville, Noble Co., OH. He came to Indiana in 1861 with his son, Ephraim, two unmarried daughters and his wife, Jane Clark (Aug. 7, 1805-Jan. 25, 1881). They had two boys and six girls:

Seated: Joseph Alonzo, Ida May, Ephraim, Martha Elizabeth, Lucetta Jane, and Mary Alice Downey. Standing: William Otis, Elisha James, Ephraim Tracy, Nancy Minerva, Vincent O., John Wallace, Thomas Humphrey and Sarah Rebecca Downey.

1. Ephraim Downey (July 31, 1838-Feb. 6, 1917) married Martha Elizabeth Emenhizer (Sept. 23, 1843-Feb. 3, 1937) when she was age 16. Her father died when she was a child and she was raised by the Thomas Humphrey Downey family. Ephraim Downey married, second, to Rebecca Kinkade.

2. Benjamin A. Downey (Nov. 24, 1850-March 3, 1874) married Malissa "Massie" Cooper. They had one child who died in infancy.

3. Margaret; she and sisters, 4. Cloey Jane who married Wm. Jordan, then Elisha Piper on Dec. 12, 1861 and 7. Mary Downey, did not come to Indiana.

5. Nancy Downey married Edmond Falkinburg on Sept. 11, 1862, they divorced. Nancy then married George Watson.

6. Rebecca Downey married on Sept. 11, 1862 to Mahlon Ward, went to Kansas after 1870.

8. Eliza C. "Lide" Downey married on March 1, 1877 to Michael West, stayed in Brown County. Three of Joseph Downey's daughters went to Kansas with their families. Two daughters came to Indiana with their parents.

Ephraim Downey (1838-1917) son of Joseph Downey, was born in Noble Co., OH. His wife, Martha Elizabeth Emenhizer (1843-1937) was the daughter of a German father and Irish mother. Ephraim and Martha came to Brown County in 1861. They had 12 children.

1. Lucetta Jane Downey (Oct. 13, 1861-March 8, 1935), married Charles Miles Patterson (Sept. 25, 1860-1956, Franklin, IN).

2. Mary Alice Downey (March 21, 1864-Nov. 27, 1932), married John Moore, died March 11, 1895; married Robert Henry Henderson on April 9, 1903.

3. Nancy Minerva Downey (Nov. 25, 1866-Nov. 25, 1955), married Wm. Ohio Grant Moore (Feb. 5, 1865-May 13, 1942) on Dec. 30, 1886, Pleasant Valley, Brown County.

4. Ida May Downey (June 9, 1869-Jan. 3, 1971), married on Sept. 19, 1892 to John Trenner (Dec. 30, 1867, Noble Co., OH-June 4, 1956, Bison, SD).

5. Vincent Ofanbaugh Downey (Oct. 13, 1871-Oct. 15, 1965), married Jan. 22, 1896 to Rebecca Jane Parker (April 22, 1868-Dec. 9, 1945), both buried Christiansburg Cemetery.

6. Joseph Alonzo Downey (Feb. 8, 1874-March 22, 1914), married on April 18, 1904 to Myra Josephine Moore (July 17, 1884, Ohio-Feb. 13, 1924).

7. Elisha James Downey (April 22, 1876-Nov. 28, 1966), married on Aug. 20, 1901 to Rose Ettie Powell (born 1878-Dec. 6, 1908); married second, on Sept. 20, 1913 to Lydia Louise Floyd (Dec. 26, 1883-Sept. 24, 1974).

8. Sarah Rebecca Downey (April 20, 1878-Jan. 25, 1967), married on July 20, 1902 to Sanford Lee Taggart (Oct. 30, 1870-Feb. 14, 1926).

9. Ephraim Tracy Downey (Feb. 9, 1881-Jan. 1, 1964), married first, on Aug. 10, 1904 to Mabel Green who died April 11, 1923; married second, to Zoe Bacherd, June 13, 1926.

10. Thomas Humphrey Downey (March 11, 1883-March 23, 1966), married on Aug. 22, 1905 to Amanda Elizabeth Waltz.

11. John Wallace Downey (Dec. 25, 1885-June 21, 1972), married September 23, to Pearl G. Weigel (Nov. 26, 1893-July 5, 1966), both buried Milan, MI.

12. William Otis Downey (March 15, 1889-June 10, 1969), married first, on May 16, 1910 to Maude Elma Barker (Jan. 1, 1889-Sept. 28, 1914); married second, on June 13, 1916 to Pearl Maude Fisher.

Ephraim Downey and his wife, Martha Elizabeth had a farm of about 500 acres. One summer he had 40 acres of wheat to cut with a cradle scythe. He also was a fruit grower, preparing as many as 40 bushels of dried peaches in a week. Their flower gardens perfumed the air. The Downey family had many friends and was liked by everyone. Ephraim was a Justice of the Peace and many of his family of 12 children became teachers. (see ROBERT HENRY HENDERSON) *Submitted by Robert Ephraim Henderson*

EPHRAIM DOWNEY FAMILY

Ephraim, son of Joseph and Jane Clark Downey, was born in Noble Co., OH (1838). He came with his wife, Martha Elizabeth Emenhizer; a daughter, Lucetta Jane; his parents, a brother, Benjamin, and sisters, Nancy, Rebecca, and Eliza to the Mt. Liberty area of Brown County in late 1861.

Ephraim and Martha had 12 children. Daughter, Lucetta Jane, married Charles Miles Patterson (son of Samuel Patterson and Eliza Gable) Nov. 6, 1881. They had nine children — Oliver Tracy, Dora Jane, Jesse Wallace, Charles Roy, Louie Walton, Daisy, Ephraim Alphonso, Rosie Mae, and Alma Etta.

1st Row: Vincent, Nancy Minerva, Ephraim Downey, Martha Downey, Mary Alice. 2nd Row: William Otis, Lucetta Jane, James, Ida Mae, Sarah Rebecca, Joseph. 3rd Row: John Wallace, Tracy, Thomas.

Daughter, Mary Alice Downey, married John W. Moore (son of David Moore and Elizabeth Correll) Nov. 10, 1886. They had four children — James Worley, Harley Everett, Myrtie Ethel, and Joseph Nathaniel. She later married Robert Henry Henderson (son of William H. Henderson and Emmeline King), and had two sons, Robert Ephraim and Louis Frederick.

Daughter, Nancy Minerva Downey, married William Grant Moore (son of Nathaniel Moore and Sarah Anna Watson) Dec. 30, 1886. Six children were born to this union — Loretta, Harrison Hovey, Lester Ernest, Orville F., Lowell H., and William Dean.

Daughter, Ida Mae Downey, married John Trenner (son of Nathan Trenner and Mary Ellen VanDyke) Sept. 19, 1892. They had one son — Ephraim Trenner.

Son, Vincent Osbold Downey, married Rebecca Jane Parker (daughter of John Parker and Mary Moore) Jan. 22, 1896. They had eight children — James Otis, Martha Edith, Mary Elizabeth, infant, Effie May, Verna Opal, Herma Faye, and Leona Grace.

Son, Joseph Alonzo Downey, married Myra Josephine Moore (daughter of Jason Moore and Amelia Johns) April 18, 1904. They had five children — Ica Amelia, Ena Myrl, Kenneth Paul, Quay, and Joseph Alonzo, Jr. Ena Myrl Downey married Harry Foster Steele. They are the parents of Patricia Horton.

Son, Elisha James "Jim" Downey, married Rose Ettie Powell on Aug. 20, 1901. They had a daughter, Ethel. Jim later married Lydia Louise Floyd (daughter of Milton Jefferson Floyd and Mary C. Deist) Sept. 20, 1913, and had four children — Mae Catherine, Floyd B., Zola C., and Owen K.

Daughter, Sarah Rebecca Downey, married Sanford Lee Taggart (son of Thomas J. Taggert and Evaline S. Strahl) July 20, 1902. Three children were born to this union — Ruth, Earl and Orval Tracy.

Son, Ephraim Tracy Downey, married Mabel Green on Aug. 10, 1904. He later married Zoe Bacherd on June 13, 1926.

Son, Thomas Humphrey Downey, married Amanda Elizabeth Waltz (daughter of Harrison Waltz and Alice Royse) Aug. 22, 1905. They had two children — Raymond Ferrell and Cornelia Fern.

Son, John Wallace Downey, married Roxena Carmichael (daughter of John W. Carmichael and Manda Fleetwood) on Dec. 26, 1906. They had one son, Max Hoyt. John later married Pearl G. Weigel.

Son, William Otis Downey, married Maude Alma Barker (daughter of James Barker and Martha Rudolph) May 16, 1910. They had two children, Wanetta and Ferrell. His second marriage was to Pearl Maude Fisher on June 13, 1916, and they had two daughters, Thelma and Wilma Jean.

Ephraim and Martha Downey are buried in the New Bellsville Cemetery as are his parents. (see WILSON MOORE FAMILY) *Submitted by Patricia Horton, great-granddaughter of Ephraim Downey*

THE EICKLEBERRY FAMILY HISTORY

It is almost 150 years since the first of the Eickleberry clan came to Brown County; the exact date is shrouded in the fog that obscures so much of early family histories.

All that is known of George Eickleberry, the earliest known of the family, is that he was a bonded servant in Pennsylvania. His wife's name is unknown. Their son Martin was born in 1819 in Pennsylvania or Ohio. He married Catharine Truex (born in 1818 or 1819). They had eight known children: John, Julia Ann, Rebecca, Susanna, Henry, Silas Evan (called Ivan, rhymes with "driven"), Francis Marion, and George. Silas Evan and Rebecca Rambo were married here in Brown County in 1875; he was recorded as being born here in the county in 1854. They had five children: Catherine Elisabeth (Bess), (married name Rambo), James Daniel, Martha Ann (married Sprague), Mary Frances (Mollie), (married Stillabower), and Charles Hugh. Charles Hugh married Iva Bevins; their children were Roy, Carl, and Lorene (married Daniels). Carl's son Steven and his son Steven Jr. both live outside the county at the present. Roy had no children. James Daniel married Margaret Emma Hendershot and had three children: Hazel (married Settle), Ethel (married Truex), and James Ernest, who married Loretta Jearldine Williams. They had three children; Carol Kay (married Waggoner), Gary Ernest, and Peggy (married Sims).

Silas Evan and Rebecca Ann (Rambo) Eickleberry

Gary Ernest, a self-employed carpenter, is the only male Eickleberry living in Brown County at this time. In 1981 he married Christine Deprez, who is a quiltmaker; she has one daughter from a previous marriage. (Renee Carlson) Renee now has a daughter, Shannon Marie, born Dec. 9, 1989. Renee is married to Charles Hobson and they live on Seelmaer Hill.

In 1989, Gary and Chris bought property and built a home on 20 acres on Grandview Ridge. It's about one mile north of the original homeplace mentioned in an old family reunion notebook as where Silas and Rebecca "went to housekeeping" after their marriage in 1875.

As they have had no children together, this branch of the Eickleberry family may find it's end in the same area where it started so long ago. Hopefully this record will help to keep the memory of the name alive a little longer.

NOAH JOSEPH ELLIS FAMILY

The first generation of the Ellis family migrated from England into Virginia. Samuel Ellis was born in Ohio in 1815. His wife, Sarah was born in Ohio in 1818. Their son, Noah Joseph Ellis was born in Ohio, Dec. 19, 1839. Noah Joseph Ellis moved to Brown Co., IN and married Henrietta McCord on Feb. 26, 1863. They had five children, Grover Cleveland Ellis, (1884) Homer Ellis, Lydia Ellis Joliff, Barbara Ellis Hutchinson and Margaret Ellis Sleighter. Homer Ellis served in War I in France.

Noah Joseph Ellis homesteaded and bought several acres of land near Bean Blossom, IN in 1859. Noah was a man of great faith. His dream was to be able to give some of these properties to each of his children. This land was passed down through the generations.

Grover Cleveland Ellis married Easter Tracy in 1918. They had four children: Howard, Grover II, Noah Joseph II, and Elly. Howard served in World

War II (1941-1945) and was killed on Okinawa, Aug. 19, 1945. Grover II died at age 25 years, April 30, 1947.

In 1924 Grover and Easter Tracy Ellis moved across the road from the Noah Joseph Ellis properties to a log cabin. This property was called Ridgeview Orchard owned by J.L. Keach of Indianapolis, IN, and tended by Grover Ellis. He worked on this farm and raised apples, sheep, cows and cattle. Grover served as County Road Commissioner in Brown Co., IN. His work consisted of constructing gravel roads. He would work with iron drags and readied all the mud soil. The roads from Unity Church and the roads leading to Spearsville were graveled under the supervision of Grover Ellis. He spent his early years building the railroads in Helmsburg. He died in 1931 and left his widow, Easter Tracy Ellis (1889-1981) with four children to be raised. Easter, a great "pioneer woman," raised the family off the various crops produced on this land. Howard, Noah II, and Grover II would cut wood for the fireplace. At daybreak you would find Easter and her three sons in the wagon off to work in the fields. They would plow the fields and plant corn. In the evening there would be milking of cows, feeding chickens, canning fruit and vegetables. At this time, there were no electric light poles in Brown County. They would light a lantern and spend time finishing daily chores.

On Sundays the family attended the Spearsville Christian Church. It was through this fellowship the Ellis faith was kept alive. The old family Bible is 100 years old and Elly has this in Sarasota, FL.

Today Noah Joseph Ellis II owns 60 acres where the original log cabin was built. He dedicates his time and energy to this land. There is pride and great memories in being connected to Brown Co., IN. There is great concern for the environment and keeping our air pure.

Noah and Janet Mahan Ellis live in Indianapolis. They have five children: Mark Ellis, Nancy Ellis (Tatum), Matthew Ellis, Jim Kidwell and Jayna Kidwell. Their seven grandchildren are: Amy and Abby Tatum (twins), Joshua and Benjamin Tatum.

Mark Ellis and Joan (Field) Ellis have three children: Nichole, Alissa, and Mark II.

Manual High School and Perry Meridian High School, Indianapolis, IN have established a Noah J. Ellis Scholarship Foundation in honor of his services to athletics.

Elly Ellis lives in Sarasota, FL with her husband, Archibald McGilvery Mann. They have five children: Rehea, Jeffrey, Marcia, Donna (Wernet) and Kim. They have two grandsons, Scott and Brian Wernet.

Our hopes and dreams are to see Brown County remain a great example of pride for our Country. We should be the "leaders" for future generations in ecology and "caring for people."

"We have this treasure in earthen vessels, that the excellence of the power may be of God, and not of us." II Cor. 4:7. *Submitted by Elly Ellis Mann*

ENES-WALLS-NOBLITT - Frederick Enes, the son of Adam and Barbara Zinzer Enes, was born in 1828, in Manheim, located in what is now Germany. Jacob Wilhelm and Katherine Renner Bergdoll were the parents of a daughter, Saloma Bergdoll, who was born in Darmstadt, Province of Hanover, Germany. Both families migrated to America. The Enes family landed at New York City, in July, 1846, and then moved to Baltimore, MD, where they met the Bergdolls, who had just landed there. Thus, Frederick Enes and Saloma met, fell in love, and were married at the immigration depot on Feb. 2, 1854.

The Enes family, except for the newlyweds, moved to Dearborn Co., IN. The Bergdolls moved to Jackson Co., IN. Frederick and Saloma Enes joined a group of German-speaking pioneers and moved westward into the recently-opened government lands of Brown Co., IN, and settled near Christiansburg. Here they established their home, and by 1856, had cleared their lands for farming. Eight children were born here.

Charlene Noblitt Rockhold

On Aug. 30, 1862, Frederick Enes joined the army and served for almost three years, participating in more than 12 major battles, including General Sherman's march through Georgia. On June 9, 1865, he was discharged from the service at Washington, and started home. He travelled by train to Columbus, IN, and walked the last 16 miles to Christiansburg. After an absence of nearly three years without a furlough, it was no wonder that when his children saw a strange soldier coming up the long lane toward the house, they ran behind the house, screaming to their mother that a soldier was coming. The family dog, excited by the noise, ran to protect "his" family from the stranger, but his barking changed to yelps of joy, when he recognized his master's scent.

Frederick and Saloma Enes' fourth child was Lucy Anna, who, along with the rest of her family attended the Christiansburg Methodist Church. It was here that she met, fell in love with, and married Reverend Jacob Holmes Walls, the church pastor. Not long after their wedding in the Enes home, Jacob and his wife, Lucy Anna, moved to Orange Co., IN, where they established their permanent home near French Lick. Minnie Walls was the third child of the six born to this family. She grew up there in Orange County, and then attended the just-organized Indiana Central College in 1905, to prepare for a career in teaching. Her father was an itinerant preacher, who was a trustee of the new college, encouraged young people to attend the college. One of these was Loren S. Noblitt, who lived near Ogilville, in Bartholomew Co., IN. Thus, Loren S. Noblitt and Minnie Walls met and were married there at the college on June 25, 1908. The ceremony was performed by her father.

The author of this account, Charlene Noblitt Rockhold, is the daughter of the youngest child of Loren S. and Minnie Walls Noblitt, Charles Robert Noblitt. Thus, Charlene is the great-granddaughter of Lucy Anna Enes and Jacob Holmes Walls. The Rockholds live in Hamilton Co., IN, where she is a former teacher of elementary education, and continues to teach piano to many local pupils. She is also a graduate of Indiana Central College.

IAN ANDREW ENGLE - Ian is a fairly recent addition to Brown County. He was born in Louisville, KY, in 1959 to George Richard Engle and Jacquelyn Dyer Engle. The Engle Family had come into Floyd and Harrison Cos., IN, from the Rhineland Palatinate in the mid 1800s. The Dyer Family, from Somerset in England originally, came into Harrison County via Virginia and Kentucky.

George and Jacquelyn grew up within a few blocks of one another in New Albany, IN, and met when she was working at the public library. Needless to say, libraries were a big part of Ian's childhood. He and his two brothers, Nathan William and Christopher Blair, were raised for a short time in New Albany, but later moved into the country around Edwardsville, IN.

During high school, Ian played cello for the Floyd Central High School orchestra, the Louisville Youth Orchestra, and the Floyd County Youth Symphony. He also toyed with learning languages. It was at this time that he started working as a volunteer at his high school library.

Ian attended Indiana University, graduating with a B.A. in Near Eastern Languages and Literatures (Arabic concentration) and in History (Mediaeval concentration) in 1981, and with a Masters of Library Science in 1982. He worked for a year for IU, then moved back to New Albany to take the position of Head of the Technical Services Department at the New Albany-Floyd County Public Library. In 1989, he applied for and was hired as the Director of the Brown County Public Library and moved into the Hamilton residence up Jackson Branch Hollow.

Ian's interests include science fiction and fantasy literature (he dabbles in writing,) historical dancing, especially 15th and 16th century (he leads a troupe in Bloomington,) mediaeval history (he is the current president, or seneschal, of the Bloomington area branch of a mediaeval recreationist organization, the Society for Creative Anachronism, and a peer of the realm as a Master of the Laurel for his work in dance history in the same,) eating (he's a natural at Historical Society meetings,) and gossiping (that is after all what most of history is!) He still thinks that the Liars' Bench should have been on the cover of this book.

AMANDA JANE PARSLEY EVANS - "The **Best** fried chicken in the **World** and the **Highest** meringue you ever **Saw** on her cream pies - all fixed on an old wood stove that smoked and hissed; but she wouldn't let Papaw smoke in the house! Loved to fish, used an old cane pole and pie dough for bait. She raised her chickens and sold the eggs in Franklin to the grocery and the bakery; had flowers in her garden, liked pink, and crocheted. They never owned their own place - always rented. If you'd known Mandy like I did . . ."

Amanda Jane (1888-1959) was the daughter of Robert Newton (1862-1908) and Anna Waltman (1867-1906) PARSLEY; Hamblen Township farmers. Her father was the son of Columbus (1830-1914) and Elizabeth Chappel (1832-1871) Parsley. Her mother was the daughter of Hiram 'Mac' and Eliza Frownfelter Waltman; granddaughter of Michael Waltman (1808-1877) who came to this county from Maryland in 1837.

This Brown County farm girl known to her family and friends as Mandy was 18, eldest of nine children, when her mother died and age 20 when her father died after a farm accident. She worked hard and was devoted to her family. Mandy and Roscoe Evans were married for 50 years; resided in Johnson County and had one child; Frank Dale Evans (1913-1979); one grandchild John Dale Evans.

An annual summer pitch-in of Mandy, her brothers and sisters has grown and expanded into "The Parsley Reunion" held each July which welcomes all Parsley descendants. ("If you'd known Mandy like I did . . .") *Submitted by Katherine Evans*

THE EWERS FAMILY - David Ewers, Sr., born in 1828, married Clarissa Moore in Ohio. He died in 1855 and is buried in New Bellsville Cemetery in Van Buren Township, Brown County. It appears that after David died, Clarissa returned to Ohio and married John David Melott, a widower with nine children. John and Clarissa moved from Ohio to Brown Co., IN after 1861.

David and Clarissa Ewers had four children: (1) Mary Ellen Ewers (1846-1886); (2) William G. Ewers (1847-1932) went to Illinois but died in Columbus, IN and is buried in New Bellsville Cemetery, Brown County. There was a Billy Ewers Place on Hurricane, a small creek which enters Salt Creek halfway between Pikes Peak and New Bellsville. Its name came from a storm which went through in the 1880s and leveled all the trees up the hollow. (3) Benjamin E. Ewers (1851-1926) went to Oklahoma and is buried there at Pond Creek, Grant County. (4) David Ewers, Jr. was born July 26, 1855 at Pikes Peak and died Dec. 12, 1923 and is buried in Christiansburg Cemetery, Van Buren Township, Brown County. He was a big powerful man, and ran a sawmill. He married Sarah Margaret Haines on Jan. 27, 1875. She was born Aug. 14, 1859 in Ohio, a daughter of William and Martha Haines. William Haines died in the Civil War and his daughter Sarah never saw him. Her mother then married a Fravel. Sarah had a sister Mary and a brother Henry. She had a half sister Arlie Fravel Garnett and a half brother Tommy Fravel who was killed when a sawmill blew up at Pikes Peak. After the death of David Ewers, Jr., his widow, Sarah, married John T. Poland.

Front: Charley, Myrt, Ep, Martha, Ell and John Ewers. Back: Mag and Clara (all children of David and Sarah Ewers. George deceased.

David and Sarah Ewers had ten children: (1) John W. Ewers (Oct. 24, 1875-Dec. 10, 1960) lived at Ft. Wayne, IN, died New Mexico, had a son. (2) Sarah Margaret "Mag" Ewers (Aug. 2, 1877-Nov. 4, 1964) lived in Brown and Bartholomew Counties, married first to David Nickerson, married second to Bill Huffstutler, had three children. (3) Ella Ewers (Nov. 29, 1879-Dec. 19, 1962) lived at Christiansburg, married first to Will Nickerson, had four children, married second John Moore. (4) Eppie Ewers (March 13, 1882-July 15, 1971) lived at Richmond, IN, married Bill Cooper, had ten children. (5) George Ewers (Dec. 20, 1884-Dec. 29, 1932) lived in Brown and Owen Counties, married Barbara Estella Wilson, had seven children. (6) Charles E. Ewers (Jan. 29, 1887-Jan. 26, 1968), lived Chicago Heights, had two children. (7) Myrtle E. Ewers (June 13, 1889-May 20, 1978), lived Knox County, married first to Ed Hughes, had six children, married second Gabe Green. (8) Clara Alice Ewers (May 14, 1892-May 22, 1985), lived all her life in Brown County, married Otto Ping and had two children: B. Irene Ping Sluss, now of Harlingen, TX and Bryce D. Ping, now of Brownstown, IN. Bryce was reared on the old Melott Place on Poplar Grove Road, near the Melott Cemetery, in Van Buren Township. (9) Martha J. Ewers (Nov. 26, 1894-Nov. 21, 1984) married Dora Murphy, lived at Kurtz in Jackson County, had seven children. (10) Bryon D. Ewers (1897-1898). *Submitted by Bryce D. Ping*

JOSEPH FEARS FAMILY - Joseph and Frances Fears made their move to Brown County from Indianapolis in 1962, seeking a rural life style and the quiet beauty of the village and wooded hills. They brought with them their entourage of two dachshunds, two wily alley cats and granddaughter Cynthia, age 12.

Joe was a native of Terre Haute, IN, and, having received his education there, he did a short stint in the Marines before going to work as Quality Control Supervisor at Stewart-Warner Plant in Indianapolis during World War II. It was there he met Frances, who had joined the many women who were called upon to replace men in the war-related industries.

Frances was reared by her paternal grandparents, Frank and Etta Carlin, and lived all her life in Indianapolis, attending Shortridge High School and Butler University. When they married in 1947, Frances and Joe both had children by previous marriages — Mary Jo, Sandra and Joseph Fears, Jr., and Jacquelyn and Elizabeth Byerly.

Joe and Fran Fears, 1990

While Frances was researching the real estate possibilities in Brown County, she met Bill Gore and found both a home and employment in one day. She purchased the property on 135 N. from William and Hortense Gore consisting of some 99 acres of wooded valley and a house with a view. At the same time she went to work for Bill in his Real Estate Office at the Old Calvin House on Van Buren Street. Joe was a Methods and Standards Engineer at Allison's Division of General Motors in Indianapolis at that time and, although he swore he absolutely would **not** drive that 120-mile round trip to work each day, he soon found life on the ridge worth it and did so until he retired in 1977.

Joe and Fran opened a little shop called **Granny's Cranny** in the Franklin House complex and Joe played shopkeeper for the next two years. After the shop was sold, Andy Rogers, owner of the building, asked that Joe continue to go down every morning and keep the corner neat and clean. Joe loved doing this and looked forward to watching the village gradually awaken to each new day.

Their granddaughter, Cindy, graduated from Brown County High School and attended Indiana State at Terre Haute. She now lives in Florida and is employed as Decorator and Visual Merchandise Assistant in Sears Display Department. Her son, C.J. Roberts, considers himself a Brown Countian and moved back to the County at age 12 to live with Joe and Fran. He graduated from Brown County High School and lives on 135 N. while attending Indiana University.

Both Fran and Joe were actively interested in all aspects of living in Brown County. Joe is a member of the Lions Club, a Past Master of the Masonic Lodge and is a member of the Brown County Humane Society. Fran continued to work in Real Estate and after Bill Gore retired she and Frank Russo joined forces in June, 1970, to form the Hills O'Brown Realty. She is a member and Past President of the Brown County Business and Professional Women's Club, a member of League of Women Voters, Audubon Society, Brown County Republican Women's Club, Brown County Art Guild and, along with Alice Weaver and Florence Bradley, began work in 1964 to establish a Humane Society in Brown County. She grew to know and love the native Brown Countians, the rural back roads, native wild-life and general character of the real, everyday life of the County while researching material for the booklet "Tales and Trails" published in 1965 by the Business and Professional Women's Club of Brown County.

Joe and Fran now spend most of the year in Naples, FL, but retain residency at their little house on 135 N. where they return often to see old friends and commune with Nature — they know home is where the heart is.

MARIE AND STANLEY FISHEL - Josephine Marie Merriman was born on April 20, 1944, the ninth child of Hallie Fleener and Clarence Merriman, in Morgan County. She graduated with high honors from Brown County High School in 1962 and thereafter found clerical work in Indianapolis before marrying David Stanley Fishel on July 4, 1964.

Ruth and David Fishel with Stanley, 1942

Stanley was born in Brown County on Sept. 29, 1942 to David Nelson Fishel and Ruth Mae Long who live at Fruitdale. The Fishel family dates back to Johannes Fischel who was born May 12, 1703, and came from Germany on the ship *Loyal Judith* to York, PA. He married Maria Elizabeth Schmidt in Eisenheim, Germany. His son John Adam Fischel lived in North Carolina and his grandson Henry Fishel Jr., who was born in North Carolina in 1810, came to Indiana before 1825, settling in Johnson County before 1860. He married Theresa Eliza Hollandbeck. Henry's son Jacob Fishel was born Nov. 9, 1842 and married Eliza Catherine Fleener.

Henry's brother Christopher had a farm three miles north of Trevlac and was of the first men in this area to become interested in fruit growing. He had a good orchard. It was through his interest in fruit growing that the present Hickory Hill Orchard had its origins. Henry's son Nelson Bonaparte Fischel was born Jan. 24, 1868 and married Catherine Fleener, a daughter of Abraham Fleener, Jr., who was the late Ray Fleener's grandfather. Nelson's son Leonard Edwin was born Oct. 26, 1891 and married Opal Fleener, a daughter of Michael Fleener of Unionville. They lived on the acreage where Marie and Stan now have their home. Leonard and Opal were the parents of David Nelson.

Ruth Mae Long Fishel is the daughter of William Sherman Long born in 1883 and Sarah Kelly. William Sherman Long's father was William Long and he married Elizabeth Ann Marcum.

Stanley served in the U.S. Army from 1960-1963 and has been a Maintenance Supervisor for International Harvester Co. (now NAVISTAR) for many years. Stan and Marie built their home on N. Shore Drive in the 1970s. Marie is presently employed as a school bus driver for handicapped children. They are members of the Word of Life Tabernacle Church. They have two children.

Stephanie Ann was born Jan. 5, 1965 in Marion County, graduated Brown County High School and Indiana Bible College. After high school, Stephanie spent two months studying in France while living with a French family. She married Joseph Aaron Sanders, son of Rev. and Mrs. David M. Sanders, on Aug. 17, 1985. They live in Indianapolis and have two children: Joseph Aaron born Nov. 11, 1986 and Megan Desiree born Aug. 13, 1989.

Stan and Marie Fishel with Stephanie, 1965

David Michael was born in Marion County on June 17, 1967. In 1985 he graduated from Brown County High School and is now serving in the U.S. Army in Korea as a radar technician.

AARON F. FLEENER FAMILY - According to our family stories either Aaron F. Fleener or his forefathers served in the Federal Militia, Revolutionary War. In exchange for their service in the Militia they were given land grants to settle in the Indiana Territory.

Aaron arrived in Brown County in the early 1820s. He purchased property along Bear Creek in 1833.

On Oct. 8, 1829 Aaron married Mary Ann Weddle. They had eight children. One son was James Addison Fleener (Add). Add was born Jan. 27, 1837.

Mary Ann died in 1847 and Aaron married Frances Waggoner and had six more children. Aaron died in 1848 and is buried a short way from Possom Trot Road. The grave is marked by field stones. It is unknown where Mary is buried.

James Addison Fleener (Add) married Nancy McLary May 5, 1859. Nancy McLarys' family lived in the Bear Creek Area.

Left to Right: Nancy McLary Fleener, James Addison Fleener (Add), Mrs. Sam McLary, Sam McLary, Nancy's brother - late 1870s.

CIVIL WAR.....Our family supported the South. Add's brother killed a Union Soldier at Needmore and disappeared. Add and Nancy searched and found him in Kansas. On Feb. 12, 1860 near Joplin, MO Jacob Fleener was born. They returned to Bear Creek to settle just North of Waycross. There they had three more children. Add and Nancy are buried at Bear Creek Cemetery.

Jacob Fleener married Mary Agnes Archer June 4, 1879. They lived in the "Old VanCamp House" located where Yellowwood Trail crosses Bear Creek Road, on the east side.

On July 7, 1880 Jacob and Mary had Edward Wilson Fleener (Wilson). They had seven other children here. Jacob and Mary are buried at Bear Creek Cemetery.

Wilson Fleener married Martha May Reichard March 24, 1901. Martha's family was from Trevlac. Martha's brother, Archibald Reichard married Wilson's sister, Nancy Fleener.

Wilson and Martha made their home northwest of Bear Creek Lake. There they had five children. Four died at birth, including a set of twins; the only exception was Melva Agnes Fleener.

In 1910 Wilson and Martha moved from Bear Creek to Johnson County. On April 28, 1913 Woodrow Wilson Fleener was born. On July 28, 1915, Lester Edward (Mutt) and Esther Ermina Fleener were born, twins. Carey William Fleener was born Feb. 27, 1921. Wilson and Martha are buried at Bear Creek Cemetery.

Woodrow married Mable Eutha Zook July 9, 1935. Woodrow's brother Lester married Mable's sister, Florence Zook.

In 1944 Woodrow and Mable bought where they now reside on Red Bud Lane, Martinsville, Jackson Township, Morgan County, two ridges north of Carmel Ridge. There they raised six children: Richard Lee Fleener, Betty Jane Fleener Asher, Thomas Wilson Fleener, Sr. (Tom), Harry Addison Fleener, Barbara Kay Fleener Denniston and Peggy Jo Fleener.

Woodrow and Mable have 15 grandchildren. Only four bear the name FLEENER to carry it on; Thomas Wilson Jr. (Tom), Paul Matthew (Matt), Daniel Harry and Adam Richard. Woodrow and Mable have three great-grandchildren, but Tom Jr. and wife are expecting the first to be named FLEENER. *Submitted by Peggy Jo Fleener*

FREDERICK FLEENER FAMILY - Frederick was born on Sept. 5, 1821 in Washington County. His parents were Nicholas and Nancy (Johnson) Fleener. About 1824 the family moved to Monroe County where they put together a large farm. Frederick married Angeline Kelly of Kentucky on March 15, 1841 and started farming 80 acres in Jackson Township, Brown County. Frederick and Angeline had eight children, all born in Brown County: Milton (1841), James (1843), Nancy (1845), Martha (1848), Sarah Margaret (1850), Mary (1852), Alexander (1855), and Julia Frances (1857).

Frederick died in late 1859 and Joseph N. Fleener was appointed guardian of the children. Nancy married Wallace Norman and lived her life in Morgan County. Frederick's great-great-grandmother, Sarah Margaret married John Wesley Rinker in 1869 and raised four children in Morgan County. Mary married Mr. Swift and lived in Harrison County. Julia married William Dix and lived in Illinois. *Submitted by Larry W. Vehorn*

GEORGE R. FLEENER HISTORY - George R. and Anna Campbell Fleener were married on June 4, 1922 and lived most of their married life on a 20-acre farm just east of Trevlac on State Road 45 along the railroad. Ray and Anna were teachers and taught in several schools in Jackson Township, Brown Co., IN.

Ray provided for his family through the depression years by teaching, raising farm animals, making large gardens, and taking outside jobs. He helped build Camp Atterbury when WWII came along. One summer he worked at Crane Naval Depot. He made chicken feed with his large grinder for neighboring farmers. When a WWI Bonus was given to those veterans Ray built a nice barn with his $500.00.

Ray and Anna both taught school. Anna went back to teaching when there was a teacher shortage because of WWII. Later they went to Indiana University to get more education. Ray taught 44 years and Anna taught 19 years in Brown County schools. Ray received a BS Degree from IU in 1952 and a MS Degree in 1954. He was given a "Teacher of the Century" honor in 1985 from Brown County School Corporation. Ray contributed many articles to the book **Brown County Remembers.** Many articles have been written about him in newspapers and magazines. *Indianapolis Magazine,* November 1987 features two pages in color of him on his Trevlac farm.

Ray and Anna had five daughters. Alice, the oldest, was born at Trevlac in 1925. She graduated from Helmsburg High School, attended Franklin College and received a BS and MS degree from Indiana University in 1965 and 1968. She married in 1946 Dale Smith, 1921-1969, and they had four children: Brenda Joyce, born 1947; Cynthia Ann, born 1949; Kevin Dale, born 1953; Timothy Ocle, born 1960. Alice married W. Dale Parmerlee on April 21, 1990. She taught school at Morgantown and Indian Creek, Johnson County, for twenty-one and a half years.

1st row: Wilma Fleener, Anna E. (Campbell), Fleener, George R. Fleener, Alice Fleener. 2nd Carol, Virginia, Marjorie Fleener

Brenda, oldest daughter of Alice and Dale Smith, graduated from Morgantown High School, Morgan County and Indiana University. She taught in the Morgantown Elementary School. Brenda married Eugene Hill in 1968, and they had three children: Jason, born 1973; Jeremy, born 1975; and Elizabeth Ann, born 1978.

Cynthia graduated from Morgantown High School. She married Robert Betts. They had one son, Robert Dale, born 1972. Cynthia married Steve Pottorff in 1978.

Kevin graduated from Indian Creek High School. He married Yvonne Ellis in 1975. Timothy, youngest son of Alice Fleener and Dale Smith, graduated from Indian Creek High School, attended Indiana State University, and Heritage Baptist University. He married LuAnn Whetstine in 1980, and they have one daughter, Julie Elizabeth, born July 18, 1988. LuAnn and Julie are tenth and 11th generation descendants of Job Hamblen.

Marjorie, second daughter of Ray and Anna Fleener, was born in 1927. She also graduated from Helmsburg High School. She married Guy L. Fleener in 1948, and they had two children: Norman A. born 1951 and Linda C. born 1954.

Wilma, third daughter, born 1929, graduated from Helmsburg High School and married first Lawrence Parker in 1948. They had two children: Connie Ann born 1951 and Larry Lee born 1949. Wilma married second Neil Gilliam.

Carol, fourth daughter of Ray and Anna, was born in 1931. She graduated from Helmsburg. She married Richard McCracken in 1951. They had three children: Ronna Kay born 1952, Richard Ray born 1955, Robert A. born 1957.

Virginia, youngest daughter of Ray and Anna, born 1932, married James Dale Moore in 1951. Her family story appears on another page of this book. *Submitted by Alice (Fleener) Smith-Parmerlee*

JOHN FLEENER - The pioneer grandfather of most of the southern Indiana Fleeners was John Fleener born 1769-1853, who came to Indiana from Washington Co., VA, where he had married Elizabeth Hensley. They settled near Salem, IN where they raised eight children.

One son Jacob, 1803-1865, came here and lived in northern Jackson Township. Another son Abraham, Sr., 1786-1874, married Nancy Greene and stayed in Washington Co., IN. Abraham, Sr., had a son named Abraham, Jr., 1819-1897, nicknamed "Crocket Abe", who obtained land from the government and farmed on the present site of Lake Lemon in Jackson Township, Brown County.

Abraham, Jr., married Sarah Jane Alexander (1830-1899) on Sept. 30, 1846. "Crocket Abe" and Sarah Jane had 11 children. Nancy Jane (1848-1918) married Wm. Spriggs. James A. (1850-1925) married Rosanna Weddle, April 5, 1874. He knew she was dying when they were married. She did live until Sept. 22, 1874. James A. then married Permelia Thompson on April 20, 1879 in Monroe County. Alexander (1855-1948) married Margaret Masters. William T. (1858-1912) married Sarah Isabelle Stout (1861-1926). Mary Elizabeth (1862) married Albert Mann (Wm.). Sarah A.M. (1866) married Kelly. Andrew Jackson (1863-1929) married Nan Huckleberry. "Lanny" (1869-1936) married Rebecca McClary. Catherine (1871-1929) married Nelson Fishel. Martha Ellen (1873-1920) married John McGown. George married Gabriella Robertson and moved west early in life. *Submitted by Alice M. Parmerlee*

WILLIAM T. FLEENER - The father of the late George R. Fleener of Trevlac was William T. Fleener, one of Abraham "Crocket Abe's" sons. Geo. R. remembered his grandfather having gray hair and a beard. Geo. R. "Ray" was only four years old when "Crocket Abe" died.

Abe's will designated his great-grandchildren as his heirs after his wife's needs were met. His wife survived him and passed the property on to their children. Most of the children sold their shares except one son, Lanny Fleener. Finally as the years went by some of Abe's great-grandchildren did benefit from his land because they lived on it and sold lots on the North Shore of Lake Lemon in Jackson Township, Brown County.

Fred, William and Sarah (parents), Janie Fleener

William T. and Sarah Isabelle Stout (1861-1926) lived on part of the old homestead and raised seven children to adulthood. Fredrick (1885-1946) married first Mary Polley and second Christine Canary. Martha Jane "Janie" (1887-1945) married James Mann. George Raymond (1893-1989) married Anna Elizabeth Campbell (1896-1982). Leo L. (1896-1963) married Ruby Campbell (1897-1980), a sister to Anna. Minnie (1898-1981) married Otis Richards (1896-1970). Emma (1901-1963) married William Richards (1901-1959), a brother to Otis. Anna (1904-1989) married Thurl Warford (1905-1957). The nearly 250 descendants of William and Sarah Fleener are scattered over the United States with some as far away as Alaska.

George R. and Anna Campbell Fleener were married on June 4, 1922 and lived most of their married life on a 20-acre farm just east of Trevlac on State Road 45 along the railroad. Ray and Anna were teachers and taught in several schools in Jackson Township, Brown Co., IN. *Submitted by Alice (Fleener) Smith-Parmerlee*

CHESTER AND MAXINE (CARMICHAEL) FLEETWOOD - Chester's great-great-great-grandfather was Isaac Fleetwood, and their family has documentation that he served in the Revolutionary War under General George Washington. His grandson, General James, was a Civil War veteran who had two children before his death in 1867. His son, Solomon Fleetwood, was Chester's grandfather. He and his wife Sarah lived around Elkinsville from the time of their marriage in 1878 until their deaths between 1937 and 1944. They raised ten children, one of whom was Chester's father, Richard Howard Fleetwood. He was born in 1891, and married Chester's mother, Sharlot Wilkerson, in 1917. Chester's mom and dad moved to LaSalle Co., Ottawa, IL, shortly after their marriage, and that's where Chester was born. Around 1930, they moved back to Brown County near Elkinsville, to buy his mother's parents' farm. That is where Chester was raised until he married later on.

Howard and Sharlot (Wilkerson) Fleetwood

Chester's mother, Sharlot Wilkerson, was the great-granddaughter of James Wilkerson, born around 1821. Her grandfather was William Riley, born in 1853, whose wife was Hulda Stogdill. Sharlot's father and mother were Isom Wilkerson and Sally Arwine, whose farm Chester's parents bought around 1930.

Chloie Marie (Pruitt) and Icel Zelmer Carmichael, 1923

Chester's family lived on and worked the farm on Elkinsville Road until Chester's marriage to Maxine Carmichael in 1941. He served in World War II in the Navy on board the destroyer, *U.S.S. Anthony* in the South Pacific. He served as president of the union for three terms at Cummins Engine Co., Columbus, IN, and retired in 1982. Chester and Maxine live in the house her father and Chester built in the early 1950s. Brown County has always been his home.

Maxine and Chester Fleetwood

The ancestors on Maxine's mother's side trace back to Archibald Pruitt, who was a Revolutionary War soldier from North Carolina. Six of his grandsons were soldiers in the Civil War. Samuel Richard Pruitt was Maxine's grandfather; he married her grandmother, Florence Emma (Helms) Cross in 1899. They had Maxine's mother, Chloie Marie, in 1901. Chloie married Maxine's father, Icel Carmichael, in 1922. Maxine's father was the great-grandson of Thomas and Elizabeth (Holts) Carmichael who moved to Brown County to farm somewhere between 1840-1850. Their son, Robert Carmichael, was born in 1824, and married Hannah

Powell in 1851. The home that they lived in is still standing and occupied on St. Rd. 135 South. One of his sons, Otto Kenny, was Maxine's grandfather. He married Clara Alice Barker in Becks Grove in 1894. The home where they raised their family is also still standing and occupied on Elkinsville Road, just south of Story. Maxine's father, Icel, was born in that house in 1896. When he married Chloie, they moved to Story to the white house on the hill (Dr. Story's house) where Maxine was born in 1924. Maxine's parents farmed, and she had a pleasant childhood in the same area where most of her ancestors were raised. Her father drove a surrey with fringe on top to collect the children for school. She used to ride with him long before she ever attended the Story School. Maxine married the boy down the road, Chester Fleetwood. They settled in their home on St. Rd. 46 and raised their two children there, Patti and Ron. Patti lives in Brown County in Annandale Estates, and Ron, his wife, Becky, (Rejko) and their two children, Joshua and Jenny, live on the farm where Chester was raised. Submitted by Becky Fleetwood

RON AND BECKY (REJKO) FLEETWOOD -
Ron was born in 1949 in Brown County to Chester and Maxine Fleetwood. He attended Brown County High School where he met his future wife, Becky Rejko. Working in auto mechanics has always been his favorite thing. He raced a dirt bike for awhile and always wished he could get into auto racing. Ron married Becky in 1973, and they moved to Williamsburg, VA, the next year. Their son, Joshua, was born there. Ron worked as a mechanic on heavy equipment. They moved then to London, OH, where their daughter, Jenny, was born. Ron was working for a Cummins' Distributor there. Then he was transferred to Fenton, MI, where he worked for Cummins Engine Co. as a technical representative at General Motors Truck and Coach. They moved back to Brown County in 1981, where Ron began working at Cummins in Columbus. He still does mechanical work on the side because it's something he enjoys doing.

Front: Joshua, Becky, Jenny. Back: Ron Fleetwood

Becky (Rejko) Fleetwood was born in Wanamaker, IN, in 1949 to Paul and Wanda Rejko. The family moved to Brown County her freshman year in high school. There she met her future husband, Ron Fleetwood. After high school, Becky attended Beauty School in Indianapolis, IN. The next year she left for college in Statesboro, GA. After one year, she came home and worked a year before going to Tennessee Temple College in Chattanooga, TN, for the next three years. The next summer, 1973, Becky married Ron, and they lived in a log cabin in Brown County. They left the county for seven years and returned with their two children to buy Ron's grandparents' farm on Elkinsville Road. Their children are the fifth generation to live here.

They've named the place "The Old Homestead". Becky teaches their children, Joshua and Jenny, at home. They're on their ninth year of school now and have found it to be a very rewarding experience. The family is very active in the Parkview Church of the Nazarene, and they count it a blessing from God to live in such a loving community. Brown County will always be home to her, and its history is now intermingled with that of her family forever. Submitted by Becky Fleetwood

DEMPSEY D. AND EDELL R. (MOORE) FORD -
Uriah Ford, the patriarch of the Fords across America, was born in Hunterstown near Gettysburg, PA, in 1821 to Alexander and Susanna Ford. Uriah's father was a shoemaker by trade, but he was a generation which time forgot—little known data. Uriah married Catharine Schisler in 1845 and moved to Belmont Co., OH.

A few years and several children later, Uriah and Catharine, Evelyn M. Ford Thrall's great-grandparents, migrated westward across the Ohio wilderness in a covered wagon, a lantern in their hand, on the way to Kansas. Near Indianapolis, IN they heard rumors of Indian uprisings and feared venturing further into dangerous and unknown territory. They decided to "settle in" along Salt Creek in Hamblen Township among the Brown County hills about 1855.

Uriah sired 16 children, but only ten survived to adulthood. The ten children who survived were Henry, Nelson, Ezekial, Dempsey U., Grant, Joseph, James, Ammsey, Lavinia and Jane. They were a prolific family, and hundreds of Fords are descendents of those ten children.

The Fords had their own personal history of love, joy, tragedy and sorrow, living life to the fullest. From humble beginnings they raised families, tilled the soil, and lived out their lives as farmers, blacksmiths, sawmill workers and carpenters.

Uriah and Catharine Schisler Ford

Uriah was a Civil War soldier, and many of his descendents have dedicated their lives to their country and died on the battlefields. Each marched to the beat of a different drummer.

Evelyn's grandfather, Ezekial Bundy Ford, married Mosena Alice Admire. They lived most of their lifetime in Hamblen Township. Thirteen children were born to them.

Evelyn's father, Dempsey D. Ford, was born on the family homestead near Sprunica in 1891. He married Edell Rachel Moore in 1920, and to them were born six children: Thurston Dempsey, Morris, Hilbert Ezekial, Richard, Norman, and Evelyn Ford Thrall. The firstborn child, Thurston Dempsey, died as an infant. Morris was killed at St. Lo, France, during World War II at the age of 19.

Dempsey Ford loved the land of his birthplace very much. He traveled through almost every state in the Union. He was once nominated Republican candidate for sheriff of Brown County, but was defeated in the political race because the county was almost entirely Democrat.

Dempsey was a World War I soldier. He was a carpenter and woodworker by trade. He treasured Indian artifacts, Indianhead pennies, arrowheads, and totem poles. When Brown County hills beckoned he returned to meander down dusty roads and wooded hills of his childhood. He knew the hills, and he knew the people well. Oftentimes by happenchance when Evelyn meets a stranger in Brown County they will say, "Who are you kin to?" When she says Dempsey D. Ford, they will always know and remember as they go backward in time recalling days of yore and memories past.

Life is summed into seven words, "We are born, we live, we die." Each generation in its own time will continue the legacy of our Ford Family heritage. Submitted by Evelyn M. (Ford) Thrall

SAMUEL FORDYCE -
Samuel Fordyce was born March, 1818 in the Carolinas, and died in 1900 at age 82. His daughter was Cinderella Fordyce, born Sept. 25, 1840 and died July 24, 1920 in Brown County. She married Wm. P. Slevin, born October 1834 in W. Virginia. He died October 1922, also in Brown County.

Their children were: Anna Slevin (Teague), Will, Marietta (Moser), Myrtle (McLvaine), Cora (Parsley), Ed and Sam Slevin.

Anna Slevin was married to Wm. Beauregard (named after a Southern general in the civil war) Teague on April 11, 1885 in Brown County. He was born Dec. 15, 1861 and died Feb. 10, 1928 in Brown County and was buried at Zion Cemetery in Brown County. His father was from North Carolina, and his mother was Sarah Fleener Teague Anderson.

Anna and Wm. Beauregard had four children: Cinderella (Porter), Clifford, Roy and Sarah 'Sally' (Porter). Wm. B. took his family, from the Sprunica area, east of the school house, and went to Texas in a covered wagon to work on the railroads with Sam Fordyce. There are two small towns in Texas named Fordyce and Sam Fordyce. Sam Fordyce was a boss on the railroad. Audrey Fay was born there in 1903. Cinderella helped her relatives cook in the cook's car for the railroad hands at a very young age. From there they went to North Dakota to homestead. Thelma Anna was born there in 1907.

They became acquainted with the Porters from Iowa there, and Cinderella and Will Rae Porter, also Sarah 'Sally' and John Henry Porter were married in North Dakota.

Will Rae Porter died May 11, 1957 and was buried at Washington Park in Indianapolis. Cinderella Teague Porter died Sept. 24, 1969 and was buried at Bean Blossom cemetery in Brown County. *Written by Mary Derringer Porter*

FOREMAN/SKIRVIN -
Emma Jane Foreman was born in Brown Co., IN, on Feb. 23, 1883. She was a daughter of Aaron L. Foreman and Sarah Ellen Kinsey. Other children of Aaron and Sarah Foreman were Myrtle A. Foreman, who married Harley Shepherd; Charles W. Foreman, who married Rhoda Parsley and Ida May Foreman, who married Ora Johnson.

Emma Jane Foreman married Samuel Alva Skirvin in Monroe Co., IN on Nov. 29, 1904. After their marriage they lived in several small towns, including Stinesville and Jasonville, where Samuel worked in the stone quarries. Emma Jane and Samuel A. Skirvin had eight children: (1) Frances Olive, died at age three months; (2) Clovis Quentin (born July 12, 1906) married Goldie Daniels; (3) Charles Sylvester (born Aug. 19, 1907) married Myrtle McCarty; (4) Lola Mae (born Sept. 1, 1908) married Harley Hamm on Nov. 24, 1928; (5) Lucille Madeline (born March 18, 1911) married first to Robert Bault, married second to Bernard Herrin; (6) James Winfred (born Feb. 2, 1918) married in Deland, FL, to Joan Deckard; (7) Elofa Irene (July 7, 1915-Nov. 10, 1926); (8) Pauline Alvina, who died as an infant.

Aaron Foreman and family homeplace near Story, IN

Emma Jane Foreman Skirvin lost her husband in a quarry accident on Sept. 10, 1929. She remained in Bloomington where she raised her children by herself. To earn income she cleaned homes for others and always raised a garden and canned food to feed her family. She was a member of the Church of Christ. Emma Skirvin died on Christmas Day of 1971.

Emma's parents lived and died in Brown County. Her father, Aaron L. Foreman, born in Brown County in 1857, died Jan. 10, 1928. Her mother, Sarah Ellen (Kinsey) Foreman, died Dec. 14, 1949. Both are buried in Duncan Cemetery in Brown County. *Submitted by Dorothy Hamm (Mrs. James W. Hamm)*

FOX FAMILY - "Jonathan Fox was the founder of this family in Brown County. He came from Kentucky, where he was born and raised. His wife was Fanny Clark. Their children were: John, born April 16, 1811, Nancy, Samuel, Joseph, Isaac and Uriah, all born in Kentucky. His wife died there.

"He moved his children to Lawrence Co., IN, where he married Martha (Hutson) Porter, a widow. She had come from Kentucky and also had children: Henry, Mary, Vicey, Violet and Elizabeth. They moved with their children, to Big Salt Creek, Washington Township, Brown County, where he entered land (Sect. 14, Twp. 9, R3E) 1831, where they resided until their death.

"Of the Fox children: John married Eliza (Louiza) Pike and had children, Fanny, Philip, Joseph, William, Samuel, Jane, Thomas, Lewis, John, Mary, Ira and Emma. Nancy married John King, lived Washington Township, Brown County and had eight children..." (**The Hamblen and Allied Families** by A. Porter Hamblen)

John Fox and Louiza Pike had the following children: Fanny, married Robert Hamblen; Philip; Joseph; William; Samuel; Sarah Jane (Janie), married John Hedger; Thomas, married Eunice Arbell (Bell) Hoover; Lewis, married Jenny Gates; Mary, married Isaac Pruitt; Ira, died as infant; Emma, married George Rainwater; John Wesley, married Laura L. Brown, daughter of James Brown and Mary Reeves. James Brown was the son of Jesse and Mary (Polly) Brown.

John Wesley Fox, born Sept. 16, 1861, died Jan. 21, 1951, and Laura Luedillie Brown, born May 5, 1874, died April 17, 1944, had 14 children. James O., born April 1892, died 1976, married Mable Bolton. Sarepta Olive, born 1893, died 1980, married first Wheeler Smith, married second Gilber Riggs. Isaac, born November 1895, died 1985, married first Edith Walker, married second Dorothy Poole. Dillard, born 1898, died 1970, married Lena Ellen Riley. Willard born 1902, died April 1979, married first Cora Zimmerman, married second Dolly Poynter. Raymond, born 1904, died 1983, married first Susey Snyder, married second Bessier Stott. Rosa A., born 1906, died 1975. Arnold A., born 1909, died 1970, married Beatrice Roberts. Goldie M., born 1912, married Eustayce Leonard. Charley W., born 1916, married Frances Louise Friend. William, Dessie, Bessie and Mary all died in infancy.

Ca. 1900, John Wesley and Laura (Brown) Fox built the log cabin that is now Camp Palowopec and owned by Mike Nickels. Ca. 1870, John Wesley's father, John, built the older log cabin on the same property.

Charley and Frances (Friend) Fox operated a small grocery and gas station (1948-1967) on their property on Gatesville Road where the road forks. This store was called Fox's Corner Grocery and even though the store has been closed since 1967, the area is still known as Fox's Corner. It was known as Tinerville ca. 1857 and the land was deeded to the County for a school by Solomon Parsley in 1857. *Submitted by Charley W. Fox*

ARTIE E. FOX FAMILY - Artie E. Fox was the great-grandson of the first Fox settler of Brown County, Jonathan Fox. It is believed that this family migrated from Northern Europe, and had spelled their name Fuchs. Jonathan was born in 1786 in Pennsylvania. He had traveled through North Carolina, Virginia, to Poplar Grove, MO, then back through the Cumberland Mountains of Tennessee to Clay Co., KY. This was around the year 1810. There he and his wife Fanny began a family. The 1820 Clay County census listed seven children living in this household. Among them were: Nancy (1814); Joseph (1815); Samuel (1816); John (1817); Uriah, and then later in 1822, Isaac. After Fanny died, Jonathan moved his family to Lawrence Co., IN. There he married second, Mrs. Martha Hutson Porter, a widow and mother of six children. This family then moved to Big Salt Creek, Washington Township, Brown County. They purchased and entered land (Sect. 14, Twp. 9, R3E) in 1831. Jonathan and Martha resided there until their deaths. This land was then part of Bartholomew County until 1836, when it became a part of Brown County. Their son Uriah died at the age of 16. Jonathan conducted a horse mill in the eastern part of Washington Township near Salt Creek.

John Fox, son of Jonathan, married Louisa Pike in 1844, and purchased around 280 acres of land throughout Brown County. John and Louisa had 12 children. Among those 12 was fifth-born Samuel (Oct. 25, 1853).

Samuel married Clara Mae Roberts on Oct. 7, 1880, and homesteaded on Clay Lick Road, raising five of seven children: Rosey; Aire W. (1881); Cora (1886); Artie E. (1888); Leslie (1893); and two who died at an early age. Samuel conducted a sawmill on Salt Creek Road where he made crossties and clapboard shingles. He and his son Artie loaded the merchandise and hauled it to Columbus, IN to sell. This trip took them two days. Samuel died in 1909. Artie was 17 at that time.

Artie Everett Fox married Amanda J. Waltz on July 12, 1911, daughter of Pleasant and Lucy Waltz of Brown County. Shortly after their marriage, they moved to Columbus and raised three children: Dorothy I. (1915); Ralph M. (1917); and Marion D. (1924). Artie was a contract farmer most of his life, harvesting corn, soybeans, and wheat. After retiring from farming, he became a self-employed carpenter. Artie and his son Marion built a brick home on Rocky Ford Road in Columbus in 1948, where Artie and his wife lived until Artie's death in 1975. Artie and his daughter Dorothy, had purchased eight acres of land and a log cabin off Four-mile Ridge Road in Brown County in 1968. They used this cabin as a weekend and summer home. After Artie's death, this cabin and land was sold.

Marion married JoAnn Sims Feb. 16, 1947 in Columbus. During their first years of marriage, they lived in the brick home Marion and his father had built. They then moved to the Sim's homestead on River Road in Columbus, which had been built in 1835. Marion and JoAnn had six children: Roger D. (1950); Randell L. (1951); Sharon J. (1953); Michael S. (1958); Keith A. (1962); and Kevin L. (1963). Kevin died in 1964. Marion retired from Cummins Engine Company in 1983, and moved with his wife to a home on Central Ave. in Columbus.

Roger married Betty Phegley in 1979 and has two children: Gregory A. (1985); and Emily D. (1987).

Randy married Nancy Byrd in 1974, and has a daughter Kelley R. (1980).

Sharon married Tom Thixton and has a daughter Heather A. (1974).

Mike married Margie Brewer in 1983, and has five step-children.

Keith married Susie Loyd in 1983, and has a son Justin C. (1987).

There are over 96 families in this line of Foxes. A Fox genealogy is being constructed and more information is needed. Please contact Susie Fox at 812-376-3127.

LOUIS CHARLES AND ALBERTA FOX - Louis was born to Frances May (Ford) Fox and Charles Wilson Fox on Feb. 8, 1912. Alberta May (Waterman) Fox was born to Mary Mirian (Lumsford) Waterman and Cary Abraham Waterman on May 9, 1915. Louis was raised in Johnson County and Alberta in Hamilton and Brown Counties. After their marriage they chose to make their home in Brown County, a spot that became very dear to both of them.

The early years of marriage were spent living near Yellow Wood Lake and Louis worked in a local orchard. In August of 1933 they were blessed with their first daughter Barbara Jean (Fox) Burgess and together they lived a happy and simple life making plans for their future. In February of 1939 they were again blessed with a second daughter, Carole Sue (Fox) Beauchamp Van Slyke.

In 1942 the family bought a log house on State Road 45 just south of Needmore, and that was home for nearly 20 years. Many fond memories were made there, and it was there in May of 1942 that blessing number three was born, Julia Ann (Fox) Nesbit. With this growing family having growing needs, Louis took a position as a carpenter with General Motors Chevrolet Plant in Indianapolis. Here he worked until his retirement in 1971. This meant long hours on the road to and from work, but the family agreed it was worth it to live in their beloved Brown County.

Back: Julia, Louis, Jean. Front: Carole, Alberta, Zelma, Fay and Kay

Early in 1944, Louis received "greetings" from Uncle Sam. Even though he had a family, he served his country in the United States Navy. It was hard to leave Alberta and the three little girls, but the sacrifice was made. Alberta was brave and very capable of caring for herself and the girls, and she did just that.

In April of 1944 Louis came home on leave from the Navy to greet two new little girls, twins, Lois Fay (Fox) Carlin and Leanna Kay (Fox) Kinser. What a joy! Once again in February of 1946 Louis and Alberta were blessed with a little girl, their sixth, Zelma Irene (Fox) Kangas. Everybody thought Louis was disappointed at not having a son, but he, gracious and kind as he was, always said he would not trade one of the girls, nor have it any other way. He said his only problem was getting to use the bathroom with seven women in the house!

Alberta devoted her life to the family; as you might imagine six girls needed a lot of devotion and guidance. She saw to it that they got to church and had a proper upbringing. Nobody in the county had a mother who cared more. She was the best "band-booster," "taxi driver," "cook," "clothes maker," "cake baker," and "room mother" ever!

Early in the 60s, Louis suffered a heart attack, and the family moved to Indianapolis, IN, to be closer to his work at General Motors. This was a difficult move as Brown County was "home" and held cherished memories for all of the family.

The girls blessed their parents with the following grandchildren: Jacqueline Gay Burgess, Vicki Leigh Burgess, Bruce Duwain Burgess, Brent Willard Burgess, Terri Lynn Burgess, Charles Wendell Beauchamp, Cynthia Sue Beauchamp, Louis De Wayne Van Slyke, Richard William Van Slyke, Juliet J. Nesbit, Arnold Andrew Nesbit, David Sanford Nesbit, Winifred Leigh Carlin, Weldon Carlin, Whitney Jay Carlin, Larry Joe Kinser, David Devry Kangas and Kristen Raney Kangas.

Alberta in 1981 and Louis in 1984 went to be with the Lord and are together in their final resting place at East Hill Cemetery in Morgantown, IN. *Submitted by Leanna Kay (Fox) Kinser*

CARL HEYDON AND MARGARET ANN FRANZÉN

The Rev. Sven Carl Franzén, grandfather of Carl Heydon, immigrated to the United States from Uppsala, Sweden in 1866. He joined the U.S. Army and saw service in the Indian Wars. He served under General George Custer with the party that surveyed the Great Divide in the Northwest and was discharged with the rank of sergeant. Later he studied for the ministry and became a Luthern clergyman. He married Mary Florence Kugler of Ardmore, PA in 1885. They had seven children.

The eldest, Carl G.F., Professor of Secondary Education at Indiana University at Bloomington, IN, was born in Worthington, MN in 1886. He married Florence Josephine Buker, of Hartford, CT, in 1921. They had three children; Carl Heydon, Charles Kugler and Richard Scheaf. Carl Heydon was born on Nov. 20, 1922 in Beloit, WI. A few months later the family moved to Bloomington, IN. During WWII he served with the 13th Air Force in the Southwest Pacific. He was employed by Western Electric (AT&T) in Indianapolis, IN as an Engineer Associate, Factory Planning, Material Handling and retired after 36 years in August 1985.

Carl Heydon and Margaret Ann Franzén

Margaret Ann (Peg) Gustin Franzén is the daughter of Omar E. and Mildred L. Gustin. She was born on Sept. 9, 1928 in Anderson, IN, the eldest of four daughters. Omar E. was the son of Jonathon and Kate Parker Gustin of Hamilton Co., IN. Mildred L. was the daughter of Stephen Ozro and Elnora Decca Cox. The Cox family lived in Madison County, where they received a Federal Land Grant. Peg attended Ball State University. Carl Heydon and Peg are the parents of four children; Ann Louise Franzén-Roha, Susan Christine Franzén Osborne, Carl Heydon II and Joel Gustin.

Carl Heydon was active in The International Material Management Society and was International President in 1982-83. He was active in the Episcopal Church, The Shadeland Civic League (Indianapolis) and the Indianapolis Hiking Club. Peg was also active in the Indianapolis Hiking Club and the Episcopal Church. She served her community with volunteer work.

Upon Carl Heydon's retirement, Carl Heydon and Peg moved to Brown Co., IN in November 1985. For Carl Heydon it was coming home; for Peg it was the wooded hills and hiking trails that attracted her to the area. They bought a home formerly owned by Elmer and Rosemary Gilson on Beanblossom Ridge Lane, Freeman Ridge. Carl Heydon and Peg are members of St. David's Episcopal Church and are active members of the Brown County Historical Society, Friends of Brown County and Friends of the Brown County Library. Carl Heydon and Peg believe that Beautiful Brown County is indeed a special place to live.

FREESE FAMILY

Germany was the original home of the Freese family. The first to come to Brown County was John Freese who was born 1806 in Maryland to John Freese Sr. and Mary Schriver.

In 1829, John married Nancy Jane McFarland in Coshocton, OH. Their home was a farm in Coshocton County where all ten of their children were born. These children survived infancy: Jane (1830); William (1832); Joseph (1835); George (1839); John C. (1842); James (1844); Ruey (1851).

In 1852 John, Nancy and the seven children, ages one to 22 years moved to Brown County, making their home on a farm near Story, Van Buren Township. Two of the sons, John Calvin and James were in the Civil War. After the War most of John's children married and moved to other counties or other states. William remained in Brown County. John died in 1879; Nancy, in 1882. They are buried in Mt. Zion Cemetery where three of their sons, William, James, and George are buried also.

William and Abigail (Deaver) Freese, 1876

In 1862 William married Abigail Deaver, daughter of Lewis Jackson Deaver and Elizabeth Read. They had five children: John Calvin, Jr. (1863); Nancy (1866); Ruey (1869); Catherine (1872); Cora (1876). Ruey married James Hurley and moved to Illinois. Catherine married Andrew Morrison and moved to Bartholomew County. Calvin, Nancy and Cora remained in Brown County and reared families.

Calvin married Nancy Kirts, daughter of William Kirts and Hannah Taylor. They had six children, three of whom lived to adulthood: Ray (1894-1980); Walter (1904), now living in Maryland; Ernest (1913), a retired teacher living in Columbus.

Nancy married (1884) James Brown, son of Thomas Brown and Elizabeth Hurley. They had five children who lived to adulthood: Grover (1886-1967); Eathel (1890-1964); Minnie (1895-1953); Delores (1900-1981); Malcolm (1904-1975).

Cora Freese married (1895) George W. Anthony, son of Samuel Anthony and Mary Elizabeth Roush. They had five children only two of whom survived infancy: Herbert Anthony (1897), WWI veteran and retired teacher, still living in Edmonton, Alberta, Canada; and Cloyd Anthony, retired teacher, living in Terre Haute.

Six of the 31 grandchildren of William Henry Freese still live. In addition to the four grandsons mentioned above, Walter Freese, Ernest Freese, Herbert Anthony and Cloyd Anthony, there are two granddaughters: Beulah Hurley (1902), living in California and Ida Hurley (1907), Bement, IL, daughters of Ruey Freese and James Hurley.

The only descendents of William Freese presently living in Brown County are three great-granddaughters and their children: Geneva Freese Hobson, and Paula Freese Dembo, daughters of Ray Freese; and Wilma Brown Pittman, daughter of Grover G. Brown. *Submitted by Cloyd Anthony*

JOHN FREESE FAMILY

John was born Oct. 8, 1806 in Maryland, married in Coshocton Co., OH on May 14, 1829, to Nancy McFarland, born May 20, 1809 in Pennsylvania. John purchased land in Bedford Township in that county on May 11, 1830. They had seven children, all born Coshocton County: Wm. Henry, Joseph A., George W., John Calvin, James W., Jane and Ruey Freese. This family came to Brown County just before 1860 and settled near Story. John and Nancy Freese are buried in Mt. Zion Cemetery.

Child #1 of John and Nancy Freese, Wm. Henry (Sept. 2, 1832-Oct. 30, 1895) married in Brown

County on Dec. 7, 1862 to Abigail Deaver (1841-1912), daughter of Lewis Jackson Deaver and Elizabeth Read. Wm. Henry and Abby had six children: John Calvin, Nancy Elizabeth, Ruey A., Mary Catherine, Cora Belle and William Freese. William Henry and Abigail Freese are buried in Mt. Zion Cemetery.

Front: Mother, Vira Freese, Pauline, Geneva, Crystal, Neal. Back: Paul, Pearl, Glen, 1938.

Child #1 of Wm. Henry and Abigail Freese, John Calvin (Aug. 19, 1863-Feb. 1, 1938) married in Brown County on Oct. 31, 1889 to Nancy Elizabeth Kirts (1874-1963), daughter of Wm. Kirts and Hannah Taylor. John Calvin and Nancy Elizabeth had six sons: (1) Willie Otto (1890-1893); (2) Ray (Oct. 18, 1894-July 8, 1980); (3) Infant (born and died July 29, 1897); (4) Earl (1899-1912); (5) Walter Edward (born June 20, 1905) married Edna Mae Wilkerson; their children, Chester D., Norma Jean, Marvin Dean, Donald E. Freese. Walter and Edna divorced. He married second Verna (Wycoff) Cress; (6) Ernest Elmer (born Sept. 13, 1913) married Christina Grace Curran; their children, Phyllis Joann, Barbara Louise and Ronald Lee Freese. Ernest and Christina divorced. He married second Viola Dunn. John Calvin and Nancy Elizabeth Freese are buried at Mt. Zion.

Child #2 of John Calvin and Nancy Elizabeth Freese, Ray married on Jan. 11, 1916 in Brown County to Vira Hazel Greathouse (July 15, 1898-March 12, 1979), daughter of Jacob A. Greathouse and Emily A. Ayers. Ray and Vira had eight children: (1) Pearl (born 1916) married Keith Thompson; their children, Phyllis Kay. (2) Paul (1918-1980) married Dorval Pauline Roberts; their children, Paula Kay and Michael Lee. (3) Glen (born 1921) married Wilma Lois Roberts; their children, Oddis Lee and Kevin Ray. (4) Howard (born and died 1923). (5) Pauline (born 1924) married Charles N. Smith. (6) Neal (born 1927) married Marie Kelly; their children, Kathleen. (7) Crystal (born 1930) married Glenn Roscoe. (8) Geneva (born 1935) married Oris Hobson.

Many Freese family members are buried in the Mt. Zion Cemetery in Van Buren Township. The first Freese to be buried there was James V. Freese, child #5 of John and Nancy Freese. He died May 7, 1873 at age 28, leaving his widow, Nancy Jane (Ogle) Freese with three small children. She married second to Benjamin F. Whitehorn. *Submitted by Crystal (Freese) Roscoe*

RAY FREESE FAMILY - Ray, son of John Calvin Freese and Nancy Elizabeth Kirts, was born Oct. 18, 1894 near Story in Van Buren Township, Brown Co., IN. On Jan. 11, 1916, in Nashville, IN, he was married to Vira Hazel Greathouse. Ray and Vira traveled to Nashville in a horse drawn buggy, with her father accompanying the couple on horseback to give the bride away. Vira, born July 18, 1898, was a daughter of Jacob A. Greathouse and Emily A. Ayers, also of Van Buren Township.

Ray and Vira lived their entire lives in Brown County except for about two years when they lived in Illinois around Hoopeston and Bement where their son Paul was born.

Besides farming, Ray and Vira managed the Charles Spurgeon fruit orchard at Spurgeon's Corner in Van Buren Township for several years in the late 1930s and early 1940s, and Ray worked for the County Highway Department when needed in the 1950s and 1960s.

Vira (Greathouse) and Ray Freese, 1916

Ray and Vira Freese had eight children: (1) Pearl, born 1916, married Keith Thompson. Their daughter Phyllis Kay Thompson, born 1940, was killed in a car accident in 1941. (2) Paul (1918-1980) married Dorval Pauline Roberts and had children Paula Kay and Michael Lee. (3) Glen, born 1921, married Wilma Lois Roberts and had children Oddis Lee and Kevin Ray. (4) Howard (born and died 1923). (5) Pauline, born 1924, married Charles N. Smith. (6) Neal, born 1927, married Marie Kelly and had a daughter, Kathleen. (7) Crystal, born 1930, married Glenn Roscoe. (8) Geneva, born 1935, married Oris Hobson.

The Freese house was always open to family, friends and neighbors. Mrs. Freese was noted for her delicious cooking and ability to prepare a meal on short notice. Mr. and Mrs. Freese were loved by their children and their families very much, and every weekend was like a family reunion at the Freese house.

Ray Freese died Oct. 15, 1984 and his wife, Vira, died March 12, 1979. Both are buried in the Christiansburg Cemetery in Van Buren Township. *Submitted by Crystal (Freese) Roscoe*

LEWIS FRITCH AND DESCENDANTS - Lewis was born in Germany, March 13, 1816. In 1837 he came to the U.S. by way of New Orleans, traveled to Hamilton Co., OH, resettling in Brown County, Jackson Township on the corner of North Shore Drive and Slippery Elm Shoot Road. He owned 255 acres and gave land to his children. Lewis married Sarah Ann Prail, April 13, 1839; and had three children: Margaret Jane, James and Francis. He married a second wife, Ellen Aldrich, March 18, 1845 and had seven children: Joseph, Nathaniel, Hannah, McAllen, Andrew, John and Conrad. He married a third wife, Elizabeth Stump Geary, Nov. 23, 1858 and had one step-son, William Geary, and seven children: Catharine, Nancy, Christopher, Frederick, Isaac, Mary and Martha.

Lewis was a Justice of Peace in Brown County from 1858 until 1873. He was a farmer and raised sheep. Elizabeth spun yarn on her spinning wheel, wove and dyed cloth. She made men's pants from this woolen fabric and used scraps for quilts. Lewis died May 15, 1891, and is buried at Bear Creek Cemetery.

The Fritch homestead is still occupied. Originally the house was sided with whitewashed boards. It had high ceilings and a winding stairway—13 steps to landing and seven steps to the hall. The banister was made of solid cherry. The north wall of the living room had a fireplace with a wooden mantel and bookcases with doors on each side. The house included an entry way, bedroom, pantry, kitchen, back porch, two upstairs bedrooms and a cellar.

William and Phyllis Rotino

Catharine Fritch (born 1859) married James Neal; two children, William (born 1879) and Lewis (born 1880). Lewis had an accident leaving him crippled. He died at age 23. After James' death, Catherine taught school in Brown County for ten years. She married George Tutterrow in 1892 and had three children: Elmer (born 1893), John (born 1897) and Elva (born 1901).

They dried fruit and vegetables between cheesecloth on the roof of their house. George traveled by horse and wagon for supplies at Martinsville. George and John cut timber and hauled logs up Bear Creek Road and Gosport Hollow Road to the Gosport sawmill. Catharine died Aug. 16, 1937 and is buried at Needmore Cemetery. John and family had the pleasure of living in the homeplace from 1937 until George's death in 1940, when the place was sold.

John attended Brock School and Helmsburg High School. When weather permitted he ice-skated to school up Bean Blossom Creek. He was an excellent carpenter, building numerous homes in Brown County. He enjoyed nature, coon hunting and was a genius in mathematics. Young children immediately loved him. John married Dolores Gee in 1930 and had five children: Twins Marilyn and Margilyne (born 1932), Billy (born 1933), Phyllis (born 1935) and Alice (born 1938). John died Sept. 13, 1978 and is buried at Bear Creek Cemetery.

Phyllis Tutterrow married William Joseph Rotino in 1958 and they reside on Bear Creek Road. They have six children: Diana (born 1959), William II (born 1960), Rick (born 1961), Kevin (born 1963), Alice (born 1965) and Margee (born 1971). Their six grandchildren are: Joshua, Rachel, twins Courtney and Charlotte Turner, Krystal and Morgan Rotino.

Phyllis is a member of Bear Creek Church, Nashville Eastern Star, Cottonwood Homemakers Club and Brown County Historical Society. William is semi-retired from Precision Litho Services, Inc., an offset printing company at St. Petersburg, FL, which he partially owns. He is a member of Nashville Masons Lodge, Nashville Eastern Star, Brown County Shrine Club and is a Trustee of Bear Creek Cemetery.

Mabel Logsdon is the oldest Fritch descendant living in Brown County, and Mandy Cody is the youngest. *Submitted by Phyllis J. Rotino*

ROE FRITCH - Isaac Monroe "Roe" Fritch was born April 27, 1865 in Brown County, Jackson Township in the area now mostly covered by Lake Lemon. He was the 14th child of Lewis Fritch (1816-1891) who immigrated to the United States from Germany in 1837 via New Orleans. Lewis settled in Hamilton Co., OH, where he found work on the Erie Canal. In 1839 he married Sarah Ann Crail. Born to the union were Margaret Jane, James William, and Francis. Sarah passed away in 1843. The family purchased 60 acres in Shelby Co., IN, and Lewis in 1845 was married to Ellen Folsom Aldrich (1822-1857). Seven children were born to this union: Joseph F., Nathaniel, Hannah Ellen, McAllen, Andrew, John, and Conrad. Lewis sold the farm in 1849 and moved to Brown County where he purchased 130 acres of land. Ellen passed away in 1857. Lewis cleared, improved and added to his land which now totaled 255 acres. Elizabeth Stump Gary (1827-1896) became his third wife in 1858. The couple built a comfortable home which still stands overlooking Bean Blossom Valley, now Lake Lemon. Lewis and Elizabeth had seven children: Catherine Arminte, Nancy Elizabeth, Isaac Monroe "Roe," Frederick, Mary, and Martha Ann.

"Roe" Fritch

Roe married at age 25 Laura McKee (1872-1907) in February 1890. Her parents were Silas and Ann McKee, formally Ann McGee. Roe lost his father, Lewis, in 1891 and inherited 30 acres of bottomland where he built a small house and raised his family. The couple lost their first baby, Ernest, at eight months and had four other children. James Earl served in the Navy during World War I, married, and moved to the state of Washington. Lena May married Floyd Young, farmed in Brown and Johnson Counties and had two children: Virginia and Leon. Harold Monroe joined the Army and later moved to Idaho. He and wife, Mattie, had three children: Donna, William, and Carol. Clay married Dolly Fritch. They lost their son, Forest, but had a daughter, Mary Colleen. Clay and Dolly still reside in Morgantown, IN.

In 1902 a Needmore physician told Roe he had only a short time to live and needed to change climates. Roe traveled to Greeley, CO where he worked harvesting potatoes. The potatoes were dug and stored in underground "dugouts." He loved the west. Although he returned to Indiana when his health was restored, Roe made other trips west, especially to Washington where his son, Earl had settled. Roe was almost 90 when he passed away in January 1955.

Roe liked to loaf in Poling's Store at Needmore. His son, Clay, recalls a time in the spring of 1907 when he had accompanied his father in their team and wagon to the store. They were loafing as usual when the store received a call for help. Melk Hawley's daughter was in danger of drowning as she was caught between two streams of water. She had climbed into a willow bush but the flood-swollen creek was rising to her level. Roe lost no time as he unhitched one horse from his wagon and rode quickly to rescue the girl.

Driving oxen was both a challenge and joy for Roe, and he also made the yokes for them. The bows were made from split hickory and the yokes from soft maple. He drove the last big oxen for W.S. Richards, who brought them from Kentucky. They weighed over a ton each, were well broken, and could move a railroad car loaded with logs on the switch track at Trevlac. The time was about 1911. Roe broke two yokes of steers of his own years later, but they served mainly as companions or pets.

Roe supplemented his farming income working as a teamster mainly hauling logs. He took his horses to Indianapolis and did grade work there. He helped to build the 500 Racetrack and also a building for Ely Lilly Co.

Laura passed away in 1907, but Roe never remarried. He was independent and a wanderer much to the chagrin of his family at times. He had only four years of schooling, but he was a self-educated man. He spent much time reading and remembered much of what he read. He was well-versed in National and World affairs, and in his later years could be found loafing in local stores expounding his philosophy.

GENOLIN FAMILY - John Genolin, Sr., born in France, arrived in New York on Nov. 12, 1844 from Marseilles. On Sept. 19, 1850, at age 35, he received his Naturalization Papers in the Brown County Court. He married Elizabeth Clark, born in Ireland. Family tradition says he had a business in Dublin before coming to America. They came to Columbus, IN, then to Brown County. Of their ten children information has been found on these: John F., Glodine, Lucy Jane, Charles, Thomas, Mary, and Clementine. Two sons, Lewis and William, died young, buried Greenlawn Cemetery. Their father was a wine merchant and had a three story building built for his business on Lot #5 in Nashville in 1866-67. He was a dealer in horses as well. He died on a burning ship in New Orleans harbor in 1874. His wife, Elizabeth, died in 1889 and is buried in Greenlawn Cemetery, Nashville, Brown County.

His son, John F. Genolin, MD, practiced medicine in Nashville. He married in 1884 to Susie Watton, daughter of George and Josephine Watton. He died in 1912, she, in 1922; both are buried in Greenlawn Cemetery. They had two daughters, Verna (Mrs. Alonzo Allison) and Maude (Mrs. Lowell C. Day). Their father had been a member of the Nashville Christian Church, a trustee, elected for the purpose of building the church, which was accomplished in 1888.

Glodine Genolin married George Welch of Monroe County. Their children were Mrs. Charles C. Bender, Mrs. Henry Rogers, Osborn G. Welch, Albert C. Welch, Nolan Welch and Mrs. Isaac Meyers.

Lucy Jane Genolin married James McGrayel of Mayo Co., Ireland. Their children: John A., Mary Elizabeth, James H. (died young), Charles M. and James Matson McGrayel. James Matson married Ruby Campbell, daughter of Clark Campbell and Harriet Poling. Their four children were John Michael, Meredith Jane (Rogers), Ruth Eloise (Sherwood), and William Harry. Some of Lucy Jane's grandchildren, great-grandchildren and great-great grandchildren live in Brown County.

Charles Genolin was a pharmacist. He served in the Indiana Legislature as joint representative for Brown and Monroe Counties in 1913. He married Mary Jennie Prosser in 1885. Their children were Hesper (Mrs. Guy Patterson), Jessie (Mrs. Crowell), John M., who died in infancy, and Max who married Susan Weddle. Max and Susan Genolin had a son Charles. Max and Susan, who had served as a nurse in France in WWI, divorced and he married an Illinois girl.

After the death of his wife, Mary Jennie, Charles Genolin married Ola Lackey, daughter of Oscar L. Lackey and Sarah R. Rightmier, on Aug. 19, 1901. Charles and Ola ran a drugstore in Nashville until his death on Dec. 16, 1921. Ola then married the famous artist, Will Vawter.

Thomas married first to Lib Watton, daughter of George and Josephine Watton. They had a daughter, Ruby. Thomas and Lib divorced. He later married Jeanne Antoinette Cibial of Bordeaux, France; the marriage arranged by his friend, Jeanne's father. They met at New York Harbor, each wearing a white carnation to identify themselves to each other. They were married in Plainfield, IN on Oct. 31, 1922. Thomas died of heart attack at their home in Indianapolis in 1933 and she returned home to France.

Mary Genolin (Mrs. Wilson) and her husband moved to Oklahoma. They had one daughter, Mrs. Roy Graves, of Norman, OK.

Clementine Genolin married John E. Kennedy on June 17, 1875 in Nashville.

(See the Rogers family) (see the McGrayel family)
Submitted by Meredith McGrayel Rogers

GEORGE FAMILY - James David George was born Dec. 16, 1837 in Clark Co., IN. James moved to Jackson Co., IN with his parents Jess and Mercy Anderson George. His brothers and sisters were America Jane who married Edwin Callaham, William P. who married Irenay Davis, Mary E. who married Francis M. Jones, Jess who married Nancy Emmons, Maria, Zuelda, Margaret who married George Huber, Semantha who married George W. Newcomb and Francis L. George.

James David George, married Margaret Stogdill July 10, 1856 at Clear Springs, Jackson Co., IN. They were married by Reverend John Cummings, a Methodist minister, and witnesses were Joseph Elkins and Gibson Cummings. Margaret Stogdill George was the daughter of early settlers William Sherman Stogdill and Mariah (Elkins) (Stogdill). James David and Margaret had 14 children. William Andrew who married Sarah Jane Sexton, Jess Madison who married Florence Belle Robertson, James Edward, born Aug. 18, 1863, Brown County who married Sarah Tabitha Curry, Thomas J. who married Ida Leach, Mercy M. who married J.P. Anglin, Francis M., Clarinda who married Fellars, Laura B. who married George Williams, Margaret R., Walter J. and Iva who married Hendricks and several children that died early in life.

James David George enlisted in the Civil War from Elkinsville, Brown County. He was in Co. F, Regiment 145 Indiana Volunteers Infantry and Co. G, 21st Indiana Volunteers. He was discharged from Ft. McHenry, MD. James and Margaret moved to Brown County after the war and lived at Elkinsville having been deeded land by William Elkins.

In 1881 James and Margaret George were one of the Brown County families that moved to Tarrant Co., TX. In 1963 Annie Robertson Souder (90 years old at that time) said that the trip from Brown County took ten weeks by wagon to Tarrant Co., TX. Bramble Stogdill, Margaret's nephew said that James George was one of the leaders of the trip and they called him Captain Jim George. The government gave them mules and land to come to Texas. Bramble said that the wagon train gathered at Browning Hill at Elkinsville. Some of the Brown County families that went to Texas were the Sextons, Robertsons, Wilkersons, Lutes, George and the Arwines.

James Edward George and daughters Clara Ellen (left) and Hattie Belle George (right)

Two of James and Margaret George's children Jess Madison and James Edward George went to Tarrant Co., TX on the train and remembered the date because they bought a newspaper in the St. Louis Harvey House and read that President James A. Garfield had been assassinated July 2, 1881.

From Texas, James and Margaret George went to Arkansas around 1885 to homestead in Washington Co., AR with their son William Andrew George. Their son William and family remained in Washington Co., AR and there are many descendants up to this day in Springdale, AR.

James and Margaret returned to Texas in the 1890s. James died in Texas Nov. 8, 1912 and Margaret George died March 11, 1924 while she was living with her son Jess George. They are buried in the Arwine Cemetery in Tarrant County where other families are buried from Brown Co., IN. The last remaining child in 1963 of James and Margaret Iva, said that her mother was a wonderful woman who never went to school a day in her life but was smart, a good Christian, a good mother and a faithful wife.

The above picture shows two daughters of James Edward George: Clara Ellen born Nov. 30, 1887 in Tarrant Co., TX and Linda Zablatnik's grandmother Hattie Belle George born Oct. 31, 1885 also in Tarrant Co., TX. Linda Zablatnik is great great granddaughter of James David and Margaret (Stogdill) George. *Submitted by Linda Zablatnik*

CLAYTON AND ANNA GEORGE - Harry George is a true Brown County native. Born in a log home still standing on Rt. 46 West of Nashville, his lineage intersects with other Brown County natives. On Jan. 18, 1923 Harry's parents, Clayton and Anna Jane Bitter were married in Nashville. Witnesses to the marriage were Maude and Duard Calvin, owners of Calvin Hardware. Anna was born in Storm Lake, IA on March 9, 1896. Her mother, Martha Jane Brials Bitter moved back to Brown County after the death of her husband Christian. Martha had been born on a farm east of Nashville on Dec. 6, 1854. It was in Brown County then that Anna met Clayton, married and became stepmother to his four children, a son James and three daughters, Bessie, Dessie and Jessie.

Clayton George Family (1923). Martha Bitter, Clayton George, Anna George

They then had three more children, Harold, Franklin and Harry. The latter was named after his mother's beloved younger brother, Harry Bitter, who died at 28 years of age from what was probably consumption. Clayton George was well known as a log cabin builder in Brown County. He left the construction business eventually and owned a poultry and feed store where the Shell/Bigfoot station now stands in Nashville. He then ran a grocery store where Knight's Grocery near Yellowwood is now located. In 1949-1952 and again in 1957-1960 he served as County Recorder. At his death in 1964 he was serving his second two year term as County Councilman. Anna continued living in the log home until her death on Aug. 16, 1982. Harry George was the only one of the seven children to remain in the county. Except for his military service during the Korean conflict he has lived here all his life. When he returned he worked in a furniture store, helped manage the Old Hickory Restaurant, worked for Al Robertson Construction, then began his own construction business.

DAVID DEANE AND MARY ALICE (BUTLER) GIRARD - Over 40 years after they first met at Franklin College, David and Mary Alice Girard returned to enjoy southern Indiana living at its best — Brown County.

Mary Alice was born in Oakland City, IN (Gibson County) to Curtis and Etta (Pfohl) Butler. She graduated from Knightstown, IN high school.

David was born in Calion, AR (Union County) to James R. and Ruth Estella (Coonrod) Girard while they were conducting logging operations away from their White Co., IN home. David grew up in South Bend, IN and graduated from Riley High School.

David and Mary Alice were married at the Quantico, VA Marine Corps Base Chapel during World War II. Dave's service career took him throughout the Pacific, China, Arctic Ocean, numerous bases in the U.S. and Caribbean and finally to the National Military Command Center in the Pentagon. Mary Alice set up housekeeping in over 40 locations.

After retirement from the Marine Corps in 1965 David joined IBM. Again the family was on the move with assignments in Hawaii, Washington DC, Germany, Minnesota, and Arizona.

Retirement from IBM has included life in the Southern California desert and extensive travel in the U.S. and abroad.

David and Mary Alice have two children: Susan G. Waege with three grandchildren in St. Paul, MN and David B. in Seattle, WA.

EVANS GLADDING FAMILY - The Gladding family originally came from Warrick Co., IN near Boonville. Evans L. Gladding was born at Sullivan, IN. He was the son of Amanda and B. Frank Gladding.

Evelyn (Foster) Gladding was born and grew up in Vincennes, IN. Her parents were Lillie (Scales) Foster and Clarence Huston Foster. Huston, as he was called, was the youngest son of Sarah C. (Taylor) and Thomas Foster.

Evelyn remembers of her grandmother Sarah C. telling stories about her own childhood along the Ohio River in Harrison Co., IN. Grandmother, at an early age, helped carry water to Union soldiers passing through the area.

Evans and Evelyn were married in Vincennes, Knox Co., IN. Their four children were born in Vincennes. The oldest was Stephen E. Gladding who is a pastor in the Church of the Nazarene. Cathryn J. (Gladding) Eyre is a teacher in Clearwater, FL. Timothy F. Gladding lives at Columbus, IN. Elizabeth Jane (Gladding) Muncie works in church ministry with her husband. There are nine grandchildren.

Evans and Evelyn Gladding

In 1966 the family moved from Vincennes to Bourbonnais, IL where Evans was involved in car sales and Evelyn taught first grade. On retirement in 1981 they moved back to the Hoosier State and built a home on Sweetwater Lake in Brown County. At that time Evans joined the Horseshoe Club that met in Johnson County Park at Camp Atterbury. He was a member of the National Horseshoe Pitchers Association and the Indiana State Horseshoe Pitchers Association. He had been on teams in Vincennes and Bourbonnais when living there. Evans pitched with the Atterbury Team at the Indiana State Fair. He was Johnson County Horseshoe Champion in 1983.

Evelyn taught a number of years in the Vincennes Public School System and in the Momence, IL Community Schools. On moving to Brown County she continued as supply teacher in both Johnson and Brown Counties.

Two important contacts needed to be made when they moved to Brown County. One was to find a church home and the other was to get a library card. They are avid readers.

Parkview Church with its caring friends proved to be a pleasure to attend and a comfort during illness. In 1988 Evans had a severe stroke. Improvement was a slow process. It became necessary to move to Nashville. Evans still keeps in touch with horseshoe pitchers from the Atterbury Club. He is also a dedicated bird watcher. Much of his time is spent with a backyard bird sanctuary.

Evelyn is a member of the Brown County Genealogical Society, Homemakers Nashville Daytime Club and Society of Children's Book Writers. Evelyn has done some writing for publication.

The Gladdings enjoy their home on Parkview Road and entertain friends when they come to visit Brown County.

ARNOLD GOLDMAN - Arnold the son of Albert and Lillian Goldman, was born on a farm in

Ashtabula, OH, on Dec. 7, 1922. He graduated from Glenville High School in Cleveland, OH and attended Ohio State University. When Pearl Harbor was attacked on his birthday, he enlisted in the U.S. Air Force. In 1943 he married Anita Clark, the daughter of Holland and Olive Henderson Clark of Brown County, in Wilmington, DE. Upon his discharge from the service in 1945, he came to Brown County and with the urging of his father-in-law—a much respected teacher in Brown County—he enrolled at Indiana University. After receiving his degree in education, he taught for three years at Clark's School, a one-room school near Gnawbone. After a few more years of teaching at the old Nashville High School, he moved to Monroe County, obtained a Master's degree and principal's license from I.U., and taught one year in Lawrence County and two years in Monroe County. Upon completion of the new building at Nashville, he returned as principal of the elementary school. After three years there, he became a science and math teacher in the Junior High School. He then accepted a position as principal of Helmsburg Elementary School and remained there for 20 years until he retired.

Arnold Goldman

Mrs. Goldman was the granddaughter of Richard M. (Bub) Henderson (one of the men in Hohenberger's famous "Liar's Bench" photograph) and Ida Kent Henderson, daughter of Samuel Kent, well-known early pioneer families in Brown County. She was also the granddaughter of Omer Clark, a master carpenter, and Lena Bradley Clark.

The Goldmans are parents of two daughters: Mrs. Sharon Yeley of Columbus, mother of Brian and Allison, and Mrs. Sandra Burton of Indianapolis, mother of Mrs. DeAnn Frye (who is the mother of Christopher Allen and Anthony Scott) and Stephanie Burton.

DONALD K. AND MARJORIE GOODWIN
Donald and Marjorie bought their first 40 acres in Brown County on Highway 135 South from Sam Poer in 1952 and started their Christmas tree farm, adding more acreage through the years, including the Ernest Garlach farm. They had planted their first Christmas trees in Morgan County while Don was a student at Purdue.

Donald Keith, born on Sept. 3, 1928, in Lafayette, IN, is the youngest of two sons of Sheldon and Helen R. Goodwin. Sheldon was born in Shelby County to Alva and Mary S. Bentley Goodwin. He graduated from Purdue in 1925 and worked for Rauh Fertilizer Co., later purchased by International Minerals Corp., until retirement. One of the first areas covered as salesman was Brown County, where he traveled by hired wagon to call on Dealers after taking the train to Helmsburg. Helen Ruth was the only child of Wilbur and Edna N. Keen of Lafayette, IN. Her father was a former Chief of the Lafayette Fire Department.

Marjorie June, born on April 20, 1931, in Marion Co., IN, is a daughter of Garry Madison and Blanche Z. Kennedy. Garry was born in Franklin County to George Riley and Annabelle S. Kennedy. He attended school in Rush County, then moved to Marion County where he worked for Indianapolis Power & Light Co. for 46 years. Blanche Zoeth, age 90, lives with a daughter in Indianapolis and was born in Shelby County to Jacob and Cora Anderson Spurlin.

After graduation from Purdue University Forestry School in 1950, Don became the first private Consulting Forester in Indiana. He planted trees and helped landowners manage their timberland. Over 30 years, Don estimates he planted 17 million trees for plantations and reforestation for landowners. He no longer plants trees for others but continues as a Consulting Forester with son, Steven, a 1984 Purdue Forestry graduate. Don is a Charter member of the Indiana State Christmas Tree Grower's and the Mid-America Christmas Tree Association. He is a member of the Society of American Foresters and served on the Indiana Tree Farm Committee. He helped plan the first Forestry Field Day, in cooperation with State and Industry foresters, which was held on the Meyer farm in Brown County.

Don and June are parents of Terry Shane, Cynthia K. Goodwin Price, and twins, James Stuart and Steven Shawn. When the children were young, both parents were active in scouting, church, and school activities. They are members of Eastminster Presbyterian Church, Indianapolis. Don, an Eagle Scout, was a Boy Scout leader and merit badge counselor for over 40 years, and all three sons earned Eagle Rank.

Using timbers from a 100 year old barn, native stone, trees cut from their property, with the help of Contractor Jim Mara, and other Brown County craftsmen, Don and June built a home overlooking the lake on the Christmas tree farm where they spend much of the year. They also maintain a home in Indianapolis where their business office is located. *Submitted by Marjorie J. Goodwin and Donald K. Goodwin*

WILLIAM AND MARGOT GORE
William Adolph Gore, Sr. was born in Goreville, IL in 1883; Hortense Campbell Gore in Marion, IL in 1887. He was a graduate of the University of Illinois, and became a teacher in Oak Park, IL where William A. Gore, Jr. was born in 1910; later a school principal in St. Louis, MO. The Gores moved to New York City where W.A., Sr. earned his Ph.D degree at New York University and became Superintendent of Schools at Hempstead, NY, retiring in 1947. Hortense attended McMurray College in Illinois as a music major.

Steve, Dave, Bill, Margot Gore, 1959

After his retirement Dolph and Hortense spent several years traveling from Long Island, through Illinois, to Scottsdale, AZ and back again. On one of their trips East they stopped in Cincinnati and saw an article about Brown County in a 1950 issue of "Holiday" magazine. They visited here and through Walter Snodgrass bought acreage north on State Road 135 where they built a house in 1951.

That year William A., Jr. (Bill) and Margot Gore came with their two sons, Stephen (7) and David (4) to see the new acreage. Margot Young Gore was born in Brooklyn, NY in 1917 and had lived in Hempstead and Garden City, NY. Bill and Margot had bought a home in Huntington Station, NY soon after Bill returned from serving in the Pacific in Army Ordnance during World War II. They decided to "go West" and bought a few acres north of Nashville, and with Al Robertson, as the builder, "Gore's Orchard Hill Motel" was completed and opened in the spring of 1952. Bill helped in the new Chamber of Commerce and was later given a life membership. He also served on the Selective Service Board.

The motel was sold seven years later and Bill became a real estate salesman in Walter Snodgrass' office, then opened his own office in the old Calvin house at the corner of Van Buren and Franklin Streets. That building was sold by Bill and his father, and Bill opened "Bill Gore Realty" in the Allison House on Jefferson Street, retiring from there in 1972. The building is now owned by Bob and Tammy Galm.

The Gores became affiliated with Nashville Methodist Church where Margot is still active. Nina Taggart, who sang in the choir, asked Bill to play the organ, which he did, playing and directing the choir as long as his health permitted. Dolph and Hortense sang in the choir many years.

Margot worked as a receptionist at the Brown County Art Gallery for about ten years after Bill's retirement. Bill died in June 1988 at the Brown County Community Care Center.

Stephen William Gore and David Young Gore were both born in Mineola, NY and at the present time both live in Brown County. Steve has an accounting and tax preparation business with his wife the former Stefanie Binkley. Dave is a builder, and his wife, the former Carol Greene of Bloomington, is Supervisor in the County Welfare Department.

Steve has two sons, Bryan and Kevin, both born in Vero Beach, FL. Their mother is the former Jane Newman.

Dave has three children, Abi, Sarah, and Alex. Abigayle was born in Bloomington in 1968. Her mother is the former Sherry Dewey. Sarah was born in Bloomington in 1978 and Alex in Bloomington in 1985. *Submitted by Margot Y. Gore*

VIDA SIPES GRAPE - Singleton Sipes received a land grant of 455 acres. He divided the land between his six children.

Daniel Sipes the youngest child married Grace Robertson, daughter of John Wesley and Nancy Ann (Lucas) Robertson, Jan. 10, 1900. They were married by Rev. Harrison at the brides home in a buggy. They were the parents of six children. The eldest Vida (Sipes) Grape born in 1903. Her brothers and sisters are Lova Sipes, Pearl (Sipes) Nilson, Clarence Sipes, Edith (Sipes) Deckard and Doshie (Sipes) Wilkerson. All are still living.

They lived off the land tending a garden, milking cows, feeding chickens and hogs. Corn had to be taken to the grist mill to be ground.

The nearest store was Elkinsville, two miles

away. Stores at Storyville and Maumee were four miles away. Cream and eggs were sold or exchanged for sugar, flour, baking powder, soda, oatmeal, etc.

Estes, Margaret B. and Vida (Sipes) Grape (sitting on car is Ruth)

Vida remembers riding a horse and holding a basket of eggs which she was taking to Elkinsville. The road was muddy and as the horse was going down a grade it fell to its knees and slid down the grade, Vida's fear was that the eggs would be broken and she wouldn't be able to get her supplies, fortunately the eggs weren't broken.

Money was earned by cutting crossties, 8'x6"x8", from white oak and hauling them to Kurts, a 24 mile round trip. Potatoes, sweet and irish, also navy beans which sold for 10¢ a pound were taken to the market at Bedford. This was a three-day 50 mile round trip and the money was used to purchase overshoes and school clothes for the children.

In 1917 a cyclone hit their home and blew most of the roof off their log home, one section was left where Grace was in bed with Edith who was six days old.

Vida attended the Browning School. She had over a two-mile walk each way. During the war years when flour was scarce cornbread was used to make sandwiches to take to school.

Vida's first job away from home was at Storyville as a housekeeper for the Wheelers.

Vida married Clarence Estes Grape, June 3, 1922, whom she met after coming to work at Bloomington.

This period of time which was the depression made it hard to make a living. They tended a garden, had chickens and a cow. Vida helped by washing and ironing for people and had hotbeds from which they sold plants. Estes worked at several different jobs during this time. Estes passed away in 1970. Vida is still living in Bloomington and loves to read the Brown County Democrat paper.

They had two daughters: Margaret B. who married Fred Kerr and Ruth, who married Richard C. Zimmerman. Richard and Ruth had three children, Donald, Victoria and Debora. *Submitted by Ruth C. Zimmerman*

LOUIS GRAY FAMILY - William John and Alfred Gray moved from Virginia to Indiana. William married Della Ballard, their son Oliver was born in 1873. Oliver married Mary Ellen Johnson, daughter of Nathan Johnson. Nathan served in the Civil War and married Phoebe Jane Scott. Oliver and Mary Ellen had Louis Garfield, 1894, Edith, Louisa and Laura. Louis is the only child living in 1990. Louis was put in a Noblesville, IN children's home after his parents separated. Louis was taken from the home by Ernest and Delpha Cave and lived around Washington, IN until he enlisted in World War I. Louis was a wagon master. Louis received a citation from General Pershing. After the war Louis returned to Westfield, IN, and married Mabel Maude Hines in 1920. Louis and Mabel had eight children, Delpha Jo, 1921; Samuel Ernest, 1922; Carl Nathan, 1927; Sylvia Edith, 1929; Nellie Sue, 1930; all born in Westfield, Hamilton County. Louis and Mabel moved to a one room log cabin near Fruitdale, in Brown County, in 1932, here Alfred Lowell, 1932, and Robert Louis, 1934, were born. Louis and Mabel then moved to the Sprunica area where Richard Gale was born was born 1938. In 1950, Louis and Mabel moved to Putnam County where they still live in their own home and take care of each other.

While in Brown County, Louis was hired as a foreman for the Bean Blossom Bridge on State Road 135. Louis and Mabel joined the Unity Baptist Church and were baptized in the creek west of the church. Louis started preaching in 1932. Louis was ordained at the Unionville Church in 1937, licensed at Unity. Louis has been associated with several American Baptist Churches throughout Indiana. Louis retired in 1977.

Louis and Mabel Hines Gray, 50th Anniversary

Delpha Jo, Samuel Ernest, and Carl Nathan's widow live in Brown County. The rest of the children reside in Putnam County.

Delpha and Samuel attended Spearsville's one-room school. Delpha went to Morgantown for her freshman and sophomore years. The trustee sent Delpha to Nashville High School for her junior year. Delpha graduated from Helmsburg High School in 1939.

In 1942, Delpha married Homer Amos Oliver in Spearsville, in the house they still live in today. Delpha has worked as secretary at Sprunica and Helmsburg Elementaries. In 1963, Delpha took the bookkeeping job in the Superintendent's office where she is still employed.

Samuel married Lorean Fox and had five children: Mabel, Howard, Gerald, Raylean, and Becky.

Carl Nathan married Dixie Huddleson and had two children, Diana Kay and Nathan. Carl died in 1976.

Nellie married George Fox, they had seven children: Karen Sue, Lucinda Ann, Sandra Lynn, Judy Jean, Larry Joe, Donald Dayton, David Louis, and Patricia. They operate a hog farm.

Alfred married Waneta Nichols, they had two children: Luella and Louis Alfred. Alfred operates a hog farm.

Robert Louis married Carol Mitchell, they had two children: Jennifer and Mark. Robert is retired from I.B.M.

Richard married Donna Miller, they had three children: Ginger, Danny and Andy. They operate a store and restaurant in Reelsville.

PETER GREATHOUSE - Peter was a son of Solomon Greathouse and Catharine Little who had married in Belmont Co., OH on May 25, 1821. Peter was born Nov. 12, 1837 in Washington Co., OH. He married first, before 1860, in Ohio, to Barbara Wilcox, daughter of Absolom Carr Wilcox and Elizabeth Barkhimer. He enlisted Aug. 6, 1862 to serve three years in the Civil War as a private in Co. C and F, 92nd Regt., Ohio Vol. Inf. Discharged for disability April 26, 1864, he returned home to find his wife had disappeared leaving their infant son William. Peter filed for divorce, then married Barbara's sister Zedorah on Oct. 27, 1864 in Washington Co., OH. Peter and "Dora" Greathouse had children: Leonard (born 1865), John (1867-1949), George Washington (1868-1945), Maria Jane (born 1870), Jacob Alexander (1872-1943), Mary Elizabeth (1874-1934), Hezekiah (born 1876), Anna E. (1878-1930), Rachel T. (1880-1961), Peter T. (born 1882), Barbara E. (1885-1961), Charles Greathouse (1890-1958).

Front Row: Goldie, Edith, Buelah Greathouse; Back row: Frances, holding Clifford, Alra, Ray Greathouse, Faye Hatton in George Greathouse arm's, 1924

George Washington Greathouse, child #4 of Peter Greathouse, was born in Ohio but came to Brown Co., IN at an early age with his parents. Peter died in 1906, his wife Dora died in 1924. Both are buried in Christiansburg Cemetery, Brown County.

George Washington Greathouse married in the fall of 1892 in Brown County to Frances Adaline Ayers, born Jan. 18, 1872, daughters of James Ayers and Jane Stevens. George and Frances Greathouse had 12 children: Lemuel James (1893-1935) married Laura Hatton; Maley Amos (1895-1972) married Mabel Timberman; Ressie Jane (1897-1979) married John Henry Hatton; Ira E. (1899-1985) married Ada Carter; Charlie Clifford (1901-1983) married Nellie Elizabeth Shelton; Marion Alonzo (1904-1953) married Thelma Myrtle Williams; William Thomas (1906-1952) married Mary Carter; Lester Ernest (born 1908) married Beulah May Shelton; Roy (born 1911) married Florence Wilma Martin; Ray (1914-1987) married Mildred Lawson; Alra (born 1916) married Inez Lenora Guthrie; Goldie (born 1918) married Melvin Rumph.

Ressie Jane Greathouse, child #3 of George W. and Frances Greathouse, married in Brown County on Jan. 14, 1914 to John Henry Hatton, born Dec. 10, 1887, son of Samuel E. Hatton and Matilda Tabor. Ressie and Henry Hatton had five children: Carl, Cloyd, Faye Naomi, Doyle and Donald. Henry Hatton had been a teacher. He died in 1946 and Ressie died in 1979; both are buried in Christiansburg Cemetery.

Donald Hatton, child #5 of John Henry Hatton and Ressie Jane Greathouse, married in Nashville on May 11, 1957 to Rose Marie Cross, daughter of Albert Henry Cross and Kathryn May Stogdill. Donald and Rose Hatton had four sons: Gregory Lee, Andrew Ray, Alan Dale, and Michael Keith. Donald recently retired after 31 years at Cummins

Engine Co. in Columbus. He and Rose also operated Spurgeon's Corner Grocery in Van Buren Twp. for eight years, retiring in 1989. *Submitted by Donald Hatton, great-grandson of Peter Greathouse* (See Samuel and Lucinda Allman Hatton)

JAMES G. AND MARGARET E. (BOOTS) GREGORY

Jim was born in Beech Grove, IN to Melvin and Mattie Gregory on April 9, 1929. His parents were both born and raised in Kentucky. They moved to Beech Grove after their marriage when Melvin was employed at the New York Central Railroad. Jim is a graduate of the Beech Grove Grade and High Schools.

Boots was born in Indianapolis to Leonard and Elsie Meisberger on Feb. 19, 1937. She was raised in the Fountain Square area on the southside of Indianapolis. After graduating from St. Patrick's Grade School and St. Mary's Academy, she went to work for an insurance company and later worked for insurance agents.

Jim and Boots were married on June 11, 1955 at St. Patrick's Catholic Church, built a home in Beech Grove and lived there until moving to Brown County.

Boots and Jim Gregory, 1973

On July 28, 1989, Jim and Boots moved to Nashville, but prior to that time had a home on Sweetwater Lake in northeast Brown County, since May, 1976. Before moving to Sweetwater full time in December, 1981, they owned and operated the Beech Grove Dog Center and various real estate holdings.

After moving to Nashville, Jim opened a Clock Repair Shop in their home. His interest started when they purchased two vintage clocks in 1974. He became interested in the working mechanism and subsequently took a course in Clock Repair and Restoration, which he completed in 1976. He is a member of the National Association of Watch and Clock Collectors, Inc.

Boots Gregory as "Tulip"

For 14 years before opening the Dog Center, Jim was employed at Eli Lilly, where he worked in plastic design and production control.

Boots is an active member of St. Agnes Catholic Church and various organizations, including the Pioneer Woman, and is known as "Tulip" the Clown.

IRVIN AND LIZZIE GRIFFIN

Irvin Griffin married Elizabeth "Lizzie" Steinbarger on Aug. 15, 1884. Irvin (March 25, 1862-Sept. 29, 1937) and Lizzie (Oct. 19, 1864-Feb. 7, 1950) came to Brown County from Bartholomew County about 1890. Their children were: Bertha May Griffin (Oct. 9, 1886-Nov. 26, 1967) married John Siegle Hyde (April 11, 1873-June 15, 1954); Edith Mary Griffin (May 29, 1889-July 22, 1956) married Carry Cummings (Oct. 10, 1889-March 12, 1962); Raymond Griffin (Jan. 1, 1892-June 2, 1965) married Bessie Rogers (Sept. 2, 1895-Sept. 6, 1965); Ralph E. Griffin (Jan. 22, 1897-July 8, 1946) married Fern Boaz; Laura Maude Griffin (Sept. 4, 1901-March 6, 1970) married John P. Wright (March 15, 1874-Oct. 3, 1949); Myrtle Iva Griffin (born Jan. 3, 1905) married Roy Dowell (Nov. 8, 1899-Aug. 21, 1982); Mildred Griffin, died young and Irvin and Lizzie Griffin both died in Brown County and are buried in Lanam Ridge Cemetery.

Front Row: Edna S. Richardson, Mary A. David, Bertha (Griffin) Hyde, Wilma J. Watson (behind) Back row: Wayne, Rex, John S., and Vernon Hyde

Bertha May Griffin, oldest child of Irvin and Lizzie, attended Jackson Creek School and Howard Ridge Church where she met John Siegle Hyde whom she married on Oct. 13, 1906. Their son William recalled that his father liked a good horse and buggy and remembered hearing the story of the horse named Tops that got scared one day and took his mother and his sisters for a fast ride to Belmont for groceries.

Bertha May and John Siegle Hyde had nine children, all born in Brown County: Lela Pearl, Edna Sophronia, Lizzie Estle, Virgil Chester, James Vernon, Irvin Wayne, Mary Alice, William Rex and Wilma Jean Hyde.

Lela Pearl Hyde, born Sept. 18, 1907, died Sept. 18, 1907, buried DuBois Cemetery, Brown County. Edna Sophronia Hyde, born June 14, 1909, married Glenn Richardson (1908-1988). Lizzie Estle Hyde, born March 19, 1911, married Ralph Woolridge. She died April 28, 1943 at Plainfield, IN where she is buried.

Virgil Chester Hyde, born July 27, 1913, died July 31, 1915, buried DuBois Cemetery James Vernon Hyde, born Aug. 15, 1915, married twice.

Irvin Hyde, born April 7, 1918, died Aug. 26, 1988; married Jesse Eloise Reese. Mary Alice Hyde, born Nov. 5, 1919, married Theodore Glen Davis, born April 5, 1918. William Rex Hyde, born June 8, 1922, Brown County, married Zella Margaret Frye, born June 23, 1927, Monroe Co., IN.

Wilma Jean Hyde, born Oct. 1, 1925, married Howard Frank Watson, born June 29, 1922, died Oct. 1, 1967. *Submitted by William Rex Hyde*

GRIMM FAMILY

The Grimm family began with John Gottfried Grimm, born 1878 in Switzerland and migrating to New York City about 1897. Settling first in New York City then in Massapequa, Long Island. He was a butcher by trade and an amateur wrestler. He married Margaretha Erni from Interlaken, Switzerland in 1905. They had four children: Henry, Helen, Edward and Elsie. The depression years did not hurt them as they did not believe in credit or banks. Money was actually kept in a jar buried in the basement of their home.

Edward, born April 4, 1909 in Queens County became a printer. He married Marguerita Catsanos, a writer in 1931 and had five children: Edward, John, **Marguerita,** Richard and Roy. They lived in the Massapequa area several years, then moved to up-state New York. They bought a small farm to fulfill a life-long dream to be a farmer, only to have that dream come to an end with his sudden death in 1945.

Marguerita, faced with raising five children, moved to Gloversville, NY and acquired a job as columnist for a local newspaper. She remarried and later became interested in antiques. She began an antique shop, specializing in antique books. She corresponded with people world wide concerning her books.

Marguerita Grimm

Daughter **Marguerita,** (Marge) born June 2, 1936 in Amityville, Long Island, graduated from Gloversville High School in 1954. She attended the University of Miami for one year, studying accounting, then met and married Don Mason from Princeton, IN. After their marriage, they moved to Indiana, settled in Indianapolis and later moved to Mooresville. They had four children: Marguerita, Donald, Jon and Robert. Marge was a homemaker, volunteering in church work, scouting and Little League.

In 1970 Marge and Don divorced and she attended the LPN School in Indianapolis, receiving her LPN license. She worked eight years at St. Francis Hospital in Beech Grove and there learned of Brown County. After visiting the area she moved to Princes Lakes, at the north-east edge of Brown County. Obtaining a part-time job in one of the shop, she fell in love with the county. Once a friend said to her "don't you ever get tired of driving those windy roads to Nashville?" Her response was "Heaven's no, I enjoy every minute it takes me to get there and back. It's the only job I've ever had that I've enjoyed traveling to and from work."

Marge moved to Nashville in 1984, her children grown, she had dreams of owning a shop. Two years later that became a reality by opening one in Antique Alley and later moving to the Artist Colony Shops. She currently has combined her hobby of family genealogy and business by operating THE FAMILY TREE. She resides at 30 Johnson Street, Nashville with her constant companion, Pompi, her dog. She enjoys her children, grandchild, friends, sports, hiking, outdoor activities, reading, playing her dulcimer, working in county genealogy and of course constantly working on her own family history. *Submitted by Marge Grimm*

GARRISON GROVE - Garrison was born in Brown Co., IN on August 1823, a son of George and Lavina Grove. His childhood years were probably spent helping his father operate the mill at Georgetown. On Nov. 11, 1843, Garrison married Sally Ann Stivers (born 1825, Kentucky) and about five years later they migrated to Jasper Co., IL, where Sally died on June 4, 1874. Garrison remarried to Elizabeth Shupert in 1875 and again in 1883 to Louisa McMannis Hamilton; but died on Dec. 9, 1901 in Jasper County. He and Sally are buried at Tate Cemetery near Bogota. Garrison and Sally's children were: Lavina (born 1845, married Nathan Boldrey), John H. (born 1847, married Matilda Elizabeth Nottingham), Margaret (born 1849, married Newberry Tate), Malinda (born 1852, married John Lipscomb), Elizabeth (born 1855, married John Lancaster), Malissa (born 1856, married James Tate), Nancy Jane (born 1858, married Thomas B. Tate), Sarah (born 1862, married Enoch Reed), Matthew L. (born 1863), Mary Etta (born 1866). *Submitted by Randall Grove*

Garrison Grove
1823-1901

GEORGE GROVE - George was born in Pennsylvania around 1798 and was in the Brown/Monroe Co., IN area before 1820. He married around 1818 to Lavina Barnes (born ca. 1798, North Carolina) and until about 1847, ran a mill at Georgetown, a village named after himself but since changed to Bean Blossom. Around 1847, George moved east to Jasper Co., IL where he died sometime around 1855. Lavina died in Jasper County in September 1877. All of George and Lavina's children migrated to Jasper Co., IL except for Anna, who married Jesse Richards in 1836. She and Jesse remained in Brown County. George and Lavina's other children were: Michael (born 1822, married to Patience Boldrey), Garrison (born 1823, married Sally Ann Stivers), Rebecca (born 1827, married David Richards), Silas (born 1830, married Martha Ervin), George W. (born 1832, married Anna Smallwood Milburn), Daniel (born 1835, married Mary J. Jackson), Jesse (born 1835, married Angeline Mardis). *Submitted by Randall Grove*

CHARLES AND MARGARET GUY - It was August 1973 when this couple took up residence in VanBuren Township of Brown County, coming here from Jackson County. Charles Guy (more familiarily known as Bud) was born at Crothersville, IN, July 26, 1929. His parents were Joseph Curtis Guy and Maggie Naomi (Young) Guy. Margaret Guy was born in Jackson County Nov. 11, 1930. Her parents are Ross Stigdon and Doris (Mellencamp) Stigdon.

Charles served in the Air Force and was honorably discharged Sept. 20, 1949. It was during furlough time that he met Margaret and they were married Dec. 23, 1948 at Seymour, IN.

The children born to Charles and Margaret are: (1) Barbara Lou Gurhl of Hope, IN, born March 26, 1950; (2) Marlene Elaine Cross, lives in Seymour, IN and was born March 1, 1951; (3) Lisa Ann Terry, born Crothersville, IN Sept. 12, 1952; and (4) Curtis Ross, Columbus, IN born May 27, 1954.

Charles is retired from Cummins Engine Company. He and Margaret have a great time riding their motorcycle on various trips and have even gone twice to California on it.

Charles and Margaret Guy, June, 1987

Charles and Margaret have the joy of seven grandchildren and two great-grandchildren. Two of the grandchildren are in college and one is a missionary in Guatamala.

Margaret Guy has four sisters and one brother. These are listed under Ross Stigdon.

Charles Guy has one brother, Olover Guy of Crothersville, IN, and sisters Mary Schrader, Medora, IN; Audrea Summa, Seymour, IN and Phyllis Lamb, North Vernon, IN. He had two sisters and two brothers deceased. *Submitted by Mrs. Charles Guy*

CHARLES WM. AND MARY (SWAN) HAGEN - Charles and Mary moved to Brown County in 1965, settling on 65 acres adjacent to Yellowwood State Forest. They were drawn to Brown County because of its physical beauty and abundance of plant and animal life.

Charles' childhood was spent in East Orange, NJ and during visits to his grandparents' farm near Port Jervis, NY he developed a love of nature. He majored in Botany at Cornell, graduated in 1939, and was elected to Phi Beta Kappa. At Indiana University he earned his PhD in 1944. After World War II research at the Manhattan Project in Chicago, he returned to the Indiana University Botany Department as a faculty member. His ranks at I.U. included Professor, Associate Dean of Arts and Science, Associate Dean of Academic Affairs, Dean for Resource Development, and Director of Long Range Planning. For many years his biography appeared in Who's Who. After retiring in 1983, he served on the Board of the Hilltop Education Foundation, on the Environmental Resource Advisory Committee for the Bloomington Park Board, the Boards of Directors for the Meadowood Retirement Community and the Mathers Museum, and was Chairman of the Planning Committee for the Arboretum at I.U. His hobbies included photographing wildflowers, maintaining several gardens, growing plants of special interest, primarily Bromeliads, in his greenhouse and solarium, and weaving tapestries and baskets.

Mary and Charles Hagen, 1990

An Indianapolis native, Mary Swan graduated from Shortridge High School, majored in Botany at DePauw, joined Kappa Alpha Theta, and graduated in 1942. During Summer Sessions she studied Field Biology at the Universities of Colorado and Wyoming. She came to Indiana University as a research assistant in Botany and started her graduate studies. Here she met Charles and marriage followed in December 1942. Their first son, Charles III, was born in 1945 while they were living in Chicago. After returning to Bloomington, David was born in 1947, Ronald in 1948.

Mary engaged in many child-oriented volunteer services and earned her Masters Degree in Elementary Education in 1956 at I.U. In 1957 Charles was awarded Guggenheim and Fulbright Scholarships to study at the Imperial College of Tropical Agriculture in Trinidad, British West Indies. While there, Charles did research, Mary taught in a girls' high school, and the boys attended British schools. On returning to Bloomington, Mary taught at Hunter Elementary, was elected President of the Monroe County teachers' association, taught at Unionville, took a Sabbatical Leave to study Educational Psychology, and spent the next ten years teaching at Arlington Elementary. After retiring in 1982, she pursued weaving and quilt-making, taught her crafts at workshops throughout the Midwest, and participated in several weaving and quilting guilds.

Travel was an important part of the Hagens' lives. Professional consultation took Charles to the Philippines and Afghanistan. Later, pleasure trips took them to Mexico, Europe, Japan, Hong Kong, Hawaii, Canada, Peru, Bolivia, Trinidad, the Bahamas, the Virgin Islands, and to many locations in the United States.

JOHN PAUL HAGGARD - John's family migrated from Kentucky when he was around four years old. They settled close to Nashville, Brown Co., IN. John Paul Haggard was born in 1856 and the family came to Brown County in 1860.

Indians were living in tepees along Indian Creek just south of Morgantown at that time. John Paul married Edith Ann Percifield. They built their home in northern Brown County. In fact, the Morgan and Brown County line ran through the middle of their house. They ate in Brown County and slept in Morgan County. Their house was built on what is now called the Haggard Road, named after John Paul Haggard.

They had seven living children: three boys and four girls. One of the girls was named Minnie Agnus Haggard, who later married a Jacobs. They had 52 living grandchildren.

John Paul Haggard was a farmer. He also had what was called a stink factory. Dead animals were brought in, skinned and then they cooked the meat from the bones, dried the bones and hauled them to

Indianapolis by horse and wagon to make what was called bone dust. He also cured the hides and took them to make shoes and harness. It took him three to five days to make the trip to Indianapolis and back home.

John Paul played tug of war with the grandchildren. He'd say "pull real hard" and then he would let his end loose. He really got a bang out of the deal when the kids went tumbling down.

John Paul and Edith Ann (Percifield) Haggard

One day while Bonnie Jacobs Walker was at grandpa's house four Indians came riding by on horses. One was a girl riding a paint horse. Her name was "Humming Bird." They stopped and talked to John Paul. They were hunting a silver mine. They said it was on a pine bluff between Helmsburg and Trevlac. They said "it had enough silver to shoe all the white man's horses but white man no find, he no have sense enough." Bonnie was standing close by listening in. There must have been one because a few years later an article came out about the mine in the Farmer's Guide Magazine saying it had never been found. The Indians talking with John Paul were from northern Indiana.

John Paul became real sick a couple years before he passed away in the 1920s or 30s. Two years after that his wife, Edith, died. *Written by Bonnie Jacobs Walker*

WILLIAM THOMAS HAGGARD FAMILY
- William Thomas Haggard was born Sept. 8, 1942 in Beech Grove, IN. His father was William Francis Haggard and he married Mildred Melvina Miller in 1939. His paternal grandfather was Francis Marion Haggard and he married Indiana Stinnet. The family home has been in Marion County at Acton, IN since the early 1900s where William's mother still resides.

The Haggard family originated in England. William's great-grandfather was a wagon maker. William's paternal grandfather settled in Morgantown, IN before moving to Acton, IN.

William's wife Ann Cecelia Bauder Haggard was born March 25, 1947 in Indianapolis. Her father was Joseph Francis Bauder and he married Patricia McNevin in 1946. Ann's paternal grandfather was John Dominic Bauder and was married to Helen Cecelia Walker. The Bauder family is of German Descent.

William and Ann were married May 14, 1966 in Indianapolis. William started in 1962 as an upholsterer with the New York Central System and is a graduate of Kansas City School of Watchmaking. He is a Master Watchmaker listed with the American Watchmakers Institute. He is now employed as a cabinetmaker for Amtrack Railroad at Beech Grove, IN.

Ann has been a Licensed Practical Nurse since 1981 and now works in Brown County.

William and Ann have two children. Michael Thomas Haggard was born Feb. 3, 1970. He lives at home and is a full-time student in the School of Business at Indiana University. William Joseph Haggard was born March 17, 1967. He married Kimberly Ann Hebauf and they are the parents of a daughter Lauren Celeste Haggard born Oct. 10, 1986. They live and work in Indianapolis.

The Haggard family moved from Acton, IN to Brown County and lived in the Wabash Village Apartments in June 1988. They resided there while William and his son Michael began building the family home three miles North of S.R. 46 on Salt Creek Road. They constructed the home using native yellow poplar logs sawed at the Morgan Sawmill in Gatesville. In spite of the heat and drought in the summer of 1988, they were able to complete all four exterior log walls and had the home under roof by the year's end. The family continued to work throughout 1989 on their project and finally moved into their home called "Smokepole" in January of 1990.

The Haggards are members of the National Muzzle-Loading Rifle Association and the St. Agnes Catholic Church in Nashville.

HALL-SINN - Jesse Hall, Jr. was born Nov. 12, 1823 in Kentucky. He was the son of Jesse Hall, Sr. and Rebecca (Fleetwood) Hall. His parents were early settlers to Brown County; coming up from the Blue Ridge Mountains of Kentucky. Jesse, Jr. was over six feet tall and Jesse, Sr. was about seven feet tall. Jesse Hall, Sr. came to Brown County by 1850. Jesse Hall, Sr. built log houses in Brown County. Jesse Hall, Sr. was the father of 25 children by two marriages. He married first, on Jan. 15, 1812 in Floyd Co., KY to Rebecca Fleetwood. He married second, on May 13, 1841 in Lawrence Co., IN to Melinda Hanson/Henson.

Jesse Hall, Jr. and Rebecca Aynes were the parents of: Nancy Jane born Aug. 18, 1848, died Jan. 25, 1911 married to Frederick Sinn; Sarah Ann, born Sept. 28, 1849, died Sept. 13, 1886, married June 18, 1871 to Henry Rose; Nathan Alexander, born Aug. 19, 1851, died April 24, 1926, married Jane Setser; John H., born Sept. 26, 1853, died Jan. 26, 1912, married Elizabeth Lutes; Isaac, born March 11, 1855 died March 30, 1855; Peter, born Jan. 27, 1856 died Feb. 24, 1941 married April 22, 1877 to Pheobe Sipes; Mary Elizabeth, born July 23, 1858 died Dec. 2, 1927 married Joe Helms; William David, born July 24, 1861 died Aug. 16, 1890 married Feb. 22, 1880 to Mary Elizabeth Hedrick; Jesse Hall, III, born April 15, 1864 died Sept. 21, 1874; Rebecca Frances, born May 27, 1869 died March 31, 1939 married in 1889 to Stanley Axsom; and Izila, born May 12, 1871 died Sept. 23, 1871.

Frederick and Nancy Jane (Hall) Sinn

Jesse Hall, Jr. died March 14, 1901 and Rebecca (Aynes) Hall died Oct. 4, 1891 in Brown County. They are both buried in the Elkinsville Cemetery. Nancy Jane Hall, eldest daughter of Jesse and Rebecca Aynes Hall, married on May 9, 1869 in Brown County to Frederick Sinn. He was born in Ohio on April 1, 1845, a son of Morris and Norma Carolina (Caroline Rose) Sinn/Sind. He lived at Belmont, in Brown County, where he had a General Store. Years later he moved to Third Street in Bloomington, IN. Fred hunted ginseng with Gabriel Aynes. Nancy Jane and Fredrick Sinn were the parents of eight children: Savannah born March 28, 1870, Laura born Feb. 2, 1872, Jesse born Aug. 25, 1873, Mary Rosetta born March 30, 1876, Rebecca born Feb. 26, 1878, Lila born Jan. 26, 1881, Grace born Dec. 21, 1883 and Frederick Wesley born Sept. 29, 1887.

Savannah married Monroe Mobley; their children were: Jesse William, Grace, Myrtle, Nancy Anna, Fred Monroe, Nathan Orval, Charles Raymond, Estes Herman, Martha Savannah and Lester Earl.

Laura married Arl Bruner; their children were: Oma, Lobie, Jake, Stella, Ray, Buleh, Wayne, Ruth and Wesley.

Jesse married Lula Wilson; their children were: Estle, Earl, Ernest and Ray.

Mary Rosetta married Cecil Deckard; their children were: Iva, Lonnie, Wesley, Janie, Rachel, Estella, Ella and Mary Ellen.

Rebecca married Milton Floyd; their children were: Ivan and Orval.

Lila married Harley Wilson; their children were: Hester, Chester, Olive, Oliver and Dorval.

Grace married Charles Rose; their children were: Blanche, Oma, Dorothy and Betty.

Frederick Wesley married Grace Galyan; their children were: Cleo, Olive, Samuel, May, Wesley Junior, Charles and Paul.

Frederick Sinn died May 22, 1928 and Nancy Jane (Hall) Sinn died Jan. 25, 1911. Both are buried in the Duncan Cemetery in Brown County near Yellowwood Lake. *Submitted by Mary (Deckard) Bond, granddaughter of Frederick Sinn*

GEORGE W. AND MARGARET (SHIPLEY) HAMBLEN
- George W. was born Jan. 12, 1857 in Marion Co., IA about one year after his parents, William and Elizabeth Huff Hamblen, moved to Iowa from Brown Co., IN. William died while serving in Co. C, 34th Iowa Infantry, on March 7, 1864. George's mother, Elizabeth, returned to Brown County with four small children ranging from one month to nine years of age. William is buried in the Taggart Cemetery. Elizabeth received an $8.00 per month pension as a widow and $2.00 per month for each of the four children. This provided her with some independence and this led to accusations of her being a loose woman. The children's grandfather, Pleasant, eventually obtained custody of the three younger ones just before he died in 1874. Mary, the oldest, had reached the age of 16. Upon the death of Pleasant custody of the three, George, John William and Maneca Jane, was transferred to John C. Hester who had assisted Pleasant in his custody battle. Elizabeth is reported to have married a — Smith and moved to Morgan Co., IN. What happened to her is not known as of July 1990.

On April 2, 1878 George married Margaret May Shipley Nelson, the widow of Samuel Nelson and the daughter of Jesse W. Shipley and Mary Ann Hall. Margaret was born Feb. 25, 1854 and her mother, Mary Ann, died the following April 30. Mary Ann is buried in Deckard Cemetery in Brown Co., IN. Sam Nelson died March 25, 1876 at age 28 and is buried in the Elkinsville cemetery.

Margaret May Shipley Nelson Hamblen, ca. 1873

George and Margaret had sons, Pleasant, born Sept. 25, 1879, and James William, born April 9, 1888, and daughters, Mary Jane, born May 16, 1881, and Lula, born July 31, 1882, all in Brown County. In 1892 while returning from Nashville George apparently had a heart attack. When he did not return home as expected they searched for him along the path he was expected to take, found his body and buried him where they found him. The location of his grave has been told to his grandchildren as being "up in back of the old Browning School." This is near Elkinsville.

Jimmy Hamblen's Huckster Truck ca. 1925

Margaret lived with her youngest son, James William (Jimmy) Hamblen, on what is now the Brown County State Park until 1924 when they sold to the State and moved to Story in Van Buren Township. She died July 14, 1929 and is buried in the Elkinsville Cemetery. At her request her casket was taken to the Cemetery from the Elkinsville Road on a wagon drawn by two horses. While the family was at the Cemetery the house in Story was broken into and the accounts for the huckster routes were stolen. This event hastened the demise of Jimmy Hamblen's huckster business.

Pleasant married Ada Emeline Brown, born Dec. 16, 1879, the daughter of Polk Brown and Malinda Jane Stevens of Brown County. Mary Jane married James Mullis, born July 16, 1865, the son of Franklin Mullis and Margaret Rogers of Brown County. Lula married George C. Hobbs, born March 3, 1860, son of Thomas Hobbs and Mary Bird of Brown County. James William married Mary Etta Morrison, born Sept. 28, 1897 in Adams Co., OH. *Submitted by grandson John W. Hamblen*

J.B. AND VIRGINIA HAMBLEN - The Hamblen family ancestors migrated to Indiana from eastern Virginia prior to 1818, when Job Hamblen and his family of five first settled in Jennings County. A soldier in the Revolutionary War, young Job saw the British soldiers under General Cornwallis stack their arms after the battle of Yorktown (1781). To escape sickness found in Indiana's low lands, Job's family later homesteaded along Sweetwater Creek, Brown County. As a seventh generation descendant of Job, Jennings Bryan "Bill" Hamblen was born in a log cabin on Nov. 7, 1897, in what is now Hamblen Township. He was the son of Armeanous Porter Hamblen, who did extensive research on the Hamblen and associated families, which culminated in the publishing of a family history, *The Hamblen and Allied Families* (1940).

Following the pioneer spirit of his forefathers, Armeanous Porter left Brown County for Indian Territory, now the western half of Oklahoma (1901). He built a one room frame house for his wife, the former Mary Jane Anderson, and their children, Bill and Mable. There the family prospered on their claim, operating a grocery store, installing the first telephone exchange and running a post office. Bill's father also built the first grade school, serving as headmaster. He was a secret member of the *Anti Horse Thief Association*, a necessity for law and order in the wild west. Bill left the broad prairie and cow punching when he and his sister returned to Franklin, IN to attend high school, staying with their grandparents. His wild west stories earned him the name of *Bronco Bill* by his class mates. In 1917 Bill entered the University of Wisconsin to study a new field called Chemical Engineering. These studies were interrupted upon entering Army as a 2nd Lieutenant Field Artillery (1918).

J.B. and Virginia Hamblen

After graduating from the University of Wisconsin (1921) Bill worked three years in Nova Scotia for the U.S. Gypsum Co. He then received a Masters degree in Chemical Engineering at M.I.T. (1926). It was at the start of Bill's career with the Standard Oil Company in Whiting, IN that he met Ivis Virginia Fateley, who was working part time in his dad's general store in Franklin. Virginia, born March 11, 1904, is a native of Needham Township in Johnson County, the daughter of Worth Peter and Anna (Fisher) Fateley. She and her sisters Carrie and Mary, and brothers, Winthrop, Nolan, and Clinton, were raised on the Fateley farm located about four miles south of Franklin on route 44, near Sugar Creek. Following her graduation from Franklin College with a degree in Education she married Bill (1927). Virginia and Bill have one son, David Philip, born in 1928.

Bill received a job transfer, so they moved to Destrehan, LA (1933), to an oil refinery built on an old sugar plantation along the banks of the Mississippi River, about ten miles upriver from New Orleans. Another transfer took them to Texas City, TX (1935), where Bill was assistant manager of the Pan American oil refinery. The three weathered cold Texas *"blue northers"* in the winter and several hurricanes in the summer, living on the prairie along the Gulf coast. David went to college (1947), served in the Army (1951), and married Frances Anne Winfree of Oak Ridge, TN (1959). Anne is a descendant of pioneer families from middle Tennessee. Her folks moved to Oak Ridge where her father was with the security forces during development of the Atomic Bomb. David and Anne now live in Rochester, NY, where he is completing 23 years as a research physicist at Eastman Kodak Co.

Bill and Virginia returned to New Orleans (1955), to the charm of the floral city and its Mardi Gras, where Bill was vice president and manager of manufacturing of the petroleum corporation. A next stop was to the Amoco offices in New York, living in Irvington-on-Hudson, then on to the corporate office, living in LaGrange, IL, where he retired (1962). Both returned to the land of their forefathers, their home being on Artist's Drive in Nashville for 22 years. They participated in many local activities: belonging to the Methodist church, the Art Gallery, Historical Society, and both commanders of the World War I Veterans club. Bill was an avid photographer and Virginia is well known for her artistic touch in making hooked rugs. They moved to the Methodist Home in Franklin three years ago, where Virginia still resides in their cottage following Bill's death March 3, 1989. *Submitted by David P. Hamblen*

JAMES W. AND MARY E. HAMBLEN - Jimmy (James William) Hamblen, a great-great-great-grandson of Job Hamblen through Uriah, Pleasant, William and George, was born near Nashville on April 2, 1888. By 1900 he was living with his mother, Margaret Shipley Nelson Hamblen, and his brother, Pleasant, in Johnson Township. A few years later he moved with his mother to Van Buren Township, Sec. 4, T8N, R3E, where they purchased 125 acres. This property is just southeast of the Lookout Tower in Brown County State Park. On March 19, 1915 he married Mary Etta Morrison who had recently moved to the area with her mother, Laura Belle Duffey Morrison Rybolt and her stepfather, James Rybolt, from Dunkirk, IN. (The Rybolts had been in Columbus. They came from Adams Co., OH ca. 1913.) From this 125 acres James cut crossties which Mary hauled to Gnaw Bone by mule team. Later James began to peddle and drove a huckster wagon, truck and later a car through southern Brown County. In July, 1924, he moved his family to Story and continued his peddling business. At the height of his business in the mid-1920s he purchased a new Model-T truck. An accurate painting of this truck is shown above as commissioned by his son, John, and painted by the Brown County Artist, Kenneth Reeve. The roads were very hard on motor vehicles. Stumps and jutting rocks in the middle of the road were not uncommon. During the late 20s when money became scarce he was forced to curtail his routes and resorted to the gathering of roots, primarily sassafras, and the peddling of Brown County items such as sassafras, horseradish, potatoes, sorghum molasses, and bittersweet in surrounding towns, even so far as Richmond. Most of the sassafras was shipped East to be used in medicines. He moved his family to Columbus in September 1932 and died there on Oct. 16, 1933. Mary died 1974. Both are buried in Mt. Zion Cemetery.

Twelve children were born to James and Mary Hamblen. Six were born at what is now the Park, five at Story and one in Columbus. Tressa (died Dec. 1, 1989) married Garland Ayers and lived in

Van Buren Township most of her life. Jesse married Pauline Marshall and Plessie married Helen Marshall. Both are retired from Cummins and live in Columbus. Three died as infants.

Family, back row: James, Mary, Margaret. Front row: Jesse, Tressa. Taken about 1921 at the homeplace in the Park.

John was the first to be born at Story on Sept. 25, 1924. He married first Brenda F. Harrod of Noble County (divorced 1979) and married second (1987) Marianne Muhlbauer. He retired in 1987 from the University of Missouri-Rolla with the rank of Professor Emeritus of Computer Science. After spending two years in Maryland doing genealogical research they moved to Columbus for their permanent retirement residence in August 1989.

Children: Flora, Raymond, Wanda, John, Wilma, Tressa, Plessie, Jesse, Donald - taken 1984

Flora married Clarence Otte of Jackson County. He died 1980. Donald married Clara Baker of Geneva, IN and lives in Lanesville. Raymond married Peggy Smith of Brown County and lives near Scottsburg. Wilma married Wm. Fleetwood (divorced 1968). She died March 7, 1989 in Columbus. Wanda was adopted by Paul and Kathryn Bayne, married Dale Wilson and lives in Indianapolis.

Mary E. was the daughter of Thomas Mifflin Morrison and Laura Belle Duffey of Adams Co., OH. Thomas was the son of William W. Morrison and Susan A. Raleigh. Tradition is that Susan was a full blooded Indian but this has not been confirmed. William was probably the son of Joseph Morrison of Mifflin Co., PA. Laura Belle descended from Michael Duffey, born 1753 in Londonderry, Ireland. Other names in her ancestry are Swisher, Ramsay and Cross. Other names in James' ancestry are Shipley, Hall, Huff, Brummett, Weddle, Mason, Mullins, Washington, Carey, and Holloway.
Submitted by son, John

JESSE E. AND F. PAULINE HAMBLEN -
Jesse Eugene, born Nov. 14, 1917, just southeast of the Lookout Tower in Brown County State Park, is the son of James Wm. and Mary E. Hamblen. Until about 1940 he lived in Van Buren Township, spending much of his time fishing and hunting. The skills acquired through hunting in Brown County may have contributed to his survival in the jungles of the South Pacific during WWII. Jesse served in Co. K, 147th Infantry of the U.S. Army for 38 months in the Southwest Pacific, including Tonga, Guadalcanal, British Samoa, New Caledonia, and Emmaru(?). While on Guadalcanal, Jesse had just returned one evening with his company from the hills when he was asked to serve as a guide for two other companies going to where he had just been. While he was doing this, his own Company was ambushed on the Banika(?) River and badly shot up.

Jesse and Pauline Hamblen

During his teens, Jesse spent almost three years in the CCC Camps of Freetown and Henryville, IN; Short Creek, AZ; and Hurricane, UT. During this time he paid off a note at the Irwin Union Bank and Trust Company which his Dad, James Wm., had left when he died in 1933.

Jesse worked at Cummins for 34 years and eight months from 1945 until he retired in 1980, and worked part-time for Columbus Tool and later for Midwest Tool and Engineering in Columbus.

On June 7, 1941, Jesse m. Frances Pauline Marshall, born May 23, 1921, daughter of John Marshall, Sr. and Leona Idessa Reed. They have two children, Douglas Eugene and Karen Jo.

Douglas, born July 20, 1955, in Columbus, IN, married Karen York, born July 31, 1957, in Belleville, IL, daughter of William D. York and Frances Diane Wyatt, who now live in Taylorsville, IN. Their children are Megan Diane, born April 14, 1977, and Katelyn Nicole, born July 29, 1983. Divorced 1988, Doug married second Sherry Lewis Wehmiller on July 5, 1989.

Karen, born Sept. 11, 1960, married Greg Nichter in 1981 and was divorced in 1984, no children. Karen married second Jeff Davis on Aug. 3, 1985, son of Robert Davis and Mary Reed of Columbus. They have one son, Dillon, born Feb. 25, 1988, and live near Grandview Church.

Jesse and Pauline are members of St. Peters Lutheran Church in Columbus.

JOB HAMBLEN -
Job moved his family into what is now Hamblen Township, Brown County, in 1825 from near what is now Clifford, IN where he had settled by 1821 after leaving Lee Co., VA ca. 1816.

Job was born in Worcester Co., MD in 1762 to George and Piercy Carey Hamblen. In 1771 the family moved to Halifax Co., VA, then to Charlotte Co., VA by 1777, to Pittsylvania Co., VA by 1780 and to Rockingham Co., NC in 1786. Job served in the Virginia Militia and was present for the surrender of Cornwallis at Yorktown. He married (1782) Eleanor Mullins, daughter of John and Jane (Washington) Russell Mullins, who was related to George Washington, according to A. Porter Hamblen in his book **The Hamblen and Allied Families**. Job and Eleanor spent time in the Carolinas before settling in Lee Co., VA ca. 1795. They were still there in 1812 when their son, George, enlisted and was killed in the war on Mackinac Island, MI in 1814. Their children were: John Mullins, Uriah, William, George, Eliakim, Eleanor, Sarah and Mary.

Job Hamblen Monument

The descendants of Job and Eleanor now number in the thousands and are spread over most of the states. Although their eldest, John M., stayed in Lee Co., VA, his descendants also came to Brown Co. and several, including his wife, Mary Campbell, are buried in Taggart Cemetery. The late J.B. (Bill) Hamblen who lived on Artist Drive in Nashville for many years was John's great-great-grandson.

Job's second son, Uriah, married Clarissa Casey after losing his first wife, Keziah Mason, and moved to Jefferson Co., IL ca. 1830. However, his children remained in Brown County with Job and Eleanor. The eldest of Uriah, Pleasant, married Milly Weddle ca. 1831 and homesteaded in Hamblen Township (NE 1/4 of NW 1/4 Sec. 35, T10N, R3E) by patent dated 1836. Part of the original log cabin is included in the present home located on this property. Pleasant also lost his wife and mother of seven. He married again to Angeline Murphy in 1851 and they had five children. Some of Pleasant's children followed their grandfather to Illinois and from there they moved westward.

Job's youngest son, Eliakim, is said to have suggested that Hamblen Township be named after his father, Job, who was the first permanent settler in the locality. By 1880 there were 25 Households with the name Hamblen in Brown County.

Bob and Lester Hamblen, great-grandsons of Pleasant Hamblen, grandson of Job, beside Pleasant Hamblen's homestead on Upper Salt Creek Road, 1988 (House burned August 1990)

Job's son-in-law, William Taylor, filed for the homestead in 1836 and lived there with his wife, Sarah (Hamblen) Barnett. She died 1875, he died 1876. They are both buried in the Hamblen-Taylor Cemetery on the Job Hamblen homestead north of Gatesville. In 1929 the Hamblen Family Association erected a monument to Job Hamblen at this location honoring the Revolutionary War Veteran. The event was spearheaded and chaired by the Hamblen Genealogist, Armeanous Porter Hamblen. The cemetery has been in the custody of Porter's son, the late J.B. Hamblen, for many years. *Written by great-great-great-great-grandson, John Wesley Hamblen, descended through Uriah, Pleasant, William, George and James Wm. (Jimmy)*

JOHN WESLEY HAMBLEN - John, computer scientist and genealogist, was born at Story on Sept. 25, 1924 to James William and Mary Etta (Morrison) Hamblen. He attended elementary school at Story, Columbus, Laulis, Indianapolis (Nos. 4 and 21), Waymansville and Meyers (Jackson County). He lived with Mrs. Henry Meyer, Jr. in Jackson County, 1937-41, Alfred Naffe fall of 1941 and Ralph McKain spring of 1942. He graduated from Cortland High School (Jackson County) as valedictorian in 1942.

John worked at W.D. Springer Elevator in Kennard (Henry Co.), IN and the Farm Bureau in Columbus before entering Indiana University in May, 1943. He earned a B.A. degree in Mathematics (1947) at IU and M.S. and Ph.D. degrees in Mathematics and Statistics at Purdue in 1952 and 1955. He taught high school at Kingsbury (LaPorte County, 1946-48) and Bluffton (1948-51). He was on the faculties of Oklahoma State, as Assistant and Associate Professor of Mathematics (1955-58), of the University of Kentucky, as Associate Professor of Statistics (1958-1961), of Southern Illinois University, as Professor of Mathematics and Technology (1961-65), of Georgia Tech., as Adjunct Professor of Information Science (1965-66), and of the University of Missouri-Rolla, as Professor of Computer Science (1972-87).

Dr. John W. Hamblen, taken: 1984

Dr. Hamblen started computer centers at Oklahoma State University (1956) and the University of Kentucky (1958), and was Director of the Data Processing and Computing Center at Southern Illinois University before going to the Southern Regional Education Board in Atlanta as Project Director for Computer Sciences (1965-72). He then moved to Rolla, MO to become Chairman of the Computer Science Department of the University of Missouri-Rolla (1972-81). During 1981-82 and half-time during 1982-83 he was a Visiting Scientist at the National Bureau of Standards with the Office of the Associate Director of Computing. For the other half-time of 1982-83 he was awarded a Development Grant from the University of Missouri-Rolla to attend Computer Science classes at the University of Maryland. He returned to UMR and taught for two years (1983-85). He then went to the National Science Foundation as Associate Program Director for Advanced Applications of Technology to Education (1985-86) and returned to UMR to teach during 1986-87.

Dr. Hamblen retired from UMR in 1987 with the title of Professor Emeritus of Computer Science. He then moved to Gaithersburg, MD for two years to do genealogical research. In August 1989 he and his wife, Marianne, moved to Tipton Lakes in Columbus, IN for their permanent retirement residence.

John has one son, James Ovid, by his first marriage to Brenda F. Harrod (1947-79), of Noble County. James has a BSEE degree from Georgia Tech, an MSEE from Purdue and a PhD in EE from Georgia Tech. He is now a professor of EE at Georgia Tech.

John is a life member of the American Association for the Advancement of Science and was elected a Fellow in 1963. He was President of the Association for Educational Data Systems, 1968-69, founding Editor of the AEDS Journal, and received the Aid to AEDS Award in 1971. In 1988 he was awarded the National Educational Computing Conference's first Distinguished Service Award.

John served as Secretary of the Association for Computing Machinery, 1972-76, was a member of the committee which developed recommendations for an Undergraduate Curriculum in Computer Science, 1960-68, was chairman of this Committee, 1976-81, and developed recommendations for an MS program in Computer Science (1981) and updated the undergraduate recommendations (1978). He was a recipient of the 1990 ACM/SIGCSE Award for Outstanding Contributions to Computer Science Education. He was Chairman for the 1981 and 1987 ACM Computer Science Conferences held in St. Louis and was Program Chairman for the 1985 World Conference on Computers in Education. He was on the Board of Directors of the American Federation of Information Processing Societies, 1981-86, Chairman of the AFIPS Education Committee, 1971-72, 1979-84, and received the AFIPS Education Award for 1985.

John is Editor and Publisher of **The Hamblen Connector**, a Newsletter for the Hamblen, Hamblin, Hamlin, Hamlen and related families and Publisher of the second printing of **The Hamblen and Allied Families** by A. Porter Hamblen. He was lead consultant for evaluating all computer related curricula for the State University System of Florida, 1979, and was consultant to the NBS, NSF, ETS, IBM, FTC, SREB, Systems Development Corp., Sunray-DX and numerous colleges and universities. He has proposed and administered approx. 20 grants and contracts from NBS, NSF, IBM, Exxon Education Foundation and Wright Patterson AF Base for over 1.5 million dollars. He has published over 80 papers and books, mostly dealing with the status of computing, computer science education and computer manpower in the U.S. He is an Associate Editor of the Journal of Computer Science Education. His vitae have been published in **American Men of Science, Who's Who in America, Who's Who in the World,** and **Who's Who in Frontiers of Science and Technology**. He was a member of Rotary Clubs in Lexington, KY, Carbondale, IL and Rolla, MO for 20 years.

NEWTON HAMBLEN - Newton, a fifth-generation descendant of Job Hamblen, was born Aug. 7, 1901 in Hamblen Township, Brown Co., IN. Louis Napoleon Hamblen and Laura (Roberts) Hamblen's sixth child (and sixth son), Newton, was born in the log cabin owned by his grandfather, Pleasant Hamblen, which was located on the Upper Salt Creek Road. The cabin burned in August, 1990. John Condon lived close by and the Quilley family lived just across the creek. Behind the cabin was Chinchbug Hill. The Fowler place was located on top of the hill.

Newton and Bertha (Allman) Hamblen, 1927

As a toddler Newton accidentally fell into the fireplace and was burned about the head, although no disfigurement resulted. His father, who had been paralyzed in 1906, rescued him by pulling him out of the fireplace with his cane. Newton later went to school at the Taggart School, just across from the Gatesville store. In fact, it was in Gatesville that he first saw an automobile. In the summer all six of the Hamblen brothers worked "out". They picked blackberries where Camp Attebury is now located and sold them in Edinburg. In the winter his brothers cut railroad ties, a job in which the women of the family occasionally assisted.

In 1908 Louis Hamblen died. In 1912 Laura Hamblen and her children moved to Knox Co., IN. In 1916 the family moved again, this time to Iowa. Then in 1918 Newton and his brother Carl moved to Phoenix, AZ. Newton found employment as a cook and, on Oct. 13, 1918, he married Marian McBrown. They lived on a farm near Phoenix and had one daughter, Nodine (born May 25, 1919) before divorcing.

On Jan. 12, 1926 Newton married a second time. He met his bride, Bertha Louise (Allman) Edgett, (born Jan. 12, 1905), in Los Angeles, CA. Newton and Bertha had seven children: Bob Hugh (May 13, 1929), Louis Mervin (Feb. 19, 1932), Lester Maurice (Feb. 3, 1935), Sandra Janell (Oct. 9, 1937), Laura Belle (Dec. 26, 1940), Sharon Carline (April 26, 1943), and Mary Ruth (June 30, 1945). During these years Newton continued to work as a cook. Later he found employment as a carpenter.

Louis Napoleon Hamblen (father of Newton (Hugh) Hamblen)

As of 1990 Newton and Bertha still live in Citrus Heights, CA. Retired now, Newton has spent many of the last years raising a large vegetable garden and teaching his grandchildren and great-grandchildren the history of the Hamblen family. His extended family forms a close-knit group that still centers around the house that Newton built in 1947. His family has grown to 23 grandchildren and 31 great-grandchildren. Some members of the family return each year to visit the old homestead in Brown County and attend the annual Hamblen Family Reunion in Columbus. While none of Newton

Hamblen's family currently reside in Brown County, the heritage of the county has richly rewarded all family members.

PLESSIE T. AND HELEN L. HAMBLEN

- Plessie Thomas Hamblen, born June 12, 1922 just southeast of the Lookout Tower in Brown County State Park, is the son of James Wm. and Mary E. Hamblen. Plessie first worked for the Otte General Store in Waymansville, then for 35 years at Cummins Engine Company. He retired from Cummins in 1978 and worked full time as a self-employed Electrician. He retired from his Electrician business in 1984.

Plessie married Helen L. Marshall on Nov. 28, 1942. Helen, born Oct. 1, 1923 in Cannelton (Perry), IN, is the daughter of John Marshall, Sr. and Leona Idessa Reed. For a few years Plessie and Helen ran the Hamblen Grocery at Grandview and have been active in the Harmony Baptist Church at New Belleville since 1955. Most of this time Plessie served as Deacon and Sunday School Teacher. They have three children, Jimmy Dean, Tommy Wayne and Janice Elaine.

Helen and Plessie Hamblen

Jimmy Dean, born Oct. 17, 1944, is a Tool and Die Maker and is now employed by Progressive Tool and Die in Columbus. He married Norma Jean Bruner on Nov. 3, 1963 and divorced 1984. They had three children, Sandra K., Gary D., and Brian K.

Sandra, born Nov. 17, 1964, graduated from Ball State University and is employed by The Republic in Columbus. She married James Rhodes, son of Mr. and Mrs. James Rhodes of Bartholomew County, on June 11, 1988.

Gary, born July 23, 1967, is a Tool and Die Apprentice at Hartup Tool and Die in Columbus. He married Kim Bowman, Feb. 28, 1989, daughter of Mike and Linda Bowman. They live in Van Buren Township, near Christiansburg.

Brian, born June 29, 1972, just graduated from Columbus North High School and is working at Penway in Edinburg.

Jimmy Dean married second to Jane Patrick of North Vernon.

Tommy Wayne, born July 6, 1947, married Betty Louise Lee in Brown County on Nov. 18, 1967. Betty, born May 3, 1942, is the daughter of Haskell Clay Lee and Mary Verna Likens of Tennessee. Tommy works at Cummins Engine Co. and is a Baptist Minister. He conducts the Sunday services at the Nature Center in the Brown County State Park during the summer. His father, Plessie, fills in for him when he cannot be there. Tom and Betty have a son, Anthony Wayne (Tony), born Sept. 22, 1970. Tony graduated from Columbus North High School in 1988 and is employed at WalMart in Columbus.

Janice, born Aug. 4, 1949, graduated from Parkview Methodist Hospital Nursing School in Ft. Wayne as a Registered Nurse. She worked at the Bartholomew County Hospital for eight years and eight and one-half years as surgical nurse for Dr. Lipson until he retired from private practice. She is now doing graduate study at IUPUI in Indianapolis. On June 14, 1970 Janice married Lloyd Edward Bruner, born Feb. 28, 1948 in Brown County, son of Lee Bruner and Altha Houshour. Lloyd is a Journeyman in Machine Repair at Cummins. They have two daughters, Jana Loraine, born Sept. 20, 1972, and Tina Elaine, born Sept. 11, 1975. Tina is employed at Cameo Studios in Columbus.

REV. WILLIAM HAMBLEN

- William Hamblen was born in 1814 in Lee Co., VA, where he lived with his parents, John Mullins and Mary (Campbell) Hamblen, until age 22, working as an apprentice shoe and bootmaker in his father's shop. In 1836 William migrated to Hamblen Township, Brown County, riding on horseback. There he worked as a shoemaker in the establishment of James Parmerlee who operated a tannery on Beanblossom Creek in Brown County. William married in 1839 in Brown County to Nancy Ann Goforth (1818-1894), daughter of William Goforth and Geriah Barnes Mullis.

Tiring of shoemaking, William moved to a farm in 1844. In 1846 he joined Capt. James Taggart's Co. E, 3rd Indiana Infantry as one of six Corporals for duty in the Mexican War. This company had the distinction of being the tallest in the army, its members averaging over six feet in height. They encountered seasickness and measles and other ills on the ship from New Orleans to Mexico. William never regained his health to actively serve and was sent home December 1846. His recovery took a year.

Rev. William Hamblen

William moved his family to a farm near Zion Church in Hamblen Township and built a log home on Government land, having been issued a military bounty land warrant for 160 acres.

During the late 1840s and early 1850s William joined the United Brethren Church, became a minister, travelled to surrounding counties serving various churches. In 1869 he joined the Methodist Episcopal Church. He was known as a circuit rider preacher. The farm was maintained by his wife and children. His last charges were Liberty Chapel at Taggart; Nashville, Green Valley; and Spearsville Churches. Scores of people came to hear the noted preacher.

Rev. Hamblen later lived with his children, died at the home of his daughter and son-in-law, John Burnett Craven. He was buried at Taggart Cemetery beside his devoted wife.

Rev. William Hamblen and his wife Nancy Ann had seven children: 1. Elizabeth Jane (1839-1905) married Michael Weddle in 1856; 2. Mary "Polly" (1841-1923) married John Gillaspy in 1861; 3. John William (1844-1870) married Julia Stilgenbauer in 1864; 4. Richard Preston (1846-1920) married Evaline Cordill in 1875; 5. Williamson (1849-1916) married Loretta Jane Wisenburg in 1872; 6. Sarah Catherine (1852-1899) married Oliver Perry Wheaton in 1870; 7. Martha Adline (1854-1902) married John Burnett Craven in 1872. All the Hamblen children married in Brown County. *Submitted by Marcedes L. Walker Joslin, great-great-granddaughter of Rev. Wm. Hamblen* (See John Burnett Craven; Samuel Walker; and Lowell and Marcedes Joslin)

BOB AND NEL HAMILTON

- It was August 1982 when Bob and Nel Hamilton purchased their home on West Drive in Nashville from Ferrol and Rosalie Arney who had already vacated the house and moved to their new residence in Bloomington. The Hamiltons, planning for retirement the following spring, had noticed the house with its house number - 444 - posted on the carport entry during a stopover on their way to Florida. They arranged with Bob Galm Realty to look at it, and since "4" was Bob's "lucky number," it seemed obvious that this was meant to be their home.

Bob and Nel Hamilton

From an abstract given to the Hamiltons by the Arneys, it was learned that the lot on which this pleasant, spacious, and well-located home was built was a part of a Government Land Grant purchased by Silvanus and Lorena Manville (brother and sister) on Jan. 1, 1844, and July 3, 1846, respectively. There followed a number of owners and on Sept. 7, 1911, a portion of the land called the "Patrick J. Mullaney Addition" was incorporated into the town of Nashville. On Aug. 5, 1940, Philip and Fern Bessire and William and Grace Bessire, then owners, had the land further subdivided and recorded as the "Sayer Subdivision." The next owners of this particular lot were Ival and Stella McDonald (September 1940), Grace Woody and Marguerite Oliver (September 1944), Donald and Jeanetta Hatten (June 1961), and Henry and Evelyn Kazimier (August 1963). It was during 1963 that the house was built, possibly begun by the Hattens and finished by the Kazimiers. William and Marguerite Claybaugh were the next owners (February 1965), Lucille Snead (August 1966), and then the Arneys (October 1967). The abstract contains interesting statements made to verify ownership particularly following the courthouse fire in 1873 which destroyed so many of the land records.

Now back to the current owners. Bob (Robert Eugene) was born in Mansfield, OH, Oct. 4, 1920, to Hedwig (Roth) and John Courtney Hamilton. He had one sister four years older, Ruth Hamilton McBride. Following high school graduation, Bob worked for the Perfect Rubber Company in Mansfield and in 1942 joined the U.S. Navy as a V-5 Aviation Cadet and later was transferred to the aircraft carrier, USS Cowpens. Bob's entire Navy career was spent on that ship, and he was considered a plank owner since he was aboard at the time of commissioning. He saw World War II action in the South Pacific and was mustered out on March 18, 1946, as First Class Petty Officer. He began working at Republic Steel Corporation in Cleveland, OH, later transferring to the South Chicago plant. He completed transportation studies at the College of Advanced Traffic and Northwestern University (Chicago), was a Certified Member of the American Society of Traffic and Transportation, was President of the Calumet Transportation Association serving as Secretary/Treasurer for ten years. At the time of his retirement he was District Traffic Manager of Republic's South Chicago works.

Nel (Annella Holmes) was the only child of Regena (Wynn) and Thurston Holmes born in Avalon, PA, Nov. 24, 1930. In the middle of her senior year at Ambridge (Pennsylvania) High School, the family moved to Lakewood, OH, where she graduated. After completing the secretarial course at Dyke Spencerian School of Business (Cleveland, OH), she worked for Dalton-Dalton Associates, Architects and Engineers, located on the 9th floor of the Old Arcade Building (an historic landmark) on Euclid Avenue in downtown Cleveland.

Bob and Nel were married May 5, 1956, and moved from Ohio to Whiting (Lake Co.) IN, in August of that year.

On March 28, 1983, they and their possessions arrived in Nashville. The concern of their friends was how the Hamiltons were going to "survive" in a town of only 700, a county of 12,000, when they had lived so many years in the large metropolitan area of Chicago and the Calumet region. It did not take long for them to find a "niche" among the outgoing and friendly people of the Brown County area.

They became members of the Nashville United Methodist Church, served on the Sesquicentennial Committee, and were active in the Brown County Historical Society participating as docents at the museum complex. Bob joined the Brown County Lions Club serving as President in 1989-90; volunteered at the Chamber of Commerce office and as a park tour guide for the Convention and Visitors Bureau.

Hambone the Clown

Bob has been able to continue his love of clowning which began when he joined Orak Shrine Temple (Hammond, IN) in 1974 and became a member of the Orak Shrine Clowns. As "Hambone, the Clown" he entertained with members of Church of the Lakes at the Brown County Care Center monthly birthday parties. He also appeared at local birthday parties; continued his participation with the Great Lakes Shrine Clown Association and the International Shrine Clown Association serving as education chairman and editor of **Clown Chatter**; and presented seminars at Shrine Clown and Clowns of America conventions. His specialty was teaching the art of paper cutting and the construction of large parade props, but probably most importantly was his ability to stimulate creativity in others.

Brown County - its hills, its residents and its history - have been a delight to the Hamiltons and made "retirement" a stimulating and interesting time in their lives.

HAMILTON-BOND - David Morgan Hamilton, born July 21, 1860, Lexington, KY, was a son of Jesse Turner Hamilton and Martha Neal. He married Sarah Arminia Baker of Bloomington, IN; she died leaving nine children: Alpha, Frank Grover, Bruce Harley, Clyde Stanhope, Wilfred Roy, Paul Morgan, Ruth, Gail and Pearl. He married second on Sept. 10, 1902 to Ella Florence Bond, born Feb. 9, 1877 in Brown County, daughter of James and Sarah Patton Bond. Ella Florence had first married Hiram Griner and lived about five years at Morgantown, IN. David and Ella Hamilton made their home in So. Tunnel, TN in 1903. He had attended Elletsville College and Louisville Medical College. He completed his Doctor's degree but became a traveling minister of the Church of Christ. He established many congregations in Indiana, Tennessee, Kentucky and Texas. He donated land for a school, church and family-community cemetery. Bushes Chapel Church and cemetery are still in use. David and Ella had children: Faith (May 4, 1903-July 6, 1909), Blanche Margaret (Dec. 9, 1904-Jan. 26, 1989), Bonde Louise born May 18, 1907, Florence Ella (Feb. 24, 1909-May 4, 1981), Sarah Madge (Feb. 18, 1911-Oct. 11, 1985), Martha Neal (March 22, 1913-May 22, 1981), Iris (Sept. 10, 1917-Oct. 4, 1921), George David born Sept. 1, 1915, Helen Hunt born Nov. 4, 1919; four children died in infancy. David Hamilton died Feb. 28, 1924. His widow, Ella Florence Hamilton, married third, to Burley Pearson. She died March 18, 1951.

Standing at Back: Ruth and Paul Hamilton. Father: David Morgan Hamilton. Mother: Ella Florence Bond Hamilton Pearson. Front: Bonde, Ella F., Madge and Blanche.

Blanche M. Hamilton married Paul Pilkenton, Indianapolis. Their daughter, Betty Jean Pilkenton, born Feb. 2, 1927, married Charles Goodman. Their sons were (1) Charles Michael who married Elaine White and had daughter, Dawn. Charles Michael then married Audrey Drake and had Brooke and Brett Goodman; (2) David Morgan Goodman married Tammy Rogers. Blanche M. Hamilton married second to Albert A. Carlson and had a son, Ronald, born May 14, 1938, who married Joyce (?) and had children, Dawn, Debbie and Al. Ronald and Joyce divorced; he then married Sandra (?). Blanche M. Hamilton once had a store in So. Tunnel, TN.

Bonde Louise Hamilton married Vernon G. Cooper, Indianapolis, Dec. 4, 1926. Later they worked the family farm at So. Tunnel which is now owned by George Hamilton. Bonde and Vernon Cooper had three children: (1) Gwendolyn Marie, born Oct. 26, 1930, married Fred Watson and had children, Stan, Amy and Bonnie who married Daniel Keen and had children, Graham and Courtney Bond Keen. (2) Hilda Joyce who married Clem McDearman and had children, Debbie, Connie, Janice and Tammy. Debbie McDearman married Andy McClarney and had one child; Connie married Allen Porter and had children, Angela and Beth Ann; Connie married second to Dewell Scruggs and had a son David. Janice married Joe Johnson and had a daughter Emily. (3) Vernon Gilbert Cooper, Jr. married Sandra Garrett and had children, Cynthia Renee and Charles Phillip Cooper.

Florence Ella Hamilton married Henry Key on June 29, 1924 and had five children: (1) Joy Muriel, born Aug. 31, 1925, who married Tom Woodward and has children, Jimmy and Kenny Dale; (2) Clarice Hope, born and died Sept. 25, 1927; (3) Tawanda, born Feb. 17, 1930, who married Raymond Trammel and has children, Randall and Denise; (4) Sandra Dean, born Sept. 26, 1939, who married Robert Butler, Jr. and has sons, David and Daniel; (5) Patricia, born Oct. 10, 1944, who married Mike Deasy and has a son, Kevin.

Sarah Madge Hamilton married Monte Heun in Chicago, and they had five children, Carol, Joseph, David, Stephen and Linda.

Martha Neal Hamilton married Wesley Cron on Nov. 1, 1930, Franklin, KY and had children (1) Wilbur Mayzelle, born July 22, 1931, who married James Vernon Wilson on June 10, 1950, Franklin, KY. Their son, James Byron Wilson, born Nov. 11, 1956, married Marian Denise Harper; (2) Gary Neal Cron, July 10, 1943-Feb. 21, 1987, married Eva Nell White, and had daughters Donna who married Jerry Ladd and had a son Christopher; and Ronda who married Stanley Perry and had a daughter, Tori; (3) Horace Wendell Cron was born July 14, 1952, married Anita Crouch and had sons, Phillip, Joel and Jared; (4) David Walter Cron, born and died.

George David Hamilton, Judge of Sumner Co., TN Circuit Court, married Margaret Bruce Baker, Feb. 15, 1941, had sons, George David Hamilton, Jr., born Sept. 14, 1942 and John Howard Hamilton, born Nov. 5, 1948, who married Beth Jones, had two daughters.

Helen Hunt Hamilton married Everett Champney of Chicago, had two daughters, Greta Gayle and Cathy Champney. *Submitted by Wilbur Cron Wilson*

MADGE A. HARLAN - Madge A. Younghans (Junghans) McAllister Harlan came to Brown Co., IN from Ohio in the early 1970s after the death of her second husband, Daulbert D. Harlan looking for peace and quiet. She knew Brown Co., IN for she was raised in Indianapolis, IN and had lived in Indianapolis during her first marriage to Carl E. McAllister, now deceased. They had one son, Carl E. McAllister II who has three children: Jeffery E., Eddy Dewayne, and Dinah married to Chris Common. Her father, Richard E. Younghans (Junghans) who emigrated to America in the 1880s with his father, Wilhelm F., born June 24, 1846, his mother, Anna F., born Aug. 5, 1943, and four unmarried brothers: Arno, Emil, Hugo and Oscar. Her grandfather died July 17, 1904 and the grandmother Jan. 19, 1914. Both are buried in Pennsylvania.

Her grandfather was a clock maker in Germany. He worked in the factory that was started by his ancestors and is still in operation and bears the family name: Junghans Uhren BmbH Postfach, D 7230 Schramberg, West Germany.

In 1903 it became the world's largest manufacturer of clocks in the world. 1963 the first solar-powered battery-free quartz operated clock in the world arrived from Schramberg, Germany. Junghans also released the first radio-controlled analog clock.

Her father, Richard E. living in Pennsylvania, unmarried and a glass blower heard about natural gas needed in blowing glass, being discovered in Grant Co., IN so he moved there. Other brothers moved to Chicago, IL, Gowanda, NY and two remained in Pennsylvania.

In Grant County her father met and married B.A. Parsons whose father was a farmer. They had six children, five born in Grant County and one in Cincinnati, OH: Frederick, Carmen, Lucille, Madge, Norma and an infant unnamed that died soon after birth.

Her mother died May 21, 1913 and is buried in Converse, IN.

After much struggling to keep the family together her father took the family to Indianapolis where there was a German Orphanage and a glass factory where he could work and be near his children. Frederick was too old to go to the orphanage so he went to live with an Aunt Maude in Terre Haute, IN. Norma, the youngest, was too young for the orphanage so friends, the Strickler family took her.

Carmen, Lucille and Madge were placed in the orphanage which had its own school. They remained there until they reached 16 years of age when they were supposed to leave and find a job. Madge found one and continued her schooling including some college. Then she met a nice young man that became her first husband (Carl E. McAllister). Her father Richard E. Younghans, died in 1940 and is buried in Washington Park Cemetery in Indianapolis.

Madge worked as a secretary at the Indiana Department of State Revenue. She was a 50 year member of the International Travel Study Club, and belongs to the Nashville United Methodist Church, Brown County Historical Society and the Brown County Genealogical Society. *Submitted by Madge A. Harlan*

KENNETH AND RUTH WARFORD HARRIS - Ruth K. Warford was born in Brown County on Aug. 22, 1915, the youngest daughter of Frank and Ola Warford of Trevlac. Ruth married Kenneth E. Harris Nov. 14, 1934 in Newton, IL. Kenneth was born in Jasper Co., IL. Kenneth passed away Nov. 4, 1984 in Tucson, AZ.

Kenneth's parents are Elmer and Ola (Fritschle) Harris. Ola Fritschle was born in Baden-Baden, Germany on Sept. 25, 1814 and died in 1897. Ola's grandfather was Jacob Fritschle. The Harris family of Alberman Co., VA trace to William Harris (1706-Aug. 25, 1788).

The Harris family also lived in Bean Blossom and Kenneth worked at Camp Atterbury for the government as a plumber. Children Marlene and Larry went to the Mennonite Church in Bean Blossom.

Ruth and Kenneth had six children: (1) Peggy Marlene Harris born in Newton, IL on Feb. 21, 1936 married Robert Livesay Dec. 26, 1952 in Philo, IL. Robert is retired from government work and Marlene from secretarial work. They had one daughter Jill who married Brad Yockall and they have a son Nickalas Yockall. Brad is a minister and they all live in Knoxville, TN.

Ruth and Kenneth Harris 50th Wedding Anniversary, 1984

(2) Sandra Sue Harris born in Malta, MT Feb. 28, 1939 passed away April 7, 1945 in Terre Haute, IN.

(3) Larry Allen Harris born in Malta, MT on Feb. 1, 1940 is married and lives in Mahomet, IL. Larry works for University of Illinois as a plumber. He has one daughter, Kimberly Ann Grave. She also has one daughter Amandy and they live in Philo, IL.

(4) Janet Ruth Harris was born in Jasper Co., IL on Dec. 30, 1947. She married Leslie O'Banion in Champaign, IL on Jan. 14, 1965. He was stationed at Chanute Air Force base in Rantoul, IL. They have three children: Brian, born in Lubbock, TX; Corina in Stateville, NC; and L.T. born in Maryville, TN. They all live in Maryville, TN.

(5) Pamela Jean Harris born in Urbana, IL, Nov. 13, 1951. Pamela married Vance Stacy on June 16, 1978 in Tucson, AZ. They have a daughter Melany and a son Matthew. They now live in Lima, Peru where he works for the government Embassy on drugs and D.E.A. work. Pamela works in the Embassy on housing.

(6) Deruses Meree Harris was born in Champaign, IL on Dec. 13, 1956 and married William Swindle on April 10, 1979 in LeRoy, IL. They have two daughters: Rayna and Ronna. They live in LeRoy, IL where Bill is an electrician and Dee works for Novak flowers in Bloomington, IL. *Submitted by Mrs. Ruth K. Harris*

WILLIAM HENRY AND JULIANA (TRUAX) HARRISON - William was born Sept. 13, 1840, Bartholomew Co., IN, the first child and oldest son of Carter J. and Julianna (St. Clair) Harrison.

William Henry Harrison and Julianna (Truax) Harrison

Carter J. Harrison was born Jan. 30, 1812. Julianna St. Clair was born Oct. 30, 1819. They married Jan. 12, 1840 at Columbus, (Bartholomew Co.) IN. They had 12 children. Julianna died and Carter J. married (second) Barbara Matson April 11, 1865 in Brown County and they had six known children. They are buried in South Bethany Cemetery, Bartholomew Co., IN. Carter V. Harrison, the ninth child of Carter J. and Julianna Harrison was a teacher in Brown and Bartholomew Counties.

William Henry Harrison and Julianna Truax (born Aug. 12, 1844) were married Sept. 26, 1861 at the home of her step-father, B.W. Cook, in Brown Co., IN. Her mother was Catherine Sipe(s).

William H. and Julianna Harrison lived on the Three-Notch road in Brown County. They had seven children. Their second child, Martha Ellen, born Oct. 6, 1864, married Jacob Douglas R(h)ude, born Nov. 26, 1858 in Brown County.

William Henry and Julianna (Truax) Harrison home located on Three Notch Road, three miles south of Peoga.

William H. was a circuit riding preacher of the Christian faith and served Sprunica, Haw Creek, Nashville, and South Bethany churches.

William H. died Dec. 31, 1912. Julianna died Jan. 3, 1923 at the age of 83 years. Both are buried at Sprunica Church Cemetery, Hamblen Township, Brown Co., IN. *Submitted by Mrs. Doris Wilson*

OTIS B. HATCHETT - Otis B. Hatchett was born April 30, 1895 near Belmont in Brown Co., IN, to William Green Hatchett and Martha K. (Varney) Hatchett, his wife by a second marriage. Otis had one brother, Homer, older than he and two half-sisters: Alice and Laura, from his father's former marriage.

On Aug. 9, 1916 Otis was married to Glenna E. Mosburg in Martinsville. To them were born three children: James A., Wilma Faye and William H. Hatchett. Otis and Glenna lived out their lives in Morgantown, IN. He died in 1982 and she in 1983.

Otis' great-grandfather, Thomas Hatchett was born in Virginia about 1760. Bowen's **Bartholomew and Brown Counties**, IN states that he was in the American Revolutionary War as a driver of a baggage wagon. Many of the services of the quartermasters corp at the time of that war were performed by contract with private owners of a means of transport. Thomas, then only in his early teens, may well have been hired to drive a baggage wagon hauling supplies for the American Revolutionary forces.

Otis B. and Glenna Hatchett

Thomas was in Bartholomew County by 1830. His oldest known son, John B. Hatchett, was born in Kentucky on Jan. 7, 1824 to his wife, Betsy Cox, of

Virginia. At that time Thomas was 64 years of age. Little is known of his history before he was in Kentucky. He may have been married with a family before his marriage to Betsy Cox in his early 60s.

Betsy gave him six other children: William Green, Patty, Bartlett, Malinda, Jane and Emily. William Green served his country in the Mexican War and Bartlett in the War Between the States.

The 1860 Federal Census indicates that Thomas was then 100 years of age, and, it is believed, he died about 1863. No stone marks his grave in the Duncan Cemetery in Brown County, but it is near that of his son Bartlett.

Thomas' son John B. Hatchett had several children by his two marriages. William Green was born to his wife Nancy (Jeffers) Hatchett.

William Green Hatchett was also married twice. His marriage to Mary Margaret Henthorn resulted in two daughters: Alice and Laura. By his marriage to Martha K. Varney, he had two sons, Homer and Otis.

Otis' mother, Martha, was the daughter of Reuben Varney. Reuben, the father of six girls by his wife, Amanda Abercrombie, was born Aug. 26, 1818 in New Hampshire. He worked his way to Cincinnati, OH, possibly by canal boat. After nearly drowning while working on a canal, Amanda, whom he married in Cincinnati on July 20, 1848, begged him to leave this type of work. With their two oldest daughters they followed Amanda's sister and her husband Mary and Henry Swain, to Seymour, IN. From there they came west and lived in and around Elkinsville where Reuben worked as a carpenter. Otis' mother Martha was born in Brown County Sept. 29, 1860.

Reuben built a house for each of two Deckard brothers. One house is now covered by the waters of Lake Monroe the other, now restored, proudly stands on high ground not far from the present lakeshore—a reminder of the "Old Varney House" near Dover, NH.

Most of Otis' forebears, as well as Aunts, Uncles and Cousins are buried in Duncan Cemetery, Brown Co., IN.

ASA AND SUSAN DAMRELL HATTON -

The Hatton family of Brown, Bartholomew and Jackson Counties descend from Samuel Hatton, Sr. and Rosanna Queen. Samuel (1749-1839), born in London, came to Virginia as a young man and was in the Virginia militia during the Revolutionary War. He settled in Washington Co., MD, later in Hampshire Co., VA (now Mineral Co., WV). Among the children born to Samuel and Rosanna were John, Samuel, Jr., Asa, Levi, David, Jonah, William, Margaret, Phillip, Elijah and Elizabeth Hatton. Samuel went to Big Sandy River Valley near Huntington, WV about 1815 where his sons had gone to get land grants in 1806. He is buried at Prichard in Wayne Co., WV.

The Hattons of Brown County trace to Asa Hatton (1775-1830) son of Samuel and Rosanna, and his wife, Susan Damrell, who left Cabell Co., VA (WV) about 1820 and settled in Martin Co., IN at Loogootee. Asa's children were Samuel (1794), Philip (1800), William (1806), Asahel (1808), Ephraim (1809), Levi (1810), Charles (1811), Sarah (1813), Jane (1814), Allen (1816), Cynthia (1816), Elizabeth (1818), Marshall (1820), Edmond (1821) and Frank (1829).

Six adult male Hattons were in Van Buren and Hamblen Townships, Brown County by the 1840-50 censuses. They were sons of Asa: Asahel, Philip, William, Ephraim, Levi and Samuel, the older sons, and probably stepsons of Susan Damrell. By 1860, only Samuel and Lucinda (Allman) Hatton were in Brown County. Among their children were Philip, Jonas, Samuel, Malinda, Sarah, Pernetta, William, Catherine and Benjamin.

Philip A., son of Asa Hatton, went to Jackson Co., IN. He and his wife Nancy had nine children: Minerva, John, Alfred, Cynthia, Samuel S., Marion, Robert, Rachel and Mary. Ephraim, son of Asa Hatton, married Elizabeth Bailey and had eight children: Elizabeth, Sally, Alexander, Mitchell, Abigail, Catherine, Rosannah and Ellen. This family relocated before 1860. Asahel, son of Asa Hatton, married Elizabeth Williamson, no children. Sarah, daughter of Asa Hatton, married John Kinworthy and moved to Jackson County with children: Nancy, Sarah, John, Levi, Asa, Elizabeth, Susan, Mary and James. Levi, son of Asa Hatton, and his wife Catherine had children: Jeriah, Malinda, William and Nancy. William, son of Asa Hatton, married Amy Hampton and had eight children: Elizabeth, Asa, Marian, Jemimah, Margaret, Allen, Julia and Martha.

Marshall, son of Asa Hatton, left Brown County with his wife, Harriett Carmichael and their children and were not traceable. Jonathan Hatton may have been a son of Asa but possibly was a son of Samuel, oldest son of Asa. Jonathan married Sarah Ayers and had William, Mary and James Hatton.

Four children of Asa Hatton, Sr. and Susan Damrell who settled in New Albany, Floyd Co., IN were: 1. Charles who married Elizabeth Graham and had Susan, Charles, Ann, Clay and Freelin. 2. Edmond who married Mary Gardner and had Thomas, Frank, Ellen, Mary, Edmond and Pinkney. 3. Frank who married Miranda Burke and had Edith. 4. Cynthia Ann who married George Bartlett and had Elzora, Georgiana, George, Cicero, Kate, Susan, Elizabeth, Charles, Salem and Alma.

Allen, son of Asa Hatton, moved to Monroe Co., MO. He and his wife Martha raised seven children: John, Michael, Susan, Martha, Cynthia, Andrew and Ellzora. Elizabeth, daughter of Asa Hatton, died in Missouri, unmarried. *Submitted by Dr. Walter E. Hatten*

HAROLD AND LOIS CROUCH HATTON -

Harold, born near Storyville, Brown Co., IN on April 18, 1919, was a son of James Oscar Hatton (1875-1943) and Nora Aynes (1886-1978). His grandparents were Philip H. Hatton, born 1830, and Lovina Percifield, born 1840. Harold Hatton's great-grandparents were Samuel Hatton (1797-1839) and Lucinda Allman, early settlers of Brown County, who had come from West Virginia. Harold's parents raised a large family with eight children living to adulthood. Harold Hatton's brothers and sisters were:

Clotha Cordella Hatton, (1895-1963), daughter of James Oscar Hatton and his first wife, Anna E. Greathouse. Clotha married John Mitchner.

Edith Hatton (1904-1987), unmarried; Dora Hatton (1906-1987), married John H. Hill; Leeco Hatton (1911-1977), married Helen Krause; Norma Dell Hatton, born Dec. 21, 1921, married Wilbur Imel; Olive Hatton, born Feb. 11, 1924, married Samuel Scott; Ronald Keith Hatton, born 1929, married Wilma J. Mobley; Lucille Hatton who married William Waddle.

The James Oscar Hatton family was raised in a log home and attended school and church at Mt. Nebo in Brown County, which was a three mile walk through the woods to the one-room school and little country church. When the family walked to church, it was not unusual for nearly 50 people to show up for Sunday dinner on the return trip. Sunday dinner required much cooking on the woodstove by the mother of the family and was quite a feat, one that modern women would probably not attempt without much notice.

On Sept. 19, 1942 Harold Hatton was married to Miss Lois D. Crouch, the daughter of Alfred and Nellie (Moore) Crouch of Pikes Peak in Brown County. Harold and Lois Hatton had three sons:

Larry Leon Hatton who married Janet Leslie; their child, Leon Harold, born 1981.

Harold and Lois (Crouch) Hatton December 1980

Larry helps farm near Westport, IN. Lanny Lee Hatton who married Diane Golden; their children are Jonathan Thomas, born 1974 and Gregory Allen, born 1979. Lanny has worked at Cummins Engine Company for 25 years, lives near Columbus, IN.

Jackie Dean Hatton works at Bakalar Air Base and is Sergeant over maintenance in the National Guard. He lives at Freetown, IN, is unmarried. Harold worked on a sheep farm for 16 years for Quentin G. Noblitt of Noblitt and Sparks Industries. Lois is retired from Cummins Engine Company. After Harold's passing in 1980, Lois later married Charles N. Brown, now also deceased. Lois resides in Columbus where she looks after her 93 year old mother, Mrs. Nellie Crouch Gentry, and is involved in church work. *Submitted by Lois (Crouch) Hatton Brown*

JOHN HENRY AND RESSIE (GREATHOUSE) HATTON -

John Henry was born on Dec. 10, 1887 in Brown County, the son of Samuel E. Hatton (1863-1933) and Matilda Tabor (1861-1906). His grandfather was Philip Hatton, born 1830, son of Samuel Hatton and Lucinda Allman, early settlers of Brown County who migrated, about 1820, from Cabell Co., VA, near Huntington. Philip's wife, Lovina Percifield, born 1840, was a daughter of Thomas and Jemimah Percifield of Kentucky. John Henry Hatton had six brothers and sisters who lived to adulthood: James Oscar Hatton (1891-1966) who married Lela Woods; Charlotte A. Hatton (1893-1970) who married William Lutes; Charles Murphy Hatton (1884-1946) who married Ada Alice Mobley; Laura M. Hatton (born Aug. 29, 1896) who married Lemuel Greathouse; Ora Ray Hatton (1898-1973) who married Eva Carmichael, then Lucille Crider; and Florence Hatton (1900-1920).

John Henry Hatton married on Jan. 14, 1914 in Brown County to Ressie Jane Greathouse. Ressie, born Sept. 9, 1897, was a daughter of George W. Greathouse and Frances Ayers.

John Henry and Ressie Hatton's children were: Carl Hatton, born Dec. 18, 1914, died Nov. 9, 1989, unmarried; Cloyd Hatton, born March 3, 1917, died

Aug. 9, 1989, unmarried; Naomi Faye Hatton, born March 19, 1923, married Glen Gorbett, resides at Seymour; Doyle Hatton, born May 14, 1925, resides in Columbus, unmarried; Donald Hatton, born Sept. 17, 1937, married Rose M. Cross. They live in Van Buren Township, Brown County and had four children: (1) Gregory Lee Hatton, born 1957, died 1972; (2) Andrew Ray Hatton, born 1958, married Carla Colson, had sons, Ben and Jacob; (3) Alan Dale Hatton, born 1960; (4) Michael Keith Hatton, born 1962.

Henry and Ressie Hatton

John Henry Hatton passed away on March 28, 1946 in Madison, IN and was buried in the Christiansburg Cemetery in Brown County. His wife, Ressie, died on Nov. 26, 1979 in Seymour and was buried alongside her husband. *Submitted by Rose Cross Hatton*

JOHN WILLIAM HATTON

John (1869-1948) was a son of Philip H. Hatton, born 1829, and Lovina Percifield, born 1840. John's siblings were Samuel E., Amanda, George P., Jesse, James and Valentine. John's grandparents were Samuel and Lucinda Allman Hatton, in Brown County before 1850. John's great-grandparents were Asa and Susan Hatton of Cabell Co., VA (WV) and then of Martin Co., IN. Asa's father, born in England came to Virginia and was a Revolutionary War veteran from Virginia.

John William Hatton and family

John Wm. Hatton married Rachel Greathouse (1880-1961), daughter of Peter and Dora Wilcox Greathouse. John and Rachel Hatton had 14 children; this family moved from Brown to Knox Co., IN about 1915. (1) Roy Hatton (1896-1968) married Bonnie Bowers and had four children: 1. Joseph who married Robertine Goodwin and had four children: (1) Gayle who married Royce Huffer and had Royce III, Stephanie and Joseph; 2) Penny who married Arthur Tedrow and had Arthur III, Kristen and Kathleen. 3) Cindy who married Ricky Compton and 4) Kellie Hatton. 2. Gladys who married Jerry Lamb and had Ricky, Rodney who married Michelle McGee, Pamela who married Paul Sturgeon and had Tamara. 3. John who married Billie Deisher and had Debra who married Darrell Reeves, David who married Angela Kern and Douglas. 4. Mary who married Leroy Michaelis and had Dianne who married David Bartram.

(2) Sheridan Hatton (1898-1976) married Ressie Long and had four children: 1. Evelyn who married Carl Otten; 2. Aline who married Robert Harting; 3. Howard who married Arline Johnson and Sharon Wells; 4. Frank who married Sue Pilz. (3) Peter Hatton (1901-1973) married Eva George and had Phylis who married Joseph Pollock and had Mark and Richard. (4) Samuel E. Hatton (1903-1975) married Frances Williams and had four children: 1. Vera who married Merlin Faught; 2. Rachel who married Paul Hughes; 3. Herman who married Sondra Reed; 4. Wanda who married Lawrence Reed. (5) Mary Elizabeth (1905-1977) married Opal Kays and Roy Long. Mary's children: Opal, Jr. who married Beverly Zineman and Nancy Small; and William who married Ann Blakely and Linda Spence. (6) Charles Hatton (1907-1957) married Ethel Evans and had 13 children: 1. Charles, Jr. who married Lorna O'Brian; 2. John who married Mona Bradfield; 3. James; 4. Marjorie who married Edward Lindsey; 5. Olive who married David Alvis; 6. Edward who married Arline Johnson; 7. Richard who married Linda Smith; 8. Rosemary; 9. Herbert who married Mary Lettzell; 10. Larry who married Debbie King; 11. Billie; 12. Brenda who married Fred Davis; 13. Jackie, unmarried. (7) Emma Hatton born 1909, married Oves Long and had Jack who married Grace Goslin and Jerald who married Linda Elliott. (8) Earnest Hatton (1912-1982) married Jadwiga Wojciechowski and had four children: 1. Earnest, Jr. who married Ellen Griffin; 2. Christine who married Edward Gyure; 3. Thomas who married Audrey ....; 4. Barbara. (9) Garland Hatton (1913-1980) who married Velma Stevenson and had five children: 1. Garnet who married Robert Eyre; 2. Donald who married Anita Edwards; 3. Alice who married James Roberson; 4. Margaret who married John York; 5. Garland, Jr. who married Judy Haubeil and Rhonda Johnson. (10) Clyde Hatton born 1915, married Edith Erickson and had six children: 1. Donna who married Jay Williams; 2. Robert who married Barbara Nickless and Frances Woodward; 3. Dianna; 4. Roseanna who married Carl Wheeler; 5. James who married Joyce Beard; 6. Stephen who married Sherry Palmer. (11) Lloyd Hatton (1918-1981) who married Eva Holt who died 1963 and Ann Boyd; Lloyd had a daughter, Sandra; he operated a store and farm in Shoals, Martin County. (12) William Earl Hatton born 1925, married Bessie M. Andrews, a daughter of Rev. N.V. Andrews and Winifred Hutchins, and had four children: 1. Beverly who married Robert Donovan and had children: Jeffrey, Andrea and Ryan; 2. Charlotte who married Michael Thompson and had three children: Julia, Jennifer and Andrew; 3. Bruce who married Kathleen Gregg and Cindy Parmenter and had three children: William, Nathan and Drew; 4. Ray who married Teresa Williams and had Shannon Rae and Daniel Hatton. Two sons of John and Rachel Hatton died in infancy; Noah born 1899 and John born 1917. *Submitted by William Earl Hatton*

SAMUEL AND LUCINDA ALLMAN HATTON

Samuel was a grandson of Samuel and Rosanna Queen Hatton of Virginia. The oldest son of Asa and Susan (Damrell) Hatton, he was born about 1794 in Hampshire Co., VA (WV). He went to western Virginia, near Huntington, WV, where he received a land grant in 1811. His parents had moved to Indiana by 1820 and soon thereafter, Samuel and his wife Lucinda Allman settled there also. The 1840 census lists Samuel as a resident of Van Buren Township, Brown Co., IN.

Samuel and Lucinda Hatton had nine children: (1) Philip H. Hatton born 1830, married Lovina Percifield and had seven children: Samuel E., Amanda, George, John William, Jesse, James and Valentine. (2) Jonas Hatton, born 1828, married Margaret Sullivan and had six children: George, William T., Sarah, Ezekiel, Alfred and Marion. (3) Samuel, Jr. born 1834, married Hannah Mobley and had eight children: Margaret, Lovina, Sarah, John, Samuel, Hannah, Philip and Elizabeth. (4) Malinda born 1837, married John Weddle. (5) Sarah born 1838, married John Krebbs. (6) Pernetta. (7) William H. (1845-1876) married Margaret Mobley and had three children: Clarissa, Lucinda and Lovina. (8) Catharine. (9) Benjamin (1854-1917) married Viola Sullivan and had five children: Samuel, Mary, Amanda, Rosa and Jonah.

John William Hatton

Among the grandchildren of Samuel and Lucinda Hatton who remained in Brown County were: Philip Hatton (1876-1907), son of Samuel and Hannah, married Sarah Ayers and had five children: Malissa, Leona, Alice, Estal and Lillie; John Wesley Hatton (1872-1920), son of Samuel and Hannah, married Margaret Carmichael and had 11 children: Samuel, Arnold, Harlan, Ford, James, Clora, Elzia, Elsie, Anna, Charles and Henry; Arnold (1899-1959), son of John Wesley Hatton, married Susan Carmichael and had five children: Vivian, Velma, Stella, Arnold, Jr. and Arthur (1931-1981) who married Mary Kelly and had three children: Susie Jane who married David Renner and had a child, Eric, who died in infancy; Mary and Marilyn.

Samuel E. Hatton (1863-1933), son of Philip and Lovina, married Matilda Tabor and had ten children: (1) Charlotte; (2) Ora Ray (1898-1973) married Eva Carmichael and had two daughters, Geneva and Thelma; (3) James Oscar (1891-1966) married Lela Woods and had five children: Estella, Ganell, Harry, James and Gwendolyn; (4) John Henry (1887-1946) married Ressie Greathouse and had five children: Carl, Cloyd, Faye, Doyle and Donald; (5) Charles Murphy (1894-1946) married Ada Alice Mobley and raised children: Charles, Gerald and Kathryn; (6) Laura; (7) Florence; (8) Bertha; (9) Clarence; (10) Delpha. Samuel E. Hatton, after Matilda's death in 1906, married Sarah Ault Meeks and had a daughter, Nora.

James Hatton (1875-1943), son of Philip and Lovina, married Anna Greathouse and had a daughter, Clotha Cordella. James married second Nora Aynes and had 11 children: (1) Fanny; (2) Sylvia; (3) Berniece; (4) Leeco "Bud" (1911-1977) married Helen Krause and had three children: Joseph, Donald and Donna; (5) Edith; (6) Dora; (7) Norma; (8) Olive; (9) Lucille; (10) Harold (1919-1980) married Lois Crouch and had three children: Larry,

Lanny and Jackie; (11) Keith, born 1929, married Wilma Mobley and had five children: Jerald, Darrell, Gary, Kevin and Cheryl. *Submitted by Joseph Leroy Hatton*

ALVA CLARENCE HAWLEY FAMILY -
Alva was born Aug. 30, 1901 in Monroe Co., IN, son of William Morgan and Millie Francis (Richardson) Hawley. He was the third child of Morgan and Millie Hawley and was raised on a farm in Jackson Township in Brown County. He had two sisters, Ada Opal, born in 1893, died Nov. 20, 1908 of Typhoid Fever at the age of 15. Ola Ellen, born in 1895, married Frank Allen Warford, Aug. 17, 1912, son of Oscar and Sarah (Branstetter) Warford.

Floyd, Alva, Bertha and Robert Hawley May 19, 1944

After the death of his father in 1907, Alva and his mother went to Farmland, IL and lived with her brother and family. After about a year they returned to Indiana. In 1908 he witnessed the shooting of Frank McCoy and Joel McCoy, his father, by Edward Ford near the Brown and Monroe County line. In the 1910 census he lived with John A. Martin in Washington Township, Brown Co., IN. In March 25, 1922 he married Bertha Mae Elkins, daughter of Carl Edgar Elkins and Daisy Mae (Fitzpatrick) in Franklin, IN. Two children were born, Robert William Hawley, born June 7, 1924, in Franklin, IN and Floyd Edgar born, Feb. 14, 1927, in Rock Lane, IN.

Robert William married Wilma Ilene Cline, April 21, 1944, daughter of Fred Raymond Cline and June Mildred Spencer and three children were born, Robert Allen, Dec. 15, 1944, Larry Lee, Aug. 13, 1946, and Judith Elaine, May 19, 1948.

Floyd Edgar Hawley married Violet G. Worthington, Aug. 14, 1948, daughter of Luther Jefferson and Bertha Whilamena (Hill) and five children were born, Floyd Anthony, Feb. 17, 1949, Linda Joyce, Dec. 11, 1950, Timothy Dale, May 13, 1954, Cynthia Jean, June 8, 1957, and Kathleen Mae, Nov. 25, 1962.

Alva was a farmer, ran a milk route, and raised vegetables and sold them to the City Market. He raised and showed Belgian horses. He trained horses, breaking them to lead, drive, ride and hitched to race carts. He also liked to hunt and fish. They lived most of their married life within the four adjoining counties. He retired from Sharp Brothers and Watermans Implement Company. He died March 9, 1980 at his home in Smith Valley, IN. Bertha died Sept. 21, 1980. They are buried at Greenlawn Cemetery in Franklin, IN. *Submitted by Larry Lee Hawley*

JACOB OMER HAWLEY FAMILY -
Jacob, son of Malachi and Mary Alice (Bruner) Hawley, was born in Needmore, Dec. 16, 1884. He attended Valparaiso University in Northern Indiana and taught in the Brown County schools. Omer married a schoolmate sweetheart, Maude Lillian Miller, daughter of Luther Miller and Hester (Squires) Miller on May 30, 1906. Maude was born July 29, 1888. There were three children born to this union: Mabel Clare, Leonard Omer and Ruth.

Mabel Clare Hawley born Aug. 10, 1908 at Needmore married Robert Lee Arthur, son of Dempsey and Della (Dow) Arthur. They were married at the Monrovia Christian Church, May 13, 1939 and lived in Paragon, IN until Lee's death Sept. 17, 1960. Mabel Clare graduated from Butler University in Indianapolis and earned a Master's Degree in Education from Indiana University. Lee graduated from Teacher's College of Terre Haute. Both taught school many years. After Mabel Clare's retirement from 44 years as a teacher she travelled extensively in many countries of the world.

L-R, Mabel Clare (Hawley) Arthur, Ruth (Hawley) Walk, Leonard Omer Hawley, Maude (Miller) Hawley.

Leonard Omer Hawley was born in Needmore Jan. 7, 1911. He married Helen Burns, (born Sept. 8, 1911), daughter of Irvin and Eva (Wills) Burns on July 25, 1937. Leonard was a teacher, basketball coach, and supervisor in the Indiana school system. He graduated from Butler University with a Master's Degree in Education. He died Nov. 10, 1977. Leonard is listed in the Indiana Basketball Hall of Fame at New Castle, IN.

Ruth Hawley was born April 4, 1917 after the Omer Hawley family moved to Paragon, IN. She graduated from the Methodist Hospital in Indianapolis as a Registered Nurse. She married Marvin Walk, son of Carl and Joy (Cooper) Walk on Sept. 12, 1951. Ruth died Sept. 1, 1962 and Marvin died Jan. 4, 1986. A daughter, Marchie Lou Walk, was born June 18, 1953. She married Roger Brown on July 30, 1971 and they divorced in 1976. Three daughters were born during her marriage with Roger Brown: (1) Lora Marie born May 5, 1972; (2) Angela Joy born July 21, 1973; (3) Cheryl Renee born Feb. 28, 1975.

A daughter of Ruth and Marvin Walk, Mary Ellen, married Jeff Collins on Dec. 20, 1975 and moved to Huntington Beach, CA. They have Dawn Ann Collins born Feb. 8, 1981 and Blake Vincent Collins born Jan. 3, 1984. Blake and Dawn were born in California.

After Omer and Maude Hawley moved to Paragon, IN, she was in partnership with Claud Potter in the grocery store and was postmaster at the time of Omer's death Oct. 9, 1924. Maude married Alonza Knight Dec. 2, 1934. Maude died April 1, 1972. Omer and Maude are both buried in the Friendship Park Cemetery near Paragon. Mr. Knight is buried with his first wife in Morgantown. *Submitted by Mabel Clare Arthur*

THOMAS HAWLEY FAMILY -
Thomas was born in 1812, in what is now Preston Co., WV, to Amos and Elizabeth Hawley. He married Elizabeth Poling, born 1819 in Randolph Co., VA (now WV) to John Poling and Mary (Pitzer) Poling.

Thomas and Elizabeth lived in Noble Co., OH from about 1847 and had seven children. By 1876, all the children except the oldest, Martin, were in Needmore, Brown Co., IN. Most bought small parcels of land, raised produce and animals for their own use, worked in the woods and other jobs. These were Bible believing people and wished they had received better education. They were pleased when churches and schools were built at Needmore and at Howard Ridge. Polings, Pitzers, Prathers, McGees, Shields and other families kept coming from Noble Co., OH to Brown Co., IN. The later ones came by train to Indianapolis or Mahalesville. They used to gather at Elmer Smith's parents' place near Needmore and talk about the mines, trees and people in Noble Co., OH.

The third son of Thomas and Elizabeth was known as "Melk." It is usually written Melker (riches), but sometimes Malakhi (to be king).

Melk married Alice M. Bruner. They had nine children, all born in Brown County and many of their descendants still live here. A son, William "Bummer", lived some time in Tennessee. Robert was crippled. Louisa "Lud" never married. Jacob (Omer) married and had two children. He was known as "White Top". Lilly married Clyde Legge and moved to Illinois. Charles married Abby Pearl Lithicum and had children in Monroe County. Anna married Ben Pryor, had family and moved to Florida. John Hobart "Hob" married Anna Lucille Ball and raised children in Indiana. Elizabeth "Lid" married Ed Snider, son of William "Tobacco Bill" Snider, remained in Brown County and raised a large family.

Thomas' daughter, Elizabeth, married William Parks and had: Henry, Sam, George and a daughter.

Thomas' daughter, Sarah, married Henry Burton, Jr., son of Henry Burton Sr. and Nancy Rice of Ohio, a descendant of Sir Edmund Rice (Rhys), as they were told by Dr. Charles Rice. Son, Carl, was born in Indiana and married a Brown County girl, Dorothy Miller. The Henry Burtons are listed as charter members of the Brush Creek Church of Christ.

Thomas' youngest son, George, a cripple, married Nanc ?.

The Parks family, the Henry Burtons, the Carl Burtons and the George Hawleys went to Cumberland Co., IL. Later the Parks and Hawleys went to Tennessee.

Thomas' daughter, Mary Ellen, married John Arnold and two of their children lived to marry. A son, William F., married Belle Chitwood. They and other relatives were musicians at Needmore. A daughter, Salena "Seen" married ? Giles and had two daughters, Sadie and Lula. Mary, "Seen," and the two girls lived together in Needmore where "Seen" operated the telephone exchange.

Thomas' son, William Morgan and his family are elsewhere in this book.

WILLIAM MORGAN HAWLEY FAMILY -
William Morgan second son of Thomas Hawley came with his brothers and sisters from Noble Co., OH and bought land in Brown Co., IN. He married Arah (Mary) Poling in 1878. They had three children, Mayme, Grace and Harry. Mary died while the children were small.

"Morg," as he was known, married second Millie Frances (Richardson) Martin. Millie was a descendent of Thomas and Nancy Richardson of Virginia. John Weddle, who served in the Revolutionary War from Pennsylvania, and John Richardson, War of 1812, were some of her ancestors. She had married Hiram Martin. They had a nice farm in Benton Township, Monroe County, near Brummet's Creek with Baby Creek, a branch, running through the farm. Three daughters and two sons were born to them. Mr. Martin met a tragic death when a log rolling down a hill crushed him. Morg and Millie and their children lived at the Martin farm which became known as the Hawley place. Two daughters and a son were added to the family.

William Morgan Hawley

The children attended school in Benton township just west of the Brown County line. Morg was more "care free" than Hiram Martin had been—he was given to making music with what he could find and teaching the little ones, especially Ola, to dance Irish folk steps. He farmed and loved animals, especially horses, as did Millie's brother, "John A.". Millie was a good home-maker and taught all the girls well. They sewed, mended and "made over" garments, did embroidery work especially on comfort tops. She loved to garden having garden greens ready as soon as the wild greens were too old to use.

They attended church just northeast of their home at Howard Ridge in Brown County near Needmore, so when marrying time came many picked Brown County mates.

John Martin married Maude Chitwood. Will Martin married Lena Westbrook. Before moving to Johnson County both families lived on what is now Yellow Wood lake and the older children came up the hill to Howard Ridge to school. Maude Martin married Charles Bock, section foreman for the railroad at Trevlac. Myrtle married "Johny" Legg, living in Needmore, then Bloomington. Nora married Walter Dresslar of Marion County.

Mayme Hawley married "Alf" Fleener and lived in Arizona in later years. Grace married Everett Browning and moved to Monroe County. Both Harry and Ada Hawley died early deaths, Alva and Bertha Hawley lived in Marion County. Ola Hawley married Frank Warford. They lived in what was known as the "weaning house" (extra house on the Warford farm on Rt. 45 by Weddle Lane where each newlywed Warford could set up house keeping). Frank worked in the Trevlac depot and was transferred to Oblong, IL I.C. depot.

After Morg's early death Millie and two younger children spent a year with her brother's family in Camargo, IL. Returning to Indiana, Millie often helped the older ones with new babies.

A few years before death Millie married Mr. Ritchey and lived in Greenwood.

JOHN MASON HEDGER - John and Permelia Jane (Fox) King were married in Brown County on Jan. 12, 1880. Among their children were Alford William Hedger and Clara F. Hedger. Alford William Hedger was born March 26, 1881 in Brown County. He married in 1902 to Elizabeth Rouse, daughter of Thomas and Elvira Reynolds Rouse of Bartholomew County. Elizabeth was born June 7, 1885 and died Jan. 30, 1965. Her husband, Alford Hedger died Oct. 26, 1954 at his home eight miles west of Columbus on Georgetown Road. They were members of Shiloh Separate Baptist Church and are buried there. Alford and Elizabeth had only one child, Floyd E. Hedger (Aug. 21, 1904-July 18, 1964), married Mona Hendershot. They had two children, Dale and Betty: (1) Dale Lacount Hedger, born Sept. 17, 1926, died Jan. 30, 1974. Dale married on Sept. 17, 1949 to Carolyn Joan Chapman, born April 9, 1929, daughter of Claud L. Chapman and Almedia Tracy. Dale and Carolyn Hedger had a son, Jackie Dale Hedger who married Shirley Jean Neat, daughter of Robert and June Neat. These Hedger families are very active members of the Morgantown Baptist Church. Jackie and Shirley Hedger have three children: Andrew Scott Hedger, Paul Gregory Hedger and Joy Hedger. Dale and Carolyn Hedger also had a daughter, Pamela Sue, who married Teddy John Sichting, son of Chester Sichting and Margaret Hensley. Teddy and Pamela Sichting had two children: 1. Mandi Lynn Sichting who married Charles Brock; 2. Matthew John Sichting. Teddy and Pamela divorced and Pamela married Michael Ferguson and had a daughter, Michelle JoAnna Ferguson. (2) Betty Hedger, born March 30, 1929, died Sept. 7, 1966. She had been a victim of polio for 12 years. Floyd and Mona Hedger divorced. He married Mildred Irene Legan, daughter of Clancy Legan and Dora Littleton. Mildred Hedger died Nov. 25, 1975, 11 years after Floyd's death. They were members of the Christian Church and are buried at Garland Brook Cemetery, Columbus, IN. Mona (Hendershot) Hedger married Harvey Needler.

Front: Carolyn and Dale Hedger. Back: Jackie Dale and Pamela Hedger.

Alford Hedger's sister, Clara F. Hedger, born April 7, 1884, died Sept. 16, 1962, married Walter Ashley on July 3, 1901. He was a son of William Ashley and Sarah E. Christman and was born in Brown County on May 28, 1880. Walter and Clara Ashley had six children: (1) Hazel Ashley who married Frank Wells; (2) Ina Ashley who married Otis Dunn; (3) Alta Ashley who married Earcle Freese, then ..... Copenhaver; (4) Estal Ashley married Dorothy Donahue; (5) Cora May Ashley married Dwight Talley; (6) Ralph G. Ashley, born Jan. 14, 1907, Brown County, died July 1, 1961. He married Ruth Morris Ashley on Sept. 5, 1949. *Submitted by Jackie Dale Hedger*

BURNELL HEDRICK FAMILY - The Peter Hedrick family migrated from Germany, in the early 1700s, to Virginia. Peter Hedrick was born in 1790 and died Aug. 6, 1854. He married Anna Zenor (born 1805 and died in 1898). They came from Virginia and settled on a 79.83 acre farm on Gravel Creek in Brown Co., IN. Their children were Benjiman Franklin, Joseph, Calvin and Shelby Hedrick.

After Peter and Anna died, son Calvin Hedrick, born Feb. 29, 1840, purchased the farm from the heirs on Feb. 13, 1861. Calvin married Sarah E. Ogle on Sept. 24, 1865. Seventeen children were born to them. Sixteen grew to maturity. One died in infancy. They were James, Louisa, Franklin, Walter, Oscar, Jane, Mahalia, John, Levi, Jason, Rosa, Henreitta, Minnie, (twins) Anna and Asa, William and Clara. Not more than one third of the farm was tillable. They never called for charity, but many times were short of the bare necessities, but they made their own way. They did custom work for neighbors and raised their own sorghum, wheat and corn for bread. They also raised chickens, hogs, cows, vegetables and fruits they ate.

Mary Jane, Burnell and Michael Hedrick

A large number of these children died in their late teens or early 20s. Jane, Mahalia, John, Walter, and Anna died of tuberculosis. Levi was killed by train in Camargo, IL. Oscar either fell, jumped, or was knocked from a train, crossing a high bridge in Sedalia, MO and was killed. Jason (while a patient in the hospital) choked to death on a bone. The mother lingered nearly a year with inward cancer. The father, in his late 80s became mentally unbalanced. One February night, unknown to the rest of the family, he wandered out of the house. The next morning they found him with frozen hands and feet. He died Sept. 6, 1923. Sarah was born 1849, died 1907 or 1908.

After Calvin's death, son William Hedrick, who married Lena Fulks (Dec. 16, 1916) purchased the farm in 1926. He farmed as his father in the past. Six children were born to them. They were Beatrice, Edelle, Burnell, Virgil, Belva (died in infancy), and Pauline. William died June 18, 1972. Lena died March 16, 1967.

After William's death, son Burnell Hedrick, who married Mary Jane Harris, purchased the farm in 1971. Burnell served in the armed forces in World War II. He now farms and lives on the home place. They have four children, Ronald, Bernard, Teresa and Michael. This makes four generations that have owned the Hedrick farm on Gravel Creek, Van Buren Township, Brown Co., IN. *Compiled by Edelle (Hedrick) Axsom, daughter of William Hedrick*

BRIAN AND RITA HELLER - One of the early homesteads in Jackson Township, the Masoner property, was subdivided a number of years ago. They live right next to the original homesite on a seven acre parcel on what is now called Lost Branch Road, Featherbed Lane.

In October 1982 Cecil Cunningham came to Chicago from his home in Los Angeles, CA to visit his daughter Rita and her husband Brian Heller. It was a cold and gloomy month in Chicago, and the three decided to get away to some place they had never been to before, and decided to try Brown County. They came here for a few days, walked the roads, visited the parks and all agreed that the land felt open and inviting and that they should look for a place here to make their new home.

Less than a year later Brian and Rita bought their property and Cecil moved out from California. Cecil took care of the place and made many of the improvements on the property. Brian and Rita commuted from Chicago on weekends and every other vacation and spare time they could take from their jobs.

In 1988 they made the decision to relocate permanently, and moved to Brown County in January, 1989. Cecil passed away in June of 1989. They were sustained by the beauty and warmth of the County and its people both then and now.

Brian and Rita find that other places are now measured by how they compare with their home county with its benign, gentle beauty, friendliness and very special "something" that they haven't quite exactly figured out yet, but are truly enjoying.

HENDERSON FAMILY - Joseph Henderson of Montgomery Co., VA, moved down river to Kentucky in 1810, lived there for five years, then moved to Jackson Co., IN. His son, Robert Henderson, born Feb. 14, 1795 (while George Washington was President), picked up his rifle and walked back to see his grandfather John Henderson before he married.

Robert returned, married on March 22, 1821 to Elizabeth Taggart (Nov. 2, 1798-Dec. 10, 1825) at Leesburg, Jackson Co., IN. They had three children: Nancy Henderson, born Jan. 12, 1822, died young; Rachel Henderson born Aug. 13, 1823; she married Joseph Rice on Feb. 9, 1840; they went to Shelby Co., IL. Jane Henderson, born April 22, 1825; married on Sept. 20, 1840 to Daniel McKinney (May 5, 1822-April 22, 1898); they went to Menlo, KS; had ten boys and one girl. After the death of his wife, Elizabeth, in 1825, Robert Henderson married Permelia Newkirk (Feb. 20, 1806-Jan. 17, 1865). Robert spent the winter of 1826-27 hunting in Brown County. He loved it so much that he brought his family over the top of Weed Patch Hill in the spring of 1828 and built a log cabin east of Gnawbone where he farmed and raised his family. It was a wilderness, no roads and no one lived nearby. He helped build roads. The first school was built by the creek east of New Bellsville. His children walked from Gnawbone carrying their rifles for protection. A school was finally built on his land between the Henderson Cemetery and the road. This early school had a six foot wide fireplace whose huge backlog required the efforts of the teacher and the largest boys to bring it in and place it properly. Another school was built on top of the hill at Mt. Liberty Rd. and Harrison Ridge Rd., called the Stull School. Students' benches were split open logs with legs. Children attended school until age 21. A record, written by W.A. King on March 2, 1888: "Francis Marion Henderson, born May 28, 1846, died July 13, 1853. Robert Henderson, born 1795, died March 2, 1885, age 90 years and 16 days." Family tradition says that Robert Henderson had a heart attack while feeding horses (throwing hay for them).

Robert and Permelia (Newkirk) Henderson had ten children: (1) Robert Henderson (Aug. 28, 1827-Aug. 10, 1910) married on Dec. 13, 1849 to Mary Ann Davis (Aug. 27, 1830-Jan. 29, 1892); both buried Henderson Cemetery; (2) William Henderson (Jan. 20, 1829-Aug. 15, 1898), married on Jan. 18, 1852 to Emaline King (Nov. 4, 1832-Feb. 5, 1868); both buried Henderson Cemetery; (3) James M. Henderson (Nov. 7, 1831-July 13, 1917) married on Aug. 19, 1855 to Jane Bright (March 12, 1835-Dec. 28, 1915); both are buried Henderson Cemetery; (4) Elizabeth Henderson (Feb. 27, 1833-??) married on March 19, 1852 to Isaac King; (5) Richard Henderson, born Feb. 7, 1835; married on June 9, 1861 to Mary Jane King; (6) Elcy Jane Henderson (March 19, 1837-Dec. 30, 1909) married on March 13, 1859 to Wesley Kirts (Aug. 22, 1836-Sept. 27, 1916); both are buried Henderson Cemetery; (7) Malinda Henderson (Feb. 19, 1839-Jan. 14, 1872) married on April 21, 1859 to Logan Ping (Aug. 9, 1830-March 26, 1912); both buried New Bellsville Cemetery; (8) Delila Henderson, born Jan. 12, 1842; married on Nov. 26, 1866 to Louis Burkhart; (9) Amanda Henderson, twin of Delila; married on March 16, 1862 to George Burkhart; (10) Harriet Henderson (March 26, 1844-Feb. 5, 1909) married, first, on April 22, 1866 to Jasper Job Ping (May 16, 1846-May 25, 1867).

William Henderson, child two of Robert and Permelia (Newkirk) Henderson, and his wife, Emaline (King) Henderson, had nine children: (1) Robert Henry Henderson (Dec. 5, 1852-April 3, 1937) married, first, on Jan. 18, 1874 to Marietta Truex (March 31, 1854-Dec. 15, 1900); married second, on April 9, 1903 to Mary Alice Downey (March 21, 1864-Nov. 27, 1932); all buried New Bellsville Cemetery; (2) Mary Elizabeth Henderson (April 2, 1854-May 6, 1931) married on March 30, 1876 to John Strange Joslin (Dec. 11, 1850-June 25, 1928); (3) John Richard Henderson (Dec. 19, 1855-Feb. 21, 1930) married on April 29, 1877 to Iva Elizabeth Morrison, born Jan. 11, 1858; (4) Sarah Jane Henderson (Oct. 30, 1857-August 1936) married on June 12, 1878 to Oren Womack; they moved to Oklahoma; (5) Martha Ann Henderson (Sept. 30, 1859-Sept. 9, 1922) had a daughter, Minerva E. Nelson, born Sept. 12, 1878, raised by grandfather, William H. Henderson; Martha Ann married on Nov. 16, 1881 to Elisha Davis (May 10, 1860-April 29, 1947); (6) James Henderson (Sept. 10, 1862-March 15, 1863); (7) William Benjamin Henderson (Nov. 6, 1864-April 9, 1946) married on April 23, 1885 to Alpha B. Frazer (Sept. 4, 1864-Feb. 21, 1953); (8) Lucinda Abarilla Henderson (born March 23, 1866), married on Feb. 28, 1881 to James Lucas; they had a child who died at birth; (9) Hugh Stewart Henderson (Aug. 23, 1867-Feb. 2, 1955, Bison, SD) married on Jan. 5, 1890 to Mary Jane Trenner.

After the death of his wife, Emaline, William Henderson (1829-1898), married on Nov. 8, 1868 to Mariah Rambo (1839-June 6, 1877). Their children were: (10) Thomas Jefferson Henderson (Feb. 4, 1871-March 30, 1948) married on Nov. 2, 1892 to Nettie Marshal (November 1875-June 11, 1941); (11) Sivala Alice Henderson (Jan. 24, 1873-Dec. 21, 1896) married March 14, 1896 to Hannibal Pingry Taggart (1868-1937); (12) Solomon Willard Henderson (July 22, 1875-April 22, 1895, in Illinois, of typhoid).

After the death of his wife Mariah, William Henderson (1829-1898) married for the third time, on Nov. 1, 1877, to Hannah Rambo, sister of Mariah. Hannah (Jan. 9, 1844-Sept 19, 1925) and Mariah were daughters of Solomon Rambo and Elizabeth Moore. (see ROBERT HENRY HENDERSON)
Submitted by Robert Ephraim Henderson

ROBERT HENRY HENDERSON - Robert was child one of William and Emaline King Henderson. Robert was born Dec. 5, 1852 and lived all his life in Brown County. He married, first, on Jan. 18, 1874 to Marietta Truex (March 31, 1854-Dec. 15, 1900), daughter of Henry Truex and Saloma Moore. Robert and Marietta Henderson had nine children: (1) Henry Willard Henderson (Jan. 6, 1875-March 28, 1956) married on Feb. 15, 1899 to Ella Campbell, divorced; married on Oct. 19, 1905 to Emma Lucinda Truex; (2) Ida Salome Henderson (Dec. 28, 1876-Sept. 15, 1938) married Daniel Webster Bennett on Dec. 28, 1898; (3) Lucinda Henderson (Dec. 25, 1878-Oct. 12, 1951) married on Dec. 27, 1898 to Judson Carter (Sept. 19, 1873-June 21, 1942); (4) Hannah Melissa Henderson (March 9, 1882-May 4, 1966) married on May 17, 1902 to William George Moore (Jan. 13, 1882-Aug. 28, 1964); (5) Mary Alice Henderson (June 25, 1884-June 7, 1939) married on March 9, 1904 to John Albert McCoy (Sept. 20, 1869-April 28, 1945); (6) George Earnest Henderson (April 20, 1887-Oct. 14, 1893); (7) Newton Ray Henderson (Sept. 28, 1892-Feb. 28, 1893); (8) Iva Bertha Nola Henderson (Sept. 28, 1895-March 20, 1978) married on May 13, 1916 to Joe Adam Miller (April 24, 1883-1958); (9) Ora Chester Henderson (Jan. 14, 1900-Nov. 29, 1904).

After the death of his wife, Marietta, Robert Henry Henderson (1852-1937) married, second, on April 9, 1903 to Mary Alice (Downey) Moore, widow of John Moore. Their children: (10) Robert Ephraim Henderson (Jan. 18, 1904, Brown County) married on June 21, 1928 to Violet May Lively (May 12, 1908-July 16, 1972); (11) Louis Frederick Henderson (Dec. 4, 1905, Brown County) married on Dec. 24, 1927 to Mabel Newmister (Aug. 2, 1909-Aug. 16, 1988), buried New Bellsville Cemetery.

Florence Henderson Yeager

Robert Ephraim Henderson, child ten of Robert Henry Henderson (Dec. 5, 1852-April 3, 1937) and his second wife, Mary Alice Downey (March 21, 1864-Nov. 27, 1932), married at Downers Grove, IL on June 21, 1928 to Violet May Lively (May 12, 1908-July 16, 1972) daughter of Harvey Talbert Lively and Carrie Etta (Ross) Lively. Robert Ephraim Henderson and his wife, Violet May, had children: Florence Elizabeth Henderson (Feb. 26, 1930-Sept. 20, 1984) who married on Jan. 27, 1956 to Benjamin F. Yeager, Jr., born April 20, 1923. Lowell Robert Henderson (July 31, 1931-July 4, 1950) married on Nov. 16, 1949 to Marilyn Jo

Miles, born Jan. 15, 1932, daughter of Charles Kendall Miles and Harriet J. Snider. Lowell and Marilyn had a son, Steven Lowell Henderson, born March 7, 1950. After Lowell's death in 1950, his widow, Marilyn, married Kelly Walter Maier, born Feb. 21, 1934. They had three children: Theresa Diane Maier, born May 8, 1954, married Philip Dean Bentz; Randall Kirk Maier, born June 28, 1955 and Julia Ann Maier, born April 28, 1957.

Robert Ephraim Henderson took into his home Lula Loree Frazer, daughter of William Oscar Frazer and Margaret Gibson (Bell) Frazer, after the death of her father in 1958. Lula, born Oct. 24, 1948, became the legal ward of Mr. Henderson. She has lived as a member of the Henderson family for over 30 years. Married to Richard Carley, she has two children, Charlotte L. Carley, born Aug. 19, 1969 and Richard S. Carley, born Nov. 8, 1973. (see THE HENDERSON FAMILY) (see THE DOWNEY FAMILY) *Submitted by Robert Ephraim Henderson*

GLEN COOPER HENSHAW - Arthur Glen Hinshaw was born in Windfall, IN, Tipton County, in 1880, the son of Andrew and Mary Ellen Cooper Hinshaw. His mother died one year later, in 1881. He graduated from Windfall High School in 1897, along with classmate Pearl Cue Hinshaw, grandmother to Nashville resident, Judith Lawless, and great-grandmother of Heather Celestina Hinshaw Lawless. Dr. Wood of Windfall sponsored him to study in Europe. Before studying abroad, he was one of the first students to enroll in the John Herron Art Institute, Indianapolis. He paid for his schooling by cleaning out brushes. He studied for one year in Munich, Germany, then went on to Paris and studied with Jean Paul Laurens at the École des Beaux Artes. There he met and married Olive Ballucia Roberts, a sculptress and one-time pupil of Rodin. Henshaw exhibited at the Paris Salon and was commissioned to do illustrations for a deluxe edition of Charles Lamb's **Essays**. For this he went to London, but World War I forced him to return to the states. About this time he no longer used Arthur, his given name, and added his mother's maiden name, Cooper, to his. After researching the Hinshaws in England, he also reverted to the older spelling, Henshaw.

Glen Cooper Henshaw, Nashville artist

After returning to America, Glen Cooper Henshaw established studios in New York and Baltimore. After the death of his first wife in New York, he married Carolyn Hastings of Baltimore. Together they established a home gallery in Nashville, IN, in the old Odd Fellows Hall on West Main, opening it on July 1, 1941. It had earlier been studios to Gustave Bauman and photographer, Frank M. Hohenberger.

Henshaw's work is Impressionistic, and it has been said that he bridged the gap between Impressionism and Expressionism. He suggests more than he defines, and painted not only what he saw, but what he felt about what he saw. With a few quick strokes of the brush he captured a fleeting moment. He painted both oils and pastels, the latter being his favorite medium. He enjoyed painting derelicts, the elderly, blacks, and small children, as well as nocturnal scenes of a cityscape or of Venice. One of his portraits hangs in the National Portrait Gallery in Washington, D.C.

Henshaw died in 1946 in Baltimore. Carolyn continued to live out her life in Nashville, where she added a concrete block firesafe building behind the Odd Fellows Hall to house her husband's paintings. The Odd Fellows Hall did burn down in the early 60s. Until 1990 their fireplace still stood beside the sidewalk leading to the Torchlight Shops. His paintings are now housed in the Glen Cooper Henshaw Memorial Room of the Brown County Art Gallery. *Submitted by Judith Lawless*

HENTHORN FAMILY - Isaac Henthorn was born Feb. 14, 1826 and married Margaret Brown, born Oct. 22, 1828. Their children were born in Brown Co., IN and included: Jonathon, born Dec. 15, 1848, died Feb. 20, 1872, may be buried at Duncan Cemetery; Cassey, born July 15, 1850, died Jan. 14, 1938, married Alvin Bradley; Elizabeth, born June 7, 1852 in Brown County, died July 12, 1931, married Chessley Bradley (brother of Alvin Bradley); Mary Margaret, born April 23, 1854, died Sept. 3, 1879; Henry Isaac, born July 6, 1856, died Aug. 28, 1877; George, born and died Sept. 9, 1858; Sarah born Aug. 10, 1859, died Feb. 5, 1895; William, born March 3, 1862, died Feb. 7, 1890 from drowning while taking someone across high waters in Brown County; Robert, born Aug. 21, 1864, died 1962, is buried at Duncan Cemetery; Minerva, born July 9, 1867, died April 10, 1933, married Gilbert "Gil" Sturgeon; Rebecca A., born Feb. 17, 1870, died March 1, 1928, and married Jim Woods whose son was also named Jim; Dora Alice, born Nov. 29, 1873, married James Stevenson Owens. Many of these Henthorns including Isaac and Margaret Brown Henthorn are buried at Duncan Cemetery in Brown Co., IN. *Submitted by Pearl Nugent*

DICK AND SARA HESS - The Hesses purchased their home on Town Hill in 1987. The old log structure had been christened "Lookout Cabin" when it was part of the Hilltop Camp from the 1920s to the 1940s, having been erected in 1928 from two "pioneer" cabins moved from the Helmsburg area. Reports at that time dated the hand hewn logs back to the 1850s.

Dick was born in 1934 in eastern Pennsylvania (Columbia County), the first of two children (sister, Janet) of Martin J. and Belva Pealer Hess, both descendants of German immigrants (Pennsylvania "Dutch"). All of his forefathers had immigrated by the early 1800s and all remained modest farm folk, working the land, until his father left the scenic Fishingcreek Valley, where stand the gravestones of five earlier generations of the Hess and Pealer families. Dick's maternal grandmother, a fifth generation American, spoke only German until starting school.

Hess family tradition states that the immigrating ancestor was Heinrich Johann Hess, a Hessian mercenary captured by Washington's forces at the Battle of Trenton on Christmas Eve 1776.

Sara's paternal immigrating ancestor, Symon Jansen Van Arsdalen, came to New Amsterdam in 1653, reportedly commissioned to investigate establishing a pottery business. He remained in Flatlands, Long Island and became a leader in the Dutch community. His descendants moved on to Somerset Co., NJ, later to the Dutch community in Conewago, PA, and after the Revolution, to the Harrodsburg, KY area. There they lived for generations as farmers and millers until Sara's father, Sanford Boyer Van Arsdale, Jr., moved with his parents to Indiana in 1908. His mother's family were also Kentucky pioneers, of English descent (Horn and Wilkerson).

Sara and Dick Hess, March, 1990

S.B.V. married Sara Lucele Hodges in 1926. In 1936, Sara was born in Indianapolis, the second of three daughters (sisters Gretchen and Nan). Sara Lucele Hodges was the first of two daughters (sister Elizabeth) of Curtis Aaron Hodges and Lulu Myrtle Hastings. The Hodges were from Paragon, IN and the Hastings from Martinsville. Curtis Hodges was a journalist and his wife a teacher and social activist. In 1922, Curtis became managing editor of the Indianapolis News and was blessed with having his friend, Kin Hubbard, creator of Abe Martin, on his staff.

Sara's mother died in 1946 and two years later her father married Rosemary Eller whose family was from the Noblesville area. They continue to reside in Indianapolis.

Dick graduated from Kokomo High School in 1952 and Butler University in 1956. At Butler, he met Sara, a 1954 graduate of Shortridge High School. They were married in 1956 and have three children: Todd, an M.D. married to Gudrun (Emmel) whom he met in Germany; Laura, a Ph.D. in Human Development; and Richard, a senior at the University of Wisconsin.

Dick is a marketing manager at Kimberly-Clark Corporation, where he has been for more than 30 years. Sara is a real estate broker managing a sales office. Early in their marriage they lived in Taiwan where Dick was an Air Force Intelligence Officer, and, subsequently, with Kimberly-Clark, they lived in West Germany.

HETHERINGTON - This history could not be authentic without mention of the Hetherington family and its vital contributions to Brown County.

Frederick Alexander Hetherington (1859-1931) was a prime instigator of the first artist colony and was an early resident of Peaceful Valley. Fred was one of six children of Benjamin Franklin Hetherington who was born in Carlisle, England in 1828 to John Hetherington, a son of a member of the English parliament. Ben first came to Massachusetts and lived in Ohio before coming to Indiana in 1852. He co-founded Hetherington and Berner, Inc., which engaged in iron foundry and machine work in Indianapolis. Fred became president upon Ben's death in 1906. It is believed that Ben perfected the Gatling gun under Gatling's specifications. Fred was a genius of invention. He devised a huge asphalt-paving machine. He was an advocate of photography as well as art and invented the first portable magazine camera which could hold a dozen plates which flopped into position by a turn of a key. Fred and Ben are buried with their wives in Crown Hill Cemetery, Indianapolis.

Frederick A. Hetherington

Fred Hetherington attended the Indiana School of Art as a student of John Love. In 1879 he produced the first cartoons to appear in Indianapolis papers or periodicals. He also illustrated for advertisements and for the early publications of the Hoosier poet, James Whitcomb Riley. He was a contemporary and personal friend of T.C. Steele and William Forsyth. Together they helped form the Bohemian or "Bohe" Club which was composed of art students of the early 1880s.

Fred maintained a cabin on Jackson branch about a quarter-mile northwest of Nashville where he carried on his artistic sketching and community service. He was among the nature-lovers who discovered the vast beauty of Brown County and he attracted hundreds to the county by arranging tours for people as far away as Chicago. Frank Hohenberger in his column "Down in the Hills O'Brown", (Sept. 8, 1939, Indianapolis Sunday Star), called Brown County "Fred Hetherington's ideal playground". A friend, Richard Lieber, and others, met in Fred's cabin to initiate the formation of the Indiana State Park system and its Fish and Game Department. It is the present site of a bronze-plaque memorial to Lieber.

Fred was twice married, first to Emma Lucretia Boardman (1852-1909) who was also an art student. After her death he married Emma Beatrice Baker. His four children, all by his first wife, were: Rosalind, Aug. 20, 1881 (married Willard Bottome); Frederick Carl, Nov. 3, 1882 (married Anna Margaret Tharp); Valentine, Feb. 14, 1886 (who died young); and Marian Grace, Jan. 12, 1890. In 1909 Marian married James Harvey Marsh, the Brown County artist and sculptor who painted and exhibited under the pseudonym John Paul Marsh. (See Marsh history elsewhere). Marian's father, Fred, and Marsh's father, Courtland, helped erect the Indianapolis Soldiers and Sailors monument about 1902. The Hetherington company installed the iron staircase and Courtland Marsh, a carpenter, helped build the scaffolding. *Submitted by Ms. Mary Louise Alter*

ALICE WARFORD HIGHSMITH -
Alice Carrie, born June 26, 1914, on Carmel Ridge Road, middle daughter of Frank and Ola (Hawley) Warford, Trevlac, IN. At age four, her family moved by rail to Oblong, IL, where her father was employed by the N.Y. Central Railroad, which made a daily run from Effingham, IL, to Indianapolis. She soon became familiar with the flagman and conductor. Grandfather, Oscar Warford, was asthma sufferer, so once monthly (Sundays) the family would travel by rail to visit him (an eight-hour ride roundtrip).

Alice greatly enjoyed her grandparent's home atop a hill on Carmel Ridge Road—a chicken farm with cows, turkeys, and bees. Old well was covered by small house whose window was always locked. On the side was a crank for moving bucket up and down with thirst-quenching cold water. A large, covered dish holding honeycomb always sat on dining table where step-Grandma Olive provided this sweet-tasting treat. Delicious, large, mouth-watering melons from neighbor "Chick" Weddle's farm during summer months held fond memories.

Oscar and Sarah (Branstetter) Warford

Big hill was south of Alice's little home—the "Bluff"—and was beautiful year round. Grandpa Oscar's old, open touring car was always there when we departed the train. Grandma Olive provided good care for him.

Alice and sisters, Gladys and Ruth, attended school in Oblong; Gladys attended college and taught. Her daughter, Nancy, also taught in Nashville. Two Uncles, Walter and Ed, along with cousins Eva Alberding, Norma Moore, Lucy Mann, and her son, Fred, have been/are teachers. Other relatives pursued nursing including: Mildred Warford Yaws, Glenda Mann, Mary Jane Richards and daughter, Clover Phillips and granddaughter, Ana del Rio. Alice is equally proud of them.

Frank A. Warford attended high school and college. Worked at his brother Ed's store and post office in Trevlac. (Incidentally, Trevlac acquired its name from the first settlers, the Calvert family, who operated hotel and bath house across the road. They reversed spelling of their last name; hence, Trevlac.) Later Frank, along with his brother, Homer, and brother-in-law, Charles Bock and nephew Thurle, went to work on N.Y.C. Railroad. After several years with R.R. and "bumping," Frank managed his own movie theater in Newton, IL. Although a successful venture, he chose semi-retirement and moved back near his childhood home on Route 45 close to Carmel Ridge Road to the house his brother, Cary, built for his son, Thurle. Frank also became active in local government—a staunch Democrat.

On June 30, 1932, in Olney, IL, Alice Warford married Orman Highsmith of Robinson, IL and became parents of four daughters: Marianne Hill, Orma Jean Treft, Barbara Alice del Rio, Kay Lynn Siebeneck and a son, Richard Owen, a computer supervisor at Littleton, CO. Of 18 grandchildren, two are doctors in Madrid; oldest grandson, radio personality in Dallas; youngest granddaughter attending The American University in Washington, D.C.; while youngest grandson will attend Duke University in the Fall 1990. Ten grandchildren have/are attending college. Three grandchildren— including two great—are among Alice's namesakes: Alisa Siebeneck, Carrie Suman, and Alice Cervera (Madrid). Eleven great-grandchildren, including Jason Dorman, nine years, who is our "special" boy. Another special person is Alice's great-nephew, Brian, who provided great joy and companionship to the Highsmith family while they lived in Brown County. One of Frank's great-grandsons, Frank Rodgers, and his family, currently live on a portion of the original Branstetter/Warford estate.

Alice is proud to be a Hoosier, blessed with many close relatives and friends: Hawleys, Lawson, Dr. Murphy family, Jane Gore family and Dr. Seibel family. Also, two ladies very close to the Warford family years ago are Dote and Cord Richardson. God has richly blessed our family (Hawleys, Warfords and Highsmiths) with children and grandchildren who love Him.

DAILY F. HILL FAMILY -
As one drives past the Brown County High School Athletic Field he will notice that the field is called the DAILY HILL FIELD, so named in tribute to Daily F. Hill, beloved Athletic Director and Interim Superintendent and Administrator in the Brown County Schools from 1968-1980. Daily Hill, with his friendly smile and helpful personality, was an avid Coach who played "to win" and was respected and loved by students and teachers alike. He inspired confidence and self-esteem in those with whom he worked. As he put it, "If you can't do **great** things, you can do **small** things in a **great** way."

Daily Francis, born May 28, 1918, of German and French ancestry, was the eldest son of George and Grace Ruby Means Hill and brother of Paul and Sara Virginia. He grew up on the Ohio River at Madison, IN, then a thriving Pork Center where hogs were driven on foot to market down old "Hog Trough Road." Sports were important in Daily's life as Varsity player on the basketball, baseball and track teams of Madison High School, Ball State University and Hanover College.

Daily, Bobbie and Daily Stephen Hill

At Hanover College he met Carrie Roberta (Bobbie) Jones of Norwood, OH, whom he married on Oct. 10, 1944. After graduating in 1942, Daily served in the Navy's V-7 and Army's Engineer Programs; Bobbie kept busy teaching Physical Education and Dance at Hanover College, Wilson College for Women and the Covington Y.M.C.A. After marriage he coached and she taught in several high schools of Milan, Eaton, Royerton, New Castle and Madison. During the Madison Period of the 1950s, two important events took place: the majestic old LaGrange home at Hanover, where the Hills were living, burned to the ground; and Daily Stephen Hill was born Jan. 29, 1957.

The three moved north to Gary and Griffith, IN, where they were neighbors of Ed and Rosemary

McMinds (who came to Brown County in 1976 to live on five acres of Daily Hill's Pine Acres) and where Daily became a Principal of Schools; then to Cedar Lake, where he served as Superintendent; and back south to Ellettsville as Superintendent. In each Corporation a successful building program became an important item and, as each program was completed, Daily Hill looked ahead to other pastures, the greatest being with the Brown County School Corporation.

The Hill Family, with their three dogs, settled for 18 years on Helmsburg Road, on top of beautiful Hill's Pine Acres, in the red house formerly owned by John and Carrie Kensler. The property, which lies just beyond Art Smith's farm and Grandma Barnes Road, is now owned by Nashville Glass-Blower Jim Lawrence, his wife and concert-pianist Jennifer and two children Hannah Rae and Brian Tyler. The Daily Hill Family bought the property in 1968 when Cox's Drug Store (then the gathering place for coffee) was jam-packed into the Storeroom that became Jay Kilgore's Colonial Restaurant. The Totem Post and Nashville House seemed to be the only shops open during the Winter months (a far-cry from the many shops open year-round 20 years later in 1988).

Daily Stephen Hill attended Rose-Hulman Institute of Technology at Terre Haute, graduating in 1979 with a Degree in Mechanical Engineering. He presently is an Engineer for Kopin Optical Industries in Taunton, MA, where he resides with his Long Island wife and Art Teacher Mary Ann and daughters Justine and Alexandra.

Daily was an active person: Elder in the Bloomington Presbyterian Church, 13th. President of the Hanover College Alumni Association, member of the Indiana Basketball Hall of Fame (a brick on the courtyard map at the new Indiana Basketball Hall of Fame in New Castle is dedicated to him from Irvin Stoner, a member of Madison's State Finals Team), member of Lambda Chi Alpha Fraternity, and member of the Indiana High School Athletic Association.

The Brown County Lions sponsored Lion Hill as Governor of District 25E for the Hoosier Lions Council of 1988 and he and Deputy District Governor Lou Macon traveled many miles to further worthwhile community projects in Brown County and other areas in the District. Perhaps his greatest accomplishment was the splitting of District E into E 1 and E 2.

Bobbie, too, was active in the Brown County as member and President of the Business and Professional Women and Delta Kappa Gamma. It was she who started the Elementary Physical Education Program for **every class** in all four Elementary Schools, promoting physical fitness for **every** child and, with Bob Weir, first introduced a Tennis Program to Brown County.

Yes, the Daily Hill Family loved the hills and valleys of Brown County and the people who traversed their roads and paths. How appropriate that the Daily Hill Field is nestled in the middle of such beauty!

NELL CHITWOOD HILL - Nellie Ann Chitwood, daughter of Richard and Ida May Chitwood, was born Oct. 13, 1898, near Needmore, Brown County, and later moved to the farm with her parents near what is now Lake Lemon. She married Edward Hill and they had four sons, Richard (born 1919) married Joyce Linters and second Delores Lossin; Edward, died as an infant; Maurice (born 1921) married Thelma ?; and James who died when two years old.

Chitwood home, west of Needmore about 1909. Back L-R: Martha Chitwood, Richard C., Ida May C., Maude C. Martin holding Ethel Martin, John Martin, Ora Chitwood, Belle Chitwood. Front: Clarence Martin, Ralph Chitwood, Edith Martin, Nelle Chitwood, Blanche Chitwood.

The Hills lived in Ohio, California, and Chicago. Ed died in 1961 and Nell in 1987.

ROBERT HIMES FAMILY - Robert White Himes and Frances (Wallace) Himes moved to Brown Co., IN in September 1963. Robert was the County Extension Agent in Brown County from 1963 to May 1977. Before coming to Brown County, Himes was Extension Agent in Fountain County, County Seat, Covington, IN for 12 years. They lived in Veedersburg, IN. Prior to that he was Extension Agent in Johnson County at Franklin, IN.

Robert White Himes was born in Scott Township, Montgomery Co., IN, Nov. 12, 1917, to Perry Robert and Mabel White Himes. Robert lived on a farm until he entered the United States Army Air Force, during World War II, in March 1942. He attended White School for five years. This was a one room brick school building on land donated by Benjamine White, his great-grandfather. He graduated from New Market Indiana High School in 1935, and attended two agriculture Short Classes at Purdue University in 1936 and 1937.

Frances and Robert Himes

Before entering the U.S. Army Air Force he worked at Allisons Division of General Motors at Indianapolis. After airplane mechanics training he was in Hawaii for one year and then returned to the States for Air Force Cadet Training. It was during this training at the University of Tennessee in Knoxville, that he met Frances Lucille Wallace. They were married April 6, 1945, in Knoxville, TN. Frances was born in Knoxville, TN on April 2, 1922 to Archie Jett and Eva (Brown) Wallace. She was their only child. Frances had worked at Western Union Telegraph and the Hamilton National Bank. After Robert was discharged from the Air Force in November 1945, he attended the University of Tennessee where he graduated in Agriculture Engineering in 1949.

Robert and Frances had four children: Roger, born 1948; Carolyn, born 1952; Warren, born 1955 and Richard, born 1961. All four children graduated from Brown County High School. Roger graduated in 1966 and from Purdue University in 1971. He is employed by Turner Management Construction Company of New York. Roger married Patricia Erickson, a Purdue University graduate, from Indianapolis, IN, in 1969. They have twins, Ryan and Jennifer, born 1976.

Carolyn graduated from Brown County High School in 1971, and from Purdue University School of Nursing in 1974. Carolyn married Drake Dingeman, a Purdue Electrical Engineering Graduate, from Grand Rapids, MI, in 1975. They have two children, David, born 1979 and Drew, born 1982.

Warren graduated from Brown County High School in 1974. After taking training in City Water Management, he worked in Nashville, IN and is presently employed by Indiana Cities Water Co. in Shelbyville, IN. In 1982 he married Lynn LeClerc Critser from Shelbyville, IN. They have three children, Katie, born 1983 and twins, Samantha and Courtney born 1985.

Richard graduated from Brown County High School in 1961 and from Cedarville College, Cedarville, OH, in 1985. Richard married Julie Brockage, a University of Ohio Graduate, from Cincinnati, OH in 1990.

Richard has worked as a Youth Minister, and is presently employed by Paper Mint Company in Columbus, OH.

The Robert Himes Family home is located on a five acre tract with a 3/4 acre lake located 1.6 miles north of the courthouse on State Road 135N.

The Himes lived in a mobile home on the property while Robert built their ranch style house.

RICHARD AND ELLEN HUFFMAN - There was a mass migration of residents of Belmont and Monroe Counties of Ohio to Van Buren Township, Brown Co., IN in the 1850s and 1860s. Among them were Richard and Ellen Huffman and daughter, Mary J., born July 10, 1852. They came to Brown County about 1853. Richard Huffman was born July 29, 1826 in Greene Co., PA, son of Phillip Huffman, born Virginia, and Letitia Stewart, born Pennsylvania. This family later moved across the Ohio River to Greene Township, Monroe Co., OH about 1828. Richard, the oldest of eight children at home, married March 13, 1851 to Sue Ellen Moore, born March 21, 1830, daughter of Solomon Moore and Mary Truex (born Feb. 15, 1798, Pennsylvania), residents of Belmont Co., OH, where they had married Jan. 26, 1815.

Richard and Ellen Huffman had seven more children: Thomas E. (born Feb. 9, 1854); Frederick Nelson (born Feb. 28, 1856, died age three); Sarah Letitia (born June 24, 1858); John Willard (born Feb. 28, 1861); Alice Adelia (born Sept. 7, 1867); Lula Genetta (born April 12, 1869); and Bertha E. Huffman (born Feb. 1, 1873).

Richard Huffman was a private in Co. G, 6th Reg't. Indiana Vol. Inf. from Dec. 31, 1861 to Nov. 29, 1864. Wounded at Resaca, GA, May 15, 1864, he was a patient in Clay U.S.A. General Hospital, Louisville, KY, for over two months.

In 1873, the Huffman family joined the covered wagon trains of travelers to the Kansas prairies. There they purchased 160 acres of railroad land five miles southwest of Bushton, in Farmer Township, Rice Co., KS. Only three years before, Rice County census listed only five qualified residents.

Mrs. Huffman's sister's family took land north of Ellinwood in Barton Co., KS in 1884. They were Moses and Matilda (Moore) Ward formerly of Belmont and Monroe Counties of Ohio and Bartholomew and Brown Counties of Indiana. Their son, Mahlon Ward had taken a soldier's claim in S10, T19, R11, securing the southwest quarter in Barton County in 1873, less than ten miles from the Huffman home.

Of Richard and Ellen's seven children who grew up in northwest Rice County, Mary J. married Mr. Rees and was living in Bowman, CA in 1911.

Thomas E. Huffman married Hulda Jane Joy on May 29, 1878, lived south of Holyrood and at Jetmore, KS where his wife died Sept. 27, 1918. Thomas died Jan. 3, 1919 at Medford, OK.

Sarah Letitia "Tish" Huffman (June 24, 1858-June 27, 1933) married Charles Wesley "Wes" Shepherd in Brown Co., IN. They had five children.

John Willard Huffman married Eliza (Lawlor/Lollar) Ratliff of Fayetteville, AR some years after he made the 1893 Cherokee Strip race into Oklahoma. Eliza was a young widow with three daughters and a son. John and Eliza had a daughter, Alice. John was living at Jefferson, OK at the time of his death Feb. 9, 1933.

Alice Adelia Huffman died Sept. 3, 1887 at age 19 years 11 months.

Lula Genetta Huffman married Walter Edmond Jung. She died Sept. 11, 1892 at age 23 leaving three daughters.

Bertha E. Huffman married April 8, 1890 to James E. Evans. She died Sept. 9, 1922, the mother of nine children. She is buried in Lyons Cemetery in Rice Co., KS.

In the early 1890s Richard and Ellen Huffman sold their land and moved to Fayetteville, AR. In time, poor health brought them back to Rice County and to the home of their daughter, Tish Shepherd. There on June 13, 1907, Ellen passed away at age 77. Richard Huffman joined his wife in death on April 7, 1911 at age 84. They are buried in the Lyons Cemetery, Rice Co., KS.

Richard and Ellen Huffman have three living grandchildren: Mable E. (Evans) Smith, El Dorado, KS, and Milton Lowell Evans, Colorado Springs, CO who grew up in Rice County, and Alice Huffman Lackey, Spearman, TX. Mrs. Lackey still owns the land in Grant Co., OK which her father won in the Cherokee Strip race in 1893. *Submitted by a great-granddaughter, Agnes Drake Bedient*

HUFFORD-PATE - Frances Hufford Pate born Aug. 1, 1920 in Indianapolis, IN is the daughter of Warren and Ida Spencer Hufford. Warren born April 1, 1880, died March 29, 1957, buried at Greenlawn Cemetery, Brown County. Ida was born Jan. 1, 1891 in Ohio, died April 26, 1979, buried at Bear Creek, in Brown County.

Frances Pate Family. Back row: Kenneth A., David H., Francis M., Sandra, and Kenneth K. Front row: Ernest D., Judy E., Wayne F., Charles W., and Forest R.

The Hufford ancestors were from Schwartzenan, Germany. They came to the United States in company with other families who fled for liberty of conscience being under religious persecution in 1729. They were Old German Baptist Dunkards.

Warren and Ida came from Ohio to Indianapolis. He worked at Kinghan Meat Packing Company. They came to Brown County in 1931. They lived on Salt Creek Road, Frances was 11 years old, she went to Turner School on Clay Lick Road. Charlie and Herbert Campbell were her teachers. Fred Taylor was mail carrier. Frances attended Goshen Church.

Herb McDonald ran a huckster wagon. On the day he came on the Old Georgetown Road, Frances and her mother would meet him.

Frances remembers after coming to Brown County the first wood tick that she saw, she jumped up and down and screamed.

Her home had no electricity and the roads were dirt. After a rain or snow they would get muddy. Frances' mother thought about having her wear boy's shoes since she walked to school. To her, this was horrible. Her mother didn't do this and Frances laughs about all this now, city girl turned country.

After two years the Huffords moved back to Indianapolis but returned in 1938. They remained here the rest of their lives.

Frances married Kenneth Pate in Indianapolis. Kenneth was born Aug. 20, 1918 in Robards, KY.

In 1952 they decided to move to Brown County at Camp Roberts. The house is no longer there. Kenneth worked at Shumaker Brothers, a road paving company until he retired.

They had eight children, Kenneth A. born April 13, 1939, Charles W. born May 8, 1943, Wayne F. born July 21, 1947, died May 19, 1962, buried Brown County Memorial Park. He was the first person to be buried there. Ernest D. born Nov. 25, 1948, Forest R. born Feb. 18, 1951, Judy E. born Nov. 1, 1952, David H. born Jan. 6, 1955, Sandra K. born June 15, 1957. Judy and David were born at home in Brown County. Mrs. Lory was midwife.

Charles Haarer, minister of Bean Blossom Mennonite Church at that time, was the first minister to visit their home. He started picking up the children for Sunday School, Youth and Bible School.

Warren and Ida Hufford

In 1971 Kenneth and Frances divorced. Frances worked at the Masonic Home in Franklin, IN for 15 years. She retired in 1985.

She is an Eastern Star, Chapter 579 Morgantown, IN. She went back to school and got her G.E.D. in 1988. Her family gave her a surprise get-together and presented her with a Ryre Study Bible. She has a strong faith in God.

In 1983 Frances' house burned. The Mennonite Church, Frances' family and friends helped rebuild it. Frances thanks God for all these people.

Charles served in the Army in Hawaii and David in Panama.

Ernest, Forest and David live in Brown County. Frances lives on Gatesville Road. She has 17 grandchildren and eight great-grandchildren. She attends Bean Blossom Mennonite Church. (see Judy (Pate) Toney) *Submitted by Frances M. Pate*

TONYA HUNT - Tonya liked living in Brown County in the early 1980s where she attended Helmsburg Elementary. She and her two brothers, David and Billy are the children of Linda and David Hunt. Tonya now lives in Morgan County and enjoys visiting her Brown County friends.

Tonya Hunt

HUTCHISON FAMILY - William Hutchison and his wife Sarah migrated to the United States at the close of the Revolutionary War from the County of Tryonne, Ireland, and settled in Huntington Co., PA. Prior to 1813 the family moved to Ohio, settling in Belmont and Morgan Counties, except for his son Archibald who remained in Warriors Mark, PA.

Leonard, John Wm., Newton, Charles, Addie, Sarah and Seward Hutchison

It was his son James Hutchison (born May 8, 1789, died July 16, 1873, Brown County) who married Anne Pennington, daughter of Amos and Elizabeth Barre Pennington, on Dec. 26, 1809 in Huntington Co., PA. James brought his family to Brown County around 1855. He and Anne were the parents of 12 children: Amos (born June 16, 1811, Barnesville, OH, died June 1, 1823, Ohio), William D. (born Oct. 1, 1813, Ohio, died Jan. 19, 1857, Brown County), Matilda (born Feb. 24, 1815, Ohio, died Nov. 23, 1824, Ohio), Edith (Ada) (Mrs. Thomas Ogden), (born Aug. 9, 1816, died June 1866, Brown County), Elizabeth C. (Mrs. Jonathon P. Johnson) (born Aug. 9, 18??, died ?), John W. (born Feb. 7, 1820, died April 6, 1867, Indiana), Asbury (born Aug. 3, 1821, died June 3, 1907, Belmont Co., OH), George Miles (born March 14, 1823, died Dec. 26, 1896, Brown County), Jarrett (born July 17, 1825, Ohio, died July 2, 1870 Brown County), Emily (Mrs. Jesse Williams), (born July 17, 1828, died March 7, 1912, Brown County), Rebecca Ann (born April 1829, died Nov. 16, 1828, Ohio), James Finley (born June 2, 1831, Ohio, died ?).

James, son of William and Sarah, served in the War of 1812 in Capt. Shannon's Company of the Ohio Militia. On March 3, 1855 he made his declaration for bounty land under the Act of Congress, Sept. 28, 1850. He received 80 acres of land in Brown County which passed to his son Grammar Hutchison. John W. son of James and Anne, served in the Civil War, Co. G 27th Indiana Inf. His brother Asbury served as Private in Deen's Co., Dept'l. Corps., Pennsylvania Inf.

James Hutchison and his wife Anne and their son Jarrett are buried at the Unity Church Cemetery in Hamblen Township, Brown County. It is the belief that Edith (Ada) Ogden, daughter of James and Anne, is also buried there without a marker. Many of the other Hutchison descendants are also buried there.

The early money box of the Unity Church, made by Jarret Hutchison, was given to the family of Seward Hutchison, son of Grammar Hutchison. Seward's daughter Ruth passed it on to Cornelia Hutchison Korte who lives in the area. *Submitted by Ruth Hutchison, daughter of Seward Hutchison*

JAMES V. AND MILDRED F. HYDE -

James Vernon, fifth child of John Siegle Hyde and Bertha May Griffin, was born Aug. 13, 1915, Brown County. He married first to Mildred Florence Mayo, born March 3, 1922, died May 6, 1982. He married second to Joan Ann Hill Savage. His children by his first marriage were Virginia Mae, Marilyn Kay, James Vernon, Jr., Brenda Faye, John Michael and Joseph Marion Hyde.

Joe, Florence, Vernon with son Michael and Brenda Hyde

1. Virginia Mae Hyde, born Aug. 13, 1940, married Donald Clyde Smith, born June 18, 1936. Their four children are Steven Smith, born Oct. 6, 1962; Amy Lea Smith, born Nov. 8, 1964; Donald Scott Smith, born Nov. 5, 1965; Susan Lynn Smith who married David Childress. Their son, Travis Donald Childress was born April 15, 1988.

2. Marilyn Kay Hyde, born Nov. 7, 1942, married Paul Burton Smallwood, born Jan. 18, 1940. Their four children are (1) Paul Douglas Smallwood, born Nov. 28, 1962, married Carman Michelle Goodwin, born July 31, 1969. (2) Malinda Jo Smallwood, born Sept. 6, 1964, who married Jeffery Bruce Mills born July 13, 1960. Their children are Jacob Thomas Mills, born Sept. 29, 1986 and Annah Marie Mills, born Feb. 20, 1990. (3) Dee Ann Smallwood, born Oct. 28, 1966, married Thomas Edgar Raley, born September 1962. Their children are Kathleen Elizabeth Raley, born Aug. 7, 1986 and Cafele Thomas Raley, born February 1989. (4) Lora Jane Smallwood, born May 8, 1972.

3. James Vernon Hyde, Jr., born Jan. 10, 1944, married Rose Leeann Jones, born Aug. 10, 19—. Their children are James Andrew Hyde, born June 11, 1967 who married Julie Scott; and Audrey Ann Hyde, born Sept. 29, 1969.

4. Brenda Faye Hyde, born March 16, 1952, married James William Chandler, born June 13, 1951. Their children are William Griffin Chandler, born Aug. 11, 1976 and Emily Elizabeth Chandler, born July of 1978.

5. John Michael Hyde, born Nov. 6, 1964, married Ginney ....., they divorced. They had a son, Michael Jorden Hyde, born Nov. 26, 1986.

6. Joseph Marion Hyde, born Dec. 12, 1965.
Submitted by Marilyn Hyde Smallwood

FRED BATES JOHNSON -

Sometime between 1898 and 1902, Fred Bates Johnson, an undergraduate student at Indiana University in Bloomington, discovered Brown County. Although Mr. Johnson never had a legal residency in Brown County, he loved it and was preoccupied with Brown County during much of his life. He was one of the first who foresaw the economic potential of this early development.

Mr. Johnson was born on May 17, 1889 in Kokomo, IN, the son of Benjamin Bates and Clara Albaugh Johnson. Benjamin Bates Johnson was born on a farm near Canton, OH in 1852. Fred Bates Johnson had one sibling, an older sister, Edna Johnson, who was born in Kokomo in 1876.

After receiving his undergraduate degree at Indiana University, Mr. Johnson's first job was as superintendent and high school teacher in Carlisle (Sullivan County, Southern Indiana), where he taught from 1902 to 1904. In 1903, the last but one lynching in Indiana took place in the Evansville area, and according to family history, Mr. Johnson was locked up in a businessman's office to keep him from trying to stop the lynching lest he be harmed, too.

From 1904 to 1907, he worked as a newspaper reporter in Indianapolis, working variously on the Indianapolis Sun (Times), Sentinel and News. One of his "jobs" was to see to it that Kin Hubbard, the creator of Abe Martin, got home without mishap. Mr. Johnson was a diligent reporter...good both in "legwork" (ferreting out the news), and in writing good expository prose under the pressure of the deadline. He became the number one political reporter for the News. One day in 1907, the City Editor of the News was sick, and his replacement for that day was not Mr. Johnson, who ordinarily should have been. He quit the newspaper business, and persuaded Dr. William Lowe Bryan, then President of Indiana University, to hire him to teach a course in journalism while he studied law. Thus, Indiana became one of the first universities to teach journalism; from his courses the School of Journalism developed. In 1910 he received his law degree and opened his office at 1414-16 Fletcher Trust Building in Indianapolis.

Soon after World War I broke out in Europe, Mr. Johnson perceived that the U.S. might become involved, and, if so, he wanted to be ready. He was the first to enlist in Indianapolis when the Indiana National Guard was called up for service along the Mexican border. He was the first of a line of Johnson Quakers to serve in the military since his great grandfather Johnson, a strict Quaker, along with 30 or 40 other Quakers, were inducted during the War of 1812. They were released after a few months.

Mr. Johnson rose rapidly through the ranks from private to major. He saw service first along the Mexican border in 1916 and 1917, then in Hattiesburg, MS as Captain and Company Commander, and finally in the Judge-Advocate-General's Office in Washington, D.C. He resigned his commission in 1919 to return to Indianapolis to take up his law practice.

It was during this service with the Army in April 1917 he met his bride, Priscilla Moeller Wagner, of Terre Haute, IN. Miss Wagner was the daughter of Professor and Mrs. Frank Casper Wagner. Miss Wagner was born in Ann Arbor, MI, on Sept. 17, 1895.

Mr. Johnson met his bride through unusual circumstances. Miss Wagner had been engaged to a young man in Terre Haute of whom her parents disapproved. An acquaintance of the Wagners, Sam Garber, suggested his friend, Mr. Johnson, be asked to dissuade her from this engagement. Mr. Johnson not only succeeded in this mission, but also persuaded her to become his bride. A short time later, Captain Johnson took the train to Terre Haute to meet his in-laws-to-be. When the train arrived, Miss Wagner saw a puny man with bowed legs, large protruding ears and a pocked face coming towards her. She wondered whether she had made a mistake after all, but as soon as he started talking she realized she hadn't.

Fred Bates Johnson

After the war, Governor James P. Goodrich appointed Mr. Johnson to the Public Service Commission of Indiana in 1919 to 1925. His pay while on the commission eased his financial situation. He also became a member of the Indianapolis Board of Commissioners where, according to family history, he sought to eliminate the influence of the Ku Klux Klan from the Indianapolis school system.

Mr. Johnson never lost his early enthusiasm for Brown County during World War I. Before the war he had gotten into such good physical condition by hiking over the Brown County hills that the Army marches did not overtax him; he weighed under 140 pounds at this time. He and Jack (Andrew Jackson) Rogers, a former student of Mr. Johnson at Indiana University, spent much of their free time there. The trip down, before there were cars, involved a train ride to Helmsburg and then a hackney ride to Nashville. They became acquainted with Dale Bessire in Nashville, who had come to Brown County to paint. Mr. Johnson and Mr. Rogers joined Mr. Bessire in his orchard business. In the Spring of 1930, after a particularly severe frost, Mr. Johnson and Mr. Rogers became discouraged with the orchard business and sold out, each receiving the amount of $9,000—the amounts they had invested.

During this period, Mr. Johnson's law practice began to flourish. He sold most of his stock before the Crash of 1929. During the Depression, Brown County land was extremely cheap, five dollars or less an acre, and he began investing in real estate there.

While staying in the Pittman Inn on Main Street in Nashville one day in December of 1926, Mr. Johnson was overheard remarking, "What Brown

County needs is a modern hotel." This remark led to some burning of the midnight oil, and before the next morning, a deal was struck for him to buy the Pittman Inn for $6,000. Mr. Rogers picked up half the tax and Mr. Johnson the other half. The following spring the Inn was extensively remodeled and was renamed the Nashville House.

In the year 1936, Mr. Johnson and Mr. Rogers divided their Brown County holdings, Mr. Rogers taking the hotel and Mr. Johnson the outlying land. In September 1943, the hotel caught fire and burned to the ground. At one point the flames had been under control, but the water supply gave out. (See Dorothy Bailey's article on the remodeling and history of the hotel.)

The Johnsons had two cabins during these years: the first was primitive, with no electricity nor running water. This cabin was on the second ridge past the Carl Lieber house at the end of Jackson Creek Road. The second cabin, now owned by the Martin family, was a couple of miles north of Nashville on State Highway 135. It was said to have been built of one of the largest set of logs ever found in southern Indiana. It was modern in every respect, except for city water. Ernie Pyle, the war correspondent, stayed several weeks at this cabin before World War II.

By the mid-30s, Mr. Johnson had become one of the largest landowners in Brown County. Three separate parcels of land included the bulk of this land: the Hitz-Johnson development along Freeman Ridge Road, a subdivision north and slightly west of Nashville, and the "Big Place" south of Gnaw Bone on Seilenmeier Ridge.

Mr. Benjamin Hitz was a fresh food wholesaler from Indianapolis. He and Mr. Johnson put up five or six log cabins in the 1930s which were either rented or sold. At one point, they had horses and a genuine Texas cowboy named Scott. After one of the horses threw a lady rider, they decided running a Dude Ranch was not for them.

Sections of the subdivision north of Nashville were partially sold off in the late 30s. The last land of this subdivision was sold after Mrs. Johnson's death in 1983, leaving Brown County without any land owned by the Johnson family.

The "Big Place" Mr. Johnson's informal name for the acreage along the Seilenmeier Ridge, included the Gnaw Bone Hunt & Kennel Club, a rather grandiose name for a very primitive establishment. Friends of Mr. Johnson used it for rabbit hunting. One of his friends was the "Hoosier Cartoonist" Gaar Williams, Mr. Johnson's best and oldest friend from high school days in Richmond. Eddie Voland, Mr. Johnson's Man Friday, took care of the beagle hounds and went hunting with them. During the Depression, the "Club" was used by the local welfare authorities to house the needy. Later Fred Lorenz, a shop teacher at Orchard School in Indianapolis, started the Gnaw Bone Camp for boys there. Mr. Johnson was glad to let Mr. Lorenz use the facility. Later he paid Mr. Johnson $3,500 for the camp and 40 acres, and the camp was well on its way. In 1957, Mr. Johnson sold over 1,100 acres along the Seilenmeier Ridge to Earle S. and Olivia Cascadden of LaPorte, IN.

During the late 50s and early 60s, Mr. Johnson had a series of strokes which progressively incapacitated him, leaving him at the end without significant speech. A sad end for a man who loved life and particularly enjoyed exchanging ideas, or "yammering" as he used to call it. He died in his home at 4115 North Illinois Street in Indianapolis on April 3, 1963. His widow died at the home of her daughter, Mrs. Charles B. Doak, in Malvern, PA. Mr. and Mrs. Doak now reside in Devon, PA. Other survivors are Mr. and Mrs. Bates Johnson of Essex, CT, Mr. and Mrs. Gaar Williams Johnson of Indianapolis, and Dr. Frank Wagner Johnson and Britt Lipson, who reside at Crystal Lake, Benzie Co., MI.
Submitted by Gaar W. Johnson

SAM AND HARRIET JOHNSON - Harriet Frank Johnson, born at Hibbing, MN to Harry Edwin and Ersie Storms Frank, is a descendent of Henry Whitney who came from England to Connecticut in 1649. Raised on a farm near Detroit Lakes, she graduated from Hibbing High School and Junior College, then attended Purdue University in a program sponsored by Curtiss-Wright Company, and worked as a draftsman in Columbus, OH during World War II.

Samuel Gideon Johnson, Jr. was born at Fort Wayne, IN to Samuel Gideon and Caroline "Jessie" Loomis Johnson of Sweetwater, TN. He is descended on his mother's side from Joseph Loomis who came from England to Windsor, CT in 1638, and on his father's side from Thomas Savage, who came to Jamestown, VA in 1607 with Captain John Smith's Adventurers. He graduated from Purdue University with a B.S. in Metallurgical Engineering, attended Midshipman's School at Notre Dame, was commissioned an Ensign and assigned to sea duty on a Naval Transport in the Pacific in World War II.

Sam and Harriet Johnson

Upon discharge from the service, Sam worked briefly in the steel industry, then returned to Purdue and received a M.S. in Engineering. He and Harriet met when she was a student in a class that he was teaching. They were married in Hibbing, MN, June 25, 1949, then moved to Indianapolis where he began a 33-year career with International Harvester Company, starting in the foundry.

During the Korean War, Sam was recalled by the Navy and spent two years of sea-duty in the Atlantic and Mediterranean Fleets. He returned to International Harvester, working at many locations including five years as Manager of the Indianapolis Engine Plant, and holding a series of manufacturing and executive positions in the General Office in Chicago before retiring in 1982. Sam is a Registered Professional Engineer in Indiana and Ohio. He received a Distinguished Alumni Award from Purdue University and the Sagamore of the Wabash Award from Governor Whitcomb.

Sam and Harriet have three children, and three grandchildren. Ann, Susan and Samuel III all graduated from Purdue. Ann is Professor of Veterinary Surgery at the University of Illinois. She is married to Professor Walter Hoffman of Monroe Co., IL and has a son, Wesley. Susan is Professor of Veterinary Medicine at Ohio State University. She is married to Professor David A. Wilkie of Toronto, Canada and has a son James. Sam III is an Industrial Engineer with TRW in West Lafayette. He married Kimberly Sinclair, an Elementary School Teacher from Huntington, IN and has a daughter, Caroline. Twenty years after leaving college, Harriet returned to Purdue and received a B.S. in Mathematics and taught at IUPUI.

Sam and Harriet have owned land in Brown County since 1957, and since retiring have operated a 260 acre farm on Salt Creek. The farm is the site of the historic Hoover/Howard mill and the original homesite of the Alfred McGuire family, well-known Brown County pioneers. In 1983 they built a contemporary home, incorporating the old two-room house built on the site by Joseph Heckman in 1880. They are members of the Nashville Methodist Church and have been involved in many Brown County activities including the Lions Club, Humane Society, P.E.O., Historical Society, Literary Club, Friends of the Library, 4-H, Agriculture Extension Board, Arbor Day Committee and the County Plan Commission.

ALEXANDER JONES - Alexander was born at Greencastle in Putnam County on April 29, 1835. He was raised by his mother and took her last name. He was always known as "Alec."

Alec came to Brown County in the early 1850s and Homesteaded in the Southwestern part of the county. The post office and store came later at a place called Youno.

Alec first married in 1860 to Margaret Fleetwood, born June 17, 1837. They had eight children: Sarah, born June 19, 1861, married John Browning, died Aug. 3, 1942; Thomas, born Feb. 6, 1863, married Mary Mitchaner, died Oct. 21, 1945; William, born Jan. 29, 1865, married Mary Browning, died Dec. 16, 1941; Cynthia, born Feb. 28, 1867, married Marion Lutes, died Feb. 2, 1920; James, born March 28, 1869, married Mary Hopper, died March 31, 1961; Rosetti, born April 4, 1870, died Aug. 15, 1951; Jerry, born Jan. 5, 1874, married Teresa Kirk, died July 4, 1951; Charles, born May 3, 1877, married Addie Pyles, died March 4, 1910. All these children were born at Youno in Brown County.

Elizabeth Jones

Margaret died Feb. 8, 1880 at Youno and is buried in the Fleetwood Cemetery in Jackson County.

Alec then married Elizabeth "Lizzie" Bates Todd in May 1882. Elizabeth who was of German descent, was born July 22, 1845 to Wiley and Susan Zornes Bates. She was married first to a man named Todd. After she was divorced, she moved her family to Burgoon Ridge in Monroe County to teach at the Burgoon School. This is where she met Alexander Jones.

Children of Alexander and "Lizzie" were: Mabel, born June 9, 1883, married John Mitchell, died Oct.

13, 1970; Fredrick Alexander, born Aug. 27, 1884, married Lillie Combs, died Dec. 3, 1945; Otto Jones, born March 18, 1886, married Dorval Hedrick, died Jan. 12, 1979; John, born Jan. 28, 1889, married Pearl Axom; Henry, born July 8, 1891, married Ruth Deckard, died Dec. 3, 1978. All the children were born at Youno in Brown County.

"Lizzie" always regarded the last seven children as "The third litter." She said her children escaped the 1918 flu epidemic, diphtheria, measles and other killer diseases of that time because she regularly fed them a mixture of sulfur and sorghum molasses and quinine. Her children even escaped the occasional outbreak of head lice most common in school rooms in those early years.

Alexander died April 28, 1894 at Youno and is buried in the Fleetwood Cemetery in Jackson County. After his death, each child received ten acres of ground. His other possessions, including four ewes and four lambs, a stand of bees, a trundle bed, a scythe and cradle and one red cow were sold at auction.

Elizabeth died Feb. 13, 1916 at Youno and is buried in Bloomington, IN. *Submitted by Ruth Hansen*

ERNEST JONES -
Ernest was born a half mile north of Youno on the Old Family Homestead in Brown County on Jan. 15, 1914. He is the son of Fredrick Alexander and Lillie (Combs) Jones. Lillie, the daughter of John H. and Mary Jane Elkins Combs, was born Sept. 2, 1890 in Jackson County. She later married Charles Fox and died in Bartholomew County on Jan. 20, 1981. She is buried at Garland Brook Cemetery in Columbus. Fred, son of Alexander and Elizabeth (Bates) Todd Jones, was born in Youno, Brown County on Aug. 27, 1884. He and Lillie were married on Dec. 9, 1906. Fred died in Terre Haute, IN on Dec. 3, 1945 and is buried at the Rose Hill Cemetery in Bloomington. Two other children were born to Fred and Lillie: Jessie Mae, born Dec. 9, 1907, married Marion Todd; she has five children and Walsie Fern, born Feb. 26, 1920, married Paul Clark; she has one son.

Ernest Jones and Helen Beeman Jones

Ernest walked a mile and a half to the Browning School House on a dirt and creek gravel road across the Lively Ford Bridge until he was 14 years old. His folks then sold the old homestead where all the Jones family had been born and moved to a farm near Surprise, IN. He graduated from Surprise 8th grade in the Spring of 1929. Ernest went to Freetown High School for two and one half years before transferring to Wellington High School in Illinois, where he graduated in 1933.

Ernest came back to Indiana in 1934 and went to work for Noblitt Sparks in Seymour. In 1942, he quit Noblitts and went to work at Cummins Diesel for the next 27 years. Retiring with a total 45 years of factory work.

On Oct. 18, 1936, he married Helen Beeman, daughter of Oscar and Sarah Grace (Holsclaw) Beeman. Helen was born Sept. 30, 1909 in Jennings County. She has been a secretary and bookkeeper and is also a poet.

Children of Ernest and Helen are: (1) Marilyn, born Nov. 30, 1939, married July 16, 1957 to Roger Brown: children, Anthony and Robert; Marilyn and Roger are divorced; (2) Rebecca, born Aug. 30, 1943, married July 28, 1962 to Jimmy Cornette: children, James Brion and Gina; (3) John P., born April 8, 1945, married May 30, 1964 to Janet Welch: one child, J. Eric; (4) Ruth, born May 11, 1947, married May 22, 1965 to Jerome York: children, Christopher and Geoffrey, Ruth married Robert Hansen on May 21, 1981; (5) Martha, born Nov. 30, 1948, married Jan. 28, 1967 to Donald Kelley: children, Brad and Deann. Marty and Don are divorced. All the children of Ernest and Helen were born in Jackson County.

Ernest has served in several fraternal organizations and presently belongs to the Masons, Shrine and is an ordained Priest and Elder in the Church of Jesus Christ of the Latter Day Saints. He and Helen live in Jennings County at R.R. 5, North Vernon. *Submitted by Janet Jones*

JAMES M. AND WILLIAM M. JONES -
James Marshall Jones, son of Alexander and Margaret Fleetwood, was born March 28, 1869. His ancestors came from Virginia. He attended a one-room school in Brown County. Because he was slightly crippled from birth, his family considered him unable to do heavy farm work; and so his sister in Bloomington helped him in attending I.U. He graduated from the School of Law, 1895.

He began his law practice in Nashville, where he met Mildred Hopper, whom he married in October, 1895. Mildred was a daughter of William Marmaduke "Duke" Hopper and Nancy Ann Morse, their families migrating to Brown County from southern Ohio.

William M. Jones and parents Mildred and James M. Jones

James practiced law in Nashville for more than 50 years. During that time he became the attorney for The Nashville State Bank, and later the bank president, before his retirement in 1956.

James and Mildred had six children, for each of whom they desired education above the elementary and secondary level. They helped provide advanced education for their first son, Newland, "Dick" at the Atkins Embalming School, Indianapolis; for their first daughter, Lucille, at the Louisville Conservatory of Music; for their second son, James, Jr., at the University of Louisville, which led to his becoming a successful dentist at Columbus, IN; and for their third son, William, at New York University, and later at Indiana University. The two other daughters, Aletha and Margaret, died in their early years.

After college, William taught and coached athletics in high school in Benton Co., IN, for six years until he joined the U.S. Navy, 1942, serving as a Chief Petty Officer for almost four years. After Navy service, he returned to teaching and coaching for 33 more years.

In 1943, William married Ada Marie Schieler, a native of Benton Co., IN. Her parents were John and Marie Schieler, whose ancestors had come from Switzerland and settled on the rich farm lands of Illinois and Indiana.

William and Ada had two sons, Kerry Marshall, born Sept. 6, 1948; and Ross Mitchell, born June 17, 1953. As with the preceding generation, the parents continued the tradition of encouraging and helping their children towards opportunities in advanced education.

Kerry earned a Master of Science Degree in Electrical Engineering, Purdue University. He is a projects engineer at Hewlett-Packard Corporation, Chelmsford, MA, and he and his wife Deb live in Winchester, MA.

Ross also attended Purdue, where he received a Bachelor of Science Degree in Aeronautical and Astronautical Engineering, and later added a Master's Degree in the same study at Massachusetts Institute of Technology. He is employed at JPL (Jet Propulsion Laboratory), Pasadena, CA. He and his wife Ana and their two daughters, Laura, and Jennifer, live in La Canada, CA.

After the two sons had finished most of their higher education, Ada completed the education tradition by securing her own Master's Degree in Education from Indiana University and taught kindergarten in the Kokomo (IN) Public Schools for ten years.

In 1981, after retiring from teaching, William and Ada moved to Nashville to manage a small shops complex at the Jones Homestead, where William had been raised. The complex is named Honeysuckle Place in memory of Mildred Jones, who was devoted to flowers, flowering shrubs, and vines of many kinds. *Submitted by William M. Jones*

ISRAEL AND PHEBE (OWEN) JOSLIN -
Israel Joslin born 1820 Ohio, son of Ezekiel and Nancy (Higgins) Joslin, married Phebe Owen born 1822 Ohio, in 1844 in Brown Co., OH. Six children were born in Ohio before coming to Brown Co., IN in the mid 1850s.

Israel was a farmer, chair-maker and butcher, married four times. First to Phebe in 1844, Sarah Reeves in 1867, Sarah Wright in 1868, and to Susan Dougherty in 1880. Israel left Brown County and settled in Bartholomew in 1865.

Children of Israel and Phebe were: William W. (1844-1900) married Alcinda Gates; Harriett born 1847; Perry (1847-1882) married Mary L. Clark, Harriet and Perry were twins; Enoch Ellsberry (1848-1904) married Louisa Joslin (1844-1917) (Lowell Joslin's grandparents); John Strange (1850-1928) married Mary Henderson; Ezekiel born 1853; Henry Eleazor (1855-1928) married Lydia Ann Nielson; Mary Etta born 1858 married Charles Reeves; Martha Jane (1861-1898) married John Waltz; Phebe Luella born 1863, married George Beatty.

Children of Israel and third wife, Sarah Wright were: Lorena (Emma) born 1868 married Charles Elliott and Winifred born 1871 married A.L. Smith.

Sons William, Enoch Ellsberry and John and daughter Martha Jane married and remained in Brown County and raised families, and to this date have several descendants living in Brown and Bartholomew Counties.

Israel died in Bartholomew County in 1894 and is buried in the Dobbs Cemetery in Brown County. Sons William and Enoch Ellsberry are buried there also. *Submitted by Lowell Joslin, great-grandson of Israel Joslin*

LOWELL AND MARCEDES (WALKER) JOSLIN

Lowell Ray Joslin was born in Brown County in 1918, son of Clarence E. and Nelle Gertrude (King) Joslin who married in Brown County in 1911. Lowell was a grandson of Enoch Ellsberry and Louisa (Joslin) Joslin who married in Brown County in 1869; and George and Ianthia Ann (Fox) King who married in Brown County in 1889. Lowell was a great-grandson of Israel and Phebe (Owen) Joslin who married in Ohio in 1844; John and Christann (Smith) Joslin who married in Ohio in 1841; Conrad and Eliza (Shafer) King who married in Brown County in 1854; Joseph and Julia Ann (Lister) Fox who married in Brown County in 1869.

Lowell was a great-great-grandson of Ezekiel and Nancy (Higgins) Joslin who married in Ohio in 1815. Ezekiel Joslin entered land in Brown County, Van Buren Township 1849. He had come from Ohio to Shelby Co., IN, then to Brown County. Ezekiel's son, Israel Joslin, sold land to his second cousin, John Joslin in the early 1850s. Israel's son, Enoch Ellsberry Joslin, married John Joslin's daughter, Louisa Joslin. Ezekiel Joslin married Jemima Breedlove Percifield in 1860 in Brown County, after the death of his first wife, Nancy.

Clarence and Nellie (King) Joslin

Enoch Ellsberry and Louisa Joslin had a son Clarence who was Lowell's father. Lowell had two brothers and two sisters: Evelyn Louise, born 1920, married Woodrow Tays; Howard Lester, born 1925, married Betty Longnecker Ervine; Mary Alice, born 1928, married Chester Roberts; Rev. Hurschel Paul, born 1932, married Carol Dobbs. Lowell married Marcedes L. Walker in 1946. She was the daughter of Jennings Atla and Lucy (Sells) Walker, granddaughter of William and Mary Alma (Craven) Walker who married in Brown County in 1893; great-granddaughter of James Knox and Rebecca Catherine (Campbell) Walker; great-great-granddaughter of Samuel and Nancy (Young) Walker; great-great-granddaughter of Rev. William Hamblen.

Lowell and Marcy Joslin had two sons: (1) Duane E., born 1948, had two children by his first wife: Anthony Joseph Joslin, born 1968 and Jill Michelle Joslin Sweeney, born 1970. Duane married second to Deborah Williams who is also a Hamblen descendent. (2) Donald Ray Joslin born 1949, died 1986. He married Sharon K. Morgan and they had two children: Hollie Ann Joslin, born 1977 and Joshua C. Joslin, born 1981.

Lowell graduated from Nashville High School in 1936. He served during World War II, South Pacific, Navy Seabees. He retired as a millwright from R.S.R. Quemetco Inc. of Indianapolis in 1981. He and Marcy moved back to Brown County on S.R. #46 E, on land that has been in the Joslin name since the early 1850s.

Lowell and Marcy are members of the Brown County Historical Society and are charter members of the Brown County Genealogical Society.

Lowell's great-grandparents, John and Christann Joslin deeded land in 1860 to the Methodist Episcopal Church, which is now the North Salem United Methodist Church on S.R. 46 E. John and his wife also deeded land to the Washington Township Trustee, where the North Salem School was located in 1858. *Submitted by Lowell and Marcy (Walker) Joslin*

JOHN GATES KAIN

John (Oct. 29, 1816-Feb. 2, 1875) and his wife, Elizabeth Neidigh (April 16, 1815-Feb. 4, 1896) are buried in Bean Blossom Cemetery, Brown County. Their son, Charles Kain, born March 14, 1851, married on Oct. 19, 1870 to Rhoda Jane McNeely, born Aug. 31, 1848. Charles died Nov. 15, 1925; his wife died July 20, 1910, both are buried in Bean Blossom Cemetery. They are the parents of Jesse, Oscar, Fred W., Oral Gates, and Evan Wiley Kain.

Oral Gates Kain, fourth child of Charles and Rhoda Kain, was born Oct. 10, 1874 and died April 9, 1951. He married Ollie Dean Turner, sister of Lena Turner who had married his brother, Evan Kain. Oral and Dean Kain had children:

(1) Theadore Fay Kain who died in December of 1981 in Minnesota; (2) Paul Fredrick Kain who married Ruby Jureal May in 1929. Their child was Paul Fredrick Kain II, born in December of 1937, who married Ruth C. Tinsley, daughter of Frank W. Tinsley. Children of Paul and Ruth Kain are Carol Lynn, Ruth Ann and Charles Lawrence Kain.

Evan Wiley Kain, fifth child of Charles and Rhoda Kain, was born in Brown County on Jan. 22, 1878 and died Jan. 15, 1936. He married Lena Bell Turner, daughter of Lewis A. Turner and Latona Frances Tracy. Lena Bell was born Oct. 8, 1880 in Brown County and died June 27, 1976. Evan and Lena had a son, Maurice Kain who was born July 9, 1909 and died Dec. 21, 1981. He married Mildred Naomi Bond, daughter of Alonzo "Lon" Bond and Olive Skaggs. Maurice and Mildred had two sons:

(1) Steven Michael Kain who married Sharon Platt, daughter of Irvin Platt and Elizabeth Woods. Steven and Sharon Kain had children, Barbara Ann Kain, Bryan Steven Kain and David Richard Kain; (2) J. Richard Kain who married Judith Mae Lanquist. Their children are: Janett Marie Kain, Jeannie Louise Kain, Phillip Matthew Kain and Michael Kain.

Oral Gates Kain and his wife Ollie Dean are buried at East Hill Cemetery in Morgantown. His brother Evan Kain and his wife Lena Bell are also buried there. *Submitted by Sharon Kain*

JAMES AND CLEOPATHRA KAKAVECOS

Benjamin Boren, the great-grandfather of James Kakavecos, was of Scottish descent. He served in the union army in the Civil War. He took part in "The Battle above the Clouds" on Lookout Mountain, Chattanooga, TN. His wife's name was Julia (Lamb) Boren, who lived on a farm on the outskirts of Noblesville, IN with her two sons Calvin and Wilson K. Boren. After the death of Benjamin, Julia with her sons migrated to Brown County buying a farm at Fruitdale from the Tucker Family in 1918. Calvin Boren had married Katherine Louise Craig (of Irish Descent) and they had four children. All lived on the farm at Fruitdale after moving from Noblesville. The children were Ruth May (married Charles Barnes of Brown County); Dorothy Amelia (married James Kakavecos, an immigrant from Edipsos, Greece); Benjamin Franklin (married Lola Devore of Franklin) and George (Wash) Boren.

Cleo and Bud Kakavecos - 1956

To the marriage of James and Dorothy Kakavecos were born six children, Eileen Elizabeth (married Forbus Hatfield-Indianapolis); Ruth Mary; James Kakavecos (married Cleopathra Lawson-Elverton, TN); Constance Ann (married Kenneth Riggs-Indianapolis); Georgiana (married John S. Kimberlin-Brown County); and Catherine Jane (married Robert Hensley-Franklin).

James Kakavecos was born on the farm at Fruitdale and went to school in Indianapolis until graduating from George Washington H.S. in Indianapolis. Then served in U.S. Army as a Mortar Gunner in the 13th Armored Division in WWII in France, Germany and Austria. After discharge in 1946 from Service, James moved back to Brown County to the Farm at Fruitdale. He commuted to and from Indianapolis where he was employed as a printer until his retirement in 1988.

Boren family (1918) at Fruitdale. Ruth, Ben, Dorothy, Katherine Louise (mother), Calvin (father) and George Boren.

Cleopathra (Lawson) Kakavecos was born in Elverton, TN, to High and Sally Lawson. High Lawson was of English and Dutch descent and Sally (Adkins) Lawson was of English and Indian Descent. Cleopathra moved to Indianapolis in the early 1950s living with a sister until her marriage to James Kakavecos in 1956. Then to Brown County.

James and Cleo have made their home on the farm at Fruitdale since their marriage. The Lord has blessed them with five children. Rex Donald (adopted-married Donna Sparks, Decatur, AL);

Thalia (Kakavecos) Combs (married Karl Combs of Bargersville); James Jr. (married Deanna Ashbrook of Martinsville); Christopher (married Lisa Emerson of Franklin) and Stephen Nathaniel. All of the children attended schools in Brown County, Helmsburg, Sprunica, and BCHS.

James, Cleo and their son Stephen still live on part of the Farm where James was born in 1926. The farm at Fruitdale had mostly been sold off as building sites, by Calvin Boren before his death. Most of the homes along the east side of 135 at Fruitdale are built on the family farm. James Jr. and his family also live on part of the farm.

Although we may leave Brown County for a while, we always return. Its charm and beauty forever draws us back. Brown County, it's our home and we love it.

KANTER-CANTER FAMILY -
Great-great-grandfather Truman Canter came to America from France with the Marquis de Lafayette when the Marquis came to help the colonists during the American Revolution. Truman's son was Thomas Anthony. Thomas Anthony's eldest son, William Carlyle Canter, was born Aug. 17, 1817. William had a large first family. Then he married Mary Frances (Rader) Portwood (born 1847) in 1883. William Carlyle and Mary Frances had three children - Benjamin Franklin, born April 23, 1887, an older brother, George Washington, who died at age 16 from a hunting accident, and a younger sister, Nancy Elizabeth. William died in 1910 and Mary Frances in 1923.

William Carlyle served in the Mexican and in the Union Army during the Civil War.

Hallie Tate Thomas, daughter of Alpha Adele Flannery and Vincent T. Thomas, was born Oct. 17, 1891. The Flannery family, of Irish origin, and the Thomas family, of Welsh origin, moved from Virginia to Kentucky. He had been a teacher, superintendent of schools, and county judge of Owsley Co., KY. Hallie was a teacher.

Hallie and Ben Kanter, 1960

Benjamin Franklin Kanter and Hallie Tate Thomas were married Dec. 27, 1912. Ben worked for a timbering company so they moved often. In the 1920s he quit timbering and moved to Indianapolis. The family moved to Brown County (Needmore) May 1, 1927. Ben was buying land in Jackson Township. When Marmon Motor Company failed in the depression, Ben was without a job and lost the land. In 1931 the family moved to Georgetown (Beanblossom). Later in the 1930s Ben worked for WPA as a supervisor during the development of the Yellowwood Forest area.

There were nine Kanter children: (1) James Euwin (from an earlier marriage) was born Dec. 17, 1906; died in 1970; (2) Mary Frances, born Nov. 21, 1913; (3) Thomas Truman, born June 26, 1916; (4) Victor Franklin, born March 22, 1918; (5) Joy Paul, born April 8, 1920, died in 1987; (6) Helen Adena, born July 9, 1923; (7) William Carlyle, born Feb. 14, 1928, died in 1982; (8) Robert Bruce, born Jan. 30, 1930; and (9) Margaret Louise, born March 9, 1932.

Ben Kanter died in 1963 and Hallie in 1970.

Thomas and Victor served in the navy during World War II. Thomas was in the Pacific theater. Paul was in the army. Later, William and Robert served in the army in Germany.

Mary Frances was a teacher in Brown County and Center Grove schools. Victor was a principal in Indianapolis schools.

James and Thomas worked for General Motors Truck and Bus Company as skilled tradesmen. Robert worked for Chrysler Corporation as a supervisor. Paul was an electrician and William a car salesman. After her husband's death Helen worked for the town of Willow Springs, IL.

The escaped convict, Joseph Jenkins, arrived in Bean Blossom near dusk, Sept. 30, 1933. Some older boys had gathered and were questioning Jenkins. Herbert McDonald and Ivan Bond drove across the road to talk to the man.

Ben Kanter's son ran home and told his dad about the man. Ben loaded his shotgun and went down onto the road near the man. When Jenkins was asked for identification, he pulled his gun and shot Herb in the shoulder, turned and saw Ben with the shotgun and fired his pistol, Ben dropped down so the bullet went over his head. Ben shot back as he dropped down and hit Jenkins at the top of the head. Jenkins was taken to Dr. Crabtree's office where he died. *Submitted by Mary Frances Davis and Victor Kanter*

KEATON FAMILY -
The first generation of the Keaton family migrated from England in the early 1700s. William Keaton, the forefather, was a soldier in the Revolutionary War at the age of 17. His brother, James Keaton, born in 1803, went to Kentucky in 1808, with his parents and on to Indiana. The family settled first in Johnson County, where James married Cloe Ann Adams (Nov. 13, 1834). James Keaton wanted to come to Brown County, because of the timberland, as well as the hills. He could find work cutting timber and sawing crossties. He came to Brown County in the 1840s, where he built a two room log cabin from the virgin trees. There was one room downstairs and a second room upstairs. How rugged these pioneers were: James Keaton and wife, Cloe, to brave the wilderness, to cut the trees for their cabin and clear a road to the cabin.

Keaton Family, 1935. Front: Olive (Watson), Lena (mom), Betty (Harris), Roy (dad), Ethel (Alvey). Back: James, Garnet (Parsley), Gaynelle (Yount), Lennis, Claris, Earl, Irene (Canter).

The Keaton homestead consisted of 137 acres, purchased by a land grant from the government. The acreage was between Spearsville and Fruitdale. It was good bottom land near Beanblossom Creek in Hamblen Township.

James and wife, Cloe, were the parents of six children: George, Jacob, Polly, Scofield, Jackson and Catherine; and all the children died young except Scofield, who was raised in the log cabin.

Cloe and James deeded the farm (1887) to their son Scofield, where the two families of Keatons continued to live together, after young Scofield married Elizabeth Long (1848-1899). Four of Scofield and Elizabeth's children (Bluford, Jessie, Julia and Rose) are buried in the Unity Cemetery beside their parents. The children of Scofield and Elizabeth who survived and raised a family were Delia, Roy and Ida. At Scofield's death, his son Roy Miller Keaton bought the land from the other members of the family.

House built by Roy Keaton, 1916

Roy married Lena Olive Richardson July 4, 1905. To this union 12 children were born: Earl, Claris, Mary, Harold, Gaynelle, Lennis, Garnet, Irene, James, Ethel, Olive and Betty. All the children were born at home (no prenatal care for the mother) and delivered by Dr. Pat Murphy. Garnet (Keaton) Parsley was born the middle child of the family of 12, Dec. 1, 1917, in the same log cabin her great-grandfather, James, had built (1840s) and where her grandfather Scofield Keaton was raised the century before.

When Garnet was about a year old, her father Roy decided to build a new house from virgin timber—huge, beautiful oak and black walnut logs (see house above). All 12 children were raised in this house with kerosene lamps, no running water, carrying water from the neighbor's spring (Ed Walker), walked to a one-room school (West Spearsville), with one teacher for eight grades. Next they attended Morgantown High School and some went on to college.

1975 - Front: Olive (Keaton) Watson, Gaynelle (Keaton) Yount, Betty (Keaton) Harris, Irene (Keaton) Canter, Garnet (Keaton) Parsley, Ethel (Keaton) Alvey. Back: Claris, James and Lennis Keaton. Missing from picture: Earl C. Keaton.

The father made their living from the land—learning to be a good farmer from his father, Scofield.

These God-fearing, parents, Roy (1884-1936) and Lena Richardson Keaton (1888-1950) and their large, happy family survived the great depression without any emotional or physical scars, but must have said many times, "I can do all things through Christ who strengthens me." *Submitted by Garnet (Keaton) Parsley*

CLARIS AND LAURA KEATON -
James Keaton born 1803 and his wife, Chloe, settled in northeast Brown County in 1840. He lived on a farm in a log cabin. They had a son, Scoffield, born 1844. He married Elizabeth Long. Their son Roy born 1882, died 1936. He married Lena Richardson born 1888, died 1950. They had 12 children: two died young, then Earl, Claris, Gaynelle, Lennis, Garnet, Irene, James, Ethel, Olive and Betty.

Claris born 1908 in the log cabin where his grandfather lived. In 1917 they built a new house at a different location. Claris attended Spearsville school and graduated from grade eight. He did not go to high school, but worked on the farm.

When he was old enough he went to Anderson and worked at Delco Remey. After a short time he came home and worked at the Brown County State Park, which was a new park in 1928-1929. They cleared the right of way and built roads. Paid 30¢ an hour.

In 1933 Claris married Laura (Mathis) Keaton, born 1909. Daughter of William and Mary Ann (McLary) Mathis. At this time he accepted a job with the Conservation of Fish & Game Department. They lived in the park until 1940 when the administration changed and he went to Columbus to work at Cummin's Engine. His father was killed in a car wreck in 1936 and his mother was left with the farm. She moved to Franklin to live and Claris and family moved to the farm and farmed during World War II. He was elected County Assessor in 1946-1950. Elected Democratic County Chairman and held that position for 19 years.

Claris Keaton Family 1979

In 1950 his mother died and the farm was sold. Claris and Laura moved to the Clark farm three and one-half miles S.W. Nashville in 1951. In 1953, he was appointed Superintendent of Brown County State Park and they lived there eight years. After leaving the park, they moved to their present home which was built in 1880 by grandfather Samuel McLary. Claris is still active in community affairs. He belongs to Historical Society, Lion's Club, Masonic Lodge, is on the board for Senior Citizens, and was elected to board of directors for R.E.M.C.

They have three children, ten grandchildren and four great-grandchildren.

William Roy married Donna Bennett. They have two children: Jerry married Debra Taylor and Melanie. They live in Phoenix, AZ.

Phillip Ray married Shelby Shipley. They have five children: Douglas Ray married Lisa Woods. Two children, Joe and Danielle. Jeffrey married Penny Ayres. Two children, Nicole and Ashley. Jill married Joe Wray. Neal and Barry at home in Brown County.

Linda Kay married Jack Hinkle. They have three children: Jennifer, Jonathan and Kelley, live in Carmel, IN.

DEMPSEY AND SUSAN KELLER -
Dempsey E. "Gene" Keller, the third son of six children of Roy G. and Minda K. Keller, was born in Coalmont, Clay Co., IN on Jan. 13, 1918. The Kellers came from Germany in early 1800, located in Cincinnati, OH then moved to Brown County. Roy is the son of George and Emma Browning Keller. Emma was the daughter of Wm. W. and Lucinda Browning. Mr. Browning was Editor of The Brown County Democrat in 1883. Other Brown County branches of The Keller Family Tree are the Kelp & Ralphy families. Roy, as a young man, moved to the western Indiana coal-fields to find work. While living in Alum Cave, Sullivan County, he met Minda Katherine Tucker, a Tennessee Lady, daughter of Anderson and Mary C. Tucker, they were married Oct. 12, 1903.

Susan E. Keller was born Aug. 9, 1922 in Cass, Sullivan Co., IN the second daughter of 13 children of Noah C. and Ethel Moore Keene. The Keene family, of Irish descent, arrived in this country in the early 1600s; moved to Sullivan County from Virginia, via Tennessee and Kentucky in 1857, purchasing 225 acres. Noah is the son of Flemmon and Susan Gambill Keene. Ethel is the daughter of James W. and Mary E. Morgan Moore.

Susan E. and Dempsey E. Keller

The Roy Keller family had a four-room house, located adjacent to a railroad serving the Big and Little Dirty Coal Mines, with six kids, a girl and five boys, looking for a place to sleep. They raised the majority of their food; supplemented by fishing, hunting, trapping, and harvesting wild berries, fruits and nuts; also dug coal which was used for cooking and fuel. All six kids graduated from High School; one son Max, who owns "Friendship Haven" on Brown County's Greasy Creek Road, obtained a degree in pharmacy. Four sons served their Country in WWII. After graduating in 1935, in the middle of The Great Depression, Gene couldn't find steady work; in October 1936 he joined the Civilian Conservation Corps (CCC); the pay was $30 a month with $25 sent home to your family. He rose, through the ranks, from private to Camp Commander. He met Susan at a Square Dance in 1938; they were married April 21, 1941. He was the last Commander of the CCC Camp in The Brown County State Park; transferred to Camp Atterbury. Their son Michael Eugene "Mickie" was born Nov. 14, 1942. Gene entered the U.S. Army December 1942; he was assigned to K Company, 333rd Infantry, 84th Infantry Division, trained in Texas and Louisiana; was promoted to 1st Sergeant in nine months. Their daughter, Jacqueline Sue "Jackie" was born in Alexandria, LA April 9, 1944. After 13 months in Europe, Gene came home, returned to Camp Atterbury; was Deputy Post Commander when the Camp was de-activated; retired from the U.S. Army Finance and Accounting Center in 1976.

A very large house was required for Susan's family of 15; all kids were required to perform the myriad of daily chores. The biggest task, to help their mother stretch the available food to satisfy all the hungry mouths. Susan worked, outside the home, to help pay her way through High School, graduating from Dugger High School in 1940.

Jackie and Mickie were active in scouting and church youth groups. Gene served as Scoutmaster and Susan as Den Mother, Mickie has a BS degree from the University of Evansville, a DD degree from United Theological Seminary, Dayton, OH; served 16 years in the Parish Ministry of the United Methodist Church; is now a successful businessman in Indianapolis. He has a son Randy and daughters Lisa and Nikki. Many remember him as the "Friendly Butcher" at Walkers IGA in Nashville. Jackie entered nurses training at Wishard Hospital in Indianapolis; worked as a Salesperson; the Reservationist at The Brown County Inn and now is Dr. Bill Howard's "Girl Friday." She is active in Psi Iota Xi Philanthropical Sorority. She is now married to Lee Roberts. Her daughter Susann, who has a BS degree from IU, lives in Kenai, AK.

The family are all members of the United Methodist Church. Susan and Gene are active in their WWII Outfit; led a trip to Europe in 1979 and were featured on the CBS "Sunday Morning" TV program. They helped write a book about their WWII Outfit, entitled "The Men of Company K."

BENJAMIN R. AND MARY JANE KELLEY -
Benjamin Roten, son of Joseph and Mary Kelley, was born in Mercer Co., KY, in 1817. After the death of his first wife, Ann Clemens, he came to Brown County in the early 1840s. In 1847 he married Mary Jane Marshall, daughter of Samuel and Abigail Fowler Marshall, in Barren Co., KY. Mary Jane's brother, Samuel; half-brother, John C.; and uncle, Robert Marshall, also came to Brown County.

B.R. and Mary Jane lived in Jackson Township until the 1860s, when they moved to the location that became known as Kelley Hill, two miles west of Nashville. The log cabin in which they lived is still standing and is owned by Dorothy Kelley, widow of their great-grandson, Dwight. B.R. served in the Mexican War and the Civil War, and was named a 2nd Lieutenant during the latter. He was sheriff of Brown County two years during the 1850s, and was a farmer, blacksmith, justice of the peace, United Brethren minister, and superintendent of the poor farm 1877-79. He died in 1894 and is buried in Greenlawn Cemetery at Nashville. Mary Jane died in 1900 and is also buried at Greenlawn.

Benjamin R. Kelley

B.R. and Mary Jane's children were William Harrison, Joseph Fowler, Rachel Ellen, Sarah Ann Elizabeth, John Fowler Caleb, James Scott Hester, Samuel G.W., Mary Roten, and Nancy Jane. William and Joseph died when they were small boys, and John and James both died in their early 20s.

Rachel married Eli Howland and moved to California. They had no children.

Sarah married Henry Lester. They lived in Newberry, Green County, and had one son, Grover Cleveland. "Cleve" married, but had no children. He carried the mail in Indianapolis nearly 40 years, then retired to Florida.

Samuel married Lydia Percifield, daughter of George and Elizabeth Clapton Percifield. Lydia died in 1893, leaving Harry, nine; Richard; seven; and Eudora, five.

Neither Mary nor Nancy married. Mary was killed in a run-away horse accident in 1907. Nancy owned a millinery shop in Nashville. She died in 1916. *Submitted by Dale Kelley*

DALE AND MARGUERITE KELLEY -
Dale Kelley and Marguerite Spangler were married in Chicago May 3, 1946. Dale was associate editor of *Poultry Supply World*, a business magazine affiliated with *Prairie Farmer*-WLS, and had a weekly program on WLS when it was farm-oriented. Marguerite was working at Scott Foresman & Co.

In 1947 Dale and Marguerite moved to Mt. Morris, IL, where they worked for Watt Publishing Co. Dale served as associate editor of *Poultry Tribune* one year, and as advertising manager of *Hatchery and Feed* two years. Marguerite worked in the advertising department. In 1950 they moved to Indiana, where Dale became assistant county agricultural agent in Elkhart County. The following year they moved back to Chicago, where he rejoined *Poultry Supply World* as managing editor, later becoming editor and publisher of that publication and of *Broiler World* and *Blue Book of the Poultry Industry*. He also served as executive secretary of the National Broiler Association three years.

Marguerite and Dale Kelley, 1946

In 1960 the Kelleys purchased a farm in Van Buren Township, and moved to Brown County. In addition to farming, Dale attended Indiana University and became a teacher at Brown County High School, where he taught 11 years. Marguerite worked in the Brown County Auditor's and Treasurer's offices and at Brown County Abstract Co. at various times.

Dale quit teaching in 1972, when he and Marguerite purchased Spink's Greenhouse. They changed the name to Kelley Greenhouse and continue to operate it, as well as their Van Buren Township farm and part of the old Kelley farm on Green Valley Road, which has been in the Kelley family more than 100 years.

Dale and Marguerite have four children: Richard Dale Jr., Marianne, John Morrison, and Robin Lee. "Rick" is married to Brenda Hale, daughter of Robert and Wilma Dowell Hale, and they have two daughters—Jennifer Marie and Elizabeth Ann. Rick holds BA and MA degrees from Indiana University and is employed by the U.S. Department of Agriculture in Indianapolis. He is a captain in the Air Force Reserves. Brenda is employed by USAir.

Marianne holds BS and MS degrees from Purdue University, and formerly taught handicapped children in Indianapolis. She and her husband, Dr. Stanton G. Schultz, a nephrologist, live in Evansville. They have three children—Kelley Erin, Jesse Elizabeth, and William Morrison.

John and his wife, the former Debbie Thompson, live in Bloomington. A graduate of Indiana University, John is a senior adjustor for USF&G Insurance in Bedford, and Debbie manages Pizza Express stores in Bloomington.

Robin holds a business degree from Indiana University, and works as a warehouse supervisor for Kroger in Indianapolis.

Dale was born at Story, Brown County and was graduated from Nashville High School and from Purdue University. Richard and Jessie Morrison Kelley were his parents.

Marguerite was born in Chicago, daughter of Earl and Marguerite Van Der Hoven Spangler. She is a graduate of Highland Park (Illinois) High School and attended business college in Chicago.

JOSEPH AND MARY KELLEY -
Joseph was born in Virginia Jan. 17, 1789, came to Johnson Co., IN, in 1833 and to Brown County in 1836 from Mercer Co., KY. Joseph died Nov. 7, 1853, and is buried in Bean Blossom Cemetery. His wife's name in 1850 was Mary; her surname and date and place of marriage are unknown. Joseph was a veteran of the war of 1812. The census lists his occupation as "trader," and he served as Brown County coroner in 1841 and as a commissioner in 1845 and 1848.

Joseph's children included Benjamin Roten, William Jackson, Margaret Jane, Elizabeth, Mary, John C., Minerva, Ann, and probably William. B.R.'s family is covered in a separate sketch.

William Jackson is probably the William J. who married Martha Jane Tracey in Johnson County in 1842. William J. and Martha Jane had Eliza Ann, Benjamin W., James K.P., Mary and John L.

Eliza married (1) George Bowden, and (2) Alexander Wilson. Her children were James and William Bowden and Jennie, Charles and Frank Wilson.

Benjamin W. enlisted in Co. H, 82nd Indiana Infantry Aug. 7, 1862, at age 18. Three months later he died of typhoid fever.

James K.P. married Susan McDonald. Their children were John L., Ida, Amanda, Sarah, Courtland and Joseph.

Margaret Jane married James Prosser. They had 11 children. Manerva, Martha and Nancy died in infancy and are buried in Bean Blossom Cemetery, where their parents also are buried. Sarah Ann married Jacob Neely. Paul V. McNutt, former governor of Indiana, was their grandson. Rebecca married George Turner. Dr. James Allen Turner, who practiced medicine in Nashville several years, was their son. Daughter Dorval married Fremont Miller, a prominent attorney in Brown and Johnson Counties.

Joseph's daughter Elizabeth married Issac Prosser, who died in Louisville during the Civil War. Their children included George W., Joseph Kelley, Sarah Catherine, and Minerva Destimony. Elizabeth, George and other family members are buried in East View Cemetery, Morgantown.

Mary Kelley married Wilson Price, who also died in the Civil War. Mary drew a widow's pension and was a seamstress in Nashville. Two children, Ida May and Lincoln, died in infancy and are buried in South View Cemetery, Nashville. Mary and Wilson's other children were Wilson S., William, John and Charles. Wilson, born in 1863, died in 1900 and is buried in Greenlawn Cemetery, Nashville. Charles was a barber in Nashville many years, but died in California in 1935 at age 75. William was living with his mother in 1900, with a wife Sarah and a daughter Hazel. When and where Mary died is unknown.

John C. Kelley, a Civil War veteran, married Hannah Cox. They apparently were divorced. John is buried at Bean Blossom, next to James and Margaret Prosser.

Minerva married William D. Roberts in 1856. They had one son, Joseph W. Minerva apparently died soon after his birth, as William married Mary Navity in 1871.

Ann married Caleb Crane, Jr., and probably a Prosser later. *Submitted by Dale Kelley*

RICHARD AND JESSIE KELLEY -
Benjamin Richard Kelley, son of Samuel and Lydia Percifield Kelley, was born on the Kelley farm three miles west of Nashville in 1886. His mother died when he was seven years old. Richard spent his early years on that farm and the one on Kelley Hill, which had been in the Kelley family since the 1860s.

In 1909 Richard married Jessie Morrison, daughter of J.S. and Sarah Rude Morrison. Jessie was born and reared at Belmont, where her father had a store 40 years. After their marriage Richard and Jessie lived in Benton Co., IN, where he worked on a farm. However, the hills of Brown County and family ties called them back after a year or so. They spent most of the next 35 years on farms in Brown County, including J.S. Morrison's farm at Belmont, Samuel Kelley's farm on Green Valley Road, and three farms they owned at different times in the Christiansburg, Story and Oak Grove communities.

Jessie and Richard Kelley

In the early 1920s Richard and his father-in-law bought the general store at Story and ran it a few years. Richard was postmaster during that period.

While he was farming Richard sought employment off the farm whenever possible. He hauled gravel for the county roads, plowed neighbors' gardens, worked on the bridge just south of Nashville when it was constructed, and measured fields for the agricultural program. He operated a road grader when the main road through Brown County State Park was built as well as on several county

213

roads. At that time graders were pulled by horses or caterpillar tractors.

In the mid 1940s Richard and Jessie sold their last farm and moved to Bloomington. Richard died in 1964 and Jessie in 1967. They are buried at Duncan Cemetery.

Richard and Jessie had six children: Cleo Beryl, Leo Pearl, Dwight, Nellie Marie, Beulah Jean and Richard Dale. Leo Pearl (Cleo's twin) and Nellie Marie died in infancy.

Cleo attended business college and Indiana University, and taught school in Brown County several years. She married Eugene Willoughby and worked with him in Nashville Hardware many years before his death in 1990.

Dwight married Dorothy Prebster soon after they graduated from Butler University and earned a master's degree at Indiana University. He worked for the Indiana Employment Security Division nearly 40 years before his death in 1976, at which time he was chief of research and statistics.

Beulah Jean married Lester "Bill" Percifield. She served as jail matron during his two terms as sheriff in the 1950s and 1960s, and helped him run Jerry's Drive-In in Nashville several years after that.

Dale graduated from Purdue University, and spent 15 years in agricultural journalism before returning to Brown County in 1960. He taught at Brown County High School 11 years, and has been operating Kelley Greenhouse with his wife Marguerite since 1972. *Submitted by Dale Kelley*

SAMUEL AND LYDIA KELLEY - Samuel George Washington Kelley, son of B.R. and Mary Jane Marshall Kelley, was born in Jackson Township in 1860. When he was a small child his parents moved to the site two miles west of Nashville which became known as Kelley Hill. He spent practically his entire life in Brown County, and died in 1945. Samuel was a farmer, blacksmith, and mail carrier, and served one term as county assessor. He donated the land on which the west entrance to Brown County State Park is located to the State when the park was created.

Samuel and Lydia Percifield, daughter of George and Elizabeth Clapton Percifield, were married in Brown County in 1883. Two sons and a daughter—Harry, Richard and Eudora—were born to them. Lydia died in 1893.

Samuel Kelley

After attending an institute at Beck's Grove, Harry started teaching in Brown County schools at age 17. Later he was graduated from Central Normal College. His last teaching assignment was as principal at the school which later became Warren Central in Marion County. Leaving the teaching profession to become a salesman, he lived at various times in Indianapolis and Danville, IN and Kankakee and Bloomington, IL.

Harry and Margaret Green were married in 1812. Their two sons, Keith and Thomas, both died at age eight, Keith from a sledding accident and Tom from pneumonia.

In 1931 Harry and Margaret moved to Brown County. For a short time Harry was a partner in the Star Store in Nashville, then operated a service station opposite the Brown County State Park entrance on Kelley Hill. For 15 years before his death in 1956 he was an inspector for the Indiana Highway Department. Margaret died in 1962.

Richard married Jessie Morrison, daughter of J.S. and Sarah Rude Morrison, and became a farmer.

Eudora was asked to leave Nashville High School before her graduation to teach in one-room schools. She taught in a number of these schools, eventually earning a degree from Central Normal College, and taught at Helmsburg and Nashville high schools. In about 1930 she moved to Ben Davis High School in Indianapolis and remained there until her retirement after 40 years of teaching.

Active in Democratic politics, Eudora was Brown County and Ninth District vice-chairman of the party several years. In 1948 she was elected Indiana Supreme and Appelate Court Reporter, the first and only Brown County person to be elected to state office. She was also a delegate and alternate to the party's national conventions.

Eudora and her father lived in Nashville many years, but moved to the old Kelley cabin on Kelley Hill in 1939 and spent the rest of their lives there. Eudora died in 1973 at 85 years of age. *Submitted by Dale Kelley*

KENNEDY FAMILY - John D. Kennedy (1802-1864) and his wife, Mary Alexander (1804-1887), natives of East Tennessee and of Scotch-Irish extraction, came to Brown County in 1837. They had a farm near Georgetown and were the parents of 11 children.

Steven A. Kennedy (1826-1911) was the second of these children. He was a veteran of the Mexican War and served under Capt. James Taggart at the Battle of Buena Vista. He married Susanna Taggart (1829-1892), daughter of Capt. Taggart and Jane Weddle, in 1847 and was the father of seven children, James Winfield, John E., Margaret E., William M., Patterson S., Wesford L., and Cordelia. In July of 1861, he enlisted in the 22nd Indiana Volunteer Infantry and took part in the battles of Mission Ridge, Stone River, Pea Ridge, and others and was commissioned a Second Lieutenant. He was a farmer, a school teacher, and served several terms as Sheriff of Brown County.

James Winfield Kennedy (1848-1928)

James Winfield Kennedy (1848-1928) married Sarah Jane Snider in 1869. There were 11 children born to them, among whom were, R. Claude, Alonzo, James, Jacob, Bertha, Gertrude, Emma, Elsie, Mayme and Teenie. Sarah Jane was a daughter of William Snider (1802-1875) and Elizabeth Brummett (1812-1867). James was an early sheriff of Brown County and their home, a two-story house on Gould St., just west of Van Buren is still standing.

Jacob T. Kennedy (1890-1971) and Freda Nell (Ted) Percifield (1894-1988) were married in 1913 and were the parents of seven children. Thelma Cudahy (1914), Dorothy Litherland (1916), Laura Jane Smith (1919), Helen Huber (1920), Robert M. Kennedy (1923), Betty Abbett (1925), and Peggy Woods (1930). The family lived in Brown County until the 1930s when they moved to Indianapolis. Prior to that time, Jacob was County Recorder. Ted Percifield was the youngest of six children of William Henry Percifield (1856-1925) and Laura Ellen Mann (1865-1930).

Betty Kennedy Abbett and Walter C. Abbett lived in Indianapolis and Shelbyville, IN before moving to Lake La Salle in 1988. They have three children, six grandchildren, four step-grandchildren and four step-great-grandchildren.

Michael S. (1942) and his wife, Martha Butler Ehret, live in Brownsburg, IN with Michael D. (1970), Holly L. (1972) and Martha's son, Jason Ehret. Michael is a realtor and insurance broker. Michael D. and Holly's mother was Janet Macy (1942-1978).

David C. (1946) is an employee of A T & T and lives on Helmsburg Road with his wife, Judy Hester and sons, John C. (1968) and Mark T. (1971).

Jacquelyn Abbett May (1949) is a nurse at Johnson County Hospital and lives in Whiteland, IN with her children, Amy C. (1967) and James T. (1971). The children's father is Thomas A. May.

Walt Abbett (1922) was born in Indianapolis to Walter Cleveland Abbett (1892-1956) and Nellie Marie Lohman (1894-1984). They were natives of Indianapolis and came from German and Irish backgrounds. He has a sister, Anita Ball, and a brother, Corydon D. Abbett.

Betty Abbett, an artist, is a volunteer at the Brown County Art Gallery and remembers when the gallery was on West Main Street. As children, she and her sisters posed for the early artists. Ada W. Shulz did a series of paintings of her sister, Helen, one of which is owned by the gallery. They also posed for Will Vawter, who was a favorite of all the children.

Betty and Walt, who is a retired electrician, love Brown County and made many visits here before finally coming to stay. *Submitted by Betty Kennedy Abbett*

LOBIE D. AND IVA (DECKARD) KENT - Lobie Daniel Kent was born Oct. 31, 1891. He was the son of Sam and Elnora (Kliendorfer) Kent. The Kents' originated to Brown County from Belmont Co., OH, settling in the community today known as Belmont. Here Sam Kent set up a mill (possibly two) along Salt Creek. His mill was located at the small stream which feeds into Salt Creek, just below the present iron bridge on the T.C. Steele Road. From this operation, many families kept supplied with flour and meal. Elnora Ann Kliendorfer's sister, Othelia (Tilla) was married to Dr. Thomas Warring. (First cousin to band leader, Fred Warring). His doctor office was located on the bank of Salt Creek also. He visited patients by foot, horseback or by boat down Salt Creek. He deeded land to Brown County and named it "Belmont." The Kliendorfers came to Indiana in 1851. Thomas Kliendorfer and family sailed from Munich, Germany landing near Baltimore, MD, and proceeded by stagecoach to Indiana. Here they had 14 children with eight survivors. A daughter Elnora Ann married Issac Samuel Kent and begat Charles, James, Lobie, Minnie Effie (Floyd), Thomas and Agnes (Webb).

Lobie was a very quiet hard working farmer. Iva Deckard was the daughter of Cecil and Mary Rosetta ("Settie," Sinn), Deckard. Lobie and Iva had three sons: Cecil Samuel Kent. Cecil married Virginia Mercer of Brown County. Another son, Edward Kent graduated from Nashville High School in 1938. He married Doris Eloise Stevens of Monroe Co., IN. To them were born five children: Bette Joyce (Kent) Walden of Evansville, IN; Robert Edward Kent of North Vernon, IN; Thomas Wayne Kent also of North Vernon, IN; Nancy Eloise Kent of Seymour, IN and Mary Beth (Kent) Woods of Bloomington, IN. Edward died September 1979. Harry Clifford Kent was the youngest of Lobie and Iva's family. He graduated in 1942 from Nashville. In April of 1943 he was called to the service of his country. In October, 1944 he was sent overseas to Belgium. On Jan. 15, 1945 during battle his life was taken. Back at home Ruth (Stevens, a sister to Edward's wife) had given birth to their son Gary on Jan. 12, 1945. It was never known if Clifford received word of the birth of his son. Gary and Ruth now live in Bloomington. Clifford also was a Purple Heart recipient.

The only daughter of Lobie and Iva was Edna, who married Elbert Dewar of Brown County. They lived on Crooked Creek Road until the state bought the farm for the Monroe Reservoir. They had six children: Phyllis Miller of Gosport, IN; Donald Dewar of Brown County; Daniel of North Vernon, IN; Judy Dewar of Seymour, IN; Kenneth of Seymour and Iva Jane Ray of Hayden, IN.

From Brown County they moved in 1963 to a brothers' farm (Edward) in Jennings County. After retiring they moved into Seymour near to the church they attended for many years. In 1987 Edna died of cancer and heaven gained a wonderful precious soul.

Cecil worked much of his life in real estate and house construction. Virginia and Cecil both reside now on 10th Street in Bloomington, IN.

LEWIS HENRY KERN - Lewis Henry Kern born April 21, 1892 (died Dec. 22, 1980) and Gladys Decina Gasho Kern, born Sept. 29, 1900 (died March 25, 1989) moved to Brown County in 1939. They bought acreage from Mrs. George, north of Bean Blossom (approximately one mile north, left side of the road, across from Rund property) where a small restaurant now stands. Lewis and Gladys named their land "Wild Cat Knob."

Lewis was an electrician and Gladys was a nurse. She retired after 50 years in her nursing career.

Their three children, all living now in California are: George Roland McCay, Rebecca Jane McCay Derringer, and Delcina Ann Kern Cassella.

Lewis and Gladys moved to California, at the end of World War II, as did their three children and their spouses.

Mr. and Mrs. Kern had eight grandchildren and 23 great-grandchildren, all living.

Both Lewis and Gladys maintained their love for Beautiful Brown County, and visited friends and relatives quite often. There is now another "Wild Cat Knob," which is the name given to the vacation residence of Walter Asa Derringer's widow, at the end of the "Three Brothers' Road." *Submitted by Rebecca Derringer (Mrs. Walter Asa Derringer)*

KESLER FAMILY - Ora Kesler lived in the Sprunica area for a time then moved on to Indianapolis. There he met Janie Kitteringer. Later they moved to Brooklyn, IN where Wilbur Carl was born on June 11, 1917. Wilbur married Tressie Clarke in Indianapolis on June 11, 1939. His parents lived in Broad Ripple and Tressie's lived in Indianapolis.

Wilbur worked at Mitchell & Scott Machine Shop for 20 years and at Milturn Corporation for 14 years. He retired in 1982.

In 1950 Wilbur and Tressie purchased 24 acres on Spearsville Road in Brown County. They moved from Indianapolis with their three children: Carl, Larry and Janet in order to raise them away from the city. At that time there was no electricity or telephone lines on Spearsville Road. Later due to a water shortage they returned to Indianapolis to live for a year.

After returning to Brown County their daughter Viva was born in 1953, six years later their youngest son Ross was born. Their oldest son Carl graduated from Helmsburg High School. Larry, Viva and Ross graduated from Brown County High School. Carl married a local woman her name was Mabel Fox. Larry married Sharon Petrow from Johnson County. As a wedding gift Wilbur and Tressie gave each couple seven and a half acres of land on which they built homes. Both couples had two children. Janet married Irvin Payson who was born and raised in Pennsylvania. They purchased a home in Trevlac and had three children. Viva married Dick Thompson from Indianapolis and now they live in Greenwood with their three children. Ross married Donna Coffey of Johnson County and they have three children.

Wilbur and Tressie still live in their original home on Spearsville Road. They have 13 grandchildren and three great-grandchildren. In June of 1989 Tressie and Wilbur celebrated their 50th wedding anniversary. Their oldest son Carl was killed in an automobile accident caused by a drunk driver. He left behind two small children. All the other children are still living. *Submitted by Tressie Kesler*

KING FAMILY - The progenitor of the King's line in Brown Co., IN was Daniel King with wife Aberilla. Daniel was born 1785 in North Carolina. Aberilla born 1783 in South Carolina. They married 1806, lived in Tennessee, then Kentucky and on to Indiana. Daniel and family in 1830 census of Bartholomew; Brown County not formed until April 1836. Daniel went to Illinois in 1832 and served in Black Hawk Indian War with Abraham Lincoln. He returned to Indiana and entered land 1834. Daniel King died 1848 and is buried at Taggart Cemetery, Hamblen Township, Brown County. Aberilla died 1864, and is buried at Taggart also. Their stone is still standing. Daniel's eldest son, William King, born 1807, married Elizabeth and came to Brown Co., IN. He had six children by Elizabeth (three sons and three daughters). Elizabeth died 1845. William then married Mary Ann Park and had five children by 1869. He then sold his property and family has no knowledge of him since.

Children in Daviess Co., MO. William's three sons by first marriage were: Daniel born 1829, Conrad born 1833 and George Washington King born 1836. Daniel served in Mexican War and owned between 200 and 300 acres of land in Hamblen Township. Daniel died Feb. 29, 1912, lived on Clay Street, Edinburgh, IN. Conrad King entered the Union Army March 13, 1865. Conrad died March 19, 1865, buried in Dalton, GA. George Washington King, third son, walked behind an ox team and wagon to Harrison Co., MO and married, March 1, 1856, the girl who rode in the wagon. He also served in the Union Army. George Washington King died Oct. 25, 1898 in Sullivan Co., MO.

George and Jane Ellen (Jones) King

George Washington King and Jane Ellen Jones were married March 1, 1856 at the home of her parents in Bethany, MO. They had five children. George Washington was inducted into the Civil War (Union Army) in October 1861 and served with an infantry regiment. He contacted measles and was wounded in the shoulder by gunshot and spent a great deal of time in the hospital in St. Louis and was a partial invalid until his death at Milan, MO. Some descendants migrated farther west but there remains a large number still in those two Missouri counties.

William Thomas King son of George Washington and Jane Ellen (Jones) King is the father of Gertrude King Storts who comes occasionally to Brown County to visit the home of her ancestors and their graves.

Conrad King married Elizabeth Shafer May 28, 1854. Six children were born to this marriage. Mary E. King (never married), William Joseph King married Mary E. Hankins, Martha Rebecca King married Michael McKee, John Jacob King (never married), George King married Ianthia Ann Fox and Julia Ann King married Umphrey Stillabower.

George King and Ianthia Ann Fox lived their entire lives in Brown County and 11 children grew to adulthood. The 11th child, Russell Lee King married Doris Marie Waggoner Feb. 22, 1948. They had two children: Jerald Leon King born 1948 and Josie Ann (King) Henneke born 1955. Doris Marie King died Sept. 10, 1990. Russell has one grandchild Karin Jo Oard. *Submitted by Russell Lee King and Lucille King*

CECIL FRANKLIN AND RACHEL SOPHRONIA (ROBERTS) KING - Cecil is the 12th child of George and Ianthia Ann (Fox) King. Cecil was born May 12, 1913 in Brown County, about seven miles east of Nashville on Hoover Road at Knob Hill. Cecil first attended Knob School, then attended Taggart School on Salt Creek at Gatesville. Cecil's mother Ianthia Ann (Fox) King died Dec. 16, 1919 and is buried at Henderson Cemetery in Washington Township. Cecil then stayed with his older sister Vinnie (King) Simonton in Lafayette, IN. When school was out he lived with his Dad, George King every summer. Cecil also attended Neville School at Camp Atterbury. George and Ianthia Ann had 13 children. It was hard on George raising the family after Ianthia Ann died. Children who survived childhood are: (1) Irene (died early),

(2) Dora born Nov. 17, 1891, (3) Nelle born March 24, 1893, (4) Vinnie born March 12, 1895, (5) Harley born July 21, 1897, (6) Elmer Joseph born March 29, 1899, (7) Theodore born April 19, 1901, (8) Carl born Jan. 29, 1903, (9) James Emery born March 21, 1905, (10) Virgil Gerald born Aug. 1, 1907, (11) Russell Lee born June 26, 1910 and (12) Cecil born May 12, 1913, all were born in Brown County. George King died Aug. 22, 1949 and is buried at Henderson Cemetery.

Front: Cecil Franklin King, Rachel Sophronia (Roberts) King, Judith (King) Williamson. Back: Carmen (King) Altop, Karen (King) Olmsted

Cecil met and married a neighbor girl, Rachel Sophronia (Fronia) Roberts the daughter of Otha and Rosa (Reeves) Roberts. Rachel was born Feb. 2, 1916. Cecil and Rachel raised three girls. Carmen Rosetta who was born May 28, 1935 in Brown County, Judith Ann born March 25, 1941 in Brown County and Karen Sue born April 30, 1943 in Columbus, IN. Rachel retired from Arvin Industries and Cecil retired from Golden Foundry both in Columbus, IN. Rachel died May 25, 1986 and is buried in Greenlawn Cemetery.

Carmen married (1) Philip Deckard and they have one daughter, Denise K. Deckard born Feb. 23, 1957. Denise married John Douglas Campbell and they have two daughters: Crystal K. Campbell born Nov. 30, 1980 and Leslie Nicole Campbell born Oct. 22, 1987, both were born in Columbus, IN. Carmen married (2) Jack Altop and they have one daughter, Demetria Dawn (DD) Altop born March 22, 1960 in Columbus, IN. DD married Michael Watkins and they have two sons: Travis Michael Watkins born Feb. 28, 1978 and Ty Landon Watkins born June 23, 1980. Carmen Altop and her daughters and their families live on Hoover Road.

Judith Ann King was married to Paul Oliver Williamson Dec. 31, 1961, by Rev. Howard Small in Nashville, and they have five children: Brett Franklin Williamson born Aug. 1, 1963, Bartley Dwight Williamson born July 23, 1964, Benita Faith Williamson born Jan. 22, 1966, Brad Lee Williamson born Nov. 23, 1968 and Beth Ann Williamson born May 23, 1970. All were born in Columbus, IN. Benita Williamson married Thomas Issac Fox and they have a daughter Rachel Rachelle Fox born Feb. 13, 1989 in Bloomington, IN. They live in Bean Blossom. Beth Ann Williamson married Robert Mulry and they have a son Malcomb Lee Mulry born Nov. 15, 1988 in Bloomington, IN. They live in Helmsburg. Judith and Paul and their sons live on Hoover Road. Judith and Paul are avid fishermen.

Karen Sue King married Robert Joe Olmsted Sept. 21, 1961 at the North Salem Methodist Church on Highway 46 eight miles east of Nashville. They have three children: Kayla Sue Olmsted born Sept. 2, 1962, Eric Joseph Olmsted born Feb. 21, 1965 and Todd Robert Olmsted born Feb. 2, 1968, all were born in Columbus, IN. Kayla Sue Olmsted married Scott Richardson July 9, 1983, at the North Salem United Methodist Church. They live on Spearsville Road. Eric Joseph Olmsted and Beth Knapp have one daughter Marra Ashley Olmsted born Aug. 9, 1990 in Bloomington, IN. Eric Olmsted and Todd Olmsted are building a log cabin on Knob Hill on a part of the land where their grandfather Cecil King grew up. Cecil F. King died Sunday, Jan. 20, 1991 and is buried at Greenlawn Cemetery, Nashville. *Submitted by Karen Olmsted*

DOROTHY AND MARION KING -
The year was 1959, in the month of April, that the name "King's Retreat" was established for a round log cabin, which was the beginning of a new chapter in Dorothy and Marion King's book of life.

The cabin was built in 1932 on beautiful Morrison Road. An Indiana University student who desired to live and study in these hills erected it with the help of Ralph Yoder and Elmer Smith. A spot was selected close to the gravel road. Pine and oak trees had to come down. They were measured and cut to go into the building of a one-room cabin. A mason was hired to build a native stone fireplace with a "spit" for cooking and heating.

Dorothy and Marion King - 25th Anniversary

The gravel roads from Morrison Road to I.U. became more than the student could cope with, especially that first winter. Before his second winter started, he sold his cozy cabin and 12 acres to Ralph and Wilma Woods from Terre Haute. Their friends, also from Terre Haute, Floyd and Katherine Wrightsman, had a cabin across the road. The four of them had 26 years of happy week-end fellowshipping.

A small lake and a winding stream in the valley adorned this 12 acres dotted with many dogwood and redbud trees. This beautiful hilly forest was graced by oak, pine, beech, gum and sycamore. "God's beautiful creation," says Dorothy.

The dirt road ambled up, and around and over the ridge to Road 45. The roadside produced wild grapes, hazel nut bushes, mushrooms, daisies, Queen Anne's lace, and huckleberry. Aleetha Chitwood was born and raised on this road. She and Frank Chitwood met each other, fell in love and married. Aleetha was a graduate of Indiana University and became a teacher. Frank was a born farmer, so together they enjoyed their lives together, and still do, in the same place. During this era there was Johnny and Mary Morrison. The road was named after them. On back up the ridge slowly came the Howard and Birt DeGolyers, the Jimmy Harrisons and Alice Lloyd.

Down the other end of this beautiful road was the cabin where the LaMar's folks lived. During the lifetime of their parents, Bess and Marguerite enjoyed happy growing-up years here. Marguerite was schooled to be a teacher; was a professor at several colleges including Kent University. Bess was schooled for a Third Grade teacher on far Northside Indianapolis. Their home they shared was in this area. After their folks died, they modernized the cabin. They were world travelers. They were loved. They both died while summering in their sweet Brown County cabin. Mrs. King says, "We were honored to share their friendship." Their place is still alive with a niece, Dianne, and her husband, Don King, and their boy and girl. The LaMar sisters gave them the joy of willing "Rebel Acres" to them.

Going back to April of 1959, Dorothy King learned that Wilma Woods was selling their cabin. Her husband had died and she had lost her sight. Dorothy was a Red Cross driver and Wilma was one of her blind passengers. Both lived in Indianapolis at this time. Dorothy was returning her passengers home when she heard Wilma announce that she was selling her cabin in Brown County. Dorothy and Marion made a date with her, picked her up, and got on the road to Brown County. It was a dark and rainy day. Upon arriving and entering the cabin a damp and musty air surrounded them; the cabin had been vacant for five years. As they led Wilma from room to room she told them of this and that of the 22 happy years they had enjoyed there. Still raining, she wanted to walk the paths which were grown up in weeds and also to show us the outhouse, the lake, and the well. Her reminiscing was sweet and contagious. As Marion inquired about this and that as men need, Dorothy was falling in love with everything. As they walked back to the cabin Marion explained to Wilma that he and Dorothy were leaving for Alaska in a few days and asked what would she accept as a token of faith until they returned. Wilma answered, "Nothing, my faith has been in 'Dot' as my driver and I have faith in you."

Dorothy recalls, "Later at home Marion and I told each other of how we both slowly realized that this beautiful spot had been waiting for us and we had been waiting for it! Suffice to say, we bought it, we loved it." Five King children, Maynard, Andy, Don, Nan Coddington, and Annabelle Shanks, all married, 17 grandchildren, their spouses, and 13 great-grandchildren all loved it too, and shared the joy for 30 years. Dorothy adds, "We have praised our Lord and thanked Him for loaning us a small part of His creation. Our friends and loving neighbors, so dear to us, have gone on Home with the exception of Aleetha and Frank Chitwood." Many new friends who have chosen Morrison Road have come and gone as the years have passed.

Dorothy says they had no "PAST" here before April 1959, but they have experienced and established a "PAST." Their first friends, Howard and Birt DeGolyer welcomed them and invited them to the Historical Society. Howard was President at that time. From here on the "Village" blossomed into many activities and lasting friendships. Early 1960 they chose Nashville Christian Church and were welcomed as members. Don Whetstine was the minister at that time. He and his family, Jennie, Sharrianne and Brent, gave of their love and service. Dorothy acknowledges, "God has blessed every one as the years have come and gone. Our path was inviting as we started walking into our 30 years; into our Future."

In the mid-70s, Robert Himes called a meeting in view of establishing a Senior Citizen organization. He asked for a volunteer to act as President. Marion volunteered and was accepted. Marion enjoyed organizing and working with senior citizen for four years. Area 11 based in Columbus was legal assistants. Meals would be prepared and delivered to Nashville for senior citizens five times a week; mainly for people who needed fellowshipping and a balanced meal. The Historical Society loaned space for the noontime lunch.

"Our path was strewn with historical and interesting doings, says Dorothy. "There was the Lions Club with Robert Gregg's grapefruit sales; Pioneer Women and the work involved in the museum; Garden Club with its beautification plans; Lions selling sundries at the Playhouse; the Art Gallery and Guild with its "teas" and "hangings"; the hayrides and narrating to tourists concerning historical places. There was mushrooming, deer hunting, fishing, whippoorwills, raccoons, mourning doves, many other birds, and the smell of sassafras. There was also the rich smell and beauty of smoke curling from fireplace chimneys curling toward the heavens for artists to capture on their canvasses. Our paths became joyously full of what Brown County is about."

Mrs. King concludes, "Brown County, lovingly we 'gave' and we 'took' memories. Thanks for our sharing 30 years of your 'PAST'; a beautiful and fulfilling inheritance."

MARIE KING

MARIE KING - Marie and her husband, Marion, were married in 1936 while she was an English College teacher and he was one of her pupils. She continued to teach two more years until he finished his pastor studies. They had one child which was never allowed to leave the hospital. She got to hold the three lb. infant once before his death. Later they were thrilled to be able to adopt a four-year old son whom they loved very much. She remembers every detail of the day's event when they were allowed to bring their child home from the orphanage.

Marie and Rev. Marion King

Being a pastor involved a lot of moving and traveling. Later in God's service, the Methodist World Conference sent them as delegates to London, England; Denver, CO; and Dublin, Ireland. Those were wonderful years as compared to the earlier ones when a pastor's salary was very meager. She recalls one Christmas Eve when a lady in their church brought them a baked chicken. After talking for a few minutes she left. Mrs. King walked to the counter and said to the chicken, "Well, Biddy, you'll have to last us several days!" and the old hen did just that. They had baked chicken Christmas Day, then chicken and dumplings and by New Years were finishing with chicken flavored gravy and biscuits.

The following are churches that Marie and Marion served: (1) Maxwell Curry (1938-39); (2) Wesley Foundation (1939); (3) Farmland (1940-41); (4) Tippecanoe (1942); (5) Milford (1942-45) with Clunette (1943); (6) Elwood (1946); (7) LaGrange (1951); (8) Leesburg (1959); (9) Lapel (1961); (10) Loogootee (1967) and (11) North Salem (1973-74).

They retired in Brown County on Lick Creek Road on June 19, 1979. The beloved pastor and husband died from a garden tractor that had turned over on him. Her son later died when he was only 38. Marie moved to Nashville living in a rented home of Von Williamson for several years. She said the people in Nashville were very kind. About two years ago she moved to the Franklin United Methodist Home and has made many friends there.
Submitted by M.J. Richards

DALTON AND VEARL (MOBLEY) KREBBS

DALTON AND VEARL (MOBLEY) KREBBS - Dalton and Vearl have always lived close to the home where they now live. They both were raised within a couple of miles of their present home.

Dalton's parents were Andrew and Marie (Farlin) Krebbs. He is from a family of six children, four of which died at an early age. He has one brother, Virgil Krebbs living.

Vearl's parents were John and Laura (Nickerson) Mobley. She is also from a family of six children. She has two sisters, Pauline Greenlee and Thelma Long, and one brother Russell Mobley. There was also a sister, Mina Krebbs and a brother Keith Mobley now deceased.

Dalton and Vearl were married in 1947. In 1950 they built their home which is located on the Mt. Nebo Road in southern Brown County. They lived in that home until 1989, at which time they had a new home constructed on their farm.

Dalton and Vearl Krebbs and children Larry, Karen and Ray-1961

They had three children, Larry, Karen, and Ray.

Larry (deceased, automobile accident in September 1989) married Barbara Kinney. Barbara lives at Pikes Peak in Brown County. She works for Quinco Consulting. They have three children, Doug, Lori, and Robbie.

Karen married Morris Rouse. They reside in the Whitecreek area in southwestern Bartholomew County. Karen is a homemaker and Morris is an agent for Farm Bureau Insurance. They also do some farming and raise livestock. They have one son, Freddie.

Ray married Susan Woodmansee. They live at the Brown County State Park. Ray is a maintenance supervisor at the park. Susan works at Yellowwood State Forrest. They have one daughter, Sandy.

Dalton and Vearl have five grandchildren. They are very proud of their family.

They attend the Mt. Nebo United Methodist Church. They have been regular members of the church since they were young. Dalton worked at Arvins for 30 years before retiring. He also was a part time farmer. Vearl spent most of her time as a homemaker, and also helping on the farm.

Dalton and Vearl have always been very proud of their Brown County heritage.

SARAH (ADAMS) KRITZER

SARAH (ADAMS) KRITZER - Sarah L. Kritzer's roots run deep into the county with both parents well established families. Her father, Paul Adams was a land baron of sorts in the town of Nashville. His earliest ancestor in the county, Thomas Martin Adams, set the precident. He came to Brown County by way of Johnson County from Greene Co., TN in 1836. He obtained a land grant for several hundred acres of land with part of that being where the school administration building is now located in Nashville. He was very civic minded not only locally holding many political positions but was also an Indiana State Senator. Thomas had 12 children. Sarah L. branch of the family is from the eighth child, John Walter, who was born in Brown County in 1848. His marriage to Mariah Butler, in 1866 produced her grandfather, Hugh Thomas. He married into a German family that came to the United States in 1856. Conrad and Mary Deist and son, John, lived in Ohio until the late 1860s. When John's first wife died he remarried and left Ohio for Brown County. Eight of John's 11 children were born in Brown County. Hugh Thomas married one of the daughters, Wilhelminia, and they lived on a farm on Clay Lick and raised three boys, Harold, Paul, and Maurice. Hugh Thomas was the first mail carrier for Brown County and a 50 year member of the Nashville Masonic Lodge.

Adams boys: Maurice, Paul, Harold and Hugh Thomas, Main Street, Nashville. House still stands in 1990.

As Hugh and Minnie were raising their sons, there was another family in the county raising a family. This was John and Leota Bond who had a beautiful red-headed daughter, Sarah Jane, who would marry Paul Adams in June, 1919.

Sarah Jane's earliest Brown County ancestor was Joshua and Catherine Bond who probably brought their eight children to Brown County in 1850s. Their son, James married Sarah Patton in 1865, in the county. It was their union that produced seven children, the fourth being John F., grandfather to Sarah Louise. As a prominent resident of the county, John was county clerk, postmaster, and editor of the Brown County Democrat. He and Sarah's father Paul Adams, were active as Elder and Deacon of the early Nashville Christian Church.

Sarah Louise Adams, Sarah Jane Bond Adams and Vernita Bond Adams, 1927.

Paul and Sarah Jane had two daughters, Vernita and Sarah Louise. In 1939 Sarah Louise married Preston Crabtree, son of Dr. L.R. Crabtree who came to Nashville from Monroe Co., KY. Dr. Crabtree's office was located above the Star Store. His most famous patient was one of John Dillinger's men wounded in a shoot out in Bean Blossom.

Preston and Sarah L. had five children, Larry, Dan, Sheila, Deborah and Steve. Preston worked as butcher for his father-in-law, Paul Adams, who owned and operated the Star Store in Nashville.

Preston supported his family after WWII as part owner of the Gables Restaurant, but was soon elected Brown County Sheriff and two and a half years later became Indiana State Policeman.

With Preston's sudden death at age 38, Sarah Louise later married Rex Kritzer, another Brown County family. *Submitted by Sarah Louise Kritzer*

GEORGE AND BETTY JANE KYLE -

They moved to Brown County in April 1980 in search of a cleaner environment in which to live and found the ideal location on Little Fox Lake. George is the third child of George and Phoebe (Wake) Kyle of Clinton, IN. George, Sr., the son of John and Margaret (Houston) Kyle who came from Lark Hall, Scotland in 1882 and was born in Pennsylvania and migrated with his parents to Indiana in 1890. They worked in the coal mines near Clinton.

Phoebe was the daughter of George Lee and Louisa Wilson Wake. Her grandparents had immigrated from England in 1866. Young George spent his early years in Clinton, served his country as a Radio Operator with the U.S. Army in Panama during World War II and graduated with a bachelor of science degree in Electrical Engineering from Rose Polytechnic Institute in Terre Haute in 1948. George was employed by Indiana Bell Telephone in Indianapolis for the next 34 years and retired as district manager of Equipment Engineering in 1982.

George and Betty Jane Kyle

Betty Jane, the youngest of nine children of Joseph and Hazel (Smith) Moulton, was reared on a 600 acre farm near Vandalia, IL. She is the tenth generation since 22 year old William Moulton arrived in Newburyport, MA in 1637 from the small village of Ormsby, northeast of London. The next 200 years found the Moultons as silver and goldsmiths and in 1860, apprentices Anthony F. Towle and William Jones purchased the business.

The Towle company is the oldest continuing silver company in the United States. Fourth generation, William, came west at age 68 and was a cofounder of Marietta, OH. Great-grandfather Nathan Noyes Moulton came to Vandalia, IL in 1839 and dealt in horses (possibly furnishing Abraham Lincoln with transportation when he came for Legislative duties). Nathan married a local girl, Mary Jane McKinney, and raised two sons and a daughter.

The Kyles were married on Easter Sunday 1949, lived on the northside of Indianapolis, and have three lovely daughters. (1) Laura, the eldest, graduated from Purdue and later acquired a masters degree in Clinical Psychology and is in private practice in the Detroit Area. (2) Leslie, also graduated from Purdue and lives in Carmel, IN. She is married and has a daughter Sarah, age nine, a son Joel age four and twin daughters Rachel Marie and Rebecca Lynn arrived Nov. 13, 1990. She is a successful sales representative for a major fragrance company. (3) Her twin sister Lynn has a masters degree in Psychology from Evansville University and serves as head of "Stepping Stone," a new substance-abuse facility in Evansville. She is presently serving on Governor Bayh's Commission on drugs.

George and Betty Jane enjoy Brown County and love the birds and flowers and working to beautify their little bit of heaven. Betty Jane enjoys sewing and dress designing, loves to cook and entertain. She organized the Central Indiana Chapter of H.E.A.L. in 1979 (Environmental Illness related) and both she and George are active in the national organization. George is also very busy with a second career as a therapist, which he finds very rewarding as he is able to help people to improve their health.

LYNN AND SHELLEY (SMITH) LAW -

Lynn was born on Oct. 7, 1962 in Martinsville, IN to Milton and Lowana (Chandler) Law, the youngest of six children. Lynn has one twin brother (Ken), two additional brothers, Jeff and Michael, and two sisters, Gayle and Carol.

Lynn received his diploma from Brown County High School. He is presently employed at True Value Hardware in Nashville.

Lynn and Shelley Law: 1989

On Nov. 17, 1984 he married Shelley Smith in Brown Co., IN. The youngest of four children, Shelley was born in Columbus, IN on Dec. 18, 1964 to Richard and Rosella (Shiley) Smith. Her family's origination in Brown County dates back to the early 1800s when her grandmother's, Helen Smith, great-grandfather, Edward David settled in Brown County after migrating from Kentucky.

Shelley's grandfather's family, the Smiths and the Settles came from Virginia and England respectively and in the mid 1800s both families settled in Brown County.

Shelley graduated from Brown County High School in 1983. For several years after her marriage to Lynn, she worked outside the home, presently, however, she is at home with their three children: (1) Kole born July 8, 1986 and twins, Rebecca and Levi, born March 3, 1990.

LAWLES-LAWLESS FAMILY - A group of Lawlesses, all cousins, came from Ireland, settling in Bartholemew, Ripley and Brown Counties in Indiana. Jacob Lawles (born 1794, probably in Delaware, died before the 1870 census) and his six children came to Van Buren Township in Brown County from Maryland about 1838. He was an Inspector for Van Buren Township. At that time residents were paid for wolf scalps by the County Auditor. Bear and panthers were also killed in the county.

Jacob Lawles had lost his first wife and remarried on May 31, 1844, to Elizabeth Mabe Matney. Jacob Jr., a son from this marriage, married Viola Day on Feb. 9, 1888. They owned property which we now know as the Village Motel. The main building was originally a two-story house. It is now owned by Mr. and Mrs. S. Koons. There was also a Lawless-Day marriage in Ripley County, and Lawless-Day Reunions were held up until the 1940s.

Heather Celestina Hinshaw Lawless

Jacob Lawles, Jr., widowed, married a third time at age 77 to Miss Charlotte (Skinner) Bruce. Mrs. Charlotte Lawles and her former husband, Mr. Bruce, owned Weedpatch Hill, now in the Brown County State Park. Charlotte's home became the Post Office of Kelp Village, population 11.

The Razor's Edge Building on Old State Road 46 East, owned by Robert R. Lawless, was begun in 1948 by renowned potter, Karl Martz, now Professor Emeritus from Indiana University. The Martz family worked on their building project for 12 years, living at first in two tents on the site.

John Lawless, son of Jacob Lawles, Jr., changed the spelling of the name to Lawless.

Robert R. Lawless (born 1924) came to Brown County from Ripley County in 1960. He opened the first men's hairstyling shop in the Midwest, after training in Paris, France. He married Judith Hinshaw Leach (born Oct. 12, 1944) on Oct. 13, 1973. Judith is a cousin to artist Glen Cooper Henshaw (born 1880-died 1946). The artist changed the spelling from Hinshaw back to the original English spelling of Henshaw in 1911-12. There are Henshaw castle ruins in England.

Robert and Judith Lawless have one daughter, Heather Celestina Henshaw Lawless (born Jan. 18, 1979).

Their studio home in Brown County, located on Old State Road 46 East, was built in the late 40s by

Karl and Backy Martz. Karl Martz, an internationally known potter, had his early pottery studio in this home in Brown County. While building the house, the Martz's put out a sign, "We Need Help". Indiana University students returning to classes in Bloomington stopped, and helped the Martz's to raise a huge barn beam into place, which is exposed in the home today. This house and Razor's Edge shop are a tourist attraction, housing early Indiana art and a collection of the photography of Brown County photographer, Frank M. Hohenberger.

The Lawless residence home is at the upper end of Shultz Lane (Locust Lane). It was built by a well-known Indianapolis architect, Frank Hunter, in 1955. It was later the home of artist George Baum and his artist daughter, Elizabeth (Libby) Baum. It now has tourist rentals and houses a Henshaw Gallery; hence it has been named the Henshaw House; which originally was named "Trails End" and the family continues to call their home "Trails End."

LAWSON FAMILY - James Lawson married Brown County native Phoebe Lyons (May 14, 1862-Jan. 16, 1943) in 1879 or 1880. They had eight children.

James, Jr. - 1889-1967. He served in World War I. Married Bertha Griner, a widow with four children—Settie, Bill, Noah, and Alonzo. Together Bertha and James had two daughters—Dorothy and Bertha (who died in a house fire when she was 18); Charley - moved to Illinois and was never heard from again; Mellie - 1884-1926. Married Ben Scrogham. Some of their children are Emmett, Columbus, Irene, and Florabelle; Hiram - married. No children; Riley - Nov. 23, 1892-March 12, 1979. Married Grace Bay (April 1, 1900-July 31, 1970) ten children, two of whom died in infancy; Viola - 1893-1972. Married Cleave Pitcher and had seven children; Harley - 1898-1971, never married; Willie - 1904-1980, never married.

Lawson Family, 1944: Allen, Jim, Frank, Riley, Mabel, Dale, Margie and Edell (Charley was in the Army).

Riley married Grace, daughter of James and Evalina (David) Bay Jan. 31, 1921. Grace had a son, Joseph Allen, born July 22, 1920. He has six children. Together Riley and Grace had: Pearlie May - died in infancy 1922; Charles - Three children from a first marriage. Then married Ann Childress, a widow with two children. Together Ann and Charley have two sons—Charley and Billy; Marjorie - Jan. 16, 1925. Married Verlis Derringer (Sept. 12, 1926-Aug. 18, 1989) on July 3, 1950 in Elizabethtown, KY. Six children: James Ray (died in infancy October 1951), Mary Ruth, William, Marjorie Ann, Rebecca and Daniel Asa (died in infancy November 1965). Mary Ruth married Bill Fox son of Charley and Frances Fox. Their children are: Joseph, David, Sarah and Micah. William has two sons Scott and Josh from a first marriage. He then married Ludeana (Lu) Sanders daughter of Dean and Wanda Shroyer. She has a daughter, Shaunna. Marjorie married David Underwood son of Ron and Patty (George) Underwood. They have a daughter, Holly. Rebecca married Mike Smith son of Jim and Betty Jo (Ficklin) Smith. They have two daughters Kristen and Ashley; Opel Leona Ruth - died in infancy 1926; Edell - has four children: Connie, Doris, Florence, and John. She married Owen McAnelly; Mabel - married Leonard Brockman. Eleven children: Betty Jean, Judy, Barbara, Leroy, Patty, Diana, Regina, David, Darlene and Marlene, and Greg. Leonard died in a house fire; James - married Margaret Lewis. Seven children - Jerry, Nora (died in infancy), Lucille, Susie, Christina, Jimmy and Saundra. Jim was chief mechanic at Bill McDonald's Chevrolet in Nashville many years; Francis (Frank) married Wanda Rohl. Two children Charles (Chuck) and Ronald. Chuck has a son Trevor and Ron has two daughters Ronna and Melissa. Frank worked for the Illinois Central Railroad for many years; A. Dale - married with children. Currently living in Baton Rouge, LA. When Dale was ten, he tried to cut a loose string from his jacket with a pocket knife. The knife slipped and an eye was put out.

Charley, Margie, Jim and Frank live in Brown County. Edell and Mabel live in Columbus, IN.

Riley farmed all his life in Brown County. He also drove a wagon to take children to Turner School on Clay Lick during winter when snow was high and roads were bad. *Submitted by Mary Ruth (Derringer) Fox*

LEE FAMILY - After May Lee's divorce in 1907 she purchased 80 acres in northwestern Brown County when their son, Mordie, was three years of age. Mordie had whooping cough as the family moved from Indianapolis to Brown County in a horse-drawn wagon. Mordie grew up in the old farm house with two brothers and a sister. Mordie was a traveling salesman, who was rarely home, and raising the family was mainly his wife's responsibility. Mordie remembers Halley's Comet in 1910, the Titanic disaster of 1912, World War I, various snowstorms and attending Ray School on Peoga Ridge Road. Living in Brown County during those formative years fostered an appreciation for rural living and values which can never be forgotten. Mordie's father passed away in 1920 and shortly thereafter the family moved back to Indianapolis. Sadly, the family's pet dog, Boone, had to be left in Brown County because the mover would not allow him in the truck.

Mordie completed his education at Tech High School and Butler University, but always enjoyed returning to the country. He and his best friend, Henry Wilson, from Indianapolis spent many outings exploring the area. He married Mildred Aug. 15, 1937, and shared his love of the locale and together they built a small cabin in 1943. Their son Richard H. Lee arrived at the end of the second World War on May 5, 1945, and many of his happiest childhood memories originate in Brown County. The cabin, the woods, the pond, all have been a constant source of joy and refreshment. As Richard looks to retirement, he eagerly anticipates the day when Brown County will no longer be a place of weekends but a place called home. *Submitted by Richard H. Lee*

LEONARD W. LEHMAN - The Lehman family background is Swiss-German, with recorded roots in the Rhine Valley in the 1700s.

Leonard's great-grandmother, Elizabeth Christophel Lehman (1833-1932) was the first born of John Jacob and Barbara Bare Christophel's seven, in a family of 14. Two previous (European) wives of John Jacob Christophel (1783-1868) had faithfully mothered and died abroad: Gertrude Berg bore Catherine (1814-1829); Susan Neff was mother to six: (1) Elizabeth lived only one month (Nov. 18, 1818 to Dec. 2, 1818); (2) Christian (Feb. 16, 1820 to 1883); (3) Johannes (John) lived 1822-1901; (4) Maria (Mary) (1824-1897); (5) Peter (1826) and (6) Barbara (1828).

Leonard Lehman

Leonard's parents are Arthur Lehman (1895-1967) and Nora Weaver Lehman (1896-1970) and they were in midlife during the Great American Depression of the '30s.

Leonard's grandfather, Simeon Lehman, was from a family of ten and Leonard's father was one of seven and bore Leonard, Ernest and Esther. Esther died age nine years, ten months, four days in 1934.

Leonard married Marie Martin, May 7, 1939, and they had two children: (1) Keith Lehman born in Goshen, Elkhart Co., IN, Aug. 23, 1940 and died Feb. 10, 1985, and (2) Letha Lehman born May 20, 1943 at Goshen, Elkhart Co., IN.

Keith Lehman had two children: Kirk Arthur Lehman born Feb. 18, 1965 and Natalie Lehman born Jan. 7, 1967 at Goshen, Elkhart Co., IN. Natalie married Lonnie Mast and had a son named Andrew Michael born April 20, 1986 at Elkhart Co., IN. They have a daughter, Kelsey Marie, born May 2, 1990 also in Elkhart Co., IN.

Leonard's great-grandfathers, Issac Weaver and Abraham Lehman owned hundreds of acres, his grandparents owned 80 acres, Arthur Lehman owned 50 acres, Leonard Lehman owns four acres and today children of these ancestors must walk their children from their urban lots to green grass in the parks.

Leonard completed an undergraduate degree at Goshen College with a major in Biology-English and received his M.S. in Education in 1947 at Indiana University. Following this study, Leonard taught biology, English, automobile driving, and health at the Helmsburg High School.

Leonard began teaching at age 19 and drove a sturdy '36 Ford in 1938 exploring Indiana. During the family's two years in Brown County, Leonard was active in youth work, political affairs, school, and the State Park during the summer.

Great Uncle Jacob Lehman (1860-1931) son of Abraham Lehman and Elizabeth Christophel Lehman was a homesteader in Dakota Territory around 1883. Great Uncle Joel (1866-1932) son of Abraham and Elizabeth above was an educator at Hinds Co., MS, after graduation from Tri-State at Angola, IN.

Leonard's father's mother's line were named

Buzzard. Joe Buzzard (son of Jacob C. Buzzard and Elizabeth Kreider (March 1, 1840 to Sept. 29, 1909) graduated as an electrical engineer, Northwestern University, Evanston, IL, but died soon after of tuberculosis. David Buzzard was born Dec. 20, 1863, son of Jacob above and was a graduate veterinarian. The ancestors in this line are: Lehman, Christophel, Buzzard, Weaver, Muser, Hess, Kreider and Martin. Submitted by Leonard W. Lehman

PETER I. LINDSEY - The Peter Lindsey family moved to Indiana from Georgetown, WV in 1871. They moved from Brown County to Monroe County in the fall of 1871. They had three sons and four daughters. Two of the daughters, Minerva (Tomlinson) and Martha — along with sister, Hannah (Campbell), all lived in Brown County. Nathaniel stayed in West Virginia. Many of his descendants are still living there. Some of his descendants are now living in Bloomington.

Nathaniel Lindsey

Hannah married Cornelius S. Campbell but not much is known about the other children of Peter and Rachel Lindsey. A letter to cousin Anna Campbell Fleener in 1964 from Mae Moore stated that she was born on Jackson Creek, above the present Yellowood Lake, July 1, 1890. She stated that her mother was the only child that lived out of six children born to Alexander N. Lindsey, perhaps a brother of Hannah. The other small children are buried in Needmore cemetery along with her grandfather Alexander. Mae further stated that her grandmother whose initials are M.A. came to North Dakota with the rest of her family in 1909.

There was much sickness due to the swampy lowlands and many people moved to North Dakota and formed a little town named Grenora.

Mae wrote that there were nine children in her family and that all were living except Lora and Elma. The grandmother of Mae was buried in Grenora, ND far from her husband in Needmore Cemetery. Submitted by Alice Fleener-Smith-Parmerlee

LEROY AND MABEL LOGSDON - "Roy" Logsdon was born in Hart Co., KY, June 12, 1898, the second son of John Consolver and Elizabeth (Kenney) Logsdon, the seventh generation of Logsdons in America. The first Logsdon ancestor we have record of was William Logsdon, Sr. reportedly born in Northern Ireland 1652. He arrived in America near Baltimore, MD in 1673 and in 1702 selected Honora O'Flynn from a boatload of girls brought from Ireland (some had been kidnapped) to be his wife.

The Logsdon ancestors were Irish Catholic and began emigrating westward to Kentucky in the late 1700s after Jesuit missions had been burned in Maryland.

When "Roy" was quite a young man his family moved from Kentucky to Indianapolis where he met Mabel Edith Richards (1901), daughter of Milton and Viola (Robertson) Richards. "Roy" and Mabel were married in Indianapolis, March 4, 1918 and moved to Brown County where Mabel was a native, the same year.

Mabel Richards and Leroy Logsdon before their 1918 marriage.

Ivy Logsdon (1897-1971) followed his younger brother, "Roy," to Brown County in the early 1930s after serving overseas in World War I. He raised Elsie (1921), Margie (1922), and Edward (1925), the children of his first marriage May 17, 1920 to Muriel Taylor (1902-1926). Ivy, Jr. (1930), Marilyn (1933), Lena Jean (1936), and Jenny (1941) are the children of his second marriage March 20, 1929 to Dorothy Sweetwood (1912-1980) daughter of Harry Sweetwood and Lena McIntire.

"Roy" became an accomplished carpenter and enjoyed fishing, fox hunting, ginseng digging, and mushroom hunting among the beautiful hills of Brown County. Mabel worked in Camp Atterbury during World War II and the Korean Conflict. She was given a special commendation for her outstanding work in the Clothing and Equipage Shop. She has been active in Republican Politics and in her churchwork. In their retirement years they spent many winters fishing in the Florida sunshine.

Four children were born to this couple: (1) Paul Richard (1919-1981) who served in the Army during World War II and graduated from Indiana University School of Law in 1955. He married Vivian B. Fenicle (1914) on Oct. 9, 1940 in Monroe County. They had Paul Edward (1941) and identical twins, Robert Dale and Richard Gale (1945). (2) Wilma Laverne (1921) married George L. Leggins, Oct. 27, 1940 in Monroe County. They had Russell Leroy (1941-1946) who died of a brain tumor. (3) Mildred Edith (1923-1926) died of tuberculosis. (4) Marvin Leroy (1928-1979) was an Industrial Insulation Engineer for 25 years. He married Lila J. Blois (1931) on Nov. 28, 1948 in Monroe County. They had Gary (1951), Denise (1954), and Galen (1960).

"Roy" passed away April 15, 1969 shortly after their 51st wedding anniversary, but not before he was introduced to his first great-grandchild, Mark Edwin, son of Paul Edward and Joanne (Olsen) Logsdon.

Mabel presently resides in Trevlac with his sister, Helen Rund, where she enjoys reading, crocheting and cooking for friends and relatives who visit them. Submitted by Lila J. Logsdon

LONG FAMILY - Aaron Hodges born July 24, 1810 married Martha Hannah Lee born May 20, 1823, died May 11, 1867. Their daughter, Louise Frances, born July 25, 1845, died Oct. 27, 1917 married Robert Long. They had a son, William Long born Oct. 30, 1875, died Dec. 22, 1959 who married Arkie Barnard. Their children were Jessie, Lillard, Sonny, Laura, James, Lucille, Mary, Lester and Chester (twins), Joann and Betty.

William and Arkie moved from the Clinch Mountains in Morristown, TN, to a farm in Hendricks County in the 1900s. They later moved to Brown County where they farmed and William worked in timber.

Lillard and Mary (Robertson) Long

Their son, Lillard (Buck) Long born Aug. 3, 1902, died March 1, 1976, married Mary Robertson born July 19, 1904, died Nov. 4, 1973. They owned and operated a large country store in Helmsburg from April 1948 to August 1977. Son, Lillard Jr. ran the store after Mary's death from 1973-1977. The store was known to many people throughout Indiana who loved to come and try to find something they didn't carry, which was rare. They sold hardware, clothes, shoes, feed for animals, fuel oil, kerosene, meats, vegetables and groceries. Lillard worked for the county as highway superintendent and Ralph Rogers Company for many years, leaving the running of the store to Mary. She loved the people and saw to their many needs. Groceries were delivered weekly to older people, the sick and the snow bound. Living over the store, she had many calls very late on cold nights for fuel oil and cold remedies for the sick. They had three sons and one daughter. William C. born Sept. 21, 1922, married Gloria Caruso born July 11, 1925, died April 29, 1974. They had one son James William born May 10, 1945. James married Linda Stockwell born Jan. 19, 1948. They have one daughter, Amanda C. born July 2, 1975. William was married a second time to Lucille Thompkins. The second son, James F. born Dec. 3, 1924 was killed in WWII April 1945 in Germany, returned and buried in Morgantown, IN Cemetery in 1948. Their daughter, May Ann (Long) Walker born July 24, 1933 married Lawrence Dean Walker born Oct. 28, 1924 and they live in Brown County on Highway 135 near Bean Blossom, IN. Their third son, Lillard E. (Buckshot) Jr. born July 26, 1936, died June 29, 1989, married Geraldine Poore born Feb. 15, 1936. They had one daughter and one son, Brenda (Long) Canary born April 17, 1954 married Mark Canary born Nov. 10, 1956. Mark and Brenda have one daughter, Michelle Lynn born Sept. 14, 1981. Their son, Gary E. Long was born March 29, 1958. Lillard Jr. was married a second time to Charlotte Asdell Lancaster born May 29, 1946. Charlotte has one daughter, Kelli born Dec. 7, 1966. Submitted by Mary Ann Walker

ALBERT E. AND LILLIAN LONG - About 90 years ago, Albert E. Long better known as "Bert" by his friends and neighbors and Lillian (Feigel) Long moved to Brown County from Indianapolis and lived in a house built by Mr. Long off the Old Nashville road better known as the "Red House."

At that time they had two little boys Finley and Lacell (Toots). They both went to the Old Dolsberry school off the old Nashville road at the left at the foot of Baker Hill. The school has been gone for many years.

Finley graduated from Helemsburg High School.

From there, they moved to the Old Dale Bessire orchard at the top of Plum Creek Hill that Mr. Long took care of. He worked in apple orchards all of his life in Brown County.

There a daughter was born Doris (Betty Belle) on Jan. 14, 1920.

From there they moved across the Old Gibson orchard. Where he spent the rest of his life.

Bert passed away at age 80 and is buried in the Oak Ridge Cemetery.

Lillian Long then made a living by having a milk route to Helemsburg where she sold milk for 10¢ a quart. She also cooked one meal a day for Phil Baker that lived on top of Baker hill.

Later she moved to Needmore, IN where she lost her youngest son "Toots." She passed away August of 1954. Both Toots and Lillian are buried in the Needmore Cemetery.

Finley Long passed away in April of 1984 at age 77. He is also buried in the Needmore cemetery.

Betty Belle is still living at Loogootee, IN.

When Lillian Long passed on, she had three grandchildren.

The boys never married so the Long family had no one left to carry on the name of Long. *Written by Doris (Betty Belle) Sabatier*

FINLEY H. LONG
- Was born to Albert (Bert) Long and Lillian Louise (Fiegel) Long Nov. 18, 1906 at Indianapolis, IN.

When he was a boy of about four they moved to Brown County. In a house his father built off the old Nashville road known by many as the "Red House."

He spent all the years of his life in Brown County. He attended the old Dolsberry grade school off the old Nashville Road to the right and at the foot of Baker Hill. The school is now gone. He graduated from Helmsburg High School at the age of 21.

Finley H. Long

He lived at home for many years because he never got married. He finally bought a few acres of ground at the edge of Yellowwood Forest. There he built a small cabin where he spent the rest of his life. He took a young boy to raise who built him a big bird house, chimney, fireplace and an out house. The boy then got married.

Everyone that knew Finley liked him for he was very kind and helped everyone. But he lived in his own little World of Nature. I believe he knew every wildflower and tree that grew.

He worked at Indianapolis for different families as a gardener and made and planted wildflower gardens for many. Some of them in Nashville, IN. He planted a lot of Myrtle, which he dug up by the bushel.

He also loved hunting mushrooms and he was always hunting ginseng. He had a big ginseng patch near his cabin. He also had a yard full of wildflowers - Red Bud and Dogwood trees. He knew all the herbs and what they were used for.

He loved animals and I don't think he could of killed one if he was starving. He only killed the poisonous snakes, for most snakes are harmless.

In his last years of life he lived alone with his dog, a big half St. Bernard and half Irish Setter.

Finley hadn't felt good for about one year and it was getting mushroom season. His legs were swelling so he checked into the hospital to find out what was wrong.

He never returned to the home and dog he loved so much. He died April 19, 1984 and is buried in the Needmore Cemetery.

After Finley passed away the dog grieved himself to death. There is nothing more faithful as a dog to their master.

WILLIAM LONG AND DESCENDANTS
- William, born around 1836, was in Co. D 25th Indiana Infantry, Civil War. He married Elizabeth ?, they had five children: Arra Jane, Mary Ellen, Willard, Scott, and Sherman. They lived near Helmsburg, IN on Railroad Road, Jackson Township. William was a coroner in 1878.

Willard (born Aug. 8, 1861) married Malcenia Stevens (born July 25, 1865) July 26, 1883. They had four children (one dying in infancy): John, Minnie and Martha. Willard lived his entire life at the Long Homestead. He belonged to the Unity Baptist Church. His favorite subject was the Bible and he could talk to the best authorities on that book. Willard had a long white beard and mustache. He used a mustache cup to drink his coffee. Willard and Malcenia were married for 55 years. He died Feb. 9, 1941; buried at Oak Ridge Cemetery.

John and Dolores Tutterrow

Minnie (born 1884) married Walter Gee (born 1880). They lived in Hamblen Township at the Gee Homestead. Seven children were born: Beryle, Dolores, Berniece, Dale, Walter Clifton (died in infancy), Marjorie and Raymond. Minnie graduated from Danville Central Normal Teachers College and taught school. She played the organ, and was a member of Unity Baptist Church, Eastern Star and Ladies Auxiliary. She was a homemaker, canning all their food, made their clothes, baked bread, pies and cakes. Minnie loved and cared for her neighbors. Many nights she sat up with the sick. She always had a quilt on her quilting frame; also the neighbors had quilting bees. They gave these quilts to the needy or people who lost their home from fires. Minnie walked from Weber Hill to Spearsville Road and met the huckster wagon and carried her groceries back. She died 1959 and is buried at Unity Cemetery. She had 24 grandchildren and 56 great-grandchildren.

Minnie narrowly escaped death from runaway horses. She was gathering vegetables from her garden; a neighbor was disking with a team of horses. He left them standing and went to get a drink of water; something spooked them, they ran and just as they got to Minnie the disk went up on one side, knocking her down, bruised from head to toe.

Dolores Gee (born 1910) married John Tutterrow Dec. 24, 1930. They lived in Jackson Township near Trevlac. Five children were born: Twins Marilyn and Margilyne (1932), Billy (born 1933), Phyllis (born 1935), and Alice (born 1938). Dolores was one of the best seamstresses in the county. In later years, she worked in foods at I.U. and Bloomington Hospital. As a young girl, she joined Unity Baptist Church. She was a member of Trevlac Homemakers Club and Nashville Eastern Star. She died in 1989 leaving five children, 20 grandchildren and 27 great-grandchildren. Dolores is buried at Bear Creek Cemetery.

Marilyn Tutterrow, born June 24, 1932, graduated from Helmsburg High School in 1951. She married Phillip Rotino in January 1952. They have two daughters: Brenda and Cherlynn; three grandchildren: Wendy Sadler and Chad and Brady Sparks. Marilyn has worked as a bookkeeper accountant for 31 years. Phillip is a stone mason and shoe repairman. Marilyn attended Bear Creek Church. *Submitted by Marilyn Rotino*

LORENZ FAMILY
- Frederick G. Lorenz, Jr. and Mary Jane Lorenz were born and lived in Indianapolis, IN, until their move to a permanent home in Brown County in 1972. Frederick G. Lorenz, Sr. and Bessie Sherman Lorenz became parents of Fred, Jr., born April 18, 1914. Mary Jane Lorenz was born July 28, 1914 to Carl W., Sr. and Marie Howe Steeg. Their families were of British and German descent. Fred and Mary Jane were married in Central Christian Church Feb. 17, 1940. At the time Fred was employed by Indiana Bell Telephone Co., and Mary Jane worked at Indianapolis Life Insurance Co.

Frederick and Mary Jane Lorenz

Fred was active in Boy Scouts from age 12, becoming an Eagle Scout, Scoutmaster, Cubmaster and receiving the Scoutmaster Key and Silver Beaver Award for distinguished service to boyhood. In 1976 he was presented with a 50 Year Pin by Richard G. Lugar, one of his former Scouts.

In 1944 Fred bought property in Brown County which was the beginning of Gnaw Bone Camp. While operating the Camp in the summer, he was a teacher of Industrial Arts and Science at Orchard Country Day School the rest of the year. In 1972 after 25 years he retired from teaching but returned to the campus each spring to conduct a maple syrup camp. He became a member of the American Camping Association in 1945 and served on state and national boards. He was a Certified Camp Director, Lifetime Instructor of Outdoor Living

Skills, was named a Pioneer in Camping in 1989, and received the Heart and Soul Award of the Indiana Section of the Association in 1990.

Fred was a member of the Nashville Masonic Lodge, transferring in 1973 from Oriental Lodge in Indianapolis. He was also a 32° mason of the Indianapolis Valley of Scottish Rite. In 1989 he was honored as a Sagamore of the Wabash. He served for many years on the Zoning Appeals, Soil and Water Conservation, and Agricultural Soil Conservation Service boards in Brown County.

As their daughters were growing up, Mary Jane was a Girl Scout leader and PTA officer and active in several volunteer, charitable and social groups, including The Indianapolis Propylaeum. She also assumed the office duties for the Camp. In Brown County she was a member of the Business and Professional Women, the Nashville Literary Club, and the Nashville Christian Church Missionary Group. In 1988 she transferred her PEO affiliation to the Nashville Chapter.

Fred and Mary Jane were Charter Members of The Brown County Historical Society and belonged to the Friends of the Library and the Brown County Art Gallery.

They had three daughters and four grandchildren: Helen Marie Holdeman, born 1941, lives in Muncie, has a son, Roger Andrew, born 1973, and a daughter, Amy Lynn Holdeman Riggins, born 1967; Alice Sue Lorenz, born 1945, lives in Brown County and manages Gnaw Bone Camp; Linda Jane Norton, born 1951, lives in Franklin, has a daughter, Jennifer Marie, born 1977, and a son, Peter Jonathan, born 1980.

BEULAH "TAB" LOW - Beulah Mae Clark, younger daughter of Raymond Julius and Bertha (Wolpert) Clark, was born May 7, 1921, in Belleville, St. Clair Co., IL. She married John Edward Low, son of Charles Grandison and Mabelle Edith (Nixon) Low, in Lawrenceville, IL, June 22, 1940, and they had Charles Raymond Low, born Nov. 27, 1941. John, having spent his adult years in oil field work, died December 1967 in Houston, TX.

Charles "Chuck" graduated from Vincennes High School, attended Vincennes University and in 1965, graduated from Indiana State University, Terre Haute. There he met fellow-student, Beverly Ann "Becky" Hert, daughter of Robert William and Mildred Maxine (Atkinson) Hert. "Chuck" and "Becky" married June 26, 1965, in Richmond, IN. Their two children, Stacey Anne born Oct. 12, 1967, and Robert Charles born Sept. 13, 1969, are both college students. A resident of Indianapolis, Charles was recently honored as a 25-year employee of Indiana Bell Telephone Co. Beverly Ann is a secretary.

Beverly Ann, Stacey and Robert trace their ancestry to Daniel Brower who served with the 4th Regiment Light Dragoons, Continental Army (Pennsylvania) (DAR # 567,349) and to Daniel's ancestor Anneka (Jans) Bogardus, wife of Rev. Everardus Bogardus, ordained minister in the 1600s of the first church in New Amsterdam, NY. Anneke, daughter of Manhattan's first midwife, Tryn Jansen, was a famous participant in the New Amsterdam "Trinity Episcopal Church" court battle of the 1600s - a battle which resurfaces even today.

Beulah "Tab," Charles "Chuck" and Beverly Ann "Becky" all trace their roots to common ancestors Theunis Thomazen Quick deMatzelaer (the Mason) and his wife, Belitjen Jacobus of Van Naarden, Holland, who lived in the 1630s in Nieuw Amsterdam, (NY) and where in 1645, they received a grant from Gov. Peter Stuyvesant for land partly covered by the present Produce Exchange Building, New York City, and where Theunis aided in the construction of the "Old Trinity Church" in New York City. Theunis' son, Jacob Theuniszen Quick deLooper (the Runner) received a 4,000 acre tract of Manhattan land in the 1640s signed by His Majesty George II and Indian chiefs of the Delaware tribe.

Charles and Beulah's ancestor, Canzaday Quick, descendant of Theunis Thomaszen and Belitjen (Jacobus) Quick, married William Rittenhouse, Sr., in 1772. William was a descendant of progenitor Willem Rüddinghüysen van Mulheim, papermaker, born in 1644 near Rhenish Prussia, who emigrated to Germantown, PA, where about 1680 he built the first paper mill in the Colonies and was Germantown's first Mennonite minister. William and Canzaday's daughter Hannah married Joshua Clark whose grandson, John Glover Clark, married Louisa Espenschied whose ancestors came from Marnheim, Rheinpfalz (Palatinate) Germany.

Beulah settled in Indiana after many years of traveling from state to state as an "oil Johnny's wife." She received an Associate degree from Vincennes University, a Bachelor's degree in Elementary Education and a Master's degree in Audiovisual Communications from Indiana State University, Terre Haute. After her retirement from teaching, she continued her interest in genealogy.

Beulah's one grandfather, Frederick William Wolpert, earned his apprenticeship in Hesse-Darmsted, Germany. Another grandfather, Joshua Stoneman, married Elizabeth Adams whose ancestry is traced to Sir Gilbert de Johnstone, Laird of Caskieban in the 1480s, thence to Margaret, second wife of Malcolm III, 19th King of Scotland. Margaret, who died in 1093, was canonized in 1250 as St. Margaret and was declared Patron Saint of Scotland in 1673.

A lesser known Stockholm ancestor, Margaret Matson (Mrs. Nils) was found guilty in 1683 of "having the reputation of being a witch." Her accuser claimed Margaret had caused a herd of cows to go dry. The hearing, the only one of its kind ever held in Pennsylvania, was presided over by William Penn. After he acquitted her of "actually being a witch," the Matson family moved to Gloucester, NJ.

Beulah and other Brown Countians trace their ancestries to Nicholas Hutchins, a Society of Friends (Quaker) minister, who in 1711 worked on the breastworks of the Battery at Jamestown (CDXVIIC #23303) and whose son Strangeman is credited with Public Service in Virginia during the Revolutionary War (DAR #671,953).

Little did the Dutch-Reformed Church Quick families, the Rhenish Prussia - Mennonite Rittenhouses, the German Rheinpfalz Espenschieds or the Hesse-Darmsted Wolperts, Scotland's Johnsons and St. Margaret, the Swedish Matsons, or the Quaker Hutchins' envision that their adventuresome trails would wind their ways down through the centuries to weave a tapestry of life which would today be the heritage of the present Brown Countian, Beulah "Tab" Low.

ROBERT W. LOYD FAMILY - Robert's great-grandfather William Loyd first came to Indiana in 1850 from Kentucky where he was born Dec. 25, 1830. William farmed in Knox Co., IN and he and his wife Mary Chambers Loyd had eight children raising only two of them to adulthood. Their son Edmond born Feb. 15, 1868 continued farming and married his first wife Annie Moffitt Nov. 6, 1889. He and Annie had two children; however this marriage didn't work out and Annie and her son and daughter moved to the Terre Haute area. Edmond then married Elizabeth Southerland Dec. 25, 1894 and they had six children, Ralph born 1895, Edith born 1897, Willard born 1900, Willis born 1903, Clarence born 1905, and Thelma born 1907. With four sons and only 40 acres to Farm in Knox County, Edmond sold his farm and purchased 270 acres in Jefferson County. Robert's father, Willard Loyd didn't care about farming and he sold out his interests to his brother Clarence so that he could attend Barber College in Indianapolis. Willard graduated and barbered for 35 years before going to Newsom Industries in Columbus, IN. Willard was married to Ida Pearl Boardman Dec. 19, 1919 in Jefferson County and they had two sons Leroy Earl Loyd born 1920 and Robert Willard Loyd born 1934. Robert was married to Mary Margaret Burton Dec. 31, 1956. Of this union three children were born; Victoria Lynn born 1958, Reginald Bob born 1961 and Mary Suella born 1962. Vickie was married to Gary Cook Sept. 21, 1985. Mary Suella married Keith Fox July 2, 1983 and they have one son Justin Craig Fox born Aug. 16, 1987.

Robert Loyd Family, June 22, 1985

Robert married Marilyn A. Repp the daughter of Gilfred and Janet Marsh of Decatur County June 22, 1985 in a pioneer type wedding at the Hoosier National Forest in Southeastern Brown County. Marilyn has two children Jonathan Willis Repp born 1973 and Pamela Sue Repp born 1975. Robert and Marilyn purchased the Van Osdol property on Beck's Grove Road in October of 1985. Robert retired in April of 1987 from Cummins Engine Company to pursue his hobbies of Blacksmithing and Copper work as well as hunting. Marilyn has interests in reading, sewing and genealogy and is actively pursuing the Loyd family roots as well as the Boardman, King and Marsh family lines. The Loyd family enjoys Brown County very much. Though we came late we hope to stay long.

DAN AND KATIE LUCAS - Daniel Jonathan Lucas was born at Gnawbone, IN on Feb. 20, 1894. He was the 11th child of Elijah Lucas and Sabra Hawkins whose story is told elsewhere in this book.

Dan lived in Brown County until September 1917 when he was "mustered in" to the U.S. Army and boarded the train at Helmsburg to go to Camp Taylor. In October he was sent to Camp Shelby in Mississippi and remained there until Sept. 14, 1918. On that date, Dan left for service in France, by way of Quebec, Canada and England. He was in France from Oct. 30, 1918 until Jan. 2, 1919. He then returned to the United States and was discharged at Camp Sherman in Ohio on Feb. 15, 1919. He arrived home in Gnawbone the next day. While he was on his way home from France, his favorite sister, Rhoda, died.

Wedding picture of Katie Mae Gates and Daniel Jonathan Lucas

During his Army service, he corresponded with Katie Mae Gates, daughter of John J. and Sarah Georgianna (Anna) Stitt Gates, both of whom were born in Brown County. At various times, the Gates family lived in Brown and Bartholomew Counties. Katie, the fifth of 11 children, was born in Bartholomew County on April 6, 1898.

Dan and Katie were married on May 17, 1919 at Williamsport in Warren County, IN by Methodist minister John E. McCloud. Dr. Frank Tilton of Brown County was living in Williamsport at the time and was a witness to the ceremony.

Dan went to work farming the rich soil of Warren County which is at the eastern edge of the great prairie. In March 1928, the family moved from Warren County to near Alvin, IL and in March 1932, they moved back again to live north of West Lebanon. Dan and Katie had four children, all of whom are still living. Edith Katheryn was born March 9, 1920 and was followed by Laura Jean on May 21, 1922, Manuel Elmer on Aug. 4, 1924, and Paul Dwayne on Sept. 24, 1932. Katie was an excellent housekeeper and cook. After the children grew up, she enjoyed many handicrafts, especially crochet. It seemed she was always in the middle of a lacy doily of some sort.

In 1955, Dan and Katie bought a farm near Ladoga in Montgomery County and lived there for the rest of their lives. They were sociable people, attending church regularly and participating in the World War I Barricks (veterans' organization). In the summer they always had a garden and Katie canned and froze the products of it. They were also always delighted with visits by their children and 11 grandchildren.

Laura Jean, Edith Katheryn (standing) and Manuel Elmer Lucas

Katie died of a heart ailment at home on Feb. 23, 1966. Dan lived until Jan. 13, 1977 when he died of cancer.

Although they left Brown County at an early age, Dan and Katie returned often to visit relatives and friends. Katheryn remembers attending the Old Settlers' Reunion and Paul's earliest recollection of a vacation was "going to visit the relatives."

Dan never lost his love of Brown County and passed it on to his granddaughter, Julia Ottenweller, who was born in Warren County but now lives near Fruitdale with her husband Carl. *Submitted by Julia M. Ottenweller, granddaughter of Dan and Katie Lucas*

ELIJAH AND SABRA (HAWKINS) LUCAS

Elijah was the grandfather of Edgar S. Lucas. He was born April 20, 1844 in Brown Co., IN. He was the first child of Jonathan Lucas and Elizabeth Petro. The family moved to Missouri after 1848 and lived in Wright and then Miller County over the next decade. Three brothers and a sister were born before the family returned to Brown County between 1862 and 1866. A major impetus in their exodus was the civil war. Elijah was 18 in 1862 and the family feared he would be taken into the Confederate Army. My mother told me that Elijah described hearing cannon 'thunder' as they departed. Elijah walked most of the way and hid in the woods if strangers were encountered. They returned to Brown County by covered wagons pulled by oxen. Elijah grew up in the Mt. Liberty area with his six siblings. He married Sabra Hawkins of Brown County on April 28, 1872. She was the daughter of Daniel Hawkins who was born May 26, 1824 in Virginia and Rebecca A. Petro who was born in Indiana March 9, 1834. They had 12 children as follows: Charles (ca. 1873-1938) who married Elizabeth Evelyn "Eva" Pittman (1877-1962) and had three children, Elizabeth (1874-1951) who married Elva Clifford (1871-?) and had six children. After his death, she married Alfred Eddy 9 (1855-1936) and had one child, Frederick D. (1877-1939) who married Emma Lucetta "Setta" Pittman (1882-1975) and had five children, Clara (1878-1912) who married John F. Boffing (?-?) and had eight children, Rebecca (1880-1957) who married Elvie Lane (1881-?) and had three sons, Perry Commodore (1838-1958) who married Flossie E. Rambo (1891-?) and had two sons, Anna A. (1886-1953) who married William Samuel Jolly (1880-1924) and had five children, Rhoda C. (1888-1919) who married Albert Whittinghill and had two daughters, Eva (1890-1890) who died at seven months of age from the whooping cough, Manuel C. (1891-19??) who married Mina Evalyn Curtis (1892-?), Daniel (1894-1977) who married Katie Mae Gates (1891-1966) and had four children and Isaac Sampson (1896-1965), my father, who married Catherine Geneva Helms (1903-1978) and had eight children. Most of these spouses were also Brown County residents at the time of marriage. Charles and Frederick married sisters (Elizabeth and Emma Pittman).

Sabra Hawkins Lucas

Elijah was a carpenter and blacksmith and also kept a peach and apple orchard. They had a long house that required going outside to move from room to room. He once posted bail (1877) and later gave up a 3000 pound load of tobacco and a two horse wagon in 1878 to rescue his father-in-law from a bad debt suit. He served as Brown County Recorder as a Democrat following the 1916 election. Elijah built the Clark Church near Gnaw Bone. He and Sabra are buried in the Clark Cemetery in Washington Township along with their infant daughter Eva and Elijah's parents. Elijah died April 14, 1926 at the home of his daughter, Mrs. Elvie Lane, from chronic myocarditis. Sabra died from nephritis at home on Aug. 8, 1920, eight miles NE of Nashville. She was a member of the Clark Church and was active in church circles. *Submitted by Edgar S. Lucas*

JONATHAN AND ELIZABETH ANN (PETRO) LUCAS

Jonathan was born in Indiana, July 1821. His father was born in New Jersey and his mother in New York (1900 census) but their names remain unknown. Jonathan also once used the name of Thomas Lucas (1870 Brown County census). He married Elizabeth Ann Petro, daughter of Paul Petro and Mary "Polly" Davis, in Brown County (license issued April 5, 1844). She was born July 1827 in Bartholomew County. Paul (born 1793) was the youngest child of Phillip and Nancy Petro of Bartholomew County. Mary (born 1800) was a full-blooded Indian from Kentucky. Their first child, Elijah was born April 20, 1844 and they paid poll tax in Van Buren Township in 1848. These three are next found in Wright Co., MO (1850 census). They purchased property in Osage Township of Miller Co., MO in 1855 and sold it in 1857. By the 1860 census they are in Wright County and have added children as follows: John H. 9 (November 1850), George 6 (June 20, 1854), Jonathan 3 (Jan. 28, 1857 in Miller County), and William (Jan. 6, 1860).

Elizabeth and Thomas Jonathan Lucas

Family tradition relates that they returned to Brown County in the early 1860s after the birth of Mary Elizabeth (born in Poplar Bluff, MO Jan. 26, 1862) to evade Elijah's involuntary Confederate Army duty. It is said that they could hear cannon shots as they departed. Elijah walked most of the way and hid in the woods at the appearance of strangers. They returned via covered wagon pulled by oxen and crossed rivers by ferry boat. Their last child, Armilda, was born in Brown Co., IN on Sept. 5, 1867. The family resided in the Mt. Liberty area of Washington Township (1870, 1880 and 1900 censuses) until his death on Feb. 21, 1904. His estate listed one bee stand, 20 acres of property and miscellaneous personal effects. His wife, "Betsy" Petro, died Feb. 15, 1911 at the home of her son-in-law, William P. Taylor. She had nine children, seven of whom are known. They are thought to be buried in the Henderson Cemetery at Gnaw Bone but no marker has been found.

Jonathan was a farmer, cupboard maker, hunter and respected community member. All of his children but one, John Henry (who was blind and single), married in Brown County. His oldest son (grandfather of Edgar A. Lucas), Elijah, married Sabra Hawkins (born April 9, 1855) on April 28, 1872 and they had 12 children. Sabra was the granddaughter of Paul Petro's brother, Nicholas Petro. Elijah was elected Brown County recorder in 1916. He was a farmer and a blacksmith. John Henry never married. George married Anna Louisa "Amy" Taylor (born March 23, 1859), daughter of Benjamin and Mary Elizabeth Taylor. They had five children. Amy died Jan. 29, 1914 and he married Clara Phoebe Brock and died May 29, 1921. George was a blacksmith. Jonathan L. Lucas, Jr. married Louisa Robinson (born about 1866 in Indiana) daughter of George Robinson and Mary Marlett and had three children. He was a blacksmith and a grocery salesman. After her death about 1895, he married Caroline Bell Orman, widow of Willis Paris, about 1898 and they had two children. William married (Dec. 23, 1883) Mary Sullivan and they divorced. He then (July 11, 1886) married Martha Elizabeth Petro, daughter of Joseph Petro and Jemima Jane Taylor, and they had 15 children. Mary Elizabeth married Daniel William Gates (born Nov. 6, 1857 in Indiana), son of David Gates and Sidney Shanon, on Oct. 9, 1884 and they had 11 children. She died Sept. 21, 1925 after being hit by a car. Anna Armilda married Michael P. "Pete" Taylor, son of Archibald Taylor and Elizabeth King on Aug. 28, 1890 and they had four children. She died March 2, 1951. Most of their descendents still reside in Indiana. *Submitted by Edgar A. Lucas*

MABE FAMILY - The family dates back to William and Elizabeth Mabe who came from England to Albemarle Co., VA in 1738. On Feb. 1, 1738 William received a land grant of 204 acres in Hanover Co., VA from King George II. They had four sons and three daughters. One of his sons was Robert Mabe who according to a will dated in 1762 received land in Virginia from his father, William, which he later sold, and settled near Danbury (Stokes Co.) NC prior to 1771. In 1778 Robert, both a miner and a farmer, received a land grant of 150 acres and later in 1795 he received a second grant of 50 acres. A voucher dated in 1782 listed in Treasurer and Controller's Records, Vol. XII, page 3, folio 4 records payment for services during the Revolutionary War.

Robert Mabe's family consisted of either seven or eight children, one of whom was Sarah, who had four children. Hiram Mabe born about 1798 in Stokes Co., NC was one of her two sons. Sarah died in 1807 and Hiram was placed by the court in the home of Wm. Pafford, a Revolutionary War Veteran. Mr. Pafford agreed to provide food, clothing, lodging, and to educate him to read, write and cipher. At age 21 years, Hiram was to receive a new suit of clothes, a horse, a bridle and saddle, 50 dollars and his freedom. The court placed his two sisters and an older brother, Ambrose Wheeler Mabe, in other Stokes Co., NC family homes. It is believed that his brother Ambrose, died in the War of 1812.

Hiram Mabe was married to Lusenda Barrott in Stokes Co., NC on Feb. 17, 1818. Hiram's marriage bond was signed by Taylor Mabe, the son of John Mabe, a Kentucky War Veteran. In 1833 Hiram and family settled in Brown County, where he acquired land. He died in Brown County on Dec. 24, 1855.

James Madison Mabe was one of six children born to Hiram and Lusenda. He was born in Stokes Co., NC on Oct. 23, 1820. All these children were born in Stokes County with the exception of his youngest sister, Nancy, who was born in Brown County. James served in Co. H, 82nd Indiana Volunteer Infantry, during the Civil War. He married Ann Noblet, Nov. 3, 1842 and died in Hendricks Co., IN, March 5, 1896. He held the rank of Corporal when mustered out of service on July 9, 1865, after serving almost three years.

Sylvanus Mabe, born May 31, 1844, in Brown County was one of 13 children born to James Madison Mabe and Ann (Noblet) Mabe. Like his father, James Madison, he also volunteered for service in the Civil War serving over three years in Co. C, 6th Indiana Volunteer Infantry. He was the last Civil War Veteran in Hendricks Co., IN. He died June 30, 1940 at age 96. He was married on March 14, 1869 to Harriet C. (Bartholomew) Mabe who preceded him in death on Oct. 24, 1929.

Lorenzo Fuller Mabe was one of two sons born to Sylvanus and Harriet (Bartholomew) Mabe. He was born in Brown County on Nov. 14, 1869. On Oct. 7, 1900 he married Aurelia Hurley in Brown County where she was born on Nov. 19, 1872. They had only one son and Lorenzo died in Clayton, Headricks Co., IN on Dec. 1, 1942. Lorenzo Mabe was a businessman and a farmer, remaining an active farmer until a few months before his passing.

Lyle Lorenzo Mabe, only child of Lorenzo and Aurelia Hurley Mabe was born in Clayton, IN (Hendricks Co.) on Oct. 6, 1911. He was married on Aug. 26, 1934 to Virginia (Meyers) Mabe in Clayton, IN. They were the parents of two children. Judith Lyle, born April 25, 1938 and Stephen Kent born April 7, 1941 in Indianapolis, IN.

Judith (Mabe) Buser now resides in Houston, TX. She and her husband, B.J. Buser, have two children: Curtis Lyle living in Maryland and Amy Jo now living in Kansas City, MO. Curt is married to Janine (Walton) Buser and Amy Jo is unmarried.

After the death of his first wife on April 8, 1969 Lyle married Aleitha (Hedge) Mabe and they now reside in Indianapolis.

HIRAM MABE FAMILY - Researchers think the Mabe family goes back to Birdstow, Herfordshire, England. The first Mabe (William) to come to America, migrated to Hanover Co., VA in 1738.

Hiram Mabe (1794) (1855) born in Surry Co. (now Stokes Co.) NC, married Lucinda Barret (Barrot) Feb. 18, 1818. Van Buren Township lists Hiram Mabe as a landowner in 1833. In the History book, counties of Morgan, Monroe, and Brown, Hiram is listed as First overseer of the poor, first inspector and first Constable for Van Buren Township. His reports are well written and his signatures are very good. William F. Mabe, son and Aaron Crouch, son-in-law were also land owners in Brown County.

James Madison Mabe (1829) (1895) son of Hiram and Lucinda was a land owner in 1841 in Van Buren Township. He moved with parents to Brown County where he married Ann Noblet. They were blest with 13 children. Sylvanus (1844) (1940) first son enlisted in the Civil War in Company C, 6th Regiment Infantry. Also Vandiver Ray Mabe (1847) (1909) third son enlisted in Company D, 43rd Indiana Infantry. Their father James Madison Mabe served in Company H Indiana Volunteers.

Four sons of James Madison and Ann Mabe. Front: David Wilson Mabe. Back: William, Vandiver Ray and Sylvanus Mabe.

The first home of the James Madison's was a log home. A new home was built in 1861. It was considered very attractive and convenient for that time. Brown County rumors are that the home was an underground station for escaped slaves. The home now is owned by Kenneth and Helen Reeve. They have restored and modernized the home and discovered a secret passage which would give support to the rumor about the underground station.

Often places that David Wilson Mabe (1868) (1956) (Grandfather of this writer and 12th child of the James Madison Mabes) spoke of were Gnawbone, Stone Head, Pikes Peak, New Bellsville, Becks Grove, Story and Christiansburg. David received a good education which enabled him to become a school teacher. He also helped farm for the family. In 1890 he married Mary Etta Gates. Soon after the marriage they and James Madison Mabes moved to Hendricks Co., IN. A son Carl was born (1892), another son Harold Cecil born (1896) (1988) and a third son Floyd (1900).

After the death of James and Ann their farm was sold to settle the estate.

David W. and Mary Etta Mabe then purchased a farm in Bartholomew County. After World War I they purchased a larger farm in Shelby Co., IN which they lost during the Depression. Their remaining lives were spent in Bartholomew County.

Harold Cecil Mabe married Hazel Hester Mounts on Valentines Day 1917. They had two children, Lawrence (1919) and Mildred (1921). Lawrence served as an Infantry Man in World War II. He and Anna Faye Mabe were married in 1941, and a son David Charles Mabe was born in 1942.

After graduating from Purdue, David married Susan Alexander 1965, and they had two children, a son David Todd (1969) and a daughter Christina Laura Mabe (1973). *Submitted by Lawrence Mabe*

MACKEY - From Germany came the Mackey family. John Henry Mackey and Gertude Miller Mackey both were born in Germany. By way of Ohio they came to Brown County to live on Valley Branch Road. They had nine children. The second oldest was Caroline born Feb. 2, 1857 who married James Leroy Moore the son of Wilson and Ally Butler Moore. Caroline was a midwife and was with Dr. Alfred Ralphy when he delivered babies in the community. She was asked for advice for cough remedies by making a tea of hickory bark, horehound and mullen or wild cherry with sugar or honey and lemon juice. Sometimes white pine tar was added. For worms you mixed a few drops of turpentine with sugar. A good salve for sores was unsalted butter and sulphur. Caroline and James Leroy had 13 children including a set of twins named Nellie and Della.

Nellie E. Crouch Gentry

Nellie Esther made home-baked bread on a wood stove when she had to stand on a chair. She also did a lot of the cooking since her mother was busy with someone sick or having a baby. In the winter time, her father, James Leroy, helped get ice ready for storage in Tipton's ice house so in the summer her brother would drive his matched team of horses and get a block of ice to make ice cream. Nellie Esther married Alfred Ralphy "Doc" Crouch, son of Joseph W. and Lillian Mae Crouch. They had three children: Gwendola, Lois, and Harry Wendell. "Doc" Crouch died in 1941. In 1963 Nellie Esther married Raymond Gentry, who died in 1987. Nellie loved to crochet. In 1988 at age 90 she entered a pillow in the Brown County fair and received a blue ribbon and reserve grand champion, and in 1989 she entered the pillow in picture and received a blue ribbon and grand champion. *Submitted by Norma R. Crouch*

ROGER MARKLEY FAMILY - Roger B. Markley was the eldest son of Dr. Herman and Beulah Markley and was born in Wells Co., IN on Feb. 25, 1921. The Markley's came from the Ruhr Valley in Germany in 1740 and located in Pennsylvania, then moved to Wells Co., IN where they received a Federal Land Grant signed by Benjamin Franklin for 4,000 acres. As each generation came along the children were given parcels of land when they married. Herman was the son of George and Lillian Markley. Beulah was the daughter of William and Alice Harmon of Elwood, IN. Herman and Beulah moved to Portland, IN in 1921 and set up practice.

Betty and Roger Markley

Betty J. Sheffer Markley was the daughter of Ervin and Faye Cole Sheffer of Portland, IN. She was born on April 15, 1924 in Jay County. Ervin was the son of Albert and Hattie Sheffer of Jay County. Faye was the daughter of Alva and Mae Cole of Jay County. Roger and Betty were married on Feb. 14, 1942 at which time Roger entered the United States Air Force and upon graduation from Flight School was joined by Betty. After 23 years in the military Roger retired as Major and they returned to Portland and opened a CPA office. Betty became a teachers aid in the Elementary schools. They had three children, Jeffrey, born in 1947, Patrice, born in 1951 and Rodney, born in 1955. Patrice moved to Nashville in 1973 after graduation from Art college and became an artist. After several visits to Brown County, Roger and Betty decided that it was a nice place in which to retire and they moved to Brown County in October of 1974 and purchased the Burkett Property on Artist Drive. Mr. Underwood wanted Roger and Betty to take over the management of Wabash Village Apts. and to this date they still manage the Apartments. Their youngest son, Rodney, is Head of the Maintenance and Patrice is the Night Manager of the Apartments. Their eldest son, Jeffrey, was a physical Therapist at Parkview Hospital in Fort Wayne, and moved to Nashville in 1976. He worked in the nursing home at Franklin and later came to the Brown County Community Center in Nashville where he is presently employed as a Q.M.A. None of the three children have married.

The family are all members of the Nashville United Methodist church and Roger was active in the Jay County Cancer Society and is now active in the Brown County Cancer Society. Roger has a limited practice in Tax Return Preparation. He graduated from Ball State University, attended Oxford University in England while recuperating from war injuries, and is a graduate of War College. He is listed in "Whos Who" and "Personalities of America" and earned 16 Medals in the military. He is a Mason, Eastern Star, and is a member of American Legion. Betty is a member of the Eastern Star, American Legion Auxiliary, and the United Methodist Church Women. *Submitted by Roger B. Markley*

MILDRED (BRUMMETT) MARSHALL - Mildred's roots are in Franklin Co., VA where George, her great-grandfather (one of six children of James and Agnes Brummett) was born in December 1780.

In early manhood, he and his brothers, James and Renna and sister Anne, moved into the Kentucky Territory. Here, in Adair County, he married, on July 22, 1802, Mary French. Mildred has birth records of six children: Joab, Langston, Elizabeth, William (Whispering Billy), Robert and Solomon. The latter two were born after the division of the territory. Their records state they were born in Tennessee.

These four families: George, James, Renna and Anne, came to Monroe Co., IN around 1819. They settled in the valley which is known as Brummetts Creek.

George entered 40 acres of land in Washington Township, Brown County April 4, 1838. He moved his family here and lived here until his death in 1891, being 111 years of age.

Mildred Olive Brummett Marshall

Mildred's grandfather, Robert, who was born April 18, 1820, and Amanda Harris born 1830, daughter of John Harris, were issued a marriage license Dec. 18, 1845.

Robert and Amanda lived on a farm of 320 acres in Washington Township, at the southern end of Dubois Road. They were the parents of 11 children: James K., John, George, Elizabeth, Solomon, Lucinda (died 1872), Robert Hester, Felix, Sarah, Joseph and Christopher.

Robert died in March 1875 leaving Amanda with seven children living at home. She died in 1891 at the age of 61. Her daughter, Elizabeth, contributed her death to hard work and life in a cold cabin which led to pneumonia resulting in her death.

Mildred's father, Joseph, except for a few years spent in Texas with his brother, John, continued living with Felix and Chris until his marriage to Emma, daughter of Harvey and Sarah Jane (Neal) Moore, June 7, 1907.

After Amanda's death, the farm was divided into 40 acre tracts—one for each of the eight children. Mildred's parents lived on one of these where Mary was born June 21, 1908. In 1909 they moved to a farm on Jackson Creek. It was here that Mildred Olive was born Feb. 1, 1910 during one of the biggest snowstorms ever recorded in Brown County. David was born June 26, 1912. He died in August, 1935. Martha was born Feb. 28, 1916. She died in August 1977.

Mildred and siblings attended Jackson Creek Elementary School. Mildred attended Nashville High School, then Indiana University for two years and began teaching in a one-room school in 1930. She continued her education while teaching and received a B.S. degree in Education in 1941. In 1960 she received her M.S. in Education. In 1972 she retired from teaching after 40-1/2 years, thinking she would now be able to travel before retiring to an old rocking chair. Her dreams failed to materialize because of knee and hip surgeries (eight combined) which kept her very busy since 1977 supporting the orthopedic surgeons. Her last hip replacement was done February 1990. It refuses to remain in place so her crutches are her constant companion for the rest of her life. Both knees are artificial, so are her teeth. She doesn't wear a wig, but has an appointment with the eye doctor. She manages to keep busy with knitting, sewing, and caring for house plants. She hopes to get her genealogy of the Brummett Family all recorded and ready for publication within the next year.

With so many new discoveries in medical science being made each year, she may manage to stay around and run her great-grandfather a race for longevity—111 years is 31 years into the future. "Well, it doesn't hurt to dream. Who knows? One might just come there; anyway it would give her two nieces, one nephew, eight great nieces, two great nephews and one great-great niece something to talk about." *Submitted by Mildred Olive Brummett Marshall*

JOHN AND MAUDE (CHITWOOD) MARTIN - Maude May, daughter of Richard and Ida May Chitwood, was born near Needmore, Brown County, June 12, 1886 and married John A. Martin, son of Hiram and Millie Richardson Martin of Monroe Co., IN. They farmed near Yellow Wood Lake before moving to the Greenwood area in 1916 where they successfully raised corn, wheat, soybeans and seven children, Clarence Richard (born 1905) married Genevieve Gillum; Edith Pearl (born

1907) married (1) Mr. Miller, (2) Steve Kennedy; Ethel May (born 1909) married Melvin Jack Myers; Olive Viola (born 1910) married Earl Neese; Hazel Ida (born 1912) married Paul Ryker; Julia Belle (born 1916) married Harold Doty; and Myrdith Marie (born 1920) married Howard Brummener.

Back: Ora and Ira Chitwood, about 1927. Front: Blanche Neal, Belle Arnold, Maude Martin, Ida May Chitwood Ritchey, Nell Hill.

Maude and John were devoted parents who worked very hard to provide not only for their own large family but there seemed always to be extras at the Martin table. An orphan, Arthur Winkler, made his home with them for two years and also nephew Robert Arnold spent many summers at the Martin home after the death of his mother, Belle Arnold, as well as others for shorter periods of time.

Maude passed away in 1947 and John in 1962.

LISA HOUSE MASSEY - Was born to Laurence and Dorothy House on March 30, 1962 in Indianapolis, IN. The family moved to Lake Lemon when Lisa was in second grade.

Dorothy and Laurence also have another daughter Lori, and two sons, David and Dennis. Lisa graduated from American Christian Academy in Bloomington, IN in 1980. She went to college in Springfield, MO where she met Ray Massey. They later married and have one son, Jeremy. Lisa graduated from nursing school with her RN and works for a major hospital in Springfield. They still reside in Springfield but enjoy coming back to Brown County to visit.

Lisa House Massey

MARSH - John Paul Marsh, a Brown County landscape artist and sculptor of national prominence, was born as James Harvey Marsh on Jan. 12, 1886 to Courtland Marsh (1842-1917), a Civil War lieutenant, and Jemima Jones Marsh (1853-1933), whose 1870 marriage took place in Boone Co., IN. Both were buried in Crown Hill Cemetery, Indianapolis. Courtland's father was Milton and he was a son of David Marsh, a pioneer of Boone County. The early Marsh family came through North Carolina, Virginia and Cynthiana, KY. The Marsh family has been traced genealogically to the Mayflower pilgrim Stephen Hopkins (1581-1644) who sailed from England and landed at Plymouth Rock, MA in 1620. This line flows from Hopkins through Snow, Doane (several) and Jones to Marsh.

James Courtland Marsh, Sr. 1970

James Harvey (John Paul) Marsh was married in 1909 to Marian Grace Hetherington (1890-1961) whom he met in art school. She specialized in pen and ink drawings and later taught school in Sullivan, New Harmony and Huntington, IN. Her parents, Frederick Alexander Hetherington (1859-1931) and Emma Lucretia Boardman Hetherington (1852-1909), were early residents of Brown County. (See Hetherington history elsewhere). James Harvey died Jan. 8, 1939 and was buried in Holy Cross Cemetery, Indianapolis. The couple lived in Morgan Co., IN and in Geneva, IL before being divorced in 1922. Marsh later married Flora Reinsperg.

John Paul studied at the John Herron Art Institute, Indianapolis, and the Art Student League of New York City. He studied sculpture in Florence, Italy. He once lived in New Orleans, LA. The Indiana Limestone Company in Bloomington employed him as a stonecarver and he designed the clay models for carvings used on the Tribune building in Chicago. His exhibits are listed in an article, "In The World of Art", by Lucille Morehouse (Indianapolis Star, May 5, 1929).

Locally Marsh had a farm southeast of Nashville. His six children, all by his first wife, were: Emma Jemima, Feb. 1, 1910; James Courtland, Oct. 8, 1911; Frederick Louis, May 4, 1914; Carl Milton, March 22, 1916; Rosemary, March 24, 1918; and Daniel Zaru, July 1, 1921. Louis, Carl and Daniel served in World War II, and Daniel also served in Korea. Carl became a medical doctor in Indianapolis. Artistically talented, Louis produced a number of oil paintings.

Their eldest son, James Courtland Marsh, lived for six years at the Hetherington place northwest of Nashville. He was graduated from Nashville High School, attended Purdue University and worked on a survey team and as an electrical engineer at RCA, as does his son. Jim was married in 1937 to Beatrice Marie Alter (1917-1976), a daughter of John Harris Alter (1875-1960) and Bernadetta Murphy Alter (1888-1978). The five children of Jim and Bea are: James Courtland, Jr., June 30, 1939; Marian Jeanne, Oct. 5, 1942; Viola Louise, Feb. 12, 1944; Rebecca Bernadette, Nov. 30, 1945; and Constance Alter, Jan. 26, 1947. *Submitted by James Courtland Marsh, Jr.*

MATHIS FAMILY - Jeremiah and Elizabeth Mathis came from Illinois. He was a civil war veteran. Entered the army in 1864. He died in 1891. They had one son, William, born 1872, died 1933. He married Mary Ann McLary, daughter of Samuel and Mary Ann Branstetter McLary, born 1880 died 1961. Her father owned several acres of land around Green Valley and she eventually inherited several acres of land and the homestead which he built in 1883.

They had 11 children. Harry, born 1899, died 1987. He taught school in one room schools in Brown County. Later moved to Bloomington and was a carpenter.

Back Row: Maurice, Mary Jane, Harry, Alpha, Richard, Eudora, Ray, Laura and Samuel. Front Row: Olive, Jeremiah (Dad), Elizabeth (Mom) and Dale.

Ray, born 1900, died 1986 married Charlotte Lutes. He taught school in Brown County. Later moved to Bloomington and taught in school system there for 50 years.

Alpha, born 1902, died 1988 married Frank Sipes. She taught in the one room schools. Later moved to Bloomington.

Richard, born 1905, married Nancy Ray. Lives in Iowa City. Works at a dairy there.

Samuel, born 1907, died 1987 married Emma Snyder. Farmed three miles W. Nashville.

Laura, born 1909, married Claris Keaton. She was a housewife and later worked for Farm Bureau Ins. 15 years.

Eudora, born 1912, married William Steinke, who lives on a farm in North Dakota.

Mary Jane, born 1914, married Walter Weisman. Served as nurse overseas during war. Lives in San Diego, CA.

Maurice, born 1916, married Eva Harden and Eunice Zink. Served in army overseas. Now farms on his farm three miles S.W. Nashville.

Dale, born 1921, married Hilda Ann (Betty) Bond. Served in air force during war. Later was basketball coach at Helmsburg; athletic director at Nashville; and is now retired at home.

Olive, born 1923, married Ted Steinke. Worked at Cummin's Engine Co. during war. Now a homemaker. Lives in South Bend, IN.

The children all went to school at Green Valley where their mother also attended when she was young. After the 8th grade they went to Nashville High School. After graduation, they were married and went separate ways. Four still live in Brown County. They get together for a family reunion every year.

DALE AND BETTY MATHIS FAMILY - William Dale Mathis was born Feb. 5, 1921 to William and Mary Ann (McLary) Mathis in Brown Co., IN. He was the tenth of 11 children. He graduated from Nashville High School in 1940, spent four years in the Army Air Force, then attended and graduated from Indiana University in 1950.

Dale met Hilda Ann (Betty) Bond at a ball game (where else). Betty was born Oct. 21, 1926 to Earl and Grace (Barkes) Bond, the fourth of eight children. Her mother and father named her "Hilda Ann" but when Grandma Barkes came to help out with the new baby, she did not like the name and it was quickly changed to "Betty Jo", but by that time the doctor had already gone and the name remained Hilda Ann on her birth certificate. Betty attended first grade at Goshen (Fox's Corner). The school house burned one morning and Betty grieved over the loss of her two new "penny pencils". School was finished in the church house there. The second grade was at Sprunica and then the family moved to Helmsburg, and she finished her schooling there. After graduating from high school in 1944 she worked for Grover G. Brown, the County School Superintendent at that time.

Dale and Betty Mathis

Dale and Betty were married Sept. 13, 1947 at her home with Reverend deGafferelly officiating. Jack Bond was best man and Joan Hoeany was bridesmaid. After the bride and groom had left on their wedding trip, along came an Electro-Lux vacuum sweeper salesman (Wilbur Sellars) just in time to sweep up all the rice. Just before the wedding was to take place, two bushels of grapes were delivered to Mrs. Bond, ready to be worked up. What a busy day!

While Dale attended Indiana University they lived with his mother until they could afford a home of their own. On Aug. 28, 1948 they were blessed with a beautiful baby daughter, Joyce Ann Mathis (Boulton). In 1952 they moved to Hope, IN, where Dale taught school and coached basketball. On Oct. 28, 1952 they were again blessed with a wonderful baby son, John William Mathis. In 1953 they moved back to Nashville and Dale continued to coach and teach school until his retirement in 1983. When both children were in school Betty was deputy clerk while Ralph Parsley was Clerk of the Brown Circuit Court. After Ralph's eight years in office, Millard (Mid) Thickstun was elected Clerk and Betty continued to work for him until his death in 1972. In May, 1972 Betty started working for Arressia Allender and the Brown County Abstract Company where she is still employed.

They are the proud grandparents of Melissa Anne Boulton, born Sept. 8, 1968 and Matthew Chasteen Boulton, born April 8, 1971 to Joyce Ann and Michael Roy Boulton; and Nathan Andrew Mathis born June 24, 1974 and Eliza Ann Mathis, born June 18, 1976 to John William and Amanda (Wallace) Mathis. *Submitted by Hilda Ann (Betty) Mathis*

GARY AND CHARLOTTE (MERCER) MCCLURG

Gary and Charlotte bought property on Little Fox Lake on Bittersweet Road in 1973. Eight years later they built a cabin to use on weekends and summer. In August 1985, the McClurgs built on to the cabin and permanently moved to Brown County from Greenfield.

Gary A. McClurg, born on March 21, 1939, is the son of Marcus and Mary Ellen McClurg. He was born and grew up in Carthage, IN, in Rush County. He served in the U.S. Army and was a paratrooper in the 101st Division. After serving three years in the Army including a tour of duty in Korea, Gary attended Ball State University, graduating in 1967 with a degree in Business Administration.

Gary and Charlotte (Mercer) McClurg; 1987.

Born on June 21, 1939, Charlotte grew up in LaGrange County in northern Indiana. She is the daughter of Samuel and Thelma Mercer. Charlotte attended Anderson University and graduated in 1961 with a degree in Business Education.

After graduation Charlotte began a teaching career in Carthage in 1961. She taught there for ten years and is currently teaching at Knightstown High School. This is her 29th year of teaching high school business subjects.

Charlotte and Gary were married in 1962 in Anderson, IN. They have always lived in Indiana. Before coming to Brown County in 1985, they lived in Knightstown, Carthage and Greenfield. Gary is a school photographer and takes athletic pictures and proms in his territory in southern Indiana and southern Ohio.

The McClurgs are busy with the activities at Little Fox Lake and they enjoy traveling. They are looking forward to participating in more Brown County activities in a few years when they retire.

MCCOY FAMILY - Migration from the stormy ridges of Kentucky's McCoy-Hatfield feud brought the Joel McCoy family to the Brown-Monroe County area. James, their fourth child of seven, grew up in a Brown County atmosphere usually described as primitive. His work as a farmer, logger, and carpenter was his education; and much work was required to raise the nine children born to him and Martha Ellen Fleener.

James and Martha, known as "Jim" and "Matt", were slight of build and their nine children followed the pattern - except for their second son, Lawrence, who was fair haired, fair skinned and robust. This family was humorous, quick-witted, sharp-tongued and loved practical jokes; growing up was considered an accomplishment in itself! Lawrence was often singled out (or so he said) because of his different stature and his good nature. Of course, he returned every indignity two-fold. Story-telling was family entertainment; and as the practical jokes and the results of them were described over and over, they became just that - stories! Therefore, there was much laughter intermingled with hardship of grubbing out a living for a large family in the wilds of Brown County. Lawrence McCoy learned early in life that hard work had its rewards and pushed himself to excel in everything he did, whether it be shucking corn, playing cornet in the local band or story-telling.

Martha Ellen and James McCoy   Ida Mabel and Lawrence McCoy

Lawrence proudly served as Bugler during World War I where he spent two years near Brest, France; and as a carpenter, he was assigned to the 35th Engineers to build railroad cars for transporting men, food, equipment and supplies to the war front. A poem he wrote states, "Oh, armies in the fields of France, we owe you gratitude; we see you haven't got a chance unless we send you food. We'll build more cars than all the wars will need to haul supplies; we'll build a train from here to Mars and lay the rails and ties!" Stories from this experience were told often, but even the most humorous contained regret that it had been necessary.

He married Ida Mabel Fleener on Oct. 20, 1919, a lifelong neighbor and one of seven daughters of F.E.V. (Fleming Elvin Volandingham) and Rebecca Savannah McClary Fleener ("Lannie" and "Vannie"). Lawrence and Ida purchased the farm where his father, James, was born and raised, then adjacent farmland until 220 acres and Brown County's largest dairy farm resulted. One tract was Ida's childhood home and had been owned by her ancestors since acquisition through Federal Land Grant.

After raising five daughters, Clarice, Geneva, Ruby, Dorothea and Wanda; then a son Lawrence Aaron, Lawrence and Ida sold the farm (which became Lake Lemon) and traveled extensively for several years. As Ida never learned to drive after the Model T, Lawrence motored through every state but Hawaii, much of Mexico and most Canadian provinces. At age 71, Lawrence drove to Alaska via the unpaved Alcan Highway. This trip and others were material for many interesting, humorous stories.

While farming, carpentry, owning a concrete business in Helmsburg and traveling, Lawrence was foremost a member and elder of the Church of Christ in Unionville; he also served as Director of Brown County Water Utilities which he helped organize, and as a member of the Trustee's Advisory Board. He constantly improved his mind and education through reading; he was an avid crossword puzzle fan and a good typist. He also did considerable McCoy genealogy research.

Ida Mabel Fleener McCoy died on Aug. 11, 1982, when Lawrence was 90 years old. Although crushed by the loss of his companion of 63 years, Lawrence's stories were enjoyed until Feb. 22, 1989, when he died at the age of 96. Lawrence had planned to live to be 100, and always claimed he was "born 20 years too soon." *Submitted by Ruby I. (McCoy) Clay, daughter of Lawrence McCoy*

MARIA JANE (SHERWOOD) MCCURDY - Maria was born on Oct. 16, 1853 in Ohio, the daughter of John and Comfort (Simons) Sherwood.

She was united in marriage to John McCurdy in 1872 and to this union were born Mary Alice and Leota. John McCurdy died in Ohio. Maria Jane later married John S. Foster (1835-1924) in Ohio on Jan. 12, 1890. To this union was born two daughters: Blanche (Foster) Sherwood and Nellie (Foster) Snider.

John William and Mary (McCurdy) Turner and daughter Eva Belle.

Maria Jane died October 1945, and was buried in the Greenlawn Cemetery, Nashville, Brown County.

Mary Alice was born on March 24, 1873 in Ohio. She was married on Jan. 28, 1891 for a short time to John Kent. No children. She then married John William Turner on June 29, 1895, and they had four daughters: (1) Lottie Marie Landers - (born Sept. 7, 1896 and died in October 1975), (2,3) twin girls born April 7, 1898 were Ruby Letha Derringer (died Aug. 29, 1949) and Pearl Lelia Schrock (died October 1964) and (4) Eva Bell Bennett (born Jan. 1, 1914 and died 1935).

Five Generations of Turners: Front: Thelma M. (Porter) Arvin, Lois M. (Porter) Sanders, and Audrey A. (Porter) Beasley. Center: William A. and James E. Porter. Back: James W. Derringer holding Janet; Mary (Derringer) Porter, Ruby (Turner) Derringer, Mary (McCurdy) Turner and Jane (Sherwood) McCurdy Foster.

Mary Alice, also known as Mollie, lived with Uncle Adam and Aunt Elizabeth "Lib" Porter Sherwood most of her life on Country Club road, and was known by the name of Mollie Sherwood. A lot of her records are under the name of Mollie Sherwood.

Mary Alice/Mollie Turner, age 72, passed away at the home of her daughter, Mrs. Ruby Derringer, in Bean Blossom on April 25, 1945, with burial in Bean Blossom cemetery. See John Wesley Turner.
Submitted by Mary (Derringer) Porter

CECIL HERBERT AND GLADYS MAYME (CHRISTIE) MCDONALD -
Cecil, better known as Herb or Herbie, was born on June 2, 1898, the son of Charles Kessler and Flora May (Rund) McDonald. Herb grew up helping his father in the grocery business and driving a huckster truck similar to a store on wheels.

In 1917, Herb left Kess and enlisted in the United States Navy. Shortly after finishing his training the armistice was signed. Instead of returning to Bean Blossom, Herb settled in Indianapolis and worked for a poultry house.

Herb McDonald

Herb met Gladys Mayme Christie (born Sept. 15, 1906 in Indianapolis) whom he married Aug. 13, 1930, Pine City, MN.

Herb, Gladys, and Jack, their son born in 1932, returned to Bean Blossom in 1933. Kess' (Herb's father) health had been poor for some time before his death in 1933. The store was also not in very good shape.

Herb bought a 1933 Chevy truck chassis from his brother Ival, who by this time had established a Chevrolet dealership in Nashville. Ival's son, Bill, continued in his father's business until around 1984.

Herb's huckster routes didn't change too much over the years. Many of his customers had been his dad's customers in earlier years. During most of these years Gladys worked in the store, and son, Jack, helped load the truck in the evenings after school. Jack later drove the truck in 1951 for about a year, before leaving home for the Air Force. Herb finally pulled his truck off the road in 1954.

Herb's first love was for the huckster route, he had worked for nearly 30 years on the road and felt that it was time to slow down and ease up a little. He continued to get up at 5:00 AM each morning, go to the store, put on a pot of coffee and wait for some of his early rising friends to drop in for conversation, tobacco, or a free cup of coffee.

Gladys, Jack and Herb McDonald

On Jan. 11, 1966, Herb was helping to take the store inventory when he became ill. He had suffered an aneurism and spent the next four months in the hospital recovering. He returned to the store in May 1966, Herb spent most of his time in the store talking to customers and visiting with old friends. He could remember everything about his early life, but from that time on had some difficulty remembering things that had happened yesterday or last week. His doctors had said that he might not be able to walk or care for himself after his stroke, but he was soon able to drive to the store and got along quite well.

In 1971 after a two month illness Herb died on Oct. 17, 1971; buried at Weeping Willow Cemetery at Bean Blossom. Gladys, along with Jack and his wife Nina Jo continued to operate the store. Gladys worked in the store regularly until she suffered a slight heart problem in 1984, then she decided to slow down a little. Today (1990) you can still find Gladys in the store helping from time to time, but even at age 83 she doesn't seem to have slowed down much.

CHARLES KESSLER AND FLORA MAY (RUND) MCDONALD -
Charles, known as Kess or Cass, was born on Aug. 8, 1876 to John Tom and Melvina (Mead) McDonald of Georgetown (Bean Blossom), IN. He was married to Flora May Rund (1878-1905) on March 7, 1898 and they had three children Cecil Herbert (1898-1971), Ival (1900-1975), and Jennie (1905-1918). Flora May (Rund) McDonald died on June 11, 1905 shortly after the birth of Jennie.

In 1891, Kess decided to go into business. He purchased a small building one lot north of what is now the intersection of State Roads 135 & 45. Part of that building is still standing today (1990). Kess traded a watch and a bicycle for a pair of mules and a spring wagon and began what is now known as McDonald's IGA.

Charles Kessler (Kess) McDonald

Kess bought some staple food including among other things salt, sugar, beans, flour meal, tobacco, spices, coffee, and tea, from Aaron Zody who also operated a grocery store in Bean Blossom.

Kess recognized the need of people in that day to have some kind of grocery delivery service. Many people lived out in the country with no convenient way to trade their small crops and poultry for other staples. Kess loaded his wagon and headed for the country to sell his products house to house. He would sell people products and would then buy their eggs, chickens, rabbit furs, and anything else that they had to trade for his products. He would in turn resell the items either on his route or take them to Indianapolis to trade on his two day trip there to restock his wagon. Kess continued in his huckster grocery business until his death on May 1, 1933.

Kess had been ill for quite some time and his son Herbie took over the family business shortly before Kess' death. Kess's other son Ival began an automobile sales business in 1923.

IVAL AND STELLA (COPE) MCDONALD -
Ival was born on Oct. 4, 1900 the son of Charles Kessler and Flora May (Rund) McDonald. Ival married Stella Cope on April 30, 1924. They had one son Bill McDonald who was born on July 6, 1931.

Ival began working for his father, who owned a general store in Bean Blossom, when he was just a youngster. His first permanent job was driving a Model T taxi for Jim Allison of Indianapolis for about three years from 1918 to 1921. His taxi route ran from Columbus to the railroad station in Helmsburg.

Ival's taxi job marked the beginning of 57 years devoted to automobiles. Ival began selling Overlands at Helmsburg from 1923 to 1925. In the very beginning Ival would take the train to Indianapolis buy an Overland, drive it back to Brown County and sell it for a little profit he would even take livestock and buggies as trade. Then he would get back on the train and go back to Indianapolis for another car.

Ival switched to Chevrolets when the Overland was no longer made. In 1926 he built a 40' x 50' building where the old livery stable had been in Nashville.

Ival was honored by the General Motors Corporation in June of 1972 for having completed 50 years as a Chevrolet dealer. After Ival's death on Feb. 26, 1975, his son Bill continued the business until it closed around 1985.

JACK HERBERT AND NINA JO (LEWIS) MCDONALD

Jack was born on March 20, 1932, the son of Cecil Herbert and Gladys Mayme (Christie) McDonald. Jack grew up helping his parents in their family grocery business in Bean Blossom.

While attending Indiana University, Jack met Nina Jo Lewis (1939) whose family had a general store in Lewisville, IN. Lewis & Co. was in business for over 100 years, before closing its doors in 1982.

Jack and Nina Jo married shortly after graduating from IU in 1961 and they moved to Indianapolis. The following summer Herb decided it was time to retire and turned the grocery business over to Jack and Nina Jo.

Soon they planned to build a new store building just north of Kess's and Herb's original store. That building was completed and opened in November 1962. At this same time the C.H. McDonald Grocery became McDonald's IGA.

In 1963, Jack and Nina Jo began their family. Diana Lynn was born on December 26th of that year. James Kessler came along July 9, 1965 and Michael Lewis was born on Aug. 27, 1968.

In 1970, the store was doubled in size and it was at this same time that Herb's health began to slide again and after a two month illness he died on Oct. 17, 1971. Jack, Nina Jo and Gladys continued to operate the store.

Nina Jo and Jack McDonald with Diana Lynn (center back) and Michael (left) and James Kessler McDonald (right).

In 1976, Nina Jo opened her own business, Village Real Estate in Bean Blossom. In 1989, Nina Jo joined the Century 21 Real Estate Company and became Century 21-Village of Bean Blossom.

Jack and Nina Jo's three children have all been actively involved in working at the store. Diana Lynn began working as a cashier after school, beginning in the fifth grade (1975). Diana continued working in the store throughout high school and on weekends and summers through college. On Nov. 24, 1984 she married Brent Lee Biddle of Sheridan, IN. On Feb. 1, 1988 Abigail Marie Biddle was born, the first grandchild for Jack and Nina Jo. Diana and Brent both graduated from Maranatha Baptist Bible College in Watertown, WI in 1990 with degrees in teaching, but they still continue to come back to Bean Blossom and help out at the store during the summer months, when not teaching. A second daughter was born Aug. 22, 1990, Hannah Jo Biddle at Watertown, WI. Diana now lives in Florida.

James Kessler (Jim) McDonald also helped out in the store during his high school years and while going to college. Jim graduated from Franklin College in Franklin, IN in 1987 and married Kathy Lynn Scrougham of Helmsburg on Oct. 3, 1987. Jim assumed managerial duties at the store in 1988. On Oct. 26, 1989 Jim and Kathy became the proud parents of Megan Elizabeth McDonald.

Michael Lewis (Mike) McDonald, Jack and Nina Jo's youngest son, also helped out in the store during his high school years, but his love for the outdoors and sunshine has since directed him into the construction business. Mike has a daughter Tricia Elaine, who was born on Jan. 4, 1989.

Jack and Nina Jo continue to be very active in community work, helping out with several local groups including Kiwanis, BPW, Board of Realtors, DAR, Brown County Youth Baseball, and the Weeping Willow (Bean Blossom) Cemetery Association.

The McDonald family will celebrate 100 years in the grocery business in 1991 in the same community.

JOHN AND MARY B. (ADAMS) MCDONALD

John (1817 to Nov. 13, 1894) and Mary B. Adams, born 1819, were married in Oldham Co., KY with the consent of her father, Joel Adams of Oldham County, in 1843.

In 1854 John and Mary McDonald arrived in Georgetown, known now as Bean Blossom. They came from Oldham County and brought with them four children: William (1844), John Tom (1846), Martha (1851) and Mary (1852). A fifth child, George, was born in Brown County in 1855. Their mother died Oct. 10, 1869 and was buried in the Unity Church Cemetery. Their father remarried on Sept. 9, 1870 to Sarah Reeves, widow of James Reeves. Sarah was a daughter of John L. and Anna Dew. Sarah and John McDonald had six children: Sarah E., Louis D., Mack, Hattie, Essie D. and Desdemona R. McDonald.

John Tom, child number two of John and Mary B. (Adams) McDonald, was born May 7, 1846. John Tom, a boot and shoe maker, married in Brown County, on Oct. 26, 1869, to Melvina M. Mead, daughter of Joseph and Rebecca Mead. The 1860, 1870, and 1880 census indicates Melvina was born in 1852, though the tombstone date looks like 1857. John Tom and Melvina McDonald had eight children: Ida, Fred, John, Edward S. (1870-1946), Charles Kessler (1876-1933) who married Flora May Rund, Samuel J. (1888-1957) who married Mary Elva Baughman, Nellie Opal (1887-1939) who married Sylvester Barnes, James William (1877-1939) who married Nellie (Huffer) Eaton.

It was Charles Kessler McDonald (Kess) who began the McDonald Grocery business in 1891 in Georgetown. Kess traded a watch and bicycle for a spring wagon and mule and began selling groceries house to house in the area. A short time later he opened the store—an enterprise which grew over the years with several generations of McDonalds contributing to its success.

MCGRAYEL FAMILY

James McGrayel, born in Mayo Co., Ireland on July 25, 1842, came with his brothers, John, Pat and Michael and their widowed mother, to Connecticut in 1845. After her death the brothers went to Lafayette, IN. James settled in Nashville, where he was active in Community affairs, serving in several official capacities. He was a Civil War veteran, serving as 1st Lieutenant in Regt. 22, Co. G. He married Lucy Jane, daughter of John and Elizabeth Clark Genolin, on Aug. 19, 1874. James died May 24, 1885; Lucy Jane, born Jan. 7, 1856, died April of 1938. Both are buried in Greenlawn Cemetery, Nashville. Their children were: Mary Elizabeth (1875-1875), James H. (1876-1878), John Anthony (Dec. 19, 1879-Jan. 10, 1953), Charles M. (Sept. 9, 1881-Feb. 10, 1919) and James Matson McGrayel (Feb. 2, 1885-Oct. 20, 1917).

John Anthony McGrayel married Della Griffitt, daughter of Dr. Reuben C. Griffitt, of Morgantown. They had three children, Margaret, Mary and James G. McGrayel.

Charles M. McGrayel married Catherine Maloney, a milliner, from Seymour, IN.

James Matson McGrayel married Ruby, daughter of Clark Campbell and Harriet Poling, on Oct. 27, 1909 in Nashville. Their children were: John Michael (Aug. 10, 1910-Oct. 9, 1916), Meredith Jane, born Nov. 2, 1912 (Mrs. Wm. Paul Rogers), Ruth Eloise (April 24, 1914-Aug. 31, 1986), Mrs. Vincent A. Sherwood, and William Harry McGrayel (April 17, 1916-Aug. 26, 1988). James Matson McGrayel and his family lived with his parents in the large white house, surrounded by pine trees, which later became the Singing Pines Motel. James Matson McGrayel, a school teacher, died at age 32, leaving his wife, Ruby, a widow at age 26 with three small children. Ruby died in June of 1967, she and James are buried Greenlawn Cemetery.

Meredith Jane, daughter of James Matson McGrayel and Ruby Campbell, married on Sept. 5, 1931 to William Paul Rogers, son of Cecil R. and Mildred Clark Rogers. Paul, as he was known, was born Jan. 17, 1912, died May 26, 1983 and is buried in Greenlawn Cemetery. Paul and Meredith Rogers had two daughters, Cynthia Caroline, born May 26, 1937 and Celia, born Aug. 22, 1945. Cynthia married James Louie Miller, son of Frances and Louie Miller. Children of Cynthia and James are Casey Lee, James Scott and Clark Rogers Miller. Celia married Dan Davis, Aug. 16, 1964 in Nashville. They divorced. Celia then married James Kraatz June 12, 1982.

Ruth Eloise, daughter of James Matson and Ruby Campbell McGrayel, married Vincent A. Sherwood on May 6, 1939, Hollywood, FL. Their children are Jane Antoinette and William Vincent Sherwood. Jane is unmarried; William married Linda Pane; their children are Michael, Maureen, Melinda Lee and Monica.

William Harry, son of James Matson McGrayel married Mary Elizabeth Cain on July 3, 1948. Their family consists of Charles Cain Greller, Mary's son by a former marriage and Lucy Jane, James William, Elisabeth Ann McGrayel. Charles Greller married Diana Seely in 1970. Their children are Matthew Charles and Sarah Kathryn. Lucy Jane McGrayel married Richard Snider in 1974. Their child is Jennifer Snider. Lucy Jane and Richard divorced and she married Ray Seyfried on July 19, 1987. James McGrayel married Christine Towne in 1982. Their children are Abraham Michael, Kate Kardynall, Hannah and David James McGrayel. Mary Elizabeth Cain McGrayel, widow of William Harry McGrayel, lives in Brown County as do all her children and grandchildren. (see THE GENOLIN FAMILY) (see THE ROGERS FAMILY) *Submitted by Meredith McGrayel Rogers*

ELMER LESTER AND MARY GENEVA (YOUNG) MCGUIRE -
Alfred McGuire, great-great-grandfather of Lester McGuire, was born in Montgomery, KY, in January 1812. His parents are not known, however it is said they came from Ireland. Alfred was married to Anne Jackson, and they settled at Howard Mill on Salt Creek. Alfred served in the U.S. Army during the Mexican and Civil Wars. He and Anne had 11 children, the seventh being Alfred Seralvo, Lester's great-grandfather. Seralvo was named for a small village in Mexico where his father had served during the Mexican War. Seralvo is married to Lucy Jane Hackett with whom he had six children. The eldest was Hugh, Lester's grandfather. Hugh was married to Laura Ellen McLary, the daughter of Sam McLary and Mary Ann (Branstetter) McLary. Mary Ann's father, Daniel Branstetter, entered 80 acres of land from the government in 1842. This land was in Jackson Township near Trevlac. Today, Lester and Geneva own and reside on 40+ acres of that entry. It is believed that descendants of Daniel Branstetter have lived on this portion of the farm since its entry.

Hugh and Laura McGuire had three children, the eldest being Lester's father, Roy Elmer. He married Ruby Pearl Hodges of Indianapolis, and they had five children: Elmer Lester, Thomas "Pat", Dorothy Jean, Norma Ruth, and Robert Lee "Sonny". Ruby was the daughter of Gilbert and Harriet Emaline (Beasley) Hodges.

During World War II, Lester served in the U.S. Army, European Theater, as a commissioned officer. He was recalled to active duty in 1952, serving in Korea, and remained on active duty until retirement as a Lieutenant Colonel with over 26 years service. Upon retirement from the Army he was employed by the Federal Supply Service, General Services Administration, in Washington, D.C. He attended Purdue University and the University of Maryland. He has numerous professional, civic and social affiliations.

Elmer Lester and Mary Geneva (Young) McGuire

The great-great-grandfather of Geneva, Banner Brummett, came from Kentucky to Monroe Co., IN, near Unionville. He married Eva Stephens. In 1823 he journeyed through the wilderness to what is now Nashville. He built the first log house there, laid out the plans for Nashville and ran a store. His daughter Charon, at the age of 19, married a widower, Isaac Cox near Unionville. Isaac had six children, and he and Charon had 11 more. Their daughter Martha married John Young and had six children. Courtland, the father of Geneva, married Estella (Sluss) Peterson. All of these ancestors are buried at Unionville. Geneva had four brothers and four sisters.

Geneva attended Indiana University and held a primary teacher's license. She taught and substituted over a period of many years, and has been active in Church and club work at all the locations where her husband was stationed.

When Lester retired from his Government career in 1979, he and Geneva moved to their new home at Branstetter Villa. They are the parents of Jacqueline Sue (McGuire) Kremer, and Joyce Lea (McGuire) Stuber. They are active members of the Nashville Christian Church and the Historical Society. *Submitted by Elmer L. McGuire*

REV. DANIEL AND JANE MCKINNEY -
Daniel and Jane (Henderson) McKinney, married Sept. 20, 1840, Brown Co., IN. Their families were early Indiana settlers. Daniel, son of John D.W. and Elizabeth (Mullis) McKinney, married March 5, 1818 in Bullitt Co., KY. Daniel's grandfather, Daniel, came ca 1780 to America, from Ireland with brothers, James and Archibald, probably to Virginia. Daniel settled in Pennsylvania; married Permelia Douthitt.

Jane, a daughter of Robert and Elizabeth (Taggart) Henderson; born April 22, 1825 in Jackson Co., IN. Elizabeth was married by her father, James Taggart, in 1821. She died 1825, leaving small daughters, Nancy, Rachel (Joseph Rice) and Jane. Robert remarried to Permelia Newkirk, were in Brown County by 1829 and had a large family. The Hendersons were in Montgomery Co., VA by 1766 and a descendant still owns the land on Roanoke Creek.

Rev. Daniel and Jane McKinney: ca. 1880

Daniel and Jane had 13 children; 11 born in Indiana; James 1841, Robert 1844, Elizabeth Jane 1845 died an infant, John D. 1846, William Preston 1848, Williamson 1851, Joseph Samuel 1853, Charles Marion 1855, Daniel Stewart 1858, George Taggart 1860 and Missouri Frances 1862.

Daniel and family were farmers on the 1850 census; in 1852 inherited 80 acres of land from James Taggart. Daniel started studying law, became a Justice of the Peace in 1853, serving three and one-half years; was offered a Law partnership with James Hester in Nashville and a seat in the Indiana Legislature but preferred ministry.

Daniel started preaching 1855, joining the Evangelical United Brethern Church Itinerary in 1856. The denomination, established in early 1850s led by Taggarts, Hamblens and Waddells; Daniel being one of the Taggart Church ministers. Jane accompanied Daniel on his ministries to surrounding counties.

In Brown County, the family lived amid relatives of Taggart, Henderson, McKinney, Hamblen, Rice, Mullis-Goforth, Wadell, McGee and Ayres until 1863. Daniel, Jane, sons and families, Daniel's grandmother, Geriah Mullis (remarried to William Goforth) and family, migrated to Shelby Co., IL. Daniel's parents, John and Elizabeth moved with their son, William, and family to Vermillion Co., IL, dying December 1863.

Daniel continued his ministry until spring of 1885, when he, Jane, sons and families and other relatives boarded an immigrant train to Harlan Co., NE. Daniel, Jane and families moved to Halford, Thomas Co., KS. They filed homestead claims and built prairie homes of Buffalo grass sod. They ministeried until Daniel's death.

Jane, a small, energetic lady, made quick decisions, her instructions were followed. She married at 15 years, had 13 children in 27 years, kept her family well clothed, did laundry by hand, made homemade soap and candles and other home cares, besides accompanying her husband. It was said she rested while cooking. Her birthdays were fondly remembered by her grandchildren and were celebrated with the first rhubarb pie of the season. Her birthday on April 22, 1890, was saddened by Daniel's death. Jane died June 1, 1909.

Samuel (Daniel's brother) and wife, Catherine, Daniel, Jane, five sons and families now rest in the Menlo, KS Fairview Cemetery. *Submitted by great-granddaughters Dolores McKinney Brenenstall and Ila Gatons Eckstadt*

JOHN AND ANNA MCKINNEY -
John D. was born Sept. 15, 1846 in Brown County, son of Rev. Daniel and Jane (Henderson) McKinney. The McKinneys and Hendersons were early Indiana settlers. Daniel and Jane served the Itinerary ministry in Brown and surrounding counties, a mobile life, but it and Brown County were fondly remembered by the family.

John's father, also studied law and politics and with the pre-Civil War unrest, kept aware of the social and political climate. The adults engaged in public speakings. John recalled debates held from train platforms and he engaged in debating his young peers.

John became a carpenter, an occupation he served well. He had a caring family sense, being from a large family and near-by relatives. His paternal grandparents lived with them at times.

Standing: Emery, Francis, Florence and May. Seated: Omar, John D. and Anna: ca. 1915.

In 1863, John, his family and other relatives moved to Shelby Co., IL and his parents continued the ministry. When a young adult, the lure of the west took John to Oklahoma before the land rush. He followed the buffalo hunters as a skinner, a dirty and weather endangering chore. He nearly lost his life and frosted feet from an ice storm. In southeast Kansas, John helped fell and use walnut trees to build an entire house. He felt lucky to not encounter the James Gang when they came across the line into Kansas to escape the Missouri Bounty hunters.

In 1873, John bought a family Bible in Des Moines, IA and kept family records; now a family treasure.

He returned to Illinois, marrying May 4, 1882, Anna Luella Jones; born Aug. 29, 1858, a daughter of Dr. James and Elizabeth (Johnston) Jones in Moccasin, IL. Son, Walter, was born October 1883.

The McKinney Boys (as John and his nine brothers were referred) were approached to become a circus attraction; instead, they with families, parents and relatives moved to Harlan Co., NE.

John and family moved to Bird City, KS; John was a welcome carpenter. A daughter, May, was born there in 1886. Other family members homesteaded in Thomas Co., KS. John's family joined them 1889. John learned a new construction; building a sod home, cool in summer and warm in winter. Their children born there were Francis, 1890; Florence, 1894; Emery, 1897 and Omar, 1899. Beloved son, Walter, died June 1889. They attended local church services and when a minister was unavailable, John helped lead the services.

The family moved to Fruita, CO 1907 and had a fruit orchard there for ten years before moving to Menlo, KS where John and Anna spent their remaining years. John and sons built a church and town hall. On his 18th birthday he was helping son, Omar, build his home.

Anna's family had a pioneering background. Her great-grandfather, Thomas Jones came from Wales, enlisting at age 16, in the Revolutionary War. The Jones and Johnstons were early settlers in Ohio. Anna lovingly cared for her family and added to the family income by sewing.

Anna died 1934 and John 1935 and are buried with family members in the Menlo cemetery. *Submitted by granddaughter Dolores McKinney Brenenstall*

WILLIAMSON MCKINNEY
- Williamson McKinney was born Feb. 24, 1851 in Brown Co., IN. He was the son of Rev. Daniel McKinney and Jane Henderson McKinney. He lived his first 12 years in Indiana when his father's itinerary ministering took the family to Shelby Co., IL, in 1863. Williamson died Sept. 12, 1926, at Salina, KS while visiting his niece, Mrs. William Cockey. With him was his wife, who was also ill and was unable to accompany the body of her husband back to his home for burial. William died of leukemia. He married Feb. 25, 1877, in Shelbyville, Shelby Co., IL, to Sarah Luella Adams, born Dec. 12, 1860 in Moultrie Co., IL. She was the daughter of Samuel W. Adams and Amanda Sackrider. She spent her early life in Illinois, uniting with the Methodist Church at Shelbyville. She remained a loyal member during her lifetime. Sarah died May 4, 1927 at the home of her daughter, Mrs. Henry Schroeder, in Colby, Thomas Co., KS. She was buried in Fairview Cemetery, Menlo, KS beside her husband and son.

Williamson and Sarah had four children: Charles, Daniel Webster, Ethel Amanda, and Frances. Williamson and Sarah spent their early married life in Shelby Co., IL. When Rev. Daniel McKinney, Will's father, and all the family moved to Nebraska in the spring of 1885, Will and Sarah and son Daniel filed for a homestead at McCook, NE and settled near Stratton, Hitchcock Co., NE. Later they moved to western Kansas.

William McKinney; Sarah Adams McKinney

By 1890, they had gone back to Illinois, to live in Chicago. There, Will was a weigh master. This meant he kept records of the grain as it was weighed in. When Sarah developed lung trouble, they returned to western Kansas where they bought a general merchandise store. After they sold the store, Will and Sarah spent their remaining years in Colby, KS. According to his obituary, Will was "a member of the Methodist church at Colby, KS. He was a man of strong character and integrity, ambitious and the last number of years a close observer and student of the history of mankind and the wonderful things of nature and received a great deal of enjoyment in conversing with others on this subject. Sarah had been in ill health for several months and had been lovingly attended at the home of her daughter Frances." They pioneered together and rest together. *Submitted by Mary K. Hubbard*

GEORGE W. MELOTT - On April 24, 1882 George Washington Melott (1861-1922) married Mary Alice Shepherd (1864-1893) in the home of her parents, William and Elizabeth (Hanvey) Shepherd of Pikes Peak, Brown County. George was a son of John D. Melott and Clarissa (Moore) Ewers. Mary Alice Melott died at age 29, leaving four children: Clara Nettie who died at age 12 of pneumonia; John William who died in a hunting accident as a young teenager; Pearl Mae and Virgil Ray Melott.

On April 18, 1897, George married, second, to Minerva Jane Keller, mother of two daughters. In March of 1904, George and Minerva Melott left Shelbyville, IN by train with his children, Pearl and Virgil Melott, her two children, Mae and Opal Keller and the children of their second marriage, Floyd E., Zella L. and Mary M. Melott. The family dog, Bounce, got off the train at a stop in Chicago and was never seen again. The youngest daughter of George and Minerva, Blanche B. Melott, was born on the Lewis farm three miles east of Jefferson, OK, where the family lived for 11 years.

George Washington and Minerva Jane (Keller) Melott

The George W. Melott family bought a farm from Luther Hodge on July 13, 1913. This farm had the Fairview District #78 school house on the southeast corner. It had two rooms and about 40 students with grades one through seven on one side of the building and grades eight through ten on the other side of folding doors.

The Melott family drove a buggy or carriage to the Church of Christ four miles east of the farm. The buggy horse, named Pet, was very high-spirited and would shy at anything that moved. She was a race horse, very pretty and high-stepping. One day Zella and Mary were driving to their home from Jefferson and Pet got scared of something and ran away. They didn't get her slowed down until they got home. Floyd and Zella used their little wagon to go to the pasture and pick up cow chips to burn in the stove. Their mother used to tell that her great-great-grandmother was kidnapped in England, along with other young women, and put on a boat bound for America where there were men who wanted wives.

Pearl Melott died May 21, 1911 at Anthony, KS, less than a year after her marriage to Virgil Scamahorn. She left a baby son Cleo.

Virgil Melott married Velma Hanan of Pond Creek, OK. Virgil died Dec. 15, 1964. Their children were: Vincent, Kenneth, George, Alice Maude and Nita Melott.

Mae Keller married Will Shepherd. She died May 15, 1912. Their children were: Wilma, Victor and Pearl Mae Shepherd.

Opal Keller proved up a claim near Clayton, NM. She lived alone in a small cabin built near the Scammerhorn family about 1912 to 1914 when she returned to Oklahoma. She married Erve Bules of Jefferson. She died Dec. 28, 1969. Their children were: Herschel, Berniece, Lola B. and Marvin Bules.

Floyd Melott married Clara Mae Parkinson of Texas. He died Oct. 18, 1972.

Zella Melott married Ivan Armstrong. She lives in Medford, OK. Their children were: Lloyd, Bruce, Alan Kent (A.K.) and Dennis Armstrong.

Mary Melott married Earl Lamb. She died March 28, 1989. Their children were: Malcolm, Yuki Dean and Earlene Lamb.

Blanche B. Melott married Arthur Watsek. She lives at Pond Creek, OK. *Submitted by Zella Melott Armstrong*

MERIDA FAMILY - Both Elbert Merida and his wife, Mary McCullen, were born in Tennessee in the 1820s. They came to live in Hamblen Township, Brown Co., IN about 1841. They later moved to a cabin north east of Nashville. They were parents of two sons and one daughter. Mary passed away about 1875. Elbert continued living alone in the cabin until his health failed. He was not an outgoing person, but was known for helping the poor. Regardless of weather he walked to Nashville frequently, carrying a basket of eggs to pay for needed supplies. In his home were the remains of some rattle snakes he had killed; he believed wearing a rattle snake belt helped ward off sickness. Elbert had never shaved nor been to a barber. Though he was a bit eccentric he was well-liked. He died of typhoid fever in 1910 at the home of son, John, in Helmsburg. Another son, Nathaniel, and a daughter survived.

This Nathaniel in later years lived alone in the Bear Wallow vicinity. While liking his father's life style he had many friends.

John Merida married Mary Chesher and they were parents of nine children. Both John and Nathaniel earned their living working with machinery in timber and farm work. John had a sawmill a short distance east of Bean Blossom at the present sight of the Drag Strip. They also made hickory chairs and wove baskets. The chairs were very solid but rustic looking. The woven seats of the chairs were "special" showing the basket making talent. The chairs were sold in Indianapolis and Kentucky.

John moved his family to northern Monroe County and continued the wood working projects there. One of his sons, Aurand, was named for a Brown County family, Aurndt, it is said.

One of John's sons, Arthur, died in 1981 in Brown County. He had married Patricia McKee and was a carpenter and also a member of the Methodist Church. Two sons James and John and three daughters Mary, Edith and Tina survived his passing. These children were a credit to the Brown County ancestors. One who had employed the children for summer jobs said they were very dependable workers. (Their father had an antique and fruit market business in Fruitdale and Bean Blossom - a good start.) *Submitted by Patricia Merida Smith*

NAT AND JOHN MERIDA

Nat who lived on the old home place on Bear Wallow Hill spent weeks hunting rattlesnakes and ginseng. He sold this to Eli Lilly for venom and medicine. This was how he made a living. He had a forked stick to catch the snakes which he put in sacks then at home he had pens built for them. His highest pay was $75.00 for a large rattler. That was good money in those days. He was never married. He had a sister, Moll that stayed with him when he was sick. Nat deeded the property to Eli Lilly at his death and later Eli Lilly deeded it to Indiana University.

John Merida a brother to Nat came from Spain to Mexico. Later he came to Tennessee. As a small boy he had a negro lady to raise him. He could print Merida and she supposed that to be his name. Later we found out there was a Merida Mexico. So we wondered about this, if it was his name or where he lived.

John married Mary Chessir and her people came from England. Her people were pleasant but Grandpa Merida's Mother and Dad were harsh and strict, rather solemn. My mother Verna Zimmerman (one of their children) always said Grandpa's people were Republicans and Grandma's people were Democrats. She said if there was that much difference in Republicans and Democrats she wanted to be a Democrat and she was.

John Merida had a furniture factory in Helmsburg and later moved north of Dolan, IN on the Dixie Highway. He had quite a success making hickory furniture and selling it in Martinsville. They also lived on the south side of Bear Wallow Hill while raising their family of seven children. They were Margaret (Maggie), Everett, Verna, Agnes, Sarah and Aurand and Alvin (all deceased).

They also lived at Georgetown, now called Bean Blossom and at Greasy Creek. It was told Grandpa Merida bought the first new Model T Ford in Brown County. He paid $750.00 cash for it. When he came to visit all of the kids came running down the lane and also followed them as they went home. *Written by Helen Zimmerman Sanders, daughter of Verna Merida Zimmerman*

HALLIE AND CLARENCE MERRIMAN

- Merrimans came from England to Virginia in 1600s. Francis, grandson of John Merryman, Goochland County (born 1700, thought to be descendant of John coming in 1638 to Charles City County) with his two brothers and an uncle served in the Revolutionary War. Francis was at Yorktown when Cornwallis surrendered. He married Mary Sublett and inherited a slave, "Hannah." In 1804 he left Powhatan County for Knoxville, TN. Dr. John Thomas Merryman, a descendant of Francis' father Thomas, died in the Civil War. His bible and diary are at the Confederate Museum in Richmond. Thomas wed the great-great-granddaughter of Capt. Thomas Harris, who was a member of the Virginia Company in 1609, a Burgess, and second in command of Indian War 1622.

Francis' son William married Catherine Hudiburgh and in 1828, to escape slavery, migrated to Indiana with Hudiburgh family, settling southwest of Morgantown. Catherine's grandfather, Thomas Hudiburgh, Sr., was a Baptist minister. The Hudiburghs were silk merchants in London, and their history dates back to 1650 as communicants of Church of Walloons, Canterbury. Their coat of arms indicates Crusaders. The family left Indiana for the west, and many of their descendants are in educational, religious, and medical fields.

Clarence and Hallie Merriman, 1942

William's son, William John (born 1833), married Rachel Franklin and moved to Three Story in Brown County about 1870. He had a large fruit orchard, panned for gold and precious stones. In GOLD AND DIAMONDS IN INDIANA, Indiana Department of Geology, William John is pictured along with his findings cited.

Nine children. Ira - Minister, Church of First Born.

Lewis (born 1860), William John's oldest son, married Frances Tutterow Reichard whose father George Tutterow settled on Carmel Ridge (1846). Frances first married Charles Reichard, son of Samuel who came to Carmel Ridge (1860s) and traded his wife's black horse for 40 acres. (Reichards and Tutterows originally from Germany.) Lewis' children: Harvey, Edgar, Clarence, Roy; stepchildren: Archibald, Martha, Joseph.

Clarence (born 1898) built his home on Bear Creek. He married Hallie Fleener (daughter of Artie and Amanda) whose earliest ancestor Johannes Flinner, horsebreeder from Wurttemberg, Germany, arrived in Philadelphia 1754. Johannes' descendants migrated to Maryland, Virginia and Washington Co., IN. Nicholas and son Milton came to Monroe and Brown Counties (1823). Milton married Eliza Jane Davidson. They had three children. He served Brown County as Constable, Associate Judge and County Commissioner and helped begin Old Settlers. His son, Dr. Joseph (born 1838), married Elizabeth Campbell. They had seven children. For a fee, he sometimes accepted farm products. He built the large house west of Needmore. (Dr. Joseph, brothers James and uncle Isaac were Civil War Vets.) Joseph's son James Martin (Artie's father) moved to Bloomington after raising his family. Artie's children: Charles, Dorothy, Hallie, Dora, Mary, Martin, Daniel, Bessie, Pearl, Louise, Beulah, Donald Everett.

Clarence and Hallie's children: Dora, Esther, Louise, Wayne, Franklin, George, Rosey, Clarence, Marie, James. (Picture - Hallie wears husband's shoes and socks, WWII custom).

Dora attended Branstetter (where teacher Ray Fleener was a distant cousin and her mother's teacher) graduated from Helmsburg High School (1947); worked at UCLA and in Indianapolis as a legal secretary. She has visited her ancestors' countries.

GEORGE VIRGIL MERRIMAN

- George was born in Brown County on Oct. 6, 1937, the sixth son of Clarence Merriman and Hallie Fleener. He attended the Brown County schools and joined the United States Marines in 1954. He was stationed at Camp Pendleton, San Diego, CA. At Escondido, CA, he met and married Jeanne Vanderheiden on June 6, 1959. They had three children: Joyce Jennine, Robert Doyle and Teresa Ann. They divorced and George came back to Indiana where he married Nadine Wall in December of 1966, daughter of Donald and Alberta Beaver Wall. They had two children, George Virgil and John Clarence. After Nadine's death in a tragic auto accident in October 1975, he met and married Tammy McCreary, May 18, 1982.

George Virgil Merriman

George moved from Indianapolis where he worked at Central Supply Company to Trevlac where he purchased a home from Nadine's parents. He installs gas and water equipment for Warford Gas.

Joyce Jennine was born March 22, 1961 and married Lawrence Ardoin. She lives in Louisiana and has two children: Sherrie and Christine Renee. Robert Doyle was born Jan. 8, 1960 and lives with his wife Lisa in Louisiana. They have several children. Teresa Ann was born April 18, 1962 and married Gaza Kovach. She lives in Louisiana and has one child, Gaza, Jr.

George Virgil was born in Marion County, graduated from Helmsburg High School in 1987 and lives at home.

John Clarence attended Brown County schools and lives at home, presently working with his father.

MARY AND CLARENCE MERRIMAN, JR.

- Clarence was born Aug. 31, 1941, in Brown County, the eighth child to his parents, Clarence Merriman and Hallie Josephine Fleener. He attended Brown County schools graduating from Helmsburg High School in 1959. He then attended classes at Indiana Central College and later studied computer technology. He has worked at National Starch in Indianapolis since 1963, having become a supervisor in 1967.

Clarence Merriman, Jr. eighth grade, December, 1954

He met Mary Kenipe and they married Oct. 9, 1971 in Johnson County. Mary is the daughter of Jennings Kenipe, Sr. and Goldie Gladys Ottinger Kenipe. Goldie was born in Lizton, IN. Mary has several brothers and sisters: Thelma Craig, Betty Barnes, Judith O'Neill, Pauline Tex, Jennings, Jr., Donald, Kenneth, William and Robert Kenipe.

Mary worked as a legal secretary before her marriage to Clarence. They live in a second home in Whiteland, IN which is solar-heated with a swimming pool. At present, Mary is a teaching assistant.

Mary and Clarence have two sons: Mark Allen and Michael Andrew.

Mark was born Feb. 9, 1972 in Johnson County. He graduated from Whiteland High School in 1990 as a valedictorian and plans to enter Purdue University in the fall.

Michael was born June 30, 1974 in Johnson County and is attending high school.

WAYNE AND LEODA MERRIMAN -

Wayne was born March 7, 1933, in Brown County. He was the fourth child of Hallie Fleener and Clarence Merriman. After graduating from Helmsburg High School, he met Leoda Burton at Chitwood's Grocery Store in Needmore and married her on May 31, 1952. He served in the U.S. Army 1953-1955 as Personnel Specialist. Leoda joined him in Oahua, HI where he was stationed. With this experience Wayne obtained a time keeping job at Allisons in Indianapolis where he lived for several years before purchasing a home in Quincy, IN. He retired from Allisons after working there for 30 years.

Leoda Ann was born Oct. 2, 1935 to Ernest Cleo Burton and Laura Eva Holding who lived near Needmore. Ernest's parents were Charles Burton and Lucy Offutt also from Brown County.

Wayne Merriman

Wayne and Leoda have four living children: Ralph Lee, David Wayne, Charles Eugene, and Susan Ann.

Ralph Lee was born May 25, 1955 in Marion County. He married Debra Neuhausel in 1975 and they divorced. They had two children: Benjamin Wayne and Rachel Leah. Ralph lives in Indianapolis and is a Hiring Supervisor for Nationwise Autoparts.

David Wayne was born Sept. 25, 1957 in Marion County. He married Julie McKamey in 1975 and they divorced. They had one daughter: Stacey Jo. David lives in Indianapolis and works for Hammons Lasers.

Charles Eugene was born Nov. 23, 1960 in Marion County. He married Debra Grider in 1983. He works at a Photo Lab in Plainfield. They own a trailer in Quincy, and are raising three daughters there: Crystal Eugenia, Jessica Cay, and Amber Michelle.

Susan Ann was born Sept. 26, 1968 in Marion County. She married Richard Green in 1986. Richard is employed at Shenandoah Industries. They are buying a home in Cunot, IN where they are raising their only daughter, Tove Josephine.

ALOYSIUS MEYER FAMILY -

Aloysius H., youngest of ten children of Joseph and Agnes Elizabeth Ehrbar Meyer, was born April 6, 1923. The Meyers came from Bad Griesbach, Baden in the Black Forest of Germany in 1880, settling in Cuyahoga Co., OH where Joseph met and married Agnes Ehrbar. The Ehrbars settled there in 1845, migrated from Untermelsenforf, Bavaria. The Ehrbars were foresters and farmers. The Meyers were foresters and bakers. The name Mayer was changed to Meyer by the immigration office in New York.

Following World War II and service in the 8th Air Force Fighter Command Aloysius completed his education, having attended Cambridge University, England, South Dakota State University and graduate study at Wayne University.

The wooded Hamblen Township forestry lands challenged "Al" and he made his home on his Wolfpen Hollow farm in 1951 while commuting to Indianapolis at his employment as District Inspector of the Eastern Railroad Association from which he retired in 1983.

On April 16, 1955 he married Ida Rose Caito daughter of August and Mary Ann Mercurio Caito. The Caitos were Banana importers and made the first Banana deliveries into Brown County. The Caito and Mercurio families migrated to Indianapolis from Termine, Sicily in the 1870s where they were fishermen with routes from Sicily, coast of Africa, Portugal, Corsica and return. Their main catch being sardines.

A.H. and Ida Rose Meyer

The homestead of August and Mary Ann Caito (Circa 1927) and the homestead of August's parents Philip Ardizzone Caito and Michelina Miceli Caito (Circa 1870) are on the Indiana Historic Register and are located in the Fletcher Addition on the Indianapolis South Side.

Aloysius and Ida Rose had four children, Mary Agnes born in 1956, Michael Anthony born in 1958, Joanne Marie born in 1959 and John August born in 1964. All of whom are married.

Aloysius was captivated by the "Hills O' Brown" in Hamblen Township. From 1951 and later with the help of Ida and the children the challenge of Soil Stewardship and re-forestration of the badly abused lands was utmost in their minds. The Meyers championed the Banner of Good Forestry Practices and considered themselves self made conservationists. Through the years they acquired over 800 acres of land, improving the timber stands, planting the abused and eroded lands. Now they have an enviable Tree Farm which has become a showplace for which they have received many awards. Including, the Tom Wallace Farmer of the Year in Brown County, Tom Wallace Grand Award in Kentucky and Indiana, Conservation of the Year Award, Buffalo Riders Award by our Department of Natural Resources, both Johnson County and Brown County Conservation Farmers Awards, Distinguished Service Award from Johnson County Soil and Water Conservation District and the Mid-Central States Tree Farmer of the Year.

Their Tree Farm was an educational tour place for many years for various education, forestry, conservation and youth groups. Aloysius is a founder and original chairman of the Hoosier Heartland Association of Soil and Water Conservation Districts; also, The Indiana Forestry and Woodland Owners Association.

CARL AND IDA ALICE MILLER -

Hezkiah Deckard, married to Bashie Pennington, grandfather and grandmother of Mary Alice Deckard, came to Brown County about 1839. Three Deckard brothers (Peter, Michael and Jacob) arrived in America from Lorraine, France in the year 1775. Jacob Jeckard was the grandfather of Hezekiah Deckard, born in 1822.

Mary Alice Deckard married Daniel Miller April 9, 1882. They had four children—Carl, Carrie, Kiah, and John. They lived on Miller Ridge where they had a truck farm.

Carl Miller married Ida Alice Carter, daughter of Thomas and Susan Carter of Story, in 1904. They had nine children—Clyde, Glen, Leoma, George, Raymond, Lorene, Wayne and twins, Jurene and Josephine. They lived in the holler below Miller Ridge. Carl and Ida raised vegetables, which they canned and sold in town. The labels read "Miller and Sons." They also took fresh vegetables and fruit to sell in Bloomington. Hogs were raised for butchering, the ham and bacon smoked and sold to stores and the Graham Hotel in Bloomington. It would take Carl and Ida two days by horse and wagon to go to and from Bloomington to sell their goods and get supplies that were needed.

Top Row: Ida Alice Miller, Clyde Miller, small child Wayne Miller, Carl Miller. Front: Lorene (Miller) Callahan, Raymond Miller, George Miller.

The Millers bought the Alwine Place in 1928. It was about a mile down the holler, a quarter mile from Browning School, which the children attended.

Carl Miller served as County Assessor for 16 years. He rode horseback to get around to all of the farms and homes.

As a child, Josephine remembers going to church at Elkinsville and Crooked Creek by horse and wagon. Her Daddy would fill the wagon with hay and her Mother put in comforters for the children to sit or sleep on along the way.

Ida Alice passed away in 1936 at the age of 48.

The family had very special neighbors—Fred and Bell Thickston. The Miller children have very fond memories of them. They helped watch over the children after their Mother passed away. Bell would walk over through the field and yell to us until someone answered that everything was all right. She would do this three or four times a day when she knew Carl was away for the day and school wasn't in session.

Bell also watched over Lorene, Wayne, Jurene, and Josephine when heavy rains caused the creek to rise while we were in school. They would take them to their home and keep them there until it was safe enough to return home. Then Fred would get the horse and take each child, one by one, until all were safely across the creek.

Bell always remembered birthdays with a gift, that was always special.

In 1939 Carl married Jessie Furgeson, a widow with seven children. They had one son, Donald. Carl passed away on Christmas Day, 1952.

The families remembered from Browning School are: Deckard, Bruce, Crider, Henderson, Axsom, Lucas, Fulk, and George.

The ground on which the Millers' made their living now belongs to the State as part of the Hoosier National Forest. The remainder is under water as part of Lake Monroe. Submitted by *Josephine Miller Aubin*

DARRELL AND CATHERINE MILLER -
Amzy Miller, grandfather of Darrel Miller, moved to Illinois from Holmes Co., OH in the late 1800s. Amzy was an Amish farmer. He married Anna Hershberger, who was also Amish. They had nine children.

The next to the youngest child, Elmer A., an Amish farmer in Arthur, IL was born in 1918. He married Theda Maydell Strader of Champaign, IL in 1947. Theda's father, Earl Strader was born in 1904 in Oakland, IL. Earl was a farmer and also worked for the University of Illinois in horticultural research. Earl married Lucille Brading in 1923. Lucille was born in 1901 in Oakland, IL. Earl and Lucille had two daughters, the youngest was Theda. Theda married Elmer Miller and they had five children: Larry, Darrel, Judy, Scott and Tim.

Darrel was born on April 6, 1951 in Decatur, IL. He spent his childhood growing up on a grain and livestock farm in Arthur, IL. Upon graduation from High School he attended Southern Illinois University where he completed work on a degree in Agronomy. In 1974 he attended Florida Bible College, then went on for further study at Grace Seminary in Winona Lake, IN.

Catherine (Cassell) Miller is the daughter of Edward H. Cassell and Kathleen (Fuhrman) Cassell. She was born on Feb. 12, 1952 in Freeport, PA, the second of four children: Connie, Catherine, Edward and Harvey.

Edward H. Cassell was born in 1918 to Harvey and Mary Rick Cassell of Freeport. Edward H. worked as an Engineer for the Pennsylvania Railroad for 30 years. Edward's father, Harvey, was also a railroadman. Kathleen (Fuhrman) Cassell was born in 1918 to Charles Fuhrman and Anna Martina (Kerr). Kathleen attended Beauty School upon completion of high school and worked in her own shop for several years. The Fuhrman family lived in Freeport where Charles worked as a paymaster for Allegheny Ludlum Steel Mill.

Darrel Miller Family: Chris, Mark, Brett, Michael and David; December, 1989.

Catherine grew up in Freeport and spent much of her time in or near the Allegheny River. Upon graduation from high school she attended the University of Pittsburgh and received a degree in nursing. Then she attended Grace Seminary in Winona Lake, IN and received a certificate in Biblical Studies.

Darrel and Cathy met in Winona Lake, IN, while attending school. They were married April 2, 1977 and moved to Chattanooga, TN. While in Chattanooga, Darrel worked as a Painting Contractor and Cathy at a local hospital. They were involved with a local church and hoped to one day get into the ministry full-time. In October, 1981 they received a call from Village Missions, a rural missions organization, concerning a church in Brown Co., IN that was looking for a pastor. Darrel had visited Brown County State Park as a child with his family so he was familiar with the area.

In November 1981, Darrel, Cathy and their 20-month old son arrived in Brown County at Cottonwood Church. The following month another son arrived at the Miller home. The Millers' have five sons: Christopher James, Mark Andrew, Brett Scott, Michael Paul and David Victor. The Miller family all agree—growing up in Brown County has its special joys and indeed is a wonderful privilege.

FRANCES MILLER FAMILY -
Frances was the oldest daughter of Thomas Novellett Messina and Nellie her mother. She had four sisters and two brothers. One brother died before he was one year old. Her mother's parents, James L. Rickard and R. Mina, moved to Brown County in 1928, the same year her parents moved here from Kankakee, IL.

Her father came to the United States when he was 17 years old, from Italy. A brother came with him and was killed in World War I. She never knew any of her father's family. Her mother was from Tennessee.

Her folks bought a farm off Salt Creek Road, which used to be called Bay place. She and her sisters and brother went to Brown School on Salt Creek. She married Louie Miller in 1930, son of John and Myrtle Miller. To this union were born 13 children, Norma, Mary, Vivian, Margaret, James, Gerald, Kay, John, Brenda, Dean, Steve, Peggy and Kevin. Margaret was killed in a car accident in 1943, and Dean was killed in a car accident in 1964. He was a senior in high school.

Frances and Louise Miller, 1960

They raised their family on Miller Road. Gerald and Kevin still live on this road on acreage from the homestead. Tobacco was the crop they raised to sell. They had their own milk cows, hogs and chickens. They always had a large garden, Frances canned many quarts of fruit and vegetables.

Frances made all their butter and cottage cheese. She washed on the board until their first son was born. Louie bought a gasoline washer for her and life was so much easier. He was employed at Cummins Engine Co. for 29 years. He died in 1971 with cancer.

Electricity was made available in 1949. What a blessing, no more lamp chimneys to clean, or filling kerosene lamps. Louie loved to hunt and fish and kept meat on the table for his family. The children had to walk to school and take their lunches. There were seven in school at one time. In 1956, Frances went to the commissioners meeting and asked if possible, for their road to be accepted into the county road system. The commissioners gave their permission, and .526 mile was taken over by the county. The school bus came, and a mail route created.

Frances' father was Catholic, she and one sister had gone to a convent in Bourbonnais, IL, before moving here. There was no Catholic church here, her mother had been raised a Protestant, so they went to Clarks Baptist Church on St. Rd. 46 when possible.

Her husband, mother and father, grandmother and grandfather, son Dean and daughter Margaret, are all buried in Nashville, Greenlawn cemetery. *Submitted by Frances Miller Hiatt*

MAURICE AND MARIANNE MILLER -
The Miller family first came to Indiana in the early 19th century. The parents of William B. Miller emigrated from Lancashire, England soon after William was born in 1812. They settled in the coastal area of America's New England. Some years later William married Sarah Gullett (born 1813), a Delaware native, and brought his young bride to southern Indiana, settling on Hogans Creek in Dearborn County. There he built their home and a grist mill out of the fossilized limestone found in the area. The house is still being used almost a century and a half later.

Rheuben H. Miller was born in the stone house on Hogans Creek in 1854. After helping in the family mill as a young man he enrolled in the Ohio Medical College at Cincinnati, graduated in 1876 and began the practice of medicine in Friendship in Ripley County. While there he married Sarah Elizabeth McGee of Cross Plains. To this union were born two sons, Herbert and Harry, both of whom later became pharmacists.

After Herbert had graduated from Moores Hill College and married Clara Mae Ward, a native of Switzerland County, Dr. Miller moved his family to Cross Plains, where he continued his practice of medicine, and where Herbert opened a drugstore in the year 1899. Here in the large house that served as home, doctor's office and drugstore Herbert and Clara raised their four children: Charles (born 1912), Nina (born 1914), Maurice (born 1916) and Herbert, Jr. (born 1923).

Both doctor and son were successful in the practice of their professions. But Cross Plains had no high school, and when Charles graduated from the eighth grade Herbert moved his family to Nashville, Brown Co., IN where a high school and an established drug business awaited.

In 1926 Doctor Miller and wife followed the elder son to Nashville where he continued his medical practice. Both of them died in 1930, Sarah in May and Rheuben in December. They both lie buried in the cemetery behind the Cross Plains United Methodist Church.

In March, 1947 Herbert Miller was injured fatally in an auto accident near Elwood, IN. Maurice, a pharmacy school graduate, assumed the operation of the Miller Pharmacy until it was sold in 1972. Clara died in March of 1977. She and Herbert are buried in the Greenlawn Cemetery at Nashville.

In the meantime the four children of Herbert and Clara Miller had married into Brown County families. Charles, a civil engineer, married Mae Crabtree. They raised seven children. Charles died in 1978. Nina married Keith Taggart. They had three children, one of whom died in infancy. Nina died of leukemia in 1985. Herbert, Jr. married Cora Louise Murphy. They maintain their home in Nashville. Maurice married Marianne Ruth Bessire, daughter of Dale and Ruth Bessire, in 1939. They live in the Nashville house they built in 1940. There are four children, ten grandchildren and six great-grandchildren. John has Sandra (Freshour), Greg, Sara (Balcerak) and Ryan; Susie Roush has Kevin and Craig; Stephen has Jill and Jeffrey; and Marilyn Rudd has Aaron and Andy.

The Millers have followed the Methodist tradition from their time in England, William having built the Mount Tabor Methodist Church near Dillsboro in 1854. Their faith has brought them to the present moment in history.

MINK FAMILY - Harvey Thompson Mink came to Indiana as an infant in 1870. He was born near Barboursville, KY while his parents were traveling to Indiana from Virginia. His father, Thompson Mink, was born in Ashe Co., NC in 1815. In 1837 he married Rhoda Plummer of Grayson Co., VA. With one or two children the Minks left North Carolina and traveled along the Virginia-Tennessee border, eventually residing in Jonesville, VA. Rhoda died a month after their ninth child was stillborn (1860).

Thompson then married Nancy (Andis) Taylor, widow of George, and mother of Mattie and Pat. When Pat was about 12 he ran away and wasn't heard from again. Thompson and Nancy had three children (Susan, Samuel, and Harry) at Jonesville. Leaving behind sons David and William, who were married, and the graves of five or six children, the parents and remaining children came to Indiana settling near Noblesville in Hamilton County. Nancy died in May 1875. Harvey, who was four, and Harry, about seven, were cared for by their father and older sisters, Caroline, Jane, Mattie and Susan, until the boys were grown.

Harvey Thompson Mink and wife Louellen (Richardson) Mink

Harvey met Louellen Richardson while they were working on adjoining farms south of Glenns Valley. They were married at the home of Louellen's great-aunt and -uncle, Will and Cymentha (Fleener) Richards. Harvey was 22 and Louellen 15 years of age. Louellen was the daughter of William Mack Allen and Permelia Jane (Peoples) Richardson. Mack's parents were Jeremiah and Mary Ellen (Fleener) Richardson of Monroe County, and the Fleeners were from Brown County, Mary Ellen being of Aaron Fleener's family. Louellen lived in Brown County in her childhood.

Harvey and Louellen lived in Indianapolis 21 years but around 1920 they moved to eastern Brown County in Washington Township. They gathered with their neighbors, the Hopkins, Rileys, Grahams and others and had square dances, taffy pulls, picnics, suppers, songfests and visiting for entertainment. These were "horse and buggy days"—and people walked a lot, too! Horses were used to plough gardens and farm land but Brown County soil was not well adapted to farming. Tobacco seemed to do well so there were several tobacco fields and barns.

Though their stay in Brown County was rather short, since the Minks moved to Shelby County in 1922, their family connections and friendships made it a much-remembered place; and in later years they enjoyed attending the Brown County Reunions at Garfield Park (Indianapolis) where they could have contacts with relatives and friends and reminisce about Brown County and its good people.

Harvey and Louellen died at Bloomington, he in 1954 and she in 1951. Both are buried at Mt. Pleasant Cemetery near Glenns Valley in Johnson County. *Submitted by Esther Mink*

MAY (ROBERTS) MONROE - May, born 1909, was the oldest child of Nicholas Roberts and Cora Simons. Nicholas was one of ten children of Suzanne Petro and George Melvin Roberts, and was a twin to Otha. In 1908, he married Cora who was one-quarter Cherokee Indian, descended from the branch of the tribe still found in North Carolina. They had four other children: Edell (1911), Wayne (1912), Hazel (1914), and Charles (1916).

George Melvin and Suzanne (Petro) Roberts

Just before Charles was born, Nicholas and Cora Roberts established the area now known as Camp Roberts by constructing two houses—one for themselves and one for Johnny Roberts, married to Cora's sister, Samaria. Both of these houses were connected to the famous Clarence Roberts case. Clarence, a nephew to Nicholas and Cora, was thought to have died in a fire in 1970, but a body found several years later in another fire was also declared to be Clarence. The location of the second fire was one of the original Camp Roberts houses built by Nicholas. The other house was burned in a re-enactment of the fire made for a television program about the case.

As they farmed, Nicholas and Cora also ground grain and operated a sawmill. Cora was the head sawyer and she also drove a Model T Ford truck in the creekbeds, which were often in better condition than the roads. The truck had to be backed up the steep hills of Brown County; otherwise gasoline would not flow to the engine!

Because Nicholas was thought to be very trustworthy, Brown Countians asked him to haul groceries into the area for them. Nicholas soon expanded his business to include the delivery of ice and coal throughout the County. Many projects Nicholas worked on are still in operation. He helped build Camp Atterbury in the northeast part of the County and moved several log houses from southern Indiana and Kentucky to the Conner Prairie living history museum at Noblesville, IN. He hauled the materials for the construction of Nashville's Village Green Building from the Helmsburg railroad station and built the June Gray cabin near St. Agnes Chapel on St. Rd. 135 North.

In 1924, he moved his family to Franklin and Johnson Streets in Nashville so that two of his daughters could begin high school. May Roberts Monroe continues to make her home at that Nashville location. Prior to moving to town, they had most recently attended Clark Elementary School on Old State Road 46, transported there and back each day by a horse-drawn covered wagon driven by their Uncle Otha.

May married Boyd Monroe in 1927, and bore two children: George Emerson (1928) and Mary Agnes (1930). George is a clinical psychologist in Evanston, IL and Mary Agnes is a client at Developmental Services Inc., in Columbus, IN. May has five granddaughters and six great-grandchildren.

May began working at The Brown County Folks Shop during the Depression, and filled the roles of buyer and assistant manager until her retirement in 1974. In the 1930s, together with her two sisters, she owned and managed the town's only movie theater, the Melodeon Hall, located on West Main Street. She continues to be active in the community through her participation in the Brown County Historical Society, Pioneer Women, Business and Professional Women, and the Nashville Christian Church. *Submitted by Merle and May Monroe*

BENJAMIN FRANKLIN AND REBECCA (BREECH) MOORE - Tobias Moore, born 1761, died March 18, 1839, born on the "south bank of the Potomac River," was the grandfather of Benjamin Moore. Tobias at age 17 was at Ten-Mile Creek in western Pennsylvania. In the American Revolution, Tobias substituted as an Indian spy in 1778 for his brother John. He was in the Crawford Defeat at Sandusky and slightly wounded. He also served at Jansetta Fort and Jackson Fort, PA. After the war he moved to Lexington, KY, and from there to Brown Co., OH. His wife was Elizabeth. Their fifth child was Solomon, born 1795, died Oct. 19, 1856.

Solomon Moore moved to Southeast Ohio where he married Mary Truax whose father was also a Revolutionary soldier. There is evidence in the Truax family that there was an ancestor of pure Turkish blood. Solomon moved to South Bethany, Brown County with all his family except Benjamin. Solomon and his wife are buried in the Bellsville Cemetery.

In 1850, having been married in Ohio, Benjamin Moore and his wife Rebecca Breech, born July 4, 1828, with their two children, Samuel and Mary Ellen, came down the Ohio River from Wheeling, WV, and moved to Bellsville, Brown County. He entered a farm of 100 acres from the Federal Government. (One of his crops was tobacco.) Reuben and Sarah Jane were born in Brown County.

Benjamin Franklin Moore   Rebecca (Breech) Moore

Rebecca had been told that her great-grandfather had been the captain of a ship that with all its crew was lost at sea. The trustee of his son, Thomas, changed his name from Beech to Breech to deprive him of his fortune.

Thomas, Rebecca's grandfather, migrated from England to Pennsylvania. From there he crossed the Allegheny Mountains in a wagon train to eastern Ohio. His son, Simeon Breech, was Rebecca's father.

Simeon Breech, born 1778, died 1874, spent his early years in central Pennsylvania and moved to Belmont Co., OH. He served in the War of 1812. His wife, Mary Miller, born Sept. 30, 1792, died Dec. 19, 1850 was of Dutch and Colonial ancestry. After the death of his wife, he came to live with his daughter, Rebecca.

Rebecca did not learn to read until Samuel, her first child, taught her after he started to school. She was extremely near-sighted and could not read without glasses. A very intelligent woman, who loved poetry, she made a scrapbook of articles she wanted to save, including articles of Sam's ministry. Buried in the Bellsville Cemetery are Simeon Breech and Benjamin and Rebecca Moore.

Samuel became a minister of the Christian Church. At the first Christian Church of Denver, CO, he had the largest membership at that time of any of the denominations. When his church was at Hagerstown, MD, he was visiting minister at the President's church. President Garfield was present. The ladies of the church presented Samuel with flowers that he sent to his mother, Rebecca, in Brown County. President Garfield was shot soon after.

Samuel and his wife, Nanie J. Thomas, had two sons, Howard and Frank, who became doctors. After graduating from medical school, Howard went to Germany for further study. There he attended the same Masonic Lodge with Wilhelm II, Emperor of Germany. Frank Moore graduated from medical school with honors. He practiced in Danbury, CT. When he visited the Tiltons in Nashville in the early 30s, his son, Howard, was in school at Illinois University.

Reuben and his wife Edith Lawless from Brown County had one daughter, May, who married Otis Limpus. They had one son, Robert, who at the age of 22 earned his doctorate in English from Chicago University. He was Professor of English and Dean of the department at Western Michigan College.

Mary Ellen, born April 4, 1848, died June 21, 1929, married Emanuel Haghn Moore (Mohr), born September 1846 and died at the age of 42. They set up housekeeping at Greeley, MO. Their children were Edmond, Linnie, Clara, and Frank. After her husband's death, she moved to Moore's Hill, IN, where her children were in school. Linnie and Clara were interested in music.

After her children were married and her husband had died, Mary lived with her mother. She took care of her through her last years. Rebecca was confined to her bed for four years. She was 94 when she died in 1919.

Edmond Laban, Mary's older son, married Clara Josephine Schabel of Moore's Hill. They had one son, Earl, who graduated from Purdue and had a position with Bell Telephone in Indianapolis until he retired.

Linnie May Moore married Rev. Stanton Morrow. At one time he was minister at the Broadway Methodist Church, Indianapolis. They had one daughter, Hilda, who died with pneumonia in her junior year of college.

Benjamin Franklin (Frank) Moore married Bessie Davis. He had a grocery store in Columbus. Their one son, Reynolds, had no children. His work has been with Cummins.

Ruth Katherine Tilton on bed made by Simeon Breech father of Rebecca Moore.

Clara married Joe Seal. Their children were William Dale and Mary Helen. Dale married Margaret Haley. He graduated from Purdue University in electrical engineering and worked for the Indianapolis Power and Light Company until he retired. He held a very responsible position. They had two children, Barbara and Thomas William. Barbara married Joseph Hilton, dentist in Florida. In World War II, Tom served in the Air Force at Thule, Greenland. He worked in electronics at Naval Avionics until he was killed in an automobile accident. His two sons, John Thomas and David William Seal, seem to have inherited their father's and grandfather's talents. They both graduated from Poly-Tech.

Mary Helen Seal, Clara's daughter, studied at Arthur Jordan Conservatory. She was a public school music teacher in the Marion County Schools.

Benjamin and Rebecca Moore's youngest daughter, Sarah Jane Moore, married James Lewis Tilton. Their grandchildren will never forget the memorable, good times spent overnight at Aunt Mary's and great-grandmother Rebecca's house, nor playing "Fox and Geese" under the pines in the snow. *Submitted by Ruth Tilton*

HARVEY MOORE FAMILY - Harvey is first found in Brown County records on Oct. 10, 1867 when he married Sarah Jane A. Neal. His gravestone shows that he served in the Civil War in Co. C, 186th Ohio Infantry. He evidently did not move to Brown County with his parents, Timothy and Catharine Moore, who were living in Washington Township by 1860. Harvey Moore (June 10, 1841-July 2, 1906) was born Noble Co., OH.

Harvey and Sarah Moore had 11 children: (1) William Isaac Moore (1869-1923), (2) Rachel E. (1870-1898), (3) Emma Ann (1872-1957), (4) James W. (1874-1924), (5) Mary Ellen (1876-1949), (6) Rosa Cordelia (1880-1942), (7) Rena (1884-1967), (8) Artie (1887-1918) the first boy from Brown County to be killed on the battlefields of France. (9) Estella (1891-1984). Two Moore children died as infants and are buried next to their sister Rachel in Lanam Cemetery, Brown County.

William Isaac Moore, first child of Harvey and Sarah Moore, married Minerva Jane (Followell) Moore on Nov. 25, 1894. Minerva had married John Moore in 1892; they divorced. William Isaac and Minerva Moore had seven children: (1) Minnie (Alltop), (1892-1966), (2) Edell Rachel (Ford) (1895-1981), (3) Roy (1901-1986), (4) Ruth (Snyder) (1902-1974), (5) Hazel (Dunnick) (ca. 1907-1973), (6) Sarah Esther born ca. 1909, (7) Frank Moore (1911-1975). Minerva and William died within two weeks of each other, in 1923. They are buried in Bean Blossom Cemetery.

Front: Aunt Hazel Dunnick, Mildred Wilkerson Moore and Dad, Roy Moore. Back: Aunt Edell Ford, Aunt Minnie Alltop, Uncle "Buck" Frank Moore, Aunt Ruth Snyder, 1957.

Roy Moore, third child of William and Minerva, was born Feb. 16, 1901. He married Etta Marie Beauchamp, born March 21, 1911 at Spinook, OK. They had seven children: Geraldine (Ping), Leroy, Betty (Graham), Billy, Marietta (Henderson), Lula Pearl "Dude," Donna (Petro). Leroy, Billy, "Dude" and Marietta live in Brown County. Roy Moore married second to Mildred Wilkerson who also lives in Brown County.

Geraldine, first child of Roy and Etta Marie Moore, married Bryce Ping on June 1, 1947. They had eight children: Gloria Starr (Reitzel) born 1948; Gerald Bryce born 1949; Rebecca Sue (Simpson) born 1951; Betty Ann (Compton) born 1952; Anita Kaye (Owens) born 1953; Lois Faye (Steinberger) born 1954; Kenneth Dwight born 1958; Edwin Paul born 1961.

On Aug. 11, 1963 Geraldine (Moore) Ping died in a car wreck on Mauxferry Rd. in Bartholomew County, a quarter mile from home. She is buried at New Bellsville Cemetery in Brown County. Four years later Gerald Bryce Ping, aged 17, died in a car wreck also. He was driving with his cousins Larry and Jerry Moore. He is buried at New Bellsville Cemetery near his mother.

The Moores of Brown County have seen a lot of hardships and a lot of joys, but they are still prospering. *Submitted by Rhonda Owens*

JIMMIE D. AND VIRGINIA R. MOORE -
Jimmie was born in Allen Co., KY, March 14, 1930. He married Virginia Ruth Fleener who was born in Brown County Dec. 29, 1932. Jim graduated from Helmsburg High School in 1949 and Virginia in 1951. They are parents of (1) James Dale Moore born at Camp Atterbury Sept. 19, 1951, (2) Jeffery Curtis Moore born at Franklin, IN March 21, 1957, (3) John David Moore born at Franklin, IN April 2, 1960. The Lord has blessed them with grandsons: Todd Jamison Moore born July 17, 1974 and Scott Alexander Moore born May 19, 1976 who are sons of James Dale and Beth Ann Collett Moore who was born Jan. 5, 1952. Also Joshua Daniel Moore born Feb. 14, 1982 son of John David Moore and Connie Sue Warren. One step-grandson, Ryan Scott Pool born March 23, 1982, son of Brenda Lee (Biles) Moore (born July 29, 1965), wife of John David Moore.

Jimmie D. and Virginia R. Moore

Jimmie moved to Brown County, Hamblen Township in 1945 at age 15 with his parents Arvel J. and Fannie F. Moore (originally from Allen Co., KY).

Virginia is the daughter of George R. and Anna E. (Campbell) Fleener from Trevlac, Brown County. Jimmie served in the U.S. Army during the Korean War with 8166th A.U. Sendai, Japan.

Jimmie and Virginia operated a grocery store in Peoga from 1958 to 1978. They now own property on Mt. Moriah Road, Hamblen Township. They are active in the Mt. Olive Methodist Church which is located in Brown County at Peoga.

LEVI JOHNSON MOORE -
Michael Moore, (1787-1847) was the father of Henry, Wilson, Lemuel, Eli, Levi and Sylvanus Moore. He owned and operated a government distillery in Belmont Co., OH. His son, Levi Johnson Moore, (1828-1908) and Mary Ann Moore (1827-1905) were married Dec. 25, 1850 at St. Clairsville, OH. He moved his family from Belmont Co., OH to Brown Co., IN about 1855.

Levi Moore volunteered to serve in the Civil War on Feb. 7, 1865 at Columbus, IN. He was a member of Company K, 145th Indiana Reg't. He spent most of his tour of duty in Dalton, GA and was mustered out of service on Jan. 21, 1866 at Macon, GA.

Children born to Levi and Mary Ann Moore were Cinderella, Beady, Elizabeth, Sarah, Augustus, Levi, Clint, Jackson and Genevery Moore. Dewitt Clinton "Clint" Moore was born in Van Buren Township, Brown County. Clint and Abigail Deaver were married in 1900. They spent most of their lives on the Levi Moore homestead. After their retirement they moved to Columbus to live with their daughter, Imo Moore.

Children born to Clint and Abigail Moore were Imo, born 1901; Aquilla Ert, born 1902; Albert, born 1905; Vivian, born 1911 and Julius Moore, born 1921. Imo and Julius live in Columbus, IN; Ert lives in Nevada; Vivian lives in Van Buren Township, Brown County; Albert is deceased.

Vivian Moore and Francis Lutes (1912-1982), son of William Lutes and Charlotte Hatton, were married June 13, 1930 at New Albany, IN and lived in Brown and Monroe Counties all their lives. They have four children: (1) Wandalyn Marie, born 1931, who married William Engleman, Jr. and had children, Robert Steven and Patricia Lynn Engleman. (2) Bill Dean, born 1933, who married Dorothy Lou Cross and had children, Valerie Ann, Cynthia Sue, Julie Kay, Betsy Jo, Suzanne and Jennifer Lynn. (3) Ted Loren, born 1937, who married Eunice (Aldrich) Neal and has adopted twins, Gary and Terry Lutes. (4) Jack Lee, born 1939, who married Carol Ann Wright and has a daughter Stephanie Ann Lutes. *Submitted by Jack Lee Lutes*

LOREN AND RUTH MOORE -
Loren Robert was born Oct. 29, 1924, the third of four sons born to Harold and Elma Moore, in the same house that his father was born, (Washington Township, 135 South). Loren's great-grandparents, Henry Bernhard Seitz and Catherine Burkhart Seitz, were born in Bavaria where they fell in love. When Catherine's folks decided to leave Bavaria for greater freedom and opportunities, Henry was determined to come also. He did, as a stow-away on their ship. He presented himself to the family in New York. Loren's grandparents were Brown Countians, Henry and Mary Catherine Seitz and Oddy and Frances Ardella Stitt Bright. A special treat that Loren remembers was visiting his Grandmother Bright's grocery store and enjoying a sack of candy.

Loren attended his first six years of school at Clark School and graduated from Nashville High School in 1943.

Ruth Irene Bond was born May 1, 1928, the fifth of eight children born to Earl and Grace Barkes Bond on a farm near Goshen (now Fox's Corner). Six years later the family moved to a farm near Helmsburg where Ruth attended all 12 years of schooling. Ruth remembers getting lost in Nashville when she was six years old, trying to get to her grandparents' home on South Jefferson Street from her Grandfather's restaurant on East Main Street. She made it in two attempts. Her grandparents were Joshua and Myrtle Yoder Bond and John and Hester Ann Brown Barkes.

Loren and Ruth were married Sept. 1, 1951 in the Nashville Christian Church while Loren was on Navy leave. Loren served in both World War II and the Korean War. After his discharge from service they moved to Columbus where Loren was employed at Hamilton Cosco and Ruth at Irwin Union Bank. They soon grew homesick for Brown County and came "home". Loren bought the Rogers Brothers Grocery Store and went into the grocery business, but this was not to be, for within the year the building was destroyed by fire. Before being called to service, Loren had worked for his uncle, Courtney Moore, in the plumbing business, so he put his experience to work in Brown County in 1954. They did not have a telephone so a neighbor, Sarah Louise Crabtree Kritzer, would take their calls for them. Loren is still in the plumbing business.

They were blessed with three daughters: (1) Marcia Kay Boyd, born June 25, 1953, is a nurse at Bloomington Hospital. She is married to John Boyd and has three daughters, Jennifer Kay and Christie Jolene Beery, Lauren Grace Boyd, and a stepdaughter, Contessa Boyd. (2) Marilyn Sue Ayers, born July 8, 1954, is a teacher, married to Michael Ayers. They are parents of (triplets) born May 23, 1990; Allyson Sue, Brooks Michael, Conner Keith. (3) Mary Beth Fisher was born June 28, 1956 and works at Railroadmen's Federal Savings and Loan Association. She is married to Steven Craig Fisher and they have two children, Daniel Lee and Holly Nicole Fisher.

Loren and Ruth have centered their lives around their family and their church family at the Nashville Christian Church and other community activities. *Submitted by Ruth Moore*

WILSON MOORE FAMILY -
Son of Michael and Lucretia Matheny Moore, was born in Belmont Co., OH (1809). He along with his wife, Ally Butler, six of his ten children, and brothers, Henry, Lemuel, Eli, and Levi migrated to Brown Co., IN.

Daughter, Lucretia Moore, married Samuel Moffitt on Dec. 15, 1853 in Ohio. They had ten children.

Son, Henry Floyd Moore, married Lucinda Fogle on July 21, 1860 in Ohio. Nine children were born to this union—Filena, Mary E., John W., Charles W., Eli T., Sandy M., George W., Grant, and Willie. Henry later married Eliza Jane Lutes Moffitt and had a son, Charles Otto.

Daughter, Nancy J. Moore, married John D. Moore (son of Benjamin M. Moore and Cassie Ann Butler) on Dec. 24, 1863, in Ohio. They had one surviving child, Jason Ellsworth Moore.

Son, Jason Moore, married Amelia Johns (daughter of William Johns and Nancy King) on Jan. 14, 1873 in Ohio. Only one of their eight children migrated to Brown County - Myra Josephine Moore, who married Joseph Alonzo Downey. Their daughter, Ena Myrl Downey married Harry Foster Steele. Ena and Harry Steele are the parents of Patricia Steele Horton.

Son, Isaac Peters Moore, married Mary Elizabeth Deaver (daughter of John Deaver and Sarah Ann Hanna) on July 11, 1872 in Brown County. They had three children—Sarah Alice, Ida Jane, and John Deaver Moore.

Daughter, Elizabeth Marshall Peters Moore, married William Leonard Deaver (son of John Deaver and Sarah Ann Hanna) on April 23, 1872 in Brown County. They had four children—Minerva, Jane, Mary Elizabeth and Sarah Anna.

Son, James Leroy Moore, married Caroline Mackey (daughter of John Henry Mackey and Catherine Miller) on Aug. 18, 1880 in Brown County. Thirteen children were born to this union—Mary Ann, Lewis Jason, Minnie Louise, Gertrude Alta, Clarence E., Clyde, Dollie Pearl, Maude Elizabeth, twins, Della Esta and Nellie Esther, Earl, Ernest E., and Mackey F. Moore.

Wilson's brother, Henry, married Rachel M. Skinner (daughter of Nathaniel Skinner and Hannah King) on Dec. 14, 1826 in Ohio. They had 11 children—Andrew, Michael, Nathaniel, Hannah, Lemuel, William, Lucretia, Janet, James, Phebe, and Nancy.

Brother, Lemuel R. Moore, married Catherine Skinner (daughter of Nathaniel Skinner and Hannah King) in 1832 in Ohio. They had three children, Nancy, Michael, and Rachel.

Brother, Eli T. Moore, married Ellen J. Shults (daughter of Henry and Elizabeth Shults) before 1847 in Ohio. Nine children were born to this union—Dewitt C., Sarah Elizabeth, Henry Jackson, Mary Lucretia, Wilson Shannon, Ally Jane, Eli Ellsworth, William Sherman, and Cora Ellen Moore.

Brother, Levi Johnson Moore, married Mary Ann Patterson on Dec. 25, 1850 in Belmont Co., OH. They had eight children, six of whom were living in 1900—Lilly Ann Genevra, Eli Jackson, Elizabeth Helen, Sarah Frances, Augustus Marion, and Dewitt Clinton Moore.

Wilson and Ally Moore are buried in Melott Cemetery, Van Buren Township, on Poplar Grove Road. Also buried there are his sons, Henry and Isaac, and daughter, Nancy J. Moore, and brothers, Lemuel and Levi. (see Ephraim Downey Family) *Submitted by Patricia Horton, great-granddaughter of Jason Moore*

J.S. AND SARAH MORRISON - John Swayze Morrison owned general stores at three locations in the Belmont area over a period of nearly 40 years starting in 1880. He also named Belmont and served as its postmaster.

Swayze, as he was known, started his mercantile business at Needmore as a peddler with a pack on his back and a partnership in a store with his brother-in-law, Jacob Bruner. In later years he owned, or was a partner in, stores at Youno, Crooked Creek and Gent. After he sold the Belmont store he lived in Nashville a short time, then bought the Story store and operated it a few years in the early 1920s in partnership with his son-in-law, Richard Kelley.

Sarah and J.S. Morrison

Swayze was born in Noble Co., OH, in 1858 to John and Phoebe Poling Morrison. A Methodist minister, his father died when Swayze was two years old, leaving the widow, two sons and two daughters by Phoebe and a son and five daughters from a previous marriage. Phoebe brought her children—Martin Luther, Elizabeth, Swayze and Emma—to Needmore in the early 1860s when some Polings migrated to that area.

Swayze married Sarah Elizabeth Rude, daughter of Thomas and Mary Jane Blair Rude of Morgan County, in 1883. They had seven children, two of whom died in infancy. The others were Omer, Jessie, Della, William and Nellie.

Omer married Grace Payne. He served one term as Brown County auditor and was a partner in a Nashville grocery store before moving to Bloomington, where he was a wholesale grocery salesman. Jessie married Richard Kelley. They lived in Brown County until the mid 1950s, then moved to Bloomington. Della married Clyde Rogers and moved to North Dakota. William went to Illinois to work when he was 18. He married Hazel Williamson and remained in Illinois until the early 1930s, when he moved his family to Bloomington. He was a farmer and truck driver. Nellie married Dr. R.L. Kleindorfer. They lived in Washington, IN, and later in Evansville, where he was a surgeon.

While the Morrisons were at Belmont Sarah and her daughters and her unmarried sister, Martha Rude, cooked meals for "drummers" and store customers. Swayze had a safe in the store in which he kept money and other valuables. Some customers took advantage of this facility, storing their "extra" money in it.

A huckster wagon kept people in the surrounding area supplied with merchandise. As he made his rounds the driver also bought or traded for produce. The produce included geese, which were kept until they numbered about 100, at which time Swayze and one helper drove them to market in Indianapolis.

After they left Story the Morrisons lived on a farm on Brummetts Creek Road, Monroe County. Later they bought a house in Bloomington, and spent winters in it and summers on the farm. Sarah died in 1934 and Swayze in 1940. They are buried at Needmore. *Submitted by Dale Kelley*

NEAL-KISSLING FAMILY - John and Lula Neal lived from the late 1800s to 1922 on the grounds now known as the Brown County Country Club. This property is located on Country Club Road about two miles west of Nashville.

They had ten children, only seven survived childhood. In order of their birth they are: Mabel, John, Omer Ray, Mary Emily, Pauline, Ida May and James.

Mable was a teacher in Atlanta, GA. She married Bennet Hunter who was a businessman and had no children. John married Hannah Walker, also from Brown County. John and Hannah lived in Indianapolis and had five children: Leon, Beulah, Emerson, Mildred and Wilmer. Omer Ray became a restauranteur and married Alberta Phillips from Monrovia. Omer Ray and Alberta had three daughters, only one survived, Mildred Louise (Kissling). She now lives in Brown County with her family. Mary Emily was a teacher and married John Dee Cantrell from Bloomington. Mr. Cantrell became a teacher and later a principal in Lakewood, OH. They had two children: John Dee Jr. and Burton Neal. Pauline married Walter Andrew Kettle from New Jersey. He was president of New York University. They had one child, Walter Andrew Jr. Ida May married Glen Wilson from Indianapolis, a painter and businessman. They had three children: Alice, Norman and Velva Loris. James married Ruth Morgan from Speedway, IN. James worked at Allisons and was also a musician. He and Ruth had one child, Donald James.

Front: Kathleen Ray, Louise and George Kissling. Back: Karen Sue and Michael George Kissling.

Omer Ray returned to Brown County in 1921 with his wife, Alberta and there on his old home place where he and his brothers and sisters were born, his daughter Mildred Louise was born. After two months, they returned to Indianapolis where he and Alberta worked in restaurants and later owned three of their own. In 1942, Louise (as she is known) married George Kissling. George was born in Koblenz, Germany and had come to America when he was nine days old. He had grown up in Indianapolis and was engaged in the construction and electrical business. George is now Project Manager for Everett I. Brown & Company based out of Indianapolis. George & Louise had three children: Karen Sue, Michael George and Kathleen Ray. Karen married William Norman and has two children, Dawn Michelle and Anthony Michael. Michael married Ronda Alstott and had no children. He is now deceased. Kathleen married Kenneth Ray Seitz from Helmsburg. They now live in Noblesville and have two children, Kourtney Robert and Kristina Rebecca.

In 1966, the Kissling family moved to their farm on New Bellsville Road in the southeastern part of Brown County. Louise had studied art in Indianapolis and opened her own studio in Nashville. The oldest granddaughter, Dawn works for an advertising agency in Indianapolis and lives in Carmel. The other three grandchildren are still in school.

George, Louise, Karen and Tony are now living on Lake La Salle, eight miles north of Nashville. *Submitted by Louise and Dawn Kissling*

NEAT - Delvin T. and Florence Herring Neat moved to Brown County from Indianapolis in 1942. Both were natives of Hendricks Co., IN. Delvin was born Aug. 18, 1886, the son of George Washington Neat and Matilda Brewer Neat. Florence, daughter of John William Herring and Lillian Evelyn Sweeney Herring, was born July 12, 1888. Delvin and Florence were married in Indianapolis on June 24, 1909, in what had been planned to be an outdoor garden wedding which was delayed four hours because of a torrential rainstorm.

Other than a World War II stint at Allison's in Indianapolis, Delvin worked as a brick and stone mason, and was still actively working at age 84. Florence was a homemaker.

They were members of Brown County Historical Society, Brown County Senior Citizens, and Hamblen-Jackson Unit of Farm Bureau. They attended Morgantown Methodist Church.

Delvin was a member of North Park F. & A.M. Lodge in Indianapolis. He visited the Nashville Masonic Lodge frequently. He received his 50-year certificate and pin from Grand Lodge in November 1970.

Florence H. Neat, Kathryn Neat Harvey, Bob Neat, Harry Neat, Delvin T. Neat, and Herring Neat. February 28, 1943.

After Florence died Oct. 31, 1969, Delvin lived alone for many years. At the time of his death, on

March 7, 1984, he was a resident of the Heritage House Convalescent Center in Martinsville. They are buried in East Hill Cemetery, Morgantown.

Herring Neat, their oldest child, married Ernestine Sutton and they lived in Speedway. Their sons, Tom and Dick, enjoyed visiting their grandparents in Brown County and riding the pony Billy. A daughter, Victoria, died when she was four.

Delvin and Florence's only daughter, Kathryn, and husband, Owen J. Harvey, moved to Brown County in 1959. Owen died the following year. They had no children. She is now married to Keith Donaldson and they live in Van Buren Township.

In the fall of 1942, not long after coming to Brown County, Harry, the third child, joined the U.S. Navy and served aboard a destroyer escort in the Pacific. He returned to his parents' home and commuted to Indianapolis to work at Farm Bureau Insurance and rode the "old" Nashville to Indianapolis bus. He married Marian Batman of Bargersville. They built a home on S.R. 135 north of Fruitdale. Not long after Harry's death in 1957, Marian and their two children, Harry Thomas and Cheryl Kay, moved away. Both children are now married and live in the Greenwood area.

The youngest child, Bob, married June Arnold. Their new home was ready for them on their return from a wedding trip and they still live in "downtown" Fruitdale. They are parents of Shirley Jean, now Mrs. Jackie Hedger, and of David Neat. Both Shirley and David are graduates of Brown County High School. While in elementary school at Helmsburg, during the construction of the new school building, Shirley attended Branstetter School in Jackson Township. Shirley was active in Rainbow Girls Assembly and served as Mother Adviser. The Hedgers have three children, Andrew, Paul, and Joy. They live near Woodland Lake in Hamblen Township. David Neat served as a Commissioner of Brown County for four years. He has one daughter, Michelle.

NOBLITT - John W. Noblitt was the son of William Noblitt, who moved in 1847, from Jonesville, Bartholomew County to Brown County. William settled near New Bellsville, where he cleared nearly 15 acres of land and erected a cabin. After a year's time, he returned to Jonesville, where he married Lucinda Womack and settled down on a 64 acre farm. It was here that John W. Noblitt was born on July 23, 1853. At the age of eight years, John joined with the other children in keeping the family together. This was necessary because his father, William, was killed during the Civil War. For the next 25 years John helped with family affairs and finally helped his mother move to his father's claim near New Bellsville, where she died and was buried in the cemetery there.

Charles Robert Noblitt

John married Hannah Cain of Brown County. A year later on July 1, 1873, she died, and was buried near Beck's Grove.

John married Hannah E. Barkes on April 12, 1874. Hannah was from Van Buren Township, Brown County. She was the daughter of George and Delilah Stucky Barkes, who lived near Grandview Church, having settled there on Dec. 13, 1864.

John and Hannah Barkes Noblitt eventually settled in the nearby community of Ogilville, Bartholomew County, where they raised a family of nine children. Although John and Hannah never returned to live in Brown County, their son, Loren S. Noblitt and his family lived near Grandview Church during the late 1930s and early 1940s. The church was located on land donated by George and Delilah Barkes.

Loren S. Noblitt was born only a mile east of Grandview Church. He was raised in the Ogilville area and attended the local schools and also the United Bretheran Church there. It was there that Reverend Jacob Holmes Walls, the presiding elder of the church, recruited Loren to become a student at Indiana Central College, just organized. Minnie Walls, Reverend Walls' daughter, was also a student there. On the college campus there, Loren and Minnie fell in love and were married on June 25, 1908. This was one of the very first college romances.

Both Loren and Minnie Noblitt became teachers and then later were Methodist preachers. Many years later they served as pastors of the Grandview Church. They became the parents of three children, all of whom graduated from Indiana Central College and became teachers. Alma Noblitt O'Dell lives in Lubbock, TX; Loren W. Noblitt lives in Brownstown, IN.

Charles Robert Noblitt, the author of this account, lives in Hamilton Co., IN where, following his retirement from teaching, he continues serving as a Methodist pastor. Like his parents before him, Charles Robert met his wife, Lucille Valentine Noblitt, at Indiana Central College, and they have shared a lifetime of teaching. Two of their children, Kelly R. Noblitt, and Charlene Noblitt Rockhold, are, or have been, teachers.

Minnie Walls Noblitt died in 1969, and is buried in Garland Brook Cemetery, Columbus, IN. Loren S. Noblitt, aged 101 years, resides with his daughter in Lubbock, TX.

WARREN AND EDITH OGLE - The earliest known OGLE ancestor came from England to Delaware in the late 1600s. Later generations went from Maryland westward to western and southern states including Kentucky and Ohio. Warren's great-grandfather, James Ogle was born in Clark Co., IN in 1824. He was the son of Levi Ogle and Sarah Cooper. Later he was married in Decatur Co., IN to Louisa J. McClary, the daughter of Robert McClary and Nancy Dickey.

Warren's grandfather, James Perry Ogle, was born in Decatur Co., IN on Nov. 19, 1846. On July 21, 1872, he was married to Elizabeth Matilda Roush. To this marriage were born 12 children, one of which was Warren's father, Conner C. Ogle. Two of the children died in infancy.

They farmed about 200 acres of land for the support of this large family. Besides farming, they cut timber to be used for lumber and cross-ties. In the late 1920s the State of Indiana purchased the farm as a part of Brown County State Park. Warren's grandfather had passed away in 1909, leaving his grandmother to live in the home just below what is now Ogle Lake. She later was married to John Crouch. After his death she married Henry Rose, and lived with him until her death in January of 1927. Conner C. Ogle was married to Herma E. Chafin on Dec. 13, 1902. To this marriage were born three sons: Clarence, Wayne and Warren. In the early 1900s Conner and the Ogle family moved to Gnawbone where he operated a blacksmith shop and a small grocery store. In April of 1921 he bought a 280 acre farm about two miles south of Pike's Peak. Here he farmed and worked part time in the blacksmith shop.

Warren and Edith Ogle

Warren's mother Herma, was the daughter of Isaac and Mary Woods Chafin. Her family owned the land where the north entrance to Brown County State Park is now located. Warren's grandfather Chafin was at one time part-owner of the Brown County Democrat. He was active in community affairs and at one time was elected to a county office.

Clarence (son of Conner Ogle) was married to Lela Evon Tracy. They lived in Nashville until he passed away in May 13, 1956.

Conner and Herma moved from the farm to Nashville where they lived until their death. Their son, Wayne, operated a garage in Nashville until his death on Feb. 18, 1974. He was never married. He served his country for four years during World War II.

Warren was married to Edith M. Beauchamp, whose family moved here from near Tulsa, OK. They have two children: James Ogle and Mary L. Fleetwood. Also they have four grandchildren and four great-grandchildren. Warren has been a teacher, principal and school Superintendent in Brown County.

Edith and Warren celebrated their 60th wedding anniversary on Aug. 12, 1989, with an open house at the Brown County Inn.

Their daughter Mary Louise married Winfer E. Fleetwood who passed away on Aug. 13, 1980. Their son, James Ogle, was married to Rosalie Rose on May 10, 1957. Four grandchildren are: Jerry Fleetwood and Donita Fleetwood Potts and Mark Ogle and Lori Ogle Myers. The four great-grandchildren are Daniel and Brad Fleetwood, Madeline Myers and Camden Lee Ogle. *Submitted by Warren Ogle*

ANNE OLSEN - Anne was born in Bremen-Germany as second daughter of Heinrich and Wilhelmine Frank. Wilhelmine was the daughter of Gerhard Meyer and Emilie Ziehms from Bremen-Germany. Heinrich was the son of Johann Frank and Anne Langner from Austria. Heinrich came for a visit to Bremen-Germany, met Wilhelmine and married her. He became a German citizen.

Anne attended school in Bremen, finished with a

Certificate in Physical Education. She experienced the horrors of WWII while living in Germany.

Anne met Robert McAdams in 1946. He was stationed in Bremen-Germany with the U.S. Army. Robert was the son of Bert and Mary McAdams of Indianapolis, IN. Anne and Robert married in Nurenberg, Germany, and came to the U.S. in 1948. They resided in Indianapolis for a while until discovery of Brown Co., IN. Moved to this beautiful area in 1952. Purchased property and lived in the Cabin on Carmel Ridge until the untimely death of Robert in 1977.

Anne Olsen

Anne married Gene Olsen in 1981 but was soon widowed again. Gene was the son of Ora and Alvina Olsen from Anderson, IN. Ora had left Norway as a young boy to come to the United States. This area in Norway, Drontheim, is especially dear to Anne since she lived there for a while prior to coming to the States.

Anne purchased a small cabin in Annandale Estate where she still lives. Her cabin on Carmel Ridge has been taken over by her only daughter Ginnvor and husband Norman Bullard. Ginnvor attended Helmsburg High School (1961) and the University of Indianapolis. Here she met her future husband Norman (Pete). Both have a BA degree in Physical Education from there and a MA from Indiana University. They have two children, Will, a sophomore at Wabash College, and Kathy, a Freshman at Georgetown University.

Anne is very active in the Historical Society and the Pioneer Women. She loves to play golf and picked up old hobby of Folkdancing again. She is a member of German Society in Indianapolis where this dancing group is performing. They are very much in demand to perform for other organizations and have travelled all over Indiana and neighboring states. She was always very active in Sports having won medals in different categories. She was in training for gymnastic competition for the 1940 Olympics in Tokyo. However, WWII cancelled that.

Anne returns to the land of her birth every few years for a visit—her home is here in beautiful Brown County.

GEORGE SCOTT OLIVE, JR.

George, Jr. born Indianapolis May 20, 1918, to George S. Olive, Sr., born Indiana and Louise Carpenter born North Carolina. They met and married in Rutherford Co., NC, June 8, 1909.

Scott has early connections in Brown County. His family built a log cabin south of Nineveh when he was about 13. The logs were cut from the 45 acre property.

Scott met and married Sally Resseguie while attending Harvard University at Cambridge, MA. He graduated there 1940 with John F. Kennedy, entered the U.S. Army and became a Major, after starting as a Private. He taught Accounting at the Army-Navy Industrial College at the Pentagon in D.C. One of his students was a young Naval Officer named Richard Nixon.

After receiving a Medical Discharge due to severe surgery in 1946, he returned to Indianapolis where he entered the accounting firm of Geo. S. Olive & Co. When George Sr. retired, Scott became Chairman of the Policy Committee until retiring in 1981 to become Professor of Accounting at Butler University in Indianapolis. He retired from the classroom 1988, but is still at Butler University with the Internship Program.

Scott and Sally had three sons and one daughter: Scott III, David, James and Anne, and maintained a weekend/vacation home at several different areas around Brown County. Their children attended Gnawbone Camp for several years. Sally died October 1982.

Scott is a Board Member of several organizations in Indianapolis. He was a Founding Board Member of the Indianapolis Zoo, and St. Richards Episcopal School, becoming its first Treasurer. He's a former President of Indiana CPA Society—was Board Member and Treasurer of Indianapolis Chamber of Commerce when Senator Lugar was the Mayor.

Scott, an only child, has nine grandchildren, two sets of twins, and two great-grandchildren. Hazel Lemmons Olive, his second wife, has two grandsons.

Hazel's great-great-grandfather came from Pennsylvania by way of Kentucky to Vigo Co., IN, where he bought 164 acres at the General land office, Vincennes. The deeds say Sec 30 and 31, township 12, dated Feb. 25, 1836—from President Martin Van Buren—City of Washington, by a Van Buren Sec'y. Her great-grandfather, Thomas B. Lemmons took his family to Missouri, 1884. Her grandfather, William Henry Lemmons, brought his family back to Indiana about 1915. *Submitted by Hazel (Lemmons) Olive*

HAZEL (LEMMONS) OLIVE

Born Aug. 20, 1923, in "Goose Pond" near Linton, Greene Co., IN, second of eight daughters born to George W. Lemmons, born in Missouri, and Nana A. Griffith born Virginia. They met and married in Sullivan Co., IN, April 7, 1919. Hazel graduated from Linton High School 1940 age 16. She went to Indianapolis during WWII and worked in a war plant (now Naval Avionics) making Norden Bombsight for the Navy. After the war ended in 1945 she worked for Eli Lilly & Company. She married Charles M.D. Smith born in Indianapolis, Dec. 5, 1918, on June 30, 1951. One son, Marvey David Smith, born Indianapolis, Sept. 10, 1965. Hazel retired 1968 after 23 years at Lilly.

G. Scott and David Olive, M. David Smith, Hazel L. Olive, April, 1989

Her connection with Brown County began 1956 when they bought a lot on Lake Lemon from Lawrence and Ida Fleener McCoy. They built a weekend/vacation home there and after Mr. Smith died January 1981, Hazel and son David, age 15, moved to the lakehouse. David finished high school at Brown County, class of 1983—after two years at Perry Meridian in Indianapolis. David entered the U.S. Army for four years at schools and served in Germany. His father, Charles was in five major battles in Europe during WWII.

In 1983, Hazel met Scott Olive and married him in Brown County, Dec. 30, 1983 at St. David's Episcopal Church, where she is Treasurer. She moved back to Indianapolis, January 1984, but they still spend most weekends at their lakehouses.

Brown County reminds the Olives of Grayson Co., VA in the Blue Ridge Mountains where her mother was born in a log cabin.

HOMER OLIVER STORY

The Oliver family immigrated from England to Pennsylvania in the early 1700s. Andrew F. Oliver born in 1815 in Pennsylvania. Later he moved to Ohio where the 1850 census listed him as a carpenter worth $810. He married Jane Taylor; their first born was James Henry in 1844, Wm. A. in 1847, Sarah Ellen in 1849, Samuel E. in 1854 and Martha Jane in 1858. James Henry married Nancy Ann Watson in 1869 and lived in Bean Blossom. They had Effie 1870, Omer Hendricks, 1872, Chalmer Victor, 1874, Andrew Herbert, 1875, Otis Jonathan, 1878, and Franklin Myrven (Peach) 1883.

Andrew Herbert married Emma Ruth Parsley in 1899; they had five children, Leo Vernon 1889, James Parsley, 1904, Iva Lena, 1907, Thurl Dennis, 1910, and Homer Amos 1913.

Homer and Delpha Gray Oliver

Homer helped his family farm while he attended one-room schools at Gold Point and Spearsville. Homer rode a horse to Morgantown High School and graduated in 1932. Homer drove a school bus for Brown County for 29 years. Homer and Delpha Jo Gray were married in May 1942. Delpha moved to Brown County in 1932 from Hamilton Co., IN. Homer served in World War II from November 1942 until January 1946. Their children are Marcia Kay, born July, 1943, Gary Andrew, born after Homer returned from the war, November 1946, and Nancy Jo, born May 1952. Marcia graduated from Helmsburg High School in 1961 along with Robert Layton (Boots) Deckard whom she married in August 1961. Their children are Rodney Layton and Andrea Jane. Rodney attends I.U.P.U.I. and Andrea attends I.U. Gary Andrew attended one room schools in Brown County; his first grade was at Bean Blossom; he started second grade at Spearsville. The Spearsville school burned down two weeks after school started. The county fixed Bethel Church so they could finish the school year. Gary entered the new Sprunica Elementary School in 1953 for the third grade. Due to Sprunica's overcrowding problem, Gary attended Helmsburg until eighth grade. In 1961, he was one of the first classes to attend the new Brown County High School. Gary started college at Indiana State University where he completed his first year. Gary transferred to I.U., graduated 1969; he received his masters from I.U. 1973. Gary teaches science in the new Brown County Jr. High. Gary married Sheila Jane Crabtree in 1968. Sheila graduated from I.U. with a B.A. in 1968 and Masters. Sheila is the principal of Sprunica Elementary. Their children are Ryan Andrew, born in 1973, Jannaka Jane, born in 1976. Ryan attends Brown County High School; Jannaka attends Brown County Jr. High. They live in Van Buren township.

Nancy Jo attended BCHS, graduating in 1970. For nine years, Nancy worked in Dr. Robert Seibel's clinic. Nancy married Lee Fleetwood; they had one daughter, Heidi, who attends Bloomington North High School. Nancy is now married to Gary Bruce, and they live in Bloomington. Nancy sells Longaberger baskets.

After 48 years of marriage, Homer and Delpha still own and farm where Homer was born east of Spearsville in Hamblen Township.

LOWELL OLIVER FAMILY

- The Oliver family migrated from England to Pennsylvania in the 1700s. Here, Lowell's great-grandfather, Andrew Oliver, was born (1815). Later the family blazed a trail to Ohio and then on to Indiana. Andrew married Jane Taylor (1819). They had five children; James, William (Lowell's grandfather), Sarah, Samuel and Martha.

William married Mary Schaffer. They purchased land in Hamblen Township, Brown County (1880). They deeded a tract off the northwest corner for a Methodist Church (Bethel). William and Mary had four children; John Darvin, Anna, Maggie and Chalmer Samuel.

John Darvin married Effie Poulton. They owned a grocery store in Nineveh. Anna passed away in 1876. Maggie never married, living at home with her parents. She was very religious, keeping the Bethel Church and Sunday School going for years.

Marie and Lowell Oliver 50th (Golden) Wedding Anniversary, 1982.

Tim, Deb and Jim (back), Derrick Oliver (front).

Chalmer Samuel (1881) married Rosa Louella Hutchison (1883). He was a farmer and a dealer for North American Fertilize. In his spare time he hauled gravel with his horses and wagon for the county roads.

Chalmer (Chall) and Rosa had three children, Muriel Gladys (1903), Lowell Travers (1905) and Rosa Luceila (1907). Rosa and Baby Rosa passed away in 1907. Chall took Muriel and Lowell back to the family homestead on the corner of what is now Bittersweet and Woodland Lake Roads. Maggie helped raise the children. Muriel and Lowell walked to a one-room elementary school. Muriel became a school teacher. She taught in one-room schools in Brown County.

Lowell helped his father farm and worked for neighbors, including William Waltman, who had an orchard on Bean Blossom Ridge. He rode a horse to Helmsburg High School, leaving his horse at the Bond's Livery Stable in Helmsburg. He graduated in 1926. After graduation, he ventured out west in a Model A Ford, working in the wheat harvest and also for Puget Sound Power and Light Company. Upon his return, Lowell entered Central Normal College in Danville, IN. While here, he met his future wife Marie Beck from Putnam County. They graduated in 1932 and married the same year.

Lowell began teaching in one-room schools in Hamblen Township. After graduation from Butler University, he taught at Helmsburg High School, later becoming Principal. He was Principal also in Clark Township and Trafalgar. Lowell taught school for 42 years. His wife, Marie, graduated from Indiana University. She taught 32 years in Putnam, Brown and Johnson counties.

The Oliver's were also farmers raising Hereford Cattle with the help of their only son, Lee William (1939). In the summer they traveled to many states including Alaska, Canada, Mexico and South America. They celebrated their 50th wedding Anniversary in 1982.

Lee graduated from Helmsburg High School and Indiana Central Business College. He worked for Burford Printing, Carpenters and McClean Trucking. He married Donna White (1961). They worked on the family Farm raising pigs and chickens. Lee and Donna have three children; Debora Lee (1962), James Lowell (1964) and Timothy Robert (1971). In their spare time the family traveled across the country collecting antiques. They purchased a Model T from Clarence Chitwood, refinished it and showed it in parades and shows.

Debbie, Jim and Tim graduated from Brown County High School. Debbie graduated from Indiana University. She and her son Derrick are remodeling the Oliver homestead (being five generations living there). Jim is attending Indiana University. Tim has joined the U.S. Navy and is stationed in California. *Submitted by Marie Oliver*

JAMES HARRY OWENS AND GENEVRA (DERRINGER) OWENS

- Jim's family (Owens) traveled from Ireland to Ohio and then to Brown County, where they bought 45 acres of land for $1.00 and the deed was written on a piece of tree bark. The Owens family farmed and operated a sawmill and grocery at Belmont for 45 years.

The Belmont School was two rooms—one for lower grades and the other room for higher grades. Jim graduated from Nashville High School and played basketball on the team. They played in an old church building and dressed across the street.

He married Genevra Derringer on June 5, 1935 at Columbus. She was the daughter of Rex and Vinnie (Rariden) Derringer. Her grandparents and great-grandparents were from Ireland, Wales and Holland. Her great-grandfather, James W. Derringer was an undertaker, notary and carpenter in Bean Blossom, then called Georgetown.

Genevra attended a one-room (Owl Creek) School for one year, when the school closed she went to Helmsburg School. In the winter, in the first few years they rode in a sled with a horse pulling it, then on to an automobile and then to a bus. Genevra's first year was accomplished by walking to school and the mud was so bad and she so small that she would bog down and her mother would have to come and get her. They lived on Helmsburg Road. In later years the people on the road each paid so much and had the road chipped and sealed (about 1961).

James H. and Genevra (Derringer) Owens

When Genevra was a child, Helmsburg was a thriving town with a hotel, a meat shop, two restaurants and three groceries. One night a fire swept through the town and as there was no fire protection most of the businesses burned and it was never rebuilt.

Everyone raised a garden and had a root cellar and did home canning and their own butchering.

After Jim and Genevra were married, he worked at Cummins Engine Company in Columbus. He enlisted in the Navy and served for two years in the Pacific in World War II.

After he retired from Cummins, he ran for political office, Commissioner, and served for six years until his death in 1984 on Thanksgiving Day. The family was very politically minded and Genevra was appointed to finish his term by the Democrat Central Committee. She then was elected for four years to the same office. Genevra has served in various political committees for the Democratic Party since she was old enough to vote.

Jim and Genevra lived in Helmsburg for several years and later on in 1959 they built a home near her parents on Helmsburg Road.

Jim was born at home on March 23, 1916, the youngest of ten children to Dora (Henthorne) Owens and James S. Owens. Jim died Nov. 22, 1984.

Genevra was born Aug. 24, 1917, to Vinnie (Rariden) Derringer and Rex Derringer at Helmsburg. She was so small her grandfather compared her to a red chigger—hence the nickname of "Chig."

At that time all babies were born at home and if lucky there was a Doctor not too far away. A Dr. Selfridge had an office in Helmsburg for several years.

JAMES STEVENSON OWENS

- James was born Jan. 21, 1870, in Brown Co., IN, a son of Samuel Owens and his first wife. Samuel Owens was a farmer and about Aug. 17, 1907, was buried at Duncan Cemetery near Knight's Corner. James S. Owens' mother died when he was young and she may be buried at Green Valley Cemetery in Brown County. James S. Owens married Dora Alice Henthorn, daughter of Isaac and Margaret Brown Henthorn. Dora A. Henthorn Owens was born Nov. 29, 1863, in Brown County. When James S. and Dora A. Owens were first married, they farmed near Belmont, IN. They hired a hand (maybe Jim Willoughby from Kentucky) of the timber business to help with the farmwork while James S. also worked in timber and Dora A. did the selling in their store, Owens Grocery.

James S. and Dora A. Owens Family, ca. 1909. Back: Albert Alfred and Mary Margaret. Middle: Wm. Robert, James S., Dora A., Pearl Elizabeth and Rose Nellie. Front: John Ross and Samuel Isaac.

Owens Grocery started as a room attached to James S. and Dora A. Owens' home before 1908. They had counters and wall shelving with bulk products ordered from drummers who traveled in the area. They kept kerosene for lamps in a 50 gallon barrel and in the spring of 1913 high waters rose into the store. The kerosene barrel was overturned and the kerosene went into the living area. Neighbors came in boats to clean up the mess and their legs were burned by the kerosene. Eventually they built a store in Belmont in the late 1920s or early 1930s.

Besides working his farm, timbering, and co-owning the Owens Grocery with his wife, James S. Owens was also a blacksmith and his daughter, Pearl, can remember working the bellows. In his shop he shod horses for neighbors. James S. was a Baptist and belonged to The Glee Club. He was a beautiful singer and when he died Nov. 15, 1934, the only two remaining members of the Glee Club sang at his funeral. James S. was also a strong Democrat and lived to see Franklin D. Roosevelt elected as he wished. James S. was a wonderful father and husband.

Dora A. (Henthorn) Owens in Owens Grocery in Belmont

Dora A. Owens was a member of the Church of Christ at Belmont. She also was a wonderful singer and had an organ at home for family and friends to play on Sundays after church. The single minister, Henry Griffin, used to come to the Owens home after church for Sunday dinner and to share music with the family.

After her husband died in 1934 Dora A. Owens kept up the Owens Grocery business in Belmont until early May of 1939 when she became ill and died Aug. 25, 1939. She along with her husband is buried at Duncan Cemetery.

The ten children of James S. and Dora A. Owens include: Mary Margaret (Mrs. Willard Bush) born 1893; Albert Alfred, born 1894, who married Mary Brock; Wm. Robert, born 1896, who married Goldie Stevens; Rose Nellie (Mrs. Ivan Bartley) born 1898; Samuel Isaac, born 1901, who married Blanch Mercer; John Rose, born 1903, who married Dorval Fleetwood; Grace, born and died Jan. 31, 1907; Pearl Elizabeth (Mrs. Wade A. Stevens) born June 19, 1908; Ruth (Mrs. Maurice Stevens) born 1913; and James Harry, born 1916, who married Genevra "Chig" Derringer. *Submitted by Pearl Nugent*

CHARLOTTE AND ARTHUR PADISH -
Arthur William Padish and Charlotte Ruth Padish moved to Brown Co., IN, in 1985.

Arthur was born in 1921 in Vermillion County to John Francis Padish and Hulda Mae Padish. John was born in Vermillion County. His parents, Paul and Mary Padish, were natives of Austria. Hulda's mother was Cora Lee Spurr, nee Starrett, and her father was Charles Spurr. The Spurrs are Scotch-Irish. Both Paul Padish and Charles Spurr were coal miners. John Padish moved his family to Lake County in 1925 and was head of the Electrical Line Department at U.S. Steel in Gary. Arthur's sister, Maxine, (1923) resides in Glen Cove, NY.

Charlotte and Arthur Padish

Charlotte was born in 1929 in Noble County to Charles Fairbanks Strait and Fanny Rita Strait. Charles was born in Noble County, and his parents, Abraham and Lena Strait, nee Swihart, were born in Ohio. Straits are of Scotch descent. Fanny was born in LaGrange County to Simon Peter and Stella Yoder, nee Niles. Simon's mother's maiden name was Zook (Zug). Her sister was Jerome Smucker's (of apple butter fame) mother. Stella was of English descent. Her mother's name was Chapman, of the "Johnny Appleseed" line. Fanny was a direct descendant of John Hertzler, one of two sons of Jacob Hertzler, who came from Switzerland prior to the Revolutionary War. John was a captain in the Pennsylvania militia during the Revolutionary War. Charlotte's brothers are Byron (1923), John (1924), and Carl (1927). Byron died in 1945 (World War II). Carl lives in Wabash County and John in Salisbury, MD.

Arthur and Charlotte married in Allen County in 1950. They lived in Lake County until 1980, then moved to Gibson County. They have three children, William Charles (1953), James Edward (1956), and Gail Ruth (1958). William married Beatriz Chin, and they have a son, Jonathan (1988). James married Gay Lynn Varner, and their daughters are Erica Lynn (1985) and Megan Elizabeth (1990). Gail married James Alan Clarin.

Both William and James are attorneys. William practices law in Wheaton and resides in Roselle, IL. James practices in Phoenix and resides in Scottsdale, AZ. Gail is a certified audiologist employed in a pediatric E.N.T. practice in Chicago, IL, where she resides.

Arthur and Charlotte are graduates of Indiana University, where they met. Their children are also. Charlotte has a master's degree from Valparaiso University, and both Gail and William earned master's degrees from Indiana University. Both sons are graduates of John Marshall Law School.

Arthur was an industrial salesman and became branch manager of an electrical supply firm. He later joined U.S. Steel's Electrical Cable Department and Wire Rope Division. Charlotte taught English in secondary schools in Lake, Gibson, and Brown Counties.

During World War II, Arthur served in the Army Air Force. He is a member of the United Methodist Church, Lions Club, Historical Society, I.U. Alumni Association, Varsity Club, and Iron and Steel Institute.

Charlotte has membership in the United Methodist Church, Nashville Literary Club, Psi Iota Xi, Delta Kappa Gamma, Historical Society, and the I.U. Alumni Association.

EARL AND ALICE PAGE -
The Pages, Earl, Alice and son Paul discovered Brown County in the summer of 1937. They were spending the summer in Evanston, IL, where Earl was guest instructor at Northwestern University. They heard of Brown Co., IN and decided to make a visit on their way to Kansas to visit their families before returning to their home in New Jersey. Earl was on the faculty of State Teachers College located in Newark, NJ. (In those days his field was called Industrial Arts.) Before leaving Brown County that summer, they had purchased acreage across from the North entrance to Brown County State Park. Arrangements were made for a shell of a summer cottage to be built by Fred Rains and Walter Rariden. "Chud" Roberts was responsible for having a well dug. This little spot back in the woods was loved and enjoyed for several summers and then World War II stopped the Pages from coming to Brown County.

Alice Page, 1928; Earl Page, 1928

Earl was from Independence, KS; Alice's home was Girard, KS. They met at Pittsburg State University, Pittsburg, KS, where both received their B.S. Degrees. Earl attended Iowa State University, Ames, IA, for his Masters Degree.

Earl's grandfather Greer grew up in Morgantown, IN, but moved his family to Independence, KS, in 1880. Upon hearing that his grandson had purchased land in Brown County, he let it be known there were no roads into Brown County! Grandfather Page was born in Nebraska but moved with his family in 1885 to Independence, KS.

Alice's family, the Hossacks, came from Scotland to Canada in the middle 1700s. Her father, Walter C. Hossack, was born in Odell, IL, and at age four moved with his family to Girard, KS. He was a farmer and auctioneer. Her mother, Jessie Falwell Hossack, was born in Chillicothe, MO. When she was 12, she traveled with her parents in a covered wagon to Girard to make their home.

In 1945 the Pages moved to Brown County, restored a log cabin for a home, built a workshop on old State Road 46 across from the North entrance to the park, and Earl's dream of having a shop for the building of early American furniture reproductions and restoring antique furniture was realized.

The Hossacks came to Brown County to live in 1948.

The Pages' son Paul, attended Indiana University and is a graduate of Chicago College of Osteopathy. He is an Osteopathic Physician in Seymour, IN, where he lives with his wife Carole. They have five adult children and one grandchild.

After the death of Earl in 1958, Alice studied for Real Estate Salesman License and after a few years of working in other offices, she decided to get her Broker's License and open her own office in her home in Nashville. Known as "Alice Page Real Estate Service", this business was very satisfactory, and she had the office until her retirement. She lives in that home at this time. *Submitted by Alice Page*

WOODROW AND HELEN PAINTER -

The first generation of the Painter family came from the Northern part of Germany and Holland. They came to Virginia in 1789, married, and started their families. In the early 1800s, his great-grandparents moved his family to Powell Valley, TN. They bought land and built their homes, which were handed down through five generations.

His great-grandparents had 500 acres of land and ten slaves. When the Civil War started in 1861, three young boys, two negroes, and his cousins tended the crops for four years and were overseen by Great Grandpa. Every year the Army would come to collect the corn.

Woodrow and Helen Painter

During the war, there was not any church or school. Students studied the old blue backed speller; the only book except for the Bible. After the Civil War was over in 1865, church and school started up again. After Sunday school, the young folks would meet and go horseback riding for four or five miles. When the slaves were finally freed, they wanted to stay.

His grandparents were married in 1869 and had eight children. After his grandfather's death in 1909, he willed each child a farm. The old homestead was later sold to his father, Louis Painter. The homestead is where Woodrow spent his childhood. They had to carry water from a spring and kept their milk and butter cool in the spring house. They also had a grist mill which ground the corn and wheat. For each bushel of corn or wheat they ground, they kept a peck for payment.

During the Depression in the mid 30s, times were hard. His father sold the farm and became a share cropper. The family moved to Burrville, TN. Being a young man at this time, Woodrow became restless and joined the army in 1940 and was discharged in 1945. After serving two years overseas, Woodrow joined the Civil Service and came back to Camp Atterbury near Edinburgh, IN. He soon met Francis Cooley, and they were married in 1946. She died childless in 1952.

Helen (Powers) Painter was the daughter of Kennel and Hattie Powers of Prestonsburg, KY. Woodie and Helen met in Edinburgh, IN. They were married in April of 1953. At that time, Woodie had gone to work for Cosco Inc. of Columbus as an electrician. They had two children — Theresa was born in 1958, and David was born in 1961. Helen later went to work for Cosco Inc. also. They lived in Edinburgh until 1969. They then bought 40 acres of land in Freetown on rural route number one in Brown County and built their home. The real reason they love Brown County is due to the many hills which remind them of their native states, Kentucky and Tennessee.

Woodie retired from Cosco Inc., in March of 1981. Helen quit a few years later. Their daughter, Theresa, and her family live on the 40 acres. Their son, David, lives in northern Indiana. They have two wonderful grandsons. Woodie is enjoying his retirement by fishing, hunting, and traveling. They are both members of the American Legion and of the Veterans of Foreign Wars. *Submitted by Teresa G. Dowden*

PARKER FAMILY - William M. Parker, (whose father was born in Pennsylvania and his mother born in Ohio), was born in Belmont Co., OH, on Feb. 29, 1812, married Mary Polly Collins, born Dec. 5, 1813, also in Belmont County. Mary was the daughter of Elijah and Mary Collins. William and Mary lived in Belmont County several years, rearing eight of their 11 children. They moved to Hamblen Township, Brown County, to an area called Ginger Ridge, near Goshen Church. The three youngest children were born there. William and Mary's children were: (1) James Alexander Parker (born Oct. 23, 1834, died Oct. 13, 1903), (2) Washington A. (born Jan. 23, 1836), (3) Nancy J. (born May 30, 1837), (4) Abner G. (born March 22, 1839), (5) Martin Van Buren (born Oct. 11, 1840, died Jan. 11, 1916), (6) Mary Jane (born Feb. 2, 1842), (7) Sarah A. (born May 19, 1843), (8) Louisa A. (born June 22, 1845), (9) William J. (born May 24, 1847, died April 6, 1921), (10) Susan A. (born Aug. 22, 1848), (11) Amelia (born Oct. 14, 1849, died Sept. 26, 1910), (12) Mary Anna (born Jan. 8, 1851), (13) Sampson R. (born Nov. 26, 1853), (14) Leander (born March 13, 1855).

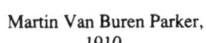

Martin Van Buren Parker, 1910.   Hannah Mary (Settles) Parker, (wife of Martin Van Buren Parker), 1910.

William and Mary Parker spent the rest of their lives there in Hamblen Township. William died after 1880 and Mary died of pneumonia on March 31, 1891.

Several of the Parker children remained in Brown County and some moved to other areas of the country. Martin Van Buren stayed and married Hannah Mary Settles. This union produced seven children. Their children were: (1) James Parker (born 1873, died 1915), (2) Ida May (born July 4, 1875, died 1951), (3) Leona (born 1880, died 1903), (4) Myrtle Ellen (born 1884, died 1912), (5) Lydia Ann (born 1870, died 1882), (6) William (born 1869, died ?), (7) Mary ("Molly") Isabelle (born 1871, died 1953).

Martin was a very well-liked man who loved children. He was remembered for his long, white beard. He was a farmer and once served in the Army. He died in 1916 and Hannah died 14 years later, in 1930. They are buried in Goshen Church Cemetery.

Three children in front: Omar Schrougham with sisters Nellie and Mabel. Middle: Artie Parker, Hannah Mary Parker, Martin Van Buren Parker, Edith Parker (holding baby Jim Parker), Ida May (Parker) Schrougham, Glen Allender. Back: Harry Schrougham, Walter (Toots) Parker, Reba Schrougham, Ethel Parker, Charles Schrougham, Hazel Snider, Mrs. Scripture (mother of Edith Parker), Ruth (Snider) Allender (holding baby Cecil), 1914.

Some of Martin and Hannah's children died in early childhood. Some moved to other areas. One who stayed in Brown County was Ida May who married a local man, Charles Schrougham, the son of early settlers. He was born to Vincent and Catherine (Alders) Schrougham, on Sept. 9, 1871, died Sept. 13, 1951. Charles and Ida were married Dec. 14, 1895. They lived in a log house owned by his parents. Their first two children were born there. Charles built a new home on Clay Lick Road, where they lived for many years and where their three other children were born. Charles and Ida's children were: (1) Harry Schrougham (born Oct. 31, 1896, died February 1981, married Mabel Condon), (2) Reba (born March 7, 1899, still living October 1990, married Ralph W. Condon), (3) Mabel (born Dec. 30, 1905, died April 1926 of Scarlet Fever, married Harley Waltz), (4) Omar (born Aug. 26, 1907, still living October 1990, married Dorothy Bush (Helmsburg) deceased, then married Elsea Neal), (5) Nellie (born June 22, 1910, died April 1988, married several times, no children).

Charles worked at several things to support his family. He farmed, taught school in both Brown and Morgan Counties. He was an excellent carpenter and worked at that trade in Brown County and, later, in Indianapolis (for the Grinslade Construction Co., building many homes on Indianapolis' south side). Other family activities the Schrougham family pursued in helping to make a living, included hunting ginseng, which they sold, gathering nuts and berries and hunting wild game. When it became increasingly difficult to make a living, Charles and Ida sold their home and brought the family to Edinburgh, IN, where they lived a few years, then moving to Indianapolis, where Charles did carpenter work until he retired. They died within two months of each other in 1951, a few months before their 56th wedding anniversary. They are buried together at Rest Haven Cemetery in Edinburgh, IN.

Charles and Ida lived near their daughter, Reba, who had married Ralph W. Condon (son of Oliver Perry Morton Condon and Mahala Ellen (Weaver) Condon), also born and raised in Brown County. Their children were: (1) Victor Eugene Condon (born Feb. 17, 1921, died September 1988), (2) Violet Elaine Condon (Bartram) Walton (born Nov. 19, 1923, living October 1990), (3) Donald Duane Condon (born July 26, 1934, living October 1990). *Submitted by Don Condon*

BUD PARKER - Brown Park Lake is a mile north of Becks Grove in southeastern Brown County. The 12 acre lake was planned and developed by Bud Parker. The 40 acre tract was purchased from Sertoma Club of east side Indianapolis in January 1970. Bud had the lake and road constructed shortly after he purchased the property. He developed 16 lots surrounding the lake. He has speculated in two other real estate deals in Brown County. Bud still maintains a cottage on the Keith Donaldson Road where he spends much of his time since retirement. The remaining time is spent at his home in Indianapolis. Bud has thoroughly enjoyed mixing business with pleasure in Brown County.

Garnet "Bud" Parker was born in Shelbyville, IN on March 31, 1929. He was the youngest of five children. Mother was Edna Pearl Parker (Richardson). Father was Floyd Parker from Shelbyville, IN.

Bud Parker at Brown Park Lake

Bud graduated from Lebanon High School in 1948. He attended Western Michigan State Teachers College and Purdue University. He joined the United States Air Force in January 1950. Bud graduated from the Air Force Airplane and Engine school at Shepard Air Force base, Wichita Falls, TX. He was stationed at O'Hare Air Field in Chicago and General Mitchell Field in Milwaukee, WI.

Bud married Margaret Teboe in June 1958. She is the daughter of Kathryn and Orval Teboe from Lebanon, IN. Bud and Margaret have a daughter, Corinne Kay who married Rickie DeBaun in February 1984. Corinne and Rick have two children, a girl, Tory Nichole and a boy, Taylor Allen. They live in Indianapolis, IN.

Bud worked as an engineer for Rock Island Refinery for ten years and a Plant Engineer for Chrysler Corporation for 25 years. He retired from Chrysler in December 1987.

GEORGE WASHINGTON PARKS - On July 2, 1839, George Washington Parks was born to Stephen and Amanda Parks. He led an uneventful life in Brown County until the onset of the Civil War. On Aug. 15, 1861, he was enlisted at Madison, IN as a private in the 22nd Indiana Infantry regiment. The 22nd was a much traveled regiment. Among the more familiar actions in which they were involved were as follows: Battle of Stone River, Murfreesboro, TN, Chickamauga, GA campaign, Missionary Ridge, TN, and many more. The action ended for George at Kenesaw Mountain on June 27, 1864, when he received a severe wound to the arm. He spent the rest of the war in military hospitals, and was mustered out of service as a Corporal on July 24, 1865.

George returned to Brown County and on April 26, 1873, married Caroline Sinn, daughter of Morris Sinn and Carolyn Rose. Morris Sinn was born in Bavaria, Germany, in 1808, and died in Brown County on July 27, 1870. He was buried on the old Fleetwood farm on Crooked Creek Road. Carolyn Rose was born in Baden, Germany, in 1838 date of death unknown.

Carolyn Parks; George Washington Parks

Carolyn (Sinn) Parks was born in Pennsylvania in 1854, and migrated with her parents to Brown County, date unknown. George and Caroline's union produced nine children: Sarah Francis, George Elmer, Rosetta, Edward, Lena, Stella, Homer, James Morris, and William, who died in infancy.

In The House of the Singing Winds, a book written about T.C. Steele by his wife, Selma Steele. Mrs. Steele wrote on page 105: "I found a particular friend in the person of Mrs. Parks." "The Parks were our nearest neighbors adjoining us to the North." "We grew very fond of them." "The two sons, Homer and Jimmy, hauled our daily water supply from Belmont, and took care of our horse." "I saw much of Mrs. Parks and depended upon her for advice concerning the perplexing problems with which I had to deal." "Through her I learned much about the history of the neighborhood." "I learned the tragic side of life as it existed in the hills." "I drove with her to distant neighbor friends, and learned much about the ways of living among the better households." "I took many walks with her through the woods in search of herbs and plants with which she compounded her medicines." "Being interested in bird life, she took me to see a pair of eagles nesting in a large tree on the banks of Salt Creek." "Many an hour I sat in the woods listening to her telling stories out of her youth." "She had the strength and character of the pioneer women - buoyant and uncomplaining." "Her outlook on life was commanding and yet generous." "Her interpretations, with her advice, became indispensable to me." "She helped me through many a difficulty, and I owed her much."

George and Caroline spent most of their married years on a farm which now is part of the T.C. Steele sanctuary. T.C. Steele as a young artist boarded with the Parks family, and later after his great success as an artist, built a home there with his second wife, Selma Steele, which they called The House of the Singing Winds.

On April 2, 1900, George was appointed Post Master of Belmont, IN. The length he held that post is unknown. George died Oct. 31, 1911. Caroline died May 5, 1946. Both are interred at Duncan Cemetery, Brown Co., IN. *Submitted by Robert P. Strickland and Gloria Mainord*

PARMERLEE HISTORY - The family of Marcus Beecher Parmelee came to Indiana from Connecticut with their mother Lois (Fairchild) Parmelee Shepard in the 1840s. James Clark Parmelee, son of Marcus and Lois Parmelee, moved westward before his siblings to Ohio. James Clark and Mary (Burgett) Parmelee were joined by his brother and sister-in-law, Marcus Hurlbutt and Rebecca Jane (Staples) Parmelee and by his sister and brother-in-law, Louise (Parmelee) and George Botsford. With their mother, they moved to the northern part of Indiana. Not finding it to their liking they came to Brown County which reminded them of Fairfield Co., CT.

James Clark Parmelee and his family settled in Hamblen Twp. where he operated a tannery. George and Louise (Parmelee) Botsford settled in Nineveh, Johnson County.

Marcus Hurlbutt Parmelee (1808-1866) and his wife Rebecca (1811-1883) also settled in Hamblen Twp., where, on a hill north of Fox's Corner, he built a two-story house in which three generations of Parmerlees were raised. Marcus and Rebecca had five children: (1) Anna, born in Connecticut, 1832; (2) Harriet Louisa, born in Connecticut, 1834; (3) George, born Connecticut, 1840; (4) Amos, born in Brown County, 1845; (5) Anna Eliza, born in Brown County, 1848. In the 1860 census the second "r" was added to the name of the family which has been called Parmerlee ever since.

George Parmerlee, third child of Marcus and Rebecca Parmerlee, enlisted in the army in 1861 and died that year of fever in Jefferson City, MO. Amos Parmerlee, fourth child of Marcus and Rebecca Parmerlee, married in 1869 to Sarah Ellen Oliver, born 1849. She had come with her parents to Brown County in 1865. Amos and Sarah Parmerlee had six children: (1) Alva T. (1870-1871); (2) Rebecca J. (1872-1873); (3) Ida (1874-1952); (4) May (1879-1955); (5) George Cleveland (1884-1968); (6) Andrew Marcus (1888-1970). Amos died in 1895 and Sarah Ellen in 1936; both are buried in Weeping Willow (Bean Blossom) Cemetery.

George Cleveland Parmerlee, 5th child of Amos and Sarah Ellen Parmerlee, married Amanda Ethel Stout (1886-1979). George and Ethel moved to Nineveh Twp., Johnson County, in 1906 to work a farm. Their children: Ruby (1908-1961), Pansy (1910-1945), Doris (1914-1981) and Warren Dale (born 1920). Members of this family are buried in Franklin, Johnson County.

Warren Dale Parmerlee, only son of George and Ethel Parmerlee, married LaDeama M. Essex (1922-1989). Their children: Roberta (born 1943), Connie (born 1946) and Dana (born 1951) who married Charlotte Hubbard (born 1951) and had Amanda (born 1977) and Alan (born 1981). *Submitted by Charlotte (Hubbard) Parmerlee*

PARSLEY FAMILY - The first generation of the Parsley family migrated from England two centuries ago. In the late 1700s, they came to Virginia and then on to Kentucky. Some came to Indiana and settled for a while in Jackson County. Because of a typhoid epidemic and for the value of the forests, they started to the hill country.

Robert Martyr Parsley, a school teacher, came from Richmond, VA to Brown County by wagon and oxen, blazing a trail in the wooded hills near Bear Wallow Hill east of Georgetown, now known as Bean Blossom. Here, he staked out a section (Sec. 33, Twp. 10) homesteading in the early 1800s before this county was organized. He built a primitive log cabin with a dirt floor, wooden, windows and a fireplace. Some of the tools they had were an axe, mattock, double shovel, loom, and spinning wheel.

Columbus Parsley, 1881

Solomon S. Parsley, son of Robert Martyr, was born in Virginia (1803). He came with his father and lived his lifetime in the Brown County pioneer cabin on the Parsley Farm. He married Susannah Staples. They had eight children: Ralph's grandfather Columbus (1830), Mary (1833); William (1834); Rachel (1835); Jasper (1836); Newton (1838); Robert (1840); and Henry (1842). In 1883, aged 45, Newton was killed on the farm by a horse and wagon tragedy, leaving ten children from the ages of two to 21.

The Parsley family was deeply religious. Faith had brought them a long way. Their prized possession was the family Bible. Solomon founded and helped build the Unity Baptist Church (1845) where he was a trustee. He was civic-minded, as the Justice of Peace (1841) and as the County Commissioner (1845). He thought they needed a church and a school. He and Susannah gave the land for a school called "Goshen #4" which is now Foxes Corner. Charlie and Frances Fox still have the deed from Solomon and Susannah Staples Parsley.

Old Parsley Home built by Columbus Parsley on Gatesville Road

The family lived off the land, depending on the natural resources. They carried water from a spring in the hill. Besides farming, they cut the timber—mostly white oak and hickory—to make crossties. The railroad came through in 1909. They made hoopbands from hickory to go around barrels and hauled them to Martinsville, where the barrels were made.

They drove cattle to Cincinnati on foot for sale in the stockyards. The family decided to build a new house, barn and other buildings on level bottom ground from native virgin timber. In this house Columbus Parsley, son of Solomon S., raised eight children (four by his first wife, Elizabeth Chapell, who died in 1871): Sylvester, Amanda, Susan and Newton. He and his second wife Sarah Steven had Clarence, John, Elsie and Otto (Ralph's father). Ralph is the great-great-grandson of Robert Martyr Parsley.

Ralph and Garnet still own and raise cattle on the Parsley Farm, east of Bean Blossom, Hamblen Township. They have two children and five grandchildren. Daughter Wanda Parsley Bunge, a school teacher, has Trudy, Polly and Angela; their son John C. is a Baptist minister, has sons Jason and John Robert.

Ralph and Garnet received the 1986 Homestead Award from the Governor for continuous family living on the same farm for 150 years. *Submitted by Garnet (Keaton) Parsley*

ELMER, JR. AND FRANCES PARSLEY -

Elmer, Jr. and Frances Parsley live on a farm in Hamblen Township on Upper Salt Creek about two miles north of Sprunica School. This farm was purchased by his parents (Elmer and Ruth C. (Condon) Parsley) in 1921 from James Walker. The land had been farmed by members of the Walker family since it had been purchased from the United States Government in 1829. Elmer, Sr. taught school in Hamblen Township until 1952. Ruth was a homemaker, raised chickens, as well as helping with the cows and horses. They were the parents of two children: Elmer, Jr. and Eileen Eubank. The children attended grade school in Hamblen Township and graduated from Helmsburg High School and Trafalgar High School, respectively. Eileen Eubanks retired from RCA in Indianapolis where she had worked 46 years. She and her husband, Raymond, own and operate a farm near Gatesville that was at one time owned by her grandfather, John Henry Condon.

Elmer, Jr. is the grandson of William and Anna Parsley and the great-grandson of Jasper Parsley who was born in 1836 on the land his grandfather, Robert Parsley had homesteaded in the early 1800s near Fox's Corner. His maternal grandparents were John Henry and Louisa (Meade) Condon, who lived on Goshen Ridge in Hamblen Township. Frances is the daughter of John and Josephine Zupancic of Mt. Zion Road off of Carmel Ridge in Jackson Township, Brown County.

Elmer, Jr. has been a bus driver for Brown County School Corporation for 35 years. Frances has retired after 40 years as a school teacher. On the farm they raise beef cattle and sell feeder calves. Much of the farm is used for pasture and raising hay. In the past 16 years they have raised from one to three acres of tobacco.

They are the parents of one daughter, Robin Elizabeth, who is a graduate of Brown County High School and Purdue University. She is married to William Esarey and lives in Plainfield, IN. They both work at the Gas Turbine Division of Allison's in Indianapolis as metallurgical engineers.

Elmer, Jr. and Frances are active in local Farm Bureau Organization serving as officers and members of the Farm Bureau County Board. He has served as Township Trustee and she has been a member of Hamblen Township Advisory Board. They attend St. Agnes Church in Nashville. Frances has served on the Board of Health of Brown County since 1966. Elmer, Jr. has spent many years working on the County ASCS Committee.

ORVAL PARSLEY - Orval was born Jan. 8, 1904 approximately two miles east of Bean Blossom (Georgetown), IN on what is now the Ralph and Garnet Parsley farm. He was the ninth of ten children born to Robert Newton and Anna (Waltman) Parsley.

Orval was two years old when his mother died, May 26, 1906, two months after giving birth to her tenth child Daisey. Orval's father died April 22, 1908, from a farm related accident.

Amanda (Parsley) Evans, Orval's sister took care of Orval and his brothers and sisters as best she could after their father's accident. At age 12, Orval went to live with a farm family north of Nineveh, IN where he did chores before and after school and worked summers in exchange for room and board while he was going to school at Nineveh.

Orval and Gladys Parsley

Orval then moved to Indianapolis, where he worked for the Stutz's auto company as a painter. Tiring of city life, he moved to Franklin, IN in the early 1920s, where he met Gladys Leota Chandler and they were married on May 26, 1928. Later two sons were born to them, Walter Chandler Parsley (1929) and Edwin Eugene Parsley (1932).

Orval worked as a Yard Foreman for 22 years at Central Lumber and Supply and later he worked 23 years as a foreman for Graham Manufacturing Company. Orval was an avid outdoorsman. Many oldtimers said he could catch fish and find mushrooms when no one else could. He liked to take both sons with him, when he went fishing. He was also a long time member of the Franklin Masonic Lodge #107.

On Thanksgiving day 1958 Orval's wife died of a massive brain hemorrhage; she was 50 years old. After Gladys' death Orval built a house on Princes Lake, not far from where he lived and worked as a small boy.

In June 1969 Orval's oldest son, Walter, died while living in Florida; he was 40 years old and was a veteran of the Korean War. He was never married. Orval's youngest son, Edwin, while serving in the Army, married Marjorie L. Koons Dec. 24, 1953, and they moved to Washington, DC while Edwin finished his Army enlistment. Edwin and Marjorie returned to Franklin, IN, and they had a son born to them, Edwin E. Parsley II, and a daughter Sandra S. Parsley. Edwin II married Denise A. Floyd from Bloomington, and they have two sons Joshua Michael and Blair Justin Parsley. Sandra married Charles N. Sturkie in South Carolina, where they now live. They have one daughter Kyla Eva Sturkie.

Orval enjoyed living at Princes Lake and having his grandson Edwin E. II visit him for many fishing trips. Although Orval's life was extremely hard, with many hardships and tragedies, he never complained. He put his family above everything else. He was always proud that his roots were in Brown County, and he returned there whenever he could.

He was known by his family, friends and colleagues as being an honest, hard-working man.

Orval died Thanksgiving evening 1971 of a massive stroke. *Submitted by Edwin E. Parsley, son*

RALPH AND GARNET (KEATON) PARSLEY
Ralph and Garnet (whose Brown County family background goes back to the early settlers, before the County was organized) were both born, reared, and educated here.

Ralph Dale Parsley, son of Otto and Olive (Burris) Parsley married Garnet M. Keaton, daughter of Roy and Lena (Richardson) Keaton in 1938, moved into their home east of Beanblossom that was purchased from Ralph's Aunt Susan and Harry Noe (1937), where they have lived for 52 years. To this union two children were born: Wanda Rose (1939) and John C. (1956).

Ralph and Garnet (Keaton) Parsley

Wanda was born at home, delivered by Dr. Pat Murphy, the same family doctor who delivered her mother and father, also home deliveries. Wanda Rose, a beautiful girl, grew up on the Parsley farm, attended Sprunica's one room school where Jesse Neff taught all eight grades. All the students called him Jesse! Wanda graduated from Helmsburg High School (1956) and Franklin College (1960), majoring in Secondary Education; received her master's degree at IUPUI; and now teaches in the Martinsville Schools.

Kenneth Bunge, a Brown County boy, married Wanda Dec. 22, 1960. They live north of Martinsville. They are the parents of three girls: Trudy Mae (1963), Polly Ann (1965) and Angela Rose (1970). The Bunge's oldest daughter, Trudy, attended Green Township elementary and graduated from Martinsville High School and Ball State University. She also studied in France. Trudy is associated with American Rowing as the Managing Editor of the magazine. She lives in Indianapolis.

Polly Ann, the Bunge's second daughter, graduated from Martinsville High School, attended Indiana Central (Indianapolis University) and is now employed by American Airlines. She married Mark Seibert, Nov. 11, 1989. They live in Dallas, TX.

Angela Rose, the Bunge's youngest, attended Green Township grade school, graduated from Martinsville High School and attends Franklin College. Angie is an avid sports fan.

Ralph and Garnet's son John C. was born 17 years after his sister Wanda. He attended Sprunica and Helmsburg schools, graduating from Nashville High School in 1974. John went on to graduate from Butler University and a Baptist Theological Seminary. He was ordained to the ministry in his beloved home church (Unity Baptist) on April 21, 1980. He has served as youth minister in Little Union Baptist Church under Rev. Wally Jeffs. He also served in Crawfordsville as Associate Pastor under Rev. Jim Ranard, then served as Pastor of First Baptist of Brazil. He is now pastor of the First Baptist Church in Plainfield.

John married Susan Rose Kuhn from Shelbyville (1980) and to this union three sons were born: Jason Daniel (1987), James Timothy (1985) deceased and John Robert (1987). They live at N. Broadway, Plainfield, IN.

Ralph and Garnet have always been civic minded, actively involved in church and community affairs, such as Farm Bureau, Home Extension, Historical Society, A.S.C.S., Beanblossom Boosters, Interfaith, Family History Book Committee, Cancer Crusade, Library Board, Historical Board, Church offices, Unity Cemetery Board and Politics. Also Ralph is President of the "Old Settlers Association" which is 115 years old and is held north of Beanblossom annually, the first Saturday in September. Garnet also serves on the Committee as Chairperson of the hymn sing. She also collects monies and sale items to fund the "Old Settlers" projects. They both have worked many years for the Old Settlers Reunion, one of the oldest organizations in Brown County, but their greatest contribution to society are their children and grandchildren.

Front: 1984, John Robert, John C., Jason, and Susan (Kuhn) Parsley. Center: Angela Bunge. Back: Garnet (Keaton) Parsley, Polly (Bunge) Seibert, Wanda Rose (Parsley) Bunge, Kenneth Bunge, Trudy Bunge, Ralph Parsley.

Since some of the Keaton and Parsley family have been active members of the Unity Baptist Church for over 100 years and the Parsley family have owned and operated the same farm over 150 years, Ralph and Garnet (Keaton) Parsley hope their offspring will carry on these traditions. *Submitted by Garnet (Keaton) Parsley*

ROBERT M. PARSLEY - TONYA A. CARLTON
The early Parsleys journeyed to this country from England, nearly 200 years ago. They settled in Virginia, Kentucky and Indiana.

Robert Martyr Parsley, a school teacher, settled in Brown County, along with his wife, Mary E. Haggart, from Virginia. They had three sons, Solomon S., Daniel J., James and John A. The first three born in Virginia, and John was born in Kentucky. The third son, James was, in fact, recorded living in 1850 with his mother in Hamblen Township.

James was married to Mary Ann Waltman, of Maryland, in 1856. They lived on a farm outside of "Georgetown" (now Bean Blossom) and raised eight children, Mary Margaret, (born 1857), Daniel T., (born 1859), Robert, (born 1860), Elizabeth, (born 1861), Edwin H., (born 1864), William, (born 1869), Joseph, (born 1873), and Simeon (unk).

In September of 1880, eight years before he died, James purchased a 40 acre tract of land that had been offered at tax sale with no bidders. He bought the 40 acres for the tidy sum of $9.68!

James' daughter, Elizabeth, married Ashley David Fergason, of Johnson County, who, with his son, Hallard, operated a house moving business. In those days, they moved houses with logs and a team of horses. Ashley had two other sons, Haskell and Irvin, and a daughter Hazel.

Standing: Hazel Ferguson and Elizabeth Parsley Ferguson. Seated: Mary Ann Waltman, James Parsley's wife.

Haskell married Bertha Susan Jane Kemp in November, 1908. He was a contractor in Franklin, IN and surrounding areas. He built some of the shelter houses in Brown County State Park, Turkey Run State Park, as well as others.

Haskell and "Jane" were the parents of eight children, Clara G., Henry A., Mary G., David H., Kathryn J., Elizabeth A., and two babies who died in infancy. One of their daughters, Kathryn, married Homer G. Mitchell, of Shelbyville. They were the parents of Tonya A., Philip A. and Barbara D.

Tonya and her husband, Robert E. Carlton, are now living in a 110 year old barn, restored by them, near Gwynneville, IN. The barn is furnished with many primitive antiques which they enjoy collecting.

Tonya, and her aunt, Clara Fergason Cox, have spent many fascinating hours researching their family history. They say that "Memories and stories are the threads that weave a family tapestry."

RORK-COLUMBUS-PARSLEY
Marjorie Rork, a former high school teacher of Latin in schools in Indianapolis, New Trier in Illinois, and Richmond, IN is the great-granddaughter of Columbus Parsley. Her grandmother was Amanda, daughter of Columbus. Amanda married Zachary Taylor Staples, Feb. 6, 1879, an optician whose workshop was on a parcel of land immediately adjacent to Ralph Parsley's house. Amanda and Zachary lived in Bean Blossom, later moving to Morgantown. They had three daughters: Olive Elizabeth, Feb. 3, 1880, Anna Leora, Aug. 17, 1888, and Nova Gladys, born May 10, 1890. Olive married Doctor Reuben Parker in 1916, a dentist from Cleveland, OH. Anna had previously married Dan Anderson who died tragically of tuberculosis a year later. Gladys, Marjorie's mother, married Elmer James Rork in 1914, a mechanical engineer with the Prest-O-Lite Company in Indianapolis. The Staples family had moved to Indianapolis some years before Gladys entered Manual Training High School in Indianapolis.

Marjorie Rork, 1966

Years later, Zachary, who had had an optical shop in downtown Indianapolis, decided to retire to Brown County, purchasing 11 acres of land adjacent to Ralph Parsley's land and which included the site on which he had had his optical shop. After only the garage was built, Zachary passed away (1924). Amanda and her daughter, Anna, however, decided to continue construction by adding on a bedroom and living room so they could spend their summers there. They continued to do this until Anna's death in 1937. During all those years Marjorie and her family spent many weekends in Brown County. After Amanda's death in 1944, Gladys spent the greater part of every summer at the cottage (as it was called), always planting a large garden with Ralph Parsley's help. Marjorie also would spend time there. One summer Marjorie stayed at the cottage, commuting each day to Indiana University for several courses. When Gladys passed away in 1960, her sister, Olive, decided to sell as she could not take care of the cottage from so far a distance. She sold it to Florence Tjomsland, daughter of Roonie Wilkerson (nee Clark) whose grandmother was a Parsley. So, in a strange way, this land still remains in Parsley hands.

LEONA I. PATTERSON FAMILY -
Leona was first introduced to Brown County when she brought her daughters to Girl Scout Camp Gallahue in the 1960s. She was a Girl Scout Leader for ten years and had many overnights at Gallahue. It reminded her of the forests and hills of Upper Michigan where she grew up.

The paternal grandparents, Lars and Josephina Carlson emigrated from Sweden in the 1880s to Minnesota. The maternal grandparents, Rudolph and Minnie Just, emigrated from Germany in the 1880s and also settled in Minnesota.

Her mother, Leona Just Carlson and her father, Oscar Carlson, moved from the Iron Range in Minnesota to Iron River, MI. Oscar Carlson was a blacksmith for the Iron Mine. The Carlsons brought their three daughters, Surella, and twins Leona and Leora to Michigan in 1923.

The twins, Leona and Leora Carlson, graduated from Iron River High School and then graduated from Northern Michigan University in 1944 with a Bachelor of Science Degree and a License to teach Elementary Education. They taught school in Traverse City, MI where Leona met Patrick O. Patterson who was stationed there in the U.S. Navy Air Force. They were married and moved to Indianapolis after his discharge from the Navy. They had four children, a son, Patrick O. Patterson, Jr. who resides in Los Angeles, CA; and three daughters, Peggy Jean Naile who resides in Trafalgar, IN; Wendy Jo Ott who resides in Franklin, IN and Vicky Lee Wilson who resides in Warsaw, IN. Leona Patterson has seven grandchildren.

Leona I. Patterson

After the death of her husband in 1964, Leona attended Butler University in Indianapolis and received her Masters Degree in Education and Library Science. She was a grade school librarian at Harrison Hill Elementary School in Lawrence, IN for eight years and for the last 15 years she has been a librarian at Indian Creek Middle School in Trafalgar, IN.

In 1972, Leona sold her home in Indianapolis and moved to Brown County. She hired a local contractor to build a home on Lick Creek Road and added a two acre lake so that she could enjoy the Canadian Honkers, Mallards and Wood Ducks. During the 18 years she has lived in Brown County, she has planted over 1000 evergreen seedlings for wildlife, soil erosion and windbreak. The deer, fox, raccoons, opossums and squirrels are regular visitors.

When she retires, she plans to have more time for her hobbies: crafts, needlework, gardening - vegetable, perennial and wild flowers and she hopes to improve her hobby of bird identification as they visit her numerous bird feeders. She hopes to find time to master her Dulcimer. She belongs to the Brown County Spinners and Weavers Guild. Her favorite food is anything chocolate.

PELTON AND PANGBORN FAMILIES -
In the midst of thunderstorms, on July 3, 1985, John and Mary Pelton, newly-retired from long teaching careers in the Indianapolis area, moved to Southeastern Brown County one mile north of New Bellesville. The moving van burned out a part and stalled on a highway 135 south hill, and even on its arrival a small truck was needed to shuttle belongings up the steep driveway from the van to the house on the top of the ridge. The 21 acre property was a typical Brown County eroded hill farm, reverting to a beautiful mix of meadows and woods. It is now a registered "Classified Wildlife Habitat Area," christened "Juniper Ridge," left undisturbed except for a network of trails and small swimming pond.

John and Mary Pelton

John's paternal Pelton ancestors came from England in the 1630s, served in the Revolutionary and Civil Wars (a grandfather, Benjamin H. losing his life in the latter), various ones of them living in Massachusetts, Vermont, Connecticut, Ohio, Indiana (Cottage Grove), Colorado, and California (where John was raised). His father, George Seeley, was in mining with his father in Nevada, and automobile dealerships in Los Angeles. John's paternal great-grandparents Andrew A. and Christina (Ericson) Anderson, migrated from Arvika, Sweden to Colorado where daughter Katy met his grandfather John E. Pelton, who was a farmer-rancher near Montrose. On his mother's side are the Forresters and McCarthys (both of Scotch and Irish origin), who reached California in the last century. His mother, Luella, who is still living, was born in Los Angeles 95 years ago, and as a girl rode her horse in open fields in now downtown 7th and Figueroa Streets. John attended UCLA (major-subtropical horticulture) and received graduate degrees from the University of Minnesota in botany and plant ecology. He taught at University of California at L.A. and Berkeley, Oberlin College, and for 32 years at Butler University, Indianapolis, where he also served as head, Dept. of Botany. He is a charter member of the Indiana Chapter of The Nature Conservancy, and is listed in Who's Who in America. His interests continue in science and ecology, conservation, environmental ethics, and naturalistic landscaping.

Mary's paternal ancestors, the Pangborns, came from England in 1668 to New York, some moving to Vermont, and then later Iowa. Both her great-grandfather (Charles Benjamin) and his father Cyrus, served in the Civil War, Cyrus being a Graybeard in the Iowa volunteers and dying enroute home to Mt. Pleasant, IA. Mary's father, a veteran of World War I, worked as a railroad mail-clerk. Mary's maternal line, the Arbogasts, came from Germany in 1749. Michael Sr. served in the Revolutionary War and was a farmer in Highland Co., VA. Mary's great-grandfather, John Quincy Adams Arbogast, a Civil War veteran, migrated from Springfield, OH, to a farm in Randolph Co., IN. His son Clinton Dewitt, also a farmer, married Matilda Turfinger, and raised two daughters, one of which, Anna Mae, was Mary's mother. Anna Mae worked her way through Depauw University, and Chicago Training School, finding employment there as a social worker. In Chicago she met Mary's father, Frank Leroy, bore Mary and three brothers, John, Frank, and Charles William and moved to the suburb of Downers Grove, IL. After her father's death when Mary was eight, the family moved to her grandfather Clinton's farm north of Losantville, IN. Mary worked her way through Ball State University (major-Speech and Hearing Therapy) and was employed for 28 years as a speech pathologist in the Noblesville and Washington Township, Indianapolis, schools. She currently serves on Council of the Indiana Speech and Hearing Association and is active in local volunteer work, including the Nashville United Methodist Church and the Historical Society museum as docent and weaver.

John and Mary have three adult children, George Steven Pelton (wife Sherry Gauntt), James Daniel Eudaly, and Joan (Eudaly) Lietz (Mrs. Stephen Lietz), the parents of James and Jonathon. All live in the Indianapolis area.

BEULAH JEAN (KELLEY) PERCIFIELD
- Beulah was born at Belmont in Brown County, on May 1, 1919. She is the daughter of Benjamin Richard and Jessie Morrison Kelley. Beulah Jean's grandfather, Samuel George Washington Kelley, grandmother Lydia Percifield Kelley, and their two other children, Harry and Eudora, lived on Kelley Hill in Brown County much of their lives. Beulah Jean's Aunt Eudora Kelley was the first woman from Brown County elected to a state office. She was elected Reporter of the Supreme and Appellate Court during Henry Schricker's term of Governor in 1948.

Beulah Jean grew up in various areas of Brown County. At one time, her father and grandfather, John Swayze Morrison owned the Story General Store and lived near there for a short time. Her grandfather Morrison also owned the general store in Belmont. There, he would buy the neighbor's geese and drive them by foot to market at Indianapolis periodically.

Beulah Jean Percifield, ca: 1923

Lydia Percifield Kelley

Beulah Jean and her parents, along with brothers, Dwight Denzil, Richard Dale, and sister, Cleo Beryl, lived around the Green Valley area much of their lives. The Kelley children walked one and one-half miles to the Green Valley School, many times having to walk over the bluff because of high water. When Beulah Jean started high school, bus service started and she began riding to school.

The Kelley's neighbors and friends were the Grover C. Percifield family. Beulah Jean married Lester Percifield who was called "Bill." Lester Percifield's mother was Lottie L. Fleener Percifield.

Lester and Beulah Jean had three children, William Lester was born in Brown County, Richard Glen was born in Brownsburg, and Janice Kay (Crabtree) was born in the Bartholomew County Hospital.

After the children were born, Lester and Beulah Jean moved back to Brown County and along with her sister and husband, A. Eugene and Cleo Kelley Willoughby, bought the Nashville Hardware from Ralph and Mable Calvin Burkholder. Later they sold their share to the Willoughby's and opened an electrical appliance and variety store in the Star Store Building.

Lester was elected Sheriff of Brown County in 1954 and was the first sheriff to serve two four-year terms. He, Beulah Jean, their children and one deputy, "ran" the sheriff's office. The telephone and radio were in their dining room in the sheriff's residence and prisoner's meals were prepared in the family kitchen.

In 1959, the family bought Jerry's Drive In, a root beer stand and favorite spot for Brown Countians to come and sit, eat, and visit. Lester "Bill" loved to talk and if he wasn't real busy would visit with everyone who came in. Lester "Bill" and Beulah Jean retired from this business in 1979 and opened a small shop on their Kelley Hill property across from the west Park Entrance.

Lester "Bill" died suddenly Oct. 30, 1980. Beulah Jean still lives at their home on Salt Creek Road in Brown County. *Submitted by J. Kay Percifield Crabtree*

GEORGE AND ELIZABETH PERCIFIELD

George came to that part of Monroe County which later became part of Brown County with his father, Gilbert, in 1831. George was born in Tennessee, March 11, 1822 (probably in Grainger County). Gilbert married Sally Spires in Grainger County on March 13, 1821. She apparently died before Gilbert and George came to Indiana.

Other Percifields who came to this area at, or about, the same time included Samuel, Thomas and Sampson and their families. Thomas later moved to Bartholomew County. Samuel, Thomas and Gilbert were in Clay Co., KY, in 1830.

Gilbert settled on a tract of land about six miles west of Nashville. George grew to maturity on that farm and eventually purchased a farm on Owl Creek three miles west of Nashville, where he spent the remainder of his life. The Percifield Cemetery, which contains a few marked stones and many unmarked graves, is located on that farm. On March 27, 1847, in Brown County, George married Elizabeth "Betsy" Clapton, born April 1, 1823, in Kentucky. They were active members of the Christian Church.

George and Elizabeth had 12 children: Martha Ann, who married Robert Robertson; Sarah, who married (1) Moses Wooten and (2) John Robertson; Marcus Lafayette, who married Susannah Rogers; Lucy J., who married Joseph Heckman; Anderson, who married Barbara Campbell; Blevins, who married Mary Alice Rogers; Nancy "Nan," who married (1) John Heckman and (2) a Mr. Petty; William Henry, who married Laura Ellen Mann; Eliza, who married William L. Moser; Watson "Jack," who married Catherine Shipley; Lydia Mary Ellen, who married Samuel G.W. Kelley; and Sherman, who married Lucinda Poulter.

After Elizabeth's death Jan. 1, 1881, George married Rachael Hurley Followell, and they had two children, Pearl and Lawrence. *Submitted by Dale Kelley*

GILBERT PERCIFIELD

Gilbert homesteaded a farm in Brown County in 1831, about six miles west of Nashville. Gilbert and his son George who was born earlier in 1822 in Tennessee worked to build the homestead.

George later in adulthood cleared and maintained his own farm about three miles west of Nashville, where he and his wife, Elizabeth (Clapton) Percifield (born April 1, 1825 in Kentucky), raised their 13 children. The fifth child being Anderson Percifield, born on the parental homestead March 22, 1853.

Anderson at a tender age devoted his life to serve the community fervently in the field of law. Letting God's word rule in all, he began using his vacation and free time to teach. Taking an academic course at Bloomington and later entering the State University working as an educator awaiting his formal admission to the bar. In 1874 from his own office he forged to the ultimate of his profession. Having few equals and no superiors in the southern part of Indiana and having a success of over 90 percent in nearly every major criminal trial within a several county range, the records show a 90 percent acquittal rate. The 30 years of success for Anderson was magnificent since he was elected twice to the Prosecuting Attorney's Office.

Anderson married Barbara M. Campbell of Belmont Co., OH, a woman of grace and excellent repute. They were blessed with five children: the oldest a daughter, Daisy (Irwin Guthries' wife); a second daughter, Lula, who died as a child; and sons Thurman, George and Paul.

Paul, born Sept. 15, 1897, in Brown County was a steel worker and a union carpenter. He served in WW I with the Army and again heard a calling and served again in WWII as Boatswains Mate, First Class USNR. Paul had one son, George, born Oct. 6, 1930, who's mother was Amelia Lee (she died shortly after this childbirth). Paul married Louise (Clarkston-Young) of Mooresville, IN, June 26, 1948, and raised their family in Nashville. The oldest, Loretta (Jan) Young Smith, lives with her husband Silas on the Bartholomew Brown County line as they have for 20 years, after living their childhood in Nashville.

Michael William Percifield born Sept. 14, 1948, is a graduate from Brown County High School and is now a union carpenter in Johnson County after serving his country with the U.S. Army.

Son Steven Andrew Percifield born March 17, 1953, lived his life in Brown County and became a union carpenter and is also now living in Johnson County. He is also a very talented artist.

Penny Joan (Percifield) Beasley born Oct. 17, 1960, married Don Beasley and now lives on the Bartholomew-Brown County line. They have one daughter: Amber Dawn Beasley born July 9, 1988.

James Anthony Percifield born March 23, 1962, died April 1, 1962.

Paul had the pioneer spirit of Brown County and loved the area as his family, remembering the days of a sweet country village and precious memories of home. *Submitted by Penny Joan (Percifield) Beasley*

MARY (DILTZ) PEREZ

Mary was born the middle child of Isabel Fisher and Ernie Diltz in Buchanan Co., IA on Dec. 7, 1937. The Diltz's (Dilts) came to Troy Mills, IA in 1853, moving west from Pennsylvania and Ohio. Her mother's family, the Fishers and Pikes, came to Iowa from Hamilton, OH, and Vermont around the 1860s. Grandfather Peter Diltz was a carpenter and farmer. Grandmother Zilpha Isaacs was a cook who could make wonderful pies. Ernie was the second of eight children. He left home at age 14 to work on the railroad. Grandfather Edwin Fisher was a painter and paper hanger, a game warden, and farmer. Grandmother Julia Pike was widowed young, left to raise ten children by herself. Isabel, being the fourth child and first daughter, shared the responsibility of the large family. Isabel attended six weeks of normal training at University of Iowa, then became a country school teacher, where many of the students were larger than she.

Mary's parents, Ernie and Isabel, married in May, 1930 and lived in Troy Mills, IA, where they farmed. During his later years Ernie carpentered like his father and grandfather before him. He died in 1981. Isabel, along with helping on the farm, devoted a large part of her life to various community services and organizations, always reaching out to the less fortunate. Together they raised three children, Anne, Mary, and Peter.

Mary grew up on the farm, attended the University of Iowa, graduating in 1960. She moved to Chicago to work as a social worker in public and child welfare. She received a master's degree in social work from the University of Chicago in 1973, continuing her career as a school social worker. She married Robert J. Perez in 1961 and lived in Elmhurst, IL. Robert's parents, Jose and Jesusita

Ortega both came from Chihuahua, Mexico, as young teens. They met and married in Mason City, IA, and moved to Chicago in the late 1920s. Robert, born March, 1930, was the ninth child, a twin, of ten children. He worked in the insurance business until his death in 1981. Mary and Robert had two children, Maria, born 1961 and Robert, born 1964. Maria is an officer in the United States Army and Robert is a roofer and lives in Lombard, IL.

Mary Perez

In 1986, with the children grown and having had a successful career as a social work supervisor, she felt it was time to return to her heritage, the country. After several visits to Brown County, she resigned her job, sold her home, and moved here. She lived the first few months with a friend on Oak Grove Road. She moved to a cabin on Mt. Nebo Ridge, in an isolated area in Hoosier National Forest. Heating with a wood stove, fixing frozen pipes, having a kitchen with no cupboards or drawers, which often was 32° at 7:00 A.M., was quite an adventure. The hot summer came with accompanying hordes of wasps, wood roaches, and other flying insects. During this time her search for land proved to be a stroke of luck, as she found 40 acres with a beautiful ten acre lake in southern Brown County, on the Mckinney Cemetery Road. This was the Zody lake built by the Howard Zody family in the early 1970s. Their families used it as a recreational area, fishing, boating, swimming, and camping until the grandchildren were grown and many had moved away. She enjoyed building her own home, making certain that each room had an ample view of the lake and woods.

Mary works part-time as a manager/hostess at the Story Inn, substitute teacher in the Brown County schools, especially enjoying the special education classes, and also as a clerk at Orion's Belt during the tourist season in the fall. She likes to travel, for friends to visit, or to work in the gardens and watch the birds. She does volunteer work with the Agency on Aging, Health Department, Habitat for Humanity and has been a member of Extension Homemakers, and is active in conservation environmental projects. *Submitted by Mary I. Perez*

RACHEL B. PERRY AND MICHAEL R. DUFF - Rachel (Aug. 29, 1949) first moved to Brown County in 1975 to inhabit a cottage located on Lake Somerset north of Knight's Corner on Highway 46 between Bloomington and Nashville. The lakeside house was a week-end retreat belonging to her parents, Bernard and Elizabeth Perry. A Bostonian, Mr. Perry (1910-1985) and his wife Betty (Aug. 5, 1916) who was a native of Southold, Long Island, NY, settled with their three children in Bloomington, IN in 1950. At that time Bernard founded the Indiana University Press, and directed it until his retirement in 1981.

The Lake Somerset summer cottage lured Rachel to its year-round charm with swimming and canoeing in warm months and peace and wooded beauty in winter. In 1977 she left her job at the Oliver Winery (Monroe County) and attended horseshoeing school at the Oklahoma Farrier's College in Sperry, OK. Upon her return to Brown County, her horseshoeing business quickly flourished, and the major shortcoming of the lake house became evident - there was no place to keep a horse!

Rachel bought a 16 acre tract of land on T.C. Steele Road, one mile north of the Crooked Creek Boat Ramp, and began construction of a 24' x 40' frame house (dark stained rip-rap siding) on Easter Sunday of 1980. A few weeks later she met her husband-to-be on a blind date at the Porthole Inn on Lake Lemon. Michael R. Duff is a Bloomington native and eldest of 11 children of Robert and Anne Duff of LaPorte, IN and Auburn, IN respectively. Mike and Rachel were married Feb. 14, 1981 and Mike commuted to Bloomington as Vice President/General Manager of Monroe Beverage Company while Rachel continued to travel the back roads of Brown and Monroe Counties shoeing horses.

Improvements on the property continued with the addition of a small barn, split rail fencing, a garage, and a footbridge over their picturesque but volatile creek. One November morning in 1985 a large tree fell across T.C. Steele Road, making the driveway through the T.C. Steele State Historic Site the only passage to the boat ramp. When Rachel was driving up the site driveway, a man wearing a suit and tie flagged her down, asking for a ride to the Steele house. He introduced himself as the new curator of the site, and asked if she knew anyone who would like to work there. Being the off-season for horseshoeing, Rachel took the job herself.

She continued to work at the historic site on a part-time basis until December of 1988 when she was promoted to Assistant Curator, and gave up shoeing horses. Simultaneously, Mike experienced a job change when his company merged with another. He's now pursuing a career in free-lance writing.

Throughout the nine years of rural residency the Perry/Duffs have enjoyed the charm of the area in every season and have found serenity in being tucked away in a hollow in Brown Co., IN. At the same time, they're near their families and hometown of Bloomington and able to enjoy the advantages of living close to Indiana University. *Submitted by Rachel Perry*

PRESTON AND ELLEN PETRO - Preston was born June 5, 1861, in Brown County and died at Shelbyville, IN on Feb. 14, 1947. A preacher, Preston Petro married Ellen Sullivan in Brown County on Sept. 4, 1880. Ellen was born July 27, 1863, at Story and died Feb. 27, 1940. She was a daughter of Hiram Sullivan and Jane Graham, both of whom are buried in Duncan Cemetery in Brown County. Jane Graham Sullivan was known as "Grandma Graham" and lived on Dry Branch Road. Frank Hohenberger, early photographer of Brown County, took pictures and wrote about both Ellen Petro and "Grandma Graham". A photograph of Ellen Petro is among the collection of portraits of Brown Countians displayed on a large wall in the Nashville House. Dillon Bustin, folklorist, devotes a chapter to Ellen Petro and Grandma Graham in his book, *If You Don't Outdie Me*.

Preston and Ellen Sullivan Petro had 11 children, three of whom died at birth. One of their daughters,

Ora Flossie Petro, born Aug. 27, 1898, Brown County, married Joseph Crouch, son of John R. Crouch and Rebecca Reeves. Ora's sister, Lula K. Petro, married Thomas Martin Crouch, brother of Joseph Crouch.

Ellen Petro, 1930

Ora Flossie Petro and Joseph Crouch married on Sept. 9, 1914, and had six children, two of whom died at birth. Joseph and Ora lived and started their family on their farm which later became the Horsemen's Camp in Brown County State Park. They also had lived in the Kelp Post Office where their youngest son, Donald, was born. The other children were Grover, John and Kenneth Woodrow. Ora's husband, Joseph, died March 3, 1930, at the age of 54 of TB. After his death the family was separated. Donald was adopted at the age of nine months by the Samuel Chandler family of Columbus. His older brothers, Grover, John and Woodrow became wards of the County Home in Columbus. Woodrow was adopted by the Claud Robbins family of Indianapolis.

Ora, widow of Joseph Crouch, married Elza Albert Polley on Jan. 19, 1932. They had five children: Evelyn, born 1932, Phyllis, born and died 1934, Jesse L., born 1935, died Aug. 21, 1979, Irene, born 1937 and Janet, born 1944. Evelyn, Janet and Irene live in the Brown County area. Elza Polley died April 22, 1945, and is buried in Unionville, IN. Ora Polley then married William M. Petro. They had no children. William Petro died in 1962 and is buried in Green Valley Cemetery in Brown County. Ora Petro then married John Mathis. They lived in Brown County where Mr. Mathis worked for the Yellowwood State Forest and the T.C. Steele Memorial. After retirement, John and Ora Mathis lived at Trevlac, then moved to Columbus. John was seriously injured in a fall and died at the Columbus Hospital on June 10, 1985.

After 50 years of separation, Ora's family was reunited. She lives at the Community Care Center in Nashville, IN. She has always been a devout Christian and read her Bible every day until her sight failed. (see Joseph William Crouch) *Submitted by Don and Carol Chandler*

WENDELL C. PHILLIPPI - In 1975 Wendell bought a long dreamed of cabin on a hill on Jackson Branch Hollow. Wendell first heard of Brown County early in life in grade school. The superintendent of schools in Zionsville, IN was quite a humorist. He kept referring to the win-ding roads of Brown County. Wendell swallowed his pronunciation of win-ding early in life much to the amusement of fellow students in grade school. In fact win-ding roads became a common saying in the household and still is. Wendell was so curious that his parents took him to Brown County State Park at an early age and allowed him to purchase an expensive pine box for treasures, as meager as they were, and as small as the box was. It probably cost 50¢ but that was a hunk of dough in the depression days.

M.G. Wendell Phillippi

In high school the park was a favorite place for daytime dates if you could get the family car for an outing. Then it was college at Indiana University and on rare occasions a drive to Brown County for a decent meal. If one looked old enough one could buy a beer—a real treat. Wendell was a Sigma Nu fraternity brother of Bill and Phil Bessire. They even spiked a drink in the old tavern if any one had enough money to buy a half pint of apple or peach brandy. A year after graduation, Wendell started dating a girl, Georgiana Pittman, whose parents had a cabin on Jackson Branch Hollow and they had many picnics before he went into the Army in 1941, after one year at The Indianapolis News—an early draftee. The big treat was to buy cider and apples at the Bessire orchard, which adjoined the cabin property. A drop or two of whiskey was really living it up. As a young newspaperman he was not flushed with cash.

Wendell married that girl during the war and in the postwar years his new family spent many weekends at the cabin until his in-laws, George and Netta Pittman, sold the cabin in 1957. Georgiana always regretted the sale of the cabin. Wendell was too involved with work at The Indianapolis News as managing editor and also as an officer in the 38th Division, Indiana National Guard, to buy the cabin and visit Brown County very often at this time.

The Pittmans were good friends of Fred Bates and Priscilla (Queenie) Johnson who had Eddie Voland build three cabins on the ridge. They bought their cabin in 1937 from Ida Anderson, a mutual friend. She also owned the two cabins below. Ida, a teacher at Tech High School, who later sold one to the University of Chicago professor Herbert Green and his wife, Winnie. They sold occult books from their cabin address and planted many flowers.

The third cabin was sold to Harry E. Burketts in 1939. They had the "nicest" one on the hill. It is the one Wendell now owns. The WPA built outside privies for all three during the depression—some call them Franklins and others Roosevelt. They were luxury in their day—two still standing, which were used by hikers over the years also.

Wendell and Georgiana bought it in 1975 from Grace Roland (late husband John) who were encouraged to buy it from the Pittmans who were old friends in the grocery business. It was thought to be an expensive adventure and too hot in the summer time but since they were coming down to Leila David's cabins and later the Ramada Inn so often on weekends that they decided to buy. The day they stopped to see it they had been in Bloomington for an alumni meeting and it was hot as Hades. But a strong breeze came up as they were sitting at the picnic table with Grace, and Wendell knew his wife would get her dream—a cabin in County Brown.

Wendell and Georgiana fell in love again with Nashville and the beautiful hills surrounding them in Washington township. Georgiana died in 1978 after many good times at the cabin. The cabin was kept and when Wendell married again to Barbara Jean Howden (a widowed school teacher in his native Zionsville) in 1980, he found that she also had visited Brown County often with her parents from nearby Gibson County and while attending I.U. She fell in love with the cabin and has written reviews on the Playhouse shows for the Brown County Democrat.

At The News over the years, Wendell heard a lot about Brown County from Wayne Guthrie, a fellow editor and later columnist, who wrote many a yarn about their beloved hill, art and recreation paradise. The News started the Abe Martin cartoons and Wendell became well acquainted with the Kin Hubbard family over the years with copyright, reproduction, syndication problems.

Wendell's Brown County art collection, which includes Marie Goth, Cariani, Graff, Bessire, Griffith, Williamson, Adolph Schulz, Hohenberger, LaChance, Evelynne and George Mess enhances their Indianapolis residence.

They live in Brown County as much as possible. Wendell made the front pages of the Brown County Democrat when he was attacked by Hornets in 1987 (Dr. Tim Alward saved his life with adrenaline injections in the main intersection of town) and again in 1988.

When Dan Quayle was nominated for vice president, the press hordes swarmed on the cabin because Wendell had made one call to one person in Quayle's behalf in 1969. Otherwise, their Brown County stays are treasures in their memory lane on Jackson Branch Hollow.

Phillippi is former managing editor of The Indianapolis News and a retired Army major general. He has two children by his first marriage: Frank Phillippi, and Ann Perry. Barbara has four children by a previous marriage: Miranda Biber, Michelle Laconi and Mike and Marc Howden. *Submitted by Wendell C. Phillippi*

PHILLIPS - Clover Lorraine (Rogers) Phillips was born on May 6, 1960 to Mary Jane and Jewel Wayne Rogers. She was the first of three daughters. Her two younger sisters are Diane Lee Scott and Shana LaVerne Swabb. Clover spent her early years in Trevlac. Some of her childhood friends include: Thalia Kakavecos and the Finch sisters Susan, Cindy and Honnalora. Clover had two sons from Robert (Bobbie) Arthur Phillips. They are Robert (Robbie) Arthur the third and Matthew Allen. Both boys have attended school in Brown County.

Matthew Allen and Robert Arthur III Phillips. Rob holding wood animal bank.

RICHARD AND NANCY PHILLIPS -
Richard M. Phillips and Nancy E. Carmichael raised their family in southern Brown County. He was the son of George and Joanna Phillips and she was the daughter of William and Louisa Carmichael.

Richard and Nancy had five children: Martha, Mary, Albert R., Richard Wiley, and Rufus P.

Richard Wiley Phillips married Laura B. Hamilton on Feb. 16, 1895. She was the daughter of Morton Hamilton and Nancy F. Pruitt, and the granddaughter of Martin and Sarah Pruitt.

Wiley and Laura had one child, Leatha Lucille, before Laura's death in 1897. Wiley then married Anna Waggoner and had two more children: Fay and Ray.

Leatha Phillips married Clinton Allen Winkler on May 15, 1915. He was the son of William Winkler and Nancy Catherine Lutes.

Clinton and Leatha had three children: Emil, Harold, and Vivian Loretta. *Submitted by Larry Dean Wayt*

THE PICKARD FAMILY - John Pickard, from whom Allen Higgins Pickard descends, settled in Rowley, MA, from England prior to 1644. His great-great-grandson, Thomas Pickard, Jr., served in the American Revolution in the Rhode Island Campaign under his future father-in-law, First Lieutenant James Lord. Lord was also a veteran of Bunker Hill and the Long Island Campaign. After the War, this branch of the family moved to Litchfield, ME, where they remained until the 20th century when Mr. Pickard's father, Guy Allen Pickard, son of Algernon William and Annie Sophia (Ring) Pickard, of Hollowell, ME, a graduate of Bates College, left to study at Yale. While in New Haven, he met and married Caroline Darby Higgins. She was the daughter of Dr. Archibald Sage Higgins of Manasquan, NJ, and his wife Annie Taylor Darby of Lutherville, MD.

Allen Pickard was born on March 7, 1922, at 169 Livingston St., New Haven, CT. He is a graduate of Dartmouth College and received his M.A. in History from the University of Connecticut. He served with the U.S. Army in World War II, and for most of his career was employed by the Department of Defense at the Defense Information School at Fort Harrison where he was a professor of public affairs and a department head. He retired to Brown County in 1982.

Allen H. and Ruth E. (Gormley) Pickard

In 1946 Mr. Pickard married Judith S. Sloane of New York City. Two children resulted from this marriage: Janet Carole, born April 22, 1948, at Newburgh, NY, now Mrs. Michael B. Bernstein of Thousand Oaks, CA, and Todd Sloane, born Oct. 9, 1949, at Middletown, NY. This marriage terminated in divorce. Mr. and Mrs. Bernstein are the parents of Shayne Jessica, born Oct. 16, 1976, and Keith Bryan, born Feb. 22, 1983. Mrs. Bernstein, an elementary school teacher, is a graduate of California State University at Northridge, and completed her graduate work at California Lutheran University.

Todd Sloane Pickard and his wife, the former Chahee Choi of South Korea, are the parents of Sarah N., born June 21, 1979, and Benjamin L., born Oct. 6, 1981, at New York City. Todd Pickard, a graduate of Dartmouth College and Stanford University Law School, resides with his family in New York.

Allen Pickard subsequently married on April 28, 1951 at Foxon, East Haven, CT, Ruth Elizabeth Gormley of New Haven. She is the daughter of Paul Dresser Gormley of Schenectady, NY, and Ruth Amy Rider, daughter of Frank A. and Hattie Calista (Powers) Rider of Forestville, NY. She was born at Schenectady on Oct. 15, 1927. The children of this marriage are: David Sage, born May 26, 1956, and Henry Rider, born July 3, 1959, both at New Haven, CT.

On Sept. 30, 1978 David Pickard married his DePauw University classmate, Kim Forster Howard, daughter of Edward Allen and Phyllis (Vincent) Howard of Evansville. He subsequently served for four years in the U.S. Air Force attaining the rank of captain. While in the Air Force he completed his masters degree in computer science at the University of Colorado. David and Kim, who presently reside in Cincinnati, OH, have one son, Alexander Forster, born June 10, 1988, at Dayton, OH.

Henry Pickard, a graduate of Indiana University, is unmarried and lives in Indianapolis where he is employed by the Radisson Hotel.

Mrs. Pickard is a descendant in the maternal line from two Mayflower passengers, the Elder William Brewster and Stephen Hopkins. Her paternal grandparents were Harry V. Gormley of Baltimore and Claire Dreiser of Terre Haute, IN. Among her grandmother's brothers were the noted American author, Theodore Dreiser, and Paul Dresser, the composer of "On the Banks of the Wabash," the Indiana state song.

Mrs. Pickard is a graduate of Brown University, Providence, RI, and holds a masters degree from the State University of New York at New Paltz. She represents the fifth generation in her family to have taught in the public schools of the state of New York. She retired from the Indianapolis school system in 1981 after a teaching career of 21 years—15 of them as a teacher of the gifted.

Mr. and Mrs. Pickard share an interest in history and genealogy as well as an enthusiasm for country living and for the birds and animals that inhabit their secluded 19 acre farmstead bordering Bean Blossom Creek.

Since their retirement the Pickards have been active in various organizations. Mrs. Pickard is a member and past president of the Nashville Literary Club and currently serves as president of the Brown County Retired Teachers Association. She is also a member of the Bloomington Chapter DAR and the Lydia Prescott Chapter, Colonial Dames of the XVII Century. For the past two years she has worked part-time at the Brown County Public Library.

Mr. Pickard lists among his memberships the Brown County Kiwanis Club and the Hugh Thomas Miller Chapter, SAR. He is the immediate past president of the Spencer Family Association and serves on its board of directors.

Mr. Pickard has maintained a life-long interest in local politics and prior to coming to Indiana was village trustee and later mayor of Montgomery, NY. He is presently in his third term as Republican Precinct Committeeman for the second precinct of Jackson Township and serves as a member of the Brown County Board of Tax Review.

LOREN AND PHYLLIS PING FAMILY -
Edgar Loren Ping, born June 29, 1929, in Van Buren Township, south of Story in Brown County. He was the son of Charles Solomon Ping (1883-1952) and Iva Iona Tabor (1886-1957).

Loren Ping

Loren had three sisters; Fern, Blanche and Clodean. Thelma Fern Ping (1905-1987) married Wesley Leroy Pruitt (born 1905). Blanche Olive Ping (1908-1962) married Virgil Greathouse (1906-1970). Altha Clodean Ping (1914-1975) married Herschel Glenn Taylor (born 1909).

On July 3, 1948, Loren married Phyllis Lovenia Browning (born 1928) daughter of Leonard J. Browning (1906-1973) and Edith Mae Lewis (1908-1989) of Jackson County. They had two children: Gary Wayne and Lana Diane.

Gary Wayne Ping (born June 21, 1952), married Kathleen Joan Craig (born 1953) of Bedford, IN. Gary adopted five children: Amy Lynn Ping (born Feb. 26, 1976); Michelle Joan Ping (born Oct. 15, 1977); Robert Wayne Ping (born Feb. 14, 1980); Cassandra Lovenia Ping (born March 6, 1986); and Zabrina Marylou Ping (born March 6, 1986). Gary lives near Bedford, IN.

Lana Diane Ping, (born Aug. 15, 1953) married Ernest Lee Dickmeyer (born Aug, 8, 1951) of Ogilville, IN. They have three children: Ernest Lee II (born July 13, 1978); Jason Lee (born Oct. 22, 1980); and Miranda Dawn (born May 21, 1982). Lana lives near Pikes Peak in Brown County.

Loren and Phyllis both worked and put Loren through college. He attended Indiana University at Bloomington, IN. In 1961 after completing three years of college Loren started teaching at Freetown High School in Freetown, IN.

He taught several subjects. He was also the Basketball coach for Varsity and reserve teams. He taught at Freetown three years and then Freetown consolidated with Brownstown. Loren continued his Education to receive a B.A. in Education and a Masters degree. He has several hours beyond his Masters degree.

In 1964-65 he taught at Brown Co. High School in Nashville, IN. He coached the reserve basketball team and taught Social Studies.

In 1965-66 he taught at Azalia (Gr. 5-6-7-8) and coached all four grades in basketball. He taught at Azalia until again consolidation took place in Bartholomew County. He then taught at Southside Jr. High in Bartholomew County starting in 1969-70. He also coached Cross Country. Loren taught at Southside until May 16, 1973, when he had a heart attack which left him disabled.

In January 1979 Loren became trustee of Van Buren Township and was trustee at the time of his death in November 1985. He used the same old desk his father, Charles Ping, used when he was trustee of Van Buren Township.

Loren's wife, Phyllis became the school secretary at Van Buren Elementary in 1963-64, in Van Buren Township. This year, 1989-90, she will have completed 26 years of service to the school.

OTTO PING FAMILY -
Otto Ping, born April 3, 1883 in Brown County, died Oct. 28, 1975, married on June 19, 1910, to Clara Alice Ewers, born May 14, 1892, daughter of David and Sarah (Haines) Ewers. Otto and Clara lived all their lives in Brown County; both were members of the Harmony Baptist Church, New Bellsville. Otto's occupation was farming. He also raised chickens and he owned a canning factory on Poplar Grove Ridge during World War I. As Otto travelled selling canning equipment, he found he could also work as a photographer. There is an article about him in the book "Things Invisible To See" by W. Douglas Hartley who also wrote an article for the Indiana Historical Society magazine, "Traces", Winter 1990, Vol. 2, No. 1. Otto's glass negatives have recently been donated to the Indiana Historical Society.

Otto and Clara Ping made their home on Poplar Grove Ridge near Pikes Peak. They had two children: Bernice Irene who married Eldon Sluss (deceased). She lives in Harlingen, TX; Bryce Dwight Ping who married first to Geraldine Moore (deceased), then married second to Wilma J. (Sutton) Wayt. They reside at Rt. 2, Brownstown, Jackson County. Irene and Eldon Sluss had two children: Patricia and Curtis. Bryce and Geraldine Ping had eight children: Gloria Starr, Gerald Bryce (deceased), Rebecca Sue, Betty Ann, Anita Kaye, Lois Faye, Kenneth Dwight and Edwin Paul.

Irene, Clara, Otto and Bryce Ping

Otto Ping wrote the following: "My grandfather Job Ping and grandmother Christena moved from Crab Orchard, KY in the year 1830, and settled in the Hawpatch just north of Columbus, before Columbus was. They lived there for some time and during this time they lost their son (William) and buried him on Road 46 just east of Columbus in Sandhill Cemetery. My father, Logan Ping, was six months old when they came to Bartholomew County. In 1830s moved to Brown County east of New

Bellsville. There were just three families for some distance around for some time. Hancher and Lawles were the other families. The first Deacon in the Harmony Baptist Church was a brother of Grandfather."

Logan Ping, father of Otto Ping, was born Aug. 9, 1830, and in 1857 married Malinda Henderson born Feb. 19, 1839, in Washington Township, Brown County. She was a daughter of Robert Henderson and Permelia Newkirk. Logan and Malinda had four children: John Thomas, Christina M., Permelia and William Logan Ping. Malinda died on Jan. 27, 1872. Logan then married Emaline Henderson, born Dec. 28, 1850, of Gnawbone. She was a daughter of Robert Henderson, Jr. and Mary Ann Davis. Emaline was a member of the Harmony Baptist Church for over 75 years.

Logan and Emaline Ping raised their family on Poplar Grove Ridge. They had eight children: Freeman, Mary Ann, Charles Wesley, Lewis Franklin, Otto, Walker, Carrie Ethel and Earl who is the only one still living at this writing. He was 98 years of age on April 1, 1990, and resides at the Lake Worth Nursing Home in Ft. Worth, TX. (see Ewers Family)
Submitted by Wilma Ping (Mrs. Bryce Ping)

PITTMAN FAMILY - The earliest Pittman ancestors arrived here from Virginia in 1867 and purchased a farm of about 117+ acres six miles east of Nashville. In 1872 Absalom and Sarah Jane Pittman were living on the family farm with at least two sons, Andrew J. (Jerry) who was born in 1860, and William H. (Bill) born in 1869. At about 30 years of age Bill Pittman became Clerk of Brown County, a position he held for eight years. In 1907 he purchased the Sanitarium which was next to the Nashville Christian Church, built in 1890 which specialized in treatments with the use of mineral water, which was quite the vogue in this area in those days. He changed the name to the Pittman Inn and operated it as a 25 room hotel. With its six bathrooms it was quite unusual in those days. After eight years of successful operation he sold the property and moved to the southeast corner of Main and Van Buren Streets to reopen the Pittman Inn for another eight years of operation. Bill Pittman had a son Orville who helped him and his wife Amanda in their business. Bill Pittman died in 1923.

The Pittman Farm

In 1916 Andrew J. (Jerry) Pittman acquired the family farm east of Nashville from his mother, Sarah Jane. Jerry and his wife Maude had three children: Blanche, Grover, and Delbert (Butch). Grover worked for his uncle, William H. (Bill), driving a buggy to Helmsburg to pick up guests at the railroad and bringing them back to the Pittman Inn. His pay was 25 cents per day. Grover married Mayme Mobley, daughter of "Bummer" Mobley of Nashville. They moved to the family farm and cared for Andrew J. (Jerry) until his death in 1936, at which time they inherited the farm. To them were born three children; a stillborn daughter, Earnest who died at age eight, and William L. (Bill). Grover was killed on the farm in a tractor accident in 1951. In 1956 ownership of the farm passed from Mayme to her son William L. (Bill) and his wife Wilma, who own the farm to this day. To them were born four children: Leon, Jerry, and twins Brenda and Linda. Leon who died in 1982 had two sons, Greg and Brad. Jerry has two daughters, Leigh Ann and Jerrica Lynn. Brenda has a son, Derek Ray. Greg has a daughter Lisa Marie. The farm is currently 230 acres and operated by Jerry and his nephews, Greg and Brad. A barn is still in use on the farm that was built prior to 1867. The original log home burned in 1947.

In 1976 the Pittman Farm received the Hoosier Homestead Award, which honors farms that have operated in the same family for 100 or more years, emphasizing the important role which these farms have played in Indiana's economy.

In 1976 Bill and Jerry started a petroleum business that operates from the farm, providing fuel delivery and heating and air conditioning service to more than 1400 customers in five counties.

THE POOL FAMILY - The Pools originally came from England and Wales. William Taylor (Aug. 20, 1910-Sept. 2, 1974) and Kathryn (Kaye) Evelyn Virginia (Nicolle) Pool (June 13, 1912) came to Brown County in 1955. Their elder son, Kurtis Eugene (1933-1972) had bought property in Gnawbone and then joined the Navy so William, Kaye and William Everett (Aug. 20, 1940 Des Moines, IA) moved to this property. Their daughter Merrie Margaret (Pool) MacNabb was married and away from home.

The move to Gnawbone was a bonus for Kaye who was an aspiring artist who went on to study under Leota Loop. William worked for Chrysler Corporation and young Bill graduated from Nashville High School in 1959. He attended I.U., worked briefly at Arvin's then joined the Air Force in 1962.

In 1960 William and Kaye moved near Gatesville where William grew Christmas trees and started a firewood business. Young Bill bought some property north of Bean Blossom and also grew Christmas trees.

Susan, Willie, Kevin, Melanie and Bill Pool 1980. Note Kaye Pool's landscape in background.

In 1963 Bill was sent to Kirknewton Air Force Base near Edinburgh, Scotland, as a medic. One night he heard square dance music drifting up from the Airmen's Club so went to investigate. There, he met Susan Esther Stevenson Gavin. She had come to the square dance with a church group under the leadership of an exchange Canadian minister who thought it would be a good cultural experience for the young Scots.

Susan, a medical secretary, was the daughter of Ian Sinclair (March 10, 1912) and Mary Ramsay Walker (Gow) Gavin (April 23, 1912). She was born in Dunfermline, Scotland, April 23, 1942 on her mother's 30th birthday as Bill had been born on his father's 30th birthday! She had two brothers, Neil Gow Sinclair (1946) and Donald Fleming Sinclair (1947-1989). Bill and Susan were married Sept. 26, 1964 in Colinton Parish Church, Edinburgh. Their first child William Ian (Willie) was born Sept. 22, 1965 in Edinburgh. They came to Brown County in November, 1965.

William and Kaye were now living on Artists' Drive in Nashville where Kaye maintained a studio, held art classes and was very active with the Brown County Art Gallery. Bill started work at Chrysler in 1966 and also raised Christmas trees. Bill and Susan had two more children, Melanie Mary (May 2, 1967) and Kevin Sean (April 1, 1969).

In 1969 Merrie (MacNabb) moved to Brown County with her five children. She met Cecil Inman and they married in 1973. They moved to Indianapolis in 1979. Cecil died April, 1990.

William retired from Chrysler in 1971 and worked as a Town Marshall in Nashville. He and Kaye came to a parting of the ways and William moved to Arizona where he died Sept. 2, 1974.

Kurtis Eugene Pool died Nov. 3, 1972, in California leaving a wife and three daughters.

Bill bought the Helmsburg Sawmill in 1973 from Charles Richards and he and Susan expanded it in 1979. This structure was destroyed by fire Oct. 13, 1987. Undaunted, they rebuilt once more and are still operating the family business with sons Willie and Kevin. Kevin is also a Specialist in the Indiana National Guard and a football coach for B.C.J.H.S. Melanie is a private duty nurse in Indianapolis and also works at J.C.M.H. Bill has been a Mason since 1962. *Submitted by Susan E.S. Pool*

EDWARD K. PORTER - Edward was born Nov. 10, 1846, in Pennsylvania, the son of Edward and Jane Watt Porter. His ancestors came from England to Pennsylvania, then later moved to Clinton, IA in 1862, where he married Melissa Jane Morgan on Feb. 10, 1879. Their children were: Will Rae, John Henry, Edward, Clara and Mary.

In Grundy Co., IA the Porter's farmed, sold farm machinery and Will was a school teacher for several years.

This third generation of Porter's from England, moved on to McKenzie Co., ND, about 1905.

In North Dakota they tilled the heavy prairie sod, and lived in sod houses. About every two or three years the crops were a failure, no moisture. They planted potatoes late in the fall by plowing a furrow and turning the sod over it for warmth under the snows. The sod was so heavy the potatoes weren't nice and round, but flat sides.

While in North Dakota, Will Rae married Cinderella Teague on Jan. 12, 1909. Ray Allen Porter was born Oct. 9, 1910, near Charleson, McKenzie Co., ND.

Edward K. and Melissa Jane went on to near Richmound, Sask. Canada, with the Will and John Porter families about 1911. While there, Will and Cinderella had another son, Earl Walker Porter, born March 27, 1915.

Edward K. and Melissa both died and were buried in Alberta, Canada.

Will Rae Porter died May 11, 1957, and was buried at Washington Park in Indianapolis. Cinderella Teague Porter died Sept. 24, 1969, and was buried at Bean Blossom cemetery in Brown County.

Their oldest son, Ray Allen Porter, married Mary Cordelia Derringer on Oct. 31, 1932, and lived in Brown County. Their children are: William Allen, James Earl, Thelma Mae, Lois Marie, Audrey Anna and Richard Leo.

Ray Allen died Jan. 12, 1980, and was buried at Bean Blossom cemetery in Brown County. *Written by Mary (Derringer) Porter*

MARY CORDELIA (DERRINGER) PORTER

- The first child of Willie and Ruby Derringer, was born on July 17, 1915, in Brown County. She was married in Indianiapolis, IN on Oct. 31, 1932 to Ray Allen Porter. Their children are William Allen, James Earl, Thelma May (Arvin), Lois Marie (Sanders), Audrey Anna (Beasley) and Richard Leo who died in infancy.

Ray Porter and children Audrey, Thelma, Lois, Allen and Jimmy. The Fordson tractor made in Ireland.

William Allen Porter married Doris Ann Albright Sept. 19, 1954, and they have four children: (1) Nancy Ann Porter born Oct. 21, 1955, who married Gary Lamont Manning June 28, 1980 and they have two children; Grant Allen Manning born May 7, 1983, and Megan Leann Manning, born March 1, 1986. (2) Donna Sue Porter born Feb. 12, 1957, who married Richard Allen Lucal on July 5, 1980, and they have two children; Kyle Allen Porter Lucal born Aug. 6, 1986 and Devon Charles Porter Lucal born March 8, 1990. (3) Kenneth Allen Porter born Jan. 10, 1960, (unmarried). (4) Betty Jean Porter born June 26, 1961, who married Kevin Lee Grelle on Aug. 14, 1982, and they have three children; Austin Lee Grelle born June 20, 1988; Jaclyn Ann Grelle born Aug. 28, 1989; and Lauren Marie Grelle born Sept. 21, 1990.

James Earl Porter married Barbara Ann Hayworth Dec. 11, 1955, and they have two children: (1) Stephanie Kay Porter born May 27, 1956, who married Kendall Lee Kritzer on Dec. 31, 1981, and have two children: Kristopher Michael Talmadge Kritzer born Aug. 21, 1984, and Kaitlyn Mary Louise Kritzer born May 9, 1990. (2) Michael Eugene Porter born may 25, 1958, who married Jill Elaine Ison Sept. 26, 1981, and have three children: (1) Mandy Leigh Porter born March 16, 1982; (2) David James Porter born Jan. 28, 1985; (3) Steven Michael Porter born March 10, 1988.

House built by Porter in 1939 on Porter Road. Mary had a school bus route for 28 years.

Thelma May Porter married Gene Otis Arvin on Feb. 10, 1961, and have three children: (1) Sheila Marie Arvin born Sept. 2, 1967, (unmarried); (2) Sheryl May Arvin born April 16, 1969, who married Daniel E. Sharpe on May 19, 1990; (3) Gene Porter (Bud) Arvin born Sept. 11, 1973 (unmarried).

Lois Marie Porter married Leslie Marlowe Sanders on Dec. 3, 1955, and they have four children: (1) Marvin Leslie Sanders born July 6, 1957, who married Pamela Jo Haugh Brummett April 28, 1977, and have three children; Steven Lee Brummett born Dec. 20, 1975; Elizabeth Ann Sanders born March 18, 1980; and Brian Leslie Sanders born March 3, 1983. (2) Dennis Wayne Sanders born July 16, 1958, who married Debra Sue Sumpter Sept. 19, 1977, and have one daughter Jennifer Marie Sanders born Dec. 5, 1983. (3) Roy Nathan Sanders born May 11, 1962, who married Esther Caroline Dodson on Dec. 31, 1981, and have one son, Nathan Daniel Sanders, born Dec. 23, 1984. (4) Terry Leon Sanders born Dec. 18, 1966 (unmarried).

Audrey Anna Porter married Harold Eugene Beasley June 17, 1961, and have two children: Brian Eugene Beasley born July 30, 1962, (unmarried) and Brent Douglas Beasley born May 10, 1964, (unmarried). *Submitted by Mary (Derringer) Porter*

LUTHER POWELL FAMILY

- The Powell family came into Powell Valley, VA from England in the 1600s. Jessie Powell married Nancy Waters in Kentucky and raised his family of seven children: (1) Joe, (2) Clora, (3) Ancil, (4) Liza, (5) Lilly, (6) Sadie, and (7) Clydia. Jessie received a land grant of 1000 acres in Kentucky and on his death each child received 160 acres each.

The Powells came from Montgomery County and Powell Co., KY to Trevlac, IN in January of 1921. They knew people that were already here: John Harmon Neal and Grover Willoughby and Ancil Powell, timberman came to work for Mr. Neal. The family moved to a "holler" named Davis Creek and they built a shack 18 foot square in size for their family of five.

Homer Powell   Luther, Herman and Wesley Powell.

Miriam (Warmouth) and Ancil Powell's children are: (1) Jessie (born 1909 and died December 1988); (2) Edna (Williamson) (born 1912) and present owner of the Red Door Restaurant; (3) Ollie, (4) Luther Crokett (born Dec. 12, 1915) married 1937 to Mary Olive Bush and divorced 1979; (5) Herman Oliver (born 1918 and died 1981) all born in Montgomery Co., KY. (6) Homer (born 1923 and died 1945, January 7, the first casualty from Brown County in WWII was on Ship St. Augustine); (7) Joseph Arthur; (8) John Wesley (born 1925); (9) Elberta (born 1928) and (10) Annie Lorraine (born 1932). The last five children all born in Brown County.

Luther Powell, the fourth child of Ancil remembers vividly coming to Brown County first by wagon and then train to Trevlac, a journey of two days by train. They next traveled by wagon from Trevlac to Belmont on Davis Creek. Luther went to the Belmont School, his first teacher was Virginia Leonard.

After high school Luther was a carpenter for Houser Construction Company for about four years then he joined the Navy for four years and was again back at Houser Company for about four years more. He accepted the Lord on Dec. 8, 1946 and entered the ministry in 1947 for the Church of God. Then he served churches in four states, and was District Superintendent in three states (Indiana, Illinois and West Virginia).

Luther's memories of Nashville includes the livery stable on the corner where the Pine Room is now and at that time the creek ran across the street between Calvin's Hardware and Nashville State Bank. The large trees by the Court House were planted by Luther and others on one Arbor Day when he was around 16, which makes these trees a little over 58 years old.

To the best of Luther's memory only four folks owned cars in 1921. Several of the family entered the service: Luther (Navy), Herman (Army Sergeant), Homer (Navy) and Wesley (Navy) and so gave 16 years in service in WWII. Luther is a charter member of the U.S. Commission for the Battle of Normandy Museum.

In 1937 Luther married Mary Olive Bush and they have three children: (1) Sharon Lynn (born April 13, 1938) and (2) Luther Allen (born Aug. 13, 1944) and (3) Nancy Lee (born Jan. 4, 1948). Allen and Nancy were born in Bartholomew County and Sharon was born in Marion County. Today Luther has 14 grandchildren and seven great-grandchildren.

Luther's grandfather on his mother's side is Oliver Warmouth, who was a volunteer in the 14th Kentucky Calvary. He is buried in Powell Co., KY. His grandmother is Rebecca Barnett. Oliver and Rebecca both were half Cherokee Indian. Oliver's mother was born on the Cherokee Indian Reservation in North Carolina. *Submitted by Luther Powell*

HOWARD PRINCE FAMILY

- The young man, Howard Prince, who was destined to affect the future of both Ruby Ford and Hamblen Township did not come to live there until 1908. Howard's father, James M. Prince, came from a family that originated in England, and had been in West Virginia for only two generations. Events in West Virginia made James Prince decide to move further west and in the early 1890s he settled in Madison Co., IN, married Laura Frazier, and began to raise a family. However, about 1908, for reasons unknown, he moved the family to Brown County.

Ruby Ford (1897-1945) and Howard Prince (1896-1962), were married on Oct. 25, 1917. Howard was operating a canning factory in Helmsburg under the name Brown County Products Company. The brand name of the canned foods was "Abe Martin." Although only 20 or 21 years old at the time he started into this business, Howard did have previous experience. The Prince family home was on Porter Road near Sprunica. (see James M. Prince Family). As a teenager he had raised vegetables and picked wild berries and canned them. He used a corn crib for his first commercial canning "factory."

In this trial venture he produced canned tomatoes, greenbeans, and blackberry jam. When he expanded into a building in Helmsburg, it is understood that he had a financial partner from Indianapolis, but the details of this arrangement are unknown. It is believed that Howard was the first to commercially can green beans in Indiana. Most individuals canned their own, but there was a need for canned goods for the armed forces.

Howard and Ruby Ford Prince

Howard and Ruby moved out of Brown County after a while and Howard tried other enterprises including farming, gas stations, coal mines, and heavy equipment construction contracting as the years went by.

Five children were born before Rudy died. Their children were: Ruby Alice, Marlin, Joan, Donald, and Carolyn. Ruby did not live to see Howard involved in the final project of his life that affected Hamblen Township. By then he was married to Riley Boswell. In 1949 Howard was in business with his son Marlin, owning earth moving equipment in the name Prince & Prince, Inc. Howard envisioned building a man-made lake and selling the lots around the lake. At that time there were no man-made lakes in southern Indiana, other than farm ponds—no place where a family could own a lot on a lake as they did around the natural lakes in northern Indiana.

Prince & Prince, Inc. did not have the capital to finance a project of this magnitude, so Howard originated the idea of asking people to buy a lot before the lake was built, and using that money for building the lake. An option was taken on land in Nineveh Township, Johnson County and Hamblen Township, Brown County, in September, 1949.

The time was right for an offering of this kind and many people responded to the advertising. Lots on the first lake were sold out in ten days for $250 each. This was the beginning of the area now known as the Town of Prince's Lakes. With the exception of a very small parcel, the town is in Johnson County.

The demand for lake front lots continued so Howard planned another project further south of the Brown/Johnson County line in Hamblen Township. He planned, promoted, and started the construction of Cordry and Sweetwater lakes and roads. However, he failed to realize the extent of expenditures this dream would involve. In 1956 he was forced into bankruptcy. It was many years, and many problems later when the area was incorporated into the Cordry-Sweetwater Conservancy District, and the project was completed.

Howard Prince was a man who dreamed of things that might be. Without his dream, the planning, the option of land, the promotional advertising, the start-up work of clearing the trees, laying out the roads, starting the dams, and selling some lots, the project never would have begun, and the beautiful lakes of Cordry and Sweetwater might not exist.

Howard did not live to see this cherished dream completed. The disappointment and failure he felt hastened his death from heart failure. But how it would please him to see so many people enjoying the lakes, and the value of the property he was instrumental in bringing to Hamblen Township, Brown County, where he spent his youth and met his bride Ruby. *Submitted by Joan (Prince) Lattimore Ankney and Ruby Alice (Prince) Brown*

JAMES M. PRINCE FAMILY - In 1908 James Martin Prince and his wife Laura Frazier Prince purchased 60 acres of land in Hamblen Township on Porter Road near the Sprunica community from George A. Jewell. The house and all outbuildings have been torn down in recent years.

When the family moved from Elwood in Madison County there were three children in the family: Howard, Lola, and Mary. Two more children were born after the move: Everett and Beatrice.

Then Sprunica had a school, church, grocery store, canning factory and a Red Men's Lodge. A few houses were close by.

The canning factory and lodge were at a curve in the road a short distance east of the grocery store and not far from Salt Creek. Laura worked at the factory in the fall when tomatoes were being canned. While she and the other ladies peeled tomatoes her youngest daughter was allowed to help carry the clean, empty metal cans to them to be filled, sealed, and cooked.

Prince Family Reunion Prince's Lakes Aug. 12, 1956

During this era the Sprunica School was a one room school where they taught eight grades. There was a family who lived near the Prince's whose last name was "Campbell." They had two young grown daughters and two young married sons that were all school teachers. Their names were Anna, Ruby, Charlie, and Herbert. The first grade teacher at Sprunica School was Anna Campbell when Bea Prince started to school. Her second grade teacher was Charlie Campbell; third grade teacher was Herbert Campbell.

In 1925 the Sprunica school was closed because there were not enough students to justify hiring a teacher. Bea was transferred to the one room Goshen School, which was about three miles from the family home. The school building is no longer there, and the place is called "Fox's Corner." It was too far for students to walk to school when transferred out of their own school district so the township trustee paid 50 cents a day for transportation, and the student had to find their own way.

The Prince family had no auto for transportation, and the Goshen school was too far for Bea to walk, so she rode a horse. The "Stephensen's" who were family friends lived a short distance north of Goshen School and they allowed Bea to leave the horse at their place while she was in class.

In those days, telephones were few and far between, however the Prince family had a telephone even though they did not have a motorized vehicle.

Whenever some of the family needed to go to Indianapolis, or someone was coming down to "Brown" from the "City" they would take the train and get off at Bean Blossom. From there they took Georgetown Road and walked to the Prince home. *Submitted by Beatrice (Prince) Hicks*

PRUETT AND McCOY - Nathan P. Pruett (1812-1863), son of Samuel Pruett and Mary Ann Wilson, was born in Knox Co., KY. On Jan. 19, 1839 he married Jane McCoy in Monroe Co., IN and entered land in western Washington Township, Brown County in 1839. His wife (1814-1878) was born in Tennessee, a daughter of William McCoy and Jane Richardson. Nathan and Jane Pruett had ten children: 1. Wm. Henry (1836-1919) 2. Mary (1837-1919) 3. John R. (1840-1920) 4. Hiram (1842-1909) 5. David (born 1843) 6. Elizabeth (1845-1917) 7. Elisa Ann (born 1847) 8. Joseph (1848-1917) 9. Nancy (born 1849) 10. Pleasant (1850-1903). Some family members spelled their surname "Pruitt."

By 1860 Nathan Pruett and his family were in Webster Co., MO. Nathan was too old to serve in the Civil War but nevertheless he was hunted down by bushwackers who came to the Pruett home on Oct. 20, 1863. They ordered him to go to Little Rock. Jane held on to him, crying for him not to go. She was told she could go with him and to go get her shawl. When she went into the house the bushwackers shot Nathan, leaving him dead. Jane and her children carried him onto the porch. They never forgot the tragic scene.

Joseph Pruett

Four of Nathan's sons served in the Union Army: Wm. Henry, John, Hiram and David. Joseph was too young to serve. Large for his age, he was persuaded to let his hair grow and wear a dress to avoid being hunted down by bushwackers as his father had been.

After the war the family went north to Harrison Co., MO where Jane died on July 21, 1878 and was buried in Longsdon Cemetery in that county. Nathan was buried in the Harvel Cemetery in Christian Co., MO. Many family members returned to Webster and nearby counties in Missouri after 1880. Elizabeth, "Aunt Betsey", child #6 of Nathan and Jane, told stories about the difficulties of travel from Indiana to Missouri, among them scarcity of food and encounters with outlaws. They hid their few valuables in holes dug in the ground at each encampment.

William Henry, child #1 of Nathan and Jane Pruett, had a son John who was a Baptist preacher, called "Dogwood John". John's son John also became a Baptist preacher and was called "Hi lonesome John". "Aunt Betsey" was a gifted organist and played for the Church. Some of John's descendents are playing now at Branson, MO Music Shows.

Although Jane McCoy went to Missouri with her husband, Nathan Pruett, some of her siblings remained in Brown County. Among them was Cornelius McCoy, progenitor of a large family with links to many early Brown County families: Fleener, Robertson, McLary, Rogers, Chitwood. *Submitted by Maxine Brown, great-great-granddaughter of Nathan and Jane Pruett*

DR. ALFRED JONES RALPHY FAMILY

- Dr. Ralphy (1854-1928) was the youngest child of John and Sarah Jones Ralphy. John Ralphy (1797-1886) a ship builder from London, England immigrated through New Orleans to Cincinnati in 1846 with his teenage children Mary Ann and John, wife Sarah and their children Emma and James. The family moved to the healthier environment of Brown County in 1853, without Mary Ann and John who had married.

Emma married Capt. William Harrison Taggart. Their children were Willard, Horace A. and Oscar. Widowed, Emma married Dr. Arnold S. Griffitt. James died on a trip to the South. Dr. Ralphy, a Nashville native, married Adeline (daughter of Michael Eugene and Catharine Stabb Keller, both from Germany) in 1878. Their children are Clifford (1880-1961), Grace (1886-1972), Edith Evangeline "Eva" (1892-1972), and Gladys (1897-1982). They reared a niece Alpha Taggart (Mrs. Isaac) Evans (1875-1966).

Gladys, Eva, Grace, Clifford, Addie and Dr. A.J. Ralphy

Dr. Ralphy began employment at age 12 in a printing business. He was teaching school winter seasons nine years, but became interested in study of medicine as he clerked in a drug store during summers. He began medical practice in the early 1870s with his brother-in-law Dr. Arnold S. Griffitt. In 1878 he graduated from the Cincinnati School of Medicine and Surgery and in 1884 from the Kentucky School of Medicine in Louisville. He practiced in Nashville, helping organize the Brown County Medical Society in 1879. (See Whitaker, Gladys, "Reminiscences of a Country Doctor", Journal of the Indiana State Medical Association, Indianapolis, Vol. 65, No. 11, Nov. 1972, 1156 ff.) The Dr. Ralphys relocated to New Bellsville in 1891, where they became active members of the New Harmony Baptist Church. In 1902 when telephones came to that section of the county the switchboard was located in their home. Making house calls by horse and buggy, he delivered 2049 Brown County babies without losing one mother. He was also a naturalist and taxidermist. His two-room office is on display as part of the Historical Society Complex in Nashville, IN.

Clifford, who married Anna daughter of William and Mary Petro Newmister was secretary-treasurer of Gates Marble and Tile in Indianapolis. Their children are Wm. Alfred (1908-1986) and Ragene (Mrs. Charles) Williams (1910-). Alfred's wife Eloise (McCoy), their daughter Diane Ralphy Mayes, a teacher, and grandchildren Bill, James, and Martha reside in Indianapolis.

Grace married Bert Campbell.

Eva married James H. Brown, son of William Henry and Ruth Williamson Brown of Elkinsville and had two sons Robert (1920-1984) and Loyd Ralphy (1925-). Eva, James and Robert were school teachers. Loyd was a missionary in Zaire in the 1950s and is a professional engineer. Robert married Angela Tranowski, had two daughters: Charmaine (Mrs. Eugene Zschernitz) and Jeannine (Mrs. James Nicosia), and three grandchildren. Loyd and wife Marie (Diller) adopted Carol (Mrs. Douglas) Hoffman, Jerald, Ruth (Mrs. William) Dameron, Jeffrey, and Nancy (Mrs. Jeffery) Reynolds. They have 12 grandchildren.

Gladys taught in several Brown County schools, retiring from Helmsburg. She married Walter Young and after his death, Ira Whitaker. *Submitted by Loyd Ralphy Brown*

JEFFERSON RARIDEN

- John Rariden was born in Ireland. In 1804 he came to America and settled in Brown County. He was married and his son, Jefferson Rariden, was born Dec. 11, 1828.

Jefferson Rariden was married to Minerva Chappel (born Jan. 24, 1826). They lived on Carmel Ridge. They had two sons: John William and Frank.

Minerva died and he married Minerva's sister, Eleanor Chappel (born Nov. 1, 1837). He left his two sons with her and went off to the Civil War. He was a private, Company H, 25th Regiment, Indiana Volunteers. He told of the fighting and in the freezing temperatures his beard was frozen to the ground. He stayed awake to keep the hungry soldiers from stealing the corn from the horses. He returned home with a pension and when Eleanor died he married Margaret Hormel Kaserman, widow of Samuel Kaserman. After her death he was married for a fourth time to Martha Newcomb. Jefferson Rariden died April 18, 1913 and is buried at Unity Cemetery.

Jefferson's son John William was born Dec. 29, 1857. He was married to Anna Kaserman on Aug. 1, 1880. She was born Sept. 22, 1861 to Samuel and Margaret Honnel Kaserman. Margaret and Samuel both came to America from Holland. They married shortly after arriving here and settled in Kansas. The dust storms were so bad there they came East and made their home in Brown County. They had six children: Anna Kaserman Rariden; George, David, John, Emma (Kaserman) Shrock and Sarah (Kaserman) Kinnet.

John and Anna Rariden were also parents of six children: Rosa, who died very young; Margaret (Deckard, Mrs. Charles); Walter Rariden, Charles, William and Vinnie Minerva who married Rex Derringer Jan. 3, 1916 at Nashville. Rex and Vinnie had one child, Genevra Irene (Owens).

John William Rariden worked most of his life in timber: hauling cross ties for the railroad after it came through Brown County. He built his growing family a big log house on Morrison Road and they lived there for six or seven years until it burned. He drove his horses to Morgantown for some supplies before Helmsburg became a thriving community. The roads mostly followed the creek beds or were on a ridgetop. Everyone either walked or rode horses or drove a "buggy." Helmsburg Road was in the East Fork of Owl Creek. Baptisms were held in the Creek where the East Fork of Owl Creek joined the West Fork.

Lots of trading was done. John once traded a load of corn for enough carpet for the living room. Bean Blossom (then Georgetown) was an easy walk up over the hill to the store. Pie socials were big things as was Sunday School and Church.

Anna Rariden died Feb. 24, 1928. John died March 10, 1944. Both are buried at Oak Ridge Cemetery in Jackson Township.

JAMES DELBERT READ

- Joseph Read married Elizabeth Ward in Belmont Co., OH where they had two children, Elizabeth, born 1818 and James, born 1824.

James Read married Margaret Ann Jarrett in 1850 in Belmont Co., OH. They had eight children: Mary E., Wilson Ross, Amanda Isabel, James Harvey, William Lonzo, Annis Caroline, Allis/Alice Jane and Ida L.M. Read. James and Margaret Read settled near Kelp in Brown County between 1869 and 1873. Their children settled near Kelp and around Storyville, now known as Story. James and Margaret are buried at Mt. Zion Cemetery as are some of their children.

Rosa Pearl, James Delbert, Bertha A., and Mary Estella Read

William Lonzo Read, born July 22, 1864, married Elizabeth Caroline Kritzer on Oct. 29, 1883 in Brown County where they had nine children: Myrtie Mae, Prudy Ann, Mary Estella, Bessie Bell, Bertha A., James Delbert, Ora Ellis, William Oval and Rosa Pearl Read. Their mother, Elizabeth Read, died Jan. 19, 1923. William Lonzo Read then married Margaret (Smith) Schrock on June 30, 1926; they had two sons, Alonzo Wilson "Lonnie" and Louie Eugene Read. Some of William's children changed their name from Read to Reed when they were older. William's home place was just up from Kelp Branch, now in the State Park. Just behind the bath house at the Horsemans Camp is where William Lonzo had his home and Blacksmith Shop. His brother, James Read, had his home at the bottom of Mt. Zion in the State Park, where the Horsemans Camp entrance is today. William Lonzo, his wife Elizabeth and some of their children are buried at Mt. Zion Cemetery. Alonzo Wilson Read, son of William Lonzo, lives in Edinburg, Johnson County, with his wife and two sons.

James Delbert Read, born Dec. 25, 1892, married Meta Lavida Tabor in 1913. Meta was born Dec. 20, 1890 to Isaac and Loretta Carmichael Tabor. James and Meta had twin sons born Sept. 10, 1915, Lester Noel who died in 1920 and Chester Lowell Read. James Delbert Read was the founder and past owner of the Pine Room Tavern in Nashville. In 1949 he bought the Old Ferguson House from his son, Chester. James Delbert and his wife

Meta moved to Florida in 1954. Meta died on May 7, 1973 in Dade City, FL; James Delbert passed away on July 6, 1980 in Columbus, IN. They are buried next to their son Lester, at Christiansburg Cemetery in Brown County. James Delbert and Meta Read were long time members of the Masonic Order.

Chester Lowell Read, son of James Delbert and Meta Read, married Margerette Rosetta Flint on Dec. 10, 1936. She was born Sept. 14, 1919. They had four daughters: Evonne Lou, Rita Arlene, Margie Sue and Candace Lynn. Chester Read died on March 30, 1962 and is buried in Schererville, IN. He was a 32nd degree Mason, his daughters and two granddaughters are Eastern Stars. He had ten grandchildren and two great-grandchildren.

Rita Arlene, daughter of Chester Lowell and Margerette Read, was born May 2, 1944. She married in 1961 to Harold Hutsell. They had one daughter, Jo Ann, born Jan. 2, 1964, and were divorced in 1967. Rita then married Jimmy R. Green on May 17, 1969. They have two children: John Reid, born June 5, 1972, and Sonya Marlyn, born July 12, 1973. They live in Dade City, FL.

Jo Ann Hutsell, daughter of Rita Read and Harold Hutsell, married Roger Dale Mills on March 17, 1979; they have a son Steven Allen Mills, born May 31, 1981. *Submitted by Rita Read Green*

WILSON R. AND NANCY E. READ -

Wilson Rosley Read (known as Ross), oldest son of James and Margaret Read was born Sept. 4, 1854 in Belmont Co., OH. In 1872 at the age of 18, Ross migrated to Brown Co., IN. He was accompanied by two sisters, Mary and Amanda and a brother, Jim. An older cousin came with them. This overland journey was made by wagon train consisting of two wagons, one of which was covered for sleeping, the other one carried supplies. Each wagon was drawn by two horses. A young colt was also brought along. They camped out each night, and if possible, near a farm house to avoid any danger which might occur. Occasionally the sisters were invited into a farmhouse to spend the night. Enroute they encountered a variety of experiences, one of which could have been tragic. One day, two men appeared driving two horses to a buggy. They offered to trade horses with Ross but he refused. They were disappointed and remarked as they left that they would "get them" that night. The horses were sequestered in a way to provide better protection should these men return, and sometime after midnight they did return and were making their way towards the horses. Ross was awakened by his dog which was very alert and vicious and slept near him every night. Ross was armed but the faithful dog frightened the men and they did not return. They arrived in Brown County, about two miles west of Stone Head on Oct. 12, 1872.

Ross married Irene Anthony, daughter of Peter Anthony. To this union were born two children, Alonzo and a baby girl. Irene and the baby died within a few days of each other and were buried in the same casket. Ross later married Nancy E. Noblet, oldest daughter of John and Amandy Noblet. To this union were born six children: four girls, Grace, Dolla, Laura and Edith and two boys, Murnal and Beryle. Ross and his brother Jim operated a Cane Mill for several years making Sorghum Molasses. During September and October each year you could smell the aroma of sorghum molasses coming from the mill. In 1911, Jim was appointed Superintendent of the Brown County Poor Farm and moved to Nashville dissolving this partnership. The cane mill never operated again but was known for its friendly atmosphere that accompanied the making of the molasses. Ross was a resident of Brown County for 57 years and was a farmer during those years until his death June 6, 1929.

Nancy, his wife, was born in Brown County and was a resident for 80 years. Her last ten years were spent in Indianapolis with her daughter, Edith. She died March 16, 1955. Both became Christians early in life and remained true to their God and church. Their home church was the Mt. Zion Christian Church, erected in 1876 with lumber from the James Read farm. All the family is deceased except Edith who lives in Indianapolis and Beryle who lives in Brooksville, FL. *Submitted by Beryle R. Read*

KENNETH J. AND HELEN H. REEVE -

The Reeve family moved to Brown Co., IN from Western Springs, IL in 1949. Their "new" home, on Christiansburg Road, south of Pikes Peak, dates to 1861, the farm home of James M. and Anna Noblet Mabe whose original land grant was in 1841.

Kenneth was born July 2, 1910 in Western Springs. He graduated from Lyons Township High School in 1928 and the Chicago Academy of Fine Arts in 1930. Subsequently he was a commercial artist and art director in Chicago advertising agencies until 1949. He and Helen Estelle Hessler were married in Western Springs Nov. 30, 1935. Their children are Susan, born June 30, 1939, now Mrs. George J. Cash, of Chesterfield, VA and Daniel Hart Reeve, born Feb. 11, 1943, of near Belfast, ME. Susan has one son, Gregory D. Miles, by her first marriage. Daniel married Martha S. "Marnie" Legg; they have a son, Andrew Hart, born March 27, 1982 and a daughter, Lee DeCourcy, born March 21, 1985.

Kenneth and Helen Reeve

In 1952, Ken became a member of the Brown County Art Gallery, served the association as a director for many years and as its president for four years. He is a member also of the Indiana Artists Club, the Hoosier Salon and Indiana Heritage Arts. He is known for his watercolor landscapes and aquatint etchings. His works have won many awards and are in homes here and abroad.

Helen Hessler was born Sept. 11, 1915 in Cicero, IL, moving with her parents to Western Springs in 1924. She also graduated from Lyons Township High School, 1933. Both Helen and Ken are charter members of the Brown County Historical Society. Since 1972 they have been active as the Society's Genealogical Committee and have assembled a large collection of information on Brown County families.

The Reeve lineage has been traced to (1) John Reeve (1730-1811) and wife Sarah (1736-1818) of Chatham, CT; (2) John Reeve (1764-1806) of Catskill, NY, blacksmith, and wife Hannah Hall; (3) Hiram Reeve (1804-1865) and wife Catherine Clum (1807-1876) of Germantown, NY; (4) Edwin Reeve (1831-1893), born Germantown, married March 19, 1862, Bristol, IN, Julia Jeanneret, daughter of Robert J. Jeanneret and Amanda Allworth. Edwin had a farm produce business in Ligonier, IN; (5) Henry Jeanneret Reeve (1871-1951), born Ligonier, married April 20, 1899, Chicago, to Eva Elizabeth Hart (1874-1956), daughter of Edwin R.F. Hart and Margaret E. Kull. Children of Henry and Eva Reeve were: Edwin A., Norman H., Kenneth Jeanneret and Muriel E. Reeve.

The Hessler lineage goes back to (1) August Andreas Hessler and Dorothe Christiane Osterloh of Holstedt, Germany; (2) Gottlieb Christian Hessler (1828-1895) and Marie Sophia Fritze (1835-1915) who emigrated to Chicago in 1885; (3) Ernst Charles Hessler (1858-1891) and Elizabeth Paus (1859-1924); (4) Otto Joseph Hessler (1890-1969) and Estelle Horn (1892-1975), who had Evelyn, Orville, Helen and Robert. Helen's parents moved to Brown County in 1952. *Submitted by Kenneth J. Reeve*

EBERHARD AND RUTH REICHMANN -

In 1967 the Reichmanns fell in love with a farm behind the present "Opry" and moved to Brown County. Eberhard ("Eb") was born Dec. 8, 1926 in Stuttgart, Germany. His father, Augustus R., an Austrian violin virtuoso, had married the Stuttgarter Maria Koehler. Eb was to follow his father's footsteps to become "the world's greatest violinist." But one day, Augustus busted the "Wunderkind's" violin, because Eb hadn't practiced his full four hours. Eb attended a teachers prepschool before spending the last year of WWII at the Russian front. He escaped from the Soviets but almost died in an American P.O.W. camp. In late 1945 at 19, he started teaching: 226 children, grades one through eight. He finished teacher training in 1949 and came to the U.S. in 1951 as a fellow of the U.S. Office of Education. One year in America wasn't enough; in 1953 he came again—for about five years, he thought. He arrived via Quebec with $4 in his pocket and first worked at a friend's Mill in Troy, NH. This made almost a Yankee out of him. But he decided to accept an assistantship at the German Dept. of the University of Cincinnati, where he received his M.A. (1955) and Ph.D. (1959)—and married Ruth in 1956.

Prof. Eberhard and Ruth Reichmann

Ruth was born in Munich, July 29, 1928, the daughter of the prominent Bavarian physician Dr. Karlheinz Backmund and his wife Lillianne. With the anti-Nazi disposition of her family, Ruth grew up in difficult circumstances in Nuremberg. From her Third Reich experience she learned that you have to fight for what's right, before it is too late. In postwar Munich she tried her hand in acting and the export business. In 1952 she immigrated and worked in medical research while attending the University of Cincinnati.

In 1959 Eb joined the faculty at IU's German Dept. He became internationally known as research director "for the Improvement of the Teaching of German in the U.S." (1966-1969)—which did not stop him from raising white-face Herefords on his farm. In the 1970s he became director of the IU Institute of German Studies. For the Tricentennial of German Immigration in 1983, he and Ruth served on the State Commission, appointed by the Governor, to assist communities with their celebrations. This led to what Eb calls "my last professional passion"—the documentation of "The Hoosier German Heritage" (title of one of his forthcoming books dealing with the Indiana Germans; others include an illustrated edition of "The Germans in Indianapolis" (1989), "Hoosier German Tales" (1991)).

In Bloomington, Ruth first helped with the new I.U. Language Laboratory. She finished her B.A. cum laude in Speech and Theatre and an M.A. in German—all while raising their adopted children, Robert Anthony and Maria Ingrid. The environmental dawn found Ruth involved in organizing the *Sassafras Chapter* of the *National Audubon Society*. From 1972-74 she served as its president and helped build it into an environmental task force with several hundred members. Her work was recognized with a National Arbor Day award (1974). In 1970 Ruth helped organize the *League of Women Voters of Brown County* and has been its president since 1985. She is active in the people-to-people oriented *Sister Cities International* and serves on the board of *Indiana Sister Cities*. Together with Eb she was a co-founder of the *Indiana German Heritage Society* and its first president while Eb chairs its publications program. Both have been active with the *Society for German American Studies*; Eb as vice president and Ruth as education chair. Ruth received her Ph.D. at IU in 1986; her dissertation is a theory on adult and multicultural education. She is an Adjunct Asst. Professor at IUPUI, organizing exchange programs, conferences, and establishing a German-American Center.

Ruth was elected *Phi Beta Kappa* (1964), received *The Federal Republic of Germany Friendship Award* (1985), and was chosen *Sagamore of the Wabash* (1987). Eb received the *Humboldt Medal for International Scientific and Cultural Cooperation* (1976) and the *Cross of Merit*, First Class (1990) from Germany's President.

Both became U.S. citizens in 1963 and subscribe to President Kennedy's challenge, "...ask, what you can do for your country."

JESSE AND SUE REJKO - Jesse Joseph Rejko was the last child born to the parents of Paul and Wanda Rejko on March 20, 1961 in Fort Myers, FL. Jesse, his two sisters Karen and Becky and brother Darryl moved with their parents to Brown County in 1963 on Lick Creek Road. Jesse grew up in a log cabin surrounded by the beautiful woods of Brown County. As a child he often recreated the civil war in those woods. He attended Baptist High School in Indianapolis and finished his last year of school at Brown County High School. There he graduated in 1978 majoring in drafting. He began working in construction and today works part time drafting with his father. His fascination with airplanes inspired him to get his private pilot license.

Katharine (Sue) Davis was born in Lubbock, TX on March 24, 1958. Sue's parents and sister Marlene (Marti) moved to Brown County on Oak Ridge Road in 1965, only one-half mile away from Sue's future husband Jesse. Sue graduated from Brown County High School in 1976 and the School of Practical Nursing in 1978. She received her R.N. degree in 1984 and now specializes in critical care and substance abuse.

Jesse and Sue Rejko, 1986

It wasn't until 1985 that Sue and Jesse met through a mutual friend (Margarey Musgrove Armstrong). They were married at Beck's Chapel on the Indiana University Campus on July 4, 1986. They each brought a child from their previous marriage; Jesse's daughter Casey Jo and Sue's daughter Christin Michelle (Chris). Family and friends enjoy hearing Sue's new name appointed by Casey Jo, Momma Sue.

Sue, Jesse, Chris Rejko and below Casey Jo Rejko August, 1990.

In 1988 the Rejko family moved to West Palm Beach, FL for two years. They missed the trees and the beautiful country views in Brown County. So they moved home in June of 1990. They have a true appreciation for Brown County. There's truly no place like home!

PAUL AND WANDA (MORRIS) REJKO - Veronica Fazekas, Paul's mother, was born outside of Budapest, Hungary, in 1890. As a widow, she came to America in 1912, where she met and married another immigrant from Hungary, Mike Rejko (Paul's father). He was a shoe maker in Indianapolis, IN, and they lived on a small farm in Warren Township. Paul spoke only Hungarian as a child, and when he started the first grade of school, he couldn't speak enough English to be understood. Paul's older brother, Mike, had to help him learn the "new" language. Paul attended Warren Central High School where he became interested in drafting. His brothers worked together as carpenters and builders, and he learned by helping them. After high school he married Wanda Morris and continued to work in construction, doing drafting on the side. Later on, he began doing drafting full time, and still does to this day.

Veronica and Mike Rejko, 1912 wedding picture

Nannie and Howard Morris wedding picture, 1904

Brown County was always a place they enjoyed visiting together. They had talked of moving there someday when they retired. Then they decided why should they wait until they were old and couldn't do as much. So they moved while the children were young and they could enjoy their years together in the log home in the woods that they still love.

Wanda's mother, Nannie Stuard, moved to Shirley, IN, from Georgetown, KY with her father and step-mother in the early 1900s. At 14 years of age, Nannie hired on at a boarding house where she cooked and cleaned and would later meet her future husband, Howard Morris. Howard (Wanda's father) came on horseback from the Appalachian Mountain area of eastern Kentucky, to Shirley, to find work also. They met there and courted a short while. Howard's brother-in-law married them, and they settled in Indianapolis. Wanda was born and raised in the same house and never left it until she married. She attended Warren Central High School where she met Paul Rejko. They graduated in 1946 and married in 1947. They settled in the Wanamaker area. The stories she had heard as a child about her father's home in a log cabin in the mountains, always inspired her to want to do the same. Their honeymoon at Springmill State Park, just gave her more of a desire to live in the woods someday. She would drag her husband and now four children to Brown County each fall to visit.

Paul and Wanda Rejko and Family. Back: Jesse, Paul and Darryl. Front: Karen, Wanda and Becky.

Finally, they found the cabin of their dreams on Lick Creek Road, and there they moved in 1963. All four of their children, Karen, Becky, Darryl, and Jesse, have graduated from Brown County High School. Karen now lives in Chicago with her husband, Chris, and her daughter, Beth. Becky married a Brown County native, Ron Fleetwood, and they reside here in Brown County with their two children, Joshua and Jenny. Darryl and his wife, Joanne, live in Florida with their son, Christopher. Jesse lives here in Brown County with his wife, Sue (Davis), and her daughter, Chris. He also has a daughter, Casey Jo, who lives in Franklin, with her mother, Kyle. Brown County is still the love of their life, and their home in the woods is their dream come true. *Submitted by Becky Fleetwood*

RICHARDS FAMILY - John Richards, Sr. patented land in 1792 and owned 400 acres in Cany Valley on Possum Creek of Hawkins Co., TN at the time of his death there in 1829. His two known sons were John Jr., who was located in Clark Co., IN in 1829, and Michael (1783-1862) who married Charity Hubbard and moved to Washington Co., IN in 1816. In 1818 Michael built the first house ever in Little York, IN. His known children were: John (1808), Anna (1810), David (1813), Jesse (1816), Steven (1817), Mary (1819), Lucinda (1824), and Abigail.

Michael entered land 1835 in Hamblen Township, Brown County. His eldest son, John, had already located (1833) in Jackson Township on Bear Creek. John married (1832) Priscilla Parks and they had seven children: Steven (1833), Marion (1835), Columbus (1837), Commodore Perry (1839), Mary (1841), Michael (1843), and John (1846).

Winfield and Hannah (Fritch) Richards

John first lived in a log cabin on the west side of Bear Creek just north of Slippery Elm Shoot Road, then later built a frame house on the east side of the creek. Priscilla died 1846 and John married 1847 to Joanah Stepp (1824-1901), daughter of Reuben Stepp and Sabra Chappell. John and Joanah's children were: Winfield Scott (1847), Angeline (1850), Eli (1852), George (1858).

John ran a flour mill on Bear Creek, was Constable, County Commissioner, Justice of the Peace, and elected Representative to the Indiana State Legislature on the Democrat ticket in 1864 and served two terms. He attended the first Old Settlers in 1877. His wife, Joanah, was listed a midwife among the county physicians of 1881-83.

John and his son, Winfield, were both timber men, buying large tracts of land, logging off the trees, selling the land and buying another tract. John at one time owned 1500 acres along Bear Creek.

Winfield Scott Richards (1847-1934) married 1866 Hannah Ellen Fritch (1849-1931), daughter of Lewis and Ellen Folsom Fritch. Winfield and Hannah's children were: John (1867), Naomi (1869), Julius (1872), Mary (1873), Scott (1875), Milton (1878), Conrad (1882), Calvin (1884), Anna (1887).

Winfield panned gold, tried to perfect a perpetual motion machine and in later years tended large berry patches and orchards with his trusted dog, "Si-Colly."

Milton, son of Winfield married 1899 Viola Lucretia Rachel Robertson (1878-1932), daughter of Daniel and Elizabeth Lampkins Robertson. They raised seven children: Mabel (1901), Melvin (1903), Jesse (1906), Helen (1908), Naomi (1910), Robert (1912) and Harold (1921).

Milton followed his father and grandfather running a sawmill most of his life and assisted in building the Bear Creek Church 1917. Milton married 1933/4 Flossie Collins (1912-1964). They raised: Elmer (1935), Fay (1937), Darlene (1942), and Viola (1947).

Milton and Flossie were proprietors of a grocery in Trevlac and later held weekly auctions in the building that caught afire January 1961. Milton died of a heart attack as he stepped out of the burning building.

Many of the descendants of this Richards family still populate Brown County and Indiana. Milton was grandfather of Marvin Logsdon (1928-1979). His mother was Mabel Richards Logsdon. (see Leroy Logsdon) *Submitted by Lila J. Logsdon*

BOB AND ELAINE RICHARDS - Robert (Bob) and Elaine (Shortie) Richards are both Brown County natives. Bob is the son of Leo and Velma (Waltman) Richards. Elaine is the daughter of Thurman and Verna (Myers) Percifield.

The Richards family came from Hawkins Co., TN in 1816 and entered land in what is now Washington Township, and soon after, the family moved to Bear Creek in what is now Jackson Township. There have been some members of the Richards family living on Bear Creek since before Brown County came into being in 1836.

The Waltman family lived in the Bean Blossom area and came here from Maryland before or shortly after Brown County was formed.

Bob Richards, England, July 1945

The Percifield family came to Brown County from Belmont Co., OH. Gilbert Percifield entered land in Washington Township in 1839.

Elaine's grandfather was Anderson Percifield—a well-known Attorney in Nashville, and is still remembered by some of the older residents of Nashville. Her father was Thurman Percifield who was known as a fiddle player for square dances all over the county.

The Myers family entered land in Jackson Township in 1836 near what is now Helmsburg. Some descendents still live there.

After being classified 4F in the United States Army during World War II, Bob hitch-hiked to Windsor, Ontario, Canada in June 1943 and enlisted in the Canadian Army. He is a Veteran of the D Day landing in France and served in a French Canadian Regiment, Le Regiment De La Chaudiere and the Highland Light Infantry of Canada. He was honorably discharged, Nov. 17, 1945.

Bob and Elaine were married on May 1, 1948 and have three sons: (1) Alan, who married Darlene Roberts and they have two sons Neil and Jamie; (2) Phillip, who married Julie Law and they have a son Joshua; (3) William, who married Alice Hutchison and they have a daughter Sarah. The sons and families all live on Bear Creek also.

Bob and Elaine have traveled widely on a motorcycle and at this time have ridden in 31 States and six Provinces in Canada.

DONALD AND SANDRA RICHARDS - Donald "Don" was born in Sommerset, KY, July 13, 1939. Son of Leroy Foster and Jeanette Richards. Don was a member of the 101st Airborne Division out of Fort Campbell, KY. He served during 1957-1960, stationed in Wurtzburg, Germany. Grandson, of Joseph R. and Lockie Richards of Kentucky.

Don is employed as a professional Truck Driver for 28 years, and currently a Reserve Deputy for the Brown County Sheriff's Department. Married, Sandra (Sandy) Smith on April 14, 1962 in Indianapolis, IN at Edwin Ray Methodist Church. Sandy is the daughter of Clayton and Eileen (Moberly) Smith of Shelbyville, IN born in Indianapolis on Feb. 12, 1941, granddaughter of Gary and Mary Smith, and Oris and Margaret (Williams) Moberly all of Shelbyville, IN. Sandy graduated in 1958 from Harry E. Wood High School in Indianapolis, and is employed at Patty's Porch in Nashville, IN.

Children born to Don and Sandy are daughter Claytanna Jean, born July 13, 1966, and son Donald (Don) Jr. born on July 18, 1972. Claytanna married Kenneth McNeely in 1987 and have two children, Kenneth Donald and Jennifer Chantel McNeely.

In the 1950s growing up and dating, they would visit Brown County several times and the Brown County State Park. They enjoyed this beautiful area so much they decided this was the place to move and plan on Don's retirement from trucking. They took up residence in Brown County on Oct. 31, 1987. *Submitted by Sandra Richards*

RICHARDSON FAMILY - The Richardson Family begins with John and Mary Richardson of Grayson Co., VA; of English descent and owning a 250 acre plantation. To this family were born 14 children, Elizabeth, Lettila, Lewis, Joshua, Mary, Sarah, Milly, John, Lettus, Thomas, Anne, William, Jane, and Jonathan. John died about 1800 leaving his estate to his wife and children.

Thomas, born about 1769 married Nancy Anne Quensberry in Grayson County, moved to Tennessee, Kentucky and Monroe County, Unionville area in 1827. Their children were John, George, William, Elizabeth, Joshua, Sarah, Mary, Andrew, Margaret and Milly.

John born 1792 in Virginia married Milly O'Daniel Aug. 20, 1818 in Anderson, TN. Their children were Jeremiah, Joel, Lucretia, John, Thomas, Mary Jane, Andrew, and Nancy. John and his family came to Unionville with his parents.

Jeremiah born 1825 in Tennessee married Mary Ellen Fleenor Aug. 25, 1848 in Brown County, settling eventually in the Needmore area. Their children were John A., Samuel, William, Milly, Joel and Jacob. Jeremiah and Mary Ellen died four days apart in 1875 of yellow fever.

Vivian and Wendall Richardson

John A. born July 24, 1853 in Monroe County went as a young man to Vermillion Co., IL to look for work. It was an area where broom corn was grown. He boarded with the Cooper family and married one of their daughters, Deborah Ann. Their children were Laura, Jessie, <u>Bert</u>, Milly and Lester. John and Deborah moved between Brown County and Vermillion County during their lifetime with John dying in Brown County.

Bert born Sept. 3, 1883 in Vermillion County, moved to Brown County with his family. Married Mrytle Rogers Dec. 1, 1909. Their children were <u>Wendell</u>, Wilma, Iris, Orville, Mary Lou and Cecil. Bert and Mrytle lived in Brown County approximately ten years. He had various jobs to support his family, one being a taxi driver. He owned an Empire car, made in Indianapolis. Taxied people to Columbus and the train station in Helmsburg. He also owned a steam engine tractor, which he used for custom farming. In 1918 Bert moved his family, Mother and steam engine to Vermillion County to join his family in the farming business. He and Mrytle both died there.

Wendell was born Dec. 30, 1910, on Jackson Creek Road in Brown County. He started to school in 1916 at the Nashville School and also attended Jackson Creek and Van Studder Schools. In 1918 he went to Vermillion County with his family, growing up there and marrying Vivian Davis in Sept. 21, 1935. He worked with his father in farming and equipment repairing. In 1948 Wendell's cousin Paul Rogers asked him to move back to Brown County to help him in his Regal Grocery store in Nashville. He and Vivian did and lived here since. He worked at the Regal Store, Cummins, Calvins Hardware and the Brown County State Park. He retired as an air-cooled engine mechanic from Indiana University in 1975 and lives at 74 Johnson Street Nashville, has one daughter, Sharon Jean Middleton and four grandchildren. *Written by Marge Grimm*

RICHARDSON GIRLS AND GRANNY -

Between Trevlac and Helmsburg on route 45 on the north side of the road a little west of Lost Branch (it was formerly called Daggy Haller, being the lowland home of Jake Daggy) is a private graveyard, Richardson Cemetery. The above named persons along with other relatives are buried here.

Granny was third wife of John Richardson born 1820 in Tennessee, a grandson of Thomas and Nancy Richardson of Virginia. She was Anna Stephens, an aunt of Jordan (Jerd L. Stephens) and his sister, Thaney. The "girls" were Anna's daughters—Theodoshia (Dote) and Cordelia (Cord). The Stephens lived on Slippery Elm Chute road. The Richardson women lived close to the Richardson Cemetery. Both families were economical, raised gardens, helped each other and their neighbors.

Thaney's bread board had a deeply worn place from years of biscuit making. The Richardson girls preferred cornbread—Dote made bread without "cracklins" and Cord made bread with "cracklins."

The walls of the Richardson home were papered with many layers of yellowed newspaper. The wooden floors were unfinished but were worn smooth and shiny where the rag rugs did not cover them.

The Girls worked at jobs in surrounding towns: this was especially true during World War when jobs and transportation to them was not a major problem (the Girls did not drive).

Granny kept house, befriended the neighbors who had sickness or troubles and cared for new babies with love and old fashioned remedies.

Few people may stop and look at their stones but many will continue to hear and read about them. *Submitted by Gladys M. Rodgers*

GLENN AND EDNA SOPHRONIA RICHARDSON -

Glenn was born Feb. 29, 1908, died Nov. 18, 1988, married in March of 1933 to Edna Sophronia Hyde. She was born June 14, 1909, the second child of John Siegle Hyde and Bertha M. Griffin. Glenn and Edna had four sons and a daughter: William Glenn, Johnny Dale, Harold Ray, Max Lee and Edna Mae Richardson.

Edna S. and Glenn Richardson, 1985

(1) William Glenn Richardson, born Feb. 5, 1934, married first to Linda Rivers, second to Neomie ...., third to Kathy Young. His first two marriages ended in divorce. He has three children: (1) Sara Joella Richardson, born April 27, 1957 in Maryland, married Donald Brock. Their children, all born in Michigan, are Brad Dean Brock, born Oct. 29, 1981; Dana Marie Brock, born March 5, 1983; Magan Louann Brock, born Jan. 17, 1987. (2) Daniel Ray Richardson, born Oct. 28, 1961, married Sara Margaret Doyle. (3) Robert Glenn Richardson, born Feb. 5, 1968.

(2) Johnny Dale Richardson, born March 23, 1935, died May 22, 1960; married Clara Lugar, had sons: (1) Michael Dale Richardson, born Feb. 14, 1956, married Kathy Jo Dillion. They have children, Andrea Jo, born Nov. 13, 1982 and Josh Dale, born March 22, 1988. (2) Jeffery Patrick Richardson who married .... Stick.

(3) Harold Ray Richardson, born March 23, 1936, died May 22, 1955, unmarried.

(4) Max Lee Richardson, born Nov. 3, 1940; married Carol Campbell. They have two sons: James Dale, born Oct. 13, 1963 and Steven Lee, born Dec. 16, 1968.

(5) Edna Mae Richardson, born April 9, 1945, married first to Ronald Flick. They divorced and she married second to Wayne Yeager. They also divorced. Her children are Timothy Allen Flick, born July 30, 1966 and Charles Matthew Yeager, born Jan. 15, 1970. *Submitted by Edna Mae Yeager*

WILLIAM MACK ALLEN RICHARDSON -

The Richardsons of Indiana date back to about 1827 when Thomas, Lewis and their sister Jane (married to William McCoy) came to Indiana, settling in Benton Township, Monroe County, in the community now called Unionville. These children of John and Mary Richardson were originally of Christiansburg, VA, but later of Tennessee and Kentucky.

Mary Agnes, William Mack Allen, Martha Ann, Jacob Hiram, Louellen, Permelia Jane (Peoples) and Della Frances Richardson

The writer's maternal grandfather was William Mack Allen Richardson, son of Jeremiah and Mary Ellen (Fleener) Richardson, Jeremiah being the son of John and Millie (O'Daniel) Richardson. Mack, as he was called, was born in eastern Monroe County but lived several years in Brown County. He was born June 22, 1858. His boyhood and youth were spent in the country where he helped his father farm. On Feb. 27, 1877 he married Permelia Jane Peoples, whose sister Martha had married Mack's Uncle Thomas (Jeremiah's brother) several years earlier. Jane, born in Tennessee July 6, 1846, and Mack had five children: Louellen (1878); Martha Ann (1879); Jacob Hiram (1882); Mary Agnes (1884); and Della Frances (1886).

The family lived on Howard Ridge near Needmore in Brown County. They went to Illinois to work in broom corn about 1887. Jane took German measles and died Feb. 27, 1888 and is buried in High Ridge Cemetery near Villa Grove, IL. Mack returned to Howard Ridge where he and Louellen (ten years old) cared for the younger children. They managed to get by for a year or so but it was difficult for the children as Mack had to be away at work; and sometimes when taking grain to the mill at Bloomington it was necessary to stay overnight. In a busy season the wagons would line up at the mill and wait their turns. When night came those who were still waiting would sleep on the wagons or nearby after caring for their horses or oxen.

A fireplace warmed the household and was used for cooking the meals. A long iron rod stretched over the coals and on it hung a big, black iron pot for cooking beans for supper. Louellen asked Martha to hold her skirts back so she could get close enough to reach the pot to add seasoning. Martha lost hold of the skirts and as they swung forward Louellen jumped back. The dress luckily did not get into the fire but it was a frightening moment.

On Feb. 19, 1889, Mack married Abrilla (Stepp) Mozee, a widow with four children: John, Eliza, Sadie, and Willie. They all moved to Glenns Valley (1890) where Mack continued farming. Willie died (1912) but the other children grew up and married. Mack was working with a threshing crew in 1914. The men went to the farmhouse, ate a hearty meal and returned to the field. Mack was on the reaper and when he didn't come on around the field the other men went to see what was wrong. They discovered that Mack had apparently had a heart attack and died. He was buried in Mt. Pleasant Cemetery near Glenns Valley on his birthday— June 22, 1914. Abrilla died in 1928 and is buried beside Mack. *Submitted by Esther Mink, daughter of Louellen (Richardson) Mink*

BLANCHE CHITWOOD NEAL RIGGINS

- Daughter of Richard and Ida May Chitwood, was born Dec. 5, 1900, in the log inn on the property west of Needmore that her parents bought in 1899. She married in 1918 Orville Neal, son of Linzey and Addie Smith Neal of Brown County, and had four children, La Vere Ward (born 1919) married Nina McGlocklin; Lowell Vernace (born 1921) married Dorothy Gilmore; Roger Lee (born 1930) married Shirley Hahn; and Marie Anne (born 1933) married Robert Owens.

Orville and Blanche helped his brother, Vernace, develop a chain of Neal Cafeteria's in Dayton, OH; Indianapolis, Washington, D.C., and other locations. After Orville died in 1942, Blanche had mouths to feed at home in Bloomington and so she drove the 54 miles into Indianapolis to work in the GM factory rather than uproot her kids. Several years later she moved to Speedway.

Blanche Chitwood Neal Riggins and Ralph Chitwood, 1982

Blanche was one of the first women to join Rosie the Riveter as a tool crib worker at Allisons GM Corporation in Indianapolis. Women were a novel sight at the plant when she first went to work and the men would line up along the jumbo cafeteria wall to watch the women go by. The women responded by saying, "Never mind, we'll be lining up to watch you before the war is over!" And at the end of the war there were as many women as men workers and the men quit looking. The whole crew working together could produce 100 airplane engines every 24 hours during World War II.

Blanche held the job for 23 years until age 65. She married a fellow worker, Andy Riggins, in 1951. He died in 1976. Her mother, Ida May Ritchey, made her home with Blanche and Andy for some time before her death in 1958. Blanche still lives in her home in Speedway with her daughter, Marie Owens.

FREDERICK W. AND JEANNETTE G. RIGLEY

- Frederick, artist and teacher, was born in 1914 in Owosso, MI. His formal art education began at the age of 18 when he took summer courses at Saugatuck, MI. From 1932-1936 he studied at the Ringling School of Art in Sarasota, FL, majoring in Sculpture. While studying there he met Adolph and Alberta Schulz, who introduced him to Brown County. After that he frequently returned here to paint.

During this time he also studied with George Bridgman at the Art Students League in New York City and in landscape painting with Emile Gruppe and John F. Carlson in Gloucester, MA.

In 1942 he married Jeannette Greene in Owosso and moved to Gloucester. In 1946 their first daughter, Ellen (now Carter) was born and in 1951 they moved to Nashville and bought the Taggart-Hopper house on North Jefferson. He soon became a member of the Brown County Art Gallery, Hoosier Salon, the 20 Club and the Indiana Artist Club. In 1955 he helped organize the Brown County Art Guild and is now its only remaining founder and oldest continuous member. He served as president and secretary of the Guild several times.

Sketch by Frederick Rigley

In 1955 their youngest daughter, Joan, was born. Joan is married to former Brown County resident, William S. Wells, son of Melba and Bert Wells. They now live in Arkansas and have two children: Brandise Nicole, age seven and Brent Mahlon age one.

Mr. Rigley taught for 25 years with the Indianapolis Art League as well as private classes in Brown County and other Indiana towns. In 1964 he was artist in residence at the University of Delaware, working on campus and leaving the paintings to the University. He has received numerous awards and prizes.

The Rigleys operated a tourist home for several years and in 1957 opened Nashville's first Art Store and Frame Shop. It was located first in their living room, then between Woody's Barber Shop and the Star Store and finally in the Mathis house next to the summer playhouse. They closed the store in 1978. Jeannette retired but Fred continues to paint and teach.

Jeannette substituted in the schools when they first came to Nashville. She was also active in forming the Psi Iota Xi Sorority.

CARL RITTER FAMILY

- Christmas, 1909, delivered a special gift to the Ritter Family of Louisville, KY in the form of a son, named Carl Harry Ritter. Parents of this special Christmas package were Harry and Elizabeth (Kaster) Ritter, both of German descent. Carl was raised in Louisville, KY where his grandfather, Richard Ritter, founded and ran the Ritter Tanning Company, located at 34th and Herman Streets. Between 1890 and the end of the World War I, Louisville was a major "leather center."

William C. Kimmel, also of Louisville met Henrietta Heim while working at the Menne Candy Company. They married and in 1913 gave birth to their fifth child, Madeline, born October 28. She was given the unusual name of Madeline Martha America Kimmel - "Martha America" was the name of an Indian friend of the family. Madeline can also boast of strong German heritage. Madeline's great uncle, Edward Kimmel, owned and operated two candy stores in the Highlands area in the early 1900s called "Kimmel's Highland Sweets."

Madeline and Carl Ritter

Carl and Madeline were married in 1935 in Louisville. Two sons and seven years later they moved to Indianapolis, IN. Carl was a Conveyor Engineer and Sales Representative for Logan Conveyors for 50 years. They were very active in their Church, Carrolton Avenue United Church of Christ, later changing its name to St. Peters United Church of Christ. Leisure time found them very active in family activities, one favorite hobby being bowling. It was through one of their good bowling friends that they started visiting Brown County and started dreaming of one day living there. In 1949, Carl and Madeline purchased ground in Hamblen Township and named their retreat "Wonder Woods."

They started with a one-room summer house used on weekends and during summer vacations. They had no electricity until 1950, used kerosene lights and carried water from the well. Weekends often found them on Lake Lemon participating in sailing regattas in a sailboat they built themselves.

In 1966 Carl and Madeline decided to build a permanent home at Wonder Woods. They purchased adjoining ground to their property and Carl commuted to Indianapolis for work until he retired in 1981.

Madeline made homemaking her career. Since Carl's death in 1982, Madeline continues to keep very active in the Brown County Historical Society, is a member of the Pioneer Women and the Hickory Ridge Senior Citizens and has belonged to the Hopeful Planters Garden Club for many years. Weekends often find her as a docent at the Brown County Museum. She is a charter member of the Prince of Peace United Church of Christ in Johnson County and enjoys many hobbies such as knitting, growing and arranging flowers and plays in a weekly bridge group.

Both sons are married. Carl Jr., the eldest, lives with his wife, Leslie in Merritt Island, FL. They have two sons, also married and residing in Arizona. Mark, born Nov. 4, 1961 has one son, Thomas James (1984), and Glenn, Sept. 11, 1963 has one daughter, Breanna (1988).

Madeline's second son, Eugene and Joan have five sons. Gene Jr. (1964) is married and lives in Michigan. Kurt (1967), Jade (1970), Hans (1974) and Brandon (1979) live with their parents in Batesville, IN. *Submitted by Madeline Ritter*

GLEN OTIS ROBERTS FAMILY

- Glenn O. (1911-1989) eldest of Otha Roberts Sr. (1885-1980) married Rosa (Reeves) Roberts (1887-1963) in 1905 and had nine children: (1) Annie Irene (born and died 1914), (2) Dorothy (1905-1972), (3) Rhoda Pearl (1908-1976), (4) Clara (1909), (5) Glenn (1911-1989), (6) Rachel (1915-1985), (7) Wanda (1917), (8) Winifred (1922), and (9) Otha, Jr. (1928).

Glenn was born in Brown County, Dec. 8, 1911. His father Otha was the fifth child of George Melvin Roberts (1859-1952) and Susan (Petro) Roberts (1860-1948). George Melvin and Susan were married in 1877 and had six sons and four daughters: (1) Joseph (1879-1959), (2) Sarah E. (1881-1908), (3) Anna Belle (1882-1915), (4) Sandy W. (1890-1927), (5) twins Otha (1885-1980) and (6) Nicholas (1885-1943), (7) John W. (1887-1916), (8) Roy (1894-1978), (9) Rebecca (1897-1921), and (10) Mamie (1900-). George and Susan lived on purchased property that was part of the Brown County State Park. Otha, Sr. also owned property in Brown County State Park and sold it around 1928 for $10.00 an acre. Later Otha bought the Henry Miller farm on Green Valley (Hoover Road) around 1928-29. In 1917 they moved to Illinois for two years, where he worked for the railroad. He worked as a logger and farmer most of his life. Rosa was the first woman school bus driver in Brown County in 1936 and she was also the first woman County Recorder in 1932.

Front: Anita, Jack, Lois and Janet. Back: Tom, Mary (mother) and Glenn (father).

Mr. William S. Roberts had a son born in 1821 who was Glenn's great-grandfather Otha Roberts (born in Virginia and married Rebecca Pittman). Six of their children were born in Virginia: Elmer, Anna, Clara, Hugh D., Lucy B., and Homer C. The family moved to West Virginia where George Melvin was born. From there they came to Madison, IN by boat by way of the Ohio River, then to Brown County by covered wagon where they settled between 1872-1877, where Lewis was born (1877). Glenn married Mary Steele on June 24, 1933. She was the daughter of Clifford and Vina Steele and whose great-grandfather Eugenius purchased the farm in 1875 from Squire and Raney West and where Mary still resides today. Glenn spent most of his life as a logger, school bus driver, Trustee, farmer and carpenter, retiring from Dunlap's in 1980. He wrote about his memories of traveling by covered wagon; his first train ride; 1917 the Year of the Locust; 1918's Armistice where men burned their hats in the street, bells and whistles blowing; about the terrible flu epidemic; how he tried to clean a horse's hoof at three years of age; of Daddy Cane who had a peg-leg and raised tobacco; at 12 he was drawing a man's wages ($5.00 per day); their first new car (1923) Model T Touring Car with side windows and a lantern for floor-board light and heat (car cost $700); when he lost two wheels off his wagon and had wildest chariot ride ever.

Glenn and Mary had five children: (1) Thomas Leon (1934), (2) Janet Rosalyn (1935), (3) Jackie Glenn (1936), (4) Anita Malvina (1938), and (5) Lois Ann (1941). They have 15 grandchildren and 24 great-grandchildren and have been married for 56 years. They attended North Salem United Methodist Church located on highway 46 since the early 50s and were actively involved with church and community. *Submitted by Anita Pope and Janet Taggart*

ROBERTSON FAMILY - The name Robertson is of Scotch-Irish origin. The Robertsons were one of the oldest and most eminent family of Scotland. Stephen Robertson was born about 1775 and his son, Lazarus Robertson born 1801 came to Brown County among the earliest settlers. The time was around 1825. His land and log cabin was located near the present cut of Railroad near Trevlac. Lazarus's son, Claiborne Robertson 1822-1912 was married twice. First to Mary Stephens who died when 50 years old. They had nine children. Later he married Sarah Dillingham. They had two children, first one, Ora and the other, Clarence, grandfather of Mary Ann Walker. Claiborne left an old worn Bible with many passages marked as he and Sarah read it often. He was a Baptist and she a Methodist. She also had seven girls, so it was quite a large family.

Clarence and Catherine (Cullen) Robertson

Clarence Robertson, born March 15, 1876, as a young man, taught several terms of school in Jackson Township. In 1898 he married Catherine Cullen. They had eight children, (1) Fred Robertson born Nov. 6, 1899, (2) Francis Robertson born Feb. 19, 1902, died April 18, 1985, (3) Mary Robertson Long born July 19, 1904, died Nov. 4, 1973, (4) William C. Robertson born Nov. 7, 1906, died Nov. 6, 1966, Esther E. Robertson Callahan born June 2, 1910, died Sept. 17, 1987, (6) Sarah Alice Robertson Zody born March 23, 1912, died March 3, 1990, (7) Arthur J. Robertson born June 2, 1914, (8) Charles E. Robertson born Aug. 5, 1919. They lived at Needmore, IN and farmed until 1933 when Clarence became postmaster at Nashville, IN. The mail was delivered through Helmsburg, IN and would be picked up and delivered in a truck to Nashville. In the summer Mary Ann Walker and her brother, Junior, as young kids, would ride back with the mail person and spend the night with grandparents, Clarence and Kate, which they really looked forward to. Clarence was quite a fisherman, too. Grandma Kate lived to be 96 years old and was loved by all. She was born April 17, 1879, died July 29, 1975. Grandpa Clarence was looking forward to retirement when he died on Dec. 24, 1948. *Submitted by Mary Ann Walker*

ELSIE ROBINSON - Ivy Logsdon and his brother, Roy, lived in Missouri, moved to Kentucky then to Brown Co., IN, before 1920. Ivy married Muriel Taylor and they were parents of three children: Margie Gray, Ed Logsdon, and Elsie Robinson. When Elsie was seven years old her mother died, Ivy later married a second time.

Elsie grew up and married Marvin Abbott, who was born in Arkansas to Charles and Gertrude Abbott. Elsie and Marvin were parents of Donald Abbott, Jean Smith and Dorothy Joan Sipes. They divorced.

Robert and Elsie Robinson

Ivy Logsdon and his second wife, Dorothy, were parents of Ivy Logsdon, Jr., Marilyn Jordan, Jean Chitwood, and Jenny Wheatly. They divorced.

Marvin Abbott then married Dorothy Logsdon.

Elsie is now married to Robert E. Robinson son of Robert Thomas Robinson and Viola Ballinger Robinson, who grew up in Brown County. Elsie and Robert live on Lick Creek Road where Richard Road joins it.

Elsie says "I have lived in Brown County for most of my life—I wouldn't want to live anywhere else."

GEORGE W. ROGERS AND SARAMAE (LOESCH) ROGERS - George W. and Saramae Rogers have property on R.R. 4, Creamer Road, (top of first hill) Township No. IX North (Washington Township), Range No. III, East of 2nd Med. The land (120 acres) was surveyed by James Hedges in 1820. Forty acres were acquired by M. Reddington in 1854 through a U.S.A. Land Grant. In 1873 the remaining 80 acres were deeded to William L. Cox and later sold to Luther Pool. Records show that in 1893, Frances Hutchinson purchased the original 120 acres and subsequently sold them in 1900 to William Leffler. A deed is recorded in 1911 for the purchase of 80 acres by Fay and Sara Leffler, and this property was acquired by Virgil and Thelma Leffler in 1943 with a quitclaim deed.

George W. and Saramae Rogers

Further division of the Leffler's 80 acres were made through a warranty deed of 63 acres to Thomas and Ruth Woods, of one and one-half acres to Thomas and Frances Creamer, and of 15-1/2 acres to Denis and Barbara Albert. In 1976 the Alberts modernized the log home (circa 1935) built of hand-hewn native logs. The logs were first scored with a hand axe, then flattened with a broad axe and smoothed with an adze. The dovetail corner notches, a centuries old design of Scandinavian origin, required skillful hewing and notching and literally lock the walls together. The original log home had a dirt floor, so the Alberts raised the home to provide for a crawl space for ducts and pipes and floor construction, and they added a half story for two bedrooms. In 1980 the home and ten acres were purchased by Terry and Sara Sullivan, who further expanded the home and built an acre pond. George and Saramae purchased the Sullivan property in September, 1989.

The Rogers Home on Creamer Road.

George is a direct descendant of James Rogers, who arrived in the United States from England in 1635, as documented by his genealogy book written by James Swift Rogers—book entitled "James Rogers of New London, CT and His Descendants." The family still has his "license to go beyond the seas," dated April 15, 1635.

Saramae is a native of Columbus, IN. Her maternal great-grandparents came from Germany and raised nine children on a farm northwest of Columbus. The Schnatzmeier farm remains in the family. Her paternal great-grandparents also came from Germany. Her parents, William C. and Opal Schnatzmeier Loesch, after many years in the retail heating business, founded South Central Co., a Columbus wholesale supply business.

George and Saramae are in the executive placement business. They have five adult children.

RAY AND GLADYS RODGERS FAMILY

- From an apartment in the windy city of Chicago to a small house in the quiet town of Trevlac came the Ray and Gladys Rodgers family on July 3, 1943. Ray Edgar Rodgers was born in Illinois (December, 1913). His mother, Nellie Jane Harris was a daughter of Martha Ellen Shieley (of Green Co., OH) and Samuel Harris of Illinois. His father, John Wesley Rodgers was a son of Mary Crum (daughter of William and Mary Crum of Owen Co., IN) and John R. Rodgers (born in Calloway Co., KY) (his mother, Anna Turner of Tennessee). The history of Gladys Warford Rodgers is elsewhere in this book.

Ray Rodgers holding Nancy; Ruth sucking her thumb; Mary Jane and Sonny Ray 1946

The four children of the Rodgers family: Mary Jane (adventurous, always trying something new); Ray Warford (Sonny) (inventive and good at it); Ruth Marie (very shy); and Nancy Ellen (friendly, outgoing, she was special to all) grew up happy despite hard times along the way.

Ruth has many fond memories of those days. Among them: going to the Bean Blossom Creek (that was in the woods behind their house at that time); having apple time with Mom (her grandmother Warford) and setting in their front porch swing; listening to the birds in the evening with Dad (her grandfather Warford) after working in the cornfield; the whole family doing things together making Valentines, playing games and listening to stories her mother would read over and over to them.

Ruth married George Edward Hopkins of Beech Grove, IN (a son of Louisa Jane Collins from Brown County and Robert Wilson Hopkins from Minnesota). She is the mother of Gail Marie Henrick (a nurse in Indianapolis). Her husband is Brian R. Hendrick; their son is Michael Reed; David Donald Fetty (a Sergeant in the Air Force); and Brian Ray Hopkins (Army Airborne Special Forces) and his wife Loura S., daughter of David and Laverne Manning of Brown County.

Gladys Rodgers still lives in the same house (being a resident of Trevlac longer than most anyone else). She enjoys genealogy, spending time with her grand and great-grandchildren and doing things for others. Her daughter Ruth is very proud of Gladys and happy that she grew up in Beautiful Brown County. *Submitted by Ruth M. Hopkins*

WILLIAM AND NANCY ROGERS FAMILY

- Lewis Rogers (Jan. 22, 1819-July 8, 1892) and his wife Perilda Sciscoe (Jan. 22, 1820-March 3, 1897) came to Brown County about 1848. They came from Bloomington. They homesteaded land on Jackson Creek. Their son, William was born on Feb. 10, 1860. He married Nancy "Nannie" Welch (1860-1926) in 1878. They had seven children. Two, Lucile and Ralph, died in infancy. The other children, Walter (1878-1956), Orval (1881-1956), Cecil Ray (July 13, 1883-Feb. 19, 1947), Mable (Mrs. Cummings and later Mrs. Carson), and Myrtle (Mrs. Richardson) grew up on the place their grandparents had homesteaded. William committed suicide in October of 1928.

William Rogers (1860-1928) and Nancy (Welch) Rogers (1860-1926)

Cecil Ray married Mildred Rose Clark on Aug. 24, 1905. His brother, Walter, married Mildred's sister, Cora. Another Clark sister, Mary, married Wilbur M. Rogers, a cousin of Walter and Cecil. Cecil and Mildred had four children, Ruth (Aug. 16, 1906-March 1988), Helen (Aug. 12, 1909-Jan. 31, 1936), William Paul (Paul) (Jan. 17, 1912-May 26, 1983), and Loyd Eugene (Trigger) (April 17, 1915-December 1989). After their marriage Cecil and Mildred farmed for a time at the home place on Jackson Creek. Then they moved to Bloomington where Cecil opened a restaurant. They returned to Brown County to open a grocery store with Cecil's brother, Orval, in Trevlac. In 1916 they returned to farming on Jackson Creek. In 1921 Cecil opened a grocery store in Nashville and moved into town. Cecil ran the store until 1938, when he retired. After that his son, Paul, ran the store until the 1950s. Helen died after being badly burned in 1936.

Lewis and Perilda had received the sheepskin deed from the government for their property on Jackson Creek. It is still in the family. The family lived on and farmed the land until 1938, when they sold it to the state of Indiana. Yellowood Lake is now on the site.

On Nov. 26, 1926 Ruth married George Ennis. Their child, Rosalie Mildred was born on Nov. 8, 1932. She married Lloyd Barnhill on Nov. 30, 1952. Their children are Mark and Roseann.

Paul married Meredith McGrayel on Sept. 5, 1931. Their children are Cynthia Caroline (May 26, 1937-), and Celia (Aug. 22, 1945-). Cynthia married James Louie Miller (son of Lounie and Frances (Novelette) Miller on Sept. 9, 1956. Their children are Casey Lee, James Scott, and Clark Rogers. Celia married Dan Davis on Aug. 18, 1964. They were divorced. She married Jim Kraatz on June 12, 1982. After Paul sold the grocery store he worked for the state as a tax inspector, then opened his own accounting firm and was the Justice of the Peace for nine years. Meredith worked in the store, then at the Brown County Democrat, then at Cummins Engine Company.

Trigger married Ethel Snider. They were married 25 years and had no children. After her death, he married Catherine Brown Burkhart. *Submitted by Cynthia Miller*

GLENN W. ROSCOE - Glenn was born in Jennings Co., IN, April 22, 1922. He died July 3, 1989. He was the son of Charles and Carrie (McNicholas) Roscoe. His brothers are: (1) Paul Roscoe (Scipio, IN), (2) Lloyd Roscoe (died as an infant) and (3) Harold Roscoe (deceased at age 40 in November, 1966. He was adopted by a family by the name of Storm). His sister is Helen (Roscoe) Clampitt, now living in Niceville, FL. He had the following half brothers and sisters: (1) Reba (Roscoe) Moore (Scipio, IN); (2) Fred Ward (Columbus); (3) Dorothy (Roscoe) Carson (Calipatria, CA); (4) Beryl (Roscoe) Hundley (Columbus); (5) Sharon (Roscoe) Jaggers (Columbus) and (6) Judy (Ward) Simms, Columbus; (7) a half brother, Sherman Roscoe passed away in 1967.

Glenn Roscoe

At an early age Glenn, Paul, Harold and Helen were put in the orphans home in Columbus, IN. At the age of 12, Glenn was taken out of the orphans home by a family by the name of Sutton, who lived in Hamblen Township. He attended grade schools in the Grammer area, East Columbus and later

Brown County and the Brown County High School in Nashville. He was baptized at the East Columbus Christian Church when a young man. In 1944, he married Frances Condon, daughter of Virgil and Hazel (Sutton) Condon, and to this union were borne two children: (1) Judy, (2) Dickie, who was killed in an auto accident in 1964. Frances passed away in January 1965.

In September 1966, Glenn married Crystal Freese, daughter of Ray and Vira (Greathouse) Freese of Van Buren Township. Glenn, along with his first wife, Frances, when she was living, drove the Route #1 school bus route for more than 20 years. Glenn was county commissioner from 1969 through 1972 and served on the Brown County Welfare Department. A Brown County farmer for some 30 years, he retired from Burnside Ready Mix in 1977 due to heart problems, after 25 years employment. Glenn and Crystal moved from Brown County to Columbus, IN in November, 1977.

Glenn was interested in history and traced down his grandfather's history and toured the Murfreesboro battleground where his grandfather was wounded in the Civil War, and also found his grave marked with a Civil War stone at the Bethel Cemetery in Bloomington.

Glenn's grandfather, Robert Roscoe, enlisted in the Civil War as a private of Company F in the 39th 8th Cavalry regiment Indiana Volunteers at Indianapolis on Aug. 29, 1861, at the age of 18. He was discharged on May 5, 1862 because of injuries. On Oct. 7, 1864, he enrolled as a private of Company D, 140th Regiment Indiana Volunteers at Columbus, IN at the age of 22. He was wounded on picket duty at Murfreesboro, TN on Dec. 8, 1864, and had his hand amputated. He was in a hospital at Indianapolis and discharged May 8, 1865. Several years ago, Glenn was given the government issue of the iron hook his grandfather wore after his hand was amputated.

Glenn Roscoe was a well known and respected individual and was always remembered by his friends and family as a man who never met a stranger and was always there to help a friend or neighbor. See article in Brown County Democrat of Aug. 16, 1989 about his work to repair and improve the Goshen Church on the Bean Blossom/Georgetown Road.

ROUSH FAMILY -
The name "Rausch" came from the old German words "rouzo" and "ruozjan" which means to rout out the forest or to dig in the ground and this was surely the name of an old farm family.

The earliest actual date that the name appears was 1190 during the time of the crusades. Originally they were Christians of the Catholic faith but then became Calvinists and eventually Lutherans.

The area from which they came was called the "Palatinate," the name of two German states along both sides of the Rhine river.

Wars, terrorism, political reasons, scarcity of fertile lands, and the death of their ruler left the peoples of this area quite disheartened and discouraged. After a very severe winter of 1703 they were ready to leave.

John Adam Rausch, one of the first of the Roush line in America came with a group of 110 from the Palatinate by the way of Rotterdam on the Brigantine John of Perth Amboy landing at Philadelphia in 1736.

It is believed that Nicholas Roush (1723-1777) was a younger brother in this group. He married Elizabeth Kek in 1750 in Berks Co., PA and later moved to Hagerstown, MD.

One of their sons, George, led a very interesting life. He was a Revolutionary War soldier, justice of the peace, land owner, and an educated man. When he was 17 he walked or rode horseback 120 miles through the mountains to Ft. Pitt to enlist in the militia. After serving three years as a scout and Indian spy, he married Elizabeth Reischer and settled near Pittsburg. He was always interested in education and saw that his children went to school. In 1819, after his children were grown, he and his neighbors leased a tract of land and built a school.

One of his 12 children, Boston, (1790-1829) married Matilda Fisher and moved to Harrison Co., OH which was new land. He died in 1829 and Matilda raised their four sons. It is from this line that the Roushes of Brown Co., IN came. See George Washington Roush.

GEORGE WASHINGTON ROUSH -
George (1817-1907), son of Boston and Matilda Roush grew up in Belmont Co., OH. After a brief marriage to Elizabeth Workman, he married Mary Powell in 1848.

In 1850 they moved to Brown County settling in the Christiansburg area. George signed a land grant for two parcels of 40 acres of public land and the sheep skin deeds were signed by president Zachary Taylor. These deeds are still displayed in the home of his great-grandson. The cemetery at Christiansburg was land given by George and one of the first graves is a son, William Roush, dated 1853.

Roush Farm painted by Kenneth Reeve

Children were Mary Elizabeth (Anthony), Thomas Jefferson, William H., George Washington, Hanna Jane (Noblitt), James Boston, Lottie Alice (Setser), and Amanda Emma (Brown). Son James Boston inherited the 80 acres plus more that had been purchased and lived there all his life as a farmer. The house he lived in was built by him and his father about 1900 and is still in use. Jim as he was known, married Eva Carmichael and children were Blanche (Pruitt), Jessie (McKain), Mary (Curtis) (Beam), Grace (Allen), Ada (King), and Paul. Jessie is the only member still living. Jim and Eva raised sheep, chickens, cattle and hogs. They sold milk and cream, made maple syrup and had big butchering days when several hogs would be processed. Jim never owned a tractor or a car and did all his farming with teams of horses or mules. One of his favorite teams was a big strong pair of mules known as "Buck" and "Kate."

Son Paul (1905-1974) inherited the land and lived there all his life as a farmer and school teacher. In 1925 he married Elizabeth Phillips and their children are Betty Jean Manuel (1926) and Charles Edward (1940).

Paul began his teaching career of 40-1/2 years at age 18 in 1923 at Mt. Nebo school. He completed an eight week course at old Central Normal College and rode horseback to the $800 per year job.

He was quite athletic as a young man, playing on an independent basketball team and different times winning pole vault and hop-skip and jump contests in the county. He could clear 9' with a beech pole he cut from the woods and then 10' when he finally got a bamboo pole.

After about ten years of summer school, Paul took a year off and finally received his four years Bachelors Degree in 1937.

Being too old for WWII, Paul instead signed up for the Camp Canol Project in 1943. This was a construction project by the Army Corps of Engineers in the N.W. Territory of Canada to construct roads and an air base.

Each summer from 1947-1973 Paul and Elizabeth travelled extensively in the western U.S.A. Paul became a fan of the Cheyenne Frontier Days Rodeo and went more than 20 years to it. He worked two summers in Yellowstone Park and in 1972 they drove to Alaska and back.

Elizabeth, (1909-1983) was a housewife and then later the Farm Bureau Insurance Agent for 19 years in Brown County. Everyone knew her as a stalwart Christian (Beck's Grove Church) and as a person always willing to help anyone in need. Her reputation of a good cook was widely known at family reunions, church, and community pitchins.

Daughter Betty married Bob Manuel (1926-1980), in 1947 and lives on an adjoining farm. She has three grown children, Marcella White, Robert Manuel II, and Dean Manuel. Community service work, the Beck's Grove Church and eight grandchildren keep her active and on the go.

Son Charlie married Susie Miller in 1964 and they had two sons, Charles Kevin (1968) and Craig Edward (1972). Kevin is a senior at Ball State University majoring in marketing and advertising and Craig is a senior at Brown County High School with plans to attend Ball State in art education.

Divorced in 1983, Charlie married Brenda Brumley in 1989 and now lives on 167 acres of family land being the fourth generation Roush to live there. Charlie graduated from Nashville High School in 1959 after its consolidation with Van Buren and played on the sectional championship basketball team. He also played for Branch McCracken at Indiana University graduating in 1963 with a degree in biology and earth science. He received his masters degree in biology in 1968 and has taught 27 years at Central Middle School in Columbus. He is currently teaching earth science and horticulture and is in the position of activities/athletic director, a post he has held for 20 years. See Roush Family.

JACOB DOUGLASS AND CASSIE MABLE (TRISLER) RHUDE, JR. -
Jacob Douglass Rhude, Jr. was the oldest son and third child of 13 children of Jacob Douglass Rhude and Martha Ellen Harrison. He was born in Brown County on Jan. 21, 1888. He married Cassie Mable (Trisler) Zimmerman on May 18, 1921 in Nashville, Brown Co., IN. Cassie was the third of nine children of Ward W. and Mary (Adair) Trisler. She was born Oct. 5, 1900 in Brown County.

Cassie, first married Colonel Elsworth Zimmerman, son of Abraham and Catherine (Kate) (Mullinix) Zimmerman. They had one son, Grover Elsworth born March 2, 1920. They divorced.

Jacob Douglass Rhude, Jr., also known as Bob,

and Cassie Trisler had five children, all born in Brown County:

Jacob D. and Cassie (Trisler) Rhude, Jr., 1937

(1) Mary Martha, born April 1, 1922, married Loyd Clifford Brock of Crab Orchard, KY. Mary lives in Hamblen Township, Brown County; (2) Wilma Marie, born Feb. 1, 1925, married Bert Elmer Witham of Franklin, IN, and lives in Franklin; (3) Doris Louise, born April 17, 1927, married Robert Earl Wilson of Ware Co., GA and lives in Jacksonville, FL; (4) Norma Arlene, born Sept. 20, 1930, married (first) Robert H. Stickford, and (second) Fred H. Wilson. Norma lives in Springville, IN; (5) Gerald Leon, born Aug. 10, 1936. Gerald (Sonny) was killed in an automobile accident west of Trafalgar, IN on June 16, 1941. He is buried in Greenlawn Cemetery, Franklin, IN.

Grover Zimmerman married Anna Mae Cline, March 13, 1939. They had seven children. Grover died July 26, 1981.

Jacob D. Jr. was a land-owner in Brown and Johnson Cos., IN. He farmed, worked in timber, and later worked for Morgan Packing Company and Stokely-Van Camps. He was a U.S. Navy veteran of World War I. He had served on the Brown County draft board prior to enlisting in the U.S. Navy, where he served as a shipwright. He saw active duty in France and England, participating in the Battle of Eastleigh.

Bob and Cassie spent some winters in Florida. There he worked for Blue Goose Packing Company and did some building-construction.

They were both members of The General Assembly and Church of the Firstborn; both were registered Democrats.

After their son, Gerald, died, they separated and later divorced. Cassie married for the third time to Edmund J. Stephens of Florida and they later divorced.

Jacob D. Rhude, Jr. died Dec. 2, 1949 at Billings VA Hospital, Fort Harrison, IN. Cassie died Oct. 19, 1972 at Johnson County Hospital, Franklin, IN. Both died of cancer. Both are buried near their son, Gerald, at Greenlawn Cemetery, Franklin, IN. *Submitted by Doris (Rhude) Wilson*

WILLIAM AND SARAH RUDE - William, son of Asher and Elizabeth Rude, and Sarah Merrifield, daughter of Thomas and Rachel Kennedy Merrifield, were married in Hardin (now LaRue) Co., KY, Dec. 29, 1819. William was born March 4, 1789, in Fayette Co., PA.

A Revolutionary War veteran, Asher Rude moved his family to Nelson Co., KY, when William was an infant, then to Hardin County about 1802. Asher died in 1803, but his widow and family were close neighbors of the Thomas Lincoln family when Abraham was born in 1809. Both families lived on the South Fork of Nolin Creek near Hodgenville.

Sarah Merrifield was born Feb. 6, 1802, in Hardin County. She and William came to Indiana about 1822, first to Marion County. By 1850 they were living in Brown County on a farm in Jackson Township near the Morgan County line. They had 11 children: Syntha Ann (Cynthia), Thomas Andrew, Elizabeth, Rachel, Mary Jane, Martha Ann, Sarah, Nancy, Ruth Matilda, William, and Zachariah James. The first two were born in Kentucky and the others in Indiana.

Elizabeth, born May 28, 1824, died about three weeks before her seventh birthday, and William, born Jan. 8, 1841, died at about three weeks of age.

Syntha Ann was born Oct. 28, 1820; married 1838 to Benjamin Boles; and died Nov. 20, 1842. Thomas was born May 27, 1822; married July 13, 1848, Mary Jane Blair, died July 28, 1881. Rachel was born April 12, 1826; married (1) March 28, 1844, James H. Whitaker; married (2) May 15, 1881, Thomas Owens. Mary Jane was born March 17, 1828; married Sept. 30, 1844, Jesse Moore; died July 4, 1904. Martha Ann was born Oct. 19, 1830; married Sept. 30, 1849, to William H. McCarty; died July 13, 1919. Sarah was born May 27, 1833; married Sept. 10, 1854, Jacob Henry Fleener; died Jan. 24, 1857. Nancy was born Aug. 5, 1835; married (1) Jan. 1, 1852, Samuel W. Fleener; married (2) Oct. 14, 1863, Charles Whitaker; died Oct. 24, 1865. Ruth Matilda was born July 13, 1837; married Oct. 16, 1856, Joshua Whitaker, Jr.; died Aug. 29, 1907. Zacchariah James was born March 10, 1842; married Lily Quintilla Wayt.

William, a farmer, died Jan. 6, 1869, and Sarah died June 21, 1868. They are buried in Fleener Cemetery, along with several family members. Still other family members are buried in Old Boles Cemetery and; East Hill, Morgantown; and Taggart, Brown County. *Submitted by Dale Kelley*

RUDE/RHUDE - Jacob Douglas Rude Sr. was born Sept. 6, 1860 in Bartholomew Co., IN the son of Worden and Lavina Anna (West) (Reynolds) Rude. Worden Rude was born in Illinois, the son of John and Cela Rude. Before coming to Bartholomew County, he lived in Jackson Co., IN. Worden and Lavina (widow of Wm. H. Reynolds) Rude were married in Nashville April 7, 1854. They resided in Harrison Township, Bartholomew County where their children were born. Jacob Douglas Rude was one of seven brothers and two half-brothers. Later they lived in Clifford. Lavina Anna West was the daughter of William and Sarah (Sary) West from Ohio. She was born there in 1830. William West received Bounty land for his service in the War of 1812. This was located in Bartholomew Co., IN. Lavina Anna (West) Rude is buried in the Liberty Cemetery, Bartholomew County.

Jacob Douglas Rhude Sr. and Martha Ellen (Harrison) Rhude/Rude

Jacob D. Rude Sr. married Martha Ellen Harrison in Brown Co., IN Nov. 26, 1882. He operated a General store, farmed, and operated a sawmill in Hamblen Township, Brown County. They were the parents of 13 children. All deceased. Martha Ellen was the daughter of William Henry Harrison and Julia Ann (Truax) Harrison. Wm. H. Harrison was a circuit riding preacher. He served in the Haw Creek, South Bethany, Nashville, and Sprunica churches. Wm. H. Harrison was born Sept. 18, 1840 in Bartholomew County, this State. Both, he and his wife are buried in Sprunica Cemetery, Hamblen Township. Wm. H. was the son of Carter J. Harrison and Julianne (Sinclair/St. Clair) Harrison. Julianne being the daughter of Thomas Sinclair of Jackson Co., IN. Thomas Sinclair, formerly of Kentucky, came to Indiana before 1830. Wm. H. Harrison and Julia Ann Truax were married Oct. 12, 1860 in Nashville, Brown County at the home of the bride's step-father. Julia Ann Truax was the daughter of Aaron Truax and Catherine Sipe(s) and came with the mother and stepfather from Ohio to Brown County about 1850/60. Catherine Sipe(s) born in Maryland was the daughter of Christopher Sipe(s) and Nancy McCalley of Maryland and Ohio. Catherine came with her second husband (B.W. Cook) to Indiana. They lived not too far from the Brown County and Bartholomew County line. Many descendants live in the area as well as scattered throughout the United States. Also see Robert Earl and Doris Wilson.

DELMER E. AND ELIZABETH RUND FAMILY - Delmer was born June 11, 1916 in the same log house that his paternal grandparents had set up housekeeping when they were married in 1876. Rund attended the one room Greenwood School in 1922-1924. His first teacher was Clarence Zody.

In 1924 Mr. Rund's parents moved to Hickory Hill about two miles north of Trevlac. He finished his grade school at the one room Cottonwood School.

During World War II he spent five years in the Army and Air Force. While in the Air Force he met and married Elizabeth Farison. They were married on March 4, 1944. Sons are Arthur and Robert. Samuel is only grandchild, son of Robert.

Front: Delmer E. Rund, Elizabeth Rund, Mun Eu (daughter-in-law) and Samuel (grandson). Back: Lee and Robert.

The late columnist for the Indianapolis News, Wayne Guthrie, in his column, Ringside in Hoosierland, ran an article in April 1976 about Mr. Rund. A few of the excerpts of his article follow:

"To pay for his clothing and school books from the time he was ten years old he picked berries and dug ginseng.

"Walked one and one-half miles to catch a school hack to go to grade school: At completion of grade school he ranked third in county on written tests that were required of all students. Walked about five miles to high school the first two years. Last two years he walked one mile to catch school bus when it was first provided. Graduated from Helmsburg High School second in County. He entered Indiana University in fall of 1933 with a one year tuition scholarship. Worked eight hour weekly to pay for room rent. Worked 28 hours a week for meals at Leonard's restaurant in Bloomington. Talk about inflation! He took a two year elementary teachers' course. Began student teaching with a broken arm. Earned an elementary teacher's license and began teaching in the one room Cottonwood school."

"During summers he often worked a 60 hour week and was paid ten cents per hour."

"By taking extra classes and with summer courses he received his B.S. degree in math and education in the year 1938. After teaching experiences in South Bend and Pendleton, he enlisted in the army and air force until his discharge on Nov. 15, 1945."

"Following military service he resumed his teaching career teaching grade six at Edinburg. By attending summer school and night school he obtained a M.S. and an administrative license in 1948. His first two years of administration was at Columbus, IN as a teaching principal. This was followed by two years principal of a junior high school in Lawrenceburg, IN. He took over a full time elementary principalship in 1953 at Beech Grove, IN, where he remained until his retirement in 1976. Including military service he was credited with 41 years as a teacher and administrator." *Submitted by Delmer E. Rund*

FRANCIS AND SALLY (LEE) RUND -

Bert Rund and Flora Rund, children of Francis Rund and his second wife, Sally, resided their entire life in Brown County. Son, Bert, married Emma Long. In this marriage five children were born. Hubert, Edith, Evelyn, Jessie and James. The two oldest children are now deceased. Son, James, still resides on his father's farm and house just north of Helmsburg.

Parts of both families are shown in picture taken at Garfield Park in Indianapolis ca. 1939.

Daughter Flora married Cass McDonald. Flora's son Herb operated a general store for many years in Bean Blossom. Herb's son, Jack, presently operates the I.G.A. store in Bean Blossom. Their son Ival probably had the first auto dealership in Brown County. *Submitted by Delmer E. Rund*

FRANCIS THERESA RUND FAMILY -

Mr. and Mrs. Franz (Francis) Rund left Wittenberg, Germany with their four oldest children to America in 1848. Only Maria (Mary) is their only child that came with them from Germany that there is little known. Mary lived to an advanced age in Morgantown. Mr. Rund was a tanner by trade. The Runds settled near Bean Blossom around 1852. Mr. Rund continued his tanning in cave or cellar near his home.

Three other children were born to this family after coming to America. Louis Albert was born 1852, Herman (Hammond) Hayer 1855 and Theresa 1858.

Mary (Rund) Knight

Mr. Rund's first wife died Sept. 2, 1869. A few years later he married Sally Lee, a niece of Robert Lee. His second wife gave birth to a son, Bert, and daughter Flora.

Many of the descendants of Mr. Rund and his two wives became successful business persons, farmers, doctors, lawyers, missionaries, ministers, educators among other successful occupations.

Hammond Rund, who married Jane Snider ran a general store for many years in Bean Blossom. To this couple were born four sons, Francis, Forest, Roy, and Theodore. Each of these sons at one time operated a grocery store as their livelihood. A daughter, Grace, also married a grocerman.

The late Wayne Guthrie, a long time columnist for the Indianapolis Newspapers grew up in the Bean Blossom community. He once related the story of his early life in Bean Blossom and his association with Hammond Rund to the writer of this Rund history. To supply Hammond's grocery store, he would drive a team of horses and a wagon to Indianapolis to secure his needed supplies. It was nearly a 24 hour trip. Mr. Guthrie says that as a boy he often would accompany Hammond on this journey. After securing their groceries the team would be driven out south Meridian Street to the edge of town. The teams lines would be tied to front of wagon. Mr. Rund and Wayne would then lie down in the wagon and sleep. Around midnight the horses would pull up to their barn door and come to a halt. Son, Forest Rund, has been considered the last person to operate a huckster route in Indiana. *Submitted by Delmer E. Rund*

LOUIS AND HANNAH RUND FAMILY -

Louis Albert was born in 1852 and married Hannah Horner in 1876. To this union were born five sons, Elmer - 1877; Oscar Barzillar who was a rancher in New Mexico; Earl who died at a young age; Lee Otis Rund, who married Eva Fleener, who was a native of Brown County; Ora Rund born 1890, who married Bessie Davis.

Louis and Hannah Rund with sons Oscar and Elmer.

Only Lee Otis and Ora E. had any children. Margaret, James, and Robert were born to Mr. and Mrs. Lee Otis Rund. James died quite young. Margaret taught art and music a few years. She now resides in New Whiteland; son Robert became an aviator and retired from the Air Corps as a colonel. After retiring he became a commercial pilot. The accompanying picture shows Otis Rund as one of the first principals of the Helmsburg High School.

Helmsburg High School

Mr. Louis Rund was a successful farmer and orchardist. The Louis Runds resided about two miles north of Helmsburg until Mr. Rund's death on Feb. 22, 1916. *Submitted by Delmer E. Rund*

ORA E. AND BESSIE RUND FAMILY -

Ora E. Rund born 1890 married Bessie Davis in 1915. Three sons were born to this couple. Delmer - June 11, 1916; Melvin - June 10, 1922; Victor - Oct. 10, 1932. Ora and Bessie Rund lived in his father's homestead until 1924 when he and his wife moved to the Hickory Hill orchard about one and one-half miles north of Trevlac. Ora Rund attended the old Greenwood School. He is shown in school picture taken around 1907. Ora was a farmer.

Greenwood School ca. 1907, Ora Rund is back row middle.

Son, Delmer married Elizabeth Marie Farison on March 4, 1944. This couple reared two sons, Arthur Lee and Robert Wayne.

Son, Melvin married Martha Smythe Nov. 12, 1949. This couple have a daughter Donna and a son David. Donna married James Bond and presently live on Morrison Road. James is grandson of Earl Bond, a long time Brown County mortician.

Elmer, Ora and Bessie Rund

Son, Victor Rund married Carolyn Parish. Two children, Victor Glenn and Annette were born to this couple.

BETTY BELLE (LONG) SABATIER -

Doris Betty Belle (Long) Sabatier was born in the beautiful hills of Brown County on a cold snowy night, Jan. 14, 1920, to Albert E. Long, better known as "Bert" by friends, and Lillian (Fiegel) Long.

Lillian named her "Doris" on record but a few days later she renamed her "Betty Belle" but she didn't change it on the record. At school and by her friends she was known as "Betty Belle."

Betty Belle was born top of Plum Creek hill on the late Dale Bessire orchard which her father, Albert E. Long, took care of. When Betty was two, the Long family moved to an old log cabin across the Ole Gibson orchard owned at that time by the Long family. There Betty spent 18 years of her life. There her father died and was buried in the Oak Ridge Cemetery near Helmsburg.

Doris (Betty B. Long) Sabatier on cabin step where she had lived for almost 20 years.

Betty attended the Helmsburg school. She traveled first to school by covered wagon and sometimes in the winter in a bobsled covered with horse blankets. Betty met and married Maurice Sabatier, better known as "Frenchie." Their oldest girl, Carmileta was born there. She married Ronald Emberton and they live in Morgantown. When Carmileta was one and a half years old, the family moved to Needmore. There Betty and Maurice lived for 27 years and Ramona, David and Michael were born.

Betty (Doris) had two brothers, Finley and Lacell (Toots) Long. There Toots died along with his grandmother, Lillian Long, and are both buried in the Needmore Cemetery.

Betty's daughter Ramona married the late Kenneth Weddle. They had two sons and were divorced. She then married Carl Byrd and they now live at Martinsville, IN.

In 1964 Maurice and Betty were divorced and Betty left Brown County and moved to Bloomington, IN. She worked as a cook for years.

Michael Sabatier married Lu Ann Coy and now lives in Falls Church, VA.

In 1978 Betty moved to Loogootee, IN where David had started a restaurant. Here he married Janet Inman. Betty lost her brother Finley while living in Loogootee. He is buried in the Needmore Cemetery.

Betty lives in Loogootee, IN and has never remarried. She has 11 grandchildren and nine great-grandchildren.

Many happy things and many sad things have happened while Betty grew up but in her heart Brown County will always be home. (See Long history.) *Submitted by Doris (Betty Belle) (Long) Sabatier*

SANDERS FAMILY - Nathan Sanders and Emma Pierce Sanders were from southern Indiana. They lived in Mitchell, French Lick, Oolitic and Bedford. They had four children of their own. Arthur, Leslie, Grace and Rex. They also raised Nate's brother Wright's son Raymond from 12 days old and also two other boys. Arthur's wife died and left Dale Sanders, two years of age. Arthur died five months later. Both died of tuberculosis. Leslie's first wife died leaving them Deloris and Napolean to raise. Grace, their only daughter, died at 18 years of age. They then moved to Minnesota but returned in 1924 after trading the place in Minnesota for Frank Coons' 160 acre farm. They had a branch of the Brown County Library in their home.

Leslie married Marvel Wesene (who had one child named Edith Mae) and to this union were born Marlowe and Richard who still live on the home place and Myrtis who lives in Indianapolis.

Leslie and Marvel Sanders, 1984.

Rex and his wife Doris are deceased. They had three children Bobby and Marlene who live in California and Raymond who is in the Air Force.

Arthur's son Dale married Helen Zimmerman July 19, 1930 at Mitchell, IN. They were married by the same Minister that married his Mom and Dad. His name was Warren Sanders. To this union were born Arthur Dale, Kenneth, Eileen, Gary also Darryl, Faith, Bette and Esther Sanders. Dale died of Cancer on Oct. 5, 1979.

Nate would often look at Arthur Dale when he was a baby and say, "You don't care how much corn is in a bushel." At that time in the 30s corn was only .09¢ a bushel. He had a farm loan to pay every six months, it was hard to meet the payments but he always did. Leslie and Marvel were married in Minnesota on July 19, 1930. Dale and Helen and Deloris and Roland Heller had a double wedding on the same date as Leslie and Marvel. *Written by Helen (Zimmerman) Sanders (wife of Dale Sanders)*

KENNETH E. SANDERS FAMILY - Kenneth was born close to Spearsville, IN on June 6, 1933. His parents were Dale Veloris and Helen Ione Zimmerman Sanders. Kenneth attended Brown County Schools and also served in the United States Army. He was stationed in Germany. He married Ada Louise Vaught on Aug. 6, 1955. Ada's parents were Clyde Bell and Emma Rose Little Vaught.

Kenneth and Ada had seven children. They are Randy Joe, Kenneth Ray, Roger Dale (deceased), Pamela Corinne Sanders Hochstetler, also John Dennis, Deborah Elaine Sanders Hilligoss, and William Darren. All were born at Johnson County Hospital in Franklin, IN except for William who was born at Columbus, IN. All of the children except Randy live within three miles of the family farm. Randy along with his wife Robin and three daughters reside in Okeechobee, FL. All together Kenneth and Ada have 17 grandchildren.

Kenneth and Ada Sanders

Kenneth and Ada purchased part of the family farm which has been in the family for over 50 years. They also purchased part of the Mitchell farm. They raise cattle and farm a little. Kenneth also has been in Bridge Construction for almost 30 years. He is now Bridge Superintendent for Robertson Construction in Franklin, IN. Ada helps around the farm and also along with her children raise a large garden which they all can and freeze from. The entire family enjoys getting together quite often for games, cookouts and singing country music. Every year all friends and family look forward to the annual corn roast held by Kenneth and Ada. *Written by Pam Sanders Hochstetler*

LESLIE SANDERS FAMILY - Leslie was born July 10, 1892 in Orange Co., IN. He was born to Nathan, son of Joseph Sanders and Emma Pierce, daughter of Napoleon Pierce. Leslie had one sister, Gracie, also brothers Arthur Lee and Rex. His family also raised Raymond who was actually a cousin but considered a brother.

Napoleon (standing), Richard, Leslie and Marlowe Sanders

Leslie married Carrie Dorsett. They had two children. Delores died at the age of 18 from complications of a tooth extraction. She is buried at Unity Baptist Cemetery in Brown County. They also had one son named Napoleon Miles. Napoleon married Dorothy Verhines and of this marriage were born David, Donna and Larry. There are nine grandchildren from this marriage. Napoleon and Dorothy are both buried at Morgantown, IN. Carrie Sanders died so Leslie traded Frank Coons his farm in return for Frank's Minnesota farm. While in Minnesota Leslie met and married Marvel Wesen. They married July 19, 1930 in Hibbing, MN. Later that year they again traded with Frank Coons and returned to their farm on Spearsville road. Marvel's daughter Edith Mae also returned with them. After moving back to Brown County Leslie and Marvel had three more children. They are Marlowe and Richard born in Columbus at Bartholomew County Hospital and daughter Myrtis, born at home. The boys still live on the farm while Myrtis resides in Indianapolis. There are 15 grandchildren from this marriage.

Leslie and Marvel (Wesen) Sanders

Leslie was one of the first in the area to have electricity. He had a generator and an electric fence which the children hated to get shocked on. Like many, Leslie farmed with a horse. Leslie's father Nathan also did a lot of the hoeing. Leslie's mother Emma also helped out by washing the clothes on a washboard and watching the children while Marvel helped milk the cows. She also canned and made butter, which she sold along with milk and eggs to make extra money. Marvel also took in laundry and did babysitting. Leslie worked for the state highway department and also for the county highway. He also did blacksmithing.

Leslie passed away Dec. 2, 1984 at his home. He was 92 years, five months and seven days old. After a service at Bond Funeral Home in Nashville, Leslie was buried in Liberty, IN along with other family members.

Marvel is now in Brown County Community Care Center in Nashville. Marvel had fallen and broken her leg and is unable to remain at home, although she does return home for short visits. Marvel also attends church on Sundays in Morgantown with her family.

MARVEL (WESEN) SANDERS - Marvel Estella was born April 24, 1905 in Starbuck, MN to Victor and Edith Jones Wesen. Marvel's grandpa, George Washington Jones, was born in Wales. He was a sailor. He moved to Minnesota where he met and married Hattie Ray. They had four daughters, Nellie Josephine, Abby Jane, Mary Jane and Edith Mae which is Marvel's mother.

Front: Edith Mae, Marvel and Myrtis Sanders. Back: Napolean, Marlowe and Richard Sanders.

When Marvel was four her mother passed away. She also left behind Myrtis who was two and a half and Hazel aged six months. Marvel and Myrtis went to live with their Aunt Mary in Montana. While living in Montana their family used to lay cloth diapers in the grass to dry. Since there were so many rattlesnakes, before picking up the diapers, they would lift a corner to see if there was a snake under them (which happened quite often). On the way home from school Marvel and cousin Edith along with other children would kill the snakes and put them in buckets. Marvel moved back to Minnesota when she was 12 or 13. She lived with her Aunt Abby and Uncle Elmer Wesen who was a brother to Victor.

Marvel Sanders and Judy Mendes (granddaughter)

Marvel met and married Leslie Sanders in Meadowlands, MN. They married July 19, 1930 and moved to Brown County later that year. Leslie had two children, Napolean Miles and Delores. Marvel had a daughter named Edith Mae. Leslie and Marvel then had three children together. They were Marlowe, Richard and Myrtis. There are 15 grandchildren altogether.

Marvel always helped out on the farm. She would milk cows, raise chickens and worked in the tobacco fields. She and Helen Sanders would take the little children along to pick blackberries. Of course being children they would always eat and spill many of them. Marvel always did a lot of mending and sewing clothes for the kids. She also did plenty of canning.

Marvel is now in the Brown County Community Care Center. She makes quilts, attends church in Morgantown, reads her Bible every day and visits her family at home. *Written by Marvel (Wesen) Sanders*

JOHN AND SARAH SAUNDERS - John (1806-1875) was born in Cornwall, England in the small town of Stratton. As a young man he made the trip to the United States in 1832 on a sailing vessel, taking six weeks to do so. He brought along his wife, Isabella, and small daughter, Mary Ann. In his journal he tells of the motion sickness and how each family had to do their own cooking.

The vessel landed at St. John's, Newfoundland and then he went to Honesdale, PA for a short time. John was a shoe cobbler by trade, so followed the men laying the tracks for the first trains in this country. When a canal was built, he lived nearby to make the boots for the men.

John Saunders

It was while he was living in Columbiana Co., OH that his first wife died after giving birth to six children. Soon he married Sarah Robbins Smith, a widow and they were the parents of six children.

During the Civil war, John joined the army and while he was away Morgan and his raiders were captured on the farm adjacent to Sarah Saunders. This not only scared Sarah, but also many of the other women living nearby and when someone suggested they trade their farm land for land in Brown Co., IN, where "there was no fighting," they agreed. Many packed up and moved to Brown County.

After John was wounded and discharged from service, he found Sarah in her new home. She became pregnant and at the time of delivery, the doctor, who was drunk, lost both the mother and the twins, in 1866. Sarah is buried in Lick Spring cemetery.

In 1869 John married Mary Pitcher, a widow. Meantime John could not care for his six small children and they were put out into homes to be taken care of. Eventually all the children moved to Johnson County when they wanted more schooling or were married. Martha Jane Caywood moved to Palestine, IL; Daniel became a doctor in Franklin; Peter went to Colorado for the gold rush; James was a school teacher and farmer; Agnes married Dr. John Records and lived in Franklin; and Sarah Matilda Alexander moved to Oklahoma with her family. *Submitted by Rachel (Saunders) Henry*

RAY SCALF AND JUDIE HURT SCALF - Ray was born in Himyar, KY, on Oct. 17, 1938, to Beulah and Dudley Scalf. They had three other sons, Jim, Ronny, and Danny. Ray married Bertha Davis in 1957. They had two children, Judy and Randy. Ray and Bertha were divorced in 1977. He married Judie Hurt on Oct. 30, 1986. He is a musician and artist.

Judie Bivins Hurt Scalf was born Sept. 3, 1943 to Mary Lou Fisher Mensi Bivins and Silas J. Bivins. They had five other children together, Iris, Larry, Alma, Paul, and Betty. She also has a brother and sister, Irene and Pete Jr. from her Mother's previous marriage to Pete Mensi. Judie moved from where she was born in Phoenix, AZ to a small town in northern Arizona called Ash Fork. She lived there with her family from age three until she was 14 years old, when the family moved back to Phoenix, AZ. She married Brent Plonkey in 1962, who passed away at an early age of 23, with kidney failure. Judie moved to Indianapolis, IN in 1966. She married Jack Hurt there and commuted to Nashville for her art business. Judie's niece, Kristy Richardson, living in Nashville, IN is the only relative living near her. Kristy is one of five children born to Judie's sister Irene. Kristy is married to Jeff Richardson of Nashville, IN.

Judie moved to Nashville, IN in 1984 after her separation from Jack Hurt. She was divorced in 1985 and later married her present husband, Ray Scalf, on Oct. 30, 1986. They are both artists and have a lot in common. They love living here and painting the historical scenes in this beautiful artist's colony. They are art supporters and also make their living selling their paintings from the Gallery known as The Brown County Art Barn.

WILLIAM AND HERMAN SCHNEIDER - One of Brown County's earliest pioneer citizens was William Snider, known as "Kentucky Bill." He arrived here in 1825 after the treaty for the "Land Purchase" of 1818 was made with the Indians. William's father was Herman Schneider, a native of

Hesse, a state in Germany previous to 1871. The German leader, Bismarck, united the states into one military country. Any state could send soldiers to be paid for service or "hired out" commercially by another country. England hired the Hessian soldiers to fight Gen. George Washington. They surrendered at Trenton, NJ on Christmas Eve, 1777.

Herman never returned to Germany after his furlough in the United States, but "hid out" until 20 years passed when his allegiance was completed.

During his hideout he worked for a Pennsylvania Dutch family with whose daughter he fell in love with and married. Her father disinherited her.

In 1789 a group of Pennsylvania Dutch sailed down the Miami River into Kentucky. Herman and Betty Bowman Schneider came along and settled near Bloomfield but later moved to Taylorsville. There they established a plantation. Seven children were born to them. Herman willed the farm to William, his favorite son. For unknown reasons, William never claimed it. Instead he followed others to the "Land Purchase" in 1825. Our government had just (1818) made a treaty with the Indians for some land including what would later be Brown and Monroe counties.

William left his wife, Jane and their two children, Eliza Jane and Harmon in Kentucky. When he was settled in his new home he returned to Kentucky to kidnap his two children. Shortly after that Jane had another son, George Washington Snider, whom she sent to live with his father. William then was united in a common law marriage with Elizabeth Brummett, daughter of pioneer citizen Banner Brummett. They had nine children: George, Joshua, John, William, Jacob, Jane, Sarah, Martha, and Rachel.

Jane Evans Snider stayed in Kentucky running the plantation until she was unable to care for herself. Then Eliza Jane Baughman and her husband Jacob, brought her to live with them on Lanam Ridge.

A few of Eliza Jane's descendants are Millard Dale Baughman and Lennis Baughman; John's grandson is Elmer of Columbus; Jacob's grandson is Lester Jerome Snider of Indianapolis; one of George's grandsons is James. The daughters married names were: Jane Myers, Sarah Kennedy, Martha Brummett, and Rachel Knauber.

William and Elizabeth are buried in the old Snider cemetery in the hills south of Bean Blossom, now grown up in briars and brush. Just recently Carl Brummett, of Bean Blossom, has begun a clean-up move to show respect to these brave pioneer souls. *Submitted by Aletha (Snider) Chitwood*

SCHOENTRUP - Lyman, Elizabeth and son, Robert, moved to Brown County, Jackson Township, June 1960 from New Bethel, Franklin Township, Marion Co., IN. All are graduates of New Bethel or Franklin Township School.

Lyman's family, the Schoentrups, and Andersons were from Hanover, Germany and Holland. They settled in VeVay, IN, coming to the U.S.A. in 1847, first to Cincinnati, then on farms in Kelso Co., IN in 1854.

Anderson family landed in Virginia and migrated to Pennsylvania, then to Indiana.

Elizabeth (Toon) Schoentrup is related to the Toon, Collins, Hittle, Maze, Rabourn, and Craft families and are Irish, Danish decent and all living in Franklin Township, Marion Co., IN.

Robert (unmarried) was 30 when he came to Brown County with his parents. He served four years in the Korean War, attended Indianapolis Electronic College, and two years at IUPUI. He graduated as an Electrical Engineer from Purdue University two years later (1962). In his school years he started working for RCA and is still working there. In 1963 he married Mary Margaret Meyer and moved back to Marion County. They have two children: Dale and Iraina.

Elizabeth and Lyman Schoentrup

Schoentrup's daughter, Rita Marie was married to Robert Shaffer and they have two children, Daniel and Patricia. Daniel and family live in Marion County and all the rest live on Lake Freeman, Monticello, IN.

Schoentrup's second son William Rhea was married to Dorothy Lou McConnald and they have three children: Karla, William, Jr. and Lori and all live in Marion County.

Schoentrup's third son, Carl Joseph, was married to Sandra Warrenburg. They have five children: Leisa, Leslee, Andrew, Lynne and Samuel and all live in Marion County.

Elizabeth and Lyman have 20 great-grandchildren. They bought 32 acres on Lick Creek Road, Jackson Township, Brown County, which they sold in 1971 and moved to Lake LaSalle, four miles south of Morgantown. Lyman worked at Allison and retired in 1970 at age 62. Elizabeth is active in the Cottonwood Homemakers, Brown County Homemakers, and Franklin Center Junior Homemakers. Both belong to St. Agnes Church. They were married 61 years on Oct. 20, 1989. Both have enjoyed trips all over the U.S.A., Canada, and Alaska. Elizabeth has visited every state except Hawaii, and both enjoy fishing, sports cards, clubs, family get-to-gethers, church, neighbors and friends.

SCHROUGHAM FAMILY - The Schrougham family name was first introduced into Brown County in the late 1820s or early 1830s when two brothers, Daniel and William, journeyed here from Kentucky.

Daniel, born circa 1806 in Kentucky, married the widow Parnelia Pike, mother of Phillip and Eliza, of Brown County. Children are James, Thomas, Jackson, Lewis, William, and Mary.

Vincent and Catherine Schrougham, ca. 1920

William, born circa 1787 in Virginia, married his second wife, Jane Day, in 1831. Their sons were: (1) Isaac Marshall born 1835 married four times; (2) Pierson Murphy born ca 1837 married Mary Dragoo and Mary Furguson. In 1837, William married the widow Mary "Polly" Goodwin (Gooden). Mary "Polly" (Pierce) Goodwin, according to family tradition was the niece of President Franklin Pierce. Mary "Polly," born circa 1814 in Tennessee had two children: (1) Samuel M. Gooden born 1832 married Nancy Henry, (2) Lydia Gooden ca. 1835. William and "Polly" had four children: (1) George Washington born 1840 married Nancy Shoemaker, (2) Mary "Polly" born 1842 married Thomas Stewart, (3) Nancy "Jane" born 1846 married Thomas Benton Stucker, (4) Vincent born 1849 married Catherine E. Alders.

In the 1840s, William and Mary were homesteading a tract of land north of Bear Wallow Hill. On June 10, 1848, President Polk signed the sheepskin deed granting William 80 acres of land, because William's oldest son from his first marriage, William H., lost his life at Metamora, Mexico while serving his country during the Mexican War.

This deed is in the possession of William's great-granddaughter, Eva Ford. William died in 1850. In November, 1851, Mary married Joel Havens.

William and Mary "Polly" along with her daughter Lydia are buried on the crest of the hill back of the house in the Family Plot. The graves are marked by large, granite boulders placed there by their son, Vincent.

Vincent inherited the homeplace. He married Catherine Elizabeth Alders, daughter of the Reverend Anderson Alders and Martha Hubbard in 1870. They had seven children: (1) Charles married Ida Parker, (2) William, unmarried, (3) Albert, unmarried, (4) Benton, married Pearl O'Haven, (5) Prudence, married Andrew Robertson, (6) Minnie, married Ulysses "Jake" Settles, (7) Omar, married Alta Clark.

Vincent was one of three Postmasters appointed to serve the Wake Up Post Office that was in his home. He was a farmer, one of the founders and builders of the Goshen M.E. Church. His son, Benton, was a school teacher and auditor of Brown County. Vincent and "Kate" are buried in Goshen Cemetery.

In 1932, Vincent died. Son Omar and wife Alta inherited the homeplace. They had sons, Ralph, Warren, Clovis, Raymond, Merril, and Edwin. Daughters are Eva Ford and Fay Johnson.

Omar, who raised tobacco for a living, told how he witnessed the killing of a Dillinger gang member on the street in Bean Blossom.

Omar and Alta are buried in the Goshen Cemetery. The "home place" is now owned by one of their granddaughters and her husband. The home that was the birthplace of so many Schroughams has been torn down and replaced by a two-story frame house. *Submitted by Christine (Settles) Contos*

ERNEST AND VELMA SCROUGHAM FAMILY - Both born, raised and spent their entire life in Brown County. They both attended Helmsburg School. They were married Nov. 1, 1941. They were blessed with two daughters, Judith Mae Scrougham born Jan. 28, 1943 and Sharon Anne Scrougham born Dec. 23, 1951. Both daughters were school teachers in the Brown County School system. Sharon Scrougham taught the fourth grade at Nashville Elementary for 14 years before her death April 30, 1988. Judith Mae (Scrougham)

Clupper has taught the fourth grade at Helmsburg Elementary for 25 years and is still employed there.

Velma Scrougham was born Sept. 29, 1920, the daughter of Ershel Wayman Turner and Charles Turner (Sept. 30, 1887-Jan. 28, 1948). She was raised on what is now named "Turner Road" which was named after the Turner family. It is just off Railroad Rd. near Helmsburg. The Turner farm was handed down for three generations; from her great-grandfather, Dan Turner, to her grandfather John Turner, then divided between his children which included her father Charles Turner. Charles Turner's mother was Martha Belle Waltman.

Sharon, Ernest, Judith and Velma Schrougham

Ershel Wayman Turner, Velma's mother, was born near Fox's Corner Sept. 5, 1892 and died in 1965. Her mother Jannie Parsley Wayman (1874-1913) and step-father Joseph Wayman lived on Greasy-Creek where she grew up. Velma had one brother, Glenn Turner who was born Aug. 29, 1916 and was married to Helen Long. Glenn died in 1979 and Helen died in 1975, Glenn drove a huckster truck for several years delivering groceries to the doors of many Brown County people. He lived near Helmsburg. Velma had two sisters, Ruth Turner (Sept. 28, 1912-Jan. 13, 1923) and Irene Turner (Dec. 8, 1922-Dec. 20, 1922).

Ernest was the youngest son of Henry and Jane Settles Scrougham. He has retired from Navistar International after working there for 32 years. He is a veteran of Foreign Wars, having served in World War II. His father Henry Scrougham (1868-1957) came to Brown County from Illinois in the late 1800s and settled on Dollsbury Lane, just south of Helmsburg. His mother was born 1889 and died 1965. Jane's father, James Settles born 1852, died 1935. Her mother, Amelia Parker Settles born 1852, died 1910. Jane was raised on Bear-Wallow Hill.

Ernest was raised in a family of 11 children. He had five sisters and one brother, one half-sister and three half-brothers. He has three sisters living; Grace Turner of Indianapolis born Nov. 8, 1909; Ruby Bennet of Michigan born April 6, 1924; Hazel Clark of Texas born Feb. 4, 1913; the other sisters and brothers that have passed away are: Wanda Worden (Aug. 30, 1924-1985); Mary Kelp (Dec. 27, 1918-Sept. 29, 1980); Millard Scrougham (Jan. 31, 1911-July 13, 1987). Half-brothers and half-sister are: Ray Scrougham (March 15, 1900-Aug. 3, 1979); Blanch Holeman (April 24, 1905-1968); Merle Scrougham (Oct. 10, 1907-May 8, 1975); Muncie Scrougham (Feb. 13, 1902-1973).

SCOTT-ROGERS - On Jan. 26, 1962 Jewel Wayne and Mary Jane (Rodgers) Rogers had their second of three daughters, Diane Lee. Clover Lorraine was the oldest and Shana LaVerne was the youngest. There was always much confusion between the two last names Rodgers and Rogers being so similar. Jewel was born in the Ozark Mountain area of Arkansas, his family moved to Brown County in the early 1940s. He attended the one-room school house in Bean Blossom. Mary Jane was born in Willow Hill, IL, she also came to Brown County in the early 40s. For Mary Jane she was "coming home" as most of her mother's relatives already lived in Brown County. She also attended a one-room school, Branstetter's, until the schools consolidated in Helmsburg.

Diane and her two sisters lived in Trevlac until 1976 when Mary Jane married Charles Glen Richards and they moved to the family farmhouse on Richards Road just off of Lick Creek. The Richards have a rich heritage in Brown County and Charlie was partly known for the big pumpkin patch he would plant in the garden next to the house. The move gave the three girls lots of new woods to explore and roam.

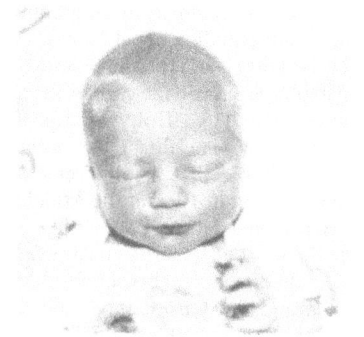

Ethan Evan Scott

On Oct. 20, 1984 Diane married James (Jay) William Scott from Conservation Club Road near Morgantown in Morgan County. Jay is an avid hunter and fisherman, he especially enjoys hunting with dogs. He and Diane have one son Ethan Evan. Jay is employed with Gradex in Indianapolis and Diane with Indiana Bell in Bloomington. They live close to Diane's parents on Richards Road and both feel that Ethan and any future children will enjoy growing up able to admire the beauty and uniqueness that God created in Brown County.

HENRY AND KATARINA SEITZ - Henry Bernhardt Seitz stowed away on a ship sailing from LeHavre, France on May 3, 1854. His fiancee Katarina Ablunda Burchhardt always said that she didn't know that he was on the ship carrying them to America. They were both born in Bavaria, Germany.

They were married in New York after Henry became a United States citizen. They moved to Monroe County and Cincinnati, OH, then to Columbus, IN and, in 1859, bought land in Washington Township, Brown Co., IN.

They had ten children, five boys and five girls. Each boy had "Henry" in his name and each girl had "Mary" in her name, in respect for the German Kaiser and his wife. German was spoken in their home and it was difficult for the children when they went to school because they couldn't speak English. They lived off the land, farming, raising their own chickens, pigs and cows.

Henry died when the youngest child was two years old, making it difficult for Katarina to raise the children alone. However, the children were hired out and upon marriage each was given a parcel of land to work and live on.

Charles Henry Seitz, ninth child of Henry and Katarina Seitz, married Jeannette Viola "Nettie" Stull, daughter of Granville Stull and Sarah Ann Rice, on Dec. 14, 1898. They had two daughters, Leatha Elizabeth Seitz, born 1899 and Ferne Lucille, born 1900.

Charles donated the land where Clark School once stood and where Pleasant Valley Church now stands. Leatha and Ferne attended grade school at Clark School and high school in Nashville. Charlie drove them into town on Sunday evenings by horse and wagon and picked them up on Friday evening. They boarded at the Minor home in Nashville with several other girls.

Leatha attended Indiana University and became a teacher. She taught all eight grades at Clark School for several years, and at Bethany School. Later she taught in Nashville. She married Lawrence Leslie Walker, son of Charles F. Walker and Marietta "Manie" Slevin, in December of 1921. They had two children, Charles Leslie, born 1922 and Joan Elizabeth, born 1927. Leatha and Les ran the Rustic Parlor Restaurant in the old Nashville House for a couple of years after marrying, then he went to work for the Indiana State Highway Dept.

Ferne became a beauty operator, working at L.S. Ayers Co. Prior to that she was the receptionist at the old Brown County Art Gallery and was working there when Eleanor Roosevelt came for a visit. Ferne married Chelce "Dan" Whitaker Williams, son of Nelson Williams and Belle Whitaker of Morgantown. Ferne and Dan Williams had no children. He was a barber for a few years and later became an insurance salesman. Ferne worked at the Morgantown Post Office for several years. After Dan died, she moved back to Nashville and worked for the new Art Gallery for many years. (see Charles F. and Marietta Walker) *Submitted by Joan (Walker) Williams*

SEITZ AND BURKHART FAMILIES - Catherine Burkhart's family arrived in New York on June 1, 1854 after leaving their native Bavaria for the opportunities and freedom of America. Upon docking of their ship Henry Bernard Seitz presented himself to the family of his beloved Catherine. He had deserted from the Prussian Army and stowed away on the same ship. Two years later they were married and moved to Cincinnati where their three oldest children were born. They then came to the Mt. Liberty area of Brown Co., IN. Henry's health began to fail and he died July 13, 1874 at the age of 47. Catherine was left with ten children and a debt of $300. She was wise in business and reared and educated her children well. The boys worked the farm and as the girls became old enough, they went out to work for $2.00 a week to help support the family. Catherine died May 13, 1903 at age 70. She and Henry are buried in Burkhart Cemetery as are other family members.

The children of Henry and Catherine Seitz were: (1) Mary Catherine (1857-1915); (2) Mary O. (1859-1902); (3) Josephine Mary (1860-1934); (4) Filomena Mary (1861-1952); (5) William Henry (1863-1945); (6) Lucetta Mary Elizabeth (1864-1956); (7) Henry William (1865-1930); (8) Anna Mary (born ca. 1867); (9) Charles Henry (1870-1962); (10) John Bernard (1872-1957).

William Henry, child #5 of Henry and Catherine Seitz, married in Brown County on Aug. 28, 1892 to Caroline Clark (Nov. 12, 1870-Dec. 9, 1956), daughter of Andrew J. Clark and Patsy David. William Henry and Caroline Seitz had six children: (1) Hesper Leona (1893-1968); (2) Warren G. (1895-1916); (3) Cecil Ray (1897-1959); (4) Hildreth (1900-1910); (5) Irene Blanche (1903-1958); (6) Ruth (1909-1989).

Cecil Ray, child #3 of William Henry and Caroline Seitz, married in Brown County on March 30, 1923 to Rinnie Bright (Dec. 23, 1900-Dec. 20, 1982), daughter of Oddy L. Bright and Ardilla L. Stitt. Cecil Ray and Rinnie Seitz had two sons: William Cecil and Charles Ray.

William Cecil Seitz (1925-1978) married Barbara Jean Taylor, daughter of Chauncey Taylor and Nettie Smithers of Johnson County, on Aug. 31, 1945. William Cecil and Barbara Seitz had two children: Kenneth Ray born Nov. 26, 1946 and Karen Lynn born May 5, 1956. Kenneth Ray Seitz, an educator, married Kathleen Ray Kissling, daughter of George Kissling and Louise Neal, on Aug. 21, 1971. Kenneth Ray and Kathleen had two children: Kortney Robert born May 3, 1977 nd Kristina Rebecca born Sept. 24, 1978. *Submitted by Kathleen (Kissling) Seitz*

KENNETH RAY SEITZ - Kenneth was born at Wishard Hospital Nov. 26, 1946 in Indianapolis. He returned to Brown County at the age of one year and lived on Mt. Liberty Road. He was involved in Little League Sports with his parents Barbara and William. They along with Maurice "Pods" Miller and Mike Links, were active in starting the Little League in Brown County. Kenneth's mother, Barbara, started the Cub Scouts in the county. He spent many fun hours riding his bicycle through Nashville with Clyde and Lance McDonald and Buddy Greller. They had many exciting baseball games in the lot next to Clyde's house which was across from the Old Bond Funeral Home. They also played in Blood Alley—which was called that because it was behind the Bond Funeral Home where the blood was drained from the dead people (rumor has it). Their favorite swimming hole was by the big bridge over Salt Creek. They would spend hot summer days there keeping cool.

In the high school days Kenny was involved in cross country, basketball and baseball. He also worked his summers at the Brown County Park pool. He had many fun times there with his friends who would come daily to swim and try to meet girls from out of town.

Kenneth graduated with the Brown County class of 1965 and proceeded to go to Indiana State where he stayed for a year and a half. He returned home to join the Air Force Reserves. This was during the Vietnam War. He was in the Personnel Department at Bakalar Air Force base. His unit was called to go to Vietnam. He was already to go when they informed him that only the Flight units would be going. Later Bakalar was closed and he didn't live within the range to travel to Grissom Air Force base. So he was relieved of any further obligation to his unit. So he was very lucky that he wasn't called to Vietnam.

He worked at the Old Hickory as a waiter and then later as a bartender. He also frequented Millers Drug Store where he befriended a teenage girl named Kathy Kissling. He and Bill Voland were best buddies and they used to come in for a cherry coke and a hug. Later Kenny married Kathy Kissling who had been a cheerleader for Brown County. She married at 18 and Kenny was 24. They both entered I.U. the next semester after their Aug. 21, 1971 wedding. One memorable event of their wedding was the police escort and convertible ride through town given them by "Punk" Snyder and his wife Betty. Punk was Sheriff at that time.

Kenny and Kathy graduated from IU in 1974-75 respectively. They both majored in the Health and Physical Education Department (HYPER) with teaching careers in mind.

Kenny was hired by Hamilton Southeastern Schools which is located near Fishes, IN. He has taught Biology, Physical Education, Health and Contemporary living. He has coached cross country, basketball and for the last 15 years baseball, where he has won six sectional championships against bigger schools like Noblesville, Tipton and Carmel; seven range-line conference championships; and three coach of the year awards. His best team in 1988 made it to the final eight in the state.

He and Kathy have two children: Kortney Robert, born May 3, 1977 and Kristina Rebecca born Sept. 24, 1978. They are both active in sports also. Kristy carries on with her mother's love for horses. Kory's middle name is "Robert" after Robert Knight our famous IU coach.

Kenny's job has changed to an administrative assistant and athletic director at Hamilton Southeastern. He is at the school for long hours during the school year to supervise all the various events going on. He often feels like a Hollywood producer to make sure events are coordinated smoothly.

Kathy stayed home while the children were young and started teaching in 1989 at the Middle School level in Health and Home Economics. She also directs the Fellowship of Christian Athletes and co-sponsors the cheerleaders at her school and is a class sponsor. Kim and Kathy are members of Clarksville Christian Church near Noblesville.

SETSER (SETZER) FAMILY - Caleb Setser and Levina Crump, born in North Carolina, of German ancestry. They were married July 12, 1846 in North Carolina. His occupation was wagonmaker, coffin maker, sawmill worker and farmer.

Three children were born in that state: William Paten (1847), John Pinkney (1848), Albert Joshua (1850).

They traveled through the wilderness by wagon, with their belongings and livestock. No fine roads in those days. The people they met on the way treated them very nicely.

Albert J. and Maranda Jane (Spurgeon) Setser

In Indiana, they settled for awhile near a river that flows through what is now called Rockford. It was the best place to cross because of the rock bed. The Morgan Raider rebels were in the vicinity. They demanded milk, eggs and meals from the family. Sometimes, they would pay.

Caleb, Levina and boys settled in Houston. Seven more children were born: Elisha (1852), Elizabeth (1854), Mary (1856), Joseph (1858), George (1860), Marthey (1862), Thomas (1865), Walter (1868).

William Paten married Katie Elkins. Born: John, George and Pearly. John and George were teachers. John's picture hangs in the Nashville House. He and George were influential in bringing the railroad to Helmsburg, where John established the post office, in his house. He was superintendent of the State Park, owner of the Star Store in Nashville. The brothers were very civic minded. John married Lizzie Hedric. She died. He married Amanda Hedric. Pearley married Winfrey Lutes. George married Ida Carter.

Albert Joshua Setser married Maranda Jane Spurgeon (pictured) in 1873 in Brown County. Born: John (1874), William (1875), Charles, teacher and banker, (1877), Albertis, farmer (1879), Mary (1881), Scott, teacher and banker (1883), Luzetta (1885), Nora Edna (1891).

William's education for teaching was interrupted by the death of his father. He was the oldest living son and so was "breadwinner" for the family. Married Rachel Olmstead. She died. As conductor on the interurban trains, he met Ruth Bowman. They married in 1914. He, then, farmed. Born: Beatrice (pictured), married E. Norwood Leslie; Cale, married Ruth Smith; Naomi, married Floyd Morgan; Paul, married Dean Ward; Pauline, married James Wasson; Charles, married Betty Atwood; Chase, married Catherine Carey; Martha, married Roger Goff; Miriam, married Wayne Land; Lillian, married Dale Jones; Dean, married Joan Spahr; Paul and Pauline, twins. Chase and Charles, twins.

Beatrice (Setser) Leslie, 1981

E. Norwood, Sr. and Beatrice had six children: E. Norwood, Jr., married Judy Favero, 1958, mechanical engineer in his own international business, "Micro Dynamics," Dallas, TX. Children: Robert and Michael. Richard, married Diane Long, 1966, salesman for "Digital Equipment." Daughter: Christie. Married Barbara Pitman, 1976. William, married Sue Maines, 1970. Daughter: Beth. Married Sharon Siddons, 1978. In law enforcement near Cartersburg, IN. Steven, married Denese Blue, 1970. Children: Ryan and Dana. Professor in "Pharmaceutical Research," University of Texas. Cheryl, married Rudy Crabtree, 1968. Daughters: Lisa and Amy. Married Darwin Scott, 1987. He is a member of Indiana State Police. Elaine, married Robert Austin, 1975. Children: Trenton, Chad, Lindsey. He is a mechanic.

E. Norwood, Sr., died in 1970. His and Beatrice's children were raised in Brown County. *Compiled by Beatrice (Setser) Leslie*

SETTLE - SETTLES FAMILY - The Settle, Settles family of English Origin were in Yorkshire prior to the Norman Invasion, the ancestoral seat probably in Settle, West Riding Yorkshire. Records indicate the Settle population had shifted to "Barick-In-Elmet" parish in the 16th Century.

Francis Settle, first known ancestor, emigrated to the "The Province of Virginia in the 1650s." A descendant of this line, probably a fourth great-grandson, William Settle and his wife Frances James (daughter of Thomas James) of Facquier Co., VA had son William who married Charlotte Corely (daughter of Menoah Corely). Of this family a son,

James William Settle, born 1815 Virginia, died 1884 Van Buren Township, Brown Co., IN. James Wm. and father William left Virginia late 1820/30s. They were in Belmont, Monroe, Noble Counties, OH where employed in construction of the Baltimore and Ohio Railroad from Bellaire to Zanesville. The 1840 Census for Belmont Co., OH lists James and William Settle's families living next door to each other. The 1850 U.S. Census lists James Settle and John Hancher neighbors. James William Settle and Lydia Ann Hancher were married Dec. 11, 1835, Harrison Co., OH. The trip to their new home in 1853 made by covered wagon, owned and driven by Alfred Hamilton, a relative, who later brought Lydia's brother John Hancher and family. James Wm. Settle had entered land in Van Buren Township, Brown Co., IN. Here he built the old homestead where they reared their family as well as some of their children's families. Jim Settle was conscientious and a hard working family man who made his living from the land and its environment. James Wm., Lydia and many members of their families are buried in the New Bellsville Cemetery, Van Buren Township. James and Lydia died 1884 in the area where they settled with their family.

Settle home on Bearwallow Hill. This house was dismantled, taken to the Conner Prairie Settlement and reconstructed as the "Still" House in the Colonial Settlement. It was donated to Conner Prairie by Eli Lilly. Photo by Frank Hohenberger, Indianapolis Star Reporter. Jim Settle in foreground.

Children born in Ohio: Sarrah married Ulysses Kinsey 1858; Thomas married Eliza Kinsey 1861; Elaner Jane married Thomas Snider 1859; John married Sarah Snyder 1863; Lewis married Mary E. White 1866; Isabell married Martin Hardin 1866; Hannah Mary married Martin V. Parker 1869; James Alexander married Amelia Parker 1873. Born in Brown County: Daniel Robertson married Sarah A. Truex; Walker ?; Hiram married Mary Martha Curry 1873.

James A. Settle, born 1852, Belmont Co., OH and his wife Amelia moved to the Bear Wallow Hill, reared a large family. Their first three children died within two months of each other: Cora A., Thomas and John died August 1 through Oct. 8, 1897 in Hamblen Township, buried Goshen Cemetery. Son Ulysses Jake Settle(s) married Minnie Schrougham (1899): daughter of Vincent and Catherine E. Alder Schrougham. Other issue were Ella May, James Wesley, Charles E., Margaret Jane, Bertha Viola and Jesse Oral. They reared the grandson, Ora Snow, son of Cora and Thomas Snow.

Jake and Minnie Settle(s) reared eight sons and three daughters. Their first home was upon the Bearwallow Hill near the former home of Marcus Dickey. Their son Morris Settles was elected first Mayor of Lawrence, IN, November 1959, was re-elected five more terms serving 24 years. Son Ray E. returned to Brown County, commuting to RCA in Indianapolis. He died Nov. 1, 1986, is buried in Henderson Cemetery. His wife Helen still lives R.R. 4, Nashville on the Green Valley Road. *Submitted by Mable Van Osdol*

LAURA B. (DUFFEY) MORRISON RYBOLT SEXTON
Laura Belle Duffey, born Nov. 11, 1869 in Adams Co., OH was the daughter of Thomas R. Duffey and Martha Ann Swisher of Adams Co., OH. Around 1895 Laura married Thomas Mifflin Morrison, born February 1859 in Adams Co., OH. Thomas M. was the son of William W. Morrison and Susan A. Raleigh. Thomas R. and William were both Civil War Veterans. Thomas M. died in Adams County from a heart attack after fighting a fire sometime between 1904 and early 1906. There was a huge fire in downtown Manchester on New Year's morning of 1906. However, records show that only one man lost his life in the fire and that he was a black man. Dying in the fire and dying from the fire may be two different things. A search of the local newspapers may reveal something more.

Milton Sexton, Ray Rybolt, James A. and Laura B. (Duffey) Morrison Rybolt Sexton, and John Edward Morrison.

Thomas M. Morrison and Laura Belle Duffey had three children, William, born and died 1900, Mary Etta, born Sept. 28, 1897, and John Edward, born ca. 1902, died Dec. 17, 1955. John Edward spent most of his adult life in the Wooster and Mansfield, OH areas. Mary Etta married James William (Jimmy) Hamblen of Brown Co., IN. Family tradition is that Mary Etta was 1/4 Indian and that her father, Thomas Mifflin Morrison was 1/2 Indian. However, no evidence of this has been found as of 1990. The Morrisons came from Ireland to Pennsylvania. Therefore, Mary Etta's grandmother, Susan A. Raleigh Morrison must have been a full blooded Indian. Further research may verify this.

Laura Belle remarried Nov. 5, 1906 to James Rybolt, whose father had come from Ireland to Ohio. Shortly after they were married they moved to Dunkirk or New Castle, IN for a while, then to Columbus, IN, and back to New Castle. They had two children, Ray and Mae. Mae was born ca. 1907 and died May 8, 1969. She married Joe Moore ca. 1925 and they had nine children. Ray was born in New Castle, IN in 1910 and married Martha Folks, daughter of Franklin Folks and Margret E. Carter of Brown County on March 19, 1938. Ray and Martha were living in Columbus, IN in 1990 and have three children, Wanda, Franklin James and Linda Lou. James Rybolt died in 1922 in New Castle, IN and is buried in South Mound Cemetery.

Laura Belle and the children returned to Brown Co., IN and she married James A. Sexton of Elkinsville in 1924. James is buried in the Elkinsville Cemetery. Laura Belle died June 27, 1944 and is buried in the Mt. Zion Cemetery. James Sexton was known as "Jim Aught" and was well known and highly respected in Johnson and Van Buren Townships. This is expressed eloquently in his obituary which appeared in the Brown County Democrat on Oct. 8, 1936, "— Mr. Sexton was a devout Christian and held in high reverence by all who knew him. He was always eager to lend a helping hand, and will be missed by friends and neighbors." He and his son, Milton, were known to have walked miles at night, carrying a lantern, in response to a request from a sick friend "—to come and pray for me." *Submitted by Laura Belle's grandson, John W. Hamblen*

JAMES F. & ALICE (HENDERSHOT) SHAFER
James Faucett Shafer, born Sept. 16, 1877 in Brown Co., IN and Alice Hendershot, born June 9, 1894, were married June 15, 1912 in Brown Co., IN. He was the son of Joseph and Campsadell Amelia Stull Shafer. She is the daughter of William Peter and Margaret Elizabeth Moore Hendershot. They are both of German descent. He was a letter carrier for many years, using a motorcycle part of the time and a mail hack the rest of the time. There were many instances when the motorcycle had to be pushed up the hill as it did not have enough power to carry him and the mail to the top of the Brown County hills. They also raised peaches, apples, berries and pears for selling at their home. The fall of the year was a family affair for harvesting these crops.

They had nine children: Floyd Harland, born June 10, 1913; Mary Margaret, born April 24, 1915; Ira William, born Oct. 1, 1916; Hilda Mae, born July 7, 1920; Hesper Louise, born Feb. 22, 1922; James Junior, born June 28, 1925; June Rose, born June 22, 1927; Alice, born May 30, 1930 and Robert Herrod, born Sept. 11, 1932. Floyd Harland operated his own tool and die shop in Edinburgh, IN. He is married to Nola Priddy. Mary Margaret married John Perry. John worked in construction for Repp & Mundt. Ira William, who had his own trucking business for many years, married (1) Edna Pauline Loy (2) Virginia Hill. Hilda Mae married Dr. Henry E. Lee. He had his practice in Detroit and she lived there until his death. James, who has been a contractor for many years, married Mary Jane Barker. June Rose married Jack Johnson and lived in Mansfield, OH for many years. Alice married Richard Nieman and they have lived in and around Houston, TX for many years. Robert Herrod married Betty C. Lovins. He is retired from Cummins Engine Company.

James Faucett Shafer died in his sleep July 22, 1967 at his home in Brown County. Alice Hendershot Shafer died at Bartholomew County Hospital March 26, 1969; they are both buried at Garland Brook Cemetery, Columbus, IN. *Submitted by granddaughter, Karen Neptune*

JOSEPH JR. AND CAMPSADELL (STULL) SHAFER
Joseph Schaeffer was born in Germany in 1797. He and five other boys wanted to go to America and the only way they could do this was to go through Switzerland. The five families that traveled with them were: Stull, Hodler, Gutknecht, Gressel and Wolfe. It was here that Joseph met his wife, Elizabeth Carney. She was born in 1810 and was only 15 when they married...he was 28. They landed in America around April 1826.

Four children were born to Elizabeth and Joseph near the east coast, probably Pennsylvania. They then moved to Chillicothe, OH, and became parents of four more children; they had a total of five girls and three boys. Jacob, born 1830; Margaret, born 1832; Elizabeth, born 1836; Mary, born 1838; John William, born 1840; Isabell, born 1843; Joseph, Jr., born 1845; Julia Ann, born 1848. When they moved to Indiana Joseph homesteaded 640 acres in Brown County. When he applied for citizenship papers, he had the spelling of the last name changed to Shafer.

Joseph and Campsadell Stull Shafer

Joseph Sr. died April 1, 1874 and Elizabeth died in the spring of 1889. He is buried at Roth Cemetery by Grandview Lake as he was a member of the Lutheran church. However, Elizabeth was a member of the Methodist Church and was buried at the Haislup Cemetery. Joseph helped to build the log church near where the graveyard is located; the church burned about 1905. All five men who came to this country with Joseph are buried in a row.

Joseph Jr. married Campsadell Amelia Stull Feb. 10, 1870; she was 19; he was 25. He was a fine citizen, one who made friends easily and retained those friendships. He was honest, and a gentleman in every sense of the word. They operated a grocery store in Columbus for a number of years but sold it and moved to Mt. Liberty. They farmed the 640 acres his father homesteaded. They were members of the Methodist church at South Bethany. Campsadell's mother and father were William Palmer Stull and Mary Ann Maring; Mary Ann Maring lived to be 101 years old.

Joseph and Campsadell had eight children: Charles Franklin and Joseph "Dode" were never married. Viola married John E. Summa, a prominent attorney in Columbus. Blanche married Grover Hurley; James Faucett married Alice Hendershot; Cora married Harley Barkes; Hazel married James E. Howard; Al married Anna Shirk in Idaho. "Dode" and Al went west in a covered wagon to try out sheep herding. They both ended up back home but it was later that Al took a railroad job and moved to Idaho. Charles had his own photography business and even developed his own film. His old camera is still in the possession of the Shafer family. *Submitted by Karen Neptune*

ALLEN SHARP - Allen Sharp is a descendant of two Hoosier pioneer families. The first members of the Sharp family moved from Kentucky to the Carr Hill area of Bartholomew Co., IN about 1840. One member of that family, Samuel Sharp, was a lifelong educator in the Columbus area and served as Bartholomew County Superintendent of schools during the World War I period. His son, Robert L. Sharp, is the father of Allen Sharp. Robert owned a 20-acre farm in the very south part of VanBuren Township, land which had belonged to the pioneer McKinney family, and which was adjacent to the McKinney Cemetery.

The mother of Allen Sharp was Frances Louise Williams of Johnson County. The Williams family moved from New England to Johnson County about the time of the Civil War.

Allen Sharp was born in Washington, D.C. on Feb. 11, 1932 at a time when his parents were temporarily residing there. In 1947, he moved with his father and stepmother to this small, 20-acre farm which was also close to an area once known as Buffalo approximately a mile north of the Jackson-Brown County line just off of State Highway 135. Later that year, his father and stepmother moved to Chicago to take employment and Allen stayed on the family farm, living alone, the rest of that winter and attended VanBuren High School.

The next summer he worked for Virgil Greathouse as a farmhand. At that time, Virgil Greathouse owned a farm on the creek between Christiansburg and Highway 135 and also owned the store at the corner on 135 at Spurgeon's Corner. Allen had always had an intense interest in history and politics and the Greathouse store was a beehive of political discussion during the Truman versus Dewey election of 1948. He attended his first political meeting in 1948 at the Hamblen Township School with Bill Carmichael, who was then running for Brown County Treasurer and Kenneth Kritzer who was then VanBuren Township Trustee.

The following winter, he lived in the guest house on the Cherry Hill Farm owned by Harriet and "Buck" Widmer while continuing to attend VanBuren High School. At the end of his junior year of high school, the County Superintendent of Schools, Grover G. Brown, arranged for Allen to have employment as a bellboy at the Abe Martin Lodge, then managed by Mr. and Mrs. Pat J. Cain. This employment lasted from the summers of 1949, 1950 to 1951. Allen graduated from VanBuren High School in a class of eight in the spring of 1950 and through the good offices of Superintendent Brown, he was awarded a state scholarship to Indiana State Teachers College in Terre Haute, IN, where he commenced his schooling in September, 1950.

In November, 1949, he was invited into the home of Reverend and Mrs. James W. Hendricks of the New Bellsville community, where he stayed during the rest of the winter of 1949-1950, until he graduated from high school. He has remained close to the Hendricks family for the last 40 years, and has been considered by them as one of their family. He has often publicly and privately expressed his deepest respect and gratitude to the kindness and generosity shown by Jim and Blanche Hendricks during his formative years and throughout his adult life.

He attended Indiana State Teachers College for approximately three years, was awarded membership in several honor societies, and was elected President of the Student Council and the Indiana Student Government Association.

In 1953, he transferred to the George Washington University in Washington, D.C. where he received the B.A. Degree in 1954. While there, he worked full time in the United States Senate Post Office.

Allen was also awarded a prestigious Root-Tilden scholarship from New York University School of Law in 1954, but declined it in favor of a scholarship to a school of law in Indiana University in Bloomington, where he commenced his legal education in September, 1954. He graduated with a Doctor of Jurisprudence Degree from Indiana University in 1957, and in 1959 was awarded an Honorary Doctor of Civil Law by Indiana State University. He also attended night classes at Ball State University and Butler University, and was awarded a Master of Arts Degree in History by Butler University in 1986. He has taught classes in the law school at Valparaiso University and in the History Department at Butler University.

Allen served for more than 28 years in the United States Air Force Reserve at Bakalar Air Force Base near Columbus, IN and at Grissom Air Force Base near Peru, IN. He achieved the rank of Lieutenant Colonel in the Judge Advocate's Department.

He is the father of two daughters, Crystal Catholyn Sharp, born Aug. 2, 1965, and Scarlet Frances Sharp, born Aug. 24, 1966. Crystal is a graduate of Purdue University and at this writing, Scarlet is attending Ambassador College in Pasadena, CA.

Following his active service in the United States Air Force, Allen engaged in the general practice of law for 11 years beginning on December, 1957 in Williamsport, IN. During that time, he had the unusual honor and opportunity to successfully argue a case before the Supreme Court of the United States in 1968.

In 1968, Allen was nominated in the Republican State Convention for a seat on the then Appellate Court of Indiana which is now known as the Court of Appeals of Indiana. At the age of 36, he was one of the youngest judges ever to serve on either the Supreme Court of Indiana or the Appellate Court of Indiana. As an appellate court judge, he developed a reputation by writing a record number of opinions which won praise for their clarity. Following a change in the Indiana Constitution which became effective in 1972, he was retained as a judge of the Court of Appeals with approximately 80% approval. He also received approximately that same percentage of approval in a poll of the lawyers throughout Indiana conducted by the Indiana State Bar Association in 1972.

In September, 1973, he was nominated as a United States District Judge by the President of the United States and was confirmed by the United States Senate commencing his term as a Judge of the United States District Court for the Northern District of Indiana on Nov. 1, 1973.

In 1981 he became the Chief Judge of the United States District Court, which presently has five active judges, a senior district judge, four bankruptcy judges and three United States magistrates and has five federal courthouses where court proceedings are conducted.

He has traveled extensively in the Middle East and in Europe and has a long-standing intensive interest in both American and European history. One of his greatest joys is to return to VanBuren Township and to revisit on foot and by automobile the scenes of his childhood.

He has maintained his membership in the Masonic Lodge in Nashville, IN, and was a long-time close friend of Wayne Guthrie, who wrote several articles about him when Mr. Guthrie was a columnist for the *Indianapolis News*.

CHARLES WESLEY AND LETITIA SHEPHERD - A few years after Sarah Letitia "Tish" arrived in Rice Co., KS, in 1873 with her parents, Richard and Ellen (Moore) Huffman, she returned to Brown Co., IN, where she had been born June 24, 1858. She came to visit her uncle and aunt, John D. and Clarissa (Moore-Ewers) Melott and that special boy friend, Charles Wesley "Wes" Shepherd whom she married Dec. 18, 1879 in the Melott home. Wes was a son of William and Elizabeth (Hanvey) Shepherd of Van Buren Township, Brown County. Wes was born Sept. 29, 1858 at Steubenville, Jefferson Co., OH. Witnesses at the wedding of Wes Shepherd and Tish Huffman were her cousin, Mary Ellen (Ewers) and her husband, Jacob Lawles.

Wes and Tish Shepherd set up housekeeping on his father's place, in a second house. Wes and his brother, William F., helped their father, William Shepherd, with working up trees for barrel making, cutting firewood, raising livestock, butchering and growing foodstuff. Wes and Tish's first two children, Bertha Alice (1881) and George Melvin (1883) were born in Brown County. In 1884, Wes, Tish and their small children left Brown County for Farmer Township, Rice Co., KS. They bought railroad land southwest of Bushton near Tish's parents. It was on this farm that William Clyde (1887), Charles Auburn (1890) and Clara May Shepherd (1895) were born. Wes' father, William Shepherd, died in 1888.

Back: Willie, Charley, Melvin Shepherd. Front: Tish, Clara (Shepherd) Drake, Wes, and Bertha (Shepherd) Jung.

Wes and Tish's daughter, Bertha Shepherd, was married in 1901 to Theodore Jung. They lived at Waukomis, OK and near Arlington and Lyons, KS. Their children were Melvin, Ethel Sailor and Floyd Jung. Bertha died April 15, 1952. Melvin Shepherd married Sarah Teresa "Sadie" Blakely at Lyons, 1906. Their children: Lowell, Elwin, Virginia Goudy and Georgia Molder. Melvin died July 12, 1955. William "Will" Shepherd married Mabel Willard in 1909. Their children were Ansel and Lola Wolf Hopkins. Will died on Sept. 10, 1964 at Lyons Hospital. Charles Shepherd married Ida Kellogg in 1910 at Sharon Springs, KS. After Charles' death on May 17, 1921, his widow, that fall, took her young family to California where they still live. They are Thelma Keiser, Grace Modie and Charles Shepherd. Clara Shepherd married Homer Drake on Dec. 9, 1914 at the home of her parents, near Saxman. Clara died on March 24, 1925 at Hutchinson, KS at age 29, leaving three children, Harold, Francis and Agnes Drake. Clara's family lived in Reno, Co., KS.

In the spring of 1904, Wes and Tish Shepherd purchased 360 acres in Wilson Township, southeast of Lyons and there built a new home. It was here that Tish died on June 27, 1933. After his wife's death, Wes planned an extended visit to Brown Co., IN to see his sister, his and his wife's many cousins and childhood friends. While doing business in preparation for this trip he was killed in a car/train accident near Lyons on Aug. 9, 1933. He had enjoyed good health and was a man of great industry and thrift. At the time of their deaths they owned 1,080 acres of Rice County land. The five Shepherd children all lived on farms as did their parents. Wes and Tish Shepherd and four of their children, Bertha, Melvin, William and Charles are buried in the Lyons Cemetery. Their daughter, Clara, is buried in Peace Valley, Walnut Township, Reno County. The Shepherd family attended the Christian Church in Lyons. The Shepherd grandchildren cherish many memories of accompanying their parents and grandparents to visit relatives. Pikes Peak school friends, Addie Story and her sister, Phoebe Banks of Co-

lumbus, visited in Kansas several times. They were known as "Aunt" Addie and "Aunt" Phoebe to the children. South of Lyons was the Santa Fe Trail marker. Grandmother Tish Shepherd often said, "I traveled on that trail in a covered wagon when there were still Indians here." That historic trail crossed their farm. *Submitted by a granddaughter, Agnes Drake Bedient*

ELIZABETH MAY SHEPHERD -
Born May 5, 1874, at Pikes Peak, Brown County, was the daughter of William and Elizabeth Ann Hanvey Shepherd. Three of Elizabeth May's young sisters, Margaret Jane, Julia Ann and Martha, and a brother, Alexander, died in a measles epidemic. Five siblings survived to adulthood: Wesley, William F., Clara Bell who married John Brown, residents of Jackson County all their lives; Mary Alice who married George W. Melott and died at age 29 leaving several small children; and Elizabeth May, called "Lizzie May."

Lizzie May was proud of the Scotch, Irish and English ancestry of her grandparents, Thos. and Mary Lazenby Shepherd. Her parents came from Belmont Co., OH to homestead in Brown County in the 1850s. Lizzie remembered her early years in Brown County with fondness and her pride in her father's service in the Civil War as a Union soldier.

About 1891, Lizzie May went to visit her brother Wesley Shepherd who had homesteaded in Rice Co., KS. While there she met Eli Albert Shire, native of Crawford Co., IL, who was teaching at Hoisington, KS. On Sept. 24, 1893 they were married in the Christian Church at Claflin, KS. By 1895, the couple returned to Crawford Co., IL where they engaged in farming. Four sons were born there: Wesley, Paul, Ivan and Fred Shire.

Elizabeth May Shepherd

In 1901, the Shire family leased an immigrant railway car and loaded their livestock, machinery and worldly goods on the car and travelled by train to Grant Co., OK Territory, where they purchased a homestead near Nashville. They resided in Grant County until 1919 when they moved to Wellington, KS, where they operated a Dairy until 1941 when they retired. While in Oklahoma, four more children were born: Lucy, Glynn, Clara and Durward Shire. Their five youngest children attended and graduated from Wellington High School.

In 1930 and 1934, Paul Shire and his family took his parents, Lizzie May and Eli Albert Shire, to Illinois and Indiana to see their old family homes and relatives they had not seen since 1901. The writer, a grandson, was privileged to be on the trips and remembered the visits to his grandmother's sister, Clara Bell Shepherd Brown and her husband John. In the early 1930s rail fences were common to the area and logging operations in the heavy timber areas were being carried out.

Lizzie May Shire died Dec. 1, 1952 at age 78 in Enid, OK, and is buried beside her mother, Elizabeth Ann Hanvey Shepherd, at Pond Creek, OK, not far from where they homesteaded in 1901. Eli Albert Shire, Lizzie May's husband, died in 1964 at age 97 at Enid.

Lizzie May often recounted stories of early experiences while growing up in Brown County; her early years there were important in her life. She liked to write poetry. One of her poems was about an old quilt that had warmed her in her bed in her youth in Brown County. It was a patchwork quilt made by her mother's grandmother and was her mother's pride. Many times she told her daughter Lizzie May, the stories behind each patch of different color and hue that made up the "Pine Tree Quilt."

Paul Shire, son of Elizabeth May Shepherd and Eli Albert Shire, wrote of the Shepherd-Hanvey ancestry: "The Shepherd-Hanvey people were of a jolly disposition with a sense of humor. They were hard-working people. There was a talent for music and poetry. They had imaginative minds and could have been successful writers of stories and poetry." Lizzie May had been active in WCTU, Daughters of Union Veterans and Quill and Arts Club. *Submitted by Lowell W. Shire, eldest grandson*

WILLIAM SHEPHERD -
This Shepherd family had its origin in England. Thomas and Mary (Lazenby) Shepherd were married in Bubwith parish, East Riding, Yorkshire in 1821. They arrived in America shortly before July 1822 at Norfolk, VA. His application on July 29, 1822 for 80 acres of government land in Belmont Co., OH (S12, T5, R4) was signed by William Thornbrough for "Thomas Shepherd." Mr. Thornbrough and his wife, Matilda Lazenby, had arrived in 1818 from England. Their government land was in the adjoining section.

Thomas and Mary Shepherd's 13 children (nine sons and four daughters) grew up on the family farm northeast of Armstrongs Mills in Washington Township, Belmont Co., OH. This farm remained in the Shepherd family at least until 1915.

William Shepherd | John W. and Clara Bell (Shepherd) Brown

Child #4 of Thomas and Mary Shepherd, named William, was born Jan. 2, 1827. He married on Sept. 30, 1852 to Elizabeth Ann Hanvey, born July 22, 1834. She was a twin daughter of neighbors, William and Mary Hanvey. William and Elizabeth Ann Shepherd joined the adventurous persons of Belmont County who were migrating to Brown Co., IN where their first child, Margaret Jane, was born July 1853. Their other children were Julia Ann (1855), Alexander Asbery (1856), Charles Wesley (1858), Clara Bell (1861), Martha (1862), Mary Alice (1864), William Franklin (1867) and Elizabeth May Shepherd (1874). Julia, a single lady, died sometime after age 24, Margaret died of measles, Martha died very young and Alexander died of summer complaint. This list of nine children, birth dates and notations of early deaths, was found in William Franklin Shepherd's trunk after his death.

Elizabeth Ann Shepherd's twin sister, Margaret J. Hanvey and her husband, Hiram King, also came to Brown County. With their hard life in primitive times William and Elizabeth Ann Shepherd moved back to Steubenville, Jefferson Co., OH for two or three years. It was there that their son, Charles Wesley, was born. But they were back in Brown County in 1860.

William, at age 38, served as a private in Co. C, 25th Regt. of Indiana Vol. Inft. He was drafted in November 1864. While in the line of duty on April 10, 1865 near Raleigh, NC, he was kicked by a pack mule. He suffered poor health during his remaining life from this injury to the abdominal area. After the war his younger brother Thomas came to live in Brown County.

William had arrived too late to be a first-time owner of Van Buren Township land in Brown County. But in the following 35 years he bought several parcels of land until he owned 200 acres. He often employed other men and with the help of his sons they worked the timber for barrel making. He also raised fine livestock of which his family was proud.

William Shepherd passed away on July 18, 1888 at age 61 and was buried in the New Bellsville Cemetery in Van Buren Township, Brown County. In settling his estate 40 acres were sold to a Mr. Brand and 160 acres to Joshua and Emma J. Tipton. James Gredy and his family now live on the Tipton place at Pikes Peak.

A few years later William's widow, Elizabeth Ann Shepherd, went to live with her youngest daughter in Oklahoma. The families of four of her children were living in Kansas and northern Oklahoma. Elizabeth Ann died Sept. 8, 1903 and was buried at Pond Creek, OK, far from the grave of her husband and her beloved hills of Brown County. *Submitted by Agnes Drake Bedient, granddaughter of Charles Wesley Shepherd*

WILLIAM FRANKLIN SHEPHERD - Born Nov. 7, 1867 in Pikes Peak, Brown Co., IN, was the son of William and Elizabeth (Hanvey) Shepherd. (William Shepherd born, Ohio; died in Brown County July 18, 1888, aged 61 years, six months, 16 days and is buried in New Bellsville Cemetery. Elizabeth Ann Hanvey born July 22, 1834; married William Shepherd, Sept. 30, 1852, Belmont Co., OH; died Sept. 8, 1903, buried Pond Creek, OK.) In the spring of 1892, he went to Rice Co., KS to the farm of his brother, Charles Wesley Shepherd, to help with planting and harvesting of wheat and oats. He spent the winter there, feeding cattle and making plans to run into Oklahoma. Wesley and Tish Shepherd loaned their brothers, William F. Shepherd and John Willard Huffman, born Brown County, their fast and sure-footed surrey horses. They waited on the line east of Manchester for the signal "go." With them was a cowboy from Ness City, KS who had driven on the Chisholm Trail. He assured the boys he knew that the good land was just west of the trail and north of the Salt Fork River, south of the red hill brakes. Shepherd staked his claim, SE6, T26, R6, Huffman joining on the north. They slept on their saddle blankets with the saddle for pillow. Shepherd stayed to watch their claims while Huffman rode to Enid to file on his. Then he stayed to watch while Shepherd went to Enid to file and bring back supplies such as shovels and axes. Together they made a dugout for shelter on the Shepherd Claim.

Then John Huffman returned to Kansas with both ponies and brought back a wagon and team, an extra riding horse, plow, and household and food supplies. They had a hard time finding water near the dugout. So a neighbor witched a site on the south side of the farm and that's where they plowed sod for a house.

Elizabeth Ann (Hanvey) Shepherd

It was a hard winter. They cooked over a campfire and hunted for most of their food. Their friend, Jack Ebbe, taught them to roll their quail, prairie chicken, ducks and geese in the soft red clay and roast them in the ashes of their fire. Lumber was hauled from Caldwell, KS and Jefferson, OK and a one-room house was built before the next winter. There was no timber on the homestead so all posts and fencing had to be brought in. William made many trips back to Kansas for supplies and home cooked meals at his brother's table. By 1898 he had the farm fenced, a crop growing and a new three room house built and furnished.

He went to Kansas and brought his bride, Mary Elizabeth Stone, to Oklahoma on Aug. 11, 1898. Their daughter, Stella Alice, was born April 27, 1900. On the 18th day of May 1903, William Shepherd received in the mail his homestead papers signed by President Theodore Roosevelt. In August of 1903, a son was born, only living the day. On Oct. 8, 1903, William's wife, Mary Elizabeth, died and was buried in Klondike Cemetery.

On April 7, 1905, William Franklin Shepherd married Pearl Mae Keller at the home of her stepfather and mother, Mr. and Mrs. George W. Melott. That summer William sold his homestead and bought the SW16-26-8, four miles north and two miles west of Nash, OK where he built a new five room house. Corn, watermelons and lots of good prairie hay were raised on this farm and also on land, SE17, T26, R8. William F. and Pearl Mae Shepherd had three children: Wilma, Victor and Pearl Mae Shepherd. William's wife died May 17, 1912.

In August of 1917 he rented his farms and moved to the Medford area so his daughter, Alice, could go to high school. Then in 1921 he moved back to his farm. He retired to a home in Jefferson in 1936 and passed away June 29, 1951 at age 84 years and six months. *Submitted by his daughter, Wilma Shepherd Kindred*

JESSE W. SHIPLEY, SR. - Jesse was born April 7, 1821 in Knox Co., KY, the son of Isaac Shipley, born ca. 1790 in Kentucky or Tennessee, and Elizabeth Polly, born ca. 1790 in Tennessee. Isaac brought his family to Brown Co., IN, and entered land in Van Buren Township in 1834. Jesse married Mary Ann Hall on March 23, 1845 at Nashville, IN and was listed as a poll tax payer in Johnson Township in 1848 where he had purchased 40 A. from the U.S. Government on May 10, 1848. He and Mary Ann sold this land to James Chafin on Dec. 21, 1850. Mary Ann, born Aug. 9, 1825, died April 30, 1854, was the daughter of Jesse Hall, Sr. and Rebecca Fleetwood. Mary Ann is buried in Deckard Cemetery in Brown Co., IN. Jesse and Mary Ann had children: Bashaba, born 1848; Sarah E., born 1849; John W., born Dec. 2, 1851 and Margaret May, born Feb. 25, 1854. All children were born in Brown Co., IN.

Jesse W. Shipley, Sr. ca. 1863

Margaret May married first Samuel Nelson and second George W. Hamblen. Sam Nelson died March 25, 1876 at age 28 and is buried in the Elkinsville Cemetery. Sam and Margaret had two daughters, Vanie, born 1869, died 1894, and Evaline. Vanie is buried in the Elkinsville Cemetery between her mother and father.

Evaline Nelson married Jacob Roberts and they had three children, Ida, May and Fred. Ida Roberts married Chester Taylor and had two children, Hazel and Albert. They lived on farms as tenants around Franklin and Columbus. Ida died in a nursing home in Edinburgh. Hazel is still living in Indianapolis. Albert's first wife, Elizabeth (Harrison) Coy lives in Columbus and their children are Barbara and Alberta. Alberta married Robert Green.

May Roberts married Ray Ford. They lived on farms around Franklin, IN. Fred Roberts married Mamie Evans and married second Ruth Schrougham. His obituary stated that he had a total of 14 children.

Jesse married second Emmarine Wilkerson Hash, daughter of William Wilkerson, on Nov. 24, 1854 in Brown Co., IN. They were divorced and had no children.

Jesse enlisted at Bloomington, IN on Sept. 20, 1861 in Co. E, 31st Regiment, Indiana Volunteer Infantry. He later was transferred to Co. B, 15th Regiment, Veteran Reserve Corps and was discharged Sept. 21, 1864.

Jesse married third Sylvania Ann Crider, daughter of George Crider and Elizabeth Fleetwood, Jan. 4, 1863. Sylvania was born ca. 1844 in Johnson Township since she was listed in the 1850 Census there as being six years old. Jesse and Sylvania had ten children: Catherine, Mary, Levi, Isaac, Elender, James Jacob, Charles, Nora, Florence Minerva, and Jesse W. Jr. Jesse W. Shipley, Jr.'s son, Marriot, of Columbus, has the original tintype of Jesse W. Shipley, Sr.

Jesse, Sr. died June 3, 1882 and Sylvania died March 28, 1918. Both are buried in the Shipley Cemetery on Jackson Branch Ridge Road northwest of Nashville.

(Much of the information on Jesse W. Shipley and his families came from Helen and Kenneth Reeve's research and from Janet K. (Venice) Dixon, a great-great-great-granddaughter of Jesse and Mary

Ann, who lives in Kokomo.) *Submitted by great-grandson John W. Hamblen*

ISAAC AND ELIZABETH SHIPLEY -
Isaac fell in love with the young Elizabeth Polley, and received her father's blessing, as he was present when his future son-in-law, and daughter, applied for a marriage bond, in Monticello, Wayne Co., KY, July 15, 1809. Shortly after, Isaac, and Elizabeth were married, and moved to Knox Co., KY where they remained until they moved north to Indiana, in 1827. With all their worldly goods, and five children: Hiram (1811), Margaret (1812), Jesse W. (1821), Mary Polly (1825), John (1826). With wagons loaded beyond compacity, the Shipleys moved out, with some of his in-laws, (the Polleys). They settled into Jackson Co., IN where three more children were born to them: Nelson (1828), Elizabeth (1832), Samuel J. (1834). The Shipleys entered land, in Brown County, in 1834, on section 32, which is south of Story. Nothing more is known of Isaac after 1834, and his third child, Jesse W.; 13 years of age, had the responsibilities of the family farm, along with his brothers, and sisters, who varied in ages. Jesse W. Shipley, married, March 23, 1845, to Mary Ann Hall, in Brown County, where four children were born to them, before Mary passed away April 30, 1854 and is buried in Deckard Cemetery. Abasha (1848), Sarah E. (1849), John W. (1851), Margaret May (1854).

Sylvania Ann (Crider) Shipley and Florence Minerva (Shipley) Brown about 1910.

Jesse, remarried shortly after the death of his wife, to Emmarine Wilkerson Hash, Nov. 24, 1854, and family legend has it, that Jesse, married this lady to have someone to take care of his children, and after he joined the Army, Sept. 20, 1861, Emmarine, left him for another man. Jesse, was in Company G, 31st Regt. Indiana Volunteer Infantry, and was later transferred to Company B, 15th Regt. Veteran Reserve Corps, and was discharged Sept. 21, 1864. Jesse, married a third time, to Sylvania Ann Crider, while on sick leave from the Army, Jan. 4, 1863, in Brown County, where ten children were born to them: Catherine (1863), Mary Polly (1866), Levi (1868), Isaac (1870), Ellender Ella (1871), James Jacob (1875), Charles (1876), Nora (1877), Florence Minerva (1880), Jesse W. Jr. (1881). Jesse died shortly after the birth of his son, Jesse Jr., and was buried in the Shipley Cemetery, Washington Township, Brown County, where his wife, Sylvania Ann joined him, March 24, 1918.

Jesse W. Shipley, Jr., was raised by his mother, and married Aug. 4, 1906, to Elizabeth Ellen Shick, in Lawrence Co., IL, where she was born Sept. 15, 1888. Jesse Jr., died Sept. 13, 1956, in Clifford, Bartholomew Co., IN, and is the grandfather to Vickie Lynn (Jackson) Sullivan, whose mother was Florence E. (Shipley) Jackson, daughter of Jesse Jr. Vickie, and her husband Gary L. (Myler) Sullivan were married March 31, 1973, in Berrien Co., MI, and now reside in Woodstock, IL with their three sons: Jason, Shad, and Michael.

Vickie, and her husband Gary are Shipley Family Researchers, and publish a Shipley Family Newsletter. Vickie's mother, Florence E. (Shipley) Jackson passed away, Aug. 17, 1988, in Saint Joseph, MI.

MIR AND PAT SIDDIQ -
Mir and Pat moved to Brown County in 1980, with their three sons, Sharif, Tim and Bob. Mir has been doing research for Indiana University in Afghan studies. Since October, 1988, he and Pat have owned and operated the Nashville Frame Company on East Main Street. The business includes frames, art supplies, art classes and an art gallery. They live on Hoover Road.

Mir helped start the Brown County Park and Recreation Soccer program. Pat has been active in Psi Iota Xi, Indiana Heritage Arts, and the United Methodist Church. She enjoys painting and has exhibited in several art exhibits locally and abroad. Her illustrations have appeared in several books published in Afghanistan, and she recently finished illustrating a book on Afghanistan to be published in the United States.

Mir's ancestry traces back to the prophet Mohammed, more recently his ancestors are from Afghanistan. Mir's father, Mohammed Siddiq-Hussaini, the first Afghan to receive a University degree, was employed with the Afghan Foreign Ministry. He developed a shorthand for the language, Farsi, and spoke seven languages. Mir played on the Afghan National Soccer Team; he graduated from Kabul University and later received his doctorate in Educational Planning from Indiana University. His experience includes teaching management and planning, being advisor to the Prime Ministry, President of Planning in the Ministry of Education, Deputy Minister of Education, and he introduced an educational reform in the Afghan schools in 1973.

Tim, Mir, Bob, Pat and Sharif Siddiq

Patricia Foley Siddiq's ancestors immigrated from Ireland in the 1700s; she is a descendant of John Cory who came over on the Mayflower. She was born in Indianapolis. She has spent 20 years as an art teacher in Indiana, Illinois, and Afghanistan. She graduated from DePauw University and has her masters degree from Indiana University.

Mir and Pat met in 1964 at Indiana University. They lived 13 years in Kabul, Afghanistan.

In April, 1978, a communist coup occurred in Afghanistan, making it necessary to leave Afghanistan. After over a year of living under communism and being in a war zone, Pat and the boys came to the U.S., followed by Mir, nine months later. Mir was under house arrest, so it was especially difficult for him to leave. The communist government, which was backed by the Russians took the Siddiq's home, land and other property. They left Afghanistan with only their suitcases to start life again in the United States. Mir's brothers and sisters and family have also been able to come to the U.S. to live.

Through the Afghan experience of being in the midst of the spread of communism, the Siddiqs see a great need for concern about the spread of communism and a need for how to control it. They see a need to channel our energy and creativity toward a more peaceful and humane world.

CLARENCE AND JOSEPHINE SIMMONS FAMILY -
Patrick and Eliza (Stone) Simmons moved to Brown County in 1918. They were in their 60s. Since they were exchanging properties with Lucinda Meddors, the decision was made to exchange furniture also. The journey from Knox County was over deeply rutted dirt roads, and was made by horse and wagon. This couple was the first of five generations to make Brown County their home.

Patrick was born in Martin County on Jan. 3, 1853. He married Eliza Stone on April 19, 1888. They had five children: Clarence, Emma, Mamie (died in infancy), Mary, and Wallace.

Patrick died May 5, 1928. Eliza died in 1935. They are buried in Old Unionville Cemetery. They had been farmers throughout their lives.

Clarence Simmons was born in Knox County on Feb. 25, 1889. He worked on his father's farm. At age 18 he joined the United States Marine Corps. He was stationed in the Virgin Islands, Santo Domingo, France, Fort Ozoma, Mexico, Quantico, Panama, Nicaragua, and Haiti. After 23 years of serving his country, he retired in 1932, with the rank of Sergeant Major. He bought his father's farm, and brought his family to Brown County (Howard Ridge).

Josephine Myrtle (Williams) Simmons was born in Indianapolis on July 25, 1896. Her parents were William and Catherine Lavina (Bowers) Williams. She had six sisters. They were descendants of John Hart (one of the signers of the Declaration of Independence).

Clarence and Josephine were married at Greensburg on Jan. 20, 1918. They had four children: Dorothy Rae, Clarence Patrick, Joanna Lee, and Carole Lynn. Dorothy's history is recorded under Arthur and Dorothy Smith. Joanna's history is recorded under Simmons-Moore.

Patrick was born in Santo Domingo on Feb. 24, 1923. He was a joy to all that knew him. His bright red hair, blue eyes, and freckles were an exterior for a loving, gentle boy. His life was all too short. He died on Feb. 11, 1938. His funeral was held in Helmsburg Gymnasium, and he is buried in Old Unionville Cemetery. He is still sadly missed.

Carole was born at home on Aug. 8, 1934. She has a son, Larry Dale Bennett, born Feb. 5, 1956. Larry owns 18 acres of the Simmons' original 20 acres. Joanna's daughter, Cindee, owns the remaining two acres. This contains the log home, built in 1938, for Josephine's mother, Catherine Gatheman. She lived here until 1954. The Simmons' log home (125 years old) burned to the ground in 1968.

Clarence and Josephine lived on this land for 31 years. They wanted to raise their children in the country, and own their own land. And they loved this land. They looked forward to each Spring, to plant and grow their own food. In Autumn, they were in awe of these beautiful hills.

The Simmons family attended the Old Unionville Baptist Church for several years. They then

SIMMONS - MOORE - Joanna Lee Simmons was born on Feb. 26, 1926, in Quantico, VA. Her father, Sergeant Major Clarence Simmons, served in the United States Marine Corps. Her mother, Josephine Myrtle (Williams) Simmons, traveled with her husband. The family had an interesting life in a time when few people traveled extensively. In March 1932, the family returned to Quantico, having lived in Haiti for a year. Clarence retired from the Marine Corps, and the family moved to Brown County.

Joanna's sister, Dorothy Rae, and brother, Clarence Patrick, and their parents, made the long arduous trip to Indiana in an Essex automobile. The narrow mountain roads were a real challenge for an inexperienced driver.

There was a tremendous amount of work to do on their log cabin. The home had been vacant for some time. Summer went by quickly.

In September, Dorothy, Patrick, and Joanna attended school at Needmore (a one-room school). Three years later they attended Helmsburg School. Mart Brown was their bus driver. He and his wife, Pearl, were good friends throughout these years.

On Aug. 8, 1934, another family member was added. Carole Lynn was born in the family home.

Hot summer days were spent hoeing fields of corn, perhaps on the way home, getting to wade in the creek, and trying to catch crawdads. Patrick and Joanna worked and played together. Happy childhood ended on Feb. 11, 1938. Patrick died (after a short illness) and the family's lives were never the same after this tragedy.

Joanna's seventh grade teacher, Sylvester Barnes, taught English and History - what a wonderful teacher! He had a tremendous impact on Joanna's love for English, Literature, and History throughout her life.

Joanna graduated from Helmsburg High School in 1944. That autumn she attended Indiana University. Many friends were serving their country—World War II claimed several friends—thank you, dear friends. It was a sad time for our country.

On June 30, 1945, Joanna married Richard Badgley Moody. They had three children: Michael Jan (April 8, 1946); Patrick Richard (July 27, 1948), and Toni Lee (April 4, 1951, deceased). Richard died May 24, 1954. Michael and his wife, Jo Clare, have one son, Christopher Michael (March 10, 1974). Michael is a career Navy man and serves aboard the Aircraft Carrier USS Kennedy. He was a radioman on the destroyer USS O'Brien during the Vietnam War, which was hit with missiles.

Joanna married Walter Paul Moore on Sept. 10, 1955. They have one daughter, Cindee Camille (Feb. 14, 1958). Cindee married Robert Alan Laughlin. They have three sons: Jason Alan (July 8, 1977), Alexander Patrick (Sept. 13, 1985), and Kirk Andrew (July 15, 1988). Alan is an architect and Cindee a registered nurse. They live in Cincinnati.

Paul has worked for Civil Service for 34 years. Joanna retired in 1981. They bought ten acres in Boone County and built a two-story A-frame home (with all work done by themselves). Landscaping was a challenge, with beautiful results.

Paul and Joanna are active members of Old Union Church of Christ.

THE SIPES FAMILY - The ancestors of Henry Sipes, an early settler of Brown County, were from Untergimpern, Baden. Johann Carl Seib emigrated from there to Lancaster Co., PA in 1732. His son George Michael Sipes of York Co., PA was too old and infirm to serve in the Revolutionary War, so his son, George served in his place. George Michael was a miller near Gettysberg and he is buried in the National Cemetery at Gettysburg.

Front Row: Frank Sipes, Anna Lucas, Henry Sipes, A.F. Sipes, Henry Clevenger, Blanche Clevenger. Back Row: Edgar Clevenger, Rose Sipes Taggart, Sarah Sipes Adams, Emma Susan Sipes Clevenger, Cyrus R. Clevenger, H. Franklin Clevenger.

After the war George Sipes and his wife Rachel Mellinger moved to Western Pennsylvania, then to Elizabethtown, KY, and then to Henderson Creek in Northern Lawrence County. There he built a mill. George and Rachel had eight children: John (1792-1869) who never married; George (1794-1884) who married Elizabeth Hardin; Henry (1796-1877) who married Mary Howell; William (1800-ca. 1877) who married Elizabeth; Elizabeth (1802-?) who never married; Charles (1805-?) who never married; Catherine (1807-?) who married John Stephenson; and Patsy (1811-1852) who was the second wife of Edward David. Charles Sipes who was physically handicapped served as school teacher in the Brown County schools.

Henry and Mary Howell were married in Elizabethtown, KY and moved to Brown County about 1836 when they entered land in Washington Township just south of State Road 46. By 1839 Henry was operating a small distillery, among the first in Brown County. Henry and Mary had eight children: Henry and Mary (twins) died in infancy; Drewilla Ann (1829-1909) who married Joseph Mead (no issue); Albert Franklin (1831-1916); George Washington (1833-1913) (no issue); James Marion (1836-1865); Charles Van Buren (1838-1898) who married Jennie Pegg (no issue); Rachel Jane (1840-1875) who never married. While most parents recorded the births of their children in a Bible, Henry and Mary recorded theirs on the fly leaf of a shapenote songbook! Family tradition has it that James Marion was not killed in the Civil War, but married a Southern belle and came home twice to Brown County after he was officially dead. Henry was active in the early government of the county and served as a grand juror during the second court session in 1837.

Albert Franklin Sipes married Elizabeth Jane Adams on April 2, 1857. Elizabeth was the daughter of Thomas and Elizabeth Rose (High) Adams. Albert Franklin and Elizabeth Jane had five children who reached maturity: Mary Rose (1862-1948) who married Walter A. Taggart; Sarah Jane (1865-1948) who married Charles Gess Adams; Henry Adams (1867-1947) who married Addie Claude Lane; Emma Susan (1873-1927) who married Franklin Henry Clevenger; and Edgar Thomas (1880-1964) who married Zella Myers. Albert Franklin was sheriff at the old log jail from 1872 to 1876. For more descendants see the Clevenger Family of Brown County.

VIRGIL AND NELLIE SISSON - William Sisson came from Yorkshire, England to America in the late 1700s. The wife's family name "Hudeburg," from Knox Co., TN. A son, William, Jr. resided in Madison Co., IN before coming to Brown County. William, Jr.'s son, Sam, married Margaret Merriman and had a son Virgil.

Virgil married Nellie Chitwood, daughter of Sam and Emma Crowdy Chitwood. About 1910 the Chitwood family came to Indiana from Taswell Co., IL. Virgil attended Cottonwood School and Nellie attended Brock School. Both worked at Douglas Orchard (off Bear Creek) when teenagers.

Virgil and Nellie settled on the Sam Wade farm. Their children and spouses: Marjorie married George Collett; Alvin married Mable Voland; Catherine never married (deceased); Emma married Junior Butler; Chelsea married Rosemary Bay; Mary married Ralph Frownfelter; Lloyd married Donna Steinneger; Phyllis married Thomas O'Quinn; Virginia married George Mathis; Lester married Brenda Wilson; Marolyn married Omar Kirts; Helen married Curtis Underwood; Harry married Lula Mae Douty; Carolyn married Richard Mathis; Robert married Cora Burton; Rebecca married Gerald Scrougham; Thurl married Myla Faye; Thelma June (deceased).

Virgil owned mules at times and once had a mule cart but most travelling was by foot until the boys could get bicycles. A two-door Model T and a Model A were the only cars he had. Virgil made a living by tenant farming, raising tomatoes for the canning factory and working in the woods. They kept chickens and livestock for their own use and raised a large garden.

Nellie made kraut by the barrel, hominy, canned beans, apple butter and soap.

Toys were mostly "thought up" and hand made—cars made of cardboard and paper dolls from catalogues. They could not afford to keep pets but did have a dog as Virgil and Chelsea liked to 'coon hunt. The children went to the Helmsburg School; the younger ones going to Nashville High School when the schools consolidated. It was often stated among the Helmsburg students that if you did not know a pupil's name you called him "Sisson" and it would probably be correct.

They attended various country churches. Paul Knight was one of their favorite ministers. In later years Nellie became a member of the Nashville Nazarene Church.

Nellie worked at the canning factory, Camp Atterbury and Nashville School cafeteria. Later she was making candy for special friends.

There are 57 living grandchildren and one grandchild deceased; 56 living great-grandchildren and one great-grandchild deceased; two living great-great-grandchildren and two great-great-grandchildren deceased. *Submitted by Mary Frownfelter*

HAROLD AND LEOTA (BRUNER) SKIRVIN - George and Elizabeth (Betsy) Smith Skirvin, the great-great-grandparents of Harold Skirvin, were one of the early settlers of Monroe County. They purchased a farm east of Bloomington for 12 cents an acre. He was a farmer but later gave most of his time to his cooper shop located where the Arbutus Apartments are today. He fought in the War of 1812. George and his brother, Joel, were captured by the Indians during the French and Indian War. George escaped by swimming across the Ohio River but Joel was held several years. Upon becoming ill, he was traded to the British for a keg of whiskey. The British gave him his freedom. George died in 1879 at age 86.

George and Betsy had six children. The second, Simpson S. (1819-1898) was a farmer settling near his father. He married Catherine Rader in 1822. He fought in the Mexican War. His son, Newton Smith Skirvin, married Clara Kent, related to the Kents in Brown County. He was a farmer and lived his life on the homestead east of Bloomington, dying at age 89. Newton's son, Obel Estes, the father of Harold, lived most of his life near the Skirvin homestead. He married Goldie Cecil Shields in 1910. Her lineage is documented back to William Shields (1600-1654) born in County Antrim, Ireland. His grandson, William Shields, was born in Kent Co., MD in 1668.

Harold and Leota (Bruner) Skirvin

Harold was born in 1917 and died in 1971. He married Leota Bruner in 1945. They had five children: Michael, Morris, Theresa (Terry), Marc and Patrick. They moved to Nashville in 1953, purchasing the P.O. Jones log cabin on Old SR 46. This burned in 1966 and they moved to the H. Brooks house (built 1929) on South SR 46 where Leota still lives after marrying Francis Felknor Smith in 1983. The extraordinary kindness the people of Brown County extended to the Skirvin family during this period of extreme illness, fire, and death characterizes its citizens. The family has been so very grateful.

It is believed the Bruner family migrated from Switzerland to Schifferstadt in the Palatinate area of Germany and then to Fredricksburg, MD, in 1728. The house Joseph Bruner built there is now owned by the historical society. He later moved to Kentucky.

James William Bruner was born in Kentucky in 1822 and married Sarah Jane Edwards in 1839. Both died in Illinois within weeks of each other leaving two sons, 18 and 15 years old. Upon the death of their parents both enlisted in the Union Army and fought in the Civil War, the older brother, Thomas Riley, in the 27th Indiana Volunteers at Gettysburg. Thomas lived from 1841 to 1930. He married Rebecca Freeman in 1864. It is through Rebecca's grandmother, Elsa Margaret Fincannon, that the lineage can be traced to Johnathon Peter Von Kannen who arrived from Rotterdam on the HMS Edinburg in 1748. The name was changed to Fincannon later. He had one son who was a Tory loyal to the British and one son a Revolutionary War soldier.

Thomas and Rebecca had one daughter and seven sons, the youngest, Adrian Dorsey, was the father of Leota. He married Mabel Clara Green and they lived most of their lives in Bloomington. Leota taught for 20 years at Brown County High School and retired in 1984 at age 64. She has four grandchildren, Matthew, Kate, Benjamin and David. *Submitted by Leota Skirvin Smith*

SLAYBAUGH FAMILY - Jack L. Slaybaugh was born in Fulton Co., IN on Feb. 1, 1932, the last of three children born to Lewis and Margaret (Smoker) Slaybaugh. Jack has a brother Richard and a sister Julia. Ancestry for both the Slaybaugh and Smoker families began in Germany. Jack's father, Lewis, owned Slaybaugh Trucking in Akron, IN for which both his sons drove. Leaving his father's business, Jack began a career in law enforcement with the Indiana State Police, retiring with the rank of Lieutenant. In recognition of his work and service as a police officer, among many citations, Jack was named a Sagamore of the Wabash by Governor Edgar Whitcomb, an Honorary Kentucky Colonel by the State of Kentucky, and an Honorary Aide-de-Camp by the State of Alabama. Now presently in Sales as Security Specialist, Jack is a member of the American Society for Industrial Security. He is also a member of the Masonic Lodge, Murat Temple and the Scottish Rite.

Jack, Georgeanna and Kelly Slaybaugh, 1985

Jack married Georgeanna Lewis of Indianapolis, IN on Nov. 3, 1973. Georgeanna was born March 30, 1948 in Marion Co., IN, the third of seven children born to Paul Robert and Irma (Cook) Lewis. She has one brother, Paul, Jr. and five sisters: Connie, Sherry, Lynda, Terri and Nita. Both of Georgeanna's parents also trace their ancestry to Germany.

After 21 years of employment as a civilian with the Indiana State Police, Georgeanna retired and worked as a Teacher's Aide at Sprunica Elementary. She also designs and creates silk and dried floral arrangements, specializing in Victorian styles, and sells her work through The Designing Woman in Nashville.

In 1977, Jack and Georgeanna moved to Brown County and live on Goldpoint Road in Hamblen Township. True to its name, gold is often found in the creek that courses through their property (although the specks are quite miniscule!) and the Slaybaughs have entertained visitors from around the state who've heard of the lore and come to see and pan for themselves.

Jack has two children from a previous marriage: a son, Kevin, who is employed at Indiana Bell and a daughter, Kris, who is in Nursing School. There are five grandchildren: Corey, Nikki, Robbie, Jennifer and Michael. Jack and Georgeanna were blessed with another daughter, Kelly, who resides at home with her parents. She attends Sprunica Elementary School.

The Slaybaugh family are members of Cottonwood Church and are active in local and community affairs. *Written by Georgeanna Slaybaugh*

ARTHUR AND DOROTHY SMITH FAMILY - Arthur Walter was born near Vincennes on Aug. 6, 1914. His grandparents had immigrated to the United States from Germany. His parents were Clarence and Marie (Ellerman) Smith. They lived in a German community, and all were farmers. Their specialty was raising melons. Arthur and his brothers and sisters worked on the family farm. He had two brothers, Clarence and Luther, and five sisters: Beulah, Mary, D'Lema, Luellen, and Donna. During the depression, the family lost their farm and moved to Martinsville. They then moved to Fruitdale, and later, to Bean Blossom.

Arthur married Dorothy Rae Simmons on Sept. 24, 1939. They have lived on farms with in a five mile radius since their marriage. Arthur has always farmed, and sold produce, since childhood. Each summer he and his family have worked at the Farmer's Market (on the south side of Indianapolis). This market was closed two years ago. It brought an end to an era of "country in city." Many people depended on this market to supply them with fresh fruit and vegetables. Arthur is now retired from his lifelong vocation.

Dorothy Rae Simmons' (Nov. 26, 1919) parents were Clarence and Josephine Myrtle (Williams) Simmons. She has two sisters: Joanna Lee and Carole Lynn. She had one brother, Clarence Patrick (deceased). Her family moved to the Howard Ridge area in 1932 from Haiti. Her father was a career Marine, and the family had lived in several countries. Dorothy had lived in Quantico, Santo Domingo, Nicaragua, and Haiti. Dorothy, Patrick, and Joanna attended Needmore School. Three years later they attended Helmsburg School. Dorothy graduated in 1939.

Arthur and Dorothy have three children: Nancy Gay (Nov. 21, 1940), Ronald Arthur (March 29, 1945), and Steven Mark (Nov. 11, 1960).

Nancy married Robert Oliver Hafner. They have three children: Kenneth, Douglas, and Laurie, and five grandchildren: Dustin, Matthew, Alisha, Jesse, and Timothy. Ronald and his wife Linda have one daughter, Rona Lorraine. They live in Brown County. Steven has one son, Joshua Steven.

Dorothy raises purebred Himalayan and Persian cats. She also raises purebred Airedale and Rottweiler dogs. She works full time as Case Manager of Brown County for Senior Citizens. She has been a real estate agent for seven years. She was a 4-H leader for 17 years, and the 4-H County Agent for seven years. She has worked for the Area Agency on Aging for eight years. She was a "Big Sister" for several years. She helped to organize the Agency for Planned Parenthood. Her sister, Joanna (the person writing this history), is very proud of her, and her generosity in helping others.

Arthur and Dorothy celebrated their 50th wedding anniversary in September 1989. Two hundred people were present to celebrate the occasion with them.

They are members of the Lutheran Church and for many years, Dorothy created floral arrangements for Sunday services. And they love their 150 acres of beautiful Brown County.

ELMER SMITH FAMILY - Elmer and Catherine (Bodenreider) Smith moved to their home near Needmore in 1948, but their ties to Brown County go back much farther. In September 1885,

Elmer's grandparents, William and Susan Leonard Shields, moved to a 40 acre farm south of Needmore. They came from Noble Co., OH with their three children—Rosa May, Hugh, and Benjamin Warner. Mr. Shields was a farmer and carpenter. In the 1890s he was Jackson Township Justice of the Peace. The family has some of his records showing fines of one or two cents levied for drunkenness. In 1897, the house burned and the family rebuilt on a hill closer to a good spring. In 1897, Rosa May married Hervey O'Dell Smith. He was from Johnson County, but had been staying with his cousin, Robert Smith, a Civil War Veteran who lived and is buried in Needmore. They had five children: Irene, Ralph, Elmer, Oren, and John Walter, and lived in the Whiteland area. Benjamin Warner married Bertha Hyde from near New Unionville. They had seven children: Beatrice, Jenny, Clarence, Earl, Evelyn, Helen, and Ben.

Elmer often visited his grandparents. Sometimes he would ride the train to Trevlac then catch a ride with his Uncle Will Poling who worked for the railroad. Sometimes he and his Mother came to pick and preserve blackberries. He rode his bike down in the fall to gather nuts and mailed them home. Mr. Shields had very strong opinions about many things. At one time he refused to trade at the Needmore store, so he and Elmer walked the hot, dusty road to Trevlac with a basket of eggs to trade. Elmer had to carry back the 25 pound sack of flour. At the foot of a long hill, a man driving a Model T Roadster offered them a ride, but Mr. Shields refused saying he never intended to ride in a car. When he died in 1925, a horse drawn hearse was used to carry his body to the Needmore Cemetery. Susan died in 1932 and is also buried at Needmore.

In 1936, Elmer married Catherine Bodenreider in Franklin and they bought his grandparents' farm. She was born in Indianapolis. Her parents were Camille and Katie Johantges Bodenreider. Camille was born in Alsace Lorraine and Katie in Schwich, Germany. In 1944 they bought another 40 acres west of Needmore. Elmer farmed in Johnson County and was an "Omar Man." After moving to Brown County in 1948, they farmed. When Lake Lemon was built, all but ten acres of their farm was sold, but his grandparents' farm is intact. In the 1950s Elmer was the janitor at the Helmsburg schools. He was also a carpenter on many projects throughout Brown County. Catherine has become very well known for her strawberries, garden produce, and beautiful yard. They built their tidy limestone house in the 1950s. Their two children, Catherine and Jerry, graduated from Helmsburg High School. Jerry retired from the Navy and he and his wife, Dorothy, live in McHenry, IL. Jerry's two children, Melanie Dawn and Jeff, live in Florida. Melanie is married to Terry Tibbetts and has a daughter Mandy Catlyn. Catherine graduated from IU, is married to Alan Donaldson and lives in Van Buren Township with her youngest daughter Susie. Catherine's son, Mark Donaldson, lives in Plainfield, is married to Jane Roe and has two children, Amanda Beth and Daniel Paul. A daughter, Lynn Donaldson, is married to Philip Adams, lives in Tennessee and has a son Nicholas Adams.

GUY E. SMITH - Guy was born May 22, 1907 in Barren Co., KY came to Camby, IN in 1924 with migrant corn huskers. He met his future wife, Lucille M. Harper, in Mooresville in 1928. They lived across the creek from each other but he had to go three miles around to reach her home. Due to the Great Depression, with the shortage of jobs and money, they courted for seven years before they married on March 31, 1935.

Their only child, Guylia Lucille, was three months old when they moved to Brown County to manage the neglected Cottey Orchard on Spearsville Rd. The first two years, while bringing the orchard back into production, they continued to truck farm; taking produce to the Southside Market **every** night except weekends. This involved taking their young daughter in the 1926 one-and-half-ton Ford truck as there was no such thing as a baby-sitter! This was even before R.E.M.C. "turned on the lights in the country." They were one of the seven original families to sign up for electricity for that part of Spearsville Road.

Guy E., Lucille and Guylia Smith

The home entertainment of square dancing and live music became too large for the Smith's dining room, so they moved it to Kelp's Grove, south of Nashville, where dances were held every Saturday night with live music for 25¢ per person. Guy was sworn in as Deputy Sheriff by Harry Kelp, Justice of Peace to help keep the dances orderly. The dances became so popular that it led to Guy forming several music groups: The Hoosier Farm Hands, The Brown County Buckroos & The Brown County String Band with Guy as M.C. and all playing in and around Bean Blossom in the late 30s and early 40s. The shows were performed outside, sometimes from the back of a flatbed truck, the local Williams' gas station and on top of the Beanblossom Lunch Room, presently Short's Mkt. There was a drawing for a basket of free groceries from Herb McDonald's grocery store every weekend. The crowds became so large, a tent was placed on the Frances Rund property on the north side of town where the Blue Grass Festival is held today. The first show "Under the Big Top" of the Brown County Jamboree was Sept. 28, 1941 with admission 25¢. A copyright for the name Brown County Jamboree issued to Len Trissell Nov. 15, 1941 led to a dispute over the name, but the shows with Guy as M.C. continued under Beanblossom Jamboree through 1942.

By the time WWII came, the orchard was prospering, Camp Atterbury was being constructed and Guy, missing the Draft because of his age and family, went to work as a plumber at the Camp. Many good and interesting experiences came from this time. (1941-1945) Camp Atterbury leased out POWs to do manual labor. Guy hired both Italian and Germans to pick apples and cut corn for shocks in the field. Several friendships were made and some continued after the POWs were returned to their homelands.

In the spring of 1943, Guy and family moved from the orchard to a new little house a mile west of Spearsville and in 1948 he opened a small country store on the corner of Spearsville and Horseshoe Roads. This became a neighborhood loafing and "spinning of tall tales" meeting place where many families stopped each evening from work to pick up a few things and exchange the news. A party-line telephone was kept busy as very few people had phones.

They moved to Nashville in 1952 on old 46 east to open the Circle View Appliance store. One of Guy's dreams was to travel to Florida, "the rich man's paradise," he said. In September 1954 he sold the store to Roberts Bros. In January 1955 their daughter married Philip Richards Bunge and in February he began to realize his Florida dream.

A new home and several winters in Ft. Pierce, FL were enjoyed by Guy and Lucille. The summers were spent operating "The Family Restaurant" in Beanblossom, presently Short's Mkt., which was famous for Lucille's peach cobbler and persimmon pudding. After retiring from the restaurant, time was spent selling real estate, traveling to Florida and enjoying their three grandchildren: Loretta Kay, David Michael and Robin Lee at the converted Old Brandstetter School House until his death on Dec. 12, 1964. His widow, Lucille M. Smith Rufly, now resides in downtown Helmsburg on the property of the birthplace of her son-in-law, Philip R. Bunge. *Submitted by Guylia Bunge*

HELEN M. SMITH - Born Helen M. White, Helen was the ninth child born of James Milton (Milt) and Laura Kay David White. She was born Aug. 8, 1915 in Brown County.

Helen attended Nashville High School and graduated in 1932. On Oct. 16, 1933, she married Ora Arto Smith. (see "Ora Arto Smith, Sr.")

Helen's great-grandfather, Edward David, Sr., came from Kentucky to Brown County around 1822. Land grant records show that Edward David entered 80 acres of land on March 6, 1828, in section 28, township 9 north, range 3 east. This land is on present State Road 135 south a short distance from its junction with State Road 46 east. Until 1836 when Brown County was established Ed David's land was located in Bartholomew Co., IN.

Helen M. (White) Smith

Quite a character was Edward David. In his 96 years he married four times, and fathered a record 29 children. His 21st child, by wife number two; Patsey Sipes David, was William David, Helen's grandfather.

According to a 1941 article in the *Brown County Democrat*, Edward David was offered "all the land he wanted" near Columbus, IN, in exchange for a pony he brought from Kentucky. The article also states that he made the first bricks in Brown County.

Edward David supported himself and his family by operating a combined grist and saw mill in the eastern part of Washington township. He was also a horseman. He owned fast horses and was often a participant in the oldtime horse races at Georgetown, which is now present-day Bean Blossom.

Helen's paternal grandfather, John Greenleaf White, was born in 1850. On Oct. 20, 1870, he married Naoma Floyd. To this union there were nine children born. Their first born son was Helen's father James Milton.

After her marriage to Ora Smith, Helen settled into the role of wife and mother. When her children were older, Helen went to work at the Abe Martin Lodge as a cook, sharing the talent she had fine-tuned over the years. She also worked at the Brown County State Park Pool for a time.

By the time the majority of her grandchildren were born, Helen was again home full time.

Helen Smith died on Feb. 29, 1988, leaving behind a husband of 54 years, six children, 14 grandchildren and four great-grandchildren. She is buried in the David Family Cemetery on the farm that she and Ora called home for many years.
Submitted by Shelley Law

MILDRED SMITH - Mildred was born Aug. 17, 1914 in Oxford, KS to Dollie and Turner Armstrong. Her husband, Raymond, was born in Posey County on Jan. 20, 1907. They met at a school box supper. They lived in Kansas until 1935 (this was during the dust bowl years) and then they moved to Evansville, IN and on to Indianapolis in 1959 where Raymond worked for Trailmobile until he passed away October, 1970. Mildred continued working at R.C.A. until she retired. She then worked at Johnson County Memorial Hospital until retirement. In 1971 she moved to Brown County and loves it. After 14 years of rough roads on Three Notch Road, she decided it was best to live in Johnson County. Not content to be idle she went to work six years ago at the Franklin United Methodist Home where she is loved by all the residents. Her hobbies are gardening, flowers, and quilt making plus occasional trips to Brown County. At age 56 she decided to learn how to drive and felt this was a big accomplishment.
Submitted by M.J. Richards

ORA ARTO SMITH, SR. - Ora was born in Brown County, April 8, 1912, to Shadrack (Shade) and Margaret (Maggie) Settle Smith.

Ora's great-grandparents Elijah and Lucinda Walker Smith, along with their four children, migrated from Virginia through Ohio to Tippecanoe Co., IN, where they lived among the Indians. Here Elijah built and operated a small water-powered grist mill.

About 1848 Elijah and his family, now consisting of eight children, moved to Brown Co., IN, where he bought a large farm on "Big Salt Creek." Here in Brown County Elijah and Lucinda had two more children, enlarging their family to ten. Elijah and Lucinda remained in Brown County until their deaths in 1881 and 1874 respectively. Both are buried in Taggart cemetery.

Ora Arto Smith, Jr.

Their second eldest son, Gordon, was born in Virginia ca. 1830. On Jan. 9, 1862 he married Martha Jane Brown. Together they had six sons, five of whom lived to adulthood. Their third born was Ora's father, Shadrack. Shadrack Monroe Smith was born Feb. 25, 1868.

In the year 1657 Francis Settle migrated from Yorkshire, England to Fauquier Co., VA. Around the year 1830 his descendant, James William Settle would leave Fauquier County and travel with his father, his sister and her husband to Ohio. Here in Harrison County he married Lydia Ann Hancher on Dec. 11, 1835. Together they moved on to Van Buren Township in Brown Co., IN. The old log home that James built for his family still remained standing until about 1928 when Governor Jackson purchased it and moved it to a new location on his farm. In this cabin James and Lydia raised ten of their 11 children to adulthood. Their seventh child, and first of the 11 born in Brown County, was Ora's grandfather Daniel.

In 1875 the red-headed Daniel Settle married Sarah Truex, and their fifth born Margaret Olive Settle would tie together the Settle and Smith families by marrying Shadrack Monroe Smith on Dec. 29, 1900.

Shade and Maggie had six children: Arlie E., Byron, Lelan Oresa, Verlis Raymond, Ora Arto, and Helen Josephine. Ora is their only surviving child.

On Oct. 16, 1933 Ora wed Brown County native Helen White. She was born Aug. 8, 1915, the daughter of Milt and Laura David White. (For more information on Helen and her families see "Helen M. Smith.")

During their married life they lived several places in Brown County including a log cabin built by Ora on Salt Creek and the Edward (Ned) David homestead located on 135 south, where Ora, Sr. and Ora, Jr. still live today.

Ora's occupations throughout his working years were quite diverse. When the Brown County State Park was being established Ora worked with the WPA building the first roadways into the park. He retired from Cummins Engine, and also worked as a carpenter. For three years he held the position of manager at Yellowwood State Forest.

Ora and Helen had six children. They are: Richard Smith, Betty McMasters, Geneva Dinsmore, Judy Burroughs, Kathy Smith and Ora Smith, Jr.
Submitted by Shelley (Smith) Law

SNIDER FAMILY - The progenitor of the Snider family is believed to be a certain Herman Snider who originally came from Germany to America during the Revolutionary War as a hired Hessian soldier for the British Army. Captured by the American Army, he requested to stay in America following the war. Living in a Pennsylvania Dutch settlement, Herman later moved to the State of Kentucky sometime after 1790.

William Snider, a son of Herman, was born April 9, 1802. He came to Indiana by horseback settling in Brown County in the year 1832. William served as Grand Juror in 1837 and was a leading businessman until his death on Oct. 18, 1875. To William was born a son named Harmon Snider in approximately the year 1822. Harmon married Sarah (Sally) Long and had two children: William W. and Mary Jane Snider Kemp. Born Sept. 18, 1843, William W. was Harold's grandfather. William W. served with Company "D" 25th Regiment of the Indiana volunteers during the Civil War and was with General Sherman in his march to the sea. William W. also donated the land where the Oak Ridge Cemetery and Church are presently located.

Harold and Wilma Snider

To William W. and Emmaline (Helms) Snider were born five children, Mary Jane (Snider) Wade, James Edgar, Rosabelle, Rutherford Clinton, and Edwin Arlington. Rutherford Clinton was Harold's father and farmed his lifetime in Jackson Township of Brown County. Rutherford was a graduate of the old Long School, completing grade school and four years of finishing school. Rutherford was first married to Myrtle (Morrison) Snider by whom two children, Aletha and Emma, were born.

Rutherford's second wife was Bessie Bailey to whom were born ten children. They are by name: Mary Gaynall, Elwin Earl known as "Buck", Harold Roscoe, Lester, Paul Arnold, Olive Branch, Ermal Faith, Naomi Ruth, Eva Ester, and Laurel Clinton. All children of Rutherford are now deceased with the exception of: Aletha Chitwood who currently resides in Brown County, Harold Roscoe who resides in Morgantown, IN, Eva Connell who lives in Evans, WA, and Ruth Dewitt, who lives on the old homeplace on Oak Ridge near Helmsburg.

Harold, who is Rutherford's only living son, entered World War II and remained until he was honorably discharged at the rank of 1st Lieutenant following the end of the war. Returning to Brown County, Harold took again his trade of carpentry and married Wilma Fesler Snider of Morgantown. To them was born one son Harold Lee Snider. Residing in Morgantown, Harold and Wilma are now retired. Their son Lee is presently in management within an Indianapolis-based corporation and married to Cheryl Kincaid Snider, formerly of Kokomo, IN. Residing also in Morgantown, they have two children: Rachel Leigh and Ryan Daniel. All the Snider family are active in Christian service. Recently Harold received an award for poetry written on Christian themes.

GEORGE AND NANCY (BAKER) SNIDER - George was born Oct. 10, 1836, to Brown County pioneers William and Elizabeth (Brummett) Snider. Members of both the Snider and Brummett families are included in the 1884, Historical and Biographical publication of Brown County by Weston A. Goodspeed.

George Snider married Nancy Baker Sept. 3, 1856, in Brown County and settled on a farm in the same neighborhood as his parents and many of his siblings. Evidence of the Snider children settling in same area is found in Brown County census of 1860, 1870, 1880, and 1900.

Some of George Snider's story was learned from his obituary. "After a long illness of a complication of diseases, George Snyder, an old and well-known citizen of Jackson township died ...at the home of his son, Joshua Snyder, one mile south of Helmsburg.

Mr. Snyder was 70 years old and was a son of William Snyder, one of the earliest settlers in this county, who located on the farm now owned by John M. Winchester, 3-1/2 miles east of Nashville." He died July 29, 1908. George and Nancy are buried in Lanam Ridge Cemetery, Brown County.

1908 Standing: Jane Rund, Dessie Squires, Ella Mathis, Maggie Zook, Kate Murphy and Cordelia Derringer. Seated: Lewis Joshua and Nancy (Baker) Snider.

The spelling of Snider/Snyder was interchangeable; people in same families used either or both spellings.

Nancy Baker's parentage is unproven. She was born Jan. 4, 1838, in either Indiana or Missouri; died March 4, 1912, in Brown County. Among survivors listed in her obituary, three sisters and one brother were included, but didn't give names or places.

Twelve children were born to George and Nancy; most remained in Indiana, where descendants still live. They were: (1) Mary Elizabeth, June 14, 1858-Dec. 16, 1926, married Johnson Gilbert; lived in Johnson County; one child; (2) Almira, Sept. 5, 1860-before 1912, married Franklin Reardon; five children; whereabouts unknown; (3) George Ella, July 24, 1862-unknown, married William Mathis; unknown issue and whereabouts; (4) Eliza Jane, June 14, 1863-Nov. 15, 1934, married Hammond Rund; lived in Brown and Johnson counties; seven children; (5) Lida Ann, Dec. 27, 1864-Oct. 29, 1865; (6) Lucinda Catherine, April 30, 1866-June 14, 1911, first married William Murphy, second married James Murphy; had five children, all died as infants; (7) James William, July 16, 1868-Aug. 23, 1870; (8) Cordelia, March 27, 1870-May 9, 1920, married James Derringer; five children; (9) Lewis Joshua, Feb. 1, 1872-Dec. 16, 1948, married Bertha Richardson, 12 children; (10) Maggie May, Oct. 26, 1874-Feb. 25, 1952, married James A. Zook; ten children; (11) Ollie, Jan. 4, 1876-April 30, 1908, married Henry Scrogham; four children; (12) Dessie, Oct. 11, 1878-Dec. 14, 1963, married Asa Squires; homesteaded in eastern Montana 1909; eight children; buried at Stevensville, MT. *Submitted by Marian Waters Challender, great-granddaughter*

HERMAN SNIDER (SCHNAITER)

Herman Schnaiter (or Herman Schneider or Harmon Snider), the progenitor of these Sniders may have been born in Hesse, a State in West Germany, in the years approximately 1750 to 1755. He was one of the hired soldiers furnished Britain to fight in the American Revolution. Before becoming a soldier, he had been a weaver.

He went to a Pennsylvania Dutch Settlement and married Elizabeth Bowman (also known as Betsy and 'Dutch Granny'). About 1779 they came down the Ohio River and settled near Bloomfield, KY, sometime after 1790 and later moved to Taylorsville, KY.

Elizabeth Bowman Snider was born in 1758 and died at the home of her grandson, George Washington, son of Jacob. Records of 1952 show she was buried in Glass burying ground on a farm owned by her great-great-great-great-granddaughter, Mable Burge Lewis, at an age of above 92 years. Herman died in 1824.

To Herman and Elizabeth were born seven children between the years of 1781 and 1802; Jacob, John Allen, Polly, Terry (Tina), Sally, Betsey and William.

William, the seventh child was born April 9, 1802. He married Jane Evans on Sept. 11, 1820 in Nelson Co., KY, (later became Spencer Co., KY). For some unknown reason, William left Jane and with his two older children came on horseback to Indiana, settling in Brown County. He made an entry of land in Brown County in 1832. He served as Grand Juror in 1837. Surplus Revenue and 3% Commissioner, and was the First Claimant under the county order that one dollar be paid for each wolf scalp presented.

After William left Jane and came to Indiana, he married Elizabeth Brummett, a Brown County girl of German extraction - born Feb. 20, 1812 in Tennessee, the daughter of George Brummett. To this union were born 11 children: John, James, George, William, Martha, Joshua, Jacob, Sarah, Rachael, and two died in infancy.

William died Oct. 18, 1875 at the age of 73 years, six months and nine days. He is buried by the side of his second wife, Elizabeth in the Snider Cemetery, Brown County. Elizabeth died April 4, 1867.

George Snider, the third child of William and Elizabeth was born Oct. 10, 1836. He married Nancy Baker (born Jan. 4, 1838) on Sept. 3, 1856 in Brown County. They had 12 children between the years of 1858 and 1878: Mary Elizabeth Gilbert, Almira Rariden, George Ella Mathis, Eliza Jane Rund, Lida Ann died in infancy, Lucinda Catherine Murphy, James William, Cordelia Derringer, Lewis Joshua, Maggie May Zook, Ollie Scrogham, and Emma Destimona Squires.

George died July 29, 1908, and Nancy died March 4, 1912, both are buried in Lanam Ridge Cemetery, Brown County.

Cordelia Snider, the eighth child of George and Nancy was born March 27, 1870. On March 16, 1890 she married James Napoleon Derringer. His parents were James W. Derringer, born Jan. 5, 1836 in Wales; and Hannah Jane Markum. His second wife, Mary Phillips Waltman is buried beside him at Bean Blossom cemetery. *Written by Mary Derringer Porter*

SNYDER FAMILY

Charles W. Snyder (Paul's grandfather) (1850-1912) was born in Ohio, one of 11 children born to John and Mary Brand Snyder. They moved from Ohio to southern Brown County between 1858 and 1860.

Charles W. married Mary E. Gatten, daughter of Richard and Hannah Gatten in 1871. They bought the Snyder Farm located just east of Nashville which has been owned and operated by the Snyder family since that time. He was Brown County School Superintendent. They had one child, Charles Louis.

Louie married Mary Olive Moore, daughter of Henry and Mary Catherine (Seitz) Moore. For many years Louie was a teacher in the one room schools scattered over Brown County. He later became attendance officer. He was a member of the Masonic Lodge and Louie and Olive were both members of the Nashville Christian Church. Olive was in the Garden Club and the Ladies Aid Society, a group that met each week and quilted. They had two sons, Raymond Moore and Paul Charles.

Paul and Betty Snyder

Upon graduation from high school, Raymond married Emma Marsh and moved to Bloomington where he was employed by Showers Brothers Furniture Company. When Showers closed, Raymond went to Arkansas and found employment. He had a son, Robert, and two daughters, Kathy and Sharon. He still resides in Arkansas.

Paul, after graduation from high school, attended Coyne Electrical School in Chicago, where he learned the trade of electrician. In addition to the electrical work, Paul helped his parents farm and manage a dairy herd. Paul delivered milk to stores and eating places in Nashville for seven cents a quart. While delivering milk to a small eating place, called The Grill, Paul met Elizabeth (Betty) Quilliam, daughter of William and Maude Martin Quilliam. She came from near Terre Haute to teach in Nashville High School after graduating from Indiana State Teachers College. Paul and Betty married and built a house on the farm. Betty taught in the high school 28 years. Paul is the only living charter member of Brown County Lions Club who is still active. They are both members of the Nashville Christian Church and members and officers of Farm Bureau. Their children are: M. Marilyn and Charles W. (Chuck). The family's favorite recreational activity was boating on Lake Lemon. Paul and Betty have enjoyed many trips to Florida and other places in their travel trailer. They had two children:

(1) Marilyn married J. Eugene DeWees, son of Joe and Amelia DeWees, who taught music in Brown County Schools until a fatal accident in 1984. Marilyn lives on a part of the farm and works as a secretary. Their children are: Joseph Charles, James William, and Elizabeth Amelia. Joseph Charles married Barbara Denise Hays. Their children are Brittany Jo and Joseph Paul.

(2) Charles (Chuck) married Fanny Marie Kemp. Their children are: Kimberly Kay, Kevin Charles, and Karmen Lynn. He later married Joyce Kain and they have Jennifer Joy. Chuck is the fourth generation to be living on and farming the Snyder farm where he raises Angus cattle, Percheron horses, and Quarter horses. He is also an electrical contractor.

BOB AND CINDY SNYDER

Bob was born Nov. 23, 1921 in Lapel, IN. Cindy was born on March 14, 1923 in Marshall Co., Green Mountain, IA. Bob and Cindy were married April 28, 1945 in San Diego, CA. They moved to Lapel, IN in 1946. They purchased ten acres from Webster White, situated along Friendship Cabin Road in October 1972, and began building a log cabin August 1978 and completed it in 1980. They moved to Brown

County November, 1982 and built their garage in April, 1983. Bob has a hobby of carving birds. In the fall of 1990 they moved to Arcadia, IN.

SPARKS/DUNGAN FAMILY

In 1954 Charles G. Dungan purchased 70 acres of land on Possum Trot Road bordered by Slippery Elm Shoot and North Shore Drive. He was a railroad engineer on the New York Central between Cincinnati and Chicago. He and his wife lived in Indianapolis, but between his runs on the railroad he restored the old farm house which had not been inhabited for many years. Plumbing was impossible so he cleaned out the old dug well and built an outhouse.

After retirement the couple enjoyed their country home away from home, but when health problems arose it became apparent that mowing was no longer fun.

Mr. Dungan's niece, Leora Dungan, was married to Ben Sparks, a U.S. Naval Aviator. As his retirement was on the horizon, the Sparks family with four sons were looking for a place to call a permanent home. Leora (Lee) had grown up in Cincinnati, but had many kin folk in central Indiana. Ben was a native of Rushville, IN. During the 27 years in military life the couple had lived up and down the east coast, west coast, Hawaii and Iceland. Hawaii is great but they missed the changing seasons. When Mr. Dungan decided to sell, the time and price were right.

The Sparks family moved to Possum Trot in January 1968. Ben III had just graduated from Purdue as a Civil Engineer. Three younger sons, John, Anthony and Timothy helped cut wood to fire the wood burning stove. The following summer, Ben installed electric heat and completed a room addition. Indoor plumbing was installed. By 1973 Brown County Water Utility piped water down North Shore so water was piped to the house.

In 1970 the couple attended Purdue University Ag short course to study soils, weeds, homestead planning, marketing and kindred subjects. With all this new knowledge, a new drive and sidewalks were layed. The old barn was restored.

In 1971 the Small Wineries Act was passed in state legislature which made it possible to grow grapes and make wine on a commercial basis. Work continued in the vineyard with the goal in mind of becoming a winery.

In 1978 they received their federal approval by Bureau of Alcohol, Tobacco, and Firearms and Indiana Alcoholic Beverage Commission. The business grew and word of mouth between satisfied customers kept the family busy. The boys became adults, went to college, married and moved on to their careers. Ben and Lee continued to operate the business.

In 1986 the old farm house was moved 500' north and a new house was built on the same site. The new house is a salt box replica of the Stanley Whitman house which still stands in Farmington, CT.

At present they have announced that 1990 will be the last vintage year. The winery stainless steel tanks and equipment will be donated to Purdue University. The Sparks will be free to travel and visit with their sons and families. The grandchildren are Jane (1979), Charles (1982), Stephen (1984), Alexander (1987) and Faye (1987).

SPURGEON FAMILY

The Spurgeon ancestry is mostly of English descent. They were farmers and ministers in that country. Research is being done as to names and dates. We do know they came to the New World in the 1700s, and were farmers, preachers and teachers in this country.

They settled in the Carolinas: Josiah (1777), Elizabeth (1785), William (1805). This is taken from the Old Bible of the old Manuscript.

They traveled northward through the wilderness until they settled in Indiana.

Wiley and Mary F. Spurgeon

Wiley Spurgeon (1825) and Mary F. Spurgeon (1824) were married in 1848 and lived in Salem, where William A. was born in 1852. Wiley, wife and son moved from Salem in 1853 to their new home situated in NE1/4 of Section 1, Township 7, Range 3E, Brown Co., IN and lived there until their deaths. Six more children were born there: Maranda Jane (1855), Orville (?), Elizabeth E. (1857), Charles W. (1861), Mollie F. (1863), Harriett H. (1867).

Besides farming, their orchards, known as the "Spurgeon Orchards" were well known, far and wide, for their wonderful apples, tasty apple cider, and for delicious apple pies. The women folk were accomplished weavers on their looms that was in their house. They were very community minded and saw the need for education. The school house was built and known as the "Spurgeon School."

William and Orville were doctors and Charles was teacher and itinerant preacher. John Dillinger, in his young days, liked to visit with Charles. But, Dillinger chose not to heed the words of wisdom, but to take the wrong path.

Dr. William married Elvira Chute (1872). Miranda J. married Albert J. Setser (1873). From these, eight children were born: John (1874), died in infancy. William (1875), his 11 children named in the Setser history. Charles (1877) teacher and banker, married Emma Shaefer, no children. Albertis (1879), farmer, married Pearl Beatty. Five children: Parry, Lawrence, Ethel, Mary L., and Grace. Mary (1881), Scott (1883) teacher and banker, married Mary Gelfus. Two daughters: Bertha Mae and Mary Frances. Luzetta (1885), married John Rice, no children. Nora Edna (1891) married Clarence Beatty. Two children: Dale and Lenore.

Albert J. died from an attack of measles and pneumonia in 1895. Maranda J., then married Andrew Scott Carmichael, 1899. He died in 1907. Elizabeth married Thomas Waggoner. Orville married Mary Spurgeon. Charles W., married Olive Spurgeon. Mollie married Will Thompson. Harriett died in 1890 at age 23.

The home place and school still stand and is known as Spurgeons Corner. They were a very religious family in the Church of Christ in that community. William is author of a well-known and well-read book on the Book of Revelations of the Holy Bible. He and Orville as teachers, doctors and ministers, moved later on to Muncie, where William founded the "Muncie Gear Works."

Mary Setser tells a story about one time when she visited the Spurgeon home and saw a Model T Ford stored away. She asked Dr. Orville if "He didn't want it, could she have it?". He said "It's yours for 10¢"! She drove it for a long time! *Written by Beatrice Spurgeon Setser Leslie*

WESLEY AND GENIZA (POLING) SQUIRES

Many families in Barbour Co., WV sought better farmland and farming conditions and the Squires with their six daughters were prompted to migrate to Brown County in 1869.

On the 15th of March 1869, Wesley bought 120 acres from William and Mary Wright near Bean Blossom Creek at Needmore in Jackson Township. With the help of some Poling families, who had settled there earlier, they erected a large log cabin with an immense fireplace. There was a fine spring nearby. Eventually, Wesley built a frame house near the road running west to Needmore, which was still used as a home in 1963. He grew plums, peaches, apples and other fruits as well as grains.

Asa Squires and Dessie Snider

Wesley Squires, born Nov. 5, 1825 in Preston Co., WV, was one of 13 children born to John and Mary (Fortney) Squires. At census time in 1850 they lived in Barbour Co., WV on a farm adjacent to Elisha Poling, who had a daughter Geniza (born March 19, 1834). Wesley and Geniza were married Dec. 24, 1853 and lived in Barbour County until they moved to Indiana. They are buried in Needmore Cemetery. Wesley died April 23, 1898 and Geniza died April 1, 1907.

Land and religion were important to Wesley. On the 1860 census his occupation was listed as "farmer and Meth." He wrote to his daughter Sarah on Feb. 5, 1888, "We are still trying to live wright, to get nearer to Christ every day, discharge our every duty. We hope we have your prayrs. Our big meeting commences in two weeks. We hope to see good done and ask your prayrs for the upbuilding of the church."

Wesley and Geniza had ten children. Many descendants live in nearby Indiana counties.

(1) Matildah born and died in 1854.

(2) Mary Elizabeth, born Dec. 30, 1855, died July 7, 1936. Married Samuel Potter Feb. 6, 1873 at Needmore. They had nine children. She is buried at Paragon, IN.

(3) Hester, born March 22, 1858, died Dec. 30, 1929. Married Luther A. Miller Oct. 21, 1880 at Needmore. They had two children.

(4) Charity, born April 6, 1860, died March 29, 1932. Married Nathaniel Gregg at Needmore June 12, 1881. Moved to Montana in 1913. Both buried in Richey, MT. They had five children.

(5) Sarah, born Dec. 27, 1862, died Aug. 17, 1904. Not married.

(6) Clara Geniza, born Nov. 17, 1864, died Sept. 23, 1950. She was a schoolteacher. Married April 2, 1910 in Glendive, MT to William Poling, who

migrated from Needmore to Montana in 1909. No children. Buried in Glendive Cemetery.

(7) Melissa Jane, born June 3, 1867, died April 18, 1944. Married William Lear Feb. 27, 1893 in Tuscola, IL where they lived. She had three children.

(8) John Wesley, born Sept. 30, 1869, died July 28, 1870.

(9) Asa, born June 27, 1871, died March 11, 1945. Only son of Wesley and Geniza to grow to adulthood. Married Dessie Snider June 4, 1898 in Brown County. Homesteaded in eastern Montana 1909. Eight children.

(10) Andrew J., born Nov. 1, 1873, died May 16, 1879. *Submitted by Marian Waters Challender, great-granddaughter*

DAVID STACKHOUSE FAMILY

David W. and Shirley Pat Smith-Stackhouse moved to Brown Co., IN in the spring of 1972. They purchased their home and 21 acres of land - south of Helmsburg, and part of the original Helms homestead - from David and Lily Swift (Mr. Swift is currently the County Sheriff).

Dave was born in Cumberland, IN in 1926. His parents were Dorothy Frances (Snider) Stackhouse and David William Stackhouse, Sr. He served in the Navy in the South Pacific during World War II. In 1950 he earned his BS degree from Lawrence College.

Pat was born in 1926 in Kokomo, IN. Her parents were Julia Marita (Thompson) Smith and Clyde Cecil Smith. She is a direct descendant of the Mayflower Pilgrims William White and Edward Doty.

David W. and Shirley Pat Stackhouse and son Stefan B., 1952

At the time of their move to Brown County Dave and Pat were very active in the American Wine Society, and hoped to establish a vineyard. However, after four years of hard work they discovered that our soil, location, and weather conditions were not right for this purpose and the project was abandoned.

Pat had become permanently disabled a few years earlier and was forced to retire from her career as a Registered Nurse and Director of Health and Safety for Blue Cross/Blue Shield of Indiana. Dave was still working in Indianapolis in the office equipment business. He later traveled as a manufacturer's representative for seven years, and worked briefly in local real estate. At the beginning of 1980 he started his own business, contracting the installation of office openplan workstations and systems - he continues in this business today.

Dave and Pat have been moderately active and interested in many local organizations: Lion's Club, Historical Society, Friends of the Library, Humane Society, DAR, local politics, and the Episcopal Church. Their son Stefan B. Stackhouse completed his education while living in Brown County; he received his BS and MBA from Indiana University. After graduation he operated the Film Shack in downtown Nashville for one season. Dave and Pat established the H. & R. Block office in Nashville and Stefan also ran that for a year. Stefan and Eunice Wonderly were married at Warsaw, IN in 1978. He subsequently worked in State government for a number of years before going to Minnesota where he was Vice President of Administration for the Minneapolis College of Art and Design. Presently he is Dean of Finance and Operations for Hutchinson Community College, Hutchinson, KS.

Dave and Pat are looking forward to retirement in the not too distant future, and hope to become more active in promoting Brown County interests. *Submitted by Dave and Pat Stackhouse*

WILLIAM STEEL FAMILY

William was born 1801 in Maryland. His wife was Mariah Woodford born 1808 in Virginia. The Somerset Township, Belmont Co., OH, 1850, Census lists them with the following children: Mary, age 15 years, John J., 13 years, Samuel, age 11, J. William, nine years, Lydia, age six years, Maria, four years, Thomas, age three years, and Moses Peter, born in 1850.

William and his family migrated to Jackson Township, Brown Co., IN about the year of or before 1861. Four sons, John J., Samuel, J. William, and Thomas served in the Civil War, Co. I, 63rd Indiana Infantry.

Son, John J. Steel, born Feb. 5, 1836, married Sarah Cain on Jan. 1, 1862 in Brown Co., IN. They had a daughter, Sarah E. A son, Otis D. 1874-1881 and a daughter, Effie Agnes were born of a later marriage to Rebecca Barnes Sisson.

Son, Samuel J. Steel, born 1839, married Lucinda Baker, daughter of James A. and Elizabeth Baker, on Sept. 9, 1866, in Brown Co., IN. Four children were born to this union — William J., Florence J., Elizabeth M., and Charles E.

Son, James William Steel, born Jan. 8, 1841, married Catherine Norman, daughter of Joseph T. and Elizabeth Williams Norman, on Dec. 10, 1878, in Morgan Co., IN. They resided in Jackson Township, Brown County and had three sons and two daughters: Scott, Oscar L., Edgar D., Lillie Odessa, and Emma Caroline.

Son, Thomas Steel, born 1847, married Lydia Anna Sisson, on Sept. 17, 1874. Three children were born to this union: William Alonzo, James Walter, and Amanda Arena Steel. He was later married to Lavinna C. Jackson.

Son, Moses Peter Steel, born April 4, 1850, married Mary Catherine Stump, daughter of William and Araminta Abbey Stump, on April 5, 1877 at her father's home in Brown Co., IN. They had four children: Bertha Ione, William Oliver, Araminta Mariah, and Rosa Fern.

William Steel died 1870 in Brown County and is buried in Myers Cemetery with his wife, Mariah. Sons, John J. and James William are buried in the Oakridge Cemetery in Jackson Township, Brown County, and son, Thomas, is buried in the Carmel Ridge Cemetery, Jackson Township, Brown Co., IN.

MARY ELLEN STEELE FAMILY

Mary Ellen was born Dec. 14, 1917 and married Glenn O. Roberts (1911-1989). They were married June 24, 1933. Her parents were Clifford Steele (1883-1934) and Minnie LaVina (Wright) Steele (1885-1974). They were married in 1904. Clifford was born on his father's farm on Green Valley Road (also called Hoover Road) in Brown County. He was the only son of Eugenius Steele. They settled on his father's home place which they purchased in 1917. They had eight children: (1) Carmen Lovetta (1904-1974), (2) Lucille Pauline (1905), (3) Lee Oral (1912), (4) Hazel Lourine (1916), (5) Mary Ellen (1917), (6) Thomas Allen (1919), (7) Mabel Nadine (1922), (8) Dorothy Mae (1924). A few years after Clifford's death, Vina married A.B. Harrison and moved to Amity. She sold the farm to her daughter and son-in-law Glenn and Mary (Steele) Roberts in 1945.

Mary's grandfather Eugenius Steele (1835-1918) was born in Taylor Co., WV, the fourth son of Thomas. Before moving to Brown County with his father and family he married Margaret Dillon who died in 1878. In 1880 he married Lydia Cunningham of Taylorsville, she died in 1898. He continued on the old home place until his death in 1918. (This farm was purchased in 1875 from Squire and Raney West.) He was a member of the Green Valley Methodist Church. He deeded the land in 1915 for the church which reverted back to the farm when the church was moved to North Salem property.

Mary's great-grandfather Thomas Steele (1803-1876). Born in Monongalia Co., WV. The eldest of John, his family moved to Brown County in 1865, a year later he moved to Taylorsville, there he was elected Justice of the Peace in Bartholomew County he served this office the remainder of his life.

Back: Carmen and Lucille Steele. Front: Clifford, Hazel, Lee, Mary Ellen and Minnie LaVina Steele.

Mary's great-great-grandfather John Steele (1776-1821). Born in Brownsville, PA, the eldest son of James Sr. John served as a Private in Captain Samuel Kennedy's Company in the war of 1812 and the hardships of that war left him crippled and emaciated for life.

Mary's great-great-great-grandfather was James Steele, Sr. (1732-1840) and is the earliest paternal ancestor. He was born in Ireland of Scotch-Irish parents. He came to America on a boat as a stowaway at 18 years of age. After landing in America he was bound out to a hat maker in Philadelphia, PA, and later opened his own hat shop in Pittsburgh. The family moved to Monongalia Co., WV in 1788. He lived to be 108 years old, but at the age of 81 he quit having birthdays and claimed to be 81 until his death. Age 81 is engraved on his monument.

Mary (Steele) and Glenn Roberts had five children: (1) Thomas Leon (1934), (2) Janet Rosalyn (1935), (3) Jackie Glenn (1936), (4) Anita Melvina (1938), (5) Lois Ann (1941).

They were married 56 years. Mary still resides on the family farm on Green Valley Rd. (Hoover Rd.). They attended North Salem United Methodist on Highway 46 and they were very actively involved since the early 50s and Mary and her family still attend there today. *Submitted by Anita Pope and Janet Taggart*

THEODORE C. AND SELMA N. STEELE
- Theodore Clement, eldest of five sons of Samuel and Harriet Steele was born in Owen County in 1847. His great-grandfather, Ninian Steele, had moved to Indiana territory from Chester Co., PA. Samuel Steele's parents, James Armstrong and Anna Johnston Steele, settled in Waveland, IN in southeastern Montgomery County in 1852. Samuel and Harriet also moved their family to Waveland so that T.C. Steele could have an education at Waveland Academy. By the time Steele was 21, he made his living painting portraits. He married Mary Elizabeth Lakin, known as Libbie, on Valentine's Day in 1870.

Fulfilling his life-long dream to study abroad, T.C. Steele convinced 13 Indianapolis businessmen to sponsor his art career. In 1880 he took his wife and three young children to Munich, Germany where he studied at the Royal Academy of Art for five years. Upon his return he lived predominantly in Indianapolis and painted portraits for a living. He also traveled the countryside painting landscapes in warmer weather.

Large Studio of T.C. Steele

The Indianapolis Art Association had an exhibition of paintings by Steele, William Forsythe, R.B. Gruelle, Otto Stark, and J. Ottis Adams in 1895, which was later sent to Chicago. The work was highly praised and the Artists were coined "The Hoosier Group." In 1897 Steele moved his family to Metamora to concentrate on his landscape painting. Two years later his wife, Libbie, died of tuberculosis.

The artist first visited Brown County in 1905. He fell in love with the area for its rugged beauty and captivating scenery. He purchased 211 acres on which to build a studio home one and one-half miles south of Belmont. On Aug. 9, 1907 he married Selma Neubacher and brought her to his newly built home. Selma had been assistant superintendent of art in the Indianapolis public school system. Her parents, who were Austrian, had settled in Cincinnati before moving to Indianapolis.

Although a distance from Nashville, Steele influenced an influx of artists to the Brown County area. In the worst months of the winter the Steeles would return to the city. Their cherished "House of the Singing Winds" was expanded in 1908. The largest studio in the midwest was completed in 1916 and visitors from near and far enjoyed the Steele's hospitality. Steele became an artist in residence at Indiana University in Bloomington the last four years of his life. He died in 1926 a respected and influential artist.

Selma Steele, an avid gardener, continued to live in Brown County for 20 more years. She gave the entire estate to the state of Indiana in 1945, a year before her death.

THOMAS ALLEN AND EDNA MAE (OLMSTED) STEELE
- From Ireland and Scotland to Philadelphia, PA, by way of Brownsville, PA, Monongahela River, Morgantown, WV, the Steeles came to Brown County and Bartholomew Co., IN in 1865.

Thomas Allen Steele, Scotch-Irish, Asbury Methodist, Democrat, Blue Lodge Mason, 32nd Mason, and Shriner was born in Brown County July 26, 1919 in the house where his father, six sisters, and one brother were also born. Eugenius Steele, grandfather of Thomas, settled in Brown Co., IN on 200 acres in 1865. Mary Ellen is Thos. Allen's younger sister. Mary Ellen (Steele) Roberts, owns and still lives there. Thomas was the sixth child of Clifford Lee and Minnie Lavina (Wright) Steele. Clifford - born in Brown County July 18, 1882; died Jan. 23, 1934. Vina (LaVina, Louvina) - born in Brown County Aug. 21, 1885; died July 11, 1973. Thomas's education: Nashville High and several trade schools; worked for Arvin Industry as Master Tool and Diemaker for 42 years. July 11, 1941 Thomas married Edna Mae Olmsted at the home of Rev. Clarence Davis. Edna, born June 19, 1923 in Brown County the seventh child of Hallie Elsworth Olmsted born in Bartholomew County April 20, 1887, (on his tombstone,) birth certificate says April 25, 1888, died Feb. 11, 1955, mother was Alverna (Taylor) Olmsted born in Brown County Nov. 10, 1890; died March 18, 1958. Alverna's great-great-grandfather, Robert Henderson settled in Brown County in 1829. The Taylors also settled in Brown County at a very early date.

Edna and Thomas Steele

Thomas was inducted into the Army Dec. 1, 1943 at Indianapolis and went to Fort Thomas, OH and then took basic at Flora, MS as an Ordnance Tech., served in European Theater 3044 Ordnance until being discharged at Camp Atterbury, Johnson Co., IN Jan. 26, 1946. Medals: Good Conduct, Marksmanship, four Bronze Stars and etc. Thomas and Edna Steele's children: Stephen Allen Steele born in Bartholomew Co., IN on Aug. 20, 1944. Graduated from Columbus North High and received a degree in Philosophy from Indiana University. Stephen enlisted in the Army Sept. 1, 1966 - Aug. 31, 1970. Service School at Fort Bliss, TX November 1966-November 1967. Language-Vietnamese. Service School Goodfellow Air Force Base, Texas, December 1967-February 1968. Voice Interceptor Operator. Vietnam Services: March 22, 1968-March 20, 1969. National Defense Service Medal, Vietnam Service Medal, Campaign Medal, w/60 Service: two-0/8 Bars, Good Conduct Medal, Marksman Badge, Rifle M14 Medal. After service he received two Master Degrees; Foreign Languages and Foreign Marketing and Business from University of Texas in El Paso. Steve lives in Pocatello, ID with his wife, Barbara Jane (Norris) Steele. Very active in community affairs and owns Mutual Business Realty and Mutual Insurance.

Randall Thomas Steele was born in Bartholomew Co., IN Dec. 2, 1947, graduated from Columbus North High and attended Indiana State College, Terre Haute, IN, enlisted in the Marines Dec. 3, 1969 and discharged Dec. 2, 1971. Stationed at San Diego, CA. Randall married Peggy Ann Gunning Jan. 15, 1971 in St. Francis Catholic Church in Vista, CA. Peggy is the daughter of Kenneth Eugene and Marion Francis Davis Gunning. Randall and Peggy's children are: Kendra Kathleen Steele, born Nov. 22, 1975 and Michael Thomas Steele, born Oct. 7, 1978. Randall works for the Postal Service and Peggy works in a doctor's office. They live in Columbus, IN. *Submitted by Thomas A. Steele*

STEININGER FAMILY
- Dwight and May Steininger brought their family of three children, Donna, Bill, and Connie, to Nashville in the summer of 1955. Dwight was born in Logansport, IN, July 26, 1910, to Forest and Viola Lusher Steininger. He is the oldest of seven children: six boys and one girl. His parents left to their family the legacy of a true Christian example, vital spiritual training, and moral discipline, which their children considered to be an inheritance far greater than any earthly possession they could have left.

May was born in Logansport, Feb. 22, 1912, to Albert and Grace Cline Meinert. Her father came to the United States from Austria in the year of 1885 at the age of 17. He brought with him his most treasured Bakemaster's certificate, which introduced him to his life-long occupation as a baker in Chicago, and later in Logansport, IN.

Dwight and May Steininger

Dwight's great-grandparents, Ruben and Sophie Steininger, migrated from Holland to Lancaster, PA, about 1830, and from there to the Whipporwill community near Rochester, IN, where they raised their family of six children, one of whom was Dwight's grandfather, Howard Steininger.

After what Steininger calls his "four black years of wild life" he hit bottom on Dec. 8, 1929. It was then, at the age of 19, that his life was totally turned around. That was when he accepted Jesus Christ as his Savior and Lord. Seven months later he recognized his talent in art, which has been a part of his life ever since. In the summer of 1931 he felt his call to the Christian ministry, in which he and his wife spent 45 years, until they retired from full-time ministerial work in 1975.

Dwight and May began their ministry in Logansport, IN, during the heart of the Great Depression. Their weekly salary the first year, including their parsonage, was $3.50. They spent 28 years in the field of chalk-artist evangelism, and 17 years in pastorates in Indiana, Oregon, Jamaica, and Pennsylvania. They organized 18 Nazarene churches during the first three years of their ministry, and three more later. Mrs. Steininger served as an accomplished pianist throughout the years of their ministry. Mr. Steininger estimates that he has drawn about 10,000 colored chalk drawings in the 850 evangelistic campaigns he has conducted in many parts of the United States.

Dwight has painted nearly 4,000 oil paintings, both large and small. He has taught at least 800 art students in his two-day workshops in Brown County and many other places, and he has given about 200 art demonstrations. He became a member of the Brown County Art Gallery in the summer of 1956, and served about 14 years on the executive board, and two years as president.

Mr. Steininger has been a member of the Brown County Ministerial Fellowship over 13 years and was the president two years. He has also served on the board of the Brown County Convention and Visitors Bureau, the Brown County Area Eleven Agency on Aging, and is currently serving on the board of the Brown County Habitat for Humanity. He has also served as chaplain of the local jail most of the time since 1976.

Donna Steininger married Lloyd Sisson. To Dwight and May Steininger were born three children: Donna, Bill and Connie. Donna Steininger married Lloyd Sisson. To their union were born five children: Thomas Dwight (stillborn), Janet, Gary, Roger and Donnie. Janet has a son David Benjamin. To Gary and Misty were born Tyler and Kimber. To Bill and Judith were born three children, Bradley, Barbara and Karen. Bradley married Wanda Gorden and Karen married Dan Randall.

WADE ALLEN STEVENS - Born March 17, 1905 in Monroe Co., IN, a son of Andrew Stevens and Laura Pogue Stevens. Laura was buried at Brummett's Cemetery in Monroe Co., IN after her death on Dec. 2, 1932. Andrew Stevens was buried at the same cemetery as his wife following his death Feb. 12, 1936. Andrew's grandson, Donald James Stevens, says that his grandfather was the son of Hugh Stevens. Wade A. Stevens had the following siblings: Homer who married a Brock; Wavel (female) whose second husband was Elmer Bell; Goldie who married Aug. 26, 1916 in Brown Co., IN to William Owens (son of James S. and Dora A. Henthorn Owens); Fawn (male) who married Edna Pogue (daughter of Charlie Pogue and a relative of Laura Pogue Stevens); Harold who married Zetta Sewal; Maurice who married Ruth Owens (daughter of James S. and Dora A. Henthorn Stevens); and Alice who married Austin Crane.

On Feb. 6, 1924 in Nashville, IN Wade A. Stevens married Pearl Elizabeth Owens, daughter of James Stevenson Owens and Dora Alice Henthorn. Wade and Pearl Stevens had the following children: Ernest McClellan born June 1, 1925 in Brown Co., IN who married Emogene Wrightsman; Ruth Naomi born May 10, 1926 who married Grover Percifield; and Donald James born Sept. 23, 1931 who married Betty Stone. Wade Allen Stevens died June 1, 1957 in Columbus, IN and is buried at Duncan Cemetery in Brown Co., IN. His widow, Pearl Elizabeth, remarried Feb. 28, 1958 to Paul Nugent who died Jan. 19, 1981. *Submitted by Pearl Nugent*

STEWART - FULTON FAMILY - It is understandable that Michael Fulton has chosen the Hills 'o Brown as home. Hill Country, the Black Hills of South Dakota, and Indiana are a part of his heritage.

About 1899 Willis Carlton and Nellie (Farnham) Spindler moved from Edgerton, OH to Deadwood, SD. The Spindlers had four children, Wanda, Mildred, Helen, Carl, and Mae - born May 2, 1905. Gordon Fulton, also of Deadwood, married Mae "Mitzie" Spindler in 1928. They had one son, Robert Theodore; born Oct. 10, 1930. Gordon drowned in a boating accident in 1938 and Mitzie married Paul Guiser, originally of Richmond, IN, and moved to his homestead near Martin, SD. As of this writing, Grandpa Guiser has harvested his 62nd wheat crop.

Robert returned home, to the Black Hills, where he married Joanne Seeley of Spearfish - daughter of Kenneth Mayne Seeley and Edna (Gemmill) Seeley. They raised four sons: Kenneth Gordon, Michael Paul, Bret Robert, and Scott Brian. Michael was born Oct. 16, 1954 in Washington D.C. at the Walter Reed Army Hospital at a total cost of $1.75.

Michael Paul Fulton, Judith Ann Stewart - 1990

The Fultons returned to Indiana in 1959 where Robert completed his PhD at Purdue University. Upon graduation, Dr. Fulton became a director at the State Hospital for Retarded Children in Fort Wayne, IN. Michael completed elementary school in Ft. Wayne, before moving to Southeast Kansas. Michael graduated from Parsons, KS Senior High School and then graduated from the University of Kansas in 1977. Michael returned to KU and earned his Masters of Business Administration (MBA) - Finance in 1981. He moved to Indianapolis, IN in 1983. There he met his wife, Judith Ann Stewart, and with their mutual love for one another and nature they moved to Brown Co., IN in 1986.

Judy Stewart's love of nature and devotion to family come from her roots. Her grandfather, Charles Anderson Griffith, was born in Anderson, IN in 1892. An automotive engineer, he also served as a U.S. Marine from 1913-1915 in Mexico with the American Expeditionary Forces and in Air Force Intelligence during World War II, receiving the Commendation of Meritorious Service, the highest honor a civilian governmental employee can receive. In 1920, he married Hester Oral Swift who was born in Yorktown, IN in 1901. Hester and Charles had one daughter, Betty Jeanne, born in Muncie, IN in 1921. Following her graduation from Indiana University in 1945, Jeanne married Robert Herman Stewart. In 1946 they moved to the Stewart farm near Darlington, IN where Robert's family held the original land grant. Jeanne worked for the Air Force during World War II and later became a legal secretary and then an executive secretary with Union Carbide Corporation. Robert and Jeanne had two daughters: Nancy Jean, born Dec. 18, 1955 and Judith Ann, born Sept. 22, 1954. Both were born in Lebanon, IN. In 1959, Jeanne Stewart with Hester and Charles Griffith moved to Speedway, IN where Nancy and Judy were raised. Judy became an attorney, obtaining her B.A. from Butler University in 1979 and her Doctor of Jurisprudence from Indiana University School of Law at Indianapolis in 1982. In 1988 Judy was appointed Brown County Circuit Court Referee and was elected Brown County Circuit Court Judge in 1990.

As of the time of this writing, Hester Griffith, who has been the mainstay of this family for 70 years, and Jeanne Stewart still live in Speedway. Charles Griffith died in 1985. Nancy, an avid naturalist and conservationist, lives in Owen Co., IN and works at Union Carbide Corporation. *Submitted by Michael Fulton and Judith Stewart*

ROSS STIGDON - A lifetime dream was realized for Ross Stigdon when he bought his 40 acre farm in Brown County in 1966. He was raised on a farm and learned to appreciate that lifestyle.

He was born Sept. 9, 1904 in Geneva Township of Jennings Co., IN. His father, George William Stigdon was born Oct. 4, 1874 and died March 23, 1952. His mother, the former Charity Vanmeter was born Sept. 10, 1882 and died Jan. 13, 1970. The ten other children born in this family were Ruby Mae, born Aug. 8, 1902; Mary Elizabeth, born Aug. 20, 1906; Mildred, born Feb. 25, 1908; Harry Gordon, born Feb. 19, 1910; Dorothy Lucille, born Nov. 3, 1911; Walter "Doc", born April 6, 1913; Elmer Curtis, born Jan. 31, 1915; Oscar Lenuel, born Nov. 13, 1916; Hazel Pearl, born Oct. 19, 1919; and Geneva Fern, born May 27, 1925.

Ross Stigdon, 1987

Ross learned many of the skills of carpentry from his Father and his Grandfather, Thomas Jefferson Vanmeter, but he did not pursue that career. Instead, he did factory work to support his family. He was married March 14, 1925 at Jeffersonville, IN to Doris Mellencamp, daughter of Louis Herman and Dolly (Abell) Mellencamp. She was born in Jackson Co., IN Oct. 26, 1909. To this union were born six children: Betty Allene, born Feb. 22, 1927; Charlotte Mae, born Nov. 17, 1928; Margaret Elaine, born Nov. 11, 1930; Donna LaVerne, born May 30, 1934; Sharon Lynne, born July 28, 1941; and Louis William, born June 5, 1943. This family lived in Jackson Co., IN.

The last job Ross had was at Cummins Engine Company in Columbus, IN where he worked for 14 years, then he retired in 1970. Finally he thought he could really enjoy his farm. He raised chickens and a large garden, always having enough to give to his children and friends. His wife enjoyed the country living too and busied herself with making quilts and crocheting rugs, but her diabetic condition left her partially disabled. She died Jan. 30, 1974 and is buried at Riverview Cemetery in Seymour, IN.

Ross stayed on at his Brown County farm until his vision started to fail and it was no longer safe for him to drive a car. It was a tough decision, but he sold his farm and moved back to Seymour, IN in 1987.

Now as his 86th birthday approaches, he has many memories to keep him amused. His grandfather, Philip Stigdon emigrated from Germany in 1854 and was married to Elizabeth Clapp. His maternal grandmother was the former Harriet Miller and no memories are so precious as the ones about visiting at Grandma's house. *Submitted by his daughter, Betty Bullard*

HARRISON STIVERS - Harrison Arthur was born Dec. 24, 1812 in Kentucky and married Esther Richards (born 1815, Tennessee) around 1835. Harrison was in Brown Co., IN by at least 1843 but around 1847 he and his family migrated to Jasper Co., IL with the George Grove family. By 1860, Harrison was back in Brown County, although he died and was buried in Jasper County in 1870. Harrison and Esther's children were: Mary (born 1837), Ann (born 1839), John William (born 1840, married to Eliza Martin), Martha (born 1842), George W. (born 1844), Lucinda (born 1846), Granville (born 1849, married to Catherine Holm). *Submitted by Randall Grove*

STOGDILL - Samuel Stogdill (ca. 1767-1836) married Martha Elkins (ca. 1781-1854) in Clark Co., KY in 1799. Martha was the daughter of Drury and Margaret Elkins. The Stogdills and Elkins were from Virginia and lived in Kentucky before moving to Indiana around 1820.

Samuel and Martha Stogdill's children were: Mary; Polly married Daniel Nix; Drury married Martha Acton; Nellie married Hiram Collier; Margaret married James Acton; William Sherman married Mariah Elkins; Thomas married Margaret Shortridge; and Rebecca married Thomas Elkins.

William Sherman Stogdill, son of Samuel and Martha Stogdill, was born Aug. 18, 1809 and died in 1890. He married Mariah Elkins, daughter of William and Rhoda Stephens Elkins. Mariah was born ca. 1818 and died in 1906. Their children were: Sarah married Richard Collier; Nancy married James Weatherman; William married Mary Ann Davis; Margaret married James George; Rebecca; Martha married John Elkins; Iva; James Harvey married Amanda Sipes and second Mary Nilson; Francis Marion married Elizabeth Crider, second Amanda Greenlee and third Matilda Bush; Clarena married Gabriel Aynes; Muhulda married William Riley Wilkerson.

Front: Mary Stogdill Whitehorn, Emma Stogdill Eddy, Ethel Stogdill Davis. Back: Bramble Stogdill, Walter Stogdill, William Sherman Stogdill.

James Harvey Stogdill, son of William Sherman and Mariah Stogdill (Jan. 7, 1850-Dec. 19, 1925). He married Amanda Sipes, daughter of Singleton and Mary Jane Lutes Sipes on Dec. 7, 1873. Amanda (March 18, 1857-March 7, 1899). Their children were: William Sherman married Lula Nilson; Mary Etta married Noah Whitehorn; Phoebe Jane married James Pruitt; Jesse married Mary Ida Combs; Margaret Emma married Walter Eddy; Walter married Anna Hedrick, second Mildred Bennett, third Clara Wilkerson and fourth Mary Gillman; Ethel married Clyde Davis; Bramble married Iva Vaught, second Gertrude Beavers, third Lilly Haynes and fourth Emma Zenter.

William Sherman Stogdill, son of James Harvey and Amanda Stogdill, was born Oct. 28, 1874 and died Oct. 18, 1953. He married Lula May Nilson, daughter of John and Mary Ann Deckard Nilson. Lula was born Dec. 10, 1884 and died Jan. 15, 1949. Their children were: Otto married Beulah Wooten; Dorothy married Herschel Stines; Cecil married Ola Todd and second Emma Adams; Brady married Erma Carothers; Kathryn May married Albert Cross; Fairney married Earl Bowman, Frona married Bill Bruce; Lucy married Glen Hanner; Lester, Mary Edith, and Alvina Fern.

Kathryn May Stogdill, daughter of William Sherman and Lula Stogdill, was born Sept. 3, 1910 and died May 10, 1984. She married Albert Henry Cross, son of Jacob and Peony Langley Cross. Albert was born Aug. 2, 1894 and died Feb. 10, 1978. Kathryn and Albert's children were: Albert W. married Thelma Chambers; Dorothy married Billy D. Lutes; Fred married Virginia Fredericks; Rose married Donald Hatton; Rodney married Janet Manship; Robert married Nancy Burk and second Carol Barnhart; Beverly married Gerald Sample; Alberta married Samuel Etienne and second Larry McConnell; Linda married Gerald Baxter and second Randy Lane; and Gary Dean Cross who died at birth.

Dorothy L. Cross, daughter of Kathryn and Albert Cross, was born Nov. 1, 1933. She married Billy D. Lutes, son of Francis and Vivian Moore Lutes, on Oct. 19, 1953. Billy was born May 2, 1933. They live in Brown County. Their children are - Valerie Ann Holbrook born Oct. 31, 1956, Cynthia Sue Mood born Jan. 10, 1959, Julie Kay born Nov. 7, 1961, Betsy Jo born March 5, 1963, Suzanne born April 14, 1964, and Jennifer Lynn born April 6, 1966. Their grandchildren are Aaron Lee and Jason Michael Holbrook. *Submitted by Dorothy Lutes*

JULIA ROSS STOOPS - Julia, born April 30, 1935, was the fourth child of Dr. Ben R. Ross and Julia (Hepburn) Ross of Bloomington, IN. She has three brothers: Henry, Donal, and James. Julia grew up on her family's small farm north of Bloomington. She attended University School from first grade through the 12th, graduating in 1953. Then she went to Hanover College in Hanover, IN for two years. It was there she met and married James A. Stoops from Indianapolis. They became parents of five children: Katherine A., James D., Robert B., Mark A. and Tammy Stoops (Tjardes). The family lived in Hanover, and Bloomington, IN, Pittsburgh, PA, and Crown Point, IN.

While living in Crown Point for 30 years raising her family, Julia became very active in the 4-H program as a superintendent and project leader for the Dairy Goats, Dogs and Veterinary Science projects. She also spent many years working with other youth organizations and schools with programs for Humane Education.

In May of 1990, Julia returned to southern Indiana and the hills she loved so much. She bought an old log cabin with five acres on Plum Creek Road in Brown County. Now that she is closer to some of the family, she is able to see them more often and finds special enjoyment in visits from her two granddaughters: Leslie Stoops, born Jan. 7, 1980 (Robert's daughter) and Rebecca Stoops, born Jan. 17, 1990 (Mark's and Gillian's daughter).

Here she plans to spend her remaining years visiting family and friends, taking care of her menagerie of assorted critters and enjoying the uniqueness of Brown Co., IN.

STORY FAMILY - Dr. George P. Story married Catharine Shelenburger in Muskingum Co., OH, August 1833. On July 1835 David Shelenburger Story was born in Perry Co., OH. Dr. Story married Jane Morrison March 1839 after Catharine died, perhaps in childbirth. Enoch and George A. were born February 1840 and July 1845.

Dr. Story moved his family to Van Buren Township on land granted him in 1851 that was to be known as Storyville and now as Story. He served Brown County as a member of the Medical Association from 1881 through 1883 and as a committee member to provide relief and funds to Civil War families in 1861.

Four oldest children of David S. and Cordelia (Wadsworth) Story: Clara, Enoch Sylvester, Cyrus and Ella Story, 1918 (all born in Brown Co., IN).

David S. was school examiner and surveyor prior to joining the Indiana Volunteer Infantry Company H 82nd Regiment, August 1862. He had married Cordelia, daughter of John and Mariah (Hilt) Wadsworth, September 1856. She awaited his return from war in June 1865 with their children: Cyrus Leandander (October 1857-October 1920); Jane C. (November 1859-July 1965); and Enoch Sylvester (February 1862-March 1928). Clara Winifred (July 1866-?); Rosalie (July 1868-December 1905); Ella Orena (April 1873-?); David Robert (July 1875-July 1875); and Olive Mae (May 1878-?) were all born before the family moved to Kansas where Johny Urbin (February 1882-May 1882) was born.

Enoch married Sabra S., daughter of Philip S. and Sarah A. Brown Petro, June 1865. Cordelia (1866-?), an infant son (died 1872) and Mandy G. (1868-?) were born prior to their move to Kansas where Meda I. (January 1884) and Gracie M. (December 1886) were born. Enoch was living in McDonald Co., MO in 1906.

George A. married Mariah Wadsworth, Cordelia's sister, November 1861. David W. (November 1862-June 1865); Martha (ca. 1866-?) and Flora B. (April 1867-?) were all born before they moved to Kansas where Albert A. (November 1886-?) and Bessie W. (May 1887-?) were born. George and Mariah were in Butler Co., KS in 1910.

Dr. Story married Mrs. Sandusky Percifield after Jane Morrison died November 1872. The Indiana property was sold to John Noblet March 1882.

Emory Grant (March 1887-November 1964) and

Earston Ver (May 1888-1972) were born to Enoch Sylvester and Eva Mae Nicholson Story in Scott Co., KS. Edwin Guy (February 1891-April 1942) was born in Saint Joseph, MO. Most of the David S. Story family remained in Missouri when about 1898 Enoch S. moved his family to Claremore, OK where he owned a laundry.

Descendants of this early Van Buren Township family live throughout the U.S. today. *Submitted by Natalie Miller Orozco*

LAWRENCE AND MARGARET STRAHL

Lawrence "Jack" was born, June 4, 1908, on the site of Jimmy Strahl Lake in Brown County State Park which was named after his father, James W. Strahl, who was also born on the same site on Feb. 16, 1875, the son of Martin and Mary Reed Strahl. His mother was Minnie A. Skinner who was born April 6, 1877 on Skinner Creek in Brown County State Park, the daughter of John and Melissa Glines Skinner.

Lawrence and Margaret Strahl at their 50th Wedding Anniversary

Lawrence married Margaret Littiken, who was born Feb. 20, 1912 in Bartholomew County, on Feb. 21, 1930 in Bartholomew County. Until 1947 they lived on the Littiken homestead in Ohio Township, Bartholomew County. From 1947 to the present they have lived near Ohio Chapel Church. Margaret died Aug. 10, 1989. Their children are: Minnie (born April 10, 1931; died April 22, 1931), Esther (born Feb. 21, 1932), Mary (born May 22, 1933), Lucille (Jan. 9, 1935), Robert (born May 19, 1937), Alice (born April 28, 1939), William (born April 21, 1941), Nellie (born Sept. 18, 1944).

Esther married Robert Settle and they have sons, Randall and Gary, and daughter Jeanette; Mary married Wilbert Lovins and they have a daughter, Sharon; Lucille married Gordon Huckaby and they have sons, Joe, Eric, Theo and daughter Geth; Robert married Joan Newland and they had sons, Michael, Tony, and Darrell (divorced) married Judy Baxter, 1988; Alice married Edward Settle and they had sons, Daniel and Leonard, and daughter Camilla; William married Phyllis Crider and they had sons David, Jeffery and Brian (divorced) married Sandra Simpson; Nellie married Ronald Hill and they had sons Quent and Travis and daughter Ellen (divorced).

Lawrence had brothers Otto and Louie, and sisters Dollie Sinn, Annetta Poffenberger and Grace Adams. Lawrence recalls how he and his father made a dry kiln for drying peaches and apples. They split a hollow beech log which was about eight or ten feet long, laid the two pieces side by side, covered them with clay, placed a chimney at one end and built a fire to burn out the logs. The clay hardened to form two ridges on which the apple and peach slices were placed. A low fire was maintained to keep the kiln surface warm and the kiln was enclosed with screen to keep out the flies. The dried fruit was placed in sacks for storage in the attic. The dried fruit had to be heated periodically in the oven of the wood stove to keep it from getting wormy.

Lawrence's parents were neighbors of James and Mary Hamblen and he recalls as a youngster helping Mary load the crossties which she hauled to Gnaw Bone by muleteam.

Lawrence and his family have been largely responsible for the care of Mt. Zion Cemetery since 1973. Lawrence helped dig approximately 50 graves in Mt. Zion. He attended school at Kelp.

CHRISTOPHER FREDERICK STUMP FAMILY

Christopher was born in 1790 in Frederick Co., MD. CA 1820 he moved to Greenup, KY where he married Catherine Dommet, daughter of Robert Dommet, on Oct. 6, 1821. Their first two children, George and Elizabeth, were born in Greenup.

George Abraham Stump, born June 21, 1825, married Minerva Huff, daughter of James M. Huff, born ca. 1806 in Overton, KY, and Eleanor "Ally" Brummett, born ca. 1808 in Kentucky, in Brown County April 11, 1846. George died in Moline (Elk County) KS July 5, 1906. James M. Huff was one of the original people who gave land for the Brown County Courthouse in Nashville.

Elizabeth Stump, born Feb. 2, 1827, died Feb. 17, 1896, married Josephus Geary in 1853 and had a son, William. She married Lewis Fritch in 1858 and had seven children: Catherine A., Nancy E., Christopher, Frederick, Isaac M., Mary and Martha A. She is buried in Needmore Cemetery.

In 1828 Christopher and Catherine came to Brown Co., IN with George and Elizabeth. Christopher, Jr., born Oct. 14, 1828 in Brown County, married Millie Elizabeth Bush, born Dec. 16, 1840, on July 18, 1860. He died Oct. 11, 1893 and she died Aug. 24, 1912. Both are buried in Lanam Ridge Cemetery.

Sarah Jane (Polly) Stump, born 1831, married John Dover April 13, 1848 and died before 1860. Their daughter, Catherine Dover, married first a Chitwood and then William Brummett, son of Joab and Sarah (Sally) Brummett. William was first married to Sarah Jane Huff, daughter of James M. Huff and Ally Brummett and sister to Minerva Huff Stump.

William Stump was born Dec. 18, 1832 and married Araminta Abbey March 20, 1859. He died Aug. 21, 1911 in Brown County.

Isaiah Stump was born 1836 and married Rebecca E. Baker July 17, 1859. He died ca. 1865 and she remarried to John P. Britton Nov. 4, 1866.

Abraham Stump was born 1838, married Abigail McGlaughlin June 17, 1860 and died ca. 1891 in Brown County.

James Stump was born in 1841 and in 1860 was living in Vigo Co., IN.

Nancy C. Stump, born March 4, 1843, married March 4, 1863 and died before 1882 in Brown County.

Isaac Stump, born May 17, 1847, married Elizabeth Brummett, daughter of Joab and Sarah (Sally) Brummett, Sept. 8, 1867. He died July 27, 1877 and is buried in the Fleenor Cemetery. Elizabeth married second to George Alltop.

Several of the ten children of Christopher Frederick and Catherine (Dommet) Stump had large families which still live today in and around Brown County. William Peck's great-great-grandfather George Abraham Stump and his wife, Minerva Huff, moved to Elk Co., KS ca. 1870 where they had nine children, one of them being the great-grandmother of William D. Peck, Martha Eleanor Stump who married James Alexander Goodwin. Martha died in Kansas on April 19, 1903. James and Martha's daughter, Treasie Ann Minerva Goodwin McCalla, is William Peck's maternal grandmother.

Christopher Frederick Stump's will was probated in Brown Co., IN on June 19, 1882. He was listed in the 1880 Census as being over 90 years old. His wife Catherine died between 1770 and 1880 and both are buried in Brown County in unmarked graves. Christopher was a life-time farmer in Brown County. *Submitted by great-great-great-grandson, William D. Peck*

WILLIAM STUMP FAMILY

William, son of Christopher F. and Catherine Cusick Stump, was born in Shelby Co., IN, Dec. 18, 1832. Four years later his parents moved to Brown Co., IN (1836), where William grew to childhood and remained until late in life. On March 20, 1858 he was married to Araminta Abbey, daughter of James Pearl and Mary Hobbs Abbey, of the same county. To this union were given three sons and six daughters.

Daughter, Mary Catherine Stump, born Dec. 13, 1860, married Moses Peter Steel April 5, 1877 at her father's home in Brown Co., IN.

Daughter, Elizabeth E. Stump Stewart, passed away at her home at Worthington, IN, Nov. 11, 1893, at the age of 32 years.

Son, Lewis Fredrick Stump, born Aug. 6, 1864, died on Nov. 10, 1915.

Daughter, Nancy Anna Stump, born Aug. 3, 1866, married Mr. Merriman of Morgan Co., IN.

Son, John William Stump, born April 3, 1869, married Lillie Odessa Steel Feb. 3, 1890 in Brown County.

Son, Charles Abraham Stump, born June 12, 1871, married Emma Caroline Steel Oct. 26, 1890 in Brown County. Charles later married Lorena Carter on June 30, 1901.

Daughter, Amanda Adella Stump, born July 30, 1873, married Jefferson S. Gregory on Oct. 15, 1898.

Daughter, Emma Belle Stump, born Dec. 1, 1876, married Scott Crawford on June 6, 1898.

Daughter, Myrtle Augusta Stump, born Aug. 27, 1879 married Jasper Flint, son of Luther and Lucinda Long Flint, on Feb. 24, 1897 in Brown Co., IN.

About the year, 1861, William Stump with his wife united with the Church of Christ at Bean Blossom, being baptized (Helmsburg, IN) by the Rev. David Griffen.

When "Our Union" was threatened with dissolution, William Stump was one of the Boys who stood by the Flag. He entered the Army immediately after the "Fall of Atlanta" and followed Sherman until victory "crowned their efforts" and the Nation was Saved.

While residing in Brown County, William Stump was chosen Justice of the Peace which position he filled for over 14 years. He resigned about the middle of his last term.

It was but a short time after his identification with the Church that he became one of its pillars of support serving constantly as Elder until his removal to Martinsville, IN, which occurred in the spring of 1903. During the remainder of his life, he dwelt on a farm near Martinsville, IN. Being far advanced in years, he lived a comparatively retired, though industrious and useful life until called to that

Rest, which always rewards a life of rich service. He died Aug. 21, 1911, age 78 years, eight months, and three days. Surviving him were his wife and eight children and a host of relatives and friends who mourn the loss of his earthly companionship, but rejoice in the firm conviction that he has been faithful—unto death—therefore there awaits for him a "Crown of Life." (Some of the above is a copy of a letter from the Bible of Lillie Steel Stump.) *Submitted by James and Patricia Horton*

SHANA (ROGERS) SWABB

Shana Rogers was born Oct. 4, 1964 at the Bloomington Hospital. She is the daughter of Jewel Wayne Rogers and Mary Jane Richards. Shana grew up in Trevlac and lived close to her grandmother Gladys Rodgers, her Uncle Ray (Sonny) Rodgers, and her Aunt Becky and her two cousins Lisa and Frankie.

Shana, Jim and Kristy Swabb

When she was a teen-ager she moved to Lick Creek Road to her step-father's farm. Shana graduated from Bean Blossom School and also attended Helmsburg and Brown County High Schools. Through a pen pal booklet she started writing to James Swabb and they were married 1983 and moved to his hometown Williamsport, PA. They now have a four-year old daughter Kristy Noel, born Dec. 22, 1985. They are a cat-loving family and have taken in several. They look forward to the times when they can return to Brown County to visit since it has such a special place in Shana's life. *Submitted by Shana Swabb*

TABOR

Twenty-three families comprised the entire population of what is now Jackson County at the end of the War of 1812.

William Tabor was one family who brought his young son James and adopted children Jesse and Rebecca from Virginia around 1802-1803. James was born in 1802 in Virginia.

Joshua, son of James and Matilda lived near Story, Brown County. Joshua married Martha Elkins, who was called Granny Patsy by the Isaac Tabor family.

Isaac son of Joshua and Martha married Loretta Casandra Carmichael and were parents of four children: Iva Ione, Meta Lavida, Roxie Leota, and John Ross. Isaac Tabor was Treasurer of Brown County around 1898. Isaac moved from Nashville to Van Buren Township, one and one-half miles east of Story, close to the Shiloh Cemetery to a farm known as Brown Farm. Later he was Van Buren Township Trustee and built a new home now owned by Morie Zody and family. There was over 500 acres of land and four families at that time. Now there are nine families living on the property. The new home had carbide lights and eight rooms which included also a pantry and basement.

Isaac Tabor home

Iva Tabor married Charles Ping and are the parents of four children: Fern Ping married Wesley Pruitt; Blanch Ping married Virgil Greathouse; Cladean Ping married Hershel Taylor; Loren Ping married Phyllis Browning.

Meta Tabor married Delbert Read, and are parents of: Floyd Wheeler, Lester and Chester. Lester died at age five. Floyd married Jean ? and Chester married Marguerite Flint.

Roxie Tabor married Ralph McKinney, and are parents of five children: Hesper McKinney married Warren Parson and Bob Head; Eva McKinney married Florin Head; Kenneth McKinney deceased; Scott McKinney married Lucinda ?; Betty McKinney died in a car accident at age ten.

John Ross Tabor married Lena Fleetwood and are parents of five children: Fletcher Tabor married Sarah Spurgeon and are parents of three children; Fletcher Eugene married Sue Weddle and they have two children; Rebecca Sue married Joe Wakefield and they have two children; Ross not married; Russell Tabor married Nadine Clark and then Kathryn Scott; and Dorothy Matt (no children) but has three stepchildren.

Wendell married Jane Persinger and are parents of three children: Teresa J. married Dirk James and have a daughter; Timothy A. married Barbara Spurgeon and have no children; Carrie M. not married.

John Alan married Elizabeth McCoy and are parents of four children: Tracy L. married Don Jenkins and are parents of two children; Sherlyn J. married Michael Ducic and are parents of two children; Evans not married; Forrest married Cindy Gill and are parents of one child.

Thelma G. married Francis Paul Wilkerson and are parents of five children: Paul Eugene married Shirley Ann Carmichael and are parents of three children; Richard Leon married Patricia Kelly and are parents of one child; Myra Kathleen married Jerald Roberts and are parents of two children; Loretta Kay married Michael Wheeler and are parents of two children; Francis Alan married Jackie Louise Little and are parents of two children.

Paul passed away Aug. 21, 1988. Thelma lives in the home near Christiansburg for the last 45 years and is an active member in Christiansburg U.M. Church. Loretta Kay and Francis Alan and families live near Christiansburg and are active in Christiansburg UMC. Paul Eugene and Richard Leon live in Columbus and Myra Kathleen lives in Seymour. *Submitted by Thelma Wilkerson*

EDWIN TAGGART FAMILY

Ed and Vivian Miller Taggart were both born and raised in Brown County. Ed is the son of Keith and Nina Taggart and has one brother, Bruce.

Ed has lived in town nearly all his life. Keith and Nina owned and operated a service station for 50 years next to the Court House, and also owned the Village Motel. Keith moved to Nashville from Bluffton, IN when he was six months old. Nina moved here from Cross Plains. Her father, Herb Miller operated Miller's Drug Store for years where Ed got hooked on chocolate sodas. Since Keith loved horses, Ed had a buggy to ride in the summer, and a sleigh in winter. His dad dressed as Santa and took all the town kids for rides at Christmastime in this quaint little village.

Vivian is the daughter of Frances (Messina) and Louie Miller. Louie was born and lived his entire life in Brown County. Frances moved here from Kankakee, IL, at age 14. Vivian has 12 brothers and sisters, most of them living in this area.

Ed and Vivian graduated in 1952 from the old Nashville High School and were married in 1961. They are parents of David, Janelle and Brian who all graduated from Brown County High School and Olivet Nazarene University in Kankakee, IL. David and his wife Emilie Bassett Taggart have two children, Jori Elizabeth and Corbin Keith, who have moved back to this area from Illinois. Janelle and husband Mark Parker live in Kansas City, and Brian is in Indianapolis at this time.

Ed and Vivian first made their home in a log cabin across from the Golf Course west of town. Then lived in the North House on Van Buren Street before moving to California for two years. Upon their return, they lived on Salt Creek Road for 16 years. They now reside at 176 W. Mound Street on the old horse pasture lots.

Ed had an RCA/Zenith TV Sales and Service business for eight years across from the court house and also operated a Sport Shop for two years.

They are members of Parkview Church of the Nazarene which has been a wonderful, vital part of their lives and the lives of their children. A favorite scripture is found in Matthew "Seek first the kingdom of God and His righteousness, and all things will be added to you." Truly He has blessed our family over and over with many spiritual and physical blessings and gives us peace and joy as we serve Him in beautiful Brown County. *Submitted by Ed and Vivian Taggart*

ARCHIBALD TAYLOR

Archibald, one of 11 children, was born in Harlan Co., KY in 1813. He was the son of William, born ca. 1775 near Tom's Fork, VA and Catherine Taylor. He told of being six years old when his family came through the Cumberland Gap on their way to Brown County.

One of his brothers, William Norman, born July 10, 1802, married Sarah (Hamblen) Barnett who was the youngest daughter of Job Hamblen of Bartholomew County. All the family came from Kentucky together, probably by ox team, since Archibald never did learn to harness a team of horses.

On Jan. 26, 1837, Archibald was united in marriage to Elizabeth King. She was born about 1818 in Kentucky to Daniel and Aberilla King, prominent Brown County citizens. They lived and raised their family in Hamblen Township in the community called "Taylor Holler." Elizabeth was a determined woman, who stood up for her rights. She worked hard weaving all the family clothing from whatever material that was available, even hair.

The Taylors were tall, lank and lean. They had very dark hair and dark eyes. They came to Brown County because wild game was so plentiful. The men farmed and did public work when it was available. In 1836, Archibald, along with two of his brothers, Henry and Thomas, as well as his father, worked on the Old Sparks Ferry Rd. in Brown County.

Elizabeth (King) Taylor

Archibald and Elizabeth were the parents of 12 children: (1) Archibald, born 1838, died young; (2) William T., born 1839, married Margaret Wright, died July 19, 1910; (3) Calvinia "Cal," born 1840, never married; (4) Rachal M., born November 1843, married Dennis Khune; (5) Nancy J., born Dec. 10, 1845, married June 13, 1867 to Alex Pittman, died Feb. 20, 1915; (6) John Wesley, born April 27, 1847, married Jan. 13, 1879 to Lucinda Jane Goble, died May 16, 1921; (7) Isaac Shannon, born 1848, married April 7, 1897 to Nancy Petro; (8) Stewart, born 1852; (9) Sarah A., born 1854, married July 21, 1879 to Fredrick Hartman; (10) Mary Frances, married Feb. 15, 1882 to Willard McKee; (11) James, born June 21, 1858, married April 22, 1888 to Frances Waltz Colford; (12) Michael Peter, born September 1862, married Aug. 28, 1890 to Armilda Lucas, died Feb. 26, 1936. All the children were born in Brown County except Stewart, who was born in Grundy Co., MO.

Archibald was a very religious man and seldom missed a church meeting. He died at the home of his son, John Wesley, on a farm north of Columbus, IN on Nov. 8, 1891. Both he and Elizabeth are buried in the Ohio Ridge Cemetery in Brown County. *Submitted by Mary Welch*

EVERETT LEE AND JEANIE TAYLOR -
Everett, son of John Wesley and Lucinda Jane Goble Taylor, was born Sept. 21, 1885 in Hamblen Township in Brown Co., IN and lived there until he was five years old. He married Jeanie Thompson in Louisville, KY on May 11, 1912. She was born in Bartholomew County on June 5, 1892 to David and Alzora Jane Armstrong Thompson.

Everett Lee and Jeanie Taylor

Everett and Jeanie lived on a farm near Azalia in Bartholomew County. He belonged to the Modern Woodman Lodge of Azalia and the Red Men's Lodge of Elizabethtown. He was a member of the Azalia Friends Church and this is where his family attended services. He was a good neighbor, honest, pleasant, and friendly.

Children of Everett and Jeanie are: (1) Mary, born Jan. 7, 1913, married to Clarence Welch on Feb. 26, 1939, they have three children: Joseph, Janet and Marylynne; (2) Pauline, born Oct. 31, 1917, married Robert Stanfield on Aug. 8, 1937. They have five children: David, Patricia, Bette, Marilyn, and Larry; (3) Alzora Lucinda "Cindy," born Feb. 3, 1919, married Gail Crist on Sept. 20, 1947. They have one child: Richard; (4) Edna, born July 20, 1921, married Harold Vaughn on Jan. 20, 1940. They have four children: Ray, Steven, Christine and Logan; (5) John Everett, born May 20, 1923, married Carol Hall on Dec. 13, 1949. They have three children: Carolyn, John and Everett Lee; (6) Harry Wesley, born Sept. 6, 1927, married to Mary Lou Hawn on June 19, 1948, died Nov. 5, 1984. They have four children: Mary Jean, Patricia, Linda and Harry. All the children were born in Bartholomew County.

Everett died July 4, 1937 in Bartholomew County. Jeanie died Jan. 1, 1967 in Jennings County. She and Everett are buried at Garland Brook Cemetery in Columbus, IN. *Submitted by Marylynne Sharp*

JOHN WESLEY TAYLOR -
Born April 27, 1847 in Brown County to Archibald and Elizabeth (King) Taylor. He grew up in Hamblen Township in a place called "Taylor Holler." He married Lucinda Jane Goble on Jan. 13, 1879. Lucinda was born Oct. 23, 1860 in a covered wagon somewhere in Illinois. She was the daughter of William and Mary Jane Quinn Goble.

John, a tall, thin, dark haired farmer, and Lucinda had some acreage, a one-room house, a good team of mules, and $3,500 saved. In the winter time, they slept in one corner of their house, cooked in another, ate in the third, and the fourth corner was reserved for John's sideline, shaving hoop bands for barrel staves. He took these to Columbus to sell. He was then able to purchase apples and oranges and a gift for each child for Christmas. John made all the shoes for his family. He butchered four or five hogs at a time and Lucinda would cut the liver, heart and sweet bread into small pieces to cook for special treats for her children. They saved all their grease to make lye soap.

John Wesley and Lucinda Goble Taylor

John told of the Ohio Ridge Rd. being so steep that the family always walked behind the buggy while he led the horses, lest the buggy be overturned.

In 1890, the family moved to a farm near Taylorsville in Bartholomew County. John's father, Archibald, died at this home Nov. 8, 1891. Later, the family moved to Hope, and finally to Azalia, IN.

Children of John and Lucinda were: (1) Elizabeth Margaret, born in November 1879, married John Hayes Aug. 31, 1902, died Feb. 29, 1921; (2) William, born April 13, 1883, married Oct. 20, 1906 to Dessie Mourey, died April 24, 1955; (3) Everett Lee, born Sept. 21, 1885, married Feb. 21, 1917 to Jeanie Thompson, died July 4, 1937; (4) Dora Ethel, born Dec. 23, 1888, married Lurid Danforth, married Willis Fox, died Sept. 26, 1958; (5) Otto, born February 1891, married April 7, 1917 to Emma Smith, died 1968; (6) Mary, born Jan. 8, 1895 in Bartholomew County, married Feb. 3, 1917 to Clarence Barker, died March 1, 1986. All the children, except Mary, were born in Brown County.

John Wesley and Lucinda Jane had 23 grandchildren, 21 of these grandchildren lived to adulthood.

John Wesley died May 16, 1921 in Bartholomew County. Lucinda Jane died June 26, 1923 in Bartholomew County. They are both buried at Garland Brook Cemetery in Columbus, IN. *Submitted by Janet Jones*

WILLIAM AND CATHERINE TAYLOR
- As per census, William Taylor was born ca. 1775 in Virginia. He is listed on the tax list of Knox Co., KY 1806 through 1818. He and Thomas are listed with "males over 21" living in the section of Knox County which was set off to form Harlan Co., KY in 1819. From History of Harlan County, KY. "In 1828 William Taylor was County Judge, his wife's name was Catherine." They owned several hundred acres of land, which they started selling in 1825. November 3, 1830 William and Catherine gave power of attorney to Thomas Taylor, their son, to receive their money in Harlan County. After this date, the land sales list William and Catherine (sometimes Caty) of Bartholomew Co., IN with Thomas signing for them.

As per 1884 History of Brown Co., IN, William and sons; Thomas, Henry and Archibald helped build the Old Sparks Ferry Road, from the creek at Owen Simpson's (William's son-in-law) to sections 13 and 14 in 1836. The date for Catherine's death is unknown. The last land record Maradyn Oyler has that she signed was for a land sale in Bartholomew County March 19, 1833. This was probably when they moved to what is now Brown County on the land that was later patented by their son, William Norman Taylor.

In the 1850 Census of Brown County, William is age 75 and living with son, William Norman. Also an Elizabeth Taylor, age 65 whom it is presumed to be his second wife.

Most of the family came to north Missouri about 1840 with the exception of William Norman.

Archibald is in the 1850 Census of Harrison Co., MO, but returned to Brown Co., IN soon after—perhaps when his father died.

There are a few papers, no will, in the Administrative packet of William Taylor estate in Harrison Co., MO dated Aug. 16, 1851.

Thomas Taylor was appointed administrator of the estate of William Taylor, deceased. Due to Thomas from the estate $5 paid Burdine (Taylor, son of Thomas) for moving the deceased from Iowa, $5 for team and wagon for the Iowa trip, $24 for keeping deceased and wife 12 months @ $2, $3 paid James Brown for hauling the deceased to St. Joseph May 2, 1853.

It is presumed William died while visiting his daughters in Iowa and the body was taken back to Brown Co., IN for burial with Catherine. St. Joseph would have been the main shipping point.

Thomas Taylor, Aug. 16, 1851, County of Harrison, State of Missouri, administrator for the estate of William Taylor, deceased, lists the names and residences of the heirs of said estate to the best of my knowledge:

William N. Taylor, Brown Co., IN; Henry Taylor and Archibald Taylor both of Mercer Co., MO; Eliza Simson and Sarah Simson (Simpson) both of Harrison Co., MO; Catherine Rice of the state of Iowa (in 1860 Census Harrison Co., MO); Heirs of John Taylor, deceased, late of Harlan Co., KY; Heirs of James Taylor, deceased, late of Franklin Co., MO; Heirs of May (or Mary), deceased, late of Polk Co., IA; no information found on John, James, or May (Mary).

Thomas, born Dec. 15, 1795 Virginia, married Elizabeth Howard Feb. 2, 1818, died Dec. 27, 1853 in Harrison Co., MO.

William Norman, born July 10, 1802, married Sarah "Sally" Hamblen Barnett, March 15, 1835, died July 18, 1876 Brown Co., IN.

Henry, Maradyn Oyler's great-great-grandfather, born March 8, 1810 Knox Co., KY married April 5, 1838 in Brown Co., IN to Catharine Davidson, died June 11, 1853 Mercer Co., MO.

Archibald, born 1813 Kentucky, married Jan. 26, 1837 Brown Co., IN to Elizabeth King died Nov. 8, 1891, buried Ohio Ridge Cemetery in Camp Atterbury.

Eliza (Elizabeth) born 1815 Kentucky, married Owen Simpson May 15, 1831 Bartholomew Co., IN.

Sarah born 1817/19, married William Simpson May 2, 1841 Daviess Co., MO.

William is buried in Taylor Cemetery (Hamblen Cemetery) Brown Co., IN. *Written by Maradyn Webster Oyler*

ESTHER AND HERBERT TEAGUE -

Esther Merriman was born in Brown County Feb. 12, 1930 to Hallie and Clarence Merriman. She graduated Helmsburg High School and worked in Indianapolis before marrying 1st Sgt. Herbert L. Teague on June 17, 1950. Herb had just returned from Korea where he had been a prisoner of the Chinese Communists Forces and escaped, earning several distinguished medals.

Herbert Lemuel Teague was born in Marion County Dec. 17, 1929 to Levi Vorse Teague and Lillian Anne Louden. The Teague family has been traced to Stephen Teague (born 1813, Kentucky) who married Ollie Jane Williams. His son Levi Vorse (born 1897, Trimble Co., KY) married first Hallie Belle Louden and second Lillian Anne Louden. Levi came to Indiana in 1929. Children: G.L., Herbert, Mildred and Vivian. Levi's brother Austin and wife Dorothy Krause lived in Brown County near Needmore. Children: Mary Russ, William, Edna Fritch, Donald, Patricia Burns, James.

Herbert and Esther Teague Family

Herb became a driver for Indianapolis Transit, but reenlisted in 1955, being gyroscoped to Germany from Ft. Wood. After their third child was born, Esther traveled to Karlsruhe, Germany where they enjoyed the country for six months. After three years at Ft. Benning, GA, they lived three years in Chinon, France, southwest of Paris in the Loire Valley, a land lined with castles and chalets. They rented an 1850 stone house with marble fireplaces and floors. Family entertainment consisted of movies on Base, playing games and reading aloud. Children had uneasy adventures: Howard got lost on wrong school bus, Richard tossed his toy truck onto power line knocking out community electricity. In 1963 they returned to Ft. Wood. Herb was a Supply Sergeant, Military Advisor to Iran, with Engr. Bn. in Vietnam, returning as Combat Engr. at Ft. Wood, and retiring in 1972 when he purchased their first home in Waynesville. He managed Empire Gas Co. Esther secured Civil Service position retiring in 1988.

Betty Joan Teague, born July 7, 1952 married Dennis Thompson Oct. 13, 1973. They divorced and she married Jeffrey Breedlove, June 17, 1977. They had Charles Dale Breedlove April 4, 1980 and divorced. Betty is a college student and manages a book store at Fort Wood. Richard Herbert Teague, born Sept. 20, 1953, married Cheryl Ann Leuthen Oct. 25, 1975. They had Jason Richard April 24, 1978 and Jessica Ann Nov. 24, 1981. Richard, a licensed mechanic, works at St. Roberts, MO. Howard Lyndall Teague, born June 12, 1955, married Tisha Snelling Oct. 17, 1975. They had Amy Deanine Dec. 18, 1976 and Rebecca Lynn July 26, 1979. They divorced. Howard married Kristy Lynn Smith Aug. 18, 1986 and they had son Ryan Anthony Nov. 31, 1986. Howard is a licensed mechanic and moved to Casselberry, FL in 1989. *Submitted by Esther Merriman Teague*

TERHUNE FAMILY -

Albert Terhune, born about 1615 in Holland of a Huguenot family, came to America about 1637, settling in Flatlands, NJ. In early 1793, a migration of many families from New Jersey to Kentucky took place. Among those who settled in Mercer Co., KY were William and Garret Terhune, third great-grandsons of Albert Terhune, the emigrating ancestor. William and Garret were sons of Stephen and Marget (Cornell) Terhune. Garret and William bought land on Harrod's Run and it was there that William died June 18, 1828, and his wife, Maria (Van Nuys) Terhune died Aug. 4, 1848. Their sons Garret, William and James Terhune migrated to central Indiana, settling in Johnson and Brown Counties, about 1830.

William and Deborah (Zook) Terhune

Garret Terhune (1791-1851) married Nancy Davis on Aug. 15, 1813. Their fifth child, James Terhune (1821-1892) married Eusebia Nay on March 17, 1842. Their grandson was Dr. Rufus Webster Terhune who served as Resident Physician, from 1919, at the Home Lawn Sanitarium in Martinsville, IN. Martha, a daughter of James and Eusebia Terhune married William Robert Hunt. Their daughter, Cynthia Jane Hunt married James McNutt. Their son, John McNutt married Ruth Nealy in 1886. Their son, Paul Voris McNutt was elected Governor of Indiana in 1932.

William Terhune (March 22, 1819-Feb. 3, 1880), fourth child of Garret and Nancy Terhune, married Deborah Zook (March 1, 1822-April 10, 1895). Both are buried in Unity Church Cemetery, Brown County. William Terhune, a preacher, and his wife, Deborah, had five children:

1. Margaret Ellen Terhune (1839-1920) married George Madison Anderson. Their children were: (1) Amanda Caroline Anderson who married Thomas R. Tracy; (2) America Adaline Anderson who married Hiram Waltman; (3) Dora Esteline Anderson who married Willis Baughman; (4) Alonzo Whitcomb Anderson.

2. Mary Elizabeth Terhune (1842-1901) married Sampson Joseph Anderson. Their children were: (1) Rozilla Anderson Beatty; (2) Lorena Anderson Adams; (3) Walter Anderson; (4) Etta Anderson Miller; (5) Nova Anderson Knight; (6) Edward S. Anderson.

3. Nancy Jane Terhune (1848-1939) married Samuel Turner, lived in Nashville. Their children: Arvine, Edgar, Effie, Claud, John and Mary Turner.

4. Simon Peter Terhune (1853-1871).

5. Julia Ann Terhune (1855-1933) married Henry Phillips. They had two children: Raymond Phillips and Maxie Phillips who married Jim Campbell. *Submitted by Ida Chapman Smith*

JEREMIAH TERRILL - Jeremiah, son of Robert Terrill and Mary Henderson, was in Brown County by 1844 when he entered land in Section 9 in Johnson Township. Jeremiah (1822-1875) married Mary Martin (1822-1882); both are buried in Deckard Cemetery, Brown County. Jeremiah and Mary Terrill had eight children: (1) John (1846-1903) married Sarah Fleetwood (1846-1920), daughter of Isaac Fleetwood and Melvina Hall. John served in the Civil War from Sept. 30, 1864 to Aug. 20, 1865 when he was discharged at Camp Stanley, TX. He and Sarah had two sons: Jeremiah (1867-1932) who married Leota Fleetwood, daughter of John Fleetwood and Elizabeth Combs; and Charles (1874-1896) who married Lydia Mikels. Charles died of pneumonia after putting up horses during a storm. He and Lydia had two sons, John Wes and Leonard, who were cared for by his parents until Lydia remarried. Charles is buried in Terrill Cemetery, Lydia is buried in Knightridge Cemetery, Monroe County with her second husband, Alexander Reeves. (2) Susan (1849-1903) married Josiah Snow; (3) William (born 1851); (4) Lurana (1854-1929) married Wm. Riley Fleetwood (1842-1932); (5) Robert (1856-1919) married Elzira Axsom (1866-1945); (6) Adeline (1858-1941) married Wm. Elkins (1853-1929); (7) Samuel (1863-1865); (8) Jeremiah H. (1865-1867).

Edna, Ethel, Roxie, Seba, Jerry, Wes, Leonard, John Ford, Leota, Carrie Terrill

About 1908 John and Sarah moved to the house that had belonged to Jeremiah and Mary. It was a log structure with a barn and spring house on a ridge near the Terrill Cemetery. The house now stands near the Catholic Church, Nashville.

Jeremiah, son of John and Sarah Terrill, and his wife, Leota, had ten children: (1) son (born and died 1890); (2) Roxie (1892-1912) married Frank Ewing; (3 & 4) twins, Edna (1895-1943) married Eli Stevens and Ethel (1895-1926) married George Winkler; (5) Seba (1898-1981) married Leonard Crider; (6) John (born 1900) married Flora Deckard; (7) Cecil (1903-1908); (8) Carrie (1907-1989) married Guy Mitchell; (9) Ford (1910-1990) married Ruby Mitchner; (10) Ruth (1913-1959) married Olin White.

The Terrill children attended the Axsom Branch School which was over a mile from home. For entertainment there were free shows at Freetown, trips to the Maumee store to trade eggs and milk for staples and penny candies. In the 1940s the government bought Terrill Ridge which became part of the Deam Wilderness Preserve. The Terrill Cemetery is now about two miles within the Preserve. Hickory Grove Church was a favorite center for social activities where many of the young people did their courting. Working from sunup to sundown was the way of life. Callers were never turned away from the table. In winter bedtime came early; each home had three beds, one for the parents, one for the boys and one for the girls. If the bed wasn't wide enough for all of them they slept crossways. *Submitted by Mrs. Richard L. Mitchell*

MARIE J. THOMPSON - It was in the year of 1973 that life began in Brown County for Marie J. Thompson and her two youngest sons. Her husband, Wayne E., born Aug. 17, 1921, died in 1972. His parents, Horace E. and Hazel G. Thompson were from Indiana and Wayne and his elder brother Norman were born in Indianapolis. Wayne was a graduate of Indiana University and held a B.S. degree in organic Chemistry. He served in the U.S. Navy during WWII as a chief petty officer in Bomb Disposal. At the end of the war, he returned to Eli Lilly Co. where he worked in the pilot development plant. Some years later he was awarded an honorary Ph.D. for his distinguished contributions. Marie was born in 1921 in St. Paul, MN and was the eldest of three girls. Herman G. and Rose A. Juergens and family moved to Indiana in 1927. Marie remembers being given a farewell party by her classmates in the first grade of school. They lived in Fort Wayne for one year before moving to Indianapolis' east side. Her father worked for the Indianapolis Engraving Co. as a photoengraver. The Thompson family lived in the Broadripple area. Horace Thompson (father of Wayne E.) was in business with two of his brothers known as the Thompson Brothers Pattern Works. It was located on West Washington Street in Indianapolis.

Marie J. Thompson

The company designed and built many of the early automobiles—one in particular was the Duesenburg. In August 1941 Marie was employed at Eli Lilly Co. in the advertising department. The following Christmas the company celebrated the opening of a new building with a party and dance band. It was there that Wayne and Marie met. A romance blossomed and they were married June 5, 1944—after Wayne's overseas duty in the South Pacific. Indianapolis later became their home. They had five sons: Michael E. 1945; William N. 1951; Robert W. 1953; James R. 1955; and Joseph E. 1957. The year following Wayne's death, Marie and sons James and Joseph moved to Nashville, IN. The boys continued their schooling—James at I.U. and Joseph at the Brown County High School and later I.T.T. in Indianapolis. Marie resumed her interest in Art which began in the late '50s. For a time she was a teacher for painting classes at the Northside Y; the Indianapolis Art League and North Central High School (adult education program). In Nashville she served as president of the Brown County Art Gallery Association during 1974 and 1975. She later established her own studio and gallery in the Village Green building. She remains at that location at the time of this writing. Her focus of attention had become portrait painting. During the years much time was devoted to studies with portrait painters of renown to perfect her skills. During her 35 years of painting many awards were received. Her portraits include bank presidents; TV and radio personalities; "500" festival and state fair queens and champion horses. Works are located in educational institutions, corporations, government buildings and many private collections. *Submitted by Marie J. Thompson*

MIKE THOMPSON FAMILY - Michael E. grandson of Maurice and Ruth Thompson and son of Mrs. Charlotte Litzelman grew up in Fountain County at Newtown, IN. His grandparents and great-grandfather Clifford Pogue ran the Newtown Horse Farm raising trotting and pacing race horses. Born 1951, Michael attended Richland Township school and graduated in 1969 from Fountain Central High School.

Michael attended Franklin College where he met Peggy Bond. A year later they were married in August 1970 at the Nashville Christian Church.

Michael Thompson holding Brayton with Becky and Greg Thompson

Peggy grew up in Brown County, the eldest daughter of Pat and Jack Bond in Nashville. She had three sisters, Susie, Becky and Cindy. Peggy was active in scouting, church, school activities and 4-H. She was the 1969 Brown County Good Citizen D.A.R. winner, the 1968 Girls State Representative, and 1969 Brown County Fair Queen. She was also a 1969 Hoosier Scholar. A year after Peggy married, her only brother Jeff was born.

Mike graduated from Franklin College in 1973 with a B.A. in Education, in P.E., Health, and English. Peggy graduated with a B.A. in Elementary Education.

Mike began a teaching coaching career at Brownstown Central. Their first son Michael Jr. (known as Tigger) was born October 1973. Peggy taught Kindergarten following his birth.

Mike took his first varsity basketball coaching position in 1975 and the young family moved to Milan, IN. Here Mike was known as the youngest head basketball coach in Indiana at that time. In July of 1976, "Bicentennial Baby" - Greg was born. Proud mother watched the national historic fireworks from a hospital bed in Dearborn Co., IN.

In 1978 Mike took another varsity coaching position at Southwood High School near Wabash, IN and the family again moved. Their daughter, Rebecca Ann (Becky) was born in October 1978. Peggy taught kindergarten and third grade at Southwood Elementary. While coaching there Mike was named County Coach of the Year three times.

Leaving Wabash County in 1982 the family moved to Churubusco, IN for one year. Mike again coached and Peggy was the Whitley County Day Care Center Director.

The family returned to Brown County in 1983 where Mike taught English and coached and Peggy taught kindergarten at Van Buren Elementary.

A third son, Bryce Andrew was born in January of 1986, but died at age seven weeks from a fatal birth defect.

Following a stint as High School Athletic Director, Mike became the Vice-Principal at Brown County High School in August 1986.

Brayton Patrick Thompson was born in July 1987, the heavyweight of the family.

Mike accepted the Van Buren Elementary principalship in the fall of 1989 and Peggy moved to Nashville Elementary to teach fourth grade - a position she presently holds. Mike has been hired to begin the duties of Assistant Superintendent of the Brown County Schools in July 1990. Peggy laughs and says Brown County is a good place to raise kids. We have a child in every building level in the corporation and a preschooler too.

JAMES LEWIS AND SARAH JANE (MOORE) TILTON - James, born Jan. 6, 1851 was the only one of Lewis Cass Tilton's children to remain in Brown County. He attended the county schools in Van Buren Township and helped his father farm. Then he attended teacher training school in Columbus, and taught 15 years in the county. He married Sarah Jane Moore, daughter of Benjamin Franklin Moore and Rebecca (Breech) Moore of Bellsville.

For several years James had a grocery store in Bellsville. After being elected treasurer of the county, he moved to Nashville where he opened a general merchandise store. He became involved in several businesses: furniture store, an undertaking establishment, Ford sales, and lumber. In 1911 he became president of the Nashville State Bank, retaining that position until his death in 1950 at the age of 99.

James attended the Methodist Church faithfully. After her work was finished every day, one could find James's wife, Sarah, sitting by the window reading her Bible.

They were family people. When their daughter Mamie's husband, James Bryon Walker, died with appendicitis, they invited Mamie and her five children to make their home with them. It was always a happy home, welcoming all their grandchildren.

James Lewis Tilton and Sarah Jane (Moore) Tilton

Their sons, Frank Lewis and Raymond (Ray) Moore Tilton graduated in 1902 from Indiana Medical School. Their grandmother, Rebecca Moore, now had four grandsons that were doctors. A physician's work was not easy in Brown County in those days. Many times they had to tie up the horse and walk. After cars came on the scene, they could be stuck in the Brown County mud. Many times with critical patients they stayed overnight or longer. As it was a long 50 miles to Indianapolis, they took care of everything except major surgery. A trip to Columbus involved camping overnight in Stoney Lonesome.

Frank married Rachel Gore of Paducah, KY; Ray married Ida David of Nashville. Frank and Ray both practiced in Nashville. Rachel, whose brother was also a physician, became a good nurse, helping Frank in his office.

Before World War I, Ray moved to Columbus where he had a large practice. Volunteering for service, he was stationed in the States. Frank was turned down because of his age and a heart condition. In 1919 Frank moved with his family to Williamsport, IN, where the roads were good. He practiced for over 50 years. Ray died in 1924 as a result of exposure during the flu epidemic. In 1932 Frank returned to Nashville to be with his father who was 82. Sarah Jane had died in 1921 after breaking her hip.

Frank and Rachel had three children: (1) Frank Gore born Aug. 11, 1904, married Margaret Gatten and retired from Shell Oil in Houston. They have two daughters: Margaret Ann Sicola of Houston who has three children: Kenneth, Cary and Tracy Sicola Ashley. Claudia Ruth Martin of Minneapolis who has three children: Leah Martin Betterman, Rebecca and Bert.

(2) Ruth Tilton born Aug. 12, 1906 taught Band and Vocal Music in the schools for 40 years. She lives in the Tilton House in Nashville.

(3) Fredric Lewis born March 14, 1913 is an I.U. graduate of chemistry. He served in the Navy in World War II and was in Tokyo at the close of the war. He is a retired rural mail carrier and businessman, owning a Western Auto Store. He married Gladys Setter of Morgantown. They have three children: Frank William, a farmer, raises pumpkins, cantaloupes, corn, soybeans, and Christmas trees; Janice Elaine, a teacher, married Dennis Foster. Their two children are Rachel Lorraine and Benjamin Lewis; Thomas Ray has a serpentarium in Nashville. He married Pamela Grever of Fort Wayne. Their four children are James Jacob, Andrew William, Luke Josiah, and Ruth Katherine. They are the 12th generation of the Tilton line in the United States.

After the death of her husband, Mamie Tilton Walker was a clerk in her father, James Lewis Tilton's store. When her children, Byron and Dorothy were in school at I.U., she had a rooming house for students. Her children are Hazel, Mabel, James Byron, Dorothy, and Sarah Elizabeth (Betty).

(1) Hazel, a teacher, married Walter Calvin, who served in WWI. Beulah Jean Calvin, Hazel's daughter, lives in Florida with her mother who is now 97.

(2) Mabel, a teacher, married Paul Corter, who served in WWI. Susabelle (Sue) Corter, Mabel's daughter, married Richard Schmalz. They have three daughters: Mary Beth Schmalz, a professor at Madison, WI. Her husband, Urban Wemmedov is a professor of business at Madison. Deborah is a nurse at Milwaukee, WI. She has five sons, including twins: Jason, Joshua, Adam, and Nick and Tony Goodolf. Sarah Jane, a special education teacher, married Thomas Templin, an Athletic Dept. Professor. Their children are: Katherine Corter and Andrew Thomas.

(3) James Byron, a dentist served in WWI and married Kathleen Barger. James Richard Walker, James' son, married Jean Palmer. They adopted two children: Jim and Jody.

(4) Dorothy became totally blind at the age of 40. She was a woman of great courage. She was given an award by the governor of California for her work with the legislature to pass a law to protect the blind from poorly trained seeing-eye dogs. She and her husband, Scotty, raised funds to build an apartment complex for the blind behind the Braille Club in Pasadena. She died in 1989 at the age of 87. They had two children: Kay Scott Cook, a teacher, and her first husband, Bruce Roberts, have four children: Bruce, Becky, Steven and Penny Roberts. Phil Gordon Scott, a Doctor of Pharmacy, now teaching chemistry, and his wife, Harriet, have two children: Phil and Marcelyn Scott Beckwith. Both Harriet and Marcie are special education teachers.

Back Row: James Byron Walker holding Dorothy Walker, Mamie Tilton Walker, Dr. Ray Tilton holding James Lee Walker, Ida David Tilton, Dr. Frank Lewis Tilton holding Frank Gore Tilton and Rachel Gore Tilton. Front Row: Hazel Walker, James Byron Walker II, Mabel Walker, Sarah Jane Tilton and James Lewis Tilton.

(5) Sarah Elizabeth married William H. Thomas, who was mayor of Martinsville. They have three children: Patricia Ann married Julius (Jude) Forbes. They have two daughters: (1) Jana Kay married William Robert Syrus. They have two sons and a daughter: Robert Walker Syrus married Kimberly Lemons. They have a son Zachary William Walker Syrus and a son William Christopher Syrus. Beth Ann Syrus married Paul Brummett. They have two children: Matthew Spencer and Paul Christopher. (2) Carol Ann married Thomas Palmer. They have two daughters: Lisa Ann and Sarah Elizabeth Palmer.

Sarah and William Thomas' second daughter, Phyllis C. married Robert D. Poppino. They have two sons: Robert Thomas married Cindy and David

D. married Susan J. Russell. Sarah and William Thomas' son, William W. married Marlene F. Lemons. They have two sons: William Michael married Betty Wellerer. They have two sons: Trenton Walker and Bradley Scheiner Thomas. William W.'s second son is Jeffery Walker who married Susan Lake.

Dr. Ray and Ida Tilton had one son, James Lee Tilton, dentist in Columbus. He married Elizabeth Cutsinger. They had two children: (1) James Richard born July 9, 1927, serving for 25 years as Executive Director of the Wabash Center for the Retarded. He married Mary Margaret Cox, Administrative Counselor of Sagamore of the Wabash Indiana Vocational College. James Richard retired June 30, 1990. On July 10, 1990 he was honored at a reception and award ceremony. "He was named a Marquis of Lafayette by Lafayette Mayor Jim Riehle and also a Sagamore of the Wabash by Governor Evan Bayh, the highest award a civilian can receive from the State of Indiana." (2) Elizabeth Ann and her husband, Benjamin Mitchell Couch have four children: William Bradford Couch married Merydith Phillips. Stephen Couch married Carol Young. Thomas E. Couch married Cheryl L. Gentry and their children are Sarah Elizabeth and Emily Katherine. Linda Couch married Mark R. Gates, a descendant of General Horatio Gates. Their children are Casey Christine Gates and Mark R. Gates and Mitchell Ryan Gates born Aug. 12, 1990.

During the 1976 Bicentennial Ruth Tilton received from the American Historical Society, for a nominal fee, the Tilton Coat-of-Arms. If James Lewis had been told about it he would have said, "It's who YOU are that counts." Dr. Frank would continue reading his medical journal without a word. Janice said, "Don't tell anybody," and four year old, redheaded Luke might say, "O, boy! I like to fight!" Nonetheless, a knowledge of your ancestors' accomplishments might inspire you to achieve.

Many of the Brown County Tiltons have believed that with education, a love for mankind and a belief in a Higher Power, the quality of Life can be improved. In different ways, they have served this community and their country. *Submitted by Ruth Tilton*

LEWIS CASS AND ELIZABETH TILTON

- The name Tilton was given to a hill in Leicestershire, England, by the Anglo Saxons because they found the fortifications left by the Romans when they invaded England. It was recorded before 1086 in the Domesday Book.

The Tilton Church in Leicestershire was founded in 1190 by the Tiltons and rebuilt by them in the 16th century. According to tradition the lives of Edward I and Edward III were saved by the Tiltons. Several held positions under Henry VII with several losing their lives.

The Brown County Tiltons may be traced to William Tilton, christened Feb. 29, 1586 at Wolston, Warwickshire, England. He married Elizabeth Focell at Claybrook, Leicestershire. His father was Robert, his mother, Ursula Pycroft.

During troublesome times with Charles I, of whom they did not approve, the Puritans, William and his two sons, Peter and John, emigrated from England to Lynn, MA in 1636-40.

It was said Peter gave information to the two judges, General William Goffe and General Edward Whaley, cousins of Oliver Cromwell, who convicted Charles I to execution. Peter and Parson Russel were given credit for keeping these two in hiding for 16 years in their homes in Hadley, MA. It was rumored that General Whaley died in Peter's house and was buried in his garden. The story is that General Goffe saved the Hadley citizens when he rushed to the church to warn them of an Indian attack.

Lewis Cass and Elizabeth Lacey

William, the founder of the New England branch of the Tiltons, through Abigail, daughter of Abraham and Deliverance Tilton, was an ancestor of Millard Fillmore, 13th President of the United States.

William's son, Peter, born in England married Elizabeth. Their daughter, Mary Tilton, married Joseph Eastman. In 1910 the Eastman descendants erected the Eastman-Tilton Memorial at Hadley, MA. The inscription reads: Honorable Peter Tilton/Died July 1, 1696/He Was One of the Founders of Hadley/A Man of Great Influence/In Church and State/He Was Also One of Those Who Assisted In/Concealing the Genicide/Joseph Eastman/Born Jan. 8, 1651/married Mary Tilton 1682/Died April 4, 1692. Erected by Their Descendants/August 2, 1910.

Generation I

John Tilton, born March 4, 1612, considered the first generation in Colonial Times of the Brown County Line, believed in religious freedom. He defended the Quakers against persecution by the Puritans. John's brother, Peter, a faithful Puritan, didn't agree with John's religious ideas. When John's wife, Mary "Goodie" Tilton, refused to have their son, Peter, baptized, it caused the Puritans displeasure, resulting in John and Mary and their friend, Deborah Moodie, leaving Lynn. Eventually they removed to Gravesend, King's County, Long Island.

John was prominent in the government of Gravesend, established in 1646, serving for ten years as town clerk, the most important office. He enjoyed the respect of the Dutch authorities until the Quakers appeared. He and his friend, Samuel Spicer, were fined for "Quaking with the Quakers" and "Harboring a Quaker female preacher." John and Mary were not intimidated and joined the Quakers instead. For the fourth time they were officially banished from the colony, but were never forced to leave.

John made many purchases of land from the Indians in New York, New Jersey and Delaware. A famous Indian chief said of John's purchases, "Not a single drop of blood have you shed—not an acre of our land have you taken without our consent."

John lived in Gravesend in peace under the English rule. He died in 1688; his wife, in 1683. He left a burial ground for his descendants and friends.

William, his sons, Peter and John, were educated men. Peter's letters to his wife indicated that he was a man of great sensitivity and love for his family. William and his sons were interested in education, government, religion, and land development.

Generation II

Peter Tilton, born Jan. 16, 1642 at Lynn, was the son of John and Mary Tilton of Gravesend. When he was 17, Thomas Greedy bequeathed him his entire estate. Peter married Rebecca Brazier, born 1663, niece of Samuel Spicer, a family friend.

Peter was the first of his family to remove to Monmouth, NJ. It was his branch of the family that went West. His brother Thomas removed to Delaware, and then was the founder of the southern branch of the family, and the ancestor of Dr. James Tilton, first Surgeon General, on the staff of General George Washington in the Revolutionary War.

Peter took an active interest in public affairs. He was one of the overseers of Monmouth, a member of the Provincial Assembly, and Court of Sessions, Judge of small cases, constable, deputy, assessor, and Justice of the Peace.

John Tilton's best friend, Samuel Spicer, married John's daughter, Esther. Samuel lived a useful life, serving his church and state with honor, a man of great wealth, influence, and of the highest character. To John's great sorrow, they removed from Gravesend to an estate they named Hopewell at Rochester. He and Esther had the love and respect of many. Samuel died March 12, 1699.

On July 24, 1703 at 10:00 p.m. at Hopewell, Esther, her maid, Esther Saxley, and a young boy, Richard Thackera, were killed by lightning. In "Early Settlers in Newton," John Clement pictured Esther Tilton Spicer's funeral:

"The funeral was by night with family and friends going in boats, lighted by brands of pine to show their respect. To the Indian it was a grand and impressive sight. Araspha, the King and other Indians in their gaudy robes, the colonists in their plain apparel, and the negro slaves with almost nude bodies, made one of the grandest pageants imaginable."

Ruth and Frank Gore Tilton holding pup Penny and Sarah Elizabeth Walker with Fredric Lewis Tilton in baby buggy - 1913. (Grandchildren of James Lewis and Sarah Jane Tilton.)

Generation III

John Tilton, Sr., born Jan. 11, 1669, died 1710. John was the son of Peter and Rebecca Tilton. He was a carpenter and married Elizabeth. They removed with their family to New Castle, DE. On Nov. 2, 1710, John deeded land in Middletown, DE to his brothers, Samuel and Henry, "in consideration of ye love and good will and natural affection and other consideration." He made his will June 17, 1710 and died soon after.

Generation IV

John Tilton, Jr., born 1704 in New Castle, DE; died pre-1768. He married Elizabeth Ebtharpe from St. Peter's Parish, Cecil Co., MD.

Generation V

Thomas Tilton, born 1740 in Cecil Co., MD, married Rebecca Deborah Ferrel, born 1741 at Hopewell. Thomas's sons were: (1) John born May 17, 1768 at Talbot, MD; (2) Richard born May 30, 1774 at Redstone Fort, PA; and (3) Elijah born June 24, 1778 at Redstone Fort, PA.

Thomas and his son John came over into the Northwest Territory before it had been opened up.

When Richard was a young boy, he crossed the Ohio River from Redstone Fort to dig ginseng. It was a troublesome time with the Indians. He was captured by the Indians, taken to Sandusky, and imprisoned for six weeks. He was then released to find his own way home.

In 1805 when the British raised their flag over Redstone Fort, Richard fled to Coshocton Co., OH and was the first settler at Mill Fork. About the same time his father Thomas and his brother John came to Jefferson Co., OH, where they established Tiltonsville. Later they returned to Maryland, remaining five years. After selling some property there, Thomas returned to Redstone where he died.

Generation VI

Richard Tilton remained in Coshocton County, having four children by his first wife and nine by Mary Cass, his second wife. Around 1850, after Joseph and Elijah, his older sons, removed to Ogle Co., IL, Richard joined them.

Before leaving Ohio, he made his will, dividing his property equally among his 13 children - a horse and cow or wagon, or land to each. To his youngest son, Elisha, who was to care for his mother, Mary Cass, and his youngest sister, Sarah, he left the homestead. Upon Sarah's marriage she was to be given $500.00 or land. Richard died in Ogle Co., IL, at the age of 90. He was the sixth generation of the Brown County Tiltons in America.

Richard Tilton's seventh child, Lewis Cass Tilton and his wife, Elizabeth Lacy, came to Brown County in 1856 from Coshocton, OH. They made the trip in a covered wagon with their seven children and Lewis's inheritance: a black mare and a cow. Elizabeth inherited 40 acres in Van Buren Township and Lewis bought 40 more to clear. Their youngest son, James Lewis, was five years old at the time.

Three more children were born here: Mary Jane, Emma, and Thursa Love. Their older sons, David, William, and John served in the Civil War. John was the only one to return. Mary Jane and Emma died during a small pox epidemic. Their daughter, Maria married Lefatora Stout, Nancy married John Truax, but died later, and Thursa Love married John Angerman. (Their daughter, Sina, married a Yates. Some of her descendants live in Indianapolis).

John moved to Illinois. His first wife was Rachel Leidel; the second, Sarah. James Lewis, his youngest brother, attended John's funeral about 1933. John's children were Viola, Nancy, and Vesta. Viola corresponded with her Uncle Jim.

George Tilton married Sarah Howerth, whose father was a postmaster in Van Buren Township. Her brother, Ira Howerth, was a professor at Greeley, CO. George's sons, Ira, George, and Elmer, were born in Brown County. Ira was a lawyer and judge at Valparaiso. His daughter, Frances Weaver, also a lawyer, practiced in his office. When George moved to Collyer, KS, they lived in a sod house. They were farmers and survived the dust storms.

Lewis Cass, died Jan. 29, 1893, and Elizabeth Lacy, died Feb. 12, 1896, are buried in the Bellsville Cemetery. *Submitted by Ruth Tilton*

JUDY (PATE) TONEY - Judy was born Nov. 1, 1952 in Needmore, IN as the sixth child yet first daughter of Kenneth and Frances Pate. She lived her childhood in the rural areas near the north shore of Lake Lemon and the towns of Trevlac, Helmsburg, and Bean Blossom. Her remembrances eventually became the basis of a book of original poetry, *People & Places*, which was published in 1979. Many of the poems in the book first appeared in issues of the *Brown County Democrat*.

Other childhood memories mentioned in this book centered around the relationship she had with her maternal grandmother, Ida Hufford Cox. This woman who came to Brown County to farm in 1931 was one of the most positive influences her granddaughter ever encountered. Her strength of character, resourcefulness, and perseverance were qualities that have been handed down through the generations to the women of her family—beginning with her own daughter, Frances Hufford Pate, and so on.

Kameran Kay Toney 1989   Judy (Pate) Toney 1989

The Bean Blossom Mennonite Church was another positive influence on the young Pate girl. Several Brown County families shared their lives and homes with her as she grew up. These families included Milo and Mary Hostetler, Henry and Frances Wagler, Charles and Gladys Haarer, Joe and Opal Swartzentruber, and Jim and Wilma Stewart. These people and others were supportive as friends and influential as role models. Although most of these families have left Brown County, she still treasures the time when she has the opportunity to worship and fellowship with those who remain.

Judy attended school at Helmsburg Elementary School and Brown County Junior and Senior High School. However, after graduation, lack of job opportunities resulted in her having to leave her beloved country.

She moved to Hendricks County where she currently resides. She was married in 1973 to Terry Wesley Toney whose parents, Wes and Evelyn Toney, lived on Yellowwood Trail. A daughter, Kameran Kay Toney, was born to them in 1974.

Judy has worked in various aspects of the health care field for several years. She is currently studying to be a medical social worker through St. Mary of the Woods College in Terre Haute. (see Hufford-Pate). *Written by Judy (Pate) Toney*

EVERETT AND BLANCHE TRACY - They were life long residents of Brown County. They raised six children; Mrs. Olive Voland, Mrs. Grace Bessire, Mrs. Mary Pogue, Mrs. Robert (Ruby) Christie, George Morris Tracy and James Allen Tracy. The two sons are deceased, the other four still live in Brown County.

Everett was born near Georgetown now (Bean Blossom) in 1890 to George and Catherine Tracy. He was one of nine children. His wife was Blanche Murphy, eldest of four children born to John and Olive Gordon Murphy in 1896. Blanche and Everett were married in Nashville in 1914 in the Methodist parsonage. The parsonage was in the front part of what is now The Franklin House. They came to Nashville in a horse and buggy. They lived in Bean Blossom when all the children were born. They lived on and farmed all the bottom ground that runs from 135 back to the covered bridge. Of course 135 was not there then. In the fall Everett and other men in the area would go to Illinois to shuck corn and hopefully make extra money to see them through the winter.

Everett and Blanche Tracy

In 1930 Everett was elected treasurer of Brown County. Being the outdoor type he let Blanche run the office and he continued to farm a little and buy and sell timber and cattle.

Blanche loved books and felt the need for the neighborhood to have access to the public library. Every two or three weeks she would bring this large wooden library box home. It held 30 to 40 books and all the neighbors would read them, then she would exchange them for different books.

Everett cut the timber and milled lumber to build a new house in Nashville and moved the family there in 1932. Blanche lived in the house 58 years until her death in January 1990. Everett died in 1962.

In 1940 the Democrat Party asked Blanche to run for the Treasurer's office. She did and was the first lady elected to public office in Brown County. In those days there was no money allowance for deputies. If she needed help in May and November she paid them herself.

Blanche was raised near Fruitdale on the Riely Gordon homestead. Her grandparents were John and Ann Murphy and Riely and Elizabeth Gordon. Both of these families lived in the Unity Church community and attended church there. The Murphys and the Gordons were descendants of ancestors that came to this country in the late 1700s and early 1800s from Wales, France, Ireland and Scotland. Georgia Tracy Snider and her husband Richard live on the homestead of Riely Gordon. It's been in the family all these years. Georgia is the granddaughter of Everett and Blanche Tracy. There are nine other grandchildren living and one deceased, 21 great-grandchildren and eight great-great-grandchildren. *Submitted by Mary Pogue*

JOSHUA TRACY - Joshua, born Feb. 26, 1825, Noble Co., OH, son of Thomas Tracy, came to Indiana by 1867. In January 1851 he married Hannah Coultas, born in Ohio on March 2, 1831. They came from Ohio by wagon, walking with a grazing cow and so had fresh milk. The family settled on Owl Creek in Washington Township, then moving to a farm between Bean Blossom and Helmsburg where they reared their 13 children:

1. Nancy Angeline Tracy, born 1852, married James Findley Rose, had eight children: Alonzo, Hattie Jane, Jessie Blanch, Clarence Virgil, Alvin Findley, Oma Angeline and twins Omer C. and Clara Edith Rose.

2. Charles Tracy, born and died 1854, buried Beaver Cemetery, Batesville, OH.

3. Thomas Richard Tracy, born July 31, 1855 in Ohio, died Nov. 12, 1931 as the result of a farm accident. This family lived near Morgantown in the brick home of George Madison Anderson, father of Thomas' wife, Amanda Caroline Anderson. Thomas and Amanda Tracy had 11 children: George Clinton, Lettie Hannah Barnes, Easter Amy Ellis, Daniel Verlus, Almedia Eva Chapman, Victor, Guy William, Sarah Beryl Spahr, Earl Jennings, Florence Irene Donahue and James Kenneth Tracy. George Clinton Tracy and his wife, Hilda, had children, Harold and Georgeanna Tracy. Easter Tracy and her husband, Grover Ellis, had children, Howard, Ethel, Junior and Noah Ellis. Almedia Tracy and her husband, Claud Chapman, had children, Ida, Lester, Lawrence, Veva, Margaret and Carolyn. Guy Tracy and his wife, Laura, had children, Virginia, Betty, Telsa. Earl Tracy and his wife, Mary Way, had children, Mary Christina and Earlene Tracy.

Thomas Richard Tracy and Amanda Caroline (Anderson) Tracy

4. George Clinton Tracy married Catharine Ealy Phillips on Dec. 2, 1879, had nine children: Gertrude Miller, Walter Allen, Tommy Earl, Mabel Clark, Goldie Opal Swift-Waltman, James Everett, Hesper Alma Miller, Doris Gaynell Hayman, Claud F. Tracy.

5. Amanda E. Tracy (1859-1940), unmarried.

6. Herchel V. Tracy, born and died 1860.

7. Latona Frances Tracy, born Ohio, married Lewis A. Turner. They had five children: Ollie Dean Kain, Lena Bell Kain, Jennie Fleener, Chipp Allen, Edgel Turner.

8. William McClellan Tracy, married Cordelia Richardson on Oct. 10, 1884, no children.

9. Sonny Tracy, born and died 1866.

10. John Walter Tracy married Ella Belle Barnes on Aug. 30, 1891. He was the last of the 13 brothers and sisters to die. He and Ella had nine children: Edna Rainwater, Clarence, Olin, Virgil, Arthur, Jennings, Floyd, Cleo and Irvin Joshua Tracy.

11. Marion Tracy, died an infant; a twin of:

12. Mary Viola Tracy, twin, married Newton A. Walker, had six children: Verlis, Austin T., Hannah Neal, Clara Rooney, Susie Frazier, Tracy Calvert Walker.

13. Sarah Mattie Tracy married Seward Watson, had three children: Jettie Truesdel-Harness; Thomas E., undertaker in Morgantown and Alabama where he died; and Jessie Harding-Grayson. *Submitted by Dorinda Chapman*

EDMUND W. AND GLADYS M. TRATEBAS - Jerome Tratebas, born in Allauch, France, visited America in 1815, 1817 and 1825. In 1819 he applied for naturalization in Philadelphia. His son,

Edmund, born in France March 14, 1815, bought land in Porter Co., IN from the Government and an Indian named Nos-Wan-kee in 1835. He married Hannah Thomas, daughter of William Thomas and Anne Armstrong, who were also part of the first settlers in the area which became Chesterton, IN. Edmund died Jan. 4, 1851 and is buried in Chesterton. His youngest son, John, stayed on the farm and married Sarah (Taylor) McKibben. John bought Gossett's Mill in Liberty Township. John and Sarah's only son, John II was born there Oct. 28, 1849. The younger John learned the miller's trade and took over the business when his father died Christmas, 1918 in the flu epidemic of WWI. Later John II purchased Long's Mill in Porter Co., IN and had sons Edmund Wyatt (born Aug. 13, 1915), John III (born Aug. 7, 1919) and Russell Lewis (born Oct. 6, 1921). The Tratebas lineage comes from Allaugh near Marseille, France and is documented with Edmund's father Jerome Victor (born Sept. 3, 1773), Honoré Marie (baptized Nov. 28, 1741), Jerome (baptized April 29, 1702), Etienne (baptized Feb. 2, 1665) and Elzear (born about 1645).

Edmund W. and Gladys M. Tratebas 50th anniversary, 1990

John II married Opal Barber Nov. 17, 1914. The Barber family left Pittsylvania Co., VA for Clinton Co., OH in 1849 and Edmund's branch traveled to Michigan and Northern Indiana in 1869 and 1880s. The Barber lineage comes from Virginia to Ohio to Indiana and Edmund's mother Opal Barber (1897-1988), Alpheus James (1868-1953), Joshua Wyatt (1833-1916), Joseph (1805-1865) and Randolph (b. 1776).

Edmund Wyatt Tratebas, eldest son of John II and Opal was born Aug. 13, 1915. He studied at Valparaiso University in 1934; joined the CCCs in 1935 and worked in the Coeur d'Alene forest of Idaho; and studied at Wheaton College and Dubuque Presbyterian Seminary receiving his B.A., M.A. and B.D. degrees; plus doing further graduate study. He pastored churches, as a Presbyterian minister, in the midwest and teaching at Wheaton College, Westminster College, University of Cincinnati and Northwestern College, Iowa. He first retired from teaching in 1981.

Studying and working in Chicago in the late 30s, Edmund met Gladys Myrtle Spurr of Maywood, Cook Co., IL. Gladys' parents are Charles Joseph Spurr and Edith Bessie Russell. The Spurr lineage comes from London, England with Joseph (1841-1930), William (1817-1894), Joseph (1789-1858) and William (1700s). Gladys and Ed married on May 11, 1940 in Oak Park, IL. They have six children and three grandchildren: Pauline Jeannette born Aug. 11, 1942 in Washington, D.C.; Alice Mae born March 13, 1944 in Aurora, IL; Calvin Vincent born Jan. 1, 1948 in Aurora, IL; Patricia Ellen born Oct. 22, 1950 in Independence, IA; Deborah Sue born Jan. 1, 1953 in New Prague, MN; and Linda Marie born June 14, 1954 in New Prague, MN. Linda married Rodger Korthals and they have Sarah Joy and Dawn Elizabeth and Pauline has a daughter Lacey Beth.

While working and raising a family, Gladys completed her studies for her B.S. degree at Northwestern College, Iowa and M.A. at University of South Dakota and did some graduate studies at Indiana University. Gladys taught at St. Mary's School for Indian Girls, Springfield, SD for one year before teaching business administration courses at Northwestern College, Orange City, IA and Dakota State College, Madison, SD. She retired the summer of 1983, but taught one course in Marketing at Indiana Central, Indianapolis in 1984. She did Girl Scout volunteer work for ten years, taking her troop to Montreal, Canada with Ed's help. Gladys also directed many Daily Vacation Bible Schools being involved in various church activities.

Interest in Brown County goes as far back as Edmund's junior year in high school, when visiting the I.U. campus, Bloomington and surrounding area of southern Indiana. Gladys and Ed purchased 36 acres of land off Helmsburg Road at Low Gap in 1961 and the family spent most every summer after that in Brown County. They built their log home, Serendipity, in 1978 and retired there the end of 1983.

After retirement Edmund has been teaching Philosophy courses part time at the University of Indianapolis; IUPUI Columbus, and Franklin College and being a guest preacher in surrounding churches. Ed is a member of the Society of Indiana Pioneers. Gladys has been busy researching her English forbears besides the French side of Ed's family. Both belong to the Friends of the Library, Indiana Historical Society, Indiana Genealogical Society and Brown County Historical Society (Gladys serving as President 1988-90). Gladys also belongs to Pioneer Women, Delta Kappa Gamma, Chicago Genealogical Society, several English Family History Societies (Wiltshire and Gloucestershire) and was the founding President of the Brown County Genealogical Society.

TRISLER/TRISSLER - Joseph Trisler was born in Maryland 1790. He came at an early date to Ohio and Kentucky. He was first married to Elizabeth Snider in Jessamine Co., KY. They moved to Ohio where they divorced in 1824 in Clermont County. He secondly married Susannah Hoover Rohrer (widow of Henry Rohrer). In 1825, they moved to Shelby Co., IN. Susannah Hoover was the daughter of David and Elizabeth Hoover of Kentucky. To this marriage was born two sons, Martin R. and Francis M. Trisler. Joseph pursued farming for his vocation. He owned 148A of land in Sugar Creek Township.

Martin R. Trisler was born in 1826 in Shelby Co., IN. He married Elizabeth Catherine Daniel April 13, 1855, in Shelby Co., IN. They were the parents of eight children, of whom four sons lived to manhood. Three married and the fourth died as a young man. Elizabeth Catherine Daniel (born May 28, 1835-Shelby Co., IN, died Sept. 6, 1918) made her home with her younger son and his family in Hamblen township. Martin R. Trisler died when Ward was three years old. Elizabeth Catherine (Kate) operated a toll gate on The Old Michigan Road and Churchman's Pike and supported her family. Ward W. Trisler married Mary Etta Adair, daughter of Samuel Adair and Sarah Catherine Kessler. Samuel was the son of John Adair of Kentucky, but made his home with William Adair and wife Susannah, probably a relative. Sarah Catherine Kessler was born in Marion Co., IN Feb. 1, 1839, the daughter of Elijah Kessler and Mary. Elijah was in Marion Co., IN as early as 1830. Samuel Adair and Sarah Catherine Kessler were married May 1, 1859 in Marion County.

Ward Williamson and wife, Mary Etta (Adair) Trisler 1942

Ward and Mary Trisler were married at Needham Station, Johnson County Jan. 24, 1894. They were the parents of nine children, all deceased. They moved to Brown County about 1897 and lived in Hamblen Township. All their children were born in Brown County except one. The oldest one, a son was born in Shelby County. They were members of The General Assembly and Church of The Firstborn. Ward and Mary Trisler are both buried in Greenlawn Cemetery, Franklin, IN. Many descendants live in Brown County and surrounding counties, as well as throughout the United States. *Researched by granddaughters Mrs. Bert Witham and Mrs. Robert Wilson*

JOHN DANIEL TURNER - John was born Dec. 22, 1863 and died Feb. 12, 1940. Mary Florence Richardson was born Jan. 13, 1869 and died Oct. 26, 1958. John and Mary are buried at Bean Blossom Cemetery. They were married June 22, 1890. Both were born in Brown County and lived here all their lives. John had one brother, Harry, and no sisters. He made his living farming and doing odd jobs when called on. Mary was one of six sisters and two brothers.

In John and Mary's marriage they had two daughters: Hazel Esseny and Lona Ruth. They were raised just south of the Bean Blossom creek in a log house by what is now highway 135.

John and Mary Florence Turner

Hazel was born Dec. 28, 1890 and died and is buried at Boone, IA. She died Dec. 25, 1979 and was buried on her 88th birthday. She went to Indiana University and became a school teacher and taught at several different schools in the Brown County area. She married Lewis Knose, a lineman electrician for the Chicago and Northwestern Railroad, and spent the rest of her life in Boone, IA. To them was born one son, Lewis T., who resides in Minneapolis, MN. Hazel had three grandchildren.

Ruth and Hazel Turner, sisters

Front row, L-R: Ruby L. and Pearl L. Turner (twins). Back row, L-R: Lottie and Charles R. Tuner

Anna Lillian (Tutterow) Myers, 1912

Ruth was born April 2, 1893 in the log house in Brown County and died Jan. 12, 1929. She is buried at Oak Ridge Cemetery. She worked in Indianapolis and was a substitute teacher for her sister. She married Walter Ray Derringer June 18, 1920.

Walter Ray Derringer was born Aug. 10, 1896 and died Dec. 20, 1928. He was a farmer all his life and worked occasionally for the Illinois Central Railroad. They both died in their home (of the 1928-29 flu epidemic) on Railroad Road two miles east of Helmsburg. To this marriage was born three children: Walter Asa, Wilbur Allen and Verlis Cleo. (See Walter Derringer.) *Submitted by Wilbur A. Derringer*

JOHN WESLEY TURNER - John was born in Scotland, July 28, 1798. He died near Bean Blossom on May 16, 1871.

He came to Maryland, got married, wife unknown, had one son, George, who died in Ohio at age 92. George was married to Judy Gibbs and had 12 children.

George's mother died and John Wesley married Elizabeth Strahl and had seven children.

Front row: Ruth and Glenn Turner. Back row: Charles R., Ershel and Elisha Daniel, father of John William.

John W. and Elizabeth were loyal Republicans and a firm supporter of Lincoln. John W. freed his slaves in 1850, but they would not leave the plantation.

John W. and Elizabeth later moved to Monroe Co., OH. He was one of five sons to join the Union Army and was with Sherman on the march to the sea.

Then in 1854, John Wesley and family, and son, Elisha Daniel and family came down the Ohio River on boats and then came in a wagon to Brown County. They settled in a log cabin on Bean Blossom creek.

Elisha and wife Rebecca had seven children: John William, George Newton, Elizabeth Ellen (Allender), Lewis Allen, Mary Nettie Jane (Crouch) and Indiana Clementine ("Aunt Clem" also known as Fay) (married Hopper, then married Delph), and James L.

Rebecca died in 1898 near Bean Blossom. Elisha lived with a grandson, Charles R. Turner, then died at the home of his daughter, Mrs. Elizabeth (Thomas) Allender, northeast of Nashville.

John Wm. Turner was born in Monroe Co., OH on Nov. 14, 1852, then came to Brown County at the age of two years old. He married Nancy ? and they had four children: Wm. Perry, Bertha Jane, Lettie Frances (Mrs. Levi Parker) and Charlie D. Nancy died Feb. 24, 1884 and John Wm. married Martha Bell Waltman. They had three children: Zora J., Charles R. and Jessie Ruth. Martha Bell died on Jan. 5, 1895.

John Wm. then married Mary Alice McCurdy on June 29, 1895, and they had four daughters: Lottie Marie Landers (born Sept. 7, 1896 and died in October 1975); twin girls born April 7, 1898 were Ruby Letha Derringer (died Aug. 29, 1949) and Pearl Lelia Schrock (died October 1964); and Eva Bell Bennett (born Jan. 1, 1914 and died 1935).

John Wm. was a farmer most of his life and was known to have good teams of horses. He had 100 acres on Railroad Road, which he divided between his living children. He died Feb. 16, 1916, and is buried at the Bean Blossom cemetery. *Written by Mary Derringer Porter*

TUTTEROW/TUTTERROW FAMILY - John Tutterow (born 1769) with his son David (born 1790) migrated from Tutterow, Germany, a town in the N.E. corner of East Germany, in 1795. They settled first in Lincoln Co., NC, resettling in Rowan Co., NC in 1800. David married Ruth Bradley, Oct. 28, 1811, in Rowan Co., NC. Their son George (born 1812) married Ruth Coon (born 1822 in Hancock Co., WV) on Feb. 5, 1840 in Henry Co., WV.

George, Ruth and their son, John, traveled by covered wagon to Brown Co., IN in 1846, resettling in Carmel Ridge, Township 10 where they staked a section for their farm. They raised seven children: (1) John (born March 11, 1842 in Henry Co., NC) married Rachel Adeline Smith; (2) Sarah E. (born January 1847) married William H. Pruitt; (3) Joseph (born Oct. 15, 1848) married Sarah Ann Brittenham; (4) Abraham (born Oct. 6, 1851) married Mary Elizabeth Hale; (5) Elizabeth (born 1855) married John Baker; (6) Samuel (born 1858) married Nancy Jane Pruitt; and Francis (born Oct. 21, 1862) outlived two husbands Charles A. Reichard and Lewis Merriman. All these children were born in Brown County except for John.

Many of the children remained in Brown County area or nearby all their lives. John was a carpenter and stone mason in Brown County and helped build many of the homes around Bean Blossom and Helmsburg, as well as in other towns in Brown County.

George and Ruth Tutterow worked hard raising crops and cattle to see their family survive in the harsh winters in Indiana, as well as the cholera, flux infections of the late 1870s and early 1880s. The children were all raised in a religious God-fearing environment with which they in turn raised their own children.

Abraham Tutterow married Mary Elizabeth Hale, March 13, 1877, in Brown County. They had eight children, losing two in infancy: (1) John Ora (born 1877) married Maude Della Ridenour; (2) Cora Jane (born 1879) married Richard Smith, son of Jonathan and Mary Malissa (Howard) Smith; (3) Ira Curtis (born 1881) married Nora Scaggs; (4) Retta Belle (born 1883) outlived two husbands, Nathan Ernest Crist and Charles McCamber; (5) Mary Ethel (born 1892) married Frank Thacker; and (6) Anna Lillian (born 1895) married Wade B. Myers April 23, 1912.

Jonathan Smith (born 1830) and Mary Malissa Howard (born 1833) near Nashville, Brown County, were married March 6, 1853. Their children were: (1) Richard Smith (born 1871) married Cora Jane Tutterow; (2) Anna E. married William A. Voorheis; (3) Emma E. married twice, John F. Payton and Mr. Steele; (4) Mary E. married Robert Marshall; (5) George married Lydia A. Wise.

Cora Jane Tutterow and Richard Smith were married May 14, 1898 in Brown County. They raised five children: (1) Harry Damon Smith Sr. (born Nov. 24, 1898); (2) Frederick Glenn (born Feb. 27, 1901); (3) Herman Roscoe (born May 30, 1912), (4) Florence (born Sept. 12, 1914) and (5) Richard (born March 22, 1922).

Harry's eldest son Harry Damon Smith, Jr. (born July 22, 1922) is the father of Rodger D. Smith. *Submitted by Rodger D. Smith*

VANDERBILT FAMILY - Born in Lyons, NY in 1886, Vern Corwin Vanderbilt, Sr. came to Indiana in 1908. He set up shop which became the V.C. Vanderbilt Bakery at L.S. Ayres & Co., Indianapolis. He owned and operated it, developing and producing unusual and quality bakery goods for 48-1/2 years with the help of his wife Elizabeth Lyne Connette who had been a cashier at Ayres. Their two children, Vern, Jr. and Bertha Elizabeth (Betty) were educated in Indianapolis schools. Jr. obtained his PhD at Purdue after serving with the Air Corps in WWII. He is presently a Consulting Engineer and Adjunct Professor at Purdue Campus in Richmond. His three boys and families live on the west coast.

Betty studied Medicine, enjoyed a career in classical music, worked with her father at the shop, finished her college studies in English and Geography at Butler University. On a graduate scholarship she finished her Master's degree at Syracuse. She taught in the Evening Division at Butler, worked in Foreign Travel at Hoosier Motor Club and was

Soprano Soloist at North Methodist, 3rd Church of Christian Science, and at St. Paul's Episcopal churches in Indianapolis. She went to California to be with her aunt in her aunt's last days. During that stay she worked for both Litton and Space Technology Labs. Meanwhile her parents had retired and moved to their property in Brown County, having previously visited many times with Dale and Ruth Bessire, long time friends of Indianapolis days.

Of the 61 years of marriage Betty's parents enjoyed the last 13 in Brown County. Mrs. Vanderbilt died in 1971. Mr. Vanderbilt survived his wife by 12 years. He died in 1983 at 97 years and three months. Betty recalls how happy she was that she was able to give them 19 years of caring in their last years. Betty held various positions during that time around her parents' needs. She recalls the nearly eight years as Deputy Clerk in Nashville and her annual stint with Paul Rogers' Tax Office. Where else can one meet so many Brown County people. After her father's death she went to work at Touch of Silver selling fine jewelry where she still enjoys people. To balance her pursuits she sings with the Nashville United Methodist Church choir, is a regular volunteer at Brown County Community Care Center, and as always, tries to make something of the ever-needy garden. With the Genealogy Society she enjoys discovery of more bits and pieces of her family histories which go back to the mid-1600s in America and originate in Holland, England, Germany, France and a bit of Scandinavia. About the community she says, "Perhaps the greatest thing for me is the realization of what friendship means and how precious it is. Brown County has been good to me and for me." *Submitted by B.E. VanDerbilt*

JAMES AND ANN VARNER - James Grant Varner, II (Jim) and Ann live on State Road 135 North of Nashville and have been married for 43 years. Maude Ann was born March 9, 1918 in Columbus, Bartholomew Co., IN. Her parents are Daniel Shatto and Mary Jane Watson. Jim was born Jan. 9, 1921 in South Fork, Cambria Co., PA. Jim came to Indiana December, 1930. His parents are Emma Viola Wingard and James Grant Varner. Before Jim and Ann came to Brown County in 1969, Shelbyville was their home and Ann had an art studio there where she worked and taught. Jim worked at Western Electric Company as a machine setter. He retired in September, 1977.

Jim and Ann were married Sept. 28, 1946 at Friendswood Church at Friendswood, IN. They have three children: Daniel Clayton (1952), Jane Ann (1953), and Edward Grant (1958) all born in Indianapolis.

James and Ann Varner

Jim and Ann built their chalet style home in 1970. Ann has had an art studio since 1955 starting in Marion County, then Shelby County and continuing in Brown County. She was one of the founders of Indiana Heritage Arts. Ann worked primarily in oils in her painting, but she used acrylics for miniature pictures that sit on a table. Landscapes and florals became her specialty. Her style was to create pictures that look like a scene or yard, but she did not want them to look traced. She looked at a scene or yard and went to her studio to paint this image. Varner's Art Chalet was in Honeysuckle Place, Nashville for 15 years, but later Ann worked out of her home. Jim worked outside while she was inside working and they communicated by the use of an intercom. Jim keeps busy making shelves and frames from barnwood for Ann's paintings. Most recently Ann had been making porcelain dolls. She created full-skirted ladies trimmed in porcelain lace.

Jim and Ann have four granddaughters: Marie Ann Davis McDonald, Julie McDonald, Michelle Kay Varner and Samara Ann Varner. Ann was also active in the Historical Society and Pioneer Women's Group. Ann died March 1, 1991 and is buried in Greenlawn Cemetery.

CLYDE BELL VAUGHT FAMILY - Clyde, World War I veteran, was born in Cottontown, TN on March 17, 1896. His parents were Henry and Ada Martin Vaught. Henry's family came from Germany. Clyde married Buena Mae Poole. Four children came of this marriage. They were Mildred Belle Hutchison who now resides in Indianapolis. Also Lillian Hutchison, Clyde, Jr. and John Vaught all deceased. From these children Clyde had 22 grandchildren.

Emma and Clyde B. Vaught, 1966

Although his wife stayed in Tennessee, Clyde moved on to Evansville where he owned a Blacksmith shop. There he met Emma Rose Little and they were married on June 21, 1928. Emma was born to Abraham Lincoln and Louise Wineger Little on June 12, 1904 in Henderson, KY. The Wineger family came from Switzerland. Clyde and Emma's first son Melvin Ernest (deceased) was born in Evansville. Later they moved to Indianapolis and daughter Virginia Lee Vaught Albright was born. There Clyde worked in a body shop and the street car barns. They moved to Brown County in 1931 or 1932. He purchased 92 acres from the Ford family. This was located approximately one mile north of Sprunica. While still working in Indianapolis he would farm on the weekends. When World War II started he worked at Atterbury, then Emma started working there during the Korean War. Clyde then bought a garage in Bean Blossom, he was well known for his welding and body work. Later his brother-in-law Ewald Wolff bought into the business. He did mechanical work. Clyde did blacksmith work part time. His daughter Ada Sanders still has the forge that Clyde brought from Evansville. Ada's husband Kenny and their sons still use it. In September of 1936 Roscoe William, born in Brown County, was followed by Ada Louise in 1938, Harold Henry 1940, Donald Clyde 1943, Carl Fred 1945 and Carolyn Jane in 1947. Of these children Clyde had 28 grandchildren. In between raising the children Emma also worked at the Nashville House where she made Fried Biscuits and Apple Butter. She retired in 1967.

Life was not always easy in these times. When the roads were extremely bad which was quite often, Clyde and Emma parked at the Ott Parsley farm or Fred Walker's and walked home. If they were at home when it snowed they had to wait for it to melt before they could go out. Ada remembers how they all loved the snow. Emma would make them Ice Cream for an extra treat. They always had a big garden and daughter Carolyn Johnson still has the iron kettle her mother used for canning vegetables. For meat they butchered beef and pork and cured it in a shed. They used a cross-cut saw to cut firewood. This was a family chore. For entertainment the children found grape vines to swing on. They also played ball, tag and hide & seek. Before they got electricity in the 40s they would all listen to the Grand Ole Opry on a battery operated radio. They attended Sprunica Church where Ralph Schrougham was the Minister. It was quite a treat for relatives to come visit. They enjoyed the home cooking and the quietness of the farm.

Clyde Bell Vaught died of cancer March 11, 1967 and Emma Rose (Little) Vaught followed Oct. 28, 1980. She died of a stroke. They are both buried in Goshen Cemetery at Foxes Corner. *Written by Ada Louise Vaught Sanders*

VOORHEIS-GRAVES FAMILY - Eva Mae (Voorheis) Graves was born Sept. 19, 1932 to Wade and Nellie Jackson Voorheis on Hickory Hill at the old Ben Douglas farm house. She graduated from Helmsburg High School in 1951. In 1954 she graduated from Nursing School in Indianapolis. On March 5, 1954 Eva married Edgar E. Graves, son of Shannon and Thelma Grace (King) Graves from Salem, IN, and later Morgantown, IN. To this union two sons were born: Michael E. Graves, born April 12, 1955, Garry Lane Graves, born Dec. 26, 1956. Michael Graves married on Oct. 11, 1975 to Sonya (Hoskins) Graves. To this union two daughters were born. Katrina Carmel, born May 1, 1976, and Lisa Michael, born Sept. 3, 1978.

Back: Graves Family - Katrina (daughter of Michael Graves), Vickie (wife of Garry), Garry (son of Edgar and Eva), Edgar (father of Garry and Mike), Eva (Voorheis) Graves (daughter of Wade and Nellie). Front: Grace (King) (mother of Edgar), Shannon (son of Garry), Michael (son of Edgar and Eva) and Lisa (daughter of Michael Graves).

Garry L. Graves married Vickie (Williamson) Graves on July 14, 1979. To this union two sons were born, Shannon Lane, on April 2, 1983, and Timmothy Joseph, on Oct. 8, 1986.

VOORHEIS-JACKSON FAMILY

Wade A. Voorheis was born Oct. 9, 1907 in Brown County to William and Anna Marie (Smidth) Voorheis. In May 23, 1931 Wade was married to Nellie Gertrude Jackson of Monroe County and they made their home on Hickory Hill, northwestern Brown County at the old Ben Douglas farm house. This is now Hickory Hill Waycross Camp and was the site of Hickory Hill Canning Factory.

Front: Nellie Voorheis. Middle: Julie Voorheis, (daughter-in-law), Kay (Voorheis) Thomas, Eva (Voorheis) Graves, Wade Voorheis. Back: Edgar Graves (son-in-law) and Raymond Voorheis about 1975.

Two children were born while living there: Elmer D. Voorheis on Oct. 30, 1931, died Jan. 6, 1978; and Eva Mae (Voorheis) Graves born Sept. 10, 1932. In July, 1936 they moved from there to land owned by John McCoy who sold it to Maurice Murphy, M.D., who sold it to Wade and Nellie Voorheis. The house was built in 1917. Three other children were born to this union: Kay (Voorheis) Thomas born Nov. 30, 1941; Wade Voorheis, Jr., born Feb. 7, 1952, died Feb. 9, 1952; Raymond Lee Voorheis, born June 28, 1954, died April 10, 1979.

Elmer and Raymond served in the military service in the Army between 1952 to 1954 and the Marines between 1973 to 1977. Mrs. Nellie Voorheis still lives at the home site in northwest Brown County. Four generations of Voorheis lived in Brown County for over 60 years.

WILLIAM A. VOORHEIS FAMILY

William a native of Bellvue, OH was born on Sept. 2, 1869. Sometime after his birth, William was adopted by Simmon and Susan Voorheis. William had three children, Charles, Ida and James, from his first marriage. His first wife died.

Anna Marie (Smidth) Voorheis was born in Baden, Germany on Aug. 19, 1868. She was known as Mary Voorheis to all in Brown County. Anna Marie was the daughter of Joseph and Maria Byar Smidth. She was a member of the Lutheran Church in Germany. Her first child, Fredrick Voorheis was born April 14, 1891, and after he reached the age of one they moved to Brown County. Anna married William A. Voorheis on Feb. 16, 1896. To this union were born Henry, Harvey, Albert, Earnest, Adaline (Voorheis) Allen, Emmaline (Voorheis) McDaniel, Wade, Carolyn, and Anna who died.

William sold mineral water, raised berries and sold plants. He donated 250 dollars for the starting of Bear Creek Church. William built their home of yellow poplar.

Mary died May 29, 1958. Mary is buried at Bear Creek Cemetery. Warren Chaffin conducted the burial rites. William died June 29, 1958 at the age of 88. At the time survivors were five sons, four daughters, 30 grandchildren and 35 great-grandchildren. William was buried at Bear Creek Cemetery beside his wife, Anna Marie (Mary Smidth) Voorheis.

William A. and Anna Marie (Smidth) Voorheis

The land on which they built their home, in northwest Brown was sold to Dudley Gallahue and is now part of the Girl Scout Camp. Williams great-great-grandchildren, Katrina and Lisa Graves attended this camp in the summers of 1988-1989.

The land which is the author's home place joins her grandparents' property. It was sold at a sheriff's sale on Oct. 3, 1889. It was the property of Frederick Funk (Uncle of Anna Marie) for $654.84, it was originally sold to Jacob and Mary A. Fleener, Jr.
Submitted by Eva Graves, granddaughter

HENRY AND FRANCES WAGLER

Moved to Brown County in March, 1950 from Daviess Co., IN.

Henry was born Oct. 10, 1919 in Daviess County to Daniel and Leah (Lengacher) Wagler. Their ancestors came from Switzerland and Germany in 1750 and were of the Old Order Amish faith.

Frances was born in North Dakota, Feb. 11, 1923 to Benjamin and Anna (Swartzentruber) Slaubaugh. Their ancestors came from Germany and Switzerland, spoke German and were Amish.

Henry and Frances Wagler

Growing up 1200 miles apart of Amish faith, Henry and Frances shared similar backgrounds and experiences. Frances remembers the dust storms, grasshoppers, and crop failures of the depression in Dakota. Henry remembers his parents losing their farm in 1930 and relocating to a rental farm and different school.

Frances's parents, natives of Indiana, returned in October, 1940. This move was made when she was 17 to a farm near Loogootee, IN. She met Henry and they were married January, 1945. They changed their church affiliation and are still active members of the Mennonite Church. Their first two children, Lorene and Howard, were born there.

In March, 1950 they moved to Brown County on the Clarence Zody farm and live there at this time. Henry was a farmer, dairyman and bus driver for 24 years. He enjoyed children and getting out among people. They were active in Bean Blossom Mennonite Church and Henry was pastor there, 1970-1974. He has also served as lay pastor since that time.

Henry and Frances have eight children and 20 grandchildren. Their children attended Helmsburg Elementary and Brown County High School.

Lorene, born June, 1947, married Gary Link. They live on Woodland Lake Road with daughters Angela, Michelle, and Jennifer. Lorene teaches music. Gary is in business and at present, pastor of Bean Blossom Mennonite Church.

Howard, born January, 1949, married Cathy Headings. They live on Spearsville Road with children Kimberly, Derek, and Trenton. A son, Todd, died in a car accident at the age of three months.

Edward, born November, 1950, married Pam Carmichael. They live north of the home farm with children Lynn, Nathan, Adam, and Amanda.

David, born September, 1953, married Eulala King. They live on Spearsville Road with children Neal and Cara.

Kenneth, born June, 1955, married Lesa Moore. They live on Gatesville Road with children Shannon and Justin.

Dorothy, born May, 1957, married Ray Troyer, carpenter. They live in Goshen, IN with children Adrian and David.

Lloyd, born October, 1959, married Crystal Vaught. They live on Woodland Lake Road with children Emily, Chadd, and Brittney.

Darryl, born October, 1962, married Jacqueline Snider. They live on Spearsville Road with son, Steven.

Edward and David have an excavating business; Darryl works with them.

Howard, Kenneth, Lloyd, and families run the dairy and farming operation. Henry assists when needed.

Singing is important to this family and several family members have given many music programs in churches in this area and elsewhere. This has been a contribution to the Bean Blossom Mennonite Church, the community, and a blessing to the family.

DORIS AND VERA WALDSCHMIDT

Doris and Vera were born and raised in Harvey, IL, a suburb of Chicago. They graduated from Evanston Hospital School of Nursing and attended and graduated from Northwestern University. Their careers were spent in the occupational health field in Chicago. They have one brother, Frederick, a practicing dentist in Homewood, IL who has seven children.

Vera and Doris Waldschmidt

Their paternal grandparents migrated from Germany while in their late teens and married in Chicago. Their father, August F. Waldschmidt, was a banker and treasurer of schools in the Chicago area. Their mother, Vera Geudtner, was the daughter of Emil Geudtner and Augusta Doepp of Chicago and Homewood, IL. The Geudtner family were trunk and leather goods manufacturers in Chicago. Augusta Doepp's father, Dr. William Leonard Doepp, migrated from Germany and was a practicing physician in Chicago, located across the street from the present site of Marshall Fields. When the building burned down in 1858 he left Chicago and purchased a farm in what is now Flossmoor, IL. His practice extended for miles in all directions. He traveled the prairies on horseback as far as Crown Point, IN and New Lenox, IL.

In 1948 Doris and Vera planned a trip to New York City. However, their mother requested they accompany her on a trip to Brown County as she had corresponded with the artist, Adolph Schultz, and wanted to meet him. They were to then continue to Missouri where their mother wanted to renew some old friendships. Due to circumstances, they reluctantly acquiesced to their mother's wishes even though they had never heard of Brown County or knew where it was located! They never reached Missouri. They stayed with Mrs. Netherland at the Singing Pines Motel. They toured every back road in the county and fell in love with the unique, exquisite and unspoiled beauty, its charm and its people. Over the years they kept returning. They could not stay away. In 1965-66, they built their current home on Freeman Ridge, primarily as a place for their parents to enjoy during retirement and as a weekend and vacation retreat. Their father never lived to see it but their mother loved every nook and cranny of the county until her death in 1976. Later, Doris and Vera decided to retire here. They sold their Flossmoor, IL home and moved here in August 1988. *Submitted by Vera Waldschmidt*

WALKER FAMILY - The first generation of Walkers known of is Samuel and Martha Walker, who were in North Carolina in 1778. The children were Jacob born Aug. 8, 1778, Zephaniah born April 25, 1780, Isaac born June 16, 1782, Elinder born April 25, 1784, Rachel born Jan. 1, 1787, Elizabeth born March 15, 1790, Charles Montillion born July 28, 1798.

Benjamin Franklin Walker, son of Jacob, (1808-1890) married Frances Long in Henry Co., KY on July 6, 1834. They came to Brown County about 1840. Their children were William Daniel Walker born May 28, 1838 in Trimble Co., KY, died September 1929, married Margaret Waltman Feb. 24, 1859 in Brown County.

Dudley R. Walker born Jan. 21, 1841, died Sept. 19, 1925 married Elizabeth Waltman on Feb. 29, 1868, died Aug. 10, 1909. Children of Dudley and Elizabeth were Newton Arwine Walker (1868-1924), John W. Walker (1871-1872), Hiram Randolph Walker (1872-1931), Charles Walker (1879-1880).

Front row: David Lee, Verlis, Nancy, Gladys, Betty Walker. Back row: Maurice, Lawrence Dean, and Melvin Walker.

Newton A. Walker born Dec. 26, 1868, died May 29, 1924, second child of Dudley and Elizabeth Walker, married on March 27, 1888 to Mary V. Tracy born May 18, 1869, died Feb. 18, 1909. The children of Newton and Mary Walker were Leonard D. Walker, died in infancy, a second unnamed infant who died, Verlis Leo Walker born July 28, 1891, died March 6, 1973, Austin Thurl died May 9, 1971, Hannah Walker Neal, Clara Elizabeth Walker Rooney, Susie Lena Walker Frazier, Tracy Calvert Walker.

Newton ran a flour mill at Trevlac in the early 1900s. That foundation still stands today. He also sold lumber, hardware and grocery items in Helmsburg, IN. His son, Verlis Leo Walker married Gladys Viola Siscoe on May 30, 1917. Gladys was born March 26, 1896, died Jan. 7, 1962. They always lived in Helmsburg in a home built by Verlis and there they raised six children, (1) Maurice Avan born Jan. 29, 1923, died Oct. 31, 1985 married Betty S. Allender, (2) Lawrence Dean born Oct. 28, 1924 married Mary Ann Long, (3) Betty Delores born Sept. 20, 1926 married Delbert (Bud) Brown, (4) Melvin Eugene born Aug. 8, 1928 married Carol Wilkerson, Children - Sharon Kay born March 19, 1952, Michael Eugene born July 3, 1954, (5) David Lee born Oct. 7, 1931 married Janice Richardson, children - Kathy born Nov. 20, 1953, Dee Ann born Sept. 1, 1962, (6) Nancy Carolyn born Nov. 29, 1933 married David Coffman, children - Vicky Lynn born Nov. 14, 1950, died Dec. 21, 1978, Julie Ann born June 30, 1953, Cindy Lu born Nov. 10, 1957.

Verlis worked in timber, at one time he owned his own mill at Helmsburg. He was later superintendent over a group of men working at the CCC Camp in the late 1930s. They were instrumental in building shelters, lookouts, gate houses and roads in the Brown County State Park, all which can be seen today and visited by hundreds and hundreds of people. *Submitted by Mary Ann Walker*

CHARLES F. AND MARIETTA WALKER - Charles Franklin, son of William Samuel Walker and Nancy Young, married Marietta "Manie" Slevin, daughter of William P. Slevin and Cinderella Fordyce. They had two sons, Lawrence Leslie, born 1889 and Harold Allen, born 1892. Charles died when the boys were young. He had worked for the railroad in Illinois. After his death, Manie moved back to her parents' home with her sons. The boys had a great time growing up with all of their Irish uncles. Les used to tell of the fights the uncles would get into and that "Pap" Slevin would just say, "That's all boys," and they would settle right down. Manie taught at the Walker School.

Leslie, first son of Charles and Manie Walker, joined the Navy in 1906 and was in The Great White Fleet that sailed 46,000 miles around the world in 1907. He was still in the Navy during World War I and was given command of a captured Dutch ship, The Buglesdike, to sail to port. At the end of the war he remained in the Naval Reserve for several years.

Leslie married Leatha Seitz, daughter of Charles H. Seitz and Jeannette Viola Stull. They had two children, Charles Leslie Walker, born 1922 and Joan Elizabeth Walker, born 1927. Leslie went to work for the Indiana State Highway Dept. in 1928. He was head surveyor for State Road #46, from Nashville to Bloomington and for State Road #135, from Nashville to Bean Blossom. The men all wore heavy knee-high boots because of the snakes on Copperhead Ridge. Les retired from the Highway Dept. in 1962 as Chief Engineer of Maintenance.

Harold, second son of Charles and Manie Walker, married Fern Clark. They had two daughters, Irmalee, born 1925 and Genevieve, born 1930. He served in World War I. Later he and Fern divorced and he married Mary Alta Wilkerson.

Manie, widow of Charles Walker, married in Brown County on Nov. 26, 1899, to Roston Scott Moser. They lived in Spearsville, then moved to Nashville and ran the Pittman House. They had three children, Thelma, Clifford and Juanita Moser. Scott served Brown County as County Auditor as well as County Prosecutor. Manie was a poet and was President of the Community Club when that organization purchased and moved to Nashville the large log building known as the Community Club Building, now a part of the Museum Complex of the Brown County Historical Society. (see HENRY AND KATARINA SEITZ) *Submitted by Joan Walker Williams*

EDWARD L. WALKER - Farmer, sawmill operator and steam engine mechanic, was born Aug. 2, 1880 in Hamblen Township, Brown County. He lived his 45 years on Horseshoe Road where his parents Thomas and Hannah (Skinner) Walker had purchased land in 1870. Ed married, Jan. 20, 1900 Daisy M. Calvert, daughter of Lowrey and Melissa (James) Calvert. They went to housekeeping in the home of John Miller, sawmill owner, but later moved on down the road into their own place. Their children were: Lawrence Elliott Walker born Jan. 12, 1901 married Helen Rovine Henry on Aug. 27, 1922, and died Oct. 17, 1977; Elmer Harry Walker born Sept. 15, 1902, married Hesper Snyder Dec. 15, 1928 and died Sept. 1, 1941; Lester Nathan Walker, born Aug. 15, 1906, married the widow Vera Wayman Walker, and died Feb. 14, 1972; Sadie Florence Walker, born July 25, 1911, married Oral Sledge Oct. 6, 1928 and now lives in Franklin; twin boys Lloyd Clark and Floyd Cecil Walker born April 29, 1918, Lloyd marrying Lora Grace Eastridge on April 24, 1941 now living at Trevlac, and Floyd married Louise Smith of Indianapolis on Nov. 6, 1940 and died March 5, 1972. Ed and Daisy Walker never traveled far from Brown County and were both buried at the Bethlehem Church Cemetery.

Making sauerkraut in barrel Daisy, Lloyd and Floyd Walker, Aunt Annie White, Herman Walker, Sadie (Walker) Sledge.

The photo was taken during sauerkraut making time at the Walker home place. On the left is Daisy Calvert Walker. Twins Lloyd and Floyd Walker, Annie Calvert White, sister to Daisy, and Sadie Walker Sledge holding Herman Walker oldest son of Lawrence and Helen Walker. The cabbage was shredded by hand, layered with salt and tamped down into a wooden barrel for use during the winter. Visiting relatives were welcomed to make the task lighter with companionship and helping hands. *Submitted by Phyllis E. Walker*

LAWRENCE ELLIOTT WALKER

Lawrence was born to Edward and Daisey (Calvert) Walker on Jan. 12, 1901, in Hamblen Township, Brown County, and lived in Brown County all his early life. He married Helen Rovine Henry in 1922 and moved to Morgantown. This union produced six children: Herman, Marjorie, Earl, Helen Louise, Catherine, and Carolyn. Only Catherine lives in Brown County at the present.

Lawrence Walker standing on one of his Case engines.

While living at home, Lawrence only went to the seventh grade then worked with his father in the steam engine days, and finally owned a steam engine of his own at the age of 17. In his younger days, he always had a sawmill powered with his steam engine, and the sawmill was moved from holler to holler in Brown County. They would cut the timber in the area, then move to another area, always near a creek so the engine would have a plentiful water supply. After living at Morgantown for a few years, Lawrence and Helen moved back to the old homeplace in Brown County with the children walking to the Spearsville school across the fields and fences, sometimes in snow up to their waist. The neighbors in Brown County would gather at each other's house and play cards, or in the winter they would chop ice from the creek and make ice cream. This was done so often that they spoke of how much ice cream they made during the winter as "barrels" of ice cream instead of gallons. A relative, usually living with them, and the children would spend the winter months sleigh riding in the snow, gathering once again at the different neighbors' homes. The homes were heated with wood stoves and the cooking was done on wood range. There was no electricity, running water, or bathrooms. This was the day of oil lamps, and later gasoline lamps, and going to the Spring for water which was 500 feet or more from the house. Each child had his chore of carrying water from the spring, wood for the stove, washing the lampflues, or blackening the stove, etc. Water for clothes washing was heated outside over an open fire in a big black kettle, then dipped to a washtub with washboard. The clothes were boiled in a boiler to keep them white. In the spring the kids would watch the road grader repair the gravel roads, making them passable for the summer.

Later they moved to Trevlac then back to Morgantown where Lawrence gave up the sawmill for a living for health reasons and went into farming. He had two mules "Jack and Kate." He had a wheat threshing ring and went from place to place to thresh with his steam engine and separator. The neighbors would help and the women from the neighborhood would have dinner ready for them at each place.

Lawrence died on Oct. 17, 1977 and Helen died June 28, 1978, and both are buried at Forest Lawn Memorial Cemetery south of Indianapolis. *Written by Marjorie Ross*

SAMUEL AND NANCY WALKER

Samuel (1804-1872), son of Jacob Walker, was born in Kentucky. He married Nancy Young (1807-1887) in Henry Co., KY in 1827. They came to Johnson Co., IN, then to Upper Salt Creek, Hamblen Township, Brown County by horseback about 1829, forced to move by the prevalence of malaria. Samuel and Nancy died in Brown County and both are buried in Sprunica Cemetery, Samuel being the first person to be buried there. Samuel had entered land in 1833; the Walker School and the Walker Cemetery were located on this land.

Samuel and Nancy Walker had ten children: 1. Jacob Perry (1828-1907) married Cynthia White; 2. Franklin (1830-1922) married Nancy Curry in 1856 in Brown County; 3. Sarah Jane (1832-1915) married William Fraker in 1852 in Brown County; 4. William J. (1835-1898) married Elizabeth Taggart in 1857 in Brown County; 5. Arlanda "Landy" B. (1839-1914) married Mary Kennett in 1861 in Brown County; 6. Harrison (1841-1925) married Eliza Hurd in 1866 in Brown County; 7. Nancy (1842/44-1908) married Samuel Tracy in 1864 in Brown County; 8. James Knox (1845-1932) married Rebecca C. Campbell in 1866 in Brown County; 9. Samuel Scott (1847-1929) married first Clarissa Duhamel, second Elizabeth Wineman Bellmore; 10. Daniel born 1850, died young.

William S. Walker family: Front: Angus, Edelle, John, Earl, Jessie. Middle: William S., Herschel, Mary (Craven). Back: Marvin, Atla, Bessie, Chester.

James Knox Walker, eighth child, owned and lived on land in Brown County which he sold to Elmer Parsley in early 1900, and moved to Nineveh, IN. He and his wife Rebecca (1847-1930), had ten children: (1) Etta J. who married Sam Slevin in 1886; (2) Mary Elizabeth who married Charles Williams in 1888; (3) William S. who married in 1893 to Mary Alma Craven (1873-1945), daughter of John B. Craven and Martha A. Hamblen; (4) Lottie (died 1894, age 19 years); (5) Sarah? same as Lottie? (6) Dora A. who married John Strode; (7) James Eberley who married Myra Burton in 1898; (8) Estella Orpha who married William Titsworth in 1898; (9) Grace M. who married Frank McIlvain; (10) Opal M. who married Forest Walker, a cousin.

William S. Walker (1870-1943), third child of James and Rebecca Walker, and his wife, Mary Alma, had ten children: (1) Angus Lela (1895-1971) who married George W. Mydland; (2) Jennings Atla (1897-1985) who married Lucy Sells in 1922; (3) Marvin born 1899, married Catherine Nissen; (4) Betty born 1901, married Byron Kilgore; (5) William Earl born 1903, married Mary Armstrong; (6) Chester (1905-1957); (7) James H. born 1906, married Edith Carey; (8) John Marshall born 1908, married Charlotte Huff; (9) Mary Edelle (1911-1969), married Earl J. Wiltsee; (10) Jessie Catherine born 1913.

Jennings Atla Walker, second child of William S. and Mary Alma Walker, and his wife, Lucy, had five children. Their third child and only daughter was Marcedes Walker who married Lowell Ray Joslin in 1946. Jacob Walker (great-great-great-grandfather), Samuel Walker (great-great-grandfather), James Knox Walker (great-grandfather), William S. Walker (grandfather), Jennings Atla Walker (father), and Marcedes Walker Joslin (daughter). (See Lowell and Marcedes (Walker) Joslin). *Submitted by Marcedes L. Walker Joslin*

THOMAS WALKER

Thomas, a descendant of an old pioneer family of Orange Co., VA, was born in Wayne Co., KY April 1, 1800, a son of James and Catherine Miller Walker. The parents of Thomas and several brothers and sisters left Wayne County shortly after the 1820 census and migrated to Texas with Stephen F. Austin. Thomas, having married Miranda Collett on Dec. 24, 1827, chose to follow her parents, Samuel and Elizabeth Whitaker Collett, to Indiana. He purchased an original tract of land in Hensley Township, Johnson County and here his family of seven boys and one girl was raised. Thomas died there in 1865 and is buried at East Hill Cemetery at Morgantown. His sons, John, who never married; Granville who married Rhuhamah Skinner; and his daughter Elizabeth who married William Holeman, stayed in Johnson County. The remainder of the children, James M., William H., Samuel C., Thomas, Jr., and Charles moved to Brown County.

James M. Walker born in 1828 in Kentucky married Louisa Rawlings on Feb. 10, 1848 in Brown County. He appeared on the 1850 census with his two daughters Miranda J., who married Willis D. Holeman, and Mary Ann who later married Benjamin Pelley. Sometime before 1860 James moved to Morgantown, here another child, John, was born in 1866. John married Lucy Rush. James M. Walker died Dec. 26, 1901.

Granddad Walker's place in Brown County. At one time there were seven steam engines sitting in the holler.

William H. Walker, son of Thomas and Miranda Collett Walker was born Oct. 26, 1831 in Kentucky and died at age 29 in Morgan Co., IN. He had married Elizabeth Cooper and in 1860 was living in Hamblen Township, Brown County, with his two sons Charles M., who married Matilda Jane Richardson, and James Crawford, who never married. The widow and children moved back to Johnson County soon after the death of William H.

Samuel C. Walker, son of Thomas and Miranda Collett Walker was born May 18, 1836, in Indiana. After his marriage March 20, 1860, he came to Hamblen Township, Brown County, dying there Jan. 31, 1910. And his wife, the former Sarah E. Stewart, daughter of David Stewart, are buried at

Unity Cemetery. Their family included: Louisa J., who married Ephraim Mathney; William G. who married Cora B. Richardson; Rebecca who married Jacob Flint; Susan who married Charles G. Waltman and John.

Thomas Walker Jr., son of Thomas and Miranda Collett Walker was born Nov. 20, 1841 in Johnson Co., IN. He married Hannah Jane Skinner, daughter of Nathaniel and Matilda Slack Skinner Dec. 29, 1864 and by 1870 was living in Hamblen Township, Brown County. He died Dec. 24, 1916 and is buried at Bethlehem Cemetery. The children of Thomas and Matilda includes James N., who married Mary Ward; Ida Jane who married Joseph Dine and Edward L. who married Daisy M. Calvert.

Charles M. Walker, son of Thomas and Miranda Collett Walker was born Oct. 4, 1846 in Johnson County. He married Lydia Ann Glidden, Jan. 1, 1873 and they were living in Hamblen Township by 1880. Their children included Bessie May; who married Link Bowden; Leroy Esco who married Vonnie Renner, and then Edith Dickerson, Della Opal who married Carl G. McDaniel; and Jennie L. who never married. *Researched by Phyllis E. Walker*

THOMAS WALKER II - Thomas was born Nov. 20, 1841 in Hensley Township, Johnson County. Moved shortly after his marriage to Hannah Jane Skinner on Dec. 29, 1864 to Hamblen Township, Brown County. He lived all his life on Horseshoe Road, dying Dec. 24, 1916. He and Hannah are buried in the Bethlehem Church Cemetery. He made his living running a sawmill and farming. Their family included two daughters and twins who died young and are buried on the grandparents' lot at East Hill Cemetery at Morgantown. The other children are, James N. who married Mary Ward and died without issue. Ida Jane Walker born Feb. 24, 1877, married Oct. 31, 1894 Joseph Dine. Her children included Clarence Dine; Opal Dine who married Jasper Merriman; Nettie Marie Dine who married George Arthur Anderson; Gertrude May Dine who married Jennings Richart; Ralph E. Dine who married Mildred Burris; and Garnet Dine who married Wayne Burker. The third child of Thomas and Hannah that lived to maturity was Edward Lonzo Walker who married Daisy Melissa Calvert. (see other sketch) *Submitted by Phyllis E. Walker*

Thomas and Hannah (Skinner) Walker

WALTMAN FAMILY - Valentine Waldham was born in Alsace where his father, a Spanish count, was in charge of Spain's interests in the buffer country that Louis XIV of France coveted and eventually secured. Valentine's father was killed and he was smuggled over the border to save his life. Valentine was adopted by Count Frundsberg who gave him the name Waltman to conceal his identity. Valentine Waltman died about 1750. His only heir, Conrad Waltman, came to Philadelphia on Oct. 25, 1738. He is the progenitor of many surnamed Waltman. Conrad Waltman's son, Michael, was born about 1745 in Frederick Co., MD. Michael served as a Lieutenant in the Revolutionary War in defense of Philadelphia. He married Mary Prutzman of Frederick County. Michael Waltman, Sr. died in 1829 and is buried at Apple's Church Cemetery in Frederick County.

Michael Waltman, Jr. son of Michael, Sr., was born Aug. 11, 1808 in Frederick County. Young Michael and his wife, Susan, were in Brown County by 1837 and lived near Bean Blossom, then called Georgetown. Michael died at age 68, his wife Susan died at age 50; both are buried in Bean Blossom Cemetery.

Myron and Opal Waltman

Hiram McIntire "Mack" Waltman, son of Michael Waltman, Jr., was born Nov. 3, 1843. He married on July 1, 1866 to Eliza Frownfelter who had married in 1861 to Zephaniah Waltman. Family tradition says that Zephaniah and his brother Mack served in the Civil War. Zephaniah was killed and when Mack returned he married his brother's widow. Mack and Eliza had children: John Sylvester, Samuel, Jane and Anna. This family lived near Bean Blossom. Mack died Oct. 15, 1923. His wife Eliza, born April 5, 1841, died Feb. 22, 1905. Both are buried in Bean Blossom Cemetery.

John Sylvester Waltman, son of Mack and Eliza Waltman, was born March 9, 1869. On Sept. 20, 1891, he married Ina Evelyn Adams, daughter of John and Mary Zody Adams of Bean Blossom. John S. Waltman was a teacher and carpenter, lived on a farm east of Bean Blossom. John and Ina Waltman had three children: Elza Estell, born May 2, 1893; Lowell Carson, born Nov. 1, 1902 and Velma Vesper, born March 6, 1906. John Sylvester Waltman died Feb. 28, 1939; his wife Ina, born Jan. 4, 1871, died June 1, 1920. Both are buried in Bean Blossom Cemetery.

Elza Estell Waltman, son of John S. and Ina Waltman, was born at the family home, attended a nearby school, went to Lane Business College in Indianapolis. He continued to work his parents' farm and worked at other jobs part time. He married on Aug. 15, 1916 to Blanche Percifield, daughter of Henry and Ella Mann Percifield. Elza and Blanche had five children: Myron E. and Byron E., twins, born July 9, 1917; Marjorie N., born Dec. 4, 1918; Howard E., born May 26, 1928 and Helen J. Waltman, born May 13, 1930. Elza Estell Waltman died Oct. 23, 1988; his wife Blanche, born Nov. 23, 1891, died Aug. 11, 1976. Both are buried in Bean Blossom Cemetery.

Myron E. Waltman, son of Elza and Blanche Waltman, attended school in the Bean Blossom area. On May 23, 1936 Myron married his longtime girlfriend, Opal Marie Mead, born May 21, 1918, daughter of Marvin Mead and Pearl Condon. Myron and Opal Waltman moved to a farm near Gatesville in Hamblen Township in 1937. Until 1989 Myron worked the farm and for 30 years did other jobs as well. Myron and Opal had four children: Myron Lee, born March 16, 1937, married Lois Percifield, has four children; Marion Eugene, born June 8, 1939, married Donna Bohannon, divorced, has four children; Dorothy Marie, born March 10, 1942, married John Brester, divorced, has two children, then married Robert Goble; Walter Dale, born May 30, 1946, married Kathy Jackson, has two children. Myron and Opal Waltman have eight great-grandchildren. *Submitted by Myron E. Waltman*

MOSES AND MATILDA WARD FAMILY - Moses M. and his wife, Matilda, natives of Ohio, came to Brown County between 1846 and 1849. Moses was born in 1818, Matilda in 1819. She is said to have been part Indian. They made their new home near Salt Creek in VanBuren Township. There seems to have been a number of Wards there, and it is supposed that they were all related. A Ward man opened a store in a log building in the 1850s or 60s, in the area that came to be called Pike's Peak.

Moses and Matilda had nine children: Mahlon, Henry J., Benjamin, Mary J., Timothy, Rebecca, twins Emaline and Evaline, and Albert. Mahlon Ward, along with others from the community, served in the 6th Indiana Vol. Infantry, 1861-1864. He was discharged after the fall of Atlanta. He married Rebecca Downey in 1862, and had a second wife, named Sarah, late in life. Henry J. "Jont" Ward operated the store at Pike's Peak for several years. He married Susan Sowders in 1866. After her death, he married Margaret A. Butler in 1886. Timothy Ward married Amanda M. Gatten in 1874. Emaline Ward was married to John A. Gatten in 1874; George W. King in 1874; later to Phillip A. Moore; and finally to Daniel Keller in 1886. A fifth marriage much later to a Kansas man named Brown was annulled. Some of Emaline's King and Moore descendants still live in this region.

Ward brothers and sisters: Timothy, Mahlon, Henry J. Ward, and Emaline Ward Keller about 1915.

Evaline Ward was a beautiful, dark-eyed girl. Unfortunately she became romantically involved with a married man, and had a daughter out of wedlock in 1875. She named the child Rosa Dell Smith, Smith being the name of the father. Three years later, Evaline married Christopher S. Cook. Soon afterward, several of the Ward families moved west to Ellinwood, KS. This was on the old Santa Fe Trail, only a couple of years after all the buffalo had been killed. Chris, Evaline and Rosa made the trip in a covered wagon. A son, Joseph Cook, was born in 1879. They returned to Brown County on the train that fall, though most of the Ward family stayed on in Kansas. Chris and Evaline had two more children, Walter E., in 1881, and Iva Cordelia, in 1885. Iva died of diphtheria in 1888. Descendants of Joseph Cook remain in the region, though none are in Brown County. *Submitted by Evelyn Cook Cleland Sanborn and Donna Cleland Kuhlman*

WARFORD—FLEENER - Oscar Warford was 11 years old ca. 1865 when his widowed mother, Mary Beaty Warford moved to Brown County to be near her Uncle John Beaty. John Warford's family came from Cumbria Co., England; some of the brothers came to Ohio. John and Mary lived in Belmont County close to Barnesville, OH, south off of I-70. There is a Warford Family Cemetery close to Barnesville and this is where Mary buried John Warford in Feb. 26, 1865.

Four generations: Ilena (Warford) Buckley, Thurle Warford, Cary Warford and Oscar Warford.

Oscar married Nov. 20, 1879, Sarah Branstetter, a native Brown countian who "heired" hundreds of acres of land. One of their sons was Cary J. Warford. He lived along S.R. 45 all of his life. Cary married Mary Jane Brummett. They built a home south of brother Edward and Jesse on S.R. 45. They resided there until their death. Cary and Mary J. had one son Thurle A. Warford, who learned to be an agent-operator at Trevlac, IN on the Illinois Central Railroad and he pursued this occupation until his death on Dec. 23, 1957.

Front: Ilena and Jack Buckley. Back: Gary and Donald Buckley.

He married Anna E. Fleener a native of Brown County on Sept. 15, 1923. She was the youngest sister of Fred, George R. and Leo Fleener. Anna's parents were William T. born March 10, 1858 died Oct. 18, 1912 and Sarah I. Stout born Oct. 25, 1861 died May 31, 1926. Anna's Stout family goes back to Ivan, "The Stout." Her Stouts are from Sheffield, England. Thurle and Anna were the parents of one daughter, Doris Ilena, born May 4, 1927 at Sullivan, IN. When she was five they moved back to Brown County and built a home on S.R. 45. It was on the road at the bottom of the hill where the original Warford home place stood. Ilena attended Branstetter grade school two years. She started school in the first grade taught by her Uncle Geo. Ray Fleener. He gave her a very good start because after moving many times; she received the Citizenship Award her freshman year at New Lebanon High School. She graduated among the top ten students out of 100 in her class at Sullivan High School in 1945. She wrote a poem about Pine Bluff across from her Brown County home. She has written other poetry and is an artist which was influenced from living in Brown County. Until her grandfather's death she and her two sons returned to Brown County every summer. The homeplace built by Thurle and Anna Warford was sold to Frank Warford, her grandfather's brother. Ilena, as well as her family, will remember many Brown County years. Ilena married John William, "Jack" Buckley on March 19, 1947. They have two sons: Donald J. and Gary W. both born in Sullivan, IN. Donald married Tina M. Stanley Schofield. They have three daughters, Tammy, Jacqueline, and Kristi. Gary married Janna L. Price and they have three sons: Zachary, Kirk, and Evan. Tammy, Donald's adopted daughter married William E. Rogers and they have two children, Joselyn and Stefan. They reside in Paxton, IN on a farm. *Submitted by Mrs. John W. Buckley*

OLIVE (BLACK) WARFORD - Olive was born in Stark Co., OH in 1857 to Lafayette Black, Pennsylvania native, and Martha Roach Black. Her father's brother, Jacob married her mother's sister, Barbara Ann. Many of these Black descendants came to Brown Co., IN to live. Olive married Ausman Decatur Black. It is said these two were related but one is not sure about it. The children of Jacob, especially Andy, born 1867, and Bill, born 1873, found they could learn very little in school. But they were likeable people, worked for what was given them, and while they seemed like tramps they were really wanting attention. They did not bother Olive.

Ausman Black died in 1905. They had lived down a little lane off Carmel Ridge Road. Olive purchased a house on route 45 fairly close to Oscar Warford's home and they became friends.

Oscar's first wife had died in 1907. The next year he had married a widow lady, Henrietta Myars. Their home was somewhat unsettled-probably due partly to blending two sets of children. But one of the Warford boys had an autograph book containing a note from Henrietta saying how she approved of him. When she passed away, the children left home and Oscar was alone.

When word surfaced of Olive and Oscar's marriage the entire neighborhood along Rt. 45 gave them a chivaree.

Oscar raised chickens, farm crops and did some work in the woods. He owned various touring cars, one of which had a brass radiator. He had animal pets especially one dog and one rooster.

The couple were frequently seen on the road. While she was quiet - he was sociable and liked visiting his married children and occasional meetings with his cousin, Dr. George Beaty, lodge members and old time Barnesville, OH neighbors, as the MacAlvains.

Olive had income of her own and she was a good manager and homemaker. She dressed plainly - felt she was not properly dressed without an apron. Meals in summer were cooked and served in the summer kitchen.

Oscar's son, Homer, and wife took the old folks to the "500" race one year. Olive liked the race but she continued to clutch the car door latch as though she would jump out any moment, when she was a passenger.

Oscar had summer allergies and grandchildren visited vacation time. Though Olive had not reared children she stayed calm and looked after each one. She gave the little ones puffed cereal for snacks. Oscar gave them little tobacco sacks of pennies.

All felt a great loss when she passed away. *Submitted by Lisa Lazell*

OSCAR AND SARAH BRANSTETTER WARFORD - In Cheshire, England, the name Warford means "coming from Wier Ford." John Warford lived in Louden Co., VA, in the late 1700s. His son, Elijah, grew up there.

Elijah Warford and wife, Elizabeth, lived on a farm near Barnesville, OH for many years. A son, John, was born there in 1829. John married Mary Beaty and they lived in Belmont Co., OH. John died February 1865 as did two sons. They were buried on the farm because of fear of an epidemic.

Oscar and Sarah Warford

Mary and sons, Oscar born 1854 and John born 1865, and deaf daughter, Aurilla, came to live with Mary's brother, John Beaty, of near Fruitdale, Brown Co., IN. Mary married, second, Caleb Ferguson, a widower with several children and they lived on a farm near Nashville. Two sons were born, one dying young and the other, Green, living to adulthood. By 1872 Caleb was superintendent of the Brown County Home and it was a busy time caring for the "home" residents, a large family and Aurilla's attendance at Deaf School in Indianapolis. Mary died in 1881. She and young son are probably buried in the Unity Cemetery as there are unmarked places near the Beaty graves. The John Beatys had also lost a son, Oscar Allen.

Caleb and some of the children, including Green, went West. John lived and is buried in Bedford. Caleb contacted Oscar from Arkansas. Green and Newton were later reported in Texas. Aurilla married a deaf man, Jasper Cross, and lived in LaPorte, IN.

Oscar married Sarah Branstetter. Their house still stands on Carmel Ridge Road near SR 45. He farmed, raised cattle and chickens, worked in lumber, attended lodge and political meetings.

Sarah was glad her daughters helped with younger boys as she had been brought up to spin, weave, make feather pillows and quilts, dry apples and there was housework plus meals to prepare in the summer kitchen. The family had a garden, an orchard, bees and a row of Yucca plants along the front of the house. When opportunity came, Sarah got living room wooden walls painted in outdoor scenery by a travelling painter and her daughter, Ida.

Seven Warford children attended Branstetter School and enjoyed visits with Aunt Julia Brock in Monroe County. Walter and Ed taught school. Cary was a farmer and carpenter. Ed and Frank worked at the Turner store and at the mill when Oscar and Newt Walker had it leased. Walter and Frank worked at the Trevlac Depot and moved to similar jobs in Oblong, IL. Edgar had the Post Office and store in

Trevlac for many years. Homer was in WWII and then was a telegrapher for the railroad.

Ida married Lewis Kelso, Bertha married Walter Weddle, Edgar married Jessie Cullen, Cary married Mary Jane Brummett and they all stayed in Brown County. Walter married Ethel Richards, Frank married Ola Hawley and Homer married Joyce Purcell in Illinois.

Family Bibles were in both Elijah's and Oscar's estates.

FRANK AND WILMA HYDE WATSON -

Wilma Jean Hyde, youngest daughter of John Siegle Hyde and Bertha May Griffin, was born Oct. 1, 1925 in Brown County. She married Harold Frank Watson who was born June 29, 1924, died Oct. 1, 1967. They had two children, Nancy Charlene and Gary Frank Watson.

Front Row: Nancy Fields, Wilma Watson, Timothy Fields, Gary Watson. Back Row: Frank Watson.

Nancy Charlene Watson, born Nov. 30, 1946, married Richard Fields, born April 18, 1939. Their four children are: (1) Timothy Scott Fields, born Feb. 27, 1966, married Annette Eads. He served in the Marines. They have a son, Brandon Tyler Fields, born Dec. 9, 1989 in California. (2) Lora Kay Fields, born April 13, 1968, married Johnny Ray Smith, born March 9, 1965. (3) Darren Howard Fields, born Feb. 5, 1972. (4) Christopher Patrick Fields, born July 19, 1974.

Gary Frank Watson, born Sept. 24, 1954, married first to Pam Barrow. They had a daughter, Amber Dawn Watson, born Sept. 19, 1977. Gary married second to Kathy F. Sexton Pugh and third to Betty Jo Baxter. They divorced. *Submitted by Wilma Jean Hyde Watson*

WALTER AND ELSIE WAYMAN -

Joseph Richard Wayman, Jr., son of Joseph Richard Wayman Sr. and Rebecca Prosser, was born in Brown County in 1869. He married Rebecca Smith in 1889. They had two children: Thursa (1890) and Flossie who died in infancy.

After the death of his first wife he married Jannie Parsley (1874), daughter of Jasper Parsley and Sarah Walker, in 1898. To this marriage five children were born: Clemmie J. (1899), Elbridge (1903), Joseph Edward (1906), Walter E. (1908) and Ida M. (1911) who died in 1913. There was a stepdaughter Erschel. Joseph purchased 129 acres in Hamblen Township in 1900 for farming. A portion of this property is retained by his surviving son Walter. The men also raised cattle, ran a thrashing machine, and operated a sawmill on the property.

Joseph's second wife having died in 1913 he married Laura Belle Hurdle in 1915. She died in 1932 and he followed one month later.

Clemmie died in 1924 after being married to Ina Snider for two years.

Walter and Elsie Wayman

Elbridge married Annetta Strahl, daughter of James Strahl and Minnie Skinner, in 1923. One child, William Richard, was born in 1924. Elbridge died in 1925. His son served in Italy during WWII as an air crewman. He flew 20 combat missions in Germany and was awarded an air medal with the oak leaf cluster. After his college graduation he worked as an engineer until retirement.

Joseph Edward worked on the family farm until he entered military service in the United States Army during WWII. As a military police officer, he was stationed in North Africa. He served as a guard for President Franklin D. Roosevelt for the conference in Morocco between Roosevelt and Winston Churchill. After his discharge from service he returned to Brown County and later married Violet Bell (1917), daughter of Harry Bell and Ada Burton, in 1949. He was employed as Supt. of Brown County Highway Dept. and later as a Supt. for the town of Nashville until his death in 1962. One daughter was born, Vicki Lynn in 1957. She is the president of a retail corporation. He had one stepdaughter Nina B. Leggett (1944) a district sales manager for a Fortune 500 corporation.

Walter was a truck driver and contributed to the construction of Camp Atterbury in Johnson County and Bakalar Air Force base in Bartholomew County. He married Elsie Glick (1911), daughter of Jonathan Glick and I.V. Lawrence, in 1940. They resided on the Wayman farm until they moved to Nashville in 1957. Walter worked as a school bus driver and was employed as a grader operator for the Brown County Highway department until his retirement. Elsie served as Deputy Auditor and was later appointed Director of the Brown County Dept. of Public Welfare. They are members of the Nashville United Methodist Church, the Brown County Historical Society, and the Brown County Farm Bureau. Elsie is active in the Pioneer Women's organization and the United Methodist Church Women's group.

MILTON D. AND MATILDA WAYT -

Milton David was born in what is now West Virginia on Christmas Day of 1855. He was the son of Daniel and Lucinda Wayt. Milton and Matilda Jane Rains Wilson were married on May 12, 1882, in Brown Co., IN. Matilda, a daughter of Joel S. and Nancy Jane Rains, was a young widow at the time of her marriage to Milton.

Milton and Mattie Wayt made their home near Elkinsville in southwestern Brown County. Their four children were: (1) Nora, who was adopted, was born in 1886. She married Charlie York and they had eight children: Marie, Herman, Raymond, Helen, Myrtle, Dorothy, Althea, and Walter York. (2) Clifford Hezikiah, born in 1892, married Susan Navilla Zike and had three children: Gerald Clifford, Glen Curtis, and Gloria Sue. (3) Chester Francis, born in 1895, married Gladys Martin and had ten children: Goldie, Russell, Frank, Hazel, Nina, Kenneth, Thomas, Delores, Wilma Jean, and Laverne. (4) Clarence Joseph, born 1902, died as a child.

Most of the descendants of Milton and Matilda Wayt now live in northern Jackson Co., IN. *Submitted by Larry Dean Wayt, son of Glen Curtis Wayt*

WEDDLE FAMILY -

The Weddle family ancestors originated in Scotland and immigrated to the United States in 1774, settling in Hawkins Co., TN. Some moved north to Jackson Co., IN about the turn of the century. Thos. Wm. Weddle married Rosamond Wallen in 1796 and raised their ten children in Jackson County; however they are buried in Bear Creek Cemetery near Trevlac in Brown County.

Their second son, David Dolan Weddle, was one of the first Justices of the Peace in Brown County and also a County Commissioner. He was on the Building Committee to build the first courthouse in Nashville and furnished the first table for it. He and his family later migrated to Oregon with a covered wagon train.

The third son of Thos. and Rosamond was Daniel, born in 1801. He and his wife, Elizabeth, moved to Brown County in 1833. Daniel and his oldest son, McCallen Green Weddle, rode horseback to Indianapolis to obtain a government land grant and established a home in the vicinity of Bear Creek. Daniel and Elizabeth are the second generation of Weddles buried in Bear Creek Cemetery. McCallen was the only one of their seven children who settled in Brown County. He married Sarah Fleener in 1852 and they established their home on a 200 acre land grant just east of Trevlac, building their house on what is now Indian Hill Road. Using their ingenuity to make the most of the natural resources around them, they cleared the land, planted an orchard, and among other things, built an ice house to store the ice they cut out of Bean Blossom Creek. McCallen and Sarah are also buried in Bear Creek Cemetery. Their only child, Leander B. Weddle married Ellen Conard and lived on the family homestead, raising four children - Walter, McAllen, Ira and Grace. The three sons settled in Brown County.

Men in back row: Walter and Ira Weddle. Women Standing: Sarah McCoy, Eva (Walker) Weddle, Graice (Weddle) O'Niell, Ellen ?, Bertha (Warford) Weddle, Catherine (Weddle) McClary. Men Seated: Lenanda Weddle, Tod McClary, Doc McCoy. Boy and Girl Standing: Ervin and Norme Weddle. Children on Ground: Front is Ernie; Behind is Clarence, Frank and Horce Weddle.

Walter married Bertha A. Warford, daughter of Oscar and Sarah Branstetter Warford, and built a home on part of the original Branstetter land grant on Carmel Ridge Road, where their son, Clarence, still resides. Walter owned and operated a garage in Helmsburg, besides farming and working for the State Highway Department for a period of time. His son, Clarence, married Goldie Richards and had two children, Ruth Annette and David Leon, each living in Helmsburg with their families. Ruth and her husband, Marvin Cody, have three children and four grandchildren. David and his wife, Harrietta, had four children—their son, Gregory, died in a home fire in 1980.

Leander's second son, McAllen was a schoolteacher. He and his wife, Maud, raised their three children in Brown County. Both are buried in Bear Creek Cemetery, and their children have married and relocated.

Ira Weddle, Leander's third son, married Eva Walker and raised their five children, Irwin, Norme, Harold, Virgil, and Virginia, on the family homestead on Indian Hills Road. Ira was large in stature, but was known by the nickname, "Chicken," because most of his income came from raising chickens. His children married and relocated, except for two grandsons, Jerry L. Weddle and Rodney A. McFadden, now living in Brown County with their families. The old homestead was sold to Mr. Gallahue in 1958, after Ira's death.

To date, eight generations of Weddles have called Brown County "home." *Submitted by Harrietta Weddle and Millie McFadden*

ALVA WEST FAMILY - Alva Nathaniel, fourth and youngest child of Michael and Eliza (Downey) West, was born on June 20, 1886 in Brown Co., IN. His parents were both born in 1846 in Noble Co., OH. Michael, a Civil War veteran, came to Brown County in 1876, joining his brother and sister-in-law, Jacob and Jane (Van Dyke) West. Eliza and her parents, Joseph and Jane (Clark) Downey, also moved to Brown County in the 1870s. Michael and Eliza were married on March 1, 1877.

Alva grew up on the family farm in eastern Washington Township. He attended Pleasant Ridge (also known as Stull) and North Salem Elementary Schools, completing an eighth grade education. After leaving school he farmed, worked in timber, and cut crossties. He was a member of the Redmen's Lodge at New Bellsville for a time.

Alva and Clara West, 1960

Clara Elizabeth Howard was born in Brown County on Nov. 5, 1890, the oldest of seven children born to William Henry and Martha (Clark) Howard. William was born in Tyler Co., WV in 1866 and came to Brown County in 1873 with his parents, James and Elvira (Copenhaver) Howard. Martha was born in 1874 in Monroe Co., OH. She came to Brown County in 1879 or 1880 with her parents, Lawrence and Clarinda (Evans) Clark. William and Martha were married on May 18, 1890.

Clara was raised on her family's farm, which was located a short distance northwest of the Wests' farm. Clara received an eighth grade education at Mt. Liberty Elementary School. Her uncle, George Clark, was one of her teachers. Clara and Alva were married on Nov. 9, 1910 in Nashville. Rev. Milton Northam conducted the ceremony.

Alva and Clara set up housekeeping on a farm adjacent to Alva's birthplace. Michael West purchased this farm in 1901 and sold it to Alva in 1911. Alva and Clara's nine children were born here: Gledith (born 1911), Michael (born 1912), Ernest (born 1914), Glenn (born 1916), Ivan (born 1919), James (born 1921, died 1921), Ferrel (born 1923), Mildred (born 1925), and Frieda (born 1927). The family attended North Salem Methodist Church, and the children went to North Salem Elementary School.

Alva continued farming until 1944 when he went to work at Noblitt-Sparks (now Arvin Industries) in Columbus. He worked there until he retired in 1954. After his retirement, he raised and sold potatoes.

Alva and Clara were Democrats, and Alva served as a precinct election board clerk for several elections. He unsuccessfully ran for county commissioner on the Prohibition Party ticket in the early 1950s.

In 1979, Alva and Clara sold their home and moved to Columbus to live with their daughter, Mildred Mobley. Alva died here on Sept. 19, 1979. Clara died on June 18, 1987. Both are buried in Garland Brook Cemetery in Columbus. Of their eight surviving children, Gledith Smith, Michael, and Ivan still live in Brown County; Mildred Mobley, Glenn, and Ferrel live in Columbus; Ernest lives in Clifford, IN; and Frieda King lives in Indianapolis.

DYLAN WHITAKER FAMILY - Nelson Abbott married Ellen Rittenhouse. Among their children were Charles, William Henry and twin boys. Charles married Willa Gertrude Link, daughter of Pierce and Nancy Link. While living in Arkansas, Charles enlisted in World War II from Little Rock. Son, Marvin, was born in 1916 in Marktree, AR. They also had son Carl. Gertrude ("Gertie") lived for many years on the old Abbott home place receiving a government pension from her husband's war record. Gertie continued to piece quilt blocks and keep busy after going to stay at the Morgantown Nursing Home. She was an active member of the Morgantown Baptist Church. She lived to be 93 years old.

Angie and Dylan Whitaker and sons Jason and Dustin.

Carl Abbott married Cora Collins. Cora's mother was Tillie Mae Wilson born near Dayton, OH. Her father was Effern Allen Collins, probably from Jacksonville, KY. This couple married in Brown County and lived on land north of the old McClary farm on Branstetter Road near Trevlac in the Abbott home. His mother, daughter of the Abbotts, lives in Florida.

Several years ago Dylan set a trailer home on the old Abbott home place which is on Carmel Ridge Road just north of the junction of Bear Creek Road and Richards Road. (The two old houses on the property were already gone.) Dylan and his wife, Angie, (not a native Brown Countian) and sons Dustin age six and Jason age four live in trailer.

As Angie says, "We have lived in Brown County for ten years. We live where the land has been passed down for generations. The school is small and caring about the children. There is plenty to keep you involved with as a family".

JOHN WHITEHORN FAMILY - William and Naomi Whitehorn (great-great-grandparents of John Whitehorn) were some of the very early settlers of Brown County. They migrated from Sussex Co., VA to Grayson Co., KY between 1810 and 1820. They then settled in the eastern part of Brown County, some years before it was organized as a county in 1836. The eastern part of Brown County in which he and his family settled was in Van Buren Township, taken from the western part of Bartholomew County at that time. Marriage records for Whitehorns in 1833 and 1834 are found in Bartholomew County Courthouse for this part of Brown County.

William and Naomi had nine children. Only one of their children, David Allen, stayed in Brown County.

David Allen married Amy Cox Sept. 25, 1834. Amy was listed as a midwife in a list of Brown County Physicians, Pikes Peak, 1881-1883. David and Amy had 12 children. One of their children, David A. Whitehorn, born in 1837, fought in the Civil War. He enlisted in the Union Army in 1861, and became a member of Company C, 22nd Regiment, Indiana Volunteers. He was killed in action in 1864 at Kenesaw Mountain, GA.

Front: General and Talitha Whitehorn. Back: David Allen, Clara, Tura Luetta, Nettie Marie, Lawrence Delmas.

Another one of their children, Nathaniel Lyons Whitehorn born Nov. 28, 1861 and died May 28, 1951 was John's grandpa. Nathaniel's nickname was General. He was nicknamed General because he was named after David's commanding officer, General Nathaniel Lyons, who was killed at the battle of Wilsons Creek in Missouri.

General married Talitha Cumi Moore, daughter of Michael Moore and Sara (Cooper) Moore on Nov. 25, 1884 in Brown County. Talitha was born Jan. 15, 1867 and died May 13, 1948.

General worked as a blacksmith in Nashville for Sammy Patterson for ten years at a time when there was a well-worn path over Weed Patch Hill down into the village of Kelp where General lived. He made the round trip to town by foot (14 miles) six days a week, and he was paid the current wage of $1.00 per day. General moved to Garden City, South of Columbus in 1901. General and Talitha had nine children: (1) Harley Emmer born 1885 died 1943; (2) David Allen born 1887 died 1964; (3) Maudie Olive born 1890 died young; (4) Mary Emma born 1891 died young; (5) Clara born 1893 died 1967; (6) Benjamin Franklin, born ? died young; (7) Tura Luetta born 1896 and still living; (8) Nettie Marie born 1902 died 1980; and (9) Lawrence Delmas born 1907 died 1973.

Lawrence Delmas Whitehorn was father to John. He married Ruth Marie Kyle, the daughter of LeRoy and Hattie Imelba (Russell) Kyle from Edinburg on Feb. 11, 1941. They had two children: Marvin born March 26, 1952 and John born June 12, 1947. Marvin married Kay Montgomery from Seymour and they have one son. Marvin resides in Seymour.

John married Betty Sisson, the daughter of Chelsea and Rosemary Sisson on May 31, 1970 in Nashville, IN. They have three children: Chelsea and twin daughters Abigail and Anita. John and Betty reside on Route 2 in Morgantown. *Submitted by John Whitehorn*

GROVER AND LIZZIE (AYERS) WILKERSON

Grover Cleveland Wilkerson was born in Brown Co., IN on Aug. 11, 1887, the son of Thomas and Laura Alice (Followell) Wilkerson. Grover worked in timber much of the time. In the early 20s he worked at the Story General Store for Morrison and Kelley, including cream testing. He worked at Arvin's in Columbus for 13 years before retiring in 1957. He married Lizzie Ayers, daughter of James and Cynthia (Mitchner) Ayers, April 10, 1917. Grover and Lizzie lived at Story most of their married life and raised a daughter, Lenore, and two sons, Clifford and Amos. Lizzie worked part-time at the Freetown Canning Factory. They also dug sassafras and other roots at times and sold them. Grover died Jan. 28, 1958 and Lizzie died Sept. 23, 1967. Both are buried at the Mt. Zion Cemetery.

Grover and Lizzie Wilkerson and daughter Lenore, 1919

Grover's grandparents were Hammond and Peggy (Rogers) Wilkerson. His father, Thomas, was born in Brown County on Sept. 30, 1865. Lizzie's father, James Ayers, died Feb. 26, 1924, at his home near Story. He was a Civil War Veteran and is buried at Mt. Zion Cemetery.

Lenore, born May 8, 1917, married Donald Ayers on Oct. 4, 1933. Donald was the son of Arnold and Myrtle (Skinner) Ayers, he was a World War II Veteran who died August 1977 and is buried at Mt. Zion Cemetery. Donald was born Aug. 17, 1912. They had three sons, Mickey, Scott and Richard and one daughter, Gayle Jackson.

Clifford, born Sept. 22, 1919, died May 1981, married Vena Louise Troxell, June 1953, daughter of Fred and Ora Pendleton Troxell. He was a World War II veteran and is buried in the Mt. Zion Cemetery. They had one son, Dewayne.

Amos, born Sept. 13, 1921, married Olive Moore, daughter of Everett and Grace Bridgewater Moore. They have no children.

Lenore lives at Story and Amos lives on SR 135 south of Story.

ORVILLE WILKERSON

Henry Orville Wilkerson was born Nov. 27, 1908 and died June 21, 1974. He was born near Elkinsville in southern Brown County. His parents were George Wilkerson born April 26, 1861 and died Nov. 24, 1943 and Minnie Jane Sexton Wilkerson born March 21, 1878 and died April 29, 1940. Orville had a half brother and half sister: Albert Wilkerson and Stella (Wilkerson) Hayes. Albert died in 1973 and Stella died in 1971. Orville had two brothers who died of diphtheria: Ernest in 1900 and Wesley in 1901, a week apart. The rest of the family were Josephine (Wilkerson) Farling who died in 1941; Alta (Wilkerson) Walker died in 1978, Fada (Wilkerson) Dragoo died in 1985 and Amos Wilkerson who died in 1986.

Orville Wilkerson

Orville was a farmer and drove a high school bus to Trafalgar in 1935 and took Brown County students there. He drove a truck most of his life. He had a Ford dump truck and hauled stone for the Brown County State Park in the 1930s. He changed to Chevrolets after that and never bought any Fords.

He married Inez Everling in April 1936. They had four children: Donald Wilkerson born in 1939; David born in 1941; Jeanette (Wilkerson) Graves born in 1954 and a stillborn girl, Patricia Marie, born in 1951 and buried in East Hill Cemetery, Morgantown, near Orville's grave. He had five grandchildren and one great-granddaughter, and some adopted grandchildren.

Back: David Wilkerson, Jeannette (Wilkerson) Graves. Front: Donald Wilkerson and mother Inez.

Orville was Hamblen Township trustee for two terms in the late 1940s and early 1950s; also a county commissioner in 1962-68. Orville hauled livestock to stockyards, Brown County stone to north Indianapolis, gravel, sand and wood to Indianapolis; coal from Madison, IN. He also moved a family to Arkansas and was always busy with his truck. He enjoyed meeting people and a lot of people remember him and tell others what he hauled for them. He would help others out of ditches with tractor and was always willing to help others. *Written by Inez (Everling) Wilkerson*

WILLIAM AND JEMIMA WILKERSON

An early settler, a farmer, and the progenitor of the Wilkerson families of southern Brown County, William Wilkerson was born Jan. 11, 1735 in King George Co., VA. When he was a young boy, his father moved the family to Granville Co., NC, where years later, young William served as a soldier in the Revolutionary War. He married his first wife during this time and, by his own statement, they had 11 children.

After the war, he moved to Rowan Co., NC, and there he married his second wife, Jemima "Gemamie" Franklin. Gemamie and William moved again to Knox Co., KY, and finally, in 1830, they settled on a little farm near Crooked Creek in Monroe Co., IN (near the town of Elkinsville in what is now Brown County).

On this farm they raised ten children: Solomon, Davis, Hammond, James, Emarine, Valentine, Isom, William, Henry and Peggy. These children married into the following known neighboring families: Mary "Polly" Anderson (Solomon); Margaret Jane "Peggy" Rogers (Hammond); Mary "Polly" Rogers (James); Isaac Fleetwood, Jesse Shipley and Ahart Hash (Emarine); Nancy Rippy (Valentine).

At the time this article was written, the number of known descendants produced for William and Gemamie by the above unions are: 40 grandchildren, 119 great-grandchildren and over 180 great-great-grandchildren. These numbers are increasing, as research into this family continues.

One child of William and Gemamie, Solomon, moved to Greene Co., IN where he started a small town, was Justice of the Peace there (and Postmaster), and later the town was named in his honor: Solsbury, IN. He died in 1873 when his horse kicked him in the head at the age of 73. The town is still there to this day.

On March 4, 1835, William Wilkerson, with his sons Davis and Hammond, applied to the United States Government for revolutionary war veteran benefits made available by an Act of Congress passed June 7, 1832. He personally gave a sworn declaration of the events of his life, in particular when and where he served as a soldier.

In a letter written to the government by his granddaughter, Rebecca Jane Beightel, she stated that William "died on a little farm that he owned on Crooked Creek in Brown County" and that "awhile before he died, he went out on his little farm and located the place where he wanted to be buried." On Aug. 18, 1842, William Wilkerson died at the age of 107 years, seven months and seven days. He was buried on the spot he had chosen. She further states that he was the first person to be buried there and said it was "a right smart sized" cemetery. Rebecca Jane recorded the dates on his tombstone as Jan. 11, 1735 and Aug. 18, 1842, and she added that Gemamie died July 6, 1846. Gemamie is probably buried in the grave found next to William, though no stone has been found.

The location of these graves had eluded researchers for many years, until on July 19, 1986, his old gravestone, buried under a thin layer of dirt and leaves, was discovered in the Fleetwood Cemetery (originally the "Wilkerson Cemetery") near Crooked Creek in Brown County. The small cemetery contains approximately 30 graves, is overgrown with brush and totally neglected. It was discovered by great-great-great-great-grandson Kris D. Hardy (the author of this article). The dates were mostly illegible, except the year of birth, 1735, which confirmed the information of Jane Wilkerson Beightel.

Kris D. Hardy has lived in Chicago, IL since 1980 and currently owns and operates a publishing concern. He was born Feb. 11, 1952 (to Wilma Jean McGuire and Robert William Hardy) and was raised in Bloomington, IN. He spends much of his time in Brown County conducting genealogical research.

Currently, he is preparing to publish the *Genealogy of the Wilkerson Families of Southern Brown County, Indiana*, with co-authors Kenneth J. and Helen H. Reeve. *Submitted by Kristopher Hardy*

JOHN MERRIWETHER WILLIAMS FAMILY -

The Williams Family had its beginning on Dec. 30, 1947, in Plymouth, IN, with the marriage of Mary Lynn Seip to 1st Lt. John Merriwether Williams USAF. Mary Lynn (Mickie) born June 18, 1925 in Hayden, CO, and John born Aug. 27, 1921 in Washington, GA, set out on their itinerant lifestyle for the next few years to Georgia, New Mexico, Texas, Michigan and Indiana. John Jr. was born on June 14, 1949, in Albuquerque, NM, Ann Cavanaugh on July 7, 1952, in Texas City, TX, and Sarah Hill on Nov. 19, 1954, in Plymouth, IN.

In 1956 John left the building materials business and earned a Bachelor of Science degree in Industrial Arts from Ball State University. His first teaching position was in Brown Co., IN. The family moved there during the summer of 1958. The job was to establish an Industrial Arts program for the Nashville High School. Two years later he did the same for the new Brown County High School eventually becoming principal of that school. Mickie taught at the co-operative kindergarten in the Village Green Building and worked with Edna Frazier in the library next door. Together the family was a charter member of St. David's Episcopal Church in Bean Blossom. John, Sr. received his Masters in Education in Bloomington in 1961.

The family moved to Marshall, MI, in 1964 where John, Sr. taught at Starr Commonwealth for Boys for two years. A move to Indianapolis precipitated a stable 20 years of teaching; John, Sr. as a vocational architectural drafting teacher at Arsenal Technical High School and Mickie, who had received her Masters in Elementary Education in 1976, taught kindergarten at School 102. All three children graduated from North Central High School in Marion County. Interest in the environment flourished and John, Sr. became chairman of the newly formed Hoosier Group of the Sierra Club. This interest spread through the family and subsequently took them to many parts of the world. In addition, interest in arts and crafts and anthropology became apparent with each member choosing their own field.

John, Jr. attended Valparaiso University for three years where he began a life long interest in writing. Ann graduated from Indiana University majoring in Fine Arts. Sarah went directly into Fiber Arts and is an accomplished spinner and weaver.

Sarah married David P. Noggle of Richmond, IN. They lived in Albuquerque, NM where their first two daughters were born: Chelsea on March 11, 1976, and Leslie on July 20, 1977. They moved to Brown County in 1979 where David is a contractor. Their last two children were born here: Sarahbeth on July 22, 1980 and Theodore (Teddy) on Aug. 30, 1982.

Ann married Murray Woods in Albuquerque, NM, where their two children were born: Kjestine on Feb. 26, 1980 and Cody on Jan. 7, 1988. They are divorced. Ann and the children moved to Brown County in 1989.

John, Jr. is unmarried and lives in Tijeras, NM.

John, Sr. and Mickie retired and returned to Brown County in 1988. Mickie continues her interest in the library and St. David's Church. John, Sr. with a continued interest in archaeology has a minor faculty position at the Glenn A. Black Laboratory of Archaeology at Indiana University.

EUGENE WILLOUGHBY FAMILY -

Albert Eugene Willoughby owned and operated the Nashville Hardware for nearly 50 years. He was awarded a gold hammer for years of service in the hardware community. He bought the old Calvin Hardware Store on Main Street in 1939 and later moved to South Jefferson Street. The Hardware offered everything from shovels, hammers, and coal buckets to overalls. Gene also worked at the Brown County State Park, Ross Owens Timber Company, Gregg and Tucker Hardware and Burkholder (Calvin's) Hardware. He was Washington Township Trustee for three terms. Eugene was born March 22, 1914 in Kentucky to Grover W. and Lillian (Hainline) Willoughby. Grover W. Willoughby was born in 1885 at Mt. Sterling, KY and married Lillian, July 25, 1909 also at Mt. Sterling, KY. Grover's parents were George and Emma (Burris) Willoughby.

Eugene Willoughby, 1985

Gene's wife, Cleo Kelley, was a teacher in Brown County schools. They were married April 4, 1936. Her parents were Richard and Jessie Kelley, who were both born in Brown County. The Willoughby children, Kenneth Lee, Deanna Jean and Keith Russell, can say they are natives because they were all born in Brown County.

Kenneth Lee born Aug. 28, 1936 worked as an electronic engineer in Florida. He was at Cape Canaveral when the first space ship was sent up. He also was manager of a tracking station during the early years of space work. Kenneth married (1) Mary Louise Richard and has one son Kevin Lewis who is now in California; and one daughter Danelle (Willoughby) Boon born Feb. 28, 1958. Danelle married Castle Chan Boon and they have three children: C. Larie born Jan. 3, 1981; Tracie born March 1982; and Caleb born May 1984. Danelle and family are now living in Laie, HI.

Kenneth married (2) Chanandaye Ramsaroop from Trinidad, West Indies and had a daughter named Natasha Willoughby born Oct. 30, 1972 in Bermuda.

Deanna Jean born Nov. 12, 1938 worked in the Laundromat and the Hardware many years, being there at her father's death. Her husband, Jerry Terrill, worked at Indiana University as foreman in the tractor section and also farms. They were married Dec. 24, 1958. Deanna and Jerry have four children: (1) Jerry Lee born Sept. 7, 1961; (2) Duane born March 13, 1968; (3) Michelle born July 5, 1972 and (4) Jeffrey born Feb. 5, 1978.

Grover Willoughby Family 1939. Back: Regina (Willoughby) Springer, Grace (Willoughby) Hillenburg, Virginia M. (Willoughby) Eads, Mary (Willoughby) Clark, Iva (Willoughby) Chambers. Front: Grover Willoughby, Grover Dale Willoughby, Lillian (Hainline) Willoughby, Lois (Willoughby) Wootton, S. Harold Willoughby, Lucille (Willoughby) Sexton, and A. Eugene Willoughby.

Keith born Jan. 29, 1940 married (1) Joyce Moore and had three children: Deborah Lynn born Nov. 21, 1958, Keith Bryan born Dec. 6, 1960 and Ramona Leigh born June 6, 1969. Keith then married (2) Linda (Cole) Welch and has two stepchildren: Brian and Cindy. Keith worked at Indiana University several years. He now works at RCA in Bloomington, where he is a foreman. He has worked there 24 years. Also, he worked in his father's store while in school and afterwards for several years. He now manages the Hardware Store in Nashville. His wife, Linda, also works at RCA. Deborah Lynn married (1) Michael Bock and they had one son Keith Michael born March 14, 1978. Deborah then married (2) Clint Eastwood and now lives in Bloomington. Keith Bryan I, married (1) Rhonda Lawyer and they have two sons: Keith Bryan II born April 11, 1978 and Russell Wayne born March 31, 1980. Ramona Leigh has a daughter Kelsie Renee born Feb. 19, 1989 and they live in Bloomington.

Gene Willoughby died Sunday, April 29, 1990 and has been laid to rest in the Duncan Cemetery, which is on the road to the former Huber School and to Yellowwood Lake. *Submitted by Cleo and Keith Willoughby and Deanna Jean (Willoughby) Terrill*

CARL AND MARJORIE WILSON -

(William) Carl Wilson was a well known Brown County resident from the early 1940s until his death in June, 1946. Prior to his move to the county however, he had established himself as a poet, radio personality, writer, humorist and speaker. It was from his imagination that the poetic hobo of those times, Tramp Starr was born. The hobo Wilson created spoke about observations of human nature in vignettes of country living.

Carl was a wanderer in his early years. Prior to his marriage he used to box under the name Tug Wilson. He also earned a living as a stunt rider for a time. His father was a circuit riding Methodist preacher who was assigned to a church in Greene Co., IN. It was there that Carl met Marjorie Mitchell, a girl several years younger than he. To avoid the displeasure of her parents who objected to his age, they eloped and were married in Kansas. Their family eventually included one son Dudley, another son Robert who succumbed to the flu epidemic of 1918, and four daughters, Betty, Linda, Joan and Patsy. Carl published his work in a magazine called "Farm Life." In 1921 he published a series of small pamphlets called "The Tramp Starr Magazine" which he wrote, sold advertisements for and published in its entirety. His wife assisted by doing the actual printing. Three books of his writings had been published prior to his move to Brown County. They were *My Indiana Farm*, *Radio Rhymes* and *Pop. 359*. As a speaker and a humorist he was on the radio in the 1930s broadcasting from WLW, WOWO and WKRC. For 25 years he was a regular published writer in the *Indianapolis Star*. Making one more move, Carl and Marjorie chose Brown County as their final home. They purchased a house on Helmsburg Road from Ival McDonald and named it Curly Shingles, Jr. after their previous farm in Dearborn County.

Tramp Starr

In 1943 Carl bought the Old Hickory Tavern from Charlie Murphy in a poker game and thus led to their management of the inn (now "The Ordinary"). After Carl's death, Marjorie continued to manage the tavern. She expanded the business to include a dining room and a kitchen. She moved from Curly Shingles to a home she purchased next door to the Old Hickory. Other interests included traveling, cooking, dancing; she led a full and active life until her death in 1973. At that time she was buried next to her husband in Greenlawn Cemetery in Nashville. Their tombstones read Tramp Starr and Mrs. Starr. Her daughter Joan Birdsong, along with three of her four sons, Bob, John and Tom still reside in the county. Her oldest son Bill is a policeman in Philadelphia. Joan and her son Bob are basketweavers; their work is shown at the Brown County Craft Gallery in Nashville.

ROBERT EARL AND DORIS LOUISE (RHUDE) WILSON
- Robert, born March 22, 1925, Ware Co., GA, son of Brint and Avis (Jordan) Wilson, married Doris, of Brown Co., IN, July 21, 1945.

Robert grew up in Atkinson and Ware Cos., GA. His father, Deputy Game and Fish Warden for Atkinson County, was killed March 5, 1933. His grandfather, Albert Frederick Wilson, born Sept. 22, 1870, Coffee Co., GA, died Nov. 5, 1928. His great-grandfather, Henry Clay Wilson, son of Alexander and Francis (Cross) Wilson, born Aug. 6, 1844, Muskingum Co., OH, died March 22, 1909, married May 7, 1865, Penelope Davis, Coffee Co., GA. Henry Wilson served during the Civil War from Ohio and was taken prisoner while foraging for food along the Ogeechee River near Savannah, GA. When paroled, he remained in Georgia, married and lived out his life.

Robert retired Feb. 19, 1988, from Parker and Mick Welding and Machine Works, Jacksonville, FL, where he was Welding Shop Foreman for over 20 of his 34 years with the company.

Doris, third daughter of Jacob Dougless Rhude, Jr. and Cassie Mable Trisler, born in Brown County April 17, 1927, attended Walker and Wray Schools, Brown County; Redland Elementary and Perrine High Schools, Dade Co., FL; graduated from Nineveh High School, class of 1945. She retired from U.S. Army Corps of Engineers, Jacksonville, FL District, Sept. 3, 1983, as Chief, Office Management Branch, with almost 34 years government service. She also taught records management for Office, Chief of Engineers, Washington, D.C.

Robert Earl and Doris Louise (Rhude) Wilson, Sr. 1980

Jacob Dougless Rhude, Jr., son of Jacob Dougless Rhude, Sr. and Martha Ellen Harrison, married in Brown County May 18, 1921, Cassie Mable Trisler, daughter of Ward Trisler and Mary Adair, (born Oct. 5, 1900). They lived in Hamblen Township, Brown County; Johnson Co., IN; and Dade Co., FL. He served in U.S. Navy, World War I. He died Dec. 2, 1949. She died Oct. 19, 1972. Both are buried at Greenlawn Cemetery, Franklin, IN.

Robert and Doris had three children:

Robert Earl Wilson, Jr., graduated Paxon High School, attended Jones College, enlisted in U.S. Army and served in First Airmobile Cavalry in Vietnam. He married Margy Ellen Fuller from Oklahoma. They had three daughters, Nancy, Rachael, Rebecah, and one son, Robert Earl Wilson III. They divorced. He and his four children live in Jacksonville.

Cassie Trisler Rhude Stephens, 1963. Jacob Dougless Rhude, Jr., 1947.

Celese Murrene Wilson graduated from Paxon High School. She married John Thomas Proctor. They have two daughters, Shannon and Valerie. Shannon married Scott Graham and has two children, Brittany and Russell.

Douglas Brent Wilson graduated from Edward White High School and attended Florida Junior College. He married first, Jennifer Massey. They divorced, no issue. He married second, Meloney Jean Chaney. They have one daughter, Ashley.

Celese was born in Indiana; both boys in Florida. They were reared and presently live in Jacksonville.

Robert Wilson died Oct. 28, 1988 and is buried in Riverside Memorial Park Cemetery, Jacksonville, FL, approximately one mile from their home.

Doris has relatives living in Indiana. Her family returns for visits, reunions, and Peoga Parade. *Submitted by Doris (Rhude) Wilson*

WILLIAM EARL AND LINDA JOY WILSON
- William was born April 12, 1935 in Dayton, OH and Linda was born Dec. 24, 1938 in Indianapolis, IN. Their parents were from Indiana and Tennessee; some of their ancestors coming from France and Ireland to West Virginia, then Indiana. William is the grandson of Henry Clay Rudyard, born Nov. 23, 1866 and died Oct. 23, 1937.

William's aunt and uncle, Nellie and Roy Keyt, lived off of Lick Creek Road from 1944 to 1968. Some of their neighbors were the Frownfelters, the Sissons and the Willoughbys. The Keyts were active in the Historic Society during this period.

Henry Clay Rudyard (Nov. 23, 1866 to Oct. 23, 1937), grandfather of William E. Wilson.

William and Linda, married Jan. 27, 1957, spent most of their married life in Indianapolis and are relatively new residents to Brown County. However, they are real old timers to its magic. As William and Linda were dating, there were several "trips to Brown County" to whet their appetite for belonging there.

In 1963, the Wilsons were given an opportunity to purchase a cabin on Lake Lemon, in the Chitwood Addition, on Watson Road. This started out nothing but a boathouse, with fold out doors on each end; no plumbing of any sort. As the years went along, they added a room here, a room there, but the property was so low it would flood quite frequently. Knowing their love for Brown County, they decided to plan on retiring there. In 1986 the Wilsons and a group of friends completely tore down the old structure, salvaging some lumber, but basically burning the majority of the cabin. It was a sad day for everyone to see so many memories go up in flames, but just as exciting were the plans for a two-story gambrel barn. Now all they are waiting on is retirement.

This magic has been passed on to their children and grandchildren. They have two daughters, Lynne Marie and Joy Lynne. Lynne married Mark Medsker who had two children, David and Tammy, and they have had two children, Joshua and Alyssa. Lynne is a co-director of a church-affiliated day care center. Joy Lynne graduated from Warren Central, completed a modeling course, and is presently pursuing a career in nursing. The children and grandchildren love coming to Brown County, be it hiking through Yellowwood, kicking up the ice-cold water of the creek under the hanging bridge, listening to the winds through the pine trees and admiring all the pine cones, looking for the oldest date in the cemetery, going to Bear Wallow and looking at the flags, a slow boat ride up Beanblossom Creek, fishing at the "log jamb" or swimming in the lake!

JOHN AND JUNE WOHLER
- John and June moved to Brown County in July 1983. Their son, Jim, was operating the Country Gourmet Restaurant in Nashville at the time, (formerly Rudi's Country Kitchen).

John was the only child of John and Emma (Battermann) Wohler and was born on the farm from which he moved, in the Town of Eldorado, Fond du Lac Co., WI, on March 27, 1920. He was a dairy farmer until 1968, when he went to work as an expeditor in the Research Department of Kiekhaefer-Mercury Marine Company. Before retirement he was an assistant manager in the retail store of the J.F. Ahern Plumbing Company in Fond du Lac.

June and John Wohler

June was the youngest of two daughters born to William and Erna (Merten) Kapke. She was born in Milwaukee, WI on June 2, 1925 and was a student nurse in Oshkosh before marrying John on Dec. 8, 1945. June worked as a medical clerk at the Fond du Lac Clinic in Fond du Lac, WI for 16 years before moving to Indiana.

They have two children and two grandchildren. James, a salesman for Lawson Products, resides in Bloomington, and is married to Kellan. Their daughter, Judith (Mrs. Barry Permut), lives in Denver, CO, and has two daughters, Ashley and Tessa.

Upon deciding to retire in Indiana, John and June fell in love with the beauty of Brown County and the uniqueness of Nashville. They purchased Dr. Walker's home on Highway 135, one mile north of Nashville. They joined the Lutheran Church, at that time right next door, and became active in the church and the community. June has served as secretary and treasurer of the Brown County Republican Women, secretary of the Interfaith Committee, secretary of the Historical Society, president of the Pioneer Women, secretary of the Brown County AARP Chapter, and currently is a certified instructor of AARP's 55 Alive/Mature Driving Course. She has served in various offices of the Lutheran Women's Missionary League on the local, Columbus Zone, and Indiana District levels. She is financial secretary for the congregation. In the Sycamore Valley Senior Citizen's Club she has served as vice-president and secretary. John has served as a trustee in his church, on the Board of Directors of the Historical Society, as president of the AARP Chapter, as a volunteer AARP tax consultant for several years, and as treasurer of the Senior Citizen's Club. John and June serve as docents at the Museum Complex in Nashville with John working the Old Log Jail and June demonstrating spinning and weaving in the Loom Room. Both served on the Brown County Sesquicentennial Committee in 1986.

John and June are of German ancestry with both the Wohler and Kapke families emigrating from Pommern, Germany to Wisconsin in the late 1800s.

John attended the Agricultural Short Course at the University of Wisconsin at Madison. His hobbies are gardening, tinkering in his workshop, and reading. June attended the Mercy Hospital School of Nursing in Oshkosh and finds pleasure in crocheting, weaving, and reading.

GEORGE L. WOLFF
George's parents were: Karl Wolff (born April 24, 1876 who died April 24, 1946) and Sophie Soffner (born March 29, 1875) and who died Dec. 5, 1967. They had three children: (1) Karl died of pneumonia at age ten; (2) George L. Wolff born Sept. 12, 1904; (3) Sophie Wolff born Dec. 23, 1908. All were born in Noerdlingen, Germany. George L. Wolff's father had a coal and cutlery business in Noerdlingen, Germany.

Sophie (Wolff) Ludwig Boeckh had five children: Wilma, Marianne, Ludwig, Walter and Helga living in Noerdlingen, Ludwigsbury, Bablinger, Munich and Meckenbeuren.

George L. and Marie Wolff

Wilma is an art teacher; Dr. Marianne Baeckel, a medical psychiatrist; Ludwig an IBM engineer; Walter a landscape naturalist; and Helga an artist.

George came to the United States from Germany in 1921. He married Marie Fosmoe in Michigan in 1934.

George Wolff created the first all metal portable mailable bird bath that was ever made. They lived in Michigan City for 32 years. They moved to Nashville, IN to a nine-room house in 1978 located off Route 46E. George started making old-fashioned match boxes in the workshop that was created from a horse barn. Their son Karl, with George, made decorative tinware and did metal fabricating.

At 80 years of age George and his wife Marie purchased a four-room beautiful mobile home. It was placed near their garden below the large brick home which was rented out. There are five barrels filled with good earth along the long wall of their Mobile Home for flowering annuals. From one side of their new home they have a lovely wood scene with a small trickling waterfall.

George was an inventor. His last invention was a sliding shelf for double mail boxes and suction cup electric candles to place in windows. George played the violin and had a deep appreciation for music. George belonged to the Nashville United Methodist Church, singing in its choir; was a member of the Lions Club; Historical Society; and Craft Guild.

George died Feb. 16, 1990. *Written by Marie Wolff*

MARIE FOSMOE WOLFF
The first generation of this family of Norwegian Americans migrated to America in 1890. Ole H. Fosmoe and Marit Rye Fosmoe were married in Norway in 1889. They settled in Ishpeming, MI in the Norwegian settlement. Ole was a shoemaker and could make shoes for crippled feet. He taught other men how to repair shoes. Marit was an expert weaver.

They had nine children: Jennie 1891, Anna 1893, Henry 1895, Oscar 1896, Edward 1898, Albert 1899, Elizabeth 1904, Marie 1905, and Harold 1909. Anna died of diphtheria in 1898 and Edward also in 1900. The family lived on a farm within walking distance from town. Ole Fosmoe had a shoemaker shop in Ishpening, MI. In 1920 to improve earning his living by repairing shoes, they moved to Muskegan, MI. He built the seven-room home with the help of his son Oscar Fosmoe. Everything was made by the family that was needed for their daily living. Three of the children became teachers: Oscar, Elizabeth and Marie. The others were involved in business.

Fosmoe Family. Seated: Marit (mother) and Harold. On Lap: Marta. Standing, Center Front: Marie. Standing, Center: Albert and Elizabeth. Back Row: Henry and Jennie.

Marie married George L. Wolff, an immigrant from Germany, in 1934. They have a son, Karl A. Wolff born 1934, and lived for eight years in Detroit, then moved to Michigan City where they converted a four-stall garage into a workshop which was later expanded to making items under the name of Wolffcrest Products.

While living in Michigan, Marie managed a weaving shop called "Waterford Weavers" for eight years. People came nationally to see the weaving in process for they were interested in the bubble weaving, a west-faced rug. One could use narrower strips of material to weave with and it was more like the Indian style weaving.

In 1985 Marie was substituting in art and taught gym classes at Van Buren School. She was asked to teach her special form of tumbling. A Nashville elementary class needed a gym substitute and she was asked to teach this special gym activity. In the sixth grade class was the daughter of an exercise class leader who taught at the Methodist church sessions three times a week. Dr. Seibel was asked to find two outstanding older couples to submit for a contest of older citizens who are active. Mrs. Roger Kelso submitted George and Marie's names and after a while they were interviewed by the T.V. director from Channel 30, and participated in a film for the "Healthy, Happy and Wise Program." The T.V. personnel filmed Marie teaching tumbling to first graders, teaching art to fourth graders, took pictures at their home of George doing tin punching in his metal shop, pictures of them walking in the woods and planting in the garden. This program was shown all over Indiana and Michigan. It was produced by the Indiana State Medical Association. Marie was 79 and George 81 at the time.

Marie is an active member of the Historical Society and the Pioneer Women's group. See George L. Wolff. *Submitted by Marie Wolff*

ARTHUR AND JUNE WOLPERT
Arthur Milton Wolpert was born May 14, 1925 in Elizabeth, IN, son of William Evans Wolpert (1891-1935) and Carrye Ellen Funk (1890-1975), a descendant of George W. Wolpert (1857-1941) and George F. Wolpert (1825-1910) of Wurttemburg,

Germany. The Wolperts were in the tannery business.

Arthur graduated from Elizabeth High School in 1942 and attended Hanover College. He served in the U.S. Navy from October 1943 to December 1948.

On Oct. 5, 1951, Arthur married June Marie Sauerheber (June 22, 1932) of Corydon, IN, daughter of Dexter Patrick Sauerheber (May 30, 1892-July 1, 1977) and Bertha Dessie McCutcheon (Oct. 22, 1892-Feb. 4, 1969).

Arthur is retired from Mayflower Van Lines and Paul Arpin Van Lines and has written songs, poems (one published in Poetry Anthology) and epigrams which were published in four books. He has also written three childrens books. Arthur is a member of the Masonic Lodge, Scottish Rite, Shriner, Eastern Star, Historical Society and an avid golfer.

June and Art Wolpert, 1990.

June graduated from Corydon High School in 1950 and is a retired Executive Secretary from Cummins Engine Company, Columbus, IN, and became interested in quilting in 1979 and was published in Great American Quilts in 1989. June is President of the Columbus Star Quilters (1989-1990), member of the United Methodist Church (circle leader 1989-1990), Worthy Matron of Nashville Order of the Eastern Star in 1969 and 1970, District Deputy of OES in 1972, and member of the Pioneer Women and Historical Society and an avid bridge player.

They have two children, Blake Milton Wolpert, born Oct. 22, 1952, and Valeri Ellen Wolpert Morris, born Oct. 20, 1953. Both graduated from Nashville High School. Blake is a sales executive for Shamrock Van & Storage in Cleveland, OH, and has two children, Carson Ellery (Nov. 7, 1982) and Casey Dean (Aug. 24, 1984). Blake married Cindy Harvey Rose from Hastings, NE, on Feb. 4, 1990. They reside in Indianapolis and Brown County. Valeri is Regional Director of Marketing for Neogard Co., Dallas, TX, and married Garry Morris of Fort Worth, TX, on Jan. 11, 1990. They reside in Spring, TX.

In September 1955, Arthur and June were traveling to Southern Indiana from their New Castle home with thoughts of buying property in Art's territory in Central Indiana and found the "Citadel" log cabin in beautiful Brown County, now owned by Arthur Clouse near Beanblossom Overlook, three miles north of Nashville on Highway 135. The cabin only had a fireplace for heat when purchased. They lived there until 1959. They purchased property on Old 46 East in 1963 and purchased the Bantz/Springer property in 1970 where they still reside. Old records show this property once traded hands for a $60.00 funeral debt.

BLAKE AND CYNTHIA WOLPERT -

Blake Milton Wolpert, son of Art and June Wolpert, was born in New Albany, IN on Oct. 22, 1952. Art Wolpert was involved in a variety of sales related occupations during Blake's formative years. It was necessary for the family to move frequently throughout Southern Indiana, Kentucky and Tennessee. This accounts for Blake's peculiar accent which causes many passers-by to occasionally stop and stare.

Cynthia and Blake Wolpert

Blake graduated from Brown County High School in 1971. He pursued a journalistic education at Indiana University before entering the United States Navy during the Vietnam Era. After a decorated military career he returned to Brown County. He dabbled for a short time in retail sales and accepted the vice presidency of a production company before packing up and moving to West Texas. At the University of Texas (El Paso) he studied drama and the theatre. He became interested in the theatrical form and eventually became a regionally renowned playwright.

He returned to the midwest in 1986. As the district manager for a major truck line, Blake had the opportunity to travel the country's "heartland" and developed a poetic reverence for the area. It was during one of these sojourns he met Cynthia Harvey Rose. After a respectable courtship the two were married in February 1990 and took up residence in Indianapolis.

Cynthia received her BSN from the University of Nebraska, her MSN from the University of Illinois in Chicago and a Doctor of Jurisprudence degree from Indiana University in Indianapolis. She currently practices with an Indianapolis law firm.

Blake introduced Cynthia to the scenic splendor of Brown County one weekend at a time. It wasn't long before Cynthia was captivated by the natural beauty of the "Hills of Brown." They found a cabin hide-away on Baker Hill and are blissfully making the transition from urbanity to a country way of life.
Submitted by Cynthia S. Wolpert

JOE WOODS -

Joseph Woods is the son of James S. and Rebecca (Henthorn) Woods. He along with his brothers Noah, Dan, Issac, Felix and Jimmy and his sisters Ruth and Rebecca grew up on Howard Ridge, also known as Scarce O'Fat Ridge in Washington Township. Knowing nothing but work to survive, Joe did nothing but that all his life. He married Mary Fleetwood. To this union came Ancil and Glen of Belmont, IN; Julian (Tom) Verlis (Woods) Hayford and Pauline (Woods) Bond of Columbus, IN; Margie (Woods) Terrell of Danville, IN and Jewell (Woods) Heaton of Bloomfield, IN.

During the course of their marriage, while Mary was busy with the children and summer canning for the winter months, Joe worked many jobs. His cousin, Ross Owens' crosstie business was one of his many jobs. He also drove a school bus, was grounds keeper for Mrs. T.C. (Selma) Steele and Lenore Morgan, who owned Austin, IN's Canning Factory. He was also a carpenter and helped Glen cut timber.

Their children had chores they had to do—cook, clean, wash, cut wood, milk—anything necessary to be done daily. And when the next day came, it had to be done all over again. The family had a day where they butchered a family hog. Everything was done just to survive. This was common to all families of the hard times, but through it all Joe always found time to laugh. If it was just scaring a family member, a dog or just laughing at life's many calamities, he liked to laugh.

Mary, ten years after Joe's death in May of 1980, can still be found at the homestead at Belmont. She turned 86 on March 6, 1990. Ancil lives to the west and Glen to the east of her. Mary and her brothers Willard, Treva and Furl, sisters Dorval Owens (her twin Dorothy died at one or two years old), Myrtle Shields and Lena Tabor all grew up on Crooked Creek Road. Their parents were Thomas and Lucy (Polley) Fleetwood. Many memories are recalled of Lucy and Tom. They are told by children of Mary to her grandchildren and great-grandchildren. Some of the stories lead us to believe she was a good cook. At one meal as many as three tables were set for whoever wanted to eat. She might have four or five different kinds of pie and her chicken and dumplings (raised the chickens on the farm) were fixed in a huge dishpan. Tom died in 1952 and Lucy died in December 1949.

Memories will be cherished by all for many years for the inspiration of this busy generation, and memories also of their hardships. Their efforts helped make this world and this wonderful country.

JOSEPH G. WOODS -

Joseph, known to many as Glen or "Buster" was born Sept. 12, 1931 to Joe and Mary (Fleetwood) Woods in Belmont, IN. After his school years, he served the United States Army in the Korean Conflict. Safely returning home from active duty in the war, Glen married Phyllis Jean Robey of Bloomington on Oct. 31, 1963. After living briefly in Smithville, IN, they built a new home at Belmont where they still reside. To this couple was born Randy Wayne on Aug. 4, 1955; Darla June (Sept. 16, 1957) and Teddy Joe, who was stillborn in 1967. On Dec. 3, 1977, Randy married Mary Beth Kent of Monroe County. They have one child, Samuel Hezekiah, born March 28, 1980. Darla is unmarried and lives in Belmont.

Glen worked for Shower Bros. and later for Fleetwood Brothers. He was best known as a skilled timber cutter. In 1976 he suffered with a saw accident that about took his left leg off. With the mercy of the Lord, he made a full recovery and was soon back in the woods. In 1980 he was approached by Fred "Squeak" Snider about taking over Mr. Snider's established trash hauling business. He bought it and together with Randy (his son) today serve Brown County patrons with their valuable service. Many of his customers look forward to Glen's smiling face and the happy outlook that God has given him. Phyllis, Darla and Mary Beth currently are owners of the "Fabric Addict" Shop on Old School Way in Nashville.

WOOTTON FAMILY -

Abraham Wootton, progenitor of the Wootton family of Brown County, had arrived there before it became a county in 1836. Moses Wootton (ca. 1843-July 5, 1885), a son of Abraham and his first wife Mary, married Sarah Ann Percifield on March 26, 1869. She was born

April 1, 1845, died June 17, 1928, daughter of George Percifield. Moses and Sarah Wootton had eight children: Abraham, George T., Mary E., William Cummings, Martha Alice, Sherman, Charles and Moses Wootton, Jr.

Wm. C. Wootton, fourth child of Moses and Sarah, was born Dec. 7, 1875, died Jan. 29, 1957. He married April 4, 1903 to Estella Laverne Eddy (July 11, 1883-Nov. 1, 1914), daughter of Calvin Eddy and Clarissa Truex. William and Stella Wootton had children: Alice Faye, Beulah Edna, Mary Edra, Harry Allen, Wilma Edith and Verna Lucille.

Moses Wootton

(1) Alice Faye Wootton, born Jan. 1, 1904, married Wesley Oren Bell. Their children: Geneva Mae, Norma Dell, Max Eugene, Harold Keith and Lenora Bell. Alice married second to Otis Hanes after Wesley's death about 1964.

(2) Beulah Edna Wootton, born Sept. 23, 1905, married April 3, 1922 to Otto L. Stogdill (July 14, 1902-March 16, 1976). Their children were: Lloyd Kenneth, Wm. Sherman, Warren Allen, Thelma Jean, James Lee Ray, Betty Ann, Mary Alice, David Orin, Norma Marie, Joseph Eugene, Samuel Ray, Lou Ellen, Sarah Jane, Robert Stogdill.

(3) Mary Edra Wootton (Aug. 2, 1907-Sept. 3, 1984) married Elmer Hester Frye Nov. 6, 1926. Both are buried at Burgoon Cemetery, Monroe County. Their children were: 1. Zella Margaret Frye, born June 23, 1927, who married William Rex Hyde, son of John Siegle Hyde and Bertha May Griffin. William was born in Brown County in 1922. 2. Delight Helen Frye, born Feb. 26, 1933, who married Bobbie Jo Flater, son of Elbridge Flater and Mildred Hubble. Bobbie was born in Monroe County in 1933. Children of Delight and Bobbie Flater were: Luvilla Anne who married first to Bob House, their child, Jason Mandell House; married second to Monty Derting. Bobbie Jo Flater II, born at Ft. Benj. Harrison, married Shelly McGill. Dawn Yvette Flater, born Army Base Hosp., Germany, married Kenneth James Miller, their child, Leah Anne Miller, born Burlington Co., NJ. Lorelei Evannoe Flater, born Fort Gordon, Augusta, GA, married Gerald D. Cannata. 3. Eustace Llewellen Frye, born May 9, 1940, Brown County, died Nov. 3, 1956, Indianapolis.

(4) Harry Allen Wootton (Aug. 31, 1909-July 29, 1988) married Lois Clarice Willoughby, daughter of Grover Willoughby and Lillie Valentine Hainline. Their children were: Ralph Eustus, Denzil Allen, Robert Dale, Harry Dean, Paul Edward, Patricia Jean Wootton.

(5) Wilma Edith Wootton (Sept. 11, 1911-April 6, 1959) married Dillon Frye, son of Alexander Frye and Margaret Chandler, was born Sept. 1, 1900, died Feb. 28, 1987. Their two children: Marvin Louis Frye who married Luzetta Mae Sherlock and had three children, Wanda Carol, Martha Joyce and Marvin Eugene Frye. Frieda Marie Frye who married Raymond Terrell and had children David Ray and Rita Jean Terrell.

(6) Verna Lucille Wootton, born Jan. 7, 1914, died Aug. 11, 1914, buried in Deckard Cemetery, Brown County where some other family members are buried. *Submitted by Martha Joyce Frye McCammon*

WINSTON AND HELEN WYTHE

Winston Prentiss Wythe was born in Vigo Co., IN, Sept. 13, 1907 to Vane and Hallie Brill Wythe. The Wythes (pronounced Withe in Virginia) came from England to Virginia and his great-grandfather Prentiss Wythe was a relative of George Wythe who signed the Declaration of Independence and whose home has been restored at Williamsburg, VA. His maternal ancestors, the Brills, emigrated from England, pre-Revolutionary War, to New England and later moved to Indiana. Winston graduated from Indiana State University at Terre Haute and taught Physics and Math at Gary High School, then moved to Indianapolis and worked as a Tool Designer for Switzer-Cummins until World War II. He enlisted in the Naval Reserve in 1943 and was in Officer Indoctrination School in Hollywood, FL when he and Helen Dawson met. They were married in Norfolk, VA, March 21, 1944.

Winston and Helen Wythe

Helen Dawson Wythe was born in Tioga Co., NY, Dec. 2, 1918 to Ernest N. Dawson and Elizabeth Duncker Dawson. Her paternal grandfather, Sidney Dawson's ancestors, emigrated from England as early as 1690 to New England and settled in "upstate" New York in the 1700s or early 1800s, where five Dawson brothers purchased farms on a hill outside Spencer, NY. Her great-grandfather died in the Civil War. Sidney Dawson married Alice Benton, whose ancestor, Andrew Benton, was baptized in Epping, Essex Co., England, Oct. 15, 1620 and emigrated to New England as early as 1639, was allotted a parcel of land in Milford, CT in November, 1839, which was bought from the Indians in February of that year. Helen's great-grandfather Alvin Benton, moved to Spencer, NY and was married there in 1792. Her maternal grandparents, the Dunckers emigrated from Germany in late 1800s and settled in upstate New York.

After the War, Winston and Helen came to Indianapolis and Winston returned to Switzer-Cummins. He later went back to teaching. In the spring of 1950, they were invited by Maudell and Olive Brown to spend a weekend at their place on Owl Creek Road. It was a beautiful weekend with redbud and dogwood in bloom and they fell in love with Brown County. In June of 1950, they saw an ad in the paper for a piece of property here. They came down, brought a picnic lunch to the Park and purchased the property the same day. It was one and one-fourth acres with a shack, on Gatesville Road, east of Foxes Corner. They spent weekends and vacations there for the next 21 years remodeling and gardening. When Winston retired in 1971, they moved here permanently. Helen worked for American State Insurance Company for 27 years and continued to commute to Indianapolis until she retired in 1978. Winston passed away Dec. 6, 1983, is buried in Goshen Cemetery. He had one son, Winston Reed Wythe, three grandchildren and two great-grandchildren. *Written by Helen Dawson Wythe*

YODER FAMILY

Conrad Yoder (spelled "Yotter"), of Swiss descent, came to America in 1746. He made his home in Charlottetown, NC, until he died in 1790. Conrad Yoder was the great-great-great-great-great-great-great-grandfather of Ryan Andrew Yoder, youngest descendant of Conrad currently living in Brown County. One of Conrad's sons, Jacob, Sr., born Dec. 13, 1767, came to Indiana around 1800. Jacob, wife Catherine Dellinger, and family are listed in the 1830 Monroe County census.

Jacob Sr.'s son, Jacob Jr., 1815-1885, and his wife, Mary Jackson, moved to Brown County in 1845. Jacob Jr. and family are listed in the 1850 Brown County Census. One of their sons, James M. Yoder, 1843-1931, was married to Catherine Waltman, who died in 1872. James M. was later married to Eliza Jane Baughman, who lived from 1853-1934. James M. served with the Indiana Volunteers in the Civil War. He enlisted in 1862 with Company D, the 82nd Infantry.

One of James M.'s sons, Jacob Ira, known as "J.I.", was born in Brown County in 1873. One of J.I.'s brothers, Ralph Yoder, 1892-1980, lived in Nashville and was forever commenting on the addition of new shops in town. J.I., his wife, Rachel Deckard, and family are listed in the 1880 Brown County Census. He and Rachel raised a family of six, four girls and two boys. Around 1910, when his youngest son, William Glen, was six months old, J.I. lost both hands in a saw mill accident. J.I. worked the remainder of his years as a trader; he also worked in real estate.

William Glen Yoder was born in 1909 and continues to live in Helmsburg. He married Mary Tomlinson and raised five children; June Yvonne Yoder Davenport, Mary Jane Yoder Jensen, John David, James I., and Jenny Kathryn Yoder Austin. Glen works the Yoder farm, which has been in the Yoder family since 1912, and enjoys his livelihood of farming, raising and selling vegetables, and raising and selling livestock, including cattle, hogs, and chickens. Glen and Mary are members of the United Methodist Church.

Kay Yoder and son, Steve with Steve's log cabin, built in 1989.

Glen's youngest son, James I., born in 1950, is married to Edna Sue Riley and they continue to live in Helmsburg with their two children, Jeffrey and Jennifer Yoder. James I. is employed by Eli Lilly in

Indianapolis, and also farms the Yoder property that has been in the family since 1912. Glen's oldest son, John David, born in 1941, is married to Janet Kay Deckard. John and Kay both graduated from Helmsburg High School in 1959 and are lifelong residents of Brown County. John and Kay live on the John Tomlinson property where they raise cattle. This land has been in John's mother's family since 1845. John is employed by Cummins Engine Company, Columbus, IN. John and Kay have four children; Kathy Ann Yoder Porter, John Andrew, Steven Louis, and Nancy Jane.

One of John David's sons, Steven Louis, born in 1964, built a "new" log home on 80 acres, located on Bittersweet Road, where he now lives. John David's oldest son, John Andrew, was born in 1962. He and his wife, Mary Helen Webster, both graduated from Brown County High School. They were married in 1982. They have two children, Rachel Lynn and Ryan Andrew. They reside on Hurdle Road, in the original homeplace of Leston and Edith Deckard since 1945, maternal grandparents of John Andrew, in Hamblen Township.

Since 1746, nine generations of the Yoder family have lived in America. Since 1845, seven generations of Yoder family have lived in Brown County.

YORK-LOWRY FAMILY - In 1974 Donna York Lowry and her husband, Carl Lowry, decided there had to be a better place to raise their three children than Novato, CA, a suburb of San Francisco.

So they took their youngsters out of school and set out by camper and trailer to find it. Travelling into the American southwest, then to Western Canada, Texas, New England, Florida, they paused for the winter months. In early 1975 they found Brown County's scenic charm, reasonable land costs, and an interest in crafts like their own.

Carl and Donna (York) Lowry

So here on 32 acres just west of Helmsburg they settled down by the Lick Creek bridge on State Road 45. Carl worked in Indianapolis, including several years at Methodist Hospital.

Donna's parents, Park York and Florence (Flossie) Zellers York, left their home in Ventura, CA, upon his retirement in 1980, to live in South Carolina. There Flossie became ill with Alzheimer's Disease. Park undertook caring for her at their home, but they missed the support of family members.

On a May morning in 1984 Park phoned Donna. "Do you still want us?" he asked, remembering she had offered space on the farm when and if they wanted to share Brown County. So it resulted in the Yorks coming to "Autumn Leaves Homestead" later that year.

The York's two other children are: Paul, who lives in Dallas, and Richard, of Oakland, CA. They have ten grandchildren, four great-grandchildren, as of the time of this writing, June, 1990.

The Lowry's children are: Jason, a student at Vincennes University, Carla, in business in California, and Marcus, stationed with the Army at Ft. Lewis, WA.

Donna Lowry is a curriculum coordinator for Head Start in Bloomington, IN. Carl now lives in England.

Park's parents, Minor and Carrie Bertch York, were born in Iowa; later moved to Montana, then California. Florence's parents, Ralph Zellers and Isabelle Ancker Zellers, born in Pennsylvania, were early residents of the same Pennsylvania area where their German-born ancestors settled. The ancestors of Park's mother, Carrie Bertch, surnamed Houtz, also migrated from Germany in the late 1700s.

Recent research has revealed that members of the Houtz and Zellers families intermarried in Pennsylvania, but these Brown County Yorks and Lowry families are not the direct result of those marriages, but of other branches of the families.

Park York, retired from a career in sales, is now active in Alzheimer Support groups, in the New Life Community Church, and the Full Gospel Business Men's Fellowship. He is an alumnus of Occidental College, Los Angeles. Donna Lowry completed her college work at Indiana University in 1989. Carla was graduated from there in 1986. *Submitted by Park York*

YOUNG FAMILY - The Youngs in Jackson Township were descendants of David Young, Sr. who came to Monroe Co., IN in 1824 from Kentucky and settled near Unionville, IN. David's brother Harvey, a Baptist Minister, acquired land in Jackson Township in 1837 described as Township 10, North, Range 2, East, Section 17. He married Eleanor Weddle on Feb. 17, 1831.

David Young, Sr. was born in Virginia in 1779. Died March 11, 1863, buried at Unionville, IN. David married Christiana (last name unknown). They had seven children: (1) Elizabeth born Dec. 10, 1802; (2) Joseph born about 1806; (3) Abram born Jan. 24, 1808; (4) David, Jr. born May 3, 1810; (5) Mary born March 12, 1811; (6) Mahale, date of birth unknown; (7) John Franklin born June 18, 1822. John Franklin Young married Pernetia Richardson.

David Walter Young, son of John Franklin and Pernetia Young, was born in 1854 near Unionville, IN and came to Needmore, IN in the 1870s. He was a farmer, owning three farms near Needmore. He married Catherine Chitwood in 1877. Catherine was born at Needmore in 1859. David and Catherine had two children: Walter born July 16, 1879 and Edgar born Oct. 17, 1882. David died in 1924, Catherine in 1936. Both are buried in the Needmore Cemetery.

Walter Young married Blanche Curry. They had three children: (1) Gail born Sept. 25, 1916, Needmore, IN (married M.W. Willan); (2) Virginia born July 12, 1918, Needmore, IN (married Dr. A.L. Higdon); (3) Roger born Jan. 30, 1920, Trevlac, IN (married Jean Nevison). Blanche Young died in December 1921 and is buried in the Needmore Cemetery.

Walter Young taught school in Jackson township for 36 years. He moved to Trevlac, IN in 1919. He died in 1950 and is buried in the Needmore Cemetery.

Gail Willan died in 1988 and is buried in the Needmore Cemetery. Gail had two sons: Brent Willan, Rapid City, SD and Craig Willan, South Lake, TX. Virginia Higdon resides in Boca Raton, FL and Roger Young in Indianapolis, IN.

Edgar Young married Bessie Poling. They had five children: (1) Ruby born March 24, 1904, Needmore, IN (married Tracey Walker); (2) Wayne born Feb. 27, 1907, Needmore, IN (married Josephine Hoy); (3) Olive born Oct. 20, 1909, Needmore, IN (married Warren Hurdle); (4) Lowell born Jan. 14, 1912, Needmore, IN (married Mary Alice Calvin); and (5) David born Sept. 12, 1918, North Dakota (married Edith Everling). Edgar, a farmer, lived west of Needmore, IN. Bessie died in 1923 and Edgar in December 1958. Both are buried in the Needmore Cemetery.

Ruby Walker (1904-1930) and Wayne Young are deceased. Ruby and her husband, Tracey Walker, are buried in the Needmore Cemetery.

Olive Hurdle, Lowell Young and David Young II, reside in Morgantown, IN. Edgar Young had ten grandchildren, all living: Wilma Winberg, Indianapolis (daughter of Ruby); Patricia Young, Indianapolis (daughter of Wayne); Rebecca Young, Indianapolis (daughter of Wayne); John D. Young, Indianapolis (son of Wayne); Betty Hamilton, Morgantown (daughter of Olive); Dr. Norman Young, Indianapolis (son of Lowell); Gerald Young, Martinsville (son of David); Steven Young, Morgantown (son of David); Raymond Young, Morgantown (son of David); and Loretta Young, Morgantown (daughter of David). *Submitted by Roger Young*

ZIMMERMAN FAMILY - Jacob Zimmerman was born in 1847 and died in 1908. He was German by birth but his people moved to Switzerland. From there they moved to Virginia. Jacob married Margaret Merriman from Ohio.

The war came and Jacob went to war. he joined July 28, 1862. He was wounded and absent in 1862. He was in Company K, Ohio Infantry at 18 years of age. He signed up for three years from Dec. 31, 1863 to June 1, 1865, at Camp Steuvenville, OH. When the war ended, the soldiers had to get home the best way they could. He walked through rain and mud. By the time he got home he was a sick man. This left him with problems the rest of his life. They moved from Virginia to Brown County and settled three miles south of Spearsville. To this union were born Abraham, Bert, Laura, Ona, Anna and Daisy, Martha, Minnie and Clinton.

He took his family to Unity Church and later preached at Bethel. This is where he, his wife Minnie, and Daisy are buried.

Grandma Zimmerman lived with her youngest child Clinton and his wife Verna Merida Zimmerman. Helen always remember her with her Bible in her lap. She always talked about "Virginy," as she called Virginia where they had lived before. She died in 1921 when Helen Zimmerman Sanders was seven years old. *Written by Helen (Zimmerman) Sanders, daughter of Clinton and Verna Zimmerman*

ALBERT AND HAZEL ZIMMERMAN - Albert Zimmerman and Hazel Josephine Zeltner were born in La Porte, IN, and graduated from La Porte High School. Al's parents were Albert John Zimmerman and Laura (Maach) Zimmerman. Al retired from Bendix Corporation after 31 years spent mostly in management. Upon leaving Sidney, NY, Albert and Hazel settled in Brown County in 1973. Al retired again from Gaile's Gas and Electric in 1989.

Hazel's parents were Walter and Ada (Collings) Zeltner. Hazel graduated from Indiana State Teachers College in Terre Haute and received an M.S. degree in Counseling from Notre Dame.

Their daughter, Sara, married Robert Mayes, and has two college-age sons: James Albert Mayes and David Ralph Mayes. Sara is an elementary counselor in LaPorte, IN.

Daughter Pat, married Robert Thoresen, and has two daughters: Karina Jennifer and Abigail. Karina is a freshman at I.U. and Abigail is an eighth grader. Pat is an art teacher near Columbus, OH.

Hazel became very interested in the Collings' family history which a relative had begun years ago. Hazel's great-grandfather Daniel B. Collings, born in New Jersey, married Electa Owen in Ashtabula in 1834. Electa, daughter of Joel and Molly (Kneeland) Owen, Jr. and great-granddaughter of Dr. Joel and Anne (Buell) Owen, Sr. traced her roots to Hebron, CT. Dr. Joel Owen, Sr. was the grandson of Ensign Samuel Waters who married Anne Sterling about 1703 and was the great-great-grandson of John Owen who married Rebecca Wade about 1650.

Anne Buell, great-granddaughter of Samuel and Deborah (Griswold) Buell traced her ancestry to Matthew Griswold, Esq., who was a descendant of Sir Lancelot de Griswolde born about 1135.

Molly Kneeland, granddaughter of Isaac and Content (Rowley) Kneeland and great-great-great-granddaughter of Edward Kneeland who came to America circa 1630 and settled in Ispwich, CT, traced her ancestry to Alexander Kneeland born in Scotland about 1225.

Content Rowley's parents, John and Deborah (Fuller) Rowley both had the same grandfather, Moses Rowley, Sr. born before 1630. Among Deborah Fuller's Mayflower relatives were her parents "Little John" Fuller and Mehitable (Rowley) Fuller and her grandparent, the orphaned Samuel Fuller, who married Jane Lathrop in 1635 in a ceremony performed by Captain Miles Standish.

ELSWORTH AND DOROTHY (TRIP) ZIMMERMAN

Among Elsworth Colonal and Dorothy Louise (Trip) Zimmerman's children was Diana (Zimmerman) Sizemore. Other family members included Rosemarie, Annette, Peggy, Donald and Michael. Elsworth's parents were Elsworth senior and Sara Vivian (Frazier) Zimmerman. Dorothy's parents were Sanford Antonia and Flora Stella (Eubanks) Trip. Dorothy attended Sprunica Elementary and remembers her bus driver Merrill Schrougham. Dorothy married Virgil Sizemore who moved to Indiana from Kentucky when he was seven years old. They have two children Joseph Daniel and Clarence Robert. She and her husband enjoy camping and boating.

Elsworth, Jr. and Dorothy Zimmerman and family.

CLINTON ZIMMERMAN

Clinton was born about three miles south of Spearsville. He was the last of nine children born to Jacob and Margaret Zimmerman. His oldest brother, Abe, was the veterinarian in Brown County. He raised his family on the same farm where Clinton was born.

Clint, as he was known by most people was a horse trader, logger and farmer. He had wild horses shipped in from the West. He broke them, then sold or traded them. He always seemed to get extra boot in the trade. I remember lots of times when the horse almost got the best of him and I remember being afraid someone would get killed, especially, my older brother Glen.

Clinton married Bessie Glidden and of this marriage was born Glen, Donel and Gladys. Bessie died of Spinal Meningitis when Gladys was two. Later he married Verna Merida and to this union were born Helen, Melvin, and Basil. We never knew any difference but what we were all brothers and sisters, for we all were treated alike.

While the boys were growing up, the logging business brought in the money for the family. Ben Lukens, a family friend hauled the walnut stumps and logs to the mill to make veneer. Also every fall the boys and sometimes "Pop," as we called him, would go to Illinois and shuck corn for additional money. Money in those days was hard to come by. We always had plenty to eat because Dad always raised enough wheat for flour, pinto, short-cuts, great northerns and horticulture beans along with potatoes to last through the winter. Mom always canned lots of surplus. All of the kids had to help. It wasn't like today when kids have nothing to do.

We always made a game out of it and most of it was fun for my dad was a cut-up and always made people laugh. Clinton died at the age of 55, while undergoing an operation for a blocked kidney. *Written by Helen Zimmerman Sanders, daughter*

ZODY

The first Zodys known arrived in Brown County around 1860 named Henry Zody and wife Catherine Stover Zody. They were married in Pennsylvania (known to be Pennsylvania Dutch) and moved to Mansfield, OH and then to Brown County in 1858. Henry died Nov. 21, 1872 and Catherine died July 30, 1889, both are buried in Unity Cemetery Hamblen Township. They had the following children: (1) Mary Elizabeth born Feb. 13, 1848, died Aug. 19, 1925; (2) William Henry born Aug. 4, 1850, (3) infant son born Feb. 5, 1852, died Sept. 7, 1852; (4) Aaron Albert born Oct. 13, 1854, died 1937; (5) Benjamin Franklin born July 27, 1857; (6) John Wesley born Dec. 19, 1858, died July 16, 1882 in Brown County; (7) Leander B. born May 22, 1862, died June 12, 1940; (8) Amanda Jane, born Aug. 16, 1864 in Brown County.

Front row: Alice (Robertson) and Howard Zody. Back row: Richard, Kenneth, Frank, Melvin, Maurice and John.

Aaron A. moved with his family from Ohio to Brown County also around 1858. He married Emma Waltman Jan. 18, 1885. Emma was born Dec. 9, 1866 and died April 18, 1936 and is buried in Beanblossom Cemetery, Jackson Township. They had five children:

(1) Clarence Melville born July 31, 1885, died Dec. 3, 1958; (2) Cecil B. born May 22, 1889, died November, 1963; (3) Austin B. born Oct. 12, 1896, died May 22, 1960; (4) Artis born 1892, died 1908 in his teenage years as he was struck and killed by lightning; (5) Agnes, no dates known.

Clarence Melville married Oma Jane Campbell in 1911, she was born Feb. 7, 1885, died Feb. 21, 1976 in Brown County. Clarence's father Aaron ran a grocery store in Georgetown, now known as Bean Blossom for around 50 years and the building still stands today. He ran a huckster route for his father Aaron before he started his teaching career. He taught school for 35 years in Brown County in Jackson Township where he lived. He was elected clerk of Brown County for two terms after retiring from teaching.

Clarence and Oma Jane had one son Howard Sylvester Zody born March 19, 1913, married Sarah Alice Robertson born March 23, 1912, died March 3, 1990. They were married Feb. 29, 1932. They had seven children:

(1) Mary Jane born Aug. 25, 1932 stillborn; (2) Richard Graham born Sept. 23, 1933; (3) Kenneth Ray born March 22, 1935; (4) Charles Franklin born Sept. 18, 1936; (5) Clarence Melvin born July 2, 1938; (6) Howard Maurice born July 31, 1941; (7) John Austin born June 8, 1951.

Howard purchased the grocery store from his grandfather Aaron in the early 1930s. He sold the business to Ambrose Waltman and moved to Nashville and worked as clerk in the post office. He later worked at the Nashville State Bank as Assistant Cashier for seven years. He then returned to the grocery business purchasing the Star Store grocery in Nashville for one year after which he entered the Army infantry during World War II. Returning from the Army he built the original grocery known as IGA in Nashville around 1947, selling it to Carl Walker in 1950 and returning to the Post Office as postmaster. Enjoying retirement since 1972, he now lives in Nashville. *Submitted by Howard Zody*

ANTHONY AND JOSEPHINE ZUPANCIC

Anthony and Josephine (brother and sister) now live on the farm on Mt. Zion Road off of Carmel Ridge in Jackson Township. Their parents, John and Josephine Zupancic purchased the land in 1916. They immigrated from Austria to Indianapolis and lived there for three years before moving to Brown County.

This land was purchased from the United States Government in 1851 by Margaret See. The Zupancics bought it from Frank Smerdel and it has been in the family from that date until the present.

John Zupancic cleared small parcels of land for farming. He helped build a new home, barn and other farm buildings. During the winter months he commuted weekly by train to Indianapolis and worked as a moulder at the Link Belt Foundry. His wife drove a horse and spring wagon to Morgantown Depot to meet him on Friday night and took him back on Sunday night. This was a ten mile round trip journey. The mother stayed alone with the young children during the week taking care of the farm and farm animals. They raised five children, losing a son to death in his infancy and later a ten year old son to typhoid fever.

Anthony, the present owner is a retired carpenter and continues to farm the land.

Josephine is retired from factory work in Martinsville and takes care of the home.

Mary Haggard is retired after helping her husband, Morris, operate a small farm and Texaco Gasoline Station in Midway, Brown County.

John is a retired carpenter and he and his wife raised seven children in the Hoosetown Community in Morgan County. Frances spent several years teaching at Helmsburg High School and later as a substitute teacher in Brown County Schools. She also has helped on a farm which she and her husband, Elmer Parsley, Jr. owns in Hamblen Township. They are the parents of a daughter, Robin Elizabeth.

Even though there was no Catholic Church in Brown County until St. Agnes, Nashville was built in 1940, the family kept the faith with family prayer and occasional trips to Indianapolis by train to attend church and receive the Sacraments. Anthony and Josephine now attend St. Martin's Church in Martinsville.

The children were educated at the Cook School on Carmel Ridge and later at Helmsburg. Their parents encouraged their children to receive an education and made every effort to supply them with textbooks even if it took a 25 mile round trip to Nashville or Martinsville to purchase them with their horse and spring wagon.

The parents became naturalized American citizens and were proud of their home in Brown County.
Submitted by Anthony and Joseph Zupancic

Ellen Petro in 1920 smoking her pipe, which was "Her Most Comfort." [Photo by Frank Hohenberger]

Brown County Index

ABBETT, Anita Ball 214, Betty 214, Corydon D, 214, Helen 214, Holly 214, Iva 157, Jacquelyn 214, Martha 214, Michael D. 214, Michael S. 214, Nellie Marie 214, Walt 214, Walter C. 214 Walter Cleveland, 214.
ABBEY, Adela 132, Amanda 132, Anna 132, Araminta 282, 286, Armitta 132, Elmina 132, James 132, 286, James Pearl 132, Levi 132, Martin 132, Mary 132, Mary Hobbs 286.
ABBOTT, Carl 303, Charles 261, 303, Cora 303, Donald 261, Dorothy Joan 261, Ellen 303, Gertrude 261, Jean 261, Marvin 261, 303, Nelso 303, Willa G. 303, William H. 303.
ABELL, Dolly 284.
ABERCROMBIE, Amanda 198, Mary 198.
ABRAMS, Della Virginia 170, Ethel Lee 170, Lonzo Robert 170, Marty 170, Sue 170, Virginia 170.
ACKER, Bernadine 167.
ACKERMAN, Beulah 132, John R. 132, Stephanie 132.
ACTON, James 285, Martha 285, Richard 159.
ADAIR, John 294, Mary 306, Mary Etta 294, Samuel 294, Sarah C. 294, Susannah 294, William 294.
ADAMS, Amanda 132, Charles Gess 276, Cloe Ann 211, David McIlvan 132, Elizabeth Jane 132, Elizabeth Rose 276, Emma 285, Hugh Thomas 217, Ina Evelyn 300, J. Ottis 283, James Watt 132, Jennie 132, Joel 229, John 132, 300, John Walter 132, 217, Joseph Warren 132, Lorena 289, Maria 217, Mary B. 229, Mary Calphurnia 132, maurice 217, Nancy Maria 132, Nicholas 174, 278, Paul 217, 218, Philip 174, 278, Rachel 158, Samuel 132, Samuel W. 231, Sara Louise 166, Sarah 132, 276, Sarah Ann 132, Sarah Jane 217, Sarah Luella 231, Sarah Louise 166, 217, Susan Jane 132, T.M. 154, Thomas 276, Thomas Martin 132, 217, Thos. Jefferson 132, Vernita 218.
ADKINS, Sally 211.
ALBA, Alberta 156, Barbara Ann 156.
ALBAUGH, Clara 208.
ALBERDING, Eva 204.
ALBERT, Barbara 261, Denis 261.
ALBRIGHT, Doris Ann 253, Virginia Lee 296.
ALCORN, Gregory Scott 155, Julie Ann 155, Melanie Sue 155.
ALDERS, Anderson 268, Catherine 243, Catherine E. 268.
ALDRICH, Ellen 184, Ellen Folsom 185, Eunice 237.
ALEXANDER, James 154, Sarah Jane 180, Sarah Matilda 267, Susan 224.
ALLEN, Charles 133, Clara 133, 167, Coen Clark 133, 167, Daniel W. 133, Dorcas 132, Dorothy 133, 167, Earl 133, Earl Edgar 167, Elizabeth 132, Emily 133, Eunice 133, Evelyn 133, 167, Fern 167, Fonda Lou 167, Francis 132, Francis Coen 167, Frank Reuben 133, George Ira 133, George W. 133, Grace 263, Hannah 132, Hulda 133, James Alexander 133, Jane 132, Jemima 133, Jesse W. 133, Jesse Willard 167, John 132, Joshua 133, Marie 133, Marie Estella 167, Martha 133, Mary 133, Mary J. 132, Mary Jane 133, 140, Matilda 133, Melissa 132, Minnie Ann 133, Nancy 133, Pearl 133, Permelia Jane 235, Ray 133, Ray Edwin 167, Rebecca 132, Sarah 132, Sarah J. 132, Shirley Jean 167, Soloman B. 133, Sylvania 133, Viola 133, William 132, William Henry 133, William Mack 235.
ALLENDER, Armilia 133, Arressing 227, Beryl 133, Betty S. 298, Bob 133, Bobby 133, Cecil 133, Dolly 133, Elizabeth E. 133, Elizabeth Ellen 295, George 133, Glen 133, 243, Irene 133, Leon (Colt) 133, Mable 133, Mary Kirts 133, Ruth 133, 243, Ruth Armintie 133, Thomas A. 295, Thomas H. 133, Thomas Henry 133.
ALLISON, Alice 133, Alonzo 133, 185, Carl 133, Cecil Alonzo 133, Deborah A. 134, Dorothy 133, Ed 133, Eleanor 133, George 133, George Arthur 133, George W. 133, Glenn 173, Harriett 133, James 133, James Elmer 133, James Richard 134, Jane E. 133, Jane Elizabeth 133, Jennie 133, Jim 229, John Grover 133, Madie 133, Nancy Louise 134, Nettie 133, Olive 133, Orion 133, Paul Richard 133, Paula 134, Pauline 133, Rachel 133, Thurle 133, William 133.
ALLMAN, Bertha Louise 194, Lucinda 198, 199.
ALLTOP, Elizabeth 286, George 286, Minnie 236.
ALLWORTH, Amanda 256.
ALSTOTT, Ronda 238.
ALT, Marie Catherine 136, Valentin 136, Valentin II 136.
ALT (AULT), George 136.
ALTER, Beatrice Marie 226, Bernadetta 226, Constance 226, John Harris 226, Mary Louise 204.
ALTOP, Carmen 216, Demetria Dawn 216, Jack 216.
ALVIS, David 199.
ALWARD, Tim 250
ANDERSON, Alias 134, Allen Stover 134, Alonzo W. 289, Amanda 134, Amanda C. 293, Amanda Caroline 289, America A. 289, Andrew A. 247, Anna 247, Barbara 134, Bill 192, Caleb Henry 134, Charles Lewis 134, Christiana 134, Dan 247, Dora E. 289, Edward S. 289, Emily 134, Etta 289, Fanny 134, Florentine 134, Geo. Madison 289, 293, George Arthur 300, George Madison 134, Harriett 134, Ida 250, Isabell 134, James 134, James 134, John 134, Joseph 134, Joseph Jr. 134, Katy 247, Lorena 289, Mable 192, Madison Britt 134, Margaret 134, Maria 134, Mary 134, 141, 304, Mary Jane 192, Mercy 185, Nancy 134, Nettie Marie 300, Nova 289, Polly 134, 304, Rozilla 289, Saloma, 134, Sampson 134, Sampson Joseph 289, Sarah 134, Sarah Fleener 181, Sharon 143, Walter 289.
ANDIS, Nancy 235.
ANDREWS, Agnes 134, Bessie M. 199, Brent 134, Julie 134, Karen 134, Kim 134, Kyle 134, Louis 134, N.V. (Rev.) 199, Scott 134, Sharon L. 134, William P. 134.
ANGERMAN, John 292, Thursa Love 192.
ANGLIN, J.P. 186.
ANKNEY, Joan 254.
ANTHONY, Alice 135, Almeda 135, Amanda 135, Amos 135, Arena 135, Bert 135, Charlotte 135, Christopher 134, Cloyd 135, 183, Cora 135, David 135, Elysa Ellen 135, Emma D. 135, Gary Wayne 134, George A. 135, George W. 135, 183, Harley 135, Henry 135, Herbert 135, 183, Irene 256, James 135, Janalyn Renee 135, Janet 135, Jeanette 135, Jim 134, John 134, 135, John Daulton 135, John Wadsworth 135, Larry Gene 134, Lucretia 135, Martha 135, Mary 135, Mary Elizabeth 135, 183, 263, Mary Ellen 135, Mary Jane 134, Mildred 135, Myrtle 135, Nancy 134, Nora Ellen 135, Olive 135, Orville 135, Peter 134, 135, 256, Ray 135, Rose 135, Samuel 134, 135, 183, Sarah 135, Scott 135, Sina 135, Virta Mae 135, Wesley 135, William 134, William C. 135, William T. 135.
APPLEGATE, Linda Lee 144.
APPLESEED, Johnny 242.
ARASPHA, Indian King 292.
ARBOGAST, Anna Mae 247, Clinton Dewitt 247, John Q. Adams 247, Michael Sr. 247.
ARCHER, Mary Agnes 179.
ARDOIN, Lawrence 232.
ARDOIN, Christine Renee 232, Joyce 232, Lawrence 232, Sherrie, 232.
ARMSTRONG, Alan Kent "AK" 231, Alzora Jane 288, Bruce 231, Dennis 231, Dollie 279, Ivan 231, Lloyd 231, Margarey 257, Mary 299, Mildred 279, Turner 279, Zella 231.
ARNEY, Rosalie 195.
ARNOLD, Alice 135, Belle 200, 226, Charles (Dr.) 135, Charles Albert 135, Charles Eugene 135, Ellen 135, Iris 157, John 135, 200, June 239, Margene 135, Mary Ellen 200, Nora Belle 135, Robert 226, Robert Warren 135, Sara 135, 136, Vera 135, William 135, William F. 200.
ARTHUR, Della 200, Dempsey 200, Robert Lee 200.
ARTMAN, Teresa 153.
ARVIN, Gene (Bud) 253, Gene Otis 253, Gene Porter 253, Shelia 253, Sheryl May 253, Thelma M. 228, Thelma Mae 253.
ARWINE, Sally 180.
ASBURY, Deborah 166, Joel 166, John 166, Rett 166, Seth 166.
ASHBROCK, Deanna 211.
ASHER, Betty Jane 179, Jessie M. 165.
ASHLEY, Alta 201, Cora May 201, Estal 201, Hazel 201, Ina 201, Ralph G. 201, Ruth 201, Tracy 291, Walter 201, William 201.
ASHMAN, Ellen 161, Ethel 161, Laura 161, Robert 161.
ASHPAUGH, Brent David 155, Tamra Lynn 155.
ATKINSON, Mildred Maxine 222.
ATWOOD, Betty 270.
AUBIN, Josphine 171, 233.
AULT, Andrew 136, Cindy Louise 136, Donald 136, Donald George 136, Donald Gregory 136, Dora 151, Dorothy M. 165, Douglas Lee 136, Emma "Amy" 136, Hazel Verona 136, Henry 136, Jacob 136, Jacquelyn Lynn 136, Jane 136, Janet 136, Jesse 136, Keven Gregory 136, Lloyd Joseph 136, Margaret 136, Martha Lee 136, Martin (KIA) 136, Mary Ann 136, Nellie Francis 136, Ryan Douglas 136, Sarah 199, Stephanie 136, Thomas (Jake) 136, Thomas Gola 136, Thomas Hobart 136, Tina 136, Valentine 136, Wilma Jean 136.
AUSTIN, Chad 270, Grace 145, James (Rev.) 145, James M. (Rev.) 146, Jenny K. 310, Lindsey 270, Patricia Irene 145, 146, Robert 270, Stephen F. 299, Trenton 270.
AXOM, Pearl 209, Stanley 191.
AXSOM, Edelle 201, Elzira 289.
AYERS, Allyson Sue 145, 237, Arnold 304, Betty Jane 136, Brooks Michael 145, 237, Conner Keith 145, 237, Cynthia 304, Donald 304, Edmond 136, Edna Mae 136, Emily A. 184, Frances 198, Frances Adaline 188, Garland 136, 192, Garland Jr. 136, Gayle 304, Georgia 136, Gladys 136, Georgia 136, Helen Anita 136, Jack 136, James 188, 304, Jeffry Scott 136, Laura S. 136, Lauren Grace 145, Lillie 135, Lizzie 304, Lyndal 136, Marilyn 136, Marilyn Sue 237, Mary Louise 136, Michael 237, Michael Ketih 136, 145, Mickey 304, Myrtle 304, Neftal 136, Olive 135, Rhonda Lynn 136, Richard 304, Robert 136, Robert Leon 136, Roger Dale 136, Samuel 165, Sarah 198, 199, Scott 304, Stacy 136, Tressa 136, 192, Tressa Elizab. 136, Verlyn 165, Violet 136.
AYNES, Clarena 285, Gabriel 191, 285, Gabriel Sr. 153, Goldie 151, Nora 198, 199, Rebecca 153, 191, Sarah 153.
AYRES, Amanda J. 137, America 136, 137, Daniel R. 137, Delila 137, Delila E. 137, Dorcas 137, Edward E. 137, Elizabeth 137, Emily 158, Geo. Wash. (Mrs.) 137, Geo. Washington 137, James 137, John 136, John W. 137, Malinda G. 137, Margaret Amanda 137, Margaret C. 137, Mary Ann 137, Penny 212, Samuel C. 136, 137, Sarah 136, Susanna 137, Susannah, 137, William 137.

BACHERD, Zoe 176.
BACHMAN, Andreas 139.
BACHMUND, Karlheinz 256, Lillianne 256.
BADASZEWKI, David Joseph 175.
BAFUMO, Felicia Susann 155, Michael 155, Richard Michael 155, Stephen Allen 155.
BAILEY, Bessie 279, Charity 164, Elizabeth 198, Malora 164, Mary Elizabeth 164, Rebecca Emily 164, Selena 164.
BAINTER, Eric L. 137, Harold G. 137, Jeffrey W. 137, Juanita 137, Lynnette G. 137, Robert 137, Stella Jane 137.
BAKER, Clara 192, Elizabeth 282, Emma Beatrice 204, Georgia 136, Jas. A. 282, John 295, Lucinda 282, Margaret Bruce 196, Nancy 279, 280, Phil 220, Rebecca E. 286, Sarah Arminia 196.
BALCERAK, Sara 235.
BALDRIGE, Shirley Ann 145.
BALDWIN, Kristen Jay 175.
BALES, 137.
BALL, Anna Lucille 200.
BALLARD, Della 188.
BALLINGER, Viola 261.
BANISTER, David 166, Michelle 166, Robert 166.
BANKS, Henry 132, Phoebe 273, Sarah Ann 132.
BARBER, Alpheus James 294, Joseph 294, Joshua Wyatt 294, Opal 294, Randolph 294.
BARE, Barbara 219.
BARGEE, Kathleen 291.
BARGER, "Chainsaw" 137, "Mickey" 137, Alice 137, Allen 137, Allen Lorain 137, Anna 137, Beatrice 137, Bertha 137, Carol 137, Clarence 137, Dolly 137, Donna 137, Doris 137, Eva Ella 137, Gary 137, Hannah 137, Ira 137, James 137, Janice 137, John 137, John S. 137, Joseph 137, Judith 137, Karen 137, Lena Jane 137, Martin 137, Mary 137, Merrill 137, Oliver 137, Owen 137, Owen Mitchell 137, Tabitha 137, Verna 137, William 137.
BARKER, Clara Alice 181, Clarence 288, James 176, Jean 175, Mary 288, Mary Jane 271, Maude Alma 176, Maude Elma 176, Susanna 137.
BARKES, Cora 272, Delilah 239, George 239, Grace 227, 237, Grace Lodema 144, 145, Grandma 227, Hannah E. 239, Harley 272, Hester Ann 144, 145, John 237, John H. 144, 145.
BARKHIMER, Elizabeth 188.
BARKLEY, Ann Louise 149, James Arnold, 149, Jerry Duane 149, Jessica Lynn 149, John Kent 149, Lori Kay 149, Norma Irene 149.
BARNARD, Arkie 220.
BARNES, "Dump" 138, "Grandma" 138, Bert 138, Bertha Rose 138, Beth 138, Betty 232, Carol 138, Catherine 138, 299, Charles 138, 211, Dalton 138, Daniel Ray 144, Della 138, Demaree 138, Donald 138, Douglas 138, Elizabeth 138, Ella Belle 293, Emma 138, Florence Marie 144, George 138, Geriah 195, Hazel 138, Jason 138, Joan 138, Jodelle 138, John r. 138, Judith K. 138, Lavina 190, Leona 138, Letie Hannah 293, Madonna 138, Margaret 138, Margery 138, Mark 138, Mary Ann 138, Mary Avis 138, Maurice 138, Miles Ray 144, Morton 138, Nelda 138, Oda 138, Rebecca 282, Ruth 211, Sylvester 138, 229, 276, Washington 138, William Demaree 138.
BARNETT, Rebecca 253, Sarah 193, 289.
BARNHART, Carol 285.
BARNHILL, Lloyd 262, Mark 262, Rosalie Mildred 262, Roseann 262.
BARRE, Elizabeth 206.
BARRET, Lucinda 224.
BARRICK, Milford (Capt.) 132.
BARROTT, Lusenda 224.
BARROW, Anna 157, Pam 302.
BARTHOLOMEW, Harriet 224.
BARTLETT, Alma 198, Cicero 198, Elizabeth 198, Elzora 198, George 198, Georgiana 198, Kate 198, Salem 198, Susan 198.
BARTLEY, Ivan 242, Nellie 242.
BARTRAM, David 199, Violet Elaine 244.
BASSETT, Emilie 287, Mary 139.
BATES, Elizabeth 208, 209, Fred 250, Susan 208, Wiley 208.
BATMAN, Marian 239.
BATTERMANN, Emma 307.
BATTIN, Emma "Amy" 136.
BATTON, Marshall 150, Wanda Jean 150.
BAUDER, Ann Cecilia 191, John dominic 191.
BAUGHMAN, Amanda 139, Amanda Ellen 139, Anna 139, Bert 139"Billy" 139, Cecil 139, Clementine 139, D'Lema 139, Dale 139, Dlema 132, Eliza Jane 138, 156, 309, Frances 139, George 139, Hester 139, Jacob 138, 139, 268, Jane 139, "Jose" 139, Joseph 139, Josephine 139, Judith 139, Katherine 139, Laura 139, Lennis 139, 268, Lidda 139, Lillie May 139, "Liza" 139, Lorene 139, Lurena 139, Lydia 139, Margaret 139, Mary 139, Mary Elva 229, Mary Irene 139, Millard 139, Millard Dale 268, Millard Ray 139, Nancy 139, Nellie 139, Nellis 139, Nettie 139, Netty 139, Orin 139, Robert 139, Rosa 139, Samuel Walker 139, Sarah Catherine 139, Verna 139, Walter 139, William 139, Willis 139, 289.
BAUGHN, Anna Merle, 167.
BAULT, Robert 182.
BAUM, Elizabeth 219, George 219.
BAUMAN, Gustave 203.
BAUMGARD, Benton James 175, Craig 175, Ed 175, Otis Allen 175.
BAXTER, Anna 151, Betty Jo 302, Floyd 151, Gerald 285, Gladys 151, Judy 286, Linda 151, 285, Malissa Jane 171, William 171, Williamson 151.
BAY, Evaline 219, Grace 219, James 219, Joseph Allen 219, Rosemary 276.
BAYER, 147.
BAYNE, Kathryn 192, Paul 192.
BEAM, Mary 263.
BEARD, John (Dr.) 139, Joyce 199, Maragret 140.
BEASLEY, Amber Dawn 248, Audrey A. 228, Audrey Anna 253, Brent Douglas 253, Brian Eugene 253, Don 248, Harold Eugene 253, Harriet Emaline 230, Penny Joan 248.
BEATTY, Clarence 281, Dale 281, George 209, Lenore 281, Pearl 281,

Phebe Luella 209, Rozilla 289.
BEATY, John 301, Mary 301, Oscar Allen 301.
BEAUCHAMP, Barbara 139, Brenda Gail 140, Carole Sue 182, Charles 139, Charles Wendell 183, Cindee 140, Cynthia Sue 183, Donlad 139, Donna Jean 140, Edith M. 239, Elizabeth Ann 140, Estella 139, Etta Marie 236, George Francis 139, Hesper 135, Jeanette Kay 140, Joyce 139, Juanita 140, Leon 139, Marshall 139, Nicole 140, Rachel Lynn 140, Richard Leon 139, Rosey 139, Ryan 140, Vina Marie 139, Wendell 139, Wilma 139.
BEAVER, Ernest 138, Nancy 151.
BEAVERS, Gertrude 285.
BECK, Ashbel P. W. 140, Billy, 140, Carolinda 140, Catherine 140, Charlotte A. 140, Daniel Boone 140, David Jr. 140, David Louis 140, David Louis Jr. 140, Dewalt 140, Elizabeth 140, Elizabeth Ann 140, Emma Josephine 140, Hildegarde 174, James P. 140, John 140, John Benton 140, Kate 140, Margaret 140, Margaret Louisa 140, Marie 241, Martha 140, Mary Catherine 140, Mary J. 140, Mary Jane 140, Mary Katherine 140, Michael Sr. 140, Serane E. 140, Serelda 140, Solomon N. 140, Surilda H. 140, Willard 140, William Benton 140, William P. 140.
BECKWITH, Marcelyn 291.
BEDIENT, Agnes 273, Agnes Drake 206.
BEEMAN, Helen 209, Sarah Grace 209.
BEERY, Christie Jolene 145, 237, James 145, Jennifer Kay 145, 237, Marcia Kay 145.
BEHRMAN, Edna 164.
BEIGHTEL, Jane 305, Rebecca Jane 304.
BELCAS, George 164, 165.
BELL, Ada 302, Elmer 284, Eunice 182, Geneva Mae 309, Harold Keith 309, Harry 138, 302, Lenora 309, Lura 151, Margaret Gibson 203, Max Eugene 309, Nora 151, Norma Dell 309, Tura 151, Violet 302, Wavel 284, Wesley O. 309.
BELLMORE, Elizabeth 299.
BENDER, Mrs. Charles C. 185.
BENNET, Ruby 269.
BENNETT, Daniel Webster 202, Donna 212, Eva Belle 228, 295, Larry Dale 275, Mildred 285, Stella 156.
BENTLEY, Mary S. 187.
BENTON, Alice 309, Alvin 309, Andrew 309.
BENTZ, Philip Dean 203.
BERG, Gertrude 219.
BERGDELL, Jacob Wilhelm 177, Katherine 177, Seloma 177.
BERNIGER, Amy Susan 175, Ann 175, Annabelle Lea 175, Ariel Noelle 175, Charles Paul 174, Charles Paul Jr. 174, Gina Marie 175, Grace Elizabeth 175, Helen 175, Helen Graves 174, Jeannie Elaine 175, Matthew Scott 175, Michael Lee 175, Paul Brian 174, Robert Owen 175, Rose 174, Steven Wesley 175, Zackaire R. 175.
BERNSTEIN, Keith Bryan 251, Mrs. Mike B. 251, Shayne Jessica 251.
BERRY, John H. 158, Nancy Jane 158, Rachel 158.
BERTCH, Carrie 310.
BESS, George 134, John 134, Samuel 134, Sarah 134.
BESSIRE, Barbara 141, Bill 174, 250, Dale 140, 148, 208, 220, 235, 266, 296, Dale Philip 140, David 141, Fern 141, 195, Grace 141, 293, Jack 141, James Philip 141, Janet 141, Jed 141, Jennifer 141, Judy 141, Jules Philip 140, Kitty 141, Margaret Salome 140, Marianne Ruth 140, 235, Phil 250, Philip 195, Philip Dale 140, Richard 141, Ruth 235, 296, Ruth Sabina 140, William 195, William Sayer 140.
BETTERMAN, Leah 291.
BETTS, Robert 180, Robert Dale 180.
BEVINS, Iva 176.
BEYKE, Catherine 147, Christ, 147, Christotom 147, Dorothy 147, Joseph 147, Mary Helen 147.
BIBER, Miranda 250.
BIDDLE, Abigail Marie 229, Brent Lee 229, Diana 229, Hannah Jo 229.
BILES, Brenda Lee 237.
BILYEU, A.G. Stover 175, Arthur G. 175, Brian Arthur 175, Cynthis Lynn 175, Roy Eugene 175.
BINGHAM, Frances 141, Laura 141, Lessie 141, Robert 141, Robert Mearl 141, Sylvester.
BINKLEY, Stefanie 187.
BIRDSONG, Bob 305, Joan 305.
BIRGE, Cheryl Ann 155, Kevin Mattew 155, Matthew Scott 155, Tristan Lynn 155.
BIRKHEAD, John 153.
BIRR, Albert 162.
BISEL, Alice 141, Anna 141, Benj. Franklin 141, Dinah 141, Doc 141, Florence 141, George 141, Iva 141, John C. 141, John R. 141, Joseph 141, Joseph (Mrs.) 141, Lestie 141, Lillie 141, Mary 141, Mary Jane 141, Nancy 141, Nancy E. 141, Noah 141, Ritta 141, Rosemary 141, Ruth 141, Theodore 141, Vincent 141.
BISHOP, Alance 141, Charlie 141, Charlie 141, Dorathy M. 141, Geo. Washingon 141, Hannah 141, Larry A. 141, Lewis 141, Louise 141, Mary Ida 141, Norma J. 141, Thomas O. 141, Vicki L. 141.
BITTER, Anna Jane 186, Brials 186, Harry 186, Martha Jane 186.
BIVINS, Alma 267, Betty 267, Iris 267, Judie 267, Larry 267, Mary Lou 267, Paul 267, Silas J. 267.
BLACK, Andy 301, Ausman Decatur 301, Barbara Ann 301, Bill 301, Jacob 301, Jennie 164, Lafayette 301, Martha 301, Olive 301.
BLACKABY, Cyn. Virginia 147.
BLAIR, Mary 167, Mary Jane 264.
BLAKE, David Joshua 142, Dennis Lee 141, Mary Jane 141, Teresa 141, Timothy Wayne 142.
BLAKELY, Ann 273, Sadie 273, Sarah Teresa 273.
BLANTON, Bill 142, Olive Robin 142, Peter 142, Samuel William 142.
BLOIS, Lila J. 220.
BOARDMAN, Emma Lucretia 204, 226, Ida Pearl 222.
BOAZ, Abednego 151, Agnes 151, Fern 189, Leonard 141, Marie 151, Ruth 141, Thomas 151.
BOCK, Barbara 143, Beth 143, Charles 201, 204, Charles Edgar 142, Charles Robert 142, Emily Renae 143, Harold 142, Howard Martin 142, 143, Jason 143, John Franklin 142, John Pul 142, 143, Keith Michael 305, Lillian 142, 155, Martin 142, Martin Lee 142, 143, Mary 143, Mary Elizabeth 143, Maude 142, 201, Maude Catherine 142, Michael 305, Rebecca Hann 142, Rita Lynette 142, Rita Lynette 142, Ronni Lynn 143, Sharon 143, Tracy 142, Tracy Earl 143, Tresa 143, Zella 142.
BOCKSTAHLER, Evangeline C. 143, Harold W. (Dr.) 143, Katrin 143, Larry E (Dr.) 143, Rotraut 143, Wm. J.G. (Rev.) 143, Camille 278, Catherine 277, Jerry 278, Katie 278.
BOECKH, Helga 307, Ludwing 307, Marianne 307, Sophie 307, Walter 307, Wilma 307.
BOFFING, Clara 223, John F. 223.
BOGARDUS, Anneka 222, Everardus (Rev.) 222.
BOHANNON, Donna 300.
BOLDREY, Nathan 190, Patience 190.
BOLES, Benjamin 264.
BOLIN, Ed 161, Jean 161.
BOLT, Charles 154.
BOLTON, Aileen Marie 143, Arleen 143, Donna 143, Lee 143, Mable 182, Walter 143.
BOND, Allen Dale 145, Alonzo "Lon" 210, Alvin 146, Amanda Jo 144, Amy Lynn 144, Barbara Sue 145, Becky 146, 290, Bertha Ann 144, Bertha Pauline 146, Betty 144,145, 226, Bill 144, 146, Billy Hugh 144, 145, Blanche L. 147, Blanche Lavina 147, Bob 15, Bradley Scott 145, Brenda Susanne 145, Carl 146, Carol Sue 145, 146, Catherine 146, 217, Cindy 145, 290, Cindy Lou 145, 146, Claude 146, Clyde Arthella 146, Cyn. Virginia 147, Dale 144, 160, David Bruce 144, David Dale 144, 147, 172, Diana Marie 144, Dick 144, 145, Donna 165, Donna Elaine 145, Dorinda Kay 145, Doris Diane 144, Dorothy Marie 147, Earl 144, 145, 146, 149, 226, 237, 265, Elihu 146, Elizabeth 146, Elizabeth Ann 147, Ella Florence 146, 196, Estle 145, Estle Earl 144, Etta Marie 147, Florence Edith 146, Florence Marie 144, 147, 172, Hrothr Erit 146, Gladys 146, Glenn 146, Golden Rex 146, Grace 144, 145, 149, 226, 237, Grace Lodema 144, 145, Gregory Dale Jr. 145, Harold Edward 147, Harry 146, Harry Alvis 156, Hilda Ann 145, 226, Ira Patton 146, Ivan 144, 146, 211, Ivan Lee 156, Jack 144, 226, 290, Jack J. 145, Jack Jennison 145, James 146, 156, 196, 217, 265, James (MIA) 144, James Dale 145, James Douglas 144, James Frederick 144, 147, 172, James Noah 146, James Wilson 145, Jebadiah Allen 145, Jeff 145, 290, Jeffrey Scott 146, Jeffry Paul 144, John 217, John F. 217, John Franklin 146, Joseph Paul 144, 147, Joseph Walter 144, 146, 172, Joseph Wayne 144, Joshua 146, 156, 217, Joshua Jennison 144, 145, 146, Joshua William 144, Js. Elsworth 146, Joseph Paul 172, Judith Ann 144, Kathryn M. 156, Kathr. Margaret 156, Kathryn 156, Kathy Lyn 145, Lane 146, Leanna Renay 144, Leota 217, Linda Lee 144, Lloyd 146, Lois Ann 145, Lois Jean 145, Lorelle Marie 144, Louella 146, Lucille 144, Marilyn 144, Marilyn Joan 144, Marilyn Sue 145, Marjorie 146, Martha Joan 147, Mary 191, Mary Deckard 172, Mary Ellen 147, Mary Faith 144, 147, 172, Mary Kathryn 156, Mary Marguerite 146, Mary Olive 147, Mildred Naomi 210, Muriel 146, Myrtle 146, 156, 237, Myrtle Irene 144, 145, Nellie Pearl 146, Nona 146, Oma Jean 156, Otta 146, Pamela Sue 144, Pat 290, Patricia Irene 145, 146, Paula Lynn 144, Pauline 308, Pearl 146, Peggy 145, 146, 290, Phyllis Ann 144, 147, 290, Ralph 146, Ray 146, Rebecca 145, Rebecca Ann 146, Richard Earl 145, Robert 145, Robert Lance 145, Roger Dale 144, Ruby Gail 146, Ruth 144, Ruth Hold 146, Ruth Irene 237, Ryan Lance 145, Sally 146, Sara Loyd 156, Sarah 146, 196, Sarah Jane 146, 217, Sarah Lloyd 146, Setta 146, Sharon Kay 144, Shirley Ann 145, Sigeal Monroe 146, Susabel 145, Susie 144, 145, 146, 290, Tressa 146, Velma 146, Vernita 217, Wayne 146, William Cecil 144, 147, 172, William Everett 146, William Thomas 144, 146, 172, Wilma Faith 146.
BOOKWALTER, Karl (Dr.) 163.
BOON, C. Larie 305, Calab 305, Castle Chan 305, Danelle 305.
BOREN, Benj. Franklin 210, Benjamin 210, Calvin 210, Dorothy Amelia 210, Geo. Washington 210, Julia 210, Wilson K. 210.
BOSWELL, Riley 254.
BOTSFORD, George 244, Louise 244.
BOTTOME, Rosalind 204, Willard 204.
BOULTON, Joyce Ann, 227, Mathew Chasteen 227, Melissa Anne 145, 227, Michael Roy 145, 227.
BOWDEN, Bessie May 300, George 213, James 213, Link 300, William 213.
BOWERS, Bonnie 199, Catherine 275.
BOWLING, Barbara 150.
BOWMAN, Betty 268, Earl 171, 285, Elizabeth 280, Fairney 285, Jefferson 171, Kim 195, Linda 195, Mike 195, Ray 171, Ruth 270, Thomas R. 171.
BOYD, Ann 199, Contess (Tessa) 145, Contessa 237, John 237, Lauren Grace 145, 237, Marcia Kay 145, 237.
BOYER, Agnes 134, Amanda 147, Chas. Theodore 147, Debra Ann 147, Hazel Vivian 147, Henry Milton 147, Jacob 147, Lucy 147, Martha Jane 147, Mary Helen 147, Walter Thomas 147, William Richard 147.
BRADFIELD, Mona 199.
BRADING, Lucille 234.
BRADLEY, Alvin 203, Billie Lee 147, Cassie 203, Charles Nathan 147, Chessley 203, Elizabeth 203, Florence 178, Geneva 147, Lena 187, Mary Marguerite 147, Ruth 295.
BRADSHAW, Arthur 161, 162, Florence 161, Millard 161.
BRAND, Calsie 157, Mary 280, Mr. 273.
BRANSTETTER, Catherine 147, 148, Daniel 147, 148, 156, 230, Daniel W. 147, Julia 148, Magdalena 147, Mary 148, Mary Ann 156, 226, 230, Rebecca 147, 156, Sarah 148, 200, 301, 302.
BRANUM, Margaret 139.
BRANYAN, Margaret 139.
BRATTAIN, Jeremy 143.
BRAZIER, Rebecca 292.
BREECE, Anne 148, Charles A. Jr. 148, Charles Sr. 148, Georgia 148, Mary 236, Rebecca 236, 290, Simeon 236, Thomas 236.
BREEDLOVE, Ada Josephine 149, Albert E. 148, Albert M. 148, Alra Lawton 149, America 149, Angela Jill 149, Ashley 148, Betty Joan 289, Bonnie Sue 149, Carma Ellen 149, Chad Christop. 149, Charles Dale 289, Charles F. 148, 149, Charles G. 148, Charles K. 148, Christopher 148, Columbia B. 148, Cynthia 148, Debra Kelley 148, Doyle Duane 149, Elizabeth 148, 149, Elizabeth Ann 149, Emily 148, Esta Viola 148, Felix Preston 148, Flora Elizabeth 148, Francis M. 148, Gaylord Louie 149, Harry 148, Harry Roscoe 148, Ida Mae 148, 149, Jacob Sherman 148, Jeffrey 289, Jemima 210, Jerusha 148, John 148, John William 148, Lewis B. 148, Lori Kay 149, Louie Edward 149, Louis E. 148, Louis Edward 148, Lumie 148, Mark 148, Mary Etta 148, Mary J. 148, Melissa Ann 149, Mildred 148, Monagale 148, Myka Michelle 149, Nancy 148, Noah Anderson 149, Norma Irene 149, Oliver E. 148, Orinda 148, Ronnie Gene 149, Roscoe 148, Roscoe Jr. 148, Rosemary Elna 149, Ruth Mabel 149, Sarah 148, Sarah Ellen 148, 149, Shirley 148, Susan Alice 148, Thomas 148, Thomas Monroe 148, 149, Tommie Gayle 149, Tos. Monroe Jr. 149, Tos. Monroe Sr. 149, Ulysses Grant 128, Violet V. 148, William 148, Wm. Rossevelt 149.
BRENENSTALL, Dolores 230, 231.
BRESTER, John 300.
BREWER, Gene (Dr.) 167, Margie 182, Matilda 239.
BREWSTER, Elder William 251.
BRIDGEWATER, Deborah 136, Grace 304.
BRIDGMAN, George 260.
BRIGHT, Anna 152, Anna Belle 153, Beth Ann 149, Betty Ruth 149, Elma 145, Frances Ardella 237, Jane 152, 202, Lee 149, Lewis 152, 153, Luzannah 152, Mary 152, 153, Oddy 237, Oddy L. 270, Rinnie 270, Robert Lee 149, Ruth 149, Ruth Ellen 149, T. Flemmon (Rev.) 152, 153, Thornton (Rev.) 151, 153, William 152.
BRILL, Hallie 309.
BRINEGAR, Barbara 151, Gregory 173, Jeff 151, Jim 151, Lydia 151, Rachel Nicole 173, Robin 151, Zachar. Daniel 173, Zachariah Dani. 173.
BRINEY, Elizabeth 162.
BRINGMAN, Elias 162.
BRITT, Daniel Alan 150, Daniel Justin 150, Martha 150, Matthew Tanner 150, Seth Alan 150.
BRITTENHAM, Sarah Ann 295.
BRITTINGHAM, Ada Josphine 149.
BRITTON, John P. 286, Rebecca E. 286.
BRITZ, Christiana 134.
BROCK, Alan 150, Alfred 148, Barbara 150, Brad Dean 259, Brandon 150, Bruce Wayne 150, Charles 201, Clara Phoebe 223, Clifford 264, Dana Marie 259, Deborah Joan 150, Donald 259, Garland 150, Garland Lee 150, Heather 150, James Allen 150, Janette 150, Julia 148, 301, Justina 150, Laura 141, Lloyd 150, Loyd Clifford 150, Magan Louann 259, Martha 141, Martha Louise 150, Marvin Dale 150, Mary 148, 242, Mary Lou 150, Mary Martha 150, 264, Myrtle 141, Robin 150, Sim France 150, Virgie 150, Wanda Jean 150, Zack 141, Zuba 150.
BROCKAGE, Julie 205.
BROCKMAN, Barbara 219, Betty Jean 219, Darlene 219, David 219, Diana 219, Greg 219, Judy 219, Leonard 219, Leroy 219, Mabel 219, Marlene 219, Patty 219, Regina 219.
BROOKS, Amy 175, H. 276, 277.
BROONER, Jessie 151.
BROTY, George 301.
BROWER, Daniel 222.
BROWN, Ada Emeline 192, Alfred 151, Amanda 151, Amanda Emma 263, Andrew T. 151, Angela Joy 200, Angela Rose 151, Anna Belle 153, Anthony 209, B. Wayne 153, Barbara 151, Benny 151, Berton 151, Betty 151, Betty Delores 298, Betty Joy 151, Bonnie 151, Burrell 139, Camille 153, Carl 151, Carl "Bucky" 153, Catherine 150, Cathy 151, Charlene Jo 145, Charles 151, Charles N. 198, Charmaine 255, Cheryl Renee 200, Clarence 151, Clifford 151, Clyde 151, Connie 153, Constance 153, Daisy 155, Darla 151, Darwin 151, Delbert - (Bud) 298, Delores 183, Dorothy 151, Drusilla 151, Earl 151, Eathel 183, Eber 151, Edward (Ned) 151, Edward David 151, Elisha 151, Elizabeth 150, 151, 155, 183, Elizabeth Jane 151, Emaline 300, Emmett 153, Eva 205, 255, Fannie 151, Gary 151, Geo. Washington 151, George 150, Gerald 151, Glenn 151, Goldie 151, Grover 183, 227, Grover C. 272, Grover G. 151, 183, Harold 151, Henry 150, 151, Henry W. 151, Hester Ann 144, Hester Ann 145, 237, Ishmael 151, J. Dale 153, James 151, 182, 183, 188, 288, James H. 255, Jeannie 255, Jennifer Lynn 151, Jesse 182, Jessie 151, John 151, 155, 273, John A. 151, John H. 151, Joshua 151, Julia Ann 151, Karen 151, Karen (Kitty) 151, Kay 153, Kile 151, Kyra 151,

Laura L. 182, Lawrence Glenn 139, Lenore 151, Leonard Roland 139, Lewis 150, 151, Linda 152, Lloyd 255, Lois 198, Lora Marie 200, Lou Ann 153, Loyd Ralphy 255, Lucy 151, Lura 151, Lura D. 151, Lurena 139, Lydia 151, Malcolm 183, Malinda Jane 192, Margaret 203, 242, Marie 151, Marilyn 209, Marion Lee 139, Mark 139, Marshall 153, Mart 276, Martha 151, Martha Jane 279, Mary 150, 151, 153, Mary Ann 150, 151, Mary Jane 139, 155, Mary Kirts 133, Mary -(Polly) 182, Maude 139, Maudell 309, Maxine 151, 255, Michael 151, Minnie 183, Nancy 151, Nancy Ellen 158, Nellie 151, Noel 153, Noel M. 151, 152, Nora 151, Norma 151, Olive 139, 309, Orval 152, 155, Patricia 151, Paul 139, Pearl 276, Phebe 151, Polk 192, R. Ernestine 153, Rada 135, Ray 152, Robert 151, 209, 255, Roger 200, 209, Rose 153, Ruby Alice 254, Ruth 153, 255, Ruth E. 151, Ruth Elizabeth 153, Samuel 151, Sandy 150, Sarah 132, 150, 151, Sarah A. 285, Sarah Ann 151, Susanna 150, 151, Suzan 151, Teresa 153, Thomas 150, 151, 183, Thomas A. 151, Thomas Hill 151, Toni 153, V. Eugene 153, Vincent 151, Virgil 153, Virgil E. 153, Walena 151, Walter 151, Wanda 152, Wanita 151, Wayne 153, Wilburn E. 151, William Henry 255, William Manson 151, Wilma 151, 183.

BROWNING, Amanda Elizabeth 151, Edith Mae 251, Emma 212, Everett 201, Grace 201, John 208, Josephine 139, Leonard J. 251, Lucinda 212, Lura 151, Lura D. 151, Mary 208, Nathan 151, Nathan (Dr.) 139, 151, Obedience 151, Phyllis 287, Phyllis Lovenia 251, William W. 212.

BRUCE, Bill 285, Charlotte 218, Frona 285, Lloyd 171, Mr. 218, Nancy Jo 188, 241.

BRUKER, Garnet (Dine) 300.

BRUMLEY, Brenda 263.

BRUMMENER, Howard 226.

BRUMMETT, Agnes 153, 155, 225, Ally 286, Amanda 156, 225, Anne 153, 225, Arwine 155, Banner 230, Banner Sr. 154, Beth Ann 291, Carl 138, 154, 173, 268, Cather. (Katie) 155, Catherine 155, Charon 230, 286, Christopher 154, 225, David 225, Ed 154, Effie 155, Elenanor 286, Eli 155, Elizabeth 153, 154, 155, 156, 214, 225, 268, 279, 280, Emma 225, Eva 230, Felix 225, Geo. Grancher 153, George 153, 155, 225, 280, Geroge Ab. 155, Golda Virginia 163, Henry 154, Hiram 154, James 153, 225, James II 153, James III 153, James Payton 154, James K. 225, Joab 153, 225, 286, John 153, 225, Joseph 225, Joshua 154, Js. (Pate) 154, Langston 154, 225, Lloyd 155, Lucinda 225, Martha 225, 268, Mary 153, 154, 225, Mary Jane 301, 302, Matthew S. 291, Mildred 225, Nancy 154, Osa 155, Pamela Jo Haugh 253, Paul 291, Paul C. 291, Pierson 154, Prudence 153, Reason 153, Reice 154, Rena 153, Renna 225, Robert 154, 156, 225, Robert Hester 225, Sabra 154, Sally 153, 154, Sarah 153, 225, 286, Saral Jane 286, Solomon 154, 225, Steven Lee 253, Thena Catherine 155, V.A. Renna 153, W. Billy 154, "Whispering" Billy 154, William 154, 225, 286, William Enoch 154, Wm. (Billy) 154, Wm. E. (Nick) 154, Wm. McClelland 155.

BRUNER, Adrian Dorsey 276, Alice M. 200, Altha 195, Arl 191, Buleh 191, Jacob 238, Jake 191, James William 276, Jana Loraine 195, Joseph 276, Lee 195, Leota 276, Lloyd Edward 195, Lobie 191, Mary Alice 200, Norma Jean 195, Oma 191, Ray 191, Stella 191, Thomas Riley 276, Tina Elaine 195, Wayne 191, Wesley 191.

BRYAN, D.J. 132, Nancy Maria 132, Wm. Lowe (Dr.) 208.

BRYANT, Frank 161, James 153, Josephine 161, Sally 153, Sarah 161.

BUCKELY, Gary W. 301, Donald J. 301, Jacqueline 301, John William 301, Kirk 301, Kristi 301, Tammy 301, Zachary 301.

BUELHER, Carol June 149.

BUELL, Anne 311, Deborah 311, Samuel 311.

BUKER, Florence J. 183.

BULES, Berniece 231, Erve 231, Herschel 231, Lola b. 231, Marvin 231.

BULLARD, Baron Scott 155, Betty Allene 155, Catherine 155, Gilbert Franklin 155, Ginnvor 240, Kathy 240, Norman 240, Orlie 155, Will 240.

BUNCH, Catherine 165, John Wesley 165, Virginia Kather 165.

BUNGE, Angela 244, Angela Rose 246, Chester H. 155, David Michael 278, Dorothy Jean 155, Franklin Maurice 155, Gaylia Lucille 278, Hannah E. 155, Johnny Arthur 155, Kenneth 246, Kenneth Leon 155, Loretta Kay 278, Mary Johannah 155, Philip Richards 155, 278, Polly 244, Polly Ann 246, Rachale 155, Robin Lee 278, Sue Lynn 155, Trudy 244, Trudy Mae 246, Wanda 244, Wanda Rose 246, William 155.

BURCHHARDT, Katarina A. 269.

BURGESS, Barbara Jean 182, Brent Willard 183, Bruce Duwain 183, Jacqueline Gay 183, Terri Lynn 183, Vicki Leigh 183.

BURGETT, Mary 244.

BURK, Nancy 285.

BURKE, Miranda 198.

BURKER, Wayne 300.

BURKETTS, Harry 250.

BURKHART, Catherine 237, 269, Catherine Brown 262, George 202, Louis 202.

BURKHEAD, Eliza Jane 153.

BURKHOLDER, Mable 248, Ralph 248.

BURNETT, Mary 167.

BURNS, Eva 200, Helen 200, Irvin 200.

BURRIS, Emma 305, Mildred 300, Olive 246.

BURTON, Ada 302, Carl 200, Cora 276, DeAnn 187, Dorothy 200, Ernest Cleo. 233, Henry Sr. 200, Henry Jr. 200, Leoda Ann 233, Lucy 233, Mary Margaret 222, Myra 299, Nancy 200, Sandra 187, Sarah 200, Stephanie 187.

BUSER, Amy Jo 224, B.J. 224, Judith 224.

BUSH, Barbara Ann 156, Florence Edith 147, James Irvan 156, Dorothy 243, Elizabeth 156, Jennifer Ann 156, Lloyd 147, Margaret 156, Mary Margaret 156, 242, Mary Olvie 253, Matilda 285, Robert 156, Thomas Jonathan 156, Willard 242, William L. 156.

BUSTIN, Dillon 249.

BUTLER, Ally 237, Amanda 132, Cassie Ann 237, Curtis 196, Daniel 196, David 186, Etta 276, Junior 276, Margaret A. 300, Mariah 217, Robert Jr. 220.

BUZZARD, David 220, Elizabeth 220, Jacob C. 220, Joe 297.

BYAR, Maria 297.

BYERLY, Elizabeth 178, Jacquelyn 178.

BYRD, Carl 266, Nancy 182, Ramona 266.

CAIN, Hannah 239, Mary Elizabeth 229, Pat J. 272.

CAITO, August 233, Ida Rose 233, Mary Ann 233, Michelina Miceli 233, Philip A. 233.

CALLAHAN, Edwin 185, Ester E. 261, Lorene 233

CALVERT, Alice Charlotte 156, Amanda Melissa 156, Anne Elizabeth 156, Annie 156, 298, Captola 156, Catherine 156, Daisy M. 298, 300, Daisy Melissa 156, David Brewer 156, George Thomas 156, John N. 156, Lowrey 298, Mary Eliza 156, Melissa 298, Myrtle 156, Nancy 158, Owen Marion 156, Rachel 158, Sadie 156, Samuel Edward 156, Sarah 156, Stella 156, William 158.

CALVIN, Duard 186, Mable 248, Mary Alice 310, Maude 186, Walter 291.

CAMERON, Goldie E. 156, Robert O. 156.

CAMP, Ben 137, Elizabeth 137.

CAMPBELL, Alexander 157, Alice 156, Amanda 156, Anna 157, 220, 254, Anne E. 157, 237, Archie 156, Art 156, Barbara M. 248, Bert 255, Carol 259, Catherine E. 157, Charles 157, Charlie 206, 254, Clark 133, 185, 230, Clark Augustus 133, Cornelius 157, 220, Cornelius S. 157, Crystal K. 216, Denise 216, Effie 156, Elizabeth 156, 164, 232, Ella 202, Ella M. 169, Eva 156, Grace 156, Hannah 220, Hannah J. 157, Hattie 133, Hazel Vivian 147, Henry Harold 157, Herbert 157, 206, 254, Hortense 187, James B. 157, James B. (Dr.) 157, James P. 157, Jim 289, John Douglas 216, Leslie Nicole 216, Oon 156, Martha Edna 157, Mary 193, 195, Mary Edith 157, Mildred 156, Nathaniel C. 157, Nellie C. 157, Olive 133, Oma Jane 299, Rebecca C. 299, Rebecca Cath. 210, Robert 156, Ruby 180, 185, 230, 254, Ruby C. 157, Sarah Elizabeth 153, Thomas 157, Vera 135, William 147, 156.

CAMPFIELD, Mary Katherine 155.

CANARY, Abram 174, Brenda 220, Mark 220, Michelle Lynn 220.

CANATSEY, Nancy 134, Sampson 134, Sarah 134.

CANE, Delpha 188, Ernest 188.

CANNATA, Gerald D. 309.

CANTER, Benj. Franklin 211, Geo. Washington 211, Hallie Tate 211, Margret E. 271, Mary Frances 211, Nancy Elizabeth 211, Thomas Anthony 211, Truman 211, Wm. Carlyle 211.

CANTRELL, Burton Neal 238, John Dee 238, John Dee Jr. 238, Mary Emily 238.

CAREY, 193, Catherine 270, Edith 299, Piercy 194.

CARLEY, Charlotte L. 203, Lula 203, Richard 203, Richard S. 203.

CARLIN, Etta 178, Frank 178, Lois Fay 183, Weldon 183, Whitney Jay 183, Winifred Leigh 183.

CARLSON, Al 196, Albet A. 196, Dawn 196, Debbie 196, John F. 260, Josephine 247, Joyce 196, Lars 247, Leona 237, Leora 247, Oscar 247, Renee 176, Roandl 196, Sandra 196, Surella 247, Robert E. 246, Tonya 246.

CARMICHAEL, Ada 135, Adloph 135, Alice 158, Alta 157, Amos 135, 158, Amos Worley Rev. 158, Andrew Scott 281, Bert 158, Bessie 135, Bill 272, Blanche 158, Calsie 157, Caren 157, Charlotte 135, Christy 157, Cindy 157, Clara Alice 181, Dan 158, Delythia 157, Elizabeth 158, 180, Ellra 158, Elva Jane 157, Estel 158, Esther Kathleen 158, Eva 198, 199, 263, Fena 157, George 158, Grover 157, Hannah 180, Harley 135, 157, Harriett 198, Howard 158, Icel 180, Ira 158, Ival 158, James 158, James L. 157, James M. 158, Jewell 158, John 157, 158, John W. 176, Joseph 158, Joseph Thomas 158, Kathy 157, Kenneth C. 158, L. Cassandra 158, L. Neal 158, Leander 158, Lee 158, Leston Neal 158, Lola 157, Loren Harley 157, Loretta 256, 287, Loretta C. 158, 287, Louisa 158, 250, Lowell Gene 157, Lyle 157, Madeline 158, Maranda J. 281, Margaret 199, Mary 135, 158, Mary L. 158, Mary Louise 158, Maxine 180, Melissa 157, Meta Lena 158, Michelle 158, Nancy 158, Nancy Catherine 158, Nancy E. 250, Nancy Ellen 158, Nancy Jane 158, Noble 158, Olive 158, Orla 157, Otho Lessie 158, Otto Kenny 158, 181, Pam 297, Pearl 158, Phillip 158, Phyllis 158, Rachel 158, Robert 158, 180, Robert Lee 157, Roxena 176, Ruby 158, Ryan 158, Sarah 158, Sarah O. Anna 158, Sarah Oshie 158, Sheila 158, Sheryl Anne 159, Shirley 157, Shirley Ann 287, Stan 158, Sue Ellyn 159, Susan 199, Susan Caroline 157, Susie 158, Teresa 158, Thomas 158, 180, Vannie 157, Velma 157, Veva 157, Virgil 158, Virginia 157, Virginia A. 158, Vurlean 157, Will 158, William 158, 250, William Calvert 157, 158, William Thomas 158.

CARNEY, Elizabeth 272.

CAROTHERS, Amanda Elizabeth 151, Emma 285.

CARPENTER, Louise 240.

CARR, Vurlean 157.

CARSON, Dorothy 262, Mable 262.

CARTER, Ada 188, Cliffie 159, Courtland 159, Daisy Myrtel 159, Dean 171, Earl 159, Efram 138, Ellen K. 159, Ephraim 159, Hannah Elizabeth 159, Ida 270, Ida Alice 233, Ida Jane 159, Ira E. 188, James V. 159, Jay D. 159, Jessica Anne 159, Joel Russell 159, John W. 159, Judson 202, Lois 171, Lorena 286, Lynda Swift 159, Mary 188, Mary Lorena 159, Nancy 159, Patricia Eliza. 175, Shirley 159, Susan 233, Thomas 233, Virginia 159.

CARUSO, Gloria 220.

CASADY, Mary 151.

CASALE, Frank 151, Gabriele 151, Giancarlo 151, Mia 151, Patricia 151.

CASCADDEN, Earle S. 208, Olivia 208.

CASEY, Clarissa 193.

CASH, George J. 256.

CASS, Mary 292.

CASSADY, Mary "Polly" 133.

CASSELL, Catherine 234, Edward H. 234, Havey 234, Mary Rick 234, Kathleen 234.

CASSELLA, Delcina Ann 215.

CASSIDA, Barholomew 140, Elizabeth Ann 140, Max Wilbur 140.

CATSANOS, Marguerita 189.

CATT, Neftal 136.

CAVE, Daniel 159, Florence 159, John 159, Tina 159, Tom 159.

CAYWOOD, Martha Jane 267.

CERVERA, Alice 204, Madrid 204.

CHAFFIN, Warren 297.

CHAFIN, Herma E. 239, Isaac 239, James 274, Mary 239.

CHALLENDER, Marian 280, Marian Waters 280, Marion 282.

CHAMBERS, Ida 305, Mary 222, Thelma 285.

CHAMPNEY, Everett 196, Greta Gayle 196.

CHANDLER, Anne 153, Carol 168, 249, Don 249, Donald Fremont 168, James William 207, Lowana 218, Margaret 309, Samuel 249, Shadrack 153, William Griffin 207.

CHANEY, Meloney Jean 306.

CHAPELL, Elizabeth 245.

CHAPMAN, 242, Almedia Eva 293, Carolyn 293, Clarolyn Joan 201, Claud 293, Claud L. 201, Dorinda 293, Ida 293, Lawrence 293, Lester 293, Margaret 293, Veva 293.

CHAPPEL, Eleanor 255, Elizabeth 177, Minerva 255, Sabra 258.

CHASTEEN, Nora 171.

CHERRY, Amelia 174.

CHESHER, Mary 231.

CHESSIR, Mary 232.

CHILDRESS, Ann 219, David 207, Travis Donald 207.

CHIN, Beatriz 242.

CHITWOOD, Aleetha 216, 268, 279, Allen Eugene 160, Amanda Ellen 139, Andrew 161, Belle 200, 205, Beth 161, Blanche 205, 260, Blythe 161, Catherine 286, 310, Charles Corbitt 149, Clarence 149, 159, 241, David 160, 161, Donald 160, Elizabeth 161, Ella 160, Emanuel 161, Ethel Martin 205, Frank 216, George W. 161, Gina Lynn 168, Glodine Helen 160, Greenberry 161, Grocery 160, Guy Clifford 161, Helen 149, Helen Iris 149, Henry J. 161, Ida Day 160, Ida May 135, 160, 161, 170, 205, 226, 260, Ira 160, 161, Isaac 161, James 139, James Robert 168, Jean 160, 261, John O. 161, Jonathan 161, Josephine 161, Julia June 161, Lillian 160, Lillian Lee 145, Linzey 161, Lois Jean 145, Lois Marie 159, Mable 160, Martha 161, 205, Martin 205, Mathias 160, 161, Maude 161, 201, 205, Maude May 226, Michael E. 160, Nancy Ann 161, Nancy C. 161, Nell 205, Nellie 276, Nellie Ann 161, 205, Noah 161, Nora Belle 135, 161, Ora 205, Ora J. 160, Ora John 161, Patricia Mae 149, Ralph Ivan 145, 160, 161, Rebecca 161, Richard 135, 160, 161, 205, 226, 260, Richard Day 161, Robert 160, Ronald 160, Rosabelle 160, Sarah 161, Viola Blance 161, Violet 160, Walter 160, Walter James 161, Walter Joe 161, Walter Joseph 160, Wendell O. 160, William 161.

CHRISTIE, Gladys Mayme 228, 229, Robert 293.

CHRISTMAN, Sarah E. 201.

CHRISTOPHEL, 220, Barbara 219, Catherine 219, Christian 219, Elizabeth 219, Gertrude 219, Johannes 219, John Jacob 219, Maria 219, Peter 219, Susan 219.

CHURCHILL, Winston 302.

CHUTE, Elvira 281.

CIBIAL, J. Antoinette 185, Jeanne A. 185.

CLAIR, Janet 166.

CLAMPITT, Helen Roscoe 262.

CLAPP, Elizabeth 285.

CLAPTON, Elizabeth 213, 214, 248.

CLARIN, Gail Ruth 242, James Alan 242.

CLARK, Alva 303, Andrew J. 269, Anita 187, Bertha 222, Betty 161, Betty L. 162, Beulah Mae 222, Caroline 171, 269, Clarinda 303, Cora 262, Edward E. 164, Effie 155, Elizabeth 156, 185, 230, Emerson 155, Fern 298, George 303, Hannah 222, Hazel 269, Holland 187, James Samuel 156, Jane 175, 176, 303, Jolin Glover 222, Joshua 222, Lawrence 303, Lena Bradley 187, Lucy 162, Mabel 293, Margaret 156, Martha 303, Mary 262, 305, Mary L. 209, Mildred 229, Mildred Rose 262, Nadine 287, Olive Henderson 187, Omer 187, Paul 209, Pleasant 156, Raymond Julius 222, Richard 155, Roonie 247, Walsie Fern 209.

CLARKE, Charles 161, Ellen 161, Florence 161, Lucy 161, Samuel 161, Tressie 215, William 161.

CLARKSTON, Wilma L. 145, Wilma Lee 145.

CLARKSTON-YOUNG, Louise 248.

CLAY, Ruby I. 227.

CLAYBAUGH, Marguerite 195, William 195.

CLELENAD, Donna 16, 301, Evelyn 165, 301.

CLEMENS, Ann 213.

CLEVENGER, Alma 162, America May 162, Amy 162, Anna 162, Blancehe 162, 276, Celia 162, Charles 162, Cyrus 162, Cyrus R.

276, Edgar 162, 276, Emma Susan 162, 276, Francis 162, Franklin Henry 162, 276, Franklin Wm. 162, Geo. W. Runnels 162, Geo. Washinton 162, George 162, Henry 162, Hope Jane 162, Ida 162, James Louis 162, Janice 162, John 162, Jonathan 162, Lydia 162, Margaret 162, Mary 162, Mary Beth 162, Mary C. 162, Oliver P. Morton 162, Sarah 162, Sarah Jane 162, Sarah Margaret 162, Susannah 162, Sylv. Alexander 162, Sylvester 162, Sylvester Alex 162, William Adam 162, William Louis 162, Wm. H. Harrison 162, Wm. Henry Harr.162.
CLIFFORD, Elizabeth 223, Elva 223.
CLINE, Anna Mae 264, Charles 162, Flo 162, Fred Raymond 200, Grace 283, June Mildred 200, Nancy 162, Peter Sr. 169, Samuel Taylor 162, Susan 169, Wilma Ilene 200.
CLINTON, Lois 164.
CLOPFER, 163.
CLOUD, Bobbi 163, C. Carey 162, Donald 163, Harold 163, Mary 163, Vera 163.
CLOUSE, Amanda 175, Christopher 175, Debra Kay 175, Donald Gordon 175, Elisa 175, Eric 175, Jamie 175, Jason 175, Jeremy 175, Rechelle 175, Ronald Lee 175, Steven Michael 175.
CLUM, Catherine 156.
CLUPPER, Charles 163, Christian 163, Crace Edith 163, George Leonard 163, Harley G. 163, Harold "Doc" 163, Hugh E. 163, Judith 163, Judith Mae 269, Leona Muri 163, Lewis 163, Mae 163, Margaret 163, Maria 163, Mary 163, Ralph C. 163, Sarah Frances 163, William Frank 163.
COBB, Mary Ellen 135.
COCKEY, Mrs. William 231.
CODDINGTON, Nan 216.
CODY, Mandy 184, Maxine 303, Ruth 303.
COEN, Rebecca 133, William 133.
COFFEE, Evelyn 174.
COFFEY, Donna 215.
COFFMAN, Cindy Lu 298, David 298, Julie Ann 298, Nancy Carolyn 298, Vicky Lynn 298.
COLDREN, Chris Allan 164, David Lawrence 164, David Lynn 164, George 163, George Ruth 164, J. Riley 163, LaVonne 163, Mae 163.
COLE, Alva 225, Faye 225, Linda 305, Mae 225, Rachel 174.
COLFORD, Frances 288.
COLLETT, Beth Ann 237, Elizabeth 300, George 276, Miranda 300, Samuel 300.
COLLIER, Hiram 285, Nellie 285, Richard 285, Sarah 285.
COLLINGS, Ada 311, Daniel B. 311, Electa 311.
COLLINS, Alan 165, Allen 303, Allen Albert 150, Blake Vincent 200, Cora 303, Dawn Ann 200, Elijah 243, Ephraim 150, Flossie 258, Flossie Edith 150, Jane 262, Jeff 200, Maggie Etta 165, Mary 243, Mary Polly 243, Sara 135, Tillie Mae 150.
COLSON, Carla 199.
COMBS, Alfred 164, Benjamin 164, David 164, Dillen 164, Elizabeth 289, Eller 164, Ellis 164, George I. 164, John H. 164, 209, Karl 211, Laura 164, Lillie 209, Lilly 164, Lina 164, Lucinda 164, Lucy 164, Luda 164, Mary Ida 285, Mary Jane 164, 209, Rolley 164, Roy 168, Thalia 211, William Riley 164, Yvonne Gail 168.
COMMON, Chris 197.
COMPTON, Betty Ann 237, Ricky 199.
CONARD, Ellen 303.
CONDON, Ada 164, Alexander 164, Alvy Edward 164, Anna 164, Anna Belle 164, Carl Dolan 164, David Chandler 164, Dickie 262, Donald 164, Donald Duane 244, Elizabeth 164, Elmer Otto 164, Emma Florecne 164, Ethel 164, Frances 262, George Riley 164, Harry Alexander 164, Hattie Belle 164, Hazel 262, Jennie 164, Jesse Wayne 164, John 194, John Henry 164, 245, Joseph Campbell 164, Judy 262, Lee Omer 164, Leonard B. 164, Lois 164, Louisa E. 164, Lula 164, Mabel 243, Mabel Clare 164, Mahala 164, Mahala Ellen 244, Mary Elizabeth 164, Mary Lorena 164, Matilda 164, May 165, Minora 164, Myrtie Leona 164, Ol. P. Morton 164, Oliver Perry 164, 244, Pearl 164, 300, Perry Green 164, Perry Green Jr. 164, Rachel 164, Ralph W. 243, Ralph Weaner 164, Reba 164, Rebecca Emily 164, Ruth 165, Ruth C. 245, Samuel D. 164, Selena 164, Victor Eugene 244, Violet Elaine 244, Virgil 165, 262, William Henry 164, Willie Anderson 164.
CONNELL, Eva Ester 279, Fern 141, Latham 141, Sybil 141.
CONNETTE, Elizabeth Lyne 296.
CONSOLVER, John 220.
CONTOS, Christine 268.
COOK, B.W. 197, 264, Benjamin W. 165, Christop. Sipe 165, Christopher S. 300, Ebenezer 165, Evaline 300, Evelyn 165, Gary 222, Irma 277, Iva Cordelia 165, 300, James M. 165, Joseph 300, Joseph L. 165, Joseph M. 165, Kay 291, Lydia 165, Sarah A. 165, Sarah E. 165, Steven 165, Walter W. 165, 300, William J. 165.
COOLEY, Abraham 165, Alfred Eugene 165, Alfred Otto 165, Arth. McClellan 165, Arthur 165, Clinton McClell 165, Dessie Paulina 165, Edgar Allen 165, Elnora Ernest 165, Esta M. Marie 165, Esta Minnie M. 165, Frances 243, Geneva Nolena 165, Howard Walter 165, Kenneth 165, Loretta Mae 165, Martha 165, Mary Elizabeth 165, Orville 165, Ruey 165, Ruhama 165, Sarah Elsie 165, Walter Otha 165, William N. 165.
COON, Frank 266, Ruth 295.
COONROD, Ruth Estella 186.
COONS, Frank 266.
COOPER, Bill 178, Charles Phillip 196, Cynthia Renee 196, Deborah Ann 259, Elizabeth 300, Gwendolyn Marie 196, Hilda Joyce 196, Joy 200, Malissa E. 165, Malissa-Massie 175, Mary 203, Sarah 239, 304, Vernon G. 196, Vernon G. Jr. 196, Vernon Gilbert 196.
COPE, Olive 174, Stella 229.
COPENHAVER, Elvira 303, Mr. 201.
CORDILL, Evaline 195.
CORELY, Charlotte 271, Memoah 271, Jessie 151.
CORNEL, Margaret 289.
CORNETTE, Gina 209, James Brion 209, Jimmy 209, Rebecca 209.
CORRELL, Elizabeth 176.
CORTER, Mabel 291, Paul 291, Sarah Jane 291, Susabelle 291.
CORY, John 275.
COULTAS, Hannah 293.
COVEY, Ed 151, Hazel 151.
COX, Amy 304, Betsy 197, Charon 230, Clara Fergason 246, Courtland 230, Earnest A. 171, Elnora Decca 183, Estella 230, Hannah 213, Ida Hufford 292, Isaac 230, Martha 230, Ozro 183, William L. 261.
COY, Elizabeth 274, Lu Ann 266.
COYLE, Anita 165, Beatrice 165, Isaac Wesley 165, Jill Ann 165, John Alexander 165, John Allen 165, John Franklin 165, Sophia James 165.
CRABTREE, Amy 270, Barbara Kay 166, Benjamin Adams 166, Beula 166, Billy Richard 166, Brian 166, Cheryl Leslie 166, Clint 165, Danny 166, Debbie 166, Deborah 218, Deborah Asbury 166, Don 218, Dr. 211, Eloise "Nip" 166, Emma Mae 166, Erin 166, Garvin Preston 165, 166, Jack Alvin 166, Janet 166, Janice Kay 248, Jennifer 166, Joseph Harold 166, Joyce Ann 166, Kay Fracnes 166, Kermit Quentin 166, L.R. (Dr.) 166, 217, Larry 165, 218, Larry Denton 166, Lee Dunn 166, Lilian Pearl 166, Lisa 270, Lola 166, Loren Danny 166, Louie Richard 166, Louie Rudolph 166, Mae 235, Margaret 138, Mary Elizabeth 166, Matt 166, Preston 166, 217, Richard Lee 166, Robin 166, Ruby 270, Rudy 166, Sally 165, 166, Sara Belle 166, Sara Louise 165, 237, Sheila 218, Sheila Jane 166, 241, Steve 166, 218, Sue Caroline 166.
CRAIG, K. Louise 210, Katherine L. 210, Thelma 232.
CRAIL, Hannah 141, Sarah 185, Thomas 141.
CRAMER, Abraham 167, Alpha June 166, Bob 166, Geo. Frederick 167, Ira E. 166, James 167, Jeanadelle 166, Julia 167, Philip 167, Susan 167.
CRANE, Alice 284, Ann 213, Austin 284, Caleb Jr. 213, John Charles 155, Lauralee 155.
CRAVEN, Essie Myrtle 167, John B. 167, 299, John Burnett 195, John Christoph. 167, Martha 167, Mary Alma 167, 210, 299, Nancy Olive 167, William 167, Wm. Cleveland 167.
CRAWFORD, Scott 286.
CREAMER, Frances 261, Thomas 261.
CREEK, Catherine 155.
CRESS, Verna 184.
CRIDER, Elizabeth 274, 285, Emma 138, George 274, Leonard 290, Lucille 198, Phyllis 286, Simeon B. 165, Sylvania Ann 274, 275.
CRIST, Alzora Lucinda 288, Gail 288, Nathan 295, Retta Belle 295, Richard 288.
CRITSER, Lynn 205.
CROMWELL, Oliver 291.
CRON, David Walter 196, Donna 196, Gary Neal 196, Horace Wendell 196, Joel 196, Phillip 196, Ronda 196, Wesley 196, Wilbur Mayzelle 196.
CROSS, Albert 285, Albert H. 171, Albert Henry 188, Albert W. 285, Alberta 285, Beverly 285, Bobi Ann 140, Carol 185, Dorothy 285, Dorothy Lou 237, Elizabeth Ann 140, Florence Emma 180, Francis 306, Fred 285, Gary Dean 285, Jacob 285, Jasper 301, Kathryn May 285, Linda 285, Marlene Elaine 190, Nancy 285, Peony 285, Robert 285, Robert Michael 140, Rodney 285, Rose 285, Rose M. 199, Rose Marie 188, Thelma 285, Virginia 285.
CROUCH, Aaron 133, 167, 168, 224, Aaron (Sr.) 151, Alfred 198, Alfred Ralphy 168, 224, Amanda 133, Amanda M. 168, Amy 133, 167, Anita 196, Ann 167, Anna 167, Beulah 167, Caroline Ann 168, Cloyce 168, Daniel 133, 167, 168, David 133, 167, Doc 168, Donald 249, Effle Leanna 168, Elizabeth 167, 239, Elizabeth Jane 168, Elsworth 167, Evelyn 163, Even 167, Freeman Donald 168, George 167, George W. 167, Goldie F. 168, Grace Louise 168, Grover 249, Grover W. 168, Gwendola 168, 224, Harry Wendell 168, 224, Hila 167, Hiram E. 168, Imogenen 168, Ina May 168, Jacob Elsworth 168, James 167, 168, James A. 167, John 239, 249, John R. 168, 249, Joseph 167, 249, Joseph W. 168, 224, Joseph William 168, Kenneth Woodrow 168, 249, Lela Alice 168, Lillian Mae 224, Lillie May 168, Lois 199, 224, Lois D. 198, Lois Delphine 168, Mary 133, 151, Mary Ann 151, Mary Nettie J. 295, Melvin 168, Minnie Ann 133, 167, Ora F. 168, Polly 167, Ruth 168, Sarah E. 167, Steven Wendell 168, Thomas Martin 249, William 133, 167, 168, William R. 167.
CROUCHER, James W. 136, Margaret C. 136, Sarah 136, 137, Susannah 136, William 137.
CROWELL, Mrs. 185.
CRUM, Mary 262, Mary Jane 150, William 262.
CRUMP, Levina 270.
CUDAHY, Thelma 214.
CULLEN, Catherine 168, 261, Elizabeth 168, Emma 168, Harriet 168, Henry Terrance 168, Hester Al 168, James Emmett 168, James Henry 168, Jesse Elizabeth 168, Jessie 302, John 168, Mary A. 168, Mary Catherine 168, Peter Wilson 168, Rhoda E. 168, Rosanna 169, Samuel 168, Susan M. 168.
CULVER, Anna 157.
CUMMINGS, Carry 189, Gibson 185, John (Rev.) 185, Mable 262.
CUMMINS, James V. Jr. 171, James V. Sr. 171, Richard Cooper 171.
CUNNINGHAM, Cecil 201, Lydia 282, Rita 201.
CUPPER, 163.
CURRAN, Christina Grace 184.
CURRIAN, Nancy Reed 175.
CURRY, Blanche 310, David Hamblen 164, Henry Edgar 164, Minora 164, Nancy 299, Sarah Tabitha 186.
CURTIS, Mary 263, Mina Evalyn 223.
CUSICK, Catherine 286.
CUSTER, George (Gen.) 183.
CUTSINGER, Elizabeth 291.

DAGGY, Jake 259.
DAILEY, Edward 169, Ella M. 169, Frank 169, Helen 169, James Barton 169, James Robert 169, Joseph W. 169, Melba Pauline 169, Patrick 169, Robert J. 169.
DALE, Barbara 145, Gregory 145, Gregory Jr. 145.
DAMERON, Ruth 255.
DAMRELL, Susan 198, 199.
DANFORTH, Dora Ethel 288, Lurid 288.
DANIEL, Elizabeth C. 294.
DANIELS, Goldie 182, Jonathan 174, Margaret 140.
DARBY, Annie Taylor 250, Caroline 250.
DAVENPORT, June Yvonne 310.
DAVID, Edward 218, Edward "Ned" 279, Edward (Sr.) 279, Elizabeth 151, Evaline 219, Ida 291, Judith Ann 144, Laura Kay 279, Leila 250, Mary E. 189, Patsey 279, Patsy 269, Sampson 140, William 279.
DAVIDSON, Catherine 289, Eliza Jane 232.
DAVIS, Alice 135, Bertha 267, Bessie 236, 265, Celia 262, Charity 164, Chris 258, Clarence (Rev.) 283, Clyde 285, Dan 229, 262, Delpha 169, Dillon 193, Dudley 169, Edgar Adam 170, Elisha 202, Elmina 132, Ethel 285, Florence 169, Frank 170, Fred 199, Hazel S. 169, Irenay 185, Karen Jo 193, Katharine Sue 257, Linda 169, Marion Francis 283, Marlene 257, Mary 193, Mary "Polly" 223, Mary Ann 202, 252, 285, Mary Frances 211, Nancy 289, Orange 169, Penelope 306, Robert 170, 193, Robert Glen 170, Sarah 132, Sue 258, Theodore Glen 189, Vannie 157, Virginia 170, Vivian 259.
DAWSON, Elizabeth 309, Ernest 309, Helen 309, Sidney 309.
DAY, Alweda 170, Arlington 170, Charles 170, Hester 170, Ida May 161, Ingham 170, James Morten 170, Jane 268, John 170, Joni 170, Joseph Frank 170, Julia 170, Lowell C. 185, Margaret 161, Margaret 170, Mary Rawlings 170, Morten 170, Olive 170, Presley 170, Sarah 170, Thomas 161, Thomas R. 170, Viola 218, William 170.
DE LOOPER, Jacob T.Q. 222.
DE MATZELAER, Theunis 222, Thomazen Quick 222.
DE RIO, Barbara Alice 204.
DEBAUNE, Corinne Kay 244, Rickie 244, Taylor Allen 244, Tory Nichole 244.
DEGAFFERELLY, (Rev.) 227.
DEGOLYERS, Birt 216, Howard 216.
DEVORE, Brenda Joyce 149, Brian Keith 149, Carma Ellen 149, Carma Ellen 149, Carol June 149, Cedele Sue 149, Dale Gene 149, Janis Marie 149, Kenneth Ira 149, Lowell Kenneth 149, Mary Kathyrn 149, Richard Glen 149.
DEASY, Kevin 196, Mike 196.
DEAVER, Abigail 183, 184, 237, Jane 237, John 237, Lewis Jackson 183, 184, Mary Elizabeth 237, Minerva 237, Sarah Ann 237, William Leonard 237.
DECKARD, Aaron 171, Adam 171, Albert 171, Amanda Ellen 172, Amy Lynn 144, Andrea Jane 241, Andrew 172, Anna 171, Barsheba Ann 171, Bashie 171, Bashire 233, Beryl 133, Bessie 171, Carmen 216, Catherine 171, Cecil 144, 172, 191, 215, Charles 171, 255, Charlotte 172, Clarence Cecil 172, Daisy 171, Daniel 171, Denise 216, Dorothy Irene 172, Edith 187, Ella 191, Ella Inez 172, Enoch 172, Estella 172, 191, Flora 290, Geo. Washington 172, George 172, Henry 171, Herman 172, Hezekiah 171, 233, Isaac Dunn 172, Iva 171, 172, 191, 215, Jacob 171, 172, 233, Jacob Jr. 171, 172, Jacob Sr. 171, James Madison 172, Janet Kay 171, 310, Janie 172, 191, Jesse W. 171, Joan 182, Joe 172, John 171, John David 171, John Eliot 171, John Henry 172, John Wesley 172, Leslie 172, Leston 171, Lonie/ Lonnie 172, Lonnie 172, Lonnie Jr. 172, Louie 172, Lucille 172, Lydia Elva 171, Marcia Kay 188, 241, Margaret 255, Martha Jane 172, Martin 171, Mary 171, 172, 191, Mary Alice 172, 233, Mary Ann 285, Mary Ellen 144, 147, 172,191, Mary Rosetta 144, 215, Matilda 172, Maxine 172, May 171, Michael 171, 233, Milton 171, Minnie Irene 171, Ollie 172, Peggy 172, Peter 233, Philip 216, 172, Polly A. 171, Rachel 172, 191, 310, Raleigh 171, Robert Layton 241, Ruth 208, S. Clementine 172, Sallie 171, 172, Sara Elizabeth 172, Sarah Clemenen. 172, Sarah Elizabe. 172, Stephen 171, Thomas 171, Vernon 171, Vina Viola 171, Wade 171, Wesley 191, William 171, 172.
DEISHER, Billie 199.
DEIST, Conrad 217, Harold 217, John 217, Mary 217, Mary C. 176, Maurice 217, Paul 217, Wilhelminia 217.
DEITZ, David 154.
DEL RIO, Ava 204.
DEL VECCHIO, Dessie 165.
DELLINGER, Catherine 309.
DELPH, Indiana C. 295, Martha Edna 157.
DEMBO, Paula 183.
DENNISTON, Barbara Kay 179.
DEPREZ, Christine 176.
DERRINGER, Archie Leroy 173, Arthur Leo, Asa Ray 173, Clara 172, Corda 280, Cordelia 173, 280, Daniel Asa 173, 219, Denis Ann 173, Edgar Lewis 173, Elmer Lennis 173, Etta Joy 172, Everett Dale 173, Genevra 173, 241, 242, Hannah Jane 280, James 172, 280, James Napoleon 173, 280, James Ray 219, James W.

172, 173, 228, 241, 280, James William 173, Jane 172, Jerry Douglas 173, Jerry Wayne 173, Josh 219, Lillie Mae 173, Ludeana 219, Margie 173, Marjorie 173, 219, Marjorie Ann 219, Mary 181, 228, 295, Mary C. 253, 280, Mary Cordelia 173, 253, Mary E. 173, Mary Gladys 173, Mary Ruth 173, 219, Ray 173, Rebecca 173, 215, 219, Rebecca Jane 215, Rex 173, 214, 255, Rex Edgar 172, Roy 172, Ruby Letha 173, 228, 295, Ruth 295, Scott 219, Shawna Marie 173, Terra Annetta 173, Verlis 173, Verlis C. 173, Verlis Cleo 295, Verna 172, Vertis 219, Vinnie 173, Walter Asa 173, 215, 295, Walter Ray 173, 295, Wilbur 173, Wilbur Allen 295, William 173, 219, Willie Earl 173.
DERTING, Monty 309.
DERTERING, Albert Henry 150, Betty Ruth 149, Donald Albert 150, Ellen 150, Elnora 150, Mary 150.
DEW, Anna 229, John L. 229, Sarah 229.
DEWAR, Daniel 215, Donald 215, Edna 215, Elbert 215, Iva Jane 215, James Frederick 172, John William 172, Judy 215, Kenneth 215, Phyllis 215, Sara Annos 172, Stacy Mason 172, Wesley Dale 172, Wilma Jean 172.
DeWEES, Amelia 173, 280, Angela 174, Barbara 280, Beth 173, 174, Bette 174, Bradley 174, Brittany J. 280, Casey 174, Dallas Daniel 173, 174, Donald James 173, 174, Elizabeth A. 280, Haley 174, James Wiliam 280, Jim 173, 174, J. Eugene 280, Joe 173, 174, 280, Joseph 173, Joseph Charles 280, Joseph Eugene 173, 174, Joseph W. 173, Laurie 174, Marilyn 173, 174, 280.
DEWEY, Sherry 187.
DEWITT, Ruth 279.
DICKERSON, Edith 300.
DICKEY, Marcus 271, Nancy 239.
DICKMEYER, Ernest Lee 251, Ernest Lee II 251, Jason Lee 251, Lana Diane 251, Miranda Dawn 251.
DIGGS, Florence 169.
DILLER, Marie 255.
DILLINGER, John 149, 217, 281.
DILLINGHAM, Sarah 261.
DILLON, Margaret 282, Screlda 150.
DILTZ, Anna 248, Ernie 248, Isabel 248, Mary 248, Peter 248.
DINE, Arvilla 174, Clarence 300, Cornelius 174, Garnet 300, Gertrude May 300, Ida Jane 300, John 174, John Herman 174, John Jr. 174, Joseph 300, Mary Ann 174, Mildred 300, Nettie Marie 300, Opal 300, Peter 174, Peter Jr. 174, Ralph E. 300, Rebecca 174, Samuel 174, William M. 174.
DINGEMAN, Carolyn 205, David 205, Drake 205, Drew 205.
DITTS, Kitty 141.
DIX, William 179.
DIXON, Janet K. 274.
DONALDSON, Alan 174, Amanda 174, Catherine 174, D.C. 174, Daniel 174, Dorothy 174, Hildegarde 174, Janet 174, Kathryn 174, Ketih 174, Mark 174, Sawn 174, Vera 174, William 174.
DOUTHILL, Permelia 230.
DOVER, Catherine 286, John 286, Sarah Jane 286.
DOW, Della 200.
DOWDEN, Teresa G. 243.
DOWELL, Adam Roy 175, Albert Lee 174, 175, Anthony Edward 175, Betty Lou 174, Carol Sue 174, 175, Christina Ann 175, Danial Lee 175, David Wayne 175, Delbert Roy 174, Delissa Diann 175, Donald Wayne 174, 175, Edna Mae 174, 175, Helen 175, Helen Geneva 174, John Edward 175, Judy Ann 174, 175, Kathryn Louise 174, 175, Linda Marie 174, 175, Margaret Louise 175, Mary 175, Mary Elizabeth 174, 175, Meghan Lindsey 175, Michael Roy 175, Myrtle Iva 174, Nancy Eileen 175, Nicole Marie 175, Phyllis Joan 175, Roy 174, 175, 189, Thelma 175, Thelma Ruth 174, William Dale 174, Wilma 213.
DOWNEY, Benjamin 176, Benjamin A. 175, Cloey Jane 175, Cornelia Fern 176, Effie May 176, Elisha James 176, Eliza 176, 303, Eliza C. "Lide" 175, Ena Myrl 176, Ephraim 175, 176, Ephraim Tracy 176, Ethel 176, Ferrell 176, Floyd B. 176, Herma Faye 176, Ica Amelia 176, Ida Mae 176, Ida May 175, James Otis 176, Jane 175, 176, 303, Jim 176, John Wallace 176, Jos. Alonzo Jr. 176, Joseph 175, 176, 303, Joseph Alonzo 176, Kenneth Paul 176, Leona Grace 176, Lucetta Jane 175, 176, Mae Catherine 176, Margaret 175, Martha Edith 176, Mary 175, Mary Alice 175, 176, 202, Mary Elizabeth 176, Max Hoyt 176, Nancy 175, Nancy 176, Nancy Minerva 175, 176, Owen K. 176, Patrick 132, Patrick (Mrs.) 132, Quay 176, Raymond Ferrell 176, Rebecca 175, 176, 300, Sarah Rebecca 176, Thelma 176, Thomas Humphrey 176, Thos. Hunphrey 176, V. Ofanbaugh 176, Verna Opal 176, Vincent O. 175, Vincent Osbold 176, Wanetta 176, William Otis 176, Wilma Jean 176, Zola C. 176.
DOWSON, James 154.
DOYLE, Sara Margaret 259.
DRAGOO, Fada 304.
DRAKE, Agnes 273, Audrey 196, Francis 273, Harold 273, Homer 273.
DRAYER, Lori Kay 149.
DREISER, Clarie 251, Theodore 251.
DRESSER, Paul 251.
DRESSLAR, Walter 201.
DUCIC, Evans 287, Michael 287, Forrest 287.
DUCK, Bethel 160.
DUFF, Ann 249, Michael R. 249, Rachel B. 249, Robert 249.
DUFFEY, James A. 271, Laura B. 271, Laura Belle 192, 271, Martha Ann 271, Michael 192, Thomas R. 271.
DUHAMEL, Clarissa 299.
DUHM, Laura 149.
DUNCKER, Elizabeth 309.
DUNGAN, Charles G. 287, Lee 287, Leora 287.
DUNN, Otis 201, Viola 184.
DUNNICK, Hazel 236.
DYE, Eunice 151.
DYER, Jacquelyn 177.

EADS, Annette 302, Malinda 171, Virginia M. 305.
EARL, Alvira 148, Estle 145.
EARLL, Jodelle 138.
EASTMAN, Joseph 292.
EASTRIDGE, Lora Grace 298.
EASTWOOD, Clint 305, Deborah 305.
EATON, Donna 153, Nellie 229.
EBEE, Jack 274.
EBERSOLE, Catherine 162.
EBTHARPE, Elizabeth 292.
ECKERMAN, Brenda Gail 140, Steven Edward 140.
ECKSTADT, Ila 230.
EDDY, Alfred 223, Calvin 309, Delythia 157, Emma 285, Estella Laverne 309, Margaret Emma 285, Walter 285.
EDGETT, Bertha Louise 194.
EDMINSTON, Vera 174.
EDWARDS, Anita 199, Sarah Jane 276.
EGGEMAN, Norma Rosanna 168.
EHRBAR, Agnes Elizbeth 233.
EHRET, Jason 214, Martha Butler 214.
EICKLEBERRY, Carl 176, Carol Kay 176, Catharine 176, Catherine Eliz. 176, Charles Hugh 176, Chris 176, Ethel 176, Francis Marion 176, Gary Ernest 176, George 176, Hazel 176, Henry 176, Ivan 176, James Daniel 176, James Ernest 176, John 176, Julia Ann 176, Lorene 176, Martha Ann 176, Martin 176, Mary Frances 176, Peggy 176, Rebecca 176, Roy 176, Silas Evan 176, Steven 176, Steven Jr. 176, Susanna 176.
EISENMENGER, Nelda 138.
ELKINS, Bertha Mae 200, Carl Edgar 200, Daisy Mae 200, Drury 164, 285, John 285, John H. 209, Joseph 185, Katie 270, Margaret 285, Mariah 185, 285, Martha 285, 287, Mary Jane 164, 209, Nancy 164, Rebecca 285, Rhoda 285, Thomas 285, William 185, 285, 289.
ELLER, Rosemary 203.
ELLERMAN, Marie 132, 277.
ELLIOTT, Charles 209, Emma 209, Linda 199, Lorena 209.
ELLIS, Abby 177, Alissa 177, Amy 177, Barbara 176, Benjamin Tatum 177, Easter 176, Easter Amy 293, Elly 176, Ethel 293, G.Cleveland 176, Grover 293, Grover C. 176, Grover II 176, Henrietta 176, Homer 176, Howard 176, 293, Janet 177, Jayna Kidwell 177, Joan 177, Joshua 177, Junior 293, Lydia 176, Margaret 176, 177, Mark 177, Mark II 177, Matthew 177, Nancy 177, Nichole 177, Noah 293, Noah Joseph 176, Noah Joseph II 176, Samuel 176, Sarah 176, Tatum 177, Yvonne 180.
ELLSBERRY, Enoch 209, Louisa 209.
ELSWORTH, Hallie 283, Ira 137.
ELVERTON, Cleoparthara 210.
EMBERTON, Carmileta 266, Ronald 266.
EMCH, Cedele Sue 149, Jacq. Nicole 149, Jacqueline 149, Jennifer Marie 149, William Harold 149.
EMENHIZER, Martha Elizabe. 175, 176.
EMERSON, Boyd 150, Deborah Joan 150, Lisa 211.
EMILY, Betty Pauline 155, Charles David 155, Cody James 155, Constance 155, Darlene Jo 155, Doris Melba 155, Felicia Susann 155, Gilbert Paul 155, Gregory Allen 155, Heather 155, James Melvin 155, Lacy Dawn 155, Mary Etta 155, Mary Katherine 155, Melvin Leo 155, Rebecca Ann 155, Ross David 155, Stephen Michael 155, Steven Michael 155, Tamra Lynn 155, Timothy Allen 155, Veda 155.
EMMEL, Gudrun 203.
EMMONS, Nancy 185.
ENES, Adam 177, Barbara 177, Frederick 177, Lucy Anne 177, Seloma 177.
ENGLE, C. Blair 177, Christopher B. 177, Ian Andrew 177, Jacquelyn 177, Nathan William 177.
ENGLEMAN, Patricia Lynn 237, Robert Steven 237, William Jr. 237.
ENNIS, George 262, Rosalie Mildred 262, Ruth 262.
ENSLOW, Helen 151.
ERICKERSON, Edith 199, Nancy 146, Patricia 205.
ERICSON, Christina 247.
ERNI, Margaretha 189.
ERVIN, Martha 190.
ERVINE, Betty 210.
ESAREY, Robin Elizabeth 245, William 245.
ESPENSCHIED, Louisa 222.
ESSEX, LaDeama M. 244.
ESTES, Mary 153.
ETIENNE, Alberta 285, Samuel 285.
ETTER, Elizabeth 171.
EUBANKS, Eileen 245, Raymond 245.
EUDALY, James Daniel 247.
EVANS, Alpha 255, Amanda 245, Amanda Jane 177, Ethel 199, Frank Dale 177, James E. 206, Jane 139, 156, 268, John Dale 177, Katherine 215, Mabel E. 206, Mamie 274, Milton Lowell 206, Roscoe 177.
EVERLING, Edith 310, Inez 304, Maggie 173.
EWERS, Benjamin E. 178, Billy 178, Charles E. 178, Clara Alice 178, 251, Clarissa 178, 231, 272, David 251, David Jr. 178, David Sr. 178, Ella 178, Eppie 178, Estella 139, George 178, George W. 139, John 178, John W. 178, Mag 178, Martha 178, Mary Ellen 178, 272, Myrtle E. 178, Sarah Margaret 178, Vina Marie 139, William G. 178.
EWING, Frank 290.
EYRE, Catherine J. 186, Robert 199.

FAIRCHILD, Lois 244.
FALKINBURG, Edmond 175.
FALWELL, Jessie 242.
FARISON, Elizabeth 264, 265.
FARLIN, Marie 217.
FARLING, Josphine 304.
FARNHAM, Nellie 284.
FATELEY, Anna 192, Carrie 192, Clinton 192, Mary 192, Nolan 192, Virginia 192, Winthrop 192, Worth Peter 192.
FAUGHT, Merlin 199.
FAVERO, Judy 270.
FAY, Douty 276.
FAZEKAS, Veronica 258.
FEARS, Cynthia 178, Frances 178, Joseph 178, Joseph Jr. 178, Mary Jo 178, Sandra 178.
FECHMAN, Hugo 159.
FEHRENBACK, 147.
FEHRIBACH, Dorothy 147, George.
FEIGEL, Lilliam 220.
FELLARS, Clarinda 186.
FENDER, Brian 151, Drusilla 151, Larry 151.
FERGASON, Ashley David 246, Clara G. 246, David H. 246, Elizabeth 246, Elizabeth A. 246, Henry A. 246, Kathryn J. 246, Mary G. 246.
FERGUSON, Caleb 301, Green 301, John 301, Michael 201, Michelle JoAnna 201, Newton 301.
FERNANDES, Jennifer 141.
FERRENBURG, Bessie May 165.
FETRON, Sharon 215.
FETZER, Naomi 134.
FICKLIN, Betty Jo 219.
FIEGEL, Lillian 221, 266.
FIELD, Joan 177.
FIELDS, Branded Tyler 302, Christopher P. 302, Darren Howard 302, Lora Kay 302, Richard 302, Timothy Scott 302.
FILLMORE, Millard 292.
FINCANNON, Elsa Margaret 276.
FINCH, Cindy 250, Honnalora 250, Susan 250.
FINLAYSON, Andrew 143, Arleen 143, Lauren. 143.
FINN, Goldie Mae 145.
FIPPS, Mary Catherine 140.
FISCHEL, John Adam 178, Leonard Edwin 179, Nelson Bonapart 178.
FISHEL, Christopher 178, David Michael 179, David Stanley 178, Henry 178, Jacob 178, Johannes 178, Marie 178, Nelson 180, Ruth Mae Long 179, Stanley 178, Stephanie Ann 179.
FISHER, Anna 192, Daniel Lee 145, 237, Edwin 248, Holly Nicole 145, 237, Isabel 248, Mary Beth 145, Mary Lou 267, Matilda 263, Myrtle 237, Pearl Maude 176, Steven 237, Steven Craig 145.
FITZER, Robin 150.
FITZGERALD, Amanda 168.
FITZPATRICK, Daisy Mae 200.
FLANNERY, Alpha Adele 211.
FLATER, Bobbie Jo 309, Dawn Y. 309, Elbridge 309, Lorelei Evannoe 309, Luvilla Anne 309.
FLEENER, Aaron 235, Aaron F. 179, "Abe Crocket" 180, Abraham 180, Abraham Jr. 178, 180, Abraham Sr. 180, Adam Richard 179, Alexander 179, 180, Alf 201, Alice 157, 179, Andrew Jackson 180, Angeline 179, Anna 179, 180, 220, Anna Campbell 179, Anna E. 157, 237, 301, Anna Elizabeth 180, Artie 232, Barbara Kay 179, Bessie 232, Betty Jane 179, Beulah H. 232, Carey William 179, Catherine 178, 180, Charles 232, Christine C. 180, Cymentha 235, Daniel Harry 179, Donald Everett 232, Dora 232, Doris Ilena 301, Edward Wilson 179, Eliza Catherine 178, Elizabeth 180, Emma 180, Esther Ermina 179, Frances 179, Fred 301, Frederick 179, 180, Geo. Raymond 180, George 180, George R. 180, 237, George Ray 179, 301, Guy L. 179, Hallie 178, 232, 233, Hallie Joseph 232, Hallie Josephi. 139, Harry Addison 179, Ida 240, Ida Mabel 227, Isaac 232, Jacob 179, 180, Jacob Henry 264, Jacob Jr. 297, James 179, 232, James Addison 179, James Martin 232, Janice 154, Jennie 293, John 180, Joseph 232, Jospeh N. 179, Julia Frances 179, Lanny 180, Leo 301, Leo L. 180, Lester Edward 179, Linda 180, Lottie L. 248, Louse 232, Margaret 180, Martha 179, Martha Ellen 180, 227, Martha May 179, Martha - Janice 180, Martin 232, Mary 143, Mary 143, 179, 232, Mary A. 297, Mary Agnes 179, Mary Ann 179, Mary Elizabeth 180, Mary Ellen 235, 259, Mary -Polley 180, Mayme 210, Melva Agnes 179, Michael 179, Milton 179, 232, Minnie 180, Nan Huckleberry 180, Nancy 179, 180, 264, Nancy Jane 180, Nicholas 179, 232, Norman 180, Opal 178, Paul Matthew 179, Pearl 232, Peggy Jo 179, Permelia 180, Ray 178, 179, Rebecca 180, Rebecca Savanah 227, Richard Lee 179, Rosanna 180, Ruby 180, Ruby C. 157, Ruth Matilda 264, Samuel W. 264, Sarah 301, Sarah A. 180, Sarah Isabelle 180, Sarah Jane 180, Sarah Margaret 179, Thomas Wilson 179, Thos. Wilson (Jr.) 179, Vannie 149, Virginia Ruth 237, William T. 180, 301, Woodrow Wilson 179.
FLEETWOOD, Alexander 209, Becky 181, 258, Brad 239, Chester 180, 181, Cynthia Dalene 168, Daniel 239, Donita 239, Dorval 242, Earl 308, Elizabeth 274, Emarine 304, Eva 158, Heidi Lee 241, Isaac 180, 289, 304, James 180, James Robert 168, Jenny 181, 258, Jerry 239, John 289, Joshua 181, 258, Kate 158, Lena 287, Leota 289, Lucy 308, Manda 176, Margaret 208, 209, Mary 308, Mary L. 239, Mary Louise 239, Maxine 180, 181, Oliver 172, Patti 181, Rebecca 191, 274, Retta Isilla 171, Richard Howard 180, Ron 181, 258, Ronald James 168, Sarah 172, 180, 289, Sharlot 180, Sheryl Jolene 168, Solomon 180, Terry Mark 168, Thomas 308, Treva 308, Willard 308, William 192, William R. 158, William Riley 158, Wilma Hamblen 192, Winfer E. 239.
FLICK, Raymond, 259, Timothy Allen 259.
FLINNER, Johannes 232.
FLINT, Jacob 300, Jasper 286, Lucinda 286, Luther 286, Margerette R. 256, Rebecca 300.
FLODYCE, Cinderella, 181.
FLOYD, Cora 172, Denise A. 245, Elsie Mae 172, Ivan 191, Jerry Ralph 144, John 154, Joseph 172, Lydia Louise 176, Mary Faith 144, Milton 191, Milton Jeffers. 176, Minnie Effie 215, Naomi 279, Orval 191.
FLY, Christine 165, David 165, Julie 165, Mark 165.
FLYNN, Oral Eugene 175, Regina Ann 175, Wesley Arrin 175.

FOCELL, Elizabeth 291.
FOGLE, Lucinda 237.
FOLEY, Patricia 275.
FOLKS, Franklin 271, Margaret E. 271.
FOLLOWELL, John 154, Laura Alice 304, Minerva Jane 236, Orinda 148, Rachael 248.
FOLSOM, Ellen 258.
FOLSUM, Ellen Aldrich 150.
FORBES, Caorl Ann 291, Jana Kay 291, Julius 291, Patricia Ann 291.
FORD, Alexander 181, Ammsey 181, Catherine 181, Dempsey D. 181, Dempsey U. 181, Edell R. 181, Edward 200, Eva 268, Evelyn 181, Ezekial 181, Frances May 182, Grant 181, Henry 181, James 181, Jane 181, Joseph 181, Lavinia 181, Mamie 274, May 274, Nelson 162, 181, Ray 274, Ruby 254, Sarah 162, Susanna 181, Uriah 181.
FORDYCE, Cinderella 298, Samuel 181.
FORE, George W. 169.
FOREMAN, Aaron L. 181, Charles W. 181, Emma Jan 181, Ida May 181, Myrtle A. 181, Rhoda 181, Sarah Ellen 181.
FORRESTER, Luella 247.
FORSYTH, William 204.
FORSYTHE, William 283.
FORTNEY, Mary 281, Mort 281.
FOSHER, Pearl Maude 176.
FOSMOE, Albert 307, Anna 307, Edward 307, Elizabeth 307, Harold 307, Henry 307, Jennie, 307, Marie 307, Marit 307, Marta 307, Ole H. 307, Oscar 307.
FOSTER, Benj. Lewis 291, Blanche Nellie 228, Clarence Huston 186, Dennis 291, Evelyn 186, Janice Elaine 291, John 228, Lillie 186, Maria Jane 228, Rachel Lorraine 291, Sarah C. 186.
FOWELL, Amanda Louisa 153, Eliza Jane 153, Isaac 153, Isaac Jr. 153, Isaac Sr. 153, Martha 153, William 153.
FOWLER, 194, Abigail 213.
FOX, Aire 182, Arnold 182, Artie 182, Artie Everett 182, Barbara Jean 182, Benita 216, Bessie 182, Bill 219, Carole Sue 182, Charles 209, Charles Wilson 182, Charley 219, Charley W. 182, Charlie 244, Clara Mae 182, Cora 182, David 219, David Louis 188, Dessie 182, Dillard 182, Donald Dayton 188, Dora Ethel 288, Dorothy 182, E.A. Bell 182, Emily D. 182, Emma 182, Eunice Arbell 182, Fanny 182, Fanny Clark 182, Frances 219, 244, Frances May 182, George 188, Goldie 182, Gregory A. 182, Ianthia Ann 210, 215, 216, Ira 182, Isaac 182, James 182, Jane 182, John 182, Jonathan 182, Joseph 182, 210, Judy Jean 188, Julia Ann 182, Justin C. 182, Justin Craig 222, Karen Sue 188, Keith 222, Keith A. 182, Kelley R. 182, Kevin L. 182, Larry Joe 188, Leanna Kay 182, 183, Leslie 182, Lewis 182, Lillie 209, Lois Fay 183, Lorean 188, Louis Charles 182, Lucinda Ann 188, Mabel 215, Marion D. 182, Martha Hutson 182, Mary 182, Mary Ruth 219, Micah 219, Michael S. 182, Nancy 182, Nellie Sue Gray 188, Patricia 188, Permelia Jane 201, Phillip 182, Rachel Rachelle 216, Ralph M. 182, Randell L. 182, Raymond 182, Roger D. 182, Rosa A. 182, Rosey 182, Samuel 182, Sandra Lynn 188, Sarah 219, Sarepta Olive 182, Sharon 182, Susie 182, Thomas 182, Thomas Isaac 216, Uriah 182, Willard 182, William 182, Willis 288, Zelma Irene 183.
FOX'S CORNER GROCERY, 182.
FRAIL, Mary 151.
FRAKER, William 299.
FRANK, Anne 239, Ersie 208, Frances 219, Harriet 208, Harry Edwin 208, Heinrich 239, Johann 239, Wilhelmine 239.
FRANKLIN, Germaie 304, Jemima 304, Rachel 232.
FRANZE'N, Ann Louise 183, Carl 183, Carl Heydon II 183, Charles Kugler 183, Joel Gustin 183, Margaret Ann 183, Mary Florence 183, Peg 183, Susan Christine 183, Sven Carl (Rev.) 183.
FRANZE'N-ROHA, Ann Louise 183.
FRAVEL, Arlie 178, Martha 178, Tommy 178.
FRAZER, Alpha B. 202, Lula Loree 203, Margaret 203, Wm. Oscar 203.
FRAZIER, Laura 254, Sara Vivian 311, Susie 293, Susie L. 298.
FREDERICKS, Virginia 285.
FREEMAN, Rebecca 276.
FREESE, Abigail 183, Barbara Louise 184, Catherine 183, Chester D. 184, Cora 183, Cora Belle 184, Crystal 184, 263, Donald E. 184, Earcle 201, Earl 184, Ernest 183, Ernest Elmer 184, Geneva 183,184, George 183, Glen 184, Howard 184, James 183, Jane 183, John 183, John Calvin 183, 184, John Calvin Jr. 183, John Sr. 183, Joseph 183, Kathleen 184, Kevin Ray 184, Marvin Dean 184, Mary Catherine 184, Michael lee 184, Nancy 183, 184, Nancy Eliz. 184, Nancy Jane 183, Neal 184, Norma Jean 184, Oddis Lee 184, Paul 184, Paula 183, Paula Kay 184, Pauline 184, Pearl 184, Phyllis Joann 184, Ray 183, 184, 263, Ronald Lee 184, ruey 183, Ruey A. 184, Vira 158, 184, 263, Walter 183, Walter Edward 184, William 183, 184, William Henry 183, Willie Otto 184.
FRENCH, Mary 153, 154, 155, 225.
FRESHOUR, Sandra 235.
FRIEND, Frances Louise 182.
FRITCH, Andrew 184, 185, Catharine 184, Catherine 185, Catherine A. 286, Christopher 286, Clay 185, Conrad 184, Dolly 185, Earl 185, Edna 189, Elizabeth 185, 286, Ellen Aldrich 150, Ellen Folsom 185, Francis 185, Frederick 184, 185, 286, Hannah 184, 185, Hannah Ellen 150, 258, Harold 185, Isaac 184, Isaac M. 286, Isaac Monroe 185, James 184, 185, Joseph 184, 185, Konrad 185, Laura McKee 185, Lewis 150, 184, 185, 258, 286, Margaret 185, Margaret Jane 184, Martha 184, 185, Martha A. 286, Mary 184, 185, 286, May 185, McAllen 184, 185, Nancy 184, 185, Nancy E. 286, Nathaniel 184, 185, Roe 185, Sarah Ann 184, 185, Woodrow 160.
FRITSCHLE, Jacob 197, Ola 197.
FRITZE, Marie Sophie 256.
FROWNFELTER, Eliza 177, 300, Ralph 276.
FRUNDSBERG, Count 300.
FRYE, Alexander 309, Anthony Scott 187, Christo. Allen 187, Christopher 187, DeAnn 187, Delight Helen 309, Dillon 309, Elmer H. 309, Eustace L. 309, Frieda Marie 309, Martha Joyce 309, Marvin Eugene 309, Marvin Louis 309, Stephanie 187, Wanda Carol 309, Zella M. 309, Zella Margaret 189.
FUHRMAN, Anna Martina 234, Charles 234, Connie 234, Edward 234, Harvey 234, Kathleen 234.
FULKS, Lena 201.
FULLER, Deborah 310, Jane 310, "Little John" 310, Margy Ellen 306, Mehitable 310, Samuel 310, Virginia Ann 159.
FULTON, Bret Robert 284, Gordon 284, Joanne 284, Kenneth 284, Michael Paul 284, Robert T. 284, Scott Brian 284.
FUNK, Carryle Ellen 308, Frederick 297.
FURGESON, Jessie 233.
GABLE, Eliza 176.
GALLAHUE, Dudley 297, Mr. 303.
GALM, Bob 187, 195, Tammy.
GALYAN, Grace 191.
GAMBILL, Susan 212.
GARBER, Sam 208.
GARDNER, Mary 198.
GARFIELD, President 236.
GARLOCH, Ernest 187, Margaret 135.
GARNETT, Arlie 178, Sandra 196.
GARY, Elizabeth Stump 185.
GASHO, Gladys D. 215.
GATCHETT, Martha K. 197.
GATES, Alcinda 209, Charles 133, Daniel William 223, David 223, Jenny 182, John J. 223, Katie Mae 223, Mary Etta 224, Mary Jane 133, Sarah Georgiana 223, Sidney Sharon 224.
GATHEMAN, Catherine 275.
GATONS, Ila 230.
GATTEN, Amanda M. 300, Emaline 300, Hannah 280, John A. 300, Margaret 291, Mary E. 280, Richard 280.
GAUNTT, Sherry 247.
GAVIN, Mary Ramsay 252, Susan Esther 252.
GEARY, Elizabeth 184, 286, Josephus 286, William 184, 286.
GEE, Berniece 221, Beryle 221, Dale 221, Dolores 184, 221, Marjorie 221, Raymond 221, Walter 221, Walter Clifton 221.
GEISER, Catherine 147.
GELFUS, Mary 281.
GEMMILL, Edna 284.
GENOLIN, Charles 185, Charles M. 230, Clementine 185, Elizabeth 185, Glodine 185, Hesper 185, Jessie 185, John 230, John Jr. 185, John M. 185, John Sr. 185, Lewis 185, Lucy Jane 185, 230, Mary 185, Maude 185, Max 185, Ruby 185, Thomas 185, Verna 185, William 185.
GENTRY, Nellie Crouch 198, Nellie Esther 225, Raymond 225.
GEORGE, America Jane 185, Anna Jane 186, Bessie 186, Clara Ellen 186, Clayton 186, Dessie 186, Eva 199, Florence Belle 185, Francis L. 185, Francis M. 186, Franklin 186, Harold 186, Harry 186, Hattie Belle 186, Ida 186, Irenay 185, Iva 186, James 186, 285, James David 185, James Edward 185, Jess 185, Jess Madison 185, Jessie 186, Judy 141, Laura B. 186, Margaret 185, 285, Margaret R. 196, Maria 185, Mary E. 185, Mercy 185, Mercy M. 186, Nancy 185, Patty 219, Sarah Jane 185, Sarah Tabitha 185, Semantha 185, Thomas J. 186, Walter J. 185, William Andrew 185, William P. 185, Zuelda 185.
GEOTZ, 141.
GEUDTNER, Agusta 297, Emil 297, Vera 297.
GILBERT, George 280, Mary Elizabeth 280.
GILES, Lula 200, Sadie 200, Salena 200.
GILL, Angela Rose 151, Charles Mason 159, Chelsea 151, Conan 151, Everett 159, Goldie 159.
GILLAM, Genevieve 226.
GILLASPY, John 195.
GILLESPIE, Lenore 149.
GILLIAM, Neil 180.
GILLMAN, Mary 285.
GILMORE, Dorothy 260.
GILSON, Ellen 162, Elmer 183, Rosemary 183.
GIRARD, David 186, David B. 186, James R. 186, Mary Alice 186, Ruth Estella 186, Susan G. 186.
GISH, Todd 175.
GLADDING, Amanda 186, B. Frank 186, Cathryn J. 186, Elizabeth Jane 186, Evans L. 186, Eveyln 186, Stephen E. 186, Timothy F. 186.
GLICK, Elsie 302, Jonathan 302.
GLIDDEN, Bessie 311, Lydia Ann 300.
GLINES, Melissa 286.
GOBLE, Lucinda Jane 288, Mary Jane 288, Mary Jane 288, Robert 300, Susan Caroline 157, William 140, 288.
GODDARD, Francis 132, Hannah 132, Mary J. 132, Rebecca 132.
GOFF, Roger 270.
GOFFE, William 291.
GOFORTH, Geriah 195, Marilyn Joan 144, Nancy Ann 167, 195, William 195, 230.
GOLDEN, Diane 198.
GOLDMAN, Albert 186, Arnold 186, Lillian 186, Sandra 187, Sharon 187.
GOODEN, Lydia 268, Mary Polly 268, Samuel M. 268.
GOODMAN, Brett 196, Brooke 196, Charles 196, Charles Michael 196, David Morgan 196, Dawn 196.
GOODNIGHT, Beatrice 165, Fredrick Harvey 165, Mary Jane 165.
GOODOLF, Adam 291, Deborah 291, Jason 291, Joshua 291, Nick 291, Tony 291.
GOODRICH, James P. (Gov.) 208, Ralph 162, Ruth 162.
GOODWIN, Alva 187, Carman Michelle 207, Cynthia K. 187, Deborah Lou 162, Donald 187, Donald Keith 187, Helen R. 187, James Alexander 286, James Stuart 187, Marjorie J. 187, Martha Eleanor 286, Mary Polly 268, Mary S. 187, Robertine 199, Sheldon 187, Terry Shane 187, Treasie Ann 286.
GORBETT, Glen 199.
GORDEN, Wanda 284.
GORDON, Elizabeth 293, Evelyn 151, Faye 151, Forest 151, Forrest Ray 151, Jane 151, Jayenna Faye 151, Nancy 151, Nellie 151, Olive 293, Ray Brown 151, Riely 293.
GORE, Abigayle 187, Alex 187, Bill 178, Bryan 187, David Young 187, Hortens 178, Hortense 187, Jane 204, Kevin 187, Margot 187, Rachel 291, Sarah 187, Stephen William 187, William 159, 178, William A. Jr. 187, William Adolph 187.
GORMLEY, Harry V. 251, Paul Dresser 251, Ruth Amy 251, Ruth Elizabeth 251.
GOSLIN, Grace 199.
GOUDY, Virginia 273.
GOW, Mary Ramsay 252.
GRAHAM, Betty 237, Brittany 306, Elizabeth 148, 149, 198, Green 148, Jane 249, Margaret 148, Nancy 158, Scott 306.
GRAHAN, Russell 306.
GRAPE, Clarence Estes 187, Margaret B. 187, Ruth 187, Vida Sipes 187.
GRAPP, Ilo 135.
GRAVE, Amandy 197, Kimberly Ann 197.
GRAVES, Edgar 297, Edgar E. 296, Eva 297, Eva Mae 296, 297, Garry 296, Jeannette 304, Katrina 296, 297, Lisa 297, Lisa Michael 296, Michael E. 296, Mrs. Roy 185, Shannon 296, Shannon Lane 296, Sonya 296, Thelma Grace 296, Timothy Joseph 296, Vickie 296.
GRAY, Alfred 188, Alfred Lowell 188, Andy 188, Becky 188, Carl Nathan 188, Danny 188, Delila 137, Delpha Jo 188, Diana Kay 188, Edith 188, Gerald 188, Ginger 188, Howard 188, James T. 137, Jennifer 188, John 188, Laura 188, Louis Alfred 188, Louis Garfield 188, Louisa 188, Luella 188, Mabel 188, Margie 261, Mark 188, Nathan 188, Oliver 188, Raylean 188, Richard Gale 188, Robert Louis 188, Samuel Ernest 188, William 188.
GRAYSON, Jessie 293.
GREATHOUSE, Alra 188, Anna 199, Anna E. 188, 198, Barbara E. 188, Blanch Olive 251, Charles 188, Charlie Cliffo. 188, Della 158, Dora 158, Elva Jane 157, Emily 158, George W. 198, George Washing. 188, Goldie 188, Hezekiah 188, Jacob 158, Jacob A. 184, James 158, John 188, Laura 158, Lemuel 198, Lemuel James 188, Leonard 188, Lester 158, Lester Ernest 188, Maley Amos 188, Marion Alonzo 188, Mary 158, Mary Elizabeth 188, Melvin 158, Ollie 158, Peter 188, 199, Peter T. 188, Rachel 199, Rachel T. 188, Rady Mae 158, Ray 188, Ressie 199, Ressie Jane 188, 199, Roy 188, Solomon 188, Veva 157, Vira 158, 263, Vira Hazel 184, Virgil 251, 271, 287, William 188, Wm. Thomas 188.
GREDIG, Anna 170, Jerimiah 170, Rose Ellen 170.
GREDY, James 273.
GREEN, Alberta 274, Ernest E. 169, Gabe 178, Herbert 250, Jimmy R. 256, John Reid 256, Linda 169, Mabel 176, Mabel Clara 276, Mable 176, Margaret 214, Richard 233, Rita 256, Robert 274, Sonya Marlyn 256, Tove Josephine 233, Valerie Nicole 169, Winnie 250.
GREENE, Carol 187, Jeanette 260, Nancy 180.
GREENLEE, Amanda 285, Pauline 217.
GREER, 242.
GREGG, Helen Anita 136, Kathleen 199, Michael 136, Michelle Leigh 136, Nathaniel 281, Robert 217.
GREGORY, Boots 189, James G. 189, Jefferson 286, Margaret E. 189, Mattie 189, Melvin 189.
GRELLE, Austin Lee 253, Betty Jean 253, Jaclyn Ann, Kevin Lee 253, Lauren Marie 253.
GRELLER, Buddy 270, Charles Cain 229, Matthew Charles 229, Sarah Kathryn 229.
GREVER, Pamela 291.
GRIDER, Debra 233.
GRIFFEN, David 286.
GRIFFIN, Amanda 147, Bertha 189, Bertha May 189, 207, 259, 302, 309, Charles 147, Edith Mary 189, Ellen 199, Henry 242, Irvin 174, 189, Laura Maude 189, Lizzie 189, Myrtle 174, Myrtle Iva 175, 189, Ralph E. 189, Raymond 189.
GRIFFITH, Betty Jeanne 284, Charles A. 284, Hester Oral 284, Nana A. 240, Susan Jane 132, Valentine 132.
GRIFFITT, Arnold 134, Arnold S. (Dr.) 255, Della 230, Florentine 134, Francis Marion 134, Paris Whitcomb 134, Queen Victoria 134, Reuben C. (Dr.) 230.
GRIMM, Edward 189, Elsie 189, Helen 189, Henry 189, John Gottfried 189, Marge 189, 259, Marguerita 189, Richard 189, Roy 189.
GRINER, Alonzo 219, Bertha 219, Bill 219, Hiram 196, Noah 219, Settie 219.
GRINESSTAFF, Sara Belle 166.
GRISWOLD, Deborah 310, Matthew 310.
GRISWOLDE, Sir Lancelot de 310.
GROVE, Anna 190, Daniel 190, Elizabeth 190, Garrison 190, George 190, 285, George W. 190, Jesse 190, John H. 190, Lavina 190, Malinda 190, Malissa 190, Margaret 190, Mary Etta 190, Matthew 190, Michael 190, Nancy Jane 190, Randall 190, Rebecca 190, Sarah 190, Silas 190.
GROW, Lottie 148.
GRUELLE, R.B. 283.
GRUPPE, Emile 260.
GUISER, Mae "Mitzie" 284, Paul 284.
GULLETT, Sarah 235.
GUNNING, Kenneth Eugene 283, Marion Francis 283, Peggy Ann 283.
GURHL, Barbara Lou 190.
GUSTIN, Jonathan 183, Kate Parker

183, Mildred L. 183, Omar E. 183.
GUTHRIE, Daisy 248, Inez Lenora 188, Wayne 163, 250, 264, 265, 272.
GUTHRIES, Irwin 248.
GUY, Barbara Lou 190, Charles 190, Curtis Ross 190, Joseph Curtis 190, Lisa Ann Terry 190, Maggie Naomi 190, Margaret 190, Marlene Elaine 190, Olover 190.
GWIN, Helen Deloris 147, Quentin H. 147, Quentin H. Jr. 147, Wilma Faith 147.
GYURE, Edward 199.

HAAG, Eleanor 143.
HAAREER, Gladys 292.
HAARER, Charles 206, 292.
HAASE, Sarah 151.
HACKER, Pearl 137.
HACKETT, Lucy Jane 230.
HADDEN, Sarah 162.
HAEFFER, Rozannah 169.
HAFNER, Douglas 277, Joshua Steven 277, Kenneth 277, Laurie 277, Robert Oliver 277, Rona Lorraine 277.
HAGEN, Charles 190, Charles II 190, David 190, Mary 190, Ronald 190.
HAGGARD, Ann Cecelia 191, Edith Ann 190, Francis Marion 191, John Paul 190, Lauren Celeste 191, Mary 312, Michael Thomas 191, Mildred 191, Minnie Agnus 190, Morris 312, Wm. Francis 191, Wm. Thomas 191.
HAGGART, Mary E. 246.
HAGUE, Elza 167.
HAHN, Shari Lynn 175, Shirley 260.
HAINES, Henry 178, Martha 178, Mary 178, Matilda 151, Sarah 251, Sarah Margaret 178, William 178.
HAINLINE, Lillie V. 309.
HALE, Mary Elizabeth 295.
HALEMAN, Elizabeth 300, Miranda J. 300, William 300, Willis D. 300.
HALEY, Margaret 236.
HALL, A. Wateland 169, Adonias W. 169, Ephraim 132, Grace 135, Hannah 256, Ida Fore 169, Isaac 191, Izila 191, Jane 132, Jesse 153, Jesse III 191, Jesse Jr. 191, Jesse Sr. 153, 191, 274, John H. 191, Mary Ann 191, 192, 274, 275, Mary Elizabeth, Melba Pauline 169, Melvina 289, Nancy Jane 172, 191, Nathan Alexand. 191, Peter 169, 191, Rebecca 153, 274, Rebecca Frances 191, Sarah Ann 153, 191, Teresa 138, Virginia Susan 169, Wm. David 191.
HALSEMA, Andrea Lynn 175, Angelo Rena 175, Jack 175, Rissa Marie.
HALTON, Rosanna 198.
HAMBLEN, A. Porter 192, 193, Angeline 193, Anthony Wayne 195, Armeanous 193, Armeanous P. 192, Bob Hugh 194, Brenda F. 192, 194, Brian K. 195, Carl 194, Clara 192, Clarissa 193, David Philip 192, Donald 192, Douglas Eugene 193, Eleanor 193, Eliakim 193, Elizabeth Huff 191, Elizabeth Jane 195, Flora 192, Frances 193, Gary 195, George 191, 192, 193, 274, George W. 191, Helen J. 195, J.B. 193, James 136, 286, James Ovid 194, James William 168, 192, 271, James Wm. 193, 194, 195, Jana Loraine 195, Janice 195, Janice Elaine 195, Jennings Bryan 192, Jesse Eugne 193, Jessie 192, Jimmy 191, Jimmy Dean 195, Jimmy-James Wm. 192, Job 180, 192, 193, 194, John Mullins 193, 195, John W. 192, 271, 274, John Wesley 193, 194, John William 191, 195, Karen 193, Karen Jo 193, Katelyn Nicole 193, Keziah 193, Laura 194, Laura Belle 194, Lester Maurice 194, Louis Mervin 194, Louis Napoleon 194, Lula 192, Maneca Jane 191, Margaret 191, Margaret May 274, Marianne 193, 194, Martha A. 299, Martha Adline 167, 195, Mary 136, 168, 191, 193, 286, Mary "Polly" 195, Mary E. 193, 195, Mary Etta 192, 194, 271, Mary Jane 192, Mary Ruth 194, Megan Diane 193, Nancy Ann 195, Newton 194, Nodine 194, Pauline 193, Peggy 192, Piercy 193, Pleasant 191, 192, 193, 194, Plessie 195, Raymond 192, Richard Preston 195, Robert 182, Sandra Janell 194, Sandra K. 195, Sarah 193, 288, 289, Sarah Catherine 195, Sharon Carline 194, Sherry 193, Tina Elaine 195, Tommy Wayne 195, Tressa 136, 192, Uriah 192, 193. Virginia 192, William 191, 192, 193, 195, 210, William (Rev.) 195, Williamson 195, Wilma 192, Wm. (Rev.) 167.
HAMBLIN, Mary 162, William 162.
HAMBONE, The Clown 196.
HAMILTON, Alfred 271, Alpha 196, B. Margaret 196, Betty 310, Blanche 146, Blanche M. 196, Bob-Rbt. Eugene 195, Bonde 146, Bonde Louise 196, Bruce Harley 196, Clyde Stanhope 196, David Morgan 146, 196, Ella Florence 146, Faith 146, 196, Florence 146, Florence Ella 196, Frank Grover 196, Gail 196, George 146, 196, George David Jr. 196, Hedwig 195, Helen 146, Helen Hunt 196, Iris 146, 196, Jesse Turmer 196, John Courtney 195, John Howard 196, Laura B. 250, Louisa McMannis 190, Madge 146, Martha 196, Martha Neal 146, Morton 250, Nancy 250, Nel 195, Paul Morgan 196, Pearl 196, Ruth 195, 196, Sarah Madge 196, Wilfred Roy 196.
HAMM, Dorothy 182, Harley 182, James W. 182.
HAMMOND, Margaret Jane 305.
HAMPTON, Amy 198.
HANAN, Velma 231.
HANCHER, John 271, Lydia Ann 271, 279.
HANDLEY, Beryl 262.
HANES, Otis 309.
HANILINE, Lillian 305.
HANKINS, Mary E. 215.
HANNA, Charles 146, Sara Ann 237.
HANNER, Glen 285, Lucy 285.
HANNERS, Glen 285.
HANNEY, Elizabeth 273.
HANSEN, Robert 209, Ruth 208, 209, Sara Elizabeth 171.
HANVEY, Elizabeth 231, 272, 274, Elizabeth Ann 273, Margaret J. 273, Mary 273, William 273.
HARDEN, Aaron 158, Elizabeth 276, Eva 226, Geneva 147, Jessie 165, Lottie M. 165, Martin 271.
HARDING, Franklin 153, Harold 153, Jessie 153, 293, Mary Ann 153, Rose 153.
HARDY, Kris D. 305, Kristopher 305, Robert William 304, Wilma Jean 304.
HARKINS, Catherine 146, Kathryn 156.
HARLAN, Daulbert D. 196, Madge A. 196.
HARMON, Alice 225, Beulah 225, William 225.
HARNESS, Jettie 293.
HARNEY, Kathryn 239, Owen J. 239.
HARPER, Ellen 150, Lucille M. 278, Marian Denise 196.
HARRIS, Amanda 156, 225, Benjamin 197, Deruses Meree 197, Elmer 197, Janet Ruth 197, John 225, Kenneth E. 197, Kimberly Ann 197, Larry 197, Marlene 197, Martha Ellen 150, Mary 201, Millie Jane 150, Nellie Jane 262, Pamela Jean 197, Ruth K. 197, Samuel 150, 262, Sandra Sue 197, Thomas 232.
HARRISON, A.B. 282, Barbara 197, Carter J. 197, 264, Carter V. 197, Elizabeth 274, Julia Ann 264, Julianna 197, Julianne 264, Martha Ellen 150, 197, 263, 264, 306, (Rev.) 187, Vina 282, William H. 165, William Henry 150, 197, 264.
HARRISONS, Jimmy 216.
HARROD, Brenda F. 193, 194.
HARRY, Ann Louise 149, Steven Scott 149.
HARSHBARGER, Saloma 134.
HART, Edwin R.F. 256, Eva Elizabeth 256, John 275.
HARTING, Robert 199.
HARTLEY, W. Douglas 251.
HARTMAN, Frederick 288, Sarah A. 288.
HARVEY, James 137, Kathryn 174, Margaret Amanda 137, Paul 144.
HASH, Ahart 304, Emarine 304, Emmarine 274, 275.
HASHMAN, Nora Ellen 135.
HASTINGS, Carolyn 203, Lulu Myrtle 203, Olive 135.
HATCHETT, Alice 197, 198, Alvira 148, Bartlett 197, Betsy 197, Emily 197, Glenna E. 197, Homer 197, 198, James A. 197, Jane 197, John B. 197, Laura 197, 198, Malinda 197, Nancy 198, Otis 198, Otis B. 197, Patty 197, Sarah Ellen 148, 149, Setta 146, Thomas 197, William Green 148, 197, William H. 197, Wilma Faye 197.
HATFIElD, Forbus 210.
HATTEN, Donald 195, Jeanetta 195.
HATTON, Abigail 198, Alan Dale 188, 199, Alexander 198, Alfred 198, 199, Alice 199, Aline 199, Allen 198, Amanda 199, Andrew 198, Andrew Ray 188, 199, Ann 198, 199, Anna 199, Arnold 199, Arnold Jr. 199, Arthur 199, Asa 191, 198, 199, Asahel 198, Audrey 199, Barbara 199, Ben 199, Benjamin 198, 199, Berniece 199, Bertha 199, Beverly 199, Billie 199, Brenda 199, Bruce 199, Carl 188, 198, 199, Catharine 199, Catherine 198, Charles 198, 199, Charles Jr. 199, Charles Murphy 198, 199, Charlotte 199, 237, Charlotte A. 198, Cheryl 200, Christine 199, Cindy 199, Clarence 199, Clarissa 199, Clay 198, Clora 199, Clotha Cordella 198, 199, Cloyd 188, 198, 199, Clyde 199, Cynthia 198, Daniel 199, Darrell 200, David 198, 199, Debra 199, Delpha 199, Dianna 199, Donald 188, 199, 285, Donna 199, Dora 198, 199, Douglas 199, Doyle 188, 199, Drew 199, Earnest 199, Earnest Jr. 199, Edith 198, 199, Edmond 198, Edward 199, Elijah 198, Elizabeth 198, 199, Ellen 198, Ellzora 198, Elsie 199, Emma 199, Ephraim 198, Estal 199, Estella 199, Evelyn 199, Ezekiel 199, Fanny 199, Faye 199, Faye Naomi 188, Florence 198, 199, Ford 199, Frank 198, 199, Freelin 198, Ganell 199, Garland 199, Garland Jr. 199, Garnet 199, Gary 200, Gayle 199, Geneva 199, George 199, George P. 199, Gerald 199, Gladys 199, Gregory Allen 198, Gregory Lee 188, 199, Hannah 199, Harlan 199, Harold 168, 199, Harry 199, Herbert 199, Herman 199, Howard 199, Jackie 199, 200, Jackie Dean 198, Jacob 199, James 198, 199, James Oscar 198, 199, Jane 198, Jemimah 198, Jerald 200, Jeriah 198, Jesse 199, John 198, 199, John Henry 199, John Wesley 199, John William 199, Jonah 198, 199, Jonas 198, 199, Jonathan 198, Jonathan Thomas 198, Joseph 199, Julia 198, Kathryn 199, Keith 200, Kellie 199, Kevin 200, Lanny 200, Lanny Lee 198, Larry 199, Larry Leon 198, Laura 188, 199, Laura M. 198, Leeco 198, Leeco "Bud" 199, Leon Harold 198, Leona 199, Levi 198, Lillie 199, Lloyd 199, Lois 198, Lois Delphine 168, Lovina 199, Lucille 198, 199, Lucinda 199, Malinda 198, 199, Malissa 199, Margaret 198, 199, Marian 198, Marilyn 199, Marion 198, 199, Marjorie 199, Marshall 198, Martha 198, Mary 198, 199, Mary Elizabeth 199, Michael 198, Michael Keith 188, 199, Minerva 198, Mitchell 198, Nancy 198, Naomi Faye 199, Nathan 199, Noah 199, Nora 199, Norma 199, Norma Dell 198, Olive 198, 199, Ora Ray 198, 199, Penny 199, Pernetta 198, 199, Peter 199, Philip 198, 199, Philip A. 198, Philip H. 198, 199, Phillip 198, Phylis 199, Pinkney 198, Rachel 198, 199, Ray 199, Ressie 199, Richard 199, Robert 198, 199, Ronald Keith 198, Rosa 199, Rosannah 198, Rose 199, 200, 285, Roseanna 199, Rosemary 199, Roy 199, Sally 198, Samuel 198, 199, Samuel E. 188, 198, 199, Samuel Jr. 198, 199, Samuel S. 198, Samuel Sr. 198, 199, Sandra 199, Sarah 198, 199, Shannon Rae 199, Sheridan 199, Stella 199, Stephen 199, Susan 198, 199, Susie Jane 199, Sylvia 199, Thelma 199, Thomas 198, 199, Valentine 199, Velma 199, Vera 199, Vivian 199, Walter E. 198, Wanda 199, William 198, William Earl 199, William H. 198, 199, William T. 199, Wm. Carl 199.
HAUBEIL, Judy 199.
HAWK, Jeann Ann 175.
HAWKINS, Daniel 223, Sabra 223, 224.
HAWLEY, Abby Pearl 200, Ada 143, 200, Ada Opal 200, Alva 200, Alva Clarence 200, Alvey 143, Amos 200, Anna 200, Anna Lucille 200, Bertha 200, Charles 200, Cynthia Jean 200, Elizabeth 200, Ellen 135, Floyd Anthony 200, Floyd Edgar 200, George 200, Grace 200, Harry 135, 200, Ivan 135, Jacob 200, Jacob Omer 200, John Hobert 200, Judith Elaine 200, Kathleen Mae 200, Larry Lee 200, Leonard Omer 200, Lilly 200, Linda Joyce 200, Louisa 200, Mabel Clare 200, Malachi 200, Malakhi 200, Martin 200, Mary 200, Mary Alice 200, Maude 200, Mayme 200, Melk 185, 100, Melker, 200, Millie 143, Millie Francis 200, Morgan 143, 200, Nanc 200, Nora Belle 135, Ola 143, 200, 204, 302, Ola Ellen 200, Omer 200, Robert 200, Robert Allen 200, Robert William 200, Ruth 200, Sarah 200, Thomas 200, Timothy Dale 200, William 200, William Morgan 200.
HAWLEYS, 204.
HAWN, Mary Lou 288.
HAWS, Fena 157.
HAYES, Elizabeth M. 288, James C. 162, John 288, Sarah 162, Stella 304.
HAYFORD, Julian 308, Verlis 308.
HAYMAN, Doris Gaynell 293.
HAYNES, Lilly 285.
HAYS, Barbara Denise 280, John 171.
HAYWARD, J. (Evangelist) 151, John B. 151.
HAYWORTH, Barbara Ann 253.
HEAD, Bob 287, Florin 287.
HEADINGS, Cathy 297.
HEARTH, Grace 159
HEATON, Jewell 308.
HEBAUF, Kimberly Ann 191.
HEBERLING, Janet 136.
HECK, Esta Marie 165.
HECKMAN, John 248, Joseph 208, 248.
HEDGE, Aleitha 224.
HEDGER, Alford William 201, Andrew 239, Andrew Scott 201, Betty 201, Clara F. 201, Dale Lacount 201, Floyd E. 201, Jackie 239, Jackie Dale 201, John 182, John Mason 201, Joy 201, 239, Pamela Sue 201, Paul 239, Paul Gregory 201, Permelia Jane 201.
HEDGES, James 261.
HEDRICK, Anna 201, 285, Asa 201, B. Franklin 201, Beatrice 201, Belva 201, Benjiman Frankl 201, Bernard 201, Burnell 201, Calvin 201, Clara 201, Dorval 209, Edelle 201, Franklin 201, Henreitta 201, James 201, Jane 201, Jason 201, John 201, Joseph 201, Lena 201, Levi 201, Louisa 201, Mahalia 201, Mary Elizabeth 191, Michael 201, Minnie 201, Oscar 201, Pauline 201, Peter 201, Ronald 201, Rosa 201, Sarah 201, Shelby Hedrick 201, Teresa 201, Virgil 201, Walter 201, William 201.
HEFLIN, Hazel Verona, 136.
HEGWOOD, Tena 164.
HEILMAN, Betty Pauline 155, Gary 155, Rick 155, Steve 155.
HEIM, Henrietta 260.
HELLENBURG, Louise 141.
HELLER, Brian 201, Deloris 266, Rita 201, Roland 266.
HELLMAN, Elizabeth 156, James 156, Samuel 156.
HELMS, Emmaline 179, Florence Emma 180, Geneva 223, Joe 191, Nancy 134, Susanna 158.
HELVEY (KELVY), Susan 132.
HENDERSHOT, Alice 271, 272, Margaret E. 271, Margaret Emma 176, Mona 201, William Peter 271.
HENDERSON, Amanda 133, 202, Brent 160, Charles 160, Charles Marion 230, Daniel Stewart 230, DeMaris 160, Delila 202, Elcy Jane 202, Elizabeth 202, 230, Elizabeth Jane 230, Emaline 202, 252, Florence Eliza. 202, Francis Marion 202, George 230, George Earnest 202, Hannah 202, Hannah Melissa 202, Harriet 202, Henry Willard 202, Hugh Stewart 202, Ida Kent 187, Ida Solome 202, Ima Jean 160, Iva Bertha Nola 202, James 202, 230, James M. 202, Jane 133, 202, 230, 231, Jeffrey 160, John 133, 202, 230, John Richard 202, Joseph 202, Joseph Samuel 230, Kevin 160, Laura 160, Louis Frederick 176, 202, Lowell Robert 202, Lucinda 202, Lucinda Abarilla 202, Malinda 202, Marietta 237, Marilyn 203, Martha Ann 202, Mary 209, 289, Mary Alice 202, Mary Eliazabeth 202, Nancy 202, Nancy Rachel 230, Newton Ray 202, Olive 187, Ora Chester 202, Philip 160, R.M. (Bub) 187, Rachel 202, Rbt. Ephraim 202, Richard 202, Richard M. 187, Robert 154, 202, 230, 252, 283, Robert Ephraim 176, 202, Robert Henry 175, 176, 202, Robert Jr. 252, Sarah Jane 202, Sivala Alice 202, Solomon Willard 202, Steven Lowell 203, Thomas Jefferson 202, William 202, William B. 202, William H. 176, 202, William Preston 230, Williamson 230.
HENDREN, Susan 174.
HENDRICKS, Blanche 272, Iva 186, James W. 272, Iva 186, James W. 272.
HENDRY, John 174.
HENNEKE, Josie Ann 215.
HENNING, Clara 173.
HENRICK, Brian R. 262, David Donald 262, Gail Marie 262, Laura S. 262, Michael Reed 262.
HENRY, Armilia 133, Helen 298, Helen Rovine 299, Rachel 267, Truex 133.
HENSHAW, Andrew 203, Arthur Glen 203, Carolyn 203, Gallery 219, Glen Cooper 203, 218, H. Celestina 203, Heather C. 203, Mary Cooper 203, Pearl Cue 203.
HENSLEY, Elizabeth 180, Margaret 201, Robert 211.
HENSON, Malinda 191.
HENTHORN, Cassie 203, Dora A. 284, Dora Alice 203, 242, Elizabeth 203, George 203, Henry Isaac 203, Isaac 203, Jonathon 203, Margaret 203, 242, Mary Margaret 198, 203, Minerva 203, Rebecca 308, Rebecca A. 203, Robert 203, Sarah 203, William 203.
HENTHORNE, Dora 241, Dora Alice 156, Everett Isaac 147, Margaret 156.
HEPBURN, Julia 285.

HERRICK, Cora Mildred 137.
HERRIN, Bernard 182.
HERRING, Florence 239, John William 239.
HERSHBERGER, Anna 234.
HERSHEL, Taylor 287.
HERT, Beverly Ann 222, Mildred Maxine 222, Rbt. Wm. 222.
HERTZLER, Jacob 242, John 242.
HESS, 220, Belva 203, Dick 203, Gudrun 203, Heinrich Johann 203, Janet 203, Laura 203, Martin J. 203, Richard 203, Sara 203, Todd 203.
HESSLER, August Andreas 256, Evelyn 256, Helen Estelle 256, Orville 256, Otto Joseph 256, Robert 256, Robert 256.
HESTER, James 230, John C. 191, Judy 214.
HETHERINGTON & BERNER, INC., 204.
HETHERINGTON, Anna 204, Benjamin Frank. 204, Emma Beatrice 204, Emma Lucretia 204, 226, Frederick A. 226, Frederick Alex. 203, Frederick Carl 204, John 204, Marian Grace 204, 226, Rosalind 204, Valentine 204.
HEUN, Carol 196, David 196, Joseph 196, Linda 196, Monte 196, Stephen 196.
HIAT, Jane 141.
HIATT, Frances 234.
HIBBARD, Billy 161.
HICKERESON, Grace 145.
HICKS, Beatrice 254.
HIGDON, A.L. Dr. 310, Virginia 310.
HIGGINS, Caroline 250, Dr. Archibald 250, Janet 141, Nancy 209, 210.
HIGH, Elizaeth Rose 132.
HIGHSMITH, Alice Carrie 204, Barbara Alice 204, Kay Lynn 204, Marianne 204, Orman 204, Richard Owen 204.
HILBERT, Sundi Marie 145.
HILDONBORG, Catherine 171, Sallie 172.
HILL, Alexandra 205, Bertha W. 200, Bobbie 163, 205, Daily Francis 204, Daily Stephen 204, Delores Lossin 205, Edward 205, Elizabeth Ann 180, Eugene 180, George 204, James 205, Jason 180, Jeremy 180, Joan Ann 207, John H. 198, Joyce Linters 205, Justine 205, Marianne 204, Mary Ann 205, Maurice 205, Nell Chitwood 205, Paul 204, Richard 205, Sara Virginia 204, Thelma 205, Tina 136, Virginia 271.
HILLENBORG, Sallie, 171.
HILLENBURG, Grace 305.
HILLIGOSS, Deborah Elaine 266.
HILTON, Barbara 236, Joseph 236.
HIMES, Carolyn 205, Courtney 205, Frances 205, Jennifer 205, Julie 205, Katie 296, Lynn 205, Mabel 205, Perry Robert 205, Richard 205, Robert 216, Robert White 205, Roger 205, Ryan 205, Samantha 205, Warren.
HINE, Bob 145, Charlene Jo 145, Charles Robert 145, Marilyn Sue 145, Scott C. 145, Shirley Ann 145, William G. 145, Wilma L. 145, Wilma Lee 145.
HINES, Ann Elizabeth 159, Lucy 151, Mabel Maude 188.
HINKLE, Jack 212, Jennifer 212, Jonathan 212, Kelley 212, Linda Kay 212.
HINSHAW, Judith 218.
HITZ, Ben 148, Benjamin 208.
HOBB, Mary Bird 192.
HOBBES (HOBBS), Thomas 132.
HOBBS, Absalom 132, Beulah 168, George 168, George C. 192, Lula 168, Mary 132, Susan 132, Thomas 192, Vincent 132.
HOBSON, Charles 176, Geneva 183, Oris 184, Renee 176.
HOCHSTETLER, Pam Sanders 266, Pamela Corinne 266.
HODGE, Luther 231.
HODGES, Aaron 220, Curtis Aaron 203, Elizabeth 203, Gilbert 230, Gretchen 203, Harriet Emaline 230, Louise Frances 220, Martha Hannah 220, Nan 203, Ruby Pearl 230, Sara 203, Sara Lucele 203.
HOEANY, Joan 227.
HOFFA, Mildred 148, Shirley 148, Walter 148.
HOFFMAN, Ann 208, Carol 255, Walter 208.
HOHENBERGER, Frank 204, 249, Frank M. 203, 219.
HOLDBROOK, Aaron Lee 285, Jason Michael 285, Valerie Ann 285.
HOLDEMAN, Amy Lynn 222, Helen Marie 222, Roger Andrew 222.
HOLDING, Laura Eva 233.
HOLE, Brenda 213, Elizabeth Ann 213, Jennifer Marie 213, Robert 213, Wilma 213.
HOLEMAN, Blanch, 269.
HOLLANDBECK, Theresa Eliza 178.
HOLLOWAY, 193.
HOLM, Catherine 285.
HOLMES, Annella 196, Regena 196, Thurston 196.
HOLT, Eva 199.
HOLTON, Judy Ann 145.
HOLTS, Elizabeth 180, Elizabeth C. 158.
HONEAY, Barbara 138, Joan 138, John (Rev.) 138, Julie 138, Rebecca 138, Teresa 138.
HONEYSUCKLE PLACE, 209.
HONNEL, Margaret 255.
HOOVER, David 294, Elizabeth 294, Eunice Arbell 182, Susannah 294.
HOPE, Elizabeth 158.
HOPKINS, George Edward 262, Lola 273, Robert Wilson 262, Ruth 262, Stephen 226, 251.
HOPPER, Clem 295, Fay 295, Mary 208, Mildred 209, Nancy Ann 209, Wm. Marmaduke 209.
HORN, Estelle 256.
HORNER, George 162, Hannah 265.
HORNUNG, Mildred 148.
HORTON, James 286, Patricia 176, 238, 286.
HOSKINS, Sonya 296.
HOSSACK, Alice 242, Jessie Falwell 242, Walter C. 242.
HOSTELLER, Mary 292, Milo 292.
HOUSE, Bob 309, David 226, Dennis 226, Dorothy 226, Jason Mandell 309, Laurence 226, Lisa 226, Lori 226.
HOUSHOUR, Altha 195.
HOUTZ, Carrie 310.
HOWARD, Amy Sue 149, Brenda Joyce 149, Caren Kay 149, Carl Raymond 149, Clara E. 303, Dr. Bill 212, Edward Allen 251, Edward Paul 149, Elizabeth 289, Elvira 303, Hazel 272, James 303, James E. 272, Kim Forster 251, Martha 303, Mary Malissa 295, Phyllis-Vincent 251, Wm. Henry 303.
HOWDEN, Barbar Jean 250, Marc 250, Mike 250.
HOWE, Maria 134, Marie 222.
HOWELL, Lydia 165, Mary 276.
HOWERTH, Ira 292, Sarah 292.
HOWLAND, Eli 213, Rachel 213.
HOY, Josephine 310, Rachel Elizab. 133.
HUBBARD, Charity 258, Charlotte 244, Ken 208, Kim 151, Kin 203, 250, Martha 268, Mary K. 231, Shirley Ann 145.
HUBBLE, Mildred 309.
HUBER, George 185, Helen 214, Margaret 185.
HUCKABY, Eric 286, Geth 286, Gordon 286, Joe 286, Theo 286.
HUCKLEBERRY, Nan 180.
HUDDLESON, Dixie 188.
HUDE, Bertha 278.
HUDIBURGH, Catherine 232, Thomas 232.
HUDSON, Constance 155.
HUFF, 193, Ally 286, Eleanor 286, Elizabeth 191, 192, James 154, James M. 286, Minerva 286, Sarah Jane 286.
HUFFER, Joseph 199, Nellie 229, Royce 199, Royce II, Stephanie 199.
HUFFMAN, Alice 206, Alice Adelia 205, Ellen 206, 272, 273, F. Nelson 205, Frederick N. 205, John Willard 205, 274, Lula genetta 205, Mary J. 205, Phillip 205, Richard 205, 272, Sarah Letitia 205, 272, Thomas E. 205, Tish 272.
HUFFORD, Frances 206, Ida 206, Warren 206.
HUFFSTUTLER, Bill 178, S. Margaret 178.
HUGHES, Ed 178, Paul 199.
HULL, Dorathy M. 141.
HUNT, Billy 206, Cynthia Jane 289, David 206, Donna 137, Linda 206, Tonya 206, Vanessa Dale 137, William Robert 289.
HUNTER, Bennett 238, Georgia 238, Kenneth 219, Phoebe 151.
HURD, Charles W. 174, Eliza 299.
HURDLE, Betty 310, James 156, Laura Belle 302, Olive 310, Presha 156, Warren 310.
HURLEY, Anrelia 224, Bessie 165, Beulah 183, Elizabeth 183, Grover 272, Ida 183, James 183, Rachel 248, Ruey 183.
HURT, Jack 267, Judie 267.
HUTCHERSON, Lillian 296.
HUTCHINES, Winifred 199.
HUTCHINS, Malcolm III 222, Nicholas 222, Strangeman 222.
HUTCHINSON, Barbara 177, Frances 261, Alice 258, Ada 206, Amos 206, Archibald 206, Asbury 206, Cornelia 162, 207, Edith 206, Elizabeth C. 206, Emily 206, George Miles 206, Grammar 207, James 206, James Finley 206, Jarrett 206, John w. 206, Matilda 206, Mildred Belle 296, Newton 162, Rebecca Ann 206, Rosa Louella 241, Ruth 206, Sarah 206, Seward 207, William 206, William D. 206.
HUTSELL, Harold 256, Jo Ann 256.
HYDE, Audrey Ann 207, Bertha 189, Bertha May 301, Brenda Faye 207, Edna Sophronia 189, 259, Ginnie 207, Irvin Wayne 189, James Andrew 207, James Vernon 189, James Vernon Jr. 207, John Michael 207, John S. 189, John Siegle 189, 207, 259, 302, 309, Joseph Marion 207, Lela Pearl 189, Lizzie Estle 189, Marilyn 207, Marilyn Kay 207, Mary Alice 189, Michael Jorden 207, Mildred F. 207, Rex 189, Vernon 189, Virgil Chester 189, Virginia Mae 207, Wayne 189, William Rex 189, 309, Wilma Jean 189, 302.

IMEL, Wilbur 198.
INMAN, Cecil 252, Janet 266, Merrie 252.
ISAACS, Zilpha 248.
ISLEY, Sue Lynn 155.
ISON, Jill Elaine 253.

JACKSON, Ann 230, Drusila 140, Florence E. 275, Gayle 304, Henry 154, John 137, Kathy 300, Lavinna C. 282, Letitia 137, Mary 309, Mary J. 190, Nellie 296, Nellie G. 297, Vickie Lynn 275.
JACOB, Bonnie 190, Minnie Agnus 190.
JACOBUS, Belitjen 222.
JAGGERS, Sharon 262.
JAMES, Alice Charlotte 156, Amanda Melissa 156, Dirk 287, Elizabeth 156, Frances 271, Mary "Polly" 305, Melissa 298, Samuel Frank Jr. 156, Samuel Frank Sr. 156, Sophia 165, Thomas 271.
JANS, Anneka 222.
JANSEN, Tryn 222.
JARRETT, Margaret Ann 255.
JAY, Jacob 173.
JAYNES, Darlene Jo 155, Marty Dwain 155.
JEANNERET, Julia 256, Robert J. 256.
JEFFERS, Nancy 198.
JEFFS, Wally (Rev.) 246.
JENKINS, Jospeh 211, Sherlyn J. 287.
JENKINSON, Martha 153.
JENSEN, Mary Jane 310.
JEWELL, George A. 254.
JOHANTAGES, Katie 278.
JOHNS, Amelia 176, 237, Nancy 237, William 237.
JOHNSON, Ann 208, Arline 199, Bates 208, Benjamin Bates 207, Caroline 208, Carolyn Jane 296, Clara 207, Edna 207, Emily 196, Fay 268, Frank Wagner 208, Fred 140, Fred Bates 148, 207, Gaar Williams 208, Harriet 208, Jack 271, Jessie 208, Joe 196, Jonathon P. 207, Kimberly 208, Mary Ellen 188, Nancy 179, Nathan 188, Ora 181, Priscilla 250, Rhonda 199, Samuel Gideon 208, Samuel III 208, Susan 208.
JOHNSTON, Anna 283, Elizabeth 230.
JOHNSTONE, Sir Gilbert de 222.
JOLIFF, Lydia 177.
JOLLY, Anna A. 223, Samuel 223.
JONES, Abby Jane 267, Ada Marie 209, Aletha 209, Alexander 208, Ana 209, Anna Luella 230, Beth 196, Carrie Roberta 204, Charles 208, Cindy Jane 166, Cyntha 208, Dale 270, Deb 209, Dick 174, 209, Edith Mae 267, Elizabeth 209, 230, Ernest 209, Francis M. 185, Fredrick 164, Fredrick Alex 209, George Wash. 267, Hattie Ray 267, Hazel 138, Helen 209, Henry 208, Isaac 156, J. Eric 209, James 208, 230, James Marshall 209, Jane Ellen 215, Janet 209, 288, Jemima 226, Jennifer 209, Jennifer Ann 166, Jerry 208, Jessie 209, John 209, John P. 209, Kerry Marshall 209, Laura 209, Lillie 209, Lilly 164, Lucille 209, Mabel 208, Margaret 208, 209, Marilyn 209, Martha 209, Mary 134, Mary E. 185, Mary Eliza 156, Mary Jane 267, Mildred 209, Nellie Joseph. 267, Newland "Dick" 209, Nora 151, Oren 151, Otto 209, P.O. 276, Paul 134, Rebecca 209, Rose Leeann 207, Rosetti 208, Ross Mitchell 209, Roy 166, Ruth 209, Sarah 208, 255, Sharon 134, Thomas 208, 215, 231, Walsie Fern 209, William 208, 218, William M. 209.
JORDAN, Avis 306, Marilyn 261, William 175.
JOSLIN, Alcinda 209, Anthony Joseph 210, Clarence E. 210, Donald Ray 210, Duane E. 210, Emma 209, Enoch Ellsberry 210, Evelyn Louise 210, Ezekiel 209, 210, Harriet 209, Henry Eleazor 209, Hollie Ann 210, Howard Lester 210, Hurschel Paul 210, Israel 209, 210, Jill Michelle 210, John 210, John Strange 202, 209, Joshua C. 210, Lorena 209, Louisa 209, 210, Lowell 209, 210, Lowell Ray 299, Lydia Ann 209, Marcedes 210, Marcedes L. 195, 299, Marcedes Walker 167, Marcy 210, Martha Jane 209, 210, Mary Alice 210, Mary Etta 209, Mary L. 209, Nancy 210, Nellie 210, Perry 209, Phebe 209, Phebe Luella 209, Sarah 209, Susan 209, William 210, William W. 209, Winifred 209.
JOY, Corey 174, Hulda Jane 206, Laurie 174.
JOYNER, Bette 174.
JUERGENS, Herman g. 290, Marie 290, Rose A. 290.
JUNG, Ethel Sailor 273, Floyd 273, Melvin 273, Theodore 273, Walter Edmond 206.
JUNGHANS, 197.
JUST, Leona 247, Minnie 247, Rudolph 247.

KAIN, Barbara Ann 210, Bryan Steven 210, Carol Lynn 210, Charles 210, Charles L. 210, Chas. Lawrence 210, David Richard 210, Elizabeth 210, Evan Wiley 210, Fred W. 210, J. Richard 210, Janett Marie 210, Jeannie Louise 210, Jesse 210, Joyce 280, Maurice 210, Michael 210, Ollie Dean 210, 293, Oral Gates 210, Oscar 210, Paul Frederick II 210, Paul Fredrick I 210, Phillip Matthew 210, Ruth Ann 210, Sharon 210, Steven Michael 210, Theodore Fay 210.
KAKAVECOS, Catherine Jane 210, Christopher 211, Dorothy 210, E. Elizabeth 210, Eileen E. 210, Georgiana 210, James 210, James Jr. 211, Rex Donald 211, Ruth May 210, S. Nathaniel 211, Stephen N. 211, Thalia 211, 250.
KANE, Stephanie 136.
KANGAS, David Devry 183, Kristen Raney 183, Zelma Irene 183.
KANTER, 211, Benj. Franklin 211, Hallie 211, Helen Adena 211, James Erwin 211, Joy Paul 211, Margaret Louise 211, Mary Frances 211, Robert Bruce 211, Thomas Truman 211, Victor Franklin 211, William Carlyle 211.
KAPKE, William 307.
KASERMAN, Anna 255, David 255, George 255, John 255, Margaret 255, Samuel 255.
KASTER, Elizabeth 260.
KAZIMIER, Evelyn 195, Henry 195.
KEACH, J.L. 177.
KEATON, Ashley 212, Barry 212, Betty 211, 212, Bluford 211, Catherine 211, Chloe 212, Claris 211, 212, 226, Cloe Ann 211, Danielle 212, Debra Taylor 212, Delia 211, Donna Benett 212, Doublas Ray 212, Earl 211, 212, Elizabeth 211, 212, Ethel 211, Garnet 211, 212, 244, 246, Gaynelle 211, George 211, Guynelle 212, Harold 211, Ida 211, Irene 211, 212, Jackson 211, Jacob 211, James 211, 212, Jeffrey 212, Jerry 212, Jessie 211, Jill 212, Joey 212, Julia 211, Laura 212, 226, Lena 246, Lennis 211, 212, Leva Olive 211, Linda Kay 212, Mary 211, Melanie 212, Neal 212, Nicole 212, Olive 211, 2112, Penny 212, Phillip Ray 212, Polly 211, Rose 211, Roy 211, 212, 246, Scoffield 212, Scofield 211, Shelby 212, William 211, William Roy 212.
KEEN, Courtney Bond 196, Daniel 196, Edna N. 187, Graham 196, Wilbur 187.
KEENE, Ethel 212, Flemmon 212, Lola 166, Noah C. 212, Susan 212.
KEISER, Thelma 273.
KEK, Elizabeth 263.
KELLER, Adeline 255, Catharine 255, Daniel 300, Dempsey E. 212, Emma 212, Gene 174, George 212, Jacqueline Sue 212, Lisa 212, Mae 231, Max 212, Michael Eugene 212, 255, Minda K. 212, Minerva Jane 231, Nikki 212, Opal 231, Pearl Mae 274, Randy 212, Roy G. 212, Susan E. 212.
KELLEY, Amanda 213, Ann 212, 213, B.R. 214, Barbara Jean 168, Benj. Richard 247, Benj. Roteu 213, Benjamin 213, Benjamin Roten 212, Benjamin W. 213, Beulah Jean 214, 247, Brad 209, Cleo 305, Cleo Beryl 214, 248, Courtland 213, Dale 212, 213, 214, 264, Deann 209, Debbie 213, Donald 209, Dorothy 212, Dwight 212, 214, Dwight Denzil 248, Eliza Ann 213, Elizabeth 213, Eudora 213, 214, 247, Hannah 213, Harry 213, 214, 247, Hazel 151, 213, Irvin 151, James K.P. 213, James S. Hester

213, James Scott H. 213, Jessie 213, 214, 238, 305, Jessie Morrison 247, John 213, John C. 213, John F. Caleb 213, John Fowler C. 213, John L. 213, John Morrison 213, Joseph 212, 213, Joseph Fowler 213, Keith 214, Leo Pearl 214, Lydia 213, 214, 247, Margaret Jane 213, Marguerite 213, 214, Marianne 213, Martha 209, Mary 213, Mary Jane 212, 214, Mary Roten 213, Minerva 213, Nancy Jane 213, Nellie Marie 214, Rachel Ellen 213, Richard 213, 214, 238, 305, Richard Dale 214, 248, Richard Dale Jr. 213, Robin Lee 213, Samuel 213, Samuel G.W. 213, 247, 248, Samuel Geo. Wa. 214, Sarah 213, Sarah Ann Eliz. 213, Susan 213, Thomas 214, William 213, Wm. Harrison 213, Wm Jackson 213.
KELLOGG, Ida 273.
KELLY, Angeline 179, Marie 184, Mary 199, Patricia 287, Sarah 179, Sarah A.M. 180.
KELP, Harry 153, 278, Mary 269.
KELSO, Alexander (Rev.) 167, Alpha June 167, Daniel 138, Harriett 134, John (Rev.) 167, John Jamison 134, Leona 138, Lewis 302, Mary 167, Roger 307, Russell 138, William 138.
KEMP, Bertha Susan 246, Fanny Marie 280.
KENIPE, Betty 232, Donlad 232, Goldie Gladys 232, Jennings Sr. 232, Jennings Jr. 232, Kenneth 232, Mary 232, Pauline 232, Robert 232, Thelmas 2332, William 232.
KENNEDY, Alonzo 214, Annabelle S. 187, Bertha 214, Blanche Z. 187, Blythe 161, Cordelia 214, Dorothy 214, Elsia 214, Emma 214, Garry Madison 187, George Riley 187, Gertrude 214, Helen 214, Jacob 214, James 214, James Winfield 214, John C. 214, John D. 214, John E. 185, 214, John F. 240, Judy Hester 214, Laura Jane 214, Margaret E. 214, Mary Alexander 214, Mayme 214, Patterson S. 214, Peggy 214, R. Claudа 214, Rachel 264, Robert M. 214, Sarah 268, Steven A. 214, Teenie 214, Thelma 214, Wesford L. 214, William M. 214.
KENNETT, Mary 299.
KENNEY, Elizabeth 220.
KENNY, Sarah Ann 158.
KENSLER, Carrie 205, John 205.
KENT, Agnes 215, Belle Joyce 215, Cecil 172, Cecil Samuel 215, Charles 215, Clara 276, Clifford 172, Doris Eloise 215, Edna 172, 214, 215, Edward 172, 215, Ellen 172, Elnora Ann 215, Gary 215, Harry Clifford 215, Isaac Samuel 215, Iva 214, James 215, John 228, Lobie D. 172, Lobie Daniel 214, Mary Beth 215, 308, Minnie Effie 215, Nancy Eloise 215, Othelia (Tilla) 215, Robert Edward 215, Ruth 215, Sam 172, 214, Samuel 187, Thomas 215, Thomas Wayne 215.
KERN, Angela 199, Delcina Ann 215, George Roland 215, Gladys Delcina 215, Lewis Henry 215, Rebecca Jane 215.
KERR, Anna Martina 234, Fred 188.
KESLER, Carl 215, Janet 215, Janie 215, Larry 215, Ora 215, Ross 215, Tressie 215, Viva 215, Wilbur Carl 215.
KESSLER, Catherine 294, Elijah 294, Mary 294, Sarah 294.
KETTLE, Walter A. Jr. 238, Walter Andrew 238.
KEY, Clarice Hope 196, Henry 196, Joy Muriel 196, Patricia 196, Sandra Dean 196, Tawanda 196.
KEYS, Opal 199, Opal Jr. 199, William 199.
KEYT, Nellie 306, Roy 306.
KHONE, Rachal M. 288.
KHULMAN, Donna 301.
KHUNE, Dennis 288.
KIBLER, Arvilla 174.
KIDWELL, Jayna 177, Jim 177.
KILGORE, Byron 299.
KIMBERLIN, John S. 211.
KIMMEL, Edward 260, Henrieta 260, Madeline 260, William 260.
KINCAID, Cheryl 279.
KINDRED, Wilma Shepherd 274.
KING, Aberilla, 215, 287, Ada 263, Alfred 215, Andy 216, Annabelle 216, Carl 216, Carmen Rosetta 216, Cecil Franklin 215, Conrad 210, 215, Cracker Jack 163, Daniel 215, 287, 288, Debbie 199, Dianne 216, Don 216, Dora 216, Doris Marie 215, Dorothy 216, Elizabeth 215, 224, 288, 289, Elmer 216, Emaline 202, 300, Emmeline 176, Eulala 297, Frieda 303, Geo. Washington 215, George 210, 215, George W. 300, Hannah 238, Harley 216, Hiram 273, Ianthia Ann 215, Irene 215, Isaac 202, James Emery 216, Jerald Leon 215, John 182, John Jacob 215, Josie Ann 215, Judith Ann 215, Julia Ann 215, Karen Sue 215, Katherine 215, Lucille 215, Marie 217, Marion 216, Marion (Rev.) 217, Martha Rebecca 215, Mary E. 215, Mary Jane 202, Maynard 216, Nan 216, Nancy 237, Nelle 216, Nelle Gertrude 210, Permelia Jane 201, Rachel 216, Rachel Sophroni 215, Russell 216, Russell Lee 215, Thelma 296, Theodore 216, Vinnie 215, 216, Virgil Gerald 216, W.A. 202, William 215, William Joseph 215.
KINKADE, Rebecca 175.
KINNEAR, Tabitha 137.
KINNET, Sarah 255.
KINNEY, Barbara 217.
KINSER, Curtis Lee 183, Larry Joe 183, Leanna Kay 183.
KINSEY, Eliza 271, Elizabeth 133.
KINWORTHY, Asa 198, Elizabeth 198, James 198, John 198, Levi 198, Mary 198, Nancy 198, Sarah 198, Susan 198.
KIRK, Teresa 208.
KIRTS, Hannah 183, Nancy 183, Nancy Eliz. 184, Omar 276, Wesley 202, Wiliam 183, 184.
KISER, Catherine 165.
KISSLING, Dawn 238, George 238, Karen Sue 238, Kathleen Ray 238, Kathy 270, Louise 238, Michael George 238, Ronda 238.
KITTERINGER, Janie 215.
KLEINDORFER, R.H. (Dr.) 238.
KLIENDORFER, Elnora 215, Othelia 215, Thomas 215.
KNAPKE, Bobbie 163.
KNAPP, Beth 216.
KNAUBER, Rachel 268.
KNEELAND, Alexander 310, Content 310, Edward 310, Isaac 310, Molly 310.
KNIGHT, Alonza 200, Maude 200, Nova 289, Paul 276, Robert 270.
KNIGHTLER, Amelia 158, Lucretia 135, Margaret 158.
KNOSE, Hazel 294, Lewis 294, Lewis T. 294.
KOEHLER, Maria 256.
KOONS, Fort Joseph 174, Marjorie L. 245, S.
KORTE, Cornelia 207, Melvin 162.
KORTHALS, Dawn Elizabeth 294, Linda 294, Rodger 294, Sarah Joy 294.
KOVACH, Gaza 232, Haza Jr. 232.
KRAATZ, Celia 262, James 229, Jim 262/
KRAUSE, Dorothy 289, Helen 198, 199.
KREBBS, Andrew 217, Barbara 217, Dalton 217, Doug 217, John 199, Karen 217, Larry 217, Lori 217, Marie 217, Mina 217, Ray 217, Robbie 217, Sandy 217, Susan 217, Vearl 217.
KREIDER, Elizabeth 220.
KREMER, Jacqueline Sue 230.
KRITZER, Dora 158, Elizabeth C. 255, Kenneth 272, Oma Jean 156, Rex 218, Sarah 218, Sarah Louise 166, 217, 218, 237, Vernita 217, 218.
KROUT, Muriel 169.
KRUEGER, Cindy 157, Ilya 157, Phil 157.
KRUGER, Mary Kathryn 149, Mary Florence 183.
KUHLMAN, Donna 165.
KUHN, Susan Rose 246.
KULL, Margaret E. 256.
KUPFERER, Alysha Marie 144, Donna 144, Elgin Andrew 144, John Chester 144, Tyler Jonathan 144.
KYLE, Betty Jane 218, George 218, George Sr. 218, Hattie Imelba 304, John 218, LeRoy 304, Margaret 218, Phoebe 218, Ruth Marie 304.
KYLES, Laura 218, Leslie 218, Lynn 218.

LACEY, Cheryl Ann 155, Doris Melba 155, Leslie Allen 155, Melanie Sue 155, Merle Leslie 155, Merlina Kay 155.
LACKEY, Alice 206, John Henry 237, Ola 185, Oscar L. 185.
LACONI, Michelle 250.
LACY, Elizabeth 292.
LADD, Christopher 196, Jerry 196.
LAFAYETTE, Marquis de 211.
LAKE, Barbara 134, Mary 134, Susan 291, Timothy 134.
LAKIN, Mary E. 283.
LaMAR, Bess 216, Marguerite 216.
LAMB, Charles 203, Earl 231, Earlene 231, Jerry 199, Julia 210, Malcolm 231, Pamela 199, Phyllis 190, Ricky 199, Rodney 199, Tamara 199, Yuki Dean.
LAMPKINS, Elizabeth 258.
LANCASTER, Charlotte 220, John 190, Kelli 220.
LAND, Wayne 270.
LANDERS, Lottie Marie 228, 295.
LANE, Elizabeth 146, Elvie 223, Otta 146, Rebecca 223.
LANGLEY, Peony 285.
LANGNER, Anne 239.
LANQUIST, Judth Mae 210.
LATHROP, Jane 310.
LATTIMORE, Joan 254.
LAUGHLIN, Jason Alan 276, Kirk Andrew 276, Robert Alan 276.
LAURENS, Jean Paul 203.
LAW, Carol 218, Gayle 218, Jeff 218, Julie 258, Ken 218, Kole 218, Levi 218, Lowana 218, Lynn 218, Michael 218, Milton 218, Rebecca 218, Shelley 218, 279.
LAWLES, Charlotte, 218, Elizabeth 218, Jacob 218, Jacob Jr. 218, Mary Ann 150, Viola 218.
LAWLESS, Edith 236, H. Celestina 203, Heather C. 203, Heather Celest 218, Jacob 272, John 218, Judith 203, 218, Robert R. 218.
LAWLOR, Eliza 206.
LAWRENCE, Abdias 156, Brian Tyler 205, Hannah Rae 205, I.V. 302, Jennifer 205, Jim 205.
LAWSON, 204, A. Dale 219, Ann 219, Bertha 219, Billy 219, Charles 219, Charley 219, Christina 219, David 173, Dorothy 219, Edell 219, Francis 219, Grace 219, Harley 219, High 211, Hiram 219, Irvan 160, James 219, James Jr. 219, Jane 161, Jerry 219, Jimmy 219, Lucille 219, Mabel 219, Margaret 219, Marjorie 173, 219, Melissa 219, Mellie 219, Mildred 188, Nora 219, Opel Leona Ruth 219, Pearlie May 219, Phoebe 219, Riley 219, Ronald 219, Ronna 219, Sally 211, Sarah Delcina 173, Saundra 219, Susie 219, Trevor 219, Viola 219, Wanda 219, Willie 219.
LAWYER, Rhonda 305.
LAZELL, Lisa 301.
LAZENBY, Mary 273.
LeMOINE, Ilo 135, Margene 135, Wilford 135.
LeCLERC, Lynn 205.
LEACH, Ida 186, Judith 218.
LEAR, William 282.
LEARNER, Milton B. 160.
LEE, Amelia 248, Betty Louise 195, Haskall Clay 195, Henry E. 171, Iris 157, Martha Hannah 220, Mary Verna 195, May 219, Mildred 219, Mordie 219, Richard H. 219, Robert 265, Sally 265.
LEFFLER, Efie 172, Fay 172, 261, Leona Mae 172, Sarah 261, Virgil 261.
LEGAN, Clancy 201, Mildred Irene 201.
LEGG, Johnny 201, Martha B. 256, Myrtle 201.
LEGGE, Clyde 200, Emma 169.
LEGGETT, Nina B. 302.
LEGGINS, Denise 220, Galen 220, Gary 220, George L. 220, Lila J. 220, Lila J. 220, Marvin Leroy 220, Mildred Edith 220, Russell Leroy 220, Wilma Laverne 220.
LEHMAN, Abrahma 219, Arthur 219, Elizabeth 219, Ernest 219, Esther 219, Jacob 219, Joel 219, Keith 219, Kirk Arthur 219, Leonard W. 219, 220, Letha 219, Marie 219, Natalie 219, Nora 219, Simeon 219.
LEIDEL, Rachel 292.
LEMASTERS, Isaac C. 171, Pearl 171.
LEMMONS, George W. 240, Hazel 240, Thomas B. 240, William Henry 240.
LEMONS, Kimberly 291, Marlene F. 291.
LENGACHER, Leah 297.
LEONARD, Eustayce 182, Susan 278, Virginia 253.
LESLIE, Beatrice 270, 281, Janet 198, Norwood 270.
LESTER, Catherine 148, Grov. Cleveland 213, Grover C. 213, Henry 213, Sarah 213, T.H. 148.
LETTZELL, Mary 199.
LEUTHEN, Cheryl Ann 289.
LEWIS, Alexander 162, Connie 277, Edith Mae 251, Georgeanna 277, Irma 277, Lynda 277, Margaret 219, Nila 277, Nina Jo 229, Paul Robert 277, Paul Jr. 277, Sherry 277, Terri 277.
LIEBER, Carl 208, Richard 204.
LIETZ, Joan 247, Stephen 247.
LIKENS, Mary Verna 195.
LILLY, Eli 232.
LIMPUS, May 236, Otis 236.
LIN, Nancy 303.
LINCICOME, Violet 160.
LINCOLN, Abraham 218, 295.
LINDSEY, Alexander N. 220, Edward 199, Hannah 220, Hannah J. 157, Martha 220, Nathaniel 220, Peter I 157, 220, Rachel 220, Rachel A. 157.
LINK, Angela 297, Gary 297, Jennifer 297, Lorene 297, Michelle 297, Pierce 303, Willa Gertrude 303.
LINKS, Mike 270.
LIPSCOMB, John 190.
LIPSON, Britt 208.
LISTER, Julia Ann 210.
LITHERLAND, Dorothy 214.
LITHICUM, Abby Pearl 200.
LITTEN, Mary J. 140.
LITTIKEN, Margaret 286.
LITTLE, Abrahamn L. 296, Catharine 188, Emma Rose 266, 296, Jackie 287, Louise 296.
LITTLER, Mae 163.
LITTLETON, Dora 201.
LITZELMAN, Charlotte 290.
LIVELY, Carrie Etta 202, Harvey Talbert 202, Violet May 202.
LIVESAY, Jill 197, Peggy Marlene 197, Robert 197.
LLOYD, Alice 216.
LOCKRIDGE, Savannah 156.
LOESCH, Opal 262, Saramae 262, William C. 262.
LOGSDON, Amanda J. 137, Dorothy 220, 261, Ed 261, Edward 220, Elizabeth 220, Elsie 220, 261, Ivy 220, 261, Ivy Jr. 220, Jean 160, 261, Jenny 220, 261, Jessica Leigh 175, Joanne 220, Larry 175, Leroy 220, Lila 258, Lila J. 220, Lina Jean 220, Mabel 184, 220, 258, Margie 220, 261, Marilyn 261, Mark Edwin 220, Marylin 220, Muriel 220, 261, Paul Edward 220, Paul Richards 220, Richard Dale 220, Roy 261, Vivian 220, William Sr. 220, Wilma Laverne 220.
LOHMAN, Nellie 214.
LOLLAR, Eliza 206.
LONG, Albert (Bert) 221, Albert E. 220, 266, Amanda C. 220, Aria Jane 221, Arkie 220, Betty Belle 266, Bety 220, Brenda 220, "Buckshot", Chester 220, D. Betty Belle 220, Diane 270, Doris 220, 266, Elizabeth 211, 212, 221, Emma 265, Finley 220, 266, Finley H. 221, Frances 298, Gary E. 220, Gerladine 220, Gloria 220, Helen 269, Jack 199, James 220, James William 220, Jerald 199, Jessie 220, Joann 220, John 221, Lacell 266, Lacell (Toots) 220, Laura 220, Lester 220, Lillard (Buck) 220, Lillard E. 220, Lillard Jr. 220, Lillian 220, 266, Lillian Louise 221, Linda 220, Louise Frances 220, Lowell 170, Lucille 220, Lucinda 286, Martha 221, Mary 220, 261, Mary Ann 220, 298, Mary Ellen 221, Minnie 221, Oves 199, Ressie 199, Robert 220, Roy 199, Ruth Mae 178, Sarah "Sally" 279, Scott 221, Sherman 221, Sonny 220, Thelma 217, Toots 266, Willard 221, William 220, 221, William C. 220, William Sherman 179.
LONGNECKER, Betty 210.
LOOMIS, Caroline 208, Joseph 208.
LOOP, Leota 252.
LORD, James 250.
LORENZ, Alice Sue 221, Bessie 221, Fred 208, Frederick G. Jr. 221, Frederick G. Sr. 221, Helen Marie 221, Linda Jane 221, Mary Jane 221.
LOUDEN, Hallie Belle 289, Lillian Anne 289.
LOVE, John 204.
LOVINS, Sharon 286, Wilbert 286.
LOW, Beulah Mae 222, Beverly Ann 222, Charles G. 222, Charles Raymond 222, Chas. Grandison 222, John Edward 222, Mabelle Edith 222, Robert Charles 222, Stacey Anne 222.
LOWE, Linda 285, Randy 285.
LOWRY, Carla 310, Donna 310, Jason 310, Marcus 310.
LOY, Edna Pauline 271, Janet 174, Philip R. 174.
LOYD, Clarence 222, Edith 222, Edmond 222, Leroy Earl 222, Mary 222, Mary Suella 222, Ralph 222, Reginald Bob 222, Robert 222, Robert Willard 222, Thelma 222, Victoria Lynn 222, Willard 222, William 222, Willis 222.
LUCAL, Devon Chas. P. 253, Donna Sue 253, Kyle Allen P. 253, Richard Allen 253.
LUCAS, Aimee 158, Albert 158, Amy 223, Anna 276, Anna A. 223, Arlene 158, Armilda 224, 288, Bertha Pauline 147, Carol A. 165, Charles 223, Christena 168, Clara 223, Daniel 223, Daniel Johnathan 222, Ed 158, Edgar 223, Edgar A. 223, Edgar S. 224, Edith Katheryn 223, Elijah 222, 224, Elizabeth 223, Elizabeth Ann 223, Elizabeth Evel. 223, Elza Morton 147, Emma Lucetta 223, Flossie E. 223, Fred 165, Frederick D. 223, Geneva 223, George 224, Grace A. 165, Gwendolyn Fay 147, Issac Sampson 223, J.D.158, James 202, Jared 158, John 224, John Henry 223, Jonathan 223, 224, Katie 223, Katie Mae 223, Larry Ray 147, Laura Jean 223, Linda Kay 147, Manuel C. 223, Manuel Elmer 223, Mary 223, Mary Elizabeth 224, Mina Evalyn 223,

Nancy Ann 187, Paul Dwayne 223, Perry Commodore 223, Rebecca 223, Rhoda 222, Roda C. 223, Sabra 222, 223, Sabra Hawkins 223, Suzette 158, Thomas 223, William 165, 224.
LUGAR, Clara 259, Richard G. 222, Senator 240.
LUKENS, Ben 311.
LUMSFORD, Mary Miriam 182.
LUSHER, Viola 283.
LUTES, Betsy Jo 237, 285, Bill Dean 237, Billy D. 285, Charlotte 226, Cynthia Sue 237, 285, Dorothy 285, Eliza Jane 237, Elizabeth 164, 191, Francis 237, 285, Garry 237, Grace 164, Jack Lee 247, Jennifer 237, Jennifer Lynn 285, Jerry 237, John E. 164, Julie Kay 237, 285, June 164, Laura 164, Leatha Phillips 250, Marion 208, Mary Jane 285, Oscar 164, Ray 164, Rosetta 172, Stephanie Ann 237, Suzanne 237, 285, Ted Loren 237, Valeria Ann 285, Valerie Ann 237, Waldon 164, Wandalyn 237, William 164, 198, 237, Winfrey 164.
LYNN, Robert Canada 162, Susannah 162.
LYONS, Phoebe 219.

MAACH, Laura 310.
MABE, Aleitha 224, Ambrose Wheeler 224, Ann 224, Anna 256, Anna Faye 224, Aurelia 224, Carl 224, Christina Laura 224, David Charles 224, David Todd 224, David Wilson 224, Elizabeth 218, 224, Floyd 224, Harold Cecil 224, Harriet 224, Hazel Hester 224, Hiram 224, James Madison 224, Jeanette 135, John 224, Judith 224, Laura 224, Lawrence 224, Lorenzo Fuller 224, Lucinda 224, Lusenda 224, Lyle Lorenzo 224, Mary Etta 224, Mildred 224, Nancy 224, Robert 224, Sarah 224, Stephen Kent 224, Susan 224, Sylvanus 224, Taylor 224, Vandiver 135, Vanidver Ray 224, Virginia 224, William 224.
MACNABB,Merrie M. 252.
MACKEY, Caroline 168, 224, 237, Gertude 224, John Henry.
MACON, Lou 205.
MACY, Janet 214.
MADISON, James 224.
MAGAW, Enoch 151, Eunice 151, James 151, Matilda 151, Rebecca 151.
MAHAN, Janet 177.
MAIER, Julia Ann 203, Kelly Walter 203, Marilyn 203, Marilyn 203, Randall Kirk 203, Theresa Diane 203.
MAINORD, Gloria 244.
MAKEPEACE, Emma 147.
MALONEY, Catherine 230.
MANETTA, Robin 142.
MANLEY, Mark 145, Neill 145, Shirley Ann 145.
MANN, Albert 180, Ar. McGilvery 177, Archibald McG. 177, Donna 177, Ella 300, Ella 300, Fred 204, Glenda 204, James 180, Jeffrey 177, Kim 177, Laura Ellen 214, 248, Lucy 204, Marcia 177, Rehea 177.
MANNING, David 262, Gary Lamont 253, Grant Allen 253, Laverne 262, Megal Leann 253, Nancy Ann 253.
MANSHIP, Janet 285.
MANUEL, Betty Jean 263, Bob 263, Dean 263, Dorothy 133, 167, Marcella 263, Robert II 263.
MANVILLE, Lorena 195, Silvanus 195.
MARA, Jim 187.
MARCUM, Elizabeth Ann 179.
MARDIS, Angeline 190.
MARING, Mary Ann 272.
MARKLEY, Betty J. 225, Beulah M. 225, George 225, Herman R. (Dr.) 225, Jeffrey B. 225, Lillian 225, Patrice F. 225, Rodney L. 225, Roger B. 225.
MARKUM, Hannah Jane 280, Jane 173.
MARSH, Beatrice Marie 226, Carl Milton 226, Constance 226, Courtland 204, 226, Courtland Jr. 226, Daniel Zary 226, David 226, Emma 280, Emma Jemima 226, Frederick Louis 226, James 226, James Harvey 204, 226, Jas. Courtland 226, Jemima 226, John Paul 204, 226, Marian 204, Marian Grace 226, Marian Jeanne 226, Milton 226, Rebecca B. 226, Rosemary 226, Viola Louise 226.
MARSHAL, Nettie 202.
MARSHALL, Abigail 213, Elizabeth 237, Emma 225, Frances Pauline 193, Helen 193, Helen L. 195, John C. 213, John Sr. 193, 195, Leona Idessa 193, Mary Jane 213, 214, Mildred 225, Pauline 193, Robert 213, 295, Samuel 213.
MARTIN, 207, 220, Abe 203, 208, Alex Lindsey 142, Bert 291, Catherine 142, Charlotte 165, Clarence 205, Clarence Richard 225, Clarissa 143, Claudia Ruth 291, Edith 205, Edith Pearl 225, Eliza 285, Ethel 205, Ethel May 226, Florence Wilma 188, Genevieve 225, Gladys 302, Hannah 132, Hazel Ida 226, Hiram 142, 200, Hiram La Rue 142, Hirma 225, John 201, 205, John A. 200, 225, John Allen 143, 161, Jospeh 142, Julia Belle 226, Leah 291, Marie 219, Mary 289, Mary Ann 142, Maud 143, 280, Maude 135, 161, 201, 225, Maude Catherine 142, Millie 225, Milie Frances 142, 200, Myrdith Marie 226, Myrthe 201, Nora 201, Nora Larue 143, Olive Viola 226, Permilia 143, Rebecca 291, Sara Myrtle 143, Sarah 143, Steve Kennedy 226, Will 201, William 142, William Nelson 143.
MARTINDALE, Doris Diane 144.
MARTZ, Becky 219, Karl 219.
MASEY, Jennifer 306.
MASON, 193, Don 189, Donald 189, Jon 189, Keziah 194, Marguerita 189, Robert 189.
MASSEY, Heather 155, Jeremy 226, Lisa 226, Ray 226.
MAST, Andrew Michael 219, Kesley Marie 219, Lonnie 219, Natalie 219.
MASTERS, Margaret 180.
MATHENY, Lucretia 237.
MATHIS, Alpha 226, Amanda 145, 226, Betty 145, 226, Charlotte 226, Dale 226, Eliza Ann 145, 226, Elizabeth 226, Ella 280, Emma 226, Eudora 226, Eunice 226, Eva 226, Footsie 145, George 276, George Ella 280, Harry 226, Hilda Ann 145, 226, 227, Jeremiah 226, John 145, 249, John William 226, Joyce Ann 145, 226, Laura 212, 226, Mary Ann 145, 212, 226, Mary Jane 226, Maurice 226, Nancy Ray 226, Nathan Andrew 145, Olive 226, Ora 168, 249, Ray 226, Reuben 154, Richard 276, Richard 226, Samuel 226, William 145, 212, 226, Wm. Dale 145.
MATHNEY, Ephraim 300, Louisa J. 300.
MATNEY, Elizabeth 218, Lucinda 141, Nancy 151.
MATSON, Barbara 197, Margaret 222.
MATT, Dorothy 287.
MAY, Amy C. 214, Jacquelyn 214, James T. 214, Ruby Jurean 210, Thomas A. 214.
MAYER, 233.
MAYES, Daivd Ralph 311, Diane 255, James Albert 311, Robert 310, Sara 311.
MAYHEW, Eddie 138, Mary Avis 138.
MAYO, M. Florence 207, Mildred F. 207.
MAYS, Bobby Gene 155, Darlene Jo 155, Lauralee 155, Starlene 155.
McADAMS, Anne 239, Bert 239, Mary 239, Robert 239.
McALLISTER, Carl E. 197, Carl E. II 197, Dinah 197, Eddy Dewayne 197, Jeffery E. 197, Madge 197.
McANELLY, Connie 219, Doris 219, Edell 219, Florence 219, John 219, Owen 219.
McBRIDE, Ruth Hamilton 195.
McBROWN, Marian 194.
McCALLEY, Nancy 264.
McCALLS, Treasie Ann 286.
McCALMON, Delphine 135.
McCAMBER, Charles 295, Retta Belle 295.
McCAMMON, Martha Joyce 309.
McCARTY, Myrtle 182, William H. 264.
McCLARNEY, Andy 196.
McCLARY, Catherine 303, Louisa J. 239, Mary 148, Nancy 239, Rebecca 180, Rebecca S. 227, Robert 239, Sam 148, Tod 303.
McCLOUD, John E. 223.
McCLURG, Charlotte 227, Gary 227, Marcus 227, Mary Ellen 227.
McCONNALD, Dorothy Lou 268.
McCONNELL, Alberta 285, Larry 285.
McCORD, Henrietta 177.
McCOY, Clarice 227, Cornelius 255, Doc 303, Dave 160, Dorothea 227, Elizabeth 287, Ella 160, Eloise 255, Frank 200, Geneva 227, George Roland 215, Ida Mabel 227, James 227, Jane 254, 259, Joel 200, 227, John 297, John Albert 202, Lawrence 227, 240, Lawrence Aaron 227, Margaret 160, Martha Ellen 227, Rebecca 133, 173, Rebecca Jane 215, Ruby 227, Sarah 162, 303, Wanda 227, William 254, 259.
McCRACKEN, Richard 180, Richard Ray 180, Robert A. 180, Ronna Kay 180.
McCREARY, Tammy 232.
McCREERY, Margery 138.
McCULLEN, Mary 232.
McCURDY, Alice 227, John 228, Leota 227, Maria Jane 227, Mary Alice 228, 295 Mollie 228.
McCUTCHEON, Bertha 308.
McDANIEL, Carl G. 300, Della Opal 300, William 174.
McDEARMAN, Clem 196, Connie 196, Debbie 196, Janice 196, Tammy 196.
McDONALD, Bill 219, 228, Cass 228, 265, Cecil 229, Cecil Herbert 228, Charles Kessler 228, 229, Clyde 270, Desdemona R. 229, Diana Lynn 229, Edward S. 229, Essie D. 229, Flora 265, Flora May 228, 229, George 229, Gladys 229, Gladys Mayme 228, Hattie 229, Herb 206, 229, 265, Herbert 211, Ival 195, 265, 306, Jack 228, 265, Jack Herbert 229, James Kessler 229, James William 229, Jennie 228, John 229, John Tom 228, 229, Julie 296, Kathy Lynn 229, Kess 228, 229, Lance 270, Louis D. 229, Lynn 229, Mack 229, Marie Ann 296, Martha 229, Mary 229, Mary Elva 229, Megan Elizabeth 229, Melvin 228, Melvina 229, Michael Kessler 229, Nellie 229, Nellie Opal 229, Nina Jo 228, 229, Samuel J. 229, Sarah E. 229, Stella 195, 228, Susan 213, Tricia Elaine 229, William 229.
McFADDEN, Millie 303, Rodney A. 303.
McFARLAND, Nancy Jane 183.
McGEE, Michelle 199, Sarah Elizabeth 235.
McGILL, Shelly 309.
McGLAUGHLIN, Abigail 286.
McGLOCKLIN, Nina 260.
McGOWN, John 180, Martha Ellen 180.
McGRAYEL, Abraham Michael 230, Charles M. 185, David James 230, Elizabeth Ann 229, Hannah 230, James 185, 230, James G. 230, James H. 185, 230, James Matson 185, 230, James William 229, John 230, John A. 185, John Anthony 230, John Michael 230, Kate Kardynall 230, Margaret 230, Mary 230, Mary Elizabeth 185, 230, Meredith 230, 262, Meredith Jane 185, Michael 230, Pat 230, Ruth Eloise 230, William Harry 230.
McGUIRE, Alfred 208, 230, Alfred Seralvo 230, Anne 230, Dorothy Jean 230, Hugh 230, Jacqueline Sue 230, Joyce Lea 230, Laura Ellen 230, Lt. Col. Elmer L. 230, Lucy Jane 230, Mary Geneva 230, Norma Ruth 230, Robert Lee 230, Roy Elmer 230, Ruby Pearl 230, Thomas "Pat" 230, Wilma Jean 304.
McILVAIN, Frank 299.
McINTIRE, Lena 220.
McKAIN, Elva 135, Jessie 263, Ralph 194.
McKAMEY, Julie 233.
McKEE, 144, Laura 185, Mary Frances 288, Michael 215, Patricia 232, Willard 288.
McKIBBEN, Sarah Taylor 294.
McKINNEY, America 136, Anna 230, Archibald 230, Betty 287, Charles 231, Daniel 202, 230, Daniel (Rev.) 137, 230, 231, Daniel Webster 231, Dolores 230, 231, Elizabeth 137, 230, Emery 231, Ethel Amanda 231, Eva 287, Frances 231, Francis 231, Hesper 287, James 230, Jane 230, 231, Joan Alberta 175, John 230, John D.W. 137, 230, Mary Jane 218, May 231, Missouri F. 230, Omar 231, Prudence 153, Ralph 287, Samuel 230, Scott 287, Susanna 150, 151, Walter 231, William 231, Williamson 231.
McLARRY, Gladys M. 163.
McLARY, Allie Erseneth 156, Hugh A. 156, Jane 156, John Daniel 156, Kathe. Margaret 156, Matheryn Marga. 156, Laura Ellen 230, Mary Ann 145, 156, 212, 226, 227, 230, Nancy 179, Sam 230, Samuel 156, 226, Samuel L. 156, Savannah 156.
McLVAINE, Myrtle Slevin 181.
McMAHAN, Anna 164.
McMANNIS, Louisa 190.
McMINDS, Ed 204, Rosemary 204.
McNEAL, Mary 134.
McNEELY, Claytanna 258, Jennifer Chante 258, Kenneth 258, Kenneth Donald 258, Rhoda Jane 210.
McNEVIN, Patricia 191.
McNICHOLAS, Carrie 262.
McNUTT, James 289, John 289, Paul Voris 289.
McPHERON, Kathy 157 158.
McPIKE, John Rufus 151, Obedience 151, Phoebe.
McQUEEN, Elizabeth 137, Francis 137, Joshua 137, Joshua X. 137.
McQUIRE, Judith 169.
MEAD, Bebecca 229, Joseph 229, 276, Louisa E. 164, Marvin 300, Melvin 228, Opal Marie 300.
MEADE, Louisa 245.
MEANS, Grace Ruby 204.
MEDCALF, Admer 151, Jessie 151, Wanda 151.
MEDDORS, Lucinda 275.
MEDLEY, Mary Calphumia 132.
MEDSKER, Alyssa 306, David 306, Joshua 306, Lynn 306, Mark 306, Tammy 306.
MEEKS, Mary Jane 134, Sarah 199.
MEINERT, Albert 283, Grace 283, May 283.
MEISBERGER, Elsie 189, Leonard 189.
MELLENCAMP, Dolly 284, Doris 137, 155, 190, 284, Louis Herman 284.
MELLINGER, Rachel 276.
MELOTT, Alice 231, Alice Maude 231, Blanche B. 231, Clara Nettie 231, Clarissa 178, 272, Floyd E. 231, Geo. Washington 231, George 231, George 273, George W. 273, 274, John D. 231, 272, John David 178, John William 231, Kenneth 231, Mary M. 231, Minerva 231, Nita 231, Nita 231, Purley Mae 231, Vincent 231, Virgil Ray 231, Willie 231, Zella 231, Zella L. 231.
MELOTTE, John David 178.
MELTON, Barbara 143.
MENSI, Mary Lou 267, Pete 267, Pete Jr. 267.
MERCER, Blanch 242, Charlotte 227, Olive 165, Samuel 227, Thelma 227, Virginia 215.
MERCURIO, Mary Ann 233.
MERIDA, Agnes 232, Alvin 232, Arthur 232, Aurand 232, Eidth 232, Elbert 231, Everett 232, James 232, John 231, Margaret 232, Mary 231, 232, Moll 232, Nat 232, Nathaniel 231, Patricia 232, Sarah 232, Tina 232, Verna 232, 310, Verner 311.
MERRIFIELD, Sarah 264, Thomas 264.
MERRIMAN, Amber Michelle 233, Clarence 139, 178, 232, 233, Crystal Eugenia 233, Esther 289, Franklin 232, George 232, George Virgil 232, Hallie 233, Hallie J. 232, Hallie Josephine139, James 232, Jasper 300, Jessica Cay 233, John Clarence 232, Josephine Marie 178, Leoda 233, Lewis 295, Margaret 276, 310, Mark Allen 232, Mary 232, Michael Andrew 232, Mr. 286, Nadine 232, Opal 300, Rachel Leah 233, Ralph Lee 233, Robert Doyle 232, Rosey 232, Rosey Elizabeth 139, Stacey Jo 233, Teresa Ann, Wayne 232, 233.
MERRYMAN, Dora 232, Edgar 232, Eshter 232, Francis 232, Harvey 232, Ira 232, John 232, John Thomas 232, Lewis 232, Marie 232, Roy 232, Thomas 232, William 232, William John 232.
MERTEN, Erna 307.
MERYMAN, Clarence 232.
MESCHEDE, Elizabeth 147, Raymond 147, Rosa 147.
MESSER, Alberta 141, Frances 141, Maxine 141, Willie 141.
MESSINA, Frances 287, Nellie 234, Thomas N. 234, Thos. Novellett 234.
MEYER, 233, Anges Elizabeth 233, Aloysius H. 233, Emilie 240, Gerhard 240, Henry Jr. (Mrs.) 194, Ida Rose 233, Joanne Marie 233, John August 233, Joseph 233, Martha 142, Mary Agnes 233, Mary Margaret 268, Michael Anthony 233, Wilhelmine 240.
MEYERS, Mrs. Isaac 185, Virginia 224.
MICHAELIS, Dianne 199, Leroy 199.
MICKLE, Bessie M. 299.
MIDDLETON, Sharon Jean 259.
MIKELS, Lydia 289.
MILBURN, Anna Smallwood 190.
MILER, Michael Paul 234.
MILES, Charles Kendall 203, Gregory D. 256, Marilyn Jo 202.
MILLER, Adrian J. 137, Amzy 234, Anna 234, Birdie 137, Brenda 234, Brett Scott 234, Carl 233, Carol Jeanne 166, Carrie 233, Casey Lee 229, 262, Catherine 234, 237, 299, Charles 166, 235, Charles Norman 166, Christopher Jas 234, Clara 141, Clara Mae 235, Clark Rogers 229, 262, Clyde 233, Cora Mildred 137, Cynthia 262, Daniel 172, 233, Darrell 234, David Victor 234, Dean 234, Donald 233, Donna 188, Dorothy 200, Douglas 137, Elmer A. 234, Etta 289, Frances 229, 234, Galen G. 137, George 233, Gerald 234, Gertrude 225, 293, Glen 233, Greg 166, 235, Harriet 285, Harry 234, Henry 261, Herb 287, Herb Sr. 163, Herbert 141, 166, 234, Herbert Jr. 235, Hesper Alma 293, Hester 200, Ida Alice 233, James 234, James Louie 229, 262, James Richard 166, James Scott 229, 262, Jeffrey 235, Jerusha 148, Jill 235, Joe Adam 202, John 141, 233,

234, 298, Joseph Lee 166, Jospehine 233, Juanita 137, Judith Ann 166, Judy 234, Julie 138, Jurene 233, Katie Leona 159, Kay 234, Kenneth James 309, Kevin 234, Kiah 233, Larry 234, Leah Anne 309, Leoma 233, Lorene 233, Louie 229, 234, 262, Louise 287, Luther A. 281, Luther Miller 200, Lynnette G. 137, Mae 166, Margaret 234, Margaret Elizab 166, Marianne 141, 174, 234, Marianne Ruth 140, Marilyn 141, 235, Mark Andrew 234, Mary 234, 236, Mary Esther 166, Maude Lillian 200, Maurice 234, 270, Maurice "Pods" 141, Michael L. 137, Mildred Melvina 191, Myrtle 141, 234, Natalie 286, Nina 235, Norma 234, Peggy 234, Phyllis 215, Raymond 233, Rheuben H. 234, Rupert 137, 146, Ryan 235, Sandra 235, Sara 235, Sarah 234, Sarah Elizabeth 234, Scott 234, Stacy 166, Stephen 141, 235, Steve 234, Susannah 137, Susie 141, 235, 263, Terry 175, Theda Maydell 234, Thomas W. 137, Tim 234, Tom David 166, Vivian 234, Wayne 233, William B. 234.

MILLISON, Nancy 159.

MILLS, Annah Marie 207, Jacob Thomas 207, Jeffery Bruce 207, JoAnn 256, Roger Dale 256, Steven Allen 256.

MILNES, 141.

MINK, Caroline 235, David 235, Esther 235, 260, Harry 235, Harvey Thompson 235, Jane 235, Louellen 235, 260, Mattie 235, Nancy 235, Samuel 235, Susan 235, Thoda 235, Thompson 235, William 235.

MINOR, Hannah 132, Jane Elizabeth 133, Nelson 132, Rachel Elizab. 133, Robert N. 133.

MISNER, Veda 155.

MITCHANER, Mary 208.

MITCHELL, Barbara D. 246, CArol 188, Carrie 290, Dave 146, Guy 290, Homer g. 246, John 209, Kathryn 246, Marjoire 305, Phillip A. 246, Richard L. 290, Tonya A. 246.

MITCHNER, Cynthia 148, 304, John 198, Pearl 172, Ruby 290.

MOBERLY, Eileen 258, Kathy Lyn 145, Margaret 258, Oris 258.

MOBLEY, Ann 224, Ada Alice 198, 199, Allie Erseneth 156, Bummer 252, Charles Raymond 191, Emline 156, Estes Herman 191, Fred Monroe 191, Grace Myrtle 191, Hannah 199, James K. 156, Jessie William 191, John 217, Keith 217, Laura 217, Lester Earl 191, Margaret 199, Martha Savannah 191, Mary E. 141, Mayme 252, Mildred 303, Mina 217, Monroe 191, Nancy Anna 191, Nathan Orval 191, Pauline 217, Russell 217, Thelma 217, Vearl 217, Wilma 200, Wilma J. 198.

MODIE, Grace 273.

MOFFITT, Annie 222, Eliza Jane 237, Samuel 237.

MOHR, (Moore) 236.

MOLDER, Georgia 273.

MOLTHAN, Beth 143.

MONROE, Boyd 235. George Emerson 235, Mary Agnes 235, May 235, Merle 235.

MONTGOMERY, Kay 304.

MOOD, Cynthia Sue 285/

MOODIE, Deborah 292.

MOODY, Christopher M. 276, Jo Clare 276, Joanna 276, Michael Jan 276, Patrick Richard 276, Richard Badgley 276, Tonil Lee 276.

MOON, 141.

MOORE, Albert 237, Ally Butler 225, Andee Camille 276, Andrew 158, 238, Aquilla Ert 237, Artie 236, Arvel J. 237, Augustus 237, Augustus Marion 238, Beady 237, Benjamin 235, Benjamin F. 290, Benjamin M. 237, Bessie 236, Beth Ann 237. Betty 237, Billy 236, Brenda Lee 237, Caroline 168, 225, Cassie Ann 237, Catharine 236, Chalres Otto 237, Charles W. 237, Cinderella 237, Clara 236, Clara Josephine 236, Clarence E. 237, Clarissa 178, Clarissa 231, 272, 273, Clint 237, Clyde 238, Connie Sue 237, Cora Ellen 238, Courtney 237, David 176, Della 224, Della Esta 237, Dewitt C. 238, Dewitt Clinton 237, 238, Dollie Pearl 237, Donna 237, Dude 237, Earl 236, 237, Edell R. 181, Edell Rachel 236, Edith 236, Edmond Laban 236, Eli 237, Eli Ellsworth 238, Eli Jackson 238, Eli T. 237, Elizabeth 202, 236, 237, Elizabeth Helen 238, Ella 178, Ellen 205, 272, Elma 145, 220, 237, Emaline 300, Emanuel Haghn 236, Emma 225, Emma Ann 236, Ernest E. 237, Estella 237, Ethel 212, Everett 304, Fannie F. 237, Filena 237, Frank 236, Genevery 237, George W. 237, George Wesley 151, Geraldine 236, 251, Gertrude Alta 151, 237, Gladys 151, Gloria Starr 236, Grace 304, Grant 237, Harley Everett 176, Harold 145, 237, Harrison Hovey 176, Harvey 225, Hazel 236, Henry 237, 280, Henry Floyd 237, Henry Jackson 238, Howard 236, Ida Jane 237, Imo 237, Isaac Peters 237, Jackson 237, James 212, 238, James Dale 180, 237, James Leroy 168, 225, 237, James W. 236, James Worley 176, Janet 238, Jason Ellsworth 176, 237, Jeffery Curtis 237, Jerry 237, Jesse 264, Jimmie D. 237, Joanna 276, Joe 271, John 175, 178, 202, 235, 236, John D. 237, John David 237, John Deaver 237, John W. 176, 237, Joseph Nathaniel 176, Joshua Daniel 237, Joyce 305, Julia 175, Julius 237, Larry 237, Lemuel 237, 238, Lemuel R. 237, Leroy 237, Lesa 297, Lester Ernest 176, Levi 237, Levi Johnson 238, Lewis Jason 237, Lilly Ann G. 238, Linnie 236, Lora 220, Loren Robert 145, 237, Loretta 176, Lowell H. 176, Lucretia 237, Lula Pearl 237, Mackey F. 237, Mae 220, Marcia Kay 145, 237, Margaret E. 271, Marietta 237, Marilyn 136, Marilyn Sue 145, 237, Mary 153, 158, 176, 236, Mary (Molly) 151, Mary Alice 151, 202, Mary Ann 237, Mary Beth 145, 237, Mary Catherine 280, Mary E. 212, 237, Mary Ellen 236, Mary Lucretia 238, Mary Olive 280, Matilda 206, Maude Elizabeth 237, May 236, Michael 237, 238, 304, Mildred 236, Minerva Jane 236, Minnie 236, Minnie Louise 237, Moe 271, Myra Josephine 176, 237, Myrtie Ethel 176, Nancy 238, Nanie J. 236, Nathaniel 176, 237, Nellie 198, Nellie Esther 168, 224, 237, Norma 204, Olive 304, Orville F. 176, Paul 276, Phebe 238, Phillip A. 300, Rachel 238, Rachel E. 236, Reba Roscoe 262, Rebecca 236, 290, Rena 236, Reuben 236, Reynolds 236, Robert 236, Rosa Cordelia 236, Roy 236, Ruth 236, Ruth Irene 145, Saloma 202 Samuel 236, Sandy M. 237, Sanford, 153, Sara 304, Sarah 237, Sarah Alice 237, Sarah Alice 237, Sarah Ann 153, Sarah Elizabeth 238, Sarah Esther 236, Sarah Frances 238, Sarah Jane 225, 236, 290, Scott Alexander 237, Solomon 205, 236, Sue Ellen 205, Sylvanus 237, Talitha Cumi 304, Timothy 236, Tobias 235, Todd Jamison 237, Virginia Ruth 237, Vivian 237, 285, Walter Paul 276, William Dean 176, William George 202, William Grant 176, William Henry 153, William Isaac 236, William Sherman 238, Willie 237, Wilso 225, Wilson 237, Wilson Shannon 238, Wm. Ohia Grant 175, Hannah 238.

MORE, Saloma 133.

MOREHOUSE, Lucille 226.

MORGAN, Donald James 238, Floyd 270, Lenore 308, Mary 153, Mary E. 212, Melissa Jane 253, Ruth 238, Sharon K. 210, William 200.

MORIE, Zody 287.

MORRIS, Catherine 156, Garry 308, Howard 258, Nannie 258, Ruth 201, Valerie Ellen 308.

MORRISON, Andrew 183, Catherine 183, Della 238, Elizabeth 238, Emma 238, Iva Elizabeth 202, J.S. 214, Jane 285, Jesse 247, Jessie 213, 214, 238, John 139, 238, John Edward 271, John Swayze 238, 247, Johnny 216, Katherine 149, Laura Belle 192, 271, Luther 238, Martin 238, Martin Luther 139, Mary 136, 216, Mary E. 192, Mary Etta 192, 194, 271, Myrtle 139, 279, Nellie 238, Omer 238, Phoebe 238, Sarah 214, Sarah Catherine 139, Sarah Elizabeth 238, Susan A. 192, Susan Q. 271, Thomas M. 271, Thomas Mifflin 192, William 238, 271, William W. 192, 271.

MORROW, Hilda 236, Linnie May 236, Shanton (Rev.) 236.

MORSE, Nancy Ann 209.

MORTICE, Rebecca 147.

MOSBURG, Glenna E. 197.

MOSER, Clifford 298, Jennie 165, Juanita 298, Marietta Slevin 181, Roston Scott 298, Thelma 298, William 248.

MOSIER, Bramble 173, Verna 173.

MOULTON, Hazel 218, Joseph 218, Nathan Noyes 218, William 218.

MOUNTS, Hazel Hester 224.

MOUREY, Dessie 288.

MOZEE, Abrilla 259, Eliza 259, John 259, Sadie 259, Willie 259.

MUHLBAUER, Marianne 193.

MULHEIM, W. Ruddinghuysen 222, Willem R. 222.

MULLINGS, Eleanor 193.

MULLINS, 193, Eleanor 193, Jane Washington 193, John 193.

MULLIS, Cecil 172, Clyde 172, Dale 172, Delmar 172, Donald Wayne 172, Elizabeth 137, 141, 230, Floyd 172, Floyd Jr. 172, Franklin 192, George 172, Geriah 195, 230, Iva 141, James 192, Luvisa 165, Margaret 192, Mary Lucille 172, Pauline 172, Ruth 172, Silas 141.

MULRY, Beth ann 216, Malcomb Lee 216, Robert 216.

MUNCIE, Elizabeth Jane 186.

MURPHY, Angeline 194, Ann 293, Bernadetta 226, Blanche 293, Charlei 305, Cora Louise 235, Dr. 204, James 280, John 293, Kate 280, Lucinda C. 280, Maurcie 297, Olive 293, Pat (Dr.) 211, 246, Tammy 159, William 280.

MUSER, 220.

MUSGROVE, Margarey 257.

MUSSER, Catherine 162.

MYARS, Henrietta 301.

MYERS, Wade 295.

MYDLAND, George W. 299.

MYERS, Anna Lillian 295, Grover (Rev.) 168, James Leon 168, Jane 268, Lori Ogle 239, Madeline 239, Marcella Dorete 168, Melvin Jack 226, Nathan Robert 168, Paul Eugene 168, Stephen Wesley 168, Timothy Jack 168, Verna 258, Zella 276.

NAFFE, Alfred 194.

NAILE, Peggy Jean 247.

NANGLE, Arne Eugene 175, Bradley Steven 175, Tracy Jo 175.

NAPIER, Martha Louise 150, Zuba 150.

NASH, Evelyn 151.

NAVITY, Mary 213.

NAY, Eusebia 289.

NEAL, Abigail 161, Addie Smith 260, Al 149, Alberta 238, Beulah 238, Blanche 135, 161, 260, Dorothy 260, Elsea 243, Emerson 238, Eunice 237, Hannah 293, 298, Harmon 253, Ida May 238, James 184, 238, John 238, Leon 238, Lewis 184, Linzey 260, Lowell Vernace 260, Lula 238, Mabel 238, Mable 149, Marie 260, Martha 161, 196, Mary Ellen 169, Mary Emily 238, Mildred Louise 238, Nina 260, Omer Ray 238, Orville 260, Pauline 238, Roger Lee 260, samuel 161, Sarah Jane 225, Sarah Jane A. 236, Shirley 260, Vernace 260, William 184, Wilmer 238.

NEALY, Ruth 289.

NEAT, Bob 239, Cheryl Kay 239, David 239, Delvin T. 238, 239, Dick 239, Florence 239, Geo.Washington 238, Harry 239, Harry Thomas 239, Herring 238, June 201, Kathryn 239, Michelle 239, Robert 201, Shirley Jean 201, 239, tom 239, Victoria 239.

NEEDLER, Harvey 201.

NEESE, Earl 226.

NEFF, Amanda Louisa 153, James (Dan) 153, James Daniel 153, Jessee 153, 246, Martha Lee 136, Oliv. Alexander 153, Oliver A. 153, Ruth 153, Ruth E. 151, Ruth Elizabeth 153, Sarah Elizabeth 153, Susan 219.

NEGUS, Jacquelyn 136, Jeffrey Keith 136, Joel Kristopher 136, Jon Keith 136.

NEIDEIGH, Abraham 132, Adela 132.

NEIDIGH, Elizabeth 210.

NEITHERLAND, Mrs. 298.

NELSON, David 179, Evaline 274, Margaret May 191, 274, Minerva E. 202, Samuel 191, 274, Vanie 274.

NEPTUNE, Karen 271.

NESBIT, Arnold Andrew 183, David Sanford 183, Julia Ann 182, Julieet J. 183.

NEUBACHER, Selma 283.

NEUHAUSEL, Debra 233.

NEVILLE, Anne Elizabeth 156, John 156.

NEVISSA, Jean 310.

NEWCOMB, George W. 185, Martha 255, Samantha 185.

NEWKIRK, Alta 157, Henry 154, Permelia 202, 230, 252.

NEWLAND, Joan 286.

NEWMAN, Jane 187.

NEWMISTER, Mabel 202, Mary 255, William 255.

NICHOLS, Waneta 188.

NICHOLSON, Eva Mae 285.

NICHTER, Karen Jo 193.

NICKELS, Mike 182.

NICKERSON, David 178, Ella 178, Laura 217, S. Margaret 178, Will 178.

NICLESS, Barbara 199.

NICOSIA, Mrs. James 255.

NIELSON, Lydia Ann 209.

NIEMAN, Richard 271.

NILES, Stella 242.

NILSON, John 285, John F. 171, Lula 285, Lula Mae 171, Mary 285, Mary Ann 285, Pearl 187.

NIPPER, Mary 153.

NISSEN, Catherine 299.

NIX, Daniel 285, Polly 285.

NIXON, Mabelle Edith 222, Richard 240.

NOBLET, Amandy 256, Ann 224, Anna 256, John 256, 285, Nancy E. 256.

NOBLITT, Alma 239, Charlene 177, 239, Charles Robert 239, Hanna Jane 263, Hannah 239, John W. 239, Kelly R. 239, Loren S. 177, 239, Lucille V. 239, Lucinda 239, Minnie 239, William 239.

NOE, Harry 246, Susan 246.

NOGGLE, Chelsea 305, David P. 305, Leslie 305, Sarabeth 305, Sarah 305, Theodore 305.

NONEMAN, Rosemary Elna 149.

NORMAN, Anthony Michael 238, Dawn Michelle 238, Elizabeth W. 282, Jospeh T. 282, Karen 238, Wallace 179, William 238.

NORRIS, Barbara Jane 283.

NORTON, Jennifer Marie 222, Linda Jane 222, Peter Jonathan 222.

NORVELL, Evelyn 163, Gladys M. 163, Golda Virginia 163.

NORWOOD, Beatrice 270, Christie 270, Dana 270, E. 270, E. Jr. 270, Michael 270, Richard 270, Robert 270, Ryan 270, William.

NOS-WAN-KEE, 294.

NOTTINGHAM, Matilda Elizab. 190.

NOVELETE, Frances 262.

NUGENT, Elizabeth 242, Paul 284, Pearl 203, 242, Pearl Elizabeth 284.

O'BANION, Brian 197, Corina 197, Janet Ruth 197, L.T. 197, Leslie 197.

O'BRIAN, Loran 199.

O'DANIEL, Millie 259, Milly 259.

O'DELL, Alma 239.

O'FLYNN, Honora 220.

O'HANEN, Earl 268.

O'NEAL, Mary 151.

O'NEILL, Judith 232.

O'NIELL, Gracie 303.

O'QUINN, Thomas 276.

OARD, Karin Jo 215.

OFFUTT, Lucya Eva 233.

OGDEN, Thomas 206.

OGLE, Camden Lee 239, Clarence 239, Conner C. 239, Edith 239, Elizabeth M. 239, Herma E. 239, James 239, James Perry 239, Lela Evon 239, Levi 239, Louisa J. 239, Mark 239, Mary 239, Mary L. 239, Mary Louise 239, Nancy Jane 184, Sarah Cooper 239, Sarah E. 201, Warren 239, Wayne 239.

OHAAKSON, Sadie 156.

OLIVE, Anne 240, Geo. Scott Jr. 240, Geo. Scott Sr. 240, Hazel 240, James 240, Louise 240, Sally 240, Scott 240, Scott III 240.

OLIVER, Andrew 241, Andrew F. 240, Andrew Herbert 240, Anna 241, Chalmer Victor 240, Chalmer Samuel 241, Debora Lee 241, Delpha Jo 241, Derrick 241, Donna 241, Effie 240, Emma Ruth 240, Franklin Myrven 240, Gary 166, Gary Andrew 188, 240, Homer Amos 188, 240, Iva Lena 240, James 241, James Henry 240, James Lowell 241, James Parsley 241, Jane 241, Jannaka 166, Jannaka Jane 241, John Darvin 241, Lee William 241, Leo Vernon 240, Lowell 241, Lowell Travers 241, Maggie 241, Marcia Kay 188, 240, Marguerite 195, Marie 241, Martha 241, Mary 241, Muriel Gladys 241, Nancy Ann 240, Nancy Jo 240, Omer Hendricks 240, Otis Jonathan 240, Rosa Luceila 241, Ryan 166, Ryan Andrew 241, Samuel 241, Samuel E. 240, Sarah 241, Sarah Ellen 241, 244, Sheila Jane 166, 241, Thurl Dennis 240, Timothy Robert 241, William 241, William Andrew 241.

OLMSTEAD, Rachel 270.

OLMSTED, Alvera 283, Edna Mae 283, Eric Joseph 216, Hallie 283, Karen Sue 216, Kayla Sue 216, Marra Ashley 216, Robert Joe 216, Todd Robert 216.

OLSEN, Alvina 239, Anne 239, Gene 239, Ginnuor 240, Ora 239.

OLSON, Joanne 220.

ONEAL, Mary Lou 150.

ORTEGA, Jesusita 248.

ORMAN, Bell 223.

OROZCO, Natalie 286.

ORTEGA, Jose 248.

OSBORNE, Susan Christine 183.

OSTERLOH, Dorothea Christ 256.

OTT, Wendy Jo 247.

OTTE, Flora 192, Flora Hamblen 192.

OTTENWELLER, Carl 223, Julia 223.

OTTINGER, Goldie Gladys 232.

OWEN, Anne 311, Electa 311, Joel Jr. 311, Joel Sr. 311, John 311, Molly 311, Phebe 209, 210.

OWENS, "Chig" 241, Albert Alfred 242, Anita Kaye 237, Blanch 242,

Carol Sue 145, Darval 242, Dora A. 284, Dora Alice 203, 241, Dorval 308, Elizabeth 156, Elizabeth Ann 145, Gary Richard 145, Genevra 173, 241, 242, Genevra Irene 255, Goldie 242, 284, Grace 242, Harry 241, James 241, James Harry 241, 242, James Lawrence 137, James S. 241, 284, James Scott 145, James Stevenson 203, 241, Jim 241, John Ross 242, Joshua Ross 145, Lena Jane 137, Marie 260, Mary 242, Mary Margaret 156, 242, Nellie 242, Pearl 137, 241, Pearl Elizabeth 242, Rhonda 237, Robert 260, Rose Nellie 242, Ross 308, Ruth 242, 284, Samuel 241, Samuel Isaac 241, 242, Thomas 264, William 284, William Robert 242.
OYLER, Maradyn 289.
OZRO, Stephen 183.

PADISH, Arthur William 242, Beatriz 242, Charlotte Ruth 242, Erica Lynn 242, Gail Ruth 242, Gay Lynn 242, Hulda Mae 242, James Edward 242, John Francis 242, Jonathan 242, Mary 242, Maxine 242, Megan Elizabeth 242, Paul 242, William Charles 242.
PAFFORD, William 224.
PAGE, Alice 242, Carole 242, Earl 242, Paul 242.
PAINTER, Anna 151, David 243, Frances 243, Helen 243, Louis 243, Theresa 243, Woodie 243, Woodrow 243.
PALMER, Jean 291, Nancy 151, Sherry 199.
PANE, Linda 229.
PANGBORN, Charles Benj. 247, Charles William 247, Cyrus 247, Frank 247, Frank Leroy 247, John Clinton 247, Mary 247.
PARIS, Willis 223.
PARISH, Carolyn 266.
PARK, Mary Ann 215.
PARKER, Abner G. 243, Amelia 243, 269, 271, Artie 244, Bud 244, Connie Ann 180, Corinne Kay 244, Edith 244, Edna Pearl 244, Ethel 243, Floyd 244, Garnet 244, Hannah M. 133, Hannah Mary 243, 244, Ida 268, Ida May 243, James 243, James Alexander 243, Janelle 287, Jim 244, John 176, Larry Lee 180, Lawrence 180, Leander 243, Leona 243, Lettie Frances 295, Levi 295, Louisa A. 243, Lydia Ann 243, Margaret 244, Mark 287, Martin V. 133, 271, 243, Martin V. Buren 243, Mary Anna 243, Mary Isabelle 133, 243, Mary Jane 243, Mary Polly 243, Myrtle Ellen 243, Nancy J. 243, Olive 247, P.C. 154, Rebecca 175, Rebecca 176, Reuben (Dr.) 247, Sampson R. 242, Sarah A. 243, Susan A. 243, Walter 243, Washington A. 243, William 243, William J. 243, William M. 243.
PARKHURST, Cecil (Rev.) 150.
PARKINSON, Clara Mae 231.
PARKS, Amanda 244, Caroline 244, Edward 244, Elizabeth 200, Geo. Elmer 244, Geo. Washington 244, George 200, Henry 200, Homer 244, James Morris 244, Jimmy 244, Lena 244, Priscilla 258, Sam 200, Sarah Francis 244, Stella 244, Stephen 244, William 200, 244.
PARMENTER, Cindy 199.
PARMERLE, Agnes 155.
PARMERLEE, Alan 244, Alice 157, 179, 220, Alva T. 244, Amanda 244, Amos 244, Andrew Marcus 244, Anna 244, Anna Eliza 244, Connie 244, Dana 244, Doris 244, Geo. Cleveland 244, George 244, Harriet Louisa 244, Ida 244, James 195, James Clark 244, Lois 244, Louise 244, Marcus Beecher 244, Marcus Hurlbutt 244, Mary 244, May 244, Pansy 244, Rebecca J. 244, Roberta 244, Ruby 244, W. Dale 179, Warren Dale 244.
PARSLEY, Ada 165, Amanda 244, 245, 246, Amanda Jane 177, Ana 245, Bertha Susan 246, Blair J. 245, Clarence 244, Columbus 177, 244, 246, Cora 181, Daniel J. 246, Daniel T. 246, Denise 245, Edwin E. 245, Edwin E. II 245, Edwin H. 246, Elizabeth 244, 246, Elmer 245, 299, 312, Elmer Jr. 245, Elsie 244, Emma Ruth 241, Floyd 245, Frances 245, 312, Garnet 211, 244, Gladys 245, Hallard 246, Haskell 246, Hazel 246, Henry 244, Irvin 246, James 246, James Timothy 246, Jannie 269, 312, Jason 244, 246, Jasper 244, 245, Jasper 244, 245, 302, John 244, John A. 246, John A. 246, John C. 244, 246, John Robert 244, 246, Jospeh 246, Joshua M. 245, Mary 244, Mary Ann 246, Mary E. 246, Mary Margaret 246, Newton 244, Olive 246, Orvall 245, Ott 296, Otto 244, 246, Rachel 153, 244, Ralph 227, 244, 246, 247, 264, Ralph Dale 246, Robert 244, 245, Robert Martyn 246, Robert Martyr 153, 244, Robert Newton 177, Robin E. 312, Ruth 245, Sandra S. 245, Sarah 244, 302, Simeon 246, Solomon 182, Solomon S. 153, 244, 246, Susan 244, 246, Susannah 153, 244, Sylvester 244, Walter C. 245, Wanda 244, Wanda Rose 246, William 244, 246.
PARSON, Warren 287.
PARSONS, B.A. 197.
PASS, Claude 138, Judith K. 138.
PATE, Charles W. 206, David H. 206, Ernest D. 206, Forest R. 206, Frances 292, Frances M. 206, Judy 292, Judy E. 206, Kenneth 292, Kenneth A. 206, Kenneth K. 206, Louellen 132, Sandra K. 206, Wayne F. 206.
PATIE, Fae (Miss) 155.
PATON, Maxine 162.
PATRICK, Jane 195.
PATTERSON, Alma Etta 176, Charles Miles 175, 176, Charles Roy 176, Daisy 176, Dora Jane 176, Ephra. Alphonso 176, Guy 185, Jesse Wallace 176, Leona I. 247, Louie Walton 176, Mary Ann 238, Oliver Tracy 176, Patrick O. 247, Rosie Mae 176, Sammy 304, Samuel 176.
PATTON, Mary E. 146, Sara Loyd 146, Sarah 217, Sarah Lloyd 146.
PAUS, Elizabeth 256.
PAYNE, Grace 238.
PAYSON, Irvin 215, Janet 215.
PAYTON, Charles Anthony 145, John F. 295, Sundi Marie 145, Ty Michael 145.
PEALER, Belva 203.
PEARSON, Alex V. 142, Burley 196, Eselle 142, Mary Jane 141, Naomi 134, R. O. (Doctor) 134.
PEAVLER, Lillian Lee 145.
PECK, William D. 286.
PEEL, Celia 162.
PEEVLER, Lillian 160.
PEGG, Nancy Louise 134.
PELLEY, Benamine 300, Mary Ann 300.
PELTON, Benjamin H. 247, George Seeley 247, George Steven 237, John E. 247, John Forrester 247, Mary 247.
PENDLETON, Ora 304.
PENN, William 222.
PENNINGTON, Amos 206, Anne 206, Barsheba Ann 171, Basha Jane Ann 172, Bashie 171, 233.
PENROSE, Mary 133.
PEOPLES, Permelia Jane 235, 259.
PERCIFIELD, Alma 162, Amelia Lee 248, America May 162, Anderson 248, 258, Barbara 248, Beulah 166, Beulah Jean 248, Bill 166, Blanche 300, Catherine 248, Edith Ann 190, Eliza 248, Elizabeth 213, 214, 248, Fannie 151, Freda Nell 214, George 213, 214, 248, Gilbert 248, 258, Grover 284, Grover C. 248, Henry 300, James Anthony 248, Janice Kay 248, Jemima 210, Jemiman 198, Laura Ellen 214, 248, Lawrence 248, Lester 248, Lester "Bill" 214, Lois 300, Loretta Young 248, Lottie L. 248, Louise 248, Lovina 198, 199, Lucinda 248, Lydia 214, 247, Marcus Lafayette 248, Martha Ann 248, Mary Alice 248, Matson 162, Michael William 248, Michael Wm. 248, Nancy 248, Paul 248, Pearl 248, Penny Joan 248, Rachael 248, Richard Glen 248, Ruth Naomi 284, Sally 248, Sampson 248, Samuel 248, Sandusky 285, Sarah 248, Sarah Ann 308, 309, Sherman 248, Steven Andrew 248, Ted 214, Thomas 198, 248, Thurman 248, 258, Verna 258, Watson 248, William Henry 214, Wm. Henry 248, Wm. Lester 248.
PEREZ, Maria 248, 249, Mary 249, Mary I. 248, Robert 248, 249.
PERMUT, Ashley Tessa 307.
PERRY, Ann 250, Bernard 249, Elizabeth 249, John 271, Rachel B. 249, Stanley 196, Tori 196.
PERSINGER, Jane 287.
PETERS, Elizabeth 237, Taylor 158.
PETERSON, Estella 230, Kathleen 140, Martin 140, Mona 140, Patrick 140.
PETRO, Anna Mae 147, Bonnie Kay 147, Charles Thomas 147, Clifford 147, David Lee 147, Donna 237, Elizabeth 223, Elizabeth Ann 223, Ellen 168, 249, Elnora Adaline 165, George 174, Joseph 223, Margaret 148, Martha E. 165, Martha Elizabeth 224, Mary 255, Mary "Polly" 223, Nancy 223, 288, Nicholas 165, 223, Ora F. 168, Ora Flossie 249, Paul 223, Philip S. 285, Phillip 223, Preston 168, Preston 249, Rebecca A. 223, Ruby Gail 147, Sarah A. 285, Suzanne 235, William M. 249.
PETTY, Mr. 248.
PFOHL, Etta 186.
PHEGLEY, Betty 182.
PHELPS, Rosa 165.
PHILLIPI, M.G. Wendell 250, Wendell 249, 250.
PHILLIPS, Albert R. 250, Alberta 238, Anna 250, Catharine E. 293, Clover Lorraine 250, Elizabeth 140, 263, Fay 250, George 250, Henry 289, Joanna 250, Laura B. 250, Leatha Lucille 250, Lucille 144, Martha 250, Mary 250, 280, Mary E. 250, Matthew Allen 250, Maxie 289, Nancy E. 250, Ray 250, Raymond 289, Rbt. Arthur II 250, Richard M. 250, Richard Wiley 250, Robert Arthur 250, Rufus P. 250.
PICKARD, Alexander F. 251, Algernon Wm. 250, Allen Higgins 250, Annie Sophia 250, Caroline 250, Chahee Choi 250, David Sage 251, Guy Allen 250, Henry Rider 251, Janet Carole 251, John 250, Kim Forster 251, Ruth Elizabeth 251, Sarah N. 250, Thomas Jr. 250, Todd Sloane 250.
PIERCE, 147, Emma 266, Franklin 268, Mary Polly 268, Napoleon 266.
PIKE, Eliza 268, Eliza Louisa 182, Elizabeth 151, Julia 248, Louisa 182, Parnelia 268, Phillip 151, 268, Viola 133.
PILKENTON, Betty Jean 196, Paul 196.
PILZ, Sue 199.
PING, Altha Clodean 251, Amy Lynn 251, Anita Kay 251, Anita Kaye 237, B. Irene 178, Bernice Irene 178, Betty Ann 237, 251, Blanch 287, Blanche Olvie 251, Bryce 237, 252, Bryce D. 178, Bryce Dwight 251, Carrie Ethel 252, Cassandra L. 251, Charles 287, Charles S. 251, Charles Wesley 252, Christena 251, Christina M. 252, Clodean 287, Clara Alice 178, 252, Earl 252, Edgar Loren 251, Edwin Paul 237, 251, Fern 287, Freeman 252, Gary Wayne 251, Gerald Bryce 237, Geraldine 236, Gerland Bryce 251, Gloria Starr 251, Irene 252, Iva 287, Iva Lona 251, Jasper Job 202, Job 251, John Thomas 252, Kathleen Joan 251, Kenneth Dwight 237, 251, Lana Diane 251, Lewis Franklin 252, Logan 202, 252, Lois Faye 237, 251, Loren 287, Mary Ann 252, Michael Joan 251, Nancy 167, 171, Otto 178, 252, Permelia 252, Phyllis Lovenia 251, Rebecca Sue 237, 251, Richard 171, Robert Wayne 251, Thelma Fern 251, Wesley Pruitt 287, William Logan 252, William 251, Wilma 252, Zabrina Marylou.
PINK, Walker 252.
PIPER, Elisha 175.
PITCHER, Cleave 219, Jacob F. 174, Mary 267, Mary Ann 174.
PITTMAN, A.J. (Jerry) 252, Absalom 252, Alex 288, Amanda 252, Andrew J. 252, Blanche 252, Brad 252, Brenda 252, Delbert-Butch 252, Earnest 252, Elizabeth Evel. 223, Emma Lucetta 223, George 250, Georgiana 250, Greg 252, Grover 252, Jerrica Lynn 252, Jerry 252, Leigh Ann 252, Leon 252, Linda 252, Lisa Marie 252, Mary Ann 153, Maude 252, Nancy J. 288, Netta 250, Orville 133, 252, Rebecca 261, Sarah Jane 152, Sylvania 133, William 133, William H. 252, William L. 252, Wilma 183, 252.
PITTS, Lula 164.
PITZER, Mary 200.
PLATT, Irvin 210, Sharon 210.
PLONKEY, Brent 267, Judie 267.
PLUMMER, Rhoda 235.
POGUE, Charlie 284, Clifford 290, Edna 284, Laura 284, Mary 293.
POLAND, John T. 178.
POLING, Amanda Sue 145, Anna Irene 145, Arah (Mary) 200, Bessie 310, Brian David 145, Dustin Joseph 145, Elisha 281, Elizabeth 200, Geniza 281, Harriet 185, 230, Harry David 145, Harry Emil Jr. 145, Harry Sr. 145, Hattie 133, Jessica Lynn 145, John 200, Joseph Lee 145, Judith (Judy) 145, Judith Irene 145, Judy Ann 145, Mary 200, Mittie 145, Nancy Sue 145, Phoebe 238, Rebecca Hanna 142, Store 185, Susabel 145, Will 278, William 281.
POLLEY, Elza Albert 249, Evelyn 249, Irene 249, Janet 249, Jesse L. 249, Ora 249, Phyllis 249.
POLLOCK, Joseph 199, Mark 199, Richard 199.
POLLY, Elizabeth 274, 275.
POOL, Kathryn E.V. 252, Kaye 252, Kevin Sean 252, Kurtis Eugene 252, Luther 261, Melanie Mary 252, Merrie M. 252, Ryan Scott 237, Susan E.S. 252, William Taylor 252, Wm. Everett 252, Wm. Ian-(Willie) 252.
POOLE, Buena Mae 296, Dorothy 182.
POORE, Geraldine 220.
POPE, Anita 261, 282.
POPPINO, Cindy 291, David D. 291, Phyllis C. 291, Rbt. D. 291, Rbt. Thomas 291, Susan J. 291.
PORTER, Allen 196, Angela 196, Armeanous 192, Audrey A. 228, Audrey Anna 253, Barbra Ann 253, Beth Ann 196, Betty Jean 253, Cinderella 181, 252, Clara 252, David James 253, Donna Sue 253, Doris Ann 253, Earl Walker 253, Edward 252, Edward K. 252, Elizabeth 182, 228, Henry 182, James E. 228, James Earl 253, Jane Watt 252, Jesse 153, Jill Elaine 253, John 253, John Henry 181, 252, Kathy Ann 172, 310, Kenneth Allen 253, Lois M. 228, Lois Marie 253, Mandy Leigh 253, Martha Hutson 182, Mary 181, 182, 228, 252, 253, Mary 295, Mary (Polly) 153, Mary C. 228, 253, 280, Mary Cordelia 253, Mary Cordelia 173, Melissa Jane 252, Michael Eugene 253, Nancy Ann 253, Ray Allen 253, Richard Leo 252, Sarah 181, Steven Michael 252, Thelma M. 228, Thelma Mae 253, Vicey 182, Violet 182, Will 253, Will Rae 181, 252, William A. 228, William Allen 253, Wm. Allen 253.
PORTWOOD, Mary Frances 211.
POSTLETHWAIT, Benjamin F. 132, Sarah J. 132.
POTTER, Claud 200, Jessie 151, Jessie Brown 151, Samuel 281.
POTTORFF, Steve 180.
POTTS, Donita 239.
POULTER, Eleanor 133, Lucinda 248.
POULTON, Effie 241.
POWELL, Anvil 253, Annie Lorraine 253, Clora 253, Clydia 253, Edna 253, Elberta 253, Elizabeth 158, Hannah 158, 180, Herman Oliver 253, Homer 253, Jessie 253, Joe 253, John Wesley 253, Joseph Arthur 253, Lilly 253, Liza 253, Louisa 158, Luther 253, Luther Allen 253, Luther Crokett 253, Mary 263, Mary Olive 253, Miriam 253, Nancy 253, Nancy Lee 253, Olie 253, Rose Ettie 176, Sadie 253, Sharon Lynn 253, William (Capt.) 158.
POWERS, Hattie 243, Helen 243, Kennel 243.
POYNTER, Dolly 182.
PRAIL, Sarah Ann 184.
PREBSTER, Dorothy 214.
PRICE, Charles 213, Cynthia K. 187, Janna 301, John 213, Wilson S. 213.
PRIDDY, Nola 271.
PRINCE, Beatrice 254, Carolyn 254, Donald 254, Everett 254, Howard 253, 254, James M. 253, 254, Joan 254, Laura 253, Lola 254, Marlin 254, Mary 254, Riley Boswell 254, Ruby Alice 254, Ruby Ford 253.
PRINTZ, Evelyn 133, 167.
PROCTOR, John Thomas 306.
PROPECK, Elza 137, Mary Ann 137.
PROSSER, James 213, Manerva 213, Margaret Jan 213, Martha 213, Nancy 213, Rebecca 302.
PROSSER, Mary Jennie 185.
PRUETT, Betsey 254, David 254, Elisa Ann 254, Elizabeth 254, Hiram 254, Jane 255, John 254, John R. 254, Joseph 254, Mary 254, Nancy 254, Nathan P. 254, Pleasant 254, Samuel 254, William Henry 254.
PRUITT, Archibald 180, Blanche 263, Chloie Marie 180, Deborah 136, Florence Emma 180, George Samuel 136, Isaac 182, James 285, Jane 136, Martin 250, Nancy F. 250, Phoebe Jane 285, Samuel 136, Samuel Richard 180, Sarah 250, 295, Thelma Fern 251, Wesley 287, Wesley Leroy 251, William 295.
PRUTZMAN, Mary 300.
PRYOR, Ben 200, Della 138, Flo 162.
PUGH, Kathy F. Sexton 302.
PURCELL, Joyce 302.
PURTLEBAUGH, Marie 166.
PYCROFT, Ursula 291.
PYLE, Ernie 151, Ernie 207.
PYLES, Addie 208.

QUAYLE, Dan 250.
QUEEN, Rosana 198, 199.
QUENSBERRY, Nancy Anne 258.
QUESENBERRY, Nancy 161.
QUICK, Belitjen 222, Canzaday 222, Jacobus 222.
QUILLEY, 194.
QUILLIAN, Elizabeth 280.
QUINN, Mary Jane 288.
QUILLIAN, Maude 280, William 280.

RADER, Catherine 276, Mary

Frances 211.
RAINS, Fred 242, Joel S. 302, Matilda Jane 302, Nancy Jane 302.
RAINWATER, Edna 293, George 182.
RALEIGH, Susan A. 192, Susan Q. 271.
RALEY, Cafele Thomas 207, Kathleen Eliza 207, Thomas Edgar 207.
RALPHY, Sarah 255, Adeline 255, Alfred 255, Alfred J. (Dr.) 168, Anna 255, Bill 255, Clifford 255, Diane 255, Dr. Alfred 225, Edith E. 255, Emma 255, Gladys 255, Grace 255, James 255, John 255, Martha 255, Mary Ann 255, Ragene 255, Wm. Alfred 255
RAMBO, Catherine 176, Ernest 151, Flossie E. 223, Hannah 202, Hazel 151, Hulda 133, Mariah 202, rebecca 176, Solomon 202.
RAMSAROOP, Chanadaye 305.
RANARD, Barbara 138, Jim (Rev.) 246.
RANDALL, Dan 284, Darlene Jo 155, Hugh Francis 155, Karen 284, Mark Anthony 155.
RAREDON, William M. 174.
RARIDEN, Almira 280, Anna 255, Charles 255, Cleanor 255, Frank 255, Jefferson 255, John 255, John William 255, Margaret 255, Minerva 255, Rosa 255, Vinnie 173, Vinnie Minerva 255, Walter 243, 255, William 255.
RATLIFF, Eliza 206.
RAUSCH, John Adams 263.
RAWLINGS, Louisa 300, William 170.
RAY, Brenda 252, Derek 252, Nancy 226.
REA, Barbara Sue 145, Gregory D. 145.
READ, A. A. "Lonnie" 255, Alice 255, Allis Jane 255, Alonzo 135, 256, Alonzo Wilson 255, Amanda 256, Amanda Isabel 255, Annis Caroline 255, Arena 135, Bertha A. 256, Beryle 256, Bessie Bell 255, Candance Lynn 256, Chester, 287, Chester Lowell 256, Delbert 287, Delphine 135, Dolla 256, Edith 256, Elizabeth 183, 184, 255, Evonne Lou 256, Floyd Wheeler 287, Ida L. M. 255, James 255, 256, James Delbert 256, James Harvey 255, Jim 256, Joseph 255, Laura 256, Lester 287, Lester Noel 256, Louis Eugene 255, Margaret 256, Margie Sue 256, Mary 135, Mary 256, Mary E. 255, Mary Estella 255, 256, Murnal 256, Myrtie Mae 255, Ora Ellia 255, Prudy Ann 255, Rosa Pearl 255, Ross 256, William Lonzo 255, William Oval 255, Wilson Rosley 256, Wilson Ross 135, 255.
REARDON, Franklin 280.
RECORDS, Agnes 267, John (Dr.) 267.
RECTOR, Mary Jane 165.
REDDINGTON, M. 261.
REED, Enoch 190, Lawrence 199, Leona Idessa 193, 195, Mary 193, Sondra 199.
REES, Mr. 206.
REESE, Jesse Elois 189.
REEVE, Andrew Hart 256, Daniel Hart 256, Edwin 256, Edwin A. 256, Helen 224, 256, 275, Helen H. 305, Henry Jeanneret 256, Hiram 256, John 256, Kenneth 192, 224, 275, Kenneth J. 256, 305, Kenneth Jeanneret 256, Lee DeCourcy 256, Muriel E. 256, Norman H. 256, Sarah 256, Susan 256, Alexander 289, Charles 209, Darrell 199, Eunice 168, James 229, Lydia 289, Mary 182, Mary Etta 209, Rebecca 168, 249, Rosa 216, 261, Sarah 309, 229, William 168.
REICHARD, Archibald 179, Charles 232, Charles A. 295, Martha May 179, Samuel 232.
REICHMANN, Augustus R. 256, Eb 257, Eberhard 256, Maria 256, Maria Ingrid 256, Robert Anthony 257, Ruth 256, 257.
REISCHER, Elizabeth 263.
REITZEL, Gloria Starr 236.
REJKO, Becky 257, 258, Casey Jo 257, 258, Christen Michel 257, Christopher 258, Darryl 257, 258, Jesse 170, 257, 258, Joanne 258, Karen 257, 257, Kyle 258, Mike 257, Paul 181, 257, 257, Sue 170, 257, Sue Davis 258, Veronica 257, Wanda 181, 257.
RENIHAN, Mary Johanna 155.
RENNER, David 199, Eric 199, Katherine 177, Vonnie 300.
REPP, Jonathan Willis 222, Marilyn A. 222, Pamela Sue 222.
REPPERT, Cindy Louise 136.
RESSEGUIE, Sally 240.
REYNOLDS, Amy 133, 167, Bob 170, Celinda 170, Elvira 201, Ingham 170, Lavina Ann 264, Marlene 170, Marti 170, Mary 170, Mary Etta 155, Nancy 255, Samuel 162, William H. 264.
RHOADES, Donna 132.
RHODES, James 195 .
RHUDE, Cassie Mable 150, Doris Louise 264, 306, Gerald Leon 264, Jacob D. Jr. 150, Jacob Douglas Sr. 197, 150, 263, 306, Martha Ellen 150, 197, 263, Mary Martha 150, 264, Norma Arlene 264, Wilma Marie 264.
RICE, Catherine 288, Dr. Charles 200, John 281, Joseph 202, Nancy 200, Sarah Ann 269, Sir Edmund 200.
RICHARD, Anne 166, James Michael 166, Mary Louise 305.
RICHARDS, Abigail 258, Angeline 258, Anna 258, Anna Ellen 150, Bob 258, Calvin 150, 258, Charles 252, Charles Glen 269, Claytana Jean 258, Clover Phillips 204, Columbus 258, Commodore Perru 258, Conrad 150, 258, Cymentha 235, Darlene 258, David 190, 258, Donald 258, Elaine 258, Eli 258, Elmer 258, Elmer Ray 150, Elvira 165, Ester 285, Ethel 302, Fay 258, Faye 150, Faye Louise 150, George 258, Goldie 303, Hannah E. 155, Harold 150, 258, Helen, 150, 258, Jamie 258, Jeanette 258, Jesse 150, 190, 258, Joanna 150, John 150, 158, John Lewis 150, Joseph R. 258, Joshua 258, Julius 150, 155, 258, Kathern Darlene 150, Leo 258, Leonard 150, Leroy Foster 258, Lockie 258, Lucinda 258, M. J. 279, Mabel 150, 258, Mabel Edith 220, Marion 258, Mary 155, 258, Mary Helen 150, Mary Jane 204, 217, 269, 287, Melvin 150, 258, Michael 258, Milton 150, 220, 158, Nancy 134, Naomi 150, 258, Neil 258, Otis, 180, Phillip 258, Robert 150, 258, Sandra 158, Sarah 258, Scott 150, 258, Steven 258, Velma 258, Viola 150, 220, 258, W. S. 185, Will 235, William 180, 258, Winfield Scott 150, 258.
RICHARDSON, Abrilla 259, Andrea Jo 259, Andrew 258, Anna 259, Anne 258, Bert 258, Bertha 280, Cecil 258, Cora B. 300, Cord 204, 259, Cordelia 259, 293, Daniel Ray 259, Deborah Ann 258, Della Frances 259, Dote 204, Edna Mae 259, Edna Pearl 244, Edna S. 189, 259, Elizabeth 258, George 258, Glenn 189, 159, Granny 259, Harol Ray 259, Iris 259, Jacob 258, Jacob Hiram 259, James Dale 259, Jane 254, 258, 259, Janice 298, Jeff 267, Jeffrey Patrick 259, Jeremiah 143, 235, 258, 259, Joel 258, John 258, 259, John A. 200, 258, Johnny Dale 259, Jonathan 258, Josh Dale 259, Joshua 258, Kayla Sue 216, Kristy 267, Laura 258, Lena 212, 246, Lester 258, Lettila 258, Lettus 258, Leva Olive 211, Lewis 258, 259, Louellen 235, 259, Lucretia 258, Mack 259, 260, Margaret 258, Martha 259, Martha Ann 259, Mary 143, 258, 259, Mary Agnes 259, Mary Ellen 259, Mary Florence 294, Mary Jane 258, Mary Lou 258, Matilda Jane 300, Max Lee 259, Michael Dale 259, Millie 259, Millie Frances 142, 200, Milly 258, Myrtle 258, 262, Nancy 161, 200, 258, 259, Nancy Anne 258, Orville 258, Permelia Jane 235, 259, Pernetia 310, Robert Glenn 259, Samuel 258, Sara Joella 259, Sarah 258, Scott 216, Sharon Jean 259, Steven Lee 259, Thoman 161, 200, 258, 259, Vivian 258, Wendell 258, William 258, William Glenn 259, William Mack 259, Wilma 258.
RICHART, Gertrude May 300, Jennings 300.
RICHEY Ida May 161, Millie 143, Taylor 143, 161.
RICHART, Beth 138.
RICHLE, Mary 175.
RICHMOND, Nancy 133.
RICKARD, James L. 234, Nellie 234, R. Mina 234.
RIDDLE, James Harold 175, Janae Leeann 175, Jennifer Ann 175, Jill Susan 175.
RIDENOUR, Maude Della 295.
RIDER, Frank A. 251, Hattie Calista 251, Henry 251, Ruth Amy 251.
RIECE, Sarah 153.
RIGGINS, Amy Lynn 222, Andy 260, Blanche 161, 260.
RIGGS, Gilber 182, Kenneth 211.
RIGHTMIER, Sarah R. 185.
RIGLEN, Ellen 260.
RIGLEY, Frederick 159, Frederick W. 260, Jeanette G. 260, Jeanette 159, Joan 260.
RILEY, Edna Sue 310, James Whitcomb 204, Lena Ellen 182.
RING, Annie Sophia 251.
RINKER, John Wesley 179.
RIPPY, Nancy 304.
RITCHEY, Ida May 260, Millie 200, Mr. 200.
RITCHIE, Cathey Lynn 175, Heather Noelle 175, James Lemont 175, James Mark 175, Stephanie Lynn 175.
RITTENHOUSE, Ellen 303, William Sr. 222.
RITTER, Brandon260, Breanna 260, Carl H., Jr. 260, Carl Harry 260, Elizabeth 260, Eugene 260, Gene, Jr 260, Glenn 260, Hans 260, Harry 260, Jade 260, Joan 260, Kurt 260, Leslie 260, Madeline 260, Mark 260, Richard 260, Thomas James 260.
RITZLER, Margaret Salome 140.
RIVERS, Linda 259.
ROACH, Martha 301.
ROATH, Albert J. 143, Evangeline C. 143, Lydia 143.
ROBBINS, Claud 249, Kenneth Woodrow 168, Mary C. 168, Sarah 267.
ROBERSON, James 199.
ROBERT, Lee 212, Susann 212.
ROBERTS, Anita Malvina 261, 282, Anna 261, Anna Belle 261, Annie Irene 260, Beatrice 182, Becky 291, Bruce 291, C. J. 178, Charles 235, Chester 210, Chud 242, Clara 260, 261, Clara Mae 182, Clarence 235, Darla 151, Darlene 258, Dorothy 260, Dorval Pauline 184, Edell 235, Elmer 261, Evaline 274, Fred 274, George Melvin 235, 261, Glenn 260, Glenn O. 260, 282, Grace 162, Hazel 235, Homer c. 261, Hugh D. 261, Ida 274, Jackie Glenn 261, 282, Jacob 274, Jane 141, Janet Rosalyn 261, 282, Jerald 287, John W. 261, Johnny 235, Joseph 141, 261, Joseph w. 231, Kay 291, Laura 194, Lois Ann 261, 282, Loretta Kay 287, Lucy b. 261, Mamie 261, 274, Mary 213, 282, Mary Ellen 283, May 235, 274, Minerva 213, Nancy E. 141, Nettie Pauline 155, Nicholas 235, 261, Nick 140, Olive Ballucia 203, Otha 216, 235, Otha St. 260, Otha Jr. 260, Penny 291, Rachel 260, Rachel Sophroni 216, Rebecca 261, Rhoda Pearl 260, Rosa 216, 260, Roy 261, Ruth 274, Sarah E. 168, 261, Steven 291, Susan Petro 261, Thomas 282, Thomas Leon 261, 282, Wanda 260, Wayne 235, William D. 213, William S. 154, 261, Wilma Lois 184, Winifred 260.
ROBERTSON, Al 187, Andrew 268, Annie 185, Arthur 185, Bertha Ann 144, 146, 172, Cather. (Katie) 155, Catherine 261, Charles E. 261, Clairborne 261, Daniel 258, Esther E. 261, Florence Belle 186, France 261, Fred 261, Gabriella 180, George 172, Grace 187, James Monroe 146, John 248, John Wesley 187, Lazarus 261, Mary 220, 261, Mary Catherine 169, Nancy Ann 187, Ora 261, Perry 172, Robert 248, Sally 146, Sara Alice 311, 261, Sarah 261, Stephen 261, Viola 150, 220, 258, Walter 144, William C. 261.
ROBEY, Phyllis Jean 308.
ROBINSON, Angela Jill 149, Elsie 261, George 223, Louisa 223, Mary Marlett 223, Robert E. 261, Robert Thomas 261, Viola 261.
ROCKHOLD, Charlene 177, 239.
RODGERS, Becky 287, David 150, Fay 150, Frank 204, Frankie 287, Gladys 262, 287, Gladys M. 259, John R. 262, John Wesley 150, 262, Johnathan 150, Linda 150, Lisa 287, Martha 142, 150, Mary Jane 150, 262, 269, Millie Jane 150, Nancy 150, Nancy Ellen 262, Olive Robin 142, Ray (Sonny) 287, Ray edgar 262, Ray Edward 150, Ray Jr. 150, Ruth 150, Ruth Marie 262, Scott 150, Will James 142.
RODY, Rebecca 149.
ROE, Jane 174, 278.
ROGERS, Andrew Jackson 208, Andy 178, Anna 172, Aquilla 154, 170, Bessie 189, Catherine Brown 262, Cecil r. 230, Cecil Ray 262, Celia 229, 262, Clover Lorraine 250, 269, Clyde 238, Cora 262, Cynthia Carolin 262, Cynthis C. 229, David 170, Della 238, Diane Lee 250, Diane Lu 269, Ethel 262, George W. 261, Hannah 170, Helen 262, Henry 170, Jack 140, 208, James 170, 261, James Swift 262, Jewel Wayne 269, 287, 250, Joselyn 301, Lewis 170, 262, Loyd Eugene, 262, Lucile 262, Mabel 161, Mable 262, Margaret 170, 192, Margaret Jane 304, Mary 262, Mary 304, Mary Alice 248, Mary Jane 250, 269, 287, Mary Olive 147, Meredith 185, 230, 262, Mildred Rose 262, Mrs. Henry, 185, Myrtle 259, 262, Nancy 262, Orval 262, Parilda Siscoe 170, Parilla 170, Paul 259, 262, Peggy 304, 262, Polly 304, Rachel 133, Ralph 220, 262, Ruth 262, Sarah 171, Saramae 261, Shana 287, Shana LaVerne 250, 269, Stefan 301, Susannah 248, Tammy 196, Trigger 262, Walter 262, Wilbur 262, William 262, 301, William Paul 185, 230, 262.
ROHL, Wanda 219.
ROHRER,Henry 294, Susannah 294.
ROLAND, Grace 250, John 250.
ROLLINS, Alexander 151, Douglas 151, Emily 151, Jennifer Lynn 151, Justin 151.
ROONEY, Clara 293, 298.
ROOSEVELT, Eleanor 269, Franklin D. 302.
RORK,Elmer James 246, Gladys 246, Marjorie 246.
ROSCOE, Beryl 262, Carrie 262, Charles 262, Dorothy 262, Glenn 184, Harold 262, Helen 262, Lloyd 262, Paul 262, Reba 262, Robert 262, Sharon 262, Sherman 262.
ROSE, Alonzo 293, Alvin F. 293, Betty 191, Blanche 191, Caroline 191, Carolyn 244, Charles 191, Cindy Harvey 308, Clara Edith 293, Clarence V. 293, Cynthia Harvey 308, Dorothy 191, Elizabeth 239, Hattie Jane 293, Henry 191, 239, James Findley 293, Jessie B. 293, Olive 191, Oma 191, Oma a. 293, Omer C. 293, Rosalie 239.
ROSENBERGER, Martha 133.
ROSS, Ben R. (Dr.) 285, Carrie Etta 202, Donal 285, Henry 285, James 285, Julia 285, Marjorie 299, Mary Ellen 172.
ROTH, Hedwig 195.
ROTINO, Alice 184, Brenda 221, Cherlynn 221, Diana 184, Kevin 184, Krystal 184, Margee 184, Marilyn 221, Morgan 184, Phillip 221, Phyllis 184. Rick 184, William II 184, William Joseph 184.
ROUSE, Elizabeth 201, Freddie 217, Karen 217, Morris 217, Thomas 201.
ROUSH, Ada 263, Amanda Emma 263, Betty 263, Blanche 263, Brenda 263, Carolyn 299, Charles Edward 262, Charles Kevin 263, Craig 235, Craig Edward 263, Elizabeth 183, 263, Elizabeth M. 239, Eva 263, George 263, George W. 158, 263, Grace 263, Hannah Jane 263, James Boston 263, Jessie 263, Kevin 235, Lottie Alice 263, Margaret 158, Mary 263, Mary Elizabeth 135, 263, Mary Pearl 158, Matilda 263, Nicholas 263, Paul 263, Susie 141, 235, 263, Thomas Jeff. 263, William 263, William H. 263.
ROVINE, Helen 298.
ROWLEY, Content 310, Deborah 310, John 310, Moses, Sr. 310.
ROYSE, Alice 176.
RUBECK, Mildred 148.
RUDD, Aaron 235, Andy 235, Marilyn 141, 235.
RUDE, (See also Rhude) Andrew 264, Asher 264, Cela 264, Elizabeth 264, Jacob Douglas 264, John 264, Lavina Ann 264, Martha 238, Martha Ann 264, Martha Ellen 264, Mary Jane 238, 264, Nancy 264, Rachel 264, Ruth Matilda 264, Sarah 214, 264, Sarah Elizabeth 238, Syntha Ann 264, Thomas 238, 264, William 264, Worden 264, Zaccahariah 264.
RUDOLPH, Martha 176.
RUDYARD, Henry Clay 306.
RUGGLES, Leonard 160.
RUMPH, Melvin 188.
RUMSEY, Beryl 155.
RUND, Annette 266, Arthur 264, Arthur Lee 265, Bert 265, Bessie 265, Carolyn 266, David 265, Delmer 264, 265, Delmer E. 264, 265, Donna 265, Donna Elaine 145, Early 265, Edith 265, Eliza Jane 280, Elizabeth 264, 265, Elmer 265, Emma 265, Evelyn 265, Flora 265, Flora May 228, 229, Forest 265, France 278, Francis 265, Grace 265, Hammond 280, Hannah 265, Helen 220, Herman Hayer 265, Hubert 265, James 265, Jane 280, Jessie 265, Lee Otis 265, Louis 265, Louis Albert, 265, Margaret 265, Martha 265, Mary 265, Melvin 265, Mun Eu 264, Ora E. 265, Oscar Barzillar 265, Robert 264, 265, Robert Wayne 265, Roy 265, Sally Lee 265, Samuel 264, Theodore 265, Theresa 265, Victor 266, Victor Glenn 266.
RUSH, Lucy 300.
RUSSEL, Parson 291, Anna Merle 167, Cindy 291, Edith Bessie 294, Hattie 304, Jane Washington 193, Jeanadelle 166, Lewis Samuel 167, Susan J. 291.
RUSSO, Frank 178.
RYBLOT, Franklin James 271, James W. 271, Laura Belle 192, 271, Linda Lou 271, LMae 271, Ray 271, Wanda 271.
RYKER, Paul 226.

SABATIER, Betty Belle 220, 266, Carmileta 266, David 266, Doris 220, Janet 266, Lu Ann 266, Maurice 266, Ramona 266.
SACKRIDER, Amanda 231.
SADLER, Wendy 221.
SAFFEL, Elizabeth 141.
SAFFELL, Mary E. 165.
SAMPLE, Beverly 285, Gerald 285.
SANBORN, Evelyn 301, Evelyn Cook 165.
SANDERS, Ada Louise 266, 296, Arthur 266, Arthur Dale 266, Arthur Lee 266, Bette 266, Bobby 266, Brian Leslie 253, Carrie 266, Dale 266, Dale Veloris 266, Darryl 266, David 266, Deborah Elaine 266, Debra Sue 253, Delores 266, 267, Dennis Wayne 253, Donna 266, Doris 266, Dorothy 266, Edith Mae 266, 267, Eileen 266, Elizabeth Ann 253, Emma 266, 267, Esther 266, Esther Caroline 253, Faith 266, Gary 266, Grace 266, Gracie 266, Helen 232, 266, 267, 310, 311, Helen Ione 266, Jennifer Marie 253, John Dennis 266, Joseph 266, Joseph Aaron 179, Kenneth 266, Kenneth E. 266, Kenneth Ray 266, Kenny 266, Larry 266, Leslie 266, 267, Leslie Marlowe 253, Lois M. 228, Lois Marie 253, Ludeana 219, Marlene 266, Marolowe 266, 267, Marvel 266, 267, Marvel Estella 267, Marvin Leslie 253, Megan Desiree 179, Myrtis 266, 267, Napolean 266, Napoleon 267, Napoleon Miles 266, Nathan 266, Nathan Daniel 253, Pam 266, Pamela Corinne 266, Randy Joe 266, Raymond 266, Rev. David 179, Rex 266, Richard 266, 267, Roger Dale 266, Roy Nathan 253, Sarah 156, Shaunna 219, Terry Leon 253, Warren 266, William Darren 266, Wright 266.
SAUERHEBER, Bertha 308, Dessie 308, Dexter Patrick 308, June Marie 308
SAUNDERS, Daniel 267, Isabella 267, James 267, John 267, Kate 158, Mary Ann 267, Peter 267, Rachel 267, Sarah 267.
SAVAGE, Elizabeth 156, Joan Ann Hill 207, Thomas 208.
SAXLEY, Esther 292.
SAYER, Clara Hannah 140, William Elmer 140.
SAYERRE, Ruth Sabrina 140.
SCAGGS, Nora 295.
SCALES, Lillie 186.
SCALF, Bertha 267, Beulah 267, Donny 267, Dudley 267, Jim 267, Judie 267, Judy 267, Randy 267, Ray 267, Ronny 267.
SCAMAHORN, Cleo 231, Virgil 231.
SCHABEL, Clara Josephine 236.
SCHAEFFER, Joseph 272.
SCHAFFER, Mary 241.
SCHICKENDANTZ, M. Donald (II) 169, Mark (II) 169.
SCHIELER, Ada Marie 209, John 209, Marie 209.
SCHISLER,Catherine 181.
SCHMALZ, Deborah, 291, Mary Beth 291, Richard 291, Susabelle 291, Marie Catherine 136, Maried Elizabeth 178.
SCHNAITER, Harmon 280, Herman 280.
SCHNATZMEIER, Opan 262.
SCHNEIDER, Betty 268, Herman 267, Kenneth (Dr.) 146, William 267.
SCHOENTRUP, Andrew 268, Carl Joseph 268, Dale 268, Dorthy Lou 268, Elizabeth 268, Iraina 268, Karla 268, Leisa 268, Leslee 268, Lori 268, Lymon 268, Lynne 268, Mary Margaret 268, Rita Marie 268, Robert 268, Samuel 268, Sandra 268, William Rhea 268.
SCHOFIED, Tina M. 301.
SCHRADER, Mary 190.
SCHRICKER, Henry 247.
SCHRINER, Mary 183.
SCHROCK, Margaret 255, Pearl Leila 295, 228.
SCHROEDER, Henry (Mrs.) 231, Irene 133.
SCHROGHAM, Catherine 271, Albert 268, Benton 268, Catherine 243, 268, Charles 243, 268, Clovis 268, Daniel 268, Dorothy 174, 243, Edwin 168, Eva 268, Fay 268, George Washington 268, Harry 164, 243, Harry 243, Ida May 243, Isaac Marshall, 268, Jackson 268, James 268, Lewis 268, Mabel 243, Mabel Clare 164, Mary 268, Mary Polly 268, Merril 268, Merrill 311, Minnie 268, 271, Nancy Jane 268, Nellie 243, Omar 243, 268, Parnelia 268, Pierson Murphy 268, Prudence 268, Ralph 268, Raymond 268, Reba 164, Thomas 268, Vincent 243, 268, 271, Warren 268, William 268, William H. 268.
SCHULTZ, Jesse Elizabeth 213, Kelley Erin 213, Marianne 213, Stanton G. 213, Wm. Morrison 213.
SCHULZ, Adolph 260, Alberta 260.
SCHWAB, Ollie 158.
SCOTT, Diane Lee 250, Dorothy 291, Ethan Evan 269, Harriett 291, James William 269, Jay 269, Julie 207, Kathryn 287, Kay 291, Marcelyn 291, Margaret C. 136, Phil 291, Phil Gordon 291, Phoebe Jane 188, Samuel 198, Scotty 291.
SCOVELL, Ruth E. 167.
SCRIPTURE, Mis. 244.
SCROGHAM, Ben 219, Columbus 219, Emmett 219, Clorabell 219, Irene 219, Mellie 219, Ollie 280, Ernest 163, 268, Gerald 276, Henry 269, 280, Jane 269, Judith 163, Judith Mae 269, Lynn 229, Merle 269, Millard 269, Ralph 296, Ray 269, Ruth 274, Sharon Anne 269, Velma 163, 268.
SCRUGGS, David 196, Dewell 196.
SEAL, Barbara 236, Clara 236, David William 236, Joe 236, John Thomas 236, Margaret 236, Mary Helen 236, Solomon 165, Thomas William 236, William Dale 236.
SEE, Margaret 312.
SEELEY, Edna 284, Joanne 284, Kenneth Mayne 284.
SEELY, Diane 229.
SEIB, Johann Carl 276.
SEIBEL, Dr. 204, 307.
SEIBERT, Mark 246, Polly Ann 246.
SEILER, Elizabeth 147.
SEIP, Mary Lynn 305.
SEITZ, Anna Mary 269, Barbara 270, Catherine 237, 269, Cecil Ray 269, Charles H. 269, Charles Henry 269, Charles Ray 270, Ferne Lucille 269, Filomena Mary 269, Henry Bernard 269, Henry Bernhardt 269, Hesper Leona 269, Hildreth 270, Irene Blanche 270, John Bernard 269, Josephine Mary 269, Katarina 269, Kathleen 238, Kathy 270, Kenneth 270, Kenneth Ray 238, 270, Kortney Robert 270, Kourtney Robert 238, Kristina R. 238, 270, Leatha 298, Leatha E. 269, Lucetta M. E. 269, Mary Catherine 269, 280, Mary O. 269, Ruth 166, 270, Warren G. 269, William 270, William Cecil 270, William Henry 269.
SELLARS, Wilbur 227.
SELLS, Lucy 210, 299.
SENESAC, Amy 157, Caren 157, Don 157, Matthew 157.
SETSER, Albert J. 281, Albert Joshua 270, Albertis 270, Amanda H. 270, Beatrice 270, Cale 270, Caleb 270, Charles 270, Chase 270, Dean 270, Elisha 270, Elizabeth 270, George 159, 270, Ida Carter 270, Jane 191, John 270, John Pinkney 270, Joseph 270, Katie 270, Levina 270, Lillian 270, Lizzie 270, Lottie Alice 263, Luzetta 270, Martha 270, Marthey 270, Mary 270, Mirian 270, Naomi 270, Nona Edna 270, Paul 270, Pauline 270, Pearly 270, Rachel 270, Ruth 270, Scott 270, Thomas 270, Walter 270, William Paten 270, Winfrey Lutes 270.
SETTER, Gladys 291.
SETTLE, 218, Bertha Viola 271, Camilla 286, Charles E. 271, Cora A. 271, Daniel 286, Daniel R. 271, 279, Edward 286, Elaner Jane 271, Ella May 271, Frances 270, Francis 270, 279, Hannah M. 133, Hannah Mary 271, Helen 271, Hiram 271, Isabell 271, James Alexander 271, James Wesley 271, James William 270, 279, Jeanette 286, Jesse Oral 271, Jime, 271, John 271, Leonard 286, Lewis 271, Lydia Ann 279, Margaret Jane 271, Margaret Olive 279, Morris 271, Randall 286, Ray E. 271, Robert 286, Sarrah 271, Thomas 271, Ulysses Jake 271, Walker 271, William 270.
SETTLES, Amelia 269, Christine 268, Elnora 165, Hannah Mary 243, Harold 165, Jake 268, James 269, Jane 269, Ulysses 268, Wesley 165.
SEWAL, Zetta 284.
SEWARD, Elizabeth 153.
SEXTON, David 172, James A. 271, Kathy F. 302, Laura B. 271, Lucille 305, Milton 271, Minnie Jane 304, Rachel 172, Sarah Jane 186.
SEYFRIED, Ray 230.
SHAEFER, Emma 281.
SHAFER, Al, 272, Alice 271, Anna 272, Blanche 272, Campsadell A. 271, Charles F. 272, Cora 272, Eliza 210, Elizabeth 215, Floyd Harland 271, Hazel 272, Hesper Louise 271, Hilda Mae 271, Ira 271, Isabell 271, James Faucett 271, 272, James Junior 271, John William 271, Joseph 271, Joseph "Dode" 272, Julia Ann 271, June Rose 271, Mary Margaret 271, Robert Herrod 271, Viola 272.
SHAFFER, Daniel 268, Patricia 268, Robert 268.
SHANKS, Annabelle 216.
SHANNON, Captain 207.
SHARP, Allen 272, Crystal C. 272, Frances Louise 272, Kathleen 161, Mary Lynne 288, Robert L. 272, Samuel 272, Scarlet F. 272.
SHARPE, Daniel E. 253, Sheryl May 253.
SHATTO, Daniel 296, Mary Jane 296, Maude Ann 296.
SHAW, Betty Jane 136, Michael 136, Nellie Frances 136, Warren K. 136.
SHEFFER, Albert 225, Betty J. 225, Ervin A. 225, Faye L. 225, Hattie 225.
SHELA, Martha Ellen 150.
SHELBY, Evan 132, Isaac 132, Mary 132.
SHELENBURGER, Catharine 285.
SHELTON, Beulah May 188, Nellie Elizabeth 188.
SHEPARD, Lois 244.
SHEPHERD, Alexander 273, Alexander A. 273, Alice 272, Ansel 273, Bertha Alice 273, Blanche L. 147, Charles 273, Charles Auburn 273, Charles W. 273, Charles Wesley, 206, 272, 273, 274, Christena 168, Clara 272, Clara Bell 273, Clara May 273, Elizabeth 231, 272, 274, Elizabeth Ann 273, Elizabeth May 273, Elwin 273, George Melvin 273, Grace 273, John W. 273, Julia 272, Julia Ann 273, Letitia 273, Lillie May 168, Lowell 273, Margaret Jane 273, Martha 273, Mary Alice 231, 273, Mary Elizabeth 274, May 272, Pearl Mae 231, 274, Stella Alice 274, Thelma 273, Thomas 168, Thomas 273, Tich 206, Tish 274, Victor 231, 274, Wes 206, 272, 274, Wesley 273, Will 231, William 231, 272, 273, William 274, William Clyde 273, William F. 272, 273, Wilma 231, 274.
SHERLOCK, Luzetta Mae 309.
SHERMAN, Bessie 222, Cindee 140, General 295.
SHERRILL, Lona May 163.
SHERWOOD, Adam 227, Blanche 227, Comfort 227, Elizabeth 227, Jane 227, 228, Jane Antoinette 229, John 227, Maria Jane 227, Mary Alice 227, Maureen 229, Melinda Lee 229, Michael 229, Mollie 227, Monica 229, Vincent A. 230, William Vincent 229
SHICK, Elizabeth Ellen 275.
SHIELDS, Ben 278, Benjamin Warner 278, Bertha 278, Clarence 278, Earl 278, Evelyn 278, Goldie Cecil 276, Harold F. 172, Helen 278, Hugh 278, Jenny 278, Madeline 172, Mary Jane 172, Myrtle 308, Rosa May 278, Rosetta 172, Susan 278, William 276, 278, Martha Ellen 262.
SHILEY, Rosella 218.
SHINGLES, Curly Jr. 306.
SHIPLEY, 193, Abasha 275, Bashaba, 274, Batherin 248, 274, Charles 274, Elender 274, Elender Ella 275, Elizabeth 274, Emmarine 304, Florence E. 275, Florence M. 274, 275, Hiram 275, Isaac 274, 275, James Jacob 274, Jesse 304, Jesse W. 191, 275, Jesse W. Jr. 274, Jesse W. Sr. 274, John 275, John W. 274, 275, Levi 274, 275, Margaret 275, Margaret May 192, 274, Marriott 275, Mary 274, Mary Ann 191, 274, Mary Polly 275, Nelson 275, Nora 274, Samuel J. 275, Sarah E. 274, 275, Sylvania Ann 274, 275.
SHIPP, Martha Jane 147.
SHIRE, Clara 273, Durward 273, Eli Albert 273, Fred 273, Glynn 273, Ivan 273, Lowell W. 273, Lucy 273, Paul 273, Wesley 273.
SHIRK, Anna 272.
SHOEMAKER, Nancy 268.
SHOENFIELD, John 159, Zelma 159.
SHORT, Bart 171.
SHORTRIDGE, Margaret 285.
SHRANZE, Mary 163.
SHROCK, Emma 255.
SHROYER, Dean 219, Ludeana 219, Wanda 219.
SHULTS, Elizabeth 238, Ellen J. 238, Henry 238.
SHULZ, Ada W. 214, Alolph 148.
SHUPERT, Elizabeth 190.
SICHTING,Chester 201, Mandi Lynn 201, Matthew John 201, Pamela 201, Teddy John 201.
SICOLA, Cary 291, Kenneth 291, Margaret Ann 291, Tracy 291.
SIDDIQ, Bob 275, Mir 275, Patricia 275, Sharif 275, Tim 275.
SIDDIQ-HUSSAINI, Mohammed 275.
SIEBENECK,Alisa 204, Kay Lynn 204.
SIMMONS, Alexander P. 276, Carole Lynn 275, 276, 277, Clarence 275, Clarence P. 275, 277, Dorothy Rae 275, 276, 277, Eliza 275, Emma 275, Joanna Lee 275, 277, Joanna Leo 276, Josephine Myrtle 275, Josephine 275, Josephine M. 276, 277, Mary 275, Mamie 275, Patrick 275, Wallace 275.
SIMMS, Judy 262.
SIMONS, Comfort 228, Cora 235, Elizabeth 168, Samaria 235.
SIMONTON, Vinnie 216.
SIMPSON, Bob 170, Delpha 170, Eliza 289, Owen 288, 289, Pearl 170, Rebecca Sue 237, Ruth Mable 149, Sarah 289, Virgie 150, William 289.
SIMS, JoAnn 182, Peggy 176.
SIMSON, Eliza 288, Sarah 288.
SINCLAIR, Aaron 264, Donald Fleming 252, Ian 252, Julianna 264, Kimberly 208, Neil Gow 252, Thomas 264.
SINGLETON, Mary Ellen 169.
SINN,Caroline 244, Carolyn Rose 244, Charles 191, Earl 1919, Ernest 1919, Estle 191, F. Wesley 191, Frederick 172, 1919, Frederick W. 191, Grace 191, Jessie 191, Laura 191, Lila 191, Mary 191, Mary Rosetta 144, 172, 191, Morris 191, 244, Olive 191, Paul 191, Ray 191, Rebecca 191, Samuel 191, Savanah 191, Wesley Junior, 191, Cleo 191.
SIPE, Catherine E. 165, Christopher 165.
SIPES,Addie Claude L. 276, Albert F. 132, Albert Franklin 276, Alpha 226, Amanda 285, Catherine 197, 264, 276, Charles 276, Christopher 264, Clarence 187, Daniel 187, Dorothy Joan 261, Doshie 187, Drewilla Ann 276, Edgar Thomas 276, Edith 171, 187, Elizabeth 276, Elizabeth Jane 132, 276, Emma Susan 162, 276, Frank 226, 276, George Michael 276, George Washington 276, Grace 187, H. Franklin 276, Henry 276, Henry Adams 276, James Marion 276, Jennie Pegg 276, John 276, Lova 187, Lucinda 164, Mary 276, Mary Jane 285, Mary Rose 276, Patsey 279, Patsy 276, Peral 187, Phoebe 191, Rachel 276, Rachel Jane 276, Sarah Jane 276, Singleton 187, 285, Viola 187, William 276.
SISCOE, Gladys Viola 298, Parilda 170, Perilda 262, William 170.
SISSON, Alvin 276, Betty 304, Catherine 276, Chelsea 304, 276, David Benjamin 284, Donna 284, Donnie 284, Emma 276, Gary 284, Harry 276, Helen 276, Jant 284, Kimber 284, Lester 276, Lloyd 276, 284, Lysia Ann 282, Marolyn 276, Marjorie 276, Mary 276, Misty 284, Nellie 276, Phyllis 276, Rebecca 276, 282, Robert 276, Roger, 284, Rosemary 304, Thelma 276, Thomas Dwight 284, Tyler 284, Virgil 276, Virginia 276, William 276.
SIZEMORE, Chad 158, Clarence Robert 311, Danielle 158, Diana 311, Joseph Daniel 311, Virgil 311.
SKAGGS, Olive 210.
SKINNER, Amanda 168, Catherine 238, Charlotte 218, Hannah 298, Hannah Jane 299, 300, John 286, Keith 286, Melissa 286, Minnie 286, 302, Mitilda 300, Myrtle 304, Nathaniel 237, 300, Rachel M. 237, Rhuhama, 300.
SKIRVIN, Charles Sylvester 182, Clovis Quentin 182, Elofa Irene 182, Emma Jane 182, France Olive 181, George 277, Harold 277, James Winfred 182, Joel 277, Leota 277, Lola Mae 182, Lucille Madeline 182, Marc 277, Michael 277, Newton Smith 277, Obel Estes 277, Patrick 277, Pauline Alvina 182, Samuel Alva 181, Simpson S. 277, Theresa-Terry 277, Elizabeth 277.
SKOK, Willa 161.
SLACK, Matilda 300.
SLAUGBAUGH,Anna 297, Benjamin 297.
SLAVENS,Jenny 162.
SLAYBAUGH,Corey 277, Georgeanna 277, Jack L. 277, Jennifer 277, Julia 277, Kelly 277, Kevin 277, Kris 277, Lewis 277, Margaret 277, Michael 277, Nikki 277, Richard 277, Robbie 277.
SLEDGE,Oral 298, Sadie Florence 298.
SLEIGHTER, Margaret 176.
SLEVIN,Anna 181, Cora 181, Ed 181, Manie 269, 298, Marietta 181, 269, 298, Myrtle 181, Sam 181, 299, Will 181, William P. 181, 298.
SLOANE, Judith 251.
SLUSS,B. Irene 178, Curtis 251, Eldon 251, Estella 230, Mary 132, Patricia 251.
SMALL, Howard (Rev.) 216, Nancy 199.
SMALLWOOD, Anna 190, Dee

Ann 207, Lora Jane 207, Malinda Jo 207, Marilyn 207, Paul Burton 207, Paul Douglas 207.
SMERDEL, Frank 312.
SMIDTH, Anna Marie 297, Joseph 297.
SMITH, A.L. 209, Alice 157, 179, 180, Amy Lea 207, Anna E. 295, Arlie E. 279, Art 205, Arthor Walter 277, Arthur 132, 275, Ashley 219, Bernadine Lou 167, Betty Jo 219, Beulah 277, Brenda Joyce 179, Byron 279, Captain John 208, Catherine 174, 277, 278, Charles (M.D.) 240, Charles N. 184, Christann 210, Clarence 132, 169, 277, Clayton 258, Clyde Cecil 282, Cora Jane 295, Cynthia Ann 179, D'Lema 139, 277, Dale 179, Dlema 132, Donald Clyde 207, Donald Scott 207, Donna 132, 277, Dorothy 275, 278, Dorothy Rae 277, Dwight Richard 167, Eileen 258, Elijah 279, Elizabeth 277, Elma 277, Elmer 200,216, Elva 143, Emma 288, Emma E. 295, Florence 295, Francis Felknor 277, Frederick G. 295, Gary 258, George 295, Goldie 151, Gordon C. 279, Guy E. 278, Guylia Lucille 278, Harry Damon Jr. 295, Harry Damon Sr. 295, Harvey O'Dell 278, Hazel 218, Helen 218, 279, Helen Josephine 279, Herman Roscoe 295, Jean 261, Jeanette Kay 140, Jeff 289, Jerry 278, Jim 219, John Walter 278, Johnny Ray 302, Jonathan 295, Julia Marita 282, Julie Elizabeth 180, Kevin Dale 179, Kristen 219, Kristy Lynn 289, Laura Jane 214, Lelan Oresa 279, Leota 277, Lewis 167, Lewis P. 133, Lillie 135, Linda 135, Loretta 248, Louellen 132, Louise 298, Lucille 278, Luellon 277, Luther 132, 277, Mable E. 206, Mae 163, Margaret 255, Margaret Olive 279, Marie 132, 133, 277, Marie Allen 167, Martha Jane 279, Marvey David 240, Mary 132, 258, 277, Mary Malissa 295, Melanie Dawn 278, Mike 219, Mildred 279, Mr. 191, Muriel 169, Nancy 141, 159, Nancy Gay 277, Ora Arto 279, Ora Arto Sr. 279, Oren 278, Patricia 232, Peggy 192, Rachel Adeline 295, Ralph 278, Raymond 279, Rebecca 219, 302, Richard 218, 295, Robert 278, Rodger D. 295, Ronald Gay 277, Rosa 165, Rosa Dell 300, Rosella 218, Ruth 270, Sandra 258, Sarah 267, Shadrack Monroe 279, Shelley 218, 279, Shirely Pat 282, Silas 248, Steven 207, Steven Mark 277, Susan Lynn 207, Timothy Ocle 179, Verlis Raymond 279, Vernon Willard 167, Wallace Galen 167, Wheeler 182, Winifred 209, Zachary Lyle 140.
SMITTLE, Emline 156.
SMOKER, Margaret 277.
SMUCKER, Jerome 242.
SMYTHE, Martha 265.
SNDYDER, Mary 280.
SNEAD, Lucille 195.
SNELLING, Tisha 289.
SNIDER, Aletha 268, 279, Almira 280, Bessie 279, Betsey 280, Buck 279, Cheryl 279, Cordelia 173, 280, Dessie 280, Dorothy F. 282, Ed 200, Edwin A. 279, Eliza Jane 138, 156, 267, 280, Elizabeth 155, 200, 280, 294, Elizabeth 280, Elwin Earl 279, Emma 279, Emmaline 279, Ermal Faith 279, Ethel 262, Eva Ester 279, Fred 308, Geo. Washington 267, 280, George 279, George Ella 280, Georgia 293, Harmon 267, 279, Harold Lee 279, Harold Roscoe 279, Harriet J. 203, Hazel 243, Herman 279, 280, Ina 302, Jacob 267, 280, Jacqueline 297, James 280, James Edgar 279, James William 280, Jane 139, 265, 267, Jane Evans 280, Jennifer 230, John 267, 280, John Allen 280, Josh 280, Joshua 267, 280, Laurel Clinton 279, Lester 279, Lester Jerome 268, Lewis Joshua 280, Lida Ann 280, Lidda 139, Lucinda C. 280, Maggie May 280, Martha 155, 267, Mary Elizabeth 280, Mary Gaynall 279, Mary Jane 279, Myrtle 279, Nancy 280, Naomi Ruth 279, Nellie 228, Olive Branch 279, Ollie 280, Patterson 139, Paul Arnold 279, Polly 280, Rachel 267, 280, Rachel Leigh 279, Richard 229, 293, Rosabelle 279, Ruth 243, Rutherford C. 279, Ryan Daniel 279, Sally 280, Sarah 267, 279, 280, Sarah Jane 214, Terry-(Tina) 280, Thomas 271, William 139, 155, 200, 214, 267, 279, 280, Wilma 279, Wm. W. 279.
SNIVELY, Mary Ann 136, Rachel 158.
SNODGRASS, Walter 187.
SNOW, Cera 271, Cora 271, Josiah 289, Thomas 271.
SNYDER, Betty 270, Bob 280, Charles 280, Charles Louis 280, Charles W. 280, Cindy 280, Eliza Jane 139, Elizabeth 133, Emma 226, Fanny Marie 280, Frederick 133, George 279, Herman 133, Hesper 298, Jennifer Joy 280, John 280, Joseph E. 133, Joshua 279, Kathy 280, Kevin Charles 280, Kimberly Kay 280, M. Marilyn 280, Marilyn 174, Mary E. 280, Mary Isabelle 133, Paul 280, Paul Charles 280, Punk 270, Raymond Moore 280, Robert 280, Ruth 236, Ruth Armintie 133, Sarah 271, Sharon 280, Susey 182, Uriah 133, Vanstander 133.
SOFFNER, Sophie 307.
SOUDER, Annie 185.
SOUTHERLAND, Elizabeth 222.
SOWDERS, Susan 300.
SPAHR, Joan 270, Sarah Beryl 293.
SPANGLER, Earl 213, Marguerite 213.
SPARKS, Alexander 281, Anthony 281, Ben 281, Ben III 281, Brandy 221, Chad 221, Charles 281, Donna 211, Faye 281, Jane 281, John 281, Lee 281, Leora 281, Stephen 154, 281, Timothy 281.
SPEAS, Cindy Lou 145, Jeffery Scott 145, Kayla Brooke 145, Kevin Wilson 145, Todd Wilson 145.
SPELLMEYER, Catherine 147.
SPENCE, Linda 199.
SPENCER, Alexander C. 157, Ida 206, June Mildred 200.
SPICER, Esther 292, Samuel 292.
SPIKER, Wilma 135.
SPINDLER, Carl 284, Helen 284, Mildred 284, Nellie 284, Wanda 284, Willis C. 284.
SPIRES, Sally 248.
SPRAGUE, Martha Ann 176.
SPRAY, Virginia 157.
SPRIGGS, William 180.
SPRINGER, Regina 305.
SPROUSE, Christina 149.
SPURGEON, Albertis 281, Barbara 287, Beatrice 281, Bertha Mae 281, Charles W. 281, David 140, Elizabeth 281, Elizabeth E. 281, Elvira 281, Ethel 281, Grace 281, Harriet H. 281, Jane 281, John 281, Josia 281, Luzetta 281, Maranda Jane 270, 281, Mary Frances 281, Mary L. 281, Mollie F. 281, Nora Edna 281, Orville 281, Parry 281, Sarah 287, Scott 281, Wiley 140, 281, William 281, William A. 281.
SPURLIN, Cora Anderson 187, Jacob 187.
SPURR, Charles 242, Charles Joseph 294, Cora Lee 242, Gladys Myrtle 294, Joseph 294, William 294.
SQUIRES, Andrew J. 282, Asa 280, 282, Charity 281, Clara 281, Dessie 280, Emma Destimona 280, Geniza 281, Hesper 281, Hester 200, 281, John 281, John Wesley 282, Mary 281, Mary Eliz. 281, Matilda 281, Melissa Jane 282, Sarah 281, Wesley 281.
ST. CLAIR, Julianna 197, 264.
STABB, Catherine 255.
STACKHOUSE, David W. 282, David William 282, Eunice 282, Shirley Pat 282, Stefan B. 282.
STACY, Matthew 197, Pamela Jean 197, Vance 197.
STAMPER, Deborah A. 134.
STANDISH, Capt. Miles 310.
STANFIELD, Bette 288, David 288, Larry 288. Marilyn 288, Patricia 288, Pauline 288, Robert 288.
STANLEY, Tina M. 301.
STAPLES, Amanda 247, Anna Leora 247, Nova Gladys 247, Olive Elizabeth 247, Rebecca Jane 244, Susannah 153, 244, Zachary Taylor 247.
STARK, Otto 283, Rachel A. 157.
STARR, Mary 153, Tramp 305.
STARRETT, Cora Lee 242.
STARTS, Gertrude King 215.
STEDMAN, Catherine E. 157.
STEEG, Carl W. Sr. 222, Marie 222.
STEEL, Amanda A. 282, Araminta Mariah 282, Bertha Jane 282, Catherine 282, Catherine N. 282, Charles E. 282, Effie Agnes 282, Elizabeth M. 282, Emma Caroline 286, Eunice 168, Florence J. 282, J. William 282, James Walter 282, Jas. Wm. 282, John J. 282, Lavinna C. 282, Lillie Odessa 282, 286, Lucinda B. 282, Lydia 282, Lydia Anna S. 282, Maria 282, Mariah 282, Mary 282, Mary Catherine 282, Mary E. 283, Moses Peter 282, Oscar L. 282, Otis D. 282, Rebecca 282, Rosa Fern 282, Samuel J. 282, Sarah A. 282, Sarah Cain 282, Scott 282, Thomas 282, William 282, William Alonzo 282, William J. 282, William Oliver 282.
STEELE, Anna 283, Barbara Jane 283, Beryl 155, Bonnie 155, Carmen Louetta 282, Clifford 261, 282, Clifford Lee 283, Daisy 155, Dorothy Mae 282, Edgar 155, Edna Mae 283, Eugenius 261, 282, 283, Harriet 283, Harry Foster 176, 237, Hazel Lourine 282, James 282, James A. 283, Jane 133, John 282, Kendra Kathleen 283, Lee Oral 282, Lillian 142, 155, Lucille Pauline 282, Lydia 282, Mabel 282, Margaret 282, Mary 261, 282, Mary Elizabeth 283, Mary Ellen 282, 283, Michael Thomas 283, Minnie LaVina 282, Ninian 283, Patricia 238, Peggy Ann 283, Randall Thomas 283, Samuel 283, Selma 244, 283, Stephen 283, T.C. 204, 244, 308, Theodore C. 283, Thomas 282, Thomas Allen 282, Vina 261.
STEINBARGER, Elizabeth 174, 189.
STEINBERGER, Lois Faye 237.
STEININGER, Barbara 284, Bill 283, Bradly 284, Connie 283, Donna 276, 283, Dwight 283, Forest 283, Howard 283, Judith 284, Karen 284, May 283, Ruben 283, Sophie 283, Viola 283, Wanda 284.
STEINKE, Eudora 226, Olive 226, Ted 226, William 226.
STELL, Emma Cardine 282.
STEPHENS, Anna 259, Cassie Mable 264, Cordelia 259, Edmund J. 264, Eva 230, Jerd L. 259, Jordon L. 259, Mary 261, Mittie 145, Rhoda 259, Thaney 259, Theodoshia 259.
STEPHENSON, John 276.
STEPP, Abrilla 259, Joanah 258, Melinda 171, Reuben 258.
STERLING, Anne 311, Velma 157.
STEVENS, Alice 284, Andrew 284, Bell Wavel 284, Betty 284, Brock 284, Donald James 284, Doris E. 215, Eli 290, Emogene 284, Ernest 284, Fawn 284, Goldie 242, 284, Harold 284, Homer 284, Hugh 284, James S. 284, Jane 188, Laura 284, Malcenia 221, Malinda Jane 192, Mary Beth 162, Maurice 242, 284, Pearl E. 242, Ruth 242, 284, Ruth Naomi 284, Sarah 244, Wade A. 242, 284, Wade Allen 284, Zetta 284.
STEVENSON, Susan 252, Velma 199.
STEWART, Betty Jeanne 284, David 300, Elizabeth E. 286, Jim 292, Judith Ann 284, Letitia 205, Nancy Jean 284, Robert Herman 284, Sarah E. 300, Thomas 268, Wilma 292.
STICK, Miss 259.
STICKFORD, Norma Arlene 164, Robert H. 264.
STIDD, America 149, David 149, Rebecca 149.
STIDHAM, Catherine E. 157.
STIGDON, Betty Allene 155, 284, Charity 284, Charlotte Mae 284, Donna 137, Donna LaVerne 284, Doris 137, 155, 190, 284, Elizabeth 285, Elmer Curtis 284, Geneva Fern 284, Geo. William 284, Harry Gordon 284, Hazel Pearl 284, Louis William 284, Margaret E. 284, Mary Elizabeth 284, Mildred 284, Oscar L. 284, Philip 285, Ross 137, 155, 190, 284, Ruby Mae 284, Sharon Lynn 284, Waler "Doc" 284.
STILGENBAUER, Julia 195.
STILLABOWER, 141, Adam 162, Mary Frances 176, Umphrey 215.
STINES, Dorothy 285, Herschel 285, Hurshel 171.
STINNET, Indianna 191.
STIPP, Joanna 150, Melinda 171.
STITT, Ardilla L. 270, Frances Ardella 237, Sarah 223.
STIVERS, Ann 285, Catherine 285, Eliza 285, Esther 285, George W. 285, Granville 285, Harrison Arthur 285, John William 285, Lucinda 285, Martha 285, Mary 285, Sally Ann 190.
STOCKWELL, Linda 220.
STOGDILL, Alvina Fern 285, Amanda 285, Anna 285, Audrey Kay 159, Betty Ann 309, Beulah 159, 285, Brady E. 171, Bramble 285, Brody 285, Cecil 171, 285, Clara 285, Clarena 285, David Orin, 309, Dorothy 171, 285, Drury 285, Emma 285, Ethel 285, Fairney 171, 285, Francis Marion 285, Frona 171, 285, Gertrude 285, Grace Hearth 159, Hulda 180, Iva 285, James 159, James Harvey 285, James L.R. 309, Jessee 285, Joseph Eugene 309, Kathryn M. 171, Kathryn May 188, 285, Lester 171, 285, Lilly 285, Lloyd Kenneth 309, Lou Ellen 309, Lucy 171, 285, Lula 285, Margaret 186, 285, Mariah 186, 285, Martha 285, Mary 285, Mary A. 309, Mary Ann 285, Mary E. 171, Mary Edith 285, Mary Etta 285, Mary Ida 285, Matilda 285, Mildred 285, Muhulda 285, Nancy 285, Nellie 285, Norma Marie 309, Ola 285, Otto 171, 285, Otto L. 309, Phoebe Jane 285, Polly 285, Rebecca 285, Robert 309, Samuel 285, Samuel Ray 309, Sarah 285, Sarah Jane 309, Tammy 159, Teresa 159, Thelma Jean 309, Thomas 285, Walter 285, Warren A. 309, Warren Allen 309, William S. 309, William Sherman 171, 186, 285.
STOKESBERRY, Ethel 165.
STONE, Betty 284, Eliza 275, Mary Elizabeth 274.
STONEMAN, Elizabeth Adams 222, Joshua 222.
STONER, Irvin 205.
STOOPS, Gillian 285, James A. 285, James D. 285, Julia Ross 285, Katherine A. 285, Leslie 285, Mark A. 285, Rebecca 285, Robert B. 285, Tammy 285.
STORMS, Ersie 208.
STORY, Addie 273, Albert A. 285, Bessie W. 285, Catharine 285, Clara Winifred 285, Cordilia 285, Cyrus L. 285, David Rbt. 285, David S. 285, David W. 285, Earston Ver 285, Edwin Guy 285, 286, Ella Oreva 285, Emory Grant 285, Enoch 285, Enoch Sylvester 285, Eva Mae 285, 286, Flora B. 285, George A. 285, George P. (Dr.) 285, Gracie M. 285, Jane 285, Jane C. 285, Johnny U. 285, Mandy G. 285, Martha 285, Meda I. 285, Olive Mae 285, Rosalie 285, Sabra S. 285, Sandusky 285.
STOTT, Bessier 182.
STOUT, Amanda Ethel 244, Anna 301, Lefatora 292, Maria 292, Sarah 301, Sarah Isabelle 180.
STOVER, Catherine 311.
STRADER, Earl 234, Lucille 234, Theda Maydell 234.
STRAHL, Alice 286, Annetta 302, Darrell 286, Elizabeth 295, Esther 286, Evaline S. 176, James 286, 302, Lawrence 286, Lucille 286, Margaret 286, Martin 286, Mary 286, Michael 286, Minnie 286, 302, Nellie 286, Robert 286, Tony 286, William 286
STRAHLE, Brian 286, David 286, Jeffery 286, Lawrence 286.
STRAIN, Daisy Pearl 171.
STRAIT, Abraham 242, Byron 242, Carl 242, Charles F. 242, Charlotte Ruth 242, Fanny Rita 242, John 242, Lena 242.
STRICKLAND, Robert P. 244.
STRINGER, Billy Jo 165.
STRODE, Elmer 173, John, 299.
STRONG, Frances 141, Fred 141.
STROUGH, Faye 151, Sandford 151.
STUARD, Nannie 257.
STUART, Sarah 171.
STUBER Joyce Lea 230.
STUCKER, Thomas Benton 268.
STUCKY, Delilah 239.
STULL, School 202, Campsadell A. 271, Granville, 269, Jeannette V. 298, Jeannete Viola 269, Mary Ann 272, Nettie 269, William Palmer 272.
STULTZ, Amy 149, Daniel Paul 149, Jack 149, Patricia Mae 149, Paula Elaine 149.
STUMP, Abigail 286, Abraham 286, Amanda Adella 286, Araminta 282, 286, Armitta 132, Catherine 286, Charles 159, 286, Christopher 286, Christopher F. 286, Christopher Jr. 286, Elizabeth 184, 185, 286, Elizabeth E. 286, Emma Belle 286, George Abraham 286, Isaac 286, Isaiah 286, James 286, John William 286, Lewis Fred 286, Lillie 287, Martha Eleanor 286, Mary Cath. 286, Mary Catherine 282, Millie Eliz. 286, Minerva 286, Myrtle Augusta 286, Nancy 286, Nancy Anna 286, Rebecca 286, Rebecca E. 286, Sarah Jane 286, William 132, 282, 286.
STUMPF, George 143, Katerina 143.
STURGEON, Cecil 172, Charles 172, Chester Leonard 165, Dorothy Mae 172, Elizabeth 172, Florence Edith 146, Frank 165, Gil 172, Gilbert "Gil" 203, Harley 172, Helen Louise 144, 146, James 172, Lois Marie 172, Mary Doris 172, Minverva 203, Paul 199, Rosa 165, Venetia Rose 146, Virginia Kather 165, William Cecil 146, William Paul 146.
STURKIE, Charles N. 245, Kyla E. 245.
STUYVESANT, Peter 22.
SUBLETT, Mary 232.
SULLENS, Elizabeth 170.
SULLIVAN, Ellen 168, 249, Gary L. 275, Hiram 249, Jason 275, Margaret 199, Mary 223, Michael 275, Sara 261, Shad 275, Terry 261, Vickei Lynn 275, Viola 199.
SUMAN, Carie 204.
SUMMA, Andrea 190, John E. 272.
SUMMIT, Amy 149.
SUMPTER, Debra Sue 253.
SUTTON, Ernestine 239, Hazel 263, Wilma J. 251.
SWABB, James 287, Kristy Noel

287, Shana LaVerne 250, Shane 287.
SWAIN, Henry 198, Mary 198.
SWAN, Mary 190.
SWARTZENTRUBER, Anna 297, Joe 292, Opal 292.
SWEENEY, Jill Michelle 210, Lillian Evelyn 239.
SWEET, Clara 133, 167.
SWEETWOOD, Dorothy 220, Harry 220, Lena 220.
SWIFT, David 282, Goldie Opal 293, Hester Oral 284, Lily 282, Mary 179.
SWIHART, Lena 242.
SWINDLE, Deruses Meree 197, Rayna 197, Ronna 197, William 197.
SWISHER, Martha Ann 271.
SYRUS, Beth Ann 291, Jana Kay 291, Kimberly 291, Robert Walker 291, William Rbt. 291, Wm. Christopher 291, Zachary Wm. 291.

TABOR, Dorothy 287, Eugene 287, Fletcher 287, Isaac 256, 287, Iva Ione 287, Iva Lona 251, James 287, Jesse 287, John Alan 287, John Ross 287, Joshua 287, Lena 308, Lola 157, Loretta 287, Martha 287, Matilda 188, 198, 199, 287, Meta Lavida 256, 287, Rebecca 287, Rebecca Sue 287, Roxie Leota 287, Russell 287, Teresa J. 287, Thelma G. 287, Tracy 287, William 287.
TAGGART, Alpha 255, Beula 166, Brian 287, Bruce 287, Capt. James 195, 214, Captain 214, Corbin Keith 287, Earl 176, Edwin 287, Elizabeth 202, 230, 299, Emilie 287, George 230, Hannibal Pingry 202, Horace A. 255, Isaac 255, James 230, James (Capt.) 132, Jane 214, Janelle 287, Janet 261, 282, Jori Elizabeth 287, Keith 174, 235, 287, Nina 174, 187, 235, 287, Orval Tracy 176, Oscar 255, Robert 230, Rose 276, Ruth 176, Sandford Lee 176, Susanna 214, Thomas 154, Thomas J. 176, Vivian 287, Walter 276, Willard 255, Wm. Harrison 255.
TALLEY, Dwight 201.
TATE, Hallie 211, James 190, Newberry 190, Thomas B. 190.
TATLOCK, Sharon Kay 144.
TATUM, Abby 177, Amy 177, Benjamin 177, Joshua 177, Nancy 177.
TAYLOR, Albert 274, Alberta 274, Altah Clodean 251, Alverna 283, Alzora Lucinda 288, Ann Elizabeth 159, Anna 164, Anna Armilda 224, Anna Louisa 224, Archibald 224, 287, 288, 289, Archibald Jr. 288, Armilda 288, Barbara 274, Barbara Jean 270, Benjamin 141, 224, Burdine 288, Calvinia 288, Captola 156, Carol 288, Carolyn 288, Catherine 287, 288, Chauncey 270, Chester 274, Debra 212, Dessie 288, Dora Ethel 288, Edna 288, Elizabeth 224, 274, 288, 289, Elizabeth Jane 168, Elizabeth King 287, Elizabeth M. 288, Elsie Miranda 141, Emma 288, Everett Lee 288, Frances Waltz 288, Fred 206, George 235, Hannah 183, Hannah 184, Harry 288, Harry Wesley 288, Hazel 274, Henry 288, Herny 287, Herschel Glenn 251, Ida 274, Isaac Shannon 288, James 288, Jane 241, Jeanie 288, Jemima Jane 224, John 288, John Everett 288, John Wesley 288, Linda 288, Lucinda Jane 288, Madonna 138, Margaret 288, Mary 288, Mary E. 141, Mary Elizabeth 224, Mary Frances 288, Mary Jean 288, Mary Lou 288, Mattie 235, May or Mary 288, Michael P. 224, Michael Peter 288, Muriel 220, 261, Nancy 159, 235, 288, Nancy Petro 288, Otto 288, Pat 235, Patricia 288, Pauline 288, Rachal M. 288, Richard 288, Sally-Sarah 288, 287, Sarah 287, Sarah C. 186, Stewart 288, Thomas 287, 288, William 159, 193, 287, 288, William Norman 287, 288, William T. 288.
TAYS, Woodrow 210.
TEAGUE, Amy D. 289, Anna 181, Audrey 181, Betty Joan 289, Cherly Ann 289, Cinderella 181, 253, Clifford 181, Donald 289, Dorothy 289, Edna 289, Esther 289, G.L. 289, G.L. 289, Herbert 289, Herbert Lemuel 289, Howard Lyndall 289, James 289, Jason Richard 289, Jessica Ann 289, Kristy Lynn 289, Levi Vorse 289, Lillian Anne 289, Mary Russ 289, Mildred 289, Ollie Jane 289, Patricia B. 289, Rebecca Lynn 289, Richard H. 289, Roy 181, Ryan Anthony 289, Sarah 181, Stephen 289, Thelma 181, Tisha 289, Vivian 289, William 289, William B. 181.
TEBOE, Kathryn 244, Margaret 244, Orval 244.
TEDROW, Arthur 199, Arthur III, 199, Kathleen 199, Kristen 199.
TEMPLIN, Andrew T. 291, Katherine 291, Sara Jane 291, Thomas 291.
TERHUNE, Albert 289, Garret 289, James 289, Julia Ann 289, Margaret 134, Margaret Ellen 289, Marget 289, Martha 289, Mary E. 289, Nancy Jane 289, Rufus W. (Dr.) 289, Stephen 289, Simon Peter 289, William 289.
TERRELL, David Ray 309, Margie 308, Raymond 309, Rita Jean 309.
TERRILL, Adeline 289, Carrie 290, Cecil 290, Charles 289, Deanna Jean 305, Duane 305, Edna 290, Ethel 290, Flora 172, Ford 290, Jeffrey 305, Jeremiah 289, Jeremiah H. 289, Jerry 305, John 289, John Wes 289, Leonard 289, Lurana 289, Michelle 305, Robert 289, Roxie 290, Ruth 290, Samuel 289, Sarah 290, Seba 290, Susan 289, William 289.
TERRY, Lisa Ann 190.
TEX, Pauline 232.
THACKER, Frank 295, Mary Ethel 295.
THACKERA, Richard 292.
THARP, Anna Margaret 204, Marilyn 143.
THICKSTON, Fred 233.
THICKSTUN, Millard 227.
THIXTON, Heather A. 182, Sharon 182, Tom 182.
THOMAS, Alpha Adele 211, Betty 291, Bradley S. 291, Darrell 136, Edna Mae 136, Hallie 211, Hannah 294, Jeffery W. 291, Kay 297, Marlene F. 291, Melanie Ann 136, Minnie 217, Nanie J. 236, Patricia Ann 291, Phyllis C. 291, Sarah Elizabeth 291, Scott Darrell 136, Susan 291, Trenton W. 291, Vincent 211, William 294, William H. 291, William W. 291, Wm. Michael 291.
THOMASZEN, Theunis 222.
THOMPKINS, Lucille 220.
THOMPSON, Almon (Bill) 163, Alonzo E. 163, Alzora Jane 288, Andrew 199, Betty Joan 289, Brayton Patrick 145, 290, Bryce Andrew 145, 290, Clara Lavonne 163, David 288, Debbie 213, Dennis 289, Dick 215, Elsie Miranda 141, George W. 141, Greg 290, Gregory Lewis 145, Hazel G. 290, Horace E. 290, James R. 290, Jeanie 288, Jennifer 199, Joseph E. 290, Julia 199, Julia Marita 282, Keith 184, Lona May 163, Lucinda 141, Marie J. 290, Martin Sandy 141, Mary Ida 141, Maurice 290, Michael 199, Michael E. 290, Michael Eugene 145, Michael Eugene Jr. 145, Michael Jr. 290, Norman 290, Peggy 290, Peggy Jane 145, Permelia 180, Phyllis Kay 184, Rebecca Ann 145, 290, Robert W. 290, Ruth 290, Thomas 141, Viva 215, Wayne E. 290, Will 281, William N. 290
THORESEN, Abigail 311, Karina Jennifer 311, Pat 311, Robert 311.
THORNBROUGH, William 273.
THRALL, Evelyn 181.
TIBBETTS, Catherine 278, Mandy Cotlyn 278, Melanie 278, Terry 278.
TIETSORT, Hannah 174, Peter 174, Rebecca 174.
TILTON, Abigail 292, Abraham 292, Andrew William 291, Claudia Ruth 291, David 292, Deliverance 292, Elijah 292, Elisha 292, Elizabeth 291, 292, Elmer 292, Emma 292, Esther 292, Frances 292, Frank (Dr.) 223, Frank Gore 291, 292, Frank Lewis 291, Frank Wiliam 291, Frederic Lewis 292, 291, George 292, Gladys 291, Henry 292, Ida 291, Ira 292, James 292, James Jacob 291, James Lee 291, James Lewis 236, 290, 292, James Richard 291, Janice Elaine 291, John 291, 292, Joseph 292, Lewis Cass 290, 292, Luke Josiah 291, Mamie 290, Margaret 291, Margaret Ann 291, Mary 292, Mary Jane 292, Mary Margaret 291, Nancy 292, Pamela 291, Peter 291, Rachel 291, 292, Raymond Moore 291, Rebecca 292, Richard 292, Robert 291, Ruth 236, 291, 292, Ruth Katherine 236, 291, Samuel 292, Sarah 292, Sarah Jane 236, 290, Sina 292, Thomas 292, Thomas Ray 291, Thursa Love 292, Ursula 291, Vesta 292, Viola 292, William 291, 292.
TIMBERMAN, Mabel 188.
TINSLEY, Frank W. 210, Ruth C. 210.
TIPTON, Emma J. 273, Joshua 273.
TITSWORTH, William 299.
TJARDES, Tammy 285.
TJOMSLAND, Florence 247.
TODD, Elizabeth 208, 209, Jessie 209, Marion 209, Ola 285.
TOLLIVER, America 137, Tom 137.
TOMLINSON, Mary 310, Minerva Lindsey 220.
TONEY, Evelyn 292, Judy 206, 292, Kameran Kay 292, Terry Wesley 292, Wes 292. **TOON,** Elizabeth 268.
TOWLE, Anthony F. 218..
TOWNE, Christine 230.
TRACEY, Martha 213, Martha Jane 213.
TRACY, Almedia 201, Almedia Eva 293, Amanda E. 293, Arthur 293, Betty 293, Blanche 141, 143, 293, Catherine 293, Charles 293, Clarence 293, Claud F. 293, Cleo 293, Daniel Verlus 293, Doris Gaynell 293, Earl Jennings 293, Earlene 293, Easter 177, Easter Amy 293, Edna 293, Everett 141, 293, Florence Irene 293, Floyd 293, George 293, George Clinton 293, George Morris 293, Georgeanna 293, Georgia 293, Gertrude 293, Goldie Opal 293, Grace 141, Grace 293, Guy William 293, Harold 293, Herchel V. 293, Hesper Alma 293, Hilda 293, Irvin Joshua 293, James Allen 293, James Everett 293, James Kenneth 293, Jennings 293, John Walter, 293, Latona Frances 210, 293, Laura 293, Lela Evon 239, Lettie Hanna 293, Mabel 293, Marion 293, Mary 143, 293, Mary Christina 293, Mary Viola 293, Nancy Angeline 293, Olin 293, Olive 293, Ruby 293, Samuel 299, Sarah Beryl 293, Sarah Martha, 153, Sarah Mattie 293, Sonny 293, Telsa 293, Thomas R. 289, 293, Tommy Earl 293, Victor 293, Virgil 293, Virginia 293, Walter 293, William 293.
TRAMMEL, Denise 196, Randall 196, Raymond 196.
TRANOWSKI, Angela 255.
TRATEBAS, Alice Mae 294, Calvin Vincent 294, Deborah Sue 294, Edmund 294, Edmund W. 293, 294, Elzear 294, Etienne 294, Gladys M. 293, 294, Honore´ Marie 294, Jerome Victor 294, John 294, Linda Marie 294, Patricia Ellen 294, Pauline Jeannette 294.
TREES, Julia June 161, Verle 161.
TREFT, Orma Jean 204.
TRENNER, John 175, 176, Mary Jane 202, Nathan 176.
TRIEUX, Philippe du 133.
TRIP, Dorothy Louise 311, Flora Stella 311, Sanford Antonia 311.
TRISLER, Cassie 264, Cassie Mable 150, 263, 306, Elizabeth 294, Francis M. 294, Joseph 294, Martin R. 294, Mary 263, Mary Etta 294, Susannah 294, Ward 263, 306, Ward W. 294.
TRISSELL, Len 278.
TRISSLER, 294.
TROXELL, Fred 304, Ora 304, Vena Louise 304.
TROYER, Adrian 297, David 297, Dorothy 297, Ray 297.
TRUAX, Catherine 197, John 292, Julia Ann 254, Julianna 197, Mary 236, Nancy 292.
TRUESDAL, Jettie 293.
TRUEX, Catharine 176, Catherine E. 165, Clarissa 309, Densel Anthony 168, Emma Lucinda 202, Gwendola 168, Henry 202, Joseph 165, Julia Anne 165, Marietta 202, Mary 205, Melissa 132, Saloma 133, Sarah A. 271.
TUCKER, Anderson 212, Mable 133, Mary C. 212, Minda Katherine 212.
TURFLINGER, Matilda 247.
TURLEY, Rebecca 138.
TURNER, Anna 262, Arvine 289, Bertha Jane 295, Charles 269, Charles R. 295, Charlie D. 295, Charlotte 184, Chipp Allen 293, Claud 289, Courtney 184, Dan 269, Edgar 289, Edgel 293, Effie 289, Elisha Daniel 133, 295, Elizabeth 295, Elizabeth E. 133, Ershel 269, Eva Belle 295, Geo. Newton 295, George 295, Glenn 269, Grace 269, Grandma 149 Grandpa 149, Harry 294, Hazel Esseny 294, Helen 269, Indiana C. 295, Irene 269, James L. 295, Jennie 293, Jessie Ruth 295, John 269, 289, John Daniel 294, John Wesley 228, 295, John William 295, John Wm. 228, Joshua 184, Judy Gibbs 295, Lena Bell 210, 293, Lottie Frances 295, Lewis A. 210, 293, Lewis Allen 295, Loetie Marie 228, Lona Ruth 294, Lottie Marie 295, Martha Bell 295, Mary 289, Mary Alice 228, 295, Mary Florence 294, Mary Nettie 295, Molly 228, Nancy 295, Ollie Dean 210, Pearl 228, 295, Rachel 184, Rebecca 295, Ruby 228, Ruby Letha 173, 295, Ruth 269, Samuel 289, Velma 269, Wm. Perry 295, Zora J. 295.
TUTTEROW, Abraham 295, Anna Lillian 295, Cora Jane 295, David 295, Elizabeth 295, Francis, 232, 295, George 232, 295, Ira Curtis 295, John 295, John Ora 295, Joseph 295, Mary Elizabeth 295, Mary Ethel 295, Maude Della 295, Rachel 295, Retta Belle 295, Ruth 295, Samuel 295, Sarah 295.
TUTTERROW, Alice 184, 221, Billy 184, 221, Elmer 184, Elva 184, George 184, John 184, 221, Margilyn 221, Margilyne 184, Marilyn 184, 221, Phyllis 184, 221.

ULEY, Nancy 164.
UNDERWOOD, Curtis 276, David 219, Holly 219, Marjorie Ann 219, Patty 219, Ron 219 .
UNGER, Grace Edith 163.
UNVERSAW, Ray 143.
UTZ, Anna 162.

VALENTINE, Lucille 239, Nancy 305.
VAN ARSDALE, Lydia 162.
VAN ARSDALEN, Sanford Boyer 203, Sara 203, Symon Jansen 203.
VAN NUYS, Maria 289.
VAN OSDOL, Mable 271.
VAN de HAVEN, Earl 213, Marguerite 213.
VANDYKE, Jane 303, Mary Ellen 176.
VANSLYKE, Carole Sue 182, Louis Dewayne 183, Richard William 183.
VANCE, Mary 171.
VANDERBILT, Betty 295, Elizabeth Lyne 295, Vern Corwin Sr. 295, Vern Jr. 295.
VANDERHEIDEN, Jeanne 232
VANDIVER, Bessie 135, Lawrence 135, Willie 135.
VANMETER, Charity 284, Thos. Jefferson 284.
VARNER, Daniel Clayton 296, Edward Grant 296, Emma Viola 296, Gay Lynn 242, James Grant 296, Jane Ann 296, Maude Ann 296, Michelle Kay 296, Samara Ann 296.
VARNEY, Martha K. 198, Reuben 198.
VAUGHN, Christine 288, Edna 288, Harold 288, Logan 288, Mark 175, Ray 288, Rebecca Ann 175, Rena Marie 175, Steven 288.
VAUGHT, Ada Louise 266, 296, Ada Martin 296, Buena Mae 296, Carl 296, Carolyn Jane 296, Clyde Bell 266, 296, Clyde Jr. 296, Crystal 297, Donald 296, Emma Rose 296, Emma Rose 266, Harold 296, Henry 296, Iva 285, John 296, Lillian 296, Melvin 296, Mildred Belle 296, Roscoe 296,Virginia Lee 296.
VAWTER, Will 153, 185, 214.
VEHORN, Larry W. 179.
VENABLE, Evertle Martin 175, Joyce Eileen 175, Janet Marie 175.
VENICE, Janet K. 274.
VERHINES, Dorothy 266.
VOLAND, Bill 270, Eddie 208, Mable 276, Olive 293.
VOLANDINGHAM, Fleming Elvin 227.
VON KANNEN, Jonathon P. 277.
VON MONNINGER, Gottfried Peter 143, Lydia 143.
VOORHEES, Betty 151.
VOORHEIS, Anna Marie 297, Eva Mae 296, 297, Julie 297, Kay 297, Nellie G. 297, Raymond 297, Raymond Lee 297, Wade 296, Wade A. 297, Wade Jr. 297, William 297, William A. 295, Adaline 297, Albert 297, Anna 297, Anna Marie 297, Carolyn 297, Charles 297, Earnest 297, Elmer D. 297, Emmaline 297, Frederick 297, Harvey 297, Henry 297, Ida 297, James 297, Mary 297, Nellie 296, Simmon 297, Susan 297, Wade 297, William A. 297.

WADDLE, William 198.
WADE, Dorcas 132, James 132, Rebecca 310, Sam 276.
WADSWORTH, Cordilia 285, John 285, Mariah 285.
WAEGE, Susan G. 186.
WAGGONER, Alice 158, Anna 250, Carol Kay 176, David 140, Doris Marie 215, Frances 179, Howard 158, Jewell 158, Margaret 140, Margaret Louisa 140, Rady Mae 158, Thomas 281.
WAGLER, Adam 297, Amanda 297, Brittney 297, Cathy 297, Chadd 297, Cora 297, Crystal 297, Daniel 297, Darryl 297, David 297, Derek 297, Edward 297, Emily 297, Eulala 297, Frances 292, 297, Henry 297, Howard 297, Jacqueline 297, Justin 297, Kenneth 297, Kimberly 297, Leah 297, Lesa 297, Lloyd 297, Lorene 297, Lynn 297, Nathan 297, Neal 297, Pam 297, Shannon 297, Steven 297, Todd 297, Trenton 297, Frank Casper 208, Priscilla 208.
WAKE, George Lee 218, Louisa 218, Phoebe 218.
WAKEFIELD, Joe 287.
WALDEN, Bella Joyce 215.
WALDHAM, Valentine 300.
WALDSCHMIDT, Doris 297, Vera

297.
WALK, Carl 200, Joy 200, Marchie Lou 200, Marvin 200, Mary Ellen 200.
WALKER, Alta 304, Angus Lela 299, Arlanda B. 299, Atla 299, Austin T. 293, Benj. Franklin 298, Bessie May 299, Betty 298, Betty 299, Bonnie 191, Carl 311, Carolyn 299, Catherine 138, 299, Charles 299, Charles F. 269, 298, Charles L. 298, Charles Leslie 269, Charles M. 298, 299, Chester 299, Clara 293, Cora B. 299, Daisy M. 298, 299, Daisy Melissa 156, 300, Daniel 299, David Lee 298,Dee Ann 298, Della Opal 299
Dora A. 299, Dorcas 132, Dorothy 291, Dr. 307, Dudley R. 298, Earl 299, Ed 211, Edith 182, 299, Edward 298, Edward L. 299, Edward Lonzo 156, 300, Elinder 298, Elizabeth 298, 299, Elmer Harry 298, Emerson 238, Ernest 167, Essie 167, Estella O. 299, Etta J. 299, Eugenus 132, Eva 303, Floyd Cecil 298, Forest 299, Frances 298, Franklin 299, Fred 296, Genevieve 298, Gladys 298, Grace M. 299, Granville 299, Hannah 238, 293, 298, Hannah Jane 299, 300, Harold Allen 298, Harrison 299, Hazel 291, Helen Cecelia 191, Helen Louise 299, Helen Rovine 298, 299, Henry T. 174, Herman 298, 299, Hershel 299, Ida Jane 299, Irene 160, Isaac 298, Jacob 298, 299, Jacob C. 174, Jacob Perry 299, James 245, 300, James Bryan 290, James Eberley 299, James H. 299, James Knox 210, 299, James Richard 291, Jean 291, Jennie L. 299, Jennings Atla 210, 299, Jessie 293, Jessie C. 299, Jim 291, Joan 269, 298, Joan E. 298, Joan Elizabeth 269, Jody 291, John 299, John Marshall 299, Juanita 140, Junior 261, Kathleen 291, Kathy 298, Landy 299, Lawrence Dean 220, Lawrence E. 298, 299, Lawrence L. 298, Lawrence Leslie 269, Leatha 269, Leon 238, Leroy E. 299, Lester Nathan 298, Lloyd Clark 298, Lora Grace 298, Lottie 299, Lousie 298, Lucinda 179, Lucy 299, Lydia Ann 299, Mabel 291, Mable 238, Mamie 290, Manford 164, Marcedes 167, Marcedes L. 195, 299, Margaret 298, Marietta 269, 298, Marjorie 299, Martha 298, Marvin 299, Mary 252, 300, Mary Ann 169, 220, 261, 298, 299, 311, Mary Edelle 299, Mary Elizabeth 299, Matilda Jane 299, Melvin 298, Melving Eugene 298, Mercedes L. 210, Michael Eugene 298, Mildred 238, Mildred Louise 238, Miranda J. 299, Nancy 298, 299, Nancy Carolyn 298, Newt 301, Newton A. 293, Opal M. 299, Penny 292, Phyllis 299, Phyllis E. 298, 299, 300, Rachel 164, 298, Rebecca 299, Ruby 310, Sadie 298, Samuel 210, 298, 299, Samuel Scott 299, Sarah 299, 302, Sarah E. 292, 299, Sarah Elizabeth 291, Sara Jane 299, Susie 293, Thomas 298, 299, Thomas II 300, Tracy 310, Tracy Calvert 293, Vera 298, Verlis 293, Vonnie 299, William 210, William Earl 299, William J. 299, William S. 167, 299, Wilma 310, Wilmer 238, Wm. Daniel 298, Wm. Samuel 298, Zephaniah 298.
WALL, Alberta Beaver 232, Donald 232, Nadine 232.
WALLACE, Amanda 145, Archie Jett 205, Eva Brown 205, Frances Lucille 205.
WALLEN, Ellen 303, Rosamond 303.
WALLS, Dillon Eric, 155, J.H. (Rev.) 177, Jacob H. (Rev.) 239, Jacob Holmes 177, Minnie 177, 239, Nettie Pauline 155, Rbt. Wm. III 155, Rbt. Wm. Jr. 155, Robert William 155, Starlene 155.
WALTER, (Dr.) 148, John 217.
WALTERS, David 159, Erin Elizabeth 159, Megan Elyse 159, Sara 136.
WALTMAN, Ambrose 311, Anna 177, 300, Catherine 309, Charles G. 300, Conrad 300, Dorothy Marie 300, Elza Estell 300, Emma 311, Goldie Opal 293, Helen J. 300, Hiram 289, Hiram (Mac) 177, Hiram McIntire 300, Howard E. 300, Jane 300, John 138, John S. 300, Lowell Carson 300, Mack 300, Margaret 298, Marion Eugene 300, Marjorie N. 300, Martha Bell 295, Martha Belle 269, Mary 280, Mary Ann 246, Mary E. 173, Michael 177, Michael Jr. 300, Michael Sr. 300, Myron E. 300, Myron Lee 300, Opal 300, Samuel 300, Susan 300, Tom 163, Valentine 300, Velma 258, Velma Vesper 300, Walter Dale 300, William 241, Zephaniah 300.
WALTON, Janine 224, Violet Elaine 244.
WALTZ, 141, Amanda 182, Amanda Elizabeth 176, Amanda Elizabeth 176, Darryl 160, Dianna 160, Donna 160, Douglas 160, Frances 288, Harley 243, Harrison 176, John 209, Lucy 182, Mable 243, Martha Jane 209, Pleasant 182, Veva B. 160.
WAMPLER, Basil Glen 149, Donald Edwin 149, Ida Mae 149, John Dale 149.
WANICKI, Mary 158.
WARD, Albert 300, Amanda M. 300, Benjamin 300, Clara Mae 235, Dean 270, Elizabeth 255, Emaline 300, Fred 262, Evaline 165, 300, Henry J. 300, Jarus 162, Judy 262, Mahlon 175, 206, 300, Margaret A. 300, Mary 300, Mary J. 300, Matilda 300, Moses 206, Moses M. 300, Rebecca 300, Rebecca Downey 300, Sarah 300, Susan 300, Timothy 300.
WARFORD, Alice 204, Alice Carrie 204, Aurilla 301, Bertha 301, 303, Carey 155, Cary 204, 301, Cecil 142, Deloris Lavon 142, Donald 142, 143, Ed 204, 301, Edgar 301, Edgar D. 142, Elijah 301, Elizabeth 301, Frank 197, 201, 204, 301, Frank A. 204, Frank Allen 200, Gladys 204, 262, Henrietta 301, Homer 204, 301, Ida 301, Jessie 142, John 301, Mary 301, Mary Jane 155, 301, Mildred 204, Ola 197, 201, 204, Olive 204, 301, Osa 155, Oscar 148, 200, 204, 301, 302, Ray 262, Ruth 204, Ruth K. 197, Sarah 148, 200, 301, 302, Thurl 155, 180, Thurle A. 301, Walter 301, Zella 142, Thurle 204.
WARMOUTH, Miriam 253, Oliver 253.
WARREN, Connie Sue 237.
WARRENBURG, Sandra 268.
WARRING, (Dr.) Thomas 215, Fred 215, Tilla 215.
WASHINGTON, 193, George 202, 292, Jane 194.
WASSON, James 270.
WATERMAN, Alberta May 182, Cary Abraham 182, Mary Miriam 182.
WATERS, Anne 310, Marian 280, 282, Nancy 253, Samuel Ensign 310.
WATKINS, Michael 216, Travis Michael 216, Ty Landon 216.
WATSEK, Arthur 231.
WATSON, Amber Dawn 302, Amy 196, Bonnie 196, Elizabeth 153, Frank 302, Fred 196, Gary Frank 302, George 175, Harold Frank 302, Howard Frank 189, Jessie 153, Jettie 293, Jonathan 153, Mary Jane 296, Nancy Ann 241, Nancy Charlene 302, Sarah Anna 176, Sarah Martha 153, Seward 153, 293, Stan 196, Thomas E. 293, William Greene 153, Wilma J. 189, Wilma Jean 302.
WATT, Jane 253.
WATTERS, Nellie 157.
WATTON, George F. 185, Josephine 185, Lib 185, Susie E. 185
WAY, Mary 293.
WAYMAN, Annetta 302, Clemmie J. 302, Elbridge 302, Elsie 302, Erschel 302, Ershel 269, Flossie 302, Ida M. 302, Jannie 269, Jos. Edward 302, Joseph 269, Joseph Richard 302, Laura Belle 302, Rebecca 302, Thursa 302, Vera 298, Vicki Lynn 302, Violet 302, Walter Wayman 302, William Richard 302.
WAYT, Chester F. 302, Clarence Jos. 302, Clifford H. 302, Daniel 302, Delores 302, Frank 302, Gerald Clifford 158, Gerlad C. 302, Glenn Curtis 158, 302, Gloria Sue 158, 302, Goldie 302, Hazel 302, Kenneth 302, Larry Dean 158, 250, 302, Laverne 302, Lily Quintilla 264, Lucinda 302, Matilda 302, Milton David 302, Nina 302, Nora 302, Russell 302, Susan Navilla 158, Thomas 302, Wilma J. 251, Wilma Jean 302.
WEANER, Jacob 164, Mahala 244, Mahala Ellen 164, Sarah 164.
WEATHERFORD, Betty L. 161, Jane 161, Kathleen 161, Louis A. 161.
WEATHERMAN, James 285, Nancy 285.
WEAVER, 220, Alice 178, Frances 292, Issac 219, Nora 219.
WEBB, Agnes 215, David 162, Dorthea 162, Mary 162, Ruth 162, Walter 162.
WEBSTER, Maradyn 289, Mary Helen 172, 310.
WEDDLE, 193, Bertha A. 302, Bonnie 155, Catherine 302, Chick 204, Clarence 302, Daniel 302, David D. 154, David Dolan 302, David Leon 302, Eleanor 310, Elizabeth 302, Ellen 302, Eva 303, Frank 303, Goldie 302, Grace 302, Gregory 303, Harold 303, Harrietta 303, Horce 303, Ira 302, Irvin 303, Jane 214, Jerry L. 303, John 199, 200, Kenneth 266, Lelanda 302, Mary Ann 179, Maud 303, McAllen 302, McCallen Green 302, Michael 195, Milly 193, Norma 303, Ramona 266, Rosamond 302, Rosanna 180, Sarah 302, Susan 185, Thos. Wm. 302, Virgil 303, Virginia 174, 303, Walter 302.
WEHMILLER, Sherry Lewis 193.
WEIGEL, Pearl G. 176.
WEIR, Bob 205.
WEISMAN, Mary Jane 226, Walter 226.
WELCH, Albert C. 185, Brian 305, Cindy 305, Clarence 288, George 185, Helen Louise 144, Janet 288, Joseph 288, Linda 305, Mary 288, Marylynne 288, Nancy 262, Nolan 185, Osborn G. 185.
WELLER, Bonnie Sue 149, Christina 149, Douglas 149, Rhamsey Thor 149, Ryan Jay 149, Troy 149, Troy Linn 149.
WELLERER, Betty 191.
WELLS, Andrew 158, Bert 260, Brandise Nicole 260, Brent Mahlon 260, Elizabeth 158, Frank 201, Joan 260, Mary 158, Melba 260, Sharon 199, William S. 260.
WEMMEDOV, Mary Beth 291, Urban 291.
WERDEBAUGH, Stella Jane 137.
WERNET, Brian 177, Donna 177, Scott 177.
WERTZ, Elizabeth 162.
WESEN, Abby Jane Jones 267, Edith Mae 266, Edith Mae Jones 267, Elmer 267, Hazel 267, Marvel 266, 267, Myrtis 267, Victor 267.
WESENE, Marvel.
WEST, Alva Nathaniel 303, Eliza 303, Ernest 303, Ferrel 303, Frieda 303, Gledith 303, Glenn 303, Ivan 303, Jacob 303, James 303, Jane 303, Lavina Ann 264, Maude 162, Michael 175, 303, Mildred 303, Sarah 264, William 264.
WESTBROOK, Lena 201.
WHALEY, Edward 291.
WHEATLY, Jenny 261.
WHEATON, Oliver Perry 195.
WHEELER, Abel Alvin 140, Carl 199, Drusilla 140, Emma Josephine 140, Francis Alan 287, Louella 146, Marie 140, Mary 140, Michael 287, Mona 140, Oscar 140.
WHETSTINE, Brent 216, Don 216, Jennie 216, LuAnn 180, Sharrianne 216.
WHILARANT, Mary Agnes 175.
WHILCOMB, Edgar 277.
WHITAKER, Angie 303, Belle 269, Charles 264, David Mark 142, Dustin 303, Dylan 303, Elizabeth 300, Gladys 255, James H. 264, Jason 303, Joshua Jr. 264, Nicole Estelle 142, Teresa 142.
WHITE, Anne Elizabeth 156, Annie 156, 298, Benjamine 205, Cynthia 299, Donna 241, Elaine 196, Eva Nell 196, Helen 279, Helen M. 279, James Milton 279, John Greenleaf 279, Kristie 175, Laura David 279, Laura Kay 279, Mabel 205, Marcella 263, Mary E. 271, Mary Lou 150, Olin 290, Robert 156, Sarah Frances 163, Webster 280, William 282, Wilt 279.
WHITEHEAD, Monagale 148.
WHITEHORN, Amy Cox 303, Anita 304, Benj. Franklin 303, Benjamin F. 184, Betty 304, Chelsea 304, Clara 303, David A. 303, David Allen 303, General 303, Harley Emmer 303, John 303, Lawrence Delmas 304, Luetta 304, Marvin 304, Mary 285, Mary Emma 303, Mary Etta 285, Maudie 303, Naomi 303, Nathaniel Lyons 303, Nettie Marie 304, Noah 285, Ruth Marie 304, Talitha Cumi 303, William 303.
WHITMAN, Stanley 287.
WHITNEY, Henry 208.
WHITTINGHILL, Albert 223, Rhoda 223.
WIDMER, Buck 272, Harriet 272.
WILBURN, Ethel Lee 170.
WILCOX, Absolom Carr 188, Barbara 188, Dora 188, 199, Elizabeth 188, Zedorah 188.
WILHITE, Myrtle 156.
WILKERSON, Albert 304, Alta 304, Amos 304, Amy Lynn 145, Carol 298, Clifford 304, David 304, Davis 304, DeWayne 304, Donald 304, Doshie 187, Emarine 304, Emmarine 274, 275, Ernest 304, Fada 304, Francis Paul 287, George 304, Goldie Mae 145, Grover C. 304, Hammond 304, Henry 304, Hulda 180, Ida 162, Inez 304, Isom 180, 304, James 180, 304, Jane 304, Jeannette 304, Jemima 305, Josephine 304, laura 158, Laura Alice 304, Lenore 304, Lizzie 304, Lois Ann 145, Margaret Jane 304, Mary 304, Mary Alta 298, Melinda Lea 145, Mildred 237, Minnie Jane 304, Muhulda 285, myra Kathleen 287, Nancy 304, Olive 304, Orville 142, 304, Patricia Marie 304, Paul Eugene 287, Peggy 304, Richard Allen 145, Richard Leon 287, Rick 145, Roonie 247, Sally 180, Sharlot 180, Shirley 157, Shirley Ann 145, Solomon 304, Stella 304, Thelma 287, Thomas 304, Valentine 304, Walter Edward 184, Wesley 304, William 274, William Riley 180, 285, Winfer 145.
WILKIE, David A. 208, James 208, Susan 208.
WILLAN, Brent 310, Craig 310, Gail 310, M.W. 310.
WILLARD, Mabel 273.
WILLIAMS, Ann 305, Belle 269, Catherine 275, Charles 299, Chelce Whitaker 269, Dan 269, Deborah 210, Ferne 269, Frances 199, Frances Louise 272, Gaar 208, George 186, Jay 199, Jesse 206, Joan 269, 298, John Jr. 305, John M. 305, John S. 154, John Sr. 305, Josephine M. 275, 276, 277, L. Jearldine 176, Laura B. 186, Loretta Jeraldine 176, Margaret 258, Mary Lynn 305, Nelson 269, Ollie Jane 289, Pearl 133, Ruth 149, Sarah 305, Teresa 199, Thelma Myrtle 188, William 275.
WILLIAMSON, Bartley Dwight 216, Benita Faith 216, Beth Ann 216, Brad Lee 216, Brett Franklin 216, Edna 253, Elizabeth 198, Hazel 238, Judith Ann 216, Paul Oliver 216, Vickie 296, Von 217.
WILLMORE, Camille 153.
WILLOUGHBY, A.Eugene 248, Albert Eugene 305, Cleo 248, 305, Danelle 305, Deanna Jean 305, Deborah Lynn 305, Emma 305, Eugene 214, 305, George 305, Grace 305, Grover 253, 309, Grover Dale 305, Iva 305, Jim 242, Joyce 305, Keith Bryan 305, Keith Bryan II 305, Keith Russell 305, Kelsie Renee 305, Kenneth Lee 305, Kevin Lewis 305, Lillian 305, Linda 305, Lois 305, Lois Clarice 309, Lualle 305, Mary 305, Mary Louise 305, Natasha 305, Ramona Leigh 305, Russell Wayne 305, S. Harold 305, Virginia M. 305.
WILLS, Eva 200.
WILSON, Albert F. 306, Alexander 213, 306, Alice 238, Ashley 306, Avis 306, Barbara Estella 178, Betty 305, Brenda 276, Brent 306, Carl 305, Celese Murrene 306, Charles 213, Chester 191, Dale 192, Doris 197, 264, 306, Dorvel 191, Douglas Brent 306, Dudley 305, Estella 139, Francis 306, Frank 213, Fred H. 264, Gene 174, Glen 238, Harley 191, Henry 219, Henry Clay 306, Hester 191, Hiram 154, James Byron 196, James Judson 133, James Vernon 196, Joan 305, Joseph Woodrow 150, Joy Lynne 306, Julia 171, Velva Loris 238, Linda 305, Linda Joy 306, Leotta 172, Louisa 218, Lula 191, Lynne Marie 306, Marjorie 305, Mary Ann 254, Matilda 133, Matilda Jane 302, Meloney Jean 306, Mrs. 185, Nancy 306, Norma Arlene 264, Norman 238, Olive 191, Oliver 191, Patsy 305, Rachel 306, Robert 305, Robert Earl 306, Robert Earl II 306, Screlda 150, Tillie Mae 150, 165, 303, Tug 305, Vicky Lee 237, Wanda 192, Wilbur Cron 196, William 305, William Earl 306.
WILTSEE, Earl J. 299.
WINBERG, Wilma 310.
WINCHESTER, John M. 279.
WINEGER, Louise 296.
WINEMAN, Elizabeth 299.
WINFREE, Frances Anne 192.
WINGARD, Emma Viola 296.
WINKLER, Arthur 226, Charles 172, Clinton Allen 250, Emil 250, George 290, Harold 250, Luda 164, Nancy Catherine 250, Ora 164, Vivian Loretta 250, William 250.
WISE, Jemima 133, Lydia A. 295, William 154.
WISENBURG, Loretta Jane 195.
WITHAM, Bert Elmer 264, Doris Louise 264.
WODTKE, Dolly 133.
WOHLER, Emma 307, George 306, Jim 306, John 306, Judith 307, June 306, Kellan 307.
WOJCIECHOWSKI, Jadwiga 199.
WOLF, Lola 273.
WOLFF, Ewald 296, George 307, George L. 307, Karl 307, Karl A. 307, Marie 307, Sophie 307.
WOLPERT, Art 308, Arthur Milton 307, Bertha 222, Blake Milton 307, 308, Carrye Ellen 307, Carson Ellery 308, Casey 308, Cindy Harvey 308, Cynthia Harvey 308, Cynthia S. 308, Frederick Wm. 222, George F. 307, George W. 307, June 308, June Marie 307, Valeri Ellen 308, Wm. Evans 307.
WOMACK, Lucinda 239, Oren 202.

WONDERLY, Eunice 282.
WOOD, Dr. 203.
WOODFORD, Mariah 282.
WOODMANSEE, Susan 217.
WOODS, Ancil 308, Ann 305, Bessie 171, Cody 305, Dan 308, Darla June 308, David T.-(Judge) 159, Elizabeth 210, Felix 308, Glen 308, Helen Louise 299, Isaac 308, James 147, James Lester 147, James S. 308, Jewell 308, Jimmy 308, Joe 308, Joseph 308, Joseph G. 308, Julian 308, Kjestine 305, Lela 198, 199, Lisa 212, Margie 308, Mary 239, 308, Mary Beth 308, Murray 305, Nellie Pearl 147, Noah 308, Pauline 308, Peggy 214, Ralph 216, Randy Wayne 308, Rebecca 308, Rebecca A. 203, Robert Earl 147, Ruth 261, 308, Samuel H. 308, Teddy Joe 308, Thomas 261, Verlis 308, Wilma 216, Wilma Jean 147.
WOODWARD, Frances 199, Jimmy 196, Kenny Dale 196, Tom 196.
WOODY, Grace 195.
WOOLRIDGE, Ralph 189.
WOOTEN, Beulah 285, Moses 248.
WOOTTON, Abraham 308, Alice Faye 309, Beulah Edna 309, Charles 309, Denzil Allen 309, Estella Laverne 309, Geo. T., Harry Dean 309, Hary Allen 309, Lois 305, Martha Alice 309, Mary 308, Mary E. 309, Mary Edra 309, Moses 308, Moses, Jr. 309, Patricia Jean 309, Paul Edward 309, Ralph E. 309, Robert Dale 309, Sarah Ann 308, Sherman 309, Verna Lucille 309, Wilma Edith 309, Wm. Cunnings 309.
WORDEN, Wanda 269.
WORKMAN, Elizabeth 263.
WORTHINGTON, B. Whilamena 200, Bertha W. 200, L. Jeferson 200, Luther J. 200, Violet G. 200.
WRAY, Della 158, Joe 212.
WRIGHT, Carol Ann 237, J.E. 141, Jacob A. 174, James Allen 175, Jarrad Max 175, Jean 175, Jedidiah Paul 175, Jeffry Allen 175, John P. 189, Jonas Dale 175, Kimberly Lynn 175, Kirl Lee 175, Margaret 288, Mary 281, Mary Ann 138, Minnie LaVina 282, 283, Nancy 141, Rev. 142, Sarah 135, 209, William 281.
WRIGHTSMAN, Emogene 284, Floyd 216, Katherine 216.
WYANT, Violet 136.
WYATT, Cynthia June 164, Denise Ann 164, Frances Diane 193, LaWayne 164.
WYCOFF, Verna 184.
WYNN, Regena 196.
WYTHE, George 309, Hallie 309, Helen 309, Prentiss 309, Van 309, Winston P. 309, Winston Reed 309.

YATES, Sina 292.
YAWS, Mildred 204.
YEAGER, Benjamin F. Jr. 202, Charles Matthew 259, Edna Mae 259, Wayne 259.
YELEY, Allison 187, Brian 187, Sharon 187.
YOCKALL, Brad 197, Jill 197.
YODER, 171, Conrad 309, Cyrus 139, Daniel 139, Dorval 139, Edith 139, Eliza Jane 139, 156, Elizah Jane 156, Fanny 242, Glen 309, Ida 139, Ivan 156, J.I. 138, Jacob 139, 156, 309, James 139, James 310, James M. 138, 156, 309, Janet Kay 171, Jeffrey 310, Jennifer 310, Jenny K. 310, John 139, John Andrew 172, 310, John Daivd 171, 310, Kath. Margaret 156, Katheryn Margaret 156, Kathy Ann 171, 310, Kay 310, Leroy 139, Mary Jane 309, 310, Maude 139, Mrytle 139, 146, 156, 237, Myrtle Irene 144, 145, Nancy Jane 172, 310, Pearl 139, Rachel Lynn 172, 310, Ralph 139, 216, 309, Ryan Andrew 172, 309, 310, Simon Peter 242, Stella 242, Steven Louis 172, 310, Wm. Glen 309.
YORK, Althea 302, Carl 310, Carrie 310, Charlie 302, Christopher 209, Donna 310, Dorothy 302, Florence 310, Frances Diane 193, Geoffrey 209, Helen 302, Herman 302, Jerome 209, John 199, Karen 193, Marie 302, Minor 310, Myrtle 302, Park 310, Paul 310, Raymond 302, Richard 310, Ruth 209, Walter 302, William D. 193.
YOTTER, 309.
YOUNG, Abram 310, Bessie 310, Blanche 310, Catherine 310, Christiana 310, Colleen 185, David 310, David Jr. 310, David Walter 310, Dolly Fritch 185, Dorothy Jean 155, Edgar 310, Edith 310, Eleanor 310, Elizabeth 310, Floyd 185, Gail 310, Gerald 310, Harvey 310, Jean 310, John 230, John D. 310, John Franklin 310, Joseph 310, Kathy 259, Leon 185, Loretta 310, Louise 248, Lowell 310, Maggie Naomi 190, Mahale 310, Margot 187, Martha 230, Mary 310, Mary Alice 310, Mary Geneva 230, Nancy 210, 298, 299, Norman (Dr.) 310, Olive 310, Patricia 310, Pernetia 310, Raymond 310, Rebecca 310, Roger 310, Ruby 310, Sally 146, Steven 310, Virginia 185, 310, Walter 310, Wayne 310.
YOUNGHANS, Anna F. 196, Arno 196, B.A. Parsons 196, Carmen 197, Emil 196, Frederick 197, Hugo 196, Jan 196, Lucille 197, Madge A. 196, Norma 197, Oscar 196, Richard 197, Richard E. 196, Wilhelm 196.
YUNGHANS, Madge 196, Richard 196.

ZABLATNIK, Linda 186.
ZELLERS, Florence 310, Isabelle 310, Ralph 310.
ZELTNER, Ada 310, Hazel Josephine 310, Walter 310.
ZENOR, Anna 201.
ZENTER, Emma 285.
ZIEHMS, Emilie 240.
ZIKE, Curtis Solomon 158, Gertrude 158, Julia 158, Mary 158, Sarah O. Anna 158, Sarah Oshie 158, Susan Navilla 158, 302, William 158.
ZIMMERMAN, Abraham 263, 310, Albert 310, Albert John 310, Anna 310, Anna Mae 264, Annette 311, Basil 311, Bert 310, Bessie 311, Beverly 199, Cassie Mable 150, 263, Catherine 263, Clinton 310, 311, Cora 182, Daisy 310, Debora 188, Diana 311, Donald 188, 311, Donel 311, Dorothy L. 311, Elsworth (Col.) 263, 311, Gladys 311, Glen 311, Grover Elsworth 263, Hazel Josphine 310, Helen 232, 266, 310, 311, Helen Ione 266, Jacob 310, 311, Laura 310, Margaret 310, 311, Martha 310, Melvin 311, Michael 311, Minnie 310, Ona 310, Pat 310, Peggy 311, Richard C. 188, Rosemarie 311, Ruth C. 188, Sara 310, Sara Vivian 311, Verna 232, 310, 311, Victoria 188.
ZINK, Eunice 226.
ZINZER, Barbara 177.
ZODY, Aaron Albert 311, Agnes 311, Amanda Jane 311, Artis 311, Austin B. 311, Benj. Franklin 311, Catherine 311, Cecil B. 311, Charles F. 311, Clarence 264, 297, Clarence M. 311, Emma 311, Graham 311, Henry 311, Howard 249, 311, Howard Maurice 311, Howard S. 311, John Austin 311, John Wesley 311, Kenneth Ray 311, Leander 311, Mary 300, Mary Elizabeth 311, Mary Jane 311, Oma Jane 311, Richard 311, Sarah Alice 261, 311, William H. 311.
ZOETH, Blanche 187.
ZOOK, Deborah 289, Donna Jean 140, Emerson Cory 140, Florence 179, James A. 280, Mable Eutha 179, Maggie 280, Maggie May 280, Tim 140, Zug 242.
ZORNES, Susan 208.
ZSCHERNITZ, Mrs. Eugene 255.
ZUPANCIC, Anthony 312, Frances 312, John 245, 312, Joseph 312, Josephine 245, 312.

FAMILY TREE

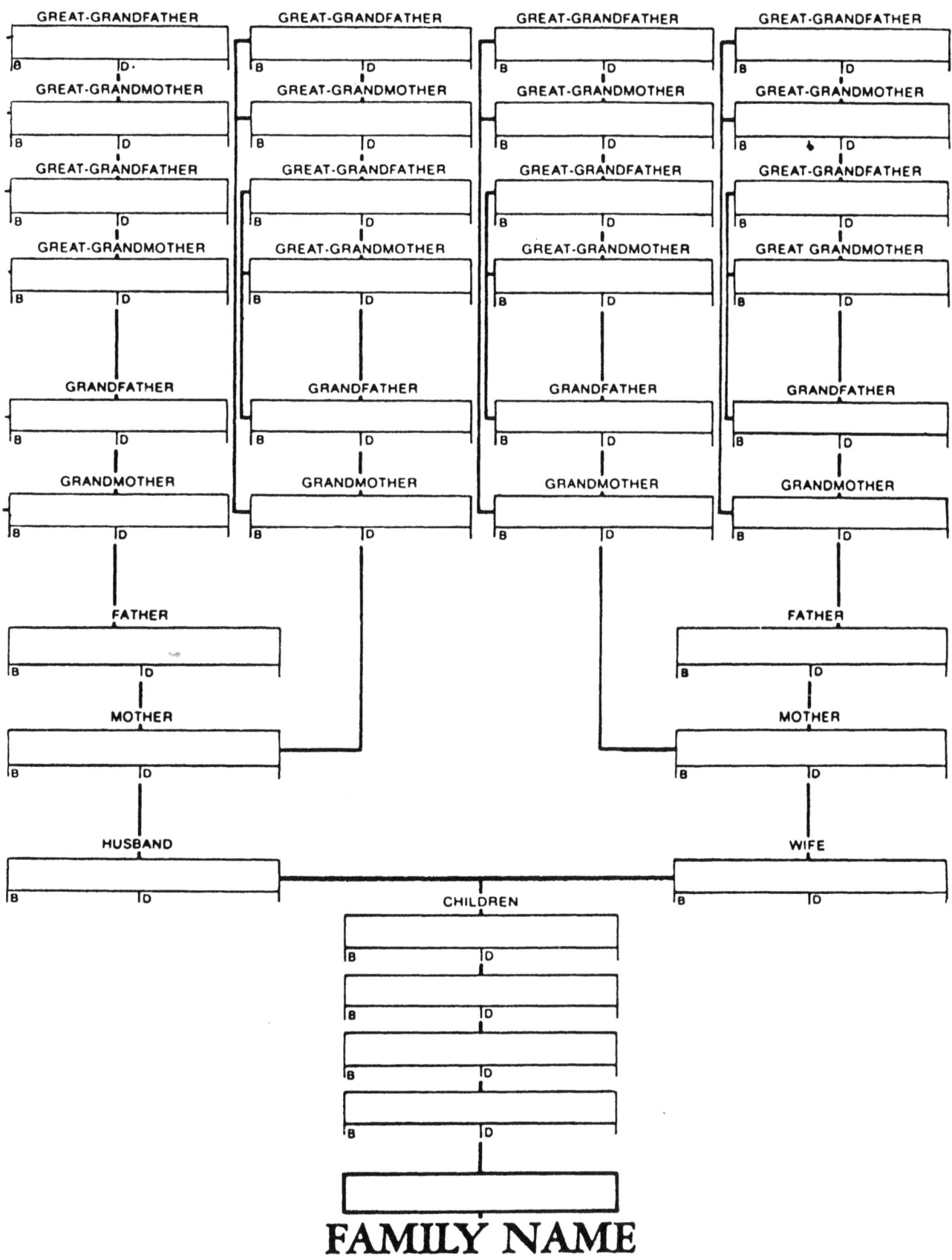

FAMILY NAME

FAMILY RECORD

NAME	BIRTH		DEATH	
	Date	Place	Date	Place

NOTES

NOTES

NOTES

NOTES

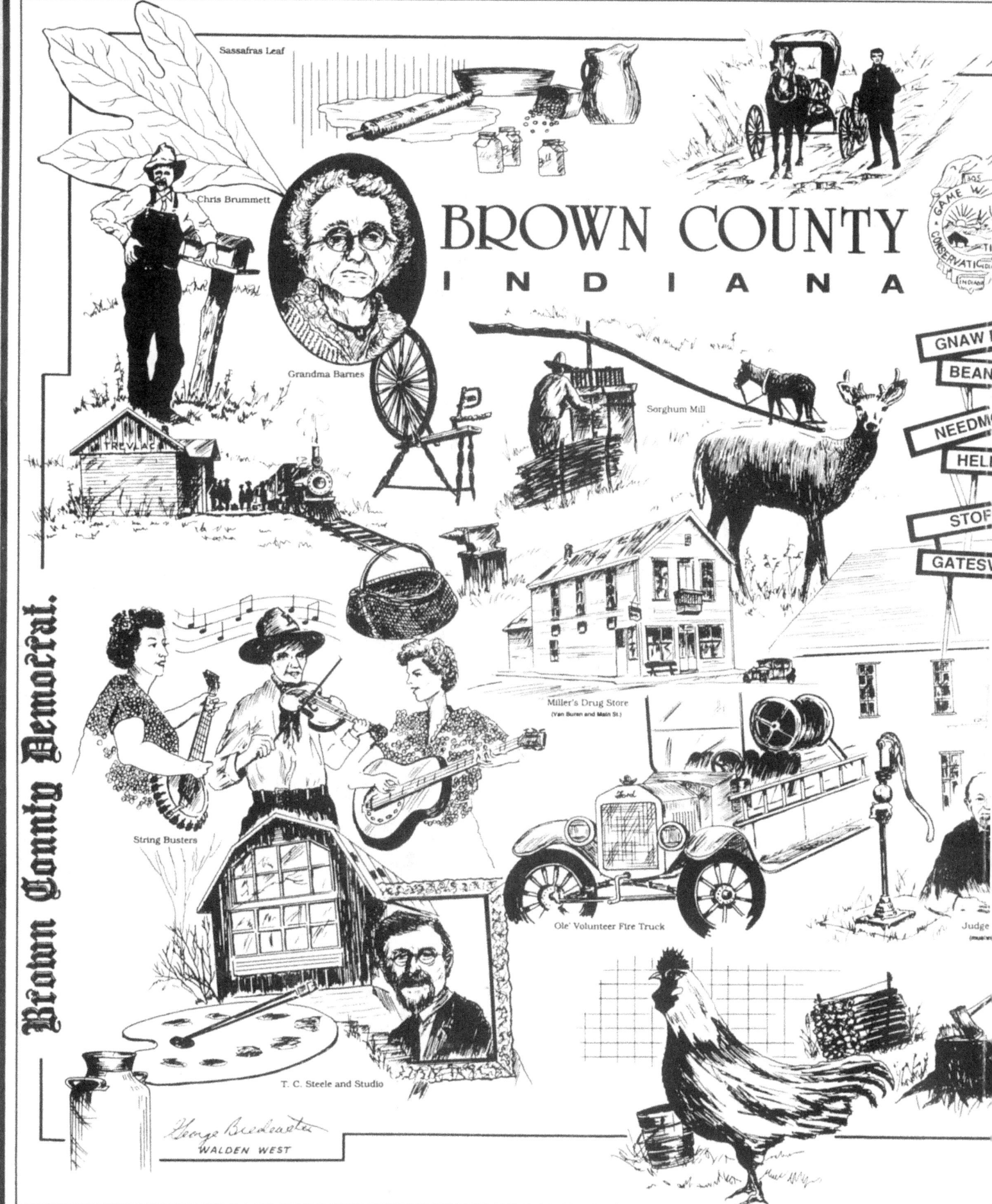

www.ingramcontent.com/pod-product-compliance
Lightning Source LLC
Chambersburg PA
CBHW062114160426

42814CB00044B/316